COLLEGE ACCOUNTING

SEVENTH EDITION

John Ellis Price, Ph.D., C.P.A.
Associate Professor of Accounting
College of Business Administration
University of North Texas
Denton, Texas

M. David Haddock, Jr., Ed.D., C.P.A.
Contributing Author
Professor of Accounting
Chattanooga State Technical Community College
Chattanooga, Tennessee

Horace R. Brock, Ph.D., C.P.A.
Distinguished Professor of Accounting Emeritus
College of Business Administration
University of North Texas
Denton, Texas

GLENCOE

Macmillan/McGraw-Hill

New York, New York   Columbus, Ohio   Mission Hills, California   Peoria, Illinois

PHOTO CREDITS: Cover and page ii, Zigy Kaluzny/Tony Stone Images; page iv, Chuck Keeler/Tony Stone Images; v, (t) Jo Riley/Tony Stone Images, (b) Michael Krasowitz/FPG International; vi, (t) Comstock, Inc., (b) © Stock Imagery, Inc. 1992; vii, (t) Hickson and Associates, (b) Comstock, Inc.; viii, (t) Comstock, Inc., (b) Andy Sacks/Tony Stone Images; ix, (t) Dick Luria/FPG International, (b) Comstock, Inc.; x, (t) Comstock, Inc., (b) Bob Mullenix; xi, Hans Peter Merten/Tony Stone Images; xii, (t) Comstock, Inc., (b) Jim Pickerell/FPG International; xiii, (t) Bob Mullenix, (b) Comstock, Inc.; xiv, (t) Tim Brown/Tony Stone Images, (b) Comstock, Inc./C. Davidson; xv, Bob Thomason/Tony Stone Images; xvi, (t) Dennis Hallinan/FPG International, (b) Comstock, Inc.; xvii, (t) Howard Grey/Tony Stone Images, (b) Tom Tracy/FPG International; xviii, Charles Thatcher/Tony Stone Images; xix, (t) Tom Tracy/FPG International, (b) Comstock, Inc./George Lepp; xx, (t) Comstock, Inc./Hartman-DeWitt, (b) Comstock, Inc.; xxi, (t) Comstock, Inc., (b) Keith Wood/Tony Stone Images; 1, Bob Mullenix; 3, Chuck Keeler/Tony Stone Images; 22, Jo Riley/Tony Stone Images; 51, Michael Krasowitz/FPG International; 85, Comstock, Inc.; 112, © Stock Imagery Inc. 1992; 145, Hickson and Associates; 174, 175, 176, Todd Yarrington; 178, 229, Comstock, Inc.; 264, Andy Sacks/Tony Stone Images; 332, Dick Luria/FPG International; 369, 409, Comstock, Inc.; 449, Bob Mullenix; 491, 492, 493, 494, 495, 496, Todd Yarrington; 497, Tim Brown/Tony Stone Images; 499, Hans Peter Merten/Tony Stone Images; 529, Comstock, Inc.; 554, Jim Pickerell/FPG International; 585, Bob Mullenix; 608, Comstock, Inc.; 642, Tim Brown/Tony Stone Images; 687, Comstock, Inc./C. Davidson; 731, Bob Thomason/Tony Stone Images; 778, Dennis Hallinan/FPG International; 811, 812, 813, 814, 815, Todd Yarrington; 817, Comstock, Inc.; 853, Howard Grey/Tony Stone Images; 889, Tom Tracy/FPG International; 929, Tim Brown/Tony Stone Images; 931, Charles Thatcher/Tony Stone Images; 966, Tom Tracy/FPG International; 993, Comstock, Inc./George Lepp; 1028, Comstock, Inc./Hartman-DeWitt; 1057, 1088, Comstock, Inc.; 1123, Keith Wood/Tony Stone Images.

Library of Congress Cataloging-in-Publication Data

Price, John Ellis.
College accounting/John E. Price, M. David Haddock, Jr., Horace R. Brock.—7th ed.
p. cm.
Rev. ed. of: Accounting: basic principles/Horace R. Brock, Charles E. Palmer, John Ellis Price, 6th ed. c1990.
Includes index.
ISBN 0-02-801441-3
1. Accounting. I. Haddock, M. David. II. Brock, Horace R. III. Brock, Horace R. Accounting. IV. Title.
HF5635.B8542 1993
657—dc20 93-19084
CIP

COLLEGE ACCOUNTING Seventh Edition

Send all inquiries to:
GLENCOE DIVISION
Macmillan/McGraw-Hill
936 Eastwind Drive
Westerville, Ohio 43081

ISBN 0-02-801441-3

Printed in the United States of America.

1 2 3 4 5 6 7 8 9 10 RRD-W 00 99 98 97 96 95 94

Brief Contents

Contents

CHAPTER 2 Analyzing Business Transactions 22

FEATURES

Ethics: It's Only a Game! 32

What Makes an Accounting Computer System Tick? 34

CHAPTER 3 Analyzing Business Transactions Using T Accounts 51

FEATURES

Characteristics of Effective Communication 62

Microcomputer Software 69

UNIT THREE
Payroll Records and Procedures 331

FEATURE

FEATURES

CHAPTER 15 Accounts Receivable and Uncollectible Accounts 529

FEATURES

Negative Messages 532

Processing Computerized Accounts Receivable 539

CHAPTER 16 Notes Payable and Notes Receivable 554

FEATURES

Persuasive Messages 562

Computer Viruses 574

CHAPTER 21 Corporate Earnings and Capital Transactions 731

FEATURES

CHAPTER 22

FEATURE

The Multinational Company 785

CHAPTER 23

FEATURES

Business Reports 820

Accounting of and Reporting International Operations 832

CHAPTER 24

FEATURES

CHAPTER 25

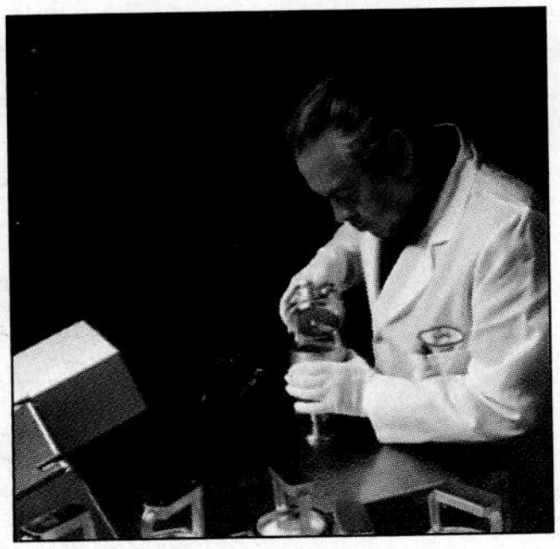

FEATURE

CHAPTER 27 Departmentalized Profit and Cost Centers 966

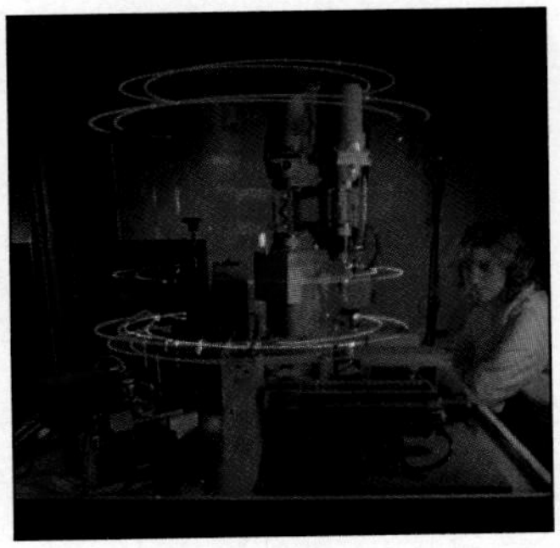

CHAPTER 28 Accounting for Manufacturing Activities 993

CHAPTER 29 Job Order Cost Accounting 1028

CHAPTER 30 Process Cost Accounting 1057

CHAPTER 31 Controlling Manufacturing Costs: Standard Costs 1088

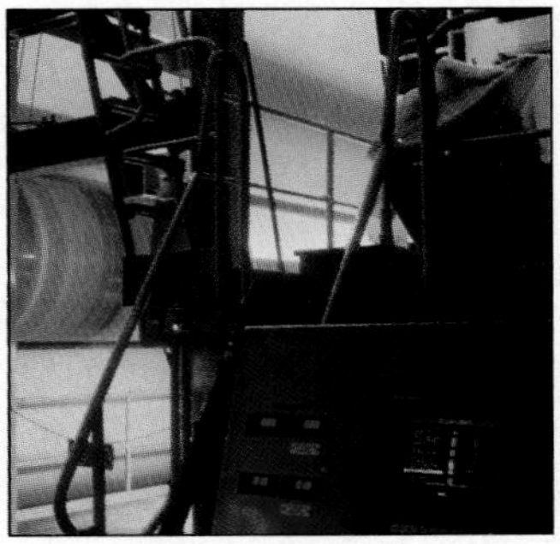

CHAPTER 32 Cost-Revenue Analysis for Decision Making 1123

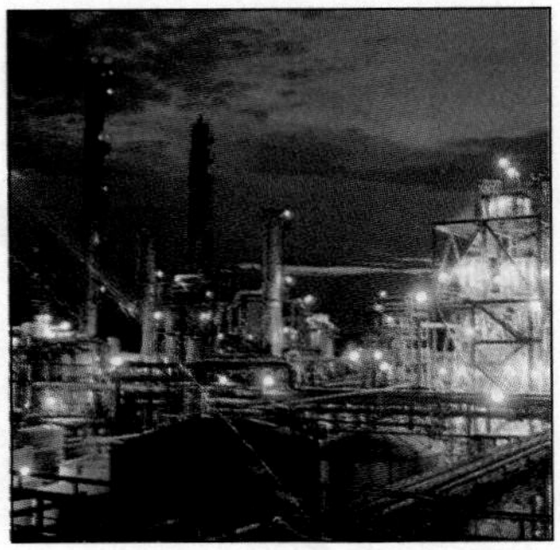

Appendix

Information Blocks

Preface

The seventh edition of *College Accounting* is the most comprehensive revision of the text ever. While retaining the key features of prior editions—short units of instruction; a clear, concise writing style; numerous illustrations and examples; and abundant questions, exercises, problems, and projects—the authors have added a number of new features to meet the needs of today's business students and instructors. These new features are the result of discussions with students, adult learners, and instructors; on-campus visits; reviews of the text by accounting instructors; and comments received from adopters. Additionally, the authors have used a more integrated approach in their writing style to demonstrate the link between accounting and computers, business ethics, communication, and the international environment. These areas are essential to a successful career in business. This approach is endorsed by the Accounting Education Change Commission, which was created in 1989 by the American Accounting Association to direct national attention to the need for change in accounting education. The authors believe that this approach will help students to become better prepared to solve real-world problems.

RETENTION AND REINFORCEMENT

This edition employs a sound pedagogy for assisting a student to learn accounting. Each chapter introduces accounting concepts through short learning modules. At the end of each module the student can reinforce understanding through self-review questions and answers. This reinforcement technique allows a student to build on a mastery of each concept. Retention and reinforcement are further enhanced through the variety of end-of-chapter activities, including questions, exercises, problems, challenge problems, critical thinking problems, and the practice sets.

SOLID ACCOUNTING COVERAGE

The seventh edition of *College Accounting* reflects a solid coverage of accounting concepts and principles. The textbook establishes a foundation of accounting procedures within the traditional proprietorship accounting cycle and builds on this framework as it examines alternative methods of accounting for assets, liabilities, and equity accounts. In addition, the textbook expands on partnership, corporation, and managerial accounting concepts. This solid accounting coverage can serve as the basis for a student to elect advanced accounting courses or serve as the basic accounting requisite for a management, marketing, or finance degree.

MAJOR TEXTBOOK CHANGES

The following summarizes the major changes that have been introduced in the student edition of the textbook.

- ***NEW*** **Four-Color Format.** A new, four-color format allows functional use of color for emphasis and in the design of diagrams, illustrations, and accounting forms. Moreover, money columns are highlighted in the accounting forms. Color is further used to distinguish journals, ledgers, and financial statements.
- ***NEW*** **Chapter Reorganization.** The new organization of chapters presents an orderly flow of accounting concepts. By reorganizing several chapters of the prior edition we offer a crisp and concise presentation of the accounting cycle, partnerships, and corporation accounting.
- ***NEW*** **Short Learning Modules.** Each chapter is divided into short learning modules. Each module is followed by a student self-check activity. The results of this activity will let students know how well they have mastered the accounting concepts in the module.
- ***NEW*** **Competency-Based Chapters.** Chapter objectives based on expected learner outcome introduce each chapter. Each objective is repeated in the margin alongside the text material that develops the objective. The objective is also keyed beside the exercises and problems that relate to the objective.
- ***NEW*** **Illustrations.** This edition makes widespread use of color illustrations. Examples of textbook illustrations include flow charts of accounting concepts, the use of T accounts to reinforce journal entries, diagrams that highlight posting procedures, and detailed financial statements.
- ***NEW*** **Vocabulary.** A new strategy to help students master accounting vocabulary is built into each chapter. All new terms are previewed on the chapter-opener page, appear in boldface type where defined, and are summarized in a glossary at the end of the chapter with page references. In addition, a master glossary appears at the end of the textbook, and the index highlights all defined terms.
- ***NEW*** **Communications, Ethics, Computers, and International Accounting Vignettes.** Short vignettes highlight timely adjunct areas of accounting suggested by the Accounting Education Change Commission of the American Accounting Association. These articles expand a student's horizon and allow the instructor to teach across the curriculum. Each article addresses a single concept and complements the chapter material without interrupting its natural flow. Selected vignettes are supported with student activities. For example, the communications activities not only illustrate business memos and letters but suggest student assignments that are typical of an accounting office envi-

ronment. The ethics vignettes are designed for lively classroom discussion and involve timely real-world events that closely identify with the chapter materials. Comprehensive instructor materials support all student activities.

- *NEW* **Margin Notes.** Major concepts are emphasized, and previously introduced concepts are reinforced in the margin. Learning objectives and points to remember are also highlighted.
- *NEW* **In-Text Worksheet Transparencies.** A special worksheet illustration using multiple overlay transparencies is bound into Chapter 5 of the textbook. This illustration highlights the procedures to prepare a worksheet on a step-by-step basis. The illustration culminates with the presentation of the financial statements that are prepared from the worksheet.
- *NEW* **Managerial Focus.** Each chapter concludes with a short discussion of real-world managerial applications. In addition, managerial questions are an integral part of every end-of-chapter activity section.
- *NEW* **End-of-Chapter Applications: Exercises, Problems A and B, Challenge Problem, and Critical Thinking Problem.** Each major concept in each chapter is supported with an exercise. The problems combine two or more major concepts and are presented in order from simple to complex. New to this edition is the introduction of a "Challenge Problem" and a "Critical Thinking Problem" for each chapter.
- *NEW* **Computer Activities.** Selected exercises and problems may be completed on a computer. These activities are designated by icons that indicate the nature of the software to be used: Tutorial, General Ledger, or Spreadsheet. The supplementary use of the computer adds a new dimension to student review and reinforcement of the material presented in the chapter.

MAJOR FEATURES OF THE STUDENT SUPPORT MATERIALS

The following summarizes the major changes and features in the student support materials. These materials will assist the student in mastering the accounting concepts introduced in the textbook.

Study Guide and Working Papers. The Study Guide and the Working Papers are combined into one workbook. The Study Guide contains a step-by-step study plan, objective questions and exercises with self-check solutions, and a demonstration problem with solution. Working papers are supplied for all the Exercises, the A or B Problems, the Challenge Problem, and the Critical Thinking Problem.

Computer Applications. A variety of student software supports *College Accounting,* including an electronic study guide for tutorial use, general ledger software, and spreadsheet software. Detailed user's guides accompany all software packages.

Electronic Study Guide. Students may use a special tutorial computer-software package that contains study guide questions and tutorial activities similar to the designated textbook exercises and problems. A special feature of the tutorial software is a computer-generated program that reports to the student the objective questions that were correctly and incorrectly answered. A basic math review program is included in this software, as well as a review of generally accepted accounting principles.

Accounting Software Systems. *College Accounting* is supported by two basic types of accounting software systems: (1) the Glencoe integrated system ACCLAIM and (2) commercial software.

ACCLAIM Software. The ACCLAIM software, an integrated Glencoe program accompanied by a template disk, assists students in solving designated chapter exercises and problems. This software also allows students to solve the mini-practice sets in the textbook and the stand-alone practice sets that are available with *College Accounting.*

Commercial Software. Template disks are available to provide opportunities to solve selected chapter problems and practice sets using the most commonly used commercial accounting software: ACCPAC®, Simply Accounting, Dac-Easy®, and Peachtree®.

Accounting Spreadsheet Software. Two types of spreadsheet template disks are available for solving designated textbook problems: (1) a self-booting spreadsheet template disk and (2) a Lotus spreadsheet template disk.

Dictionary of Accounting Terms. A quick, easy reference to accounting and computer terms is offered in a separately bound dictionary of accounting terms. Each term has been defined using the terminology found in *College Accounting.* The computer terms will assist students who elect a microcomputer accounting course after completing the basic course.

MAJOR FEATURES OF THE INSTRUCTOR'S SUPPORT MATERIAL

The following summarizes the major changes that have been made to the instructor's support materials. All these materials provide a variety of innovative teaching suggestions and alternative methods in presenting accounting concepts.

Instructor's Wraparound Edition of the Textbook

For the first time, the college accounting instructor has a comprehensive teaching guide. This unique and innovative four-color textbook teaching guide combines the student edition with the instructor's edition to provide a wealth of teaching support. Teaching suggestions and strategies specifically focus on each major concept. Interesting business connections and real-world accounting facts and figures provide a learning link. Course management tips, program components, pop quizzes, cooperative-learning strategies, life experience applications, reteaching strategies, and special-needs strategies are combined into this unprecedented publication.

Instructor's Resource Portfolio

A variety of individual booklets designed to support multiple teaching needs are housed in a handsome, tabbed portfolio.

Lesson Plans/Lecture Outlines. Lesson plans and lecture outlines for each chapter are provided in a separately bound booklet. The booklet contains teaching objectives, student objectives, a list of instructor's tools, key terms, major concepts, assignments, and evaluation. The materials are perforated and can be duplicated as needed.

How to Study Accounting. A separate booklet offers specific techniques and suggestions to help students develop good study skills. The suggestions focus on methods that students can use when reading technical materials such as those found in accounting to aid them in sorting out key concepts that will facilitate their comprehension.

Math Review. A booklet of activities designed to help students review and develop their basic math skills is provided. It includes a pretest, specific instructions for solving problems, practice problems, and demonstration masters for use with the overhead projector. The activities are provided as blackline masters to facilitate their reproduction and distribution to students or conversion to overhead transparencies.

Blackline Teaching Masters. A set of blackline teaching masters that support the major concepts in each chapter, as well as a comprehensive set of accounting form masters, are provided in booklet form. These masters may be converted into transparencies to be used with the overhead projector or duplicated and distributed to students for classroom use.

Strategies for Using Teaching Transparencies. Another booklet offers suggestions on the most effective way to use each of the transparencies that are described below under "Teaching Transparencies." Suggestions are included for using the overhead projector and for duplicating the transparency for individual student use in conjunction with illustrations in the textbook.

Strategies for Integrating Computers in Accounting. A general discussion on using computers in the classroom, combined with specific strategies for incorporating computers in an accounting classroom, is provided in a self-contained booklet. A detailed review of the student and instructor software that accompanies *College Accounting* provides suggestions to maximize the effectiveness of each accounting software package in classroom or lab situations.

Strategies for Teaching Ethics in Accounting. This booklet begins with an overview of the importance of teaching ethics in the accounting classroom. The booklet also contains specific ways of introducing the textbook vignettes on ethics, as well as providing a decision model with solutions. Each student activity contains specific teaching guides for classroom discussion.

Strategies for Infusing Communications in Accounting. As a discussion of the importance of communications in accounting, this booklet provides general suggestions for helping students sharpen their skills in reading, analyzing, and reporting financial information. This booklet also contains rationales for communication projects, features, strategies, and evaluation guidelines. There are specific instructor solutions for each communication project. These solutions contain detailed background information and additional teaching suggestions.

Strategies for Teaching Global Perspectives in Accounting. An overview of the role of accounting in a global environment, as well as specific vignette discussion questions and answers, are provided in this instructor booklet. Also, there is a series of optional student activities that will broaden a student's international horizon.

Testing Package

A variety of testing resources are available with *College Accounting.* The flexibility of these resources will allow an instructor to design a testing program specifically tailored to the aims and objectives of the course.

Test Bank. The test-bank book contains true-false questions, multiple-choice questions, fill-in questions, and problems and solutions for each chapter. Each solution immediately follows its question.

Test Bank Software. This test bank is an electronic version of the test-bank book. Its software program allows an instructor either to select individual test questions or to select randomly and customize a test. Moreover, the software has the flexibility to allow instructors to incorporate additional testing materials into the program.

Achievement Tests. A and B versions of an achievement test have been developed for each chapter. These tests contain a combination of objective questions and problems to measure the student's understanding of the major concepts of the chapter.

Solutions Manuals

Annotated editions of the Student Study Guide and Working Papers provide solutions to the exercises and problems at the end of each chapter. For clarity, student solutions appear in a second color.

Solutions Transparencies

Boxed volumes of solution transparencies are available for all exercises and problems. The large-type format will project well using an overhead projector.

Teaching Transparencies

Four-color teaching transparencies that illustrate selected major accounting concepts in the textbook are supplied in a separate package. They summarize concepts and enhance textbook illustrations.

Accounting Cycle Reinforcement Video

A video discusses the major concepts introduced in the accounting-cycle section of *College Accounting.* The step-by-step presentation of each concept offers an excellent method of introducing a specific accounting topic or of reviewing it.

MANUAL AND COMPUTER-ASSISTED PRACTICE SETS

Three practice sets are designed to accompany *College Accounting.* Each practice set may be completed manually or on the computer.

Whitewater Wilderness Canoe Livery is a sole proprietorship service business that uses source documents, general journals, general ledgers, work sheets, and a filing system. This set can be completed after Chapter 6.

Wood n' Things is a sole proprietorship merchandise business that uses source documents, special journals, general ledger, subsidiary ledger, work sheet, accounting forms, and a filing system. This set can be completed after Chapter 13.

SoftBooks, Inc. is a corporation practice set that summarizes annual events and concentrates on the financial analysis of the data recorded. Through it, the student will also gain experience in the preparation of adjustments, financial statements, and closing entries.

AUTHOR ACKNOWLEDGMENTS

The authors wish to express their appreciation to all of the following professionals for their generous contributions:

Dr. Michael R. Lane, CPA, Director, MBA Program, Bradley University
Ms. Nina Watson, MSBE, Consultant in Language Arts
Mr. Howard Donaldson, CPA, Glencoe Publishing
Ms. Linda Herrington, CPA, Community College of Allegheny County
Dr. Carolyn Hagler, Associate Professor, The University of Southern Mississippi

A special note of appreciation is in order for Dr. Charles E. Palmer, Professor Emeritus, for the many years that he has been associated with accounting education and the writing and editing of many quality accounting publications.

Acknowledgments

The authors are deeply grateful to the following accounting educators for their ongoing involvement with the *College Accounting* program. As the program moves from edition to edition, the efforts of these knowledgeable and dedicated instructors provide the authors with extremely valuable assistance in meeting the changing needs of the college accounting classroom.

George Allen
Bishop State Community College

Andy Anderson
Bryan Institute

Jere Anderson
Alexandria Technical College

John Nigro
Stone Academy

Richard Arlen
Schoolcraft College

Judy Austin
Shelton State Community College

Marilyn Beebe
Kirkwood Community College

Carol Cardone
The Cittone Institute

George Carter
New Hampshire Technical College

Mike Choma
New Kensington Commercial School

Craig Christopherson
Richland College

Carol Ciulli
The Sawyer Schools

George Converse
Stone Academy

Harvey Cooke
Penn Valley Community College

Kathy Denham
Edmunds Community College

Lela Eldridge Denson
Volunteer State Community College

Elsie Dubac
Stuart School

Sherry Dusch
Barnes Business College

Dave Evans
Johnson County Community College

Kim Frantz
CTBI

William D. Freund
Tampa College

Jack Gurney
Casco Bay College

Sharon Gough
Labette Community College

Rich Green
Burdett School

Carolyn Hairston
Faulkner State Community College

BeeBee Hall
Executive Secretarial School

Linda Herrington
Community College of Allegheny County

Brenda Earle Ray Hester
Volunteer State Community College

Paul Hogan
Shoals Community College

Nancy Hogg
Davenport College

Cynthia Holloway
Tarrant County Junior College-Northeast

Jay Hollowell
Commonwealth College

George Huffman
Tacoma Community College

Richard Irvine
Pensacola Junior College

Vernamae Johnson
Brown Mackie Business College

Marilyn Jones
Friends University

Carol Keltner
Manhattan AVTS

Don King
ITT

Frank Korman
Mountain View College

Dr. Tom Land
Bessemer State Technical College

Gene Lefort
Thibodaux Technical Institute

Carol Lemen
Odessa College

Lenny Long
Fisher College

Susie Mackey
Charter College

Dr. Ty Mathews
Broward Community College-S

Bill McDowell
Central Alabama Community College

Connie McGee
American Institute of Commerce

William Mittelstadt
American Institute of Commerce

Paul Morgan
Mississippi Gulf Coast Community College

William D. Newsom
State Technical Institute at Memphis

George Olson
New England Banking Institute

Rick Orszulak
Pittsburgh Office Management Center

Robert Painter
St. Petersburg Junior College

Jean Roberts
Opelika State Technical College

Dr. Francis Sakiey
Mercer County Community College

Carmen Salinas
San Antonio College

Billie Scott
Northeast Kansas AVTS

Linda Scott
Ivy Tech

Nelda Shelton
Tarrant County Junior College-South

Sam Silver
Mayland Community College

Brenda Smith
State Technical Institute at Memphis

Sheridan Smith
Southwestern Community College

Calvin Snyder
Polk Community College

Carolyn Spangler
Blue Ridge Community College

Leslie Tippitt
Tarrant County Junior College-South

Steve Tipton
Indiana Business College

Don Trent
Dodge City Community College

Gary Tusing
Lord Fairfax Community College

Phil Waits
Ayers State Technical College

Naomi Ward
Northwest AVTS

Jim Weglin
North Seattle Community College

Dale Westfall
Midland College

Richard Whiteside
Mississippi Gulf Coast Community College

Mark Yurgevich
ITT

College Accounting

PART ONE

UNIT ONE

The Accounting Cycle

All types of businesses need and use financial information. Most of this information is obtained from accounting records. Frequently called the language of business, accounting is the process by which a business records, classifies, summarizes, interprets, and communicates its financial information to owners, managers, and other interested parties. Financial statements are the end result of the accounting process. To produce these statements, financial information is assembled according to the steps in the accounting cycle. Accounting records are kept for all types of businesses and follow generally accepted accounting principles that are developed to meet the needs of the many users of accounting information.

CHAPTER

1

Accounting: The Language of Business

OBJECTIVES

1. Define accounting.
2. Identify and discuss career opportunities in accounting.
3. Identify the users of financial information.
4. Compare and contrast the three types of business entities.
5. Describe the process used to develop generally accepted accounting principles.
6. Define the accounting terms new to this chapter.

The purpose of accounting is to provide financial information about a business or a nonprofit organization. This information is of interest to owners, managers, and other parties outside the business or nonprofit organization. Since accounting is used to gather and communicate financial information, it is often called the "language of business."

NEW TERMS

Accounting ▪ Accounting system ▪ Auditing ▪ Auditor's report ▪ Certified public accountant (CPA) ▪ Corporation ▪ Creditor ▪ Discussion memorandum ▪ Economic entity ▪ Entity ▪ Exposure draft ▪ Financial statements ▪ Generally accepted accounting principles (GAAPs) ▪ Governmental accounting ▪ Management advisory services ▪ Managerial accounting ▪ Partnership ▪ Public accountants ▪ Separate entity assumption ▪ Social entity ▪ Sole proprietorship ▪ Statements of Financial Accounting Standards ▪ Stock ▪ Stockholders ▪ Tax accounting

THE NEED FOR FINANCIAL INFORMATION

Suppose a relative leaves you a substantial sum of money and you decide to carry out your lifelong dream of opening a small shop to sell sportswear. You rent space in a local shopping center, purchase fixtures and equipment, purchase goods to sell, hire salespeople, and open the store to customers. Before long you realize that, to run your business successfully, you will need financial information about the business. To obtain the information you need, someone must gather data about the firm's financial affairs and analyze that data.

What type of financial information do you need to operate your business successfully? At regular intervals you will probably need answers to the following questions:

- How much cash does the business have?
- How much money do customers owe the business?
- What is the cost of the merchandise sold?
- How much did the volume of sales increase?
- What is the amount owed to suppliers?
- How much profit has the firm made?

As your business grows, you will need even more financial information to evaluate the firm's performance and make decisions about the future. An efficient accounting system allows owners and managers to obtain a wide range of useful information quickly. Timely information is one reason it is so important for a business to have a well-run accounting system directed by a professional staff.

ACCOUNTING DEFINED

OBJECTIVE 1
Define accounting.

Accounting is the process by which financial information about a business is recorded, classified, summarized, interpreted, and communicated to owners, managers, and other interested parties. An **accounting system** is designed to accumulate data about a firm's financial affairs, classify the data in a meaningful way, and summarize it in periodic reports called **financial statements.** Owners and managers receive much of the information they need from financial statements. The accountant not only establishes the records and procedures that make up the accounting system and supervises the operations of the system but also interprets the resulting financial information. Most owners and managers rely heavily on the accountant's judgment and knowledge when making financial decisions.

ACCOUNTING CAREERS

OBJECTIVE 2
Identify and discuss career opportunities in accounting.

Many jobs are available in accounting, and they require varying amounts of education and experience. Bookkeepers and accountants are responsible for keeping records and providing the financial information about the business. Generally bookkeepers are responsible for the recording of business transactions. In large firms bookkeepers may also supervise the work of accounting clerks who are responsible for the record-keeping function of part of the accounting system—perhaps payroll, accounts receivable, or accounts payable. Accountants usually supervise bookkeepers and prepare the financial statements and reports of the business.

Newspapers often carry classified advertisements for accounting clerks, bookkeepers, and accountants. Accounting clerk positions usually require a minimum of one to two semesters of accounting courses and little or no experience. Bookkeeper positions usually require a minimum of one to two years of accounting education plus experience as an accounting clerk. Accountant positions usually require a college degree but are sometimes filled by experienced bookkeepers or individuals with a two-year college degree. Most entry-level positions for accountants do not have an experience requirement; however, both the education and experience requirements for these positions will vary according to the size of the firm. Accountants usually choose to practice in one of three areas: public accounting, managerial accounting, or governmental accounting.

Public Accounting

The largest public accounting firms in the United States are referred to as the "Big Six." These firms are Arthur Andersen & Co.; Coopers and Lybrand; Deloitte and Touche; Ernst & Young; Peat, Marwick, Main & Co.; and Price Waterhouse & Co.

Public accountants belong to firms whose major business is the performance of accounting services for other companies. These firms are called public accounting firms. They offer three major types of services: auditing, tax accounting, and management advisory services. Many public accountants are **certified public accountants (CPAs).** A CPA is an independent accountant who provides accounting services to the public for a fee. To become a CPA, an individual must have earned a certain number of college credits in accounting courses, demonstrate good personal character, pass the Uniform CPA Examination, and fulfill the experience requirements of the state of practice.

Auditing is the review of financial statements to assess their fairness and adherence to generally accepted accounting principles. Auditing is performed by auditors who are CPAs. **Tax accounting** is a service offered by public accounting firms that involves tax compliance and tax planning. Tax compliance is any activity associated with the preparation of tax returns and the audit of those returns. Tax planning involves giving advice to clients on how to legally structure their financial affairs to reduce their tax liability. Providing **management advisory services** involves helping clients improve their information systems or improve their business performance.

Managerial Accounting

Managerial accounting, also referred to as private accounting, involves working on the staff of a single business in industry. Managerial accountants perform a wide range of activities. They establish a company's accounting policies, direct its accounting system, prepare its financial statements, interpret its financial information, and provide financial advice to management. In addition, managerial accountants prepare tax forms, perform tax planning services for the company, and prepare internal reports for management.

Governmental Accounting

Governmental accounting involves keeping financial records and preparing financial reports as part of the staff of federal, state, or local governmental units. Although governmental units do not earn profits, they receive and pay out huge amounts of money and must have procedures for recording and managing this money. Governmental agencies that regulate certain types of businesses or oversee their reporting procedures, such as the Securities and Exchange Commission, hire accountants to review the financial statements and records of the businesses under their jurisdiction. The Internal Revenue Service and the Federal Bureau of Investigation also have large numbers of accountants on their staffs and use them to uncover possible violations of the law.

USERS OF FINANCIAL INFORMATION

OBJECTIVE 3
Identify the users of financial information.

Earlier you read that the results of the accounting process are communicated to many individuals and organizations who are interested in the financial affairs of a business. Who are these individuals and organizations, and why might they want to obtain financial information about a particular firm?

Owners and Managers

Assume your sportswear shop is in full operation. One user of financial information about the business is obviously you, the owner. The information that you need, and that all owners and managers need, is information that will help you to evaluate the results of your operations and to plan and make decisions for the future. Should you drop long-sleeved pullover sweaters that are not selling well from your product line, or should you just reduce the price to encourage sales? How much money should you spend on advertising? How much should you charge for a new type of denim jacket that you are adding to your product line? How does this month's profit compare with the profit you earned the month before? Should you open a new store? These questions would be difficult to answer without financial information.

Suppliers

Even though your business is small, a number of people other than you, the owner, may be interested in its financial affairs. For example, when you first ask for credit from suppliers of goods, they may want financial information in order to assess the ability of your firm to pay its debts. They may also use the data to determine exactly how much credit you should be given.

Banks

What if you decide to ask your bank for a loan so that you can open a new store across town? The bank will want to assure itself that your firm will pay back the loan in a timely fashion. The bank will therefore require that you provide financial information prepared by your accountant and will use this information in determining whether to give you the loan and in setting the terms of the loan.

Tax Authorities

The Internal Revenue Service (IRS) and other tax authorities are interested in financial information about your firm because this information serves to determine the tax base. Income taxes are based on taxable income; sales taxes are based on sales income; and property taxes are based on the assessed value of buildings, equipment, and inventory (the goods available for sale). All of this information is provided by the accounting process.

Regulatory Agencies and Investors

If a firm is in an industry regulated by a governmental agency, the business may be required to supply financial information to that agency. For example, the Federal Communications Commission may obtain financial information from radio and television stations. Similarly, a public utilities commission may obtain financial information from public utilities.

If a firm is a publicly owned corporation, the Securities and Exchange Commission (SEC) will be interested in its financial information. Congress passed the Securities Act of 1933 and the Securities Exchange Act of 1934 in an effort to regulate the financial information provided by corporations that traded their stock on stock exchanges and in the over-the-counter markets. These laws were passed for the protection of potential investors who, up until that time, could not depend on the fairness of the published financial information of corporations when deciding whether to buy stock. Also, since each firm used its own particular method of accounting, it was difficult for investors to compare the financial information of different companies in order to decide which company's stock to purchase.

The SEC was created to review and oversee the accounting methods of publicly owned corporations. Although it has delegated this job to the accounting profession, the SEC still retains the right to have the final say on any matter of financial accounting by publicly owned corporations. If financial reporting that results from the accounting methods of one of these firms does not meet with the approval of the SEC, it can suspend trading of that company's stock on the stock exchanges.

Customers

In some industries customers pay special attention to financial information about the firm with which they plan to do business. They may use this information to try to estimate how long the company will be operating. The computer industry is an example of one where customers are concerned about the life of a firm. Before a customer spends a lot of money on a computer, that customer will want to feel reasonably sure that the manufacturer will be around for the next several years to service the computer, replace parts, and provide additional components. Also, the customer will want to be able to purchase programs for that computer as the need arises. If the computer manufacturer goes out of business, it is likely that programmers and software houses will stop writing programs to fit that manufacturer's computer. One way the customer can estimate the economic health of a company and the likelihood that it will remain in business is by analyzing financial information about the firm.

Employees and Unions

Employees may also be interested in having financial information about the business where they work. For example, they may be members of a profit-sharing plan and therefore be very concerned

FIGURE 1–1
Users of a Business's Financial Information

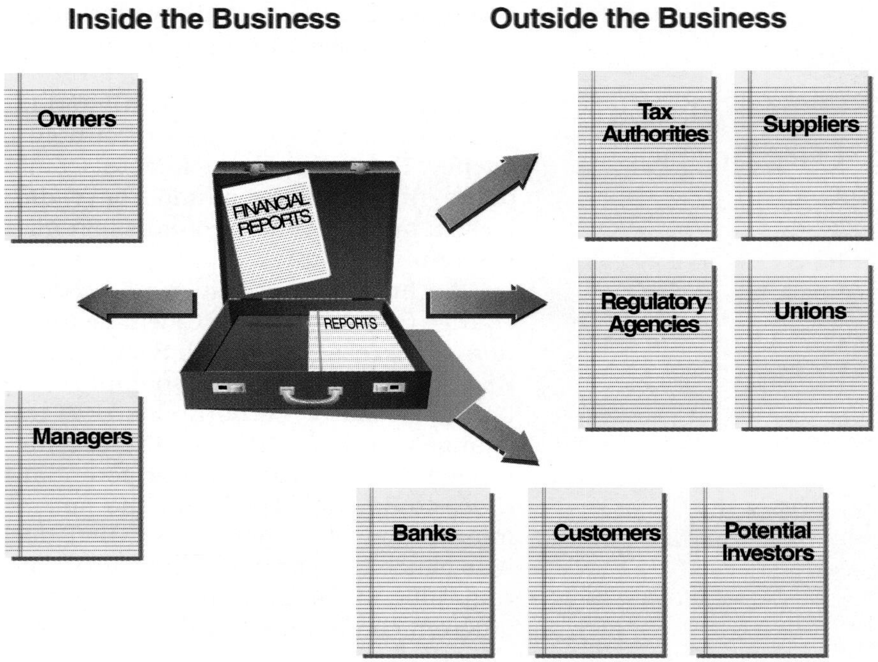

about the financial results of the firm's operations. If a large corporation has employees who belong to a labor union, the union may use financial information about the firm to assess its ability to pay higher wages and benefits when a new contract is negotiated.

Figure 1-1 illustrates the many different types of users of financial information about a business. As you learn about the accounting process, you will begin to understand why financial information is so important to these individuals and organizations and how they can use such information to meet their needs.

SELF-REVIEW

1. What is the purpose of accounting?
2. Why is accounting called "the language of business"?
3. What does the accounting process involve?
4. Name three job positions in accounting.
5. What are financial statements?

Answers to Self-Review

1. The purpose of accounting is to gather and communicate financial information about a business.
2. Accounting is often called the "language of business" because the results of the accounting process—financial statements—communicate essential information about a business to concerned individuals and organizations.

3. The accounting process involves recording, classifying, summarizing, interpreting, and communicating financial information about a business.
4. Three job positions in accounting are accounting clerk, bookkeeper, and accountant.
5. Financial statements are periodic reports that summarize the financial affairs of a business.

TYPES OF BUSINESS ENTITIES

OBJECTIVE 4
Compare and contrast the three types of business entities.

The accounting process involves recording, classifying, summarizing, interpreting, and communicating financial information about an economic or social entity. An **entity** is something that can be recognized as having its own separate identity, such as an individual, a town, a university, or a business. The term **economic entity** usually refers to a business or organization whose major purpose is to produce a profit for its owners. **Social entities** are nonprofit organizations, such as cities, public schools, and public hospitals. This book focuses on the accounting process for businesses, although nonprofit organizations need similar financial information.

There are three major legal forms of business entity: the sole proprietorship, the partnership, and the corporation. While the accounting process for all three types of business entity is generally the same, differences in their structures and in the laws that apply to these structures require some differences in the way certain aspects of their financial affairs are recorded. These specific differences in accounting procedures are presented in detail later in the book as accounting for the different business structures is discussed. However, for now you should understand the basic differences in the three types of business entities.

Sole Proprietorships

A **sole proprietorship** is a business entity owned by one person. The life of the business ends when the owner is no longer willing or able to keep the firm going. Many small businesses are operated as sole proprietorships.

The owner of a sole proprietorship is legally responsible for the debts and taxes of the business. If, for example, the firm is unable to pay its debts, the **creditors** (those people, companies, or government agencies to whom the firm owes money) can turn to the owner for payment. The owner may then have to pay the debts of the business from personal savings or other personal resources. When the time comes to pay income taxes, the owner's income and the income of the business are combined to compute the total tax responsibility of the owner.

While the owner's money and the money of the business may seem to be almost the same, it is very important that the accounting process for the business be limited to the financial transactions of the firm. Remember, accounting deals with financial information

Information Block: Communication

Communication Overview

Businesses are highly dependent on communication for making decisions, managing operations, and planning for the future. Although the primary function of accounting is to provide *financial* information about the business, accountants must often prepare written or oral presentations to accompany financial reports. Therefore, in addition to their technical and computer skills, business professionals need effective communication skills for a successful career.

Communication is the exchange of information through spoken, written, or *nonverbal* language. The communication process involves a sender initiating a message and then sharing the message with a receiver. The sender exchanges the message through a medium, which may be a letter, phone call, oral presentation, or symbol. When a receiver responds to the message, feedback occurs. Effective communication must be a two-way process with information exchanged and *understood* between the sender and the receiver.

To communicate effectively, you need skills in listening, speaking, reading, and writing. In addition, you should be aware of these communication barriers that may cause miscommunication or misunderstanding:

- *Backgrounds. Before* communicating, determine your objective for sending the spoken, written, or nonverbal message. Analyze the receiver's viewpoint, knowledge, interests, attitudes, and anticipated reaction to the subject.
- *Language.* Use standard English for your message, with special attention to appropriate vocabulary and word usage, spelling, punctua-

about an economic entity. If the owner's personal transactions are mixed up with those of the business, it will be very difficult to measure the performance of the firm. Accountants use the term **separate entity assumption** to describe this idea of separating the accounting process for a business from the accounting process for the personal finances of the owner or owners.

Partnerships

A **partnership** is a business entity owned by two or more people. The partnership structure is common in businesses that offer a professional service, such as law firms, accounting firms, architectural firms, medical practices, and dental practices. At the beginning of the partnership, two or more individuals enter into a contract that outlines how much each partner will contribute to the business;

tion, and sentence construction. The use of obscure words, slang, or wordy sentences will often confuse your message.

- *Content.* Focus on specific data related to the subject, and organize the information logically. Avoid sharing too much information, which may overload the receiver. Equally critical is the appropriateness of the type of communication: written document (letter, memorandum, report, graph, announcement) or oral presentation (speech, meeting, interview, telephone call).
- *Physical environment.* Elements of the physical environment (room temperature, noise level, lighting, seating arrangement) and timing of the message (early or late in the day, month, quarter, or year) may interfere with the communication process.

To improve your professional career, develop effective communication skills by planning, organizing, and carefully considering your message, the receiver, the medium, and potential barriers to understanding.

Project: Select a financial article in a recent issue of a business periodical, journal, or newspaper, such as *Business Week, Newsweek, Accounting Horizons,* or *The Wall Street Journal.* Applying the preceding information, analyze the article.

1. Who is the intended reader or receiver? Was the material appropriate?
2. What is the objective of the article?
3. Identify any communication barriers and appropriate means to eliminate or decrease them.
4. Evaluate the author's ability to communicate effectively.
5. Prepare a brief summary of the article.

each partner's percentage of ownership; what share of the profits each partner will receive; what duties each partner will perform; how much responsibility each partner will have to creditors and tax authorities for the amounts owed by the business; and other information detailing the rights, obligations, and limitations of each partner. The partners may share equally in the ownership and profits of the business, or they may share in any proportion agreed upon in the contract. When an individual is unwilling or unable to remain a partner, then the partnership dissolves and a new partnership may be formed with the remaining partners or with new partners.

As in a sole proprietorship, the partners are individually, and as a group, responsible for the debts and taxes of the partnership. Their personal bank accounts or other personal resources may be used to pay creditors when the partnership is unable to provide payment. Again, it is important that the accounting process for a partnership be limited to the financial transactions of the firm and not include the personal transactions of the partners.

Corporations

Although most businesses in the United States operate as sole proprietorships or partnerships, corporations contribute more to the U.S. economy. The largest corporations in the United States are referred to as the "Fortune 500."

A **corporation** is a business entity that is separate from its owners and has a legal right to own property and do business in its own name. The corporation is considerably different from the other business entities—the sole proprietorship and the partnership. The major difference has to do with the ownership of the business. There are publicly owned and privately owned corporations. The latter are often called closely held corporations. Anyone can invest in a publicly owned corporation. Shares of **stock** for such corporations are bought and sold on stock exchanges and in the over-the-counter markets. The stock represents ownership in a corporation and is issued as stock certificates. In closely held corporations, ownership is limited to specific individuals, usually family members, and its stock is not traded on an exchange.

Most large corporations have issued (sold) many thousands of shares of stock. Generally each investor's proportion of ownership is determined by the number of shares of stock purchased by that individual as compared with the total number of shares issued by the corporation. For example, assume that Nancy Ling currently owns 250 shares of the Sample Corporation's stock. If the Sample Corporation has issued 1,000 shares of stock up to this point, Ling has a 25 percent ownership interest in the corporation (250 shares divided by 1,000 shares = 0.25, or 25%). If the owners of the Sample Corporation have to make a decision by voting, then Ling will have 250 votes (one for each share of stock that she owns). The other owners will have a total of 750 votes.

The corporate form of business entity is unique in that the firm does not end when ownership changes—as through the sale of shares of stock by one individual to another. Some corporations have new owners daily because their shares are actively traded on stock exchanges. One of the advantages of a corporation is that it can last forever, whereas the maximum life of a sole proprietorship is the life of its owner. Similarly, a partnership can last only as long as the life span of any of its partners. The death or withdrawal of one partner ends the partnership.

Corporate owners, often called **stockholders,** or *shareholders,* are not responsible for the debts or taxes of the corporation. The most money a stockholder can lose if the corporation is unable to pay its bills is the total of his or her investment in the firm—the cost of the shares of stock purchased and held by the stockholder.

The corporate entity, like the sole proprietorship and the partnership, must be accounted for separately from the financial affairs of its owners. This separation is usually easier with a corporation than with a sole proprietorship or a partnership because, in most cases, stockholders do not participate in the day-to-day operations of the business.

TABLE 1–1
Major Characteristics of Business Entities

Characteristic	Type of Business Entity		
	Sole Proprietorship	Partnership	Corporation
Ownership	One owner	Two or more owners	One or several owners, even thousands
Life of the business	Ends when the owner dies, is unable to carry on operations, or decides to close the firm	Ends when one or more partners withdraw, when a partner dies, or when the partners decide to close the firm	Can continue forever; ends only when the business can no longer pay its creditors and goes bankrupt or when the stockholders vote to liquidate it
Responsibility for debts of the business	Owner is responsible for firm's debts when firm is unable to pay	Partners are responsible individually and jointly for firm's debts when firm is unable to pay	Stockholders are not responsible for firm's debts; they can lose only the amount of their investment

Some major characteristics of the three types of business entity are summarized in Table 1–1.

GENERALLY ACCEPTED ACCOUNTING PRINCIPLES

As mentioned previously, Congress has given the Securities and Exchange Commission the final say on matters of financial reporting by publicly owned corporations. The SEC has delegated the job of determining proper financial accounting standards to the accounting profession. However, the SEC has sometimes overridden decisions of the accounting profession. In accordance with its responsibility, the accounting profession has developed, and continues to develop, a set of **generally accepted accounting principles (GAAPs).** Some of these principles apply to all types of companies, and some apply only to specific industries or specific situations. Generally accepted accounting principles must be followed by publicly owned companies unless they can demonstrate that if they applied these principles to their affairs the information produced would be misleading.

The Development of Generally Accepted Accounting Principles

OBJECTIVE 5
Describe the process used to develop generally accepted accounting principles.

Currently, generally accepted accounting principles are developed by a group called the Financial Accounting Standards Board (FASB), which is composed of seven full-time members. The principles established by the FASB are called **Statements of Financial Accounting Standards.** The FASB develops statements by using a feedback process in which interested people and organizations can participate by communicating their opinions to the FASB.

First, the FASB writes a **discussion memorandum** that explains the topic under consideration. Then public hearings are held where accountants and other interested parties can express their opinions, either orally or in writing. The groups that most consistently offer opinions about proposed FASB statements are the SEC, the American Institute of Certified Public Accountants (AICPA), individual public accounting firms, the American Accounting Association (AAA), and companies with a direct interest in a particular statement proposed by the FASB.

The AICPA is a national association of professional accountants. It represents accountants in many situations, including the development of accounting principles. The AAA is a group of accounting educators. Opinions about proposed accounting principles are offered by members of the AAA to the FASB, usually after considerable research has been done about possible effects of a new principle on financial reporting and on other areas of the economy that would be directly or indirectly affected by the proposed principle.

FIGURE 1–2
The Process Used by FASB to Develop Generally Accepted Accounting Principles

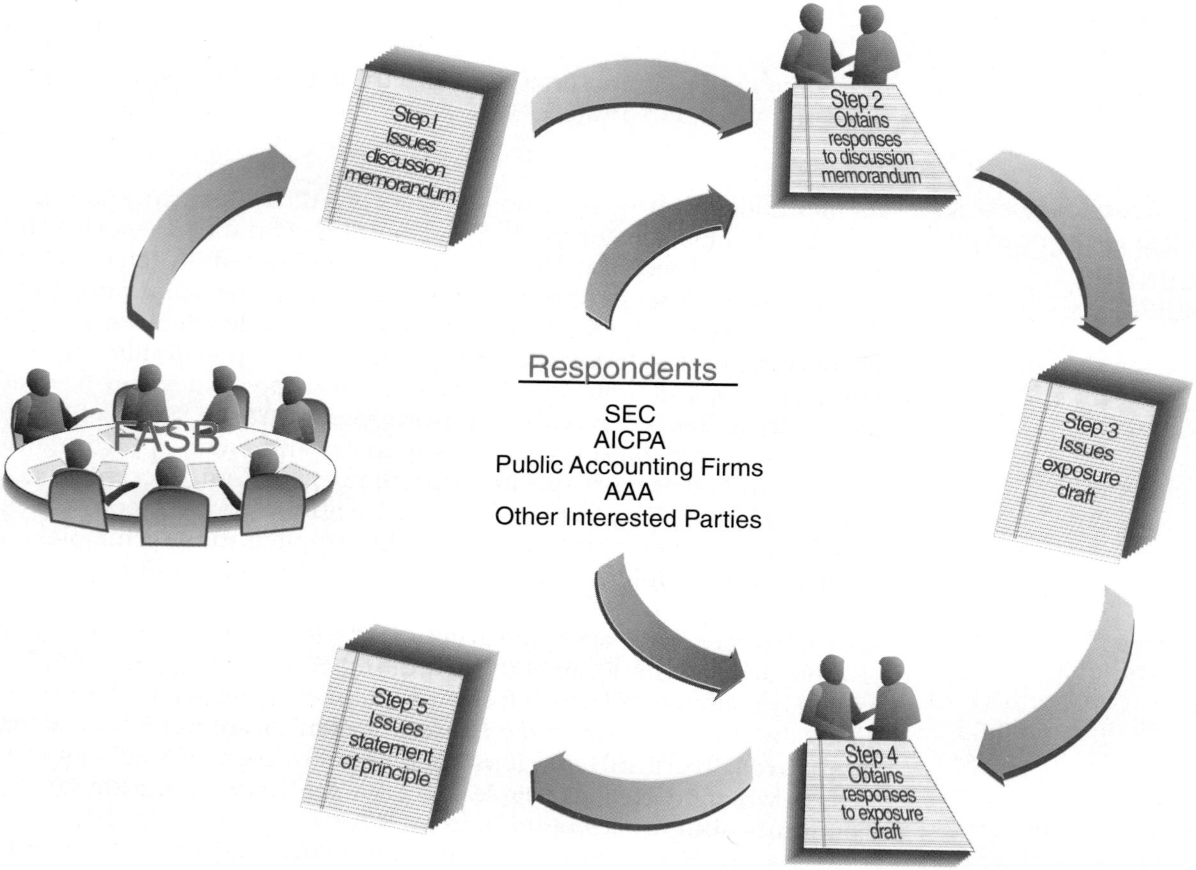

Information Block: Computers and Accounting

The Age of Computers and Accounting

Most businesses today make extensive use of computers in their accounting systems. Computers allow fast and efficient processing of large quantities of business transactions with an extremely high degree of accuracy. They can also quickly produce a wide variety of detailed financial reports when they are needed, which is especially important in providing management with the kind of financial information needed to effectively plan and control operations in a large organization.

Microcomputers are the smallest computers and the least expensive. They are often called personal computers, desktop computers, or simply micros. These computers can cost between $500 and $5,000. A microcomputer is generally used by one person at a time to handle one task. For example, one accountant can prepare the company's payroll checks on one computer while another accountant at a separate microcomputer completes the recording of the daily cash receipts.

The smallest of microcomputers are the *laptops,* or notebook computers. These portable units weigh between 4 and 18 pounds, have a *liquid crystal display (LCD),* include a self-contained battery pack, and can be used by employees almost everywhere. Laptops are currently the fastest-growing segment of the personal computer industry.

Minicomputers are somewhat larger and more powerful than microcomputers and are often called *midrange* or *midsize* computers. Minicomputers are used in medium-sized businesses as the primary computer. They are faster than microcomputers and can store more data. Minicomputers can cost from $10,000 to $150,000.

The *mainframe* computer is very large and can cost anywhere from $250,000 to several million dollars. Because of their cost, they are found in large businesses that process a high volume of data. Larger companies often connect mainframes to form a network that can support hundreds of users and process multiple tasks concurrently.

Supercomputers are the largest, most expensive computers available today. They are generally used by government agencies, research scientists, and very large corporations. Supercomputers are capable of performing over a billion arithmetic calculations per second and can cost well over $25 million. One of the most expensive supercomputers cost the U.S. government $40 million and was installed at the National Aeronautic and Space Administration's Ames Research Center in California.

After the FASB holds public hearings about a potential statement, it prepares a draft of the statement, called an **exposure draft,** which describes the FASB's proposed solution to the problem being considered. The FASB then receives and evaluates public comment about the exposure draft. Finally, its members vote on the statement. If four or more of the members approve, the proposed statement becomes one of the generally accepted accounting principles. The process used to develop GAAPs is shown in Figure 1–2, p. 14.

The Use of Generally Accepted Accounting Principles

To ensure that generally accepted accounting principles are followed by publicly owned corporations, the SEC requires that financial information, in the form of financial statements, be submitted annually by all such companies to the SEC. These financial statements must be audited, or reviewed, by an accountant who is not on the staff of the firm that issued the statements, that is, by an independent certified public accountant. In addition, the financial statements must include a report by the accountant about the review. This document is known as the **auditor's report.** The purpose of the review is to obtain the objective opinion of a professional accountant from outside the company that the financial statements fairly present the operating results and financial position of the business and that the information was prepared according to generally accepted accounting principles. The financial statements and the auditor's report must be made available to stockholders and potential stockholders of publicly owned corporations.

Businesses and the environment in which they operate are constantly changing. The economy, technology, and laws change. Therefore, financial information and the methods of presenting that information must change to meet the needs of the people who use the information. Generally accepted accounting principles are changed and refined as accountants respond to the changing environment.

MANAGERIAL IMPLICATIONS

The managers of a business must make sure that the firm has an efficient accounting system that produces financial information that is timely, accurate, and fair. Financial statements should be based on generally accepted accounting principles. Internal reports for management need not follow these principles but should provide useful information that will aid in the process of monitoring and controlling operations.

Managers also have a responsibility to use the financial information they receive about their firms. When properly studied and interpreted, financial information can help managers do a more effective job of controlling present operations, making decisions, and planning for the future. The sound use of financial information is essential to good management.

SELF-REVIEW

1. What are the three types of business entities?
2. What is the separate entity assumption, and why is it important in accounting for a business?
3. What are generally accepted accounting principles?
4. Why are generally accepted accounting principles needed?
5. How are generally accepted accounting principles developed?

Answers to Self-Review

1. The three types of business entities are the sole proprietorship, the partnership, and the corporation.
   a. A sole proprietorship has one owner, who is legally responsible for the debts and taxes of the business. The business ends when the owner is unwilling or unable to keep the firm going.
   b. A partnership is owned by two or more people. Individually and as a group, the partners are personally responsible for the debts of the partnership. The partnership dissolves when one of the individuals is unwilling or unable to remain a partner.
   c. Ownership in a corporation is obtained through purchase of shares of stock. The shareholders are not responsible for the debts and taxes of the corporation. Corporations can continue in existence indefinitely.
2. The separate entity assumption describes the idea of separating the accounting process for a business from the accounting process for the personal finances of the owner or owners. It is important in accounting because it will be very difficult to measure the performance of the business if the owner's personal transactions are mixed with those of the business.
3. Generally accepted accounting principles are financial accounting standards that are changed and refined in response to changes in the environment in which businesses operate.
4. Generally accepted accounting principles help ensure that financial information fairly presents the operating results and financial position of a business.
5. Generally accepted accounting principles are developed by the Financial Accounting Standards Board in the form of proposed statements. Interested individuals and groups such as the Securities and Exchange Commission, the American Institute of Certified Public Accountants, individual public accounting firms, the American Accounting Association, and companies with a direct interest in a particular statement all offer feedback on proposed statements. After the FASB receives and evaluates opinions from the public, the FASB members vote on the statement. If four or more of the members approve, the proposed statement becomes one of the generally accepted accounting principles.

CHAPTER 1 Review and Applications

CHAPTER SUMMARY

Accounting is the process by which financial information about a business is recorded, classified, summarized, interpreted, and communicated to owners, managers, and other interested parties. There are many job opportunities in accounting, most of which require varying amounts of education and experience. Accounting clerk positions require the least education and experience. Examples of accounting clerk positions include accounts receivable clerk, accounts payable clerk, and payroll clerk. Bookkeepers usually have experience as accounting clerks and a minimum of one to two years of accounting education. Most entry-level accounting positions require a college degree or significant experience as a bookkeeper.

All types of businesses need and use financial information. Sole proprietorships, partnerships, and corporations have different structures and operate by different rules, but the financial information needed by each is generally the same. Nonprofit organizations also need similar types of financial information in order to conduct their operations in an efficient manner.

Firms that sell stock on stock exchanges or in over-the-counter markets must publish audited financial reports annually, submit their reports to the Securities and Exchange Commission, and make the reports available to stockholders. These reports must follow generally accepted accounting principles. The SEC has delegated the authority to develop generally accepted accounting principles to the accounting profession. Currently, a group called the Financial Accounting Standards Board handles this task.

Because of the different business structures, the need for many different types of financial information, and the complex requirements of tax and regulatory agencies, accountants usually specialize in one of three major areas. Some accountants work for public accounting firms and perform auditing, tax accounting, or management advisory functions. Other accountants work in private industry where they set up and supervise accounting systems, prepare financial reports, prepare internal reports, or do internal auditing. Still other accountants work for government agencies. They keep track of public funds and expenditures, or they audit the financial records of businesses and individuals to see whether they are in compliance with regulatory laws, tax laws, and other laws.

GLOSSARY OF NEW TERMS

Accounting (p. 4) The process by which financial information about a business is recorded, classified, summarized, interpreted, and communicated to owners, managers, and other interested parties

Accounting system (p. 4) A process designed to accumulate, classify, and summarize financial data

Auditing (p. 5) The review of financial information to assess its fairness and adherence to generally accepted accounting principles

Auditor's report (p. 16) An independent accountant's review of a firm's financial information

Certified public accountant (CPA) (p. 5) An independent accountant who provides accounting services to the public for a fee

Corporation (p. 12) A publicly or privately owned business entity that is separate from its owners and has a legal right to do business in its own name; stockholders are not responsible for the debts or taxes of the business

Creditor (p. 9) One to whom money is owed

Discussion memorandum (p. 13) An explanation of a topic under consideration by the Financial Accounting Standards Board

Economic entity (p. 9) A business or organization whose major purpose is to make a profit for its owners

Entity (p. 9) Anything having its own separate identity, such as an individual, a town, a university, or a business

Exposure draft (p. 16) A proposed solution to a problem being considered by the Financial Accounting Standards Board

Financial statements (p. 4) Periodic reports of a firm's financial position or operating results

Generally accepted accounting principles (p. 13) Accounting standards developed and applied by professional accountants

Governmental accounting (p. 5) Accounting work performed for a federal, state, or local governmental unit

Management advisory services (p. 5) Services designed to help clients improve their information systems or their business performance

Managerial accounting (p. 5) Accounting work carried on by an accountant employed by a single business in industry

Partnership (p. 10) A business entity owned by two or more people who are legally responsible for the debts and taxes of the business

Public accountants (p. 5) Members of firms that perform accounting services for other businesses

Separate entity assumption (p. 10) The concept of keeping a firm's financial records separate from the owner's personal financial records

Social entity (p. 9) A nonprofit organization (a city, public school, or public hospital)

Sole proprietorship (p. 9) A business entity owned by one person who is legally responsible for the debts and taxes of the business

Statements of Financial Accounting Standards (p. 13) Accounting principles established by the Financial Accounting Standards Board

Stock (p. 12) Certificates that represent ownership of a corporation

Stockholders (p. 12) The owners of a corporation; also called shareholders

Tax accounting (p. 5) A service that involves tax compliance and tax planning

REVIEW QUESTIONS

1. What are the three major areas of accounting?
2. What types of services do public accountants provide?
3. What is tax planning?
4. What are the major functions or activities performed by accountants in private industry?
5. What types of people or organizations are interested in financial information about a firm, and why are they interested in this information?
6. What is the function of the Securities and Exchange Commission?
7. What are the three types of business entities, and how do they differ?
8. Why is it important for business records to be separate from those of the business's owner or owners? What is the term accountants use to describe this separation of personal and business records?
9. What is the purpose of the Financial Accounting Standards Board?
10. What groups consistently offer opinions about proposed FASB statements?

MANAGERIAL FOCUS

1. Why is it important for managers to have financial information?
2. Do you think a manager will obtain enough financial information to control operations effectively if he or she simply reads a set of financial statements once a year? Why or why not?
3. The owner of a small business commented to a friend that he did not see the need for an accounting system in his firm because he closely supervises day-to-day operations and knows exactly what is happening in the business. Would you agree with his statement? Why or why not?
4. This chapter listed a number of questions that the owner or manager of a firm might ask when trying to evaluate the results of the firm's operations and its financial position. If you were an owner

or manager, what other questions would you ask to judge the firm's performance, control operations, make decisions, and plan for the future?

5. The major objective of most businesses is to earn a profit. What other objectives might a business have? How can financial information help management to achieve these objectives?
6. Many business owners and managers are not accountants. Why is it useful for such people to have a basic knowledge of accounting?

CRITICAL THINKING PROBLEM

Since graduating from college five years ago, Sally Armstrong has worked for a national chain of shoe stores. She has held several positions within the company and is currently manager of a local branch store.

Over the past five years, Sally has observed a pattern in women's shoe purchases. She tells you that a large majority of the shoes sold are black and that almost every woman owns at least one pair of black shoes. Since she has always wanted to be in business for herself, Sally's idea is to open a women's shoe store that sells only black shoes. She has discussed her plan with a number of people in the industry, and they believe it is a viable one.

A new upscale shopping mall is opening nearby, and Sally has decided that now is the time to take the plunge and go into business for herself. She plans to open a shop in the new mall to sell only black shoes.

One of the things Sally must decide in the process of transforming her idea into reality is the form of ownership for her new business. Should it be organized as a sole proprietorship, a partnership, or a corporation?

What advice would you give Sally? What advantages or disadvantages are there to each choice?

CHAPTER

2 Analyzing Business Transactions

OBJECTIVES

1. Record in equation form the financial effects of a business transaction.
2. Define, identify, and understand the relationship between asset, liability, and owner's equity accounts.
3. Analyze the effects of business transactions on a firm's assets, liabilities, and owner's equity and record these effects in accounting equation form.
4. Prepare an income statement.
5. Prepare a statement of owner's equity and a balance sheet.
6. Define the accounting terms new to this chapter.

Long before there can be any recording, reporting, or interpreting of financial information, accountants have to analyze every business transaction. A **business transaction** is a financial event that that changes the resources of the firm. A business transaction may consist of a purchase, a sale, a receipt or payment of cash, or any other financial occurrence. The effects of each transaction must be studied in order to know what information to record and where to record it.

The accounting process actually begins with an analysis of the transactions of a business; thus this phase is the natural starting point for the study of accounting.

NEW TERMS

Accounts payable ▪ Accounts receivable ▪ Assets ▪ Balance sheet ▪ Break even ▪ Business transaction ▪ Capital ▪ Equity ▪ Expense ▪ Fair market value ▪ Fundamental accounting equation ▪ Income statement ▪ Liabilities ▪ Net income ▪ Net loss ▪ On account ▪ Owner's equity ▪ Revenue ▪ Statement of owner's equity ▪ Withdrawals

BEGINNING WITH ANALYSIS

Let's see how an accountant would analyze the transactions of Arrow Accounting Services, a firm that provides a wide range of bookkeeping and accounting services. This sole proprietorship business is owned by John Arrow, who has a master's degree in accounting and is also a CPA. The office is managed by Virginia Richey, who has an associate degree in business from a community college and has taken twelve semester hours of accounting. The firm is located in a large office complex that has easy public access.

To simplify record keeping and billing, Arrow permits clients to charge accounting services that are provided by the firm. He bills clients on a monthly basis for the services they have received during the period. Customers who prefer may pay in cash immediately after services are provided.

Starting a Business

OBJECTIVE 1

Record in equation form the financial effects of a business transaction.

Let's start from the beginning. John Arrow obtained the funds to start the business by withdrawing $40,000 from his personal savings account. He deposited the money in a new bank account that he opened in the name of the firm, Arrow Accounting Services. The separate bank account for the firm helps Arrow keep his financial interest in the business separate from his personal funds. The establishment of this bank account on November 6, 19X5, was the first transaction of the new firm.

In setting up his accounting records, Arrow recognized that there were two important financial facts to be recorded at the time:

a. The business had $40,000 of property in the form of cash, which was on deposit in the bank.

b. Arrow had a $40,000 financial interest in the business; this interest is called his **equity,** or **capital.**

The firm's position at that time may be expressed as a simple equation.

	Property	=	Financial Interest
	Cash	=	John Arrow, Capital
(a) Invested cash	+ **$40,000**		
(b) Increased equity			+ **$40,000**

The equation *property equals financial interest* reflects the basic fact that in a free enterprise system all property is owned by someone. In this case Arrow owns the business because he supplied the property (cash).

Renting Facilities

The first thing John Arrow did after setting up the business with his cash investment was to rent facilities. The lease he signed specified a monthly rent of $2,500 and required that he pay eight months' rent in advance. Arrow therefore issued a $20,000 check to cover the rent for December through July. Two facts must be recorded about this transaction.

c. The firm prepaid (paid in advance) the rent for the next eight months in the amount of $20,000. As a result, the firm obtained the right to occupy facilities for an eight-month period. In accounting, this right is considered a form of property.
d. The firm decreased its cash balance by $20,000.

Here is how the firm's financial position looked after this transaction.

	Property			=	Financial Interest
	Cash	+	Prepaid Rent	=	John Arrow, Capital
Previous balances	$40,000			=	$40,000
(c) Rented facilities		+	**$20,000**		
(d) Paid cash	**−20,000**				
New balances	$20,000	+	$20,000	=	$40,000

Notice that the amount of total property remains the same, even though the form of the property has changed.

Purchasing Equipment for Cash

The manager, Virginia Richey, saw that her first task was to get the business ready for business operations, which were to begin on December 1, 19X5. She bought a computer and other equipment for $10,000 and paid for it with a check drawn against the firm's bank account. Two essential elements of this transaction must be recorded.

e. The firm purchased new property (equipment) for $10,000.
f. The firm paid out $10,000 in cash.

Here is the financial position of the business after this transaction was recorded.

	Property					=	Financial Interest
	Cash	+	Prepaid Rent	+	Equipment	=	John Arrow, Capital
Previous balances	$20,000	+	$20,000			=	$40,000
(e) Purchased equipment				+	**$10,000**		
(f) Paid cash	**−10,000**						
New balances	$10,000	+	$20,000	+	$10,000	=	$40,000

Although there was a change in the form of some of the firm's property (cash to equipment), the equation that expresses the change shows that the total value of the property remained the same. John Arrow's financial interest, or equity, was also unchanged. Again, *property* (Cash, Prepaid Rent, and Equipment) *was equal to financial interest* (John Arrow, Capital).

Note carefully that these activities were recorded as financial affairs of the business entity, Arrow's Accounting Services. John Arrow's personal assets, such as his personal bank account, house, furniture, and automobile, were kept separate from the property of the firm. Nonbusiness property is not included in the accounting records of the business entity.

Purchasing Equipment on Credit

Richey also bought a copy machine, a fax machine, calculators, and other necessary equipment from Organ, Inc., at a cost of $5,000. Organ, Inc., agreed to allow 60 days for the firm to pay the bill. This arrangement is sometimes called buying **on account.** The business has a *charge account,* or *open-account credit,* with its suppliers. Amounts that a business must pay in the future under this agreement are known as **accounts payable.** The companies or individuals to whom the amounts are owed are called *creditors.* Analysis of the transaction revealed the following basic elements.

g. The firm purchased new property on account from Organ, Inc., in the form of equipment that cost $5,000.
h. The firm owed $5,000 to Organ, Inc.

This increase in equipment was made without an immediate cash payment because Organ, Inc., was willing to accept a claim against Arrow Accounting Service's property until the bill was paid. There were then two different financial interests or claims against the firm's property—the creditor's claim (Accounts Payable) and the owner's claim (John Arrow, Capital).

Here is how the transaction looked in equation form.

	Property					=	Financial Interest		
	Cash	+	Prepaid Rent	+	Equipment	=	Accounts Payable	+	John Arrow, Capital
Previous balances	$10,000	+	$20,000	+	$10,000	=		+	$40,000
(g) Purchased equipment					+ **5,000**				
(h) Incurred debt							+**$5,000**		
New balances	$10,000	+	$20,000	+	$15,000	=	$5,000	+	$40,000

Notice that when property values and financial interests increase or decrease, the total of the items on one side of the equation still equals the total on the other side. This happens because there are financial interests, or claims, against business property as soon as the property is purchased. The creditor's claim lasts until the debt is paid. The owner's claim lasts as long as he or she continues to own the business.

Purchasing Supplies

From her previous work experience, Richey was able to estimate the amount of supplies that Arrow Accounting Services would need to start operations. She placed an order for paper, diskettes, pens, pencils, folders, and other supplies that had a total cost of $1,000. The company that sold the items, Reliable Supplies, Inc., requires cash payments from businesses that are under six months old. Arrow Accounting Services therefore included a check with its order. After analyzing the transaction, the major elements listed below were identified.

i. The firm purchased supplies that cost $1,000.
j. The firm paid $1,000 in cash.

Here is how this transaction affected the business's property and financial interests.

	Property							=	Financial Interest		
	Cash	+	Supplies	+	Prepaid Rent	+	Equipment	=	Accounts Payable	+	John Arrow, Capital
Previous balances	$10,000			+	$20,000	+	$15,000	=	$5,000	+	$40,000
(i) Purchased supplies		+	**$1,000**								
(j) Paid cash	– **1,000**										
New balances	$ 9,000	+	$1,000	+	$20,000	+	$15,000	=	$5,000	+	$40,000

Paying a Creditor

Richey decided to pay $1,000 to Organ, Inc., to reduce the firm's debt to that business. The analysis of this transaction follows.

k. The firm paid $1,000 in cash.
l. The claim of Organ, Inc., against the firm decreased by $1,000.

The effect of this transaction on the firm's property and financial interests can be expressed in equation form as shown below.

	Property							=	Financial Interest		
	Cash	+	Supplies	+	Prepaid Rent	+	Equipment	=	Accounts Payable	+	John Arrow, Capital
Previous balances	$9,000	+	$1,000	+	$20,000	+	$15,000	=	$5,000	+	$40,000
(k) Paid cash	– **1,000**										
(l) Decreased debt								=	– **1,000**		
New balances	$8,000	+	$1,000	+	$20,000	+	$15,000	=	$4,000	+	$40,000

ASSETS, LIABILITIES, AND OWNER'S EQUITY

OBJECTIVE 2

Define, identify, and understand the relationship between asset, liability, and owner's equity accounts.

Accountants use special accounting terms when they refer to property and financial interests. For example, they refer to property that a business owns as the business's **assets** and to the debts or obligations of the business as its **liabilities.** The owner's financial interest is called **owner's equity;** sometimes it is called *proprietorship* or *net worth.* Owner's equity is the preferred term and is the term used throughout this book. At regular intervals John Arrow will review the status of the firm's assets, liabilities, and owner's equity in a formal report called a **balance sheet,** which is prepared to show the firm's financial position on a given date. Figure 2–1 shows how the firm's balance sheet looked on November 30, 19X5—the day before operations actually began.

FIGURE 2–1
Balance Sheet for Arrow Accounting Services

ARROW ACCOUNTING SERVICES
Balance Sheet
November 30, 19X5

Assets		*Liabilities*	
Cash	8 0 0 0 00	*Accounts Payable*	4 0 0 0 00
Supplies	1 0 0 0 00		
Prepaid Rent	20 0 0 0 00	*Owner's Equity*	
Equipment	15 0 0 0 00	*John Arrow, Capital*	40 0 0 0 00
Total Assets	44 0 0 0 00	*Total Liabilities and Owner's Equity*	44 0 0 0 00

The assets are listed on the left side of the balance sheet and the liabilities and owner's equity on the right side. This arrangement is similar to the equation *property equals financial interest* illustrated earlier. Property was shown on the left side of the equation, and financial interest appeared on the right side.

The balance sheet in Figure 2–1 shows the amount and types of property the business owned, the amount owed to creditors, and the amount of the owner's interest in the firm on November 30, 19X5. This statement therefore gives John Arrow a complete picture of the financial position of his business on a specific date.

SELF-REVIEW

1. What is a business transaction?
2. What is the difference between buying for cash and buying on account?
3. Describe a transaction that increases an asset and owner's equity.
4. Describe a transaction that will cause Accounts Payable and Cash to decrease by $400.
5. Why is Prepaid Rent considered an asset?

Answers to Self-Review

1. A business transaction is a financial event that changes the resources of the firm.
2. Buying for cash results in an immediate decrease in cash; buying on account results in a liability, which is an amount owed to a creditor. Liabilities are recorded as Accounts Payable.
3. An example of a transaction that increases an asset and owner's equity is the initial investment of cash in a business by the owner.
4. The payment of $400 to a creditor on account will cause Accounts Payable and Cash to decrease by $400.
5. Prepaid Rent is an asset because it represents a right to property.

THE FUNDAMENTAL ACCOUNTING EQUATION

OBJECTIVE 3
Analyze the effects of business transactions on a firm's assets, liabilities, and owner's equity and record these effects in accounting equation form.

The word *balance* in the title "Balance Sheet" has a very special meaning. It serves to emphasize that the total of the figures on the left side of the report must equal, or balance, the total of the figures on the right side. In accounting terms the firm's assets are equal to the total of its liabilities and owner's equity. This equality can be expressed in equation form, as illustrated below. The figures shown are for Arrow Accounting Services on November 30, 19X5.

Assets	=	**Liabilities**	+	**Owner's Equity**
$44,000	=	$4,000	+	$40,000

The relationship between assets and liabilities plus owner's equity is called the **fundamental accounting equation.** The entire accounting process of analyzing, recording, and reporting business transactions is based on the fundamental accounting equation.

As with other mathematical equations, if any two parts of the equation are known, the third part can easily be determined. For example, consider the basic accounting equation for Arrow Accounting Services on November 30, 19X5, with some items of information missing.

	Assets	=	**Liabilities**	+	**Owner's Equity**
1.	?	=	$4,000	+	$40,000
2.	$44,000	=	?	+	$40,000
3.	$44,000	=	$4,000	+	?

In the first case we can solve for assets by adding liabilities ($4,000) and owner's equity ($40,000) to determine that assets are $44,000. In the second case we can solve for liabilities by subtracting owner's equity ($40,000) from assets ($44,000) to determine that liabilities are $4,000. In the third case we can solve for owner's equity by subtracting liabilities ($4,000) from assets ($44,000) to determine that owner's equity is $40,000.

Effects of Revenue and Expenses

Shortly after Arrow Accounting Services opened for business on December 1, 19X5, some of the tenants in the office complex where the business is located became John Arrow's first clients. Arrow also used his contacts in the community to gain other clients. Services to clients began a stream of revenue for the business. **Revenue,** or *income,* is the inflow of money or other assets (including claims to money, such as sales made on credit) that results from sales of goods or services or from the use of money or property. The result of revenue is an increase in assets.

An **expense,** on the other hand, involves the outflow of money, the use of other assets, or the incurring of a liability. Expenses include the costs of any materials, labor, supplies, and services used in an effort to produce revenue. If there is an excess of revenue over expenses, the excess represents a *profit.* Making a profit is the reason that people like John Arrow risk their money by investing it in a business. A firm's accounting records show not only increases and decreases in assets, liabilities, and owner's equity but the detailed results of all transactions involving revenue and expenses. Let's use the fundamental accounting equation to show the relationship of revenue and expenses to the business.

Selling Services for Cash

During the month of December 19X5, Arrow Accounting Services earned a total of $10,500 in revenue from clients who paid cash for accounting and bookkeeping services. The receipt of this revenue is analyzed below.

m. The firm received $10,500 in cash for services provided to clients.
n. The owner's equity increased by $10,500 because of this inflow of assets from revenue. (Revenue, such as fees earned, always increases the owner's equity.)

The revenue figures are usually kept separate from the owner's equity figure until the financial statements are prepared. The revenue should appear in equation form, as follows.

	Assets							= Liabilities +		Owner's Equity		
	Cash	+	Supplies	+	Prepaid Rent	+	Equipment	=	Accounts Payable	+	John Arrow, Capital	+ Revenue
Previous balances	$ 8,000	+	$1,000	+	$20,000	+	$15,000	=	$4,000	+	$40,000	
(m) Received cash	+**10,500**											
(n) Owner's equity increased by revenue												+ **10,500**
New balances	$18,500	+	$1,000	+	$20,000	+	$15,000	=	$4,000	+	$40,000	+ $10,500
	$54,500								$54,500			

Keeping revenue separate from the owner's equity will help the firm compute the total revenue much more easily when the financial reports are prepared.

Selling Services on Credit

In December 19X5 Arrow Accounting Services earned $3,500 of revenue from charge account clients. These clients are allowed 30 days to pay. Amounts owed by such customers are known as **accounts receivable.** These accounts represent a new form of asset for the firm—claims for future collection from customers. The analysis of this transaction follows.

o. The firm acquired a new asset, accounts receivable, of $3,500.
p. The owner's equity was increased by the revenue of $3,500. The amount is recorded as revenue because the owner has made a sale and has a claim to an amount to be received in the future.

The following equation shows the effects of this transaction.

	Assets					= Liabilities +	Owner's Equity	
	Cash	+ Accounts Receivable	+ Supplies	+ Prepaid Rent	+ Equip.	= Accounts Payable	+ John Arrow, Capital	+ Revenue
Previous balances	$18,500		+ $1,000	+ $20,000	+ $15,000	= $4,000	+ $40,000	+ $10,500
(o) Received new asset		+ **$3,500**						
(p) Owner's equity increased by revenue								+ **3,500**
New balances	$18,500	+ $3,500	+ $1,000	+ $20,000	+ $15,000	= $4,000	+ $40,000	+ $14,000
	$58,000					$58,000		

Collecting Receivables

By the end of December 19X5, Arrow Accounting Services had received $1,500 from clients who had previously bought services on account. This cash was applied to their accounts. The firm therefore recognized the following changes.

q. The firm received $1,500 in cash.
r. Accounts receivable decreased by $1,500.

These changes affected the equation as shown below.

	Assets					= Liabilities +	Owner's Equity	
	Cash	+ Accounts Receivable	+ Supplies	+ Prepaid Rent	+ Equip.	= Accounts Payable	+ John Arrow, Capital	+ Revenue
Previous balances	$18,500	+ $3,500	+ $1,000	+ $20,000	+ $15,000	= $4,000	+ $40,000	+ $14,000
(q) Received cash	**+1,500**							
(r) Accounts receivable decreased		**−1,500**						
New balances	$20,000	+ $2,000	+ $1,000	+ $20,000	+ $15,000	= $4,000	+ $40,000	+ $14,000
	$58,000					$58,000		

Notice that revenue is not recorded when cash is collected from charge account clients. In this transaction there is merely a change in the type of asset (from accounts receivable to cash). Revenue was recorded when the sale on credit took place (see entry p). Notice also that the fundamental accounting equation, *assets equal liabilities plus owner's equity,* holds true regardless of the changes arising from individual transactions.

Paying Expenses

So far Arrow has done very well. His equity has increased by sizable revenues. However, keeping a business running costs money, and these expenses reduce owner's equity. The expense figures are kept separate from the figures for the owner's capital and revenue. The separate record of expenses is kept for the same reason as the separate record of revenue is kept—to help analyze operations for the period.

Employees' Salaries

During December 19X5, the first month of operations, Arrow Accounting Services hired an accounting clerk to help in the business. The firm paid $2,500 in salaries for this employee and Virginia Richey. This transaction is analyzed as follows.

s. Cash was reduced by payment of $2,500 to cover the salaries.
t. The owner's equity decreased by the $2,500 outflow of assets for salaries expense.

The effect of the salaries expense is shown below.

	Assets					= Liabilities +	Owner's Equity		
	Cash	+ Accts. Rec.	+ Supplies	+ Prepaid Rent	+ Equip.	= Accounts Payable	+ J. Arrow, Capital	+ Revenue	− Expenses
Previous balances	$20,000	+ $2,000	+ $1,000	+ $20,000	+ $15,000	= $4,000	+ $40,000	+ $14,000	
(s) Paid cash	**−2,500**								
(t) Owner's equity decreased by salaries expense									**−2,500**
New balances	$17,500	+ $2,000	+ $1,000	+ $20,000	+ $15,000	= $4,000	+ $40,000	+ $14,000	− $2,500
	$55,500					$55,500			

Utilities Expense

At the end of December 19X5, Arrow Accounting Services received a $300 bill for the utilities that it had used during the month. A check was issued to pay the bill immediately. This transaction was another business expense and its analysis follows.

u. Cash was reduced by the payment of $300 for utilities.
v. The owner's equity decreased by $300 because of the expense incurred.

The effect of the utilities expense is shown below.

	Assets					= Liabilities +	Owner's Equity		
	Cash	+ Accts. Rec.	+ Supplies	+ Prepaid Rent	+ Equip.	= Accounts Payable	+ J. Arrow, Capital	+ Revenue	− Expenses
Previous balances	$17,500	+ $2,000	+ $1,000	+ $20,000	+ $15,000	= $4,000	+ $40,000	+ $14,000	− $2,500
(u) Paid cash	**−300**								
(v) Owner's equity decreased by utilities expense									**−300**
New balances	$17,200	+ $2,000	+ $1,000	+ $20,000	+ $15,000	= $4,000	+ $40,000	+ $14,000	− $2,800
	$55,200					$55,200			

Information Block: Ethics

It's Only a Game!

You just purchased a copy of Xandress II, the hottest computer game on the market. Xandress II is a copyrighted program that is protected under United States copyright law. You and some of your friends have just finished playing the game. Chris, your best friend, asks to borrow your floppy disk of Xandress II to install the program on a computer at home.

1. What are the ethical issues?
2. What are your alternatives?
3. Who are the affected parties?
4. How do the alternatives affect the parties?
5. What is your decision?
6. Would your decision be different if you were the branch manager of a local bank and a friend who works for a competing bank asked to borrow a loan evaluation program developed especially for your bank?

Effect of Owner's Withdrawals

▲ **REMEMBER!**

The owner of the business and the business are separate economic entities. If the owner's personal transactions are mixed up with those of the business, it will be very difficult to measure the performance of the firm.

On December 30, 19X5, John Arrow withdrew $1,000 in cash from the business to pay for personal expenses. **Withdrawals** are funds taken from the business by the owner to pay for personal use. Withdrawals are not a business expense but a decrease of the owner's equity in the business. The separate entity assumption requires the recording of transactions of each entity in separate records.

The effect of John Arrow's withdrawal of $1,000 in cash for personal expenses is shown below.

w. Cash was reduced by the $1,000 withdrawal.
x. The owner's equity decreased by $1,000 because the withdrawn funds decreased the total assets of the firm.

After this transaction was recorded, the equation appeared as shown at the top of page 33.

Summary of Transactions

Figure 2–2 summarizes the transactions of Arrow Accounting Services through December 31, 19X5. Notice that after each transaction, the fundamental accounting equation is in balance. Test your understanding of analyzing business transactions by describing the nature of each transaction, then check your results by referring to the discussion of each transaction above.

	Assets					= Liabilities +	Owner's Equity		
	Cash	+ Accts. Rec.	+ Supplies	+ Prepaid Rent	+ Equip.	= Accounts Payable	+ J. Arrow, Capital	+ Revenue	− Expenses
Previous balances	$17,200	+$2,000	+$1,000	+$20,000	+$15,000	= $4,000	+$40,000	+$14,000	− $2,800
(w) Withdrew cash	**−1,000**								
(x) Owner's equity decreased by withdrawal							**− 1,000**		
New balances	$16,200	+$2,000	+$1,000	+$20,000	+$15,000	= $4,000	+$39,000	+$14,000	− $2,800
	$54,200					$54,200			

FIGURE 2–2
Transactions of Arrow Accounting Services Through December 31, 19X5

	Assets					= Liabilities +	Owner's Equity		
	Cash	+ Accts. Rec.	+ Supplies	+ Prepaid Rent	+ Equip.	= Accounts Payable	+ J. Arrow, Capital	+ Revenue	− Expenses
(a) & (b)	+40,000						+40,000		
Balances	40,000					=	40,000		
(c) & (d)	−20,000			+ 20,000					
Balances	20,000			+ 20,000		=	40,000		
(e) & (f)	−10,000				+ 10,000				
Balances	10,000			+ 20,000	+ 10,000	=	40,000		
(g) & (h)					+ 5,000	+5,000			
Balances	10,000			+ 20,000	+ 15,000	= 5,000	+ 40,000		
(i) & (j)	−1,000		+ 1,000						
Balances	9,000		+ 1,000	+ 20,000	+ 15,000	= 5,000	+ 40,000		
(k) & (l)	−1,000					−1,000			
Balances	8,000		+ 1,000	+ 20,000	+ 15,000	= 4,000	+ 40,000		
(m) & (n)	+10,500							+10,500	
Balances	18,500		+ 1,000	+ 20,000	+ 15,000	= 4,000	+ 40,000	+10,500	
(o) & (p)		+ 3,500						+3,500	
Balances	18,500	+ 3,500	+ 1,000	+ 20,000	+ 15,000	= 4,000	+ 40,000	+ 14,000	
(q) & (r)	+1,500	−1,500							
Balances	20,000	+ 2,000	+ 1,000	+ 20,000	+ 15,000	= 4,000	+ 40,000	+ 14,000	
(s) & (t)	−2,500								−2,500
Balances	17,500	+ 2,000	+ 1,000	+ 20,000	+ 15,000	= 4,000	+ 40,000	+ 14,000	− 2,500
(u) & (v)	−300								−300
Balances	17,200	+ 2,000	+ 1,000	+ 20,000	+ 15,000	= 4,000	+ 40,000	+ 14,000	− 2,800
(w) & (x)	−1,000						−1,000		
Balances	16,200	+ 2,000	+ 1,000	+ 20,000	+ 15,000	= 4,000	+ 39,000	+ 14,000	− 2,800
	$54,200					$54,200			

Information Block: Computers and Accounting

What Makes an Accounting Computer System Tick?

All computer systems contain *hardware,* which consists of input devices, a processor unit, and output devices. Input devices are usually a keyboard or a mouse. The processor unit is the "brains" of the computer system where data is actually processed. It contains two separate parts: the *central processing unit (CPU)* and the *main memory,* also known as primary storage.

The CPU contains the arithmetic/logic unit and the control unit. The arithmetic/logic unit performs mathematical calculations and logic operations such as comparing two numbers to see which one is greater. The control unit directs the activities of all components of the system including executing the computer program. A *program* is a detailed set of instructions that tell a computer exactly what to do. A payroll accounting program, for example, contains the directions for calculating the amount of an employee's gross earnings, the correct amounts for the various payroll deductions, and finally the amount of the employee's net pay. Computer programs are known as *software.*

The data to be processed by a computer is known as *input.* Most accounting data is input as raw, unorganized facts that include numbers and words. As data is entered into the system, it is processed according to the computer program. The "processed data" is known as information, which is data that is now in a meaningful and useful form. Information is the output of a computer system. For example, the amount of customers' purchases on account and the amount of customers' cash payments are entered into the computer as data. Using a software pro-

THE INCOME STATEMENT

OBJECTIVE 4
Prepare an income statement.

The **income statement** is a formal report of the results of business operations for a specific period of time such as a month, a quarter, or a year. In contrast, the balance sheet reports the financial condition of the business on a given date such as June 30 or December 31. The balance sheet shows what the business owns and owes as well as the amount of the owner's equity in the business. The income statement shows the revenue earned by the business and the expenses of doing business.

gram, the computer processes this data. The output (information) shows the balance in each customer's account as well as those customers who are late in paying their account balances.

Output devices present the output of the computer. The most common output devices are the *printer* and the *monitor.* The monitor is similar to a television screen. It is also known as a screen or a CRT (cathode ray tube). Output on a monitor is not permanent. Therefore, most output is directed to a printer that produces *hard copy.* Output can also be sent to disk drives for storage on magnetic disks or to tape drives for storage on magnetic tape. This type of storage is called *auxiliary* or *secondary storage.*

The figure below shows the elements of a computer system. These operations—input, processing, output, and storage—are called the information processing cycle.

Information Processing Cycle

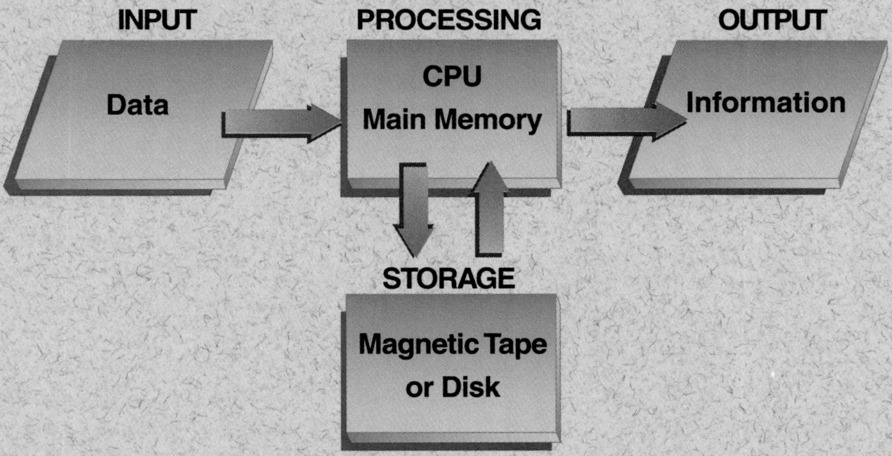

The income statement is sometimes called a *profit and loss statement* or a *statement of income and expenses.* The most common term is income statement, which is used throughout this text. The income statement shown in Figure 2–3, page 36, illustrates how Arrow Accounting Services would present the results of its first month of operation.

The difference between income from services provided or goods sold and the amount spent to operate the business is reported at the bottom of the income statement. **Net income** results when the revenue for the period is greater than the expenses. When expenses are greater than revenue, the result is a **net loss.** In the rare case when revenue and expenses are equal, the firm is said to **break even.** The income statement in Figure 2–3 shows a net income because revenue was greater than expenses.

FIGURE 2–3
Income Statement for Arrow Accounting Services

ARROW ACCOUNTING SERVICES Income Statement Month Ended December 31, 19X5		
Revenue		
Fees Income		14 000 00
Expenses		
Salaries Expense	2 500 00	
Utilities Expense	300 00	
Total Expenses		2 800 00
Net Income		11 200 00

Notice that the three-line heading of the income statement shows *who, what,* and *when.* The first line is used for the firm's name (who). The second line gives the title of the report (what). The third line tells the exact period of time covered by the report (when). The third line clearly indicates that the income statement reports the results of operations for the single month of December 19X5.

If the income statement covered the three months of January, February, and March, the third line would read, "Three-Month Period Ended March 31, 19XX." The third line of a statement reporting the results of operations for a 12-month period beginning on January 1 and ending on December 31 of the same calendar year would read, "Year Ended December 31, 19XX." In instances where the 12-month reporting period ends on a date other than December 31, the third line of the income statement would identify the period as a fiscal year; for example, "Fiscal Year Ended June 30, 19X5" or "Fiscal Year Ended November 30, 19X5."

Also note the use of single and double rules in amount columns. A single line is used to show that the figures above it are being added or subtracted. Double lines are used under the final figure in a column or section of a report to show that the figure is complete.

This income statement does not have dollar signs because it was prepared on accounting paper with ruled columns. However, dollar signs would be used on a typewritten or computer-generated income statement that is not prepared on a ruled form.

THE STATEMENT OF OWNER'S EQUITY AND THE BALANCE SHEET

OBJECTIVE 5
Prepare a statement of owner's equity and a balance sheet.

The income statement by itself is meaningful to business owners, managers, and other interested parties. However, it is even more informative when considered in relation to the assets and equities that were involved in earning the revenue. Therefore, the statement of owner's equity and the balance sheet are prepared to give the details of these assets and equities.

The **statement of owner's equity** reports the changes that have occurred in the owner's financial interest during the reporting period. This statement is prepared before the balance sheet so that the amount of the ending capital balance is available for presentation on the balance sheet. The statement of owner's equity for Arrow Accounting Services is shown in Figure 2–4.

FIGURE 2–4
Statement of Owner's Equity for Arrow Accounting Services

ARROW ACCOUNTING SERVICES Statement of Owner's Equity Month Ended December 31, 19X5		
John Arrow, Capital, December 1, 19X5		40 0 0 0 00
Net Income for December	11 2 0 0 00	
Less Withdrawals for December	1 0 0 0 00	
Increase in Capital		10 2 0 0 00
John Arrow, Capital, December 31, 19X5		50 2 0 0 00

The net income or net loss figure is the connecting link that explains the change in owner's equity during the period. Notice that the income statement is prepared before the statement of owner's equity and the balance sheet. The net income or loss is needed to complete the statement of owner's equity. The statement of owner's equity is prepared to update the change in owner's equity during the period covered by the statements. Once updated, the owner's equity balance is reported on the balance sheet.

In addition to net income and net loss, the statement of owner's equity is also affected by additional investments by the owner. Since John Arrow did not make any additional investments during the month of December, this item does not appear in the preceding statement of owner's equity.

Additional investments and net income increase owner's equity. Additional investments may be in cash or other assets such as equipment. If an investment is made in a form other than cash, the investment should be recorded at its fair market value. **Fair market value** is the present worth of an asset or the price the asset would bring if sold on the open market. Withdrawals and net losses decrease owner's equity.

The final totals in the fundamental accounting equation for the asset and liability accounts plus the statement of owner's equity supply the figures that are required for preparing a balance sheet for Arrow Accounting Services as of December 31, 19X5.

	Assets					= Liabilities +	Owner's Equity		
	Cash	+ Accts. Rec.	+ Supplies	+ Prepaid Rent	+ Equip.	= Accounts Payable	+ J. Arrow, Capital	+ Revenue	− Expenses
New balances	$16,200	+ $2,000	+ $1,000	+ $20,000	+ $15,000	= $4,000	+ $39,000	+ $14,000	− $2,800
	$54,200					$54,200			

The balance sheet in Figure 2–5 is prepared from the figures in the above equation and from the statement of owner's equity. The balance sheet shows the types and amounts of property that the business owns (assets), the amounts owed to creditors (liabilities), and the amount of the owner's equity on the reporting date.

In preparing a balance sheet, keep in mind the following details:

1. The three-line heading of the balance sheet gives the firm's name (who), the title of the report (what), and the date of the report (when). Every balance sheet heading contains these three lines.
2. On this form of balance sheet, the account form, the total of the assets always appears on the same horizontal line as the total of the liabilities and owner's equity.
3. When financial statements are handwritten or typed on accounting paper with ruled columns, dollar signs are usually omitted. However, in typewritten or computer-generated statements that are not prepared on ruled forms, dollar signs are generally used with the first amount in each column and with each total.
4. A single line is used to show that the figures above it are being added or subtracted. Double lines are used under the final figure in a column or section of a report.

Figure 2–6 shows the process of preparing financial statements.

FIGURE 2–5
Balance Sheet of Arrow Accounting Services

ARROW ACCOUNTING SERVICES
Balance Sheet
December 31, 19X5

Assets		*Liabilities*	
Cash	16 200 00	*Accounts Payable*	4 000 00
Accounts Receivable	2 000 00		
Supplies	1 000 00		
Prepaid Rent	20 000 00	*Owner's Equity*	
Equipment	15 000 00	*John Arrow, Capital*	50 200 00
Total Assets	54 200 00	*Total Liabilities and Owner's Equity*	54 200 00

FIGURE 2–6
Process for Preparing Financial Statements

Step 1: Prepare the Income Statement

ARROW ACCOUNTING SERVICES
Income Statement
Month Ended December 31, 19X5

Revenue		
Fees Income		14 000 00
Expenses		
Salaries Expense	2 500 00	
Utilities Expense	300 00	
Total Expenses		2 800 00
Net Income		11 200 00

Net income (or loss) is transferred to the statement of owner's equity.

Step 2: Prepare the Statement of Owner's Equity

ARROW ACCOUNTING SERVICES
Statement of Owner's Equity
Month Ended December 31, 19X5

John Arrow, Capital, December 1, 19X5		40 000 00
Net Income for December	11 200 00	
Less Withdrawals for December	1 000 00	
Increase in Capital		10 200 00
John Arrow, Capital, December 31, 19X5		50 200 00

The ending capital balance is transferred to the balance sheet.

Step 3: Prepare the Balance Sheet

ARROW ACCOUNTING SERVICES
Balance Sheet
December 31, 19X5

Assets		*Liabilities*	
Cash	16 200 00	*Accounts Payable*	4 000 00
Accounts Receivable	2 000 00		
Supplies	1 000 00		
Prepaid Rent	20 000 00	*Owner's Equity*	
Equipment	15 000 00	*John Arrow, Capital*	50 200 00
Total Assets	54 200 00	*Total Liabilities and Owner's Equity*	54 200 00

THE IMPORTANCE OF FINANCIAL STATEMENTS

Preparing financial statements is one of the accountant's most important jobs. All figures must be checked and double-checked to make sure they are accurate. As we discussed previously, the figures shown on the balance sheet and the income statement are used by business managers and owners to control current operations and to make plans for the future. Creditors, prospective investors, governmental agencies, and many others are also vitally interested in the profits of the business and in the asset and equity structure. Each day millions of business decisions are made on the basis of financial reports.

MANAGERIAL IMPLICATIONS

Accurate and informative financial records and statements are necessary so that businesspeople can make sound decisions. Accounting information helps to determine whether a profit has been made, the amount of the assets on hand, the amount owed to creditors, and the amount of owner's equity. Any well-run and efficiently managed business will have a good accounting system to provide timely and useful information.

SELF-REVIEW

1. What are withdrawals and how do they affect the basic accounting equation?
2. If an owner gives personal tools to the business, how is the transaction recorded?
3. Which financial statement is prepared first? Why?
4. If one side of the fundamental accounting equation is decreased, what will happen to the other side? Why?
5. What items are included in the headings of financial statements?

Answers to Self-Review

1. Withdrawals are funds taken from the business to pay for personal expenses. Withdrawals are not business expenses but they decrease the owner's equity in the business.
2. The transaction should be recorded as an additional investment by the owner. The tools should be recorded on the basis of their fair market value.
3. The income statement is prepared first because the net income or loss is needed to complete the statement of owner's equity. The statement of owner's equity is prepared next to update the change in owner's equity. The balance sheet is prepared last.
4. The opposite side of the accounting equation will decrease because a decrease in assets results in a corresponding decrease in either a liability or the owner's equity.
5. The heading of financial statements includes the firm's name (who), the title of the statement (what), and the time period covered by the report (when).

CHAPTER 2

Review and Applications

CHAPTER SUMMARY

The accounting process begins with the analysis of business transactions. The accountant analyzes each transaction to determine its effect on the fundamental accounting equation: *assets equal liabilities plus owner's equity.*

Changes in owner's equity during an accounting period result from revenue and expenses. These changes are summarized on the income statement. The difference between revenue and expenses is the net income or net loss of the business for the period.

Changes in owner's equity for the period are summarized on the statement of owner's equity. The net income for the period and additional investments by the owner increase owner's equity. A net loss for the period decreases owner's equity. Withdrawals by the owner also decrease owner's equity.

The balance sheet is a statement that shows the assets, liabilities, and owner's equity on a given date. The balance sheet is prepared after the statement of owner's equity. The ending owner's equity appears on the balance sheet. The balance sheet reflects the assets of the business and the creditors' and owner's equities in those assets.

GLOSSARY OF NEW TERMS

Accounts payable (p. 25) Amounts a company must pay in the future

Accounts receivable (p. 29) Claims for future collection from customers

Assets (p. 26) Property owned by a business

Balance sheet (p. 26) A formal report of a business's financial condition on a certain date; reports the assets, liabilities, and owner's equity of the business

Break even (p. 36) A point at which revenue equals expenses

Business transaction (p. 22) A financial event that changes the resources of a business

Capital (p. 23) Financial investment in a business; also called equity

Equity (p. 23) An owner's financial interest in a business

Expense (p. 28) An outflow of cash, use of other assets, or incurring a liability

Fair market value (p. 37) The present worth of an asset or the price the asset would bring if sold on the open market

Fundamental accounting equation (p. 28) The relationship between assets and liabilities plus owner's equity

Income statement (p. 34) A formal report of business operations covering a specific period of time; also called a profit and loss statement or a statement of income and expenses

Liabilities (p. 26) Debts or obligations of a business

Net income (p. 35) The result of an excess of revenue over expenses

Net loss (p. 36) The result of an excess of expenses over revenue

On account (p. 25) An arrangement to allow payment at a later date; also called a charge account or open-account credit

Owner's equity (p. 26) The financial interest of the owner of a business; also called proprietorship or net worth

Revenue (p. 28) An inflow of money or other assets that results from the sales of goods or services or from the use of money or property; also called income

Statement of owner's equity (p. 37) A formal report of changes that occurred in the owner's financial interest during a reporting period

Withdrawals (p. 32) Funds taken from the business by the owner for personal use

REVIEW QUESTIONS

1. What are assets, liabilities, and owner's equity?
2. What information does the balance sheet contain?
3. What is the fundamental accounting equation?
4. What is revenue?
5. What are expenses?
6. Describe the effects of each of the following business transactions on assets, liabilities, and owner's equity.
   a. Bought equipment on credit.
   b. Paid salaries to employees.
   c. Sold services for cash.
   d. Paid cash to a creditor.
   e. Bought furniture for cash.
   f. Sold services on credit.
7. What information does the income statement contain?
8. How is net income determined?
9. What information is shown in the heading of a financial statement?
10. Why does the third line of the heading differ on the balance sheet and the income statement?
11. What information does the statement of owner's equity contain?
12. How does net income affect owner's equity?

MANAGERIAL FOCUS

1. How does an accounting system help managers control operations and make sound decisions?
2. Why should managers be concerned with changes in the amount of creditors' claims against the business?

3. Is it reasonable to expect that all new businesses will have a net income from the first month's operations? From the first year's operations?
4. After examining financial data for a monthly period, the owner of a small business expressed surprise that the firm's cash balance had decreased during the month even though there was a substantial net income. Do you think that this owner is right to expect cash to increase whenever there is a net income? Why or why not?

EXERCISES

EXERCISE 2–1 (Obj. 1, 2)

Completing the accounting equation. The fundamental accounting equation for several businesses follows. Supply the missing amounts.

Assets	=	Liabilities	+	Owner's Equity
1. $87,000	=	$15,000	+	$?
2. $69,200	=	$13,500	+	$?
3. $52,000	=	$?	+	$45,900
4. $?	=	$3,500	+	$28,500
5. $25,800	=	$?	+	$18,700

EXERCISE 2–2 (Obj. 1, 2)

Determining accounting equation amounts. Just before Southside Medical Supply opened for business, French Taylor, the owner, had the following assets and liabilities. Determine the amounts that would appear in the firm's fundamental accounting equation (Assets = Liabilities + Owner's Equity).

Cash	$8,950	Laboratory Equipment	$21,250
Laboratory Supplies	1,200	Loan Payable	3,400
Accounts Payable	2,050		

EXERCISE 2–3 (Obj. 1, 2, 3)

Determining balance sheet amounts. The financial data shown below is for the dental practice of Dr. Susan Hand when she began operations on June 1, 19X2. Determine the amounts that would appear in Dr. Hand's balance sheet.

1. Owes $15,000 to the Macy Equipment Company.
2. Has cash balance of $5,650.
3. Has dental supplies of $2,340.
4. Owes $2,800 to the Wellton Furniture Company.
5. Has dental equipment of $23,700.
6. Has office furniture of $3,450.

EXERCISE 2–4 (Obj. 1, 2, 3)

Tutorial

Determining the effects of transactions on the accounting equation. Indicate the impact of each of the transactions below on the fundamental accounting equation (Assets = Liabilities + Owner's Equity) by placing a "+" to indicate an increase, and a "–" to indicate a decrease. The first transaction is entered as an example.

	Assets	=	Liabilities	+	Owner's Equity
Transaction 1	+		______		+

TRANSACTIONS

1. Owner invested $10,000 in the business.
2. Purchased $1,000 supplies on account.
3. Purchased equipment for $5,000 cash.
4. Paid $700 for rent.
5. Performed services for $1,200 cash.
6. Paid $200 for utilities.
7. Performed services for $1,500 on account.
8. Received $750 from charge customers.
9. Paid salaries of $1,200 to employees.
10. Paid $500 to a creditor on account.

EXERCISE 2–5
(Obj. 1, 2, 3)

Tutorial

Determining the effects of transactions on the accounting equation. The Professional Development Publishing Company had the transactions listed below during the month of April 19X3. Show how each transaction would be recorded in the accounting equation. Compute the totals at the end of the month. The headings to be used in the equation follow.

Assets							=	Liabilities	+	Owner's Equity				
Cash	+	Accounts Receivable	+	Equipment			=	Accounts Payable	+	A. Conn, Capital	+	Revenue	−	Expenses

TRANSACTIONS

1. Amos Conn started the business with a cash investment of $18,000.
2. Purchased equipment for $7,000 on credit.
3. Performed services for $900 in cash.
4. Purchased additional equipment for $1,500 in cash.
5. Performed services for $2,100 on credit.
6. Paid salaries of $1,600 to employees.
7. Received $700 cash from charge account customers.
8. Paid $3,500 to a creditor on account.

EXERCISE 2–6
(Obj. 1, 2, 3)

Identifying transactions. The following equation shows the effects of a number of transactions that took place at the Garden of Eden Landscaping Service during the month of August 19X3. Describe each transaction.

	Assets					=	Liabilities	+	Owner's Equity				
	Cash	+	Accounts Receivable	+	Equipment	=	Accounts Payable	+	Capital	+	Revenue	−	Expenses
Bal.	$12,000	+	$ 400	+	$25,000	=	$6,400	+	$31,000	+	0	−	0
1.	−600											−	600
2.		+	1,750							+	1,750		
3.	−1,500			+	1,500								
4.	−500						−500						
5.	+1,600									+	1,600		
6.	+800		−800										
7.	−1,300											−	1,300

EXERCISE 2–7
(Obj. 4)

Tutorial

Computing net income or net loss. The Office Supply Service Center had the following revenue and expenses during the month ended June 30, 19X4. Did the firm earn a net income or incur a net loss for the period? What was the amount?

Fees for computer repairs	$8,200
Rent Expense	900
Salaries Expense	4,275
Telephone Expense	180
Fees for typewriter repairs	1,260
Utilities Expense	375

EXERCISE 2–8
(Obj. 4)

Tutorial

Computing net income or net loss. On December 1, 19X3, Paul Vazquez opened an engineering firm. During December his firm had the following transactions involving revenue and expenses. Did the firm earn a net income or incur a net loss for the period? What was the amount?

Paid $800 for rent.
Provided services for $1,050 in cash.
Paid $150 for telephone service.
Paid salaries of $1,900 to employees.
Provided services for $1,300 on credit.
Paid $100 for office cleaning service.

EXERCISE 2–9
(Obj. 4)

Preparing an income statement. At the beginning of September 19X5, Jill Reed started Reed's Financial Services, a firm that offers advice about investing and managing money. On September 30, 19X5, the accounting records of the business showed the following information. Prepare an income statement for the month of September 19X5.

Cash	$7,600	Fees Income	$16,700
Accounts Receivable	600	Rent Expense	1,050
Office Supplies	400	Salaries Expense	3,400
Office Equipment	8,550	Telephone Expense	200
Accounts Payable	700	Withdrawals	1,000
Jill Reed, Capital, September 1, 19X5	5,400		

EXERCISE 2–10
(Obj. 5)

Preparing a statement of owner's equity and a balance sheet. Using the information provided in Exercise 2–9, prepare a statement of owner's equity and a balance sheet for Reed's Financial Services as of September 30, 19X5.

PROBLEMS

PROBLEM SET A

PROBLEM 2–1A
(Obj. 1, 2, 3)

Analyzing the effects of transactions on the accounting equation. On July 1, 19X3, John Holloway established Perfect Visions, a photography studio.

Instructions Analyze the following transactions. Record in equation form the changes in assets, liabilities, and owner's equity. (Use plus, minus, and equal signs.)

TRANSACTIONS

1. The owner invested $18,000 in cash to begin the business.
2. Paid $4,590 in cash for the purchase of equipment.
3. Purchased additional equipment for $2,800 on credit.
4. Paid $2,250 in cash to creditors.
5. The owner made an additional investment of $5,600 in cash.
6. Performed services for $1,600 in cash.
7. Performed services for $950 on account.
8. Paid $650 for rent expense.
9. Received $425 in cash from credit clients.
10. Paid $1,250 in cash for office supplies.
11. The owner withdrew $1,000 in cash for personal expenses.

PROBLEM 2–2A
(Obj. 1, 2, 3)

Tutorial

Analyzing the effects of transactions on the accounting equation. Carolyn McRae is an architect who specializes in developing plans to remodel old buildings. At the beginning of June 19X6, her firm's financial records showed the following assets, liabilities, and owner's equity.

Cash	$ 5,175	Accounts Payable	$ 1,950
Accounts Receivable	3,500	Carolyn McRae, Capital	22,500
Office Furniture	7,700	Revenue	9,300
Auto	13,000	Expenses	4,375

Instructions Set up an accounting equation form using the balances given above. Record the effects of the following transactions in the equation. (Use plus, minus, and equal signs.) Record new balances after each transaction has been entered. Prove the equality of the two sides of the final equation on a separate sheet.

TRANSACTIONS

1. Performed services for $1,200 on credit.
2. Paid $250 in cash for a new office chair.
3. Received $750 in cash from credit clients.
4. Paid $80 in cash for telephone service.
5. Sent a check for $300 in partial payment of the amount due creditors.
6. Paid salaries of $1,850 in cash.
7. Sent a check for $125 to pay electric bill.
8. Performed services for $1,950 in cash.
9. Paid $430 in cash for auto repairs.
10. Performed services for $1,750 on account.

PROBLEM 2–3A
(Obj. 5)

Preparing a balance sheet. Zant's Car Repair Service is owned by Jim Zant. The equation below shows the business's transactions during February 19X5.

Instructions Use the following figures to prepare a balance sheet dated February 28, 19X5. (You will need to compute the owner's equity.)

Cash	$ 7,625
Supplies	1,390
Accounts Receivable	2,500
Equipment	17,800
Accounts Payable	5,200

PROBLEM 2–4A (Obj. 4, 5)

Preparing an income statement, a statement of owner's equity, and a balance sheet. The following equation shows the transactions of the Everlasting Lawn Care Service during February 19X5. The business is owned by Joel Thomas.

	Assets				= Liabilities	+ Owner's Equity		
	Cash	+ Accounts Receivable	+ Supplies	+ Equip.	= Accounts Payable	+ Joel Thomas, Capital	+ Revenue	− Expenses
Balances, Feb. 1	3,500	500	1,200	8,200	1,500	11,900	0	0
Paid for utilities	−220							−220
New balances	3,280	500	1,200	8,200	1,500	11,900	0	220
Sold services for cash	+1,220						+1,220	
New balances	4,500	500	1,200	8,200	1,500	11,900	1,220	220
Paid a creditor	−400				−400			
New balances	4,100	500	1,200	8,200	1,100	11,900	1,220	220
Sold services on credit		+600					+600	
New balances	4,100	1,100	1,200	8,200	1,100	11,900	1,820	220
Paid salaries	−2,100							−2,100
New balances	2,000	1,100	1,200	8,200	1,100	11,900	1,820	2,320
Paid telephone bill	−75							−75
New balances	1,925	1,100	1,200	8,200	1,100	11,900	1,820	2,395
Withdrew cash for personal expenses	−500					−500		
New balances	1,425	1,100	1,200	8,200	1,100	11,400	1,820	2,395

Instructions Analyze each transaction carefully. Prepare an income statement and a statement of owner's equity for the month. Prepare a balance sheet for February 28, 19X5. List the expenses in detail on the income statement.

PROBLEM SET B

PROBLEM 2–1B (Obj. 1, 2, 3)

Tutorial

Analyzing the effects of transactions on the accounting equation. On September 1, 19X1, Rosa Maria Lopez opened the Little Red Riding Hood Nursery School.

Instructions Analyze the following transactions. Use the fundamental accounting equation form to record the changes in property, claims of creditors, and owner's equity. (Use plus, minus, and equal signs.)

TRANSACTIONS

1. The owner invested $12,000 in cash to begin the business.
2. Purchased equipment for $7,000 in cash.
3. Purchased $1,500 of additional equipment on credit.
4. Paid $750 in cash to creditors.
5. The owner made an additional investment of $2,500 in cash.
6. Performed services for $1,560 in cash.
7. Performed services for $780 on account.
8. Paid $900 for rent expense.
9. Received $550 in cash from credit clients.
10. Paid $1,300 in cash for office supplies.
11. The owner withdrew $1,000 in cash for personal expenses.

PROBLEM 2-2B
(Obj. 1, 2, 3)

Tutorial

Analyzing the effects of transactions on the accounting equation. Heather Turner owns Turner's Bookkeeping Service. At the beginning of September 19X3, her firm's financial records showed the following assets, liabilities, and owner's equity.

Cash	$3,875	Accounts Payable	$ 600
Accounts Receivable	750	Heather Turner, Capital	6,000
Supplies	800	Revenue	3,000
Office Furniture	2,500	Expenses	1,675

Instructions

Set up an equation using the balances given above. Record the effects of the following transactions in the equation. (Use plus, minus, and equal signs.) Record new balances after each transaction has been entered. Prove the equality of the two sides of the final equation on a separate sheet.

TRANSACTIONS

1. Performed services for $500 on credit.
2. Paid $180 in cash for utilities.
3. Performed services for $600 in cash.
4. Paid $100 in cash for office cleaning service.
5. Sent a check for $300 to a creditor.
6. Paid $120 in cash for the telephone bill.
7. Issued checks for $1,030 to pay salaries.
8. Performed services for $890 in cash.
9. Purchased additional supplies for $90 on credit.
10. Received $400 in cash from credit clients.

PROBLEM 2-3B
(Obj. 5)

Preparing a balance sheet. Ginger Chan plans to open the Information Systems Company on December 1, 19X5. This firm will develop and update accounting systems for business clients.

Instructions

Use the following figures to prepare a balance sheet dated December 1, 19X5. (You will need to compute the owner's equity.)

Cash	$11,500
Computers	75,000
Office Supplies	2,500
Office Furniture	12,000
Accounts Payable	28,000

PROBLEM 2–4B (Obj. 4, 5) **Preparing an income statement, a statement of owner's equity, and a balance sheet.** The equation below shows the transactions of Jill Peters, Attorney-at-Law, during March 19X5. This law practice is owned by Jill Peters.

	Assets				= Liabilities +	Owner's Equity		
	Cash	+ Accounts Receivable	+ Supplies	+ Equip.	= Accounts Payable	+ Jill Peters, Capital	+ Revenue	− Expenses
Balances, Mar. 1	1,200 +	300 +	900 +	1,500 =	200 +	3,700 +	0 −	0
Paid for utilities	−100							−100
New balances	1,100 +	300 +	900 +	1,500 =	200 +	3,700 +	0 −	100
Sold services for cash	+1,000						+ 1,000	
New balances	2,100 +	300 +	900 +	1,500 =	200 +	3,700 +	1,000 −	100
Paid a creditor	−100				−100			
New balances	2,000 +	300 +	900 +	1,500 =	100 +	3,700 +	1,000 −	100
Sold services on credit		+800					+800	
New balances	2,000 +	1,100 +	900 +	1,500 =	100 +	3,700 +	1,800 −	100
Paid salaries	−900							−900
New balances	1,100 +	1,100 +	900 +	1,500 =	100 +	3,700 +	1,800 −	1,000
Paid telephone bill	−100							−100
New balances	1,000 +	1,100 +	900 +	1,500 =	100 +	3,700 +	1,800 −	1,100
Withdrew cash for personal expenses	−200					−200		
New balances	800 +	1,100 +	900 +	1,500 =	100 +	3,500 +	1,800 −	1,100

Instructions Analyze each transaction carefully. Prepare an income statement and statement of owner's equity for the month. Prepare a balance sheet for March 31, 19X5. List the expenses in detail on the income statement.

CHALLENGE PROBLEM

The account balances for John Day, Attorney-at-Law, on April 30, 19X6, are reflected below in random order.

Cash	$6,500	Accounts Receivable	$2,820
Rent Expense	1,100	Advertising Expense	900
Fees Earned	9,500	John Day, Capital, April 1	?
Salaries Expense	3,000	Machinery	8,500
Accounts Payable	3,200	John Day, Drawing	1,200

Instructions Using the accounting equation form, determine the balance for John Day, Capital, April 1, 19X6. Prepare an income statement, a statement of owner's equity, and a balance sheet as of April 30, 19X6. List the expenses on the income statement in alphabetical order.

CRITICAL THINKING PROBLEM

Nancy Ford opened an exercise studio called the Get Fit Exercise Studio at the beginning of October of the current year. It is now the end of October, and Nancy is trying to determine whether she made a profit during her first month of operations. You offer to help her and ask to see her accounting records. She shows you a shoe box and tells you that every piece of paper pertaining to the business is in that box.

As you go through the material in the shoe box, you discover the following:

1. *Receipt* for $1,500 for October's rent on the exercise studio.
2. *Bank deposit slips* totaling $1,570 for money collected from customers who attended exercise classes.
3. *Invoice* for $12,000 for exercise equipment. The first payment is not due until November 30.
4. *Bill* for $450 from the maintenance service that cleans the studio. Nancy has not yet paid this bill.
5. *Parking tickets* for $25. Nancy says she was in a hurry one morning to get to the studio on time and forgot to put money in the parking meter.
6. *Handwritten list* of customers and fees for the classes they have taken. As customers pay, Nancy crosses their names off the list. Fees not crossed off the list amount to $360.
7. *Credit card receipt* for $100 for printing of flyers advertising the studio. For convenience, Nancy used her personal credit card.
8. *Credit card receipt* for $150 for two warm-up suits Nancy bought to wear at the studio. She also put this purchase on her personal credit card.

Help Nancy prepare an income statement for the first month of operation of the Get Fit Exercise Studio. How would you evaluate the results of Nancy's first month of operation? What advice would you give Nancy concerning her system of accounting?

CHAPTER

3 Analyzing Business Transactions Using T Accounts

OBJECTIVES

1. Set up T accounts for assets, liabilities, owner's equity, revenue, and expenses.
2. Analyze business transactions and enter them in the accounts affected.
3. Determine the balance of an account.
4. Prepare a trial balance from T accounts.
5. Prepare an income statement, a statement of owner's equity, and a balance sheet.
6. Develop a chart of accounts.
7. Define the accounting terms new to this chapter.

In Chapter 2 you saw how the accounting equation is used to analyze a firm's transactions and determine their effects on the firm's assets, liabilities, and owner's equity. You also saw how the firm's financial position is reported on the balance sheet and how the results of its operations for a period of time are reported on the income statement.

In this chapter you will learn how to keep records of the changes that are caused by business transactions. These records are an essential part of all accounting systems.

NEW TERMS

Account balance ▪ Accounts ▪ Chart of accounts ▪ Classification ▪ Credit ▪ Debit ▪ Double-entry system ▪ Drawing account ▪ Footing ▪ Normal balance ▪ Permanent account ▪ Slide ▪ T account ▪ Temporary account ▪ Transposition ▪ Trial balance

ACCOUNTS FOR ASSETS, LIABILITIES, AND OWNER'S EQUITY

OBJECTIVE 1
Set up T accounts for assets, liabilities, owner's equity, revenue, and expenses.

The accounting equation is a tool for analyzing the effects of business transactions. It would be awkward, though, to record every transaction in the equation format if a business had many transactions. Instead, separate written records called **accounts** are kept for the business's assets, liabilities, and owner's equity. Accounts are kept so that financial information can be analyzed, recorded, classified, summarized, and reported. Accounts are identified by their account **classification;** that is, as asset accounts (the property a business owns), liability accounts (the debts of the business), or owner's equity accounts (the owner's financial interest in the business). The title of each account describes the type of property, the debt, or the financial interest.

One type of account that accountants use to analyze transactions is a **T account.** This account consists of two lines, one vertical and one horizontal, that resemble the letter **T.** The title of the account is written on the horizontal (top) line. Increases and decreases in the account are entered on different sides of the vertical line.

T accounts for assets, liabilities and owner's equity follow.

ASSETS	
+ Record increases	– Record decreases

LIABILITIES	
– Record decreases	+ Record increases

OWNER'S EQUITY	
– Record decreases	+ Record increases

Recording a Cash Investment

OBJECTIVE 2
Analyze business transactions and enter them in the accounts affected.

Asset accounts record the items of value owned by a business. The location of items in the fundamental accounting equation determines where amounts are recorded in the T accounts. For instance, when John Arrow invested $40,000 in the business, the office manager for Arrow Accounting Services, Virginia Richey, set up a separate account for the asset Cash. The cash investment of $40,000 **(a)** is entered on the left side of the account because assets always appear on the left side of the accounting equation. The plus and minus signs shown below in the T account do not normally appear in the accounts. However, they are presented here to help you identify increases (+) and decreases (–) in accounts.

Cash	
+	–
(a) 40,000	

▲ **REMEMBER!**

ASSET ACCOUNTS	
+ Record increases	– Record decreases

Since increases are recorded on the left side of asset accounts, decreases are recorded on the right side.

Owner's equity accounts show the financial interest of the owner of the business. The account called John Arrow, Capital, is used to record John Arrow's $40,000 investment. Because owner's equity always appears on the right side of the accounting equation, Richey entered the opening balance of $40,000 **(b)** on the right side of the John Arrow, Capital account.

John Arrow, Capital	
−	+
	(b) 40,000

▲ **REMEMBER!**

OWNER'S EQUITY ACCOUNT

−	+
Record decreases	Record increases

Since the right side of the owner's equity account is used to record increases in owner's equity, the left side must be used to record decreases.

Recording Prepaid Rent

When Arrow Accounting Services rented its facilities, the lease specified that eight months' rent must be paid in advance. Arrow issued a check for $20,000 to make the necessary payment. As a result, the firm obtained the right to occupy the facilities for an eight-month period. This right is accounted for as property—an asset. Thus the transaction is analyzed as follows.

c. The firm acquired an asset, totaling $20,000, in the form of prepaid rent.
d. The firm paid $20,000 in cash.

To record the prepaid rent (c), a new asset account called Prepaid Rent is opened; the $20,000 is entered on the left, or increase, side of the Prepaid Rent account.

Prepaid Rent	
+	−
(c) 20,000	

Since the cash payment (d) reduced the firm's cash balance, the $20,000 is recorded on the right, or decrease, side of the Cash account.

Cash	
+	−
(a) 40,000	**(d) 20,000**

Recording a Cash Purchase of Equipment

When Arrow Accounting Services purchased equipment for $10,000 in cash, the transaction was analyzed as follows.

e. The firm purchased new assets in the form of equipment at a cost of $10,000.
f. The firm paid $10,000 in cash.

To record the purchase of equipment (e), a new asset account for equipment was opened and $10,000 was entered on the left, or increase, side.

Equipment	
+	–
(e) 10,000	

The payment of $10,000 in cash (f) is entered on the right side of the Cash account because decreases in assets are recorded on the right side.

Cash	
+	–
(a) 40,000	(d) 20,000
	(f) 10,000

Recording a Credit Purchase of Equipment

▲ **REMEMBER!**

LIABILITY ACCOUNTS	
–	+
Record decreases	Record increases

Liabilities are amounts owed by a business to its creditors. Like owner's equity, liabilities always appear on the right side of the accounting equation. Thus increases are recorded on the right side of liability accounts, and decreases are recorded on the left side.

When Arrow Accounting Services bought a copy machine, a fax machine, calculators, and other necessary equipment for $5,000 on credit from Organ, Inc., the transaction was analyzed as follows.

g. The firm purchased new assets in the form of equipment at a cost of $5,000.

h. The firm owed $5,000 as an account payable to Organ, Inc.

The $5,000 increase in equipment (g) is entered on the left side of the Equipment account.

Equipment	
+	–
(e) 10,000	
(g) 5,000	

▲ **REMEMBER!**

The right side of liability accounts is used for increases; the left side is used for decreases.

A new account is opened for the liability Accounts Payable to record the amount owed to Organ, Inc. (h). The $5,000 is entered on the right, or increase, side of this account because liabilities appear on the right side of the accounting equation.

Accounts Payable	
–	+
	(h) 5,000

Recording a Cash Purchase of Supplies

When Arrow Accounting Services purchased supplies for $1,000 in cash, the transaction was analyzed as follows.

i. The firm purchased new assets in the form of supplies at a cost of $1,000.
j. The firm paid $1,000 in cash.

To record this purchase of supplies (i), a new asset account for supplies was opened and $1,000 was entered on the left, or increase, side.

Supplies	
+	−
(i) 1,000	

The payment of $1,000 in cash (j) is entered on the right side of the Cash account because decreases in assets are recorded on the right side of asset accounts.

Cash	
+	−
(a) 40,000	(d) 20,000
	(f) 10,000
	(j) 1,000

Recording Payment to a Creditor

On November 30, 19X5, the business paid $1,000 to Organ, Inc., to apply against the debt of $5,000 shown in Accounts Payable. The analysis of this transaction follows.

k. The firm paid $1,000 in cash.
l. The claim of Organ, Inc., against the firm was reduced by $1,000.

The decrease in cash (k) is entered on the right (decrease) side of the Cash account. The decrease in the liability (l) is entered on the left (decrease) side of the Accounts Payable account.

Cash	
+	−
(a) 40,000	(d) 20,000
	(f) 10,000
	(j) 1,000
	(k) 1,000

Accounts Payable	
−	+
(l) 1,000	(h) 5,000

OBJECTIVE 3
Determine the balance of an account.

An **account balance** is the difference between the amounts recorded on the two sides of an account. It is computed by first adding the figures on each side of the account. When the column is added, the total is entered in small pencil figures called a **footing.** The smaller total is subtracted from the larger, and the result is the account balance. If the total of the figures on the right side is greater than the total on the left side, the balance is recorded on the right side. If the total of the figures on the left side is greater, the balance is recorded on the left side. If an account contains only one amount, that figure is the balance. If an account contains entries on only one side, the total of those entries is the account balance.

For example, the total of the figures on the left side of Arrow Accounting Service's Cash account on November 30, 19X5, is $40,000. The total of the figures on the right side is $32,000. By subtracting the footing of $32,000 from $40,000, we obtain the account balance of $8,000. The account balance is recorded on the increase (left) side of the account. The account balance for cash is shown below.

Cash	
+	–
(a) 40,000	(d) 20,000
	(f) 10,000
	(j) 1,000
	(k) 1,000
	32,000 ← Footing
Bal. 8,000	

The balance of an account is normally recorded on the increase side of the account. The increase side of the account is the **normal balance** of the account. As previously discussed, the increase side of an account depends upon whether the account is classified as an asset, liability, or owner's equity account. A summary of the procedures to increase or decrease accounts and the normal balance of accounts in the basic accounting equation follows.

ASSETS		=	LIABILITIES		+	OWNER'S EQUITY	
+	–		–	+		–	+
Increase (Normal Bal.)	Decrease		Decrease	Increase (Normal Bal.)		Decrease	Increase (Normal Bal.)

A summary of the account balances for Arrow Accounting Services is shown in Figure 3–1. The firm's position after these transactions can be given in equation form.

Assets								**= Liabilities**		**+ Owner's Equity**
Cash	+	Supplies	+	Prepaid Rent	+	Equipment	=	Accounts Payable	+	John Arrow, Capital
$8,000	+	$1,000	+	$20,000	+	$15,000	=	$4,000	+	$40,000

A formal balance sheet prepared for November 30, 19X5, is shown in Figure 3–2.

FIGURE 3–1
T-Account Balances for Arrow Accounting Services

ASSETS = **LIABILITIES** + **OWNER'S EQUITY**

ASSETS

Cash	
+	–
(a) 40,000	(d) 20,000
	(f) 10,000
	(j) 1,000
	(k) 1,000
Bal. 8,000	32,000

LIABILITIES

Accounts Payable	
–	+
(l) 1,000	(h) 5,000
	Bal. 4,000

OWNER'S EQUITY

John Arrow, Capital	
–	+
	(b) 40,000

Supplies	
+	–
(i) 1,000	

Prepaid Rent	
+	–
(c) 20,000	

Equipment	
+	–
(e) 10,000	
(g) 5,000	
Bal. 15,000	

FIGURE 3–2
Balance Sheet for Arrow Accounting Services

ARROW ACCOUNTING SERVICES
Balance Sheet
November 30, 19X5

Assets		*Liabilities*	
Cash	8 0 0 0 00	*Accounts Payable*	4 0 0 0 00
Supplies	1 0 0 0 00		
Prepaid Rent	20 0 0 0 00	*Owner's Equity*	
Equipment	15 0 0 0 00	*John Arrow, Capital*	40 0 0 0 00
Total Assets	44 0 0 0 00	*Total Liabilities and Owner's Equity*	44 0 0 0 00

SELF-REVIEW

1. On which side of asset, liability, and owner's equity accounts are increases recorded?
2. On which side of asset, liability and owner's equity accounts are decreases recorded?
3. What is a footing?
4. What is meant by the normal balance of an account? Which are normal balance sides for asset, liability, and owner's equity accounts?
5. Foot and find the balance of this account.

Cash

+	−
30,000	10,000
7,000	5,000
	2,000
	4,000

Answers to Self-Review

1. Increases in asset, liability, and owner's equity accounts are recorded on the same side on which the account appears in the fundamental accounting equation. Increases in asset accounts are recorded on the left side; increases in liability and owner's equity accounts are recorded on the right side.
2. Decreases in asset accounts are recorded on the right side; decreases in liability and owner's equity accounts are recorded on the left side.
3. A footing is the sum of several entries on either side of an account that is entered in small pencil figures.
4. The increase side of an account is the normal balance side of the account. The normal balance of an asset account is on the left side. The normal balance of liability and owner's equity accounts is on the right side.
5. The balance of the account is $16,000.

Cash

+	−
30,000	10,000
7,000	5,000
37,000	2,000
	4,000
	21,000
Bal. 16,000	

ACCOUNTS FOR REVENUE AND EXPENSES

Some owner's equity accounts can be further classified as revenue or expense accounts. Many business transactions involve revenue and expenses. Separate accounts are used to record these amounts. Let's examine the revenue and expense transactions of Arrow Accounting Services for December to see how they are recorded.

Recording Revenue from Services Sold for Cash

During December the business earned a total of $10,500 in revenue from clients who paid cash for bookkeeping and accounting services. The office manager made the following analysis.

m. The firm received $10,500 in cash.
n. The owner's equity increased by $10,500 because of this inflow of assets from revenue.

Richey recorded the receipt of cash (m) by entering $10,500 on the left (increase) side of the asset account Cash.

Cash	
+	–
Bal. 8,000	
(m) 10,500	

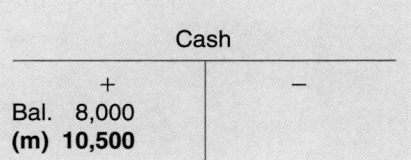

How is the increase in owner's equity recorded? One way would be to record the $10,500 on the right side of the John Arrow, Capital account. However, the preferred way is to keep the revenue figures separate from the owner's investment until the end of the month or until financial reports are prepared. Therefore, Richey opens a new account called Fees Income (a revenue account). Remember that revenue is a subdivision of owner's equity. At this point in its operations, Arrow Accounting Services needs just one revenue account, which is called Fees Income. The title of this account describes the specific type of revenue recorded in it. The revenue subdivision is used to classify and summarize various kinds of revenue of a business.

The $10,500 of revenue (n) is entered on the right side of the Fees Income account because revenue increases owner's equity and an owner's equity account is increased on the right side.

Fees Income	
–	+
	(n) 10,500

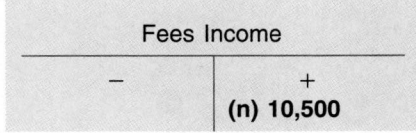

Since the right side of the revenue account is used to record increases, the left side is used to record decreases. Decreases in a revenue account may be required by corrections, by transfers to other accounts, or by refunds. However, such entries are not required often.

Different accounts are used for different types of revenue. For instance, in a business where goods are sold, an accountant would set up a revenue account called Sales. When more than one revenue account is used, the accounts are classified under the heading *Revenue* on the income statement, and the total of their balances would be the total operating revenue of the business for the accounting period.

Recording Revenue from Services Sold on Credit

During December Arrow Accounting Services also earned revenue of $3,500 from charge account clients. The office manager's analysis showed the following effects.

o. The firm obtained a new asset—accounts receivable of $3,500.
p. The owner's equity was increased by $3,500 of revenue.

To record this transaction, Richey first opened a new asset account called Accounts Receivable and entered the $3,500 (o) on the left (increase) side of the account. Richey entered the $3,500 increase in owner's equity (p) on the right (increase) side of the Fees Income account.

▲ REMEMBER!

REVENUE ACCOUNTS

–	+
Record decreases	Record increases

Accounts Receivable

+	–
(o) 3,500	

Fees Income

–	+
	(n) 10,500
	(p) 3,500

Recording Collections from Accounts Receivable

When charge account clients paid a total of $1,500 to apply to their accounts, Richey made the following analysis.

q. The firm received $1,500 in cash.
r. Accounts receivable decreased by $1,500.

Recording this information involved the use of two asset accounts. Richey entered the $1,500 increase in cash (q) on the left side of the Cash account and the $1,500 decrease in accounts receivable (r) on the right side of the Accounts Receivable account. Notice that there is no revenue from this transaction. The revenue was entered when the sales on credit were recorded (p).

Cash

+	–
Bal. 8,000	
(m) 10,500	
(q) 1,500	

Accounts Receivable

+	–
(o) 3,500	**(r) 1,500**

Recording an Expense for Salaries

Like other firms, Arrow Accounting Services had expenses in running its business. The first expense was for employees' salaries of $2,500. The office manager determined that this expense had the following effects.

s. The payment of $2,500 for salaries reduced the asset Cash.
t. Expenses increased by $2,500, specifically the Salaries Expense account.

The decrease in cash (s) is recorded on the right (decrease) side of the asset account Cash.

Cash	
+	−
Bal. 8,000	**(s) 2,500**
(m) 10,500	
(q) 1,500	

The decrease in owner's equity that results from the expense could be entered on the left (decrease) side of the John Arrow, Capital account. However, the preferred way is to keep expenses separate from the owner's equity account until the end of the month, or until financial reports are prepared. Like revenue, expenses are a subdivision of owner's equity. This subdivision is used to classify and summarize the various costs of operating the business.

A new account called Salaries Expense is opened for Arrow Accounting Services. The account title describes the specific type of expense recorded in the account.

The $2,500 for salaries (t) is entered on the left side of the Salaries Expense account because expenses decrease owner's equity and an owner's equity account is decreased on the left side. Remember that an increase in an expense brings about a decrease in owner's equity. The plus and minus signs shown in the illustration below indicate the effect on the expense account, not the effect on owner's equity.

Salaries Expense	
+	−
(t) 2,500	

Other kinds of expenses will be recorded in separate accounts, each with its own descriptive title. For example, the payment of monthly utility bills will be recorded in an account called Utilities Expense. Salaries Expense and Utilities Expense are classified under the heading *Expenses* on the income statement. The total of all such account balances is the total operating expenses of the business for the accounting period.

Recording an Expense for Utilities

During December 19X5 Arrow Accounting Services also had an expense of $300 for utilities, which it paid by issuing a check. Richey made the following analysis of this transaction.

u. The payment of $300 for utilities reduced the asset Cash.
v. The account Utilities Expense was increased by $300.

Information Block: Communication

Characteristics of Effective Communication

Just as well-run accounting systems exhibit characteristics of accuracy, promptness, and honesty, written and spoken business messages must exhibit characteristics of effective business communication. *Before communicating,* carefully analyze your message to verify that you meet your objective. You should be able to answer yes to these four questions:

- Is your message courteous? A *courteous* message shows respect and consideration for the receiver. Achieve courtesy by using positive words and an appropriate tone with emphasis on the receiver rather than the sender.
- Is your message concise? A *concise* message says exactly and only what needs to be said. Achieve conciseness by choosing specific words; eliminating repetitive material; using short sentences and paragraphs; and logically organizing each sentence, paragraph, and the overall message.
- Is your message complete? A *complete* message includes all the essential information to accomplish your objective. Achieve completeness by providing details, examples, and descriptions and by verifying that your message answers the questions your receiver may have.
- Is your message correct? A *correct* message is accurate in every detail of its content, language, and format. Achieve correctness by carefully proofreading every aspect of your message, using reference materials (dictionary, thesaurus, manuals), and correcting each error without introducing new errors.

You will accomplish your message objective only when your message incorporates each of the four characteristics of effective business communication: courteous, concise, complete, and correct. Remember that the quality of many business decisions in your career will depend on the quality of your financial information as well as the quality or effectiveness of your business communication.

Project: Applying the above information, analyze the following message to answer these questions.

1. What is the objective of the message? Is the objective accomplished?
2. Evaluate the message against the four characteristics of effective business communications.

Interoffice Communication

TRI-STATE ACCOUNTING FIRM
122 Western Avenue, Cincinnati, OH 45202-8903
Telephone: (513) 555-1234
FAX: (513) 555-1235

TO: John3 Black
FROM: Ms. Mary Johnson
DATE: April , 19--
SUBJECT: Oriention Progam

Welcome to Tristate accounting Firm! I will orient you to our co. and it's accounting system, practices, peolpe, forms, procedures, policies, hardware, and, software, by making you go threw are training program with the other new employees in our department. This program begin at 9:30 on Monday. Please be on time to the meeting.

ndw

3. Revise the message to incorporate the four characteristics of effective business communications.
4. What is the nonverbal message received with this written message?
5. Should the message have been delivered in a written or oral format?

The reduction in cash (u) was recorded by an entry on the right (decrease) side of the asset account Cash.

Cash	
+	–
Bal. 8,000	(s) 2,500
(m) 10,500	**(u) 300**
(q) 1,500	

▲ **REMEMBER!**
EXPENSE ACCOUNTS

+	–
Record increases	Record decreases

To record the expense (v), the $300 is entered on the left (increase) side of the Utilities Expense account.

Utilities Expense	
+	–
(v) 300	

Increases in expenses are recorded on the left side of expense accounts because expenses reduce owner's equity. Decreases in expenses are recorded on the right side of the accounts. Decreases in expenses may result from corrections, transfers to other expense accounts, or refunds. However, such entries are not required often.

THE DRAWING ACCOUNT

In sole proprietorships and partnerships, the owners generally do not pay themselves salaries. To obtain funds for personal living expenses, owners make withdrawals of cash against previously earned profits that have become part of their capital or against profits that are expected in the future. A special type of owner's equity account called a **drawing account** is set up to record these withdrawals. Since withdrawals of cash decrease owner's equity, withdrawals can be recorded on the left side of the Capital account. However, the preferred way is to separate withdrawals from the owner's equity account until the end of the month. On December 30, 19X5, John Arrow withdrew $1,000 in cash from the business to pay for personal expenses. The effect of the withdrawal is shown below.

Decreases in owner's equity are recorded on the left side of the Capital account.

w. Cash was reduced by the $1,000 withdrawal.
x. The amount of cash the owner withdrew from the business increased by $1,000.

The decrease in cash (w) is recorded with an entry on the right (decrease) side of the asset account Cash.

Cash	
+	–
Bal. 8,000	(s) 2,500
(m) 10,500	(u) 300
(q) 1,500	**(w) 1,000**

To record the increase in withdrawals (x), the $1,000 is entered on the left (increase) side of the John Arrow, Drawing account. The balance of the drawing account decreases the capital account and is reported on the statement of owner's equity as withdrawals for the period.

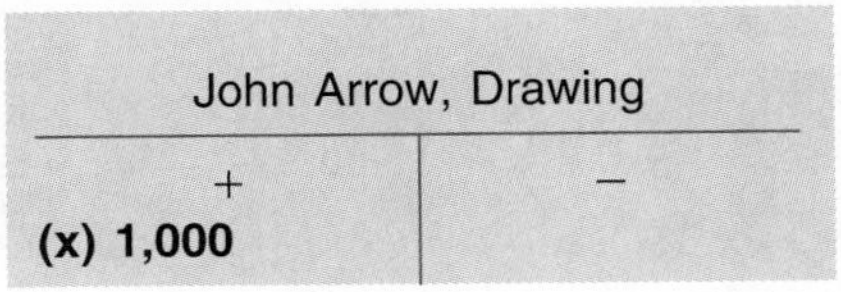

A summary of the relationship between the capital account and the revenue, expense, and drawing accounts is shown in Figure 3–3.

FIGURE 3–3
The Relationship Between Owner's Equity and Revenue, Expenses, and Withdrawals

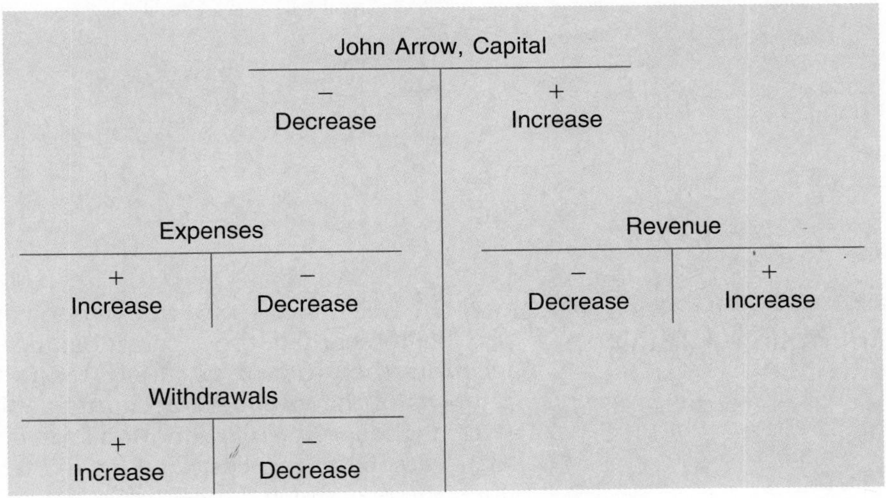

THE RULES OF DEBIT AND CREDIT

Debit = left side; Credit = right side.

Accountants do not say "left side" or "right side" when they talk about making entries in accounts. They use the term **debit** when they refer to an entry on the left side of an account and the term **credit** when they refer to an entry on the right side of an account. For example, accountants increase assets by debiting asset accounts, and they decrease assets by crediting asset accounts. However, accountants increase liabilities by crediting liability accounts and decrease liabilities by debiting liability accounts. Figure 3–4 summarizes the rules for debiting and crediting accounts.

The analysis of each transaction produces at least two effects. The effect of an entry on the debit, or left, side of one account is balanced by the effect of an entry on the credit, or right, side of another account. For this reason, the modern system of accounting is usually called the **double-entry system**. This system involves recording both effects of every transaction to present a complete picture. The balancing relationship also explains why both sides of the equations shown in Chapter 1 are always equal.

FIGURE 3–4
Rules for Debits and Credits

ASSET ACCOUNTS	
Debit + Increase Side (Normal Bal.)	Credit – Decrease Side

LIABILITY ACCOUNTS	
Debit – Decrease Side	Credit + Increase Side (Normal Bal.)

OWNER'S CAPITAL ACCOUNT	
Debit – Decrease Side	Credit + Increase Side (Normal Bal.)

OWNER'S DRAWING ACCOUNT	
Debit + Increase Side (Normal Bal.)	Credit – Decrease Side

REVENUE ACCOUNTS	
Debit – Decrease Side	Credit + Increase Side (Normal Bal.)

EXPENSE ACCOUNTS	
Debit + Increase Side (Normal Bal.)	Credit – Decrease Side

PREPARING A TRIAL BALANCE

After the December 19X5 transactions of Arrow Accounting Services have been recorded, the account balances are determined. The firm's accounts then appear as illustrated in Figure 3–5. Notice that the balances of the various T accounts at the end of December are the same as those shown in equation form on page 67. The items marked "Bal." are balances carried forward from November transactions. Once the account balances have been determined, the accuracy of the account balances must be tested.

OBJECTIVE 4
Prepare a trial balance from T accounts.

A statement to test the accuracy of the financial records is the **trial balance.** The trial balance is prepared to determine whether total debits equal total credits. When John Arrow started Arrow Accounting Services with a cash investment, we said that property equaled financial interests. Using accounting terms, we stated that assets equal liabilities plus owner's equity. Later we saw that every entry on the debit, or left, side of one account is matched by an entry of equal amount on the credit, or right, side of another account.

The firm's financial records started with an equality of debits and credits and continued that equality in the recording process. It follows that the sum of the debit balances in the accounts should equal the sum of the credit balances. If the totals do not balance, that is, the total debit balances do not equal the total credit balances, it is clear that an error has been made. To prepare a trial balance, the balance of each account is first determined. Next, the account names and their balances are listed on a trial balance as shown in Figure 3–6 on page 68. The balance of each account is written in the proper debit or credit column. Debit balances are entered in the left column, and credit balances are entered in the right column.

FIGURE 3–5
End-of-December 19X5 Account Balances

ASSETS = LIABILITIES + OWNER'S EQUITY

ASSETS

Cash

Debit	Credit
Bal. 8,000	(s) 2,500
(m) 10,500	(u) 300
(q) 1,500	(w) 1,000
20,000	3,800
Bal. 16,200	

Accounts Receivable

Debit	Credit
(o) 3,500	(r) 1,500
Bal. 2,000	

Supplies

Debit	Credit
Bal. 1,000	

Prepaid Rent

Debit	Credit
Bal. 20,000	

Equipment

Debit	Credit
Bal. 15,000	

LIABILITIES

Accounts Payable

Debit	Credit
	Bal. 4,000

OWNER'S EQUITY

John Arrow, Capital

Debit	Credit
	Bal. 40,000

John Arrow, Drawing

Debit	Credit
(x) 1,000	

Fees Income

Debit	Credit
	(n) 10,500
	(p) 3,500
	Bal. 14,000

Salaries Expense

Debit	Credit
(t) 2,500	

Utilities Expense

Debit	Credit
(v) 300	

Notice that the trial balance in Figure 3–6 has a three-line heading that shows who, what, and when. The date is the closing date for the accounting period. The accounts are listed in the following order:

- Assets
- Liabilities
- Owner's Equity
- Revenue
- Expenses

FIGURE 3–6
A Trial Balance

ARROW ACCOUNTING SERVICES
Trial Balance
December 31, 19X5

ACCOUNT NAME	DEBIT	CREDIT
Cash	16 200 00	
Accounts Receivable	2 000 00	
Supplies	1 000 00	
Prepaid Rent	20 000 00	
Equipment	15 000 00	
Accounts Payable		4 000 00
John Arrow, Capital		40 000 00
John Arrow, Drawing	1 000 00	
Fees Income		14 000 00
Salaries Expense	2 500 00	
Utilities Expense	300 00	
Totals	58 000 00	58 000 00

Errors Revealed by the Trial Balance

When the Debit and Credit columns of the trial balance are equal, we know that the financial records are in balance. We are also sure that a debit has been recorded for every credit.

If the Debit and Credit columns are not equal, it is clear that an error has been made. The error may be in the trial balance, or it may be in the financial records. Some common errors are listed below.

1. Adding amounts incorrectly on the trial balance.
2. Recording only half a transaction; for example, recording a debit without a credit, or vice versa.
3. Recording both halves of a transaction as debits or credits—for example, recording two debits or two credits in the accounts, rather than one debit and one credit.
4. Recording an amount incorrectly from a transaction.
5. Recording unequal debits and credits in a transaction.
6. Adding or subtracting amounts incorrectly when determining an account balance.

Methods of Finding Trial Balance Errors

If the trial balance is out of balance, use the following procedures to locate the error or errors.

1. Check the arithmetic on the trial balance.
2. Check to see that the balances of the accounts were correctly transferred to the trial balance.
3. Check the arithmetic used in computing the account balances.
4. Check the accuracy of recording the transactions by tracing the amounts recorded in the accounts back to the analysis of the transactions.

Information Block: Computers and Accounting

Microcomputer Software

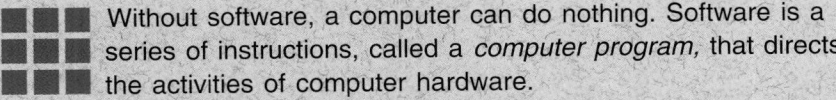

Without software, a computer can do nothing. Software is a series of instructions, called a *computer program,* that directs the activities of computer hardware.

There are two types of computer software: *system software* and *applications software.* System software is used to control the operation of application software as well as coordinate the activities of the computer equipment. Application software consists of programs that direct a computer to process input data into output information. For example, data regarding sales invoices and the number of each item sold is entered into the computer. The computer is then able to process these sales facts and print out a sales report showing total sales. Business managers can use this information to identify inventory items that are "fast selling" as well as those items that are "slow moving" or just not selling at all.

Applications software is also used for specific tasks such as processing payroll checks, creating word processed documents, calculating electronic spreadsheets, and maintaining database files. For many small business organizations, accounting application software can be purchased for as little as a few hundred dollars. Because of their relatively low cost and ease of use, these software programs offer an opportunity for efficient, economical preparation of financial reports and statements. The use of such programs is spreading quickly because they save considerable time processing data and also provide management with a wider range of information more quickly and accurately than manual accounting systems.

Accounting application programs can be purchased to maintain general journal transactions, post these transactions to ledger accounts, prepare trial balances, and prepare financial statements when needed. Specific applications programs are available for managing accounts receivable accounts by recording sales and customers' payments and preparing customer statements. Accounts payable programs maintain accurate account balances for amounts due to creditors and print necessary checks to pay those creditors when payments are due.

Computer software can be purchased to perform all accounting functions. Specialized accounting software is available for maintaining the accounting records for medical, dental, accounting, and legal offices and for various types of service businesses such as insurance and real estate agencies.

The arithmetic in the trial balance can be checked for errors by adding the columns again in the opposite direction. That is, if the columns were first added from top to bottom, they should be verified by adding from bottom to top.

Sometimes you can determine the type of error by the amount of the difference involved. For example, when the debit and credit totals on the trial balance are not equal, compute the difference by subtracting the smaller total from the larger total. If the difference is divisible by 9, there may have been a transposition ($357 for $375) or a slide ($375 for $37.50). A **transposition** is an error where the digits of a number are switched. For example, we can test for a transposition of 357 for 375 in the following manner.

$$\begin{array}{r} 375 \\ \underline{-357} \\ 18 \end{array} \qquad 18/9 = 2$$

A **slide** is an error where the decimal point is misplaced. For example, we can test for a slide of $375 for $37.50 in the following manner.

$$\begin{array}{r} 375.00 \\ \underline{-37.50} \\ 337.50 \end{array} \qquad 337.50/9 = 37.50$$

Additionally, if the difference can be divided by 2, a debit amount may have been recorded as a credit, or a credit recorded as a debit.

PREPARING FINANCIAL STATEMENTS

OBJECTIVE 5

Prepare an income statement, a statement of owner's equity, and a balance sheet.

After the account balances are determined and the trial balance prepared, the income statement, statement of owner's equity, and balance sheet are prepared. The income statement, statement of owner's equity, and balance sheet for Arrow Accounting Services are presented in Figure 3–7. As you study this illustration, note how the net income reported on the income statement is used on the statement of owner's equity to determine the new balance of the Capital account, which is used to prepare the balance sheet.

CHART OF ACCOUNTS

OBJECTIVE 6

Develop a chart of accounts.

Since most businesses have many different accounts, it is necessary to set up a system that allows the accounts to be easily identified and located. A **chart of accounts** is a list of all the accounts used by a business for recording its financial transactions. Each account is given a number as well as a name. The number is assigned on the basis of the type of account. Similar accounts are grouped within a certain block of numbers. For example, asset accounts could be numbered from 100 to 199, liability accounts from 200 to 299, owner's equity accounts from 300 to 399, and so on. These numbers help identify the type of account, no matter where it is in a firm's financial records.

Typically, accounts are numbered in the order in which they appear on the financial statements. The balance sheet accounts are listed first and then the income statement accounts, as illustrated in

FIGURE 3–7
Financial Statements for Arrow Accounting Services

ARROW ACCOUNTING SERVICES Income Statement Month Ended December 31, 19X5		
Revenue		
Fees Income		*14 000 00*
Expenses		
Salaries Expense	*2 500 00*	
Utilities Expense	*300 00*	
Total Expenses		*2 800 00*
Net Income		*11 200 00*

ARROW ACCOUNTING SERVICES Statement of Owner's Equity Month Ended December 31, 19X5		
John Arrow, Capital, December 1, 19X5		*40 000 00*
Net Income for December	*11 200 00*	
Less Withdrawals for December	*1 000 00*	
Increase in Capital		*10 200 00*
John Arrow, Capital, December 31, 19X5		*50 200 00*

ARROW ACCOUNTING SERVICES
Balance Sheet
December 31, 19X5

Assets		*Liabilities*	
Cash	*16 200 00*	*Accounts Payable*	*4 000 00*
Accounts Receivable	*2 000 00*		
Supplies	*1 000 00*		
Prepaid Rent	*20 000 00*	*Owner's Equity*	
Equipment	*15 000 00*	*John Arrow, Capital*	*50 200 00*
Total Assets	*54 200 00*	*Total Liabilities and Owner's Equity*	*54 200 00*

the chart of accounts shown in Figure 3–8. This chart of accounts was set up for Arrow Accounting Services by the firm's office manager, Virginia Richey. Notice that the accounts are not numbered consecutively. For example, the numbering under Assets jumps from 101 to 111 and then to 121, 131, and 141. These gaps are ordinarily left in each block of numbers so that additional accounts may be added when needed.

FIGURE 3–8
Chart of Accounts

ARROW ACCOUNTING SERVICES Chart of Accounts	
Account Number	Account Name
Balance Sheet Accounts	
100–199	**ASSETS**
101	Cash
111	Accounts Receivable
121	Supplies
131	Prepaid Rent
141	Equipment
200–299	**LIABILITIES**
202	Accounts Payable
300–399	**OWNER'S EQUITY**
301	John Arrow, Capital
Statement of Owner's Equity Account	
302	John Arrow, Drawing
Income Statement Accounts	
400–499	**REVENUE**
401	Fees Income
500–599	**EXPENSES**
511	Salaries Expense
514	Utilities Expense

PERMANENT AND TEMPORARY ACCOUNTS

▲ **REMEMBER!**

Permanent accounts always have a balance and are reported on the balance sheet. Temporary accounts are used to account for the changes in owner's equity during the accounting period; their balances are reported on the income statement.

The asset, liability, and owner's equity accounts appear on the balance sheet at the end of an accounting period. The balances of these accounts are then carried forward to start the new period. Such accounts are sometimes called **permanent,** or **real, accounts** because they continue from accounting period to accounting period.

In contrast to these permanent accounts are the revenue, expense, and drawing accounts, whose balances are reported on the income statement and statements of owner's equity at the end of an accounting period. Accountants use revenue, expense, and drawing accounts to classify and summarize changes in owner's equity during the period. These accounts are called **temporary,** or **nominal, accounts** because their balances are transferred to the capital account at the end of an accounting period. The accounts then have zero balances and are ready for use in recording new transactions affecting revenue and expenses for the next period.

MANAGERIAL IMPLICATIONS

Recording entries in accounts provides an efficient method of gathering data about the financial affairs of a business. A trial balance is prepared first. The income statement is prepared to report the revenue and expenses for the period and to determine the net income or loss. The statement of owner's equity is then prepared to analyze the change in owner's equity during the period. The balance sheet, which summarizes the assets, liabilities, and owner's equity of the business on a given date, is prepared last. Owners, managers, creditors, banks, and many others use these statements to make decisions about the business.

SELF-REVIEW

1. What is the increase side for each of these accounts: Cash, Accounts Payable, and Joe Dale, Capital?
2. What are withdrawals and how are they recorded?
3. What is a trial balance and what is its purpose?
4. What is a transposition? a slide? Give an example of each.
5. What is a chart of accounts and what is its purpose?

Answers to Self-Review

1. The increase side of Cash is the left, or debit, side. The increase side of Accounts Payable is the right, or credit, side. The increase side of Joe Dale, Capital is the right, or credit, side.
2. A withdrawal is cash taken from the business by the owner to obtain funds for personal living expenses. Withdrawals are recorded in a special type of owner's equity account called a drawing account.
3. The trial balance lists all the accounts and their balances. Its purpose is to prove the equality of the total debits and credits.
4. A transposition is an error in which the digits of a number are switched; for example, when 516 is recorded as 615.

$$\begin{array}{r} 615 \\ -516 \\ \hline 99 \end{array} \qquad 99/9 = 11$$

   A slide is an error where the decimal point is misplaced; for example, when 216 is written as 2.16.

$$\begin{array}{r} 216.00 \\ -2.16 \\ \hline 213.84 \end{array} \qquad 213.84/9 = 23.76$$

5. A chart of accounts is a list of the numbers and names of the accounts of a business. The purpose of the chart of accounts is to provide a system by which the accounts of the business can be easily identified and located.

CHAPTER 3 Review and Applications

CHAPTER SUMMARY

Each business transaction is analyzed to identify its effects on the fundamental accounting equation, *Assets = Liabilities + Owner's Equity*. Then the effects of each transaction are recorded in the proper accounts. Accounts are classified as assets, liabilities, or owner's equity. An increase in an asset account is shown on the debit, or left, side of the account because assets appear on the left side of the accounting equation. The credit, or right, side of an asset account is used to record decreases. In contrast, liabilities appear on the right side of the equation; thus an increase in a liability is recorded on the credit, or right, side of the account. The left, or debit, side of a liability account is used for recording decreases. Similarly, increases in owner's equity are shown on the credit side of an owner's equity account. Decreases in owner's equity appear on the debit side.

Owner's equity accounts can be subdivided into revenue, expense, and drawing accounts. Revenue accounts increase owner's equity; therefore, increases are recorded on the credit side of revenue accounts. Expenses are recorded on the debit side of the separate expense accounts because expenses decrease owner's equity. The Drawing account is used to record the withdrawal of cash from the business by the owner. Like expenses, the Drawing account decreases owner's equity; its balance is reported on the statement of owner's equity.

The list of the accounts used by a business is called its chart of accounts. Accounts are arranged in a predetermined order and numbered for handy reference and quick identification. Typically, the accounts are numbered in the order in which they appear on the financial statements. The balance sheet accounts come first and are followed by the income statement accounts.

GLOSSARY OF NEW TERMS

Account balance (p. 55) The difference between the amounts recorded on the two sides of an account

Accounts (p. 52) Written records of a business's assets, liabilities, and owner's equity

Chart of accounts (p. 69) A list of the accounts used by a business to record its financial transactions

Classification (p. 52) A means of identifying each account as an asset, liability, or owner's equity account

Credit (p. 65) An entry on the right side of an account

Debit (p. 65) An entry on the left side of an account

Double-entry system (p. 65) An accounting system that involves recording the effects of each transaction as debits and credits

Drawing account (p. 64) A special type of owner's equity account set up to record the owner's withdrawal of cash from the business

Footing (p. 55) A small penciled figure at the base of an amount column that is the sum of the entries in the column

Normal balance (p. 56) The increase side of an account

Permanent account (p. 72) An account that is kept open from one accounting period to the next

Slide (p. 69) An accounting error involving a misplaced decimal point

T account (p. 52) A type of account, resembling a T, used to analyze the effects of a business transaction

Temporary account (p. 72) An account whose balance is transferred to another account at the end of an accounting period

Transposition (p. 69) An accounting error involving misplaced digits in a number

Trial balance (p. 66) A statement to test the accuracy of total debits and credits after transactions have been recorded

REVIEW QUESTIONS

1. What are accounts?
2. Why is Prepaid Rent considered an asset account?
3. Why is the modern system of accounting usually called the double-entry system?
4. The terms debit and credit are often used in describing the effects of transactions on different accounts. What do these terms mean?
5. Decide whether each of the following types of accounts would normally have a debit balance or a credit balance.
   a. An asset account
   b. A liability account
   c. The owner's capital account
   d. A revenue account
   e. An expense account
6. How is the balance of an account determined?
7. What is a chart of accounts?
8. In what order do accounts appear in the chart of accounts?
9. When a chart of accounts is created, number gaps are left within groups of accounts. Why are these number gaps necessary?
10. Accounts are classified as permanent or temporary accounts. What do these classifications mean?

MANAGERIAL FOCUS

1. How do the income statement and the balance sheet help management make sound decisions?
2. How can management find out, at any time, whether a firm can pay its bills as they become due?
3. If a firm's expenses equal or exceed its revenue, what actions might management take?
4. In discussing a firm's latest financial statements, a manager says that it is the "results on the bottom line" that really count. What does the manager mean?

EXERCISES

EXERCISE 3–1 (Obj. 1)

Setting up T accounts. Pond Jewelry Repair Service has the following account balances on December 31, 19X3. Set up a T account for each account and enter the balance on the proper side of the account.

Cash	$2,000
Equipment	2,000
Accounts Payable	1,000
Robert Pond, Capital	3,000

EXERCISE 3–2 (Obj. 2)

Using T accounts to analyze transactions. Kathy Nelson decided to start her dental practice. The first five transactions for the business are listed below. For each transaction, (1) determine which two accounts are affected, (2) set up T accounts for the affected accounts, and (3) enter the debit and credit amounts in the T accounts.

1. Kathy invested $20,000 cash in the business.
2. Paid $5,000 in cash for equipment.
3. Performed services for cash amounting to $2,000.
4. Paid $700 in cash for rent expense.
5. Paid $500 in cash for supplies.

EXERCISE 3–3 (Obj. 3)

Identifying debits and credits. Determine whether the word *debit* or *credit* is correct for each space in the sentences below.

1. Asset accounts normally have __?__ balances. These accounts increase on the __?__ side and decrease on the __?__ side.
2. Liability accounts normally have __?__ balances. These accounts increase on the __?__ side and decrease on the __?__ side.
3. The owner's capital account normally has a __?__ balance. This account increases on the __?__ side and decreases on the __?__ side.
4. Revenue accounts normally have __?__ balances. These accounts increase on the __?__ side and decrease on the __?__ side.

5. Expense accounts normally have ___?___ balances. These accounts increase on the ___?___ side and decrease on the ___?___ side.

EXERCISE 3–4 (Obj. 3)

Determining debit and credit balances. Indicate whether each of the following accounts would normally have a debit balance or a credit balance.

1. Accounts Payable
2. Fees Income
3. Cash
4. Arthur Roberts, Capital
5. Equipment
6. Accounts Receivable
7. Salaries Expense
8. Supplies

EXERCISE 3–5 (Obj. 3)

Determining account balances. The following T accounts show transactions that were recorded at Connors' Repair Service, a firm that specializes in restoring antique furniture. The entries for the first transaction are labeled with the letter **a,** the entries for the second transaction with the letter **b,** and so on. Determine the balance for each account.

Cash	
(a) 40,000	(b) 10,000
(d) 5,000	(e) 150
(g) 500	(h) 2,500
	(i) 1,000

Equipment	
(c) 15,000	

Accounts Receivable	
(f) 2,000	(g) 500

Accounts Payable	
	(c) 15,000

Supplies	
(b) 10,000	

John Connors, Capital	
	(a) 40,000

Fees Income	
	(d) 5,000
	(f) 2,000

Telephone Expense	
(e) 150	

John Connors, Drawing	
(i) 1,000	

Salaries Expense	
(h) 2,500	

EXERCISE 3–6 (Obj. 4, 5)

Preparing a trial balance and an income statement. Using the account balances from Exercise 3–5, prepare a trial balance and an income statement for Connors' Repair Service. The trial balance is for

December 31, 19X5, and the income statement is for the month ended December 31, 19X5.

EXERCISE 3–7
(Obj. 5)

Preparing a statement of owner's equity and a balance sheet. From the trial balance and the net income or net loss determined in Exercise 3–6, prepare a statement of owner's equity and a balance sheet for Connors' Repair Service as of December 31, 19X5.

EXERCISE 3–8
(Obj. 6)

Preparing a chart of accounts. The accounts that will be used by the Zant Supply Company are listed below. Prepare a chart of accounts for the firm. Classify the accounts by type, arrange them in an appropriate order, and assign suitable account numbers.

Sue Zant, Capital	Office Supplies	Accounts Payable
Cash	Utilities Expense	Office Equipment
Salaries Expense	Prepaid Rent	Fees Income
Accounts Receivable	Telephone Expense	Sue Zant, Drawing

PROBLEMS

PROBLEM SET A

PROBLEM 3–1A
(Obj. 1, 2)

Using T accounts to record transactions involving assets, liabilities, and owner's equity. The following transactions took place at Carter's Remodeling Service.

Instructions

Set up T accounts for the following accounts: Cash, Shop Equipment, Store Equipment, Truck, Accounts Payable, and Hayden Carter, Capital. Analyze each transaction carefully. Record the effects of the transaction in the T accounts. Use plus and minus signs before the amounts to show the increases and decreases.

TRANSACTIONS
1. Hayden Carter invested $10,000 cash in the business.
2. Purchased equipment for $500 in cash.
3. Bought store fixtures for $1,200; payment is due in 30 days.
4. Purchased a used truck for $2,500 in cash.
5. Carter gave the firm his personal set of tools costing $250.
6. Bought a used cash register for $200; payment is due in 30 days.
7. Paid $450 in cash to apply to the amount owed for store fixtures.
8. Carter withdrew $1,000 in cash for personal expenses.

PROBLEM 3–2A
(Obj. 1, 2)

Using T accounts to record transactions involving assets, liabilities, and owner's equity. The following transactions occurred at several different businesses and are not related.

Instructions

Analyze each of the transactions. For each transaction, decide what accounts are affected and enter the proper titles at the top of a pair of T accounts. Record the effects of the transaction in the T accounts. Use plus and minus signs to show the increases and decreases.

TRANSACTIONS
1. A firm purchased equipment for $2,000 in cash.
2. The owner, Paul Smith, withdrew $500 cash.

3. A firm sold a piece of surplus equipment for $250 in cash.
4. A firm purchased a used delivery truck for $2,000 in cash.
5. A firm paid $400 in cash to apply against an account owed.
6. A firm purchased office equipment for $450. The amount is to be paid in 60 days.
7. Sharon Carter, owner of Builders Supply Company, made an additional investment of $2,500 in cash.
8. A firm paid $150 by check for office equipment that it had previously purchased on credit.

PROBLEM 3–3A
(Obj. 1, 2)

Using T accounts to record transactions involving revenue and expenses. The following revenue and expense transactions took place at the Industrial Cleaning Service.

Instructions

Analyze each of the transactions. Decide what accounts are affected and enter the proper titles at the top of a pair of T accounts. Record the effects of the transaction in the T accounts. Use plus and minus signs before the amounts to show the increases and decreases.

TRANSACTIONS

1. Paid $400 for one month's rent.
2. Performed services for $500 in cash.
3. Paid salaries of $600.
4. Performed additional services for $900 on credit.
5. Paid $75 for the monthly telephone bill.
6. Collected $250 from accounts receivable.
7. Received a $15 refund for an overcharge on the telephone bill.
8. Performed services for $600 on credit.
9. Paid $50 in cash for the monthly electric bill.
10. Paid $110 in cash for gasoline purchased for the firm's van during the month.
11. Received $450 from charge account customers.
12. Performed services for $900 in cash.

PROBLEM 3–4A
(Obj. 1, 2)

Using T accounts to record all business transactions. The accounts and transactions of Ron Kelly, Architect, follow.

Instructions

Analyze the transactions. Record each one in the appropriate T accounts. Use plus and minus signs in front of the amounts to show the increases and decreases. Identify each entry in the T accounts by writing the letter of the transaction next to the entry.

ASSETS

Cash
Accounts Receivable
Office Equipment
Automobile

LIABILITIES

Accounts Payable

OWNER'S EQUITY

Ron Kelly, Capital
Ron Kelly, Drawing

REVENUE

Fees Income

EXPENSES

Rent Expense
Utilities Expense
Salaries Expense
Telephone Expense
Automobile Expense

TRANSACTIONS

a. Ron Kelly invested $27,000 in cash to start the business.
b. Paid $800 for one month's rent.
c. Bought a used automobile for the firm for $8,000 in cash.
d. Performed services for $1,500 in cash.
e. Paid $200 for automobile repairs.
f. Performed services for $1,875 on credit.
g. Purchased office chairs for $1,050 on credit.
h. Received $900 from credit clients.
i. Paid $500 to reduce the amount owed for the office chairs.
j. Issued a check for $280 to pay the monthly utility bill.
k. Purchased office equipment for $4,200 and paid half of this amount in cash immediately; the balance is due in 30 days.
l. Issued a check for $2,840 to pay salaries.
m. Performed services for $925 in cash.
n. Performed services for $1,300 on credit.
o. Paid $96 for the monthly telephone bill.
p. Collected $800 on accounts receivable from charge customers.
q. Purchased additional office equipment and received a bill for $680 due in 30 days.
r. Paid $150 in cash for gasoline purchased for the automobile during the month.
s. Ron Kelly withdrew $1,000 in cash for personal expenses.

PROBLEM 3–5A
(Obj. 3, 4, 5)

Preparing financial statements from T accounts. The accountant for the firm owned by Ron Kelly prepares financial statements at the end of each month.

Instructions

Use the figures in the T accounts for Problem 3–4A to prepare a trial balance, an income statement, a statement of owner's equity, and a balance sheet. (The first line of the statement headings should read "Ron Kelly, Architect.") Assume that the transactions took place during the month ended April 30, 19X5. Determine the account balances before you start work on the financial statements.

PROBLEM SET B

PROBLEM 3–1B
(Obj. 1, 2)

Using T accounts to record transactions involving assets, liabilities, and owner's equity. The following transactions took place at the legal services business established by Susan Gale.

Instructions

Set up T accounts for these accounts: Cash, Office Furniture, Office Equipment, Automobile, Accounts Payable, and Susan Gale, Capital. Analyze each transaction carefully. Record the amounts in the T accounts affected by that transaction. Use plus and minus signs to show increases and decreases in each account.

TRANSACTIONS

1. Susan Gale invested $7,500 cash in the business.
2. Purchased office furniture for $2,000 in cash.
3. Bought a fax machine for $650; payment is due in 30 days.
4. Purchased a used car for the firm for $2,000 in cash.
5. Gale invested an additional $2,000 cash in the business.

6. Bought a new microcomputer for $2,500; payment is due in 60 days.
7. Paid $650 to settle the amount owed on the fax machine.
8. Gale withdrew $500 in cash for personal expenses.

PROBLEM 3–2B
(Obj. 1, 2)

Using T accounts to record transactions involving assets, liabilities, and owner's equity. The following transactions occurred at several different businesses and are not related.

Instructions

Analyze each of the transactions. Decide what accounts are affected and enter the proper titles at the top of a pair of T accounts. Record the effects of the transaction in the T accounts. Use plus and minus signs before the amounts to show the increases and decreases.

TRANSACTIONS

1. Bill White, an owner, made an additional investment of $6,000 in cash.
2. A firm purchased equipment for $3,500.
3. A firm sold some surplus office furniture for $300 in cash.
4. A firm purchased a microcomputer for $2,600, to be paid in 60 days.
5. A firm purchased office equipment for $3,500 on credit. The amount is due in 60 days.
6. Diane Scott, owner of Scott Travel Agency, withdrew $1,000 of her original cash investment.
7. A firm bought a delivery truck for $9,000 on credit; payment is due in 90 days.
8. A firm issued a check for $250 to a supplier in partial payment of an open account balance.

PROBLEM 3–3B
(Obj. 1, 2)

Using T accounts to record transactions involving revenue and expenses. The following revenue and expense transactions took place at the Mason Auto Repair Company.

Instructions

Analyze each of the transactions. For each transaction, decide what accounts are affected and enter the proper titles at the top of a pair of T accounts. Record the effects of the transaction in the T accounts. Use plus and minus signs before the amounts to show the increases and decreases.

TRANSACTIONS

1. Performed services for $3,600 in cash.
2. Paid $550 for the month's rent.
3. Performed services for $1,000 on credit.
4. Paid $250 in cash for the monthly utilities bill.
5. Purchased supplies that cost $1,000; payment is due in 30 days.
6. Paid salaries of $3,690.
7. Performed services for $1,750 in cash.
8. Collected $500 from credit customers.
9. Received a $50 refund for an overcharge on the electric bill.
10. Paid $120 in cash for supplies.
11. Collected $150 from credit customers.
12. Paid $475 in cash for gasoline for the firm's wrecker.

PROBLEM 3–4B
(Obj. 1, 2)

Using T accounts to record all business transactions. The accounts and transactions of Carolyn Wells, Consulting Engineer, are shown below.

Instructions

Analyze the transactions. Record each one in the appropriate T accounts. Use plus and minus signs in front of the amounts to show the increases and decreases. Identify each entry in the T accounts by writing the letter of the transaction next to the entry.

ASSETS

Cash
Accounts Receivable
Office Furniture
Office Equipment

LIABILITIES

Accounts Payable

OWNER'S EQUITY

Carolyn Wells, Capital
Carolyn Wells, Drawing

REVENUE

Fees Income

EXPENSES

Rent Expense
Utilities Expense
Salaries Expense
Telephone Expense
Miscellaneous Expense

TRANSACTIONS

a. Wells invested $15,000 in cash to start the business.
b. Paid $750 for one month's rent.
c. Bought office furniture for $2,600 in cash.
d. Performed services for $1,050 in cash.
e. Paid $225 for the monthly telephone bill.
f. Performed services for $1,275 on credit.
g. Purchased a microcomputer and copy machine for $3,950 on credit; paid $950 in cash immediately with the balance due in 30 days.
h. Received $700 from credit clients.
i. Paid $300 in cash for office cleaning services for the month.
j. Purchased additional office chairs for $800; received credit terms of 30 days.
k. Purchased office equipment for $5,500 and paid half of this amount in cash immediately; the balance is due in 30 days.
l. Issued a check for $3,250 to pay salaries.
m. Performed services for $1,025 in cash.
n. Performed services for $1,150 on credit.
o. Collected $600 on accounts receivable from charge customers.
p. Issued a check for $400 in partial payment of the amount owed for office chairs.
q. Paid $100 to a duplicating company for photocopy work performed during the month.
r. Paid $250 for the monthly electric bill.
s. Carolyn Wells withdrew $1,000 in cash for personal expenses.

PROBLEM 3–5B
(Obj. 3, 4, 5)

Preparing financial statements from T accounts. The accountant for the firm owned by Carolyn Wells prepares financial statements at the end of each month.

Instructions Use the figures in the T accounts for Problem 3–4B to prepare a trial balance, an income statement, a statement of owner's equity, and a balance sheet. (The first line of the statement headings should read "Carolyn Wells, Consulting Engineer.") Assume that the transactions took place during the month ended June 30, 19X5. Determine the account balances before you start work on the financial statements.

CHALLENGE PROBLEM

Sarah Cohen is an architect who operates her own business. The transactions and accounts for the business are shown below.

Instructions (1) Analyze the transactions for January 19X6. Record each one in the appropriate T accounts. Use plus and minus signs in front of the amounts to show the increases and decreases. Identify each entry in the T account by writing the letter of the transaction next to the entry. (2) Determine the account balances. Prepare a trial balance, an income statement, a statement of owner's equity, and a balance sheet.

ASSETS

Cash
Accounts Receivable
Office Furniture
Office Equipment

LIABILITIES

Accounts Payable

OWNER'S EQUITY

Sarah Cohen, Capital
Sarah Cohen, Drawing

REVENUE

Fees Income

EXPENSES

Rent Expense
Utilities Expense
Salaries Expense
Telephone Expense
Miscellaneous Expense

TRANSACTIONS

a. Sarah Cohen invested $10,000 in cash to start the business.
b. Paid $500 for one month's rent.
c. Purchased office furniture for $1,500 in cash.
d. Performed services for $1,200 in cash.
e. Paid $135 for the monthly telephone bill.
f. Performed services for $1,080 on credit.
g. Purchased a fax machine for $750; paid $300 in cash with the balance due in 30 days.
h. Paid a bill for $165 from the office cleaning service.
i. Received $540 from clients on account.
j. Purchased additional office chairs for $450; received credit terms of 30 days.
k. Paid $1,000 for salaries.
l. Issued a check for $275 in partial payment of the amount owed for office chairs.
m. Received $700 in cash for services performed.

n. Issued a check for $240 to pay the utility bill.
o. Performed services for $1,200 on credit.
p. Collected $200 from clients on account.
q. Sarah Cohen withdrew $700 in cash for personal expenses.
r. Paid $150 to Ed's Duplicating Service for photocopy work performed during the month.

CRITICAL THINKING PROBLEM

At the beginning of the summer, Mike Kitay was looking for a way to earn money to pay for his college tuition in the fall. On the advice of several neighbors, he decided to start a lawn-service business in his neighborhood. To get the business started, Mike used $1,500 from his savings account to open a checking account for his new business, MK Lawn Care. At a local auction, he was able to purchase two used power mowers and various lawn-care tools for $500. He also paid $900 for a second-hand truck to transport the power mowers.

Several of the neighbors who had encouraged him to start the business hired him to cut their grass on a weekly basis. He sent these customers monthly bills. By the end of the summer, they had paid him $200 in cash and owed him another $350. Mike also cut grass on an as-needed basis for other neighbors who paid him $100.

During the summer, Mike spent $100 for gasoline for the truck and mowers. He paid a friend who helped him on several occasions $250. An advertisement in the local paper cost $30. Now, at the end of the summer, Mike is concerned because he has only $20 left in his checking account. He says, "I worked hard all summer and have only $20 to show for it. It would have been better to leave the money in the bank."

Prepare an income statement, a statement of owner's equity, and a balance sheet for MK Lawn Care. Explain to Mike whether or not he is "better off" than he was at the beginning of the summer. (Hint: T accounts may be helpful in organizing the data.)

CHAPTER

4

The General Journal and the General Ledger

OBJECTIVES

1. Record transactions in the general journal.
2. Prepare compound journal entries.
3. Post journal entries to general ledger accounts.
4. Correct errors made in the journal or ledger.
5. Define the accounting terms new to this chapter.

In the last chapter, you learned that the analysis of each transaction is the basis for recording the effects of the transaction in the accounts. In business, written records are kept of each analysis for future reference. These records allow individuals to recheck their work and trace the details of any transaction long after it has happened.

The **accounting cycle** is a series of steps performed during each accounting period to classify, record, and summarize data for a business and produce needed financial information. The first step in the accounting cycle is to analyze the effects of business transactions. The second step in the cycle is preparing a record of those transactions.

NEW TERMS

Accounting cycle ▪ Audit trail ▪ Balance ledger form ▪ Chronological order ▪ Compound entry ▪ Correcting entry ▪ General journal ▪ General ledger ▪ Journal ▪ Journalizing ▪ Ledger ▪ Posting

JOURNALS

Analyzing transactions is the first step in the accounting cycle.

Business transactions are recorded in a financial record called a **journal,** which is a diary of business activities that lists events involving financial affairs—transactions—as they occur. The transactions are entered in **chronological order**—in the order in which they happen day by day.

Since the journal is the first accounting record where transactions are entered, it is sometimes referred to as a *record of original entry.* A number of different types of journals are used in business. The one that will be examined in this chapter is the general journal. As we discuss more complex accounting systems and records in later chapters, you will become familiar with other kinds of journals.

THE GENERAL JOURNAL

OBJECTIVE 1

Record transactions in the general journal.

As its name implies, the **general journal** can be used to record all types of business transactions. The process of recording transactions in the general journal is referred to as **journalizing.** To illustrate how transactions are entered in this journal, let's start with the first transaction of Arrow Accounting Services.

When the owner, John Arrow, invested $40,000 on November 6 to start the firm, the transaction was analyzed and the following effects identified.

a. Arrow Accounting Services received $40,000 of property in the form of cash.
b. John Arrow had a $40,000 financial investment in the business.

Using this analysis as a guide, Virginia Richey, the office manager, knew that the accounting transaction should be entered as follows.

Recording business transactions in a journal is the second step in the accounting cycle.

a. Debit the Cash account for $40,000 to record the increase in the asset cash.
b. Credit the John Arrow, Capital account for $40,000 to record the new ownership interest.

The written record of the analysis of the transaction appears in the general journal in Figure 4–1.

FIGURE 4–1
General Journal Entry

Record the year first, then the month and day.
Record the debit first.
Indent about half an inch and record the credit.

GENERAL JOURNAL PAGE *1*

	DATE		DESCRIPTION	POST. REF.	DEBIT	CREDIT	
1	*19X5*						1
2	*Nov.*	*6*	*Cash*		*40 0 0 0 00*		2
3			*John Arrow, Capital*			*40 0 0 0 00*	3
4			*Beginning investment*				4
5			*of owner*				5
6							6

Indent again and write the description.

Notice that each page in the general journal is given a number and that the year is recorded at the top of the Date column. The month and day are also written in the Date column on the first line of the first entry. After the first entry, the year and month are recorded only when a new page is begun or when either the year or the month changes. However, the day of each transaction is written in the Date column on the first line of each entry.

The account to be debited is always recorded first in the Description column. The account title is written close to the left margin, and the debit amount is then entered on the same line in the Debit column.

The account to be credited is always recorded on the line beneath the debit. The account title is indented about half an inch from the left margin. Next the credit amount is entered on the same line in the Credit column.

A brief explanation follows the credit part of the entry. This explanation begins on the line following the credit and is indented about one inch from the left margin of the Description column. Explanations should be complete but concise.

Whenever possible, the explanation for a journal entry should include a description of the source of the information contained in the entry. For example, if a check is written to make a payment, the explanation in the journal entry for that transaction should include the check number. Similarly, if goods are purchased on credit, the explanation in the journal entry should show the number of the supplier's invoice (bill). These source document numbers are part of an **audit trail**—a chain of references that makes it possible to trace information about transactions through the accounting system. The audit trail helps locate errors in the system. It also helps to prevent fraud because it provides a means of checking the data in a firm's financial records against the original data that appears in the source documents.

Account titles are written in the general journal exactly as they appear in the chart of accounts and in the accounts themselves. Use of the exact wording of each account title minimizes the possibility of errors when the figures are transferred to the accounts. The transfer of information from the general journal to the accounts is the next step in the accounting process and is discussed later in this chapter.

Usually a blank line is left between general journal entries. This blank line separates the transactions and makes them easier to identify and read. Some accountants prefer to use this blank line to number each general journal entry for identification purposes.

General Journal Entries for November

The journal entries made at Arrow Accounting Services during November provide a good illustration of the techniques that are used to record transactions in the general journal. For example, on November 7 the firm paid $20,000 rent in advance (Check 1001) for December through July. Analysis of the transaction and the journal entry are shown on the next page.

c. The business acquired a new asset (prepaid rent) at a cost of $20,000.

d. The business paid $20,000 in cash.

Explanations should be complete, including document numbers where appropriate to establish an audit trail.

GENERAL JOURNAL PAGE *1*

	DATE		DESCRIPTION	POST. REF.	DEBIT	CREDIT	
7	*Nov.*	*7*	*Prepaid Rent*		*20 0 0 0 00*		7
8			*Cash*			*20 0 0 0 00*	8
9			*Paid rent in advance for*				9
10			*an eight-month period*				10
11			*(December 19X5 through*				11
12			*July 19X6), Check 1001*				12
13							13

Notice the use of the check number in the explanation for the journal entry. This number will form part of the audit trail for the transaction.

When Arrow Accounting Services purchased equipment on November 9 for cash (Check 1002), the office manager made the following analysis and then recorded the journal entry that follows.

e. The firm purchased new assets in the form of equipment at a cost of $10,000.

f. The firm paid $10,000 in cash.

GENERAL JOURNAL PAGE *1*

	DATE		DESCRIPTION	POST. REF.	DEBIT	CREDIT	
14	*Nov.*	*9*	*Equipment*		*10 0 0 0 00*		14
15			*Cash*			*10 0 0 0 00*	15
16			*Purchased equipment,*				16
17			*Check 1002*				17
18							18

On November 10 the business purchased a copy machine, a fax machine, calculators, and other necessary equipment for $5,000 on credit from Organ, Inc., Invoice 2788, payable in 60 days. The transaction was analyzed and the journal entry was recorded as shown below.

g. The business purchased new assets (equipment) at a cost of $5,000.

h. The business owed $5,000 as an account payable to Organ, Inc.

GENERAL JOURNAL PAGE *1*

	DATE		DESCRIPTION	POST. REF.	DEBIT	CREDIT	
19	*Nov.*	*10*	*Equipment*		*5000 00*		19
20			*Accounts Payable*			*5000 00*	20
21			*Purchased equipment on*				21
22			*credit from Organ, Inc.,*				22
23			*Invoice 2788, payable in*				23
24			*60 days*				24

Notice how the audit trail is created for this transaction by listing the supplier's invoice number in the explanation for the journal entry.

On November 28, when the firm purchased supplies for $1,000 in cash (Check 1003), the transaction was analyzed and the journal entry was prepared as shown below.

i. The business purchased new assets (supplies) at a cost of $1,000.

j. The business paid $1,000 in cash.

GENERAL JOURNAL PAGE *1*

	DATE		DESCRIPTION	POST. REF.	DEBIT	CREDIT	
26	*Nov.*	*28*	*Supplies*		*1000 00*		26
27			*Cash*			*1000 00*	27
28			*Purchased supplies, Check*				28
29			*1003*				29

A final transaction, the payment of Invoice 2788 for $1,000 by Check 1004 to Organ, Inc., on November 30, was analyzed as shown and the journal entry that follows was made.

k. The firm paid $1,000 in cash.

l. Organ's claim against the firm was reduced by $1,000.

GENERAL JOURNAL PAGE *1*

	DATE		DESCRIPTION	POST. REF.	DEBIT	CREDIT	
31	*Nov.*	*30*	*Accounts Payable*		*1000 00*		31
32			*Cash*			*1000 00*	32
33			*Paid Organ, Inc., on*				33
34			*account for Invoice 2788,*				34
35			*Check 1004*				35

Notice that the debit item is always entered in the general journal first. This is the case even if the credit item is considered first while mentally analyzing the transaction.

General Journal Entries for December

You will recall that Arrow Accounting Services officially opened for business on December 1, 19X5. The following transactions were completed during that month. The journal entries made for these transactions provide a further illustration of the procedures used to record data in the general journal. (Refer to items m through x in Chapter 3 to review the analysis of the December transactions.)

1. Performed services for $10,500 in cash.
2. Performed services for $3,500 on credit.
3. Received $1,500 in cash from credit clients on their accounts.
4. Paid $2,500 for salaries.
5. Paid $300 for a utility bill.
6. The owner withdrew $1,000 for personal expenses.

The entries in the general journal are shown below. In actual practice the transactions involving revenue and cash received on account would be spread throughout the month and recorded as they occurred. However, for the sake of simplicity, these transactions have been summarized and recorded as of December 31 in Figure 4–2.

FIGURE 4–2
General Journal Entries for December

GENERAL JOURNAL PAGE 2

	DATE		DESCRIPTION	POST. REF.	DEBIT	CREDIT	
1	*19X5*						1
2	*Dec.*	*31*	*Cash*		*10 5 0 0 00*		2
3			*Fees Income*			*10 5 0 0 00*	3
4			*Performed services for*				4
5			*cash*				5
6							6
7		*31*	*Accounts Receivable*		*3 5 0 0 00*		7
8			*Fees Income*			*3 5 0 0 00*	8
9			*Performed services on*				9
10			*credit*				10
11							11
12		*31*	*Cash*		*1 5 0 0 00*		12
13			*Accounts Receivable*			*1 5 0 0 00*	13
14			*Received cash from credit*				14
15			*clients on account*				15
16							16
17		*31*	*Salaries Expense*		*2 5 0 0 00*		17
18			*Cash*			*2 5 0 0 00*	18
19			*Paid monthly salaries to*				19
20			*employees, Checks 1005–*				20
21			*1006*				21

FIGURE 4–2 (Continued)
General Journal Entries for December

31	*Utilities Expense*		*300 00*	
	Cash			*300 00*
	Paid monthly bill for			
	utilities, Check 1007			
31	*John Arrow, Drawing*		*1 000 00*	
	Cash			*1 000 00*
	Owner withdrew cash for			
	personal expenses, Check			
	1008			

Compound Entries

OBJECTIVE 2
Prepare compound journal entries.

Each of the journal entries shown so far consists of a single debit and a single credit. However, some transactions require a **compound entry**—a journal entry that contains several debits or several credits. In a compound entry all debits are recorded first followed by the recording of the credits.

Suppose that when Arrow Accounting Services purchased the equipment on November 9 for $10,000, John Arrow gave $5,000 in cash (Check 1002) and agreed to pay the balance in 30 days. This transaction would be analyzed as follows.

1. An asset, Equipment, is increased by $10,000.
2. An asset, Cash, is decreased by $5,000.
3. A liability, Accounts Payable, is increased by $5,000.

The compound entry shown below would be entered in the general journal.

GENERAL JOURNAL PAGE *1*

DATE		DESCRIPTION	POST. REF.	DEBIT	CREDIT
19X5					
Nov.	*9*	*Equipment*		*10 000 00*	
		Cash			*5 000 00*
		Accounts Payable			*5 000 00*
		Purchased equipment on			
		credit from Organ, Inc.,			
		Invoice 2787, issued Check			
		1002 for a $5,000 down			
		payment; bal. due 30 days			

▲ **REMEMBER!**

No matter how many accounts are involved, the total debits must equal the total credits in each entry.

Notice that this compound entry contains equal debits and credits, just as any journal entry should ($10,000 = $5,000 + $5,000).

SELF-REVIEW

1. Why is the journal referred to as the "record of original entry"?
2. Transactions are entered in the general journal in chronological order. What does this mean?
3. Why are check and invoice numbers included in the journal entry explanation?
4. If a compound journal entry has two accounts debited, will there always be two accounts credited?
5. Make a compound journal entry for the following transaction (omit an explanation): A firm purchases machinery for $3,000 with a cash down payment of $500 and with the balance payable in 30 days.

Answers to Self-Review

1. The journal is referred to as the "record of original entry" because it is the first accounting record where transactions are entered.
2. Entering transactions in chronological order means that they are entered in the order in which they occur day by day.
3. Check and invoice numbers are included in the explanation in the journal entry to provide an audit trail that makes it possible to trace information about transactions through the accounting system.
4. There is no requirement that a compound entry with two accounts debited must have two accounts credited. The only requirement is that the total debits must equal the total credits.
5. Machinery 3,000

Machinery	3,000	
Cash		500
Accounts Payable		2,500

LEDGERS

As you have seen, a journal contains a chronological (day-by-day) record of a firm's transactions. Each entry provides a written analysis of a transaction, showing what accounts should be debited and credited and the amounts involved. With the journal as a guide, data about transactions can be entered in the accounts that are affected.

Although T accounts are a good device for quickly analyzing the effects of transactions, they are not suitable for use in business as financial records. Instead, business firms keep each account on a printed form that has a heading and several columns. This arrangement makes it possible to record all the necessary data efficiently. The printed forms used for the accounts appear on separate sheets in a book or binder.

Posting to the general ledger accounts is the third step in the accounting cycle.

All the accounts together are referred to as a **ledger.** The process of transferring data from a journal to a ledger is known as **posting.** Because posting takes place after the transactions are journalized and the ledger is the last accounting record where a transaction is recorded, a ledger is sometimes called a **record of final entry.**

The General Ledger

One essential type of ledger for every business is the **general ledger.** This ledger is the master reference file for the accounting system because it provides a permanent, classified record of every financial element involved in a firm's operations. Many companies also have other kinds of ledgers that supplement the information in the general ledger. You will become familiar with some of these other ledgers in later chapters, but keep in mind that the general ledger is the main ledger of a business.

Ledger Account Forms

Several different forms are available for general ledger accounts. The office manager for Arrow Accounting Services has decided to use a **balance ledger form** for the business's general ledger accounts. With this form the balance of an account is always available because it is recorded after each entry is posted. Figure 4–3 shows how data about the first transaction of the firm—the beginning investment of the owner—was posted from the general journal to the proper general ledger accounts. The posting process will be explained in the next section, but notice the arrangement of columns in the balance ledger form and how the various columns are used.

FIGURE 4–3
Posting from the General Journal to the General Ledger

GENERAL JOURNAL PAGE *1*

	DATE		DESCRIPTION	POST. REF.	DEBIT	CREDIT	
1	*19X5*						1
2	*Nov.*	*6*	*Cash*	*101*	*40 000 00*		2
3			*John Arrow, Capital*	*301*		*40 000 00*	3
4			*Beginning investment of*				4
5			*owner*				5
6							

ACCOUNT *Cash* ACCOUNT NO. *101*

DATE		EXPLANATION	POST. REF.	DEBIT	CREDIT	BALANCE DEBIT	BALANCE CREDIT
19X5							
Nov.	*6*		*J1*	*40 000 00*		*40 000 00*	

ACCOUNT *John Arrow, Capital* ACCOUNT NO. *301*

DATE		EXPLANATION	POST. REF.	DEBIT	CREDIT	BALANCE DEBIT	BALANCE CREDIT
19X5							
Nov.	*6*		*J1*		*40 000 00*		*40 000 00*

Posting to the General Ledger

OBJECTIVE 3

Post journal entries to general ledger accounts.

To understand the posting process, examine Figure 4–4. On November 7, 19X5, the office manager for Arrow Accounting Services made an entry in the general journal to record the payment of rent in advance for an eight-month period. Next, the data from the journal was posted to the proper account in the general ledger. The debit amount in the journal was transferred to the Debit column in the Prepaid Rent account and the credit amount in the journal was transferred to the Credit column in the Cash account.

FIGURE 4–4
Posting to the General Ledger

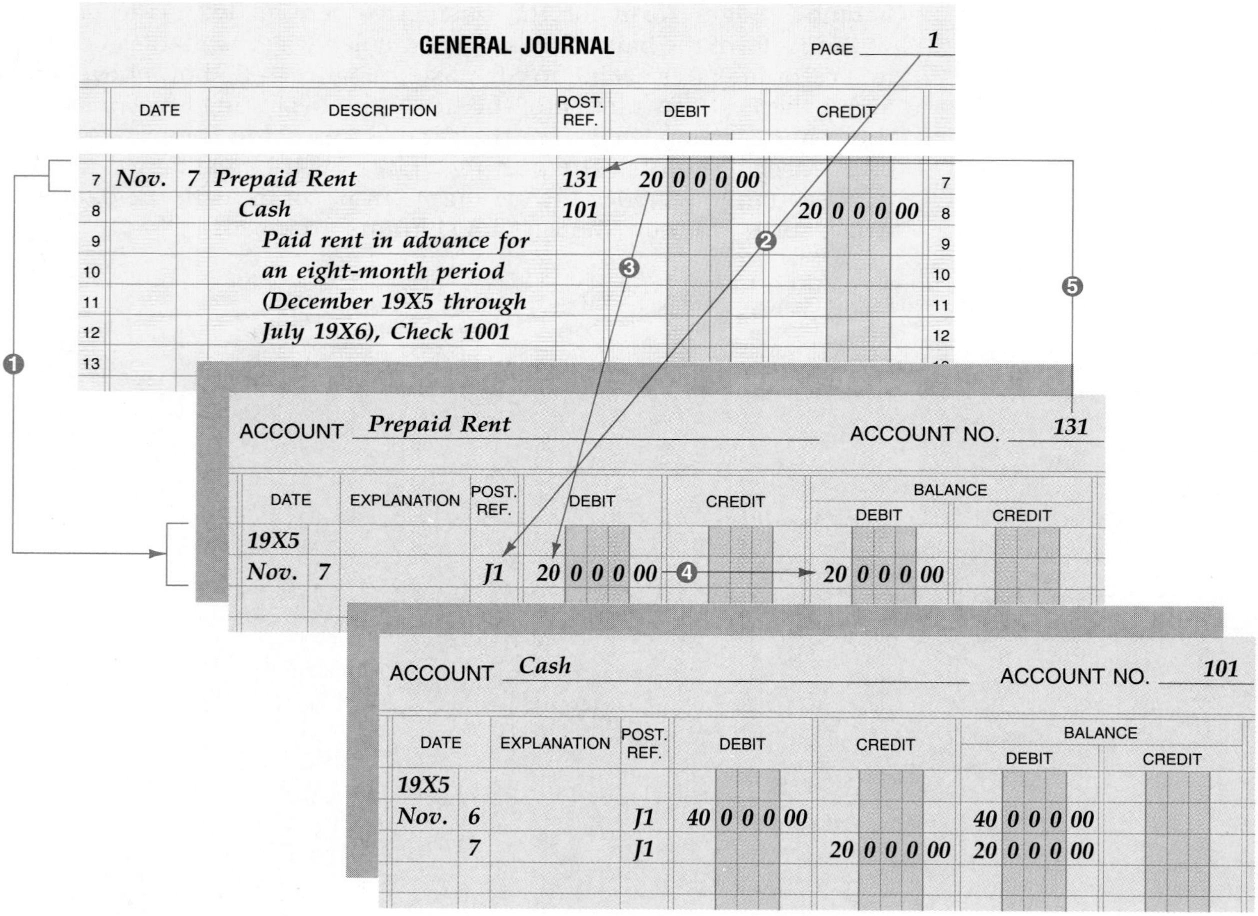

The specific procedure used in posting data from a general journal entry like the one shown in Figure 4–4 is to start with the first account listed in the journal entry, in this example, Prepaid Rent. The general ledger account for Prepaid Rent is located and the following posting steps are taken:

1. The date of the journal entry is recorded in the Date column of the ledger account. Note: If necessary, a notation explaining the

entry is made in the Explanation column of the ledger form. However, routine entries usually do not require an explanation.

2. The number of the journal page is recorded in the Posting Reference column of the ledger account. For example, **J1** is posted to the Prepaid Rent account to indicate that the entry was originally recorded on page 1 of the general journal. The letter **J** in front of the page number is an abbreviation for the general journal.
3. The debit amount in the journal is recorded in the Debit column of the ledger account.
4. The balance of the ledger account is determined and recorded in the Debit Balance column.
5. The number of the ledger account is recorded in the Posting Reference column of the journal.

Similar steps are used to post the credit amount from the general journal entry to the Cash account. Once this work is done, the posting process for the transaction is complete and the journal entry includes the numbers of the two ledger accounts.

Writing the journal page number in each ledger account and the ledger account number in the journal indicates that the entry has been posted and ensures against posting the same entry twice. The journal page numbers in the accounts and the account numbers in the journal provide a useful cross-reference when entries must be traced and transactions verified. Like the source document numbers that appear in the explanations for journal entries, posting references are part of the audit trail. These references allow accountants to trace an amount from the ledger to the proper journal entry and then to the source document that contains the original data.

After the office manager for Arrow Accounting Services had posted all the entries for November and December, the firm's general ledger accounts appeared as shown in Figure 4–5 (pages 95–97). Refer to the journal entries and trace the postings carefully.

FIGURE 4–5
Posted General Ledger Accounts

ACCOUNT *Cash* ACCOUNT NO. *101*

DATE		EXPLANATION	POST. REF.	DEBIT	CREDIT	BALANCE DEBIT	BALANCE CREDIT
19X5							
Nov.	6		J1	40 0 0 0 00		40 0 0 0 00	
	7		J1		20 0 0 0 00	20 0 0 0 00	
	9		J1		10 0 0 0 00	10 0 0 0 00	
	28		J1		1 0 0 0 00	9 0 0 0 00	
	30		J1		1 0 0 0 00	8 0 0 0 00	
Dec.	31		J2	10 5 0 0 00		18 5 0 0 00	
	31		J2	1 5 0 0 00		20 0 0 0 00	
	31		J2		2 5 0 0 00	17 5 0 0 00	
	31		J2		3 0 0 00	17 2 0 0 00	
	31		J2		1 0 0 0 00	16 2 0 0 00	

ACCOUNT *Accounts Receivable* ACCOUNT NO. *111*

DATE		EXPLANATION	POST. REF.	DEBIT	CREDIT	BALANCE DEBIT	BALANCE CREDIT
19X5							
Dec.	31		J2	3 500 00		3 500 00	
	31		J2		1 500 00	2 000 00	

ACCOUNT *Supplies* ACCOUNT NO. *121*

DATE		EXPLANATION	POST. REF.	DEBIT	CREDIT	BALANCE DEBIT	BALANCE CREDIT
19X5							
Nov.	28		J1	1 000 00		1 000 00	

ACCOUNT *Prepaid Rent* ACCOUNT NO. *131*

DATE		EXPLANATION	POST. REF.	DEBIT	CREDIT	BALANCE DEBIT	BALANCE CREDIT
19X5							
Nov.	7		J1	20 000 00		20 000 00	

ACCOUNT *Equipment* ACCOUNT NO. *141*

DATE		EXPLANATION	POST. REF.	DEBIT	CREDIT	BALANCE DEBIT	BALANCE CREDIT
19X5							
Nov.	9		J1	10 000 00		10 000 00	
	10		J1	5 000 00		15 000 00	

ACCOUNT *Accounts Payable* ACCOUNT NO. *202*

DATE		EXPLANATION	POST. REF.	DEBIT	CREDIT	BALANCE DEBIT	BALANCE CREDIT
19X5							
Nov.	10		J1		5 000 00		5 000 00
	30		J1	1 000 00			4 000 00

ACCOUNT *John Arrow, Capital* ACCOUNT NO. *301*

DATE		EXPLANATION	POST. REF.	DEBIT	CREDIT	BALANCE DEBIT	BALANCE CREDIT
19X5							
Nov.	6		J1		40 000 00		40 000 00

ACCOUNT *John Arrow, Drawing* ACCOUNT NO. *302*

DATE		EXPLANATION	POST. REF.	DEBIT	CREDIT	BALANCE DEBIT	BALANCE CREDIT
19X5							
Dec.	*31*		*J1*	*1 0 0 0 00*		*1 0 0 0 00*	

ACCOUNT *Fees Income* ACCOUNT NO. *401*

DATE		EXPLANATION	POST. REF.	DEBIT	CREDIT	BALANCE DEBIT	BALANCE CREDIT
19X5							
Dec.	*31*		*J2*		*10 5 0 0 00*		*10 5 0 0 00*
	31		*J2*		*3 5 0 0 00*		*14 0 0 0 00*

ACCOUNT *Salaries Expense* ACCOUNT NO. *511*

DATE		EXPLANATION	POST. REF.	DEBIT	CREDIT	BALANCE DEBIT	BALANCE CREDIT
19X5							
Dec.	*31*		*J2*	*2 5 0 0 00*		*2 5 0 0 00*	

ACCOUNT *Utilities Expense* ACCOUNT NO. *514*

DATE		EXPLANATION	POST. REF.	DEBIT	CREDIT	BALANCE DEBIT	BALANCE CREDIT
19X5							
Dec.	*31*		*J2*	*3 0 0 00*		*3 0 0 00*	

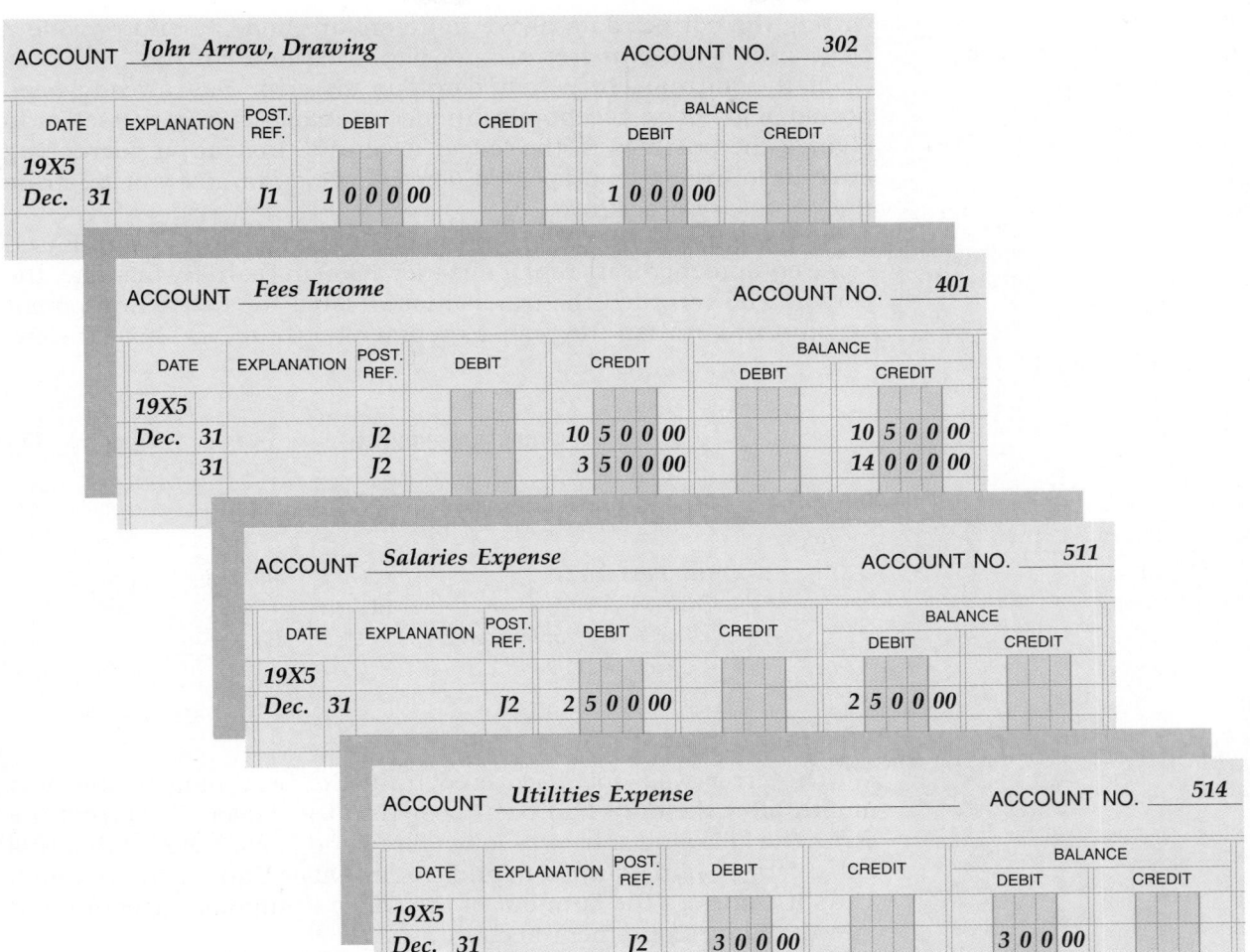

As you can see, each ledger account provides a complete running history of the increases and decreases in the item that it represents. When a balance ledger form is used, the account also shows the current balance for the account at all times.

The general ledger accounts are usually arranged so that the balance sheet accounts—assets, liabilities, and owner's equity—come first. The accounts for the income statement come next, with the revenue accounts first, followed by the expense accounts. The numbering system used in the chart of accounts follows the same order. This arrangement speeds the preparation of the trial balance, the income statement, the statement of owner's equity, and the balance sheet. All figures are found in the general ledger in the order in which they will be presented on the financial statements.

CORRECTING JOURNAL AND LEDGER ERRORS

Sometimes errors are made when recording transactions in the journal. For example, a wrong account title or amount may be used in a journal entry. If the error is discovered before the entry is posted, a correction can be made by neatly crossing out the incorrect item and

OBJECTIVE 4
Correct errors made in the journal or ledger.

writing the correct data above it. To ensure honesty and provide a clear audit trail, erasures are not permitted in a journal.

If the journal entry that contains an error has already been posted, it is not an acceptable practice to change the entry itself or to change the postings in the ledger accounts. Instead, a **correcting entry** is journalized and posted. The following example will illustrate the necessary procedure.

On August 5, 19X5, an automobile service station purchased some equipment for its repair shop for $800 in cash. By mistake, the person who recorded the transaction debited the Office Equipment account rather than the Shop Equipment account, as shown below.

GENERAL JOURNAL PAGE *15*

	DATE		DESCRIPTION	POST. REF.	DEBIT	CREDIT	
1	*19X5*						1
2	*Aug.*	*5*	*Office Equipment*	*141*	*8 0 0 00*		2
3			*Cash*	*101*		*8 0 0 00*	3
4			*Purchased equipment,*				4
5			*Check 6421*				5
6							6

The error was not discovered until the beginning of the next month after the data had been posted to the ledger. To correct the error, the following entry was journalized and posted. Notice that this entry debits Shop Equipment and credits Office Equipment for $800. Thus it transfers the sum out of the Office Equipment account and into the Shop Equipment account.

GENERAL JOURNAL PAGE *21*

	DATE		DESCRIPTION	POST. REF.	DEBIT	CREDIT	
1	*19X5*						1
2	*Sept.*	*1*	*Shop Equipment*	*151*	*8 0 0 00*		2
3			*Office Equipment*	*141*		*8 0 0 00*	3
4			*To correct error made in*				4
5			*Aug. 5 entry when a*				5
6			*purchase of shop*				6
7			*equipment was recorded*				7
8			*as office equipment*				8
9							9

MANAGERIAL IMPLICATIONS

Business managers should make sure that their firms have efficient procedures for recording transactions. A well-run accounting system provides for prompt and accurate journalizing of all transactions. It also provides for timely and accurate posting of data to the ledger accounts. The information that appears in the financial statements is taken from the general ledger. Since management uses this information for decision making, it is essential that the statements be prepared quickly at the end of each period and that they contain the correct figures. The promptness and accuracy of the statements depends heavily on the efficiency of the recording process.

Another characteristic of a well-run accounting system is that it has a strong audit trail. For the sake of accuracy and honesty, the firm should be able to trace amounts through the accounting records and back to their origin—the source documents on which the transactions were first recorded.

SELF-REVIEW

1. Why is the ledger called the "record of final entry"?
2. What is recorded in the posting reference column of a balance ledger form?
3. What is recorded in the posting reference column of the general journal?
4. What is the purpose of writing the posting reference in each ledger account and the ledger account number in the journal?
5. Is the following statement true or false? Why? "If a journal entry contains an error that has already been posted, it is an acceptable practice to change the entry or to change the posting in the ledger accounts."

Answers to Self-Review

1. The ledger is referred to as the "record of final entry" because it is the last accounting record in which a transaction is recorded.
2. The journal page number is recorded in the posting reference column of the ledger.
3. The ledger account number is recorded in the posting reference column of the journal.
4. Writing the journal page number in each ledger account and the ledger account number in the journal indicates that the entry has been posted and ensures against posting the same entry twice.
5. False. A correcting entry should be journalized and posted. To ensure honesty and provide a clear audit trail, erasures are not permitted in the journal.

CHAPTER 4 **Review and Applications**

CHAPTER SUMMARY

A journal provides a chronological (day-by-day) record of a firm's transactions. It contains a written analysis of each transaction that occurs. The process of recording transactions in a journal is called journalizing, which is the second step in the accounting cycle. The general journal is one type of journal that is widely used in business. It has the advantage of being able to accommodate all kinds of transactions that a business may have. In a general journal entry, the debit portion is always recorded first. Then the credit portion is recorded, and a brief explanation is provided. Whenever possible, the explanations for journal entries should include source document numbers in order to create an audit trail.

Data is transferred from the journal entries to the ledger accounts through a process called posting. The individual accounts together form a ledger. There are various types of ledgers, but the main ledger for every business is the general ledger. This ledger contains the accounts that are used to prepare the financial statements.

The posting references placed in the journal and the ledger accounts form another part of the audit trail. They serve to cross-reference the entries and make it possible to trace or recheck any transaction in the firm's accounting records.

GLOSSARY OF NEW TERMS

Accounting cycle (p. 85) A series of steps performed during each accounting period to classify, record, and summarize data for a business to produce needed financial information

Audit trail (p. 87) A chain of references that makes it possible to trace information through the accounting system

Balance ledger form (p. 93) A ledger account form that shows the balance of the account after each entry is posted

Chronological order (p. 86) Organized on a day-by-day basis

Compound entry (p. 91) A journal entry that contains more than one debit or credit

Correcting entry (p. 98) A journal entry made to correct an erroneous entry

General journal (p. 86) A financial record for entering all types of business transactions

General ledger (p. 93) A permanent, classified record of all accounts used in a firm's operation; a record of final entry

Journal (p. 86) The record of original entry

Journalizing (p. 86) Recording transactions in a journal

Ledger (p. 92) The record of final entry

Posting (p. 92) Transferring data from a journal to a ledger

REVIEW QUESTIONS

1. What is the purpose of a journal?
2. What procedure is used to record an entry in the general journal?
3. What is the value of having an explanation for each general journal entry?
4. Why is it important that exact account titles be used in the general journal?
5. What is a compound journal entry?
6. What is a ledger?
7. What is posting?
8. In what order are accounts arranged in the general ledger? Why?
9. What are posting references? Why are they used?
10. What is an audit trail? Why is it desirable to have an audit trail?
11. How should corrections be made in the general journal and the general ledger?
12. What is the accounting cycle? What are the first three steps in the accounting cycle?

MANAGERIAL FOCUS

1. Why should management be concerned about the efficiency of a firm's procedures for journalizing and posting transactions?
2. How might a poor set of recording procedures affect the flow of information to management?
3. The owner of a new business recently questioned the accountant about the value of having both a journal and a ledger. The owner believed that it was a waste of effort to enter data about transactions in two different records. How would you explain the value of having both records?
4. Why should management insist that a firm's accounting system have a strong audit trail?

EXERCISES

EXERCISE 4–1 (Obj. 1)

Analyzing transactions. Selected accounts from the general ledger of the Rapid Delivery Service are shown below. Analyze the following transactions and indicate by number what accounts should be debited and credited for each transaction.

101 Cash	301 Ronald Thomas, Capital
111 Accounts Receivable	401 Fees Income
121 Supplies	511 Rent Expense
131 Equipment	514 Salaries Expense
202 Accounts Payable	517 Utilities Expense

TRANSACTIONS

1. Issued a check for $850 to pay the monthly rent.
2. Purchased supplies for $500 on credit.
3. The owner made an additional investment of $8,000 in cash.

4. Collected $1,400 from credit customers.
5. Performed services for $1,950 in cash.
6. Issued a check for $750 to pay a creditor on account.
7. Purchased new equipment for $1,075 and paid for it immediately by check.
8. Provided services for $2,800 on credit.
9. Sent a check for $300 to the utility company to pay the monthly bill.
10. Gave a cash refund of $90 to a customer because of a lost package. (The customer had previously paid in cash.)

EXERCISE 4–2 (Obj. 1)

Tutorial

Recording transactions in the general journal. Selected accounts from the general ledger of the Popular Design Studio are shown below. Record the general journal entries that would be made to record the following transactions. Be sure to include dates and explanations in these entries.

101 Cash	401 Fees Income
111 Accounts Receivable	511 Rent Expense
121 Supplies	514 Salaries Expense
131 Equipment	517 Telephone Expense
141 Automobile	520 Automobile Expense
202 Accounts Payable	
301 Clark White, Capital	
302 Clark White, Drawing	

TRANSACTIONS

Sept.	1	Clark White invested $38,000 in cash to start the firm.
	4	Purchased office equipment for $8,700 on credit from Zen, Inc.; received Invoice 2398, which is payable in 30 days.
	16	Purchased an automobile that will be used to visit clients; issued Check 1001 for $15,600 in full payment.
	20	Purchased supplies for $175; paid immediately with Check 1002.
	23	Returned damaged supplies and received a cash refund of $75.
	30	Issued Check 1003 for $4,200 to Zen, Inc., as payment on account for Invoice 2398.
	30	Withdrew $1,500 in cash for personal expenses.
	30	Issued Check 1004 for $800 to pay the rent for October.
	30	Performed services for $1,275 in cash.
	30	Issued Check 1005 for $125 to pay the monthly telephone bill.

EXERCISE 4–3 (Obj. 1, 3)

Posting to the general ledger. Post the journal entries that you prepared for Popular Design Studio in Exercise 4–2 from the general journal to the general ledger. Use the account titles shown in Exercise 4–2.

EXERCISE 4–4 (Obj. 2)

Tutorial

Compound journal entries. The following transactions took place at the Talent Scout Agency during November 19X5. Give the general journal entries that would be made to record these transactions. Use a compound entry for each transaction.

TRANSACTIONS

Nov. 5 Performed services for United Artist, Inc., for $8,000; received $3,000 in cash and the client promised to pay the balance in 60 days.

18 Purchased an electronic calculator for $75 and some supplies for $100 from the Office Depot Center; issued Check 1008 for the total.

23 Received Invoice 1602 for $450 from Barry's Garage for repairs to the firm's automobile; issued Check 1009 for half the amount and arranged to pay the other half in 30 days.

EXERCISE 4–5 (Obj. 4)

Recording a correcting entry. On July 3, 19X4, an employee of the Haley Corporation mistakenly debited the Utilities Expense account rather than the Telephone Expense account when recording a bill of $225 for June telephone service. The error was discovered on July 31. Make a general journal entry to correct the error.

EXERCISE 4–6 (Obj. 4)

Recording a correcting entry. On October 15, 19X2, an employee of the Johnson Company mistakenly debited the Truck account rather than the Truck Expense account when recording a bill of $690 for repairs. The error was discovered on November 1. Make a general journal entry to correct the error.

PROBLEMS

PROBLEM SET A

PROBLEM 4–1A (Obj. 1)

Tutorial GL

Recording transactions in the general journal. The transactions listed below took place at the Fitness Tennis Center during December 19X3. This firm has indoor courts where customers can play tennis for a fee. It also rents equipment and offers tennis lessons.

Instructions

Analyze and record each transaction in the general journal. Choose the account titles from the following chart of accounts. Be sure to number the journal page 1 and to write the year at the top of the Date column. Include an explanation for each entry.

ASSETS

101 Cash
111 Accounts Receivable
121 Supplies
141 Equipment

LIABILITIES

202 Accounts Payable

OWNER'S EQUITY

301 Kevin Pyle, Capital
302 Kevin Pyle, Drawing

REVENUE

401 Fees Income

EXPENSES

511 Equipment Repair Expense
514 Telephone Expense
517 Utilities Expense
520 Salaries Expense
523 Rent Expense

TRANSACTIONS

Dec. 1 Issued Check 6921 for $1,150 to pay the December rent.

5 Performed services for $2,200 in cash.

6 Performed services for $1,950 on credit.
10 Paid the November telephone bill of $120 with Check 6922.
11 Received a bill for $105 for equipment repairs; paid the bill with Check 6923.
12 Received $600 on account from credit clients.
15 Issued Checks 6924–6929 for $3,200 for semimonthly salaries.
18 Issued Check 6930 for $250 to purchase supplies.
19 Purchased new tennis rackets for $1,850 on credit from Tennis Pros, Inc.; received Invoice 3311, payable in 30 days.
20 Issued Check 6931 for $490 to purchase new nets. (Equipment)
21 Received $650 on account from credit clients.
21 Returned a damaged net and received a cash refund of $106.
22 Performed services for $2,980 in cash.
23 Performed services for $3,520 on credit.
26 Issued Check 6932 for $280 to purchase supplies.
28 Paid the monthly electric bill of $475 with Check 6933.
31 Issued Checks 6934–6939 for $3,200 for semimonthly salaries.
31 Issued Check 6940 for $500 cash to Kevin Pyle for personal expenses.

PROBLEM 4–2A
(Obj. 1, 3)

Journalizing and posting transactions. On August 1, 19X3, Sara Kelly opened an advertising agency. She plans to use the chart of accounts listed below.

Instructions

1. Journalize the transactions. Be sure to number the journal page 1 and to write the year at the top of the Date column. Include an explanation for each entry.
2. Post to the ledger accounts. Before you start the posting process, open accounts by entering titles and numbers in the headings. Follow the order of the accounts in the chart of accounts.

ASSETS

101 Cash
111 Accounts Receivable
121 Supplies
141 Office Equipment
151 Art Equipment

LIABILITIES

202 Accounts Payable

OWNER'S EQUITY

301 Sara Kelly, Capital
302 Sara Kelly, Drawing

REVENUE

401 Fees Income

EXPENSES

511 Telephone Expense
514 Salaries Expense
517 Utilities Expense
520 Rent Expense
523 Office Cleaning Expense

TRANSACTIONS

Aug. 1 Sara Kelly invested $30,000 cash in the business.
2 Issued Check 1001 for $950 to pay the August rent for the office.

5 Purchased desks and other office furniture for $6,000 from Beals, Inc.; received Invoice 2647 payable in 60 days.
6 Issued Check 1002 for $1,950 to purchase equipment for the art department.
7 Purchased supplies for $350; paid with Check 1003.
10 Issued Check 1004 for $105 for office cleaning service.
12 Performed services for $800 in cash and $2,150 on credit. (Use a compound entry.)
15 Returned damaged supplies for a cash refund of $75.
18 Purchased an electronic typewriter for $1,050 from Electronic Office Systems, Invoice 462; issued Check 1005 to make a down payment of $525, with the balance payable in 30 days. (Use one compound entry.)
20 Issued Check 1006 for $3,000 to Beals, Inc., as payment on account for office furniture, Invoice 2647.
26 Performed services for $1,375 on credit.
27 Paid $115 for monthly telephone bill; issued Check 1007.
30 Received $800 in cash from credit customers.
30 Mailed Check 1008 to pay the monthly utility bill of $348.
30 Issued Checks 1009–1011 for $2,875 to the employees for their monthly salaries.

PROBLEM 4–3A (Obj. 4)

Recording correcting entries. The journal entries shown below contain errors. They were prepared by an employee of the Joint Venture Company who does not have an adequate knowledge of accounting.

Instructions

Examine the journal entries carefully to locate the errors. Provide a brief written description of each error.

GENERAL JOURNAL PAGE *1*

DATE		DESCRIPTION	POST. REF.	DEBIT	CREDIT
19X2					
Mar.	*1*	*Accounts Payable*		*1300 00*	
		Fees Income			*1300 00*
		Performed services on			
		credit			
	2	*Cash*		*110 00*	
		Telephone Expense			*110 00*
		Paid for February			
		telephone service, Check			
		1706			
	3	*Office Equipment*		*2250 00*	
		Office Supplies		*250 00*	
		Cash			*2600 00*
		Purchased file cabinet and			
		office supplies, Check 1707			

PROBLEM 4–4A
(Obj. 1, 2, 3)

Journalizing and posting transactions. Reflected below are five transactions for the Heritage Repair Service that took place during November 19X9, the first month of operation. Record the transactions in the general journal and post them to the appropriate ledger accounts. Be sure to number the journal page 1 and to write the year at the top of the Date column. Use the account titles and numbers listed below.

Cash	101	Accounts Payable	202
Accounts Receivable	111	Susan Clark, Capital	301
Office Supplies	121	Fees Income	401
Tools	131		
Machinery	141		
Equipment	151		
Truck	161		

TRANSACTIONS

Nov. 1 Susan Clark invested $25,000 in cash plus tools with a fair market value of $500 to start the business.

2 Purchased equipment for $1,500 and office supplies for $500 from Repair Depot, Invoice 1101; issued Check 100 for $500 as a down payment with the balance due in 30 days.

10 Performed services for Jason Taylor for $1,500, who paid $500 in cash with the balance due in 30 days.

15 Purchased a truck for $12,000 from Tyler Ford, Inc., Invoice 2210; issued Check 101 for $4,000 as a down payment with the balance due in 90 days.

20 Purchased machinery for $2,500 from Zain Machinery, Inc., Invoice 850; issued Check 102 for $500 in cash as a down payment with the balance due in 30 days.

PROBLEM SET B

PROBLEM 4–1B
(Obj. 1)

Recording transactions in the general journal. The transactions listed below took place at the Kwan Industrial Cleaning Service during September 19X3. This firm cleans industrial buildings for a fee.

Instructions

Analyze and record each transaction in the general journal. Choose the account titles from the chart of accounts shown below. Be sure to number the journal page 1 and to write the year at the top of the Date column.

ASSETS

101 Cash
111 Accounts Receivable
141 Equipment

LIABILITIES

202 Accounts Payable

OWNER'S EQUITY

301 Anna Kwan, Capital
302 Anna Kwan, Drawing

REVENUE

401 Fees Income

EXPENSES

501 Equipment Repair Expense
502 Telephone Expense
503 Utilities Expense
511 Salaries Expense
514 Rent Expense
521 Cleaning Supplies Expense
524 Office Supplies Expense

TRANSACTIONS

Sept. 1 Anna Kwan invested $18,000 in cash to start the business.
5 Performed services for $1,200 in cash.
6 Issued Check 1000 for $850 to pay the September rent.
7 Performed services for $900 on credit.
9 Issued Check 1001 for $150 to pay the September telephone bill.
10 Issued Check 1002 for $120 for equipment repairs.
12 Received $425 from credit clients.
14 Issued Checks 1003–1004 for $3,600 to pay the semimonthly salaries.
18 Issued Check 1005 for $300 for cleaning supplies.
19 Issued Check 1006 for $250 for office supplies.
20 Purchased equipment for $2,500 from Don's Equipment, Inc., Invoice 2010; issued Check 1007 for $500 with the balance due in 30 days.
22 Performed services for $1,975 in cash.
24 Issued Check 1008 for $190 for the monthly electric bill.
26 Performed services for $900 on account.
30 Issued Checks 1009–1010 for $3,600 to pay the semimonthly salaries.
30 Issued Check 1011 for $1,000 to Anna Kwan to pay for personal expenses.

PROBLEM 4–2B
(Obj. 1, 3)

Tutorial

Journalizing and posting transactions. On July 1, 19X3, Elaine Anderson opened a photographic service that works with advertising agencies. Her chart of accounts and the financial activities of her business during the first month of operations are listed below.

Instructions

1. Journalize the transactions. Be sure to number the journal page 1 and to write the year at the top of the Date column. Include an explanation for each entry.
2. Post to the ledger accounts. Before you start the posting process, open the accounts by entering the titles and numbers in the headings. Follow the order of the accounts in the chart of accounts.

ASSETS

101 Cash
111 Accounts Receivable
121 Supplies
141 Office Equipment
151 Photographic Equipment

LIABILITIES

202 Accounts Payable

OWNER'S EQUITY

301 Elaine Anderson, Capital
302 Elaine Anderson, Drawing

REVENUE

401 Fees Income

EXPENSES

511 Telephone Expense
514 Salaries Expense
517 Utilities Expense
520 Rent Expense
523 Office Cleaning Expense

TRANSACTIONS

July 1 Elaine Anderson invested $28,000 cash in the business.

2 Issued Check 1001 for $800 to pay the July rent.

5 Purchased desks and other office furniture for $6,500 from Craft, Inc.; received Invoice 2647, payable in 60 days.

6 Issued Check 1002 for $1,600 to purchase photographic equipment.

7 Purchased supplies for $415; paid with Check 1003.

10 Issued Check 1004 for $110 for office cleaning service.

12 Performed services for $600 in cash and $1,300 on credit. (Use one compound entry.)

15 Returned damaged supplies and received a cash refund of $60.

18 Purchased an electronic typewriter for $1,050 from Brown Office Supply, Invoice 330; issued Check 1005 to make a down payment of $250. The balance is payable in 30 days. (Use one compound entry.)

20 Issued Check 1006 for $3,250 to Craft, Inc., as payment on account for office furniture, Invoice 2647.

26 Performed services for $1,400 on credit.

27 Paid $120 for the monthly telephone bill; issued Check 1007.

30 Received $1,100 in cash from credit clients on account.

30 Mailed Check 1008 to pay the monthly utility bill of $250.

30 Issued Checks 1009–1011 for $4,800 to the employees for their monthly salaries.

PROBLEM 4–3B (Obj. 4)

Recording correcting entries. All the journal entries shown below contain errors. The entries were prepared by an employee of the Walker Company who does not have an adequate knowledge of accounting.

Instructions

Examine the journal entries carefully to locate the errors. Provide a brief written description of each error.

GENERAL JOURNAL — PAGE 1

	DATE		DESCRIPTION	POST. REF.	DEBIT	CREDIT	
1	*19X2*						1
2	*Jan.*	*1*	*Accounts Payable*		*1 5 0 0 00*		2
3			*Fees Income*			*1 3 0 0 00*	3
4			*Performed services on*				4
5			*credit*				5
6							6
7		*2*	*Cash*		*1 3 0 00*		7
8			*Telephone Expense*			*1 3 0 00*	8
9			*Paid for January*				9
10			*telephone service, Check*				10
11			*2706*				11

3	*Office Equipment*		*1 3 5 0 00*	
	Office Supplies		*1 5 0 00*	
	Cash			*1 4 0 0 00*
	Purchased file cabinet			
	and office supplies,			
	Check 2707			

PROBLEM 4–4B
(Obj. 1, 2, 3)

Journalizing and posting transactions. Reflected below are five transactions for Central Air Conditioning Service that occurred during December 19X9, the first month of operation. Record the transactions in the general journal and post them to the appropriate ledger accounts. Be sure to number the journal page 1 and to write the year at the top of the Date column. Use the account titles and numbers listed below.

Cash	101	Accounts Payable	202
Accounts Receivable	111	James Walker, Capital	301
Office Supplies	121	Fees Income	401
Tools	131		
Machinery	141		
Equipment	151		
Truck	161		

TRANSACTIONS

Dec. 1 James Walker invested $15,000 plus tools with a fair market value of $800 to start the business.

2 Purchased equipment for $1,800 and office supplies for $200 from Delta Air Conditioning and Supply, Invoice 831; issued Check 100 for $500 as a down payment with the balance due in 30 days.

10 Performed services for Robert Harris for $1,200, who paid $600 in cash with the balance due in 30 days.

15 Purchased a truck for $14,000 from Wood Motors, Inc., Invoice 1311; issued Check 101 for $4,000 as a cash down payment with the balance due in 90 days.

20 Purchased machinery for $1,500 from Harris Machinery Company, Invoice 550; issued Check 102 for $500 as a down payment with the balance due in 30 days.

CHALLENGE PROBLEM

On May 1, 19X4, James Tucker opened the Vocal Talent Agency. He plans to use the chart of accounts shown on page 110.

Instructions

1. Journalize the transactions. Be sure to number the journal pages and write the year at the top of the Date column. Include an explanation for each entry.

2. Post to the ledger accounts. Before you start the posting process, open the accounts by entering the titles and numbers in the headings. Using the list of accounts below, assign appropriate account numbers and place them in the correct order in the ledger.
3. Prepare a trial balance.
4. Prepare the income statement.
5. Prepare a statement of owner's equity.
6. Prepare the balance sheet.

ACCOUNTS

Accounts Payable	Office Furniture
Accounts Receivable	Recording Equipment
Advertising Expense	Rent Expense
Cash	Salaries Expense
Fees Income	Supplies
James Tucker, Capital	Telephone Expense
James Tucker, Drawing	Utilities Expense

TRANSACTIONS

May	1	James Tucker invested $20,000 cash in the business.
	2	Issued Check 501 for $800 to pay the May rent for the office.
	3	Purchased desk and other office furniture for $5,000 from Johnson Office Supply, Invoice 5310; issued Check 502 for a $1,000 down payment with the balance due in 30 days.
	4	Issued Check 503 for $900 for supplies.
	6	Performed services for $2,500 in cash.
	7	Issued Check 504 for $500 to pay for advertising expense.
	8	Purchased recording equipment for $6,000 from Hillsboro Sounds, Inc., Invoice 3333; issued Check 505 for $2,000 as a down payment with the balance payable in 30 days.
	10	Performed services for $1,850 on account.
	11	Issued Check 506 for $1,000 to Johnson Office Supply as payment on account.
	12	Performed services for $3,000 in cash.
	15	Issued Check 507 for $2,000 to pay semimonthly salary of an employee.
	18	Received $1,000 from credit clients on account.
	20	Issued Check 508 for $1,500 to Hillsboro Sounds as payment on account.
	25	Issued Check 509 for $375 for the monthly telephone bill.
	27	Issued Check 510 for $450 for the monthly electric bill.
	28	Issued Check 511 to James Tucker for $1,500 for personal living expenses.
	31	Issued Check 512 for $2,000 to pay semimonthly salary of an employee.

CRITICAL THINKING PROBLEM

Richard Hightower, the new accountant for Art Supplies Unlimited, has asked you to review the financial statements prepared for March to find and correct any errors. Review the income statement and balance sheet that follow and identify the errors Hightower made (he did not prepare a statement of owner's equity). Prepare a corrected income statement and balance sheet, as well as a statement of owner's equity, for Art Supplies Unlimited.

ART SUPPLIES UNLIMITED
Income Statement
March 31, 19X6

Revenue		
Fees Income		12 400 00
Expenses		
Salaries Expense	4 500 00	
Rent Expense	900 00	
Repair Expense	150 00	
Utilities Expense	1 300 00	
Drawing	2 000 00	
Total Expenses		8 850 00
Net Income		21 250 00

ART SUPPLIES UNLIMITED
Balance Sheet
Month Ended March 31, 19X6

Assets		*Liabilities*	
Land	10 000 00	*Accounts Receivable*	5 000 00
Building	30 000 00		
Cash	13 550 00	*Owner's Equity*	
Accounts Payable	5 000 00	*Ben Slade, Capital, March 1, 19X6*	50 000 00
Total Assets	58 550 00	*Total Liabilities and Owner's Equity*	55 000 00

CHAPTER

5

Adjustments and the Worksheet

OBJECTIVES

1. Complete a trial balance on a worksheet.
2. Prepare adjustments for unrecorded business transactions.
3. Complete the worksheet.
4. Prepare an income statement, statement of owner's equity, and balance sheet from the completed worksheet.
5. Journalize and post the adjusting entries.
6. Define the accounting terms new to this chapter.

As you already know, the purpose of having journals and ledgers is to gather the data that is needed to prepare the financial statements. After all the transactions for the operating period are posted to the ledger accounts, the trial balance is prepared to test the accuracy of the financial records. Because management will use the financial statements to make decisions, every effort must be made to ensure that these reports contain no errors.

In this chapter, you will see how the data recorded in a firm's accounting records is checked at the end of the operating period, adjusted for certain items that were not recorded during the period, and summarized in financial statements. Let's begin with the trial balance prepared on a worksheet.

NEW TERMS

Account form balance sheet ▪ Adjusting entries ▪ Adjustments ▪ Book value ▪ Contra asset account ▪ Depreciation ▪ Prepaid expenses ▪ Report form balance sheet ▪ Salvage value ▪ Straight-line depreciation ▪ Worksheet

THE WORKSHEET

When the trial balance shows that the general ledger is in balance, the financial statements for the period are prepared. These statements must be completed as soon as possible if they are to be useful. Therefore, anything that can be done to save time is important. One way to prepare the financial statements more quickly is by using a form called a worksheet. A **worksheet** is an accounting form with many columns that is used to gather all the data needed at the end of an accounting period to prepare the financial statements.

Preparation of the worksheet is the fourth step in the accounting cycle.

A common type of worksheet is shown in Figure 5–1. Notice that this worksheet contains 10 money columns, which are arranged in five sections labeled Trial Balance, Adjustments, Adjusted Trial Balance, Income Statement, and Balance Sheet. Each section includes a Debit column and a Credit column. Also notice that the third line of the worksheet heading shows the period of operations covered by the figures on the worksheet.

FIGURE 5–1
Ten-column Worksheet

ARROW ACCOUNTING SERVICES
Worksheet
Month Ended December 31, 19X5

ACCOUNT NAME	TRIAL BALANCE		ADJUSTMENTS		ADJUSTED TRIAL BALANCE		INCOME STATEMENT		BALANCE SHEET	
	DEBIT	CREDIT	DEBIT	CREDIT	DEBIT	CREDIT	DEBIT	CREDIT	DEBIT	CREDIT

The Trial Balance Section

OBJECTIVE 1
Complete a trial balance on a worksheet.

To save time and effort, many accountants prepare the trial balance on the worksheet. They list the general ledger accounts directly on the worksheet and then transfer the balances from the general ledger to the Debit and Credit columns of the Trial Balance section. After the account balances are recorded on the worksheet, the equality of the debits and credits is proved by totaling the Debit and Credit columns. The Trial Balance columns must have equal debit and credit totals, as you can see in Figure 5–2. A double ruling is placed under each column to show that the work in that column is complete.

Examine the Trial Balance section of the partial worksheet in Figure 5–2. Virginia Richey, the office manager for Arrow Accounting Services, has added four new accounts to the firm's general ledger: Accumulated Depreciation—Equipment, Supplies Expense, Rent Expense, and Depreciation Expense—Equipment. These accounts do not have balances yet, but they will be needed as other parts of the worksheet are prepared. Richey has therefore listed them in the Trial Balance section so that they can appear in numeric order with the rest of the general ledger accounts. The use of these new accounts will be explained in the discussion of the Adjustments section of the worksheet that follows.

FIGURE 5–2
A Partial Worksheet

ARROW ACCOUNTING SERVICES
Worksheet (Partial)
Month Ended December 31, 19X5

	ACCOUNT NAME	TRIAL BALANCE DEBIT	TRIAL BALANCE CREDIT	ADJUSTMENTS DEBIT	ADJUSTMENTS CREDIT
1	*Cash*	16 200 00			
2	*Accounts Receivable*	2 000 00			
3	*Supplies*	1 000 00			(a) 500 00
4	*Prepaid Rent*	20 000 00			(b) 2 500 00
5	*Equipment*	15 000 00			
6	*Accumulated Depreciation—Equipment*				(c) 250 00
7	*Accounts Payable*		4 000 00		
8	*John Arrow, Capital*		40 000 00		
9	*John Arrow, Drawing*	1 000 00			
10	*Fees Income*		14 000 00		
11	*Salaries Expense*	2 500 00			
12	*Utilities Expense*	300 00			
13	*Supplies Expense*			(a) 500 00	
14	*Rent Expense*			(b) 2 500 00	
15	*Depreciation Expense—Equipment*			(c) 250 00	
16	*Totals*	58 000 00	58 000 00	3 250 00	3 250 00
17					

The Adjustments Section

OBJECTIVE 2
Prepare adjustments for unrecorded business transactions.

Most changes in a firm's account balances are caused by transactions between the business and another business or individual. In the case of Arrow Accounting Services, all the changes in its accounts discussed so far were caused by transactions that the firm had with suppliers, customers, the landlord, and employees. These changes were easy to recognize and were journalized and posted as they occurred. However, some changes are not caused by transactions with other businesses or individuals. Instead, they arise from the internal operations of the firm itself, and they must be recognized and recorded at the end of each accounting period. The worksheet provides a convenient form for gathering the information and determining the effects of the changes on the accounts involved.

The process of updating accounts at the end of an accounting period for previously unrecorded items that belong to the period is referred to as making **adjustments,** or **adjusting entries.** Let's look at the adjustments made at Arrow Accounting Services on December 31, 19X5, the end of the business's first month of operations, to get a more detailed picture of the process.

Adjustment for Supplies Used

On November 28, 19X5, Arrow Accounting Services purchased supplies for $1,000. Some of these supplies were used during December in the course of operations. However, on the December 31 trial balance, the Supplies account still shows a balance of $1,000. In order to present an accurate and complete picture of the firm's financial affairs at the end of December, an adjustment must be made for the supplies used. Otherwise, the asset account Supplies will be overstated because fewer supplies are actually on hand. Similarly, the firm's expenses will be understated because the cost of supplies used represents an operating expense that has not been recorded.

On December 31, 19X5, Richey made a count of the remaining supplies and found that they totaled $500. This meant that supplies amounting to $500 were used during the month ($1,000 – $500 = $500). Analysis of this situation shows the following effects on the firm's accounts.

1. The Supplies Expense account has increased by $500.
2. The Supplies account has decreased by $500.

To recognize these effects, Richey makes an adjustment on the worksheet that consists of a debit of $500 to Supplies Expense and a credit of $500 to Supplies, as shown in Figure 5–2. Notice that both the debit and credit of the adjustment are labeled (a). Identifying the two parts of an adjustment is especially helpful when the adjustments are journalized after the worksheet has been completed.

Adjustment for Expired Rent

On November 7, 19X5, Arrow Accounting Services paid $20,000 rent in advance for an eight-month period (December 19X5 through July 19X6). As a result of this transaction, the firm acquired the right to occupy facilities for the specified period. Since this right is considered a form of property, the $20,000 was debited to an asset account called Prepaid Rent. On December 31, 19X5, the firm's trial balance still shows a balance of $20,000 in this account. However, the firm has used up part of its right to occupy the facilities—one month of the prepaid rent has expired.

Since the $20,000 sum covered an eight-month period, the expired rent for December amounts to $2,500 (1/8 of $20,000 = $2,500). Thus on December 31 the asset account Prepaid Rent is overstated by $2,500. At the same time the firm's expenses are understated because the $2,500 of expired rent represents an operating expense that has not been recorded. The cost of facilities used (rent) is a cost of doing business.

To update the accounts involved, an adjustment is made on December 31. The effects of this adjustment are as follows.

1. The Rent Expense account has increased by $2,500.
2. The Prepaid Rent account has decreased by $2,500.

Richey enters the adjustment on the worksheet by recording a debit of $2,500 to Rent Expense and a credit of $2,500 to Prepaid Rent. These two figures are labeled (b) as shown in the Adjustments section of the partial worksheet in Figure 5–2.

Supplies and prepaid rent are known as **prepaid expenses.** They are expense items that are acquired and paid for in advance of their use. As you have seen, at the time of their acquisition, these items represent assets for a business and are therefore recorded in asset accounts. However, as they are used, their cost is transferred to expense accounts by means of adjusting entries at the end of each accounting period.

Other common prepaid expenses are prepaid insurance and prepaid advertising. These items are debited to the asset accounts Prepaid Insurance and Prepaid Advertising when they are acquired. Later the expired cost that applies to each accounting period is debited to Insurance Expense and Advertising Expense and credited to the asset accounts in end-of-period adjusting entries.

Adjustment for Depreciation

One other adjustment must be made for Arrow Accounting Services at the end of December 19X5, its first month of operations. On November 9 and 10 the firm purchased equipment at a total cost of $15,000. This equipment was put to use in December when the firm opened for business. At the time the equipment was bought, its cost was debited to the asset account Equipment. On December 31, 19X5, the firm's trial balance therefore shows a balance of $15,000 in the Equipment account.

The various items of equipment that were purchased all have an estimated useful life of five years and no expected salvage value after that period. **Salvage value** is the amount an item can be sold for after its use by the business. Because long-term assets like the firm's equipment help to earn revenue for a business, their cost is charged to operations (transferred to expense) as they are used. This charge is made at the end of each accounting period by means of an adjusting entry. The process of allocating the cost of a long-term asset to operations during its expected useful life is known as **depreciation.** There are many different ways to determine the amount of depreciation to charge to expense in each accounting period. The method that Richey has decided on is a very simple and widely used one called **straight-line depreciation.** Under this method, depreciation is computed by the formula

$$\text{Depreciation} = \frac{\text{Cost} - \text{Salvage value}}{\text{Estimated months of useful life}}$$

This formula results in an equal amount of depreciation being charged to each accounting period during the asset's useful life.

Since the equipment purchased by Arrow Accounting Services is expected to have a useful life of five years and no salvage value, its entire cost of $15,000 must be depreciated over the five-year period. The amount of depreciation for December 19X5, the first month of operations, is computed as follows.

1. First, convert the asset's useful life from years to months: 5×12 months = 60 months.

2. Next, the total depreciation to be taken is divided by the total number of months: $15,000/60 = $250.
3. The amount of depreciation to be charged off for December 19X5 and every other month during the asset's useful life is $250.

As the cost of the equipment is gradually transferred to expense, its **book value** (recorded value) as an asset must be reduced. This procedure cannot be carried out by directly decreasing the $15,000 balance in the asset account Equipment. *Generally accepted accounting principles* require that the original cost of a long-term asset continue to appear in the asset account until the firm has used up or disposed of the asset. Thus another account called Accumulated Depreciation—Equipment is used to keep a record of the total depreciation taken and to reduce the book value of the asset.

Accumulated Depreciation—Equipment is a special type of account called a **contra asset account.** The account has a credit balance, which is contrary, or opposite, to the normal balance of an asset account. This credit balance is subtracted from the debit balance of the Equipment account on the balance sheet to report the book value of the asset.

The effects of the adjustment for depreciation at Arrow Accounting Services on December 31, 19X5, are as follows.

▲ **REMEMBER!**

Contra means opposite to the normal balance of a related account.

1. Depreciation Expense—Equipment has increased by $250.
2. Accumulated Depreciation—Equipment has increased by $250.

Richey enters the adjustment on the worksheet by recording a debit of $250 to Depreciation Expense—Equipment and a credit of $250 to Accumulated Depreciation—Equipment. These two figures are labeled (c) on the partial worksheet in Figure 5–2.

If the firm had other kinds of long-term assets, an adjustment for depreciation would be made for each one. Typical long-term assets owned by businesses in addition to equipment are land, buildings, trucks, automobiles, furniture, and fixtures. Of these items, only land is not subject to depreciation.

After the adjustment for depreciation of the equipment is recorded on the worksheet of the firm, the Adjustments columns are totaled and ruled. The totals of the Debit and Credit columns in this section must be equal. If they are not, Richey must locate and correct the error or errors before continuing. Examine the partial worksheet in Figure 5–2 to see how the Adjustments section was completed.

SELF-REVIEW

1. Why is the worksheet prepared?
2. What are adjustments?
3. A firm paid $450 for supplies during the accounting period. At the end of the accounting period the firm had $200 of supplies on hand. What information is entered on the worksheet to show this adjustment?
4. Why are prepaid items adjusted at the end of an accounting period?

5. A firm paid $6,000 for six months' rent at the beginning of its accounting period. What is the necessary adjustment for rent expense at the end of the first month of the accounting period?

Answers to Self-Review

1. A worksheet is prepared so that the financial statements can be prepared more efficiently.
2. Adjustments are made to update accounts at the end of an accounting period to include previously unrecorded items that belong to the period.
3. Supplies Expense is debited for $250. Supplies is credited for $250.
4. At the time of their acquisition, prepaid items represent assets to be used by the business. However, as they are used, their cost is transferred to an expense account to properly reflect the remaining cost to be used by the business (asset) and the amount already used (expense) by the business.
5. Rent Expense is debited for $1,000. Prepaid Rent is credited for $1,000.

FIGURE 5–3
Partial Worksheet

ARROW ACCOUNTING SERVICES
Worksheet (Partial)
Month Ended December 31, 19X5

	ACCOUNT NAME	TRIAL BALANCE		ADJUSTMENTS	
		DEBIT	CREDIT	DEBIT	CREDIT
1	*Cash*	16 2 0 0 00			
2	*Accounts Receivable*	2 0 0 0 00			
3	*Supplies*	1 0 0 0 00			(a) 5 0 0 00
4	*Prepaid Rent*	20 0 0 0 00			(b) 2 5 0 0 00
5	*Equipment*	15 0 0 0 00			
6	*Accumulated Depreciation—Equipment*				(c) 2 5 0 00
7	*Accounts Payable*		4 0 0 0 00		
8	*John Arrow, Capital*		40 0 0 0 00		
9	*John Arrow, Drawing*	1 0 0 0 00			
10	*Fees Income*		14 0 0 0 00		
11	*Salaries Expense*	2 5 0 0 00			
12	*Utilities Expense*	3 0 0 00			
13	*Supplies Expense*			(a) 5 0 0 00	
14	*Rent Expense*			(b) 2 5 0 0 00	
15	*Depreciation Expense—Equipment*			(c) 2 5 0 00	
16	*Totals*	58 0 0 0 00	58 0 0 0 00	3 2 5 0 00	3 2 5 0 00
17					

The Adjusted Trial Balance Section

OBJECTIVE 3

Complete the worksheet.

The next task is to prepare an adjusted trial balance using the worksheet. This process involves two steps:

1. First, combine the figures from the Trial Balance section and the Adjustments section to record the updated account balances in the Adjusted Trial Balance section.
2. Next, check on the equality of the debits and credits of the combined figures before extending the balances to the financial statement sections.

Refer to the Adjusted Trial Balance section of the partial worksheet shown in Figure 5–3. Notice that the balances of the accounts that did not require adjustment have simply been extended to this section from the Trial Balance section. For example, the $16,200 balance of the Cash account that appears in the Debit column of the Trial Balance section was recorded in the Debit column of the Adjusted Trial Balance section without any change.

However, the balances of all accounts that are affected by adjustments must be recomputed. For example, the Supplies account has a debit balance of $1,000 in the Trial Balance section and shows a credit entry of $500 in the Adjustments section. Thus the new balance is $500 ($1,000 − $500 = $500). This amount is recorded in the Debit column of the Adjusted Trial Balance section. In a similar manner, the updated balance of Prepaid Rent is $17,500 ($20,000 − $2,500 = $17,500).

ADJUSTED TRIAL BALANCE		INCOME STATEMENT		BALANCE SHEET		
DEBIT	CREDIT	DEBIT	CREDIT	DEBIT	CREDIT	
16 200 00						1
2 000 00						2
500 00						3
17 500 00						4
15 000 00						5
	250 00					6
	4 000 00					7
	40 000 00					8
1 000 00						9
	14 000 00					10
2 500 00						11
300 00						12
500 00						13
2 500 00						14
250 00						15
58 250 00	58 250 00					16
						17

Information Block: Communication

Planning and Developing Communication

As you have learned, the accounting cycle is a series of steps performed during each accounting period to classify, record, and summarize financial data for a business to produce needed financial information. To help you plan and develop effective *business* communication, which may accompany your financial information, learn to follow the steps below each time you communicate in writing or in oral presentations.

- *Step 1: Determine your objective.* What is the purpose of your message? What do you want to accomplish in your written or oral presentation? You must be clear in your own mind before you can communicate effectively.
- *Step 2: Analyze the receiver.* What is your receiver's viewpoint, knowledge, interests, attitudes, and anticipated reaction toward the subject of your message? The receiver's perspective will influence the details of your message, your word choice, and your approach. If a group of people will receive the message, consider each person.
- *Step 3: Gather information.* What information must you share to accomplish your objective? A variety of information may be relevant, for example, financial, procedural, staffing, technological, strategic planning and analysis, and so on.
- *Step 4: Develop an outline.* What is your plan or outline to present your message? Most messages have an introduction, an explanation section, and a closing. By developing an outline using the supporting information, your objective, and the receiver's anticipated reaction, you establish a plan to accomplish your objective. You will also decrease any tendency to ramble or suffer from writer's block.

When figures must be combined to calculate updated account balances for the adjusted trial balance, follow these rules.

1. If an account has a debit balance in the Trial Balance section and there is a debit entry in the Adjustments section, add the two amounts.
2. If an account has a debit balance in the Trial Balance section and there is a credit entry in the Adjustments section, subtract the credit amount.
3. If an account has a credit balance in the Trial Balance section and there is a credit entry in the Adjustments section, add the two amounts.

- *Step 5: Determine the medium.* How will you communicate your message? You may communicate written messages in a letter, memorandum, announcement, or report. You may communicate oral messages in a telephone conversation, meeting, conference, or teleconference.
- *Step 6: Compose your message.* Following your outline, compose sentences and paragraphs to develop your message. Focus on recording what is important and essential. Do not focus on achieving perfection at this step in the process.
- *Step 7: Critique your message.* Critique and revise your message to meet your objective by applying the four characteristics of effective business communications (courteous, concise, complete, and correct).
- *Step 8: Prepare your final message.* Since you want your final message to represent you positively, verify that the message is perfect. Most written business messages are limited to one page. Oral presentations may have time limitations; thus to ensure a positive performance, develop the habit of practicing an oral presentation *before* communicating.
- *Step 9: Communicate your message.* With your message planned and developed, you are ready to complete the communication cycle by delivering your message.

Learn to apply these nine steps for planning and developing effective business communications, and you will be successful in communicating your messages to others.

Project: Assume you are the manager of an accounting department for a mid-sized company. For several months your staff has been slow in preparing the monthly financial statements due to errors in their financial records. Apply the steps for planning and developing effective business communications to prepare an appropriate message to your staff, which includes personnel with and without accounting degrees.

4. If an account has a credit balance in the Trial Balance section and there is a debit entry in the Adjustments section, subtract the debit amount.

The other accounts affected by adjustments (Accumulated Depreciation—Equipment, Supplies Expense, Rent Expense, and Depreciation Expense—Equipment) had no balances when the Trial Balance section of the worksheet was prepared. Thus the figures shown in the Adjustments section are extended to the Adjusted Trial Balance section. For example, the $250 credit entry for Accumulated Depreciation—Equipment is recorded as the balance of that account in the Credit column of the Adjusted Trial Balance section.

Once all account balances have been recorded in the Adjusted Trial Balance section, the Debit and Credit columns are totaled and ruled. Just as with the original trial balance, the adjusted trial balance must have equal debit and credit totals. If these totals are not equal, the errors must be located. It is essential that all figures be correct before they are used to complete the financial statement sections of the worksheet.

The Income Statement and Balance Sheet Sections

The Income Statement and Balance Sheet sections of the worksheet are used to organize the figures needed for these financial reports. For example, to prepare an income statement, all the revenue and expense account balances must be in one place. It is convenient to assemble this information on the worksheet.

The process of completing the financial statement sections is quite simple. Starting at the top of the Adjusted Trial Balance section, each general ledger account is examined. If an account will appear on the balance sheet, the amount is entered in the Balance Sheet section. If an account will appear on the income statement, the amount is entered in the Income Statement section. When amounts are extended from the Adjusted Trial Balance section to the statement sections, every effort should be made not to enter a debit amount in the Credit column or a credit amount in the Debit column.

FIGURE 5–4
A Completed Worksheet

ARROW ACCOUNTING SERVICES
Worksheet
Month Ended December 31, 19X5

	ACCOUNT NAME	TRIAL BALANCE		ADJUSTMENTS	
		DEBIT	CREDIT	DEBIT	CREDIT
1	*Cash*	*16 200 00*			
2	*Accounts Receivable*	*2 000 00*			
3	*Supplies*	*1 000 00*			*(a) 500 00*
4	*Prepaid Rent*	*20 000 00*			*(b) 2 500 00*
5	*Equipment*	*15 000 00*			
6	*Accumulated Depreciation—Equipment*				*(c) 250 00*
7	*Accounts Payable*		*4 000 00*		
8	*John Arrow, Capital*		*40 000 00*		
9	*John Arrow, Drawing*	*1 000 00*			
10	*Fees Income*		*14 000 00*		
11	*Salaries Expense*	*2 500 00*			
12	*Utilities Expense*	*300 00*			
13	*Supplies Expense*			*(a) 500 00*	
14	*Rent Expense*			*(b) 2 500 00*	
15	*Depreciation Expense—Equipment*			*(c) 250 00*	
16	*Totals*	*58 000 00*	*58 000 00*	*3 250 00*	*3 250 00*
17	*Net Income*				
18					
19					

The Balance Sheet Section

Remember that the general ledger accounts are numbered according to type in the following sequence: assets, liabilities, owner's equity, revenue, and expenses. The accounts appear on the worksheet in this order. Thus the first five accounts in the Adjusted Trial Balance section of the partial worksheet shown in Figure 5–4 are assets. They are extended to the Debit column of the Balance Sheet section.

The next three accounts in the Adjusted Trial Balance section have credit balances. They are a contra asset account (Accumulated Depreciation—Equipment), a liability account (Accounts Payable), and an owner's equity account (John Arrow, Capital). The balances of these accounts are extended to the Credit column of the Balance Sheet section. The account, John Arrow, Drawing, has a debit balance that is extended to the Debit column of the Balance Sheet section, as shown in Figure 5–4.

The Income Statement Section

All revenue and expense accounts must appear on the income statement. Thus the credit balance of the Fees Income account is extended to the Credit column of the Income Statement section of the worksheet, as shown above. The last five accounts in the Adjusted Trial Balance section are expense accounts. The debit balances of

ADJUSTED TRIAL BALANCE		INCOME STATEMENT		BALANCE SHEET		
DEBIT	CREDIT	DEBIT	CREDIT	DEBIT	CREDIT	
16,200.00				16,200.00		1
2,000.00				2,000.00		2
500.00				500.00		3
17,500.00				17,500.00		4
15,000.00				15,000.00		5
	250.00				250.00	6
	4,000.00				4,000.00	7
	40,000.00				40,000.00	8
1,000.00				1,000.00		9
	14,000.00		14,000.00			10
2,500.00		2,500.00				11
300.00		300.00				12
500.00		500.00				13
2,500.00		2,500.00				14
250.00		250.00				15
58,250.00	58,250.00	6,050.00	14,000.00	52,200.00	44,250.00	16
		7,950.00			7,950.00	17
		14,000.00	14,000.00	52,200.00	52,200.00	18
						19

these accounts are extended to the Debit column of the Income Statement section, as shown in Figure 5–4.

After all account balances have been transferred from the Adjusted Trial Balance section of the worksheet to the financial statement sections, the columns in the Income Statement section are totaled. In the Income Statement columns of the worksheet for Arrow Accounting Services, the debits (expenses) total $6,050 and the credits (revenue) total $14,000.

Next the columns in the Balance Sheet section are totaled. As shown in Figure 5–4, the debits (assets and drawing account) total $52,200 and the credits (contra asset, liabilities, and owner's equity) total $44,250.

Since the Income Statement columns include all revenue and expenses, the totals of these columns are used to determine the net income or net loss. The smaller column total is subtracted from the larger one. In this case the total of the Credit column, $14,000, which represents the revenue, exceeds the total of the Debit column, $6,050, which represents the expenses. The difference between the two amounts is a net income of $7,950.

The net income causes a net increase in owner's equity as a result of the firm's operations for the month. As a check on accuracy, the amount in the Balance Sheet Debit column is subtracted from that in the Credit column and compared to net income. If the two amounts are the same, the amount of net income is added to the Credit column of the Balance Sheet section of the worksheet. The net income is also recorded on the worksheet below the total of the Debit column of the Income Statement section. The words "Net Income" are entered to identify the amount.

After the net income is recorded on the worksheet, the Income Statement and Balance Sheet columns are totaled again. All pairs of columns should then be in balance. The complete worksheet prepared at Arrow Accounting Services on December 31, 19X5, is shown in Figure 5–4.

If the business had a loss, *Net Loss* would be entered on the worksheet and the amount of loss entered in the Credit column of the Income Statement section and the Debit column of the Balance Sheet section.

PREPARING FINANCIAL STATEMENTS

OBJECTIVE 4

Prepare an income statement, statement of owner's equity, and balance sheet from the completed worksheet.

All the figures needed to prepare the financial statements are now properly organized on the worksheet. The accounts are arranged in the order in which they must appear on the income statement and the balance sheet. The net income (or loss) has been determined for use in preparing the statement of owner's equity. The next step is to prepare the income statement.

The Income Statement

The income statement is prepared directly from the data in the Income Statement section of the worksheet. Compare the income statement for Arrow Accounting Services shown in Figure 5–5 with the worksheet in Figure 5–4.

FIGURE 5–5
Income Statement

ARROW ACCOUNTING SERVICES
Income Statement
Month Ended December 31, 19X5

Revenue		
Fees Income		14 000 00
Expenses		
Salaries Expense	2 500 00	
Utilities Expense	300 00	
Supplies Expense	500 00	
Rent Expense	2 500 00	
Depreciation Expense—Equipment	250 00	
Total Expenses		6 050 00
Net Income for the Month		7 950 00

If the firm had incurred a net loss, the final amount on the income statement would be labeled "Net Loss."

The Statement of Owner's Equity

The statement of owner's equity is prepared from the data in the Balance Sheet section of the worksheet. The statement of owner's equity is prepared before the balance sheet so that the amount of the ending capital balance is available for presentation on the balance sheet. As previously discussed, the statement of owner's equity reports the changes that have occurred in the owner's financial interest during the reporting period. The statement of owner's equity for Arrow Accounting Services is shown in Figure 5–6.

FIGURE 5–6
Statement of Owner's Equity

ARROW ACCOUNTING SERVICES
Statement of Owner's Equity
Month Ended December 31, 19X5

John Arrow, Capital, December 1, 19X5		40 000 00
Net Income for December	7 950 00	
Less Withdrawals for December	1 000 00	
Increase in Capital		6 950 00
John Arrow, Capital, December 31, 19X5		46 950 00

The Balance Sheet

The accounts listed on the balance sheet are taken directly from the Balance Sheet section of the worksheet. The balance sheet for Arrow Accounting Services is shown in Figure 5–7.

FIGURE 5–7
Balance Sheet

ARROW ACCOUNTING SERVICES
Balance Sheet
December 31, 19X5

Assets		
Cash		16 200 00
Accounts Receivable		2 000 00
Supplies		500 00
Prepaid Rent		17 500 00
Equipment	15 000 00	
Less Accumulated Depreciation	250 00	14 750 00
Total Assets		50 950 00
Liabilities and Owner's Equity		
Liabilities		
Accounts Payable		4 000 00
Owner's Equity		
John Arrow, Capital		46 950 00
Total Liabilities and Owner's Equity		50 950 00

Preparation of the financial statements is the fifth step in the accounting cycle.

Notice how the equipment is reported on the balance sheet. Three figures are shown in connection with this item—the original cost of $15,000, the accumulated depreciation of $250, and the book value of $14,750. The book value is computed by subtracting the accumulated depreciation from the original cost. The book value should not be confused with the market value. The book value is simply the portion of the original cost that has not yet been depreciated. The market value may be higher or lower.

Also notice that the ending balance for John Arrow, Capital, $46,950, is transferred from the statement of owner's equity to the balance sheet for December 31, 19X5. Richey, the office manager for Arrow Accounting Services, is now using a type of balance sheet called the **report form.** Unlike the **account form,** which was illustrated in Chapters 2 and 3, the report form lists the liabilities and owner's equity under the assets rather than to the right of them. The report form is widely used because it provides more space for entering account titles and its format is easier to prepare.

JOURNALIZING AND POSTING ADJUSTING ENTRIES

OBJECTIVE 5
Journalize and post the adjusting entries.

As previously discussed, the worksheet is a tool that helps to determine the effects of adjustments on account balances and to prepare the financial statements. After the statements are completed, it is necessary to create a permanent record of any changes in account balances that are shown on the worksheet. These changes are recorded through adjusting entries made in the general journal and then posted to the general ledger. To see how the process works, let's consider again the financial affairs of Arrow Accounting Services on December 31, 19X5, the end of its first month of operations.

When the worksheet for December was prepared, the firm's office manager decided that three adjustments were necessary to provide a complete and accurate picture of the business's operating results and its financial position. Adjustments were made for supplies used, expired rent, and depreciation on the equipment that the business owns. Each adjustment must now be journalized and posted to the general ledger accounts. The entries are made in the order in which the adjustments appear on the worksheet. Thus we begin with the adjustment labeled (a). Refer to the partial worksheet in Figure 5–3 and the explanations given in the text for each of the items that appear there.

Journalizing and posting the adjusting entries is the sixth step in the accounting cycle.

Many accountants prefer to separate the adjusting entries from the routine entries that are recorded throughout the accounting period. One common method is to write the heading "Adjusting Entries" in the Description column of the general journal on the line above the first adjusting entry. This procedure was used by Arrow Accounting Services. Some accountants also prefer to start a new page when they record the adjusting entries.

As soon as all adjusting entries are recorded in the general journal, the entries are posted to the general ledger. Refer to Figure 5–8 (pages 127–128) to see how the adjusting entries made at Arrow Accounting Services on December 31, 19X5, were journalized and posted. Account numbers appear in the general journal because all the entries have been posted. Notice that the word "Adjusting" is written in the Explanation column of the accounts to identify these entries.

FIGURE 5–8
Journalized and Posted Adjusting Entries

GENERAL JOURNAL PAGE *3*

	DATE		DESCRIPTION	POST. REF.	DEBIT	CREDIT	
1	*19X5*		*Adjusting Entries*				1
2	*Dec.*	*31*	*Supplies Expense*	*517*	*500 00*		2
3			*Supplies*	*121*		*500 00*	3
4							4
5		*31*	*Rent Expense*	*520*	*2,500 00*		5
6			*Prepaid Rent*	*131*		*2,500 00*	6
7							7
8		*31*	*Depr. Expense—Equipment*	*523*	*250 00*		8
9			*Accum. Depr.—Equipment*	*142*		*250 00*	9
10							

ACCOUNT *Supplies* ACCOUNT NO. *121*

DATE		EXPLANATION	POST. REF.	DEBIT	CREDIT	BALANCE DEBIT	BALANCE CREDIT
19X5							
Nov.	*28*		*J1*	*1,000 00*		*1,000 00*	
Dec.	*31*	*Adjusting*	*J3*		*500 00*	*500 00*	

ACCOUNT *Prepaid Rent* ACCOUNT NO. *131*

DATE		EXPLANATION	POST. REF.	DEBIT	CREDIT	BALANCE DEBIT	BALANCE CREDIT
19X5							
Nov.	*7*		*J1*	*20 0 0 0 00*		*20 0 0 0 00*	
Dec.	*31*	*Adjusting*	*J3*		*2 5 0 0 00*	*17 5 0 0 00*	

ACCOUNT *Accumulated Depreciation—Equipment* ACCOUNT NO. *142*

DATE		EXPLANATION	POST. REF.	DEBIT	CREDIT	BALANCE DEBIT	BALANCE CREDIT
19X5							
Dec.	*31*	*Adjusting*	*J3*		*2 5 0 00*		*2 5 0 00*

ACCOUNT *Supplies Expense* ACCOUNT NO. *517*

DATE		EXPLANATION	POST. REF.	DEBIT	CREDIT	BALANCE DEBIT	BALANCE CREDIT
19X5							
Dec.	*31*	*Adjusting*	*J3*	*5 0 0 00*		*5 0 0 00*	

ACCOUNT *Rent Expense* ACCOUNT NO. *520*

DATE		EXPLANATION	POST. REF.	DEBIT	CREDIT	BALANCE DEBIT	BALANCE CREDIT
19X5							
Dec.	*31*	*Adjusting*	*J3*	*2 5 0 0 00*		*2 5 0 0 00*	

ACCOUNT *Depreciation Expense—Equipment* ACCOUNT NO. *523*

DATE		EXPLANATION	POST. REF.	DEBIT	CREDIT	BALANCE DEBIT	BALANCE CREDIT
19X5							
Dec.	*31*	*Adjusting*	*J3*	*2 5 0 00*		*2 5 0 00*	

MANAGERIAL IMPLICATIONS

The use of a worksheet permits quicker preparation of the financial statements. Thus management can obtain necessary information when it is still timely. This information allows management to evaluate the results of operations and the financial position of the business and to make decisions. The more accounts that a firm has in its general ledger, the more useful the worksheet is in speeding up the preparation of the financial statements.

It is important to management that the appropriate adjustments are recorded. Otherwise, the financial statements will not present a complete and accurate picture of the firm's financial affairs.

Figure 5–9A Worksheet Summary

The worksheet is used to gather all the data needed at the end of an accounting period to prepare the financial statements. The worksheet heading contains the name of the company (WHO), the title of the statement being prepared (WHAT), and the period covered (WHEN). The worksheet contains ten money columns that are arranged in five sections labeled Trial Balance, Adjustments, Adjusted Trial Balance, Income Statement, and Balance Sheet. Each section includes a Debit column and a Credit column.

The information reflected in the worksheet below is for Arrow Accounting Services for the period ended December 31, 19X5. The illustrations that follow will highlight the preparation of each part of the worksheet.

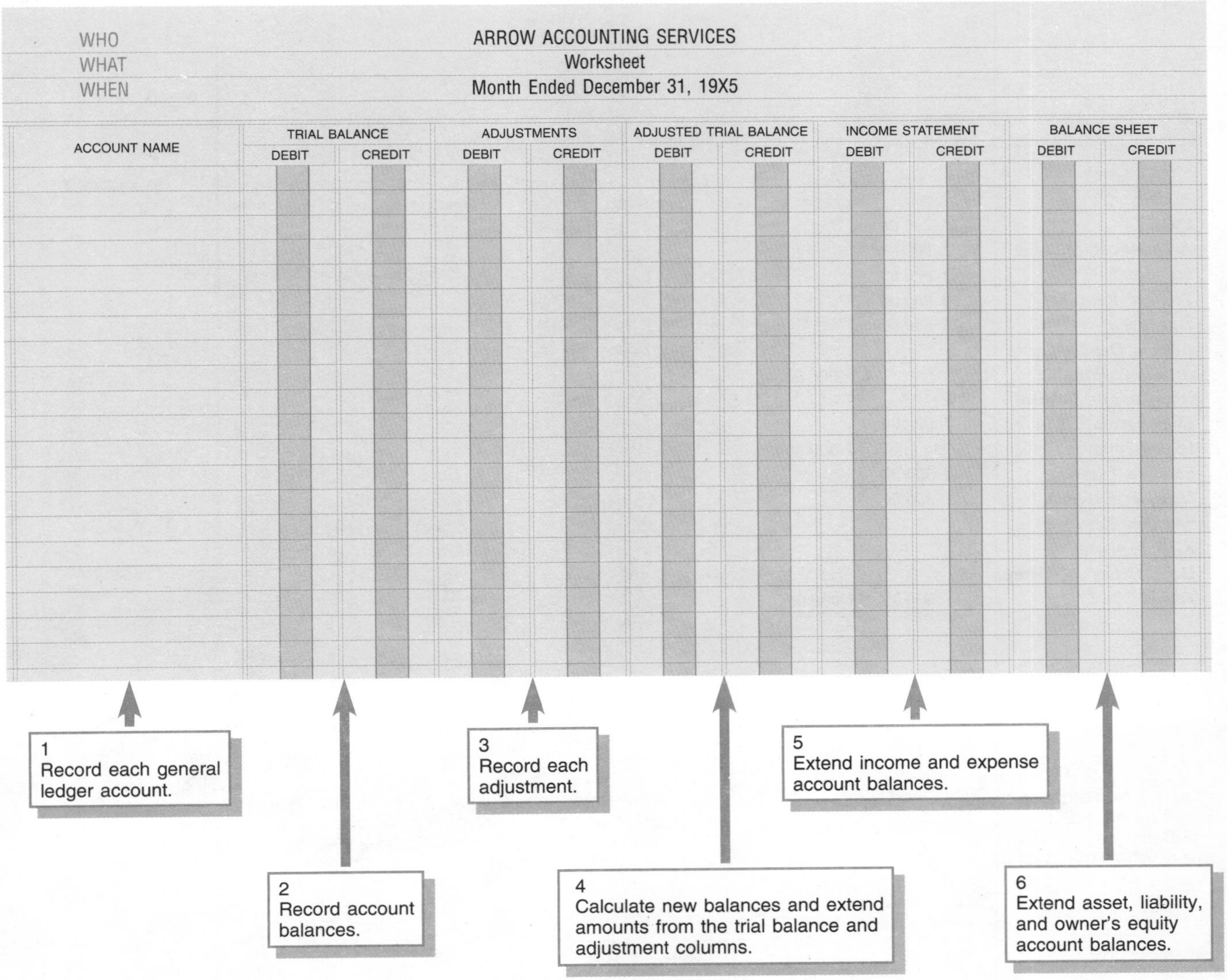

Figure 5–9B The Trial Balance Columns

The first step in preparing the worksheet for Arrow Accounting Services is to list the general ledger accounts and their balances in the Account Name and Trial Balance sections of the worksheet. The equality of total debits and credits is proved by totaling the Debit and Credit columns.

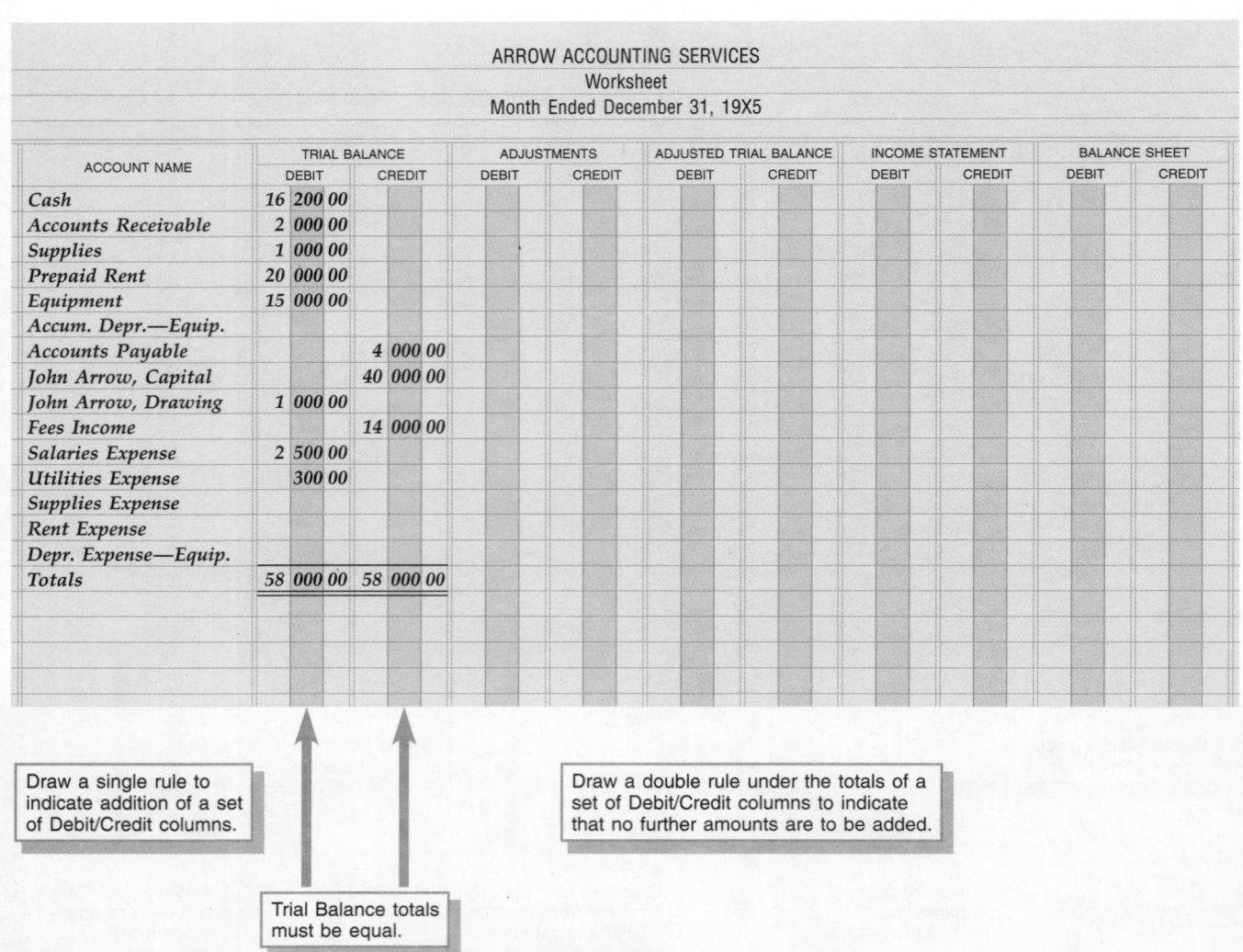

ARROW ACCOUNTING SERVICES
Worksheet
Month Ended December 31, 19X5

ACCOUNT NAME	TRIAL BALANCE		ADJUSTMENTS		ADJUSTED TRIAL BALANCE		INCOME STATEMENT		BALANCE SHEET	
	DEBIT	CREDIT	DEBIT	CREDIT	DEBIT	CREDIT	DEBIT	CREDIT	DEBIT	CREDIT
Cash	16 200 00									
Accounts Receivable	2 000 00									
Supplies	1 000 00									
Prepaid Rent	20 000 00									
Equipment	15 000 00									
Accum. Depr.—Equip.										
Accounts Payable		4 000 00								
John Arrow, Capital		40 000 00								
John Arrow, Drawing	1 000 00									
Fees Income		14 000 00								
Salaries Expense	2 500 00									
Utilities Expense	300 00									
Supplies Expense										
Rent Expense										
Depr. Expense—Equip.										
Totals	58 000 00	58 000 00								

Draw a single rule to indicate addition of a set of Debit/Credit columns.

Draw a double rule under the totals of a set of Debit/Credit columns to indicate that no further amounts are to be added.

Trial Balance totals must be equal.

Figure 5–9G Preparing the Financial Statements

The information needed to prepare the financial statements is obtained from the worksheet.

ARROW ACCOUNTING SERVICES
Income Statement
Month Ended December 31, 19X5

Revenue		
Fees Income		14000 00
Expenses		
Salaries Expense	2500 00	
Utilities Expense	300 00	
Supplies Expense	500 00	
Rent Expense	2500 00	
Depreciation Expense—Equipment	250 00	
Total Expenses		6050 00
Net Income		7950 00

When expenses for the period are less than revenue, a net income results. The net income is transferred to the statement of owner's equity.

ARROW ACCOUNTING SERVICES
Statement of Owner's Equity
Month Ended December 31, 19X5

John Arrow, Capital, December 1, 19X5		40000 00
Net Income for December	7950 00	
Withdrawals for December	1000 00	
Increase in Capital		6950 00
John Arrow, Capital, December 31, 19X5		46950 00

The withdrawals are subtracted from the net income for the period to determine the change in owner's equity.

ARROW ACCOUNTING SERVICES
Balance Sheet
December 31, 19X5

Assets		
Cash		16200 00
Accounts Receivable		2000 00
Supplies		500 00
Prepaid Rent		17500 00
Equipment	15000 00	
Less Accumulated Depreciation	250 00	14750 00
Total Assets		50950 00
Liabilities and Owner's Equity		
Liabilities		
Accounts Payable		4000 00
Owner's Equity		
John Arrow, Capital		46950 00
Total Liabilities and Owner's Equity		50950 00

The ending capital balance is transferred from the statement of owner's equity to the balance sheet.

SUMMARY OF FINANCIAL STATEMENTS

THE INCOME STATEMENT

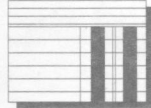

The income statement is prepared directly from the data in the Income Statement section of the worksheet. The heading of the income statement contains the name of the firm (WHO), the name of the statement (WHAT), and the period covered by the statement (WHEN). The revenue section of the statement is prepared first. The revenue account name is obtained from the Account Name column of the worksheet. The balance of the revenue account is obtained from the Credit column of the Income Statement section of the worksheet. The expenses section of the income statement is prepared next. The expense account titles are obtained from the Account Name column of the worksheet. The balance of each expense account is obtained from the Debit column of the Income Statement section of the worksheet.

Determining the net income or net loss for the period is the last step in preparing the income statement. If the firm has more revenue than expenses, a net income is reported for the period. If the firm has more expenses than revenue, a net loss is reported. The net income or net loss reported must agree with the amount calculated on the worksheet.

THE STATEMENT OF OWNER'S EQUITY

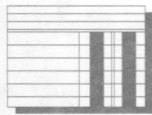

The statement of owner's equity is prepared from the data in the Balance Sheet section of the worksheet and the general ledger capital account. The statement of owner's equity is prepared before the balance sheet so that the amount of the ending capital balance is available for presentation on the balance sheet. The heading of the statement contains the name of the firm (WHO), the name of the statement (WHAT), and the date of the statement (WHEN).

The statement begins with the capital account balance at the beginning of the period. Next, the increase or decrease in the owner's capital account is determined. The increase or decrease is computed by adding the net income (or net loss) for the period to any additional investments made by the owner during the period and subtracting withdrawals for the period. The increase or decrease is added to the beginning capital balance to obtain the ending capital balance.

THE BALANCE SHEET

The balance sheet is prepared from the data in the Balance Sheet section of the worksheet and the statement of owner's equity. The balance sheet reflects the assets, liabilities, and owner's equity of the firm on the balance sheet date. The heading of the statement contains the name of the firm (WHO), the name of the statement (WHAT), and the date of the statement (WHEN).

The assets section of the statement is prepared first. The asset account titles are obtained from the Account Name column of the worksheet. The balance of each asset account is obtained from the Debit column of the Balance Sheet section of the worksheet. The liability and owner's equity section is prepared next. The liability and owner's equity account titles are obtained from the Account Name column of the worksheet. The balance of each liability account is obtained from the Credit column of the Balance Sheet section of the worksheet. The ending balance for the owner's capital account is obtained from the statement of owner's equity. Total liabilities and owner's equity must equal total assets.

Information Block: Computers and Accounting

Computerized Accounting Systems

When computers first became available on a commercial basis, large corporations quickly realized that these computers could be used to record large quantities of financial data. Unfortunately, their high cost prevented small and medium-sized businesses from buying them. This situation changed with the introduction of the microcomputer in the 1970s. These lower-priced computers now provide economical computerized accounting systems for any business—small or large.

Today computerized accounting programs are used directly or indirectly in most businesses. Computers prepare paychecks, monthly credit card statements and other bills, and keep track of bank account balances. In fact, businesses depend on computerized accounting systems to provide accurate and timely financial information daily.

After the appropriate computer hardware is acquired, a business needs to acquire the necessary software. Six common types of accounting software are available: general ledger, accounts receivable, accounts payable, customer order entry/invoice processing, inventory control, and payroll. These programs may stand alone, or they may be integrated into the general ledger system.

General ledger programs are basic to any computerized accounting system. Such software is used to record general journal entries, including adjusting entries. Posting is completed both quickly and accurately by the computer. The computer can print out a trial balance of the general ledger in a matter of seconds whenever it is needed. An accountant can quickly obtain a printed copy of the income statement, statement of owner's equity, or balance sheet.

At the end of the accounting period, the general ledger program is also able to complete closing procedures, prepare accounts for the beginning of the new accounting period, and produce a postclosing trial balance.

General ledger programs are adaptable to individual businesses since they allow a business to set up its own chart of accounts. The program maintains the chart of accounts files, allowing accounts to be added, changed, or deleted as needed by the business.

SELF-REVIEW

1. A firm purchases machinery, which has an estimated useful life of 10 years and no salvage value, for $12,000 at the beginning of the accounting period. What is the adjusting entry for depreciation at the end of one month if the firm uses the straight-line method of depreciation?
2. Why is the net income for a period recorded in the Balance Sheet section of the worksheet as well as the Income Statement section?
3. What five amounts appear on the statement of owner's equity?
4. How does a balance sheet in the report form differ from a balance sheet in the account form?
5. Why is it necessary to journalize and post adjusting entries even though the data is already recorded on the worksheet?

Answers to Self-Review

1. The amount of depreciation is: (a) 10 years × 12 months = 120 months; (b) $12,000/120 months = $100 per month. Depreciation Expense is debited for $100. Accumulated Depreciation—Machinery is credited for $100.
2. The net income for a period is recorded in both financial statement sections of the worksheet because it causes a net increase in owner's equity.
3. The five amounts that appear on the statement of owner's equity are (a) the beginning owner's equity, (b) net income or net loss for the period, (c) additional investments by the owner for the period, (d) withdrawals by the owner for the period, and (e) the ending balance of owner's equity.
4. On a report-form balance sheet, the liabilities and owner's equity are listed under the assets. On the account form, they are listed to the right of the assets.
5. It is necessary to journalize and post adjusting entries because the worksheet is only a tool that aids in the preparation of financial statements. Any changes in account balances recorded on the worksheet are not shown in the general journal and the general ledger until the adjusting entries are journalized and posted.

CHAPTER 5 Review and Applications

CHAPTER SUMMARY

A worksheet is normally used to save time in preparing the financial statements. The following procedures are used in preparing the worksheet and the financial statements.

1. The trial balance is prepared on the worksheet.
2. Any adjustments to account balances are entered.
3. An adjusted trial balance is prepared to prove the equality of the debits and credits again.
4. The figures needed for the income statement and the balance sheet are organized in the appropriate sections of the worksheet.
5. The net income or net loss for the period is determined, and the worksheet is completed.
6. The income statement, statement of owner's equity, and balance sheet are prepared.
7. The adjustments made in the Adjustments section of the worksheet are journalized and posted to the general ledger.

Adjusting entries are required in all business operations. Two items that often require adjustment are prepaid expenses and depreciation. Prepaid expenses are expense items that are acquired and paid for in advance of their use. At the time of their acquisition, these items represent assets and are therefore recorded in asset accounts. As they are used, their cost is transferred to expense by means of adjusting entries at the end of each accounting period.

Depreciation is the process of allocating the cost of a long-term asset to operations over its expected useful life. A portion of the cost of the asset is charged off as an expense at the end of each accounting period during the asset's useful life. The straight-line method is a widely used method of depreciation.

GLOSSARY OF NEW TERMS

Account-form balance sheet (p. 126) A balance sheet that lists liabilities and owner's equity to the right of assets (see Report-form balance sheet)

Adjusting entries (p. 114) Journal entries made to record business transactions that are not recorded during the accounting period

Adjustments (p. 114) See Adjusting entries

Book value (p. 117) That portion of an asset's original cost that has not yet been depreciated

Contra asset account (p. 117) An asset account with a credit balance, contrary to the normal balance of an asset account

Depreciation (p. 116) Allocation of the cost of a long-term asset to operations during its expected useful life

Prepaid expenses (p. 116) Expense items acquired and paid for in advance of their use

Report-form balance sheet (p. 126) A balance sheet that lists the asset accounts first, followed by liabilities and owner's equity

Salvage value (p. 116) An item's value to a firm at the end of the item's useful life—that is, its value as used goods or scrap

Straight-line depreciation (p. 116) Allocation of an asset's cost in equal amounts to each accounting period of the asset's useful life

Worksheet (p. 113) A form used to gather all data needed at the end of an accounting period to prepare financial statements

REVIEW QUESTIONS

1. Why is it necessary to make an adjustment for supplies used?
2. What are prepaid expenses? Give four examples.
3. What adjustment would be recorded for expired insurance?
4. What is depreciation?
5. Give three examples of assets that are subject to depreciation.
6. How does the straight-line method of depreciation work?
7. Why is an accumulated depreciation account used in making the adjustment for depreciation?
8. What is book value?
9. How does a contra asset account differ from a regular asset account?
10. What three amounts are reported on the balance sheet for a long-term asset like equipment?
11. Why is it necessary to journalize and post adjusting entries?

MANAGERIAL FOCUS

1. How does the worksheet help provide management with vital information?
2. Suppose the president of a company where you work as an accountant questions whether it is really worthwhile for you to spend time making adjustments at the end of each accounting period. How would you explain the value of the adjustments?
3. At the beginning of the year, the Williams Company purchased a new building and some expensive new machinery. An officer of the firm has asked you whether this purchase will affect the firm's year-end income statement. What answer would you give?
4. A building owned by the Santana Company was recently valued at $350,000 by a real estate expert. The president of the company is questioning the accuracy of the firm's latest balance sheet because it shows a book value of $125,000 for the building. How would you explain this situation to the president?

EXERCISES

EXERCISE 5-1 (Obj. 1)

Tutorial

Calculating adjustments. Determine the necessary adjustments for each of the following situations.

1. On June 1, 19X5, the Wright Company, a new firm, paid $6,000 rent in advance for a six-month period. The $6,000 was debited to the Prepaid Rent account.
2. On June 1, 19X5, the Wright Company purchased supplies for $1,075. The $1,075 was debited to the Supplies account. An inventory of supplies at the end of June showed that items costing $560 were on hand.
3. On June 1, 19X5, the Wright Company purchased equipment costing $6,000. The equipment is expected to have a useful life of five years and no salvage value. The firm will use the straight-line method of depreciation.

EXERCISE 5-2 (Obj. 2)

Tutorial

Calculating adjustments. For each of the following situations, determine the necessary adjustments.

1. A firm purchased a two-year insurance policy for $2,400 on July 1, 19X6. The $2,400 was debited to the Prepaid Insurance account. What adjustment should be made to record expired insurance on the firm's July 31, 19X6, worksheet?
2. On December 1, 19X6, a firm signed a contract with a local radio station for advertising that will extend over a one-year period. The firm paid $2,040 in advance and debited the amount to Prepaid Advertising. What adjustment should be made to record expired advertising on the firm's December 31, 19X6, worksheet?

EXERCISE 5-3 (Obj. 3)

Worksheet extensions. A partial worksheet is shown for the Owens Company. Complete the worksheet by extending the *X* for each account to the appropriate section of the worksheet.

	Adjusted Trial Balance		Income Statement		Balance Sheet	
Account Name	Debit	Credit	Debit	Credit	Debit	Credit
Cash	X					
Accounts Receivable	X					
Supplies	X					
Prepaid Rent	X					
Equipment	X					
Accumulated Depr.—Equip.		X				
Jane Powell, Capital		X				
Jane Powell, Drawing	X					
Fees Income		X				
Salaries Expense	X					
Utilities Expense	X					
Supplies Expense	X					
Rent Expense	X					
Depreciation Expense—Equip.	X					

EXERCISE 5-4
(Obj. 2, 3)

Correcting net income. Assume that a firm reports net income of $15,000 prior to making adjusting entries for the items that follow.

Expired rent	$1,000
Depreciation expense	1,200
Supplies used	500

Assume that the required adjusting entries are not made. What effect do these errors have on the reported net income?

EXERCISE 5-5
(Obj. 4, 5)

Post-worksheet procedures. You have just completed the worksheet of Zane Corporation for the year ended December 31, 19X6. Describe the additional procedures that you must perform after completing the worksheet.

EXERCISE 5-6
(Obj. 1, 2)

Tutorial

Worksheet through Adjusted Trial Balance. On January 31, 19X4, the general ledger of the Sanchez Company showed the following account balances. Prepare the worksheet through the Adjusted Trial Balance section. Assume that every account has the normal debit or credit balance. The worksheet covers the month of January.

ACCOUNTS

Cash	$ 9,500	Ruby Sanchez, Capital	$18,900
Accounts Receivable	3,200	Fees Income	15,000
Supplies	1,500	Rent Expense	1,200
Prepaid Insurance	2,850	Salaries Expense	1,420
Equipment	15,930	Supplies Expense	
Accum. Depr.—Equip.		Insurance Expense	
Accounts Payable	1,700	Depr. Expense—Equip.	

Additional Information:

a. On January 31, 19X4, supplies used during the month totaled $800.
b. Expired insurance totaled $250.
c. Depreciation expense for the month was $230.

EXERCISE 5-7
(Obj. 5)

Tutorial

Journalizing and posting adjustments. The following adjusting entries must be made by the Paul Company on December 31, 19X6.

a. Supplies used, $1,000; assume supplies totaling $1,500 were purchased on December 1, 19X6, and debited to the Supplies account.
b. Expired insurance, $800; on December 1, 19X6, the firm paid $4,800 for six months' insurance coverage in advance and Prepaid Insurance was debited for this amount.
c. Depreciation expense for equipment, $400.

Instructions Make the necessary journal entries for these adjustments and post the entries to their general ledger accounts. Assume that the purchase of supplies and prepaid insurance were recorded on page 1 of the general journal and that the adjusting entries were recorded on page 3. Use the accounts and numbers on page 135.

Supplies	121	Supplies Expense	517
Prepaid Insurance	131	Insurance Expense	521
Accum. Depr.—Equip.	142	Depr. Expense—Equip.	523

PROBLEMS

PROBLEM SET A

PROBLEM 5–1A
(Obj. 1, 2, 3)

Tutorial

Completing the worksheet. The trial balance of the Austin Company as of January 31, 19X5, after the company completed the first month of operations, is shown in the partial worksheet that follows.

AUSTIN COMPANY
Worksheet (Partial)
January 31, 19X5

	ACCOUNT NAME	TRIAL BALANCE DEBIT	TRIAL BALANCE CREDIT	ADJUSTMENTS DEBIT	ADJUSTMENTS CREDIT
1	*Cash*	15 5 0 0 00			
2	*Accounts Receivable*	1 3 0 0 00			
3	*Supplies*	1 4 5 0 00			
4	*Prepaid Rent*	6 0 0 0 00			
5	*Equipment*	12 0 0 0 00			
6	*Accumulated Depreciation—Equipment*				
7	*Accounts Payable*		2 0 0 0 00		
8	*Calvin Austin, Capital*		30 0 0 0 00		
9	*Calvin Austin, Drawing*	1 2 0 0 00			
10	*Fees Income*		8 1 5 0 00		
11	*Salaries Expense*	2 4 0 0 00			
12	*Utilities Expense*	3 0 0 00			
13	*Supplies Expense*				
14	*Rent Expense*				
15	*Depreciation Expense—Equipment*				
16	*Totals*	40 1 5 0 00	40 1 5 0 00		
17					

Instructions

1. Record the trial balance in the Trial Balance section of the worksheet.
2. Complete the worksheet by making the following adjustments: supplies on hand at the end of the month, $750; expired rent, $1,000; depreciation expense for the period, $100.

PROBLEM 5–2A
(Obj. 4)

Preparing financial statements from the worksheet. The completed worksheet for Wilson Corporation as of December 31, 19X5, after the company had completed the first month of operation, follows.

Instructions

1. Prepare an income statement.
2. Prepare a statement of owner's equity. The owner made no additional investments during the month.
3. Prepare a balance sheet (use the report form).

WILSON CORPORATION
Worksheet
Month Ended December 31, 19X5

	ACCOUNT NAME	TRIAL BALANCE DEBIT	TRIAL BALANCE CREDIT	ADJUSTMENTS DEBIT	ADJUSTMENTS CREDIT
1	*Cash*	*18 400 00*			
2	*Accounts Receivable*	*2 000 00*			
3	*Supplies*	*2 000 00*			*(a) 1 000 00*
4	*Prepaid Advertising*	*3 000 00*			*(b) 500 00*
5	*Equipment*	*10 000 00*			
6	*Accumulated Depreciation—Equipment*				*(c) 400 00*
7	*Accounts Payable*		*2 000 00*		
8	*Wade Wilson, Capital*		*25 000 00*		
9	*Wade Wilson, Drawing*	*1 400 00*			
10	*Fees Income*		*12 500 00*		
11	*Salaries Expense*	*2 400 00*			
12	*Utilities Expense*	*300 00*			
13	*Supplies Expense*			*(a) 1 000 00*	
14	*Advertising Expense*			*(b) 500 00*	
15	*Depreciation Expense*			*(c) 400 00*	
16	*Totals*	*39 500 00*	*39 500 00*	*1 900 00*	*1 900 00*
17	*Net Income*				
18					

PROBLEM 5–3A (Obj. 1, 2, 3)

Reconstructing a partial worksheet. The adjusted trial balance of University Computers, Inc., as of September 30, 19X6, after the company had completed the first month of operation, appears below.

UNIVERSITY COMPUTERS, INC.
Adjusted Trial Balance
September 30, 19X6

Account Name	Debit	Credit
Cash	9,500	
Accounts Receivable	1,500	
Supplies	1,200	
Prepaid Rent	7,200	
Equipment	12,000	
Accum. Depr.—Equip.		300
Accounts Payable		3,000
Norris King, Capital		16,050
Norris King, Drawing	1,000	
Fees Income		18,000
Salaries Expense	3,200	
Utilities Expense	350	
Supplies Expense	500	
Rent Expense	600	
Depr. Expense—Equip.	300	
Totals	37,350	37,350

ADJUSTED TRIAL BALANCE		INCOME STATEMENT		BALANCE SHEET		
DEBIT	CREDIT	DEBIT	CREDIT	DEBIT	CREDIT	
18,400.00				18,400.00		1
2,000.00				2,000.00		2
1,000.00				1,000.00		3
2,500.00				2,500.00		4
10,000.00				10,000.00		5
	400.00				400.00	6
	2,000.00				2,000.00	7
	25,000.00				25,000.00	8
1,400.00				1,400.00		9
	12,500.00		12,500.00			10
2,400.00		2,400.00				11
300.00		300.00				12
1,000.00		1,000.00				13
500.00		500.00				14
400.00		400.00				15
39,900.00	39,900.00	4,600.00	12,500.00	35,300.00	27,400.00	16
		7,900.00			7,900.00	17
		12,500.00	12,500.00	35,300.00	35,300.00	18

Appropriate adjustments have been made for the following items.

a. Supplies used during the month, $500.
b. Expired rent for the month, $600.
c. Depreciation expense for the month, $300.

Instructions

1. Record the Adjusted Trial Balance in the Adjusted Trial Balance columns of the worksheet.
2. Prepare the adjusting entries in the Adjustments columns of the worksheet.
3. Complete the Trial Balance columns of the worksheet prior to making the adjusting entries.

PROBLEM 5–4A
(Obj. 1, 2, 3, 4, 5)

Tutorial GL

Preparing a worksheet and financial statements, journalizing adjusting entries, and posting to ledger accounts. George Modris owns and operates an interior decorating firm called Creative Decorations. The trial balance of the firm for March 31, 19X5, the first month of operations, follows on page 138.

Instructions

1. Complete the worksheet for the month.
2. Prepare an income statement, statement of owner's equity, and balance sheet. No additional investments were made by the owner during the month.
3. Journalize and post the adjusting entries. Use J3 for the journal page number.

CREATIVE DECORATIONS
Worksheet (Partial)
Month Ended March 31, 19X5

	ACCOUNT NAME	TRIAL BALANCE DEBIT	TRIAL BALANCE CREDIT	ADJUSTMENTS DEBIT	ADJUSTMENTS CREDIT
1	*Cash*	10 2 0 0 00			
2	*Accounts Receivable*	3 6 0 0 00			
3	*Supplies*	1 1 5 0 00			
4	*Prepaid Advertising*	1 2 0 0 00			
5	*Prepaid Rent*	8 4 0 0 00			
6	*Equipment*	9 6 0 0 00			
7	*Accumulated Depreciation—Equipment*				
8	*Accounts Payable*		5 0 0 0 00		
9	*George Modris, Capital*		18 1 0 0 00		
10	*George Modris, Drawing*	1 5 0 0 00			
11	*Fees Income*		16 5 0 0 00		
12	*Salaries Expense*	3 6 0 0 00			
13	*Utilities Expense*	3 5 0 00			
14	*Supplies Expense*				
15	*Advertising Expense*				
16	*Rent Expense*				
17	*Depreciation Expense—Equipment*				
18	*Totals*	39 6 0 0 00	39 6 0 0 00		
19					

End-of-the-month adjustments must account for the following items:

a. Supplies were purchased on March 1, 19X5; inventory of supplies on March 31, 19X5, is $200.
b. The prepaid advertising contract was signed on March 1, 19X5, and covers a four-month period.
c. Rent of $700 expired during the month.
d. Depreciation is computed using the straight-line method. The equipment has an estimated useful life of 10 years with no salvage value.

PROBLEM SET B

PROBLEM 5–1B
(Obj. 1, 2, 3)
Tutorial

Completing the worksheet. The trial balance of the Henderson Company as of February 28, 19X5, follows on page 139.

HENDERSON COMPANY
Worksheet (Partial)
February 28, 19X5

	ACCOUNT NAME	TRIAL BALANCE		ADJUSTMENTS	
		DEBIT	CREDIT	DEBIT	CREDIT
1	*Cash*	*18,500.00*			
2	*Accounts Receivable*	*2,300.00*			
3	*Supplies*	*1,200.00*			
4	*Prepaid Rent*	*10,800.00*			
5	*Equipment*	*14,000.00*			
6	*Accumulated Depreciation—Equipment*				
7	*Accounts Payable*		*3,000.00*		
8	*Carl Henderson, Capital*		*33,500.00*		
9	*Carl Henderson, Drawing*	*1,000.00*			
10	*Fees Income*		*13,500.00*		
11	*Salaries Expense*	*1,800.00*			
12	*Utilities Expense*	*400.00*			
13	*Supplies Expense*				
14	*Rent Expense*				
15	*Depreciation Expense—Equipment*				
16	*Totals*	*50,000.00*	*50,000.00*		
17					

Instructions

1. Record the trial balance in the Trial Balance section of the worksheet.
2. Complete the worksheet by making the following adjustments: supplies on hand at the end of the month, $800; expired rent, $900; depreciation expense for the period, $250.

PROBLEM 5–2B (Obj. 4)

Preparing financial statements from the worksheet. The completed worksheet for the Carver Insurance Agency as of November 31, 19X5, after the company had completed the first month of operation, follows on page 140.

Instructions

1. Prepare an income statement.
2. Prepare a statement of owner's equity. The owner made no additional investments during the month.
3. Prepare a balance sheet.

CARVER INSURANCE AGENCY
Worksheet
Month Ended November 30, 19X5

	ACCOUNT NAME	TRIAL BALANCE DEBIT	TRIAL BALANCE CREDIT	ADJUSTMENTS DEBIT	ADJUSTMENTS CREDIT
1	*Cash*	15,875 00			
2	*Accounts Receivable*	2,125 00			
3	*Supplies*	2,000 00			(a) 800 00
4	*Prepaid Advertising*	1,500 00			(b) 700 00
5	*Equipment*	10,000 00			
6	*Accumulated Depreciation—Equipment*				(c) 240 00
7	*Accounts Payable*		1,500 00		
8	*Robert Carver, Capital*		19,600 00		
9	*Robert Carver, Drawing*	1,000 00			
10	*Fees Income*		14,500 00		
11	*Salaries Expense*	2,750 00			
12	*Utilities Expense*	350 00			
13	*Supplies Expense*			(a) 800 00	
14	*Advertising Expense*			(b) 700 00	
15	*Depreciation Expense*			(c) 240 00	
16	*Totals*	35,600 00	35,600 00	1,740 00	1,740 00
17	*Net Income*				
18					

PROBLEM 5–3B (Obj. 1, 2, 3)

Reconstructing a partial worksheet. The adjusted trial balance of Pauline Salsky, Attorney-at-Law, as of October 31, 19X6, after the company had completed the first month of operation, appears below.

PAULINE SALSKY, ATTORNEY-AT-LAW
Adjusted Trial Balance
October 31, 19X6

Account Name	Debit	Credit
Cash	8,240	
Accounts Receivable	1,800	
Supplies	700	
Prepaid Rent	9,900	
Equipment	12,000	
Accum. Depr.—Equip.		350
Accounts Payable		3,500
Pauline Salsky, Capital		18,765
Pauline Salsky, Drawing	1,000	
Fees Income		15,600
Salaries Expense	2,250	
Utilities Expense	275	
Supplies Expense	800	
Rent Expense	900	
Depr. Expense—Equip.	350	
Totals	38,215	38,215

ADJUSTED TRIAL BALANCE		INCOME STATEMENT		BALANCE SHEET		
DEBIT	CREDIT	DEBIT	CREDIT	DEBIT	CREDIT	
15,875.00				15,875.00		1
2,125.00				2,125.00		2
1,200.00				1,200.00		3
800.00				800.00		4
10,000.00				10,000.00		5
	240.00				240.00	6
	1,500.00				1,500.00	7
	19,600.00				19,600.00	8
1,000.00				1,000.00		9
	14,500.00		14,500.00			10
2,750.00		2,750.00				11
350.00		350.00				12
800.00		800.00				13
700.00		700.00				14
240.00		240.00				15
35,840.00	35,840.00	4,840.00	14,500.00	31,000.00	21,340.00	16
		9,660.00			9,660.00	17
		14,500.00	14,500.00	31,000.00	31,000.00	18

Appropriate adjustments have been made for the following items.

a. Supplies used during the month, $800.
b. Expired rent for the month, $900.
c. Depreciation expense for the month, $350.

Instructions

1. Record the adjusted trial balance in the Adjusted Trial Balance columns of the worksheet.
2. Prepare the adjusting entries in the Adjustments columns of the worksheet.
3. Complete the Trial Balance columns of the worksheet prior to making the adjusting entries.

PROBLEM 5–4B
(Obj. 1, 2, 3, 4, 5)

Tutorial

Preparing a worksheet and financial statements, journalizing adjusting entries, and posting to ledger accounts. Ronald West owns and operates an employment service firm called West Personnel Agency. The trial balance of the firm for April 30, 19X5, the first month of operations, is shown on page 142.

Instructions

1. Complete the worksheet for the month.
2. Prepare an income statement, statement of owner's equity, and balance sheet. No additional investments were made by the owner during the month.
3. Journalize and post the adjusting entries. Use J3 for the journal page number.

WEST PERSONNEL AGENCY
Worksheet (Partial)
Month Ended April 30, 19X5

	ACCOUNT NAME	TRIAL BALANCE DEBIT	TRIAL BALANCE CREDIT	ADJUSTMENTS DEBIT	ADJUSTMENTS CREDIT
1	*Cash*	9 4 0 0 00			
2	*Accounts Receivable*	2 6 0 0 00			
3	*Supplies*	1 2 0 0 00			
4	*Prepaid Advertising*	1 6 0 0 00			
5	*Prepaid Rent*	11 4 0 0 00			
6	*Equipment*	12 0 0 0 00			
7	*Accumulated Depreciation—Equipment*				
8	*Accounts Payable*		2 7 0 0 00		
9	*Ronald West, Capital*		25 2 9 0 00		
10	*Ronald West, Drawing*	1 0 0 0 00			
11	*Fees Income*		13 4 5 0 00		
12	*Salaries Expense*	1 9 5 0 00			
13	*Utilities Expense*	2 9 0 00			
14	*Supplies Expense*				
15	*Advertising Expense*				
16	*Rent Expense*				
17	*Depreciation Expense—Equipment*				
18	*Totals*	41 4 4 0 00	41 4 4 0 00		
19					

End-of-the-month adjustments must account for the following.

a. The supplies were purchased on April 1, 19X5; inventory of supplies on April 30, 19X5, showed a value of $400.
b. The prepaid advertising contract was signed on April 1, 19X5, and covers a four-month period.
c. Rent of $950 expired during the month.
d. Depreciation is computed using the straight-line method. The equipment has an estimated useful life of five years with no salvage value.

CHALLENGE PROBLEM

GL

The account balances for the Diaz Company on January 31, 19X3, follow. The balances shown are after the first month of operation.

101	Cash	18,475
111	Accounts Receivable	850
121	Supplies	900
131	Prepaid Insurance	5,000
141	Equipment	6,000
142	Accumulated Depreciation—Equipment	
202	Accounts Payable	1,500

301	James Diaz, Capital	30,000
302	James Diaz, Drawing	1,500
401	Fees Income	7,350
511	Advertising Expense	500
514	Rent Expense	800
517	Salaries Expense	4,000
518	Supplies Expense	
519	Insurance Expense	
520	Telephone Expense	375
523	Utilities Expense	450
524	Depreciation Expense—Equipment	

Instructions

1. Prepare the Trial Balance section of the worksheet.
2. Record the following adjustments in the Adjustments section of the worksheet.
   a. Supplies used during the month amounted to $450.
   b. The amount in the Prepaid Insurance account represents a payment made on January 1, 19X3, for four months of insurance coverage.
   c. The equipment, purchased on January 1, 19X3, has an estimated useful life of 10 years with no salvage value. The firm uses the straight-line method of depreciation.
3. Complete the worksheet.
4. Prepare an income statement, statement of owner's equity, and balance sheet (use the report form).
5. Record the balances in the general ledger accounts, then journalize and post the adjusting entries. Use J3 for the journal page number.

CRITICAL THINKING PROBLEM

Assume you are the accountant for Sloan Enterprises. Howard Sloan, the owner of the company, is in a hurry to receive the financial statements for the year and asks you how soon they will be ready. You tell him you have just completed the trial balance and are getting ready to prepare the adjusting entries. Mr. Sloan tells you not to waste time preparing adjusting entries but to complete the worksheet without them and prepare the financial statements based on the data in the trial balance. According to him, the adjusting entries will not make that much difference.

The trial balance shows the following account balances:

Prepaid Insurance	$ 4,000
Supplies	8,000
Building	180,000
Accumulated Depreciation—Building	27,000

If the income statement were prepared using trial balance amounts, the net income would be $165,000.

A review of the company's records reveals the following information:

1. A two-year insurance policy was purchased three months prior to the end of the year for $4,000.
2. Purchases of supplies during the year totaled $8,000. An inventory of supplies taken at year-end showed supplies on hand of $1,000.
3. The building was purchased three years ago and has an estimated life of 20 years.

Write a memo to Mr. Sloan explaining the effect on the financial statements of omitting the adjustments. Indicate the change to net income that results from the adjusting entries.

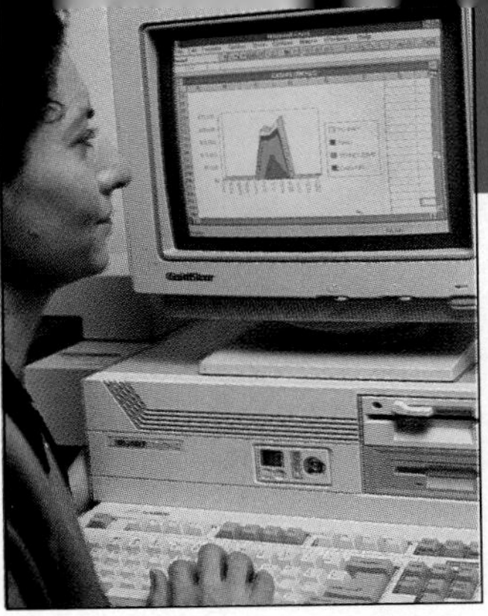

CHAPTER

6

Closing Entries and the Postclosing Trial Balance

OBJECTIVES

1. Journalize and post closing entries.
2. Prepare a postclosing trial balance.
3. Interpret financial statements.
4. Review the steps in the accounting cycle.
5. Define the accounting terms new to this chapter.

Once the worksheet and financial statements are completed, the general ledger must be updated by recording and posting the adjusting entries. As you have learned, the purpose of recording and posting the adjusting entries is to create a permanent record of the adjustments that appear on the worksheet. The next step is to journalize the entries that transfer the results of operations to owner's equity and prepare the revenue and expense accounts for use in the next accounting period.

NEW TERMS

Closing entries ▪ Income Summary account ▪ Postclosing trial balance

CLOSING ENTRIES

OBJECTIVE 1
Journalize and post closing entries.

Closing entries are journal entries that transfer the results of operations (the net income or net loss for the period) to owner's equity and reduce the balances of the revenue and expense accounts to zero so that they are ready to receive data for the next period. Like adjusting entries, closing entries are made in the general journal.

The Income Summary Account

A special owner's equity account called **Income Summary** is used to summarize the results of operations in the general ledger. It is used only at the end of a period to help with the closing procedure. The account has no balance after the closing process, and it remains without a balance until the closing procedure for the next period.

The Income Summary account is classified as a temporary owner's equity account. Other titles sometimes used for this account are *Revenue and Expense Summary* and *Income and Expense Summary.*

The Closing Process

The closing process is accomplished by performing the four steps reflected below:

1. The balance of the revenue account is transferred to the Income Summary account.

FIGURE 6–1
A Worksheet

ARROW ACCOUNTING SERVICES
Worksheet
Month Ended December 31, 19X5

	ACCOUNT NAME	TRIAL BALANCE DEBIT	TRIAL BALANCE CREDIT	ADJUSTMENTS DEBIT	ADJUSTMENTS CREDIT
1	*Cash*	16,200.00			
2	*Accounts Receivable*	2,000.00			
3	*Supplies*	1,000.00			(a) 500.00
4	*Prepaid Rent*	20,000.00			(b) 2,500.00
5	*Equipment*	15,000.00			
6	*Accumulated Depreciation—Equipment*				(c) 250.00
7	*Accounts Payable*		4,000.00		
8	*John Arrow, Capital*		40,000.00		
9	*John Arrow, Drawing*	1,000.00			
10	*Fees Income*		14,000.00		
11	*Salaries Expense*	2,500.00			
12	*Utilities Expense*	300.00			
13	*Supplies Expense*			(a) 500.00	
14	*Rent Expense*			(b) 2,500.00	
15	*Depreciation Expense—Equipment*			(c) 250.00	
16	*Totals*	58,000.00	58,000.00	3,250.00	3,250.00
17	*Net Income*				
18					
19					

2. The balances of the expense accounts are transferred to the Income Summary account.
3. The balance of the Income Summary account is transferred to the owner's Capital account.
4. The balance of the Drawing account is closed to the owner's Capital account.

The Income Statement section of the worksheet and the Drawing account balance in the Balance Sheet section of the worksheet contain the data necessary to make the closing entries. Refer to the worksheet shown in Figure 6–1 as you study each closing entry.

Step 1: Transferring Revenue Account Balances

On December 31, 19X5, the worksheet for Arrow Accounting Services shows a credit balance of $14,000 in the Fees Income account. This balance represents the total revenue for the period.

To *close* an account is simply to reduce its balance to zero. Since the Fees Income account has a credit balance, the account is debited for the same amount, which closes it. The offsetting credit is made to the Income Summary account. The effects of this closing entry are to transfer the total revenue for the period to the Income Summary account and to reduce the balance of the revenue account to zero.

ADJUSTED TRIAL BALANCE		INCOME STATEMENT		BALANCE SHEET		
DEBIT	CREDIT	DEBIT	CREDIT	DEBIT	CREDIT	
16 200 00				16 200 00		1
2 000 00				2 000 00		2
500 00				500 00		3
17 500 00				17 500 00		4
15 000 00				15 000 00		5
	250 00				250 00	6
	4 000 00				4 000 00	7
	40 000 00				40 000 00	8
1 000 00				1 000 00		9
	14 000 00		14 000 00			10
2 500 00		2 500 00				11
300 00		300 00				12
500 00		500 00				13
2 500 00		2 500 00				14
250 00		250 00				15
58 250 00	58 250 00	6 050 00	14 000 00	52 200 00	44 250 00	16
		7 950 00			7 950 00	17
		14 000 00	14 000 00	52 200 00	52 200 00	18
						19

Step 1
Close revenue

GENERAL JOURNAL PAGE 4

	DATE		DESCRIPTION	POST. REF.	DEBIT	CREDIT	
1	*19X5*		*Closing Entries*				1
2	*Dec.*	*31*	*Fees Income*		*14 0 0 0 00*		2
3			*Income Summary*			*14 0 0 0 00*	3
4							4

Fees Income

Dr. −	Cr. +
Closing 14,000	Balance 14,000

Income Summary

Dr.	Cr.
	14,000

Note that the Income Summary account does not have an increase or decrease side and thus no normal balance side.

Many accountants prefer to separate the closing entries from other types of journal entries. One common method is to write "Closing Entries" in the Description column of the general journal on the line above the first closing entry.

Step 2: Transferring Expense Account Balances

The Income Statement section of Arrow Accounting Service's worksheet lists five expense accounts and shows that the total of their balances is $6,050. Since the expense accounts have debit balances, a credit is entered in each account to close it. A compound entry in the general journal is made to close the expense accounts. The total of the expenses is debited to the Income Summary account, and each expense account is credited for the amount of its balance. The effects of this closing entry are to transfer the total of the expenses for the period to the Income Summary account and to reduce the balances of the expense accounts to zero.

When the journal entries are posted, the words "Closing Entries" are written in the Explanation column of the individual revenue and expense accounts to identify clearly the closing entries in the general ledger. Similarly, notations are often made in the Explanation column of the Income Summary account to identify entries. For example, the entries in the Income Summary account shown in Figure 6–2, page 152, have been so identified.

The Income Summary account now reflects the totals of the Income Statement columns of the worksheet (Figure 6–1). The general journal entry to close the revenue accounts summarizes and transfers the data appearing in the Credit column of the Income Statement section. The general journal entry to close the expense accounts summarizes and transfers the data appearing in the Debit column of the Income Statement section of the worksheet.

Step 2
Close expense accounts

GENERAL JOURNAL PAGE 4

	DATE		DESCRIPTION	POST. REF.	DEBIT	CREDIT	
1	*19X5*		*Closing Entries*				1
5	*Dec.*	*31*	*Income Summary*		*6 0 5 0 00*		5
6			*Salaries Expense*			*2 5 0 0 00*	6
7			*Utilities Expense*			*3 0 0 00*	7
8			*Supplies Expense*			*5 0 0 00*	8
9			*Rent Expense*			*2 5 0 0 00*	9
10			*Depr. Expense—Equipment*			*2 5 0 00*	10
11							11

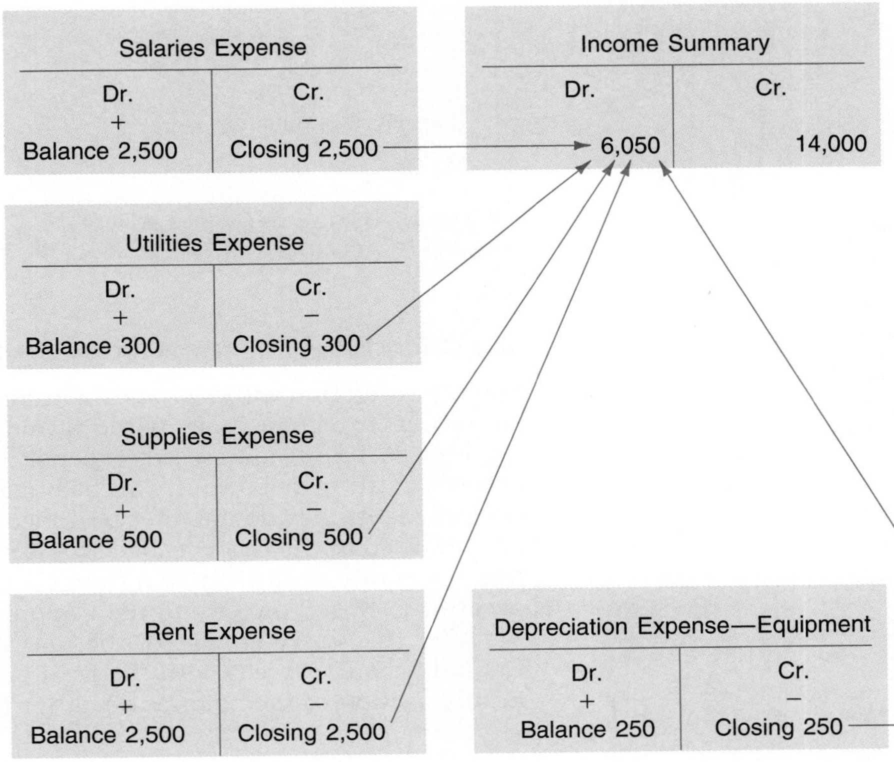

Step 3: Transferring Net Income or Net Loss to Owner's Equity

Income Summary

Dr.	Cr.
6,050	14,000
	Bal. 7,950

The next step in the closing procedure is to transfer the balance of Income Summary to the owner's capital account. On December 31, 19X5, the Income Summary account had a credit balance of $7,950. This balance represents the net income for the month (revenue of $14,000 minus expenses of $6,050).

Refer to the worksheet in Figure 6–1. The amount of net income on line 18 is $7,950. The general journal entry to record the transfer of the net income is a debit of $7,950 to the Income Summary account and a credit of $7,950 to John Arrow, Capital.

When this entry is posted, the balance of the Income Summary account is reduced to zero and the owner's capital account is increased by the amount of the net income.

Step 3
Close Income Summary

GENERAL JOURNAL PAGE *4*

	DATE		DESCRIPTION	POST. REF.	DEBIT	CREDIT	
1	*19X5*		*Closing Entries*				1
12	*Dec.*	*31*	*Income Summary*		*7 9 5 0 00*		12
13			*John Arrow, Capital*			*7 9 5 0 00*	13
14							14

Income Summary	
Dr.	Cr.
Expenses 6,050	Revenue 14,000
Closing 7,950	

John Arrow, Capital	
Dr.	Cr.
−	+
	Balance 40,000
	Net Inc. 7,950

Step 4: Transferring the Drawing Account Balance to Capital

You will recall that withdrawals are funds taken from the business by the owner for personal use. Withdrawals are recorded in the Drawing account. Withdrawals are not expenses of the business but are decreases in the owner's equity in the business. Since withdrawals are not expenses, they do not affect net income or net loss. Withdrawals are recorded in the Drawing account and appear in the statement of owner's equity as a deduction from Capital. Therefore, the Drawing account is closed directly to the Capital account.

After this entry is posted, the new balance of the John Arrow, Capital account agrees with the final amount listed in the Owner's Equity section of the balance sheet for December 31, 19X5.

Step 4
Close Drawing Account

GENERAL JOURNAL PAGE *4*

	DATE		DESCRIPTION	POST. REF.	DEBIT	CREDIT	
1	*19X5*		*Closing Entries*				1
15	*Dec.*	*31*	*John Arrow, Capital*		*1 0 0 0 00*		15
16			*John Arrow, Drawing*			*1 0 0 0 00*	16
17							17

John Arrow, Drawing	
Dr. +	Cr. −
Balance 1,000	Closing 1,000

John Arrow, Capital	
Dr. −	Cr. +
	Balance 40,000
Drawing 1,000	Net Inc. 7,950

Journalizing and posting the closing entries is the seventh step in the accounting cycle.

After the closing entries for Arrow Accounting Services are posted to the general ledger accounts, the general journal and ledger accounts appear as shown in Figure 6–2, pages 151–153.

The examples given here, which show the closing process at the end of one month, are for illustrative purposes. Normally, closing takes place only at the end of the fiscal year.

FIGURE 6–2
The Closing Process Completed: General Journal and General Ledger

Step 1
Close revenue

Step 2
Close expense accounts

Step 3
Close Income Summary

Step 4
Close Drawing account

GENERAL JOURNAL PAGE 4

	DATE		DESCRIPTION	POST. REF.	DEBIT	CREDIT	
1	*19X5*		*Closing Entries*				1
2	*Dec.*	*31*	*Fees Income*		*14,000.00*		2
3			*Income Summary*			*14,000.00*	3
4							4
5		*31*	*Income Summary*		*6,050.00*		5
6			*Salaries Expense*			*2,500.00*	6
7			*Utilities Expense*			*300.00*	7
8			*Supplies Expense*			*500.00*	8
9			*Rent Expense*			*2,500.00*	9
10			*Depr. Expense—Equipment*			*250.00*	10
11							11
12		*31*	*Income Summary*		*7,950.00*		12
13			*John Arrow, Capital*			*7,950.00*	13
14							14
15		*31*	*John Arrow, Capital*		*1,000.00*		15
16			*John Arrow, Drawing*			*1,000.00*	16
17							17

ACCOUNT *John Arrow, Capital* ACCOUNT NO. *301*

DATE		EXPLANATION	POST. REF.	DEBIT	CREDIT	BALANCE DEBIT	BALANCE CREDIT
19X5							
Nov.	*6*		*J1*		*40,000.00*		*40,000.00*
Dec.	*31*	*Closing*	*J4*		*7,950.00*		*47,950.00*
	31	*Closing*	*J4*	*1,000.00*			*46,950.00*

ACCOUNT *John Arrow, Drawing* ACCOUNT NO. *302*

DATE		EXPLANATION	POST. REF.	DEBIT	CREDIT	BALANCE DEBIT	BALANCE CREDIT
19X5							
Dec.	31		J2	1 0 0 0 00		1 0 0 0 00	
Dec.	31	Closing	J4		1 0 0 0 00	—0—	

ACCOUNT *Income Summary* ACCOUNT NO. *399*

DATE		EXPLANATION	POST. REF.	DEBIT	CREDIT	BALANCE DEBIT	BALANCE CREDIT
19X5							
Dec.	31	Closing	J4		14 0 0 0 00		14 0 0 0 00
Dec.	31	Closing	J4	6 0 5 0 00			7 9 5 0 00
	31	Closing	J4	7 9 5 0 00			—0—

ACCOUNT *Fees Income* ACCOUNT NO. *401*

DATE		EXPLANATION	POST. REF.	DEBIT	CREDIT	BALANCE DEBIT	BALANCE CREDIT
19X5							
Dec.	31		J2		10 5 0 0 00		10 5 0 0 00
Dec.	31		J2		3 5 0 0 00		14 0 0 0 00
	31	Closing	J4	14 0 0 0 00			—0—

ACCOUNT *Salaries Expense* ACCOUNT NO. *511*

DATE		EXPLANATION	POST. REF.	DEBIT	CREDIT	BALANCE DEBIT	BALANCE CREDIT
19X5							
Dec.	31		J2	2 5 0 0 00		2 5 0 0 00	
Dec.	31	Closing	J4		2 5 0 0 00	—0—	

ACCOUNT *Utilities Expense* ACCOUNT NO. *514*

DATE		EXPLANATION	POST. REF.	DEBIT	CREDIT	BALANCE DEBIT	BALANCE CREDIT
19X5							
Dec.	31		J2	3 0 0 00		3 0 0 00	
Dec.	31	Closing	J4		3 0 0 00	—0—	

ACCOUNT *Supplies Expense* ACCOUNT NO. *517*

DATE		EXPLANATION	POST. REF.	DEBIT	CREDIT	BALANCE DEBIT	BALANCE CREDIT
19X5							
Dec.	*31*	*Adjusting*	*J3*	*500 00*		*500 00*	
Dec.	*31*	*Closing*	*J4*		*500 00*	*—0—*	

ACCOUNT *Rent Expense* ACCOUNT NO. *520*

DATE		EXPLANATION	POST. REF.	DEBIT	CREDIT	BALANCE DEBIT	BALANCE CREDIT
19X5							
Dec.	*31*	*Adjusting*	*J3*	*2 500 00*		*2 500 00*	
Dec.	*31*	*Closing*	*J4*		*2 500 00*	*—0—*	

ACCOUNT *Depreciation Expense—Equipment* ACCOUNT NO. *523*

DATE		EXPLANATION	POST. REF.	DEBIT	CREDIT	BALANCE DEBIT	BALANCE CREDIT
19X5							
Dec.	*31*	*Adjusting*	*J3*	*250 00*		*250 00*	
Dec.	*31*	*Closing*	*J4*		*250 00*	*—0—*	

SELF-REVIEW

1. What type account is Income Summary?
2. What are the four steps in the closing process?
3. A firm has $18,000 in revenue for the period. Give the entry to close the Fees Income account.
4. A firm has the following expenses: Salaries Expense, 1,680; Supplies Expense, 320; and Rent Expense, 800. Give the entry to close the expense accounts.
5. What entry is made to close the Drawing account?

Answers to Self-Review

1. The Income Summary account is a temporary owner's equity account. The account is used to summarize the results of operations in the general ledger and has no normal balance.
2. The four steps in the closing procedure are
   a. The revenue account is closed to Income Summary.
   b. The expense accounts are closed to Income Summary.
   c. The Income Summary account is closed to the Capital account.
   d. The Drawing account is closed to the owner's Capital account.

3. Fees Income	18,000	
Income Summary		18,000
4. Income Summary	2,800	
Salaries Expense		1,680
Supplies Expense		320
Rent Expense		800

5. To close the Drawing account, Capital is debited and Drawing is credited for the balance of the Drawing account.

PREPARING THE POSTCLOSING TRIAL BALANCE

OBJECTIVE 2

Prepare a postclosing trial balance.

Preparing the postclosing trial balance is the eighth step in the accounting cycle.

Every effort must be made to avoid mistakes in the general ledger at the start of the new accounting period. These mistakes may arise from errors made in recording the adjusting and closing entries. If such errors occur, the general ledger will not balance at the end of the new period and it could be time-consuming to find the errors.

The **postclosing trial balance,** or *after-closing trial balance,* is prepared to test the equality of total debits and credits and is the last step in the end-of-period routine. Only the accounts with balances are listed on a postclosing trial balance. These accounts—the assets, liabilities, and owner's Capital accounts—are permanent and remain open at the end of the period. If the postclosing trial balance totals are equal, you can safely proceed with the recording of entries for the new period. The postclosing trial balance prepared for Arrow Accounting Services on December 31, 19X5, is shown in Figure 6–3.

FIGURE 6–3
Postclosing Trial Balance

ARROW ACCOUNTING SERVICES
Postclosing Trial Balance
December 31, 19X5

ACCOUNT NAME	DEBIT	CREDIT
Cash	16 200 00	
Accounts Receivable	2 000 00	
Supplies	500 00	
Prepaid Rent	17 500 00	
Equipment	15 000 00	
Accumulated Depreciation—Equipment		250 00
Accounts Payable		4 000 00
John Arrow, Capital		46 950 00
Totals	51 200 00	51 200 00

▲ **REMEMBER!**

The temporary owner's equity accounts—revenue, expenses, Drawing, and Income Summary—are closed because they apply only to one accounting period. These accounts do not appear on the postclosing trial balance or the balance sheet.

Finding and Correcting Errors

The postclosing trial balance, like the trial balance, may indicate the existence of errors in the accounting records. If an error is found, the accountant must determine where it was made and take steps to correct it. The audit trail aids in tracing data through the firm's accounting records to find errors. Refer to Chapter 5 for a discussion of some of the more common errors made in accounting records and how they may be found and corrected.

INTERPRETING THE FINANCIAL STATEMENTS

OBJECTIVE 3
Interpret financial statements.

The ninth and last step in the accounting cycle is interpreting the financial statements. Management must have timely and accurate financial information to operate the business successfully. Information obtained from the financial statements assists management in achieving this objective by providing the answers to many questions, including:

- How much cash does the business have?
- How much money do customers owe the business?
- What is the amount owed to suppliers?
- How much profit did the firm make?

The financial statements for Arrow Accounting Services at the end of its first accounting period are shown in Figure 6–4. By interpreting these statements, management can see that

- The business has $16,200 in cash.
- The business is owed $2,000 by its customers.
- The business owes $4,000 to its suppliers.
- The business has made a profit of $7,950.

FIGURE 6–4
End-of-Month Financial Statements

ARROW ACCOUNTING SERVICES
Income Statement
Month Ended December 31, 19X5

Revenue		
Fees Income		14 000 00
Expenses		
Salaries Expense	2 500 00	
Utilities Expense	300 00	
Supplies Expense	500 00	
Rent Expense	2 500 00	
Depreciation Expense—Equipment	250 00	
Total Expenses		6 050 00
Net Income for the Month		7 950 00

ARROW ACCOUNTING SERVICES
Statement of Owner's Equity
Month Ended December 31, 19X5

John Arrow, Capital, December 1, 19X5		40 000 00
Net Income for December	7 950 00	
Less Withdrawals for December	1 000 00	
Increase in Capital		6 950 00
John Arrow, Capital, December 31, 19X5		46 950 00

ARROW ACCOUNTING SERVICES Balance Sheet December 31, 19X5		
Assets		
Cash		*16 2 0 0 00*
Accounts Receivable		*2 0 0 0 00*
Supplies		*5 0 0 00*
Prepaid Rent		*17 5 0 0 00*
Equipment	*15 0 0 0 00*	
Accumulated Depreciation	*2 5 0 00*	*14 7 5 0 00*
Total Assets		*50 9 5 0 00*
Liabilities and Owner's Equity		
Liabilities		
Accounts Payable		*4 0 0 0 00*
Owner's Equity		
John Arrow, Capital		*46 9 5 0 00*
Total Liabilities and Owner's Equity		*50 9 5 0 00*

THE ACCOUNTING CYCLE

OBJECTIVE 4
Review the steps in the accounting cycle.

You have now learned that the accounting cycle is a series of steps performed during each fiscal period to classify, record, and summarize financial data for a business to produce needed financial information. You learned about the entire accounting cycle as you studied the financial affairs of Arrow Accounting Services during the first month of its operations. The steps in this cycle are summarized below and in Figure 6–5.

FIGURE 6–5
The Accounting Cycle

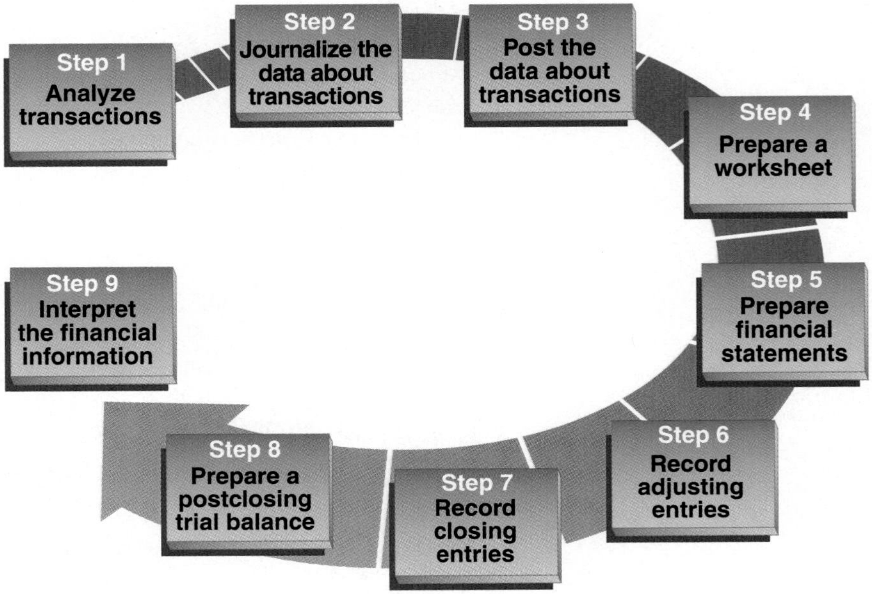

Step 1. **Analyze transactions.** The data about transactions appears on a variety of source documents—sales slips, purchase invoices, credit memorandums, check stubs, and so on. These source documents are analyzed to determine their effects on the basic accounting equation.

Step 2. **Journalize the transactions.** The effects of the transactions are recorded in a journal.

Step 3. **Post the journal entries.** The data about transactions is transferred from the journal entries to the ledger accounts.

Step 4. **Prepare a worksheet.** At the end of each period of operations, a worksheet is prepared. The Trial Balance section is used to prove the equality of total debits and credits in the general ledger. The Adjustments section is used to enter changes in account balances that may be needed to present a more accurate and complete picture of the firm's financial affairs. The Adjusted Trial Balance section provides a check on the equality of debits and credits after adjustments are made. The Income Statement and Balance Sheet sections provide data to prepare financial statements.

Step 5. **Prepare financial statements.** The financial statements are prepared to report information to owners, managers, and other interested parties. The income statement shows the results of operations for the period, the statement of owner's equity reports the changes in the owner's financial interest, and the balance sheet shows the financial position of the business at the end of the period.

Step 6. **Record adjusting entries.** The adjusting entries are journalized and posted to create a permanent record of the changes in account balances made on the worksheet when the adjustments for the period were determined.

Step 7. **Record closing entries.** The closing entries are journalized and posted to transfer the results of operations to owner's equity and to prepare the revenue and expense accounts for use in the next period. The closing entries reduce the balances of the revenue, expense, and Drawing accounts to zero.

Step 8. **Prepare a postclosing trial balance.** Another trial balance is prepared to make sure the general ledger is in balance after the adjusting and closing entries are posted.

Step 9. **Interpret the financial information.** Accountants, owners, managers, and other interested parties interpret financial statements by comparing such things as profit, revenue, and expenses from one accounting period to the next.

After studying the accounting cycle of Arrow Accounting Services, you have an understanding of how data flows through a simple accounting system for a small business. The data that comes into the system by means of source documents is analyzed; recorded in the general journal; posted to the general ledger; proved, adjusted, and summarized on the worksheet; and then reported on financial statements. This data flow is illustrated in Figure 6–6, on page 160.

Information Block: International Accounting

The International Marketplace

With improvements in technology, the world has become a smaller place, and many companies now routinely conduct business in other countries. This trend has extended the accountant's role beyond national boundaries into international areas not encountered by companies that restrict their business to the boundaries of the United States.

The United States has consistently imported and exported more goods and services than most other countries. Exports of goods and services grew an average of more than 6 percent annually during the past ten years to reach over $600 billion in the early 1990s. Similarly, imports of goods and services grew an average of more than 8 percent annually to reach over $700 billion. Foreign assets owned by U.S. citizens or businesses grew to $1.4 trillion while assets owned in the United States by foreigners increased to $2 trillion.

CHART 1
McDonald's Worldwide Restaurants

McDonald's Restaurants, 1991

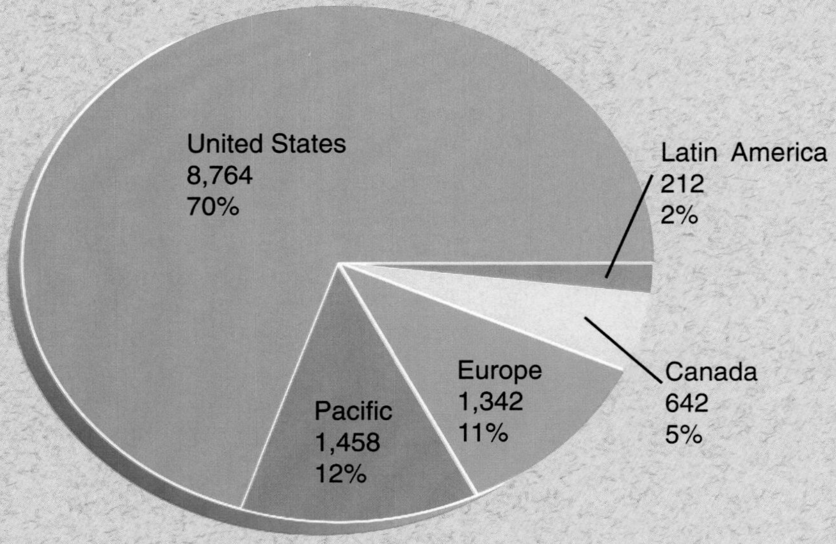

Total Restaurants = 12,418
Source: McDonald's 1991 Annual Report

CHART 2
Top Five Countries Purchasing United States Manufacturing Exports

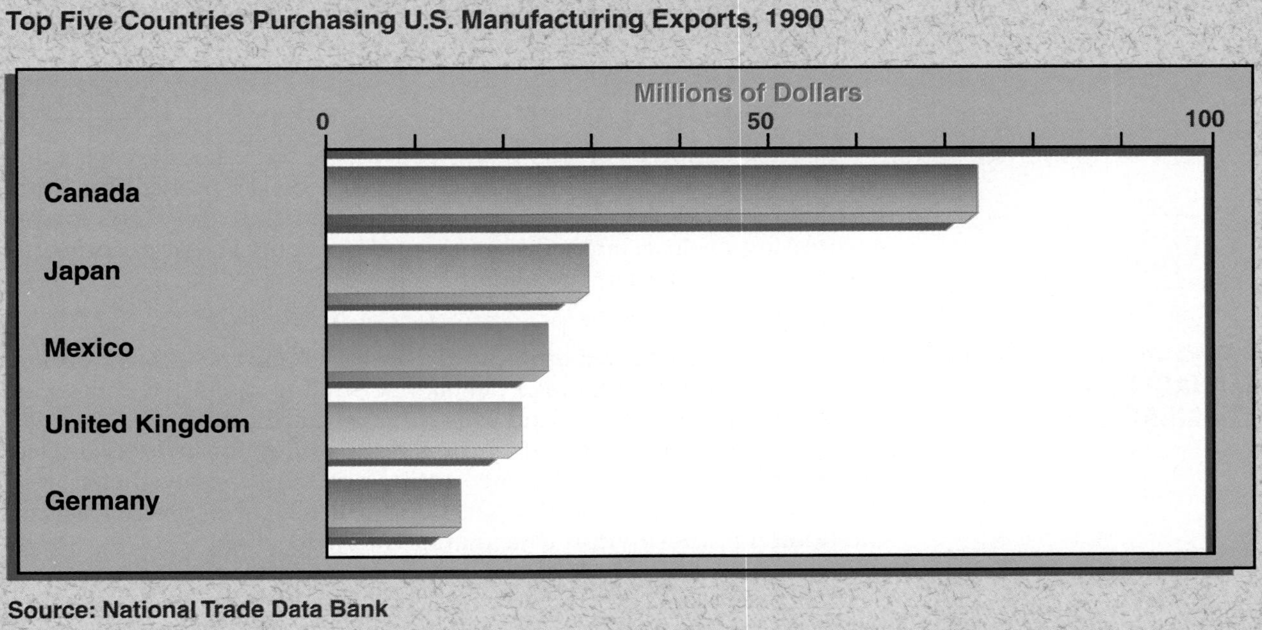

Businesses in the United States have become more global in their perspective. Over 50 percent of large U.S. manufacturers have significant international operations and are increasing the number of countries in which they do business. During the past decade, these global companies were more likely to survive, were more profitable, and increased sales faster than domestic companies. Examples of large U.S. companies with a significant percentage of international sales include AT&T with 24 percent, IBM with over 62 percent, Ford Motor Company with over 44 percent, and McDonald's with 44 percent. McDonald's now has restaurants throughout the world, as shown in Chart 1. The countries that purchase the largest proportion of U.S. manufactured goods are shown in Chart 2.

International trade will be even easier in the future. The United Nations is establishing a network of 16 cities worldwide as international trade point centers. These centers will be interconnected using computers to reduce paperwork and simplify trade. The network will eliminate the complicated and costly chore of filling out purchase orders, invoices, bills of lading, customs declarations, and payments. The centers also will assist international traders by providing referrals to banks, insurance companies, and other related businesses.

FIGURE 6–6
The Flow of Data Through a Simple Accounting System

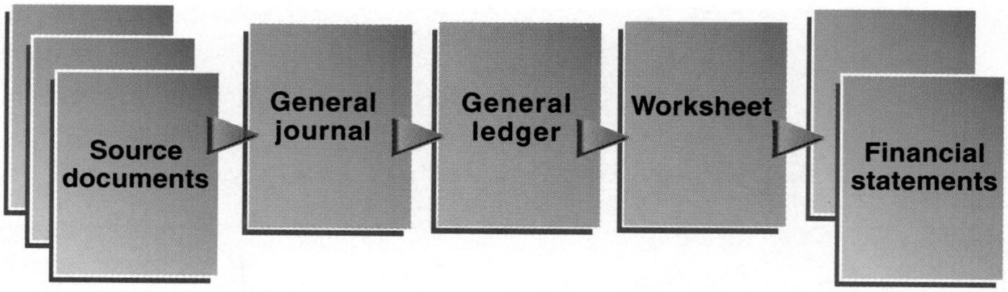

In later chapters of this book, you will become familiar with accounting systems that have more complex records, procedures, and financial statements. However, keep in mind that the steps of the accounting cycle remain the same and the underlying accounting principles also remain the same.

MANAGERIAL IMPLICATIONS

Management must have timely and accurate financial information to control operations and make decisions. Such information can come only from a well-designed and well-run accounting system. Although management is not involved in the details of day-to-day accounting procedures or end-of-period accounting procedures, the efficiency of these procedures has a major effect on the quality and promptness of the financial information that management receives.

SELF-REVIEW

1. Why is a postclosing trial balance prepared?
2. What accounts appear on the postclosing trial balance?
3. What are the first three steps in the accounting cycle?
4. What three financial statements are prepared during the accounting cycle?
5. What is the last step in the accounting cycle?

Answers to Self-Review

1. The postclosing trial balance is prepared to make sure the general ledger is in balance after the adjusting and closing entries are posted.
2. The asset, liability, and owner's Capital accounts appear on the postclosing trial balance.
3. The first three steps in the accounting cycle are: (a) analyze transactions, (b) journalize transactions in the general journal, and (c) post the journal entries to the ledger accounts.
4. The three financial statements prepared during the accounting cycle are: (a) income statement, (b) statement of owner's equity, and (c) balance sheet.
5. The last step in the accounting cycle is to interpret the financial statements.

CHAPTER 6 Review and Applications

CHAPTER SUMMARY

After the worksheet and financial statements are completed and adjusting entries are journalized and posted, the closing entries are recorded and a postclosing trial balance is prepared. The data for the closing entries is taken from the Income Statement section of the worksheet. A special temporary owner's equity account called Income Summary is used in the closing procedure. The balances of the revenue and expense accounts are transferred to this account. Then the balance of the Income Summary account, which represents the net income or net loss for the period, is transferred to the owner's Capital account. Next, the Drawing account is closed to the owner's Capital account. After the closing entries are posted, the Capital account reflects the results of operations for the period, and the revenue and expense accounts have zero balances. Thus the revenue and expense accounts are ready to accumulate data for the next period.

A postclosing trial balance is prepared to test the equality of total debit and credit balances in the general ledger after the adjusting and closing entries have been recorded. The postclosing trial balance lists only the permanent accounts that remain open at the end of the period—the asset, liability, and owner's Capital accounts.

The accounting cycle consists of a series of steps that are repeated in each fiscal period. These steps are designed to classify, record, and summarize financial data for a business to produce needed financial information.

GLOSSARY OF NEW TERMS

Closing entries (p. 146) Entries made in the general journal to transfer the results of operations to owner's equity and to prepare the revenue, expense, and drawing accounts for use in the next accounting period

Income Summary account (p. 146) A special owner's equity account that is used to summarize the results of operations and is used only in the closing process

Postclosing trial balance (p. 154) A statement that is prepared to prove the equality of total debits and credits after the closing process is completed

REVIEW QUESTIONS

1. What three procedures are performed at the end of each accounting period before the financial information is interpreted?
2. Where does the accountant obtain the data needed for the adjusting entries?
3. Why does the accountant record closing entries at the end of a period?
4. How is the Income Summary account used in the closing procedure?
5. Where does the accountant obtain the data needed for the closing entries?
6. Why is a postclosing trial balance prepared?
7. What accounts appear on a postclosing trial balance?
8. What is the accounting cycle?
9. Name the steps of the accounting cycle.
10. Briefly describe the flow of data through a simple accounting system.

MANAGERIAL FOCUS

1. Why is it important that a firm's financial records be kept up to date and that management receive the financial statements promptly after the end of each accounting period?
2. What kinds of operating and general policy decisions might be influenced by data on the financial statements?
3. An officer of the Edwards Company recently commented that when he receives the firm's financial statements, he looks at just the bottom line of the income statement—the line that shows the net income or net loss for the period. He said that he does not bother with the rest of the income statement because "it's only the bottom line that counts." He also does not read the balance sheet. Do you think this manager is correct in the way he uses the financial statements? Why or why not?
4. The president of the Mann Corporation is concerned about the firm's ability to pay its debts on time. What items on the balance sheet would help her to assess the firm's debt-paying ability?

EXERCISES

EXERCISE 6–1 (Obj. 1)

Journalize closing entries. On December 31, the end of the current year, the ledger of Williams and Company contained the following account balances.

Cash	$18,000
Accounts Receivable	1,200
Supplies	800
Equipment	15,000

Accumulated Depreciation	1,500
Accounts Payable	2,000
Jerry Williams, Capital	23,100
Jerry Williams, Drawing	12,000
Fees Income	42,500
Salaries Expense	14,000
Utilities Expense	3,600
Supplies Expense	2,000
Telephone Expense	1,800
Depreciation Expense	1,500

All the accounts have normal balances. Journalize the closing entries. Use J4 as the general journal page number.

EXERCISE 6–2
(Obj. 2)

Postclosing trial balance. Identify the accounts listed below that will appear on the postclosing trial balance.

ACCOUNTS

1. Cash
2. Accounts Receivable
3. Supplies
4. Equipment
5. Accumulated Depreciation
6. Accounts Payable
7. Steve Gray, Capital
8. Steve Gray, Drawing
9. Fees Income
10. Salaries Expense
11. Utilities Expense
12. Supplies Expense
13. Telephone Expense
14. Depreciation Expense

EXERCISE 6–3
(Obj. 4)

Accounting cycle. Reflected below are the steps in the accounting cycle. Arrange the steps in the proper sequence.

1. Journalize the data about transactions.
2. Prepare a worksheet.
3. Analyze transactions.
4. Record adjusting entries.
5. Post the data about transactions.
6. Prepare a postclosing trial balance.
7. Prepare financial statements.
8. Record closing entries.
9. Interpret the financial information.

EXERCISE 6–4
(Obj. 3)

Financial statements. Managers often consult financial statements for specific types of information. Indicate whether each of the following items of information would appear on the income statement, statement of owner's equity, or the balance sheet. Use *I* for the income statement, *E* for the statement of owner's equity, and *B* for the balance sheet. If an item appears on more than one statement, use all letters that apply to that item.

1. Cash on hand
2. Revenue earned during the period
3. Total assets of the business
4. Net income for the period
5. Owner's capital at the end of the period
6. Supplies on hand
7. Cost of supplies used during the period
8. Accounts receivable of the business
9. Accumulated depreciation on the firm's equipment
10. Amount of depreciation charged off on the firm's equipment during the period
11. Original cost of the firm's equipment
12. Book value of the firm's equipment
13. Total expenses for the period
14. Accounts payable of the business
15. Owner's withdrawals for the period

EXERCISE 6–5
(Obj. 1)
Tutorial

Closing entries. The Income Summary and Capital accounts for Apex Productions at the end of its accounting period appear below.

ACCOUNT *Income Summary* ACCOUNT NO. *399*

DATE		EXPLANATION	POST. REF.	DEBIT	CREDIT	BALANCE DEBIT	BALANCE CREDIT
19X5							
Dec.	*31*	*Closing*	*J4*		*15 5 0 0 00*		*15 5 0 0 00*
Dec.	*31*	*Closing*	*J4*	*10 1 0 0 00*			*5 4 0 0 00*
	31	*Closing*	*J4*	*5 4 0 0 00*			

ACCOUNT *Davis Robinson, Capital* ACCOUNT NO. *301*

DATE		EXPLANATION	POST. REF.	DEBIT	CREDIT	BALANCE DEBIT	BALANCE CREDIT
19X5							
Dec.	*1*		*J1*		*50 0 0 0 00*		*50 0 0 0 00*
Dec.	*31*	*Closing*	*J4*		*5 4 0 0 00*		*55 4 0 0 00*
	31	*Closing*	*J4*	*1 4 0 0 00*			*54 0 0 0 00*

Instructions: Complete the following statements.

1. Total revenue for the period is ______.
2. Total expenses for the period are ______.
3. Net income for the period is ______.
4. Owner's withdrawals for the period are ______.

EXERCISE 6–6 (Obj. 1)

Tutorial

Closing entries. The ledger accounts of Glenview Real Estate Company appear as follows on March 31, 19X5.

ACCOUNT NO.	ACCOUNT	BALANCE
101	Cash	$11,500
111	Accounts Receivable	2,200
121	Supplies	1,350
131	Prepaid Insurance	3,480
141	Equipment	16,800
142	Accum. Depr.—Equipment	3,360
202	Accounts Payable	1,800
301	Marie DeMarco, Capital	19,600
302	Marie DeMarco, Drawing	1,000
404	Fees Income	46,000
510	Rent Expense	4,800
511	Salaries Expense	23,600
514	Utilities Expense	1,200
517	Supplies Expense	650
518	Telephone Expense	900
519	Insurance Expense	1,600
523	Depr. Expense—Equipment	1,680

All of the accounts have normal balances. Journalize and post the closing entries. Use J4 as the page number for the general journal in journalizing the closing entries.

EXERCISE 6–7 (Obj. 1)

Tutorial

Closing entries. On December 31, 19X5, the Income Summary account of Henson Company has a debit balance of $18,000 after revenue of $28,000 and expenses of $46,000 were closed to the account. Jerold Henson, Drawing has a debit balance of $2,000 and Jerold Henson, Capital has a credit balance of $56,000. Record the journal entries necessary to complete closing the accounts. What is the new balance of Jerold Henson, Capital?

EXERCISE 6–8 (Obj. 4)

Accounting cycle. Complete a chart of the accounting cycle by writing the steps of the cycle in their proper sequence.

PROBLEMS

PROBLEM SET A

PROBLEM 6–1A (Obj. 1)

Tutorial

Spreadsheet

Adjusting and closing entries. The Peters Market Research Agency, owned by Ruth Peters, is employed by large companies to test customer reaction to their products. On January 31, 19X2, the firm's worksheet showed the adjustments data given below. The balances of the revenue and expense accounts listed in the Income Statement section of the worksheet and the Drawing account listed in the Balance Sheet section of the worksheet are also given.

ADJUSTMENTS

a. Supplies used, $140
b. Expired rent, $750
c. Depreciation on office equipment, $280

REVENUE AND EXPENSE ACCOUNTS

401	Fees Income	$19,250	Cr.
511	Salaries Expense	10,300	Dr.
514	Utilities Expense	115	Dr.
517	Telephone Expense	235	Dr.
520	Travel Expense	2,230	Dr.
523	Supplies Expense	140	Dr.
526	Rent Expense	750	Dr.
529	Depr. Expense—Office Equipment	280	Dr.

DRAWING ACCOUNT

302	Ruth Peters, Drawing	1,200	Dr.

Instructions

1. Record adjusting entries in the general journal, page J3.
2. Record closing entries in the general journal, page J4.

PROBLEM 6–2A (Obj. 1, 2) Tutorial

Journalizing and posting closing entries. On December 31, 19X6, after adjustments, Webster Company's ledger contains the account balances at the top of page 167.

B AND H ENTERPRISES
Worksheet
Month Ended December 31, 19X5

	ACCOUNT NAME	TRIAL BALANCE DEBIT	TRIAL BALANCE CREDIT	ADJUSTMENTS DEBIT	ADJUSTMENTS CREDIT
1	*Cash*	*15 400 00*			
2	*Accounts Receivable*	*2 000 00*			
3	*Supplies*	*1 000 00*			*(a) 500 00*
4	*Prepaid Advertising*	*4 000 00*			*(b) 500 00*
5	*Equipment*	*10 000 00*			
6	*Accumulated Depreciation—Equipment*				*(c) 400 00*
7	*Accounts Payable*		*2 000 00*		
8	*B. H. Carter, Capital*		*22 000 00*		
9	*B. H. Carter, Drawing*	*1 400 00*			
10	*Fees Income*		*12 500 00*		
11	*Salaries Expense*	*2 400 00*			
12	*Utilities Expense*	*300 00*			
13	*Supplies Expense*			*(a) 500 00*	
14	*Advertising Expense*			*(b) 500 00*	
15	*Depreciation Expense—Equipment*			*(c) 400 00*	
16	*Totals*	*36 500 00*	*36 500 00*	*1 400 00*	*1 400 00*
17	*Net Income*				
18					
19					

101	Cash	6,200	Dr.
111	Accounts Receivable	2,800	Dr.
121	Supplies	500	Dr.
131	Prepaid Rent	6,600	Dr.
141	Equipment	9,000	Dr.
142	Accumulated Depreciation—Equipment	250	Cr.
202	Accounts Payable	1,250	Cr.
301	Jim Webster, Capital (12/1/19X6)	9,270	Cr.
302	Jim Webster, Drawing	1,200	Dr.
401	Fees Income	23,000	Cr.
511	Advertising Expense	800	Dr.
514	Rent Expense	600	Dr.
517	Salaries Expense	4,800	Dr.
519	Utilities Expense	1,120	Dr.
523	Depreciation Expense—Equipment	150	Dr.

Instructions

1. Record the balances in the ledger accounts as of December 31, 19X6. The adjusting entries were recorded on journal page J3.
2. Journalize the closing entries in the general journal, page J4.
3. Post the closing entries to the general ledger accounts.

PROBLEM 6–3A
(Obj. 1, 2)
Tutorial

Journalizing and posting adjusting and closing entries and preparing a postclosing trial balance. A completed worksheet for B and H Enterprises is shown below and on page 166.

ADJUSTED TRIAL BALANCE		INCOME STATEMENT		BALANCE SHEET		
DEBIT	CREDIT	DEBIT	CREDIT	DEBIT	CREDIT	
15 400 00				15 400 00		1
2 000 00				2 000 00		2
500 00				500 00		3
3 500 00				3 500 00		4
10 000 00				10 000 00		5
	400 00				400 00	6
	2 000 00				2 000 00	7
	22 000 00				22 000 00	8
1 400 00				1 400 00		9
	12 500 00		12 500 00			10
2 400 00		2 400 00				11
300 00		300 00				12
500 00		500 00				13
500 00		500 00				14
400 00		400 00				15
36 900 00	36 900 00	4 100 00	12 500 00	32 800 00	24 400 00	16
		8 400 00			8 400 00	17
		12 500 00	12 500 00	32 800 00	32 800 00	18
						19

Instructions

1. Record balances as of December 31 in the ledger accounts.
2. Journalize (use J3 as the page number) and post the adjusting entries.
3. Journalize (use J4 as the page number) and post the closing entries.
4. Prepare a postclosing trial balance.

PROBLEM 6–4A (Obj. 1, 2, 4)

Worksheet, journalizing and posting adjusting and closing entries, and the postclosing trial balance. A partially completed worksheet for Miller Auto Customizing Service, a firm that rebuilds cars and vans to give them custom features, follows.

MILLER AUTO CUSTOMIZING SERVICE
Worksheet
Month Ended November 30, 19X5

	ACCOUNT NAME	TRIAL BALANCE DEBIT	TRIAL BALANCE CREDIT	ADJUSTMENTS DEBIT	ADJUSTMENTS CREDIT
1	*Cash*	15 525 00			
2	*Accounts Receivable*	2 475 00			
3	*Supplies*	2 000 00			(a) 800 00
4	*Prepaid Advertising*	1 500 00			(b) 700 00
5	*Equipment*	10 000 00			
6	*Accumulated Depreciation—Equipment*				(c) 240 00
7	*Accounts Payable*		2 500 00		
8	*Craig Miller, Capital*		17 750 00		
9	*Craig Miller, Drawing*	1 000 00			
10	*Fees Income*		15 000 00		
11	*Salaries Expense*	2 400 00			
12	*Utilities Expense*	350 00			
13	*Supplies Expense*			(a) 800 00	
14	*Advertising Expense*			(b) 700 00	
15	*Depreciation Expense—Equipment*			(c) 240 00	
16	*Totals*	35 250 00	35 250 00	1 740 00	1 740 00
17					

Instructions

1. Record balances as of November 30 in the ledger accounts.
2. Prepare the worksheet.
3. Journalize (use J3 as the journal page number) and post the adjusting entries.
4. Journalize (use J4 as the journal page number) and post the closing entries.
5. Prepare a postclosing trial balance.

PROBLEM SET B

PROBLEM 6–1B (Obj. 1)

Tutorial

Adjusting and closing entries. The Sanitex Commercial Laundry, owned by Wayne Thomas, provides service to hotels, motels, and hospitals. On January 31, 19X6, the firm's worksheet showed the adjustment data given below. The balances of the revenue and expense accounts listed in the Income Statement section of the worksheet and the Drawing account listed in the Balance Sheet section of the worksheet are also given.

ADJUSTMENTS

a. Supplies used, $1,430
b. Expired insurance, $185
c. Depreciation on machinery, $560

REVENUE AND EXPENSE ACCOUNTS

401	Fees Income	$16,400	Cr.
511	Rent Expense	1,500	Dr.
514	Salaries Expense	8,000	Dr.
517	Utilities Expense	320	Dr.
520	Telephone Expense	105	Dr.
523	Supplies Expense	1,430	Dr.
526	Insurance Expense	185	Dr.
529	Depr. Expense—Machinery	560	Dr.

DRAWING ACCOUNT

302	Wayne Thomas, Drawing	1,200	Dr.

Instructions

1. Record adjusting entries in the general journal, page J3.
2. Record closing entries in the general journal, page J4.

PROBLEM 6–2B
(Obj. 1, 2)

Tutorial

Journalizing and posting closing entries. On December 31, 19X6, after adjustments, Omni Pictures' ledger contains the following account balances.

ACCT NO	ACCOUNT NAME	DEBIT	CREDIT
101	Cash	9,500	
111	Accounts Receivable	2,400	
121	Supplies	1,000	
131	Prepaid Rent	7,700	
141	Equipment	12,000	
142	Accumulated Depreciation—Equipment		300
202	Accounts Payable		3,250
301	Judy Hall, Capital (12/1/19X6)		19,150
302	Judy Hall, Drawing	1,200	
401	Fees Income		18,000
511	Advertising Expense	1,100	
514	Rent Expense	700	
517	Salaries Expense	3,600	
519	Utilities Expense	1,200	
523	Depreciation Expense—Equipment	300	

Instructions

1. Record the balances in the ledger accounts as of December 31, 19X6. The adjusting entries were recorded on journal page J3.
2. Journalize the closing entries in the general journal, page J4.
3. Post the closing entries to the general ledger accounts.

PROBLEM 6–3B
(Obj. 1, 2)

Tutorial

Journalizing and posting adjusting and closing entries and preparing a postclosing trial balance. A completed worksheet for Frosty Air Conditioning Service is shown on pages 170–171.

FROSTY AIR CONDITIONING SERVICE
Worksheet
Month Ended December 31, 19X5

	ACCOUNT NAME	TRIAL BALANCE		ADJUSTMENTS	
		DEBIT	CREDIT	DEBIT	CREDIT
1	*Cash*	5 400 00			
2	*Accounts Receivable*	1 000 00			
3	*Supplies*	1 000 00			(a) 500 00
4	*Prepaid Advertising*	1 500 00			(b) 200 00
5	*Equipment*	10 000 00			
6	*Accumulated Depreciation—Equipment*				(c) 250 00
7	*Accounts Payable*		1 500 00		
8	*Paul Davis, Capital*		13 700 00		
9	*Paul Davis, Drawing*	1 400 00			
10	*Fees Income*		7 800 00		
11	*Salaries Expense*	2 400 00			
12	*Utilities Expense*	300 00			
13	*Supplies Expense*			(a) 500 00	
14	*Advertising Expense*			(b) 200 00	
15	*Depreciation Expense—Equipment*			(c) 250 00	
16	*Totals*	23 000 00	23 000 00	950 00	950 00
17	*Net Income*				
18					
19					

Instructions

1. Record balances as of December 31 in the ledger accounts.
2. Journalize (use J3 as the journal page number) and post the adjusting entries.
3. Journalize (use J4 as the journal page number) and post the closing entries.
4. Prepare a postclosing trial balance.

PROBLEM 6–4B
(Obj. 1, 2, 4)

Worksheet, journalizing and posting adjusting and closing entries, and the postclosing trial balance. A partially completed worksheet for Good Times Band, a group that provides music at weddings, dances, and other social functions, is shown on page 171.

Instructions

1. Record balances as of November 30 in the ledger accounts.
2. Prepare the worksheet.
3. Journalize (use J3 as the journal page number) and post the adjusting entries.
4. Journalize (use J4 as the journal page number) and post the closing entries.
5. Prepare a postclosing trial balance.

Adjusted Trial Balance Debit	Adjusted Trial Balance Credit	Income Statement Debit	Income Statement Credit	Balance Sheet Debit	Balance Sheet Credit	
5,400.00				5,400.00		1
1,000.00				1,000.00		2
500.00				500.00		3
1,300.00				1,300.00		4
10,000.00				10,000.00		5
	250.00				250.00	6
	1,500.00				1,500.00	7
	13,700.00				13,700.00	8
1,400.00				1,400.00		9
	7,800.00		7,800.00			10
2,400.00		2,400.00				11
300.00		300.00				12
500.00		500.00				13
200.00		200.00				14
250.00		250.00				15
23,250.00	23,250.00	3,650.00	7,800.00	19,600.00	15,450.00	16
		4,150.00			4,150.00	17
		7,800.00	7,800.00	19,600.00	19,600.00	18
						19

GOOD TIMES BAND

Worksheet

Month Ended November 30, 19X5

	Account Name	Trial Balance Debit	Trial Balance Credit	Adjustments Debit	Adjustments Credit
1	*Cash*	11,560.00			
2	*Accounts Receivable*	2,500.00			
3	*Supplies*	2,000.00			(a) 800.00
4	*Prepaid Rent*	6,000.00			(b) 1,000.00
5	*Equipment*	12,000.00			
6	*Accumulated Depreciation—Equipment*				(c) 300.00
7	*Accounts Payable*		1,000.00		
8	*Richard Holden, Capital*		25,620.00		
9	*Richard Holden, Drawing*	1,000.00			
10	*Fees Income*		10,800.00		
11	*Salaries Expense*	2,000.00			
12	*Utilities Expense*	360.00			
13	*Supplies Expense*			(a) 800.00	
14	*Rent Expense*			(b) 1,000.00	
15	*Depreciation Expense*			(c) 300.00	
16	*Totals*	37,420.00	37,420.00	2,100.00	2,100.00

CHALLENGE PROBLEM

The Trial Balance section of the worksheet for E-Z Window Washing Service for the period ended December 31, 19X5, follows. Data for adjustments is also listed.

E-Z WINDOW WASHING SERVICE
Worksheet
Month Ended December 31, 19X5

	ACCOUNT NAME	TRIAL BALANCE DEBIT	TRIAL BALANCE CREDIT	ADJUSTMENTS DEBIT	ADJUSTMENTS CREDIT
1	*Cash*	6,800 00			
2	*Accounts Receivable*	1,500 00			
3	*Supplies*	1,200 00			(a) 600 00
4	*Prepaid Insurance*	1,800 00			(b) 400 00
5	*Machinery*	14,000 00			
6	*Accumulated Depreciation—Machinery*				(c) 200 00
7	*Accounts Payable*		2,250 00		
8	*E. Z. Taylor, Capital*		12,430 00		
9	*E. Z. Taylor, Drawing*	1,000 00			
10	*Fees Income*		13,750 00		
11	*Salaries Expense*	1,850 00			
12	*Utilities Expense*	280 00			
13	*Supplies Expense*			(a) 600 00	
14	*Insurance Expense*			(b) 400 00	
15	*Depreciation Expense*			(c) 200 00	
16	*Totals*	28,430 00	28,430 00	1,200 00	1,200 00
17					

ADJUSTMENTS
a. Supplies used, $600
b. Expired insurance, $400
c. Depreciation expense for machinery, $200

Instructions

1. Complete the worksheet.
2. Prepare an income statement.
3. Prepare a statement of owner's equity.
4. Prepare a balance sheet.
5. Journalize the adjusting entries in the general journal, page J3.
6. Journalize the closing entries in the general journal, page J4.
7. Prepare a postclosing trial balance.

CRITICAL THINKING PROBLEM

Jane Swanson, the bookkeeper for the Caldo Design Company, has just finished posting the closing entries for the year to the ledger. She notes that the balance of the Capital account in the ledger is $97,100 while the ending balance of Capital on the statement of owner's equity is $55,600. She knows that these amounts should agree and asks for your assistance in reviewing her work.

Your review of the books of Caldo Design reveals a beginning Capital balance of $50,000 and the closing entries below.

GENERAL JOURNAL PAGE *15*

DATE		DESCRIPTION	POST. REF.	DEBIT	CREDIT
19X5		*Closing Entries*			
Dec.	*31*	*Fees Income*		98 000 00	
		Accumulated Depreciation		8 500 00	
		Accounts Payable		33 000 00	
		Income Summary			139 500 00
	31	*Income Summary*		92 400 00	
		Salaries Expense			78 000 00
		Supplies Expense			5 000 00
		Depreciation Expense			2 400 00
		Jane Swanson, Drawing			7 000 00
	31	*Income Summary*		47 100 00	
		Jane Swanson, Capital			47 100 00

What errors did Ms. Swanson make in preparing the closing entries? Prepare a general journal entry to correct the errors made. Explain why the balance of the Capital account in the ledger after closing entries are posted will be the same as the ending Capital balance on the statement of owner's equity.

MINI-PRACTICE SET 1

Service Business Accounting Cycle

This project will give you an opportunity to apply your knowledge of accounting principles and procedures by handling all the accounting work of Arrow Accounting Services for the month of January 19X6.

INTRODUCTION

Assume that you are the head accountant for Arrow Accounting Services. During January 19X6 the business will use the same types of records and procedures that you learned about in Chapters 1 through 6. The chart of accounts for Arrow Accounting Services has been expanded to include a few new accounts. Follow the instructions to complete the accounting records for the month of January.

ARROW ACCOUNTING SERVICES
Chart of Accounts

	ASSETS		REVENUE
101	Cash	401	Fees Income
111	Accounts Receivable		EXPENSES
121	Supplies	511	Salaries Expense
131	Prepaid Rent	514	Utilities Expense
134	Prepaid Insurance	517	Supplies Expense
141	Equipment	520	Rent Expense
142	Accumulated Depreciation—Equipment	523	Depreciation Expense—Equipment
	LIABILITIES	526	Insurance Expense
202	Accounts Payable	529	Advertising Expense
	OWNER'S EQUITY	532	Telephone Expense
301	John Arrow, Capital	535	Maintenance Expense
302	John Arrow, Drawing		
309	Income Summary		

INSTRUCTIONS

1. Open the general ledger accounts and enter the balances for January 1, 19X6. Obtain the necessary figures from the post-closing trial balance prepared on December 31, 19X5, which appears on page 154.
2. Analyze each transaction and record it in the general journal. Use page 3 to begin January's transactions.
3. Post the transactions to the general ledger accounts.

4. Prepare a trial balance in the first two columns of a ten-column worksheet.
5. Prepare the Adjustments section of the worksheet.
   a. Compute and record the adjustment for supplies used during the month. An inventory taken on January 31 showed supplies of $475 on hand.
   b. Record the adjustment for expired rent of $2,500 for the month.
   c. Compute and record the adjustment for expired insurance for the month.
   d. Record the adjustment for depreciation of $250 on the old equipment for the month. The first adjustment for depreciation for the new equipment will be recorded in February.
6. Complete the worksheet.
7. Prepare an income statement for the month.
8. Prepare a statement of owner's equity.
9. Prepare a balance sheet using the report form.
10. Journalize and post the adjusting entries.
11. Journalize and post the closing entries.
12. Prepare a postclosing trial balance.
13. Interpret the financial information.
    a. Compare the January income statement you prepared with the December income statement shown in Chapter 5. What changes occurred in total revenue, total expenses, and net income? Did the firm achieve better operating results in January? Why or why not?
    b. Compare the January 31 balance sheet you prepared with the December 31 balance sheet shown in Chapter 5. What changes occurred in total assets, liabilities, and the owner's ending capital? What changes occurred in the Cash and Accounts Receivable accounts? Has there been an improvement in the firm's financial position? Why or why not?

TRANSACTIONS

Jan. 2 Purchased supplies for $1,500, Check 1009.

7 Sold services for $5,800 in cash and $745 on credit during the first week of January.

9 Purchased a one-year insurance policy for $3,600; issued Check 1010 to pay the full amount in advance.

11 Collected a total of $295 on account from credit customers during the first week of January.

12 Issued Check 1011 for $395 to pay for advertising on the local radio station during the month.

13 Collected a total of $500 on account from credit customers during the second week of January.

14 Returned some supplies that were damaged for a cash refund of $40.

15 Sold services for $8,500 in cash and $400 on credit during the second week of January.

18 Purchased supplies for $800 from Fellowes, Inc.; received Invoice 3284, payable in 30 days.
19 Sold services for $3,890 in cash and $2,560 on credit during the third week of January.
20 Collected a total of $750 on account from credit customers during the third week of January.
21 Issued Check 1012 for $1,275 to pay for maintenance work on the office equipment.
22 Issued Check 1013 for $150 to pay for advertisements in the local newspaper.
23 Received the monthly telephone bill for $215 and paid it with Check 1014.
26 Collected a total of $1,560 on account from credit customers during the fourth week of January.
27 Issued Check 1015 for $4,000 to Olson, Inc., as payment on account for Invoice 2778.
28 Sent Check 1016 for $235 in payment of the monthly bill for utilities.
29 Sold services for $5,890 in cash and $675 on credit during the fourth week of January.
30 Issued Checks 1017–1021 for $5,400 to pay the monthly salaries of the regular employees and three part-time workers.
30 Issued Check 1022 for $2,000 for personal use.
31 Issued Check 1023 for $415 to pay for cleaning services for the month.
31 Purchased additional equipment for $6,000 from Master Equipment Company; issued Check 1024 for $1,250 and bought the rest on credit. The equipment has a five-year life and no salvage value.
31 Sold services for $545 in cash and $325 on credit on January 31.

U N I T   T W O

Recording Financial Data

A service business sells services; a merchandising business sells goods that it purchases for resale. The three critical areas of accounting for any merchandising business are: accounting for sales and accounts receivable, accounting for purchases and accounts payable, and accounting for cash. The recording of merchandising transactions demonstrates the interrelationships between these areas of accounting. Most merchandising businesses use special journals and subsidiary ledgers to save time and effort, and to reduce the cost of accounting work.

CHAPTER

7 Accounting for Sales and Accounts Receivable

OBJECTIVES

1. Record credit sales in a sales journal.
2. Post from the sales journal to the general ledger accounts.
3. Post from the sales journal to the customers' accounts in the accounts receivable subsidiary ledger.
4. Record sales returns and allowances in the general journal.
5. Post sales returns and allowances from the general journal to the general ledger and the accounts receivable subsidiary ledger.
6. Prepare a schedule of accounts receivable.
7. Compute trade discounts.
8. Record credit card sales in appropriate journals.
9. Prepare the state sales tax return.
10. Define the accounting terms new to this chapter.

Accounting systems are designed to meet the needs of individual businesses. The nature of a firm's operations, the volume and complexity of its transactions, and many other factors help to determine the types of records and procedures needed in establishing an effective accounting system. Among the goals of any accounting system are to make the recording of financial data as efficient as possible and to provide needed information quickly and accurately.

In this chapter and later chapters, we will discuss the accounting system of a clothing store called Fashion World. You will see how the accounting records and procedures of this firm differ from those used by Arrow Accounting Services. You will become familiar with other journals and ledgers besides the general journal and the general ledger, and you will learn about financial statements that are more complex than those you have encountered before. You will also learn about the controls that businesses build into their accounting systems to ensure honesty, accuracy, and efficiency in recording transactions and handling assets.

NEW TERMS

Accounting receivable ledger ▪ Charge-account sales ▪ Contra revenue account ▪ Control account ▪ Credit memorandum ▪ Invoice ▪ List price ▪ Manufacturing business ▪ Merchandise inventory ▪ Merchandising business ▪ Net price ▪ Net sales ▪ Open-account credit ▪ Retail business ▪ Sales allowance ▪ Sales journal ▪ Sales return ▪ Schedule of accounts receivable ▪ Service business ▪ Special journal ▪ Subsidiary ledger ▪ Trade discount ▪ Wholesale business

THE ACCOUNTING SYSTEM OF A MERCHANDISING BUSINESS

When an accounting system is developed for a firm, one important consideration is the nature of its operations, since different types of businesses will have different accounting needs. The three basic types of businesses are: a **service business** sells services, a **merchandising business** sells goods that it purchases for resale, and a **manufacturing business** sells goods that it produces.

Arrow Accounting Services, the firm that was described in Chapters 2 through 6, is an example of a service business. It provides accounting and tax services to clients, who pay a fee for services. The firm that we will examine in the next group of chapters, Fashion World, is a merchandising business that sells clothing for men, women, and children. It is a **retail business,** which sells goods and services directly to individual consumers. Fashion World is a sole proprietorship owned and operated by Carolyn Wells, who was formerly a sales manager for a major retail clothing store. The chart of accounts for Fashion World is shown below.

FASHION WORLD
Chart of Accounts

ASSETS

101	Cash
105	Petty Cash Fund
109	Notes Receivable
111	Accounts Receivable
112	Allowance for Doubtful Accounts
116	Interest Receivable
121	Merchandise Inventory
126	Prepaid Insurance
127	Prepaid Interest
129	Supplies
131	Store Equipment
132	Accumulated Depreciation—Store Equipment
141	Office Equipment
142	Accumulated Depreciation—Office Equipment

LIABILITIES

201	Notes Payable—Trade
202	Notes Payable—Bank
205	Accounts Payable
216	Interest Payable
221	Social Security Tax Payable
222	Medicare Tax Payable
223	Employee Income Taxes Payable
225	Federal Unemployment Tax Payable
227	State Unemployment Tax Payable
229	Salaries Payable
231	Sales Tax Payable

OWNER'S EQUITY

301	Carolyn Wells, Capital
302	Carolyn Wells, Drawing
399	Income Summary

REVENUE

401	Sales
451	Sales Returns and Allowances
491	Interest Income
493	Miscellaneous Income

EXPENSES

501	Purchases
502	Freight In
503	Purchases Returns and Allowances
504	Purchases Discounts
511	Sales Salaries Expense
514	Advertising Expense
517	Supplies Expense
520	Cash Short or Over
526	Depreciation Expense—Store Equipment
535	Rent Expense
536	Insurance Expense
538	Utilities Expense
541	Office Salaries Expense
544	Payroll Taxes Expense
553	Telephone Expense
556	Uncollectible Accounts Expense
559	Depreciation Expense—Office Equipment
591	Interest Expense
593	Miscellaneous Expense

Like Arrow Accounting Services, Fashion World is a small firm, but it requires a more complex set of financial records and statements because it must account for purchases and sales of goods and for its **merchandise inventory**—the stock of goods that it keeps on hand. Also, the business has a greater number of credit transactions with customers and suppliers.

To allow for efficient recording of financial data, the accounting systems of most merchandising businesses include special journals and subsidiary ledgers in addition to the general journal and the general ledger.

Special Journals and Subsidiary Ledgers

A **special journal** is a journal that is used to record only one type of transaction. For example, the **sales journal,** which is discussed in this chapter, is used to record only sales of merchandise on credit. A **subsidiary ledger** is a ledger that contains accounts of a single type. For example, the accounts receivable ledger, which is also discussed in this chapter, contains accounts for credit customers.

Table 7–1 lists the journals and ledgers that merchandising businesses generally use in their accounting systems.

TABLE 7–1
Journals and Ledgers Used by Merchandising Businesses

Journals	
Type of Journal	**Purpose**
Sales	To record sales of merchandise on credit
Purchases	To record purchases of merchandise on credit
Cash receipts	To record cash received from all sources
Cash payments	To record all disbursements of cash
General	To record all transactions that are not recorded in another special journal and all adjusting and closing entries

Ledgers	
Type of Ledger	**Content**
General	Assets, liabilities, owner's equity, revenue, and expense accounts
Accounts receivable	Accounts for credit customers
Accounts payable	Accounts for creditors

In this chapter and succeeding chapters, you will learn how the accounting systems of merchandising businesses operate and will become familiar with their financial records, procedures, and statements.

The Need for a Sales Journal

To understand the need for a sales journal, first consider how credit sales made at Fashion World would be entered in a general journal and posted to the general ledger, as shown in Figure 7–1.

FIGURE 7–1
Journalizing and Posting Credit Sales

GENERAL JOURNAL PAGE 2

	DATE		DESCRIPTION	POST. REF.	DEBIT	CREDIT	
1	19X3						1
2	Jan.	2	Accounts Receivable	111	106 00		2
3			Sales Tax Payable	231		6 00	3
4			Sales	401		100 00	4
5			Sold merchandise on				5
6			credit to Allen Avery,				6
7			Sales Slip 3601				7
8							8
9		7	Accounts Receivable	111	265 00		9
10			Sales Tax Payable	231		15 00	10
11			Sales	401		250 00	11
12			Sold merchandise on				12
13			credit to Helen Ballard,				13
14			Sales Slip 3602				14
15							15
16		10	Accounts Receivable	111	318 00		16
17			Sales Tax Payable	231		18 00	17
18			Sales	401		300 00	18
19			Sold merchandise on				19
20			credit to Anthony				20
21			Blackmon, Sales				21
22			Slip 3603				22
23							23
24		14	Accounts Receivable	111	212 00		24
25			Sales Tax Payable	231		12 00	25
26			Sales	401		200 00	26
27			Sold merchandise on				27
28			credit to John Hernandez,				28
29			Sales Slip 3604				29
30							

ACCOUNT *Accounts Receivable* ACCOUNT NO. 111

DATE		EXPLANATION	POST. REF.	DEBIT	CREDIT	BALANCE DEBIT	BALANCE CREDIT
19X3							
Jan.	1	Balance	✓			3,500 00	
	2		J2	106 00		3,606 00	
	7		J2	265 00		3,871 00	
	10		J2	318 00		4,189 00	
	14		J2	212 00		4,401 00	

(Continued)

FIGURE 7–1 (Continued)

ACCOUNT *Sales Tax Payable* ACCOUNT NO. *231*

DATE		EXPLANATION	POST. REF.	DEBIT	CREDIT	BALANCE DEBIT	BALANCE CREDIT
19X3							
Jan.	1	Balance	✓				712 40
	2		J2		6 00		718 40
	7		J2		15 00		733 40
	10		J2		18 00		751 40
	14		J2		12 00		763 40

ACCOUNT *Sales* ACCOUNT NO. *401*

DATE		EXPLANATION	POST. REF.	DEBIT	CREDIT	BALANCE DEBIT	BALANCE CREDIT
19X3							
Jan.	2		J2		100 00		100 00
	7		J2		250 00		350 00
	10		J2		300 00		650 00
	14		J2		200 00		850 00

As you can see, a great amount of repetition is involved in both journalizing and posting these sales. The four credit sales made on January 2, 7, 10, and 14 required four separate entries in the general journal and involved four debits to Accounts Receivable, four credits to Sales Tax Payable, four credits to Sales (the firm's revenue account), and four explanations. The posting of twelve items to the three general ledger accounts represents still further duplication of effort. This recording procedure is not efficient for a business that has a substantial number of credit sales each month.

Look again at Figure 7–1 and note the word "Balance" in the ledger accounts. To record beginning balances in accounts, the date is entered in the account, "Balance" is written in the Explanation column, a check mark is placed in the Posting Reference column, and the amount is entered either in the Debit or Credit Balance column.

Using a Sales Journal

A special journal intended only for credit sales provides a more efficient method of recording these transactions. Figure 7–2 shows the January credit sales of Fashion World recorded in a sales journal. For the sake of simplicity, the sales journal shown here includes a limited number of transactions. The firm actually has many more credit sales each month.

Notice how the headings and columns in the sales journal speed up the recording process. No account titles are entered, and only one line is needed to record the complete information for each transaction—the date, the sales slip number, the customer's name, the

FIGURE 7–2
A Sales Journal

SALES JOURNAL PAGE *1*

DATE		SALES SLIP NO.	CUSTOMER'S NAME	POST. REF.	ACCOUNTS RECEIVABLE DEBIT	SALES TAX PAYABLE CREDIT	SALES CREDIT
19X3							
Jan.	2	3601	Allen Avery		106 00	6 00	100 00
	7	3602	Helen Ballard		265 00	15 00	250 00
	10	3603	Anthony Blackmon		318 00	18 00	300 00
	14	3604	John Hernandez		212 00	12 00	200 00
	17	3605	Kim English		424 00	24 00	400 00
	20	3606	Nan Yang		159 00	9 00	150 00
	27	3607	Paul Romero		53 00	3 00	50 00
	28	3608	Laura Wilson		530 00	30 00	500 00
	31	3609	Richard Narvaez		371 00	21 00	350 00
	31	3610	Allen Avery		477 00	27 00	450 00

▲ REMEMBER!

The major advantages of using the sales journal are that it saves time in posting and it strengthens the audit trail.

debit to Accounts Receivable, the credit to Sales Tax Payable, and the credit to Sales. In addition, since the sales journal is used for a single purpose, there is no need to enter any explanations. Thus a great deal of repetition is avoided in recording the firm's credit sales.

The use of a sales journal also strengthens the audit trail. All entries for credit sales are grouped together in one place, and the Sales Slip Number column serves as a convenient reference to the source documents that contain the original transaction data.

OBJECTIVE 1
Record credit sales in a sales journal.

Recording Entries in a Sales Journal

Entries in the sales journal are usually made daily. In a retail business like Fashion World, the data needed for each entry is taken from a copy of the customer's sales slip, as shown in Figure 7–3.

FIGURE 7–3
Customer's Sales Slip

FASHION WORLD
5001 S. Portland
San Francisco, CA 94118

DATE	SALESPERSON	AUTH.
1/2/--	T. Wells	

Goods Taken ☒ To Be Delivered ☐

Send to:

Special Instructions:

Qty.	Description	Unit Price	Amount
1	Sports Jacket		100 00
		Sales Tax	6 00
		Total	106 00

NAME Allen Avery

ADDRESS 612 Henderson Circle
San Francisco, CA 94118

I authorize this purchase to be charged to my account.

Allen Avery
Signature

SALES SLIP 3601

Many state and local governments impose a sales tax on retail sales of certain goods and services. Businesses are required to collect this tax from their customers and send it to the proper tax agency at regular intervals. When goods or services are sold on credit, the sales tax is usually recorded at the time of the sale even though it will not be collected immediately. A liability account called Sales Tax Payable is credited for the sales tax charged. Since Fashion World is located in a state that has a 6 percent sales tax on retail transactions, its sales journal includes a Sales Tax Payable Credit column.

Notice how the amounts involved in a credit sale are recorded in the sales journal shown in Figure 7–2. The total owed by the customer is entered in the Accounts Receivable Debit column, the sales tax is entered in the Sales Tax Payable Credit column, and the price of the goods is entered in the Sales Credit column.

Many small retail firms use a sales journal similar to the one shown in Figure 7–2. However, keep in mind that special journals vary in format according to the needs of individual businesses. Examples of sales journals with different column headings are presented later in this chapter.

OBJECTIVE 2
Post from the sales journal to the general ledger accounts.

Posting from a Sales Journal

A sales journal not only simplifies the initial recording of credit sales, it also eliminates a great deal of repetition in posting these transactions. When a sales journal is used, it is not necessary to post each credit sale individually to the general ledger accounts affected. Instead, summary postings are made at the end of the month after the amount columns of the sales journal are totaled (see Figure 7–4).

In actual practice, before any posting takes place, the equality of the debits and credits recorded in the sales journal are proved by comparing the column totals. The proof for the sales journal in Figure 7–4 is given below. All multicolumn special journals should be proved in a similar manner before their totals are posted.

PROOF OF SALES JOURNAL

	Debits
Accounts Receivable Debit column	$2,915.00
	Credits
Sales Tax Payable Credit column	$ 165.00
Sales Credit column	2,750.00
	$2,915.00

After verifying the equality of the debits and credits, the sales journal is ruled and the column totals posted to the general ledger accounts involved. To indicate that the postings have been made, the numbers of the accounts in parentheses are entered under the column totals in the sales journal and the abbreviation *S1* is written in the Posting Reference column of the accounts (see Figure 7–4). This

FIGURE 7–4
End-of-Month Postings

SALES JOURNAL PAGE 1

DATE		SALES SLIP NO.	CUSTOMER'S NAME	POST. REF.	ACCOUNTS RECEIVABLE DEBIT	SALES TAX PAYABLE CREDIT	SALES CREDIT
19X3							
Jan.	2	3601	Allen Avery	√	106 00	6 00	100 00
	7	3602	Helen Ballard	√	265 00	15 00	250 00
	10	3603	Anthony Blackmon	√	318 00	18 00	300 00
	14	3604	John Hernandez	√	212 00	12 00	200 00
	17	3605	Kim English	√	424 00	24 00	400 00
	20	3606	Nan Yang	√	159 00	9 00	150 00
	27	3607	Paul Romero	√	53 00	3 00	50 00
	28	3608	Laura Wilson	√	530 00	30 00	500 00
	31	3609	Richard Narvaez	√	371 00	21 00	350 00
	31	3610	Allen Avery	√	477 00	27 00	450 00
	31		Totals		2915 00	165 00	2750 00
					(111)	(231)	(401)

ACCOUNT *Accounts Receivable* ACCOUNT NO. 111

DATE		EXPLANATION	POST. REF.	DEBIT	CREDIT	BALANCE DEBIT	BALANCE CREDIT
19X3							
Dec.	1	Balance	√			1590 00	
Jan.	22		J1		53 00	1537 00	
	24		J1		159 00	1378 00	
	31		S1	2915 00		4293 00	

ACCOUNT *Sales Tax Payable* ACCOUNT NO. 231

DATE		EXPLANATION	POST. REF.	DEBIT	CREDIT	BALANCE DEBIT	BALANCE CREDIT
19X3							
Jan.	1	Balance	√				712 40
	10		CP1	712 40			—0—
	31		J1	9 00		9 00	
	31		J1	3 00		12 00	
	31		S1		165 00		153 00

ACCOUNT *Sales* ACCOUNT NO. 401

DATE		EXPLANATION	POST. REF.	DEBIT	CREDIT	BALANCE DEBIT	BALANCE CREDIT
19X3							
Jan.	31		S1		2750 00		2750 00

abbreviation shows that the data was posted from page 1 of the sales journal.

During the month the individual entries in the sales journal are posted to the customer accounts in the accounts receivable ledger. The check marks in the sales journal in Figure 7–4 indicate that the amounts have been posted to the individual customer's account. Posting from the sales journal to the customer accounts in the subsidiary ledger is illustrated later in this chapter.

▲ **REMEMBER!**

When posting from the sales journal, post information moving from left to right across the ledger form.

Advantages of a Sales Journal

From the example presented here, it is clear that the use of a special journal for credit sales saves time, effort, and recording space. Both the journalizing process and the posting process become more efficient, but the advantage in the posting process is especially significant. If a business like Fashion World used the general journal to record 300 credit sales a month, the firm would have to make 900 individual postings to the general ledger—300 to Accounts Receivable, 300 to Sales Tax Payable, and 300 to Sales. With a sales journal the firm makes only three summary postings to the general ledger at the end of each month no matter how many credit sales were entered.

The use of a sales journal and other special journals also allows division of work. In a business with a fairly large volume of transactions, it is essential that several employees be able to record transactions at the same time.

Finally, the sales journal improves the audit trail by bringing together all entries for credit sales in one place and listing them by source document number as well as by date. This procedure makes it easier to trace the details of such transactions.

SELF-REVIEW

1. Explain how service, merchandising, and manufacturing businesses differ from each other.
2. Why does a smail merchandising business like Fashion World usually need a more complex set of financial records and statements than a small service business?
3. What is a special journal? Give four examples of special journals.
4. What is a subsidiary ledger? Give two examples of subsidiary ledgers.
5. What type of transaction is recorded in the sales journal?

Answers to Self-Review

1. A service business sells services, a merchandising business sells goods that it has purchased for resale, and a manufacturing business sells goods that it has produced.

2. The financial records and statements of Fashion World are more complex than those of a service business because Fashion World must account for the purchase and sale of goods and for its merchandise inventory.
3. A special journal is a journal that is used to record only one type of transaction. Four examples are the sales journal, the purchases journal, the cash receipts journal, and the cash payments journal.
4. A subsidiary ledger is a ledger that contains accounts of a single type. Two examples are the accounts receivable ledger and the accounts payable ledger.
5. Sales of merchandise on credit are recorded in the sales journal.

The Accounts Receivable Ledger

A business that extends credit to customers must manage its accounts receivable carefully. The amounts owed by credit customers must be collected promptly to provide the steady stream of cash needed for the firm's day-to-day operations. Accounts receivable represent a substantial asset for many businesses, and this asset must be converted into cash in a timely manner. Otherwise a firm may not be able to pay its bills even though it has a large volume of sales and earns a satisfactory profit.

To manage accounts receivable effectively, the accountant needs detailed information about the transactions with credit customers and the balances owed by such customers at all times. This information is provided by an **accounts receivable ledger** with individual accounts for all credit customers. The accounts receivable ledger is referred to as a subsidiary ledger because it is separate from and subordinate to the general ledger.

The information in the accounts receivable ledger makes it possible to verify that customers are paying their balances on time and that they are within their credit limits. The accounts receivable ledger also permits a business to answer questions from credit customers easily and quickly. Customers may want to know about their current balances or may think the firm has made a billing error.

The accounts for credit customers are maintained in a balance ledger form with three money columns, as shown in Figure 7–5. Notice that this form does not contain a column for indicating the type of account balance. The balances in the customer accounts are presumed to be debit balances since asset accounts normally have debit balances. However, occasionally there is a credit balance because a customer has overpaid the amount owed or has returned goods that were already paid for. One common procedure for dealing with this situation is to circle the balance in order to show that it is a credit amount.

FIGURE 7–5
Posting from the Sales Journal to the Accounts Receivable Ledger

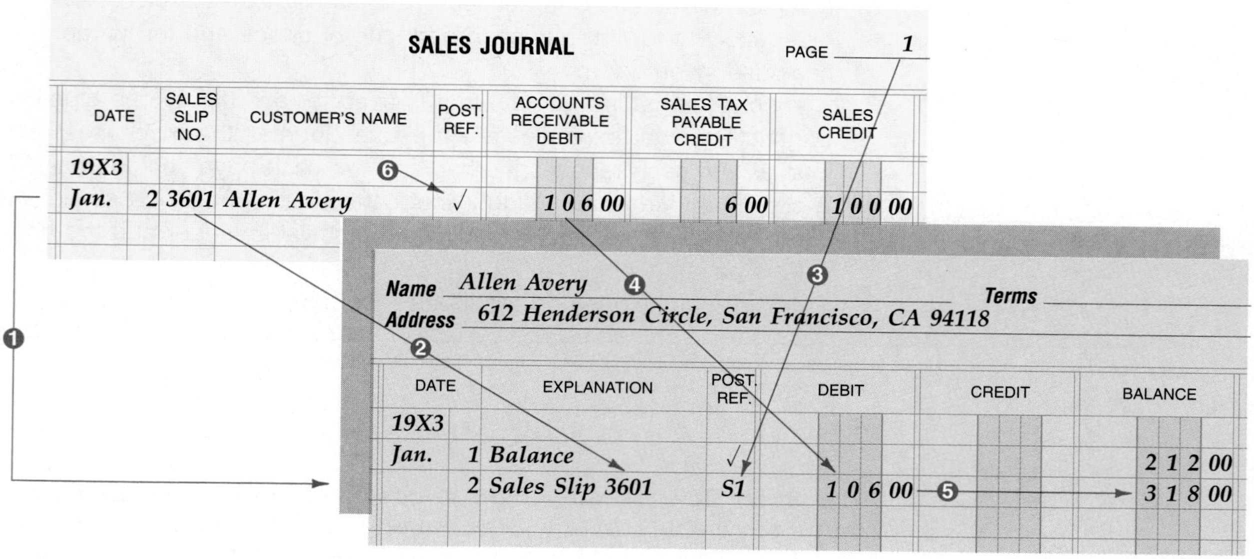

SALES JOURNAL — PAGE 1

DATE		SALES SLIP NO.	CUSTOMER'S NAME	POST. REF.	ACCOUNTS RECEIVABLE DEBIT	SALES TAX PAYABLE CREDIT	SALES CREDIT
19X3							
Jan.	2	3601	Allen Avery	√	106 00	6 00	100 00

Name: Allen Avery — Terms:
Address: 612 Henderson Circle, San Francisco, CA 94118

DATE		EXPLANATION	POST. REF.	DEBIT	CREDIT	BALANCE
19X3						
Jan.	1	Balance	√			212 00
	2	Sales Slip 3601	S1	106 00		318 00

For a small business like Fashion World, customer accounts are alphabetized in the accounts receivable ledger. Larger firms and firms that use computers to process financial data assign an account number to each credit customer and arrange the customer accounts in numeric order within the accounts receivable ledger.

Postings to the accounts receivable ledger are usually made daily so that the customer accounts can be kept up to date at all times.

OBJECTIVE 3
Post from the sales journal to the customers' accounts in the accounts receivable subsidiary ledger.

Posting a Credit Sale

Each credit sale recorded in the sales journal is posted to the appropriate customer's account in the accounts receivable ledger, as shown in Figure 7–5. The date, the sales slip number, and the amount that the customer owes as a result of the sale are transferred from the sales journal to the customer's account. The amount is taken from the Accounts Receivable Debit column of the journal and entered in the Debit column of the account. Next, the new balance is determined and recorded.

To show that the posting has been completed, a check mark (√) is entered in the sales journal and the abbreviation *S1* is entered in the Posting Reference column of the customer's account. As noted before, this abbreviation identifies page 1 of the sales journal.

Posting Cash Received on Account

When the transaction involves cash received on account from a credit customer, the cash collected is first recorded in a cash receipts journal and then posted to the individual customer accounts in the accounts receivable ledger. The account illustrated in Figure 7–6 shows a posting for cash received on January 6 from Allen Avery, a credit customer of Fashion World. (The necessary entry in the cash receipts journal is discussed in Chapter 9.)

FIGURE 7–6
A Posting for Cash Received on Account

Name *Allen Avery* **Terms**
Address *612 Henderson Circle, San Francisco, CA 94118*

DATE		EXPLANATION	POST. REF.	DEBIT	CREDIT	BALANCE
19X3						
Jan.	1	Balance	✓			212 00
	2	Sales Slip 3601	S1	106 00		318 00
	6		CR1		212 00	106 00

Sales Returns and Allowances

OBJECTIVE 4
Record sales returns and allowances in the general journal.

A sale is entered in the accounting records of a business at the time the goods are sold or the service is provided. If something is wrong with the goods or service, the firm may take back the goods, resulting in a **sales return,** or give the customer a reduction in the price of the goods or service, resulting in a **sales allowance.**

When a return or allowance is related to a credit sale, the normal practice is to issue a document called a **credit memorandum** to the customer rather than giving a cash refund. The credit memorandum states that the customer's account is being reduced by the amount of the return or allowance plus any sales tax that may be involved. A copy of the credit memorandum provides the data needed to enter the transaction in the firm's accounting records.

Depending on a business's volume of sales returns and allowances, it may use a general journal to record these transactions or it may use a special sales returns and allowances journal.

Sales Returns and Allowances Journal

In a business having many sales returns and allowances, it is efficient to use a special journal for these transactions. An example of a sales returns and allowances journal is shown in Figure 7–7.

FIGURE 7–7
A Sales Returns and Allowances Journal

SALES RETURNS AND ALLOWANCES JOURNAL PAGE 7

DATE		CREDIT MEMO. NO.	CUSTOMER'S NAME	POST. REF.	ACCOUNTS RECEIVABLE CREDIT	SALES TAX PAYABLE DEBIT	SALES RET. & ALLOW. DEBIT
19X3							
Jan.	22	191	Kim English	✓	53 00	3 00	50 00
	24	192	Nan Yang	✓	159 00	9 00	150 00
	31		Totals		1,908 00	108 00	1,800 00
					(111)	(231)	(451)

General Journal Entries for Sales Returns and Allowances

In a small firm that has a limited number of sales returns and allowances each month, there is no need to establish a special journal for such transactions. Instead, the required entries are made in the general journal.

19X3					
Jan.	*22*	*Sales Returns and Allowances*	*451*	*50 00*	
		Sales Tax Payable	*231*	*3 00*	
		Accounts Rec./Kim English	*111/√*		*53 00*
		Gave an allowance			
		for damaged merchandise,			
		Credit Memo 191; original			
		sale made on Sales Slip			
		3605 of Jan. 17			
	24	*Sales Returns and Allowances*	*451*	*150 00*	
		Sales Tax Payable	*231*	*9 00*	
		Accounts Rec./Nan Yang	*111/√*		*159 00*
		Accepted a return of			
		defective merchandise,			
		Credit Memo 192; original			
		sale made on Sales Slip			
		3606 of Jan. 20			

These entries were recorded at Fashion World for an allowance given to Kim English on January 22 for damaged but usable merchandise and a return of defective merchandise by Nan Yang on January 24. Notice that each entry includes a debit to an account called Sales Returns and Allowances for the amount of the return or allowance, a debit to Sales Tax Payable for the amount of sales tax involved, and a credit to Accounts Receivable for the reduction in the sum owed by the customer. There is also a credit to the customer's account in the accounts receivable ledger.

A Sales Returns and Allowances account is preferred to making a direct debit to Sales. This procedure gives a complete record of sales returns and allowances for each accounting period. Business managers use this record as a measure of operating efficiency.

The Sales Returns and Allowances account is a **contra revenue account** because it has a debit balance, which is contrary, or opposite, to the normal balance for a revenue account. The debit balance of Sales Returns and Allowances is used to reduce the credit balance of the Sales account on the income statement.

A customer who returns goods or receives an allowance in connection with a sale that originally involved sales tax is entitled to a

Information Block: Ethics in Accounting

Timing Is Everything!

McDoniel Computers, Inc., is a computer assembly and sales company. Alice is the sales manager for the Southwest Division of McDoniel. On December 20, Alice does a preliminary analysis of sales for the division for the current year. She discovers, much to her disappointment, that the division will not accomplish its target sales goal for the year. In fact, they will fall short by $250,000. This shortfall means that Alice will not get her bonus, and the employees of the Southwest Division will receive no profit sharing this year.

Alice calls her sales force together that afternoon to try to motivate them to meet the goal. Unfortunately, the salespeople say that their customers are suffering from the economic downturn and have canceled or delayed orders because of their slumping sales.

After spending a couple of hours trying to find a possible solution, Ben Jones, one of McDoniel's top sales representatives, makes a suggestion. He has a customer with an outstanding order that totals $277,778 and is currently scheduled for delivery on January 15. Ben suggests that he can probably convince his customer to accept delivery this year if he can offer an additional 10 percent discount.

When Alice examines the annual numbers for the Division, she finds that the total discounts given are well below the maximum allowed by the company. Alice asks Ben to talk to the customer regarding early delivery and an additional discount. Ben does so and finds the customer receptive to doing Ben this favor.

Alice knows there are only six business days remaining in this year, and there is no other way to meet the sales goal.

1. What are the ethical issues?
2. What are Alice's alternatives?
3. Who are the affected parties?
4. How do the alternatives affect the parties?
5. What should Alice do?

credit for the appropriate amount of the tax as well as a credit for the sales amount. Similarly, the business is not required to pay sales tax to the tax authority for returns and allowances. The reduction in the firm's sales tax liability is entered by debiting the Sales Tax Payable account when the return or allowance is recorded.

OBJECTIVE 5

Post sales returns and allowances from the general journal to the general ledger and the accounts receivable subsidiary ledger.

Posting a Sales Return or Allowance

Whether sales returns and allowances are recorded in the general journal or in a special sales returns and allowances journal, each of these transactions must be posted to the appropriate customer's account in the accounts receivable ledger. Figure 7–8 shows how a return of merchandise at Fashion World on January 24 was posted to the account of Nan Yang, the customer involved.

FIGURE 7–8
Posting a Sales Return to the Customer's Account

GENERAL JOURNAL PAGE *1*

	DATE		DESCRIPTION	POST. REF.	DEBIT	CREDIT	
1	*19X3*						1
2	*Jan.*	*24*	*Sales Returns and Allowances*	*451*	*150 00*		2
3			*Sales Tax Payable*	*231*	*9 00*		3
4			*Accounts Rec./Nan Yang*	*111/✓*		*159 00*	4
5			*Accepted a return of*				5
6			*defective merchandise,*				6
7			*Credit Memorandum 192;*				7
8			*original sale made on*				8
9			*Sales Slip 3606 of Jan. 20*				9
10							10

Name *Nan Yang* **Terms**
Address *1111 Mockingbird Lane, San Francisco, CA 94116*

DATE		EXPLANATION	POST. REF.	DEBIT	CREDIT	BALANCE
19X3						
Jan.	*1*	*Balance*	✓			*26 50*
	10	*Sales Slip 3606*	*S1*	*159 00*		*185 50*
	24	*CM 192*	*J1*		*159 00*	*26 50*

Because the credit amount in the general journal entry for this transaction requires two postings, the account number 111 and a check mark are entered in the Posting Reference column of the journal. The 111 indicates that the amount was posted to the Accounts Receivable account in the general ledger, and the check mark indicates that the amount was posted to the customer's account in the accounts receivable ledger. Notice that a diagonal line was used to separate the two posting references.

Reporting Net Sales

At the end of each accounting period, the balance of the Sales Returns and Allowances account is subtracted from the balance of the Sales account in the Revenue section of the income statement. The resulting figure is the **net sales** for the period.

For example, suppose the Sales Returns and Allowances account contains a balance of $200 at the end of January 19X3. Also suppose that Sales has a balance of $10,335 at the time. The Revenue section of the firm's income statement would appear as follows.

FASHION WORLD
Income Statement (Partial)
Month Ended January 31, 19X3

Revenue	
Sales	$10,335.00
Less Sales Returns and Allowances	200.00
Net Sales	$10,135.00

Schedule of Accounts Receivable

OBJECTIVE 6
Prepare a schedule of accounts receivable.

The use of an accounts receivable ledger does not eliminate the need for the Accounts Receivable account in the general ledger. This account remains in the general ledger and continues to appear on the balance sheet at the end of each fiscal period. However, the Accounts Receivable account is now considered a **control account**—an account that serves as a link between a subsidiary ledger and the general ledger because its balance summarizes the balances of its related accounts in the subsidiary ledger.

At the end of each month, after all the postings have been made from the sales journal, the cash receipts journal, and the general journal to the accounts receivable ledger, the balances in the accounts receivable ledger must be proved against the balance of the Accounts Receivable general ledger account. First a **schedule of accounts receivable,** which lists the subsidiary ledger account balances, is prepared. The total of the schedule is compared with the balance of the Accounts Receivable account. The two figures should be the same. If they are not, errors must be located and corrected.

Assume that on January 31, 19X3, the accounts receivable ledger at Fashion World contains the accounts shown in Figure 7–9. To prepare a schedule of accounts receivable, the names of all customers with account balances are listed with the amount of their unpaid balances. Next the figures are added to find the total owed to the business by its credit customers.

FIGURE 7–9
Accounts Receivable Ledger

Name *Allen Avery* **Terms**
Address *612 Henderson Circle, San Francisco, CA 94118*

DATE		EXPLANATION	POST. REF.	DEBIT	CREDIT	BALANCE
19X3						
Jan.	*1*	*Balance*	✓			*212 00*
	2	*Sales Slip 3601*	*S1*	*106 00*		*318 00*
	6		*CR1*		*212 00*	*106 00*
	31	*Sales Slip 3610*	*S1*	*477 00*		*583 00*

(Continued)

FIGURE 7–9 (Continued)

Name *Helen Ballard* **Terms**
Address *1069 Warren Street, San Francisco, CA 94116*

DATE		EXPLANATION	POST. REF.	DEBIT	CREDIT	BALANCE
19X3						
Jan.	7	Sales Slip 3602	S1	265.00		265.00

Name *John Bell* **Terms**
Address *9 Glen Road, San Francisco, CA 94116*

DATE		EXPLANATION	POST. REF.	DEBIT	CREDIT	BALANCE
19X3						
Jan.	1	Balance	√			132.50
	10		CR1		132.50	—0—

Name *Anthony Blackmon* **Terms**
Address *216 Lawson Street, San Francisco, CA 94118*

DATE		EXPLANATION	POST. REF.	DEBIT	CREDIT	BALANCE
19X3						
Jan.	1	Balance	√			530.00
	10	Sales Slip 3603	S1	318.00		848.00
	12		CR1		265.00	583.00

Name *Kim English* **Terms**
Address *4900 Vista Ridge Road, San Francisco, CA 94112*

DATE		EXPLANATION	POST. REF.	DEBIT	CREDIT	BALANCE
19X3						
Jan.	1	Balance	√			106.00
	17	Sales Slip 3605	S1	424.00		530.00
	21		CR1		100.00	430.00
	22	CM 191	J1		53.00	377.00

Name *John Hernandez* **Terms**
Address *2147 Mission Drive, San Francisco, CA 94112*

DATE		EXPLANATION	POST. REF.	DEBIT	CREDIT	BALANCE
19X3						
Jan.	1	Balance	√			318.00
	14	Sales Slip 3604	S1	212.00		530.00

Name *Richard Narvaez* **Terms**
Address *1026 Barr Street, San Francisco, CA 94116*

DATE		EXPLANATION	POST. REF.	DEBIT	CREDIT	BALANCE
19X3						
Jan.	1	Balance	✓			53 00
	15		CR1		53 00	—0—
	31	Sales Slip 3609	S1	371 00		371 00

Name *Paul Romero* **Terms**
Address *148 Fallon Street, San Francisco, CA 94116*

DATE		EXPLANATION	POST. REF.	DEBIT	CREDIT	BALANCE
19X3						
Jan.	1	Balance	✓			106 00
	27	Sales Slip 3607	S1	53 00		159 00
	31		CR1		53 00	106 00

Name *Laura Wilson* **Terms**
Address *6480 Oak Tree Drive, San Francisco, CA 94118*

DATE		EXPLANATION	POST. REF.	DEBIT	CREDIT	BALANCE
19X3						
Jan.	1	Balance	✓			106 00
	28	Sales Slip 3608	S1	530 00		636 00
	31		CR1		130 00	506 00

Name *Nan Yang* **Terms**
Address *1111 Mockingbird Lane, San Francisco, CA 94116*

DATE		EXPLANATION	POST. REF.	DEBIT	CREDIT	BALANCE
19X3						
Jan.	1	Balance	✓			26 50
	20	Sales Slip 3606	S1	159 00		185 50
	24	CM 192	J1		159 00	26 50

A comparison of the total of the schedule of accounts receivable prepared at Fashion World on January 31, 19X3, and the balance of the Accounts Receivable account in the general ledger shows that the two figures are the same, as shown in Figure 7–10.

FIGURE 7–10
Schedule of Accounts Receivable and Accounts Receivable Account

FASHION WORLD
Schedule of Accounts Receivable
January 31, 19X3

Allen Avery	583 00
Helen Ballard	265 00
Anthony Blackmon	583 00
Kim English	377 00
John Hernandez	530 00
Richard Narvaez	371 00
Paul Romero	106 00
Laura Wilson	506 00
Nan Yang	26 50
Total	3 347 50

ACCOUNT *Accounts Receivable* ACCOUNT NO. *111*

DATE		EXPLANATION	POST. REF.	DEBIT	CREDIT	BALANCE DEBIT	BALANCE CREDIT
19X3							
Dec.	*1*	*Balance*	√			*1 590 00*	
Jan.	*22*		*J1*		*53 00*	*1 537 00*	
	24		*J1*		*159 00*	*1 378 00*	
	31		*S1*	*2 915 00*		*4 293 00*	
	31		*CR1*		*945 50*	*3 347 50*	

In addition to providing a proof of the subsidiary ledger, the schedule of accounts receivable serves another function. It reports information about the firm's accounts receivable at the end of the month. Management can review the schedule to see exactly how much each customer owes and how much is due the business from all of its credit customers.

SELF-REVIEW

1. Which accounts are kept in the accounts receivable ledger?
2. Why is it useful for a firm to have an accounts receivable ledger?
3. What is a sales return? What is a sales allowance?
4. What is a control account? Explain the relationship between the Accounts Receivable account in the general ledger and the customer accounts in the accounts receivable ledger.
5. What are net sales?

Answers to Self-Review

1. Individual accounts for all credit customers are kept in the accounts receivable ledger.
2. An accounts receivable ledger is useful because it contains detailed information about the transactions with credit customers and shows the balances owed by such customers at all times.
3. A sales return results when a customer returns goods and the firm takes them back. A sales allowance results when the firm gives a customer a reduction in the price of the goods or service.
4. A control account is an account that serves as a link between a subsidiary ledger and the general ledger because its balance summarizes the balances of the accounts in the subsidiary ledger.
5. Net sales is the amount obtained when the total of sales returns and allowances is subtracted from sales.

RECORDING CREDIT SALES FOR A WHOLESALE BUSINESS

The operations of Fashion World are typical of those of many *retail businesses*—businesses that sell goods and services directly to individual consumers. In contrast, **wholesale businesses** are manufacturers or distributors of goods that sell to retailers or large consumers such as hotels and hospitals. The basic procedures used by wholesalers to handle sales and accounts receivable are the same as those used by retailers. However, many wholesalers offer cash discounts and trade discounts, which are not commonly found in retail operations.

The procedures used in connection with cash discounts are examined in Chapter 9. The handling of trade discounts is described here.

List Prices and Trade Discounts

OBJECTIVE 7
Compute trade discounts.

A wholesale business offers its goods to trade customers at less than retail prices so the trade customers can resell the goods at a profit. This price adjustment by wholesale businesses is based on the volume purchased by trade customers and takes the form of **trade discounts,** which are reductions from the **list prices**—the established retail prices. There may be a single trade discount or a series of discounts for each type of goods. The **net price** (list price less all trade discounts) is the amount the wholesaler records in its sales journal as the sales price of the goods.

The same goods may be offered to different customers at different trade discounts, depending on the size of the order and the costs of selling to the various types of customers.

Computation of a Single Trade Discount

Suppose the list price of goods is $500 and the trade discount is 40 percent. The amount of the discount is thus $200, and the net price to be shown on the invoice and recorded in the sales journal is $300.

List price	$500
Less 40% discount (500 × .40)	200
Invoice price	$300

Computation of a Series of Trade Discounts

If the list price of goods is $500 and the trade discount is quoted in a series such as 25 and 15 percent, a different net price will result.

List price	$500.00
Less first discount ($500 × .25)	125.00
Difference	$375.00
Less second discount ($375 × .15)	56.25
Invoice price	$318.75

Sales Journal Entries for Wholesale Businesses

Since sales taxes apply only to retail transactions, a wholesale business does not need to account for such taxes. Its sales journal may therefore be as simple as the one illustrated in Figure 7–11. Notice that this sales journal has a single amount column; the total of this amount column is posted to the general ledger at the end of the month as a debit to the Accounts Receivable account and a credit to the Sales account (Figure 7–12). During the month the individual entries in the sales journal are posted to the customer accounts in the accounts receivable ledger.

FIGURE 7–11
Wholesaler's Sales Journal

SALES JOURNAL PAGE 1

DATE		INVOICE NO.	CUSTOMER'S NAME	POST. REF.	ACCOUNTS RECEIVABLE DR. SALES CR.
19X3					
Jan.	2	7711	Evers Hardware Company	✓	800 00
	31	7820	Wilson Department Store	✓	1,900 00
	31		Total		15,600 00
					(111)/(401)

FIGURE 7–12
General Ledger Accounts

ACCOUNT *Accounts Receivable* ACCOUNT NO. 111

DATE		EXPLANATION	POST. REF.	DEBIT	CREDIT	BALANCE DEBIT	BALANCE CREDIT
19X3							
Jan.	1	Balance	✓			22,800 00	
	31		S1	15,600 00		38,400 00	

ACCOUNT *Sales* ACCOUNT NO. *401*

DATE		EXPLANATION	POST. REF.	DEBIT	CREDIT	BALANCE DEBIT	BALANCE CREDIT
19X3							
Jan.	*31*		*S1*		*15 6 0 0 00*		*15 6 0 0 00*

Wholesale businesses issue **invoices** to bill their customers for goods. Copies of the invoices are used to enter the transactions in the sales journal.

CREDIT POLICIES

The use of credit is considered to be one of the most important factors in the rapid growth of modern economic systems. Sales on credit are made by large numbers of wholesalers and retailers of goods and by many professional people and service businesses. The assumption is that the volume of both sales and profits will increase if buyers are given a period of a month or more to pay for the goods or services they purchase.

However, the increase in profits a business expects when it grants credit will be realized only if each customer completes the transaction by paying for the goods or services purchased. If payment is not received, the expected profits become actual losses and the purpose for granting the credit is defeated. Business firms try to protect against the possibility of such losses by investigating a customer's credit record and ability to pay for purchases before allowing any credit to the customer.

Professional people, such as doctors, lawyers, and architects, and owners of small businesses like Fashion World usually make their own decisions about granting credit. Such decisions may be based on personal judgment or on reports available from local credit bureaus, information supplied by other creditors, and credit ratings supplied by national firms such as Dun & Bradstreet.

Larger businesses maintain a credit department to determine the amounts and types of credit that should be granted to customers. In addition to using credit data supplied by institutions, the credit department may obtain financial statements and related reports from customers who have applied for credit. This information is analyzed to help determine the maximum amount of credit that may safely be granted to each customer and suitable credit terms for the customer. Financial statements that have been audited by certified public accountants are used extensively by credit departments.

Even though the credit investigation is thorough, some accounts receivable become uncollectible. Unexpected business developments, errors of judgment, incorrect financial data, and many other causes may lead to defaults in payments by customers. Experienced managers know that some uncollectible accounts are to be expected in normal business operations and that limited losses indicate that a firm's credit policies are sound. Provisions for such limited losses from uncollectible accounts are usually made in budgets and other financial projections.

Each business must reach its own decisions as to the most desirable credit policies to use to achieve maximum sales with minimum losses from uncollectible accounts. A credit policy that is too tight results in a low level of losses at the expense of increases in sales volume. A credit policy that is too lenient may result in increased sales volume accompanied by a high level of losses. Good judgment based on knowledge and experience must be used to achieve a well-balanced credit policy that is realistic and yet liberal enough to contribute to increases in profitable sales. However, the credit policy must also be conservative enough to hold losses from uncollectible accounts to an acceptable level.

Accounting for Different Types of Credit Sales

There are many different arrangements for selling goods and services on credit. The most common types of credit sales include those made through open-account credit or through use of credit cards issued by businesses, banks, or credit card companies.

Open-Account Credit

The form of credit most commonly offered by professional people and small businesses permits the sale of services or goods to the customer with the understanding that the amount is to be paid at a later date. This type of arrangement is called **open-account credit.** It is usually granted on the basis of personal acquaintance or knowledge of the customer by the professional person or the owner or manager of the business. However, formal credit checks may also be used. The amount involved in each transaction is usually small, and payment is expected within 30 days or on receipt of a monthly statement.

Fashion World is an example of a firm that uses the open-account credit arrangement. Under this arrangement, sales transactions are recorded as debits to the Accounts Receivable account and credits to the Sales account. Collections on account are recorded as debits to the Cash account and credits to the Accounts Receivable account.

Business Credit Cards

Many retail businesses, especially large ones such as department store chains, gasoline companies, and car rental companies, provide their own credit cards (sometimes called *charge cards* or *charge plates*) to customers who have established credit. The credit card serves as a means of identification and as an indicator that the customer has an account with the issuing firm. Such firms usually have a credit department that thoroughly checks each customer before an account is opened and the customer is given the credit card.

The credit card is normally made of plastic, and the name of the customer and the account number assigned are printed on it in raised letters and numbers. Whenever a sale is made, a sales slip is prepared in the usual manner. Then the sales slip and the credit card are placed in a mechanical device that prints the customer's name, account number, and other data on all copies of the sales slip. Some companies use computerized card readers and sales registers that print out a sales slip with the customer information and a line for the customer's signature. In addition to the use of the credit card, many businesses require that the salesclerk contact the credit department by telephone or computer terminal to verify the customer's credit status before completing the transaction.

The credit card sales discussed here are similar to open-account credit sales, which are also referred to as **charge-account sales.** They are recorded by debits to the Accounts Receivable account and credits to a revenue account such as Sales. Collections on account are recorded by debits to Cash and credits to Accounts Receivable.

Bank Credit Cards

A popular way for retailers to provide credit while minimizing or avoiding the risk of losses from uncollectible accounts is to accept bank credit cards. The most widely accepted bank credit cards are MasterCard and Visa. Many banks participate in one or both of these credit card programs, and other banks have their own credit cards.

Bank credit cards are issued to consumers by banks rather than by the businesses that accept the cards in sales transactions. Individuals who want such credit cards must fill out an application form. If an applicant meets the necessary requirements, a card is issued with the name and account number printed in raised characters.

Almost any type of business may participate in these credit card programs by meeting the conditions set by the bank. When a sale is made to a cardholder, the business completes a special sales slip such as the one shown in Figure 7–13.

FIGURE 7–13
Sales Slip for a Bank Credit Card Transaction

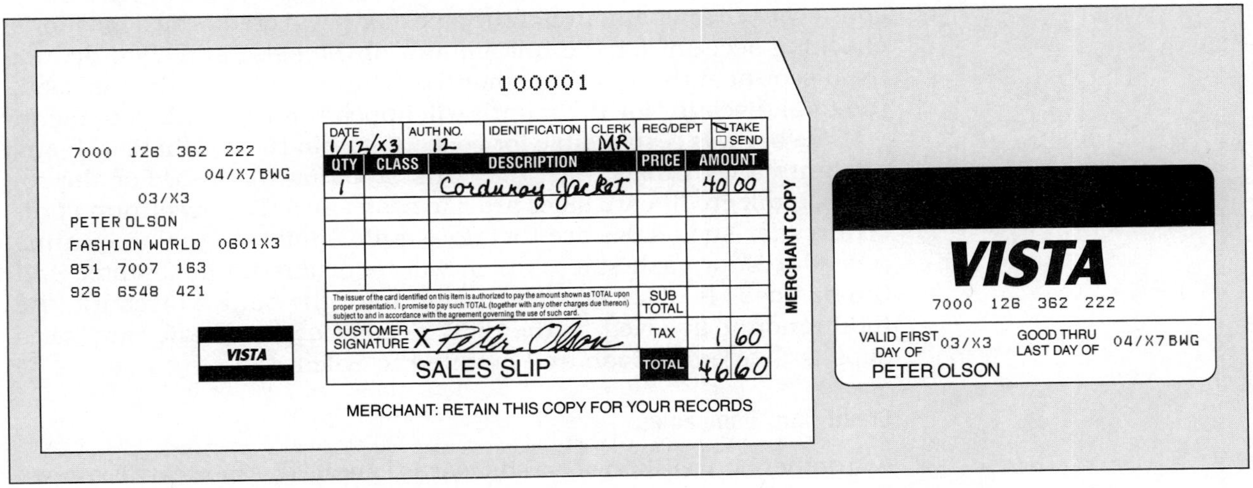

This form must be imprinted with data from the customer's bank credit card and then signed by the customer. Many businesses continue to complete their regular sales slips for internal control and other purposes in addition to preparing the special sales slip required by the bank.

When a business makes a sale on a bank credit card, it acquires an asset that can be converted into cash immediately without responsibility for later collection from the customer. Periodically (preferably each day) the completed sales slips from bank credit card sales are totaled. The number of sales slips and the total amount of the sales are recorded on a special deposit form, as shown in Figure 7–14.

FIGURE 7–14
Deposit Form for Bank Credit Card Sales

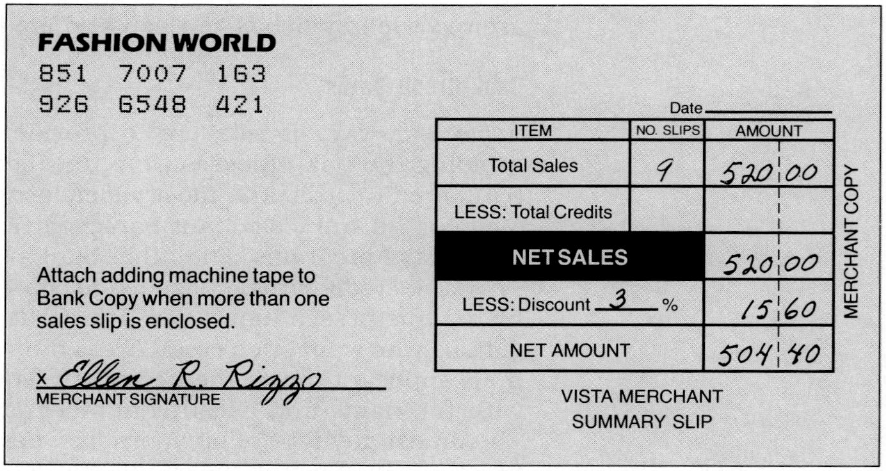
FASHION WORLD
851 7007 163
926 6548 421

Date

ITEM	NO. SLIPS	AMOUNT
Total Sales	9	520.00
LESS: Total Credits		
NET SALES		520.00
LESS: Discount 3 %		15.60
NET AMOUNT		504.40

MERCHANT COPY

Attach adding machine tape to Bank Copy when more than one sales slip is enclosed.

x Ellen R. Rizzo
MERCHANT SIGNATURE

VISTA MERCHANT
SUMMARY SLIP

The deposit form, along with the completed sales slips, is presented to the firm's bank in much the same manner as a cash deposit. Depending upon the arrangements that have been made, either the bank will deduct a fee, called a *discount* (usually between 1 and 8 percent), and immediately credit the depositor's checking account with the net amount of the sales, or it will credit the depositor's checking account for the full amount of the sales and then deduct the discount at the end of the month. If the second procedure is used, the total discount for the month will appear on the bank statement.

The bank is responsible for collecting from the cardholder. If any amounts are uncollectible, the bank sustains the loss. For the retailer, bank credit card sales are like cash sales. The accounting procedures for such sales are therefore quite similar to the accounting procedures for cash sales, which will be discussed in Chapter 9. If the business is billed once each month for the bank's discount, the total amount involved in the daily deposit of the credit card sales slips is debited to Cash and credited to Sales.

Credit Card Companies

A number of well-known credit cards, such as American Express, Diners Club, and Carte Blanche, are issued by business firms or subsidiaries of business firms that are operated for the special purpose of handling credit card transactions. The individual seeking to become a cardholder must submit an application containing the required information and must pay an annual fee to the credit card company. If the individual's credit references are satisfactory, the credit card is issued. It is normally reissued at one-year intervals so long as the company's credit experience with the cardholder remains satisfactory.

Hotels, restaurants, airline companies, many types of retail stores, and a wide variety of other businesses accept these credit cards. When making sales to cardholders, sellers usually prepare their own sales slip or bill and then complete a special sales slip required by the credit card company. As with the sales slips for bank credit cards, the forms must be imprinted with the identifying data on the customer's card and signed by the customer. Such sales slips are sometimes referred to as *sales invoices, sales drafts,* or *sales vouchers.* The term used varies from one credit card company to another.

The effect of such a sale is that the seller acquires an account receivable from the credit card company rather than from the customer. Periodically the seller summarizes the completed sales slips and submits them to the credit card company, which pays the seller promptly. At approximately one-month intervals, the credit card company bills the cardholders for all sales slips it has acquired during the period. It is the responsibility of the company to collect from the cardholders.

Accounting for Sales Involving Credit Card Companies

OBJECTIVE 8

Record credit card sales in appropriate journals.

The procedure used to account for sales made on the basis of credit cards issued by credit card companies is similar to the procedure for recording open-account credit sales. However, an important difference is that the account receivable is with the credit card company, not with the cardholders who buy the goods or services.

There are two basic methods of recording these sales. Businesses that have few transactions with credit card companies normally debit the amounts of such sales to the usual Accounts Receivable account in the general ledger and credit them to the same Sales account that is used for cash sales and other types of credit sales. An individual account for each credit card company is set up in the accounts receivable subsidiary ledger. This method of recording sales that involve credit cards issued by credit card companies is illustrated by the sales journal entries shown in Figure 7–15, page 204.

The receipt of payment from a credit card company is recorded in the cash receipts journal, a procedure discussed in Chapter 9. Fees charged by the credit card companies for processing these sales are debited to an account called Discount Expense on Credit Card Sales. For example, assume that American Express charges a 7 percent discount fee on the sale charged by James Richardson on January 2, 19X3, and remits the balance to the firm. This transaction would be recorded in the cash receipts journal by debiting Cash for $197.16,

FIGURE 7–15
Recording Credit Card Company Sales

SALES JOURNAL PAGE 4

DATE		SALES SLIP NO.	CUSTOMER'S NAME	POST. REF.	ACCOUNTS RECEIVABLE DEBIT	SALES TAX PAYABLE CREDIT	SALES CREDIT
19X3							
Jan.	2	601	American Express		212 00	12 00	200 00
			(James Richardson)				
	9	654	Diners Club		53 00	3 00	50 00
			(Brenda Davis)				

debiting Discount Expense on Credit Card Sales for $14.84, and crediting Accounts Receivable for $212.00.

Firms that do a large volume of business with credit card companies may debit all such sales to a special Accounts Receivable from Credit Card Companies account in the general ledger, thus separating this type of receivable from the accounts receivable resulting from open-account credit sales. Another special account called Sales—Credit Card Companies is credited for the revenue from these transactions. Figure 7–16 shows how the necessary entries are made in the sales journal.

Subsidiary ledger accounts may not be needed. Instead, a file is maintained of copies of the periodic summaries submitted to the credit card companies for payment. The total amount of the unpaid summaries in the file at any time should equal the balance of the Accounts Receivable from Credit Card Companies account in the general ledger at the same time.

FIGURE 7–16
Recording Sales for Accounts Receivable from Credit Card Companies

SALES JOURNAL PAGE 7

DATE		SALES SLIP NO.	CUSTOMER'S NAME	POST REF.	ACCOUNTS RECEIVABLE DEBIT	ACCT. REC.—CREDIT CARD COMPANIES DEBIT	SALES TAX PAYABLE CREDIT	SALES CREDIT	SALES—CREDIT CARD COMPANIES CREDIT
19X3									
Jan.	6		Summary of credit card						
			sales/American Express			4,240 00	240 00		4,000 00
	10		Summary of credit card						
			sales/Diners Club			2,120 00	120 00		2,000 00
	31		Totals			21,200 00	1,200 00		20,000 00
						(114)	(231)		(404)

SALES TAXES

Sales taxes imposed by city and state governments vary. However, the procedures used to account for these taxes are quite similar.

City and State Sales Taxes

Many cities and states impose a tax on retail sales. This type of tax may be levied on all retail sales, but often certain items are exempt. In most cases the amount of the sales tax is stated separately and then added to the retail price of the merchandise.

The retailer is required to collect sales tax from customers, make periodic (usually monthly) reports to the taxing authority, and pay the taxes due when the reports are filed. The government may allow the retailer to retain part of the tax as compensation for collecting it.

Preparing the State Sales Tax Return

OBJECTIVE 9

Prepare the state sales tax return.

At the end of each month, after the accounts have all been posted, Fashion World prepares the sales tax return. In some states the sales tax return is filed quarterly rather than monthly. The information required for the monthly return comes from the accounting data of the current month. Three accounts are involved: Sales Tax Payable, Sales, and Sales Returns and Allowances. The procedures to file a sales tax return are similar to those used by Fashion World on February 5, 19X3, when it filed the monthly sales tax return for January 19X3 with the state tax commissioner. The firm's sales are subject to a 6 percent state sales tax. To highlight the data needed, the January postings are shown in the ledger accounts in Figure 7–17.

FIGURE 7–17
Ledger Account Postings for Sales Tax

ACCOUNT *Sales Tax Payable* ACCOUNT NO. *231*

DATE		EXPLANATION	POST. REF.	DEBIT	CREDIT	BALANCE DEBIT	BALANCE CREDIT
19X3							
Jan.	*1*	*Balance*	√				*712 40*
	10		*CP1*	*712 40*			*—0—*
	31		*J1*	*9 00*		*9 00*	
	31		*J1*	*3 00*		*12 00*	
	31		*S1*		*165 00*		*153 00*
	31		*CR1*		*455 10*		*608 10*

ACCOUNT *Sales* ACCOUNT NO. *401*

DATE		EXPLANATION	POST. REF.	DEBIT	CREDIT	BALANCE DEBIT	BALANCE CREDIT
19X3							
Jan.	*31*		*S1*		*2750 00*		*2750 00*
	31		*CR1*		*7585 00*		*10335 00*

ACCOUNT *Sales Returns and Allowances* ACCOUNT NO. *451*

DATE		EXPLANATION	POST. REF.	DEBIT	CREDIT	BALANCE DEBIT	BALANCE CREDIT
19X3							
Jan.	*14*		*J1*	*150 00*		*150 00*	
	22		*J1*	*50 00*		*200 00*	

FIGURE 7–18
State Sales Tax Return

SALES TAX RETURN

ALWAYS REFER TO THIS NUMBER WHEN WRITING THE DIVISION →

LICENSE NUMBER
217539

—IMPORTANT—
ANY CHANGE IN OWNERSHIP REQUIRES A NEW LICENSE: NOTIFY THIS DIVISION IMMEDIATELY.

This return DUE on the 1st day of month following period covered by the return, and becomes DELINQUENT on 21st day.

37-9462315
FED. E.I. NO. OR S.S. NO.

STATE TAX COMMISSION
SALES AND USE TAX DIVISION
DRAWER 420
CAPITAL CITY, STATE 11110
RETURN REQUESTED

January 31, 19X3
—Sales For Period Ended—

OWNER NAME AND LOCATION

MAKE ALL REMITTANCES PAYABLE TO STATE TAX COMMISSION
DO NOT SEND CASH
STAMPS NOT ACCEPTED

Fashion World
5001 S. Portland
San Francisco, CA 94118

COMPUTATION OF SALES TAX	For Taxpayer's Use	Do Not Use This Column
1. TOTAL Gross proceeds of sales or Gross Receipts (to include rentals)	10,135.00	
2. Add cost of personal property Purchased on a RETAIL LICENSE FOR RESALE but USED BY YOU or YOUR EMPLOYEES, Including GIFTS and PREMIUMS	- 0 -	
3. USE TAX—Add cost of personal property purchased outside of STATE for your use, storage or consumption	- 0 -	
4. Total (Lines 1, 2 and 3)	10,135.00	
5. LESS ALLOWABLE DEDUCTIONS (Must be itemized on reverse side)	- 0 -	
6. Net taxable total (Line 4 minus Line 5)	10,135.00	
7. Sales and Use Tax Due (6% of Line 6)	608.10	
8. LESS TAXPAYER'S DISCOUNT—(Deductible only when amount of Tax due is not delinquent at time of payment) →	12.16	
IF LINE 7 IS LESS THAN $100.00 —DEDUCT 3% IF LINE 7 IS $100.00 BUT LESS THAN $1,000.00 —DEDUCT 2% IF LINE 7 IS $1,000.00 OR MORE —DEDUCT 1%		
9. NET AMOUNT OF TAX PAYABLE (Line 7 minus Line 8)	595.94	
Add the following penalty and interest if return or remittance is late 10. Specific Penalty: 25% of tax — — — — — — — — — $______ 11. Interest: 1/2 of 1% per month from due date until paid. $______ TOTAL PENALTY AND INTEREST →		
12. TOTAL TAX, PENALTY AND INTEREST	595.94	
13. Subtract credit memo No.		
14. TOTAL AMOUNT DUE (IF NO SALES MADE SO STATE)	595.94	

I certify that this return, including the accompanying schedules or statements, has been examined by me and is to the best of my knowledge and belief, a true and complete return, made in good faith, for the period stated, pursuant to the provisions of the Code of Laws, 19X3, and Acts Amendatory Thereto.

URGENT—SEE THAT LICENSE NUMBER IS ON RETURN

Carolyn Wells
SIGNATURE

Owner
Owner, partner or title

February 5, 19X3
Date

Return must be signed by owner, or if corporation, authorized person.

Division Use Only

Using these figures as a basis, the amount of the firm's taxable gross sales for January 19X3 is determined as follows:

Cash Sales	$ 7,585
Credit Sales	2,750
Total Sales	$10,335
Less Sales Returns and Allowances	200
Taxable Gross Sales for January	$10,135

The 6 percent sales tax on the gross sales of $10,135 amounts to $608.10. In the state where Fashion World is located, a retailer who files the sales tax return (see Figure 7–18) on time and who pays the tax when it is due is entitled to a discount. The discount is intended to compensate the retailer, at least in part, for acting as a collection agent for the government. The discount rate depends on the amount of tax to be paid. On amounts between $100 and $1,000, the rate is 2 percent of the tax due. For Fashion World, the January discount amounts to $12.16 ($608.10 × 0.02). With the discount deducted, the net tax due is $595.94 ($608.10 – $12.16).

The firm sends a check for the net sales tax due with the sales tax return. The accounting entry made to record this payment includes a debit to Sales Tax Payable and a credit to Cash (for $595.94 in this case). After the amount of the payment is posted, the balance in the Sales Tax Payable account should be equal to the discount, as shown in Figure 7–19. Slight differences can arise because the tax collected at the time of the sale is determined by a tax bracket method that can give results slightly more or less than the final computations on the tax return.

FIGURE 7–19
Effect of Paying Sales Taxes

ACCOUNT *Sales Tax Payable* ACCOUNT NO. *231*

DATE		EXPLANATION	POST. REF.	DEBIT	CREDIT	BALANCE DEBIT	BALANCE CREDIT
19X3							
Jan.	*1*	*Balance*	✓				*712 40*
	10		*CP1*	*712 40*			*—0—*
	31		*J1*	*9 00*		*9 00*	
	31		*J1*	*3 00*		*12 00*	
	31		*S1*		*165 00*		*153 00*
	31		*CR1*		*455 10*		*608 10*
Feb.	*5*		*CP1*	*595 94*			*12 16*

Tax payment — Amount of discount

If there is a balance in the Sales Tax Payable account after the sales tax liability is satisfied, the balance is transferred to an account called Miscellaneous Income by a general journal entry. This entry consists of a debit to Sales Tax Payable and a credit to Miscellaneous Income.

Information Block: Computers in Accounting

Computerized Sales Invoices

Business information systems produce information for individuals and managers at all levels of an organization. One major type of information system is a *transaction processing system* (TPS), which is also known as an online or real-time system. A TPS performs the tasks of recording and managing the financial information resulting from business transactions. An order entry system for recording customers' orders is an example of a transaction processing system.

The customer order entry system monitors all processing from the time an order is received until the company's products are shipped. When an order is received, data such as the customer's account number, item stock number, and quantity ordered are entered into the system. If the order is from a credit customer, the system must review the customer's credit history and status. The customer's order is then approved or denied based on this credit check.

Recording Sales Tax in the Sales Account

In some states retailers can credit the entire sales price plus tax to the Sales account. At the end of each month or quarter, they must remove from the Sales account the amount of tax included and transfer that amount to the Sales Tax Payable account. For example, assume that during January 19X3 a retailer whose sales are all taxable sells merchandise for a total price of $10,920, including a 4 percent tax. The entry to record these sales is summarized in general journal form below.

GENERAL JOURNAL PAGE 3

	DATE		DESCRIPTION	POST. REF.	DEBIT	CREDIT	
1	*19X3*						1
2	*Jan.*	*31*	*Accounts Receivable*	*111*	*10 9 2 0 00*		2
3			*Sales*	*401*		*10 9 2 0 00*	3
4			*To record total sales and*				4
5			*sales tax collected*				5
6			*during the month*				6
7							7

At the end of the month, the retailer must transfer the sales tax from the Sales account to the Sales Tax Payable account. The first step in the transfer process is to determine the amount of tax in-

The next step in the order entry system is to verify availability of the products ordered by checking inventory records for the quantities of stock on hand. If sufficient inventory exists, the TPS will print an order confirmation for the customer and a packing slip. The packing slip is sent to the company's warehouse and is used to select the ordered goods. If the product is out of stock, the system initiates a purchase order to replenish these items.

The final document printed out by the system is the *sales invoice.* This document contains all appropriate information such as cash discount terms, date of shipment, method of shipment, quantity shipped and price, freight charges, and amount of applicable sales tax. If any ordered items are not presently available, information regarding the date of future shipments can also be included. The information from the sales invoice is also posted to the customer's subsidiary ledger account, thus giving management immediate up-to-date balances in each account.

The system can also provide managers with sales reports to identify fast-selling products as well as products that are not selling. Reports can also summarize sales by geographic regions and by sales representative.

volved. The sales tax payable is computed as follows.

Sales + tax	= \$10,920
100% of sales + 4% of sales	= \$10,920
104% of sales	= \$10,920
Sales	= \$10,920/1.04
Sales	= \$10,500
Tax	= \$10,500 × 0.04 = \$420

The firm then makes the following entry to transfer the liability from the Sales account.

GENERAL JOURNAL PAGE 3

	DATE		DESCRIPTION	POST. REF.	DEBIT	CREDIT	
8	*Jan.*	*31*	*Sales*	*401*	*4 2 0 00*		8
9			*Sales Tax Payable*	*231*		*4 2 0 00*	9
10			*To transfer sales tax*				10
11			*payable from the Sales*				11
12			*account to the liability*				12
13			*account*				13
14							14

MANAGERIAL IMPLICATIONS

Management must be certain that all sales on credit and other transactions that affect accounts receivable are recorded promptly, efficiently, and accurately. Credit sales are a major source of revenue in many businesses, and accounts receivable represent a major asset. Management needs up-to-date and correct information about both sales and accounts receivable in order to monitor the financial health of the firm.

The use of a sales journal and other special journals saves time and effort and reduces the cost of accounting work. In a retail firm that must handle sales tax, the sales journal and the cash receipts journal also provide a convenient method of recording the amounts owed for this tax. When the data is posted to the Sales Tax Payable account in the general ledger, the firm has a complete and systematic record that speeds the completion of the periodic sales tax return. The firm also has detailed proof of its sales tax figures in case of a tax audit.

Management must select a well-balanced credit policy. This policy should help to increase sales volume but should also keep losses from uncollectible accounts at an acceptable level.

The use of an accounts receivable subsidiary ledger provides management and the credit department with up-to-date information about the balances owed by all customers. This information is of special value in controlling credit and collections and in evaluating the effectiveness of credit policies. Since much of the cash needed for day-to-day operations usually comes from accounts receivable, management must keep a close watch on the promptness of customer payments.

Managers of retail businesses must make sure that sales taxes are properly charged to customers and collected. Managers must also be sure that sales taxes are accurately entered in the firm's records and promptly sent to the taxing authorities along with any required reports. Retailers are liable for any undercollection of taxes. This situation can be avoided with an efficient control system.

SELF-REVIEW

1. What is the difference between list price and net price?
2. If a wholesale business offers a trade discount of 35 percent on a sale of $1,200, what is the amount of the discount?
3. A company that buys $1,500 of goods from a wholesaler offering trade discounts of 20 and 10 percent will pay what amount for the goods?
4. What are four types of credit sales?
5. What account is used to record sales tax owed by a business to a city or state?

Answers to Self-Review

1. List price is the established retail price of an item; net price is the amount left after all trade discounts are subtracted from the list price.
2. The discount is $240 ($1,200 × 0.35 = $420).
3. The goods will cost $1,080, calculated as follows: $1,500 × 0.20 = $300; $1,500 − $300 = $1,200; $1,200 × 0.10 = $120; $1,200 − $120 = $1,080.
4. Four types of credit sales are open-account credit, business credit card sales, bank credit card sales, and credit card company sales.
5. Sales Tax Payable is the account used to record the liability for sales taxes to be paid in the future.

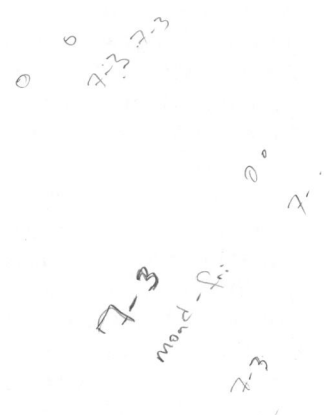

CHAPTER 7 Review and Applications

CHAPTER SUMMARY

In designing an accounting system for a business, the nature of the firm's operations, the volume of its transactions, and a number of other factors must be considered. The accounting systems of most merchandising businesses include special journals and subsidiary ledgers as well as the general journal and the general ledger. The use of these additional journals and ledgers increases the efficiency of the recording function and permits division of labor.

The sales journal is a special journal in which all sales on credit are entered. These transactions are usually recorded on a daily basis. At the end of each month, the sales journal is totaled, proved, and ruled and the column totals are posted to the general ledger. One important advantage of using a sales journal rather than a general journal to record credit sales is that there is no need to post individual entries to the general ledger during the month. A summary posting is made at the end of the month to save time and effort.

In many areas, retail sales of goods and services are subject to a sales tax. This tax is normally entered when the sale is made so that the firm has the appropriate amount of liability in its financial records. The most efficient way to record the sales tax owed on credit sales is by placing a Sales Tax Payable Credit column in the sales journal.

Sales returns and allowances are usually debited to a contra revenue account. The balance of this account is subtracted from the balance of the Sales account on the income statement in order to show the net sales for the period. If a firm has a substantial number of sales returns and allowances, it may use a special journal for these transactions. Otherwise they are entered in the general journal.

Accounts with individual credit customers are kept in a subsidiary ledger called the accounts receivable ledger. Daily postings are made to this ledger from the sales journal, the cash receipts journal, and the general journal or sales returns and allowances journal. The current balance of a customer's account is computed after each posting so that the amount owed is known at all times. At the end of each month, a schedule of accounts receivable is prepared. This schedule is used to prove the subsidiary ledger against the Accounts Receivable account in the general ledger. It also provides a report of the amounts that are due from credit customers.

Credit sales are very common, and many different credit arrangements are used. Each firm chooses a credit policy to suit its needs.

In states and cities that have a sales tax, the retailer must prepare a sales tax return and send the total tax collected to the taxing authority at regular intervals, usually monthly or quarterly. In some localities, retailers are given a discount on the sales tax in order to partially compensate them for acting as a tax collection agent.

GLOSSARY OF NEW TERMS

Accounts receivable ledger (p. 187) A subsidiary ledger that contains credit customer accounts

Charge-account sales (p. 201) Sales made through the use of open-account credit or one of various types of credit cards

Contra revenue account (p. 190) An account with a debit balance, which is contrary to the normal balance for a revenue account

Control account (p. 193) An account that links a subsidiary ledger and the general ledger since its balance summarizes the balances of the accounts in the subsidiary ledger

Credit memorandum (p. 189) A note verifying that a customer's account is being reduced by the amount of a sales return or sales allowance plus any sales tax that may have been involved

Invoice (p. 199) A customer billing for merchandise bought on credit

List price (p. 197) An established retail price

Manufacturing business (p. 179) A business that sells goods that it has produced

Merchandise inventory (p. 180) The stock of goods a merchandising business keeps on hand

Merchandising business (p. 179) A business that sells goods purchased for resale

Net price (p. 197) The list price less all trade discounts

Net sales (p. 192) The difference between the balance in the Sales account and the balance in the Sales Returns and Allowances account

Open-account credit (p. 200) A system that allows the sale of services or goods with the understanding that payment will be made at a later date

Retail business (p. 179) A business that sells directly to individual consumers

Sales allowance (p. 189) A reduction in the price originally charged to customers for goods or services

Sales journal (p. 180) A special journal used to record sales of merchandise on credit

Sales return (p. 189) A firm's acceptance of a return of goods from a customer

Schedule of accounts receivable (p. 193) A listing of all balances of the accounts in the accounts receivable subsidiary ledger

Service business (p. 179) A business that sells services

Special journal (p. 180) A journal used to record only one type of transaction

Subsidiary ledger (p. 180) A ledger dedicated to accounts of a single type and showing details to support a general ledger account
Trade discount (p. 197) A reduction from list price
Wholesale business (p. 197) A business that manufactures or distributes goods to retail businesses or large consumers such as hotels and hospitals

REVIEW QUESTIONS

1. The sales tax on a credit sale is not collected from the customer immediately. When is this tax usually entered in a firm's accounting records? What account is used to record this tax?
2. How is a multicolumn special journal proved at the end of each month?
3. What kind of account is Sales Returns and Allowances?
4. Why is a sales return or allowance usually recorded in a special Sales Returns and Allowances account rather than being debited to the Sales account?
5. How are the net sales for an accounting period determined?
6. What purposes does the schedule of accounts receivable serve?
7. How do retail and wholesale businesses differ?
8. What is a trade discount? Why do some firms offer trade discounts to their customers?
9. What is open-account credit?
10. Why are bank credit card sales similar to cash sales for a business?
11. What is the discount on credit card sales? What type of account is used to record this item?
12. When a firm makes a sale involving a credit card issued by a credit card company, does the firm have an account receivable with the cardholder or with the credit card company?
13. What procedure does a business use to collect amounts owed to it for sales on credit cards issued by credit card companies?
14. What two methods are commonly used to record sales involving credit cards issued by credit card companies?
15. In a particular state, the sales tax rate is 5 percent of sales. The retailer is allowed to record both the selling price and the tax in the same account. Explain how to compute the sales tax due when this method is used.

MANAGERIAL FOCUS

1. Why is it usually worthwhile for a business to sell on credit even though it will have some losses from uncollectible accounts?
2. How can a firm's credit policy affect its profitability?
3. Why should management insist that all sales on credit and other transactions affecting the firm's accounts receivable be journalized and posted promptly?

4. How can efficient accounting records help management maintain sound credit and collection policies?
5. How does the Sales Returns and Allowances account provide management with a measure of operating efficiency? What problems might be indicated by a high level of returns and allowances?
6. Suppose you are the accountant for a small chain of clothing stores. Up to now the firm has offered open-account credit to qualified customers but has not allowed the use of bank credit cards. The president of the chain has asked your advice about changing the firm's credit policy. What advantages might there be in eliminating the open-account credit and accepting bank credit cards instead? Do you see any disadvantages?
7. During the past year the Shelton Company has had a substantial increase in its losses from uncollectible accounts. Assume that you are the newly hired controller of this firm and that you have been asked to find the reason for the increase. What policies and procedures would you investigate?
8. Suppose a manager in your company has suggested that the firm not hire an accountant to advise it on tax matters and to file tax returns. He states that tax matters are merely procedural in nature and that anyone who can read the tax form instructions can do the necessary work. Comment on this idea.

EXERCISES

EXERCISE 7–1
(Obj. 1, 4)

Identifying the accounts used to record sales and related transactions. The transactions below took place at the Vacation Shop, a retail business that sells outdoor clothing and camping equipment. Indicate the numbers of the general ledger accounts that would be debited and credited to record each transaction.

GENERAL LEDGER ACCOUNTS

101 Cash
111 Accounts Receivable
231 Sales Tax Payable
401 Sales
451 Sales Returns and Allowances

TRANSACTIONS

1. Sold merchandise on credit; the transaction involved sales tax.
2. Received checks from credit customers on account.
3. Accepted a return of merchandise from a credit customer; the original sale involved sales tax.
4. Sold merchandise for cash; the transaction involved sales tax.
5. Gave an allowance to a credit customer for damaged merchandise; the original sale involved sales tax.
6. Provided a cash refund to a customer who returned merchandise; the original sale was made for cash and involved sales tax.

EXERCISE 7–2
(Obj. 1)

Tutorial

Identifying the journal to record transactions. The accounting system of the Vacation Shop includes the journals listed below. Indicate the specific journal in which each of the transactions listed below would be recorded.

JOURNALS

Cash receipts journal
Cash payments journal
Purchases journal
Sales journal
General journal

TRANSACTIONS

1. Sold merchandise on credit.
2. Accepted a return of merchandise from a credit customer.
3. Sold merchandise for cash.
4. Purchased merchandise on credit.
5. Gave a $100 allowance for damaged merchandise.
6. Collected sums on account from credit customers.
7. Received an additional cash investment from the owner.
8. Issued a check to pay a creditor on account.

EXERCISE 7–3
(Obj. 1)

Tutorial

Recording credit sales. The following transactions took place at the Trailways Shop during May 19X3. Indicate how these transactions would be entered in a sales journal like the one shown in Figure 7–4.

May 1 Sold a tent and other items on credit to David Walker; issued Sales Slip 1101 for $560 plus sales tax of $28.

2 Sold a backpack, an air mattress, and other items to Nancy Moore; issued Sales Slip 1102 for $240 plus sales tax of $12.

3 Sold a lantern, cooking utensils, and other items to Peter Johnson; issued Sales Slip 1103 for $200 plus sales tax of $10.

EXERCISE 7–4
(Obj. 4)

Tutorial

Recording sales returns and allowances. Record the general journal entries for the following transactions of Fashion World that occurred in May 19X3.

May 8 Accepted a return of some damaged merchandise from Paula Granbery, a credit customer; issued Credit Memorandum 129 for $318, which includes sales tax of $18; the original sale was made on Sales Slip 2605 of May 5.

21 Gave an allowance to James Wilson, a credit customer, for some merchandise that was slightly damaged but usable; issued Credit Memorandum 130 for $424, which includes sales tax of $24; the original sale was made on Sales Slip 2649 of May 19.

EXERCISE 7–5
(Obj. 2)

Posting from the sales journal. The sales journal for the Jacobs Company is shown at the top of the next page. Describe how the amounts would be posted to the general ledger accounts.

SALES JOURNAL PAGE 1

DATE		SALES SLIP NO.	CUSTOMER'S NAME	POST. REF.	ACCOUNTS RECEIVABLE DEBIT	SALES TAX PAYABLE CREDIT	SALES CREDIT
19X3							
Jan.	3	1101	James Allen	√	53 00	3 00	50 00
	5	1102	Helen Page	√	63 60	3 60	60 00
	12	1103	Anthony Bruno	√	79 50	4 50	75 00
	13	1104	Marilyn Diaz	√	106 00	6 00	100 00
	15	1105	David Foster	√	84 80	4 80	80 00
	20	1106	Karen Drake	√	42 40	2 40	40 00
	27	1107	James Allen	√	50 88	2 88	48 00
	28	1108	John Costa	√	100 70	5 70	95 00
	31	1109	Ruth Carr	√	26 50	1 50	25 00
	31		Totals		607 38	34 38	573 00
					(111)	(231)	(401)

EXERCISE 7–6 (Obj. 7)

Computing a trade discount. The Warren Distributing Company, a wholesale firm, made sales using the following list prices and trade discounts. What amount will be recorded for each sale in the sales journal?

1. List price of $700 and trade discount of 40 percent
2. List price of $1,200 and trade discount of 40 percent
3. List price of $360 and trade discount of 30 percent

EXERCISE 7–7 (Obj. 7)

Tutorial

Computing a series of trade discounts. The Asheville Corporation, a wholesale firm, made sales using the following list prices and trade discounts. What amount will be recorded for each sale in the sales journal?

1. List price of $2,000 and trade discounts of 25 and 15 percent
2. List price of $1,800 and trade discounts of 25 and 15 percent
3. List price of $940 and trade discounts of 20 and 10 percent

EXERCISE 7–8 (Obj. 9)

Tutorial

Computing the sales tax due and recording its payment. The balances of certain accounts at the Hardwood Company on February 28, 19X3, were as follows:

Sales	$425,000
Sales Returns and Allowances	3,500

All of Hardwood Company's net sales are subject to a 6 percent sales tax. Give the general journal entry to record payment of the sales tax payable on February 28, 19X3.

EXERCISE 7–9 (Obj. 6)

Preparing a schedule of accounts receivable. The accounts receivable ledger for Style Corner follows.

Instructions

1. Prepare a schedule of accounts receivable as of January 31, 19X3.
2. What should the balance in the Accounts Receivable (control) account be?

Name *Roy Anderson* Terms
Address *9 Lone Oak Trace, San Francisco, CA 94116*

DATE		EXPLANATION	POST. REF.	DEBIT	CREDIT	BALANCE
19X3						
Jan.	1	Balance	√			132 50
	31	Sales Slip 2605	S1	530 00		662 50

Name *Jeffery Baines* Terms
Address *2020 Broken Arrow, San Francisco, CA 94118*

DATE		EXPLANATION	POST. REF.	DEBIT	CREDIT	BALANCE
19X3						
Jan.	1	Balance	√			530 00
	12		CR1		265 00	265 00
	17	Sales Slip 2602	S1	212 00		477 00

Name *Karen Carter* Terms
Address *1128 Winter Street, San Francisco, CA 94112*

DATE		EXPLANATION	POST. REF.	DEBIT	CREDIT	BALANCE
19X3						
Jan.	1	Balance	√			106 00
	20	Sales Slip 2606	S1	53 00		159 00
	21		CR1		100 00	59 00
	22	Sales Slip	S1	212 00		271 00

Name *Nolan Hernandez* Terms
Address *1080 Southside Lane, San Francisco, CA 94112*

DATE		EXPLANATION	POST. REF.	DEBIT	CREDIT	BALANCE
19X3						
Jan.	1	Balance	√			318 00
	14	Sales Slip 2604	S1	106 00		424 00

Name *Sandra Nelson* Terms
Address *9926 Allen Street, San Francisco, CA 94116*

DATE		EXPLANATION	POST. REF.	DEBIT	CREDIT	BALANCE
19X3						
Jan.	1	Balance	√			53 00
	15		CR1		53 00	—0—
	31	Sales Slip 2609	S1	185 50		185 50

Name *Paula Young* **Terms** ____

Address *2211 Windsor Drive, San Francisco, CA 94116*

DATE		EXPLANATION	POST. REF.	DEBIT	CREDIT	BALANCE
19X3						
Jan.	*1*	*Balance*	√			*106 00*
	27	*Sales Slip 2607*	*S1*	*32 50*		*138 50*
	31		*CR1*		*53 00*	*85 50*

EXERCISE 7–10 (Obj. 5)

Posting sales returns and allowances. Post the journal entries below to the appropriate ledger accounts. Assume the following account balances: Accounts Receivable, $1,802; Ann Turner, $848; and Liz Davis, $954.

GENERAL JOURNAL PAGE *3*

	DATE		DESCRIPTION	POST. REF.	DEBIT	CREDIT	
1	*19X3*						1
2	*Feb.*	*14*	*Sales Returns and Allowances*		*300 00*		2
3			*Sales Tax Payable*		*18 00*		3
4			*Accounts Rec./Ann Turner*			*318 00*	4
5			*Accepted return*				5
6			*of defective merchandise,*				6
7			*Credit Memo 101; original*				7
8			*sale of Feb. 12, Sales*				8
9			*Slip 1103*				9
10							10
11		*22*	*Sales Returns and Allowances*		*100 00*		11
12			*Sales Tax Payable*		*6 00*		12
13			*Accounts Rec./Liz Davis*			*106 00*	13
14			*Gave allowance for*				14
15			*damaged merchandise,*				15
16			*Credit Memo 102; original*				16
17			*sale of Feb. 20, Sales*				17
18			*Slip 1120*				18
19							19

PROBLEMS

PROBLEM SET A

PROBLEM 7–1A (Obj. 1, 2)

Tutorial

Recording credit sales and posting from the sales journal. The Woodhaven Appliance Center is a retail store that sells household appliances. The firm's credit sales for July 19X3 are listed below, along with the general ledger accounts used to record these sales. The balance shown for Accounts Receivable is for the beginning of the month.

Instructions

1. Open the general ledger accounts and enter the balance of Accounts Receivable for July 1, 19X3.
2. Record the transactions in a sales journal like the one shown in Figure 7–4. Use 7 as the journal page number.
3. Total, prove, and rule the sales journal as of July 31.
4. Post the column totals from the sales journal to the proper general ledger accounts.

GENERAL LEDGER ACCOUNTS

111 Accounts Receivable, $7,850 Dr.
231 Sales Tax Payable
401 Sales

TRANSACTIONS

July 1 Sold a dishwasher to Alice Jenkins; issued Sales Slip 501 for $850 plus sales tax of $51.

6 Sold a washer to Marty Washburn; issued Sales Slip 502 for $600 plus sales tax of $36.

11 Sold a big-screen color television set to Austin Taylor; issued Sales Slip 503 for $2,050 plus sales tax of $123.

17 Sold an electric dryer to Earlene Hill; issued Sales Slip 504 for $400 plus sales tax of $24.

23 Sold a trash compactor to Maria Delgado; issued Sales Slip 505 for $300 plus sales tax of $18.

27 Sold a portable color television set to Carl Swenson; issued Sales Slip 506 for $300 plus sales tax of $18.

29 Sold an electric range to Jane Mabus; issued Sales Slip 507 for $600 plus sales tax of $36.

31 Sold a microwave oven to Nolan Dante; issued Sales Slip 508 for $250 plus sales tax of $15.

PROBLEM 7–2A
(Obj. 1, 2, 4)

Journalizing, posting, and reporting sales transactions. The Home Furniture Center is a retail store that specializes in modern living-room and dining-room furniture. The firm's credit sales and sales returns and allowances for March 19X3 are reflected below, along with the general ledger accounts used to record these transactions. The balances shown are for the beginning of the month.

Instructions

1. Open the general ledger accounts and enter the balances for March 1, 19X3.
2. Record the transactions in a sales journal and in a general journal. Use 8 as the page number for the sales journal and 24 as the page number for the general journal.
3. Post the entries from the general journal to the general ledger.
4. Total, prove, and rule the sales journal as of March 31.
5. Post the column totals from the sales journal.
6. Prepare the heading and the Revenue section of the firm's income statement for the month ended March 31, 19X5.

GENERAL LEDGER ACCOUNTS

111 Accounts Receivable, $2,606 Dr.
231 Sales Tax Payable, $1,195 Cr.

401 Sales
451 Sales Returns and Allowances

TRANSACTIONS

March 1 Sold a living room sofa to Mary Watson; issued Sales Slip 1483 for $875 plus sales tax of $43.75.

5 Sold three living room chairs to Robert Nixon; issued Sales Slip 1484 for $790 plus sales tax of $39.50.

9 Sold a dining room set to Kathleen Owens; issued Sales Slip 1485 for $2,600 plus sales tax of $130.

11 Accepted a return of a damaged chair from Robert Nixon that was originally sold on Sales Slip 1484 of March 5; issued Credit Memorandum 207 for $278.25, which includes sales tax of $13.25.

17 Sold living room tables and bookcases to Henry Chu; issued Sales Slip 1486 for $2,250 plus sales tax of $112.50.

23 Sold eight dining room chairs to Anita Reed; issued Sales Slip 1487 for $1,600 plus sales tax of $80.

25 Gave Henry Chu an allowance for scratches on his bookcases; issued Credit Memorandum 208 for $52.50, which includes sales taxes of $2.50; the bookcases were originally sold on Sales Slip 1486 of March 17.

27 Sold a living room sofa and four chairs to Victor Chavez; issued Sales Slip 1488 for $1,840 plus sales tax of $92.

29 Sold a dining room table to Judith Kovac; issued Sales Slip 1489 for $650 plus sales tax of $32.50.

31 Sold a living room modular wall unit to Gary Lawson; issued Sales Slip 1490 for $1,570 plus sales tax of $78.50.

PROBLEM 7–3A
(Obj. 1, 2, 3, 4, 6)

Recording sales transactions, posting to the accounts receivable ledger, and preparing a schedule of accounts receivable. The Imperial Gift Shop sells china, glassware, and other gift items that are subject to a 6 percent sales tax. The shop uses a general journal and a sales journal similar to those illustrated in this chapter.

Instructions

1. Record the transactions for November 19X4 in the proper journal. Use 5 as the page number for the sales journal and 15 as the page number for the general journal.
2. Immediately after recording each transaction, post to the accounts receivable ledger.
3. Post the amounts from the general journal daily. Post the sales journal amount as a total at the end of the month.
4. Prepare a schedule of accounts receivable. Compare the balance of the Accounts Receivable control account with the total of the schedule.

TRANSACTIONS

Nov. 1 Sold china to Michele King; issued Sales Slip 141 for $200 plus $12 sales tax.

5 Sold a brass serving tray to Robin Cooley; issued Sales Slip 142 for $300 plus $18 sales tax.

6 Sold a vase to Werner Knerr; issued Sales Slip 143 for $100 plus $6 sales tax.
10 Sold a punch bowl and glasses to Lisa Mariani; issued Sales Slip 144 for $250 plus $15 sales tax.
14 Sold a set of serving bowls to Maggie Dennis; issued Sales Slip 145 for $75 plus $4.50 sales tax.
17 Gave Lisa Mariani an allowance because of a broken glass discovered when unpacking the punch bowl and glasses sold on November 10, Sales Slip 144; issued Credit Memorandum 201 for $21.20, which includes sales tax of $1.20.
21 Sold a coffee table to Hans Rheinhold; issued Sales Slip 146 for $500 plus $30 sales tax.
24 Sold sterling silver teaspoons to Emily Gunther; issued Sales Slip 147 for $100 plus $6 sales tax.
25 Gave Hans Rheinhold an allowance for scratches on his coffee table sold on November 21, Sales Slip 146; issued Credit Memorandum 202 for $53, which includes $3 in sales tax.
30 Sold a clock to Victor Costello; issued Sales Slip 148 for $600 plus $36 sales tax.

PROBLEM 7–4A
(Obj. 1, 2, 3, 4, 6)

Recording sales transactions, posting to the accounts receivable ledger, and preparing a schedule of accounts receivable. The Greenery is a wholesale shop that sells flowers, plants, and plant supplies. The transactions shown below took place during January 19X4.

Instructions

1. Record the transactions in the proper journal. Use 6 as the page number for the sales journal and 10 as the page number for the general journal.
2. Immediately after recording each transaction, post to the accounts receivable ledger.
3. Post the amounts from the general journal daily. Post the sales journal amount as a total at the end of the month.
4. Prepare a schedule of accounts receivable. Compare the balance of the Accounts Receivable control account with the total of the schedule.

TRANSACTIONS
Jan. 3 Sold a floral arrangement to The Floral Shop; issued Invoice 1900 for $150.
8 Sold potted plants to Sorrento Garden Supply; issued Invoice 1901 for $375.50.
9 Sold floral arrangements to Heinberg Flower Shop; issued Invoice 1902 for $180.75.
10 Sold corsages to Vickers Flower Shop; issued Invoice 1903 for $265.
15 Gave Heinberg Flower Shop an allowance because of withered blossoms discovered in one of the floral arrangements sold on Invoice 1902 on January 9; issued Credit Memorandum 10 for $10.

20 Sold table arrangements to City Flower Shop; issued Invoice 1904 for $212.
22 Sold plants to Springtime Nursery; issued Invoice 1905 for $321.25.
25 Sold roses to Vickers Flower Shop; issued Invoice 1906 for $191.50.
27 Sold several floral arrangements to The Floral Shop; issued Invoice 1907 for $430.00.
31 Gave The Floral Shop an allowance because of withered blossoms discovered in one of the floral arrangements sold on Invoice 1907 on January 27; issued Credit Memorandum 11 for $53.

PROBLEM SET B

PROBLEM 7–1B
(Obj. 1, 2)

Tutorial

Recording credit sales and posting from the sales journal. The Appliance Center is a retail store that sells household appliances. The firm's credit sales for June 19X3 are listed below, along with the general ledger accounts used to record these sales. The balance shown for Accounts Receivable is for the beginning of the month.

Instructions

1. Open the general ledger accounts and enter the balance of Accounts Receivable for June 1, 19X3.
2. Record the transactions in a sales journal like the one shown in Figure 7–4. Use 7 as the journal page number.
3. Total, prove, and rule the sales journal as of July 31.
4. Post the column totals from the sales journal to the proper general ledger accounts.

GENERAL LEDGER ACCOUNTS

111 Accounts Receivable, $18,200 Dr.
231 Sales Tax Payable
401 Sales

TRANSACTIONS

June 1 Sold a dishwasher to Todd Turner; issued Sales Slip 101 for $700 plus sales tax of $42.
6 Sold a washer to Mary Hill; issued Sales Slip 102 for $500 plus sales tax of $30.
11 Sold a big-screen color television set to David Alexander; issued Sales Slip 103 for $1,800 plus sales tax of $108.
17 Sold an electric dryer to Stacee Harris; issued Sales Slip 104 for $400 plus sales tax of $24.
23 Sold a trash compactor to Ford Martinez; issued Sales Slip 105 for $350 plus sales tax of $21.
27 Sold a portable color television set to Ned Tolliver; issued Sales Slip 106 for $250 plus sales tax of $15.
29 Sold an electric range to Joe Taylor; issued Sales Slip 107 for $650 plus sales tax of $39.
30 Sold a microwave oven to Laura Alford; issued Sales Slip 108 for $200 plus sales tax of $12.

PROBLEM 7–2B
(Obj. 1, 2, 4)

Tutorial

Journalizing, posting, and reporting sales transactions. The Contemporary Furniture Center is a retail store that specializes in modern living room and dining room furniture. The firm's credit sales and sales returns and allowances for April 19X3 are reflected below, along with the general ledger accounts used to record these transactions. The balances shown are for the beginning of the month.

Instructions

1. Open the general ledger accounts and enter the balances for April 1, 19X3.
2. Record the transactions in a sales journal and a general journal. Use 8 as the page number for the sales journal and 24 as the page number for the general journal.
3. Post the entries from the general journal to the general ledger.
4. Total, prove, and rule the sales journal as of March 31.
5. Post the column totals from the sales journal.
6. Prepare the heading and the Revenue section of the firm's income statement for the month ended April 30, 19X3.

GENERAL LEDGER ACCOUNTS

111 Accounts Receivable, $2,822 Dr.
231 Sales Tax Payable, $480 Cr.
401 Sales
451 Sales Returns and Allowances

TRANSACTIONS

April 1 Sold a living room sofa to Keith Berry; issued Sales Slip 1567 for $900 plus sales tax of $54.

5 Sold three living room chairs to Glenn Kimball; issued Sales Slip 1568 for $600 plus sales tax of $36.

9 Sold a dining room set to Angela Waters; issued Sales Slip 1569 for $3,000 plus sales tax of $180.

11 Accepted a return of a damaged chair from Glenn Kimball; the chair was originally sold on Sales Slip 1568 of April 5; issued Credit Memorandum 210 for $212, which includes sales tax of $12.

17 Sold living room tables and bookcases to Pedro Salas; issued Sales Slip 1570 for $2,500 plus sales tax of $150.

23 Sold eight dining room chairs to Ann Shaw; issued Sales Slip 1571 for $1,800 plus sales tax of $108.

25 Gave Pedro Salas an allowance for scratches on his bookcases; issued Credit Memorandum 211 for $79.50, which includes sales taxes of $4.50; the bookcases were originally sold on Sales Slip 1570 of April 17.

27 Sold a living room sofa and four chairs to Harvey Reese; issued Sales Slip 1571 for $1,600 plus sales tax of $96.

29 Sold a dining room table to Janice Johnson; issued Sales Slip 1572 for $675 plus sales tax of $40.50.

30 Sold a living-room modular wall unit to Edgar Price; issued Sales Slip 1573 for $1,450 plus sales tax of $87.

PROBLEM 7–3B
(Obj. 1, 2, 3, 4, 6)

Recording sales transactions, posting to the accounts receivable ledger, and preparing a schedule of accounts receivable. The Home Interiors Gift Shop sells china, glassware, and other gift items that are subject to a 6 percent sales tax. The shop uses a general journal and a sales journal similar to those shown in the chapter.

Instructions

1. Record the transactions for October 19X5 in the proper journal. Use 4 as the page number for the sales journal and 12 as the page number for the general journal.
2. Immediately after recording each transaction, post to the accounts receivable ledger.
3. Post the amounts from the general journal daily. Post the sales journal amount as a total at the end of the month.
4. Prepare a schedule of accounts receivable. Compare the balance of the Accounts Receivable control account with the total of the schedule.

TRANSACTIONS

Oct. 1 Sold china to Bill Wilson; issued Sales Slip 101 for $100 plus $6 sales tax.

5 Sold a brass serving tray to Diane Jenson; issued Sales Slip 102 for $200 plus $12 sales tax.

6 Sold a vase to Nancy Brock; issued Sales Slip 103 for $150 plus $9 sales tax.

10 Sold a punch bowl and glasses to Wanda Evans; issued Sales Slip 104 for $125 plus $7.50 sales tax.

14 Sold a set of serving bowls to Dennis Ortiz; issued Sales Slip 105 for $75 plus $4.50 sales tax.

17 Gave Wanda Evans an allowance because of a broken glass discovered when unpacking the punch bowl and glasses sold on October 10, Sales Slip 104; issued Credit Memorandum 101 for $21.20, which includes sales tax of $1.20.

21 Sold a coffee table to Sheila Connors; issued Sales Slip 106 for $400 plus $24 sales tax.

24 Sold sterling silver teaspoons to Alison Carter; issued Sales Slip 107 for $50 plus $3 sales tax.

25 Gave Sheila Connors an allowance for scratches on her coffee table; issued Credit Memorandum 102 for $53, which includes $3 in sales tax.

31 Sold a clock to Virginia Sims; issued Sales Slip 108 for $800 plus $48 sales tax.

PROBLEM 7–4B
(Obj. 1, 2, 3, 4, 6)

Recording sales transactions, posting to the accounts receivable ledger, and preparing a schedule of accounts receivable. The Town Nursery is a wholesale shop that sells flowers, plants, and plant supplies. The transactions shown below took place during February 19X3.

Instructions

1. Record the transactions in the proper journal. Use 4 as the page number for the sales journal and 9 as the page number for the general journal.

2. Immediately after recording each transaction, post to the accounts receivable ledger.
3. Post the amounts from the general journal daily. Post the sales journal amount as a total at the end of the month.
4. Prepare a schedule of accounts receivable. Compare the balance of the Accounts Receivable control account with the total of the schedule.

TRANSACTIONS

Feb. 3 Sold a floral arrangement to Taylor Flower Shop; issued Invoice 1101 for $250.

8 Sold potted plants to Country Garden Supply; issued Invoice 1102 for $450.00.

9 Sold floral arrangements to Mary Lou's Flower Shop; issued Invoice 1103 for $580.75.

10 Sold corsages to City Flower Shop; issued Invoice 1104 for $325.

15 Gave Mary Lou's Flower Shop an allowance because of withered blossoms discovered in one of the floral arrangements sold on Invoice 1103 on February 9; issued Credit Memorandum 110 for $20.

20 Sold table arrangements to City Flower Shop; issued Invoice 1105 for $318.

22 Sold plants to Spring Nursery; issued Invoice 1106 for $375.25.

25 Sold roses to Denton Flower Shop; issued Invoice 1107 for $211.50.

27 Sold several floral arrangements to Taylor Flower Shop; issued Invoice 1108 for $475.00.

28 Gave Taylor Flower Shop an allowance because of withered blossoms discovered in one of the floral arrangements sold on Invoice 1108 on February 27; issued Credit Memorandum 111 for $53.

CHALLENGE PROBLEM

The Howard Distributing Company sells toys and games to retail stores. The firm offers a trade discount of 40 percent on toys and 30 percent on games. Its credit sales and sales returns and allowances for June 19X7 are listed below, along with the general ledger accounts used to record these transactions. The balance shown is for the beginning of June 19X7.

Instructions

1. Open the general ledger accounts and enter the balance of Accounts Receivable for June 1, 19X7.
2. Set up an accounts receivable subsidiary ledger. Open an account for each of the credit customers listed below and enter the balances as of June 1, 19X7.

Crown Department Store	$ 7,440
Elway Variety Stores	10,100
Martin Bookstores	
Rockwell Toy Center	
Toy and Game Emporium	4,210
Wilson's Toy Circus	

3. Record the transactions in a sales journal and in a general journal. Use 10 as the page number for the sales journal and 30 as the page number for the general journal. Be sure to enter each sale at its net price.
4. Post the individual entries from the sales journal and the general journal.
5. Total and rule the sales journal as of June 30.
6. Post the column total from the sales journal to the proper general ledger accounts.
7. Prepare the heading and the Revenue section of the firm's income statement for the month ended June 30, 19X7.
8. Prepare a schedule of accounts receivable for June 30, 19X7.
9. Check the total of the schedule of accounts receivable against the balance of the Accounts Receivable account in the general ledger. The two amounts should be equal.

GENERAL LEDGER ACCOUNTS

111 Accounts Receivable, $21,750 Dr.
401 Sales
451 Sales Returns and Allowances

TRANSACTIONS

June 1 Sold toys to the Crown Department Store; issued Invoice 4576, which shows a list price of $8,800 and a trade discount of 40 percent.

5 Sold games to the Martin Bookstores; issued Invoice 4577, which shows a list price of $10,650 and a trade discount of 30 percent.

9 Sold games to the Toy and Game Emporium; issued Invoice 4578, which shows a list price of $3,520 and a trade discount of 30 percent.

14 Sold toys to the Elway Variety Stores; issued Invoice 4579, which shows a list price of $12,200 and a trade discount of 40 percent.

18 Accepted a return of all the games shipped to the Toy and Game Emporium because they were damaged in transit; issued Credit Memo 362 for the original sale made on Invoice 4578 on June 9.

22 Sold toys to Wilson's Toy Circus; issued Invoice 4580, which shows a list price of $8,160 and a trade discount of 40 percent.

26 Sold games to the Crown Department Store; issued Invoice 4581, which shows a list price of $10,150 and a trade discount of 30 percent.

30 Sold toys to the Rockwell Toy Center; issued Invoice 4582, which shows a list price of $11,700 and a trade discount of 40 percent.

CRITICAL THINKING PROBLEM

Joe Jenkins is the owner of a housewares store that sells a wide variety of items for the kitchen, bathroom, and home workshop. Joe is considering replacing his manual system of recording sales with electronic point-of-sale cash register/terminals that are linked to a computer.

Cash sales are now rung up by the salesclerks on a cash register that generates a tape listing total cash sales at the end of the day. For credit sales, salesclerks prepare handwritten sales slips that are forwarded to the accountant for manual entry into the sales journal and accounts receivable ledger.

The electronic register/terminal system Joe is considering would use an optical scanner to read coded labels attached to the merchandise. As the merchandise is passed over the scanner, the code is sent to the computer. The computer is programmed to read the code and identify the item being sold, record the amount of the sale, maintain a record of total sales, update the inventory record, and keep a record of cash received. If the sale is a credit transaction, the customer's credit card number is entered into the register/terminal and the computer updates the customer's account in the accounts receivable ledger stored in computer memory. Thus many of the accounting functions are done automatically as sales are entered into the register/terminal. At the end of the day, the computer prints a complete sales journal, along with up-to-date balances for the general ledger and the accounts receivable ledger accounts related to sales transactions.

Listed below are four situations that Joe is eager to eliminate. Would use of an electronic point-of-sale system as described above reduce or prevent these problems? Why or why not?

1. The salesclerk was not aware that the item purchased was on sale and did not give the customer the sales price.
2. The customer purchased merchandise using a stolen credit card.
3. The salesclerk did not charge a customer for an item.
4. The accountant did not post a sale to the customer's subsidiary ledger account.

CHAPTER

8

Accounting for Purchases and Accounts Payable

OBJECTIVES

1. Record purchases of merchandise on credit in a three-column purchases journal.
2. Post from the three-column purchases journal to the general ledger accounts.
3. Post purchases on credit from the purchases journal to the accounts payable subsidiary ledger.
4. Record purchases returns and allowances in the general journal.
5. Post purchases returns and allowances from the general journal to the accounts payable subsidiary ledger.
6. Prepare a schedule of accounts payable.
7. Compute the net delivered cost of purchases.
8. Demonstrate a knowledge of the procedures for effective internal control of purchases.
9. Define the accounting terms new to this chapter.

Just as the management of a merchandising business needs timely and accurate information about sales and accounts receivable in order to control operations and make decisions, management must also have appropriate information about purchases and accounts payable. Buying needed goods on time, keeping track of the amounts owed to suppliers, and paying invoices promptly so that the firm can maintain a satisfactory credit rating are all vital to successful operations in a merchandising business. Thus the accounting system of a merchandising business should contain records and procedures that permit quick and efficient handling of data about purchases and accounts payable.

NEW TERMS

Accounts payable ledger ▪ Cash discounts ▪ Freight In ▪ Invoice ▪ Purchase allowance ▪ Purchase discount ▪ Purchase invoice ▪ Purchase order ▪ Purchase requisition ▪ Purchase return ▪ Purchases ▪ Purchases journal ▪ Receiving report ▪ Sales discount ▪ Sales invoice ▪ Schedule of accounts payable ▪ Transportation In

ACCOUNTING FOR PURCHASES

In this chapter we again discuss the operations of Fashion World, a small retail merchandising business. You will see how this firm manages and records its purchases of goods for resale and the accounts payable that result from such purchases.

Purchasing Procedures

Merchandising businesses normally purchase most of their goods on credit under an open-account arrangement. A large firm usually has a centralized purchasing department that is responsible for locating suitable suppliers, obtaining price quotations and credit terms, and placing orders.

When a sales department needs goods, it sends the purchasing department a form called a **purchase requisition** (Figure 8–1), which lists the items that are wanted. The purchase requisition is signed by the manager of the sales department or some other person who is authorized to approve requests for merchandise. The purchasing department selects a supplier that can furnish the necessary goods at an appropriate price and issues a form called a **purchase order** (Figure 8–2) to the supplier. The purchase order specifies exactly what items are required, the quantity, the price quoted, and the agreed-upon credit terms. This form is signed by the firm's purchasing agent or some other employee who has responsibility for approving purchases.

As soon as the goods arrive at the firm, they are examined and a form called a **receiving report** is prepared to show the quantity received and the condition of the goods. The purchasing department then compares the supplier's **invoice,** or bill (Figure 8–3), with the receiving report and the purchase order. If the invoice contains any errors or if defective goods were received, the purchasing department contacts the supplier and settles the problem.

FIGURE 8–1
A Purchase Requisition

FASHION WORLD
5001 S. Portland
San Francisco, CA 94118

No. FC-736

PURCHASE REQUISITION

DEPARTMENT Juniors — DATE OF REQUEST June 4, 19X2
ADVISE ON DELIVERY Mr. Johnson — DATE REQUIRED July 6, 19X2

QUANTITY	DESCRIPTION
100	Designer beaded jeans

APPROVED BY ______ REQUESTED BY ______

FOR PURCHASING DEPT. USE ONLY

PURCHASE ORDER NO. 8001 — ISSUED TO: LaShawn's Fashion Designs
DATE JUNE 6, 19X2 — 1010 N. Michigan
Chicago, Il 79201

FIGURE 8–2
A Purchase Order

FASHION WORLD
5001 S. Portland
San Francisco, CA 94118

PURCHASE ORDER

TO: LaShawn's Fashion Designs
1010 N. Michigan
Chicago, IL 79201

DATE: June 6, 19X2
ORDER NO.: 8001
SHIPPED BY: 2/10, n/30

QUANTITY	DESCRIPTION	UNIT PRICE		TOTAL	
100	Designer beaded jeans	40	00	4,000	00

After the invoice is checked by the purchasing department, it is sent to the accounting department, along with copies of the purchase order and the receiving report. The accounting department rechecks the quantities, prices, and extensions on the invoice and then records the purchase. Shortly before the due date of the invoice, the accounting department issues a check to the supplier and records the payment.

In a small firm purchasing activities are usually handled by a single individual. This individual may be the owner, a manager, or some other highly responsible member of the staff.

FIGURE 8–3
An Invoice

LaShawn's Fashion Designs
1010 N. Michigan
Chicago, IL 79201

No. 4201

INVOICE

SOLD TO: Fashion World
5001 S. Portland
San Francisco, CA
94118

DATE: June 31, 19X2
ORDER NO.: 8001
SHIPPED BY: North Freight Line
TERMS: 2/10, n/30

YOUR ORDER NO.	SALESPERSON	TERMS
8001		2/10, n/30
DATE SHIPPED	**SHIPPED BY**	**FOB**
June 31, 19X2	North Freight Line	Chicago

QUANTITY	DESCRIPTION	UNIT PRICE		TOTAL	
100	Designer beaded jeans	40	00	4,000	00
	Freight			40	00
	Total			4,040	00

The Purchases Account

The purchase of goods by a firm is considered a cost of doing business. During each accounting period the amounts involved in such transactions are debited to a temporary account called **Purchases.** The Purchases account is a type of expense account, as is the Freight In account (discussed below). These accounts and others related to purchases appear just before the other expense accounts in the general ledger.

Purchases	
Dr.	Cr.
+	−
252.00	

Freight In	
Dr.	Cr.
+	−
12.00	

Accounts Payable	
Dr.	Cr.
−	+
	264.00

Freight Charges for Purchases

Some purchases are made with the understanding that the buyer will pay the freight charge—the cost of shipping the goods from the seller's warehouse. In certain cases the buyer is billed directly by the transportation company for the freight charge and issues a check to that company. In other cases the freight charge is paid by the seller and then shown on the invoice that the buyer receives for the goods. The total of the invoice covers both the price of the goods and the freight charge.

No matter how the billing for a freight charge is handled, the amount involved is debited to an account called **Freight In** or **Transportation In.** When a freight charge is listed on the seller's invoice, the buyer must enter three elements in its accounting records, as indicated by the following example.

Price of goods (to be debited to Purchases)	$252
Freight charge (to be debited to Freight In)	12
Total of invoice (to be credited to Accounts Payable)	$264

THE NEED FOR A PURCHASES JOURNAL

For most merchandising businesses, it is not efficient to enter purchases of goods in a general journal. Instead, a special journal called a **purchases journal** is used to record the purchase of goods on credit. To see why a purchases journal is helpful, consider how four credit purchases made by Fashion World during the first week of January 19X3 would appear in a general journal. Each entry would involve a separate debit to Purchases and a separate credit to Accounts Payable plus a detailed explanation, as shown below.

These general journal entries would require twelve individual postings to general ledger accounts: four postings to Purchases, four postings to Freight In, and four postings to Accounts Payable.

Clearly, it would be too time-consuming to record purchases of merchandise on credit in this manner each month. A great deal of effort would be wasted in making repetitive journal entries and postings, as you can see on pages 233–234.

GENERAL JOURNAL PAGE *1*

DATE		DESCRIPTION	POST. REF.	DEBIT	CREDIT
19X3					
Jan.	*2*	*Purchases*	*501*	*1500 00*	
		Freight In	*502*	*125 00*	
		Accounts Payable	*205*		*1625 00*
		Purchased merchandise			
		from Prestige Clothing			
		Store, Invoice 43480,			
		dated Dec. 28, terms 2/10,			
		n/30			
	4	*Purchases*	*501*	*1680 00*	
		Freight In	*502*	*130 00*	
		Accounts Payable	*205*		*1810 00*
		Purchased merchandise			
		from Wholesale Fashion			
		Shop, Invoice 633, dated			
		Dec. 30, terms n/30			
	5	*Purchases*	*501*	*1350 00*	
		Freight In	*502*	*110 00*	
		Accounts Payable	*205*		*1460 00*
		Purchased merchandise			
		from Clothes-R-Us,			
		Invoice 8090, dated			
		Dec. 31, terms n/30			
	6	*Purchases*	*501*	*1925 00*	
		Freight In	*502*	*225 00*	
		Accounts Payable	*205*		*2150 00*
		Purchased merchandise			
		from Quality Clothes,			
		Invoice 1234, dated			
		Dec. 31, terms 2/10, n/30			

A special journal intended only for credit purchases of merchandise simplifies and speeds up the recording process for purchases transactions. Refer to the purchases journal shown in Figure 8–4, page 235. Notice how the various columns in this journal efficiently organize the data about the firm's credit purchases and make it possible to record each purchase on a single line. In addition, there is no need to enter account titles and explanations.

Purchases of merchandise on credit must be journalized promptly because it is essential that a business have an up-to-date record of the amounts that it owes to suppliers. Otherwise, the firm

ACCOUNT *Accounts Payable* ACCOUNT NO. *205*

DATE		EXPLANATION	POST. REF.	DEBIT	CREDIT	BALANCE DEBIT	BALANCE CREDIT
19X3							
Jan.	1	Balance	✓				2,700.00
	2		J12		1,625.00		4,325.00
	4		J12		1,810.00		6,135.00
	5		J12		1,460.00		7,595.00
	6		J12		2,150.00		9,745.00

ACCOUNT *Purchases* ACCOUNT NO. *501*

DATE		EXPLANATION	POST. REF.	DEBIT	CREDIT	BALANCE DEBIT	BALANCE CREDIT
19X3							
Jan.	2		J12	1,500.00		1,500.00	
	4		J12	1,680.00		3,180.00	
	5		J12	1,350.00		4,530.00	
	6		J12	1,925.00		6,455.00	

ACCOUNT *Freight In* ACCOUNT NO. *502*

DATE		EXPLANATION	POST. REF.	DEBIT	CREDIT	BALANCE DEBIT	BALANCE CREDIT
19X3							
Jan.	2		J12	125.00		125.00	
	4		J12	130.00		255.00	
	5		J12	110.00		365.00	
	6		J12	225.00		590.00	

might not be able to make payments on time and maintain a good credit rating. Each purchase should therefore be recorded as soon as the supplier's invoice has been verified.

Recording Entries in a Purchases Journal

OBJECTIVE 1
Record purchases of merchandise on credit in a three-column purchases journal.

The purchases journal shown in Figure 8–4 is used by Fashion World. Notice that it includes columns for recording the date of the entry, the name of the supplier, the invoice number, the invoice date, the credit terms, and three money columns—Accounts Payable, Purchases, and Freight In. The necessary information to record transactions is taken from the supplier's invoice (Figure 8–3). To the customer this document is a **purchase invoice.** To the supplier it is a **sales invoice.**

The invoice date and the credit terms must be carefully recorded because they determine when payment is due. Some suppliers require payment 30 days after the date of the invoice. These terms are usually expressed as *net 30 days* or *n/30* on the invoice. Other sup-

FIGURE 8–4
A Purchases Journal

PURCHASES JOURNAL PAGE 1

DATE		PURCHASED FROM	INVOICE NUMBER	INV. DATE	TERMS	POST. REF.	ACCOUNTS PAYABLE CREDIT	PURCHASES DEBIT	FREIGHT IN DEBIT
19X3									
Jan.	2	Prestige Clothing Store	43480	12/28	2/10, n/30		1 625 00	1 500 00	125 00
	4	Wholesale Fashion Shop	633	12/30	n/30		1 810 00	1 680 00	130 00
	5	Clothes-R-Us	8090	12/31	n/30		1 460 00	1 350 00	110 00
	6	Quality Clothes	1234	12/31	2/10, n/30		2 150 00	1 925 00	225 00
	18	Clothing Center	8979	12/27	2/10, n/30		1 050 00	965 00	85 00
	22	Family Fashions	8597	12/31	2/10, n/30		1 280 00	1 190 00	90 00
	31						9 375 00	8 610 00	765 00

pliers allow the customer to take a discount of 1 or 2 percent if payment is made within a short period of time, often 10 days. Alternatively, the customer can pay the full amount of the invoice at the end of a longer period, such as 30 days. Credit terms of this type are shown on the invoice as *2% 10 days, net 30 days,* or *2/10, n/30.* Still other suppliers have terms of *net 10 days EOM,* or *n/10 EOM,* which means that the full amount is due 10 days after the end of the month in which the invoice was issued.

The discounts mentioned here are known as **cash discounts.** They are offered by suppliers to encourage quick payment of invoices by customers. To the customer this type of price reduction is a **purchase discount.** To the supplier it is a **sales discount.** The accounting treatment of cash discounts is described in Chapter 9.

Keep in mind that the purchases journal is used to record only credit purchases of merchandise. Credit purchases of other items such as equipment and supplies that are to be used in the business and not resold to customers are entered in the general journal.

Posting to the General Ledger

OBJECTIVE 2
Post from the three-column purchases journal to the general ledger accounts.

The use of a special journal greatly simplifies the posting process for purchases of merchandise on credit. No amounts are posted from the purchases journal to the general ledger during the month. Instead, summary postings are made at the end of this period.

Figure 8–5 illustrates the procedure for posting from the purchases journal to the general ledger accounts. At the end of each month, Fashion World adds the amounts recorded in the purchases journal, enters the totals, and rules the journal. The totals are posted to the accounts in the general ledger. Then, to show that the postings were made, the account numbers are entered below the totals of the purchases journal and the abbreviation *P1* is entered in the Posting Reference column of the accounts. This abbreviation indicates that the data was posted from page 1 of the purchases journal.

FIGURE 8–5
Posting to the General Ledger

PURCHASES JOURNAL PAGE *1*

DATE		PURCHASED FROM	INVOICE NUMBER	INV. DATE	TERMS	POST. REF.	ACCOUNTS PAYABLE CREDIT	PURCHASES DEBIT	FREIGHT IN DEBIT
19X3									
Jan.	*2*	*Prestige Clothing Store*	*43480*	*12/28*	*2/10, n/30*	√	*1625 00*	*1500 00*	*125 00*
	4	*Wholesale Fashion Shop*	*633*	*12/30*	*n/30*	√	*1810 00*	*1680 00*	*130 00*
	5	*Clothes-R-Us*	*8090*	*12/31*	*n/30*	√	*1460 00*	*1350 00*	*110 00*
	6	*Quality Clothes*	*1234*	*12/31*	*2/10, n/30*	√	*2150 00*	*1925 00*	*225 00*
	18	*Clothing Center*	*8979*	*12/27*	*2/10, n/30*	√	*1050 00*	*965 00*	*85 00*
	22	*Family Fashions*	*8597*	*12/31*	*2/10, n/30*	√	*1280 00*	*1190 00*	*90 00*
	31						*9375 00*	*8610 00*	*765 00*
							(205)	*(501)*	*(502)*

ACCOUNT *Accounts Payable* ACCOUNT NO. *205*

DATE		EXPLANATION	POST. REF.	DEBIT	CREDIT	BALANCE DEBIT	BALANCE CREDIT
19X3							
Jan.	*1*	*Balance*	√				*2700 00*
	31		*P1*		*9375 00*		*12075 00*

ACCOUNT *Purchases* ACCOUNT NO. *501*

DATE		EXPLANATION	POST. REF.	DEBIT	CREDIT	BALANCE DEBIT	BALANCE CREDIT
19X3							
Jan.	*31*		*P1*	*8610 00*		*8610 00*	

ACCOUNT *Freight In* ACCOUNT NO. *502*

DATE		EXPLANATION	POST. REF.	DEBIT	CREDIT	BALANCE DEBIT	BALANCE CREDIT
19X3							
Jan.	*31*		*P1*	*765 00*		*765 00*	

For the sake of simplicity, the purchases journal shown in Figure 8–5 contains a limited number of entries. In actual practice, Fashion World would have many more entries each month. Thus the time

Information Block: Ethics in Accounting

The Price Is the Same!

Lynn is the purchasing manager for AGS Enterprises. One of Lynn's primary responsibilities is to acquire the refrigeration units that are installed in the commercial refrigeration products AGS sells. Recently, Lynn sent out requests for bids (RFBs) to about twenty prospective suppliers because the current contract with Shiver, Inc., is about to expire, and it is standard business practice to test the market.

Shiver, the current supplier, has been a good supplier during the contract period about to expire. While reviewing the bids, Lynn gets a call from Marty, the Shiver sales representative assigned to AGS. Marty asks how their bid looks. When Lynn says the bid is a little higher than the others, Marty responds by offering to match the lowest bid. Lynn hesitates, so Marty sweetens the offer. Marty tells Lynn that if AGS signs a new agreement with Shiver, Inc., they will send Lynn's family to Orlando, Florida, for a week. They would fly on Shiver's company plane. Lynn's family could stay at the Shiver condo, and Shiver would provide courtesy passes for Lynn's family to go to Disney World. Marty ends the conversation by telling Lynn that a decision is not necessary today; but, to reserve the plane in time, the contract must be signed within 30 days.

1. What are the ethical issues?
2. What are the alternatives?
3. Who are the affected parties?
4. How do the alternatives affect the parties?
5. What should Lynn do?

saved by making summary postings to the general ledger is even greater than this illustration indicates.

During the month the individual entries in the purchases journal are posted to the creditor accounts in the accounts payable ledger. The check marks in the journal shown in Figure 8–5 indicate that these postings have been completed. The procedure for posting to the accounts payable ledger is discussed later in this chapter.

Advantages of a Purchases Journal

Every business has certain types of transactions that occur over and over again. A well-designed accounting system includes journals that permit efficient recording of such transactions. In most merchandising firms, purchases of goods on credit take place often enough to make it worthwhile to use a purchases journal. This type of special journal saves time and effort by simplifying the initial entry of purchases and by eliminating repetitive postings to the general ledger. With a three-column purchases journal such as the one shown in this chapter, no matter how many transactions are recorded each month, it is necessary only to make three summary postings to the general ledger at the end of the month.

The use of a purchases journal, along with other special journals, also permits the division of accounting work among different employees. Still another advantage of a purchases journal is that it strengthens the audit trail. All purchases of goods on credit are conveniently grouped together in a single journal, and the entry for each purchase clearly shows the number and date of the supplier's invoice—the source document for the transaction.

SELF-REVIEW

1. What activities does a purchasing department perform?
2. What is the purpose of a purchase requisition? A purchase order?
3. What is the difference between a receiving report and an invoice?
4. What type of transaction is recorded in the purchases journal?
5. What are the advantages of using a purchases journal?

Answers to Self-Review

1. The purchasing department is responsible for locating suitable suppliers, obtaining price quotations and credit terms, and placing orders.
2. The purchase requisition is used by a sales department to notify the purchasing department of the items wanted. The purchase order is prepared by the purchasing department to order the necessary goods at an appropriate price from the selected supplier.
3. The receiving report is prepared by the receiving department to show the quantity of goods received and the condition of the goods. This report is also used by the purchasing department for comparison with the purchase order. The invoice provides the accounting department with information concerning quantities purchased and prices; it is the document from which checks are prepared in payment of purchases.
4. Merchandise purchased on credit for resale is recorded in the purchases journal.
5. A purchases journal saves time and effort, since the journal entries are simpler and fewer postings are required than with the general journal. The use of a purchases journal also strengthens the audit trail.

THE ACCOUNTS PAYABLE LEDGER

It is important for a business to pay invoices on time so that it can maintain a good credit reputation with its suppliers. Being able to buy merchandise on credit allows a firm to conduct more extensive operations and use its financial resources more effectively than if it were required to pay cash for all purchases.

The need for prompt payment of invoices makes it essential that businesses keep detailed records of the amounts they owe. The most efficient method of organizing this information is to set up an **accounts payable ledger** with individual accounts for all creditors. A firm's creditors may include suppliers of equipment and services as well as suppliers of merchandise.

Each account in the accounts payable ledger contains a complete record of the transactions with a creditor—purchases, payments, and returns and allowances. The balance of the account shows the amount currently owed to the creditor. Like the accounts receivable ledger, the accounts payable ledger is known as a *subsidiary ledger* because it is separate from and subordinate to the general ledger.

It is common for businesses to keep the accounts for their creditors on ledger sheets that are similar to the one shown in Figure 8–6. A balance ledger form with three money columns is usually preferred. In a small firm like Fashion World, the creditor accounts are placed in alphabetic order for convenience. Larger firms and firms that use computers for their financial record keeping assign an account number to each creditor and maintain the creditor accounts in numeric order.

FIGURE 8–6
An Accounts Payable Ledger Account

Name *Clothes-R-Us* **Terms** *n/30*
Address *1002 Valley Street, San Francisco, CA 94118*

DATE		EXPLANATION	POST. REF.	DEBIT	CREDIT	BALANCE
19X3						
Jan.	*1*	*Balance*	✓			*400 00*
	5	*Inv. 8090, 12/31/X2*	*P1*		*1,460 00*	*1,860 00*

Since liability accounts normally have credit balances, all balances in the accounts payable ledger are presumed to be credit balances. However, debit balances may occur from time to time because of an overpayment or a return of goods that were already paid for. One simple method of handling this situation is to circle the balance to show that it is a debit amount.

Posting a Credit Purchase

Because of the importance of having up-to-date information about the sums owed to creditors, postings to the accounts payable ledger should be made daily.

OBJECTIVE 3

Post purchases on credit from the purchases journal to the accounts payable subsidiary ledger.

Each credit purchase of goods recorded in the purchases journal is posted to the proper creditor's account in the accounts payable ledger, as shown in Figure 8–6.

Notice that the date the transaction was journalized, the invoice number, the date of the invoice, and the amount are transferred from the purchases journal to the creditor's account. The amount is entered in the Credit column of the account. Then the new balance is determined and recorded. To indicate that the posting process has been completed, a check mark is placed in the purchases journal and the abbreviation *P1* is entered in the Posting Reference column of the creditor's account.

Posting Cash Paid on Account

In a firm that uses special journals and subsidiary ledgers, the cash paid to creditors is first recorded in a cash payments journal and then posted to the appropriate accounts in the accounts payable ledger. The account in Figure 8–7 shows the posting of a payment made by Fashion World to one of its creditors on January 12, 19X3. The necessary entry in the cash payments journal is discussed in Chapter 9.

FIGURE 8–7
Posting a Payment Made on Account

Name *Clothes-R-Us* **Terms** *n/30*
Address *1002 Valley Street, San Francisco, CA 94118*

DATE		EXPLANATION	POST. REF.	DEBIT	CREDIT	BALANCE
19X3						
Jan.	1	Balance	✓			400 00
	5	Inv. 8090, 12/31/X2	P1		1460 00	1860 00
	12		CP1	600 00		1260 00

PURCHASES RETURNS AND ALLOWANCES

OBJECTIVE 4

Record purchases returns and allowances in the general journal.

As noted already, in a business with a good system of internal control, new merchandise is examined carefully as soon as it arrives to make sure that it is satisfactory. If the wrong goods were shipped or if any items are damaged or defective, the firm contacts the supplier and arranges to send back the merchandise, which results in a **purchase return,** or to obtain a reduced price, which results in a **purchase allowance.** The supplier then issues a credit memorandum as evidence that credit has been granted for the return or allowance.

Recording Purchases Returns and Allowances

Suppose Fashion World receives merchandise from Clothes-R-Us on January 5, 19X3, and finds that some goods are damaged. Clothes-R-Us agrees to accept a return of the items and to give credit for them as soon as they arrive back at its warehouse. Meanwhile, Fashion World records the full amount of the invoice ($1,460) in its purchases journal. On January 17 Fashion World receives a credit memorandum for $250 from Clothes-R-Us and makes an entry in its general journal as shown below.

GENERAL JOURNAL PAGE *1*

	DATE		DESCRIPTION	POST. REF.	DEBIT	CREDIT	
1	*19X3*						1
2	*Jan.*	*17*	*Accounts Pay./Clothes-R-Us*	*205/✓*	*250 00*		2
3			*Purchases Returns & Allow.*	*503*		*250 00*	3
4			*Received Credit Memo 37*				4
5			*for damaged merchandise*				5
6			*that was returned;*				6
7			*original purchase made on*				7
8			*Invoice 8090, Jan. 5, 19X3*				8
9							9

Notice that this entry includes a debit to Accounts Payable and a credit to an account called Purchases Returns and Allowances. In addition, there is a debit to the creditor's account in the accounts payable subsidiary ledger.

Purchases Returns and Allowances	
Dr.	Cr.
–	+
	250.00

Accounts Payable	
Dr.	Cr.
–	+
250.00	

Although it would be possible to credit the Purchases account for returns and allowances, the preferred procedure is to use the Purchases Returns and Allowances account to have a separate record of these transactions. Purchases Returns and Allowances is referred to as a *contra account* because it has a credit balance, which is contrary to the normal debit balance of the Purchases account. The credit balance of Purchases Returns and Allowances is subtracted from the debit balance of the Purchases account.

A business that has only a few purchases returns and allowances each month records these transactions in a general journal. However, in a firm with a sizable number of purchases returns and allowances, it is more efficient to use a special purchases returns and allowances journal.

Posting a Purchases Return or Allowance

Whether purchases returns and allowances are first entered in the general journal or in a special purchases returns and allowances journal, these transactions must be posted to the accounts payable

OBJECTIVE 5
Post purchases returns and allowances from the general journal to the accounts payable subsidiary ledger.

ledger. Figure 8–8 shows how the journal entry previously made to return damaged merchandise to Clothes-R-Us on January 17, 19X3, by Fashion World was posted from the general journal to the creditor's account.

Refer to the general journal entry previously made to record this transaction (page 241). Notice that the debit amount in the general journal entry requires two postings—one to the Accounts Payable account in the general ledger and one to the creditor's account in the subsidiary ledger. This double posting is indicated by placing the account number 205 and a check mark in the Posting Reference column of the journal. A diagonal line separates the two posting references.

FIGURE 8–8
Posting to a Creditor's Account

Name *Clothes-R-Us* **Terms** *n/30*
Address *1002 Valley Street, San Francisco, CA 94118*

DATE		EXPLANATION	POST. REF.	DEBIT	CREDIT	BALANCE
19X3						
Jan.	*1*	*Balance*	✓			*400 00*
	5	*Inv. 8090, 12/31/X2*	*P1*		*1,460 00*	*1,860 00*
	12		*CP1*	*600 00*		*1,260 00*
	17	*CM 37*	*J1*	*250 00*		*1,010 00*

SCHEDULE OF ACCOUNTS PAYABLE

OBJECTIVE 6
Prepare a schedule of accounts payable.

When an accounts payable ledger is used, the Accounts Payable account in the general ledger becomes a control account and serves as a link between the two ledgers. Its balance summarizes the balances of the creditor accounts in the subsidiary ledger.

At the end of each month, after all amounts have been posted from the purchases journal, the cash payments journal, and the general journal to the accounts payable ledger, the balances in this ledger are proved against the balance of the Accounts Payable account in the general ledger. A two-step procedure is followed. First a **schedule of accounts payable** is prepared. This schedule lists all balances owed to creditors. Next the total of the schedule is compared with the balance of the Accounts Payable account in the general ledger. The two figures should be the same.

On January 31, 19X3, the accounts payable ledger of Fashion World contained the accounts shown in Figure 8–9. The schedule of accounts payable illustrated in Figure 8–10 was prepared from these accounts. A comparison of its total with the balance of the Accounts Payable account in the firm's general ledger shows that the two amounts are equal.

FIGURE 8–9
The Accounts Payable Ledger

Name *Clothes-R-Us* Terms *n/30*
Address *1002 Valley Street, San Francisco, CA 94118*

DATE		EXPLANATION	POST. REF.	DEBIT	CREDIT	BALANCE
19X3						
Jan.	1	Balance	√			400 00
	5	Inv. 8090, 12/31/X2	P1		1460 00	1860 00
	12		CP1	600 00		1260 00
	17	CM 37	J1	250 00		1010 00

Name *Clothing Center* Terms *2/10, n/30*
Address *1111 Katie Avenue, San Francisco, CA 94116*

DATE		EXPLANATION	POST. REF.	DEBIT	CREDIT	BALANCE
19X3						
Jan.	18	Inv. 8979, 12/27/X2	P1		1050 00	1050 00

Name *Family Fashions* Terms *n/30*
Address *9927 Old Canton Road, San Francisco, CA 94116*

DATE		EXPLANATION	POST. REF.	DEBIT	CREDIT	BALANCE
19X3						
Jan.	1	Balance	√			750 00
	10		CP1	500 00		250 00
	22	Inv. 8597, 12/31/X2	P1		1280 00	1530 00
	31		CP1	1280 00		250 00

Name *Prestige Clothing Store* Terms *2/10, n/30*
Address *1220 Valley Street, San Francisco, CA 94118*

DATE		EXPLANATION	POST. REF.	DEBIT	CREDIT	BALANCE
19X3						
Jan.	1	Balance	√			550 00
	2	Inv. 43480, 12/28/X2	P1		1625 00	2175 00
	12		CP1	1625 00		550 00
	29		CP1	200 00		350 00

(Continued)

FIGURE 8–9 (Continued)
The Accounts Payable Ledger

Name *Quality Clothes* Terms *2/10, n/30*
Address *808 Spring Hill Road, San Francisco, CA 94112*

DATE		EXPLANATION	POST. REF.	DEBIT	CREDIT	BALANCE
19X3						
Jan.	1	Balance	✓			600 00
	6	Inv. 1234,12/31/X2	P1		2,150 00	2,750 00
	16		CP1	2,150 00		600 00

Name *Wholesale Fashion Shop* Terms *n/30*
Address *3300 Pacific Circle Road, San Francisco, CA 94112*

DATE		EXPLANATION	POST. REF.	DEBIT	CREDIT	BALANCE
19X3						
Jan.	1	Balance	✓			400 00
	4	Inv. 633, 12/30/X2	P1		1,810 00	2,210 00

FIGURE 8–10
A Schedule of Accounts Payable and the Accounts Payable Account

FASHION WORLD
Schedule of Accounts Payable
January 31, 19X3

Clothes-R-Us	1,010 00
Clothing Center	1,050 00
Family Fashions	250 00
Prestige Clothing Store	350 00
Quality Clothes	600 00
Wholesale Fashion Shop	2,210 00
Total	5,470 00

ACCOUNT *Accounts Payable* ACCOUNT NO. *205*

DATE		EXPLANATION	POST. REF.	DEBIT	CREDIT	BALANCE DEBIT	BALANCE CREDIT
19X3							
Jan.	1	Balance	✓				2,700 00
	17		J1	250 00			2,450 00
	31		P1		9,375 00		11,825 00
	31		CP1	6,355 00			5,470 00

DETERMINING THE COST OF PURCHASES

OBJECTIVE 7

Compute the net delivered cost of purchases.

The Purchases account accumulates the cost of merchandise bought for resale. The income statement of a merchandising business contains a section showing the total cost of purchases. This section combines information about the cost of the purchases, freight in, and purchases returns and allowances during the period. Assume that Fashion World has a January 31 balance in the purchases account of $8,610; Freight In, $765; and Purchases Returns and Allowances, $250. The net delivered cost of purchases would be computed as follows.

Purchases	$8,610
Freight In	765
Delivered Cost of Purchases	$9,375
Less Purchases Returns and Allowances	250
Net Delivered Cost of Purchases	$9,125

Notice that the balance of the Purchases account ($8,610) and the balance of the Freight In account ($765) are added to find the delivered cost of purchases ($9,375). The balance of the Purchases Returns and Allowances account ($250) is subtracted from the delivered cost of purchases to find the net delivered cost of purchases ($9,125).

If a firm has no freight charges, the computation of its cost of purchases is simpler. The balance of the Purchases Returns and Allowances account is subtracted from the balance of the Purchases account to find the net cost of purchases for the period, as in the following example.

Purchases	$8,610
Less Purchases Returns and Allowances	250
Net Purchases	$8,360

In Chapter 13 you will see how the complete income statement for a merchandising business is prepared and how the net delivered cost of purchases is used in calculating the results of operations.

INTERNAL CONTROL OF PURCHASES

OBJECTIVE 8

Demonstrate a knowledge of the procedures for effective internal control of purchases.

Because of the large amount of money spent to buy goods, most businesses develop careful procedures for the control of purchases and their payment. In Chapter 26 you will learn about the voucher system, a special system that many firms use to achieve this internal control. Whether the voucher system is in use or not, a business should be sure that its control process includes the following safeguards.

1. All purchases should be made only after proper authorization has been given in writing.
2. Goods should be carefully checked when they are received. They should then be compared with the purchase order and with the invoice received from the supplier.
3. The computations on the invoice should be checked for accuracy.

4. Authorization for payment should be made by someone other than the person who ordered the goods, and this authorization should be given only after all the verifications have been made.
5. Another person should write the check for payment.
6. Prenumbered forms should be used for purchase requisitions, purchase orders, and checks. Periodically the numbers of the documents issued should be verified to make sure that all forms can be accounted for.

One major objective of these procedures is to create written proof that all purchases and payments are properly authorized. Another major objective is to ensure that several different people are involved in the process of buying and receiving goods and making the necessary payments. This division of responsibility provides a system of checks and balances.

In a small firm with a limited number of employees, it may be difficult to achieve as much division of responsibility as is desirable. However, the business should design as effective a set of control procedures as the company's resources will allow.

MANAGERIAL IMPLICATIONS

Management and the accounting staff must work together to make sure that there is good internal control of purchasing operations. A carefully designed system of checks and balances must be set up to protect the business against fraud and errors and against excessive investment in merchandise.

The accounting staff must also make sure that all transactions related to credit purchases of goods are recorded efficiently and that up-to-date information about the amounts owed to creditors is always available. The use of a purchases journal and an accounts payable ledger helps to accomplish these goals.

Maintaining a good credit reputation with suppliers is of great concern to management, and this can be done only when there is a well-run accounting system that pays invoices on time. In addition, a well-run accounting system provides management with information that allows the planning of future cash needs so that sufficient funds are on hand for the payment of suppliers but surplus funds can be invested. Alternatively, if there will be a temporary shortage of funds, management is aware of the problem ahead of time and can arrange a loan or take other measures to handle the situation.

The use of separate accounts for recording purchases of goods, freight charges, and purchases returns and allowances also provides valuable information to management. It makes it possible to analyze all the elements involved in the cost of purchases.

SELF-REVIEW

1. What are cash discounts and why are they offered?
2. What type account is Purchases Returns and Allowances?
3. A firm has a debit balance of $27,580 in its Purchases account and a credit balance of $1,260 in its Purchases Returns and Allowances account. What is the firm's net purchases for the period?
4. What is the purpose of the Freight In account?
5. A firm receives an invoice that reflects the price of goods at $560 and the freight charge of $42. How is this transaction recorded?

Answers to Self-Review

1. A cash discount is a price reduction offered to encourage quick payment of invoices by customers.
2. Purchases Returns and Allowances is a contra asset account that is subtracted from the debit balance of the Purchases account.
3.

Purchases	$27,580
Purchases Returns and Allowances	1,260
Net Purchases	$26,320

4. The purpose of the Freight In account is to accumulate freight charges paid for purchases. Its balance is added to the balance of the Purchases account in the Cost of Goods Sold section of the income statement.
5. The transaction is recorded in the following manner:

Purchases	560	
Freight In	42	
Accounts Payable		602

CHAPTER 8 Review and Applications

CHAPTER SUMMARY

A business with a strong system of internal control will have careful procedures for approving requests for new merchandise, choosing suitable suppliers, placing orders with suppliers, checking goods after they arrive, verifying invoices, and approving payments. In addition, purchases, payments, and returns and allowances will be entered in the firm's accounting records promptly and accurately.

Merchandising businesses normally purchase the majority of their goods on credit. The most efficient way to record such transactions is to use a special purchases journal. With this type of journal, only one line is needed to enter all the data about a credit purchase. Also, the posting process is greatly simplified because no amounts are posted to the general ledger until the end of the month, when summary postings are made to the Purchases, Freight In, and Accounts Payable accounts.

Some purchases of goods are made with the understanding that the buyer will pay the freight charges. The amounts of these charges are debited to an account called Freight In. If the seller pays the freight charge in advance for the buyer, the sum involved appears on the seller's invoice and must be recorded in the purchases journal, along with the price of the goods. In such cases a multicolumn purchases journal is needed.

Returns and allowances on purchases of goods are credited to an account called Purchases Returns and Allowances. These transactions may be recorded in the general journal or in a special purchases returns and allowances journal.

The use of an accounts payable subsidiary ledger helps a firm to keep track of the amounts that it owes to creditors. Postings are made to this ledger on a daily basis. Each credit purchase of goods is posted from the purchases journal, each payment on account is posted from the cash payments journal, and each return or allowance related to a credit purchase is posted from the general journal or the purchases returns and allowances journal. At the end of the month, a schedule of accounts payable is prepared. This schedule lists the balances owed to the firm's creditors and is used in proving the accuracy of the subsidiary ledger. The total of the schedule of accounts payable is compared with the balance of the Accounts Payable account in the general ledger, which serves as a control account. The two amounts should be equal.

Purchases, Freight In, and Purchases Returns and Allowances are temporary accounts that are used to collect data about the cost of purchases during an accounting period. These accounts are reported in the Cost of Goods Sold section of the income statement.

GLOSSARY OF NEW TERMS

Accounts payable ledger (p. 239) A ledger reflecting individual accounts for all creditors

Cash discounts (p. 235) Discounts offered for payment received within a specified period of time

Freight In (p. 232) An account showing transportation charges for items purchased

Invoice (p. 230) A supplier's bill for items ordered and shipped

Purchase allowance (p. 240) A price reduction from the amount originally billed

Purchase discount (p. 235) A cash discount offered to customers buying goods for payment within a specified period

Purchase invoice (p. 234) A bill received for goods purchased

Purchase order (p. 230) An order to the supplier of goods specifying items needed, quantity, price, and credit terms

Purchase requisition (p. 230) A list sent to the purchasing department showing goods to be ordered

Purchase return (p. 240) Return of unsatisfactory goods

Purchases (p. 232) An account used to record cost of goods bought for resale during a period

Purchases journal (p. 232) A special journal used to record the purchase of goods on credit

Receiving report (p. 230) A form showing quantity and condition of goods received

Sales discount (p. 235) A supplier's reduction in price from the amount originally billed

Sales invoice (p. 234) A supplier's billing document

Schedule of accounts payable (p. 242) A list of all balances owed to creditors

Transportation In (p. 232) See Freight In

REVIEW QUESTIONS

1. What major safeguards should be built into a system of internal control for purchases of goods?
2. Why are the invoice date and terms recorded in the purchases journal?
3. A business has purchased some new equipment for use in its operations, not for resale to customers. Should this transaction be entered in the purchases journal? If not, where should it be recorded?
4. What do the following credit terms mean?
   a. n/30
   b. 2/10, n/30
   c. n/10 EOM
5. Why is the use of a Purchases Returns and Allowances account preferred to crediting these transactions to Purchases?

6. On what financial statement do the accounts related to purchases of merchandise appear? In which section of this statement are they reported?
7. How is the net delivered cost of purchases computed?
8. Why is it useful for a business to have an accounts payable ledger?
9. What type of accounts are kept in the accounts payable ledger?
10. What is the relationship of the Accounts Payable account in the general ledger to the accounts payable subsidiary ledger?
11. What is a schedule of accounts payable? Why is it prepared?
12. What is the purpose of a credit memorandum?

MANAGERIAL FOCUS

1. Why should management be concerned about internal control of purchases?
2. How can good internal control of purchases protect a firm from fraud and errors and from excessive investment in merchandise?
3. In what ways would excessive investment in merchandise harm a business?
4. Why should management be concerned about the timely payment of invoices?
5. Why is it important for a firm to maintain a satisfactory credit rating?
6. Suppose you are the new controller of a small but growing company and you find that the firm has a policy of paying cash for all purchases of goods even though it could obtain credit. The president of the company does not like the idea of having debts, but the vice president thinks this is a poor business policy that will hurt the firm in the future. The president has asked your opinion. Would you agree with the president or the vice president? Why?

EXERCISES

EXERCISE 8–1 (Obj. 1)

Tutorial

Identifying journals used to record purchases and related transactions. The transactions below took place at the Open Road Bike Shop. Indicate the numbers of the general ledger accounts that would be debited and credited to record each transaction.

GENERAL LEDGER ACCOUNTS

101 Cash
205 Accounts Payable
501 Purchases
502 Freight In
503 Purchases Returns and Allowances

TRANSACTIONS
1. Purchased merchandise for $700; the terms of the supplier's invoice are 2/10, n/30.
2. Returned some damaged merchandise to a supplier and received a credit memorandum for $125.
3. Issued a check for $400 to a supplier as a payment on account.
4. Purchased merchandise for $920 plus a freight charge of $58; the supplier's invoice is payable in 30 days.
5. Received an allowance for some merchandise that was slightly damaged but can be sold at a reduced price; the supplier's credit memorandum is for $95.
6. Purchased merchandise for $550 in cash.

EXERCISE 8–2
(Obj. 1)
Tutorial

Identifying the journals used to record purchases and related transactions. The accounting system of the Lawn Beauty Shop includes the journals listed below. Indicate which journal would be used to record each of the transactions shown.

JOURNALS

Cash receipts journal
Cash payments journal
Purchases journal
Sales journal
General journal

TRANSACTIONS
1. Purchased merchandise for $900; the terms of the supplier's invoice are 2/10, n/30.
2. Returned some damaged merchandise to a supplier and received a credit memorandum for $250.
3. Issued a check for $500 to a supplier as a payment on account.
4. Purchased merchandise for $750 plus a freight charge of $50; the supplier's invoice is payable in 30 days.
5. Received an allowance for some merchandise that was slightly damaged but can be sold at a reduced price; the supplier's credit memorandum is for $125.
6. Purchased merchandise for $650 in cash.

EXERCISE 8–3
(Obj. 1)
Tutorial

Recording credit purchases. The following transactions took place at the Autoplex Auto Parts Center during the first week of July 19X3. Indicate how these transactions would be entered in a purchases journal like the one shown in this chapter.

TRANSACTIONS

July 1 Purchased batteries for $1,950 plus a freight charge of $32 from the Auto Parts Corporation; received Invoice 8621, dated June 27, which has terms of n/30.

3 Purchased mufflers for $780 plus a freight charge of $20 from the Sterling Company; received Invoice 441, dated June 30, which has terms of 1/10, n/60.

5 Purchased car radios for $2,450 plus freight of $25 from Auto Sounds, Inc.; received Invoice 5500, dated July 1, which has terms of 2/10, n/30.

10 Purchased truck tires for $1,950 from City Tire Company; received Invoice 1120, dated July 8, which has terms of 2/10, n/30.

EXERCISE 8–4 (Obj. 4)

Tutorial

Recording a purchase return. On March 5, 19X3, Elmwood Appliance Center, a retail store, received Credit Memorandum 244 for $980 from the Arrow Corporation. The credit memorandum covered a return of damaged dishwashers originally purchased on Invoice 5566 of March 1. Give the general journal entry that would be made at Elmwood Appliance Center for this transaction.

EXERCISE 8–5 (Obj. 4)

Recording a purchase allowance. On April 3, 19X3, Home Products Company was given an allowance of $250 by Miller Appliances Inc., which issued Credit Memorandum 324. The allowance was for scratches on some stoves that were originally purchased on Invoice 689 of March 20. Give the general journal entry that would be made at Home Products for this transaction.

EXERCISE 8–6 (Obj. 4)

Tutorial

Determining the cost of purchases. On May 31, 19X3, the general ledger of Banner Fashions, a clothing store, showed a balance of $17,680 in the Purchases account, a balance of $578 in the Freight In account, and a balance of $1,810 in the Purchases Returns and Allowances account. What was the delivered cost of the purchases made during May? What was the net delivered cost of these purchases?

EXERCISE 8–7 (Obj. 1, 5)

Errors in recording purchase transactions. The following errors were made in recording transactions in the purchases journal or in posting from it. How will these errors be detected?

a. A credit of $500 to the Cooley Company account in the accounts payable ledger was posted as $50.
b. The Accounts Payable column total of the purchases journal was understated by $50.
c. An invoice of $420 for merchandise from Jones Company was recorded as having been received from James Company, another supplier.
d. A payment of $250 to James Company was debited to Jones Company.

EXERCISE 8–8 (Obj. 4)

Determining the cost of purchases. Complete the schedule below by supplying the missing information:

Net Delivered Cost of Purchases	Case A	Case B
Purchases	(a)	41,800
Freight In	1,500	(c)
Delivered Cost of Purchases	46,800	(d)
Less Purchases Returns and Allowances	(b)	1,800
Net Delivered Cost of Purchases	44,320	46,550

PROBLEMS

PROBLEM SET A

PROBLEM 8–1A
(Obj. 1, 2, 3)

Tutorial

Journalizing credit purchases and purchases returns and allowances and posting to the general ledger. The Skin Deep Photo Mart is a retail store that sells cameras, film, and photographic accessories. The firm's credit purchases and purchases returns and allowances for April 19X5 appear below, along with the general ledger accounts used to record these transactions. The balance shown in Accounts Payable is for the beginning of April.

Instructions

1. Open the general ledger accounts and enter the balance of Accounts Payable for April 1, 19X5.
2. Record the transactions in a three-column purchases journal and in a general journal. Use 12 as the page number for the purchases journal and 36 as the page number for the general journal.
3. Post the entries from the general journal to the proper general ledger accounts.
4. Total and rule the purchases journal as of April 30.
5. Post the column total from the purchases journal to the proper general ledger accounts.
6. Compute the net purchases of the firm for the month of April.

GENERAL LEDGER ACCOUNTS

205 Accounts Payable, $3,476 Cr.
501 Purchases
502 Freight In
503 Purchases Returns and Allowances

TRANSACTIONS

Apr. 1 Purchased instant cameras for $1,995 plus a freight charge of $45 from the Janus Company, Invoice 3445, dated March 26; the terms are 60 days net.

8 Purchased black and white film for $347.50 from General Photographic Products, Invoice 11021, dated April 3, net payable in 45 days.

12 Purchased lenses for $226.50 from the Allied Optical Company, Invoice 2783, dated April 9; the terms are 1/10, n/60.

18 Received Credit Memorandum 216 for $225 from the Janus Company for defective cameras that were returned; the cameras were originally purchased on Invoice 3445 of March 26.

20 Purchased color film for $1,050 plus freight of $25 from General Photographic Products, Invoice 11197, dated April 15, net payable in 45 days.

23 Purchased camera cases for $485 from Houston Leather Goods, Invoice 30138, dated April 18, net due and payable in 45 days.

28 Purchased disk cameras for $2,470 plus freight of $30 from the Briggs Corporation, Invoice 5072, dated April 24; the terms are 2/10, n/30.

30 Received Credit Memorandum 1529 for $60 from Houston Leather Goods; the amount is an allowance for slightly damaged but usable goods purchased on Invoice 30138 of April 18.

(*Note:* Save your working papers for use in Problem 8–2A.)

PROBLEM 8–2A
(Obj. 5, 7)

Posting to the accounts payable ledger and preparing a schedule of accounts payable. This problem is a continuation of Problem 8–1A.

Instructions

1. Set up an accounts payable subsidiary ledger for Skin Deep Photo Mart. Open an account for each of the creditors listed and enter the balances as of April 1, 19X5.
2. Post the individual entries from the purchases journal and the general journal prepared in Problem 8–1A.
3. Prepare a schedule of accounts payable for April 30, 19X5.
4. Check the total of the schedule of accounts payable against the balance of the Accounts Payable account in the general ledger. The two amounts should be equal.

Creditors

Name	Terms	Balance
Allied Optical Company	1/10, n/60	$ 556
Briggs Corporation	2/10, n/30	
General Photographic Products	n/45	2,620
Houston Leather Goods	n/45	300
Janus Company	n/60	

PROBLEM 8–3A
(Obj. 1, 2, 3, 4, 5, 6, 7)

Journalizing credit purchases and purchases returns and allowances, computing the net delivered cost of goods, posting to the general ledger, posting to the accounts payable ledger, and preparing a schedule of accounts payable. The Greenhouse is a retail store that sells garden equipment, furniture, and supplies. Its credit purchases and purchases returns and allowances for June 19X8 are listed below. The general ledger accounts used to record these transactions also appear below. The balance shown is for the beginning of June.

Instructions: Part I

1. Open the general ledger accounts and enter the balance of Accounts Payable for June 1, 19X8.
2. Record the transactions in a three-column purchases journal and in a general journal. Use 6 as the page number for the purchases journal and 18 as the page number for the general journal.

3. Post the entries from the general journal to the proper general ledger accounts.
4. Total, prove, and rule the purchases journal as of June 30.
5. Post the column totals from the purchases journal to the proper general ledger accounts.
6. Compute the net delivered cost of the firm's purchases for the month of June.

GENERAL LEDGER ACCOUNTS

205 Accounts Payable, $4,485 Cr.
501 Purchases
502 Freight In
503 Purchases Returns and Allowances

TRANSACTIONS

June 1 Purchased lawn mowers for $2,350 plus a freight charge of $65 from the Glenn Corporation, Invoice 7701, dated May 26, net due and payable in 60 days.

5 Purchased outdoor chairs and tables for $2,185 plus a freight charge of $69 from the Rustic Garden Furniture Company, Invoice 639, dated June 2; the net amount is due in 45 days.

9 Purchased grass seed for $475 from Superior Lawn Products, Invoice 1864, dated June 4; the credit terms are 30 days net.

16 Received Credit Memorandum 111 for $100 from Rustic Garden Furniture Company; the amount is an allowance for scratches on some of the chairs and tables originally purchased on Invoice 639 of June 2.

19 Purchased fertilizer for $600 plus a freight charge of $32 from Superior Lawn Products, Invoice 73912, dated June 15; the credit terms are 30 days net.

21 Purchased garden hoses for $460 plus a freight charge of $28 from McGill Rubber Company, Invoice 1785, dated June 17, terms of 1/15, n/60.

28 Received Credit Memorandum 223 for $150 from McGill Rubber Company for damaged hoses that were returned; the goods were purchased on Invoice 1785 of June 17.

30 Purchased lawn sprinkler systems for $2,850 plus a freight charge of $80 from the Duval Industries, Invoice 19885, dated June 26; the credit terms are 2/10, n/30.

Instructions: Part II

1. Set up an accounts payable subsidiary ledger for the Greenhouse. Open an account for each of the creditors listed below and enter the balances as of June 1, 19X8.
2. Post the individual entries from the purchases journal and the general journal prepared in Part I.
3. Prepare a schedule of accounts payable for June 30, 19X8.

4. Check the total of the schedule of accounts payable against the balance of the Accounts Payable account in the general ledger. The two amounts should be equal.

Creditors		
Name	**Terms**	**Balance**
Duval Industries	2/10, n/30	
Glenn Corporation	n/60	$2,265
McGill Rubber Company	1/15, n/60	
Rustic Garden Furniture Company	n/45	1,390
Superior Lawn Products	n/30	830

PROBLEM 8–4A
(Obj. 1, 2, 3, 5, 6, 7)

GL

Journalizing credit purchases and purchases returns and allowances, posting to the general ledger, posting to the accounts payable ledger, and preparing a schedule of accounts payable. Lexington Office Products Center is a retail business that sells office equipment, furniture, and supplies. Its credit purchases and purchases returns and allowances for September 19X3 are reflected below. The general ledger accounts and the creditors' accounts in the accounts payable subsidiary ledger used to record these transactions also appear below. The balance shown is for the beginning of September.

Instructions

1. Open the general ledger accounts and enter the balance of Accounts Payable for September 1, 19X3.
2. Open the creditors' accounts in the accounts payable ledger and enter the balances for September 1, 19X3.
3. Record the transactions in a three-column purchases journal and in a general journal. Use 4 as the page number for the purchases journal and 12 as the page number for the general journal.
4. Post to the accounts payable ledger daily.
5. Post the entries from the general journal to the proper general ledger accounts at the end of the month.
6. Total and rule the purchases journal as of September 30.
7. Post the column totals from the purchases journal to the proper general ledger accounts.
8. Prepare a schedule of accounts payable and compare the balance of the Accounts Payable controlling account with the schedule of accounts payable.

GENERAL LEDGER ACCOUNTS

205 Accounts Payable, $7,064 Cr.
501 Purchases
502 Freight In
503 Purchases Returns and Allowances

Creditors		
Name	Terms	Balance
Business Furniture, Inc.	2/10, n/30	$1,400
Carson Office Furniture Company	n/30	2,394
Grant Corporation	n/30	
Merit Paper Company	1/10, n/30	530
United Office Machines, Inc.	n/60	2,740

TRANSACTIONS

Sept. 3 Purchased desks for $1,980 plus a freight charge of $53 from the Carson Office Furniture Company, Invoice 2431, dated August 29; the credit terms are 30 days net.

7 Purchased electronic typewriters for $2,825 from United Office Machines, Inc., Invoice 42917, dated September 2, net due and payable in 60 days.

10 Received Credit Memorandum 165 for $150 from the Carson Office Furniture Company; the amount is an allowance for slightly damaged but usable desks purchased on Invoice 2431 of August 29.

16 Purchased file cabinets for $639 plus a freight charge of $31 from the Grant Corporation, Invoice 8066, dated September 11, terms of 30 days net.

20 Purchased electronic desk calculators for $250 from United Office Machines, Inc., Invoice 32456, dated September 15, net due and payable in 60 days.

23 Purchased bond paper and copying machine paper for $1,875 plus a freight charge of $25 from Merit Paper Company, Invoice 16489, dated September 18; the terms are 1/10, n/30.

28 Received Credit Memorandum 692 for $220 from United Office Machines, Inc., for defective calculators that were returned; the calculators were originally purchased on Invoice 2013 of September 15.

30 Purchased office chairs for $960 plus a freight charge of $40 from Business Furniture, Inc., Invoice 669, dated September 25, terms of 2/10, n/30.

PROBLEM SET B

PROBLEM 8-1B
(Obj. 1, 2, 3)

Tutorial

Journalizing credit purchases and purchases returns and allowances and posting to the general ledger. The Denver Ski Shop is a retail store that sells ski equipment and clothing. The firm's credit purchases and purchases returns and allowances for March 19X5 appear below, along with the general ledger accounts used to record these transactions. The balance shown in Accounts Payable is for the beginning of March.

Instructions

1. Open the general ledger accounts and enter the balance of Accounts Payable for March 1, 19X5.

2. Record the transactions in a three-column purchases journal and in a general journal. Use 12 as the page number for the purchases journal and 36 as the page number for the general journal.
3. Post the entries from the general journal to the proper general ledger accounts.
4. Total and rule the purchases journal as of March 30.
5. Post the column total from the purchases journal to the proper general ledger accounts.
6. Compute the net purchases of the firm for the month of March.

GENERAL LEDGER ACCOUNTS

205 Accounts Payable, $5,402 Cr.
501 Purchases
502 Freight In
503 Purchases Returns and Allowances

TRANSACTIONS

Mar. 1 Purchased ski boots for $1,650 plus a freight charge of $55 from the Mountainside Products, Invoice 6527, dated February 28; the terms are 45 days net.

8 Purchased skis for $2,775 from Hanover Industries, Invoice 4916, dated February 2; the terms are net payable in 30 days.

9 Received Credit Memorandum 155 for $400 from Mountainside Products for damaged ski boots that were returned; the boots were originally purchased on Invoice 6527 of February 28.

12 Purchased ski jackets for $1,250 from Winter Fashions, Inc., Invoice 968, dated February 11, net due and payable in 60 days.

16 Purchased ski poles for $790 from Hanover Industries, Invoice 6617, dated February 15; terms are n/30.

22 Purchased ski pants for $560 from the Hilton Clothing Company, Invoice 64091, dated February 16; terms are 1/10, n/60.

28 Received Credit Memorandum 38 for $105 from Hanover Industries for defective ski poles that were returned; the items were originally purchased on Invoice 6617 of February 15.

31 Purchased sweaters for $825 plus a freight charge of $25 from Century Knit Goods, Invoice 8345, dated February 27; terms are 2/10, n/30.

(*Note:* Save your working papers for use in Problem 8–2B.)

PROBLEM 8–2B (Obj. 5, 7)

Posting to the accounts payable ledger and preparing a schedule of accounts payable. This problem is a continuation of Problem 8–1B.

Instructions

1. Set up an accounts payable subsidiary ledger for Denver Ski Shop. Open an account for each of the creditors listed and enter the balances as of March 1, 19X5.

2. Post the individual entries from the purchases journal and the general journal prepared in Problem 8–1B.
3. Prepare a schedule of accounts payable for March 30, 19X5.
4. Check the total of the schedule of accounts payable against the balance of the Accounts Payable account in the general ledger. The two amounts should be equal.

Creditors		
Name	**Terms**	**Balance**
Century Knit Goods	2/10, n/30	
Hanover Industries	n/30	$ 425
Hilton Clothing Company	1/10, n/60	1,250
Mountainside Products	n/45	1,547
Winter Fashions, Inc.	n/60	2,180

PROBLEM 8–3B
(Obj. 1, 2, 3, 4, 5, 6, 7)

Journalizing credit purchases and purchases returns and allowances, computing the net delivered cost of goods, posting to the general ledger, posting to the accounts payable ledger, and preparing a schedule of accounts payable. The Town Nursery is a retail store that sells garden equipment, furniture, and supplies. Its credit purchases and purchases returns and allowances for November 19X8 are listed below. The general ledger accounts used to record these transactions also appear below. The balance shown is for the beginning of November.

Instructions: Part I

Tutorial

1. Open the general ledger accounts and enter the balance of Accounts Payable for November 1, 19X8.
2. Record the transactions in a three-column purchases journal and in a general journal. Use 6 as the page number for the purchases journal and 18 as the page number for the general journal.
3. Post the entries from the general journal to the proper general ledger accounts.
4. Total, prove, and rule the purchases journal as of November 30.
5. Post the column totals from the purchases journal to the proper general ledger accounts.
6. Compute the net delivered cost of the firm's purchases for the month of November.

GENERAL LEDGER ACCOUNTS

205 Accounts Payable, $6,745 Cr.
501 Purchases
502 Freight In
503 Purchases Returns and Allowances

TRANSACTIONS

Nov. 1 Purchased lawn mowers for $2,890 plus a freight charge of $78 from the Hazel Corporation, Invoice 1201, dated October 26, net due and payable in 45 days.

5 Purchased outdoor chairs and tables for $2,850 plus a freight charge of $50 from the Garden Furniture Shop, Invoice 336, dated October 2; the terms are 1/15, n/60.
9 Purchased grass seed for $574 from Springtime Lawn Center, Invoice 1127, dated October 4; the credit terms are 30 days net.
16 Received Credit Memorandum 011 for $200 from Garden Furniture Shop; the amount is an allowance for scratches on some of the chairs and tables originally purchased on Invoice 336 of October 5.
19 Purchased fertilizer for $800 plus a freight charge of $78 from Springtime Lawn Center, Invoice 1175, dated October 15; the credit terms are 30 days net.
21 Purchased garden hoses for $380 plus a freight charge of $38 from City Rubber Company, Invoice 5817, dated October 17, terms of n/60.
28 Received Credit Memorandum 290 for $75 from City Rubber Company for damaged hoses that were returned; the goods were purchased on Invoice 5817 of October 17.
30 Purchased lawn sprinkler systems for $1,850 plus a freight charge of $40 from the Carlton Industries, Invoice 8891, dated October 26; the credit terms are 2/10, n/30.

Instructions: Part II

1. Set up an accounts payable subsidiary ledger for the Town Nursery. Open an account for each of the creditors listed below and enter the balances as of November 1, 19X8.
2. Post the individual entries from the purchases journal and the general journal prepared in Part I.
3. Prepare a schedule of accounts payable for November 30, 19X8.
4. Check the total of the schedule of accounts payable against the balance of the Accounts Payable account in the general ledger. The two amounts should be equal.

Creditors

Name	Terms	Balance
Carlton Industries	2/10, n/30	$1,075
City Rubber Company	n/60	1,925
Garden Furniture Shop	1/15, n/60	
Hazel Corporation	n/45	2,421
Springtime Lawn Center	n/30	1,324

PROBLEM 8–4B
(Obj. 1, 2, 3, 5, 6, 7)

Journalizing credit purchases and purchases returns and allowances, posting to the general ledger, posting to the accounts payable ledger, and preparing a schedule of accounts payable. Central Office Supply is a retail business that sells office equipment, furniture, and supplies. Its credit purchases and purchases returns and allowances for October 19X3 are reflected below. The general ledger accounts and the creditors' accounts in the accounts payable subsidiary ledger used to record these transactions also appear below. The balance shown is for the beginning of October.

Instructions

1. Open the general ledger accounts and enter the balance of Accounts Payable for October 1, 19X3.
2. Open the creditors' accounts in the accounts payable ledger and enter the balances for October 1, 19X3.
3. Record the transactions in a three-column purchases journal and in a general journal. Use 4 as the page number for the purchases journal and 12 as the page number for the general journal.
4. Post to the accounts payable ledger daily.
5. Post the entries from the general journal to the proper general ledger accounts at the end of the month.
6. Total and rule the purchases journal as of October 31.
7. Post the column totals from the purchases journal to the proper general ledger accounts.
8. Prepare a schedule of accounts payable and compare the balance of the Accounts Payable controlling account with the schedule of accounts payable.

GENERAL LEDGER ACCOUNTS

205 Accounts Payable, $8,779 Cr.
501 Purchases
502 Freight In
503 Purchases Returns and Allowances

	Creditors	
Name	Terms	Balance
Business Machines, Inc.	2/10, n/30	$2,125
International Paper Company	n/30	1,015
Office Furniture Depot	n/30	2,012
Systems Corporation	1/10, n/30	3,627

TRANSACTIONS

Oct. 3 Purchased desks for $1,750 plus a freight charge of $35 from Office Furniture Depot, Invoice 2411, dated September 29; the credit terms are 30 days net.

7 Purchased electronic typewriters for $2,650 from Business Machines, Inc., Invoice 1313, dated September 2, terms of 2/10, n/30.

10 Received Credit Memorandum 1265 for $225 from Office Furniture Depot; the amount is an allowance for slightly damaged but usable desks purchased on Invoice 2411 of September 29.

16 Purchased file cabinets for $698 plus a freight charge of $32 from the Systems Corporation, Invoice 711, dated September 11, terms of 1/10, n/30.

20 Purchased electronic desk calculators for $425 from Business Machines, Inc., Invoice 1917, dated September 15, terms of 2/10, n/30.
23 Purchased bond paper and copying machine paper for $2,242 plus a freight charge of $48 from International Paper Company, Invoice 4816, dated September 18; the terms are n/30.
28 Received Credit Memorandum 296 for $198 from Business Machines, Inc., for defective calculators that were returned; the calculators were originally purchased on Invoice 1917 of September 15.
30 Purchased office chairs for $1,060 plus a freight charge of $60 from Office Furniture Depot, Invoice 2580, dated September 25, terms of n/30.

CHALLENGE PROBLEM

Carter Fashions is a ladies' retail clothing store that sells clothing to women executives. Sales of merchandise and purchases of goods on account for January 19X2, the first month of operation, follow.

Instructions

GL

1. Record the purchases of goods on account on page 4 in a three-column purchases journal.
2. Record the sales of merchandise on account on page 1 in the sales journal.
3. Post the entries from the purchases journal and the sales journal to the individual accounts in the accounts payable and accounts receivable subsidiary ledgers.
4. Total, prove, and rule the journals as of January 31, 19X2.
5. Post the column totals from the special journals to the proper general ledger accounts.
6. Prepare a schedule of accounts payable for January 31, 19X2.
7. Prepare a schedule of accounts receivable for January 31, 19X2.

PURCHASES OF GOODS ON ACCOUNT

Jan. 3 Purchased dresses for $1,250 plus a freight charge of $25 from World of Fashions, Invoice 101, dated December 26; net due and payable in 30 days.
5 Purchased handbags for $870 plus a freight charge of $20 from Handbags-to-Go, Invoice 223, dated December 24; the credit terms are 2/10, n/30.
7 Purchased blouses for $975 plus a freight charge of $15 from Fashions, Inc., Invoice 556, dated December 28; terms 2/10, n/30.
9 Purchased casual pants for $590 from Saturn Company, Invoice 901, dated December 29; terms are n/30.
12 Purchased business suits for $1,350 plus a freight charge of $25 from Executive Clothiers, Invoice 401, dated December 27; terms 2/10, n/30.

18 Purchased shoes for $780 plus freight of $20 from Larry's Shoes, Invoice 111, dated December 23; terms n/60.
25 Purchased hosiery for $350 from the Hosiery Warehouse, Invoice 012, dated January 5, 19X2; terms 2/10, n/30.
29 Purchased scarves and gloves for $400 from Saturn Company, Invoice 980, dated January 8, 19X2; terms n/30.
31 Purchased party dresses for $1,250 plus a freight charge of $25 from Sadie's Wholesale Shop, Invoice 3301, dated January 9, 19X2; terms 2/10, n/30.

SALES OF MERCHANDISE ON ACCOUNT

Jan. 4 Sold two dresses to Michele King; issued Sales Slip 141 for $200 plus $12 sales tax.
5 Sold a handbag to Diane Cooley; issued Sales Slip 142 for $100 plus $6 sales tax.
6 Sold four blouses to Brenda Smith; issued Sales Slip 143 for $100 plus $6 sales tax.
10 Sold casual pants and a blouse to Kathy Harris; issued Sales Slip 144 for $250 plus $15 sales tax.
14 Sold a business suit to Sharon Dennis; issued Sales Slip 145 for $200 plus $12 sales tax.
17 Sold hosiery, shoes, and gloves to Lisa Mariani; issued Sales Slip 146 for $300 plus $18 sales tax.
21 Sold dresses and scarves to Hilda Vasquez; issued Sales Slip 147 for $500 plus $30 sales tax.
24 Sold a business suit to Emily Gunther; issued Sales Slip 148 for $100 plus $6 sales tax.
25 Sold shoes to Helen King; issued Sales Slip 149 for $75 plus $4.50 sales tax.
29 Sold a casual pants set to Shirley Anderson; issued Sales Slip 150 for $100 plus $6 sales tax.
31 Sold a dress and handbag to Carolyn Franklin; issued Sales Slip 151 for $150 plus $9 sales tax.

CRITICAL THINKING PROBLEM

Sarah Weinman, the owner of Thrifty Bed and Bath Shop, was preparing checks for payment of the current month's purchase invoices when she realized that there were two invoices from Standard Towel Company, each for the purchase of 100 red and white striped bath towels. Weinman thinks that Standard must have billed Thrifty twice for the same shipment because she knows the shop would not have needed two orders for 100 red and white bath towels within a month.

1. How can Weinman determine whether Standard Towel Company billed Thrifty Bed and Bath Shop in error or whether Thrifty placed two identical orders for red and white towels?
2. If two orders were placed, how can Weinman prevent duplicate purchases from happening in the future?

CHAPTER

9

Cash Receipts, Cash Payments, and Banking Procedures

OBJECTIVES

1. Record cash receipts in a cash receipts journal.
2. Account for cash short or over.
3. Post from the cash receipts journal to subsidiary and general ledgers.
4. Record cash payments in a cash payments journal.
5. Post from the cash payments journal to subsidiary and general ledgers.
6. Demonstrate a knowledge of procedures for a petty cash fund.
7. Demonstrate a knowledge of internal control routines for cash.
8. Write a check, endorse checks, prepare a bank deposit slip, and maintain a checkbook balance.
9. Reconcile the monthly bank statement.
10. Record any adjusting entries required from the bank reconciliation.
11. Define accounting terms new to this chapter.

The proper handling and recording of cash receipts and cash payments are of vital concern in all types of businesses. Cash is an essential asset for every firm, but it is also the asset that is most easily stolen, lost, or mishandled. Thus a well-managed business has careful procedures to control cash and to record cash transactions.

In this chapter you will learn about the basic principles of internal control for cash receipts and cash payments. You will also see how Fashion World applies these principles to ensure accuracy, honesty, and efficiency in the handling and recording of its cash.

The proper handling of cash receipts and cash payments requires the use of a checking account. When a new business is established, a checking account for the firm should be opened at a local bank. The checking account provides a safe means of storing cash receipts and an efficient method of making cash payments. Fashion World's banking procedures will serve as an example of how businesses use a checking account to manage cash effectively.

NEW TERMS

Bank reconciliation statement ▪ Blank endorsement ▪ Bonding ▪ Canceled check ▪ Cash ▪ Cash payments journal ▪ Cash receipts journal ▪ Cash register proof ▪ Cash short or over ▪ Check ▪ Credit memorandum ▪ Debit memorandum ▪ Deposit in transit ▪ Deposit slip ▪ Dishonored (NSF) check ▪ Drawee ▪ Drawer ▪ Endorsement ▪ Full endorsement ▪ Negotiable ▪ Outstanding checks ▪ Payee ▪ Petty cash analysis ▪ Petty cash fund ▪ Petty cash voucher ▪ Postdated check ▪ Promissory note ▪ Purchases discount ▪ Restrictive endorsement ▪ Sales discount ▪ Service charge ▪ Statement of account

CASH TRANSACTIONS

In accounting, the term **cash** covers checks, money orders, and funds on deposit in a bank as well as currency and coins. A very large number of cash transactions in modern business involve checks.

Cash Receipts

The makeup of a firm's cash receipts depends on the nature of its operations. Some retail businesses, like supermarkets, obtain the bulk of their receipts in the form of currency and coins. Other retail businesses receive a large number of checks in addition to currency and coins. For example, a department store receives checks through the mail from its charge account customers when they pay their monthly bills and receives currency and coins from other customers who pay at the time they buy the goods. Wholesale firms get almost all of their cash receipts in the form of checks.

Cash Payments

For the sake of safety and convenience, businesses make almost all payments by check. In a well-managed firm, only a limited number of transactions that cannot easily be handled by check are paid with currency and coins. Carefully controlled special-purpose funds are set up to take care of payments of this type. For example, a **petty cash fund** is often used to make small payments for items like postage stamps, delivery charges, and minor purchases of office supplies. Some firms maintain a travel and entertainment fund to provide cash for business-related travel and entertainment expenses.

THE CASH RECEIPTS JOURNAL

Most businesses constantly receive and pay out cash. Since these transactions occur often, the accounting system should be designed for quick and efficient recording of cash receipts and payments.

To simplify the recording process for cash receipts, many firms use a special **cash receipts journal.** Like the other special journals, this journal speeds up the initial entry of transactions and eliminates a great deal of repetition in posting.

Recording Transactions in the Cash Receipts Journal

OBJECTIVE 1
Record cash receipts in a cash receipts journal.

The format of the cash receipts journal varies according to the needs of each business. For the sake of efficiency, separate columns are set up for the accounts used most often in recording a firm's cash receipts. In the case of Fashion World, there are two major sources of cash receipts—checks that arrive in the mail from credit customers who are making payments on account and currency and coins received from cash sales. Thus the firm uses the type of cash receipts journal shown in Figure 9–1 on page 266.

Notice that there are separate columns for recording debits to Cash and credits to Accounts Receivable, Sales Tax Payable, and Sales. The Other Accounts Credit section is used for items that do not fit into any of the special columns. The columnar arrangement in this journal greatly simplifies both the initial entry and the posting of cash receipts. Only one line is required for most transactions. In addition, posting to the accounts that are used most often can be done on a summary basis at the end of the month. The only amounts that

FIGURE 9–1
A Cash Receipts Journal

CASH RECEIPTS JOURNAL PAGE 1

DATE		EXPLANATION	POST. REF.	ACCOUNTS RECEIVABLE CREDIT	SALES TAX PAYABLE CREDIT	SALES CREDIT	OTHER ACCOUNTS CREDIT: ACCOUNT TITLE	OTHER ACCOUNTS CREDIT: POST. REF.	OTHER ACCOUNTS CREDIT: AMOUNT	CASH DEBIT
19X3										
Jan.	6	Allen Avery		212 00						212 00
	7	Cash sales			91 20	1520 00				1611 20
	10	John Bell		132 50						132 50
	11	Investment					C. Wells, Capital		5000 00	5000 00
	12	Anthony Blackmon		265 00						265 00
	14	Cash sales			117 90	1965 00	Cash Short/Over		(4 50)	2078 40
	15	Richard Narvaez		53 00						53 00
	16	Cash refund					Supplies		25 00	25 00
	21	Kim English		100 00						100 00
	21	Cash sales			126 60	2110 00				2236 60
	28	Cash sales			21 00	350 00	Cash Short/Over		1 20	372 20
	31	Paul Romero		53 00						53 00
	31	Laura Wilson		130 00						130 00
	31	Cash sales			98 40	1640 00				1738 40
	31	Collection of note					Notes Receivable		200 00	
		David Shaw					Interest Income		9 00	209 00

require individual posting to the general ledger are the ones that appear in the Other Accounts Credit section.

Cash Sales and Sales Taxes

At Fashion World a cash register is used to record the currency and coins received from cash sales and to store the funds until a bank deposit can be made. As each transaction is entered, the cash register produces a receipt for the customer and records data about the sale and the sales tax on an audit tape locked inside the machine. At the end of the day, when the machine is cleared, it prints the totals of the transactions on the audit tape. Then the manager of the store removes the tape, and a **cash register proof** is prepared. This proof is designed to reconcile the currency and coins actually in the machine with the totals shown on the audit tape. After the cash register proof is completed, it is used to enter the cash sales and sales tax in the cash receipts journal. The currency and coins are placed in the night depository of the firm's bank.

For the sake of simplicity, the cash receipts journal illustrated in Figure 9–1 shows weekly rather than daily entries for cash sales. Notice how the cash sales for the week ended January 7 are recorded. The amount of sales tax collected ($91.20) is entered in the Sales Tax Payable Credit column, the amount of sales ($1,520) is entered in the Sales Credit column, and the total amount of cash received ($1,611.20) is entered in the Cash Debit column.

OBJECTIVE 2
Account for cash short or over.

Cash Short or Over

In making change, some errors are certain to occur. When such errors are made, the cash available for deposit from cash sales is either more or less than the amount listed on the audit tape taken from the cash register. If the amount of cash available for deposit is greater than the amount shown on the tape, cash is said to be **over.** If there is less cash than the tape shows, cash is said to be **short.** In practice, cash tends to be short more often than over, perhaps because customers are more likely to notice and complain if they receive too little change than if they receive too much.

For proper control over cash receipts, amounts short or over should be recorded. Since a net shortage is expected, an expense account called Cash Short or Over is used for this purpose. If the account has a credit balance, indicating a cash overage, it becomes a revenue account. The amount short or over is determined at the end of each day when the funds in the cash register are proved against the audit tape. Information about the shortage or overage, if any, appears on the cash register proof.

Although errors in making change can be expected, large shortages or overages, or too frequent shortages or overages, should be investigated. They may indicate dishonesty or incompetence in handling cash.

At Fashion World the amount short or over is recorded in the cash receipts journal when the cash sales are entered. The account title Cash Short or Over and the amount are placed in the Other Accounts Credit section of the journal on the same line with the entry for the cash sales.

Refer to the cash receipts journal shown in Figure 9–1. The firm had a cash shortage of $4.50 for the week ended January 14. Since Cash Short or Over is debited for shortages, the amount was circled when it was entered in the Other Accounts Credit section. This procedure shows that the amount is a debit. The cash receipts journal in Figure 9–1 also shows an entry for a cash overage of $1.20 for the week ended January 28. Since Cash Short or Over is credited for overages, this amount is recorded in the Other Accounts Credit section in the normal manner. If a firm has frequent entries for cash shortages and overages, it may set up a special Cash Short or Over column in its cash receipts journal.

Cash Received on Account

Like most retail businesses that sell on credit, Fashion World bills its customers once a month. It sends a **statement of account** showing the transactions with each customer during the month and the balance owed. The customer is expected to pay within 30 days after receiving the statement.

When checks are received from credit customers, the amounts are entered in the cash receipts journal, and then the checks are deposited in the firm's bank account. Refer to the cash receipts journal shown in Figure 9–1. The entry made on January 6 is for cash received on account from Allen Avery. Notice that the amount ($212.00) is recorded in the Accounts Receivable Credit column and the Cash Debit column.

Cash Discounts on Sales

Most retail firms do not offer discounts for paying an account balance within a certain time, but many wholesale operations do offer cash discounts. For example, a wholesaler may offer a discount of 1 to 2 percent of the total invoice amount if a customer pays within a short discount period. Such a discount is called a **sales discount.**

A sales discount is entered in the cash receipts journal at the time the cash is received. A contra revenue account called Sales Discount is used to record the amount of the discount. For businesses having numerous sales discounts, a column is set up in the cash receipts journal to enter these amounts.

Additional Investment by the Owner

Sometimes the owner of a business makes an additional cash investment. For example, on January 11, 19X3, Carolyn Wells, the owner of Fashion World, invested an additional $5,000 cash because she wanted to start modernizing the store and expanding its product line. The entry for this transaction was made by recording the account title Carolyn Wells, Capital and the amount in the Other Accounts Credit section of the cash receipts journal and by recording the amount in the Cash Debit column.

Receipt of a Cash Refund

Occasionally a firm may receive a cash refund for supplies, equipment, or other assets that were purchased for cash and then returned. For example, on January 16, Fashion World obtained a cash refund of $25 for defective supplies that it returned to the seller. This transaction was recorded in the cash receipts journal shown in Figure 9–1. Notice that the credit to the Supplies account was recorded in the Other Accounts Credit section.

Collection of a Promissory Note and Interest

A **promissory note** is a written promise to pay a specified amount of money on a specific date. Most notes also require that interest be paid at a specified rate. Promissory notes serve as the basis for granting credit in certain sales transactions. In some cases they replace open-account credit when a customer has an overdue balance.

For example, on July 31, 19X2, Fashion World accepted a six-month promissory note shown in Figure 9–2 from David Shaw, a customer who owed $200. Shaw had asked for extra time to pay his balance because of financial difficulties. Fashion World agreed to the arrangement if Shaw would issue a promissory note with annual interest at 9 percent. The note provided more legal protection than Shaw's open account, and the interest gave Fashion World some compensation for the delay in receiving payment.

When the note was obtained, Fashion World made the following general journal entry to record the new asset and to remove Shaw's

FIGURE 9–2
A Promissory Note

$200.00 July 31, 19X2

Six months **AFTER DATE** I **PROMISE TO PAY**

TO THE ORDER OF Fashion World

Two hundred and no/100 - **DOLLARS**

PAYABLE AT City National Bank

VALUE RECEIVED with interest at 9%

NO. 28 **DUE** January 31, 19X3 David Shaw

balance from the firm's accounts receivable. The debit part of the entry involves an asset account called Notes Receivable. The credit part involves both the Accounts Receivable account in the general ledger and Shaw's account in the accounts receivable ledger.

GENERAL JOURNAL PAGE *15*

	DATE		DESCRIPTION	POST. REF.	DEBIT	CREDIT	
1	*19X2*						1
2	*July*	*31*	*Notes Receivable*	*109*	*200 00*		2
3			*Accounts Rec./David Shaw*	*111/✓*		*200 00*	3
4			*Received a 6-month, 9%*				4
5			*note from David Shaw to*				5
6			*replace open account*				6
7							7

On January 31, 19X3, the due date of the note, Fashion World received a check for $209 from Shaw. This sum covered the amount of the note ($200) and the interest owed for the six-month period ($9). The necessary entry is made in the cash receipts journal, as shown in Figure 9–1. Notice that the credits to both Notes Receivable and Interest Income are recorded in the Other Accounts Credit section.

Posting from the Cash Receipts Journal

During the month the amounts recorded in the Accounts Receivable Credit column of the cash receipts journal are posted individually to the appropriate customer accounts in the accounts receivable subsidiary ledger. Similarly, the amounts that appear in the Other Accounts Credit column are posted individually to the proper general ledger accounts. At the end of the month, the cash receipts journal is totaled, proved, and ruled. Then the totals of all columns except the Other Accounts Credit column are posted to the general ledger.

The proof of the cash receipts journal involves comparing column totals to make sure that total debits and credits are equal.

PROOF OF CASH RECEIPTS JOURNAL

	Debits
Cash Debit column	$14,216.30
	Credits
Accounts Receivable Credit column	$ 945.50
Sales Tax Payable Credit column	455.10
Sales Credit column	7,585.00
Other Accounts Credit column	5,230.70
Total	$14,216.30

After all posting work was completed at Fashion World, the firm's cash receipts journal appeared as shown in Figure 9–3.

OBJECTIVE 3
Post from the cash receipts journal to subsidiary and general ledgers.

Posting to the Accounts Receivable Ledger

In order to keep the accounts receivable subsidiary ledger up to date at all times, amounts are posted daily to this ledger from the cash receipts journal. Each figure listed in the Accounts Receivable Credit column is transferred to the account of the customer involved. For example, the $212 received from Allen Avery on January 6 was posted to his account in the subsidiary ledger as shown below. Notice that the posting reference *CR1* was entered in the account to indicate that the data came from page 1 of the cash receipts journal. A check mark (√) in the journal shows that the amount was posted.

FIGURE 9–3
Posted Cash Receipts Journal

CASH RECEIPTS JOURNAL PAGE 1

DATE		EXPLANATION	POST. REF.	ACCOUNTS RECEIVABLE CREDIT	SALES TAX PAYABLE CREDIT	SALES CREDIT	OTHER ACCOUNTS CREDIT: ACCOUNT TITLE	POST. REF.	AMOUNT	CASH DEBIT
19X3										
Jan.	6	Allen Avery	√	212 00						212 00
	7	Cash sales			91 20	1,520 00				1,611 20
	10	John Bell	√	132 50						132 50
	11	Investment					C. Wells, Capital	301	5,000 00	5,000 00
	12	Anthony Blackmon	√	265 00						265 00
	14	Cash sales			117 90	1,965 00	Cash Short/Over	520	(4 50)	2,078 40
	15	Richard Narvaez	√	53 00						53 00
	16	Cash refund					Supplies	129	25 00	25 00
	21	Kim English	√	100 00						100 00
	21	Cash sales			126 60	2,110 00				2,236 60
	28	Cash sales			21 00	350 00	Cash Short/Over	520	1 20	372 20
	31	Paul Romero	√	53 00						53 00
	31	Laura Wilson	√	130 00						130 00
	31	Cash sales			98 40	1,640 00				1,738 40
	31	Collection of note					Notes Receivable	109	200 00	
		David Shaw					Interest Income	491	9 00	209 00
	31	Totals		945 50	455 10	7,585 00			5,230 00	14,216 30
				(111)	(231)	(401)			(X)	(101)

Name *Allen Avery* **Terms** *n/30*
Address *612 Henderson Circle, San Francisco, CA 94118*

DATE		EXPLANATION	POST. REF.	DEBIT	CREDIT	BALANCE
19X3						
Jan.	1	Balance	✓			212 00
	2	Sales Slip 3601	S1	106 00		318 00
	6		CR1		212 00	106 00

Posting to the General Ledger

As noted already, the figures listed in the Other Accounts Credit column of the cash receipts journal are posted individually to the general ledger during the month. For example, the entries of $4.50 and $1.20 made on January 14 and 28 were posted to the Cash Short or Over account as shown below. Notice that the circled amount was posted as a debit. The abbreviation *CR1* appears in the Posting Reference column of the account to indicate the source of the entries, and the account number 520 appears in the cash receipts journal to show that the figures were posted.

ACCOUNT *Cash Short or Over* ACCOUNT NO. *520*

DATE		EXPLANATION	POST. REF.	DEBIT	CREDIT	BALANCE DEBIT	BALANCE CREDIT
19X3							
Jan.	14		CR1	4 50		4 50	
	28		CR1		1 20	3 30	

The use of a special journal for cash receipts allows the summary posting of amounts to Cash and other special amount columns in the journal. At the end of each month, the totals of these columns are posted to the general ledger. For example, the totals posted from the cash receipts journal of Fashion World to Cash, Accounts Receivable, Sales Tax Payable, and Sales are shown in Figure 9–4, page 272.

The account numbers entered beneath the totals in the journal show that the figures have been posted. Notice that an X is placed below the total of the Other Accounts Credit column to indicate that this amount is not posted.

Advantages of the Cash Receipts Journal

The cash receipts journal offers the same type of advantages as the other special journals. It saves time, effort, and recording space. The use of separate columns for the accounts most often debited and credited in recording cash receipts speeds up the initial entry of these transactions and allows summary postings to the general ledger at the end of each month. The elimination of repetitive posting work is especially important because even a small business may

FIGURE 9–4
Posting from the Cash Receipts Journal

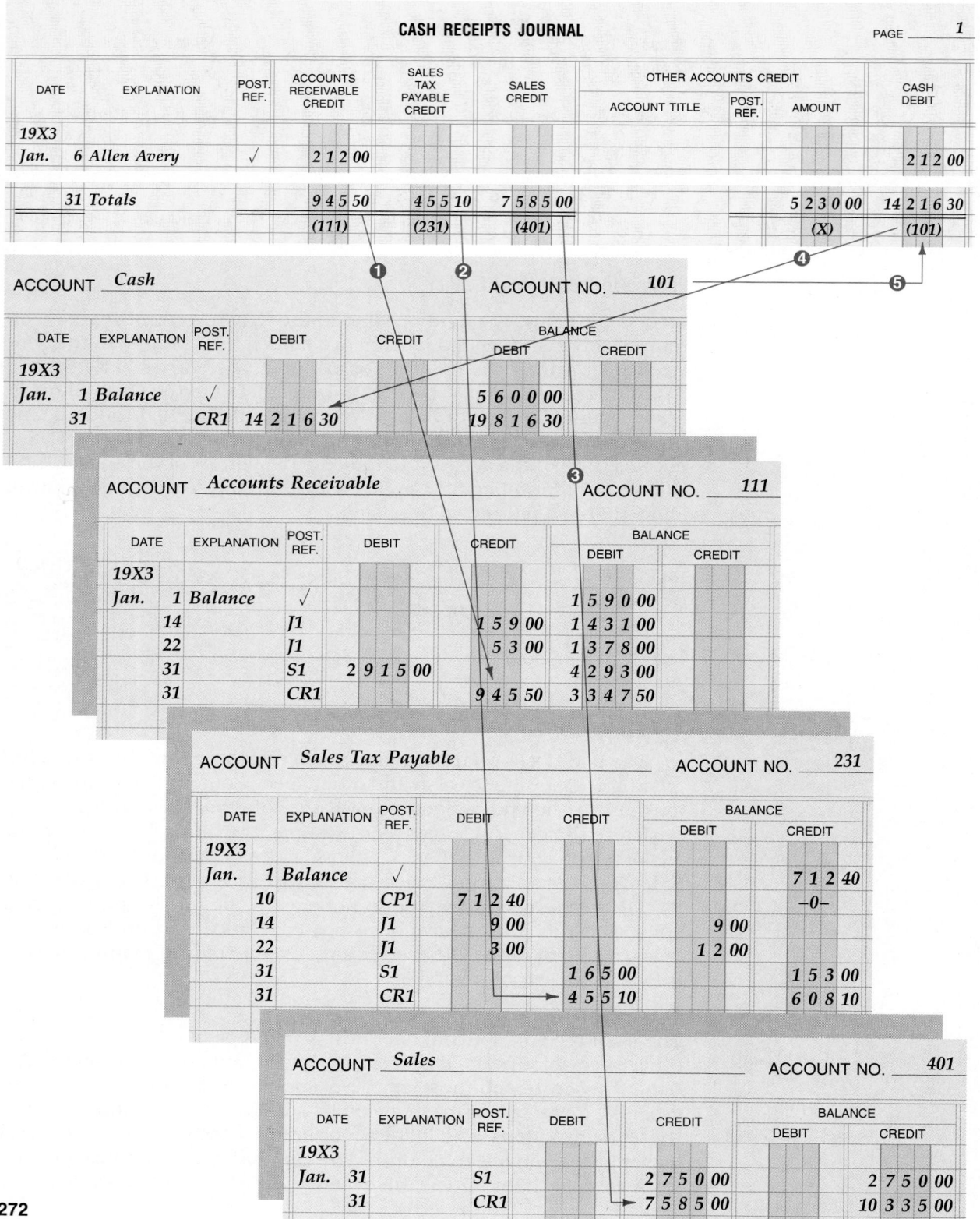

CASH RECEIPTS JOURNAL PAGE *1*

DATE		EXPLANATION	POST. REF.	ACCOUNTS RECEIVABLE CREDIT	SALES TAX PAYABLE CREDIT	SALES CREDIT	OTHER ACCOUNTS CREDIT: ACCOUNT TITLE	POST. REF.	AMOUNT	CASH DEBIT
19X3										
Jan.	*6*	*Allen Avery*	√	*212 00*						*212 00*
	31	*Totals*		*945 50*	*455 10*	*7585 00*			*5230 00*	*14216 30*
				(111)	*(231)*	*(401)*			*(X)*	*(101)*

ACCOUNT *Cash* ACCOUNT NO. *101*

DATE		EXPLANATION	POST. REF.	DEBIT	CREDIT	BALANCE DEBIT	BALANCE CREDIT
19X3							
Jan.	*1*	*Balance*	√			*5600 00*	
	31		*CR1*	*14216 30*		*19816 30*	

ACCOUNT *Accounts Receivable* ACCOUNT NO. *111*

DATE		EXPLANATION	POST. REF.	DEBIT	CREDIT	BALANCE DEBIT	BALANCE CREDIT
19X3							
Jan.	*1*	*Balance*	√			*1590 00*	
	14		*J1*		*159 00*	*1431 00*	
	22		*J1*		*53 00*	*1378 00*	
	31		*S1*	*2915 00*		*4293 00*	
	31		*CR1*		*945 50*	*3347 50*	

ACCOUNT *Sales Tax Payable* ACCOUNT NO. *231*

DATE		EXPLANATION	POST. REF.	DEBIT	CREDIT	BALANCE DEBIT	BALANCE CREDIT
19X3							
Jan.	*1*	*Balance*	√				*712 40*
	10		*CP1*	*712 40*			*–0–*
	14		*J1*	*9 00*		*9 00*	
	22		*J1*	*3 00*		*12 00*	
	31		*S1*		*165 00*		*153 00*
	31		*CR1*		*455 10*		*608 10*

ACCOUNT *Sales* ACCOUNT NO. *401*

DATE		EXPLANATION	POST. REF.	DEBIT	CREDIT	BALANCE DEBIT	BALANCE CREDIT
19X3							
Jan.	*31*		*S1*		*2750 00*		*2750 00*
	31		*CR1*		*7585 00*		*10335 00*

have numerous cash receipts transactions during a month, and individual postings would be very time consuming.

The use of a cash receipts journal along with other special journals also permits the division of labor among the accounting staff. With this arrangement, several employees can enter transactions at the same time. Finally, the cash receipts journal strengthens the audit trail by grouping all transactions involving cash receipts together in one record.

SELF-REVIEW

1. What does the term *cash* mean in business?
2. How are cash shortages and overages recorded? What type account is Cash Short or Over?
3. What is a promissory note? Under what circumstances might a firm receive a promissory note?
4. How are amounts posted from the Accounts Receivable column and the Other Accounts Debit column of the cash receipts journal? Are the totals of these columns posted? If so, how?
5. What are the advantages of using a special journal for cash receipts?

Answers to Self-Review

1. Cash includes checks, money orders, and funds on deposit in a bank as well as currency and coins.
2. Amounts short or over are recorded at the end of the day in the cash receipts journal when the cash sales are entered. If the cash is short, it is entered as Cash Short or Over in the Other Accounts Credit column and the figure is circled to show it is a debit. If the cash is over, no circle is placed around it. Cash Short or Over is an expense account if it has a debit balance and a revenue account if it has a credit balance.
3. A promissory note is a written promise to pay a specified amount of money on a specified date. Promissory notes serve as a basis for granting credit in certain sales transactions or they replace open-account credit when a customer has an overdue balance.
4. Amounts from the Accounts Receivable Credit column are posted as credits to the individual accounts of credit customers who made payments. Amounts in the Other Accounts Credit column are posted individually to the general ledger accounts involved. The total of the Accounts Receivable Credit column is posted as a credit to the Accounts Receivable control account in the general ledger. However, the total of the Other Accounts Credit column is not posted because the individual amounts were previously posted to the general ledger.
5. Using a special journal for cash receipts eliminates repetition in postings and the initial recording of transactions is faster.

Information Block: Communications

Letters

As more and more business professionals use the microcomputer to compose written communication to people within and outside their companies, acceptable document formats become critical. Since your written communication represents the company *and* you, you must be concerned with the appearance of your messages to achieve the best first impression.

Businesses primarily use two document formats for written communication: letters and memorandums. A letter is the primary document format for communication between companies or between a company and a customer. A memorandum (or memo) is the primary document format for communication between people *within* a company. Memorandums are discussed in the information block in Chapter 11.

While formats may differ from one company to the next, the most common letter format is the block format with open punctuation. As shown in the accompanying illustration, a letter in block format with open punctuation is keyed with all lines beginning at the left margin and no punctuation after the salutation and the closing.

The basic letter parts are described below and the spacing for each part is shown in the illustration.

- The **heading** for business letter stationery includes the company's name, address, and telephone number. For a personal business letter on plain paper, the heading includes the sender's address keyed on the lines directly before the date.
- The **date** of the letter shows the month, day, and year the letter is written.
- The **inside address** identifies the name, title, and complete address of the person to whom the letter is being sent. Use the appropriate courtesy title: *Mr., Ms., Miss, Mrs.,* or *Dr.*
- The **salutation** greets the receiver of the letter and must match the first line of the inside address. If you are writing to an individual, follow the word *Dear* with a courtesy title and the receiver's last name. If you are writing to a company, use *Ladies and Gentlemen.*
- The **body** of the letter contains your message, which incorporates the nine steps for planning and developing effective communication that you learned about in an earlier chapter.

- A **subject line,** if used, states the topic of the letter. For example, you may want to refer to an account number, policy number, or invoice number.
- The **closing** is the written good-bye. The most common closing is *Sincerely*.

TRI-STATE ACCOUNTING FIRM
122 Western Avenue, Cincinnati, OH 45202-8903
Telephone: (513) 555-1234
FAX: (513) 555-1235

Heading (Includes Company Name, Address, Telephone and FAX Numbers)

1″ Left and Right Margins

2 inches

May 18, 19XX (Press *Enter* 6 times) — Date

1 inch

Ms. Nancy Shiferdek
Accounts Manager
Jones Supply Company
138 Downs Road
Valparaiso, IN 46383-9382 (Press *Enter* 2 times) — Letter Address

Dear Ms. Shiferdek (Press *Enter* 2 times) — Salutation (Open Punctuation)

INVOICE NUMBER 390-2C (Press *Enter* 2 times) — Subject Line (Optional)

(Press *Enter* 2 times after each paragraph)

Thank you for sending our diskette order so promptly.

According to your recent office supplies catalog, the price for a box of 3.5" DS/HD diskettes is $17.96. The enclosed Invoice Number 390-2C shows $27.96.

After you confirm the appropriate total for our order, you may expect to receive our payment within ten days.

Body

Sincerely (Press *Enter* 4 times) — Closing (Open Punctuation)

Mary Johnson
Accounting Department Manager (Press *Enter* 2 times) — Writer's Name and Title

nm — Reference Initials
Enclosure — Enclosure Notation

- The **writer's name and title** indicate the sender of the message.
- **Reference initials** indicate the person who keyed the letter. When you key your own letter, do not include reference initials.
- An **enclosure notation** (*Enclosure*) is used to indicate that you have enclosed other material with the letter.
- A **copy notation** (*c* followed names) is used to specify the individuals who received a copy of the letter in addition to the person named in the inside address.

Just as people form impressions of you based on your personal appearance, so will they form impressions of you and your company from the appearance of your letters. A perfectly planned and developed message will lose impact in the communication process if the appearance of the message is distracting, inappropriate, or inaccurate. To achieve a favorable impression with your business letters, follow the four steps below.

1. Apply the nine steps for planning and developing messages and the four characteristics of effective business communication. (For a review, see Chapters 3 and 5.)
2. Use company stationery.
3. Confirm that your letter includes the appropriate letter parts with accurate formatting.
4. Sign a letter in the signature space only when you are convinced that you will communicate effectively, resulting in a favorable impression.

Project: Using an actual business letter that you have received or one you borrow from a friend or family member, analyze the appearance of the letter and respond to the following questions.

1. Without reading the letter, what is your initial impression of the company and the sender based on the appearance of the document?
2. After reading the letter, what is your initial impression of the company and the sender based on the appearance and the message?
3. Does the letter include the necessary letter parts with accurate formatting?
4. Is the letter in block format with open punctuation?
5. What revisions would you make to create a more favorable impression?

THE CASH PAYMENTS JOURNAL

A good system of internal control requires that payments be made by check. After approval for a payment is received, one employee prepares the check and records it in the checkbook or check register, and another employee journalizes and posts the transaction. Later in this chapter, we discuss the procedures to be used in issuing checks and maintaining bank records.

Unless a business has just a few cash payments each month, the process of recording these transactions in the general journal is very time consuming. A special **cash payments journal** provides a far more efficient method of recording these transactions.

Recording Transactions in the Cash Payments Journal

OBJECTIVE 4

Record cash payments in a cash payments journal.

The use of a cash payments journal saves a great deal of time and effort in both the journalizing and posting of cash payment transactions. To understand the reasons for this improvement in efficiency, refer to the cash payments journal shown in Figure 9–5 on page 278, which was set up for Fashion World. Notice that this journal has separate columns for the accounts the firm uses most often to record its cash payments—Cash, Accounts Payable, and Purchases Discount. The Other Accounts Debit section allows the entry of items that do not fit into any of the special columns.

The special columns eliminate the need to record the same account titles constantly, and they also eliminate the need for individual postings to Cash, Accounts Payable, and Purchases Discount throughout the month. Instead, summary postings can be made to these accounts at the end of each month. Only the amounts in the Other Accounts Debit section require individual postings to the general ledger.

The procedures for making the most common types of entries in the cash payments journal are explained below.

Payments for Expenses

Most businesses pay a variety of expenses each month. For example, Fashion World issued checks for rent, electricity, telephone service, advertising, and salaries on January 2, 16, 20, 24, and 31. Refer to these entries in the cash payments journal shown in Figure 9–5. Notice that the title of the expense account involved and the amount to be debited to this account are recorded in the Other Accounts Debit section. The offsetting credit appears in the Cash Credit column.

Payments on Account

Merchandising businesses usually make numerous payments on account to suppliers for goods that were purchased on credit. If no cash discount is involved, the entry in the cash payments journal simply requires a debit to Accounts Payable and a credit to Cash. For example, refer to the entries of January 2, 10, and 29 in the cash payments journal shown in Figure 9–5.

FIGURE 9–5
A Cash Payments Journal

CASH PAYMENTS JOURNAL PAGE *1*

DATE		CK. NO.	EXPLANATION	POST. REF.	ACCOUNTS PAYABLE DEBIT	OTHER ACCOUNTS DEBIT: ACCOUNT TITLE	OTHER ACCOUNTS DEBIT: POST. REF.	OTHER ACCOUNTS DEBIT: AMOUNT	PURCHASES DISCOUNT CREDIT	CASH CREDIT
19X3										
Jan.	*2*	*411*	*January rent*			*Rent Expense*		*700 00*		*700 00*
	2	*412*	*Clothes-R-Us*		*600 00*					*600 00*
	9	*413*	*Store fixtures*			*Store Equip.*		*600 00*		*600 00*
	10	*414*	*Tax remittance*			*Sales Tax Pay.*		*712 40*		*712 40*
	10	*415*	*Family Fashions*		*500 00*					*500 00*
	12	*416*	*Prestige Clothing*		*1625 00*				*32 50*	*1592 50*
	13	*417*	*Store supplies*			*Supplies*		*375 00*		*375 00*
	14	*418*	*Withdrawal*			*C. Wells, Draw.*		*1200 00*		*1200 00*
	16	*419*	*Electric bill*			*Utilities Exp.*		*150 00*		*150 00*
	16	*420*	*Quality Clothes*		*2150 00*				*43 00*	*2107 00*
	20	*421*	*Telephone bill*			*Telephone Exp.*		*125 00*		*125 00*
	24	*422*	*Newspaper ad*			*Adver. Exp.*		*210 00*		*210 00*
	29	*423*	*Prestige Clothing*		*200 00*					*200 00*
	31	*424*	*Family Fashions*		*1280 00*				*25 60*	*1254 40*
	31	*425*	*January payroll*			*Salaries Exp.*		*2100 00*		*2100 00*
	31	*426*	*Purchases of goods*			*Purchases*		*1200 00*		*1200 00*
	31	*427*	*Freight charge*			*Freight In*		*75 00*		*75 00*
	31	*428*	*Cash refund*			*Sales Ret. &*				
						Allow.		*40 00*		
						Sales Tax Pay.		*2 40*		*42 40*
	31	*429*	*Note paid to Allen*			*Notes Payable*		*1500 00*		
			Equipment Co.			*Interest Exp.*		*75 00*		*1575 00*
	31	*430*	*Establish petty*			*Petty Cash*		*100 00*		*100 00*
			cash fund			*Fund*				

Purchases Discount is a contra cost account that appears in the Cost of Goods Sold section of the income statement at the end of each accounting period. The credit balance of Purchases Discount is deducted from the debit balance of Purchases.

When there is a cash discount, three elements must be recorded.

1. The total amount of the purchase (as a debit to Accounts Payable)
2. The amount of the discount (as a credit to Purchases Discount)
3. The amount of cash paid out (as a credit to Cash)

The entry of January 12 illustrates the recording procedure for payments on account that involve cash discounts. For example, on January 12, 19X3, Fashion World takes advantage of a 2 percent discount for invoice 43480, dated December 28, 19X2 ($0.02 \times \$1,625 = \$32.50$).

Cash Purchases of Equipment and Supplies

When a firm makes a cash purchase of equipment, supplies, or another asset, the transaction is recorded in the cash payments journal. For example, refer to the entries made on January 9 and 13 in the cash payments journal shown in Figure 9–5. These entries are for cash purchases of store fixtures and store supplies. Notice that the debit part of each entry was recorded in the Other Accounts Debit section.

Payment of Taxes

As discussed before, many retail businesses are required to collect sales tax from their customers. This tax must be remitted periodically to the appropriate tax agency, usually on a monthly or quarterly basis. For example, on January 10, 19X3, Fashion World issued a check for $712.40 to the state sales tax commission to pay the sales tax owed for December 19X2. The necessary entry is shown in the cash payments journal in Figure 9–5. Notice that the debit to Sales Tax Payable appears in the Other Accounts Debit section.

In addition to sales tax, a firm may be required to pay a variety of other taxes, such as payroll taxes and property taxes. The entries for the payment of payroll taxes are presented in Chapter 11.

Payment of Freight Charges

Freight charges on purchases of goods can be handled in two different ways. In some cases, the seller pays the freight charge and then lists it on the invoice sent to the buyer. The total that the buyer pays includes both the price of the goods and the shipping cost. When this arrangement is used, the buyer records the freight charge in the purchases journal, as shown in Chapter 8.

Another common procedure is to have the buyer pay the transportation company directly when the goods arrive. The buyer issues a check for the freight charge and records it in the cash payments journal as shown by the entry on January 31 in Figure 9–5. Freight In is debited for the amount of the freight charge.

Payment of a Cash Refund

When a customer purchases goods for cash and then returns them or receives an allowance, the customer is usually given a cash refund. For example, on January 31, 19X3, Fashion World issued a check for $42.40 to a customer who returned a defective item that was previously sold to her for cash. The check covered the price of the item ($40) and the sales tax collected ($2.40). This transaction was entered in the cash payments journal as shown in Figure 9–5. Notice that the debits to Sales Returns and Allowances and Sales Tax Payable appear in the Other Accounts Debit section.

Cash Purchases of Merchandise

Although most merchandising businesses buy the bulk of their goods on credit, occasional purchases may be made for cash. These purchases are recorded in the cash payments journal, as shown by the entry on January 31 in the Cash Payments Journal in Figure 9–5.

Payment of a Promissory Note and Interest

As discussed already, a promissory note may be issued to settle an overdue account or to obtain goods, equipment, or other property. For example, on August 1, 19X2, Fashion World issued a 6-month promissory note for $1,500 to purchase some new store fixtures from the Allen Equipment Company. The note had an interest rate of 10 percent. This transaction was recorded in the general journal of Fashion World by debiting Store Equipment and crediting a liability account called Notes Payable, as shown below.

GENERAL JOURNAL PAGE *15*

	DATE		DESCRIPTION	POST. REF.	DEBIT	CREDIT	
1	*19X2*						1
2	*Aug.*	*1*	*Store Equipment*	*131*	*1 5 0 0 00*		2
3			*Notes Payable*	*201*		*1 5 0 0 00*	3
4			*Issued a 6-month, 10%*				4
5			*note to Allen Equipment*				5
6			*Company for purchase of*				6
7			*new store fixtures*				7
8							8

On January 31, 19X3, Fashion World issued a check for $1,575 in payment of the note ($1,500) and the interest ($75) owed to the Allen Equipment Company. This transaction was recorded in the cash payments journal, as shown in Figure 9–5. Notice that the entry includes a debit to Notes Payable and a debit to Interest Expense. Both of these amounts appear in the Other Accounts Debit section.

Posting from the Cash Payments Journal

During the month the figures in the Accounts Payable Debit column of the cash payments journal are posted individually to the accounts payable subsidiary ledger, and the figures in the Other Accounts Debit column are posted individually to the general ledger. At the end of the month, the cash payments journal is totaled, proved, and ruled. Then the totals of all columns except the Other Accounts Debit column are posted to the general ledger. The proof of the cash payments journal is prepared as shown below. The column totals are compared to be sure that the debits and credits in the journal are equal.

PROOF OF CASH PAYMENTS JOURNAL

	Debits
Accounts Payable Debit column	$ 6,355.00
Other Accounts Debit column	9,164.80
	$15,519.80

	Credits
Purchases Discount Credit column	$ 101.10
Cash Credit column	15,418.70
	$15,519.80

The cash payments journal of Fashion World for January 19X3, after all posting is completed, appears as shown in Figure 9–6.

FIGURE 9–6
Posted Cash Payments Journal

CASH PAYMENTS JOURNAL PAGE *1*

DATE	CK. NO.	EXPLANATION	POST. REF.	ACCOUNTS PAYABLE DEBIT	OTHER ACCOUNTS DEBIT: ACCOUNT TITLE	OTHER ACCOUNTS DEBIT: POST. REF.	OTHER ACCOUNTS DEBIT: AMOUNT	PURCHASES DISCOUNT CREDIT	CASH CREDIT
19X3									
Jan. 2	*411*	*January rent*			*Rent Expense*	*535*	*700 00*		*700 00*
2	*412*	*Clothes-R-Us*	√	*600 00*					*600 00*
9	*413*	*Store fixtures*			*Store Equip.*	*131*	*600 00*		*600 00*
10	*414*	*Tax remittance*			*Sales Tax Pay.*	*231*	*712 40*		*712 40*
10	*415*	*Family Fashions*	√	*500 00*					*500 00*
12	*416*	*Prestige Clothing*	√	*1 625 00*				*32 50*	*1 592 50*
13	*417*	*Store supplies*			*Supplies*	*129*	*375 00*		*375 00*
14	*418*	*Withdrawal*			*C. Wells, Draw.*	*301*	*1 200 00*		*1 200 00*
16	*419*	*Electric bill*			*Utilities Exp.*	*538*	*150 00*		*150 00*
16	*420*	*Quality Clothes*	√	*2 150 00*				*43 00*	*2 107 00*
20	*421*	*Telephone bill*			*Telephone Exp.*	*553*	*125 00*		*125 00*
24	*422*	*Newspaper ad*			*Adver. Exp.*	*514*	*210 00*		*210 00*
29	*423*	*Prestige Clothing*	√	*200 00*					*200 00*
31	*424*	*Family Fashions*	√	*1 280 00*				*25 60*	*1 254 40*
31	*425*	*January payroll*			*Salaries Exp.*	*541*	*2 100 00*		*2 100 00*
31	*426*	*Purchases of goods*			*Purchases*	*501*	*1 200 00*		*1 200 00*
31	*427*	*Freight charge*			*Freight In*	*502*	*75 00*		*75 00*
31	*428*	*Cash refund*			*Sales Ret. &*	*451*			
					Allow.		*40 00*		
					Sales Tax Pay.	*231*	*2 40*		*42 40*
31	*429*	*Note paid to Allen*			*Notes Payable*	*201*	*1 500 00*		
		Equipment Co.			*Interest Exp.*	*591*	*75 00*		*1 575 00*
31	*430*	*Establish petty*			*Petty Cash*	*105*	*100 00*		*100 00*
		cash fund			*Fund*				
31		*Totals*		*6 355 00*			*9 164 80*	*101 10*	*15 418 70*
				(205)			*(X)*	*(504)*	*(101)*

OBJECTIVE 5

Post from the cash payments journal to subsidiary and general ledgers.

Posting to the Accounts Payable Ledger

If a firm is to have current information about the amounts it owes to creditors, the accounts payable ledger must be kept up to date at all times. For this reason, the figures in the Accounts Payable Debit column of the cash payments journal are posted on a daily basis to the appropriate accounts in the accounts payable subsidiary ledger. The account for Prestige Clothing Store shows the posting of the cash payment to this creditor on January 12. To indicate that the data came from page 1 of the cash payments journal, the abbreviation *CP1* was entered in the Posting Reference column of the account. A check mark (√) in the journal shows that the sum was posted.

Name *Prestige Clothing Store* **Terms** *2/10, n/30*
Address *1220 Valley Street, San Francisco, CA 94118*

DATE		EXPLANATION	POST. REF.	DEBIT	CREDIT	BALANCE
19X3						
Jan.	*1*	*Balance*	√			*550 00*
	2		*P1*		*1,625 00*	*2,175 00*
	12		*CP1*	*1,625 00*		*550 00*
	29		*CP1*	*200 00*		*350 00*

Posting to the General Ledger

Each amount listed in the Other Accounts Debit column of the cash payments journal must be posted individually to the general ledger during the month. For example, the entry of January 2 in the cash payments journal of Fashion World was posted to the Rent Expense account, as shown in Figure 9–6. Again, the abbreviation *CP1* is placed in the account to indicate the source of the data. The account number 535 is entered in the cash payments journal to show that the amount has been posted.

ACCOUNT *Rent Expense* ACCOUNT NO. *535*

DATE		EXPLANATION	POST. REF.	DEBIT	CREDIT	BALANCE DEBIT	BALANCE CREDIT
19X3							
Jan.	*2*		*CP1*	*700 00*		*700 00*	

At the end of each month, summary postings are made to Cash and the other general ledger accounts for which there are separate columns in the cash payments journal. Figure 9–7 shows the posting of the column totals to Cash, Accounts Payable, and Purchases Discount at Fashion World on January 31. Trace these postings from the cash payments journal from Figure 9–6.

FIGURE 9–7
Posted General Ledger Accounts

CASH PAYMENTS JOURNAL PAGE *1*

DATE		CK. NO.	EXPLANATION	POST. REF.	ACCOUNTS PAYABLE DEBIT	OTHER ACCOUNTS DEBIT: ACCOUNT TITLE	OTHER ACCOUNTS DEBIT: POST. REF.	OTHER ACCOUNTS DEBIT: AMOUNT	PURCHASES DISCOUNT CREDIT	CASH CREDIT
19X3										
Jan.	*2*	*411*	*January rent*			*Rent Expense*	*535*	*700 00*		*700 00*
	2	*412*	*Clothes-R-Us*	√	*600 00*					*600 00*
	31		*Totals*		*6355 00*			*9164 80*	*101 10*	*15418 70*
					(205)			*(X)*	*(504)*	*(101)*

ACCOUNT *Cash* ACCOUNT NO. *101*

DATE		EXPLANATION	POST. REF.	DEBIT	CREDIT	BALANCE DEBIT	BALANCE CREDIT
19X3							
Jan.	*1*	*Balance*	√			*5600 00*	
	31		*CR1*	*14216 30*		*19816 30*	
	31		*CP1*		*15418 70*	*4397 60*	

ACCOUNT *Accounts Payable* ACCOUNT NO. *205*

DATE		EXPLANATION	POST. REF.	DEBIT	CREDIT	BALANCE DEBIT	BALANCE CREDIT
19X3							
Jan.	*1*	*Balance*	√				*2700 00*
	17		*J1*	*250 00*			*2450 00*
	31		*P1*		*9375 00*		*11825 00*
	31		*CP1*	*6355 00*			*5470 00*

ACCOUNT *Purchases Discount* ACCOUNT NO. *504*

DATE		EXPLANATION	POST. REF.	DEBIT	CREDIT	BALANCE DEBIT	BALANCE CREDIT
19X3							
Jan.	*31*		*CP1*		*101 10*		*101 10*

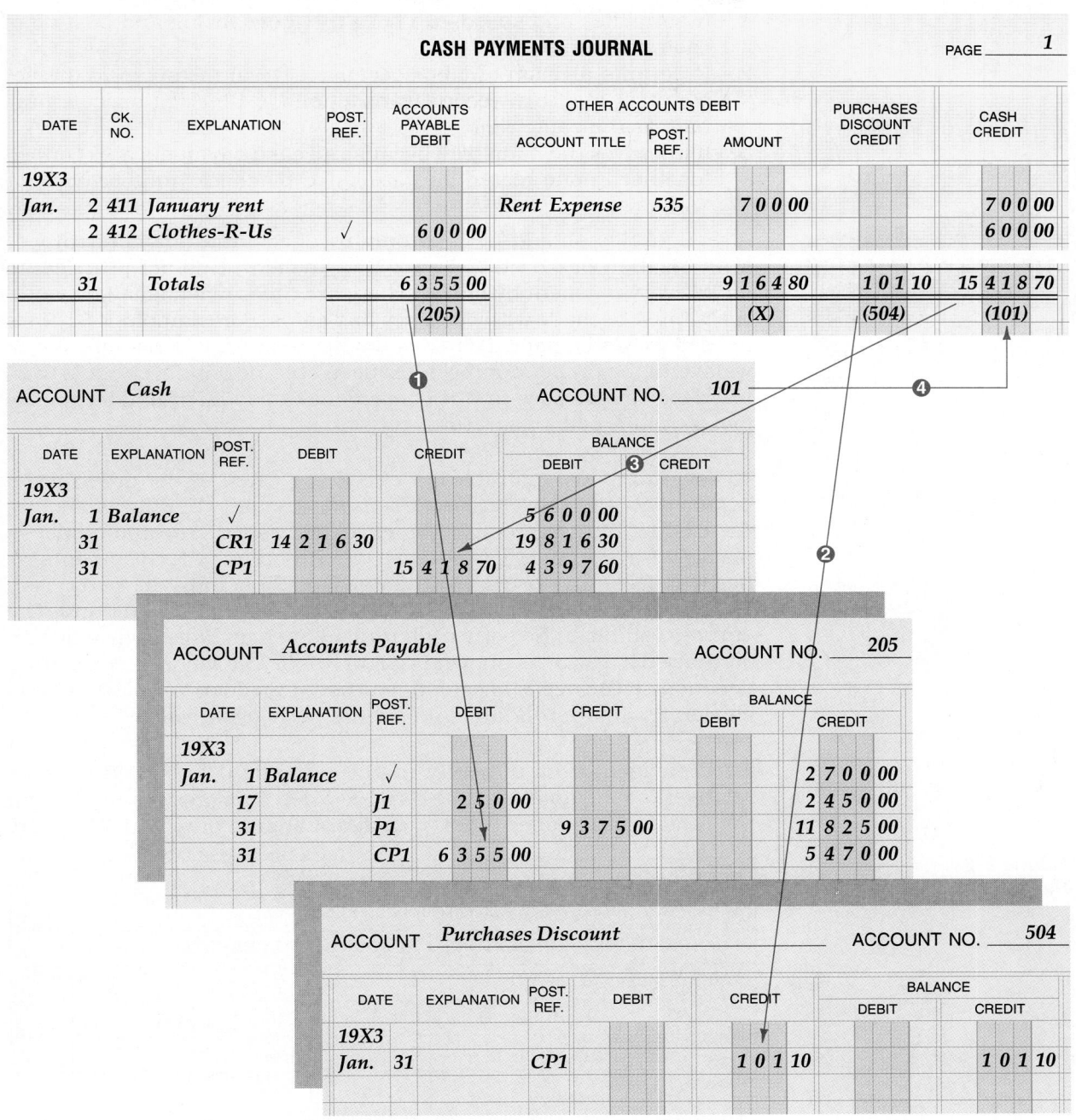

The account numbers are placed beneath the totals in the cash payments journal to indicate that the amounts have been posted. An X is entered below the total of the Other Accounts Debit column to show that this figure is not posted.

Advantages of the Cash Payments Journal

The cash payments journal provides the same kind of benefits as the cash receipts journal and the other special journals.

1. It simplifies and speeds up both the journalizing and posting of cash payments.
2. It permits division of labor because several members of the accounting staff can record transactions in different special journals at the same time.
3. It improves the audit trail because all cash payments are grouped together in one record and are listed by check number.

THE PETTY CASH FUND

OBJECTIVE 6
Demonstrate a knowledge of procedures for a petty cash fund.

Although bills should be paid only by check and only after proper authorization has been given for the payment, it is not practical to make every payment by check. There are times when small expenditures must be made with currency and coins. For example, if $1.25 is needed to send a package to a customer quickly, it is not efficient to wait until the proper approval has been obtained and a check is written. Most businesses find it convenient to pay such small expense items from a petty cash fund.

Establishing the Fund

To set up a petty cash fund, a check is written to the order of the person who will be in charge of the fund—usually the office manager, the cashier, or a secretary. The check is cashed, and the money is placed in a safe or a locked cash box to be used for payments as needed. The entry to record the check establishing the petty cash fund involves a debit to an asset account called Petty Cash Fund. The entry to establish the petty cash fund at Fashion World was made on January 31, 19X3, as shown in Figure 9–6. The amount of the fund depends on the needs of each business. At Fashion World, $100 was chosen as an appropriate sum for the petty cash fund.

Making Payments from the Fund

Each payment from the petty cash fund is usually limited to some relatively small amount, such as $15. When a payment is made from the fund, a form called a **petty cash voucher** is prepared. The petty

FIGURE 9–8
Petty Cash Voucher

PETTY CASH VOUCHER 1
NOTE: This form must be typewritten or filled out in ink.

DESCRIPTION OF EXPENDITURE	ACCOUNT TO BE CHARGED	AMOUNT		
Office Supplies	Supplies 129		8	75
	TOTAL		8	75

RECEIVED THE SUM OF Eight - - - - - - - - - - - - - - - - - - **DOLLARS AND** 75/100 **CENTS**

SIGNED A. C. Abbott **DATE** 2/3/X3 **APPROVED BY** D.W.P. **DATE** 2/3/X3
Delta Office Supply Co.

cash vouchers are numbered in sequence and are dated as they are used. When a payment is made, the amount is entered on the voucher, the purpose of the expenditure is noted, and the account to be charged is identified. The person receiving payment is asked to sign the voucher as a receipt, and the person in charge of the petty cash fund initials the voucher to indicate that it has been checked for completeness.

A petty cash voucher issued to record the payment of $8.75 for office supplies is shown in Figure 9–8.

The Petty Cash Analysis Sheet

A memorandum record of petty cash transactions is made on an **analysis sheet.** Sometimes analysis sheets are kept in a petty cash book. Cash put in the fund is listed in the Receipts column, and cash paid out is listed in the Payments column. Special columns are set up for items that occur frequently, such as Supplies, Delivery Expense, and Miscellaneous Expense. An Other Accounts Debit column is provided for accounts that are not involved in petty cash transactions often. The petty cash analysis sheet prepared at Fashion World during the month of February 19X3 is shown in Figure 9–9.

FIGURE 9–9
Petty Cash Analysis Sheet

PETTY CASH ANALYSIS SHEET — PAGE 1

DATE		VOU. NO.	EXPLANATION	RECEIPTS	PAYMENTS	DISTRIBUTION OF PAYMENTS: SUP. DEBIT	DEL. EXP. DEBIT	MISC. EXP. DEBIT	OTHER ACCOUNTS DEBIT: ACCOUNT TITLE	AMOUNT
19X3										
Feb.	1		Establish fund	100 00						
	3	1	Office supplies		8 75	8 75				
	5	2	Delivery service		12 50		12 50			
	10	3	Withdrawal		15 00				C. Wells, Drawing	15 00
	14	4	Postage stamps		10 00			10 00		
	19	5	Delivery service		9 25		9 25			
	25	6	Window washing		14 00			14 00		
	28	7	Store supplies		7 50	7 50				

Replenishing the Fund

At the end of each month (or sooner if the fund runs low), the petty cash fund is replenished so that there will be an adequate amount of money on hand to meet anticipated needs. The total of the vouchers for payments from the fund plus the cash on hand should always equal the amount of the fund—$100 in this case.

The first step in replenishing the fund is to total each column on the petty cash analysis sheet. A check is then written for an amount sufficient to restore the petty cash fund to its original balance. The amount of this check is recorded in the cash payments journal. The petty cash analysis sheet indicates the accounts to be debited when the check is entered in the cash payments journal. The column totals for February at Fashion World showed the following information.

ACCOUNTS	
Supplies	$16.25
Delivery Expense	21.75
Miscellaneous Expense	24.00
Carolyn Wells, Drawing	15.00
	$77.00

The reimbursement check for $77 is issued to the person in charge of the petty cash fund and is recorded in the cash payments journal, as shown in Figure 9–10.

FIGURE 9–10
Reimbursing the Petty Cash Fund

CASH PAYMENTS JOURNAL — PAGE 5

DATE		CK. NO.	EXPLANATION	POST. REF.	ACCOUNTS PAYABLE DEBIT	OTHER ACCOUNTS DEBIT: ACCOUNT TITLE	POST. REF.	AMOUNT	PURCHASES DISCOUNT CREDIT	CASH CREDIT
19X3										
Feb.	28	490	Replenish petty			Supplies	129	16 25		
			cash fund			C. Wells, Draw.	302	15 00		
						Delivery Exp.	523	21 75		
						Misc. Exp.	593	24 00		77 00

It is important to note that the petty cash analysis sheet is not a record of original entry and the figures on it are not posted to the general ledger accounts. The expenditures made from the petty cash fund are recorded in the cash payments journal only when the fund is replenished. The amounts are posted to the general ledger from the cash payments journal.

The reimbursement check is entered on the petty cash analysis sheet, and the sheet is balanced and ruled as shown in Figure 9–11.

The balance of $100 is brought forward on the first line of the petty cash analysis sheet for March. The amount is entered in the Receipts column. A dash is placed in the Voucher Number column, and "Brought Forward" is used as the explanation.

FIGURE 9–11
Balancing and Ruling the Petty Cash Analysis Sheet

PETTY CASH ANALYSIS SHEET PAGE *1*

DATE		VOU. NO.	EXPLANATION	RECEIPTS	PAYMENTS	DISTRIBUTION OF PAYMENTS				
						SUP. DEBIT	DEL. EXP. DEBIT	MISC. EXP. DEBIT	OTHER ACCOUNTS DEBIT	
									ACCOUNT TITLE	AMOUNT
19X3										
Feb.	*1*		*Establish fund*	*100 00*						
	3	*1*	*Office supplies*		*8 75*	*8 75*				
	5	*2*	*Delivery service*		*12 50*		*12 50*			
	10	*3*	*Withdrawal*		*15 00*				*C. Wells, Drawing*	*15 00*
	14	*4*	*Postage stamps*		*10 00*			*10 00*		
	19	*5*	*Delivery service*		*9 25*		*9 25*			
	25	*6*	*Window washing*		*14 00*			*14 00*		
	28	*7*	*Store supplies*		*7 50*	*7 50*				
	28		*Totals*	*100 00*	*77 00*	*16 25*	*21 75*	*24 00*		*15 00*
	28		*Balance on hand*		*23 00*					
				100 00	*100 00*					
	28		*Balance on hand*	*23 00*						
	28		*Replenish fund*	*77 00*						
	28		*Carried forward*	*100 00*						

Internal Control of the Petty Cash Fund

Whenever there is valuable property or cash to protect, appropriate safeguards must be established. Petty cash is no exception. The following principles of internal control are usually applied to petty cash.

1. The petty cash fund should be used only for payments of a minor nature that cannot conveniently be made by check.
2. The amount of money set aside for the fund should not exceed an approximate amount needed to cover one month's payments from the fund.
3. The check to establish the fund should be made out to the person in charge of the fund—never to the order of Cash.
4. The person in charge of the fund should have sole control of the money and should be the only one authorized to make payments from the fund.
5. The money for the petty cash fund should be kept in a safe, a locked cash box, or a locked drawer.
6. All payments made from the fund should be covered by petty cash vouchers signed by the persons who received the money. The vouchers should show the details of the payments and thus provide an audit trail for the fund.

INTERNAL CONTROL OVER CASH

Every business should have a system of internal control over cash that is specifically tailored to its needs. Accountants play a vital role in designing such a system and work with management to establish

OBJECTIVE 7
Demonstrate a knowledge of internal control routines for cash.

and monitor the system. In developing internal control procedures for the cash receipts and cash payments of a business, certain basic principles must be followed.

Control of Cash Receipts

As noted already, cash is the asset that is most easily stolen, lost, or mishandled. Yet cash is essential to carrying on business operations, so every penny received for goods or services must be protected to make sure that funds are available to pay expenses and take care of other obligations. The following precautionary routines are especially important for cash receipts.

1. Only designated employees should be allowed to receive cash, whether it consists of checks and money orders delivered by mail or currency and coins handed over in person. These employees should be carefully chosen for reliability and accuracy and should be carefully trained. In some firms all employees who handle cash are bonded. **Bonding** is the process by which employees are investigated by an insurance company, and if their characters and backgrounds are satisfactory, their employer is given insurance against losses that may occur if they steal or mishandle the firm's cash.
2. For safety's sake, cash receipts should be kept in a cash register, a locked cash drawer, or a safe while they are on the premises.
3. A record should be made of all cash receipts as the funds come into the business. Typically, for currency and coins, this record consists of an audit tape in a cash register or duplicate copies of prenumbered sales slips issued to the customers. The use of a cash register provides an especially effective means of control because the machine automatically produces a tape showing the amounts entered. This tape is locked inside the register until it is removed by a supervisor.
4. Before a bank deposit is made, the funds should be checked against the record made when the cash was received. The employee who does the checking should not be the one who received or recorded the cash.
5. All cash receipts should be deposited in the bank promptly, preferably every day or even several times a day if very large amounts are involved. The funds should be deposited intact—that is, no cash receipts should be used for payments. The person who makes the bank deposit should not be the one who received and recorded the funds.
6. All transactions involving cash receipts should be entered in the firm's accounting records promptly. The person who makes these entries should not be the one who received the funds or deposited them in the bank.
7. The monthly bank statement should be received and reconciled by someone other than the employees who handled, recorded, and deposited the funds.

One of the advantages of having efficient and speedy procedures for handling and recording cash receipts is that the funds reach the bank sooner. Cash receipts are not kept on the premises for more than a short time, which means that the funds are safer and are quickly available for paying bills owed by the firm.

Control of Cash Payments

The control procedures for cash receipts are only one part of a well-designed system of internal control. There must also be control over payments so that none of the firm's cash is spent without proper authorization or supervision. Obviously, a firm's cash is safe only if there is complete control over incoming and outgoing funds.

Internal control of cash payments can be achieved by adopting the following procedures.

1. All payments should be made by check except for payments from special-purpose cash funds such as a petty cash fund or a travel and entertainment fund.
2. No check should be issued without a properly approved bill, invoice, or other document that describes the reason for the payment.
3. Bills and invoices should be approved only by designated personnel. These individuals should be experienced and reliable.
4. Checks should be prepared and recorded in the checkbook or check register by someone other than the person who approves the payments.
5. Still another person should sign and mail the checks to creditors.
6. Prenumbered check forms should be used. Periodically the numbers of the checks that were issued and the numbers of the blank forms remaining should be verified to make sure that all forms can be accounted for.
7. When the bank statement is reconciled each month, the canceled checks should be carefully verified against the record of checks issued that appears in the checkbook or check register. The reconciliation process should be handled by someone other than the person who prepared and recorded the checks.
8. All transactions involving cash payments should be entered promptly in the firm's accounting records. The person who makes these entries should not be the one who issues the checks and records them in the checkbook or check register.

In a small business it is usually not possible to achieve as much division of responsibility in the handling of cash receipts and cash payments as is recommended here. However, no matter what the size of a firm, efforts should be made to set up effective control procedures for cash.

The subject of internal control will be discussed in more detail in Chapter 26.

SELF-REVIEW

1. What entry is made to record an additional cash investment by the owner of a sole proprietorship? What journal is used?
2. How are amounts posted from the Accounts Payable Debit column and from the Other Accounts credit column of the cash payments journal?
3. Why does a business use a petty cash fund?
4. What is the purpose of the petty cash voucher and the petty cash analysis sheet?
5. When is the petty cash fund replenished?

Answers to Self-Review

1. The entry for an additional cash investment is made by recording the title of the owner's Capital account and the amount in the Other Accounts Credit section of the cash receipts journal and the amount in the Cash Debit column.
2. The amounts in the Accounts Payable Debit column of the cash payments journal are posted as debits to the individual creditors' accounts in the accounts payable ledger. The amounts in the Other Accounts Debit column are posted individually as debits to the general ledger accounts involved. The total of the Accounts Payable Debit column is posted to the Accounts Payable control account in the general ledger. However, the total of the Other Accounts Debit column is not posted because the individual amounts were previously posted to the general ledger.
3. A business uses a petty cash fund for very small expenditures that must be made with currency and coins.
4. The petty cash voucher shows when a payment is made from petty cash, the amount and purpose of the expenditure, and the account to be charged. The petty cash analysis sheet is a memorandum record of petty cash transactions. It is not a record of original entry and no postings are made from it.
5. Petty cash can be replenished at any time if the fund runs low, but it should be replenished at the end of each month in order to have all expenses of the month recorded in the accounting records of the firm.

BANKING PROCEDURES

OBJECTIVE 8

Write a check, endorse checks, prepare a bank deposit slip, and maintain a checkbook balance.

In a firm that has a good system of internal control, cash receipts are deposited often. Keeping substantial amounts of cash on the premises for long periods of time is a dangerous practice. For this reason many businesses make a daily bank deposit, and some make two or three deposits a day. In addition to safeguarding cash, frequent bank deposits provide a steady flow of funds for the payment of expenses and other obligations.

Cash payments must also be safeguarded. Most businesses make payments by check, which provides another internal control over cash.

Writing Checks

A **check** is a written order signed by an authorized person, the **drawer,** instructing a bank, the **drawee,** to pay a specific sum of money to a designated person or firm, the **payee** (see Figure 9–12). Such a check is **negotiable,** which means that ownership of the check can be transferred to another person or firm. As you have already seen, the payee endorses a check to transfer it to a third party.

There are a number of procedures that should be followed in writing a check. For example, in a standard checkbook, the check stub should always be filled out first. Otherwise, it might be forgotten. The stub is important because it contains information that is needed for future reference. Notice that on the first check stub in Figure 9–12, the opening balance of $5,600 for January is at the top, next to the words *Balance Brought Forward.* The amount of the first check, $700, is written next to the words *Amount This Check.* The amount is then subtracted from the total to obtain the new balance of $4,900. The rest of the details recorded on the stub are the date (January 2, 19X3), the name of the payee (Bay Real Estate), and the purpose of the payment (rent for January).

Once the stub is completed, the check portion is filled out. The date, the name of the payee, and the amount in figures and words are

FIGURE 9–12
Checks and Check Stubs

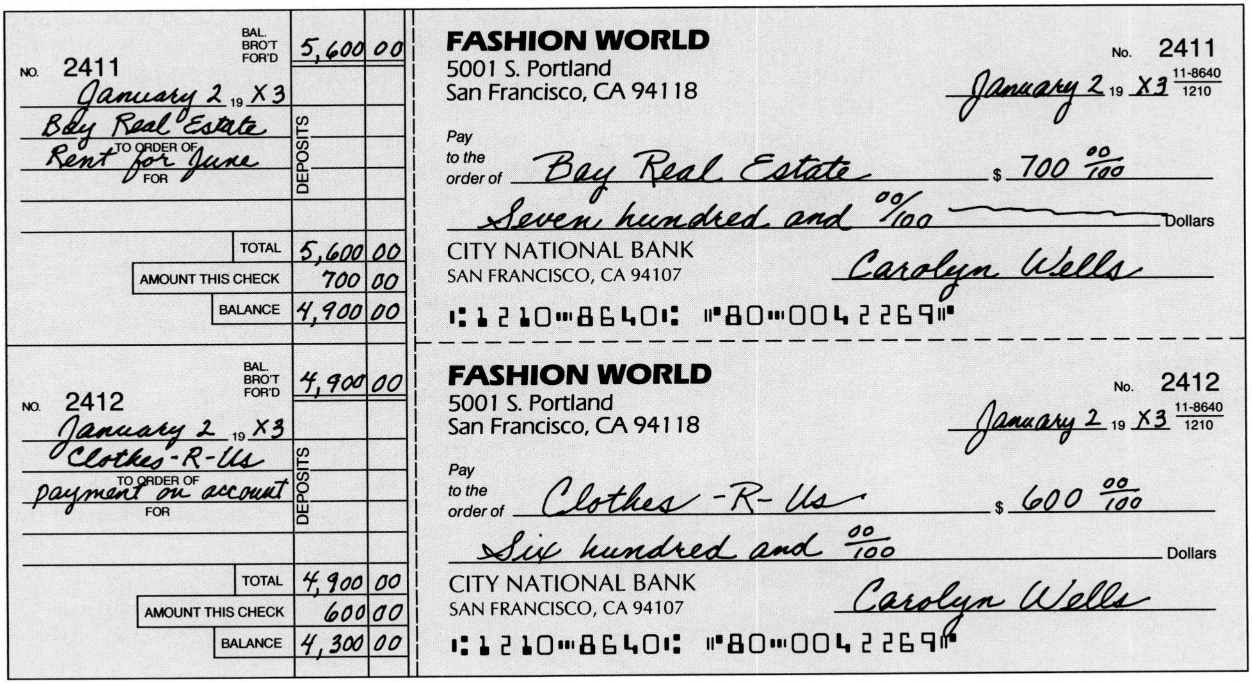
NO. 2411
BAL. BRO'T FOR'D 5,600 00
January 2 19 X3
Bay Real Estate
TO ORDER OF
Rent for June
FOR
DEPOSITS
TOTAL 5,600 00
AMOUNT THIS CHECK 700 00
BALANCE 4,900 00

FASHION WORLD
5001 S. Portland
San Francisco, CA 94118
No. 2411
January 2 19 X3
11-8640/1210
Pay to the order of Bay Real Estate $ 700 00/100
Seven hundred and 00/100 Dollars
CITY NATIONAL BANK
SAN FRANCISCO, CA 94107
Carolyn Wells
⑆1210⋯8640⑆ ⑈80⋯0042269⑈

NO. 2412
BAL. BRO'T FOR'D 4,900 00
January 2 19 X3
Clothes-R-Us
TO ORDER OF
payment on account
FOR
DEPOSITS
TOTAL 4,900 00
AMOUNT THIS CHECK 600 00
BALANCE 4,300 00

FASHION WORLD
5001 S. Portland
San Francisco, CA 94118
No. 2412
January 2 19 X3
11-8640/1210
Pay to the order of Clothes-R-Us $ 600 00/100
Six hundred and 00/100 Dollars
CITY NATIONAL BANK
SAN FRANCISCO, CA 94107
Carolyn Wells
⑆1210⋯8640⑆ ⑈80⋯0042269⑈

written very carefully. A line is drawn to fill any empty space after the payee's name and after the amount in words. When all the data is entered on the check, it should be examined for accuracy and then signed. To be valid, a check must have an authorized signature. For example, at Fashion World only Carolyn Wells, the owner, is authorized to sign checks for the business.

The second check stub in Figure 9–12 shows a payment on account to Clothes-R-Us for $600. After the second check is written, the balance of $4,300 is obtained by deducting the amount of the check, $600, from the balance of $4,900 appearing at the bottom of the first stub.

Endorsing Checks

Each check to be deposited must have an **endorsement.** The endorsement is the legal process by which the payee (the person or firm to whom the check is payable) transfers ownership of the check to the bank. The reason for transferring ownership is to give the bank the legal right to collect payment from the drawer, or payor (the person or firm that issued the check). In the event the check cannot be collected, the endorser guarantees payment to all subsequent holders.

Several forms of endorsement are in common use. Individuals often use a **blank endorsement,** which is the signature of the payee written on the back of the check, preferably at its left end (the perforated end that was torn away from the stub). A check that has a blank endorsement can be further endorsed by the bearer (anyone into whose hands it should fall by intentional transfer or through loss).

A **full endorsement** is much safer. The payee indicates, as part of the endorsement, the name of the person, firm, or bank to whom the check is to be payable. Only the person, firm, or bank named in the full endorsement can transfer it to someone else.

The most appropriate form of endorsement for business purposes is the **restrictive endorsement,** which limits further use of the check to a stated purpose. Usually the purpose is to deposit the check in the firm's bank account. For maximum safety and speedy handling, Fashion World, like most businesses, uses a rubber stamp to make a restrictive endorsement.

All three types of endorsement are illustrated in Figure 9–13.

FIGURE 9–13
Types of Check Endorsement

Preparing the Deposit Slip

A form called a **deposit slip,** or a **deposit ticket,** must be prepared for each bank deposit. These forms are usually provided to the depositor by the bank in which the account is maintained and are usually preprinted with the assigned account number. The deposit slip shown in Figure 9–14 was completed at Fashion World for a deposit made on January 7, 19X3.

FIGURE 9–14
A Deposit Slip

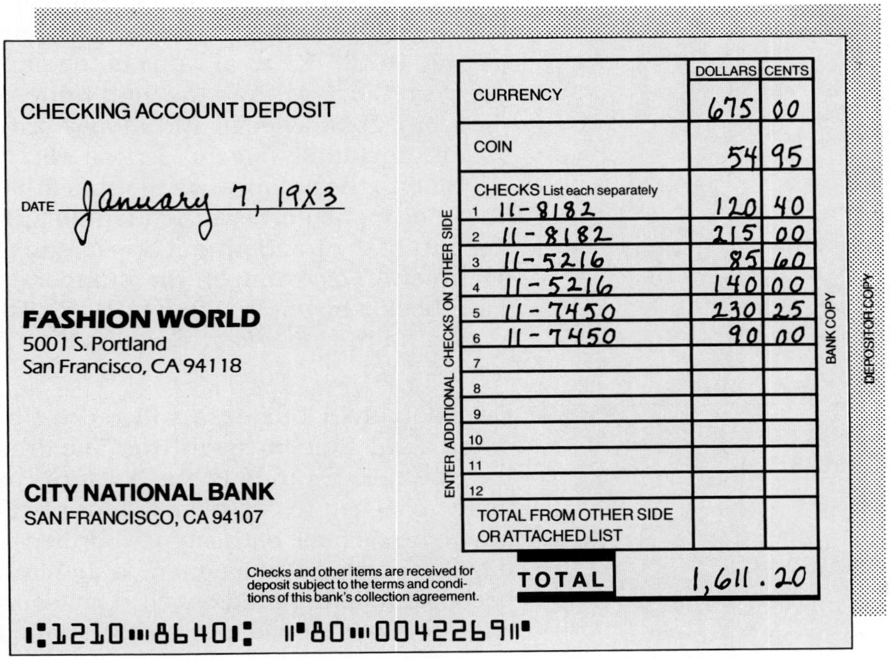

CHECKING ACCOUNT DEPOSIT

DATE January 7, 19X3

FASHION WORLD
5001 S. Portland
San Francisco, CA 94118

CITY NATIONAL BANK
SAN FRANCISCO, CA 94107

	DOLLARS	CENTS
CURRENCY	675	00
COIN	54	95
CHECKS List each separately		
1 11-8182	120	40
2 11-8182	215	00
3 11-5216	85	60
4 11-5216	140	00
5 11-7450	230	25
6 11-7450	90	00
7		
8		
9		
10		
11		
12		
TOTAL FROM OTHER SIDE OR ATTACHED LIST		
TOTAL	1,611.20	

ENTER ADDITIONAL CHECKS ON OTHER SIDE

BANK COPY

DEPOSITOR COPY

Checks and other items are received for deposit subject to the terms and conditions of this bank's collection agreement.

⑆1210⑈8640⑆ ⑈80⑈0042269⑈

Notice the series of numbers preprinted along the lower edge of the deposit slip. The same series of numbers is also preprinted along the bottom of the checks that Fashion World uses (Figure 9–12). A special kind of type called *magnetic ink character recognition (MICR)* type that can be "read" by machines is used for the preprinted numbers.

Numbers of this nature contain codes that are used in sorting and routing checks and deposit slips. The first half of the series shown on the checks and deposit slips provided to Fashion World, 1210 8640, identifies the Federal Reserve District and the bank. In this system, which was set up by the American Bankers Association, the first pair of numbers (12) indicates that the firm's bank is located in the Twelfth Federal Reserve District, and the second pair (10) is a routing number used in the processing of the document. The numbers 8640 identify the City National Bank. The next part of the series, 80 00 42269, is the number that the bank gave to the account of Fashion World.

Banks prefer to use deposit slips and checks encoded with these special numbers so that the documents can be processed rapidly and efficiently by computers and other electronic devices. Documents that are not encoded must be handled manually outside the regular processing, which is a slow and costly procedure with much greater possibility of error.

Deposit slips for checking accounts are usually prepared on multicopy sets of forms. The name of the depositor is either preprinted or handwritten on the deposit slip. Notice that the deposit slip used by Fashion World has the firm's name preprinted.

The current date is written on the deposit slip—in this case, January 7, 19X3. The total value of the paper money is entered opposite the word *Currency*, and the total value of the coins is written opposite the word *Coin.* Checks and money orders presented for deposit are listed individually on the deposit slip. Some banks require that, in addition to the amount, an identification number be entered for each check or money order. The identification number is taken from the top part of the fraction that appears in the upper right corner of each document. For example, the number 11-8640 would be taken from the check shown in Figure 9–12. This identification number is known as the *American Bankers Association (ABA) transit number.*

Handling Postdated Checks

Occasionally a business will receive a **postdated check,** a check dated some time in the future. The drawer of such a check may not have sufficient funds in the bank to cover the check but expects to make a deposit to cover the amount before the check is presented for payment. A check of this type should not be deposited before its date. If it is deposited and payment is then refused by the drawer's bank, it becomes a dishonored check. The issuing or accepting of postdated checks is not considered a proper business practice.

Reconciling the Bank Statement

OBJECTIVE 9

Reconcile the monthly bank statement.

Once a month the bank sends each individual or firm that has a checking account a statement of the deposits received and the checks paid.

The bank statement in Figure 9–15 is typical of those issued by many banks. Notice that it provides a day-by-day listing of all checking account transactions that took place during the month. A code, which is explained at the bottom of the form, identifies any transactions that do not involve checks or deposits. For example, the letters *DM* are used to indicate a debit memorandum and the letters *SC* are used to indicate a service charge. The last column of the bank statement shows the balance of the account at the beginning of the period, after each transaction was recorded, and at the end of the period.

Enclosed with the bank statement are **canceled checks**—the checks that the bank paid during the month. Any checks paid by the bank during the month are sent to the depositor with the bank statement. Banks cancel these checks by stamping the word *PAID* across the face of each one. For the depositor, canceled checks serve as proof of payment and are therefore filed after the reconciliation process is completed.

FIGURE 9–15
A Bank Statement

CITY NATIONAL BANK

FASHION WORLD
5001 S. Portland
San Francisco, CA 94118

ACCOUNT NO. 80-00-42269
PERIOD ENDING January 31, 19X3

CHECKS		DEPOSITS	DATE	BALANCE
AMOUNT BROUGHT FORWARD				5,600.00
		212.00+	January 6	5,812.00
		1,611.20+	January 7	7,423.20
700.00-		132.50+	January 10	6,855.70
600.00-		5,000.00+	January 11	11,255.70
600.00-		265.00+	January 12	10,920.70
712.40-		2,078.40+	January 14	12,286.70
500.00-		53.00+	January 16	11,839.70
1,592.50-	375.00-	25.00+	January 17	9,897.20
	1,200.00-	100.00+	January 21	8,797.20
150.00-		2,236.60+	January 21	10,883.80
2,107.00-		371.00+	January 28	9,147.80
125.00-	210.00-	53.00+	January 31	8,865.80
125.00-DM	400.00-	130.00+	January 31	8,470.80
200.00-		209.00+	January 31	8,479.80
10.00-SC			January 31	8,469.80

LAST AMOUNT IN THIS COLUMN IS YOUR BALANCE

Codes: CC Certified Check; CM Credit Memorandum; DM Deposit Correction; EC Error Correction; OD Overdrawn; SC Service Charge

PLEASE EXAMINE THIS STATEMENT UPON RECEIPT AND REPORT ANY ERRORS WITHIN TEN DAYS.

Usually there is a difference between the ending balance shown on the bank statement and the balance shown in the depositor's checkbook and Cash account. The depositor must determine why the difference exists and bring the two sets of records into agreement. This process is known as reconciling the bank statement.

Changes in the Checking Account Balance

Banks prepare a form called a **credit memorandum** to explain any amount other than a deposit that is added to a checking account. For example, when a note receivable is due, a firm may have its bank collect the note from the maker and place the proceeds in its checking account. The bank lists the amount collected on the next bank statement and encloses a credit memorandum to show the details of the transaction.

When a bank deducts any amount other than a paid check from a depositor's account, it issues a form called a **debit memorandum** and encloses it with the next bank statement. Service charges and dishonored checks are items that are often covered by a debit memorandum.

Bank **service charges** vary a great deal, but some common service charges are for account maintenance, new checkbooks, the use of a night depository, and the collection of a promissory note or another negotiable instrument. The bank uses a debit memorandum to notify the depositor of the type and amount of each service charge.

An example of a debit memorandum is shown in Figure 9–16. This form was sent to Fashion World to explain a deduction of $125 made from its account for a dishonored check. The check itself was also returned by the bank. A **dishonored check** is one that is not honored by the bank on which the check was drawn, normally because there are not sufficient funds in the drawer's account to cover the check. The bank usually stamps the letters *NSF* for *Not Sufficient Funds* on the check. The depositor's records must be adjusted (by means of a journal entry) to reflect the dishonored check. It is also necessary to correct the balance shown in the checkbook.

FIGURE 9–16
A Debit Memorandum

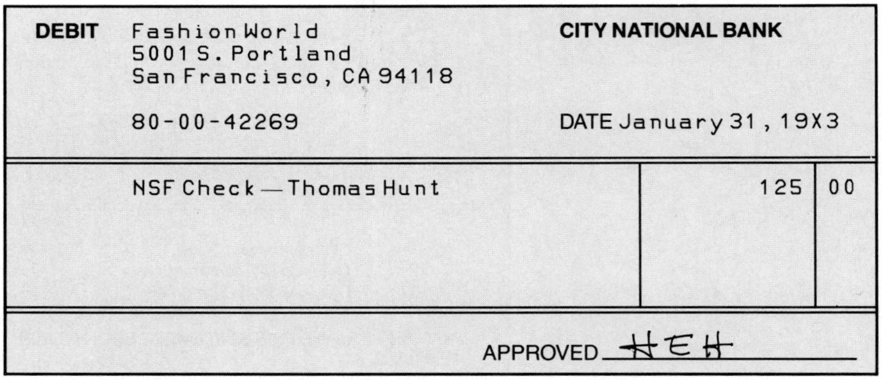
DEBIT Fashion World
5001 S. Portland
San Francisco, CA 94118
CITY NATIONAL BANK

80-00-42269
DATE January 31, 19X3

NSF Check — Thomas Hunt 125 00

APPROVED HEH

After a firm is notified of a dishonored check by its bank, it must contact the drawer to arrange for collection. The drawer may instruct the firm to redeposit the check on a certain date after it places the necessary funds in its account. The firm's records are again adjusted when the check is redeposited.

The Bank Reconciliation Process: An Illustration

Immediately after the bank statement is received, it should be reconciled with the firm's financial records. Once again we use Fashion World to illustrate the process.

On February 5, 19X3, Fashion World received the bank statement shown in Figure 9–15. This statement covers the firm's checking account transactions for the month of January 19X3 and contains an ending balance of $8,469.80. The first action is to compare this amount with the cash balance that appears in the firm's records.

An examination of the Cash account in the firm's general ledger reveals a balance of $4,397.60 on January 31, after postings have been made from the cash receipts and cash payments journals. This amount, shown below, is called the *book balance of cash.* The latest stub in the firm's checkbook also contains the same figure, but this amount is obviously different from the ending balance shown on the bank statement.

ACCOUNT *Cash* ACCOUNT NO. *101*

DATE		EXPLANATION	POST. REF.	DEBIT	CREDIT	BALANCE DEBIT	BALANCE CREDIT
19X3							
Jan.	*1*	*Balance*	√			*5 6 0 0 00*	
	31		*CR1*	*14 2 1 6 30*		*19 8 1 6 30*	
	31		*CP1*		*15 4 1 8 70*	*4 3 9 7 60*	

Since the difference between the bank balance and the book balance may be due to errors made by either the bank or the depositor, the reconciliation process must be undertaken at once. Errors in the firm's records should be corrected immediately. Errors made by the bank should be called to its attention at the earliest possible time. Many banks require that errors in the bank statement be reported within a short period of time, usually 10 days.

If no errors have been made in the calculation of the bank balance or the book balance, there are four basic reasons why the balances may not agree.

1. There may be **outstanding checks**—checks that have been written and entered in the firm's cash payments journal but have not been paid by the bank and charged to the depositor's account before the end of the month.
2. There may be a **deposit in transit**—a deposit that has been recorded in the firm's cash receipts journal but has reached the bank too late to be included in the current month's bank statement.
3. The bank may have deducted service charges or other items that have not yet been entered in the firm's records.
4. The bank may have credited the firm's account for the collection of a promissory note or for other items that have not yet been entered in the firm's records.

Differences stemming from the first two causes listed above require no entries in the firm's records. However, they must be considered in the reconciliation process. Then the next bank statement must be checked to make sure that the outstanding checks and deposits in transit have been picked up in the bank records. Differences arising from the next two causes must be corrected by making entries in the firm's records so that these records will reflect the increases or decreases of cash.

In addition to the differences already discussed, there are other differences that occur less often. The bank may have made an arithmetic error, given credit to the wrong depositor, or charged a check against the wrong depositor's account. Similarly, a check may have been entered in the firm's records at an amount different from the amount for which it was actually written, or it may not have been entered at all. Follow these steps to reconcile a bank statement.

Step 1: The canceled checks and debit memorandums sent by the bank are compared with the deductions listed on the bank statement. As noted already, debit memorandums explain any amounts paid from the account other than checks.

Two debit memorandums were enclosed with the bank statement that Fashion World received for the month of January. The first debit memorandum covered a check for $125 from Thomas Hunt, a customer, that the bank could not collect because there were not sufficient funds in Hunt's account. This NSF check was deducted from the account of Fashion World because the firm had endorsed it, deposited it, and received credit for it. The debit memorandum for Hunt's check is shown in Figure 9–16. The second debit memorandum was for a monthly service charge of $10 that the firm pays for the use of the bank's night depository. Refer to the bank statement in Figure 9–15 to see how the NSF check and the service charge were reported by the bank on this statement.

Step 2: The canceled checks are arranged in numeric order so that they can be compared with the entries in the checkbook and the cash payments journal. In making this comparison, the amount of each check and the check number must be verified. Any differences between the canceled checks and the entries in the cash payments journal must be corrected in the general journal. The endorsement on each canceled check should be examined to make sure that it agrees with the name of the payee.

In verifying canceled checks, it was discovered that a $400 check was mistakenly deducted from the firm's account on January 31. The check was issued by another business, Fashion Arena. The bank was immediately notified of the error and the check was returned to the bank. Fashion World should receive credit for $400 on the next bank statement.

While comparing the canceled checks with the entries in the checkbook and the cash payments journal, a list was made of the numbers and amounts of any outstanding checks. The list of outstanding checks for Fashion World on January 31, 19X3, is:

Check Number	Amount
424	$1,254.40
425	2,100.00
426	1,200.00
427	75.00
428	42.40
429	1,575.00
430	100.00

Step 3: The deposits shown on the bank statement are compared with the deposits recorded in the checkbook and the daily receipts that appear in the cash receipts journal. In the case of Fashion World, the bank statement agrees with the firm's records, except for the January 31 receipts of $1,739.60. The money was placed in the bank's night depository on January 31 but was not actually deposited until the following day, February 1, resulting in a deposit in transit. When the next bank statement arrives, it will be checked to see that the bank has included this deposit in its records.

Step 4: The final step is to prove that all differences between the bank balance and the book balance are accounted for. This is done by preparing a formal **bank reconciliation statement,** such as the one shown in Figure 9–17. Banks often provide a preprinted reconciliation form on the back of the bank statement, but most businesses use analysis paper and set up the reconciliation statement illustrated in the figure.

Notice that there are two main sections in the reconciliation statement. The upper section starts with the ending balance on the bank statement ($8,469.80). To this amount are added any items that increase the bank balance, such as the deposit in transit of

FIGURE 9–17
A Bank Reconciliation Statement

FASHION WORLD
Bank Reconciliation Statement
January 31, 19X3

Balance on bank statement		8 4 6 9 80
Additions:		
Deposit of January 31 in transit	1 7 3 9 60	
Check incorrectly charged to account	4 0 0 00	2 1 3 9 60
		10 6 0 9 40
Deductions for outstanding checks:		
Check 424 of January 31	1 2 5 4 40	
Check 425 of January 31	2 1 0 0 00	
Check 426 of January 31	1 2 0 0 00	
Check 427 of January 31	7 5 00	
Check 428 of January 31	4 2 40	
Check 429 of January 31	1 5 7 5 00	
Check 430 of January 31	1 0 0 00	
Total outstanding checks		6 3 4 6 80
Adjusted bank balance		4 2 6 2 60
Balance in books		4 3 9 7 60
Deductions:		
NSF check	1 2 5 00	
Bank service charge	1 0 00	1 3 5 00
Adjusted book balance		4 2 6 2 60

$1,739.60 and the $400 check that was incorrectly charged to the firm's account. These two amounts are added to the bank balance, which results in a new total of $10,609.40. From this total, items are subtracted that decrease the bank balance, such as the seven outstanding checks. After the subtraction, there is an adjusted bank balance of $4,262.60.

The second section of the reconciliation statement starts with the balance in the books, $4,397.60 in the Cash account. To this balance are added any increases not yet entered in the firm's records, such as the proceeds from a note collected by the bank. Fashion World did not have any such items during January. Next, items that were deducted by the bank but are not yet shown in the firm's records are subtracted from the previous book balance. There are two items of this type—the NSF check of $125 and the bank service charge of $10. Subtracting these amounts from the original book balance results in an adjusted book balance of $4,262.60. The adjusted bank balance and the adjusted book balance agree, as they always should at the end of the reconciliation process.

Adjusting the Financial Records

OBJECTIVE 10

Record any adjusting entries required from the bank reconciliation.

Items in the second section of the reconciliation statement now require entries in the firm's financial records to correct the Cash account balance and the checkbook balance. In the case of Fashion World, two entries must be made, as shown in the general journal illustrated below. The first entry is for the NSF check from Thomas Hunt, a credit customer. Notice that the debit part of this entry charges the amount of the check back to the Accounts Receivable account in the general ledger and Hunt's account in the accounts receivable subsidiary ledger. The second entry is for the bank service charge, which is debited to Miscellaneous Expense. Both entries involve a credit to Cash because the effect of the two items is to decrease the Cash account balance.

GENERAL JOURNAL PAGE 7

	DATE		DESCRIPTION	POST. REF.	DEBIT	CREDIT	
1	*19X3*						1
2	*Feb.*	*1*	*Accounts Rec./Thomas Hunt*	*111/√*	*125 00*		2
3			*Cash*	*101*		*125 00*	3
4			*To record NSF check*				4
5			*returned by bank*				5
6							6
7		*1*	*Miscellaneous Expense*	*593*	*10 00*		7
8			*Cash*	*101*		*10 00*	8
9			*To record bank service*				9
10			*charge for January*				10
11							11

After these entries are posted, the Cash account appears as shown below. Notice that the balance of $4,262.60 agrees with the adjusted book balance on the reconciliation statement. The checkbook balance is also corrected at this point. A notation is made on the latest check stub to explain the decreases in the balance.

ACCOUNT *Cash* ACCOUNT NO. *101*

DATE		EXPLANATION	POST. REF.	DEBIT	CREDIT	BALANCE DEBIT	BALANCE CREDIT
19X3							
Jan.	*1*	*Balance*	✓			*5 6 0 0 00*	
	31		*CR1*	*14 2 1 6 30*		*19 8 1 6 30*	
	31		*CP1*		*15 4 1 8 70*	*4 3 9 7 60*	
Feb.	*1*		*J7*		*1 2 5 00*	*4 2 7 2 60*	
	1		*J7*		*1 0 00*	*4 2 6 2 60*	

Sometimes the bank reconciliation process reveals an error in the firm's financial records. For example, on March 3, 19X3, when Fashion World compared the canceled checks for February with the entries in the firm's cash payments journal and checkbook, it was found that Check 521 of February 21, which was issued to pay for advertising, had been recorded incorrectly. The entries in the firm's records indicated the amount as $245, but the canceled check and the bank statement showed that the sum was actually $240. The error of $5 was listed on the bank reconciliation statement as an addition to the book balance of cash. After the reconciliation process was completed, the following entry was made in the general journal to correct the error. The $5 was also added to the checkbook balance on the latest check stub and an explanatory notation made there.

GENERAL JOURNAL PAGE *9*

	DATE		DESCRIPTION	POST. REF.	DEBIT	CREDIT	
1	*19X3*						1
2	*Mar.*	*3*	*Cash*	*101*	*5 00*		2
3			*Advertising Expense*	*514*		*5 00*	3
4			*To correct error for*				4
5			*Check 521 of Feb. 21*				5
6							6

Internal Control of Banking Activities

The following measures should be taken to achieve internal control over banking activities.

1. Access to the checkbook should be restricted to a few designated employees. When not in use, the checkbook should be kept in a locked drawer or cabinet.

2. Prenumbered check forms should be used. Periodically, the numbers of the checks that were issued and the numbers of the blank forms remaining should be verified to make sure that all forms can be accounted for.
3. Before checks are signed, they should be examined by a person other than the one who prepared them. Each check should be matched against the approved invoice or other payment authorization.
4. The person who prepares the checks and records them in the checkbook should not be the same one who mails them to the payees.
5. The monthly bank statement should be received and reconciled by someone other than the employees who handled, recorded, and deposited the cash receipts and issued the checks.
6. All deposit receipts, canceled checks, voided checks, and bank statements should be filed for future reference. These documents provide backup information and create a strong audit trail for the checking account.

MANAGERIAL IMPLICATIONS

Cash is an essential asset, and it must be carefully safeguarded against loss and theft. Management and the accountant must therefore work together to make sure that a firm has an effective set of controls for cash receipts and cash payments. These controls should be built into all procedures for handling and recording cash.

After a suitable control system has been established, management and the accountant must monitor the system to see that it functions properly and is not abused. Because cash is so vital to business operations, the control system should be checked periodically to be sure that it is working as intended.

Management and the accountant must also set up procedures that will ensure the quick and efficient recording of cash transactions. To make day-to-day decisions properly, management needs current information about the firm's cash position.

Because a checking account plays such a vital role in the handling of cash receipts and cash payments, management must make sure that the account is maintained properly. Management should work with the accountant to establish suitable controls over all of the firm's banking activities—depositing funds, issuing checks, recording checking account transactions, and reconciling the monthly bank statement.

Having accurate, up-to-date information about the checking account is highly important. To pay obligations on time, management must be constantly aware of the firm's cash position so that it can anticipate any shortage of funds and make arrangements to deal with the situation. Conversely, if the firm has more funds on deposit than it needs for current use, management may want to arrange for a temporary investment of the excess amount in order to earn interest.

Information Block: Computers in Accounting

Banks, Check Processing, and Automated Teller Machines

The banking industry in the United States has long been a major user of computers to process customers' checking account transactions and monthly account statements. Banks process a very large volume of such transactions, and the use of computers helps them maintain accurate records.

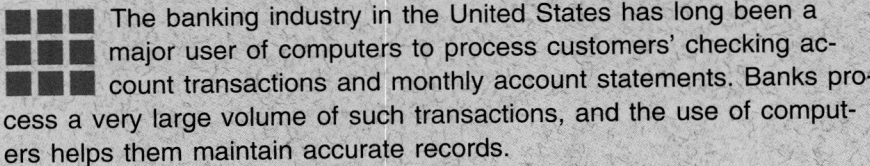

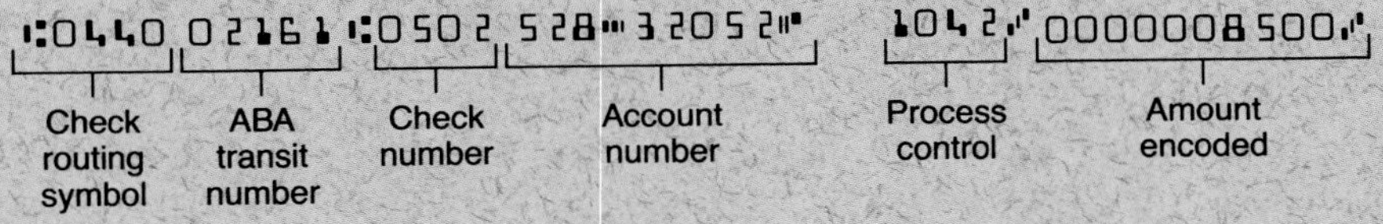

Another aid to accurate records is the special type called magnetic ink character recognition (MICR) that is printed on checks and deposit slips. MICR readers are used almost exclusively by the banking industry to input check-processing data into computers. This special code was adopted during the 1950s by the banking industry and is used on the billions of checks processed annually by banks. The accompanying illustration shows the MICR coding on a check and the meaning of the codes. With these special codings, MICR readers can process over one thousand checks per minute.

Bank computer systems use real-time processing. With this type of system, each bank workstation consists of a terminal that has a direct on-line access to the computer's accounting records. Any deposits or withdrawals are immediately entered into the computer records, and customers' account balances are instantly updated.

Automated teller machines (ATMs) also rely on computers to update accounts as bank customers withdraw cash, make account deposits, and obtain account balances. Newer ATMs allow customers to cash checks and withdraw money in bills and coins. These ATMs have special optical scanners to read checks and equipment that dispenses bills and coins to the customer.

Computers are essential in helping banks to maintain accurate accounting records of customers' accounts. Computer systems also assist bank managers in planning and controlling accounting operations as well as providing improved services to their customers.

SELF-REVIEW

1. Why must a payee endorse a check before depositing it?
2. Describe the different types of endorsement. Which type is most appropriate for a business to use?
3. What is a postdated check? When should this kind of check be deposited?
4. Which items in the bank reconciliation require entries in the firm's financial records to correct the Cash account balance?
5. The person who prepares the checks and records them in the checkbook should be the one who mails them to the payees. Do you agree or disagree, and why?

Answers to Self-Review

1. The payee must endorse a check before depositing it because endorsement is the legal process by which the person or firm to whom the check is payable transfers ownership of the check to the bank.
2. The three types of endorsements are (a) blank endorsement, which consists of the signature of the payee written on the back of the check; (b) full endorsement, which contains the name of the payee plus the name of the firm or bank to whom the check is to be payable; and (c) restrictive endorsement, which limits further use of the check to a stated purpose, usually deposit of the check in the firm's bank account. The restrictive endorsement is the most appropriate type for a business to use.
3. A postdated check is a check that is dated some time in the future. It should not be deposited before its date because the drawer of the check may not have sufficient funds in the bank to cover the check at the current time but expects to make a deposit to cover the amount before the check is presented for payment.
4. Items in the second section of the bank reconciliation statement require entries in the firm's financial records to correct the Cash account balance and make it equal to the checkbook balance.
5. Disagree. To enhance internal control, the person who prepares the checks and records them in the checkbook should not be the one who mails them to the payees.

CHAPTER 9 Review and Applications

CHAPTER SUMMARY

All businesses, whether they are large or small, should have a system of internal control for cash. This system is intended to protect funds from theft and mishandling and to make sure there are accurate records of cash receipts and cash payments.

The use of special journals leads to a more efficient recording process for cash transactions. The cash receipts and cash payments journals contain separate columns for the accounts that a firm uses most often to enter its cash transactions. The provision of these columns eliminates a great deal of repetition in both the initial recording and the posting of cash receipts and cash payments. Much of the posting work can be done on a summary basis at the end of each month.

In business, cash payments should be made by check. However, minor payments are often made in currency and coins through a petty cash fund. A petty cash voucher is prepared for each payment and signed by the person receiving the money. The person who is in charge of the fund keeps a petty cash analysis sheet as a record of the expenditures made. The fund is replenished periodically, with a check drawn for the sum that was spent. At that time, an entry is made in the cash payments journal to record the debits to the accounts involved.

The use of a checking account is essential if a business is to store its cash receipts safely and make cash payments efficiently. For the sake of security, cash receipts should be deposited daily or even several times a day when very large sums are involved. For maximum control over outgoing cash, all payments should be made by check except those that are made from carefully controlled special-purpose cash funds such as a petty cash fund.

Check writing requires careful attention to details. If a standard checkbook is used, the stub should be completed before the check so that it will not be forgotten. The stub provides the information needed to journalize the payment.

As soon as the monthly bank statement is received, it should be reconciled with the cash balance shown in the firm's financial records. Usually differences arise because of deposits in transit, outstanding checks, and bank service charges. However, many factors can lead to a lack of agreement between the bank balance and the book balance. Some differences may require that the firm's records be adjusted after the bank statement is reconciled.

GLOSSARY OF NEW TERMS

Bank reconciliation statement (p. 299) A process of proving that all differences between the bank balance and the checkbook balance are accounted for

Blank endorsement (p. 292) A signature transferring ownership of a check without specifying to whom or for what purpose

Bonding (p. 288) Insurance against losses through employee theft or mishandling of funds

Canceled check (p. 294) A check paid by the bank on which it was drawn

Cash (p. 265) In accounting, currency, coins, checks, money orders, and funds on deposit in a bank

Cash payments journal (p. 277) A special journal used to record transactions involving the payment of cash

Cash receipts journal (p. 265) A special journal used to record transactions involving the receipt of cash

Cash register proof (p. 266) A verification that the amount of currency and coins in a cash register agrees with the amount shown on the audit tape

Cash short or over (p. 267) An account used to record any discrepancies between the amount of currency and coins in the cash register and the amount shown on the audit tape

Check (p. 291) A written order signed by an authorized person instructing a bank to pay a specific sum of money to a designated payee

Credit memorandum (p. 295) A form that explains any amount other than a deposit that is added to a checking account

Debit memorandum (p. 296) A form that explains any amount other than a paid check that is deducted from a checking account

Deposit in transit (p. 297) A deposit reaching the bank too late to be shown on the monthly bank statement

Deposit slip (p. 293) A form prepared to record the deposit of cash or checks to a bank account; also called deposit ticket

Dishonored check (p. 296) A check returned to the depositor because of insufficient funds in the drawer's account; also called an NSF check

Drawee (p. 291) The bank on which a check is written

Drawer (p. 291) The person or firm issuing a check

Endorsement (p. 292) A written authorization that transfers ownership of a check

Full endorsement (p. 292) A signature transferring a check to a specific person, firm, or bank

Negotiable (p. 291) A financial instrument whose ownership can be transferred from one person to another

Outstanding checks (p. 297) Checks that have been issued but have not yet been paid by the bank on which the checks are drawn

Payee (p. 291) The person or firm to whom a check is payable

Petty cash analysis sheet (p. 285) A form used to record transactions involving petty cash

Petty cash fund (p. 265) A special-purpose fund set up to handle payments involving small amounts of money

Petty cash voucher (p. 284) A form used to record the payments made from a petty cash fund

Postdated check (p. 294) A check dated some time in the future

Promissory note (p. 268) A written promise to pay a specified amount of money on a specific date

Purchases discount (p. 278) A reduction in the cost of items purchased given as a result of large-volume purchases or to encourage quick payment of an invoice; also, the account used to record reductions in the cost of purchases

Restrictive endorsement (p. 292) A signature that transfers a check to a specific party for a stated purpose

Sales discount (p. 268) A reduction from an invoice amount offered to encourage quick payment

Service charge (p. 296) A fee charged by a bank to cover the costs of maintaining accounts and providing services

Statement of account (p. 267) A form sent to a firm's customers showing transactions during the month and the balance owed

REVIEW QUESTIONS

1. Describe the major controls for cash receipts.
2. Explain what *bonding* means.
3. Describe the major controls for cash payments.
4. What entry is made to record the collection of a promissory note and interest? What journal is used?
5. Why do some wholesale businesses offer cash discounts to their customers?
6. How does a firm record a check received on account from a customer when a cash discount is involved? What journal is used?
7. How does a firm record a payment on account to a creditor when a cash discount is involved? What journal is used?
8. What type of account is Purchases Discount? How is this account presented on the income statement?
9. When are petty cash expenditures entered in a firm's accounting records?
10. Describe the major controls for petty cash.
11. Why are MICR numbers printed on deposit slips and checks?
12. What is a check?
13. What type of information is entered on a check stub? Why should a check stub be prepared before the check is written?
14. What information is shown on the bank statement?
15. Why is a bank reconciliation prepared?

16. Explain the meaning of the following terms.
    a. Canceled check
    b. Outstanding check
    c. Deposit in transit
    d. Debit memorandum
    e. Credit memorandum
    f. Dishonored check
17. What is the book balance of cash?
18. Give some reasons why the bank balance and the book balance of cash may differ.
19. Why are journal entries sometimes needed after the bank reconciliation statement is prepared?
20. What procedures are used to achieve internal control over banking activities?

MANAGERIAL FOCUS

1. Why should management be concerned about achieving effective internal control over cash receipts and cash payments?
2. How does management benefit when cash transactions are recorded quickly and efficiently?
3. Why do some companies require that all employees who handle cash be bonded?
4. Why is it a good practice for a business to make all payments by check except for minor payments from a petty cash fund?
5. The new accountant for the Asheville Hardware Center, a large retail store, found the following weaknesses in the firm's cash-handling procedures. How would you explain to management why each of these procedures should be changed?
    a. No cash register proof is prepared at the end of each day. The amount of money in the register is considered the amount of cash sales for the day.
    b. Small payments are sometimes made from the currency and coins in the cash register. (The store has no petty cash fund.)
    c. During busy periods for the firm, cash receipts are sometimes kept on the premises for several days before a bank deposit is made.
    d. When funds are removed from the cash register at the end of each day, they are placed in an unlocked office cabinet until they are deposited.
    e. The person who makes the bank deposits also records them in the checkbook, journalizes cash receipts, and reconciles the bank statement.
6. Why should management be concerned about having accurate information about the firm's cash position available at all times?
7. Many banks now offer a variety of computer services to clients. Why is it not advisable for a firm to pay its bank to complete the reconciliation procedure at the end of each month?

8. Assume that you are the newly hired controller at the Norton Company and that you have observed the following banking procedures in use at the firm. Would you change any of these procedures? Why or why not?
   a. A blank endorsement is made on all checks to be deposited.
   b. The checkbook is kept on the top of a desk so that it will be handy.
   c. The same person prepares bank deposits, issues checks, and reconciles the bank statement.
   d. The reconciliation process usually takes place two or three weeks after the bank statement is received.
   e. The bank statement and the canceled checks are thrown away after the reconciliation process is completed.
   f. As a shortcut in the reconciliation process, there is no attempt to compare the endorsements on the back of the canceled checks with the names of the payees shown on the face of these checks.

EXERCISES

EXERCISE 9–1
(Obj. 1)

Tutorial

Recording cash receipts. The following transactions took place at the Madison Shoe Store during the first week of September 19X3. Indicate how these transactions would be entered in a cash receipts journal.

TRANSACTIONS

Sept. 1 Had cash sales of $1,400 plus sales tax of $56; there was a cash overage of $2.
2 Collected $180 on account from Joyce Levin, a credit customer.
3 Had cash sales of $1,250 plus sales tax of $50.
4 Angela Ruiz, the owner, made an additional cash investment of $7,000.
5 Had cash sales of $1,600 plus sales tax of $64; there was a cash shortage of $5.

EXERCISE 9–2
(Obj. 4)

Tutorial

Recording cash payments. The transactions below took place at the Madison Shoe Store during the first week of September 19X3. Indicate how these transactions would be entered in a cash payments journal.

TRANSACTIONS

Sept. 1 Issued Check 3805 for $600 to pay the monthly rent.
1 Issued Check 3806 for $1,220 to the Voss Company, a creditor, on account.
2 Issued Check 3807 for $2,560 to purchase new equipment.
2 Issued Check 3808 for $496 to remit sales tax to the state sales tax authority.

3 Issued Check 3809 for $686 to Hale Company, a creditor, on account for invoice of $700 less cash discount of $14.
4 Issued Check 3810 for $590 to purchase merchandise.
5 Issued Check 3811 for $750 as a cash withdrawal for personal use by Angela Ruiz, the owner.

EXERCISE 9–3 (Obj. 6) Tutorial

Recording the establishment of a petty cash fund. On January 2, 19X8, the Loomis Company issued Check 1297 for $75 to establish a petty cash fund. Indicate how this transaction would be recorded in a cash payments journal.

EXERCISE 9–4 (Obj. 6) Tutorial

Recording the replenishment of a petty cash fund. On January 31, 19X8, the Norton Company issued Check 1344 to replenish its petty cash fund. An analysis of the payments from the fund showed the following totals: Supplies, $21; Delivery Expense, $18; and Miscellaneous Expense, $15. Indicate how this transaction would be recorded in a cash payments journal.

EXERCISE 9–5 (Obj. 9) Tutorial

Analyzing bank reconciliation items. During the bank reconciliation process at the Judd Electronics Company, the items listed below were found to be causing a difference between the bank statement and the firm's records. Indicate whether each item will affect the bank balance or the book balance when the bank reconciliation statement is prepared. Also indicate which of the items would require an accounting entry after the bank reconciliation is completed.

1. An outstanding check.
2. A bank service charge.
3. A check issued by another firm that was charged to Judd's account by mistake.
4. A deposit in transit.
5. A debit memorandum for a dishonored check.
6. A credit memorandum for a promissory note that the bank collected for Judd.
7. An error found in Judd's records, which involves the amount of a check. The firm's checkbook and cash payments journal indicate $202 as the amount, but the canceled check itself and the listing on the bank statement show that $220 was the actual sum.

EXERCISE 9–6 (Obj. 9, 10) Tutorial

Determining an adjusted bank balance. On November 2, 19X4, the Santorelli Corporation received a bank statement showing a balance of $14,920 as of October 31. The firm's records showed $14,362 as the book balance of cash on October 31. The following items were found to be causing the difference between the two balances. Prepare the adjusted bank balance section and the adjusted book balance section of the firm's bank reconciliation statement. Also prepare the necessary journal entries from the bank reconciliation.

1. A bank service charge of $12.
2. A deposit in transit of $857.
3. A debit memorandum for an NSF check from Joe Day for $300.
4. Three outstanding checks: Check 4107 for $129, Check 4109 for $65, and Check 4110 for $1,533.

EXERCISE 9–7
(Obj. 9)

Tutorial

Preparing a bank reconciliation statement. On April 3, 19X7, the Ross Building Supply Company received a bank statement showing a balance of $22,635 as of March 31. The firm's records showed $23,129 as the book balance of cash on March 31. The items listed below were found to be causing the difference between the two balances. Prepare a bank reconciliation statement for the firm as of March 31, 19X7, and prepare the necessary journal entries from the statement.

1. Two outstanding checks: Check 6823 for $710 and Check 6824 for $57.
2. A credit memorandum for a $2,000 noninterest-bearing note receivable that the bank collected for the firm.
3. A debit memorandum for $7, which covers the bank's collection fee for the note.
4. A deposit in transit of $1,240.
5. A check for $89 issued by another firm that was mistakenly charged to Ross's account.
6. A debit memorandum for an NSF check of $1,925 issued by the Ames Construction Company, a credit customer.

PROBLEMS

PROBLEM SET A

PROBLEM 9–1A
(Obj. 1, 2, 3)

Tutorial GL

Journalizing cash receipts and posting to the general ledger. The Video Shack is a retail store that sells blank and prerecorded videocassettes. The firm's cash receipts for February 19X5 are listed below, along with the general ledger accounts used to record these transactions.

Instructions

1. Open the general ledger accounts and enter the balances as of February 1, 19X5.
2. Record the transactions in a cash receipts journal. Use 2 as the page number.
3. Post the individual entries from the Other Accounts Credit section of the cash receipts journal to the proper general ledger accounts.
4. Total, prove, and rule the cash receipts journal as of February 28.
5. Post the column totals from the cash receipts journal to the proper general ledger accounts.

GENERAL LEDGER ACCOUNTS

101	Cash	$ 4,960 Dr.
109	Notes Receivable	350 Dr.
111	Accounts Receivable	1,025 Dr.
129	Supplies	610 Dr.
231	Sales Tax Payable	295 Cr.

301	Kevin Walsh, Capital	34,000 Cr.
401	Sales	
491	Interest Income	
520	Cash Short or Over	

TRANSACTIONS

Feb. 3 Collected $125 from David Weiss, a credit customer, on account.

5 Received a cash refund of $30 for damaged supplies.

7 Had cash sales of $2,140 plus sales tax of $107 during the first week of February; there was a cash shortage of $5.

9 Kevin Walsh, the owner, invested an additional $5,000 cash in the business.

12 Received $95 from Janet Peters, a credit customer, in payment of her account.

14 Had cash sales of $1,760 plus sales tax of $88 during the second week of February; there was an overage of $2.

16 Collected $210 from Karen Stone, a credit customer, to apply toward her account.

19 Received a check from Douglas Moore to pay his $350 promissory note plus interest of $7.

21 Had cash sales of $1,620 plus sales tax of $81 during the third week of February.

25 Joseph Vario, a credit customer, sent a check for $145 to pay the balance he owes.

28 Had cash sales of $1,980 plus sales tax of $99 during the fourth week of February; there was a cash shortage of $3.

PROBLEM 9–2A
(Obj. 4, 5, 6)

GL

Journalizing cash payments, recording petty cash, and posting to the general ledger. The cash payments of the Regal Jewelry Store, a retail business, for July 19X3 are listed below, along with the general ledger accounts used to record these transactions.

Instructions

1. Open the general ledger accounts and enter the balances as of July 1, 19X3.
2. Record all payments by check in a cash payments journal; use 7 as the page number.
3. Record all payments from the petty cash fund on a petty cash analysis sheet; use 7 as the sheet number.
4. Post the individual entries from the Other Accounts Debit section of the cash payments journal to the proper general ledger accounts.
5. Total, prove, and rule the petty cash analysis sheet as of July 31, then record the replenishment of the fund and the final balance on the sheet.
6. Total, prove, and rule the cash payments journal as of July 31.
7. Post the column totals from the cash payments journal to the proper general ledger accounts.

GENERAL LEDGER ACCOUNTS

101	Cash	$12,240 Dr.
105	Petty Cash Fund	
129	Supplies	530 Dr.
201	Notes Payable	700 Cr.
205	Accounts Payable	4,460 Cr.
231	Sales Tax Payable	980 Cr.
302	Helen Shaw, Drawing	
451	Sales Returns and Allowances	
504	Purchases Discount	
511	Delivery Expense	
514	Miscellaneous Expense	
520	Rent Expense	
523	Salaries Expense	
526	Telephone Expense	
591	Interest Expense	

TRANSACTIONS

July 1 Issued Check 1421 for $600 to pay the monthly rent.

2 Issued Check 1422 for $980 to remit sales tax to the state tax commission.

3 Issued Check 1423 for $575 to the Digital Watch Company, a creditor, in payment of Invoice 8680, June 5.

4 Issued Check 1424 for $100 to establish a petty cash fund. (After journalizing this transaction, be sure to enter it on the first line of the petty cash analysis sheet.)

5 Paid $15 from the petty cash fund for office supplies, Petty Cash Voucher 1.

7 Issued Check 1425 for $721 to the Savoy Corporation in payment of a $700 promissory note and interest of $21.

8 Paid $10 from the petty cash fund for postage stamps, Petty Cash Voucher 2.

10 Issued Check 1426 for $130 to a customer as a cash refund for a defective watch that was returned; the original sale was made for cash.

12 Issued Check 1427 for $78 to pay the monthly telephone bill.

14 Issued Check 1428 for $1,225 to Gem Importers, a creditor, in payment of Invoice 36892 of July 6 ($1,250) less a cash discount ($25).

15 Paid $9.25 from the petty cash fund for delivery service, Petty Cash Voucher 3.

17 Issued Check 1429 for $175 to make a cash purchase of store supplies.

20 Issued Check 1430 for $686 to Designer Chains, Inc., a creditor, in payment of Invoice 5113 of July 12 ($700), less a cash discount ($14).

22 Paid $12 from the petty cash fund for a personal withdrawal by Helen Shaw, the owner, Petty Cash Voucher 4.

25 Paid $15 from the petty cash fund to have the store windows washed and repaired, Petty Cash Voucher 5.

27 Issued Check 1431 for $890 to Jewel Creations, a creditor, in payment of Invoice 656 of June 30.
30 Paid $11.75 from the petty cash fund for delivery service, Petty Cash Voucher 6.
31 Issued Check 1432 for $1,750 to pay the monthly salaries of the employees.
31 Issued Check 1433 for $1,500 to Helen Shaw, the owner, as a withdrawal for personal use.
31 Issued Check 1434 for $73 to replenish the petty cash fund. (Foot the columns of the petty cash analysis sheet in order to determine the accounts that should be debited and the amounts involved.)

PROBLEM 9–3A (Obj. 1, 2, 3)

Journalizing sales and cash receipts and posting to the general ledger. Allegro Products is a wholesale business that sells musical instruments. Transactions involving sales and cash receipts that the firm had during May 19X3 are listed below, along with the general ledger accounts used to record these transactions.

Instructions

1. Open the general ledger accounts and enter the balances as of May 1, 19X3.
2. Record the transactions in a sales journal, a cash receipts journal, and a general journal. Use 5 as the page number for each of the special journals and 15 as the page number for the general journal.
3. Post the entries from the general journal to the proper general ledger accounts.
4. Total, prove, and rule the special journals as of August 31.
5. Post the column totals from the special journals to the proper general ledger accounts.
6. Prepare the heading and the Revenue section of the firm's income statement for the month ended May 31, 19X3.

GENERAL LEDGER ACCOUNTS

101	Cash	$4,100 Dr.
109	Notes Receivable	
111	Accounts Receivable	5,250 Dr.
401	Sales	
451	Sales Returns and Allowances	
452	Sales Discount	

TRANSACTIONS

May 1 Sold merchandise for $1,850 to Harmony Music Center; issued Invoice 9321 with terms of 2/10, n/30.
3 Received a check for $715.40 from the Symphony Shop in payment of Invoice 9319 of April 24 ($730), less a cash discount ($14.60).
5 Sold merchandise for $635 in cash to a new customer who has not yet established credit.
8 Sold merchandise for $2,420 to Bob's Music Store; issued Invoice 9322 with terms of 2/10, n/30.

10 The Harmony Music Center sent a check for $1,813 in payment of Invoice 9321 of May 1 ($1,850), less a cash discount ($37).
15 Accepted a return of damaged merchandise from Bob's Music Center; issued Credit Memorandum 408 for $350; the original sale was made on Invoice 9322 of May 8.
19 Sold merchandise for $5,170 to the Music Emporium; issued Invoice 9323 with terms of 2/10, n/30.
23 Collected $1,480 from the Classic Guitar Shop for Invoice 9320 of April 25.
26 Accepted a two-month promissory note for $2,600 from Webb's Music World in settlement of its overdue account; the note has an interest rate of 12 percent.
28 Received a check for $5,066.60 from the Music Emporium in payment of Invoice 9323 of May 19 ($5,170), less a cash discount ($103.40).
31 Sold merchandise for $4,495 to Music Makers, Inc.; issued Invoice 9324 with terms of 2/10, n/30.

PROBLEM 9–4A
(Obj. 4, 5)

Journalizing purchases, cash payments, and purchases discounts; posting to the general ledger. The Runners Emporium is a retail store that sells jogging shoes and clothes. Transactions involving purchases and cash payments that the firm had during June 19X3 are listed below along with the general ledger accounts used to record these transactions.

Instructions

1. Open the general ledger accounts and enter the balances as of June 1, 19X3.
2. Record the transactions in a purchases journal, a cash payments journal, and a general journal. Use 6 as the page number for each of the special journals and 18 as the page number for the general journal.
3. Post the entries from the general journal and from the Other Accounts Debit section of the cash payments journal to the proper general ledger accounts.
4. Total, prove, and rule the special journals as of June 30.
5. Post the column totals from the special journals to the general ledger accounts.
6. Show how the firm's cost of purchases would be reported on its income statement for the month ended June 30, 19X3.

GENERAL LEDGER ACCOUNTS

101	Cash	$ 9,830 Dr.
131	Equipment	14,000 Dr.
201	Notes Payable	
205	Accounts Payable	1,220 Cr.
501	Purchases	
503	Purchases Returns and Allowances	
504	Purchases Discount	
511	Rent Expense	
514	Telephone Expense	
517	Salaries Expense	

TRANSACTIONS

June 1 Issued Check 5680 for $725 to pay the monthly rent.

3 Purchased merchandise for $1,100 from Ames Athletic Shoes, Invoice 674, dated May 30; the terms are 2/10, n/30.

5 Purchased new store equipment for $1,500 from the Wynne Company, Invoice 29076 dated June 4, net payable in 30 days.

7 Issued Check 5681 for $690 to the Outdoor Clothing Company, a creditor, in payment of Invoice 3324 of May 9.

8 Issued Check 5682 for $1,078 to Ames Athletic Shoes, a creditor, in payment of Invoice 674 of May 30 ($1,100), less a cash discount ($22).

12 Purchased merchandise for $850 from Mitchell Sportswear, Invoice 4992, dated June 9, net due and payable in 30 days.

15 Issued Check 5683 for $95 to pay the monthly telephone bill.

18 Received Credit Memorandum 324 for $265 from Mitchell Sportswear for defective goods that were returned; the original purchase was made on Invoice 4992 of June 9.

21 Purchased new store equipment for $4,000 from the Kraus Company; issued a three-month promissory note with interest at 11 percent.

23 Purchased merchandise for $2,250 from Marathon Products, Invoice 9127, dated June 20; terms of 2/10, n/30.

25 Issued Check 5684 for $530 to Mitchell Sportswear, a creditor, in payment of Invoice 4761 of May 28.

28 Issued Check 5685 for $2,205 to Marathon Products, a creditor, in payment of Invoice 9127 of June 20 ($2,250), less a cash discount ($45).

30 Purchased merchandise for $910 from Fleet Running Shoes, Invoice 37413, dated June 26; the terms are 1/10, n/30.

30 Issued Check 5686 for $1,800 to pay the monthly salaries of the employees.

PROBLEM 9–5A
(Obj. 9, 10)

Preparing a bank reconciliation statement and journalizing entries to adjust the cash balance. On May 2, 19X3, Monet Florist received its April bank statement from the Peoples National Bank. Enclosed with the bank statement, which follows, was a debit memorandum for $40 that covered an NSF check issued by Gail Reese, a credit customer. The firm's checkbook contained the following information about deposits made and checks issued during April. The balance of the Cash account and the checkbook on April 30 was $3,972.

TRANSACTIONS

Apr.	1	Balance	$6,089
	1	Check 244	100
	3	Check 245	300

5	Deposit	350
5	Check 246	275
10	Check 247	2,000
17	Check 248	50
19	Deposit	150
22	Check 249	9
23	Deposit	150
26	Check 250	200
28	Check 251	18
30	Check 252	15
30	Deposit	200

CENTURY NATIONAL BANK

MONET FLORISTS
376 KING AVENUE
ATLANTA, GA 30305

ACCOUNT NO. 454-623016
PERIOD ENDING APR 30, 19X3

CHECKS		DEPOSITS	DATE	BALANCE
AMOUNT BROUGHT FORWARD			19X3 MAR 31	6,089.00
		350.00+	APR 6	6,439.00
100.00-			APR 6	6,339.00
275.00-	300.00-		APR 10	5,764.00
2,000.00-			APR 13	3,764.00
1.65-SC			APR 14	3,762.35
		150.00+	APR 20	3,912.35
50.00-			APR 22	3,862.35
		150.00+	APR 25	4,012.35
9.00-			APR 26	4,003.35
200.00-	40.00-DM		APR 29	3,763.35

Instructions

1. Prepare a bank reconciliation statement for the firm as of April 30, 19X3.
2. Record general journal entries for any items on the bank reconciliation statement that must be journalized. Date the entries May 2, 19X3.

PROBLEM 9–6A (Obj. 9, 10)

Preparing a bank reconciliation statement and journalizing entries to adjust the cash balance. On July 31, 19X5, the balance in the checkbook and the Cash account of the Simon Company was $11,549. The balance shown on the bank statement on the same date was $11,782.05.

Notes

a. The firm's records indicate that an $879.60 deposit dated July 30 and a $476.80 deposit dated July 31 do not appear on the bank statement.
b. A service charge of $4.50 and a debit memorandum of $80 covering an NSF check have not yet been entered in the firm's records. (The check was issued by John Pell, a credit customer.)
c. The checks listed below were issued but have not yet been paid by the bank.

Check 864 for $110.50	Check 870 for $576.30
Check 865 for $11.60	Check 871 for $77.35
Check 868 for $238.20	Check 873 for $145.00

d. A credit memorandum shows that the bank has collected a $500 note receivable and interest of $15 for the firm. These amounts have not yet been entered in the firm's records.

Instructions

1. Prepare a bank reconciliation statement for the firm as of July 31, 19X5.
2. Record general journal entries for any items on the bank reconciliation statement that must be journalized. Date the entries August 4, 19X5.

PROBLEM 9–7A
(Obj. 9, 10)

Correcting errors revealed by a bank reconciliation. During the bank reconciliation process at the Moore Company on May 2, 19X5, the two errors described below were discovered in the firm's records.

a. The checkbook and the cash payments journal indicated that Check 1240 of April 10 was issued for $350 to make a cash purchase of supplies. However, examination of the canceled check and the listing on the bank statement showed that the actual amount of the check was $305.
b. The checkbook and the cash payments journal indicated that Check 1247 of April 18 was issued for $166 to pay a utility bill. However, examination of the canceled check and the listing on the bank statement showed that the actual amount of the check was $186.

Instructions

1. Prepare the adjusted book balance section of the firm's bank reconciliation statement. The book balance as of April 30 was $8,563. The errors listed above are the only two items that affect the book balance.
2. Prepare general journal entries to correct the errors. Date the entries May 2, 19X5. Check 1240 was debited to Supplies on April 10, and Check 1247 was debited to Utilities Expense on April 18.

PROBLEM SET B

PROBLEM 9–1B
(Obj. 1, 2, 3)

Tutorial

Journalizing cash receipts and posting to the general ledger. The Sound Center is a retail store that sells stereo equipment, compact discs, and tapes. The firm's cash receipts for February 19X3 are listed below, along with the general ledger accounts used to record these transactions.

Instructions

1. Open the general ledger accounts and enter the balances as of February 1, 19X3.
2. Record the transactions in a cash receipts journal. Use 2 as the page number.
3. Post the individual entries from the Other Accounts Credit section of the cash receipts journal to the proper general ledger accounts.
4. Total, prove, and rule the cash receipts journal as of February 28.

5. Post the column totals from the cash receipts journal to the general ledger.

GENERAL LEDGER ACCOUNTS

101	Cash	$ 2,320 Dr.
109	Notes Receivable	600 Dr.
111	Accounts Receivable	1,570 Dr.
141	Equipment	19,785 Dr.
231	Sales Tax Payable	469 Cr.
301	Marion Stein, Capital	42,500 Cr.
401	Sales	
491	Interest Income	
520	Cash Short or Over	

TRANSACTIONS

Feb. 2 Marion Stein, the owner, invested an additional $7,500 cash in the business.

4 Received $416 from Susan Howell, a credit customer on account.

7 Had cash sales of $3,325 plus sales tax of $133 during the first week of February; there was a cash overage of $1.

10 Collected $152 from Paul Antonovich, a credit customer, in payment of his account.

13 Received a check from Alice Mason to pay her $600 promissory note plus interest of $15.

14 Had cash sales of $2,550 plus sales tax of $102 during the second week of February.

17 Received a cash refund of $385 for some defective store equipment that was returned to the dealer; the equipment was originally bought for cash.

20 Carl Ericson, a credit customer, sent a check for $232 to pay the balance he owes.

21 Had cash sales of $2,100 plus sales tax of $84 during the third week of February; there was a cash shortage of $4.

24 Collected $541 from Jean Ashe, a credit customer, in payment of her account.

28 Had cash sales of $2,600 plus sales tax of $104 during the fourth week of February; there was a cash shortage of $6.

PROBLEM 9–2B (Obj. 4, 5, 6)

Journalizing cash payments and recording petty cash; posting to the general ledger. The cash payments of the International Gift Bazaar, a retail business, for September 19X4 are listed below, along with the general ledger accounts used to record these transactions.

Instructions

1. Open the general ledger accounts and enter the balances as of September 1, 19X4.
2. Record all payments by check in a cash payments journal. Use 9 as the page number.
3. Record all payments from the petty cash fund on a petty cash analysis sheet with special columns for Delivery Expense and Miscellaneous Expense. Use 9 as the sheet number.

4. Post the individual entries from the Other Accounts Debit section of the cash payments journal to the proper general ledger accounts.
5. Total, prove, and rule the petty cash analysis sheet as of September 30, then record the replenishment of the fund and the final balance on the sheet.
6. Total, prove, and rule the cash payments journal as of September 30.
7. Post the column totals from the cash payments journal to the proper general ledger accounts.

GENERAL LEDGER ACCOUNTS

101	Cash	$10,765 Dr.
105	Petty Cash Fund	
141	Equipment	21,500 Dr.
201	Notes Payable	840 Cr.
205	Accounts Payable	3,985 Cr.
231	Sales Tax Payable	672 Cr.
302	Peter Chen, Drawing	
451	Sales Returns and Allowances	
504	Purchases Discount	
511	Delivery Expense	
514	Miscellaneous Expense	
520	Rent Expense	
523	Salaries Expense	
526	Telephone Expense	
591	Interest Expense	

TRANSACTIONS

Sept. 1 Issued Check 934 for $672 to remit sales tax to the state tax commission.

2 Issued Check 935 for $850 to pay the monthly rent.

4 Issued Check 936 for $75 to establish a petty cash fund. (After journalizing this transaction, be sure to enter it on the first line of the petty cash analysis sheet.)

5 Issued Check 937 for $1,176 to Vantage Glassware, a creditor, in payment of Invoice 56793 of Aug. 28 ($1,200), less a cash discount ($24).

6 Paid $10.50 from the petty cash fund for delivery service, Petty Cash Voucher 1.

9 Purchased store equipment for $500; paid immediately with Check 938.

11 Paid $8 from the petty cash fund for office supplies, Petty Cash Voucher 2 (charge to Miscellaneous Expense).

13 Issued Check 939 for $485 to the Nichols Company, a creditor, in payment of Invoice 7925 of Aug. 15.

14 Issued Check 940 for $57 to a customer as a cash refund for a defective watch that was returned; the original sale was made for cash.

16 Paid $15 from the petty cash fund for a personal withdrawal by Peter Chen, the owner, Petty Cash Voucher 3.

18 Issued Check 941 for $92 to pay the monthly telephone bill.
21 Issued Check 942 for $735 to Far Eastern Imports, a creditor, in payment of Invoice 1822 of Sept. 13 ($750), less a cash discount ($15).
23 Paid $12 from the petty cash fund for postage stamps, Petty Cash Voucher 4.
24 Issued Check 943 for $854 to the Stanley Corporation in payment of an $840 promissory note and interest of $14.
26 Issued Check 944 for $620 to Pacific Ceramics, a creditor, in payment of Invoice 3510 of Aug. 29.
27 Paid $9 from the petty cash fund for delivery service, Petty Cash Voucher 5.
28 Issued Check 945 for $1,200 to Peter Chen, the owner, as a withdrawal for personal use.
29 Paid $13.50 from the petty cash fund to have a typewriter repaired, Petty Cash Voucher 6.
30 Issued Check 946 for $1,900 to pay the monthly salaries of the employees.
30 Issued Check 947 for $68 to replenish the petty cash fund. (Foot the columns of the petty cash analysis sheet in order to determine the accounts that should be debited and the amounts involved.)

PROBLEM 9–3B (Obj. 1, 2, 3)

Journalizing sales and cash receipts and posting to the general ledger. The Dawson Medical Supply Company is a wholesale business. The transactions involving sales and cash receipts that the firm had during August 19X7 are listed below, along with the general ledger accounts used to record these transactions.

Instructions

1. Open the general ledger accounts and enter the balances as of August 1, 19X7.
2. Record the transactions in a sales journal, a cash receipts journal, and a general journal. Use 8 as the page number for each of the special journals and 24 as the page number for the general journal.
3. Post the entries from the general journal to the proper general ledger accounts.
4. Total, prove, and rule the special journals as of August 31.
5. Post the column totals from the special journals to the proper general ledger accounts.
6. Prepare the heading and the Revenue section of the firm's income statement for the month ended August 31, 19X7.

GENERAL LEDGER ACCOUNTS

101	Cash	$ 6,340 Dr.
109	Notes Receivable	
111	Accounts Receivable	10,100 Dr.
401	Sales	
451	Sales Returns and Allowances	
452	Sales Discount	

TRANSACTIONS

Aug. 1 Received a check for $2,695 from the Harris Pharmacy in payment of Invoice 8277 of July 21 ($2,750), less a cash discount ($55).

2 Sold merchandise for $7,480 to United Drugstores; issued Invoice 8279 with terms of 2/10, n/30.

4 Accepted a three-month promissory note for $4,500 from the Hillside Clinic to settle its overdue account; the note has an interest rate of 11 percent.

7 Sold merchandise for $9,345 to Wayne Memorial Hospital; issued Invoice 8280 with terms of 2/10, n/30.

11 Collected $7,330.40 from United Drugstores for Invoice 8279 of August 2 ($7,480), less a cash discount ($149.60).

14 Sold merchandise for $1,750 in cash to a new customer who has not yet established credit.

16 Wayne Memorial Hospital sent a check for $9,158.10 in payment of Invoice 8280 of August 7 ($9,345), less a cash discount ($186.90).

22 Sold merchandise for $3,130 to the Leslie Drug Mart; issued Invoice 8281 with terms of 2/10, n/30.

24 Received a check for $2,500 from Grant Medical Center to pay Invoice 8278 of July 23.

26 Accepted a return of damaged merchandise from the Leslie Drug Mart; issued Credit Memorandum 311 for $210; the original sale was made on Invoice 8281 of August 22.

31 Sold merchandise for $6,370 to Lane County Hospital; issued Invoice 8282 with terms of 2/10, n/30.

PROBLEM 9–4B
(Obj. 4, 5, 6)

Journalizing purchases, cash payments, and purchase discounts; posting to the general ledger. The Top-Value Center is a retail store that sells a variety of household appliances. Transactions involving purchases and cash payments that the firm had during December 19X8 are listed below, along with the general ledger accounts used to record these transactions.

Instructions

1. Open the general ledger accounts and enter the balances in these accounts as of December 1, 19X8.
2. Record the transactions in a purchases journal, a cash payments journal, and a general journal. Use 12 as the page number for each of the special journals and 36 as the page number for the general journal.
3. Post the entries from the general journal and from the Other Accounts Debit section of the cash payments journal to the proper accounts in the general ledger.
4. Total, prove, and rule the special journals as of December 31.
5. Post the column totals from the special journals to the general ledger accounts.
6. Show how the firm's cost of purchases would be reported on its income statement for the month ended December 31, 19X8.

GENERAL LEDGER ACCOUNTS

101	Cash	$22,850 Dr.
131	Equipment	31,000 Dr.
201	Notes Payable	
205	Accounts Payable	1,900 Cr.
501	Purchases	
503	Purchases Returns and Allowances	
504	Purchases Discount	
511	Rent Expense	
514	Telephone Expense	
517	Salaries Expense	

TRANSACTIONS

Dec. 1 Purchased merchandise for $3,200 from Allied Homes Products, Invoice 76595, dated November 28; the terms are 2/10, n/30.

2 Issued Check 1563 for $1,400 to pay the monthly rent.

4 Purchased new store equipment for $6,500 from the Blair Company; issued a two-month promissory note with interest at 10 percent.

6 Issued Check 1564 for $3,136 to Allied Home Products, a creditor, in payment of Invoice 76595 of November 28 ($3,200), less a cash discount ($64).

10 Purchased merchandise for $4,450 from the Wagner Corporation Inc., Invoice 9113, dated December 7; terms of 2/10, n/30.

13 Issued Check 1565 for $120 to pay the monthly telephone bill.

15 Issued Check 1566 for $4,361 to the Wagner Corporation, a creditor, in payment of Invoice 9113 of December 7 ($4,450), less a cash discount ($89).

18 Purchased merchandise for $5,900 from the United Appliance Company, Invoice 47283, dated December 16; terms of 3/10, n/30.

20 Purchased new store equipment for $2,000 from Storage Systems Inc., Invoice 536, dated December 17, net payable in 45 days.

21 Issued Check 1567 for $1,900 to Logan Industries, a creditor, in payment of Invoice 8713 of November 23.

22 Purchased merchandise for $2,650 from the Scovill Corporation, Invoice 36131, dated December 19, net due in 30 days.

24 Issued Check 1568 for $5,723 to the United Appliance Company, a creditor, in payment of Invoice 47283 of December 16 ($5,900), less a cash discount ($177).

28 Received Credit Memorandum 821 for $450 from the Scovill Corporation for damaged goods that were returned; the original purchase was made on Invoice 36131 of December 19.

31 Issued Check 1569 for $2,700 to pay the monthly salaries of the employees.

PROBLEM 9–5B (Obj. 9, 10)

Preparing a bank reconciliation statement and journalizing entries to adjust the cash balance. On March 3, 19X3, Nakos Towing Service received its February bank statement from the Peoples National Bank. Enclosed with the bank statement, which follows, was a debit memorandum for $56 that covered an NSF check issued by Central Taxi Company, a credit customer. The firm's checkbook contained the following information about deposits made and checks issued during February. The balance of the Cash account and the checkbook on February 28 was $8,311.

TRANSACTIONS

Feb.	1	Balance	$6,500
	1	Check 421	100
	3	Check 422	10
	3	Deposit	500
	6	Check 423	225
	10	Deposit	410
	11	Check 424	200
	15	Check 425	75
	21	Check 426	60
	22	Deposit	730
	25	Check 427	4
	25	Check 428	20
	27	Check 429	35
	28	Deposit	900

PEOPLES NATIONAL BANK

NAKOS TOWING SERVICE
401 BELL STREET
CLEVELAND, OH 44106

ACCOUNT NO. 110-624-0
PERIOD ENDING FEB 28, 19X3

CHECKS		DEPOSITS	DATE	BALANCE
AMOUNT BROUGHT FORWARD			19X3 JAN 31	6,500.00
		500.00+	FEB 4	7,000.00
100.00-			FEB 6	6,900.00
200.00-	10.00-	410.00+	FEB 11	7,100.00
225.00-			FEB 15	6,875.00
60.00-			FEB 19	6,815.00
		730.00+	FEB 23	7,545.00
20.00-	4.00-		FEB 25	7,521.00
3.75-SC	56.00-DM		FEB 28	7,461.25

Instructions

1. Prepare a bank reconciliation statement for the firm as of February 28, 19X3.
2. Record general journal entries for any items on the bank reconciliation statement that must be journalized. Date the entries March 3, 19X3.

PROBLEM 9–6B
(Obj. 9, 10)

Preparing a bank reconciliation statement and journalizing entries to adjust the cash balance. On June 30, 19X5, the balance in the Haig Company's checkbook and Cash account was $6,418.59. The balance shown on the bank statement on the same date was $7,542.03.

Notes

a. The firm's records indicate that a deposit of $944.07 made on June 30 does not appear on the bank statement.
b. A service charge of $14.34 and a debit memorandum of $120 covering an NSF check have not yet been entered in the firm's records. (The check was issued by Paul Gibbs, a credit customer.)
c. The following checks were issued but have not yet been paid by the bank: Check 533 for $148.95, Check 535 for $97.50, and Check 536 for $425.40.
d. A credit memorandum shows that the bank has collected a $1,500 note receivable and interest of $30 for the firm. These amounts have not yet been entered in the firm's records.

Instructions

1. Prepare a bank reconciliation statement for the firm as of June 30, 19X5.
2. Record general journal entries for any items on the bank reconciliation statement that must be journalized. Date the entries July 2, 19X5.

PROBLEM 9–7B
(Obj. 9, 10)

Correcting errors revealed by a bank reconciliation. During the bank reconciliation process at the McKenzie Corporation on February 3, 19X6, the two errors described below were discovered in the firm's records.

a. The checkbook and the cash payments journal indicated that Check 8512 of January 7 was issued for $79 to pay for a truck repair. However, examination of the canceled check and the listing on the bank statement showed that the actual amount of the check was $77.
b. The checkbook and the cash payments journal indicated that Check 8529 of January 23 was issued for $101 to pay a telephone bill. However, examination of the canceled check and the listing on the bank statement showed that the actual amount of the check was $110.

Instructions

1. Prepare the adjusted book balance section of the firm's bank reconciliation statement. The book balance as of January 31 was $19,451. The errors listed above are the only two items that affect the book balance.
2. Prepare general journal entries to correct the errors. Date the entries February 3, 19X6. Check 8512 was debited to Truck Expense on January 7, and Check 8529 was debited to Telephone Expense on January 23.

CHALLENGE PROBLEM

PART I: During October 19X7, the Majestic Antique Shop, a retail store, had the transactions involving sales and cash receipts that are listed below. The general ledger accounts used to record these transactions are also reflected below.

Instructions

1. Open the general ledger accounts and enter the balances as of October 1, 19X7.
2. Record the transactions in a sales journal, a cash receipts journal, and a general journal. Use 10 as the page number for each of the special journals and 30 as the page number for the general journal.
3. Post the entries from the general journal and from the Other Accounts Credit section of the cash receipts journal to the proper general ledger accounts.
4. Total, prove, and rule the special journals as of October 31.
5. Post the column totals from the special journals to the proper general ledger accounts.
6. Set up an accounts receivable ledger for the Majestic Antique Shop. Open an account for each of the customers listed below, and enter the balances as of October 1, 19X7. All these customers have terms of n/30.
7. Post the individual entries from the sales journal, the cash receipts journal, and the general journal.
8. Prepare a schedule of accounts receivable for October 31, 19X7.
9. Check the total of the schedule of accounts receivable against the balance of the Accounts Receivable account in the general ledger. The two amounts should be the same.

Credit Customers

Name	Balance
Karen Cole	
Thomas DeWitt	$262.50
Donald Hall	525.00
Janet Massi	315.00
Patrick O'Connor	
Denise Richards	
Leon Roth	432.60

GENERAL LEDGER ACCOUNTS

101	Cash	$ 2,492.50 Dr.
109	Notes Receivable	
111	Accounts Receivable	1,535.10 Dr.
231	Sales Tax Payable	
301	John Valenza, Capital	45,600.00 Cr.
401	Sales	
451	Sales Returns and Allowances	
514	Cash Short or Over	

TRANSACTIONS

Oct. 1 Received a check for $262.50 from Thomas DeWitt to pay his account.

3 Sold a table on credit for $665 plus sales tax of $33.25 to Karen Cole, Sales Slip 3972.

5 John Valenza, the owner, invested an additional $7,000 cash in the business in order to expand operations.

6 Had cash sales of $1,780 plus sales tax of $89 during the period October 1–6; there was a cash shortage of $5.

8 Sold chairs on credit for $930 plus sales tax of $46.50 to Patrick O'Connor, Sales Slip 3973.

11 Accepted a two-month promissory note for $525 from Donald Hall to settle his overdue account; the note has an interest rate of 10 percent.

13 Had cash sales of $1,960 plus sales tax of $98 during the period October 8–13.

15 Collected $315 on account from Janet Massi.

19 Sold a lamp on credit to Denise Richards for $240 plus sales tax of $12, Sales Slip 3974.

20 Had cash sales of $1,650 plus sales tax of $82.50 during the period October 15–20; there was a cash shortage of $2.25.

23 Granted an allowance to Denise Richards for scratches on the lamp that she bought on Sales Slip 3974 of Oct. 19; issued Credit Memorandum 156 for $21, which includes a price reduction of $20 and sales tax of $1.

25 Leon Roth sent a check for $432.60 to pay the balance he owes.

27 Had cash sales of $2,155 plus sales tax of $107.75 during the period October 22–27.

29 Sold a cabinet on credit to Janet Massi for $590 plus sales tax of $29.50, Sales Slip 3975.

31 Had cash sales of $720 plus sales tax of $36 for October 29–31; there was a cash overage of $1.10.

PART II: During April 19X5, the Hilton Rug Mart, a retail firm, had the transactions involving purchases and cash payments that are listed below. The general ledger accounts used to record these transactions also appear below.

Instructions

1. Open the general ledger accounts and enter the balances as of April 1, 19X5.
2. Record the transactions in a purchases journal, a cash payments journal, and a general journal. Use 4 as the page number for each of the special journals and 12 as the page number for the general journal.
3. Post the entries from the general journal and from the Other Accounts Debit section of the cash payments journal to the proper general ledger accounts.
4. Total, prove, and rule the special journals as of April 30.

5. Post the column totals from the special journals to the proper general ledger accounts.
6. Set up an accounts payable ledger for Hilton Rug Mart. Open an account for each of the creditors listed below, and enter the balances as of April 1, 19X5.
7. Post the individual entries from the purchases journal, the cash payments journal, and the general journal.
8. Prepare a schedule of accounts payable for April 30, 19X5.
9. Check the total of the schedule of accounts payable against the balance of the Accounts Payable account in the general ledger. The two amounts should be the same.

Creditors

Name	Balance	Terms
Blue Ridge Company		n/45
McManus Corporation	$5,500	1/10, n/30
Northland Crafts		2/10, n/30
Reiss Company		n/30
Rosedale Mills		2/10, n/30
Superior Floor Coverings	1,940	n/30
Waverly Products	2,120	n/30

GENERAL LEDGER ACCOUNTS

101	Cash	$18,945 Dr.
121	Supplies	710 Dr.
201	Notes Payable	
205	Accounts Payable	9,560 Cr.
501	Purchases	
502	Freight In	
503	Purchases Returns and Allowances	
504	Purchases Discount	
511	Rent Expense	
514	Utilities Expense	
517	Salaries Expense	

TRANSACTIONS

Apr. 1 Issued Check 7231 for $1,940 to Superior Floor Coverings, a creditor, in payment of Invoice 56325 of March 3.

2 Issued Check 7232 for $1,200 to pay the monthly rent.

6 Purchased carpeting for $4,450 from Rosedale Mills, Invoice 827, dated April 3; terms of 2/10, n/30.

6 Issued Check 7233 for $61 to the Ace Trucking Company to pay the freight charge on goods received from Rosedale Mills.

8 Purchased store supplies for $370 from the Reiss Company, Invoice 2440, dated April 6, net amount due in 30 days.

11 Issued Check 7234 for $4,361.40 to Rosedale Mills, a creditor, in payment of Invoice 827 of April 3 ($4,450) less a cash discount ($89).

14 Purchased carpeting for $3,700 plus a freight charge of $42 from Waverly Products, Invoice 4953, dated April 11, net due and payable in 30 days.
17 Gave a two-month promissory note for $5,500 to the McManus Corporation, a creditor, to settle an overdue balance; the note bears interest at 12 percent.
21 Purchased area rugs for $2,800 from Northland Crafts, Invoice 677, dated April 18; the terms are 2/10, n/30.
22 Issued Check 7235 for $180 to pay the monthly utility bill.
24 Received Credit Memorandum 41 for $300 from Northland Crafts for a damaged rug that was returned; the original purchase was made on Invoice 677 of April 18.
25 Issued Check 7236 for $1,650 to make a cash purchase of merchandise.
26 Issued Check 7237 for $2,450 to Northland Crafts, a creditor, in payment of Invoice 677 of April 18 ($2,800), less a return ($300) and a cash discount ($50).
27 Purchased hooked rugs for $4,100 plus a freight charge of $56 from the Blue Ridge Company, Invoice 8631, dated April 23, net payable in 45 days.
28 Issued Check 7238 for $2,120 to Waverly Products, a creditor, in payment of Invoice 4811 of March 30.
30 Issued Check 7239 for $2,600 to pay the monthly salaries of the employees.

CRITICAL THINKING PROBLEM

Harry Lee is the owner of a successful small construction company. He spends most of his time out of the office supervising work at various construction sites, leaving the operation of the office to the company's cashier/bookkeeper, Grace Sierra. Grace makes bank deposits, pays the company's bills, maintains the accounting records, and prepares monthly bank reconciliations.

Recently a friend told Harry that while he was at a party he overheard Grace bragging that she paid for her new dress with money from the company's cash receipts. She said her boss would never know because he never checks the cash records.

Harry admits that he does not check on Grace's work. He now wants to know if Grace is stealing from him. He asks you to examine the company's cash records to determine whether Grace has stolen cash from the business and, if so, how much.

Your examination of the company's cash records reveals the following information.

1. Grace prepared the following July 31 bank reconciliation.

Balance in books, July 31	$18,786

Additions:		
Outstanding checks		
Check 2578	$ 792	
Check 2592	1,819	
Check 2614	384	2,695
		$21,481
Deductions:		
Deposit in transit, July 28	$4,882	
Bank service charge	10	4,892
Balance on bank statement, July 31		$16,589

2. An examination of the general ledger shows the Cash account with a balance of $18,786 on July 31.
3. The July 31 bank statement shows a balance of $16,589.
4. The July 28 deposit of $4,882 does not appear on the July 31 bank statement.
5. A comparison of canceled checks returned with the July 31 bank statement with the cash payments journal reveals the following checks as outstanding:

Check 2219	$ 263
Check 2308	1,218
Check 2524	486
Check 2578	792
Check 2592	1,819
Check 2614	384

Prepare a bank statement using the format presented in this chapter for the month of July. Assume there were no bank or bookkeeping errors in July. Did Grace take cash from the company? If so, how much and how did she try to conceal the theft? What changes would you recommend to Harry to provide better internal control over cash?

UNIT THREE

Payroll Records and Procedures

CHAPTER 10
Payroll Computations, Records, and Payment

CHAPTER 11
Payroll Taxes, Deposits, and Reports

One of the most important accounting functions for any business is to maintain accurate payroll records. These records enable salaries and wages owed to employees to be computed accurately and the amounts owed to employees to be paid promptly. Another major function of payroll accounting is to comply with the provisions of federal, state, and local employment tax laws. These laws require companies to file regular payroll reports and to pay taxes on the earnings of their employees.

CHAPTER

10 Payroll Computations, Records, and Payment

OBJECTIVES

1. Explain the major federal laws relating to employee earnings and withholding.
2. Compute gross earnings of employees.
3. Determine employee deductions for social security taxes.
4. Determine employee deductions for medicare taxes.
5. Determine employee deductions for income taxes.
6. Enter gross earnings, deductions, and net pay in the payroll register.
7. Journalize payroll transactions in the general journal.
8. Maintain an earnings record for each individual employee.
9. Define the accounting terms new to this chapter.

In the discussion of accounting records up to this point, there has been no detailed treatment of salary and wage payments to employees. A consideration of payroll accounting would have interrupted the coverage of general accounting principles and procedures. Also, payroll accounting, including the related payroll taxes and tax returns, is so important that it requires special attention.

One major objective of payroll work is to compute the wages or salaries due employees and to pay these amounts promptly. The second major objective is to compute various payroll taxes, properly report them to governmental units, and pay the taxes when due. In this chapter you will learn how earnings are computed and recorded, how various amounts that must be withheld from the employee's earnings are determined, and how to record the earnings. In the next chapter you will learn the calculation, reporting, and payment of payroll taxes.

NEW TERMS

Commission basis ▪ Compensation record ▪ Employee ▪ Employee's Withholding Allowance Certificate (Form W-4) ▪ Exempt employees ▪ Federal unemployment taxes ▪ Hourly-rate basis ▪ Independent contractor ▪ Individual earnings record ▪ Medicare tax ▪ Payroll register ▪ Piece-rate basis ▪ Salary basis ▪ Social Security Act ▪ Social security (FICA) tax ▪ State unemployment taxes ▪ Tax-exempt wages ▪ Time and a half ▪ Wage-bracket table method ▪ Workers' compensation insurance

WHO IS AN EMPLOYEE?

The discussion of payroll accounting relates only to earnings of those individuals classified as employees. An **employee** is one who is hired by the employer and who is under the control and direction of the employer. Usually the employer provides the tools or equipment used by the employee and generally controls the employee's working hours and approach to the job. The company president, the bookkeeper, the sales clerk, and the warehouse worker are examples of employees.

In contrast to an employee, an **independent contractor** is paid by the company to carry out a specific task or job. The independent contractor is not under the direct supervision and control of the company. Although the independent contractor is told what needs to be done, the means of doing the job is left to the discretion of the contractor. The accountant who performs the independent audit, the outside attorney who renders legal advice, and the computer consultant who installs a new accounting system are examples of independent contractors.

The discussion in this textbook relates to employees only. In dealing with independent contractors, the company is not bound by federal labor laws regulating minimum rates of pay and maximum hours of employment. Neither is the company required to withhold various employee taxes from amounts paid to independent contractors. Similarly, the company is not required to pay various payroll taxes on amounts paid to contractors.

Before examining the details of the process for computing the employee's earnings and deductions from the paycheck, let's first review some of the most important federal laws relating to employee earnings and withholding.

FEDERAL EMPLOYEE EARNINGS AND WITHHOLDING LAWS

OBJECTIVE 1
Explain the major federal laws relating to employee earnings and withholding.

Since the 1930s many federal and state laws have been passed that have had a crucial impact on the relationships between employers and employees. Some of these laws deal with working conditions, including hours and earnings. Others relate to taxes that must be withheld from employees' earnings and transmitted to the government by the employer. In addition, taxes are levied against the employer to provide specific employee benefits. Let's look briefly at some of these major laws, beginning with the Fair Labor Standards Act, which sets minimum wages and establishes a normal workweek. Later in this chapter and the following chapter you will learn more of the details of these rules and will see how the various laws relating to tax withholding and to employer taxes are applied.

The Fair Labor Standards Act

The *Fair Labor Standards Act* of 1938 (which has been amended frequently) applies only to firms engaged directly or indirectly in interstate commerce. This federal statute, which is often referred to as the Wage and Hour Law, fixes a minimum hourly rate of pay and maximum hours of work per week to be performed at the regular rate of pay. As of this writing, the minimum hourly rate of pay is $4.25, and

The federal government sets minimum wages and establishes the maximum normal workweek for employees.

the maximum number of hours at the employee's hourly rate is 40 hours per week. Hours worked in excess of 40 in any week must be paid for at an overtime rate of at least one and a half times the regular hourly rate of pay. This overtime rate is called **time and a half.** Many employers who are not covered by the federal law pay time and a half for overtime because of union contracts or simply as a good business practice.

The Social Security Tax

The tax levied under FICA is referred to as the social security, or FICA, tax.

The *Federal Insurance Contributions Act (FICA)* is commonly referred to as the **Social Security Act.** The act, first passed in the 1930s, has been amended frequently. It provides certain benefits for employees and their families and levies a tax, the **social security,** or **FICA, tax,** which is shared equally by the employer and employee, to finance the plan. The act provides for three major categories of benefits:

1. A retirement benefit, or pension, when a worker reaches age 62
2. Benefits for the dependents of the retired worker
3. Benefits for the worker and the worker's dependents when the worker is disabled

The rate of the social security tax and the earnings base to which it applies are both changed frequently by Congress. For the purposes of computations in this textbook, we shall assume that the amount to be withheld is 6.5 percent of the first $60,000 of salary or wages paid to each employee during the year.

The Medicare Tax

The medicare tax applies to much higher maximum earnings than does the social security tax.

The **medicare tax** is closely related to the social security tax; in fact, prior to 1992 it was a part of the social security tax. It is levied equally on the employer and employee to provide for medical care for the employee and the employee's spouse after each has reached age 65. We will assume that the medicare tax rate is 1.5 percent on the employee and 1.5 percent on the employer and that it applies to the first $140,000 of salary or wages paid during the year. Note that the maximum base for the medicare tax is much higher than that for the social security tax.

Federal Income Tax

Income tax withholding laws require the employer to withhold from the employee's pay an amount equal to the estimated income tax on earnings.

Employers are required to withhold from the employee's earnings an estimated amount of income tax that will be payable by the employee on the earnings. The amount depends on several factors. Later in this chapter you will learn how the employer determines how much income tax to withhold from an employee's paycheck.

STATE AND LOCAL TAXES

Most states, and many city governments, require employers to deduct money from their employees' earnings to prepay the employees' state and local income taxes. These rules are generally almost identical to those governing federal income tax withholding, but they require separate accounts in the firm's accounting system.

THE EMPLOYER'S PAYROLL TAXES AND INSURANCE COSTS

Employers must also pay taxes on their employees' earnings. Some taxes are required by the federal government while others are required by state government. Federal taxes are levied for social security, medicare, and unemployment benefits. State taxes are required for unemployment benefits and workers' compensation. In addition, each state requires employers to carry workers' compensation insurance.

Social Security Tax

The employer is required to pay an amount equal to the social security tax withheld from the earnings of each employee.

Under the social security rules the employer is required to pay an amount equal to the social security tax withheld from the employee's base earnings. The employer's share of tax is transmitted to the federal government along with the amounts withheld from the employee's paycheck. Remember that in this textbook we assume that the social security tax is 6.5 percent of the first $60,000 of gross earnings paid to each employee during the year, but the actual amount changes (increases) almost every year.

Medicare Tax

As in the case of the social security tax, the employer is required to "match" the medicare tax withheld from the employee's earnings and to remit both amounts to the federal government.

Federal Unemployment Tax

The *Federal Unemployment Tax Act (FUTA)* requires most employers to pay a tax based on each employee's earnings, up to a specified amount of earnings, to finance benefits for employees who become unemployed. Employees pay no part of **federal unemployment taxes (FUTA).** In this text we assume that the taxable base is the first $7,000 of each employee's earnings for the year. Note that the maximum wages to which the unemployment tax applies are much lower than the base for either social security or medicare taxes.

The federal unemployment tax can be reduced by all or a part of the unemployment tax charged by the state governments.

In this book we also assume that the rate for the federal unemployment tax is 6.5 percent. The federal tax rate can be reduced by the rate charged by the individual states, discussed below, under the state unemployment compensation laws (SUTA), not to exceed a specified maximum state rate. We shall assume that the maximum state rate that can be used to offset the federal rate is 5.4 percent. Based on this assumption, the federal rate could be as little as 1.1 percent (6.5 percent federal tax minus 5.4 percent state tax).

State Unemployment Tax

Most states require that the employer withhold a state unemployment tax from the employee's earnings.

State unemployment taxes (SUTA) are tied directly to the federal unemployment tax. The base for the state tax is usually the same as the base for the federal tax. As pointed out above, the federal unemployment tax rules permit the employer to reduce the federal rate by the rate charged by the state. In many states the rate of the SUTA is the maximum rate that is allowed by the federal law to be "credited" against the federal unemployment tax. We will assume that the maximum state rate that can be offset against the federal rate is 5.4 percent, so that the minimum federal rate is 1.1 percent.

Workers' Compensation Insurance

All the states have laws mandating **workers' compensation insurance.** These laws require employers to pay for insurance that will reimburse employees for losses suffered from job-related injuries or

Employers are required to carry workers' compensation insurance to protect employees against losses from job-related injuries or sickness.

will compensate their families if death occurs in the course of their employment. Benefits are paid directly to the injured workers or to their survivors. The insurance is generally carried through a commercial insurance company.

EMPLOYEE RECORDS REQUIRED BY LAW

Employers are required to keep a number of records relating to each employee and the employee's hours worked, earnings, and taxes withheld.

Various federal laws related to wages, hours, withholdings, and employer payroll taxes require that certain records be maintained for each employee. The most important records required are:

1. The name, address, social security number, and date of birth of each employee
2. Hours worked each day and week, wages paid at the regular rate, and overtime premium wages; certain exceptions exist for employees paid on a salary basis
3. Cumulative amount of taxable wages paid throughout the year
4. Amount of income tax, social security tax, and medicare tax withheld from each employee's earnings for each pay period

In addition, the employer is required to obtain proof from each employee that he or she is a United States citizen or has a valid work permit.

SELF-REVIEW

1. How does the Fair Labor Standards Act affect the wages paid by many firms?
2. What is "time and a half"?
3. How are social security benefits financed?
4. What is the purpose of workers' compensation insurance?
5. Name several items of information about each employee that the employer must keep in the firm's records.

Answers to Self-Review

1. The act sets a minimum hourly wage rate and requires that each employee be paid an hourly rate equal to one and one-half times the regular hourly rate for each hour worked above 40 hours in a calendar week.
2. "Time and a half" refers to the federal requirement that covered employees be paid at a rate equal to one and one-half times their normal hourly rate for each hour worked in excess of 40 hours in a week.
3. Social security benefits are financed by a tax levied equally on both employers and employees and on self-employed persons. The amount of tax is based on the amount of earnings.
4. Workers' compensation insurance is to compensate workers for

losses suffered from job-related injuries or to compensate their families if the employee's death occurs in the course of employment.

5. Among the more important items of information that must be kept are the employee's birth date, social security number, hours worked each day and week, wages paid at regular rate, wages paid at premium rate, marital status, number of exemptions, cumulative earnings, and information on withholdings from earnings.

A SAMPLE CASE

Now we are ready to see how a business computes and records the earnings of its employees and the related taxes to be deducted in computing the employees' net pay. The Ajax Mail Order Company is used in this chapter and the next to illustrate typical payroll procedures and records. This firm imports a variety of novelty items and sells them by mail. It is staffed by three packing and shipping clerks and a production supervisor, who are paid on an hourly-rate basis, and by an office clerk, who is paid a weekly salary. All employees are paid each Monday for wages and salaries earned during the week that ended on the preceding Saturday. The employees are subject to the social security tax, medicare tax, and federal income tax withholding. The owner, Jean Shaatke, manages the company and withdraws a portion of the profits from time to time to take care of her personal living expenses. Because she is the owner of a sole proprietorship, her drawings are not treated as salaries or wages. The firm itself is subject to social security tax, medicare tax, and federal and state unemployment insurance taxes. Since the mail-order business involves interstate commerce, the Ajax Mail Order Company is also subject to the Fair Labor Standards Act. In addition, the business is required by state law to carry workers' compensation insurance.

The amounts withdrawn by the owner of a sole proprietorship are not treated as a salary or wage.

Computing Total Earnings of Employees

OBJECTIVE 2

Compute gross earnings of employees.

The first step in payroll work is to determine the gross amount of wages or salary earned by each employee. There are several bases for computing the employee's earnings. Some workers are paid at a stated rate per hour, and their gross pay depends on the number of hours they work. This method is called the **hourly-rate basis.** Other workers are paid an agreed amount for each week or month or other period. This arrangement is called the **salary basis.** Salespeople are sometimes paid on the **commission basis,** usually some percentage of net sales. In manufacturing, wages are sometimes based on the number of units produced. This pay system is called the **piece-rate basis.**

Determining Gross Pay for Hourly Employees

To determine the gross pay earned by an employee on an hourly-rate basis, it is necessary to know the rate of pay and the number of hours the employee has worked during the payroll period.

Hours Worked

A record of the hours worked each day by each employee should be maintained.

There are various methods of keeping track of the hours worked by each employee. At the Ajax Company, the production supervisor keeps a weekly time sheet on which she enters the number of hours worked each day by each shop employee. At the end of the week, the office clerk uses the time sheet to determine the total hours worked and to prepare the payroll to be paid on the following Monday. Many businesses use time clocks for employees, especially for those paid on an hourly basis. Each employee has a time card and inserts it in the time clock to record the time of arrival and the time of departure. The payroll clerk collects the cards at the end of the week, determines the hours worked by each employee, multiplies the number of hours by the proper rate, and computes the gross pay. Some time cards can be fed into a computer, which determines the hours worked and makes all earnings calculations.

Gross Pay

The time sheet kept at the Ajax Mail Order Company during the week ended January 6, 19X5, shows that the first hourly employee, Cass Collins, worked 40 hours. His rate of pay is \$8 an hour. His gross pay of \$320 is found by multiplying 40 hours by \$8.

The Fair Labor Standards Act requires that employees be paid one and one-half times their regular hourly rates for all hours worked above 40 hours in one week.

The second hourly employee, Enos Echols, worked 44 hours. Four of these hours are overtime. Thus these four hours must be paid for at Echols's regular rate (\$7) plus a premium rate of one-half of his regular rate (\$7 × 0.50 = \$3.50 premium rate). Echols's gross pay is calculated as follows.

Total time × regular rate: 44 hours × \$7	\$308
Overtime premium: 4 hours × \$3.50	14
Gross pay	\$322

This method is the one specified under the Wage and Hour Law and is therefore the one used in the illustrations. Another method, which gives the same gross pay, uses the steps shown below.

Regular time earnings: 40 hours × \$7.00	\$280
Overtime earnings: 4 hours × \$10.50	42
Gross pay	\$322

The second method quickly answers the employee's question, "How much more did I earn by working overtime than I would have earned for only 40 hours of work?" The employer, however, is more concerned with the amount of premium the firm could have saved if all the hours had been paid for at the regular rate. The first method gives this information.

The third hourly employee, Carol Johansen, worked 40 hours. Her hourly rate is \$6.25. Her gross pay is therefore \$250 (40 × \$6.25). The fourth employee, Nina Sanchez, is the supervisor. She worked 40 hours, and her rate of pay is \$10 per hour. Thus her gross pay is \$400 (40 × \$10).

Withholdings for Hourly Employees Required by Law

As you learned earlier in this chapter, three principal deductions from employees' gross pay are required by federal law: FICA (social security) tax, medicare tax, and income tax withholding. These deductions are explained in greater detail below.

Social Security Tax

OBJECTIVE 3
Determine employee deductions for social security taxes.

The social security tax levied under the Federal Insurance Contributions Act is levied in an equal amount on both the employer and the employee. As we have pointed out, rates and bases change often, so a hypothetical tax rate and base are used in this discussion. We will assume that a social security tax rate of 6.5 percent is applied to a base consisting of the first $60,000 of wages paid to an employee during the calendar year. Earnings in excess of the base amount (called **tax-exempt wages**) are not taxed. If an employee works for more than one employer during the year, the FICA tax is deducted and matched by each employer. When the employee files a federal income tax return, any excess tax withheld from the employee's earnings is refunded by the government or applied to payment of the employee's federal income taxes. The employer receives no refund merely because an employee held more than one job during the year.

The amount of social security tax to be deducted can be computed either by multiplying the taxable wages by the social security rate or by referring to tax tables found in *Circular E, Employer's Tax Guide*, published by, and available from, the Internal Revenue Service. These tables also are available from commercial sources, such as office supply stores.

When the percentage method is used to compute social security tax to be withheld, the tax rate is multiplied by the employee's taxable wages for the period.

Tax Computed by the Percentage Method. When the employer uses the percentage method to compute the deduction for social security, the payroll clerk multiplies the taxable wages by the tax rate and rounds the answer to the nearest cent. The social security taxes to be deducted by the Ajax Mail Order Company on wages of hourly employees, based on the gross pay previously calculated and an assumed tax rate of 6.5 percent, are shown below.

Employee	Gross Pay	Tax Rate	Tax
Cass Collins	$320	6.5%	$20.80
Enos Echols	322	6.5	20.93
Carol Johansen	250	6.5	16.25
Rita Sanchez	400	6.5	26.00
Total			$83.98

Tax Determined from Tax Table. Social security taxes on wages can also be determined from the Social Security Employee Tax Table in *Circular E.* The table shows the tax to be withheld for different brackets of income up to $100. It also shows the social security tax on each multiple of $100. At a rate of 6.5 percent, the table would show social

	Wages	FICA Tax
On	$300	$19.50
On	20	1.30
On	$320	$20.80

security tax of $19.50 on wages of $300 and $1.30 on wages of $20. These two tax amounts are added as shown at the left to find the social security tax to be withheld from Cass Collins's paycheck.

This amount is precisely equal to the $20.80 computed earlier for Cass Collins under the percentage method.

Medicare Tax

OBJECTIVE 4
Determine employee deductions for medicare taxes.

Like the social security tax, the medicare tax is levied equally on the employee and the employer. Prior to 1992, the medicare tax was a part of the social security tax and was applied to the same tax base. Now the medicare tax is applied to a higher base and must be computed separately from the social security tax. The medicare tax to be withheld from the employee's paycheck also can be computed under either the percentage method or withholding tables.

Tax Computed by the Percentage Method. Under the assumption that the medicare tax is levied at the rate of 1.5 percent on the first $140,000 per year earned by the employee, the amount to be deducted by the Ajax Mail Order Company on the wages previously computed would be as follows.

Employee	Gross Pay	Tax Rate	Tax
Cass Collins	$320	1.5%	$ 4.80
Enos Echols	322	1.5	4.83
Carol Johansen	250	1.5	3.75
Rita Sanchez	400	1.5	6.00
Total			$19.38

Tax on $300	$4.50
Tax on $ 22	.30
Total	$4.80

Tax Determined from Tax Table. *Circular E* also contains tax tables for determining the amount of medicare tax to be calculated for various wage levels, up to $100 of wages, based on increments of 1 cent in the tax payable. A table based on a medicare tax rate of 1.5 percent would show a total medicare tax liability of $4.80 for Cass Collins, the same amount as that computed under the percentage method.

Federal Income Tax

OBJECTIVE 5
Determine employee deductions for income taxes.

A substantial portion of the federal government's revenue comes from the income tax on individuals. Many rules and regulations are used in determining the amount of federal income tax that each person must pay. Also keep in mind that rates, rules, and regulations change often. The rates used in this text are for illustrative purposes only. In actual practice, a current edition of the Internal Revenue Service's *Circular E* would be consulted for up-to-date rates and other information.

Employee income tax withholding is designed to place employees on a pay-as-you-go basis in paying their federal income tax.

Most taxpayers are on a pay-as-you-go basis. This means that an estimate of the federal income tax due from a person earning a salary or wages must be withheld by the employer and paid to the government periodically—generally at the same time that social security and medicare taxes are paid. At the end of each year, the employee files an income tax return. If the amount withheld does not cover the amount of income tax due, the employee pays the balance. If too much has been withheld, the employee will receive a refund.

Claiming Withholding Allowances. The amount of federal income tax to be withheld from an employee's earnings generally depends on the amount of income during the pay period, the length of the pay period, number of exemption allowances, and marital status. The matter of allowances for exemptions is a technical subject that cannot be fully explored here. In brief, a person is ordinarily entitled to one allowance for himself or herself, one for a spouse (unless the spouse also works and claims an exemption allowance at his or her own place of employment), and one for each dependent for whom the person provides more than half the support during the year.

In lieu of basing the withholding allowances on the number of exemptions that will be claimed on the employee's tax return, the employee can compute a number of allowances that will more nearly match the amount withheld with the income tax the employee expects to have to pay at the end of the year. These computations are quite complex and are beyond the scope of this text.

The amount of income tax to be withheld from an employee's earnings depends on the amount of pay, the length of the pay period, the number of withholding allowances, and the employee's marital status.

If the employee desires, he or she may use Form W-4 to instruct the employer to withhold each payroll period a specified amount of income tax above the amount required by law. This practice reduces the possibility that a balance may be due when the individual files the yearly income tax return.

Employees claim the number of exemption allowances to which they are entitled by completing an **Employee's Withholding Allowance Certificate, Form W-4** (see Figure 10–1). This form is filed with the employer. The first page of Cass Collins's Form W-4 is shown on page 342. If an employee fails to file a Form W-4, the employer must withhold federal income tax from the employee's wages as though there were no exemption allowances. If the number of exemptions decreases, the employee must file a new Form W-4 within 10 days. If the number of exemption allowances increases, the employee may file an amended certificate but is not required to do so.

Almost all employers compute the employees' withholding amounts by using withholding tables provided by the government in *Circular E.*

Computing Income Tax Withholding. Several methods can be used to compute the amount of federal income tax to be withheld from an employee's earnings. However, all except one require cumbersome computations. The exception is the **wage-bracket table method,** which involves the use of tables to determine the amount of tax. The simplicity of this method explains why it is used almost universally. *Circular E, Employer's Tax Guide,* contains withholding tables for weekly, biweekly, semimonthly, monthly, and daily or miscellaneous payroll periods for single and married persons. Sections of the tables for single and married persons paid weekly are illustrated in Figure 10–2.

FIGURE 10–1
Form W-4

19-- Form W-4

Department of the Treasury
Internal Revenue Service

Purpose. Complete Form W-4 so that your employer can withhold the correct amount of Federal income tax from your pay.

Exemption From Withholding. Read line 7 of the certificate below to see if you can claim exempt status. *If exempt, complete line 7; but do not complete lines 5 and 6.* No Federal income tax will be withheld from your pay. Your exemption is good for one year only. It expires February 15, 1993.

Basic Instructions. Employees who are not exempt should complete the Personal Allowances Worksheet. Additional worksheets are provided on page 2 for employees to adjust their withholding allowances based on itemized deductions, adjustments to income, or two-earner/two-job situations. Complete all worksheets that apply to your situation. The worksheets will help you figure the number of withholding allowances you are entitled to claim. However, you may claim fewer allowances than this.

Head of Household. Generally, you may claim head of household filing status on your tax return only if you are unmarried and pay more than 50% of the costs of keeping up a home for yourself and your dependent(s) or other qualifying individuals.

Nonwage Income. If you have a large amount of nonwage income, such as interest or dividends, you should consider making estimated tax payments using Form 1040-ES. Otherwise, you may find that you owe additional tax at the end of the year.

Two-Earner/Two-Jobs. If you have a working spouse or more than one job, figure the total number of allowances you are entitled to claim on all jobs using worksheets from only one Form W-4. This total should be divided among all jobs. Your withholding will usually be most accurate when all allowances are claimed on the W-4 filed for the highest paying job and zero allowances are claimed for the others.

Advance Earned Income Credit. If you are eligible for this credit, you can receive it added to your paycheck throughout the year. For details, get Form W-5 from your employer.

Check Your Withholding. After your W-4 takes effect, you can use **Pub. 919,** Is My Withholding Correct for 1992?, to see how the dollar amount you are having withheld compares to your estimated total annual tax. Call 1-800-829-3676 to order this publication. Check your local telephone directory for the IRS assistance number if you need further help.

Personal Allowances Worksheet

For 1992, the value of your personal exemption(s) is reduced if your income is over $105,250 ($157,900 if married filing jointly, $131,550 if head of household, or $78,950 if married filing separately). Get Pub. 919 for details.

A Enter "1" for **yourself** if no one else can claim you as a dependent . . . . . **A** 1

B Enter "1" if:
- You are single and have only one job; or
- You are married, have only one job, and your spouse does not work; or
- Your wages from a second job or your spouse's wages (or the total of both) are $1,000 or less.

. . **B** ____

C Enter "1" for your **spouse.** But, you may choose to enter -0- if you are married and have either a working spouse or more than one job (this may help you avoid having too little tax withheld) . . . . . **C** 0

D Enter number of **dependents** (other than your spouse or yourself) whom you will claim on your tax return . . . . . **D** ____

E Enter "1" if you will file as **head of household** on your tax return (see conditions under "Head of Household," above) . **E** ____

F Enter "1" if you have at least $1,500 of **child or dependent care expenses** for which you plan to claim a credit . . **F** ____

G Add lines A through F and enter total here. **Note:** *This amount may be different from the number of exemptions you claim on your return* ▶ **G** 1

For accuracy, do all worksheets that apply.
- If you plan to **itemize or claim adjustments to income** and want to reduce your withholding, see the Deductions and Adjustments Worksheet on page 2.
- If you are **single** and have **more than one job** and your combined earnings from all jobs exceed $29,000 OR if you are **married** and have a **working spouse or more than one job,** and the combined earnings from all jobs exceed $50,000, see the Two-Earner/Two-Job Worksheet on page 2 if you want to avoid having too little tax withheld.
- If **neither** of the above situations applies, **stop here** and enter the number from line G on line 5 of Form W-4 below.

---- **Cut here and give the certificate to your employer. Keep the top portion for your records.** ----

Form **W-4**
Department of the Treasury
Internal Revenue Service

Employee's Withholding Allowance Certificate

▶ **For Privacy Act and Paperwork Reduction Act Notice, see reverse.**

OMB No. 1545-0010
19--

1 Type or print your first name and middle initial — Last name: Cass C. Collins

2 Your social security number: 123-45-6789

Home address (number and street or rural route): 24 Oak Street

3 ☐ Single ☒ Married ☐ Married, but withhold at higher Single rate.
Note: *If married, but legally separated, or spouse is a nonresident alien, check the Single box.*

City or town, state, and ZIP code: Krum, TX 76249

4 If your last name differs from that on your social security card, check here and call 1-800-772-1213 for more information . ▶ ☐

5 Total number of allowances you are claiming (from line G above or from the Worksheets on back if they apply) **5** 1

6 Additional amount, if any, you want deducted from each paycheck . . . . . **6** $

7 I claim exemption from withholding and I certify that I meet **ALL** of the following conditions for exemption:
- Last year I had a right to a refund of **ALL** Federal income tax withheld because I had **NO** tax liability; **AND**
- This year I expect a refund of **ALL** Federal income tax withheld because I expect to have **NO** tax liability; **AND**
- This year if my income exceeds $600 and includes nonwage income, another person cannot claim me as a dependent.

If you meet all of the above conditions, enter the year effective and "EXEMPT" here . . . ▶ **7** 19

8 Are you a full-time student? (**Note:** *Full-time students are not automatically exempt.*) . . . . . **8** ☐ **Yes** ☒ **No**

Under penalties of perjury, I certify that I am entitled to the number of withholding allowances claimed on this certificate or entitled to claim exempt status.

Employee's signature ▶ Cass C. Collins **Date** ▶ December 1, 19XX

9 Employer's name and address (Employer: Complete 9 and 11 only if sending to the IRS) | **10** Office code (optional) | **11** Employer identification number

FIGURE 10–2 **(a)**
Federal Withholding Tax Tables (Partial)

In computing the employee's tax deduction, the employer may save time by using a table prepared by the government showing the amount to be withheld in various wage brackets.

SINGLE Persons—WEEKLY Payroll Period

And wages are—		And the number of withholding allowances claimed is—										
At least	But less than	0	1	2	3	4	5	6	7	8	9	10
		The amount of income tax to be withheld shall be—										
$0	$50	$0	$0	$0	$0	$0	$0	$0	$0	$0	$0	$0
50	55	1	0	0	0	0	0	0	0	0	0	0
55	60	2	0	0	0	0	0	0	0	0	0	0
60	65	2	0	0	0	0	0	0	0	0	0	0
65	70	3	0	0	0	0	0	0	0	0	0	0
70	75	4	0	0	0	0	0	0	0	0	0	0
75	80	5	0	0	0	0	0	0	0	0	0	0
80	85	5	0	0	0	0	0	0	0	0	0	0
85	90	6	0	0	0	0	0	0	0	0	0	0
90	95	7	0	0	0	0	0	0	0	0	0	0
95	100	8	1	0	0	0	0	0	0	0	0	0
100	105	8	2	0	0	0	0	0	0	0	0	0
105	110	9	2	0	0	0	0	0	0	0	0	0
110	115	10	3	0	0	0	0	0	0	0	0	0
115	120	11	4	0	0	0	0	0	0	0	0	0
120	125	11	5	0	0	0	0	0	0	0	0	0
125	130	12	5	0	0	0	0	0	0	0	0	0
130	135	13	6	0	0	0	0	0	0	0	0	0
135	140	14	7	0	0	0	0	0	0	0	0	0
140	145	14	8	1	0	0	0	0	0	0	0	0
145	150	15	8	2	0	0	0	0	0	0	0	0
150	155	16	9	3	0	0	0	0	0	0	0	0
155	160	17	10	3	0	0	0	0	0	0	0	0
160	165	17	11	4	0	0	0	0	0	0	0	0
165	170	18	11	5	0	0	0	0	0	0	0	0
170	175	19	12	6	0	0	0	0	0	0	0	0
175	180	20	13	6	0	0	0	0	0	0	0	0
180	185	20	14	7	0	0	0	0	0	0	0	0
185	190	21	14	8	1	0	0	0	0	0	0	0
190	195	22	15	9	2	0	0	0	0	0	0	0
195	200	23	16	9	3	0	0	0	0	0	0	0
200	210	24	17	10	4	0	0	0	0	0	0	0
210	220	25	19	12	5	0	0	0	0	0	0	0
220	230	27	20	13	7	0	0	0	0	0	0	0
230	240	28	22	15	8	2	0	0	0	0	0	0
240	250	30	23	16	10	3	0	0	0	0	0	0
250	260	31	25	18	11	5	0	0	0	0	0	0
260	270	33	26	19	13	6	0	0	0	0	0	0
270	280	34	28	21	14	8	1	0	0	0	0	0
280	290	36	29	22	16	9	3	0	0	0	0	0
290	300	37	31	24	17	11	4	0	0	0	0	0
300	310	39	32	25	19	12	6	0	0	0	0	0
310	320	40	34	27	20	14	7	0	0	0	0	0
320	330	42	35	28	22	15	9	2	0	0	0	0
330	340	43	37	30	23	17	10	3	0	0	0	0
340	350	45	38	31	25	18	12	5	0	0	0	0
350	360	46	40	33	26	20	13	6	0	0	0	0
360	370	48	41	34	28	21	15	8	1	0	0	0
370	380	49	43	36	29	23	16	9	3	0	0	0
380	390	51	44	37	31	24	18	11	4	0	0	0
390	400	52	46	39	32	26	19	12	6	0	0	0
400	410	54	47	40	34	27	21	14	7	1	0	0
410	420	55	49	42	35	29	22	15	9	2	0	0
420	430	57	50	43	37	30	24	17	10	4	0	0
430	440	58	52	45	38	32	25	18	12	5	0	0
440	450	61	53	46	40	33	27	20	13	7	0	0
450	460	63	55	48	41	35	28	21	15	8	1	0
460	470	66	56	49	43	36	30	23	16	10	3	0
470	480	69	58	51	44	38	31	24	18	11	4	0
480	490	72	59	52	46	39	33	26	19	13	6	0
490	500	75	62	54	47	41	34	27	21	14	7	1
500	510	77	65	55	49	42	36	29	22	16	9	2
510	520	80	68	57	50	44	37	30	24	17	10	4
520	530	83	71	58	52	45	39	32	25	19	12	5
530	540	86	73	61	53	47	40	33	27	20	13	7
540	550	89	76	64	55	48	42	35	28	22	15	8
550	560	91	79	67	56	50	43	36	30	23	16	10
560	570	94	82	69	58	51	45	38	31	25	18	11
570	580	97	85	72	60	53	46	39	33	26	19	13
580	590	100	87	75	63	54	48	41	34	28	21	14

FIGURE 10–2 (Continued) Federal Withholding Tax Tables (Partial)

(b)

MARRIED Persons—**WEEKLY** Payroll Period

And wages are—		And the number of withholding allowances claimed is—										
At least	But less than	0	1	2	3	4	5	6	7	8	9	10
		The amount of income tax to be withheld shall be—										
$0	$120	$0	$0	$0	$0	$0	$0	$0	$0	$0	$0	$0
120	125	1	0	0	0	0	0	0	0	0	0	0
125	130	2	0	0	0	0	0	0	0	0	0	0
130	135	3	0	0	0	0	0	0	0	0	0	0
135	140	3	0	0	0	0	0	0	0	0	0	0
140	145	4	0	0	0	0	0	0	0	0	0	0
145	150	5	0	0	0	0	0	0	0	0	0	0
150	155	6	0	0	0	0	0	0	0	0	0	0
155	160	6	0	0	0	0	0	0	0	0	0	0
160	165	7	0	0	0	0	0	0	0	0	0	0
165	170	8	1	0	0	0	0	0	0	0	0	0
170	175	9	2	0	0	0	0	0	0	0	0	0
175	180	9	3	0	0	0	0	0	0	0	0	0
180	185	10	3	0	0	0	0	0	0	0	0	0
185	190	11	4	0	0	0	0	0	0	0	0	0
190	195	12	5	0	0	0	0	0	0	0	0	0
195	200	12	6	0	0	0	0	0	0	0	0	0
200	210	13	7	0	0	0	0	0	0	0	0	0
210	220	15	8	2	0	0	0	0	0	0	0	0
220	230	16	10	3	0	0	0	0	0	0	0	0
230	240	18	11	5	0	0	0	0	0	0	0	0
240	250	19	13	6	0	0	0	0	0	0	0	0
250	260	21	14	8	1	0	0	0	0	0	0	0
260	270	22	16	9	3	0	0	0	0	0	0	0
270	280	24	17	11	4	0	0	0	0	0	0	0
280	290	25	19	12	6	0	0	0	0	0	0	0
290	300	27	20	14	7	0	0	0	0	0	0	0
300	310	28	22	15	9	2	0	0	0	0	0	0
310	320	30	23	17	10	3	0	0	0	0	0	0
320	330	31	25	18	12	5	0	0	0	0	0	0
330	340	33	26	20	13	6	0	0	0	0	0	0
340	350	34	28	21	15	8	1	0	0	0	0	0
350	360	36	29	23	16	9	3	0	0	0	0	0
360	370	37	31	24	18	11	4	0	0	0	0	0
370	380	39	32	26	19	12	6	0	0	0	0	0
380	390	40	34	27	21	14	7	1	0	0	0	0
390	400	42	35	29	22	15	9	2	0	0	0	0
400	410	43	37	30	24	17	10	4	0	0	0	0
410	420	45	38	32	25	18	12	5	0	0	0	0
420	430	46	40	33	27	20	13	7	0	0	0	0
430	440	48	41	35	28	21	15	8	2	0	0	0
440	450	49	43	36	30	23	16	10	3	0	0	0
450	460	51	44	38	31	24	18	11	5	0	0	0
460	470	52	46	39	33	26	19	13	6	0	0	0
470	480	54	47	41	34	27	21	14	8	1	0	0
480	490	55	49	42	36	29	22	16	9	2	0	0
490	500	57	50	44	37	30	24	17	11	4	0	0
500	510	58	52	45	39	32	25	19	12	5	0	0
510	520	60	53	47	40	33	27	20	14	7	0	0
520	530	61	55	48	42	35	28	22	15	8	2	0
530	540	63	56	50	43	36	30	23	17	10	3	0
540	550	64	58	51	45	38	31	25	18	11	5	0
550	560	66	59	53	46	39	33	26	20	13	6	0
560	570	67	61	54	48	41	34	28	21	14	8	1
570	580	69	62	56	49	42	36	29	23	16	9	3
580	590	70	64	57	51	44	37	31	24	17	11	4
590	600	72	65	59	52	45	39	32	26	19	12	6
600	610	73	67	60	54	47	40	34	27	20	14	7
610	620	75	68	62	55	48	42	35	29	22	15	9
620	630	76	70	63	57	50	43	37	30	23	17	10
630	640	78	71	65	58	51	45	38	32	25	18	12
640	650	79	73	66	60	53	46	40	33	26	20	13
650	660	81	74	68	61	54	48	41	35	28	21	15
660	670	82	76	69	63	56	49	43	36	29	23	16
670	680	84	77	71	64	57	51	44	38	31	24	18
680	690	85	79	72	66	59	52	46	39	32	26	19
690	700	87	80	74	67	60	54	47	41	34	27	21
700	710	88	82	75	69	62	55	49	42	35	29	22
710	720	90	83	77	70	63	57	50	44	37	30	24
720	730	91	85	78	72	65	58	52	45	38	32	25

The steps in determining the amount to be withheld are:

1. Choose the proper table based on the pay period and the employee's marital status.
2. Find the line in the table that covers the amount of wages the employee earned. Follow across this line until you reach the column corresponding to the number of withholding allowances claimed. The amount shown at this point in the table is the income tax to be withheld.

For example, Rita Sanchez is married, has two withholding allowances, and earned $400 for the week. In the section of the table for married persons paid weekly, Figure 10–2*b*, the appropriate line is the one covering wages between $400 and $410. On this line, under the column headed "2," the amount of tax is given as $30. The amount of federal income tax to be withheld from the wages of each hourly employee of the Ajax Mail Order Company is found in a similar manner from the sections of the weekly wage-bracket withholding tables shown in the figure. The results are summarized below.

Employee	Gross Pay	Marital Status	Withholding Allowances	Income tax Withholding
Cass Collins	$320	Married, wife works	1	$ 25.00
Enos Echols	322	Single	1	35.00
Carol Johansen	250	Single with dependents	3	11.00
Rita Sanchez	400	Married	2	30.00
				$101.00

Other Deductions Required by Law

Some states and cities require that state and local income tax be withheld from earnings of employees. The procedures are similar to those already explained for federal income tax withholding. Of course, the appropriate state or city withholding tables or tax rates must be used.

In certain states, unemployment tax or disability tax must also be deducted from employees' wages. The amounts to be deducted are determined by applying the specified rates to taxable wages as defined in the law. The procedures involved in such deductions are similar to those that have already been illustrated.

For the sake of simplicity, we will assume that no other deductions from the wages of the hourly employees of the Ajax Mail Order Company are required by law.

Withholdings Not Required by Law

Many kinds of deductions not required by law are made by agreement between the employee and the employer. For example, a specified deduction from the earnings of an employee may be made at the end of each payroll period for group life insurance or group medical insurance covering the employee's family.

The employer and employee may agree that the employer will make deductions for various purposes from the employee's pay.

Company retirement plans may be financed entirely by the employer or by the employer and employee jointly. In the latter case, employee contributions to the retirement plan are usually based on the wages or salary earned and are customarily deducted from earnings each payroll period.

In some cases, employees ask to have amounts deducted from their earnings and deposited in a bank or a company credit union, or accumulated and used to buy United States savings bonds, shares of stock, or other investments. The employee signs an authorization for such deductions and may change this authorization or terminate it at any time. Employees who have received advances from their employers or who have bought merchandise from the firm often repay such debts through payroll deductions. When employees belong to a union, the contract between the employer and the union may specify that union dues be deducted from employee wages.

These and other possible payroll deductions increase the payroll record-keeping work but do not involve any new principles or procedures. They are handled in the same way as the required deductions for social security, medicare, and income taxes.

In Ajax Company, the only recurring "other deduction" is a deduction from an employee's pay for a part of the cost of health and hospitalization insurance for dependents of employees if employees choose to have dependents covered. Ajax pays all health and hospitalization insurance premiums on each employee. In addition, it pays most of the premiums for coverage of the employee's spouse and dependents. However, the employee is required to pay a total of $10 per week for coverage of his or her spouse and other dependents. Carol Johansen has chosen to cover her dependents and Rita Sanchez has chosen to cover her spouse by this optional insurance, and $10 is deducted from each woman's pay for the week.

Determining Gross Pay for Salaried Employees

A salaried employee earns a specific sum of money for each payroll period, whether it is weekly, biweekly, semimonthly, or monthly. The office clerk at the Ajax Mail Order Company is paid a weekly salary.

Hours Worked

Salaried employees who hold supervisory or managerial positions are usually exempt from the wage and hour laws.

Salaried workers who do not hold supervisory jobs are generally covered by the provisions of the Wage and Hour Law that deal with maximum hours and overtime premium pay. The employer must keep a time record for all salaried workers of this type to make sure that their hourly earnings meet the legal requirements. Generally, salaried employees who hold supervisory or managerial positions are not subject to such requirements and are known as **exempt employees.**

Gross Earnings

During the first week of January, Mill Yamoah, the office clerk at the Ajax Mail Order Company, worked his regular schedule of 40 hours. Therefore, no overtime premium is involved and his salary of $300 is his gross pay for the week.

Withholdings for Salaried Employees Required by Law

Regardless of the method of paying an employee, the social security tax is deducted at the end of each payroll period until the base amount of earnings for the calendar year is reached. For Mill Yamoah, this tax is 6.5 percent of $300 for the week, or $19.50. Similarly, the medicare tax applies to all employees. Mill Yamoah's medicare tax is $4.50 for the week (0.015 × $300).

Yamoah is not married and claims only one personal exemption for federal income tax withholding purposes. The amount of income tax to be withheld from his earnings is found by referring to the weekly wage-bracket withholding table illustrated in Figure 10–2*a*. His gross pay of $300 is included in the line that reads "At least $300, but less than $310." Under the column for one withholding allowance, $32 is shown as the amount of income tax to be deducted.

RECORDING PAYROLL INFORMATION FOR EMPLOYEES

OBJECTIVE 6

Enter gross earnings, deductions, and net pay in the payroll register.

Payroll personnel must compute employee earnings and deductions accurately and promptly so that the net amounts can be paid at the scheduled times. After the computations are made, the payroll information for the period is entered in a record called a **payroll register.** A payroll register contains special columns for information about employees as well as other columns showing employee earnings and deductions from those earnings. A payroll register is shown in Figure 10-3 on pages 348–349.

The Payroll Register

The payroll register illustrated in Figure 10–3 shows information about the earnings and deductions of Ajax's five employees for the weekly period ended January 6, 19X5. All employees were paid at the regular hourly rate for eight hours on Monday, January 1, a holiday.

The steps in completing the payroll register are summarized below. Refer to the columns in the payroll register (Figure 10–3) as you read the descriptions given below for each column of the register.

1. *Columns A, B, C, and E.* Each employee's name (column A), withholding allowances and marital status (column B), cumulative earnings (column C) and rate of pay (column E) can be entered in the register in advance to save time in payroll preparation. In a computerized payroll system, this information would be stored in the computer and automatically retrieved when the payroll is entered.

   Column C, Cumulative Earnings, shows the total earnings for the calendar year before the current pay period for each employee. This figure is essential in determining whether the employee's current period earnings are subject to the various payroll taxes. Since this is Ajax's first payroll payment in 19X5, there are no cumulative earnings prior to the current pay period. The last payroll in December was paid early, on December 29, because of the January 1 holiday.
2. *Column D.* From the completed time records, the total hours worked in the current period are entered in column D.

FIGURE 10–3
Payroll Register

PAYROLL REGISTER **WEEK BEGINNING** *January 1, 19X5*

NAME	NO. OF ALLOW.	MARITAL STATUS	CUMULATIVE EARNINGS	NO. OF HRS.	RATE	EARNINGS			CUMULATIVE EARNINGS
						REGULAR	OVERTIME PREMIUM	GROSS AMOUNT	
Collins, Cass	*1*	*M*		*40*	*8.00*	*320 00*		*320 00*	*320 00*
Echols, Enos	*1*	*S*		*44*	*7.00*	*308 00*	*14 00*	*322 00*	*322 00*
Johansen, Carol	*3*	*S*		*40*	*6.25*	*250 00*		*250 00*	*250 00*
Sanchez, Rita	*2*	*M*		*40*	*10.00*	*400 00*		*400 00*	*400 00*
Yamoah, Mill	*1*	*S*		*40*	*300.00*	*300 00*		*300 00*	*300 00*
						1 578 00	*14 00*	*1 592 00*	*1 592 00*
(A)	└ *(B)* ┘		*(C)*	*(D)*	*(E)*	*(F)*	*(G)*	*(H)*	*(I)*

3. *Columns F, G, and H.* Gross earnings computations are made in the manner previously described and are entered in the Earnings section. These amounts are classified according to regular earnings (column F) and overtime premium earnings (column G.) In Ajax's payroll register, the sum of the earnings is entered in column H, "Gross Amount."
4. *Column I.* Column I shows the cumulative earnings of each employee through the end of the current period. It reflects the sum of the beginning cumulative earnings (column C) and the current period's gross earnings (column H).
5. *Columns J, K, and L.* To facilitate the computation of the payroll taxes to be withheld from each employee's earnings and the taxes levied on the employer, columns J, K, and L show the amount of wages subject to social security taxes, medicare taxes, and FUTA taxes. The amounts are found by comparing the cumulative wages shown in column C with the maximum amounts on which the taxes are levied.
6. *Columns M, N, O, and P.* The withholding amounts are entered in the payroll register. The social security tax (column M), medicare tax (column N), federal income tax (column O), and medical insurance (column P) withholdings are the amounts that were computed in previous illustrations. Most payroll registers also contain an additional column entitled "Other" in which nonrecurring withholdings may be recorded.
7. *Columns Q and R.* Next the deductions for each employee are subtracted from the gross earnings to find the net amount owed to the employee. This figure is recorded in the Net Amount column (column Q). Column R registers the number of the check used to pay the net amount due each employee.
8. *Columns S and T.* The last two columns of the payroll register are used to classify employee earnings as office salaries (column S) or shipping wages (column T).

AND ENDING *January 6, 19X5* PAID *January 8, 19X5*

TAXABLE WAGES			DEDUCTIONS				DISTRIBUTION			
SOCIAL SECURITY	MEDICARE	FUTA	SOCIAL SECURITY	MEDICARE	INCOME TAX	HEALTH INSURANCE	NET AMOUNT	CHECK NO.	OFFICE SALARIES	SHIPPING WAGES
320 00	320 00	320 00	20 80	4 80	25 00		269 40	4725		320 00
322 00	322 00	322 00	20 93	4 83	35 00		261 24	4726		322 00
250 00	250 00	250 00	16 25	3 75	11 00	10 00	209 00	4727		250 00
400 00	400 00	400 00	26 00	6 00	30 00	10 00	328 00	4728		400 00
300 00	300 00	300 00	19 50	4 50	32 00		244 00	4729	300 00	
1,592 00	1,592 00	1,592 00	103 48	23 88	133 00	20 00	1,311 64		300 00	1,292 00
(J)	(K)	(L)	(M)	(N)	(O)	(P)	(Q)	(R)	(S)	(T)

When the payroll information for all employees has been entered in the payroll register, the columns are totaled as shown in Figure 10–3. The total of the Regular Earnings column plus the total of the Overtime Premium column must equal the sum of the items in the Gross Amount column ($1,578.00 + $14.00 = $1,592.00). The gross amount less the sum of the deductions (social security tax, medicare tax, income tax, and health insurance) equals the total of the Net Amount column, as shown below.

DEDUCTIONS

Gross Amount		$1,592.00
Less Deductions:		
Social security	$103.48	
Medicare tax	23.88	
Income tax	133.00	
Health insurance	20.00	
Total deductions		$ 280.36
Net Amount		$1,311.64

The column totals from the payroll register supply all the necessary figures for making the journal entry to record the payroll, which we discuss in the next section.

SELF-REVIEW

1. What three deductions from employee earnings are required by federal law?
2. Give four examples of deductions from employees' earnings that are not required by law but are sometimes made by agreement between the employee and the employer.
3. What two methods can be used in determining the amount of social security tax to withhold from an employee's gross pay?

4. What factors determine how much federal income tax must be withheld from an employee's earnings?
5. What is the purpose of the payroll register?

Answers to Self-Review

1. The three deductions required are social security tax, medicare tax, and federal income tax.
2. Common withholdings are health insurance premiums, life insurance premiums, union dues, savings, and contributions to charitable organizations and/or supplemental retirement plans.
3. The two ways to compute social security withholdings are by using a withholding table provided by the government and by multiplying the wages subject to the tax by the current tax rate.
4. The employee's federal income tax withholding is determined by the amount of earnings, the period covered by the payment, the employee's marital status, and the number of withholding allowances.
5. The purpose of the payroll register is to record in one place all information about employees' earnings and withholdings for the period.

The Journal Entry for the Payroll

OBJECTIVE 7

Journalize payroll transactions in the general journal.

The general journal entry to record the payroll is simple, based as it is on the totals of the payroll register. The gross pay of the employees is charged to the appropriate expense accounts. For the packing and shipping workers at the Ajax Mail Order Company, this account is entitled Shipping Wages Expense. For the office clerk, the correct account is Office Salaries Expense. Separate liability accounts are used for each type of deduction made from the employees' earnings (social security taxes, medicare taxes, income tax withholding, and health insurance premiums). Salaries and Wages Payable is credited for the net amount due the employee, since the accounting entry for the payroll is made before the employees are actually paid.

After the payroll register is completed, a general journal entry is made to record the payroll data.

The entry made in Ajax's general journal on January 8 to record the January 6 payroll, after posting has been completed, is shown below.

1	*19X5*						1
2	*Jan.*	*8*	*Office Salaries Expense*	*541*	*300 00*		2
3			*Shipping Wages Expense*	*542*	*1 292 00*		3
4			*Social Security Tax Pay.*	*221*		*103 48*	4
5			*Medicare Tax Payable*	*222*		*23 88*	5
6			*Employee Income Tax Pay.*	*223*		*133 00*	6
7			*Health Ins. Premiums Pay.*	*224*		*20 00*	7
8			*Salaries and Wages Pay.*	*229*		*1 311 64*	8
9			*Payroll for week ending*				9
10			*January 6*				10
11							11

Paying the Payroll

Almost all businesses pay the salaries and wages of their employees by check. The canceled check provides a record of the payment and the employee's endorsement serves as a receipt. The use of checks avoids the inconvenience of obtaining the cash and putting it in pay envelopes and also eliminates the risk involved in handling large amounts of currency.

Another convenient and safe method of paying employees, which is gaining popularity, is the direct-deposit method. Under this system, the employer sends the employee's net pay to the bank to be deposited in the employee's bank account.

Paying by Check

Employees should not be paid in cash. Instead, a check may be drawn on the firm's regular checking account, or a special bank account may be opened on which only payroll checks are written.

Payments of salaries and wages should be made by check rather than in cash.

Checks Written on Regular Checking Account. When employees are paid by checks drawn on the firm's regular checking account, an individual check is prepared for each worker. The check number is entered in the Check Number column of the payroll register on the same line as the employee's other information. (See the payroll register in Figure 10–3.) Information about the employee's gross earnings, deductions, and net pay is usually shown on a stub of the payroll check. The employee detaches the stub and keeps it as a record of his or her payroll data for the period.

When the payroll check is issued to the employee for the net earnings after all deductions, an entry is made in the cash payments journal. The effect of the payment is to decrease the Salaries and Wages Payable account and to decrease the Cash account. Because there will be a substantial number of payroll checks written each month, Ajax has a special column entitled Salaries and Wages Payable in the cash payments journal. The cash payments journal for Ajax Company for January reflects the payments to the employees as shown in Figure 10–4 on the next page.

At the end of the month, the total of the Salaries and Wages Payable Dr. column is posted as a debit to the Salaries and Wages Payable account in the general ledger.

The effect of the checks written by Ajax to pay its employees on January 8 for the payroll period ending on January 6 is shown below in general journal form.

1	*19X5*						1
2	*Jan.*	*8*	*Salaries and Wages Payable*		*1 3 1 1 64*		2
3			*Cash*			*1 3 1 1 64*	3
4			*Checks to pay salaries*				4
5			*and wages, week ended*				5
6			*Jan. 6*				6
7							7

FIGURE 10–4
A Cash Payments Journal

CASH PAYMENTS JOURNAL — PAGE 1

DATE		CK. NO.	EXPLANATION	POST. REF.	ACCOUNTS PAYABLE DEBIT	SALARIES AND WAGES PAYABLE DEBIT	PURCHASES DISCOUNT CREDIT	CASH CREDIT
Jan.	2	703	*Town Supply Company*		600 00		12 00	588 00
	8	725	*Cass Collins*			269 40		269 40
	8	726	*Enos Echols*			261 24		261 24
	8	727	*Carol Johansen*			209 00		209 00
	8	728	*Rita Sanchez*			328 00		328 00
	8	729	*Mill Yamoah*			244 00		244 00
	31		*Totals*		x x x x xx	5 2 4 6 56	x x x xx	x x x x xx

Using a special payroll account on which all payroll checks are drawn facilitates the bank reconciliations and offers better internal control.

Checks Written on a Separate Payroll Account. Many firms prefer that payroll checks not be written on the regular checking account. Instead, a separate payroll bank account is maintained. One check is drawn on the regular bank account for the total amount of net wages and salaries payable and is deposited in the payroll bank account. This check is entered in the cash payments journal as a debit to Salaries and Wages Payable and a credit to Cash. Since only one check is written to the payroll account each pay period, the cash payments journal may not contain a special column for Salaries and Wages Payable Dr. If Ajax had maintained a separate payroll bank account, the effect, in general journal form, of the entry to record the check payable to the payroll account would be as follows.

1	*19X5*						1
2	*Jan.*	8	*Salaries and Wages Payable*		1 3 1 1 64		2
3			*Cash*			1 3 1 1 64	3
4			*Record check to payroll*				4
5			*bank account*				5
6							6

Individual checks totaling this amount are immediately issued from the payroll bank account to the employees.

The major benefit of using a separate payroll account if there are many employees is that it simplifies the bank reconciliation at the end of the month. There may be many payroll checks outstanding, especially if employees are paid at the end of the month, complicating the reconciliation of the regular account if that account is used for writing payroll checks. A separate payroll account eliminates this complication. In addition, a special payroll account makes it easier to quickly determine each month if there are outstanding payroll checks.

Paying by Direct Deposit

An increasingly popular method of paying employees is the direct-deposit method. Under this method, a firm has its bank transfer the net pay of each employee from the employer's own account to the employee's personal checking account at the employee's bank. The transfer is often made by "electronic transfer" rather than through the issuance of a check or other paper document. On the date of the deposit, the employee receives a statement showing his or her earnings, deductions, and net pay for the period and the date when the net pay was deposited.

Individual Earnings Records

OBJECTIVE 8

Maintain an earnings record for each individual employee.

At the beginning of each year, or when a new employee is hired during the year, an **individual earnings record** (sometimes called a **compensation record**) is set up for each worker. This record contains the employee's name, address, social security number, date of birth, number of withholding allowances claimed, rate of pay, and any other information that may be needed in computing earnings and in filing necessary tax reports. The details for each pay period are posted to the employee's individual earnings record from the payroll register. The record for Cass Collins (Figure 10–5) shows the data for each payroll in January.

Note that the details shown in this record include the payroll date (entered in the Week Ended column), the date paid, the regular and overtime hours worked, the earnings (broken down into regular earnings and overtime premium, as indicated in the payroll register),

FIGURE 10–5
An Individual Earnings Record

EARNINGS RECORD FOR *19X5*

NAME *Cass Collins* **RATE** *$8 per hour* **SOC. SEC. NO.** *123-45-6789*
ADDRESS *24 Oak Street, Krum, TX 76249* **DATE OF BIRTH** *Jan. 23, 1970*
WITHHOLDING ALLOWANCES *1* **MARITAL STATUS** *M*

PAYROLL NO.	DATE		HOURS		EARNINGS				DEDUCTIONS				NET PAY
	WK. END.	PAID	RG	OT	REGULAR	OVERTIME	TOTAL	CUMULATIVE TOTAL	SOCIAL SECURITY	MEDICARE	INCOME TAX	OTHER	
1	1/06	1/08	40		320.00		320.00	320.00	20.80	4.80	25.00		269.40
2	1/13	1/15	40		320.00		320.00	640.00	20.80	4.80	25.00		269.40
3	1/20	1/22	40		320.00		320.00	960.00	20.80	4.80	25.00		269.40
4	1/27	1/29	40		320.00		320.00	1280.00	20.80	4.80	25.00		269.40
	January				1280.00		1280.00		83.20	19.20	100.00		1077.60

Information Block: Ethics in Accounting

It's Only Another Eighteen Months!

Bob Scott is executive vice president of Graphic Truck, Inc., a major manufacturer of trucks. When he was hired two years ago, Bob was granted a two-year, $50,000 loan for the down payment on his house. This loan was given at a fair market value rate of interest and is due very soon. Bob likes to spend money freely. He earns a good salary and bonus but spends everything he earns and more. His current debts are so large that no bank will loan him any additional money. Since the loan from Graphic Truck is due soon, Bob comes to your office to discuss the situation.

An individual earnings record is set up for each employee. It contains all of the details related to the employee's earnings, deductions, and net pay for each pay period throughout the year.

each deduction, and the net pay. The cumulative total earnings after each payroll agrees with the balance shown for each employee in column I of the payroll register. It is recomputed each time a payroll entry is made in an earnings record.

The individual earnings records are usually totaled monthly and at the end of each calendar quarter. In this way, they provide information needed in making tax payments and filing tax returns, as described in the next chapter.

COMPLETING JANUARY PAYROLLS

In order to complete the January payrolls for the Ajax Mail Order Company, assume that all employees worked the same number of hours during each week of the month as they did during the first week. Thus they also had the same earnings, deductions, and net pay each week.

Journal Entries

The general journal and the cash payments journal are used to record the transactions involving the payment of the payroll and the liabilities resulting from the payroll.

Entry to Record Payroll

As explained already, one general journal entry is made to record the weekly payroll for all employees of the Ajax Mail Order Company. Since we are assuming an identical payroll for each week of the month, the four weekly payrolls require entries identical to the one shown in Figure 10–6.

As president of Graphic Truck, you must make a recommendation to the Board of Directors on extending Bob's loan or calling it. If you call the loan, Bob would be forced into bankruptcy. He probably has sufficient assets to cover most of his debts, so the company would not lose money if the loan is called. If you extend the loan, Bob promises he will get his financial house in order and repay the loan in 18 months.

Bob has been a good executive vice president, and you are aware that another organization is trying to interview him for a corporate presidency. If you force him into bankruptcy, he will lose any opportunity for that position.

1. What are the ethical issues?
2. What are the alternatives?
3. Who are the affected parties?
4. How do the alternatives affect the parties?
5. What is your decision?

FIGURE 10–6
Journalizing and Posting Payroll Data

AND ENDING *January 6, 19X5* **PAID** *January 8, 19X5*

TAXABLE WAGES			DEDUCTIONS				DISTRIBUTION			
SOCIAL SECURITY	MEDICARE	FUTA	SOCIAL SECURITY	MEDICARE	INCOME TAX	HEALTH INSURANCE	NET AMOUNT	CHECK NO.	OFFICE SALARIES	SHIPPING WAGES
320 00	320 00	320 00	20 80	4 80	25 00		269 40	4725		320 00
322 00	322 00	322 00	20 93	4 83	35 00		261 24	4726		322 00
250 00	250 00	250 00	16 25	3 75	11 00	10 00	209 00	4727		250 00
400 00	400 00	400 00	26 00	6 00	30 00	10 00	328 00	4728		400 00
300 00	300 00	300 00	19 50	4 50	32 00		244 00	4729	300 00	
1,592 00	1,592 00	1,592 00	103 48	23 88	133 00	20 00	1,311 64		300 00	1,292 00
(J)	(K)	(L)	(M)	(N)	(O)	(P)	(Q)	(R)	(S)	(T)

1	19X5					1
2	Jan. 8	*Office Salaries Expense*	541	300 00		2
3		*Shipping Wages Expense*	542	1,292 00		3
4		*Social Security Tax Pay.*	221		103 48	4
5		*Medicare Tax Payable*	222		23 88	5
6		*Employee Income Tax Pay.*	223		133 00	6
7		*Health Ins. Premiums Pay.*	224		20 00	7
8		*Salaries and Wages Pay.*	229		1,311 64	8
9		*Payroll for week ending*				9
10		*January 6*				10
11						11

FIGURE 10–6 (Continued)
Journalizing and Posting Payroll Data

	Date		Description	Post. Ref.	Debit	Credit	
1	*19X5*						1
2	*Jan.*	*8*	*Office Salaries Expense*	*541*	*3 0 0 00*		2
3			*Shipping Wages Expense*	*542*	*1 2 9 2 00*		3
4			*Social Security Tax Pay.*	*221*		*1 0 3 48*	4
5			*Medicare Tax Payable*	*222*		*2 3 88*	5
6			*Employee Income Tax Pay.*	*223*		*1 3 3 00*	6
7			*Health Ins. Premiums Pay.*	*224*		*2 0 00*	7
8			*Salaries and Wages Pay.*	*229*		*1 3 1 1 64*	8
9			*Payroll for week ending*				9
10			*January 6*				10

Office Salaries Expense

1/8	300.00		
1/15	300.00		
1/22	300.00		
1/29	300.00		

Medicare Tax Payable

		1/8	23.88
		1/15	23.88
		1/22	23.88
		1/29	23.88

Shipping Wages Expense

1/8	1,292.00		
1/15	1,292.00		
1/22	1,292.00		
1/29	1,292.00		

Employee Income Tax Pay.

		1/8	133.00
		1/15	133.00
		1/22	133.00
		1/29	133.00

Health Insurance Premiums Payable

		1/8	20.00
		1/15	20.00
		1/22	20.00
		1/29	20.00

Social Security Tax Payable

		1/8	103.48
		1/15	103.48
		1/22	103.48
		1/29	103.48

Salaries and Wages Payable

5,246.56		1/8	1,311.64
		1/15	1,311.64
		1/22	1,311.64
		1/29	1,311.64

CASH PAYMENTS JOURNAL PAGE *1*

DATE		CK. NO.	EXPLANATION	POST. REF.	ACCOUNTS PAYABLE DEBIT	SALARIES AND WAGES PAYABLE DEBIT	PURCHASES DISCOUNT CREDIT	CASH CREDIT
Jan.	*2*	*703*	*Town Supply*		*6 0 0 00*		*1 2 00*	*5 8 8 00*
	31		*Totals*		*x x x x xx*	*5 2 4 6 56*	*x x x xx*	*x x x x xx*

Entry to Record Payment of Payroll

The entries in the cash payments journal to record the checks written to employees during each payroll period will be the same as that on January 8. At the end of January, the Salaries and Wages Payable Dr. column in the cash payments journal will be totaled and the total posted to the general ledger account.

Postings to Ledger Accounts

The entries to record the weekly payroll expense and liability accounts at Ajax are posted from the general journal to the accounts in the general ledger. As previously noted, the total of the Salaries and Wages Payable Dr. column in the cash payments journal is posted to the general ledger account of that title.

The entire cycle of computing, paying, journalizing, and posting payroll data is summarized in Figure 10–6, pages 355–356.

MANAGERIAL IMPLICATIONS

Management must be very careful that a firm's payroll procedures and records comply with the provisions of federal, state, and local laws. If the business is covered by the Fair Labor Standards Act, its payments to employees must meet the minimum wage and overtime pay requirements of that law. Similarly, care should be taken that tax withholdings are made from employee earnings in accordance with any laws that apply to the business. Severe penalties are levied against employers for improper withholding of taxes and for failure to file necessary reports.

Wages and salaries form a large part of the operating expenses of most firms. Thus an adequate set of payroll records is essential as an aid to management in controlling expenses. These records pinpoint the labor cost for each area of the business by showing management exactly what amounts have been spent for sales salaries, office salaries, and factory wages. These records also indicate how much of the amount spent in each area was for overtime. Although overtime is fully justified in many cases, it may also be a sign of inefficiency. Large or frequent expenditures for overtime should therefore be investigated.

To prevent errors and fraud, management should make sure that the payroll records are audited carefully and that payroll procedures are evaluated periodically. The overstatement of hours worked and the issuance of checks to nonexistent employees are common types of fraud in the payroll area. Management must be alert to the potential for dishonesty in this area.

SELF-REVIEW

1. An employer's weekly payroll register showed that the only deductions from employees' earnings were for federal income taxes, social security taxes, and medicare tax. In the general journal entry to record the payroll, what accounts will be debited and what accounts will be credited? All employees are office workers.
2. From an accounting and internal control viewpoint, would it be preferable to pay employees by check or in cash? Explain.
3. What account is debited and what account is credited when individual payroll checks are written on the general checking account?
4. How is a payroll bank account used?
5. What information does an individual earnings record contain?

Answers to Self-Review

1. The account debited will be Office Salaries and Wages Expense. The accounts credited will be Social Security Tax Payable, Medicare Tax Payable, Employee Income Tax Payable, and Salaries and Wages Payable.
2. It would be far preferable to pay all employees by check. There is far less possibility of mistake, lost money, or fraud. The check serves as a receipt and permanent record of the transaction.
3. When payroll checks are written on the general checking account, each check results in a debit to Salaries and Wages Payable and a credit to Cash.
4. When a payroll bank account is used, one check is drawn on the general checking account, payable to the payroll account. Individual employee checks are then written on the payroll account.
5. The individual earnings record contains the employee's name and social security number; information affecting income tax withholding; the hours worked for each pay period; the regular earnings, overtime premium, and total earnings for each period; the cumulative total earnings for the year to date; and deductions and net pay for each period.

CHAPTER 10 Review and Applications

CHAPTER SUMMARY

The main objective of payroll work is to compute the gross wages or salaries earned by each employee, the proper amounts to be deducted for various taxes and other purposes, and the net amount payable.

Several federal laws affect the amount to be paid to employees. The federal wage and hour laws place a limit of 40 hours per week on the number of hours that an employee can work at the regular rate of pay. For all hours above 40 hours worked in a week, the employer must pay a rate equal to, or more than, one and one-half times the regular rate. In addition, federal laws require the employer to withhold certain taxes from the employee's earnings. The employer is required to withhold at least three taxes from the employee's pay: the employee's share of social security tax, the employee's share of medicare tax, and the federal income tax. Instructions for computing the amount of each of these taxes are provided by the government to the employer. Other required deductions may be made for state and city income taxes. In addition, some states require employees to contribute to unemployment funds and require the employer to withhold the contributions from the employee's paycheck. There may also be voluntary deductions that are made by agreement between the employee and the employer.

Daily records of the hours worked by each nonsupervisory employee are kept. Using these hourly time sheets, the payroll clerk computes the employees' earnings, deductions, and net pay for each payroll period and records the data in a payroll register. Information from the payroll record is used to prepare a payroll entry in the general journal. The general journal entry records the earnings, the withholdings, and the net amount payable.

At the beginning of each year, the employer sets up individual earnings records for the employees. The amounts that appear in the payroll register are posted to the individual earnings records throughout the year so that the firm will have detailed payroll information available for each employee. At the end of the year, the employer must report to each employee the gross amount earned and the amounts deducted for each purpose.

Salaries and wages may be paid in cash, by checks written on the regular checking account, or by checks written on a special payroll account. Using a payroll account simplifies the task of reconciling bank statements and keeping up with uncashed checks.

GLOSSARY OF NEW TERMS

Commission basis (p. 337) A method of paying employees according to a percentage of sales

Compensation record (p. 353) See Individual earnings record

Employee (p. 333) One who is under the control and direction of the employer and is paid a salary or wage

Employee's Withholding Allowance Certificate, Form W-4 (p. 341) A form used to claim exemption allowances

Exempt employees (p. 346) Salaried employees not subject to the Wage and Hour Law

Federal unemployment taxes (FUTA) (p. 335) Taxes levied by the federal government against employers to benefit unemployed workers

Hourly-rate basis (p. 337) A method of paying employees according to a stated rate of pay per hour

Independent contractor (p. 333) One who is paid to carry out a specific job outside the direct control of a company

Individual earnings record (p. 353) An employee record posted from the payroll register

Medicare tax (p. 334) A tax levied on employees and employers to provide medical benefits for elderly persons

Payroll register (p. 347) A record of payroll information for each employee for the pay period

Piece-rate basis (p. 337) A method of paying employees according to the number of units produced

Salary basis (p. 337) A method of paying employees according to an agreed-upon weekly or monthly rate

Social Security Act (p. 334) A federal act providing certain benefits for employees and their families; officially the Federal Insurance Contributions Act

Social security tax (p. 334) A tax imposed by the Federal Insurance Contributions Act and collected on employee earnings to provide retirement and disability benefits; also called FICA tax

State unemployment taxes (SUTA) (p. 335) Taxes levied by a state government against employers to benefit unemployed workers

Tax-exempt wages (p. 339) Earnings in excess of the base amount set by the Social Security Act

Time and a half (p. 334) Rate of pay for employee work in excess of 40 hours a week

Wage-bracket table method (p. 341) A simple method to determine the amount of federal income tax to be withheld using a table provided by the government

Workers' compensation insurance (p. 335) Insurance to reimburse employees for job-related injuries or illnesses or to compensate their families if death occurs in the course of their employment

REVIEW QUESTIONS

1. What is the purpose of the social security tax?
2. What is the purpose of the medicare tax?
3. How are earnings determined when employees are paid on the hourly-rate basis?
4. Does the employer bear any part of the SUTA tax? Explain.
5. How are the federal and state unemployment taxes related?
6. How does the salary basis differ from the hourly-rate basis of paying employees?
7. What publication of the Internal Revenue Service provides information about the current federal income tax rates and the procedures that employers should use to withhold this tax?
8. What is the simplest method for finding the amount of federal income tax to deduct from an employee's gross pay?
9. What are the three bases for determining employee wages?
10. How does the direct-deposit method of paying employees operate?

MANAGERIAL FOCUS

1. Why should management make sure that a firm has an adequate set of payroll records?
2. How can detailed payroll records aid management in controlling expenses?
3. Why should management carefully check the amount being spent for overtime?
4. The new controller for the Ellis Company, a manufacturing firm, has suggested to management that the business change from paying the factory employees in cash to paying them by check. What reasons would you offer to support this suggestion?

EXERCISES

EXERCISE 10-1 (Obj. 2)

Computing gross earnings. The hourly rates of four employees of the High Water Company are shown below, along with the hours that these employees worked during one week. Determine the gross earnings of each employee.

Employee No.	Hourly Rate	Regular Hours Worked
1	$8.20	38
2	8.25	40
3	6.90	40
4	9.15	35

EXERCISE 10–2 (Obj. 2)

Tutorial

Computing regular earnings, overtime premium, and gross pay. During one week, four production employees of the Aristemedes Manufacturing Company worked the number of hours shown below. All of these employees receive overtime pay at one and a half times their regular hourly rate for any hours worked beyond 40 in a week. Determine the regular earnings, overtime premium, and gross earnings for each employee.

Employee No.	Hourly Rate	Regular Hours Worked
1	$8.50	43
2	9.00	47
3	8.70	32
4	7.90	44

EXERCISE 10–3 (Obj. 3)

Tutorial

Determining social security withholdings. The monthly salaries for December and the year-to-date earnings of the employees of the Boiler Metal Works as of November 30 are listed below.

Employee No.	December Salary	Year-to-Date Earnings Through November 30
1	$6,000	$66,000
2	5,000	55,000
3	5,200	57,200
4	4,000	44,000

Determine the amount of social security tax to be withheld from each employee's gross pay for December. Assume a 6.5 percent social security tax rate and a base of $60,000 for the calendar year.

EXERCISE 10–4 (Obj. 3)

Tutorial

Determining deduction for medicare tax. Use the earnings data given in Exercise 10–3 and determine the amount of medicare tax to be withheld from each employee's gross pay for December. Assume a 1.5 percent medicare tax rate and a base of $140,000 for the calendar year.

EXERCISE 10–5 (Obj. 3)

Tutorial

Determining federal income tax withholding. Data about the marital status, withholding allowances, and weekly salaries of the four office workers at the City Answering Service are listed below. Use the tax tables in Figure 10–2 to find the amount of federal income tax to be deducted from each employee's gross pay.

Employee No.	Marital Status	Withholding Allowances	Weekly Salary
1	S	1	$440
2	M	3	575
3	S	2	380
4	M	1	320

EXERCISE 10–6
(Obj. 5)

Recording payroll transactions in general journal. O'Brien Corporation has two office employees. A summary of their earnings and the related taxes withheld from their pay for the week ending May 16, 19X2, is given below.

	Harriet Laney	Stella Smith
Gross earnings	$330.00	$410.00
Social security deduction	(21.45)	(26.65)
Medicare deduction	(4.95)	(6.15)
Income tax withholding	(37.00)	(25.00)
Net pay for week	$266.60	$352.20

Instructions

1. Give the general journal entry to record the company's payroll for the week. Use the account titles given in this chapter.
2. Give the general journal entry to summarize the checks to pay the weekly payroll.

EXERCISE 10–7
(Obj. 5)

Tutorial

Journalizing payroll transactions. On June 30, 19X3, the payroll register of the Svoda Distributing Company showed the following totals for the month: earnings, $9,600; social security tax, $624; medicare tax, $144; income tax, $760; and net amount due, $8,072. Of the total earnings, $7,500 was for sales salaries and $2,100 was for office salaries. Prepare a general journal entry to record the monthly payroll of the firm on June 30, 19X3.

PROBLEMS

PROBLEM SET A

PROBLEM 10–1A
(Obj. 2, 3, 4, 5)

Tutorial Spreadsheet

Computing gross earnings, determining deductions, preparing payroll register, journalizing payroll transactions. The Hudson Video Mart has four employees and pays them on an hourly basis. During the week beginning July 1 and ending July 7, 19X5, these employees worked the hours shown below. Information about hourly rates, marital status, withholding allowances, and cumulative earnings prior to the current pay period also appears below.

Employee	Hours Worked	Regular Hourly Rate	Marital Status	Withholding Allowances	Cumulative Earnings
Michael Cohen	44	$9.00	M	4	$9,360
Anthony Lima	42	9.30	S	1	9,400
Kelly Ryan	36	8.50	S	2	2,400
Jennifer Wills	46	8.20	M	1	8,840

Instructions

1. Enter the basic payroll information for each employee in a payroll register. Record the employee's name, number of withholding allowances, marital status, total and overtime hours, and regular hourly rate. Consider any hours worked beyond 40 in the week as overtime hours.
2. Compute the regular earnings, overtime premium, and total earnings for each employee. Enter the figures in the payroll register. Cohen, Lima, and Ryan are shop employees. Wills is an office worker.
3. Compute the amount of social security tax to be withheld from each employee's earnings. Assume a 6.5 percent social security rate on the first $60,000 earned by the employee during the year. Enter the figures in the payroll register.
4. Compute the amount of medicare tax to be withheld from each employee's earnings. Assume a 1.5 percent medicare tax rate on the first $140,000 earned by the employee during the year. Enter the figures in the payroll register.
5. Determine the amount of federal income tax to be withheld from each employee's total earnings. Use the tax tables in Figure 10–2. Enter the figures in the payroll register.
6. Compute the net pay of each employee and enter the figures in the payroll register.
7. Total the payroll register.
8. Prepare a general journal entry to record the payroll for the week ended July 7, 19X5.
9. Record the general journal entry to summarize payment of the payroll on July 10, 19X5.

PROBLEM 10–2A
(Obj. 2, 3, 4, 5)

Computing gross earnings, determining deductions, preparing payroll register, journalizing payroll transactions. Jim Alexander operates the Alexander Engineering Service. He has four employees who are paid on an hourly basis. During the work week beginning December 12 and ending December 18, 19X3, his employees worked the number of hours shown below. Information about their hourly rates, marital status, and withholding allowances also appears below, along with their cumulative earnings for the year prior to the December 12–18 payroll period.

Employee	Hours Worked	Regular Hourly Rate	Marital Status	Withholding Allowances	Cumulative Earnings
Brian DeMugeot	43	$ 8.40	M	3	$16,000
Lisa Moore	38	30.00	S	1	59,200
Ross Peters	45	20.00	M	2	40,000
Donna Sims	42	7.30	S	0	15,500

Instructions

1. Enter the basic payroll information for each employee in a payroll register. Record the employee's name, number of withholding allowances, marital status, total and overtime hours, and regular

hourly rate. Consider any hours worked beyond 40 in the week as overtime hours.

2. Compute the regular earnings, overtime premium, and gross earnings for each employee. Enter the figures in the payroll register.
3. Compute the amount of social security tax to be withheld from each employee's gross earnings. Assume a 6.5 percent social security rate on the first $60,000 earned by the employee during the year. Enter the figures in the payroll register.
4. Compute the amount of medicare tax to be withheld from each employee's gross earnings. Assume a 1.5 percent medicare tax rate on the first $140,000 earned by the employee during the year. Enter the figures in the payroll register.
5. Determine the amount of federal income tax to be withheld from each employee's total earnings. Use the tax tables in Figure 10–2. Enter the figures in the payroll register.
6. Compute the net amount due each employee and enter the figures in the payroll register.
7. Total and prove the payroll register. DeMugeot and Sims are office workers. Moore and Peters are drafting workers.
8. Prepare a general journal entry to record the payroll for the week ended December 18, 19X3.
9. Give the entry in general journal form on December 20 to summarize payment of wages for the week.

PROBLEM SET B

PROBLEM 10–1B
(Obj. 2, 3, 4, 5)

Tutorial

Computing earnings, determining deductions and net amount due, preparing payroll register, journalizing payroll transactions. The four employees of Satorical Manufacturing Company are paid on an hourly basis. During the week beginning January 6 and ending January 12, 19X3, these employees worked the number of hours shown below. Information about their hourly rates, marital status, withholding allowances, and cumulative earnings prior to the current pay period also appears below.

Employee	Hours Worked	Regular Hourly Rate	Marital Status	Withholding Allowances	Cumulative Earnings
Terry Ussery	42	$9.50	M	3	$380.00
Tim Ihloff	48	8.60	M	4	344.00
Sue Ong	36	9.75	S	1	390.00
Jane Ross	48	8.90	S	2	356.00

Instructions

1. Enter the basic payroll information for each employee in a payroll register. Record the employee's name, number of withholding allowances, marital status, total hours, overtime hours, and regular hourly rate. Consider any hours worked beyond 40 in the week as overtime hours.

2. Compute the regular earnings, overtime premium, and gross earnings for each employee. Enter the figures in the payroll register.
3. Compute the amount of social security tax to be withheld from each employee's gross earnings. Assume a 6.5 percent social security tax rate on the first $60,000 earned by each employee during the year. Enter the figures in the payroll register.
4. Compute the amount of medicare tax to be withheld from each employee's gross earnings. Assume a 1.5 percent tax rate on the first $140,000 earned by the employee during the year. Enter the figures in the payroll register.
5. Determine the amount of federal income tax to be withheld from each employee's gross earnings. Use the tax tables in Figure 10–2. Enter the figures in the payroll register.
6. Compute the net amount due each employee and enter the figures in the payroll register.
7. Complete the payroll register. Ussery, Ihloff, and Ross are shop workers; Ong is an office worker.
8. Prepare a general journal entry to record the payroll for the week ended January 12, 19X5.
9. Record the general journal entry to summarize the payment on January 15 of the net amounts due employees.

PROBLEM 10–2B
(Obj. 2, 3, 4, 5)

Tutorial

Computing earnings, determining deductions and net amount due, preparing payroll register, journalizing payroll transactions. Jesus Morales operates the Morales Consulting Service. He has four employees and pays them on an hourly basis. During the week ended December 12, 19X3, his employees worked the number of hours shown below. Information about their hourly rates, marital status, withholding allowances, and cumulative earnings for the year prior to the current pay period also appears below.

Employee	Hours Worked	Regular Hourly Rate	Marital Status	Withholding Allowances	Cumulative Earnings
Sue Able	42	$ 8.30	M	2	15,936
Don Kolbe	35	8.50	S	1	14,590
Carl Rizzo	44	32.00	M	3	58,850
Lena Staggs	40	42.00	S	1	77,280

Instructions

1. Enter the basic payroll information for each employee in a payroll register. Record the employee's name, number of withholding allowances, marital status, total hours, overtime hours, and regular hourly rate. Consider any hours worked beyond 40 in the week as overtime hours.
2. Compute the regular earnings, overtime premium, and gross earnings for each employee. Enter the figures in the payroll register.

3. Compute the amount of social security tax to be withheld from each employee's gross earnings. Assume a 6.5 percent social security rate on the first $60,000 earned by the employee during the year. Enter the figures in the payroll register.
4. Compute the amount of medicare tax to be withheld from each employee's gross earnings. Assume a 1.5 percent medicare tax rate on the first $140,000 earned during the year. Enter the figures in the payroll register.
5. The amount of federal income tax to be withheld for Rizzo is $260; for Stagg, $414. Use the tax tables in Figure 10–2 to determine withholding for Able and Kolbe. Enter the figures in the payroll register.
6. Compute the net amount due each employee and enter the figures in the payroll register.
7. Complete the payroll register. Able and Kolbe are office workers. Earnings for Rizzo and Staggs are charged to consulting wages.
8. Prepare a general journal entry to record the payroll for the week ended December 12, 19X3. Use the account titles given in this chapter.
9. Give the general journal entry to summarize payment of amounts due employees.

CHALLENGE PROBLEM

Aires Company pays salaries and wages on the last day of each month. Payments made on November 30, 19X4, for amounts incurred during November are shown below. Cumulative amounts paid prior to November 30 to the persons named are also shown.

a. Jamail Abar, president, gross monthly salary $13,000; gross earnings paid prior to November 30, $138,000
b. Joy Cummings, vice president, gross monthly salary $10,000; gross earnings paid prior to November 30, $55,000
c. Mary Spillane, independent accountant who audits the company's accounts and performs certain consulting services, $12,000; gross amount paid prior to November 30, $4,000
d. Herman Hickman, treasurer, gross monthly salary $4,000; gross earnings paid prior to November 30, $44,000
e. Payment to Acme Security Services for Alex Greene, a security guard who is on duty on Saturdays and Sundays, $800; amount paid to Acme Security prior to November 30, $8,000

Instructions

1. Using the tax rates and earnings ceilings given in this chapter, prepare a schedule showing:
   a. Each employee's cumulative earnings prior to November 30
   b. Each employee's gross earnings for November
   c. The amounts to be withheld for each payroll tax from each employee's earnings (employee income tax withholdings for Abar are $3,400; for Cummings, $3,000; and for Hickman, $820)

   d. The net amount due each employee
   e. The total gross earnings, the total of each payroll tax deduction, and the total net amount payable to employees
2. Record the general journal entry for the company's payroll on November 30.
3. Record the general journal entry for payments to employees on November 30.

CRITICAL THINKING PROBLEM

Several years ago, Carlos Gonzales opened the Fajita Grill, a restaurant specializing in homemade Mexican food. The restaurant was so successful that Gonzales was able to expand and his company, Fajita Grill, now operates seven restaurants in the local area.

Gonzales tells you that when he first started, he handled all aspects of the business himself. Now that there are seven Fajita Grills, he depends on the managers of each restaurant to make decisions and oversee day-to-day operations. Carlos oversees operations at the company's headquarters, which is located at the first Fajita Grill.

Each manager interviews and hires new employees for a restaurant. The new employee is required to complete a W-4, which is sent by the manager to the headquarters office. Each restaurant has a time clock and employees are required to clock in as they arrive or depart. Blank time cards are kept in a box under the time clock. At the beginning of each week, employees complete the top of the card they will use during the week. The manager collects the cards at the end of the week and sends them to headquarters.

Carlos hired his cousin Anita to prepare the payroll instead of assigning this task to the accounting staff. Since she is a relative, Carlos trusts her and has confidence that confidential payroll information will not be divulged to other employees.

When Anita receives a W-4 for a new employee, she sets up an individual earnings record for the employee. Each week, using the time cards sent by each restaurant's manager, she computes the gross pay, deductions, and net pay for all the employees. She then posts details to the employees' earnings records and prepares and signs the payroll checks. The checks are sent to the managers, who distribute them to the employees.

As long as Anita receives a time card for an employee, she prepares a paycheck. If she fails to get a time card for an employee, she checks with the manager to see if the employee was terminated or has quit. At the end of the month, Anita reconciles the payroll bank account and prepares quarterly and annual payroll tax returns.

1. Identify any weaknesses in Fajita Grill's payroll system.
2. Identify one way a manager could defraud Fajita Grill under the present payroll system.
3. What internal control procedures would you recommend to Carlos to protect against the fraud you identified above?

CHAPTER

11

Payroll Taxes, Deposits, and Reports

OBJECTIVES

1. Explain how and when payroll taxes are paid to the government.
2. Compute and record the employer's social security and medicare taxes.
3. Record deposit of social security, medicare, and employee income taxes.
4. Prepare an Employer's Quarterly Federal Tax Return, Form 941.
5. Prepare Wage and Tax Statement, Form W–2.
6. Prepare Annual Transmittal of Income and Tax Statement, Form W–3.
7. Compute and record liability for federal and state unemployment taxes and record payment of the taxes.
8. Prepare an Employer's Federal Unemployment Tax Return, Form 940.
9. Compute and record workers' compensation insurance premiums.
10. Define the accounting terms new to this chapter.

As we explained in Chapter 10, employers are required by law to act as collection agents for the social security, medicare, and income taxes due from employees. Employers must deduct, account for, and transmit these taxes to the federal government. They are also responsible for paying unemployment taxes and reporting employee earnings to the federal government. State and local governments also require various tax payments. This chapter explains how the accountant computes the employer's taxes, makes tax payments, and files the required tax returns and reports. The payroll procedures of the Ajax Mail Order Company will again be used as an example. You will see how this firm handles the work connected with its payroll taxes.

NEW TERMS

Employer's Quarterly Federal Tax Return, Form 941 ▪ Experience rating system ▪ Federal Tax Deposit Coupon, Form 8109 ▪ Merit rating system ▪ Transmittal of Income and Tax Statements, Form W–3 ▪ Unemployment insurance program ▪ Wage and Tax Statement Form W–2 ▪ Withholding statement

PAYMENT OF PAYROLL TAXES

The accountant secures information about wages subject to payroll taxes from the payroll register. Figure 11–1 shows a portion of the payroll register of the Ajax Mail Order Company for the week ended January 6, 19X5.

FIGURE 11–1
Portion of a Payroll Register

AND ENDING *January 6, 19X5* **PAID** *January 8, 19X5*

TAXABLE WAGES			DEDUCTIONS				DISTRIBUTION			
SOCIAL SECURITY	MEDICARE	FUTA	SOCIAL SECURITY	MEDICARE	INCOME TAX	HEALTH INSURANCE	NET AMOUNT	CHECK NO.	OFFICE SALARIES	SHIPPING WAGES
320 00	320 00	320 00	20 80	4 80	25 00		269 40	4725		320 00
322 00	322 00	322 00	20 93	4 83	35 00		261 24	4726		322 00
250 00	250 00	250 00	16 25	3 75	11 00	10 00	209 00	4727		250 00
400 00	400 00	400 00	26 00	6 00	30 00	10 00	328 00	4728		400 00
300 00	300 00	300 00	19 50	4 50	32 00		244 00	4729	300 00	
1592 00	1592 00	1592 00	103 48	23 88	133 00	20 00	1311 64		300 00	1292 00

OBJECTIVE 1

Explain how and when payroll taxes are paid to the government.

The employer must deposit federal income taxes withheld from employee earnings, along with both the employer's and employee's shares of social security and medicare taxes, in a Federal Reserve Bank or other authorized financial institution. Most commercial banks are authorized to accept such deposits. Employers usually make the tax deposits in the commercial bank with which they do business. The employer enters the amount of the deposit on a preprinted government form (a "coupon") that must be included with a check for the taxes that are due. This form is the **Federal Tax Deposit Coupon, Form 8109.** Form 8109 is issued with the employer's name, identification number, and address preprinted on the form for use in making the deposit. Form 8109 is illustrated in Figure 11–2.

FIGURE 11–2
Federal Tax Deposit Coupon, Form 8109

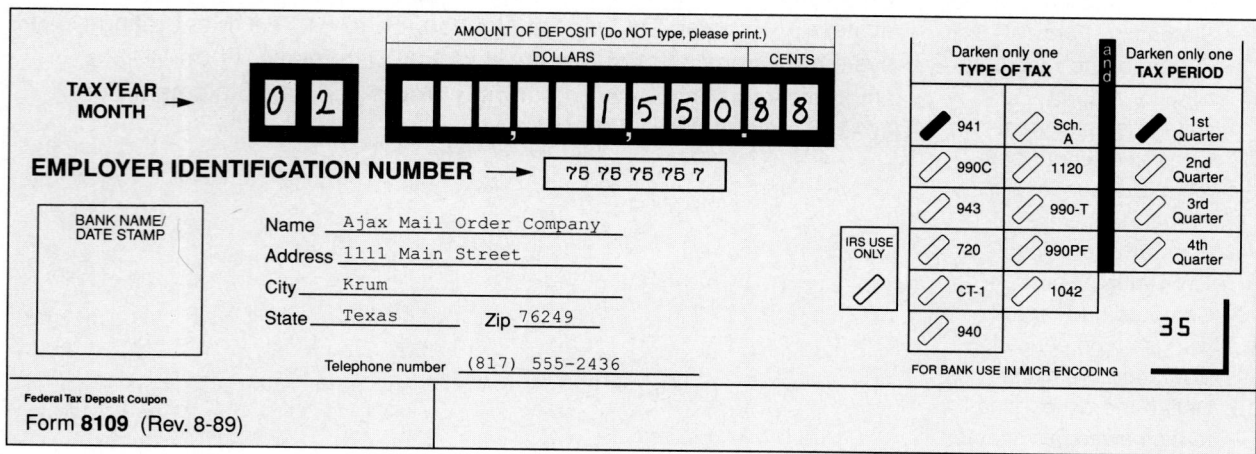

AMOUNT OF DEPOSIT (Do NOT type, please print.)
DOLLARS | CENTS

TAX YEAR MONTH → 0 2   1,550.88

EMPLOYER IDENTIFICATION NUMBER → 75 75 75 75 7

BANK NAME/ DATE STAMP

Name Ajax Mail Order Company
Address 1111 Main Street
City Krum
State Texas Zip 76249
Telephone number (817) 555-2436

IRS USE ONLY

Darken only one TYPE OF TAX: 941 (marked), Sch. A, 990C, 1120, 943, 990-T, 720, 990PF, CT-1, 1042, 940

Darken only one TAX PERIOD: 1st Quarter (marked), 2nd Quarter, 3rd Quarter, 4th Quarter

35

FOR BANK USE IN MICR ENCODING

Federal Tax Deposit Coupon
Form **8109** (Rev. 8-89)

The amount of tax liability at any time determines when payroll taxes must be deposited.

The frequency of deposits is determined by the amount owed. The rules governing the date by which social security, medicare, and income taxes must be deposited can be summarized as follows.

1. If at the end of the quarter the employer's total payroll tax liability for the quarter is less than $500, no deposit is required. The taxes may be paid to the Internal Revenue Service when Form 941 (see Figure 11–4), which contains the details of the tax computation, is filed, or they may be deposited by the end of the following month. ***Example:*** An employer's total payroll tax liability (employer's share of social security and medicare taxes, plus withholdings) for January was $125. For February it was $134, and for March the liability was $130. Since at no time during the quarter was the employer's accumulated liability equal to or greater than $500, no deposit is required. The employer may either include a check for the amount due with Form 941 or make a deposit in the regular depository by April 30.
2. If at the end of any month of the quarter, the cumulative liability for payroll taxes is $500 or more but less than $3,000, the taxes must be deposited within 15 days after the end of the month. ***Example:*** Employer taxes and withholdings on wages paid in October are $450, and taxes on wages paid in November are $550. No deposit is required for October. In November, the cumulative tax liability is $1,000 ($450 plus $550), so a deposit must be made by December 15.
3. If at the end of any "eighth-monthly period" (approximately one-eighth of a month) the total undeposited taxes for the quarter amount to $3,000 or more, they must be deposited within three banking days after the end of that eighth-monthly period. An eighth-monthly period ends on the third, seventh, eleventh, fifteenth, nineteenth, twenty-second, twenty-fifth, and last day of any month. Local holidays observed by authorized financial institutions, Saturdays, Sundays, and legal holidays are not counted as banking days. ***Example:*** The taxes on wages paid from January 4 through January 7 are $2,500; the taxes on wages paid from January 8 through January 11 are $2,000. A separate deposit is not required for the $2,500 because the cumulative liability is less than $3,000. However, the liability of $4,500 accumulated through the second eighth-month period must be deposited within three days after the eleventh of the month, that is, by January 14.
4. If at the end of any day during an eighth-monthly period the total payroll tax liability is $100,000 or more, the total amount must be deposited by the end of the next banking day. Because of the amount involved, few employers must meet this requirement.

There are various exceptions and special rules concerning deposits, making the rules complex and sometimes confusing. Because of the severe penalties for late payment and underpayments, the payroll accountant must be thoroughly familiar with the rules and conform with all requirements.

Employer's Social Security and Medicare Tax Expenses

OBJECTIVE 2
Compute and record the employer's social security and medicare taxes.

Since a business pays the social security tax and medicare tax at the same rate and on the same taxable wages as its employees do, the amount of tax the firm owes is usually the same as that deducted from the employees' earnings. Small differences can occur, however, due to rounding of individual tax deductions. When making the tax deposit, most firms simply deposit an amount equal to the amount deducted from the employees' earnings. Any final difference is settled on the quarterly tax return, Form 941.

The payroll register shown in Figure 11–1 indicates that all salaries and wages paid by the Ajax Mail Order Company for the week ending January 6, 19X5, were subject to social security tax and medicare tax. At the assumed rate of 6.5 percent for social security and 1.5 percent for the medicare tax, the employer's share of those taxes on the payroll would be $103.48 ($1,592 × 0.065) for social security and $23.88 ($1,592 × 0.015) for medicare for a total of $127.36.

These amounts are exactly the same as the total of amounts withheld from the employees' earnings for social security and medicare taxes. Refer to the total of the social security tax and medicare tax columns in the payroll register illustrated in Figure 11–1.

The employer's share of social security and medicare taxes are charged to Payroll Taxes Expense.

Ajax Mail Order Company records its expense and liability for the employer's social security tax and medicare tax in the general journal at the end of each payroll period, as shown below. The total amount of taxes is debited to an account called Payroll Taxes Expense. The individual taxes are credited to Social Security Tax Payable and Medicare Tax Payable, the same liability accounts used to record the employees' contributions. The entry illustrated below records the employer's share of social security tax and medicare tax.

1	*19X5*					1
2	*Jan.*	*6*	*Payroll Taxes Expense*	*127 36*		2
3			*Social Sec. Tax Payable*		*103 48*	3
4			*Medicare Tax Payable*		*23 88*	4
5			*Social security and*			5
6			*medicare taxes on Jan. 6*			6
7			*payroll*			7
8						8

Recording the Payment of Taxes Withheld

OBJECTIVE 3
Record deposit of social security, medicare, and employee income taxes.

At the end of January 19X5, the accounting records of the Ajax Mail Order Company contained the following information about tax deductions from employee earnings and the employer's share of social security and medicare taxes for the month.

Employees' social security tax deducted	$ 413.92
Employees' medicare tax deducted	95.52
Employees' federal income tax deducted	532.00
Employer's social security tax	413.92
Employer's medicare tax	95.52
Total	$1,550.88

Both the employee's share and employer's share of social security and medicare taxes are credited to Social Security Tax Payable and to Medicare Tax Payable.

Payroll tax deposits must be accompanied by a deposit coupon, Form 8109.

Since the total amount owed for employee income tax withheld, social security tax, and medicare tax at the end of January exceeds $500 but is less than $3,000, the amount must be deposited in an authorized bank by February 15, 19X5. As we have already pointed out, the deposit must be accompanied by a properly filled out Federal Tax Deposit Coupon, Form 8109. When this machine-readable form is processed, the amount paid is credited to the employer by the Internal Revenue Service. The Form 8109 filed in February by the Ajax Mail Order Company is shown in Figure 11–2. This form covers the payment of the January social security tax, medicare tax, and federal income tax withholdings owed by the firm. Note on Form 8109 a block in which the taxpayer indicates the type of tax being deposited. Because social security, medicare, and employee income taxes are reported on Form 941 at the end of each quarter, the space indicated as "941" is darkened by the accountant for Ajax. The form also contains a block for the preparer to indicate, when appropriate, the quarter of the year for which the deposit is being made.

Deposits of social security tax, medicare tax, and employee income tax withheld are usually made in a commercial bank.

A check is written to the depository bank, which in this case is the Security National Bank. The transaction is entered in the cash payments journal. The effect of the entry is as follows.

1	*19X5*					1
2	*Feb.*	*15*	*Social Sec. Tax Payable*	*827 84*		2
3			*Medicare Tax Payable*	*191 04*		3
4			*Employee Income Tax Payable*	*532 00*		4
5			*Cash*		*1 550 88*	5
6			*Deposit of payroll taxes*			6
7			*at Security National Bank*			7

February Payroll Records

Four weekly payroll periods occurred in February for the Ajax Mail Order Company. To simplify this example, assume that each hourly employee worked the same number of hours each week as in January and had the same gross pay and deductions. Assume also that the office clerk, Mill Yamoah, earned his regular salary and had the same deductions as in January. The individual earnings records for the employees were posted as previously described. Then a tax deposit form was prepared and the taxes deposited in the bank. Finally, an entry was made in the cash payments journal to record the deposit.

March Payroll Records

In March, Ajax Company had five weekly payroll periods, making a total of 13 weekly periods for the quarter. For the sake of simplicity, we assume that the payroll for the week ending March 31 was paid on that date. Assume again that the earnings and deductions of the employees were the same for each week as in January and February. We have seen that these amounts were as follows:

Employees' social security tax withheld	$103.48
Employer's social security tax	103.48
Employees' medicare tax withheld	23.88
Employer's medicare tax	23.88
Employees' income tax withheld	133.00
Total taxes each week	$387.72

The firm therefore owed a total of $1,938.60 for March social security tax, medicare tax, and federal income tax withholdings ($387.72 × 5 = $1,938.60). The necessary tax deposit was made before the due date of April 15 and was recorded in the cash payments journal.

Quarterly Summary of Earnings Records

At the end of each calendar quarter, the individual earnings records are totaled for the quarter. This procedure involves adding the amounts in each column in the Earnings, Deductions, and Net Pay sections of each employee's record. The sums are placed on the line for the appropriate quarter. The record for Cass Collins, completely posted and summarized for the first quarter, is illustrated in Figure

FIGURE 11–3
Individual Earnings Record

EARNINGS RECORD FOR *19X5*

NAME *Cass Collins* **RATE** *$8 per hour* **SOC. SEC. NO.** *123-45-6789*
ADDRESS *24 Oak Street, Krum, Texas 76249* **DATE OF BIRTH** *Jan. 23, 1970*
WITHHOLDING ALLOWANCES *1* **MARITAL STATUS** *M*

	DATE		HOURS		EARNINGS				DEDUCTIONS				NET PAY
	WK. END.	PAID	RG	OT	REGULAR	OVERTIME	TOTAL	CUMULATIVE TOTAL	SOCIAL SECURITY	MEDICARE	INCOME TAX	OTHER	
1	1/06	1/08	40		320 00		320 00	320 00	20 80	4 80	25 00		269 40
2	1/13	1/15	40		320 00		320 00	640 00	20 80	4 80	25 00		269 40
3	1/20	1/22	40		320 00		320 00	960 00	20 80	4 80	25 00		269 40
4	1/27	1/29	40		320 00		320 00	1280 00	20 80	4 80	25 00		269 40
January Total					1280 00		1280 00		83 20	19 20	100 00		1077 60
1	2/03	2/05	40		320 00		320 00	1600 00	20 80	4 80	25 00		269 40
2	2/10	2/12	40		320 00		320 00	1920 00	20 80	4 80	25 00		269 40
3	2/17	2/19	40		320 00		320 00	2240 00	20 80	4 80	25 00		269 40
4	2/24	2/25	40		320 00		320 00	2560 00	20 80	4 80	25 00		269 40
February Total					1280 00		1280 00		83 20	19 20	100 00		1077 60
1	3/03	3/05	40		320 00		320 00	2880 00	20 80	4 80	25 00		269 40
2	3/10	3/12	40		320 00		320 00	3200 00	20 80	4 80	25 00		269 40
3	3/17	3/19	40		320 00		320 00	3520 00	20 80	4 80	25 00		269 40
4	3/24	3/26	40		320 00		320 00	3840 00	20 80	4 80	25 00		269 40
5	3/31	3/31	40		320 00		320 00	4160 00	20 80	4 80	25 00		269 40
March Total					1600 00		1600 00		104 00	24 00	125 00		1347 00
First Quarter					4160 00		4160 00	4160 00	270 40	62 40	325 00		3502 20

11–3. Information for the other three quarters will also be entered on the record and the totals for the year computed and entered.

The quarterly totals of relevant items for each employee of the Ajax Company, taken from the individual earnings records, are shown in Table 11–1. Note that all earnings are subject to the social security tax, medicare tax, and unemployment taxes because no worker has earned more than the maximum amount subject to any of the taxes.

TABLE 11–1
Summary of Earnings, Quarter Ended March 31, 19X5

	Taxable Earnings				Deductions		
Employee	Total Earnings	Social Sec.	Medicare	SUTA & FUTA	Social Sec.	Medicare Tax	Income Tax
Cass Collins	4,160	4,160	4,160	4,160	270.40	62.40	325.00
Enos Echols	4,186	4,186	4,186	4,186	272.09	62.79	455.00
Carol Johansen	3,250	3,250	3,250	3,250	211.25	48.75	143.00
Rita Sanchez	5,200	5,200	5,200	5,200	338.00	78.00	390.00
Mill Yamoah	3,900	3,900	3,900	3,900	253.50	58.50	416.00
Totals	20,696	20,696	20,696	20,696	1,345.24	310.44	1,729.00

EMPLOYER'S QUARTERLY FEDERAL TAX RETURN

OBJECTIVE 4
Prepare an Employer's Quarterly Federal Tax Return, Form 941.

Each quarter most employers must file with the Internal Revenue Service a tax report called the **Employer's Quarterly Federal Tax Return, Form 941.** This tax report provides information about the total wages and other employee earnings subject to federal income tax withholding, the total wages and tips subject to social security tax and medicare tax, the total of the taxes owed for each of the deposit periods in the quarter, and the total of the deposits made by the employer. In effect, Form 941 serves as a verification of the employer's compliance with the applicable laws.

When to File Form 941

Form 941 must be filed quarterly by all employers subject to federal income tax withholding, social security tax, or medicare tax, with certain exceptions as specified in *Circular E.* The due date for the return and any balance of taxes owed is the last day of the month following the end of each calendar quarter. If all taxes for the quarter have been deposited when due, the employer may file the return without penalty by the tenth day of the second month following the end of the quarter. Ajax Mail Order Company's Form 941 for the first quarter of 19X5 is shown in Figure 11–4 on page 376.

Completing Form 941

Much of the data needed to complete Form 941 is obtained from the quarterly summary of earnings records shown in Table 11–1. The top of Form 941 shows the employer's name, address, and identification number, along with the date on which the quarter covered by the return ended. Let's examine each line of the completed form.

FIGURE 11–4
Employer's Quarterly Federal Tax Return, Form 941

Form **941** (Rev. January **19 --**) Department of the Treasury Internal Revenue Service

4141

Employer's Quarterly Federal Tax Return

▶ See Circular E for more information concerning employment tax returns.

Please type or print.

Type or print your name, address, employer identification number, and calendar quarter of return as shown on original. ▶

Name (as distinguished from trade name) Jean Shaatke	Date quarter ended March 31, 19X5
Trade name, if any Ajax Mail Order Company	Employer identification number 75-7575757
Address (number and street) 1111 Main Street	City, state, and ZIP code Krum, TX 76249

If you do not have to file returns in the future, check here ▶ ☐ Date final wages paid . . . ▶ ______

If you are a seasonal employer, see **Seasonal employers** on page 2 and check here . . ▶ ☐

1	Number of employees (except household) employed in the pay period that includes March 12th ▶	1	5
2	Total wages and tips subject to withholding, plus other compensation . . . . ▶	2	20,696 00
3	Total income tax withheld from wages, tips, pensions, annuities, sick pay, gambling, etc. . ▶	3	1,729 00
4	Adjustment of withheld income tax for preceding quarters of calendar year (see instructions) . ▶	4	
5	Adjusted total of income tax withheld (line 3 as adjusted by line 4—see instructions) . . .	5	1,729 00
6a	Taxable social security wages (**Complete line 7**) $ 20,696.00 x 13% (.13) =	6a	2,690 48
b	Taxable social security tips $ x 13% (.13) =	6b	
7	Taxable Medicare wages and tips . . . . $ 20,696.00 x 3% (.03) =	7	620 88
8	Total social security and Medicare taxes (add lines 6a, 6b, and 7)	8	3,311 36
9	Adjustment of social security and Medicare taxes (see instructions for required explanation) .	9	
10	Adjusted total of social security and Medicare taxes (line 8 as adjusted by line 9—see instructions) . ▶	10	3,311 36
11	Backup withholding (see instructions)	11	
12	Adjustment of backup withholding tax for preceding quarters of calendar year	12	
13	Adjusted total of backup withholding (line 11 as adjusted by line 12)	13	
14	**Total taxes** (add lines 5, 10, and 13)	14	5,040 36
15	Advance earned income credit (EIC) payments made to employees, if any . . . . . ▶	15	
16	Net taxes (subtract line 15 from line 14). **This should equal line IV below** (plus line IV of Schedule A (Form 941) if you have treated backup withholding as a separate liability) . . .	16	5,040 36
17	**Total deposits for quarter,** including overpayment applied from a prior quarter, from your records . ▶	17	5,040 36
18	**Balance due** (subtract line 17 from line 16). This should be less than $500. Pay to Internal Revenue Service . . ▶	18	
19	**Overpayment,** if line 17 is more than line 16, enter excess here ▶ $ ______ and check if to be: ☐ Applied to next return **OR** ☐ Refunded.		

Record of Federal Tax Liability (You must complete if line 16 is $500 or more and Schedule B is not attached.) See instructions before checking these boxes.

If you made deposits using the 95% rule, check here ▶ ☐ If you are a first time 3-banking-day depositor, check here . . ▶ ☐

▶ **DO NOT** Show Federal Tax Deposits Here ▶

Date wages paid		Show tax liability here, **not deposits.** The IRS gets deposit data from FTD coupons. First month of quarter		Second month of quarter		Third month of quarter
1st through 3rd	A		I		Q	
4th through 7th	B		J		R	
8th through 11th	C		K		S	
12th through 15th	D		L		T	
16th through 19th	E		M		U	
20th through 22nd	F		N		V	
23rd through 25th	G		O		W	
26th through the last	H		P		X	
Total liability for month	*I*	1,550.88	*II*	1,550.88	*III*	1,938.60

IV Total for quarter (add lines *I*, *II*, and *III*). **This should equal line 16 above** . . . . . . ▶ 5,040.36

Sign Here Under penalties of perjury, I declare that I have examined this return, including accompanying schedules and statements, and to the best of my knowledge and belief, it is true, correct, and complete.

Signature ▶ Jean Shaatke Print Your Name and Title ▶ Owner Date ▶ March 31, 19X5

- *Line 1* is completed only during the first quarter of the year and shows the number of employees employed in the pay period that includes March 12.
- *Line 2* shows total wages and tips subject to withholding, plus other compensation. For Ajax Company, the total of the wages subject to withholding is $20,696.
- *Line 3* is used to enter the total income tax withheld—$1,729—during the quarter.
- *Line 4* shows adjustments of income tax withheld in prior periods of the year. Essentially this number reflects corrections of errors made in withholding.
- *Line 5* is used to enter the adjusted income tax reported on this return. Since Ajax had no adjustments on line 4, the amount of $1,729 is also entered on line 5.
- *Line 6a* reflects the total of the wages subject to social security tax and the amount of social security tax on the wages for the quarter. For Ajax Company, taxable wages paid in the first quarter are $20,696. This amount is multiplied by 13 percent, which represents the assumed combined rate for both the employer and the employee (2 × 6.5% = 13%). The resulting social security tax on wages paid during the quarter is $2,690.48 (0.13 × $20,696 = $2,690.48).
- *Line 6b* is used when taxable tips, such as those earned by a waiter, are reported.
- *Line 7* reflects the wages and tips subject to the medicare tax and the total of the employees' and employer's medicare tax due. The taxable wages of $20,296 is multiplied by the assumed total rate of 0.03 to arrive at the total medicare tax of $620.88.
- *Line 8* shows the total amount of social security and medicare taxes. The taxes total $3,311.36.

Social security tax (from line 6a)	$2,690.48
Medicare tax (from line 7)	620.88
Total	$3,311.36

- *Line 9* is used to show adjustments, or corrections, of social security taxes reported on prior returns. Ajax has no such adjustments.
- *Line 10* reflects the total of social security taxes and medicare taxes on wages paid during the quarter, plus or minus any adjustments. Since Ajax had no adjustments related to social security taxes or medicare taxes, the amount $3,311.36 is entered on line 10 as the adjusted total of social security tax and medicare tax for the quarter.
- *Line 11* does not relate to taxes on payroll, but to withholding of income tax on interest, dividends, and certain other payments when the payee has not filed a proper identification number or under certain other conditions. Ajax has no backup withholding.
- *Lines 12 and 13* show adjustments to the backup withholding tax and the adjusted balance of backup withholding due.

- *Line 14* reflects the sum of the following two lines:

Line 5, adjusted income tax withheld	$1,729.00
Line 10, adjusted total of social security and medicare taxes	3,311.36
Total taxes	$5,040.36

- *Line 15* is used to record a special income tax provision that may be selected by certain low-income employees; it is not relevant to our discussion.
- *Line 16* reflects the total net taxes for the quarter. Since Ajax had no advanced earned income credit, the net tax is $5,040.36, the same amount shown on line 14.
- *Line 17* shows the total amounts that have been deposited during the quarter. Ajax has made deposits equal to the total of taxes due for the quarter.
- *Line 18* reflects the net balance due when the deposits have been less than the total taxes for the quarter.
- *Line 19* shows the amount by which deposits exceed the actual tax liability for the quarter.

Since Ajax's total liability for the quarter, as shown on line 16 of Form 941, is $500 or more, the section labeled "Record of Federal Tax Liability" at the bottom of Form 941 must be completed. This section shows the amount of taxes applicable to wages paid during each eighth-monthly period. Because Ajax's payroll tax liability for each month was less than $3,000, however, the company is required to show only the total tax liability for each month. It is not required to fill out lines A through X of the Record of Federal Tax Liability. The total tax liability for the quarter, $5,040.36, is entered on line IV. This amount and the amount on line 16 must be equal.

If any taxes are owed when Form 941 is completed, a check may be issued to the Internal Revenue Service for the amount due and sent with Form 941, or a deposit may be made in an authorized depository.

If the employer has not deducted enough taxes from the employees' earnings, the firm must make up any difference. This deficiency increases the charge to the firm's Payroll Taxes Expense account.

WAGE AND TAX STATEMENT, FORM W-2

OBJECTIVE 5

Prepare wage and tax statement, Form W-2.

After the end of each calendar year, employers must give each employee a **Wage and Tax Statement, Form W-2,** which is often referred to as a withholding statement. This form contains information about the employee's earnings and tax withholdings for the year. Form W-2 for each employee must be issued by January 31 of the next year. If an employee leaves the firm before the end of the year, the employer may provide Form W-2 at any time after the employee leaves, up to January 31 of the next year. However, if the employee asks for Form W-2 sooner, it must be issued within 30 days after the request or after the final wage payment, whichever is later.

The employer must provide each employee with a Wage and Tax Statement, Form W-2, by January 31 of the next year.

Although the Form W-2 illustrated in Figure 11–5 is the standard form provided by the Internal Revenue Service, employers may use a "substitute" Form W-2, provided it meets certain physical and content requirements. The substitute form is allowed to facilitate the preparation of the forms by the employer's computer system. Using a substitute form also permits the employer to list deductions other than those for tax withholdings and to reconcile the gross earnings with the deductions and net pay. Most employers with large numbers of employees use substitute forms.

FIGURE 11–5
Wage and Tax Statement, Form W-2

1 Control number 22222 | For Official Use Only ▶ | OMB No. 1545-0008

2 Employer's name, address, and ZIP code
Ajax Mail Order Company
111 Main Street
Krum, TX 76249

6 Statutory employee ☒ | Deceased ☐ | Pension plan ☐ | Legal rep ☐ | 942 emp ☐ | Subtotal ☐ | Deferred compensation ☐ | Void ☐

7 Allocated tips | 8 Advance EIC payment

9 Federal income tax withheld 1,300.00 | 10 Wages, tips, other compensation 16,640.00

3 Employer's identification number 75-7575757 | 4 Employer's state I.D. number 12-98765

11 Social security tax withheld 1,081.60 | 12 Social security wages 16,640.00

5 Employee's social security number 123-45-6789

13 Social security tips | 14 Medicare wages and tips 16,640.00

19a Employee's name (first, middle initial, last)
Cass C. Collins

15 Medicare tax withheld 249.60 | 16 Nonqualified plans

24 East Oak St.
Krum, TX 76249
19b Employee's address and ZIP code

17 See Instrs. for Form W-2 | 18 Other

20 | 21 | 22 Dependent care benefits | 23 Benefits included in Box 10

24 State income tax | 25 State wages, tips, etc. | 26 Name of state | 27 Local income tax | 28 Local wages, tips, etc. | 29 Name of locality

Copy A For Social Security Administration | Department of the Treasury—Internal Revenue Service

Form **W-2 Wage and Tax Statement 19--**

Information for Form W-2 is obtained from the individual employee earnings records.

The information for Form W-2 is obtained from the individual employee earnings records after they have been posted and summarized for the year. Assume that the individual earnings records for the employees of the Ajax Company reflect the totals shown below for the year. Notice that none of the employees earned more than the assumed social security tax and medicare tax base of $60,000 during the year. Therefore, all wages and salaries paid were subject to social security and medicare tax.

Employee	Total Earnings	Social Sec. Tax	Medicare Tax	Income Tax
Cass Collins	$16,640.00	$1,081.60	$ 249.60	$1,300.00
Enos Echols	16,744.00	1,088.36	251.16	1,820.00
Carol Johansen	13,000.00	845.00	195.00	572.00
Rita Sanchez	20,800.00	1,352.00	312.00	1,560.00
Mill Yamoah	15,600.00	1,014.00	234.00	1,664.00
Totals	$82,784.00	$5,380.96	$1,241.76	$6,916.00

The withholding statement for Cass Collins is illustrated in Figure 11–5.

At least four copies of each Form W-2 must be prepared. Two copies are given to the employee, who attaches one copy to his or her personal federal income tax return that must be filed for each year and saves the other with personal records. One of the remaining copies is transmitted to the Social Security Administration, which processes the form and sends it to the Internal Revenue Service. The transmittal of forms to the Social Security Administration is discussed in the next section. The final copy is retained for the employer's permanent files.

If there is a state income tax in addition to the federal income tax, six copies of Form W-2 are prepared. Three are given to the employee, who must attach one to the federal income tax return, attach one to the state income tax return, and keep the other for his or her own permanent records. The employer keeps one copy for the firm's records, sends one to the state tax department, and sends one to the Social Security Administration. If there is a city or county income tax as well as the state tax, the firm must prepare additional copies of Form W-2.

ANNUAL TRANSMITTAL OF INCOME AND TAX STATEMENTS, FORM W–3

OBJECTIVE 6

Prepare Annual Transmittal of Income and Tax Statement, Form W-3.

After filing the last quarterly return for the year on Form 941, the employer must also prepare a **Transmittal of Income and Tax Statements, Form W-3.** This form must be submitted with a copy of Form W-2 for each employee to the Social Security Administration. Form W-3 is due by the last day of February following the end of the calendar year. The Social Security Administration processes each Form W-2, records the employee's social security wages and medicare wages, and sends the employee's social security, medicare tax, and income tax information to the Internal Revenue Service. If an employer files 250 or more information returns, a "magnetic medium" (tape or disk) must be used for the filing.

Form W-3 reports the total social security wages; total medicare wages; total social security tax withheld; total medicare tax withheld; total wages, tips, and other compensation; total federal income tax withheld; and other information. These totals must be the same as those reported on the Forms W-2 submitted and on the quarterly Forms 941 for the year. The Forms W-2 allow the government to identify the employees from whose salaries federal income tax and FICA tax were withheld during the year and to make sure that the totals withheld agree with the amounts remitted by the employer. The completed Form W-3 for the Ajax Mail Order Company for 19X5 appears in Figure 11–6.

The filing of Form W-3 marks the end of the routine procedures needed to account for payrolls and for social security tax, medicare tax, and federal income tax withholdings.

FIGURE 11–6
Transmittal of Income and Tax Statements, Form W-3

1 Control Number		OMB No. 1545-0008
Kind of Payer ▶	2 941/941E ☒ Military ☐ 943 ☐ CT-1 ☐ 942 ☐ Medicare govt. emp. ☐	3 Employer's state I.D. number 12-98765 / 4 / 5 Total number of statements 5
6 Establishment number	7 Allocated tips	8 Advance EIC payments
9 Federal income tax withheld 6,916.00	10 Wages, tips, and other compensation 82,784.00	11 Social security tax withheld 5,380.96
12 Social security wages 82,784.00	13 Social security tips	14 Medicare wages and tips
15 Medicare tax withheld 1,241.76	16 Nonqualified plans	17 Deferred compensation
18 Employer's identification number 75-7575757		19 Other EIN used this year
20 Employer's name Ajax Mail Jean Shaatke dba Order Co.		21 Dependent care benefits
		23 Adjusted total social security wages and tips 82,784.00
		24 Adjusted total Medicare wages and tips 82,784.00
22 Employer's address and ZIP code		25 Income tax withheld by third-party payer

Form **W-3** Transmittal of Income and Tax Statements **19--** Department of the Treasury Internal Revenue Service

S E L F - R E V I E W

1. What factor determines how often deposits of social security, medicare, and income tax withholdings are made?
2. What is meant by an "eighth-monthly" period?
3. Where are deposits of federal payroll taxes made?
4. What is the purpose of Form 941? What are the due dates of Form 941?
5. What is the purpose of Form W-2? To whom is the form provided?

Answers to Self-Review

1. The amount of taxes due at any one time determines when the deposit must be made.
2. Each month is divided into periods of approximately one-eighth of a month. The period is used for determining when an employer who owes $3,000 or more in taxes must deposit the taxes.
3. Payroll taxes must be deposited in a Federal Reserve Bank or a commercial bank that is designated as a federal depository.
4. Form 941 is a form filed each quarter showing income taxes withheld, along with social security tax and medicare tax due for the quarter. The form is due on the last day of the month following the end of the quarter.
5. Form W-2 provides information to enable the employee to complete his or her personal federal income tax return. Copies are given to the employee and to the federal government (and to other governmental units that levy an income tax).

Information Block: Communication

Memorandums

As you learned in the communication project in Chapter 9, business professionals often prepare written documents to communicate with others both inside and outside their company. Applying your document formatting knowledge, along with the steps for planning and developing effective business communication, will allow you to make the best first impression with your written communication.

Memorandums (or memos) are written messages between people within a company. The format for memos may differ slightly from company to company; however, the most common memo format consists primarily of a heading and body. As with block format letters, all lines in a memo begin at the left margin.

Each of the basic memo parts is described below and the spacing for each is shown in the accompanying illustration.

- The **heading** includes the word(s) *Memorandum, Interoffice Communication,* or *Memo;* the company name and perhaps the department name; the words *To, From, Date, Subject.* Companies may use printed memo forms or a computerized memo form.

  To indicates the receiver's name and may include that person's title and/or department. Courtesy titles (Ms., Mr., etc.) are usually omitted. *From* indicates the sender's name and may include that person's title and/or department. Again, courtesy titles are omitted. *Date* shows the month, day, and year the memo is written. *Subject* states the topic of the memo.
- The **body** of the memo contains your message, which incorporates the nine steps for planning and developing effective communication.
- **Reference initials** indicate the person who keyed the memo. When you key your own memo, do not include reference initials.
- An **enclosure notation** (*Enclosure*) is used to indicate that you have included other material with the memo.
- A **copy notation** (*c* followed by names) is used to specify the individuals who receive a copy of the memo in addition to the person indicated in the *To* line.

To achieve a favorable impression with your memos, follow these four steps.

TRI-STATE ACCOUNTING FIRM
122 Western Avenue, Cincinnati, OH 45202-8903
Telephone: (513) 555-1234
FAX: (513) 555-1235

2 inches

(Press *Enter* 2 times after each part of the heading.)

1" Left and Right Margins

MEMO TO: Joy Alvarez, Vice President

FROM: Jim McNamara, Accounting Manager

DATE: July 7, 19X5

SUBJECT: Expense Account (Press *Enter* 3 times.)

Body

As the enclosed second quarter expense report indicates, the total of your expense account through June 30 is $12,459. Since your expenses are distributed fairly proportionately throughout the year and your annual budget for expenses is $25,000, you should be within your budgeted amount at the end of the year. (Press *Enter* 2 times.)

Please review this report for any inaccuracies. Call me at extension 133 if you wish to discuss your expense account report. (Press *Enter* 2 times.)

jdt
Enclosure

Reference Initials
Enclosure Notation

1. Apply the nine steps for planning and developing messages and the four characteristics of effective business communication.
2. Use the appropriate heading (printed or computerized form).
3. Confirm that your memo includes the appropriate memo parts with accurate formatting.
4. Write your initials beside your name on the *From* line and send a memo only when you are convinced that it will communicate effectively, resulting in a favorable impression.

Project: Using an actual memo that you have received or that you borrow from a friend or family member, analyze the appearance of the document.

1. Without reading the memo, describe your initial impression of the sender based on the appearance of the document.
2. After reading the memo, describe your initial impression of the sender based on the appearance and the message.
3. Does the memo include the appropriate parts with accurate formatting?
4. Did the sender choose the correct written format for the communication?
5. Identify any revisions you would make to create a more favorable impression.

UNEMPLOYMENT COMPENSATION INSURANCE TAXES

OBJECTIVE 7

Compute and record liability for federal and state unemployment taxes and record payment of the taxes.

As we have already discussed, the unemployment compensation tax program, often called the **unemployment insurance program,** provides benefits to unemployed workers. The tax is levied on the employer but not on the employee. The taxes, records, and reports that are required by federal and state unemployment insurance regulations are discussed in this section.

Coordination of Federal and State Unemployment Rates

The federal government allows a reduction in the federal unemployment tax for amounts charged by the state for unemployment taxes.

Although the unemployment tax program is essentially a federal program, it encourages the states to provide their own unemployment insurance plans for employees working within the state. Special provisions permit employers to reduce their federal tax liability by amounts charged under the state unemployment tax program, within limits. The limit on credit for charges by state unemployment compensation plans that may be offset against the federal tax is 5.4 percent of covered compensation. All states have established charges of at least that rate. In our examples, we shall assume that the basic federal rate is 6.2 percent of wages, but that a credit against the federal tax is allowed for a 5.4 percent charge by the state. The federal tax is therefore assumed to be 0.8 percent (0.008) of the first $7,000 paid each employee during the year. Remember that payroll tax rates and the bases to which they apply change frequently and payroll personnel must keep abreast of changes.

In addition to the tax on the employer, a few states also levy an unemployment tax on the employee. The amount withheld is determined by the employer at the rate and on the base earnings required by state law. The amount of state tax withheld from the employee's paycheck is sent to the appropriate state agency at the specified time and in the specified manner. The handling of this tax is similar in principle to the handling of the employee's social security and medicare taxes, discussed previously.

The reduction of state taxes because of favorable experience ratings does not affect the credit allowable against the federal tax.

One of the purposes of the unemployment insurance program is to stabilize employment and reduce unemployment. Firms that provide steady employment are granted a lower state tax rate under an **experience rating,** or **merit rating, system.** Under the experience rating system, a firm may actually pay as little as a fraction of 1 percent to the state instead of the usual 5.4 percent that would be paid without a favorable experience rating. Penalty rates, sometimes as high as 10 percent, are levied in some states if a firm has a poor record of providing steady employment. The reduction of state taxes because of favorable experience ratings does not affect the credit allowable against the federal tax. An employer may take a credit against the federal unemployment tax as though it were paid at the normal state rate, up to a maximum of 5.4 percent, even though the employer actually pays the state a lesser rate. We will assume that Ajax Company's experience rating causes it to pay a state tax of only 4.0 percent, although the basic state charge is 5.4 percent.

Computing Unemployment Taxes

Ajax records its unemployment tax expense weekly. The unemployment taxes on January 6 for the weekly payroll ending on that date are computed as follows:

Federal unemployment tax ($1,592 × 0.008)	= $12.74
State unemployment tax ($1,592 × 0.04)	= 63.68
Total unemployment taxes	= $76.42

Accounting Entries for Unemployment Taxes

Employers usually record unemployment taxes at the end of each payroll period.

Most employers record federal and state unemployment taxes at the end of each payroll period as part of the entry in which they record the employer's share of social security and medicare taxes. On page 372 we showed the entry that Ajax made on January 6, 19X5, to record the social security and medicare payroll taxes expense. The entry to record the employer's payroll taxes resulting from unemployment taxes is shown below.

We have just seen that Ajax's unemployment taxes on January 6, 19X5, included $12.74 for federal taxes and $63.68 for state taxes. The total amount is debited to Payroll Taxes Expense, and the two individual amounts are credited to separate liability accounts.

1	*19X5*						1
2	*Jan.*	*6*	*Payroll Taxes Expense*		*76 42*		2
3			*Fed. Unemp. Tax Payable*			*12 74*	3
4			*State Unemp. Tax Payable*			*63 68*	4
5			*Unemployment taxes on*				5
6			*weekly payroll*				6
7							7

Reporting and Paying State Unemployment Taxes

Most states require that the employer file the state return for each quarter by the last day of the month following the quarter. The amount owed generally must be paid at that time. For example, in April, the Ajax Mail Order Company must pay its tax for the first quarter of the year and file the proper return with the required information concerning employees and their taxable wages.

Employer's Quarterly Report

The Employer's Quarterly Report for the State of Texas filed by Ajax in April 19X5 is shown in Figure 11–7. The report forms of other states are similar to the one illustrated.

The first 12 blocks contain general information about the company. Two of these blocks warrant special attention. Block 4 provides a space for entering the state tax rate. The state notifies the taxpayer of the rate to be assessed, based on the employer's experience rating. Block 10 provides a space for entering the number of employees in the state as of the twelfth day of each month of the quarter. The remaining lines on the return are also quite simple.

FIGURE 11–7
Employer's Quarterly Report Form for State Unemployment Taxes

TEXAS EMPLOYMENT COMMISSION
AUSTIN, TEXAS 78714-9037
(512) 463-2222

11111

EMPLOYER'S QUARTERLY REPORT

1. ACCOUNT NUMBER	2. COUNTY CODE	3. TAX AREA	4. TAX RATE	5. SIC CODE	6. FEDERAL I.D. NUMBER	7. QTR. YR.
12-98765	121	2	4.0%	59	75-7575757	1st 19X5

8. EMPLOYER NAME AND ADDRESS

JEAN SHAATKE
DBA AJAX MAIL ORDER COMPANY
1111 MAIN STREET
KRUM, TX 76249

9. TELEPHONE NUMBER
(817) 383-2436

You must FILE this return even though you had no payroll this quarter. If you had no payroll show "0" in item 13 and sign the declaration (Item 24) on this form.

ALIGNMENT 9A. QUARTER ENDING 9B. PENALTIES WILL BE ASSESSED IF REPORT IS NOT POSTMARKED BY

1st Month	2nd Month	3rd Month
5		

10. Enter in the boxes above the number of employees employed in the pay periods that include the 12th day of the calendar month.

11. SHOW THE COUNTY CODE (see list on the back of this form) in which you had the greatest number of employees. 121

12. IF you have employees in more than one county in TEXAS, how many of them are outside the county shown in Item 11?

(ENTER NUMERALS ONLY)

	DOLLARS	CENTS
13. Total Wages Paid During this Quarter to Texas Employees	20,696	00
14. Taxable Wages (Paid This Quarter to Each Employee up to Annual Maximum of $7,000)	20,696	00
15. Tax Due (Multiply Taxable Wages By Tax Rate)	827	84
16. Penalty 14(a), If Tax Is Past Due	—	
17. Penalty 14(c)(1), If Report Is Past Due	—	
18. Balance Due From Prior Periods (Subtract Credit Or Add Debit)	—	
19. Total Due - Make Remittance Payable To TEXAS EMPLOYMENT COMMISSION	827	84

FOR TEC USE ONLY
PRINT YOUR NUMERALS LIKE THIS
0 1 2 3 4 5 6 7 8 9

MONTH DAY YEAR
POSTMARK DATE C3
POSTMARK DATE $
EX DATE C3
EX DATE $
DOLLARS CENTS INITIALS
AMOUNT RECEIVED

	20. SOCIAL SECURITY NUMBER	21. EMPLOYEE NAME (1ST INIT 2ND INIT LAST NAME)	22. TOTAL WAGES PAID THIS QUARTER	
1	123-45-6789	C. C. COLLINS	4,160	00
2	234-56-7890	E. E. ECHOLS	4,186	00
3	345-67-8901	C. A. JOHANSEN	3,250	00
4	456-78-9012	R. S. SANCHEZ	5,200	00
5	567-89-0123	M. YAMOAH	3,900	00
8				
9				
10				
		23. PAGE TOTAL	20,696	00

24. I DECLARE that the information herein is true and correct to the best of my knowledge and belief.

SIGNATURE Jean Shaatke

TITLE Owner DATE 04-29-X5

PREPARERS NAME Jean Shaatke

PREPARERS PHONE NUMBER 817-444-4444

MAIL REPORT AND REMITTANCE TO:
CASHIER - T.E.C.
P.O. BOX 149037
AUSTIN, TEXAS 78714-9037
DO NOT STAPLE REPORT
(Write Account No. On Check)

FORM C-3 (3-91)

- On *line 13*, the total of all wages paid during the quarter to employees in the state is entered.
- *Line 14* shows the total *taxable* wages paid during the quarter. Note that the limit on taxable wages in the state is shown as $7,000. Actually, the base in Texas was changed to $9,000 for 1989 and later years. We have used a base of $7,000 in the illustration for the sake of simplicity and because the increase to $9,000 was intended to be "temporary."
- *Line 15* reflects the total tax due for the quarter, found by multiplying the employer's rate (4 percent) by taxable wages of $20,696.
- *Line 16* shows any penalty due because the tax payment is past due.
- *Line 17* is used to report any penalty arising because the report is past due.
- *Line 18* is used to record any adjustments of amounts reported in prior quarters.
- *Line 19* shows the net tax due.

During the quarter ending March 31, Ajax Company paid wages of $20,696 to its five employees (see the summary in Table 11–1). No employee had cumulative earnings in excess of $7,000. Therefore, all wages paid were subject to the state unemployment tax. Based on our prior assumption that Ajax has earned a favorable experience rating and that its SUTA rate is 4.0 percent, the total state tax due for the quarter would be $827.84. This amount should have been entered in the State Unemployment Tax Payable account through weekly entries recording payroll taxes on the weekly payroll. The firm now issues a check payable to the proper tax collection authority for the amount due, as shown on the quarterly return.

Assume that the company files the return with the state's employment commission and sends the check for $827.84 with the tax return. The entry to record the transaction is made in the cash payments journal. The effect of the transaction, in general journal form, is shown below.

1	*19X5*						1
2	*Apr.*	*29*	*State Unemploy. Tax Payable*		*827.84*		2
3			*Cash*			*827.84*	3
4			*Paid taxes for quarter*				4
5			*ending March 31*				5
6							6

Earnings in Excess of Base Amount

The taxable wages for each quarter are obtained from the quarterly summary of earnings. Ajax's summary for the first quarter of 19X5 is shown in Table 11–1. The information from the summary is taken from the individual employee earnings records. Remember that the individual employee records show the amount of each employee's earnings each pay period that is subject to unemployment taxes. The earnings record for Cass Collins, who earns $320 a week, would show that through the pay period ending May 26 Collins would have been paid a total of $6,720. As a result, of the $320 that Collins earned for the pay period ending June 2, only $280 would be subject to state unemployment taxes, using the assumed maximum base of $7,000 of wages during the year.

Reporting and Paying Federal Unemployment Taxes

The rules for depositing federal unemployment taxes and for filing the necessary forms differ from those used for social security and medicare taxes.

Depositing Federal Unemployment Taxes

Federal unemployment taxes (FUTA) must be deposited in a Federal Reserve Bank or other authorized financial institution and must be accompanied by the preprinted tax form—Federal Tax Deposit Coupon, Form 8109. Deposits are made on a quarterly basis. Deposits of taxes due on compensation paid during the quarter must be made in a Federal Reserve Bank or designated depository by the last day of the first month following the end of the calendar quarter.

Federal unemployment taxes must be deposited quarterly.

To determine whether a deposit of FUTA must be made for any of the first three quarters, the employer multiplies by 0.8 percent that part of the first $7,000 of each employee's annual wages that was paid during the quarter. If the total tax owed for the quarter and any undeposited tax from a prior quarter amount to more than $100, the sum must be deposited by the last day of the first month following the quarter. If the amount is $100 or less, it need not be deposited but must be added to the amount subject to deposit for the next quarter. Deposits of federal unemployment taxes that Ajax must make for the first quarter of 19X5 are shown below.

Month	Taxable Earnings Paid	Rate	Tax Due	Deposit Due Date
January	$6,368	.008	$50.94	April 30
February	6,368	.008	50.94	April 30
March	7,960	.008	63.68	April 30

Since the federal unemployment tax due on compensation paid by Ajax in the first quarter exceeds $100, a deposit must be made by April 30. If the tax due on salaries paid in the first quarter is $100 or less, taxes on the first quarter payroll are not required to be deposited until July 31 if the total then exceeds $100.

The entry on April 30 for the deposit of January, February, and March taxes would be made in the cash payments journal. In general journal form, the entry follows.

19X5					
Apr.	*30*	*Federal Unemp. Tax Payable*		*165 56*	
		Cash			*165 56*
		Deposit FUTA due			

OBJECTIVE 8
Prepare an Employer's Federal Unemployment Tax Return, Form 940.

Reporting Federal Unemployment Tax, Form 940

No quarterly tax return is due for the federal unemployment tax. Instead, the employer must complete and submit an Employer's Annual Federal Unemployment Tax Return, Form 940, by January 31 of the following year. After computing the tax for the year, the employer subtracts all the amounts deposited during the year. If the remainder is more than $100, the entire sum must be deposited by January 31. If the net tax for the year minus any deposits is $100 or less, it may be deposited or it may be paid with Form 940 by January 31.

The information for this return comes partly from the annual summary of individual earnings records and partly from copies of the state unemployment tax returns that the employer has filed during the year. The Form 940 prepared at the Ajax Company for the calendar year 19X5 is shown in Figure 11–8 on page 390. Look at the figure as you read through the line-by-line description of Ajax Company's completed Form 940 for the year.

- *Lines A, B, and C* are informational and self-explanatory. Notice that line A of Ajax's Form 940 shows contributions of $455 for state unemployment tax and indicates that the required sum was actually paid. The figure of $455 reflects the firm's experience rating of 1.2 percent.
- *PART I: Computation of Taxable Wages*
- *Line 1* reports the total compensation paid to employees, $82,784.
- *Line 2* reports the amount of payments exempt from FUTA (not covered by the law). All wages paid by Ajax are subject to the law, so line 2 shows zero.
- *Line 3* shows the total compensation that is not taxable because individual employees have exceeded the $7,000 limitation on amounts subject to FUTA. For Ajax Company, the total amount subject to the federal unemployment tax is $7,000 for each of the five employees, or a total of $35,000. The remainder of the $82,784 paid employees during the year—$47,784—is not taxable.
- *Line 4* reflects the total exempt wages on lines 2 and 3.
- *Line 5* indicates the taxable wages paid by Ajax during the year. This balance must agree with the total of the amounts shown as taxable wages on the individual employee earnings records. The amount of $35,000 is the maximum taxable amount of $7,000 for each of five employees ($7,000 × 5 = $35,000).

FIGURE 11–8
Employer's Annual Federal Unemployment Tax Return, Form 940

Form **940** | **Employer's Annual Federal Unemployment (FUTA) Tax Return** | OMB No. 1545-0028

Department of the Treasury Internal Revenue Service

▶ **For Paperwork Reduction Act Notice, see separate instructions.**

19--

T	
FF	
FD	
FP	
I	
T	

If incorrect, make any necessary change. ▶

Name (as distinguished from trade name) — Jean Shaatke — Calendar year

Trade name, if any — Ajax Mail Order Company

Address and ZIP code — 1111 Main St. Krum, TX 76249

Employer identification number — 75-7575757

A Did you pay all required contributions to state unemployment funds by the due date of Form 940? (If a 0% experience rate is granted, check "Yes" and see instructions.) . . . ☒ **Yes** ☐ **No**
If you checked the "Yes" box, enter the amount of contributions paid to state unemployment funds. ▶ $ 455.00

B Are you required to pay contributions to only one state? . . . ☒ **Yes** ☐ **No**
If you checked the "Yes" box: (1) Enter the name of the state where you have to pay contributions. ▶ ________
(2) Enter your state reporting number(s) as shown on state unemployment tax return. ▶ ________
If you checked the "No" box, be sure to complete Part III and see the instructions.

C If any part of wages taxable for FUTA tax is exempt from state unemployment tax, check the box. (See the instructions.) . . . ☐

If you will not have to file returns in the future, check here, complete, and sign the return. . . . ▶ ☐
If this is an Amended Return, check here. . . . ▶ ☐

Part I **Computation of Taxable Wages** *(to be completed by all taxpayers)*

		Amount paid		
1	Total payments (including exempt payments) during the calendar year for services of employees.		1	82,784 00
2	Exempt payments. (Explain each exemption shown, attach additional sheets if necessary.) ▶	2 -0-		
3	Payments of more than $7,000 for services. Enter only the amounts over the first $7,000 paid to each employee. Do not include payments from line 2. Do not use the state wage limitation.	3 47,784 00		
4	Total exempt payments (add lines 2 and 3).		4	47,784 00
5	**Total taxable wages** (subtract line 4 from line 1). ▶		5	35,000 00
6	Additional tax resulting from credit reduction for unrepaid advances to the state of Michigan. Enter the wages included on line 5 above for that state and multiply by the rate shown. (See the instructions.) Enter the credit reduction amount here and in Part II, line 2, or Part III, line 5: Michigan wages ____ x .008 = ▶		6	–

Part II **Tax Due or Refund** *(Complete if you checked the "Yes" boxes in both questions A and B and did not check the box in C.)*

1	**FUTA tax.** Multiply the wages in Part I, line 5, by .008 and enter here.	1	280 00
2	Enter amount from Part I, line 6.	2	–
3	**Total FUTA tax** (add lines 1 and 2). ▶	3	280 00
4	Total FUTA tax deposited for the year, including any overpayment applied from a prior year.	4	280 00
5	**Balance due** (subtract line 4 from line 3). This should be $100 or less. Pay to the Internal Revenue Service. ▶	5	–
6	**Overpayment** (subtract line 3 from line 4). Check if it is to be: ☐ **Applied to next return,** or ☐ **Refunded.** ▶	6	–

Part III **Tax Due or Refund** *(Complete if you checked the "No" box in either question A or B or you checked the box in C.)*

1 Gross FUTA tax. Multiply the wages in Part I, line 5, by .062. . . . 1 ____
2 Maximum credit. Multiply the wages in Part I, line 5, by .054. . . . 2 ____
3 Computation of tentative credit

(a) Name of state	(b) State reporting number(s) as shown on employer's state contribution returns	(c) Taxable payroll (as defined in state act)	(d) State experience rate From	(d) State experience rate To	(e) State experience rate	(f) Contributions if rate had been 5.4% (col. (c) x .054)	(g) Contributions payable at experience rate (col. (c) x col. (e))	(h) Additional credit (col. (f) minus col. (g)). If 0 or less, enter 0.	(i) Contributions actually paid to the state
3a	Totals. ▶								

3b	**Total tentative credit** (add line 3a, columns (h) and (i) only–see instructions for limitations on late payments) ▶		
4	**Credit:** Enter the smaller of the amount in Part III, line 2, or line 3b	4	
5	Enter the amount from Part I, line 6.	5	
6	**Credit allowable** (subtract line 5 from line 4). (If zero or less, enter 0.).	6	
7	**Total FUTA tax** (subtract line 6 from line 1).	7	
8	Total FUTA tax deposited for the year, including any overpayment applied from a prior year.	8	
9	**Balance due** (subtract line 8 from line 7). This should be $100 or less. Pay to the Internal Revenue Service. ▶	9	
10	**Overpayment** (subtract line 7 from line 8). Check if it is to be: ☐ **Applied to next return,** or ☐ **Refunded.** ▶	10	

Part IV **Record of Quarterly Federal Tax Liability for Unemployment Tax** *(Do not include state liability)*

Quarter	First	Second	Third	Fourth	Total for year
Liability for quarter	165.56	110.44	4.00	-0-	280.00

Under penalties of perjury, I declare that I have examined this return, including accompanying schedules and statements, and to the best of my knowledge and belief, it is true, correct, and complete, and that no part of any payment made to a state unemployment fund claimed as a credit was or is to be deducted from the payments to employees.

Signature ▶ *Jean Shaatke* **Title (Owner, etc.)** ▶ *Owner* **Date** ▶ *Jan. 30, 19X6*

Cat. No. 11234O Form **940**

- *Line 6* applies only to taxpayers in the state of Michigan and is irrelevant to our case.
- *PART II: Tax Due or Refund* (for taxpayers who are covered by SUTA in only one state and who have paid all SUTA taxes)
- *Line 1* is the gross FUTA tax, except for the employers subject to FUTA in the state of Michigan. For Ajax Company, this is the product of the taxable wages of $35,000 multiplied by the applicable federal rate of 0.008, or $280.
- *Line 2* is a reduction in the credit for SUTA payable to the state of Michigan in certain instances.
- *Line 3* is simply the total of lines 1 and 2, $280.
- *Line 4* reflects the FUTA tax deposited during the year.
- *Line 5* shows the balance of tax due.
- *Line 6* is used to record any refund from overpayment of the tax. Ajax deposited $280, so there is no balance due and no net amount payable.
- *PART III: Tax Due or Refund* (for taxpayers other than those required to use Part II)
- *Line 1* shows the gross FUTA tax.
- *Line 2* reflects the maximum credit allowable because of amounts payable to state unemployment tax plans. This amount is 5.4 percent of taxable wages.
- *Line 3* is used to compute the tentative credit for charges made against the employer by state plans.
- *Line 4* reflects the credit allowable.
- *Line 5* is used to enter the special reduction in credit in the state of Michigan.
- *Line 6* records the credit allowable.
- *Line 7* records the net FUTA tax.
- *Line 8* reflects the FUTA tax deposited during the year.
- *Lines 9 and 10* show the balance of tax due, or the net amount payable, as appropriate.
- *PART IV: Record of Quarterly Federal Tax Liability for Unemployment Tax* simply summarizes the FUTA tax due for each quarter.

WORKERS' COMPENSATION INSURANCE

OBJECTIVE 9

Compute and record workers' compensation insurance premiums.

Employers who have only a few employees and who are required by state law to carry workers' compensation insurance (or do so voluntarily) generally pay an estimated premium in advance. Then, after the end of the year, they pay an additional premium (or receive credit for overpayment) based on an audit of their payroll amounts for the year. The rate of the insurance premium varies with the risk involved in the work performed. Therefore, it is important to classify employees properly according to the kind of work they do and to summarize labor costs according to the insurance premium classifications.

For the purpose of this insurance rating, there are only two different work classifications at the Ajax Mail Order Company: office work and shipping work. The premium rates are $0.40 per $100 for office work and $1.20 per $100 for shipping work. Based on em-

The premium rate on workers' compensation insurance is determined by the type of work performed.

ployee earnings for the previous year, the Ajax Company paid an estimated premium of $800 on January 15, 19X5, to cover the year 19X5. A check was issued to the insurance company for the necessary amount. The accountant then made an entry in the cash payments journal debiting Workers' Compensation Insurance Expense and crediting Cash. The entry in general journal form is shown below.

1	*19X5*					1
2	*Jan.*	*15*	*Workers' Comp. Ins. Exp.*	*800 00*		2
3			*Cash*		*800 00*	3
4			*Estimated workers'*			4
5			*compensation insurance*			5
6			*for 19X5*			6
7						7

At the end of the year, the balance of workers' compensation insurance payable or refundable is recorded.

At the end of 19X5, the accountant analyzed the payroll data for that year and applied the proper rates to determine the actual premium for the year. As a result of this analysis, the accountant found that a balance was owed for the workers' compensation insurance.

Classification	Payroll	Rate	Premium
Office Work	$15,600	$0.40/$100	$ 62.40
Shipping Work	67,184	$1.20/$100	806.21
Total Premium for Year			$868.61
Less Estimated Premium Paid			800.00
Balance of Premium Due			$ 68.61

The final balance due the insurance company, $68.61, is recorded as a liability on December 31, 19X5, by an adjusting entry.

1	*19X5*					1
2	*Dec.*	*31*	*Workers' Comp. Ins. Exp.*	*68 61*		2
3			*Workers' Compensation*			3
4			*Insurance Payable*		*68 61*	4
5						5

If the actual premium computed at yearend is less than the amount estimated and paid at the start of the year, the excess payment represents a refund receivable from the insurance company. For example, if the amount Ajax Mail Order Company had prepaid on January 15, 19X5, had been $1,000 rather than $800, the overpayment of $131.39 would have been recorded as follows.

19X1				
Dec.	*31*	*Workers' Compensation*		
		Refund Receivable	*131 39*	
		Workers' Compensation		
		Insurance Expense		*131 39*

Larger employers who have many employees are often allowed to follow a system different from that described above for paying workers' compensation insurance premiums. They may be required to make large deposits, often 25 percent of the estimated annual premium, at the beginning of the year. At the end of each of the first eleven months of the year, they pay the actual premium due for that month based on an audit of the month's wages. The premiums for the last month of the year are deducted from the initial deposit, and any balance is refunded or applied toward the next year's deposit.

INTERNAL CONTROL OVER PAYROLL OPERATIONS

Every business must develop effective internal controls over payroll operations.

Now that we have examined the basic accounting procedures used for payrolls and payroll taxes, let's look at some internal control procedures that are usually recommended to protect payroll operations.

1. Only highly responsible, well-trained employees should be involved in payroll operations.
2. Payroll records should be kept in locked files, and the employees who work with them should be cautioned to maintain confidentiality about pay rates and other information in the records.
3. No new employees should be added to the payroll system without written authorization from management. Similarly, no changes in employee pay rates should be made without written authorization from management.
4. No changes should be made in an employee's withholding allowances without obtaining a properly completed and signed Form W-4 from the employee.
5. No voluntary deductions should be made from employee earnings without obtaining a signed authorization from the employee involved.
6. The payroll checks should be examined by someone other than the person who prepares them. Each check should be compared with the entry for the employee in the payroll register.
7. The person who prepares the payroll checks should not be the one who distributes them to the employees.
8. The monthly statement for the payroll bank account should be received and reconciled by someone other than the person who prepares the payroll checks.
9. Prenumbered forms should be used for the payroll checks. Periodically, the numbers of the checks issued and the numbers of the unused checks should be verified to make sure that all checks can be accounted for.

10. All authorization forms for adding new employees to the payroll system, changing pay rates, and making voluntary deductions should be kept on file. Similarly, all Forms W-4 should be retained.

SELF-REVIEW

1. Who pays the FUTA tax? Who pays the SUTA tax?
2. How do the FUTA and SUTA taxes relate to each other?
3. How do experience ratings affect SUTA taxes?
4. Is the ceiling on earnings subject to unemployment taxes larger than, or smaller than, the ceiling on earnings subject to social security and medicare taxes?
5. Why is it important for workers' compensation purposes that wages be properly classified according to the type of work performed?

Answers to Self-Review

1. The employer pays all federal unemployment taxes. Usually the employer pays all state unemployment taxes, although some states also level SUTA on employees as well.
2. Unemployment taxes are basically imposed by the federal government. However, a credit is allowed, with limits, against the federal tax for amounts of unemployment tax charged by the state.
3. The employer's experience rating reduces the rate of SUTA tax that must actually be paid.
4. The ceiling on earnings subject to unemployment taxes is much smaller than the ceiling on earnings subject to social security tax and medicare tax.
5. The rate charged for workers' compensation insurance on each employee's wages depends on the type of work the employee performs.

MANAGERIAL IMPLICATIONS

Management must make sure that payroll taxes are computed properly and paid on time. It is also essential that payroll tax returns and forms be prepared accurately and filed promptly in order to avoid penalties imposed by law. The payroll and accounting records must allow the preparation of these reports in an efficient manner.

Managers should be familiar with the various types of payroll taxes in order to understand their impact on operating costs. In many businesses, the expense for payroll taxes amounts to a sizable sum. It is especially helpful for managers to be knowledgeable about the regulations concerning unemployment tax in their states because a favorable experience rating can substantially reduce this tax.

Information Block: Computers in Accounting

Payroll Applications for the Computer

One of the first areas of accounting to be computerized was payroll preparation and record keeping. With their speed and accuracy, computers are ideally suited for processing payroll data. A computerized payroll system performs the same operations as required for a manual system. In addition to preparing payroll registers, earnings records, and paychecks, computers also produce many special reports for management.

The same data required for a manual payroll system is needed for a computerized system. An employee master file is created first, and it contains the employee's name, address, social security number, marital status, number of withholding allowances claimed on Form W-4, gross salary or hourly wage rate, and additional information such as union membership and voluntary payroll deductions. Periodically this master file is updated to add new employees, record changes, or delete former employees.

At the end of each payroll period, a payroll transaction file is created. The data needed for this file is obtained from employees' time cards for hourly workers and from the master file for salaried workers. The computer calculates the number of regular and overtime hours worked and computes the gross pay for all employees, their voluntary and required deductions, and net pay. A payroll proof report is usually printed and reviewed by an accountant to make any changes or corrections. The computer then prepares the payroll register and posts the data to individual employee earnings records. Finally, paycheck forms are placed in the printer and the computer prints out the employee paychecks and their attached payroll stubs.

At the end of each calendar quarter and year, summary reports are prepared. These reports provide information for preparing Forms 940 and 941, as well as state unemployment compensation returns. The computer can also provide additional reports regarding employee seniority, union dues payable, pension contributions, and other employee deductions. At the end of each year, the computer prints Form W-2 statements to be sent to the Internal Revenue Service and to the employees for use in preparing their individual tax returns.

CHAPTER 11 Review and Applications

CHAPTER SUMMARY

Employers serve as collection agents for the social security tax, medicare tax, and federal income tax withheld from employee earnings and must remit these amounts, together with the employer's share of social security and medicare taxes, to the government as required by law. These taxes must be deposited in an authorized depository, usually a commercial bank. The schedule for deposits varies according to the sums involved. A Federal Tax Deposit, Form 8109, is prepared and submitted with each deposit.

At the end of each calendar quarter, the employer must file a quarterly tax return on Form 941 reporting taxable wages paid to employees during the quarter, the federal income tax withheld, and social security and medicare taxes applicable to the wages. Any balance of taxes due may be paid with this return or may be deposited.

By the end of January, each employee must be given a Wage and Tax Statement, Form W-2, showing his or her earnings for the previous year and deductions for social security and medicare taxes and employee income tax withheld. The employer prepares an annual Transmittal of Income and Tax Statements, Form W-3, and files it, together with copies of the Forms W-2 issued to the employees.

Unemployment insurance protects workers against the financial problems of temporary unemployment. It is administered by the various state governments. Taxes for this insurance are paid by the employers to both the state and federal governments. A few states also levy unemployment insurance tax on employees.

State unemployment tax returns differ in detail but usually require a list of employees, their social security numbers, and the taxable wages paid. An Employer's Annual Federal Unemployment Tax Return, Form 940, must be filed each January for the preceding calendar year. It shows the total wages paid, the amount of taxable wages, and the federal unemployment tax owed for the year. A credit is allowed against gross federal tax for unemployment tax charged under state plans, up to 5.4 percent of wages subject to the federal tax. The rate of state unemployment tax depends on the employer's experience rating. The net FUTA tax may be as low as 0.8 percent.

Employers may be required under state law to carry workers' compensation insurance. Ordinarily, an estimated premium is paid at the beginning of each year. A final settlement is made with the insurance company on the basis of an audit of the payroll after the end of the year. Premiums vary according to the type of work performed by each employee. Other premium payment plans may be used for larger employers.

GLOSSARY OF NEW TERMS

Employer's Quarterly Federal Tax Return, Form 941 (p. 375) Preprinted government form used by the employer to report payroll tax information to the Internal Revenue Service

Experience rating system (p. 384) A system that rewards an employer for maintaining steady employment conditions by reducing the firm's unemployment tax

Federal Tax Deposit Coupon, Form 8109 (p. 370) Preprinted government form that accompanies an employer's deposit of various taxes

Merit rating system (p. 384) See Experience rating system

Transmittal of Income and Tax Statements, Form W-3 (p. 380) Preprinted government form submitted with W-2 forms to the Social Security Administration

Unemployment insurance program (p. 384) A program that provides unemployment compensation through a tax levied on employers

Wage and Tax Statement, Form W-2 (p. 378) Preprinted government form that contains information about an employee's earnings and tax withholdings for the year

Withholding statement (p. 378) See Wage and Tax Statement, Form W-2

REVIEW QUESTIONS

1. How can an employer keep informed about changes in the rates and bases for the social security, medicare, and FUTA taxes?
2. What government form is prepared to accompany deposits of federal taxes?
3. What happens if the employer fails to deduct enough federal income tax or FICA tax from employee earnings?
4. When must Form W-2 be issued? To whom is it sent?
5. What is the purpose of Form W-3? When must it be issued? To whom is it sent?
6. Why was the unemployment insurance system established?
7. What is the purpose of allowing a credit against the FUTA for state unemployment taxes?
8. What is the purpose of Form 940? How often is it filed?
9. A state charges a basic SUTA tax rate of 5.4 percent. Because of an excellent experience rating,an employer in the state has to pay only 1 percent of the taxable payroll as state tax. What is the percentage to be used in computing the credit against the federal unemployment tax?
10. Is the employer required to deposit the federal unemployment tax during the year? Explain.
11. What is Form 941? How often is the form filed?

12. Who pays for workers' compensation insurance?
13. When is the premium for workers' compensation insurance usually paid?

MANAGERIAL FOCUS

1. Why should management be concerned about the accuracy and promptness of payroll tax deposits and payroll tax returns?
2. What is the significance to management of the experience rating system used to determine the employer's tax under the state unemployment insurance laws?
3. The Harris Company recently discovered that a payroll clerk had issued checks to nonexistent employees for several years and cashed the checks himself. The firm does not have any internal control procedures for its payroll operations. What specific controls might have led to the discovery of this fraud more quickly or discouraged the payroll clerk from even attempting the fraud?
4. Guess Company has 20 employees. Some employees work in the office, others in the warehouse, and still others in the retail store. In the company's records, all employees are simply referred to as "general employees." Explain to management why this is not an acceptable practice.

EXERCISES

EXERCISE 11–1
(Obj. 1)

Tutorial

Depositing payroll taxes. The amounts of federal income tax withheld and social security and medicare taxes (both employee and employer shares) shown below were owed by different businesses on the specified dates. In each case, decide whether the firm is required to deposit the sum in an authorized financial institution. If a deposit is necessary, give the date by which it should be made.

1. Total taxes of $780 owed on January 31, 19X3
2. Total taxes of $6,200 owed on February 7, 19X3
3. Total taxes of $330 owed on March 31, 19X3
4. Total taxes of $640 owed on April 30, 19X3

EXERCISE 11–2
(Obj. 3)

Tutorial

Recording deposit of social security, medicare, and income taxes. After the Wong Corporation paid its employees on May 15, 19X5, and recorded the corporation's share of payroll taxes for the payroll paid that date, the firm's general ledger showed a balance of $1,680 in the Social Security Tax Payable account, a balance of $387 in the Medicare Tax Payable account, and a balance of $1,530 in the Employee Income Tax Payable account. On May 16, 19X5, the business issued a check to deposit the taxes owed in the Valley National Bank. Record this transaction in general journal form.

EXERCISE 11–3
(Obj. 2, 6)

Computing employer's payroll taxes. At the end of the weekly payroll period on May 28, 19X6, the payroll register of the Newton Manufacturing Company showed employee earnings of $32,700. Determine the firm's payroll taxes for the period. Use an assumed social security rate of 6.5 percent, medicare rate of 1.5 percent, FUTA rate of 0.8 percent, and SUTA rate of 5.4 percent. Consider all earnings subject to social security tax and medicare tax and $16,500 subject to FUTA and SUTA taxes.

EXERCISE 11-4
(Obj. 7)

Depositing federal unemployment tax. On March 31, 19X4, the Federal Unemployment Tax Payable account in the general ledger of the Phoenix Company showed a balance of $288. This represents the FUTA tax owed for the first quarter of the year. On April 25, 19X4, the firm issued a check to deposit the amount owed in the Western Commercial Bank. Record this transaction in general journal form.

EXERCISE 11-5
(Obj. 7)

Computing SUTA tax. On April 20, 19X7, the Hughes Services Company prepared its state unemployment tax return for the first quarter of the year. The firm had taxable wages of $45,300. Because of a favorable experience rating, Hughes pays SUTA tax at a rate of 1.6 percent. How much SUTA tax did the firm owe for the quarter?

EXERCISE 11-6
(Obj. 7)

Paying SUTA tax. On June 30, 19X4, the State Unemployment Tax Payable account in the general ledger of the Gulf Book Store showed a balance of $684. This represents the SUTA tax owed for the second quarter of the year. On July 21, 19X4, the business issued a check to the state unemployment insurance fund for the amount due. Record this payment in general journal form.

EXERCISE 11-7
(Obj. 7)

Computing FUTA tax. On January 24, 19X4, the Polk Equipment Rental Company prepared its Employer's Annual Federal Unemployment Tax Return, Form 940, for the year 19X3. During 19X3, the business paid total wages of $187,200 to its eight employees. Of this amount, $56,000 was subject to FUTA tax. Using a rate of 0.8 percent, determine the FUTA tax owed for 19X3 and the balance due on January 24, 19X4, when Form 940 was filed. A deposit of $374.40 was made during the year.

EXERCISE 11-8
(Obj. 9)

Computing workers' compensation insurance premiums. The Golden Manufacturing Company estimates that its office employees will earn $80,000 next year and its factory employees will earn $420,000. The firm pays the following rates for workers' compensation insurance: $0.30 per $100 of wages for the office employees and $6.00 per $100 of wages for the factory employees. Determine the estimated premium for each group of employees and the total estimated premium for next year.

PROBLEMS

PROBLEM SET A

PROBLEM 11-1A
(Obj. 2, 7)

Computing and recording employer's payroll tax expense. The payroll register of Upper Valley Video Shop showed total employee earnings of $1,200 for the week ended July 7, 19X3.

Instructions

1. Compute the employer's payroll taxes for the period. Use an assumed rate of 6.5 percent for the employer's share of the social security tax, 1.5 percent for medicare tax, 0.8 percent for FUTA tax, and 5.4 percent for SUTA tax. All earnings are taxable.
2. Prepare a general journal entry to record the employer's payroll taxes for the period.

PROBLEM 11–2A
(Obj. 2, 3, 4, 5, 6, 7)

GL

Computing employer's social security tax, medicare tax, and unemployment taxes and recording payment of taxes; preparing employer's quarterly federal tax return. A payroll summary for Emilio Hernandez, who owns and operates the Big Apple Company, for the quarter ending September 30 appears below. The firm prepared the required tax deposit forms and issued checks as follows.

a. Federal Tax Deposit, Form 8109, check for July taxes, paid on August 13, 19X3
b. Federal Tax Deposit, Form 8109, check for August taxes, paid on September 14, 19X3

Date Wages Paid	Total Earnings	Soc. Sec. Tax Deducted	Medicare Tax Deducted	Income Tax Withheld
July 7	$ 940	$ 61.10	$ 14.10	$ 95.00
14	980	63.70	14.70	98.00
21	940	61.10	14.10	95.00
28	960	62.40	14.40	97.00
	$3,820	$248.30	$ 57.30	$385.00
Aug. 4	$ 920	$ 59.80	$ 13.80	93.00
11	940	61.10	14.10	95.00
18	940	61.10	14.10	95.00
25	960	62.40	14.40	97.00
	$3,760	$244.40	$ 56.40	380.00
Sept. 1	$ 480	$ 31.20	$ 7.20	48.00
8	440	28.60	6.60	45.00
15	460	29.90	6.90	47.00
22	440	28.60	6.60	45.00
29	420	$ 27.30	6.30	42.00
	$2,240	$145.60	$ 33.60	$227.00
Total	$9,820	$638.30	$147.30	992.00

Instructions

1. Using the tax rates given below, and assuming that all earnings are taxable, make the general journal entry on July 7 to record the employer's payroll tax expense on the payroll ending that date.

Social security	6.5 percent
Medicare	1.5
FUTA	0.8
SUTA	2.5

2. Give the entries in general journal form to record deposit of the employee income tax withheld and the social security and medicare taxes (employee and employer shares) on August 14 for July taxes and on September 14 for August taxes.
3. On October 13, the firm issued a check to deposit the federal income tax withheld and the FICA tax (both employee and employer shares) for the third month (September). In general journal form, record issuance of the check.
4. Complete Form 941 in accordance with the discussions in this chapter and the instructions on the form itself. Use the assumed 13 percent social security rate and 3.0 percent medicare rate in computations. Use the following address for the company: 2807 Brady Street, Des Moines, Iowa 52803. Use 52-2222222 as the employer identification number. Date the return October 30, 19X3.

PROBLEM 11–3A
(Obj. 7, 8)

GL

Computing and recording unemployment taxes; completing Form 940. Certain transactions and procedures relating to federal and state unemployment taxes are given below for Monica's Fashions, a retail store owned by Monica Malloy. The firm's address is 492 Clark Drive, Chicago, IL 60622. The employer's identification number is 57-1111111. Carry out the procedures as instructed in each of the following steps.

Instructions

1. Compute the state unemployment insurance tax owed on the employees' wages for the quarter ended March 31, 19X3. This information will be shown on the employer's quarterly report to the state agency that collects SUTA tax. The employer has recorded the tax on each payroll date. Although the state charges a 5.4 percent unemployment tax rate, Monica's Fashions' rate is only 1.7 percent because of its experience rating. The employee earnings for the first quarter are shown below. All earnings are subject to SUTA tax.

Social Security Number	Name of Employee	Total Earnings
333-08-4391	Kemal Jabbar	$ 2,720
444-08-9768	Rick Link	2,900
111-02-2441	Carl Oester	3,230
444-05-8967	Paul Poteet	3,700
333-04-3586	Gus Schneider	3,500
111-04-8523	Anita Tullos	3,900
222-06-3761	Steven Wise	3,150
Total		$23,100

2. On April 28, 19X3, the firm issued a check to the state employment commission for the amount computed above. In general journal form, record the issuance of the check.

3. Complete Form 940, the Employer's Annual Federal Unemployment Tax Return, on January 15, 19X4. Assume that all wages have been paid and that all quarterly payments have been submitted to the state as required. The payroll information for 19X3 appears below. The required federal tax deposit forms and checks were submitted as follows: a deposit of $184.80 on April 21, a deposit of $195.20 on July 22, and a deposit of $100 on October 21. Date the unemployment tax return January 28, 19X4. A check for the balance due will be sent with Form 940.

Quarter Ended	Total Wages Paid	Wages Paid in Excess of $7,000	State Unemployment Tax Paid
Mar. 31	$23,100.00	–0–	$ 392.70
June 30	24,400.00	–0–	414.80
Sept. 30	24,600.00	$12,100.00	212.50
Dec. 31	25,700.00	24,700.00	17.00
Totals	$97,800.00	$36,800.00	$1,037.00

4. In general journal form, record issuance of a check on January 28, 19X4, for the balance of the FUTA tax due for 19X3.

PROBLEM 11–4A
(Obj. 9)

Tutorial GL

Computing and recording workers' compensation insurance premiums. The information given below relates to the Rayzor Company's workers' compensation insurance premiums for 19X3. On January 12, 19X3, the company estimated its premium for workers' compensation insurance for the year 19X3 on the basis of that data.

Work Classification	Amount of Estimated Wages	Insurance Rates
Office work	$ 33,000	$0.30/$100
Shop work	150,000	$4.00/$100

Instructions

1. Compute the estimated premiums for 19X3.
2. Record in general journal form payment of the estimated premium on January 12, 19X3.
3. On January 4, 19X4, an audit of the firm's payroll records for 19X3 showed that it had actually paid wages of $38,000 to its office employees and wages of $151,000 to its shop employees. Compute the actual premium for the year and the balance due the insurance company or the credit due the firm.
4. Give the general journal entry to adjust the Workers' Compensation Insurance Expense as of the end of 19X3. Date the entry December 31, 19X3.

PROBLEM SET B

PROBLEM 11–1B
(Obj. 2, 7)

Tutorial

Computing and recording employer's payroll tax expense. The payroll register of the Schulz Repair Service showed total employee earnings of $1,080 for the week ended April 7, 19X3.

Instructions

1. Compute the employer's payroll taxes for the period. The tax rates are as follows:

Social security tax	6.5 percent
Medicare tax	1.5
FUTA tax	0.8
SUTA tax	2.2

2. Prepare a general journal entry to record the employer's payroll taxes for the period.

PROBLEM 11–2B
(Obj. 2, 3, 4, 5, 6, 7)

Computing employer's social security tax, medicare tax, and unemployment taxes and recording payment of taxes; preparing employer's quarterly federal tax return. A payroll summary for Toni Thompson, who owns and operates the Eazy Time Store, for the quarter ending June 30 appears below. The firm prepared the required tax deposit forms and issued checks as follows during the quarter.

a. Federal Tax Deposit, Form 8109, check for April taxes, paid on May 14, 19X3.
b. Federal Tax Deposit, Form 8109, check for May taxes, paid on June 13, 19X3.

Date Wages Paid	Total Earnings	Soc. Sec. Tax Deducted	Medicare Tax Deducted	Income Tax Withheld
Apr. 7	$ 1,080	$ 70.20	$ 16.20	$ 99.00
14	1,120	72.80	16.80	104.00
21	1,150	74.75	17.25	107.00
28	990	64.35	14.85	89.00
	$ 4,340	$282.10	$ 65.10	$ 399.00
May 5	$ 1,050	$ 68.25	$ 15.75	$ 92.00
12	1,230	79.95	18.45	118.00
19	1,190	77.35	17.85	112.00
26	1,160	75.40	17.40	107.00
	$ 4,630	$300.95	$ 69.45	$ 429.00
June 2	$ 980	$ 63.70	$ 14.70	$ 87.00
9	1,060	68.90	15.90	93.00
16	1,140	74.10	17.10	105.00
23	1,090	70.85	16.35	100.00
30	1,210	78.65	18.15	$ 115.00
	$ 5,480	$356.20	$ 82.20	$ 500.00
Totals	$14,450	$939.25	$216.75	$1,328.00

Instructions

1. Give the general journal entry on April 7 to record the employer's payroll tax expense on the payroll ending that date. All earnings are subject to the following taxes:

Social security	6.5 percent
Medicare	1.5
FUTA	0.8
SUTA	2.5

2. Give the entries in general journal form to record deposit of the employee income tax withheld and the social security and medicare taxes (employee and employer shares) on May 14 for April taxes and on June 13 for May taxes.
3. On July 14, the firm issued a check to deposit the federal income tax withheld and the FICA tax (both employee and employer shares) for the third month (June). In general journal form, record issuance of the check.
4. Complete Form 941 in accordance with the discussions in this chapter and the instructions on the form itself. Use the assumed 13 percent social security rate and 3.0 percent medicare rate in computations. Use the following address for the company: 8506 Main Street, San Mateo, CA 94403. Use 65-5555555 as the employer identification number. Date the return July 15, 19X3.

PROBLEM 11–3B
(Obj. 7, 8)

Computing and recording unemployment taxes; complete Form 940. Certain transactions and procedures relating to federal and state unemployment taxes are given below for Western Styles, a retail store owned by Lena Guerrero. The firm's address is 2817 Lewis Avenue, Butte, MT 59701. The employer's identification number is 57-7777777. Carry out the procedures as instructed in each of the following steps.

Instructions

1. Compute the state unemployment insurance tax owed for the quarter ended March 31, 19X3. This information will be shown on the employer's quarterly report to the state agency that collects SUTA tax. The employer has accrued the tax on each payroll date. Although the state charges a 5.4 percent unemployment tax rate, Western Styles has received a favorable experience rating and therefore pays only a 2.3 percent state tax rate. The employee earnings for the first quarter are given below. All earnings are subject to SUTA tax.

Social Security Number	Name of Employee	Total Earnings
333-33-3333	Susan Drake	$ 3,100
444-44-4444	Elaine Grant	3,130
222-22-8626	John Marti	3,350
222-22-7531	Maria Ramos	3,200
444-44-6408	Oliver Reed	2,980
444-44-8794	Mark Stewart	2,940
Total		$18,700

2. On April 29, 19X3, the firm issued a check for the amount computed above. Record the transaction in general journal form.
3. Complete Form 940, the Employer's Annual Federal Unemployment Tax Return. Assume that all wages have been paid and that all quarterly payments have been submitted to the state as required. FUTA deposits made in 19X3 were $149.60 on April 12, $155.20 on July 14, and $79.20 on October 12. Date the unemployment tax return January 22, 19X4. A check for the balance due will be sent with Form 940. The payroll information for 19X3 is given below.

Quarter Ended	Total Wages Paid	Wages Paid in Excess of $7,000	State Unemployment Tax Paid
Mar. 31	$18,700.00	–0–	$ 430.10
June 30	19,400.00	–0–	446.20
Sept. 30	19,100.00	9,200.00	227.70
Dec. 31	19,500.00	$18,700.00	18.40
Totals	$76,700.00	$27,900.00	$1,122.40

4. On January 22, 19X4, the firm issued a check for the amount shown on line 9, Part II, of Form 940. In general journal form, record issuance of the check.

PROBLEM 11–4B
(Obj. 9)

Tutorial

Computing and recording premiums on workers' compensation insurance. The information given below relates to the Baker Company's workers' compensation insurance premiums for 19X3. On January 10, 19X3, the company estimated its premium for workers' compensation insurance for the year 19X3 on the basis of that data.

Work Classification	Amount of Estimated Wages	Insurance Rates
Office work	$ 38,000	$0.40/$100
Factory work	185,000	$8.00/$100

Instructions

1. Use the information to compute the estimated premium for 19X3.
2. A check was issued to pay the estimated premium on January 10, 19X3. Record the transaction in general journal form.
3. On January 12, 19X4, an audit of the firm's payroll records for 19X3 showed that it had actually paid wages of $36,400 to its office employees and wages of $178,500 to its factory employees. Compute the actual premium for the year and the balance due the insurance company or the credit due the firm.
4. Give the general entry to adjust the Workers' Compensation Insurance Expense account for 19X3. Date the entry December 31, 19X3.

CHALLENGE PROBLEM

In each of the following independent situations, decide whether the business organization should treat the person being paid as an employee and should withhold social security, medicare, and employee income taxes from the payment made.

1. The Berlin Corporation carries on very little business activity. It merely holds land and certain other assets. The Board of Directors has concluded that they need no employees. They have decided instead to pay Herman Wythe, one of the shareholders, a consulting fee of $6,000 per year to serve as president, secretary, and treasurer and to manage all the affairs of the company. Wythe spends an average of one hour per week on the corporation's business affairs. However, his fee is fixed regardless of how few or how many hours he works.
2. Herman Hickman owns and operates a crafts shop, using the sole proprietorship form of business. Each week a check for $500 is written on the craft shop's bank account as a salary payment to Hickman.
3. Clariece Parker is a public stenographer, or court reporter. She has an office at the Boston Court Reporting Center but pays no rent. The manager of the center receives requests from attorneys for public stenographers to take depositions at legal hearings. The manager then chooses a stenographer who best meets the needs of the client and contacts the stenographer chosen. The stenographer has the right to refuse to take on the job, and the stenographer controls his or her working hours and days. Clients make payments to the center, which deducts a 25 percent fee for providing facilities and rendering services to support the stenographer. The balance is paid to the stenographer. During the current month, the center collected fees of $10,000 for Clariece, deducted $2,500 for the center's fee, and remitted the proper amount to Clariece.
4. Sam, a registered nurse, has retired from full-time work. However, because of his experience and special skills, on each Monday, Wednesday, and Thursday afternoon he assists Dr. Amelia Boren, a dermatologist, in her work with skin-cancer patients. Sam is paid an hourly fee by Dr. Boren. During the current week, his hourly fees totaled $400.
5. After working several years as an editor for a magazine publisher, Ramona quit her job to stay at home with her two small children. Later the publisher asked her to work in her home performing editorial work as needed. Ramona is paid an hourly fee for the work she performs. In some cases she goes to the publishing company's offices to pick up or return manuscript, and in other cases the manuscript is sent to her or returned by mail. During the current month Ramona's hourly earnings totaled $900.

CRITICAL THINKING PROBLEM

The *Times-Gazette* is a local newspaper that is published Monday through Friday and sells 60,000 copies daily. The paper is currently in a profit squeeze, and the publisher, Gretchen Malone, is looking for ways to reduce expenses.

A review of current distribution procedures reveals that the *Times-Gazette* employs 100 truck drivers to drop off bundles of newspapers to 1,200 teenagers who deliver papers to individual homes. The drivers are paid an hourly wage while the teenagers receive three cents for each paper they deliver.

Ms. Malone is considering an alternative method of distributing the papers, which she says has worked in other cities the size of Greensburg (where the *Times-Gazette* is published). Under the new system, the *Times-Gazette* would retain 25 truck drivers to transport papers to four distribution centers around the city. The distribution centers are operated by independent contractors who would be responsible for making their own arrangements to deliver papers to subscribers' homes. The 25 drivers retained by the *Times-Gazette* would receive the same hourly rate as they currently earn, and the independent contractors would receive 15 cents for each paper delivered.

1. What payroll information does Ms. Malone need to make a decision about adopting the alternative distribution method?
2. Assume the following information:
   a. The average driver earns $22,000 per year.
   b. Average federal income tax withholding is 17 percent.
   c. The social security tax is 6.5 percent of the first $60,000 of earnings.
   d. The medicare tax is 1.5 percent of the first $140,000 of earnings.
   e. The state unemployment tax is 4 percent and the federal unemployment tax is 0.8 percent of the first $7,000 of earnings.
   f. Workers' compensation insurance is 90 cents per $100 of wages.
   g. The paper pays $145 per month for health insurance for each driver and contributes $110 per month to each driver's pension plan.
   h. The paper has liability insurance coverage for all the teenage carriers that costs $60,000 per year.

   Prepare a schedule showing the costs of distributing the newspapers under the current system and the proposed new system. Based on your analysis, which system would you recommend to Ms. Malone?
3. What other factors, monetary and nonmonetary, might influence your decision?

U N I T   F O U R

Summarizing and Reporting Financial Information

CHAPTER 12

Accruals, Deferrals, and the Worksheet

CHAPTER 13

Financial Statements and Closing Procedures

The proper matching of revenue and expenses is essential to an accurate measurement of the income produced during a financial period. This objective is met through the use of the accrual basis of accounting. Applying the concepts of accrual-basis accounting, data is collected to prepare classified financial statements. In the classified format, similar accounts are grouped together and a subtotal is provided for each group. This method of presenting financial information makes financial statement data more meaningful to readers and is widely used.

CHAPTER

12

Accruals, Deferrals, and the Worksheet

OBJECTIVES

1. Determine the adjustment for merchandise inventory and enter the adjustment on the worksheet.
2. Compute adjustments for accrued and prepaid expense items and enter the adjustments on the worksheet.
3. Compute adjustments for accrued and deferred income items and enter the adjustments on the worksheet.
4. Complete a 10-column worksheet.
5. Define the accounting terms new to this chapter.

In Chapter 5 you learned that certain adjustments must be made to accounts at the end of each fiscal period so that the income statement will include all revenue and expense items that apply to the current period. In this way, the expenses of the period are matched against the revenues that they helped to produce. Because the matching principle is at the heart of financial reporting, this chapter provides detailed coverage of the techniques used to adjust the accounts so that they accurately reflect the operations of each period.

To illustrate the process of computing and recording adjustments, we again discuss the financial affairs of Fashion World, a retail merchandising business. You will see how adjustments were made at this firm at the end of its fiscal year on December 31, 19X4.

NEW TERMS

Accrual basis ▪ Accrued expenses ▪ Accrued income ▪ Deferred expenses ▪ Deferred income ▪ Inventory sheet ▪ Mixed accounts ▪ Prepaid expenses ▪ Property, plant, and equipment ▪ Unearned income

THE ACCRUAL BASIS OF ACCOUNTING

The procedure that most nearly attains the objective of matching revenues and expenses of specific fiscal periods is called the **accrual basis** of accounting. Under the accrual basis, all revenues and all expenses are recognized on the income statement for the applicable period, regardless of when the cash related to the transactions is received or paid.

Revenue is normally recognized when a sale is completed, which is usually when title to the goods passes to the customer or when the service is provided. Under the accrual basis, revenue is recorded even though accounts receivable resulting from sales on credit are not collected immediately. Similarly, the costs related to purchases of merchandise are recorded when the purchases are made—that is, when title to the goods passes to the buyer—regardless of the actual time of payment for the goods. The proper recognition of operating and nonoperating expenses requires that each expense item be assigned to the accounting period in which it helped to earn revenue for the business, even though the item may be paid for in an earlier or later period. Some expense items like rent and utilities are clearly associated with a specific period, but others are more difficult to assign.

Transactions involving revenue and expense items sometimes occur before the period to which they actually relate. For example, insurance premiums are normally paid in advance, and the coverage often extends over several periods. In other cases, the transaction involving a revenue or expense item may not take place until after the period to which the item applies. For example, employees may work during December but not be paid for this work until January of the next year.

Because there is a difference between the time certain items are recorded in the accounts and the time they are actually realized or used, each account balance is examined at the end of a fiscal period to see if it contains amounts of revenues or expenses that should be allocated to other periods. It is impossible to present an accurate picture of the financial position of a business or the results of its operations for the period until all pertinent information has been recorded and until the **mixed accounts** (accounts that contain elements of both assets and expenses or both liabilities and revenue) have been analyzed. Adjusting entries are usually needed to ensure that the revenue and expense accounts will contain amounts relating only to the current period and that the asset and liability accounts will reflect amounts properly classified as assets and liabilities.

USING THE WORKSHEET TO RECORD ADJUSTMENTS

The procedures used at Fashion World at the end of its fiscal year on December 31, 19X4, illustrate typical adjustments that are made to provide an accurate financial picture for an operating period. Remember that Fashion World is a retail merchandising business that sells clothing for men, women, and children. The firm's transactions during 19X3 were discussed in Chapters 7 through 9. Now we take into consideration the fact that Fashion World moved to a larger store and greatly expanded its operations in 19X4.

As a basis for the discussion of adjustments, look at Fashion World's trial balance as of December 31, 19X4, which has been entered in the first two amount columns of the worksheet in Figure 12–1. Notice that some accounts have no balances in the Trial Balance columns. All of these accounts will be used when the adjustments are made.

As discussed in Chapter 5, the amounts of the adjustments for a period are recorded in the Adjustments section of the worksheet. A letter is used to identify the debit and credit parts of each adjusting entry. After recording all adjustments on the worksheet, the two columns in the Adjustments section of the worksheet are totaled to check the equality of the debits and credits. Next the amounts in the Adjustments section are combined with the amounts originally recorded in the Trial Balance section. The resulting figures are entered in the Adjusted Trial Balance section as another verification of equality. Finally all figures are extended to the proper columns of the Income Statement and Balance Sheet sections and the worksheet is completed.

The worksheet is a highly useful device for assembling data about a firm's adjustments and organizing the information that will appear on the financial statements.

Adjustment for Merchandise Inventory

OBJECTIVE 1

Determine the adjustment for merchandise inventory and enter the adjustment on the worksheet.

In a merchandising business like Fashion World, the Merchandise Inventory account must be updated to present an accurate financial picture for the period. When the trial balance is taken at the end of the period, the merchandise inventory account still shows the beginning inventory. Before the financial statements are prepared, the balance of Merchandise Inventory is updated to reflect the ending inventory for the period.

Remember that the balance in the ending merchandise inventory account reflects the value of the stock of goods that a business has on hand for sale to customers. An asset account for merchandise inventory is kept in the general ledger. However, during a fiscal period, all purchases of merchandise are debited to the cost account Purchases and all sales of merchandise are credited to the revenue account Sales. No entries are made during the period in the Merchandise Inventory account. Thus, when the trial balance is prepared at the end of the period, the merchandise inventory account still shows the beginning inventory for the period.

To determine the amount of the ending inventory, a careful count is made of the goods on hand at the end of the period. Next the total cost of the items is computed. This figure must be recorded on the worksheet so that the financial statements will reflect the ending inventory.

The trial balance prepared at Fashion World on December 31, 19X4, shows a balance of $31,500 for the Merchandise Inventory account. This balance represents the stock of goods on January 1,

FIGURE 12–1
An End-of-Period Worksheet

FASHION WORLD
Worksheet (Partial)
Year Ended December 31, 19X4

	ACCOUNT NAME	TRIAL BALANCE DEBIT	TRIAL BALANCE CREDIT	ADJUSTMENTS DEBIT	ADJUSTMENTS CREDIT
1	*Cash*	28 634 00			
2	*Petty Cash Fund*	100 00			
3	*Notes Receivable*	1 200 00			
4	*Accounts Receivable*	26 000 00			
5	*Allowance for Doubtful Accounts*		100 00		(c) 630 00
6	*Interest Receivable*	136 00		(m) 24 00	
7	*Merchandise Inventory*	31 500 00		(b) 32 000 00	(a) 31 500 00
8	*Prepaid Insurance*	3 600 00			(k) 2 700 00
9	*Prepaid Interest*	225 00			(l) 150 00
10	*Supplies*	6 300 00			(j) 4 975 00
11	*Store Equipment*	12 000 00			
12	*Accum. Depr.—Store Equipment*				(d) 2 100 00
13	*Office Equipment*	3 500 00			
14	*Accum. Depr.—Office Equipment*				(e) 600 00
15	*Notes Payable—Trade*		2 000 00		
16	*Notes Payable—Bank*		9 000 00		
17	*Accounts Payable*		4 129 00		
18	*Interest Payable*				(i) 20 00
19	*Social Security Tax Payable*		1 084 00		(g) 97 50
20	*Medicare Tax Payable*		250 00		(g) 22 50
21	*Employee Income Taxes Payable*		1 490 00		
22	*Fed. Unemployment Tax Payable*				(h) 17 00
23	*State Unemployment Tax Payable*				(h) 81 00
24	*Salaries Payable*				(f) 1 500 00
25	*Sales Tax Payable*		7 200 00	(n) 144 00	
26	*Carolyn Wells, Capital*		82 921 00		
27	*Carolyn Wells, Drawing*	24 000 00			
28	*Income Summary*			(a) 31 500 00	(b) 32 000 00
29	*Sales*		409 650 00		
30	*Sales Returns and Allowances*	13 000 00			
31	*Interest Income*		136 00		(m) 24 00
32	*Miscellaneous Income*				(n) 144 00
33	*Purchases*	250 500 00			
34	*Freight In*	3 800 00			
35	*Purchases Returns and Allowances*		3 050 00		
36	*Purchases Discounts*		3 130 00		
37	*Sales Salaries Expense*	68 490 00		(f) 1 500 00	
38	*Advertising Expense*	7 425 00			
39	*Supplies Expense*			(j) 4 975 00	
40	*Cash Short or Over*	125 00			
41	*Depr. Expense—Store Equipment*			(d) 2 100 00	

FIGURE 12–1 (Continued)
An End-of-Period Worksheet

	ACCOUNT NAME	TRIAL BALANCE DEBIT	TRIAL BALANCE CREDIT	ADJUSTMENTS DEBIT	ADJUSTMENTS CREDIT
42	*Depr. Expense—Office Equipment*			(e) 600.00	
43	*Rent Expense*	13,500.00			
44	*Insurance Expense*			(k) 2,700.00	
45	*Utilities Expense*	3,925.00			
46	*Office Salaries Expense*	16,500.00			
47	*Payroll Taxes Expense*	7,705.00		(g) 120.00	
48				(h) 98.00	
49	*Telephone Expense*	1,375.00			
50	*Uncollectible Accounts Expense*			(c) 630.00	
51	*Interest Expense*	600.00		(i) 20.00	
52				(l) 150.00	
53	*Totals*	524,140.00	524,140.00	76,561.00	76,561.00
54					

19X4, the beginning of the fiscal year. However, a count taken on December 31, 19X4, indicates that the items on hand at the end of the year total $32,000.

The amount of the ending inventory is determined as follows. First the quantity of each type of goods that the firm has in stock is listed on a form called an **inventory sheet.** Next the quantity is multiplied by the unit cost to find the total cost of the item. Then the totals for all the different items on hand are added to find the cost of the entire inventory.

In order to present the correct information about merchandise inventory on the financial statements, the adjustments are made in two steps.

1. The beginning inventory ($31,500) is taken off the books by closing the account balance into the Income Summary account. Remember that the Income Summary account is a special temporary owner's equity account that is used to aid in the closing procedure. To close the beginning inventory, Income Summary is debited and Merchandise Inventory is credited for $31,500. This entry is labeled **(a)** on the worksheet in Figure 12–1 and is illustrated in the T accounts below.

Beginning inventory is removed from the records by a debit to Income Summary and a credit to Merchandise Inventory.

Merchandise Inventory			
Bal.	31,500	Adj.	31,500 (a)

Income Summary			
Adj.	31,500 (a)		

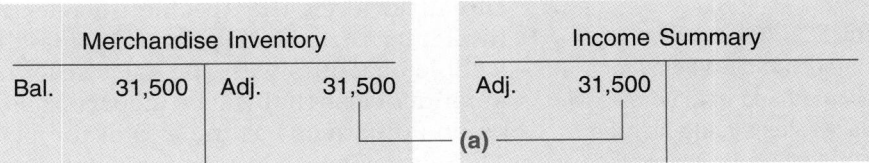

2. The ending inventory ($32,000) is placed on the books by debiting Merchandise Inventory and crediting Income Summary. This

Information Block: Ethics in Accounting

It's Not Illegal in South America

R. B. Rensink is the vice president in charge of international sales for Zephyr Chemical Company. Zephyr is a leading producer of chemicals for extermination of weeds and bugs. A recent ruling by the Environmental Protection Agency (EPA) has outlawed the production and sale of ZAP in the United States. The EPA believes ZAP to be hazardous to the health of humans if consumed in sufficient quantity in foodstuffs and water.

R. B. has just finished investigating the laws in other countries to determine whether Zephyr can sell its products containing ZAP outside the United States. R. B.'s information indicates that there are no laws

entry records the correct balance for inventory on hand on December 31, 19X4. This entry is labeled **(b)** on the worksheet in Figure 12–1.

(a) and **(b)** To record ending inventory

Merchandise Inventory

Bal.	31,500	Adj.	31,500 (a)
Adj.	32,000 (b)		

Income Summary

Adj.	31,500 (a)	Adj.	32,000 (b)

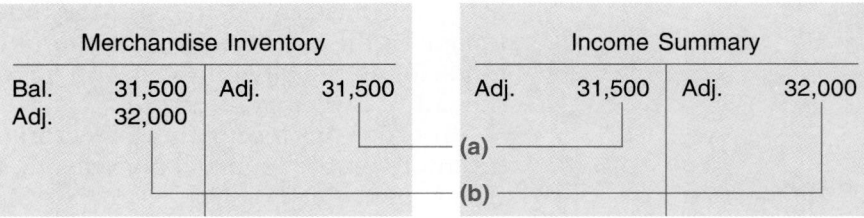

Ending inventory is recorded by a debit to Merchandise Inventory and a credit to Income Summary.

Merchandise inventory is adjusted in these two steps on the worksheet because both the beginning and ending inventory figures appear on the income statement, which is prepared directly from the worksheet.

Adjustment for Loss from Uncollectible Accounts

OBJECTIVE 2

Compute adjustments for accrued and prepaid expense items and enter the adjustments on the worksheet.

For various reasons, some of the accounts receivable that result from credit sales are never collected. The loss from uncollectible accounts represents an operating expense for a business and should be matched against the revenue recorded when the sales were made. Often, however, the specific uncollectible accounts are not known until later periods. To permit the matching of the expense for uncollectible accounts with the sales revenue for the current period, the amount of loss that will be incurred has to be estimated and recorded as an adjustment at the end of the period.

Several methods exist for estimating the amount of loss. At Fashion World the estimated loss from uncollectible accounts is calcu-

regulating the sale of ZAP in South America. Zephyr has several million pounds of ZAP on hand. Since the EPA has also regulated disposal, it would be very expensive to dispose of the product (about $25 million).

ZAP is a product that was in very high demand by farmers until this EPA ruling. Farmers in South America believe ZAP to be an effective product and may not be aware of the EPA's finding on its potential for causing cancer. R. B. estimates that the current inventory could be shipped to South America and sold at a profit of about $6 million. This sale would eliminate the supply on hand, and Zephyr would stop producing ZAP. ZAP production facilities have alternative uses for the company.

1. What are the ethical issues?
2. What are the alternatives?
3. Who are the affected parties?
4. How do the alternatives affect the parties?
5. What should R. B. do?

lated as a percent of the net credit sales for the year. The rate used is based on the firm's past experience with uncollectible accounts and the firm's assessment of current business conditions. For 19X4 the firm estimates that three-tenths of 1 percent (0.3 percent) of the firm's net credit sales of $210,000 will result in uncollectible accounts of $630 ($210,000 × 0.003 = $630). This estimated loss is recorded in the Adjustments section of the year-end worksheet, as shown in entry **(c)** of the worksheet in Figure 12–1. An expense account called Uncollectible Accounts Expense is debited for $630 and a contra asset account called Allowance for Doubtful Accounts is credited for $630. The figures are labeled **(c)** to identify the two parts of the entry for future reference.

(c) To record estimated losses from uncollectible accounts

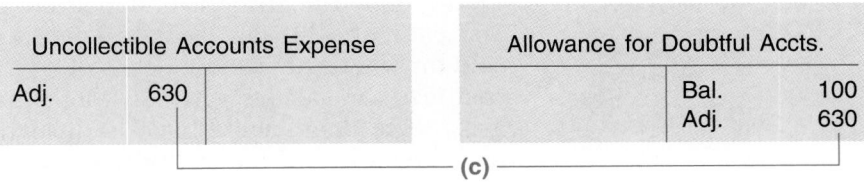

Uncollectible Accounts Expense			
Adj.	630		

Allowance for Doubtful Accts.			
		Bal.	100
		Adj.	630

(c)

Notice that Allowance for Doubtful Accounts has a credit balance of $100 in the Trial Balance section of the worksheet. When the estimate of the loss from uncollectible accounts is based on sales, the exact amount of loss calculated for each period is credited to this account. Any remaining balance from previous periods is not considered when recording the adjustment.

Uncollectible Accounts Expense appears in the Operating Expenses section of the income statement. Allowance for Doubtful Accounts is reported in the Assets section of the balance sheet, where its balance is deducted from the balance of Accounts Receivable. The resulting figure is the estimated collectible amount of the firm's accounts receivable.

In later periods, whenever the account of a specific customer becomes uncollectible, it must be written off. A general journal entry is made debiting Allowance for Doubtful Accounts and crediting Accounts Receivable and crediting the customer's account in the accounts receivable subsidiary ledger. Notice that the expense account Uncollectible Accounts Expense is not involved in this entry. It is used only when the end-of-period adjustment is recorded and is not affected by the later write-off of individual accounts that have been identified as uncollectible.

The balance of Allowance for Doubtful Accounts is reduced throughout the fiscal year as customer accounts are written off.

Adjustment for Depreciation

As discussed in Chapter 5, most businesses have long-term assets that require an end-of-period adjustment for depreciation. These assets are often referred to as **property, plant, and equipment** and include such items as buildings, trucks, automobiles, machinery, furniture, fixtures, office equipment, and land. Land is the only long-term asset that is not subject to depreciation.

Remember that depreciation is the process of allocating the cost of a long-term asset to operations during its expected useful life—the number of years the asset will be used in the business. This process involves the gradual transfer of acquisition cost to expense. Depreciation is recorded on the worksheet at the end of each fiscal period by a debit to a depreciation expense account and a credit to an accumulated depreciation account (a contra asset account).

There are a number of different methods for calculating yearly depreciation. Fashion World uses the straight-line method for the two types of long-term assets that it owns: store equipment and office equipment. With this method, an equal amount of depreciation is taken in each year of the asset's expected useful life.

To apply the straight-line method, first determine the useful life and estimate the salvage value—the amount that the asset can be sold for when the firm disposes of it at the end of its useful life. The cost less the salvage value is known as the *depreciable base* of the asset. The depreciable base is divided by the number of years in the asset's useful life to find the amount of yearly depreciation, as shown in the following formula.

$$\textbf{Cost} - \textbf{Salvage Value} = \textbf{Depreciable Base}$$

$$\frac{\text{Depreciable Base}}{\text{Useful Life}} = \text{Yearly Depreciation}$$

or

$$\frac{\text{Cost} - \text{Salvage Value}}{\text{Useful Life}} = \text{Yearly Depreciation}$$

▲ **REMEMBER!**

Depreciation may be computed on a monthly basis by dividing the depreciable base ($12,000 − $1,500) by the number of months in the estimated useful life (5 years × 12). In this case, monthly depreciation is $175 ($10,500 ÷ 60).

Depreciation of Store Equipment

At the beginning of January 19X4, when Fashion World moved to a larger store, it purchased new store equipment for $12,000. The balance of the Store Equipment account reflects this acquisition cost. Since the firm assigned a useful life of 5 years to the items and a salvage value of $1,500, the yearly depreciation is $2,100.

$$\frac{\$12{,}000 \text{ (Cost)} - \$1{,}500 \text{ (Salvage Value)}}{5 \text{ Years (Useful Life)}} = \$2{,}100 \text{ (Yearly Depreciation)}$$

The necessary adjustment for store equipment appears in entry **(d)** on the 19X4 worksheet shown in Figure 12–1.

(d) To record depreciation expense for store equipment

Depreciation Exp.—Store Equip.	
Adj. 2,100	

Accum. Depreciation—Store Equip.	
	Adj. 2,100

(d)

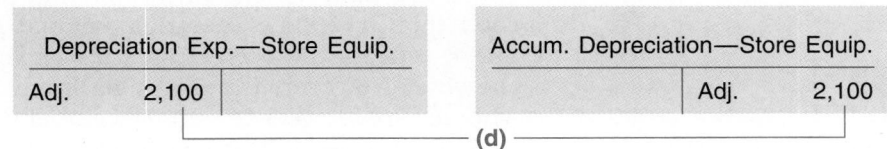

Depreciation of Office Equipment

At the beginning of 19X4, Fashion World also purchased new office equipment. The balance of the Office Equipment account shows that the items had a total cost of $3,500. The assigned useful life is five years, and the estimated salvage value is $500. Based on this data, the yearly depreciation is calculated as $600.

$$\frac{\$3{,}500 \text{ (Cost)} - \$500 \text{ (Salvage Value)}}{5 \text{ Years (Useful Life)}} = \$600 \text{ (Yearly Depreciation)}$$

The adjustment for office equipment is labeled **(e)** on the 19X4 worksheet in Figure 12–1.

(e) To record depreciation expense for office equipment

Depreciation Exp.—Office Equip.	
Adj. 600	

Accum. Depreciation—Office Equip.	
	Adj. 600

(e)

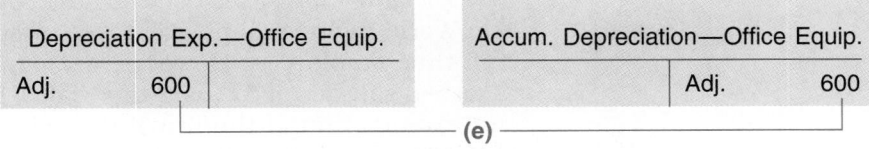

Adjustments for Accrued and Prepaid Expenses

Many expense items clearly belong to a particular fiscal period. They are paid for and used during that period and appear in the accounts at the end of the period. However, as mentioned previously, some expense items involve a more complex situation because they are paid for and recorded in one period but not fully used until a later period. Other expense items are used in one period but not paid for and recorded until a later period. When these situations occur, adjustments must be made so that the financial statements for the period will show all expenses related to the firm's current operations—no more and no less. Similar adjustments may also be required for revenue items so that the financial statements will accurately reflect the income earned during the period.

Adjustment for Accrued Expenses

Accrued expenses are expense items that relate to the current period but have not yet been paid for and do not yet appear in the accounts. On December 31, 19X4, Fashion World has three accrued expense items that require adjustments: accrued salaries, accrued payroll taxes, and accrued interest on notes payable. Because accrued expenses involve amounts that must be paid in the future, the necessary adjustment for each item consists of a debit to an expense account and a credit to a liability account.

Accrued Salaries. All full-time sales and office employees at Fashion World are paid semimonthly—on the fifteenth and the last day of each month. Hence the trial balance prepared on December 31, 19X4, reflects the correct salaries expense for these employees for the year. However, the firm also has several part-time salesclerks who are paid weekly. On December 31, 19X4, salaries totaling $1,500 are owed to these employees and have not been recorded because they are not due for payment until January 3, 19X5. Since the expense for these salaries properly belongs to 19X4, an adjustment is made debiting Sales Salaries Expense for $1,500 and crediting Salaries Payable for the same amount. This entry appears on the worksheet shown in Figure 12–1, where it is labeled **(f)**.

(f) To record accrued sales salaries expense

Sales Salaries Expense			
Adj.	1,500		

Salaries Payable			
		Adj.	1,500

(f)

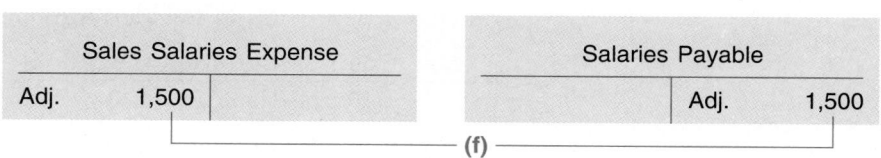

Accrued Payroll Taxes. As of December 31, 19X4, the accounts of Fashion World include all payroll taxes owed on the salaries of the firm's full-time employees. However, the employer's payroll taxes on the accrued salaries of the part-time salesclerks have not been recorded. An examination of the firm's payroll records shows that the entire $1,500 of accrued salaries is subject to the employer's share of the taxes for social security and medicare. With an assumed rate of 6.5 percent for the social security tax and a rate of 1.5 percent for medicare, the accrued payroll taxes for the period are computed as follows.

Social security tax:	$1,500 × 0.065 =	$ 97.50
Medicare tax:	$1,500 × 0.015 =	22.50
Total accrued payroll taxes	=	$120.00

The necessary adjustment for accrued payroll taxes is recorded on the worksheet by debiting Payroll Taxes Expense for $120 and crediting Social Security Tax Payable for $97.50 and Medicare Tax Payable for $22.50. The three amounts are labeled **(g)** on the worksheet in Figure 12–1.

(g) To record accrued payroll taxes on accrued sales salaries

Payroll Taxes Expense			
Adj.	120		

Social Security Tax Payable			
		Adj.	97.50

(g)

Medicare Tax Payable			
		Adj.	22.50

(g)

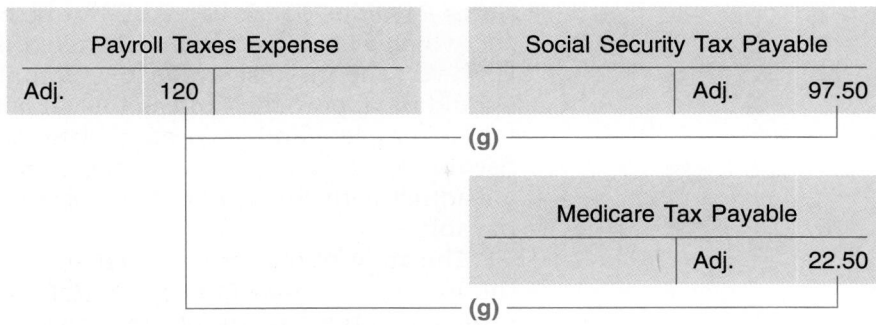

The employees of Fashion World have already reached the $7,000 wage ceiling in 19X4 for unemployment taxes. However, the accrued salaries payable will not be paid until January 3, 19X5, so the wage ceiling for 19X4 will not apply. The $1,500 of accrued salaries is for a new year and is subject to federal and state unemployment taxes.

With an assumed rate of 1.1 percent for federal and 5.4 percent for state unemployment taxes, the accrued taxes are computed as follows (rounded up to the nearest whole dollar).

Federal unemployment tax	$1,500 × 0.011 =	$17.00
State unemployment tax	$1,500 × 0.054 =	81.00
Total accrued taxes		$98.00

The necessary adjustment is recorded on the worksheet by debiting Payroll Taxes Expense for $98 and crediting Federal Unemployment Tax Payable for $17 and State Unemployment Tax Payable for $81. The three amounts are labeled **(h)** on the worksheet in Figure 12–1.

(h) To record accrued payroll taxes on accrued sales salaries

Payroll Taxes Expense			
Adj.	98.00		

Federal Unemployment Tax Payable			
		Adj.	17.00

(h)

State Unemployment Tax Payable			
		Adj.	81.00

(h)

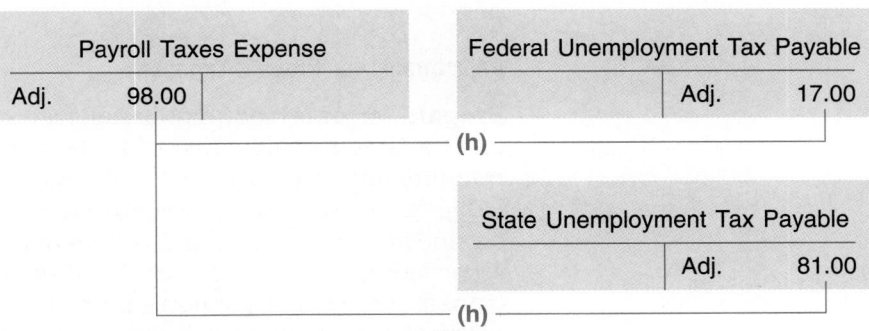

Not all businesses make an adjustment for accrued payroll taxes because the taxes are not legally owed until the salaries are paid to the employees. However, in order to match revenue and expenses as closely as possible, most firms prefer to record the expense for accrued payroll taxes at the end of the fiscal period, even though it is not technically necessary to do so.

Accrued Interest on Notes Payable. On December 1, 19X4, Fashion World issued a two-month note for $2,000, with interest at 12 percent, to a creditor. At the time the amount of the note was recorded in the

Notes Payable—Trade account, but no entry was made for the interest, which will be paid when the note matures on February 1, 19X5. However, the interest expense is actually incurred day by day and should be apportioned to each fiscal period involved in order to obtain a complete and accurate picture of expenses. At the end of the fiscal year on December 31, 19X4, Fashion World therefore makes an adjustment for a month of accrued interest on the trade note payable.

The amount of accrued interest to record is determined by using the interest formula *Principal* × *Rate* × *Time*, as shown below. The principal is the amount of the note ($2,000); the rate is 12 percent, which is expressed as the fraction 12/100; and the time is one month, which is expressed as the fraction 1/12.

$$\$2{,}000 \times 12/100 \times 1/12 = \$20$$

The adjustment consists of a debit to Interest Expense and a credit to a liability account called Interest Payable. This entry is labeled **(i)** on the firm's worksheet, shown in Figure 12–1.

(i) To record accrued interest expense

Interest Expense	
Adj. 20 (i)	

Interest Payable	
	Adj. 20 (i)

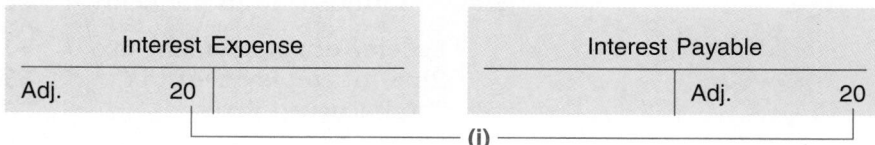

Other Accrued Expenses. Accrued property taxes represent another common accrued expense item. Many businesses are subject to property taxes imposed by state and local governments and find it necessary to accrue some of these taxes at the end of the fiscal period.

Adjustments for Prepaid Expenses

Prepaid, or **deferred, expenses** are expense items that are paid for and recorded in advance of their use. Often a portion of the item remains unused at the end of the fiscal period and is therefore applicable to future periods. Because of the nature of these items, many businesses treat them as assets when they are paid for and initially recorded. At the end of each fiscal period, an adjustment is made to transfer the cost of the portion used during the period from the asset account to an expense account. Fashion World uses this approach in handling the three prepaid expense items that it has: supplies, prepaid insurance, and prepaid interest on notes payable.

Supplies Used. At Fashion World store supplies are purchased in fairly large quantities and are debited to the asset account Supplies. On December 31, 19X4, when the trial balance was prepared, this account had a balance of $6,300. However, a count of the store supplies taken on December 31 showed that items costing $1,325 were actually on hand. This means that items costing $4,975 were used during the year ($6,300 − $1,325 = $4,975). To charge the cost of the store supplies used to the current year's operations, and to avoid overstating the firm's assets, an adjustment is made, debiting Supplies Expense for $4,975 and crediting Supplies for the same amount. This adjustment is labeled **(j)** on the firm's worksheet.

(j) To record supplies used during 19X4

Supplies Expense			
Adj.	4,975		

Supplies			
Bal.	6,300	Adj.	4,975

(j)

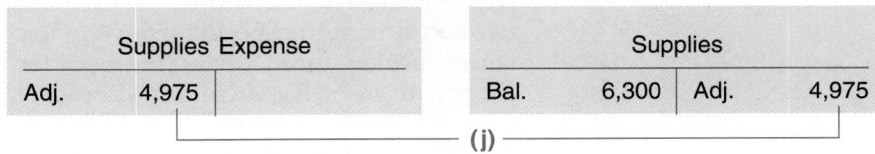

Expired Insurance. On April 1, 19X4, Fashion World purchased a one-year insurance policy for $3,600 and paid the full premium in advance. The amount was debited to the asset account Prepaid Insurance. On December 31, 19X4, this account still has a balance of $3,600, but the insurance coverage for nine months has expired. An adjustment must be made to charge the cost of the expired insurance to operations and to decrease the firm's assets so that they reflect only the insurance coverage that still remains. This is done by debiting Insurance Expense and crediting Prepaid Insurance for $2,700 (9/12 of the original premium of $3,600). The necessary adjustment is labeled **(k)** on the firm's worksheet.

(k) To record expired insurance

Insurance Expense			
Adj.	2,700		

Prepaid Insurance			
Bal.	3,600	Adj.	2,700

(k)

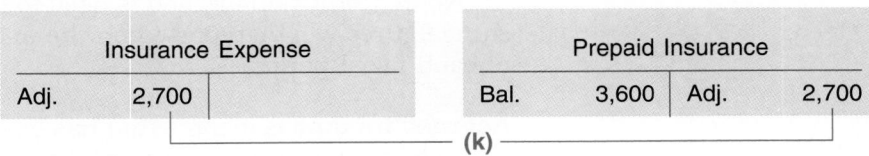

Prepaid Interest on Notes Payable. On November 1, 19X4, Fashion World borrowed money from its bank and gave a three-month note for $9,000, bearing interest at 10 percent. The bank deducted the entire amount of interest ($225) in advance, and the firm therefore received $8,775. This transaction was recorded by debiting Cash for $8,775, debiting an asset account called Prepaid Interest for $225, and crediting Notes Payable—Bank for $9,000.

By the end of the fiscal year on December 31, 19X4, two months had passed since the note was issued to the bank and one month remained until the maturity date of February 1, 19X5. Thus two-thirds of the prepaid interest should properly be recorded as an expense for 19X4. To accomplish this, an adjustment debiting Interest Expense and crediting Prepaid Interest for $150 (2/3 of $225) is made. The required adjustment is labeled (l) on the firm's worksheet in Figure 12–1.

(l) To record interest expense on Notes Payable

Interest Expense			
Adj.	150		

Prepaid Interest			
Bal.	225	Adj.	150

(l)

Other Prepaid Expenses. Prepaid rent, prepaid advertising, and prepaid taxes are other common prepaid expense items. When these items are initially paid for, the amounts are debited to asset accounts—Prepaid Rent, Prepaid Advertising, and Prepaid Taxes. At the end of each fiscal period, an adjustment is made to transfer the portion that expired during the period from the asset account to an expense account. For example, the adjustment for expired rent would consist of a debit to Rent Expense and a credit to Prepaid Rent.

Alternative Method. Some businesses use a different method to handle prepaid expense items. When they pay for the item, they debit its cost to an expense account. At the end of each fiscal period, they make an adjustment to transfer the unexpired portion from the expense account to an asset account. For example, suppose Fashion World used this method when the firm purchased the one-year insurance policy on April 1, 19X4, and paid $3,600 in advance. The transaction is recorded by debiting Insurance Expense and crediting Cash for $3,600. At the end of the firm's fiscal year on December 31, 19X4, the insurance coverage for nine months has expired and the coverage for three months remains. The firm therefore makes an adjustment debiting Prepaid Insurance and crediting Insurance Expense for $900, which is the cost of the unexpired insurance (3/12 of $3,600).

No matter which method is used to handle prepaid expenses, the same figures will be reported on the financial statements at the end of each fiscal period.

Adjustments for Accrued Income

OBJECTIVE 3
Compute adjustments for accrued and deferred income items and enter the adjustments on the worksheet.

Accrued income is income that has been earned but not yet received or recorded. If at the time the trial balance is prepared, there is any item of this nature, an adjustment is necessary so that the income statement will include all the income that belongs to the current period. The appropriate revenue account must be credited to increase its balance even though the amount will not be collected until a later period. The offsetting debit may be to an asset account or a liability account, depending on the item involved. At the end of its fiscal year on December 31, 19X4, Fashion World had two types of accrued income—accrued interest on notes receivable and accrued commission on sales tax.

Accrued Interest on Notes Receivable

Interest-bearing notes receivable are usually recorded at their face value when obtained and are carried in the accounting records at this value until they are collected. The interest income is recorded when it is received, which is normally when the note is settled at maturity. However, interest income is actually earned day by day throughout the time that the note is held. Therefore, at the end of a fiscal period, any accrued interest income that has been earned but not recorded should be recognized by means of an adjustment.

On November 1, 19X4, Fashion World accepted a four-month, 12 percent note for $1,200 from a customer with an overdue balance.

The interest is due on March 1, 19X5, when the note is paid. However, on December 31, 19X4, interest income has been earned but not received for two months (November and December). The interest income is calculated by using the formula *Principal* × *Rate* × *Time* = *Interest* ($1,200 × 12/100 × 2/12 = $24).

To record the interest income of $24 earned in 19X4 but not yet received, an adjustment debiting the asset account called Interest Receivable and crediting a revenue account called Interest Income is made. The two parts of the entry are labeled **(m)** on the worksheet shown in Figure 12–1.

(m) To record accrued interest income

Interest Receivable			
Adj.	24		

Interest Income			
		Bal.	136
		Adj.	24

(m)

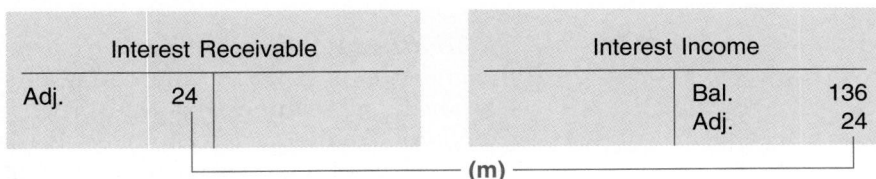

Accrued Commission on Sales Tax

Fashion World is located in a state that imposes a sales tax on retail sales. Businesses collect this tax from customers and remit it to a state agency on a quarterly basis. The sales tax law allows the firms to keep 2 percent of the tax money if they file the quarterly tax return and pay the net amount due promptly. The 2 percent tax money is treated as additional income. On December 31, 19X4, Fashion World owed sales tax of $7,200 for the fourth quarter of the year. The tax will be paid on schedule in January 19X5, and the permitted commission of $144 ($7,200 × 0.02 = $144) will be deducted at that time.

Because the commission represents income earned in 19X4, an adjustment must be made. Sales Tax Payable is debited and a revenue account called Miscellaneous Income is credited for $144. The two parts of the entry are labeled **(n).**

(n) To record accrued commission earned on sales tax

Sales Tax Payable			
Adj.	144	Bal.	7,200

Miscellaneous Income			
		Adj.	144

(n)

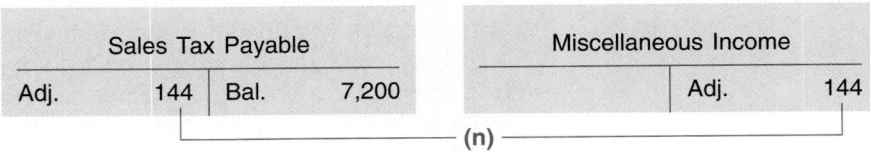

The effect of this adjustment is to decrease the firm's liability for the sales tax owed and to increase its income to reflect the sales tax commission that has been earned but not yet taken.

Adjustments for Unearned Income

Some businesses have **unearned,** or **deferred, income**—income that is received before it is earned. Under the accrual basis of accounting, any portion of a firm's income that has been received but not earned during a fiscal period should not be reported on the income statement prepared for the period. The amount should be reported as income only when it is earned. Since there are no unearned income items at Fashion World, an example from another type of business is presented here.

Unearned Subscription Income for a Publisher

Magazine publishers obtain subscriptions in advance, often several years in advance. When a publisher first receives income from subscriptions, it is unearned; and the subscriptions represent a liability because the publisher has an obligation to provide the magazines during the specified period of time. As the magazines are sent to the subscribers, the income is gradually earned and the liability decreases.

To illustrate the accounting treatment of unearned subscription income, let us consider the operations of the Braswell Publishing Corporation. Assume that this firm starts a new magazine called *Computer Trends and Techniques* at the beginning of 19X4. Whenever subscriptions are received during the year, the amounts are debited to Cash and credited to a liability account called Unearned Subscription Income. At the end of 19X4, this liability account has a balance of $112,500. An examination of the firm's records shows that $50,000 of the balance applies to subscriptions for the current year and has therefore been earned in 19X4. An adjustment is made to transfer the earned amount from the liability account to a revenue account. This adjustment involves a debit to Unearned Subscription Income and a credit to Subscription Income for $50,000.

After the adjustment is journalized and posted, the Unearned Subscription Income account has a balance of $62,500, which represents subscriptions that apply to future periods. This amount appears as a liability on the balance sheet prepared for December 31, 19X4. The balance of $50,000 in the Subscription Income account appears as revenue from operations on the 19X4 income statement.

Other Unearned Income Items

In addition to magazine publishers, many other types of business and professional firms receive unearned income. For example, management fees, rental income, legal fees, architectural fees, construction fees, and advertising income are often obtained in advance. The normal practice in each case is to record the unearned income in a liability account when it is first received and then transfer the earned amount to a revenue account at the end of the fiscal period.

Alternative Method

There is an alternative method for handling unearned income. Under this method, the funds are initially recorded in a revenue account. At the end of each fiscal period, the balance of the revenue account is analyzed, and any income that is still unearned is transferred to a liability account. For example, if unearned subscription income is treated in this manner, it is credited to the Subscription Income account when it is received. The end-of-period adjustment consists of a debit to Subscription Income and a credit to a liability account called Unearned Subscription Income for the remaining unearned amount.

No matter which method is used to handle unearned income, the same figures will appear on the financial statements at the end of the period.

SELF-REVIEW

1. What is the purpose of the accrual basis of accounting?
2. Under the accrual basis, when is revenue from sales normally recognized?
3. Under the accrual basis, when are the costs related to purchases of goods normally recorded?
4. Under the accrual basis, when are operating and nonoperating expenses normally recognized?
5. Why must the accounts be examined carefully at the end of a fiscal period before financial statements are prepared?

Answers to Self-Review

1. The purpose of the accrual basis of accounting is to match revenues and expenses of specific fiscal periods.
2. Under the accrual basis, revenue from sales is normally recognized when a sale is completed, which is usually when title to the goods passes to the customer or when the service is provided.
3. Under the accrual basis, costs related to purchases of goods are normally recorded when the purchases are made, regardless of when payment for the purchases is made.
4. Under the accrual basis, each operating and nonoperating expense item is normally recognized for the period in which it helps to earn revenue, regardless of when the expense is paid.
5. Each account must be examined carefully before financial statements are prepared to see if it contains amounts of revenue or expense that should be allocated to other periods.

COMPLETING THE WORKSHEET

OBJECTIVE 4

Complete a 10-column worksheet.

After all adjustments are entered on the worksheet, the Adjustments Debit and Credit columns are totaled to verify that debits and credits are equal. The next step is to prepare the Adjusted Trial Balance section of the worksheet.

Preparing the Adjusted Trial Balance

Preparing the adjusted trial balance involves combining the original trial balance figures and the adjustments to determine the updated account balances for the period. The columns of the adjusted trial balance are then totaled to make sure that the debits and credits are

FIGURE 12–2
A Completed 10-Column Worksheet

FASHION WORLD
Worksheet
Year Ended December 31, 19X4

	ACCOUNT NAME	TRIAL BALANCE		ADJUSTMENTS	
		DEBIT	CREDIT	DEBIT	CREDIT
1	*Cash*	28 634 00			
2	*Petty Cash Fund*	100 00			
3	*Notes Receivable*	1 200 00			
4	*Accounts Receivable*	26 000 00			
5	*Allowance for Doubtful Accounts*		100 00		(c) 630 00
6	*Interest Receivable*	136 00		(m) 24 00	
7	*Merchandise Inventory*	31 500 00		(b) 32 000 00	(a) 31 500 00
8	*Prepaid Insurance*	3 600 00			(k) 2 700 00
9	*Prepaid Interest*	225 00			(l) 150 00
10	*Supplies*	6 300 00			(j) 4 975 00
11	*Store Equipment*	12 000 00			
12	*Accum. Depr.—Store Equipment*				(d) 2 100 00
13	*Office Equipment*	3 500 00			
14	*Accum. Depr.—Office Equipment*				(e) 600 00
15	*Notes Payable—Trade*		2 000 00		
16	*Notes Payable—Bank*		9 000 00		
17	*Accounts Payable*		4 129 00		
18	*Interest Payable*				(i) 20 00
19	*Social Security Tax Payable*		1 084 00		(g) 97 50
20	*Medicare Tax Payable*		250 00		(g) 22 50
21	*Employee Income Taxes Payable*		1 490 00		
22	*Fed. Unemployment Tax Payable*				(h) 17 00
23	*State Unemployment Tax Payable*				(h) 81 00
24	*Salaries Payable*				(f) 1 500 00
25	*Sales Tax Payable*		7 200 00	(n) 144 00	
26	*Carolyn Wells, Capital*		82 921 00		
27	*Carolyn Wells, Drawing*	24 000 00			
28	*Income Summary*			(a) 31 500 00	(b) 32 000 00
29	*Sales*		409 650 00		
30	*Sales Returns and Allowances*	13 000 00			
31	*Interest Income*		136 00		(m) 24 00
32	*Miscellaneous Income*				(n) 144 00
33	*Purchases*	250 500 00			
34	*Freight In*	3 800 00			
35	*Purchases Returns and Allowances*		3 050 00		
36	*Purchases Discounts*		3 130 00		
37	*Sales Salaries Expense*	68 490 00		(f) 1 500 00	
38	*Advertising Expense*	7 425 00			
39	*Supplies Expense*			(j) 4 975 00	
40	*Cash Short or Over*	125 00			

ADJUSTED TRIAL BALANCE		INCOME STATEMENT		BALANCE SHEET		
DEBIT	CREDIT	DEBIT	CREDIT	DEBIT	CREDIT	
28,634.00				28,634.00		1
100.00				100.00		2
1,200.00				1,200.00		3
26,000.00				26,000.00		4
	730.00				730.00	5
160.00				160.00		6
32,000.00				32,000.00		7
900.00				900.00		8
75.00				75.00		9
1,325.00				1,325.00		10
12,000.00				12,000.00		11
	2,100.00				2,100.00	12
3,500.00				3,500.00		13
	600.00				600.00	14
	2,000.00				2,000.00	15
	9,000.00				9,000.00	16
	4,129.00				4,129.00	17
	20.00				20.00	18
	1,181.50				1,181.50	19
	272.50				272.50	20
	1,490.00				1,490.00	21
	17.00				17.00	22
	81.00				81.00	23
	1,500.00				1,500.00	24
	7,056.00				7,056.00	25
	82,921.00				82,921.00	26
24,000.00				24,000.00		27
31,500.00	32,000.00	31,500.00	32,000.00			28
	409,650.00		409,650.00			29
13,000.00		13,000.00				30
	160.00		160.00			31
	144.00		144.00			32
250,500.00		250,500.00				33
3,800.00		3,800.00				34
	3,050.00		3,050.00			35
	3,130.00		3,130.00			36
69,990.00		69,990.00				37
7,425.00		7,425.00				38
4,975.00		4,975.00				39
125.00		125.00				40

(Continued)

FIGURE 12–2 (Continued)
A Completed 10-Column Worksheet

FASHION WORLD
Worksheet
Year Ended December 31, 19X4

	ACCOUNT NAME	TRIAL BALANCE		ADJUSTMENTS	
		DEBIT	CREDIT	DEBIT	CREDIT
41	*Depr. Expense—Store Equipment*			*(d)* 2,100.00	
42	*Depr. Expense—Office Equipment*			*(e)* 600.00	
43	*Rent Expense*	13,500.00			
44	*Insurance Expense*			*(k)* 2,700.00	
45	*Utilities Expense*	3,925.00			
46	*Office Salaries Expense*	16,500.00			
47	*Payroll Taxes Expense*	7,705.00		*(g)* 120.00	
48				*(h)* 98.00	
49	*Telephone Expense*	1,375.00			
50	*Uncollectible Accounts Expense*			*(c)* 630.00	
51	*Interest Expense*	600.00		*(i)* 20.00	
52				*(l)* 150.00	
53	*Totals*	524,140.00	524,140.00	76,561.00	76,561.00
54	*Net Income*				
55					

equal. The worksheet illustrated in Figure 12–2 shows the completed worksheet for Fashion World on December 31, 19X4.

Notice that the balances of the accounts that did not require adjustment have simply been extended to the Adjusted Trial Balance section from the Trial Balance section. For example, the $28,634 balance of the Cash account that appears in the Debit column of the Trial Balance section was recorded in the Debit column of the Adjusted Trial Balance section without any change.

When figures must be combined to calculate updated account balances, the following procedures are used.

1. If an account has a debit balance in the Trial Balance section and there is a debit entry in the Adjustments section, the two amounts are added. For example, the original debit balance of $68,490 for Sales Salaries Expense and the adjustment of $1,500 were added to find the updated balance of $69,990.
2. If an account has a debit balance in the Trial Balance section and there is a credit entry in the Adjustments section, the credit amount is subtracted. For example, the adjustment of $4,975 for Supplies was subtracted from the original debit balance of $6,300 to find the updated balance of $1,325.
3. If an account has a credit balance in the Trial Balance section and there is a credit entry in the Adjustments section, the two

ADJUSTED TRIAL BALANCE		INCOME STATEMENT		BALANCE SHEET		
DEBIT	CREDIT	DEBIT	CREDIT	DEBIT	CREDIT	
2,100.00		2,100.00				41
600.00		600.00				42
13,500.00		13,500.00				43
2,700.00		2,700.00				44
3,925.00		3,925.00				45
16,500.00		16,500.00				46
7,923.00		7,923.00				47
						48
1,375.00		1,375.00				49
630.00		630.00				50
770.00		770.00				51
						52
561,231.50	561,232.00	431,338.00	448,134.00	129,894.00	113,098.00	53
		16,796.00			16,796.00	54
		448,134.00	448,134.00	129,894.00	129,894.00	55

amounts are added. For example, the original credit balance of $100 for Allowance for Doubtful Accounts and the adjustment of $630 were added to find the updated balance of $730.

4. If an account has a credit balance in the Trial Balance section and there is a debit entry in the Adjustments section, the debit amount is subtracted. For example, the adjustment of $144 for Sales Tax Payable was subtracted from the original credit balance of $7,200 to find the updated balance of $7,056.

Preparing the Balance Sheet Section

The accounts that will appear on the balance sheet begin with the Cash account and include all accounts through the Carolyn Wells, Drawing account. Thus all balances for these accounts are extended from the Adjusted Trial Balance section of the worksheet to the Balance Sheet section of the worksheet, as shown in Figure 12–2.

Preparing the Income Statement Section

The accounts that appear on the worksheet in Figure 12–2 appear in chart-of-account order. The accounts that will appear on the income statement begin with the Income Summary account and include all accounts through the Interest Expense account. Thus all balances for these accounts are extended from the Adjusted Trial Balance section of the worksheet to the Income Statement section, as shown in Figure 12–2.

Calculating Net Income or Net Loss

Once all the necessary account balances have been entered in the financial statement sections of the worksheet, the net income or net loss for the period is determined and the worksheet is completed. The first step is to total the debits and credits in the Income Statement section.

Refer to the worksheet shown in Figure 12–2. When the columns of the Income Statement section are added, the debits total $431,338 and the credits total $448,134. Since the credits exceed the debits, the difference of $16,796 represents a net income for the period. This figure is entered in the Debit column so that the two columns will balance. Then the final total of each column ($448,134) is recorded on the worksheet.

Because the net income represents an increase in equity, it is entered in the Credit column of the Balance Sheet section, as explained in Chapter 5. Then the debits and credits in the Balance Sheet section are added, and the totals are recorded above the net income line (to make it easier to find any errors that may occur). In this case, the total of the Debit column is $129,894 and the total of the Credit column is $113,098. The difference between the two totals is $16,796, which is the same as the net income for the year. The difference should always be equal to the net income or net loss for the period.

Next the final totals of the Balance Sheet columns, including the net income, are determined and entered. In this case, each total is $128,894 and the two columns therefore balance. The last step is to rule all money columns to show that the worksheet has been completed.

SELF-REVIEW

1. What is merchandise inventory?
2. How is the amount of the ending merchandise inventory determined?
3. What entries are made to adjust merchandise inventory on the worksheet?
4. What types of accounts appear in the Income Statement section of the worksheet?
5. What types of accounts appear in the Balance Sheet section of the worksheet?

Answers to Self-Review

1. Merchandise inventory is the stock of goods that a business has on hand for sale to customers.
2. The amount of the ending inventory is determined as follows:
   a. The quantity of each type of goods that the firm has in stock is listed on a form called an inventory sheet.
   b. The quantity is multiplied by the unit cost to find the total cost of the item.
   c. The totals for all the different items on hand are added to find the cost of the entire inventory.
3. The beginning inventory is taken off the books by closing the beginning inventory to the Income Summary account. This is accomplished by debiting the Income Summary account and crediting the beginning inventory. The ending inventory is placed on the books by debiting the ending inventory and crediting the Income Summary account.
4. The types of accounts that appear in the Income Statement section of the worksheet are the revenue, expense, and cost accounts. The figures for the beginning and ending inventory accounts also appear there in the Income Summary account.
5. The types of accounts that appear in the Balance Sheet section of the worksheet are assets, liabilities, and owner's equity accounts.

MANAGERIAL IMPLICATIONS

The matching process is necessary if managers are to know the true revenue, expenses, and net income or net loss of a period. If accrued and deferred items were not adjusted, the financial statements would be incomplete and misleading, and they would therefore be of no help in evaluating operations. Since adjustments tend to increase or decrease net income or net loss, managers should be familiar with the procedures and underlying assumptions used by their firm's accountant to handle accruals and deferrals.

Managers are keenly interested in receiving timely financial statements, especially the periodic income statement, which shows the results of operations. The worksheet is a very useful device for gathering data about adjustments and for preparing the income statement. Managers are also interested in prompt preparation of the balance sheet because it shows the financial position of the business at the end of the fiscal period.

Review and Applications

CHAPTER SUMMARY

The accrual basis of accounting requires that all revenue and expenses of a fiscal period be matched and reported on the income statement of the period to determine the net income or net loss. Typically, certain adjustments must be made to the revenue and expense accounts at the end of the period in order to make sure that they correctly reflect amounts that apply to the current period and do not include amounts that pertain to other periods. Provisions for the expense for uncollectible accounts and the expense for depreciation are common examples of such adjustments. Other typical adjustments of expense accounts involve accrued expenses and prepaid expenses.

Accrued expenses represent expense items that have been incurred or used but not yet paid or recorded. Prepaid, or deferred, expenses represent expense items that have been recorded but not yet incurred or used. A firm may also have adjustments involving accrued income and unearned income. Accrued income is income that has been earned but not yet recorded. Unearned, or deferred, income is income that has not yet been earned but has been received and recorded.

As soon as all adjustments have been entered on the worksheet, the worksheet is completed and the financial statements prepared. The first step is to combine the figures in the Trial Balance section with the adjustments in order to obtain an adjusted trial balance. Next, each item in the Adjusted Trial Balance columns is extended to the appropriate financial statement section of the worksheet.

When all figures in the Adjusted Trial Balance section have been transferred, the Income Statement columns are totaled and the net income or net loss is determined. The amount of net income or net loss is then entered in the Balance Sheet section. At this point, the total debits must equal the total credits in the Balance Sheet columns.

GLOSSARY OF NEW TERMS

Accrual basis (p. 410) A system of accounting by which all revenues and expenses are matched and reported on statements for the applicable period, regardless of when the cash related to the transaction is received or paid

Accrued expenses (p. 418) Expense items that relate to the current period but have not yet been paid for and do not yet appear in the accounts

Accrued income (p. 422) Revenue earned but not yet received and recorded
Deferred expenses (p. 420) See Prepaid expenses
Deferred income (p. 423) Income received before it is earned
Inventory sheet (p. 413) A form used to list the volume and type of goods a firm has in stock
Mixed accounts (p. 410) Accounts that contain elements of both assets and expenses or both liabilities and revenue
Prepaid expenses (p. 420) Expense items paid for and recorded in advance of their use, such as rent or insurance
Property, plant, and equipment (p. 416) Long-term assets that are used in the operation of a business and are subject to depreciation (except for land, which is not depreciated)
Unearned income (p. 423) See Deferred income

REVIEW QUESTIONS

1. What are mixed accounts?
2. Why should the estimated expense for uncollectible accounts be recorded before the losses from these accounts actually occur?
3. What adjustment is made to record the estimated expense for uncollectible accounts?
4. What is depreciation?
5. What types of assets are subject to depreciation? Give three examples of such assets.
6. Explain the meaning of the following terms that relate to depreciation.
   a. Salvage value
   b. Depreciable base
   c. Useful life
   d. Straight-line method
7. What adjustment is made for depreciation on office equipment?
8. What is an accrued expense? Give three examples of items that often become accrued expenses.
9. What adjustment is made to record accrued salaries?
10. What is a prepaid expense? Give three examples of prepaid expense items.
11. How is the cost of an insurance policy recorded when the policy is purchased?
12. What adjustment is made to record expired insurance?
13. What is the alternative method of handling prepaid expenses?
14. What is accrued income? Give an example of an item that might produce accrued income.
15. What adjustment is made for accrued interest on a note receivable?
16. What is unearned income? Give two examples of items that would be classified as unearned income.
17. How is unearned subscription income recorded when it is received?

18. What adjustment is made to record the subscription income earned during a period?
19. What is the alternative method of handling unearned income?
20. How does the worksheet help the accountant to prepare financial statements more efficiently?

MANAGERIAL FOCUS

1. Assume that you are the newly hired controller for the Bradshaw Company, a wholesale firm that sells most of its goods on credit. You have found that the business does not make an adjustment for estimated uncollectible accounts at the end of each year. Instead, the expense for uncollectible accounts is recorded during the year as individual accounts are identified as bad debts. Would you recommend that the firm continue its present accounting treatment of uncollectible accounts? Why or why not?
2. On July 1, 19X5, the Roland Company rented a portion of its warehouse to another business for a one-year period and received the full amount of $4,200 in advance. At the end of Roland's fiscal year on December 31, 19X5, the firm's income statement showed $2,100 as rental income. The other $2,100 appeared in the liabilities section of the firm's balance sheet as unearned rental income. The owner, James Roland, felt that the entire sum should have been reported on the income statement as income because all the cash was received in 19X5. How would you explain to Roland why the accountant's treatment of the $4,200 was correct?
3. Some firms initially record the cost of an insurance policy as an expense and then make an adjustment at the end of the fiscal year to transfer the unexpired amount to an asset account. Does this method produce different financial results from the method used by Fashion World? Explain.
4. Why is it important for management to understand the accounting methods used to report data on the firm's financial statements?

EXERCISES

EXERCISE 12–1 (Obj. 1) Tutorial

Determining the adjustments for inventory. The beginning inventory of a merchandising business was $63,000, and the ending inventory is $56,000. What entries are needed at the end of the fiscal period to adjust Merchandise Inventory?

EXERCISE 12–2 (Obj. 1) Tutorial

Determining the adjustments for inventory. The Income Statement columns of the worksheet of the Ryan Company for the year ended December 31, 19X3, has $72,000 recorded in the Debit column and $84,000 in the Credit column for the Income Summary account. What are the beginning and ending balances for Merchandise Inventory?

EXERCISE 12–3 (Obj. 2)

Computing adjustments for accrued and prepaid expense items. For each of the independent situations below, indicate the adjusting entry that must be made on the December 31, 19X3, worksheet. Omit explanations.

a. During the year 19X3, the Raymond Company had net credit sales of $850,000. Past experience shows that 0.9 percent of the firm's net credit sales result in uncollectible accounts.
b. Equipment purchased by Rizzoli Auto Service Center for $26,000 on January 2, 19X3, has an estimated useful life of five years and an estimated salvage value of $3,500. What adjustment for depreciation should be recorded on the firm's worksheet for the year ended December 31, 19X3?
c. On December 31, 19X3, the McConnell Toy Company owed wages of $5,200 to its factory employees, who are paid weekly.
d. On December 31, 19X3, the McConnell Toy Company owed the employer's social security (6.5%) and medicare taxes (1.5%) on the entire $5,200 of accrued wages for its factory employees.
e. On December 31, 19X3, the McConnell Toy Company owed federal (1.1%) and state (5.4%) unemployment taxes on the entire $5,200 of accrued wages for its factory employees.

EXERCISE 12–4 (Obj. 2)

Computing adjustments for accrued and prepaid expense items. For each of the independent situations below, indicate the adjusting entry that must be made on the December 31, 19X3, worksheet. Omit explanations.

a. On December 31, 19X3, the Notes Payable account at the Orion Manufacturing Company had a balance of $1,500. This balance represented a three-month, 12 percent note issued on November 1.
b. On January 2, 19X3, Valdez Word Processing Service purchased magnetic disks, paper, and other supplies for $800 in cash. On December 31, 19X3, an inventory of supplies showed that items costing $190 were on hand. The Supplies account has a balance of $800.
c. On August 1, 19X3, the Ryan Company paid a premium of $3,240 in cash for a two-year insurance policy. On December 31, 19X3, an examination of the insurance records showed that coverage for a period of five months had expired.
d. On April 1, 19X3, Harbor Seafood Restaurant signed a one-year advertising contract with a local radio station and issued a check for $1,920 to pay the total amount owed. On December 31, 19X3, the Prepaid Advertising account has a balance of $1,920.

EXERCISE 12–5 (Obj. 2)

Tutorial

Recording adjustments for accrued and prepaid expense items. On December 1, 19X3, Discount Camera Center borrowed $10,000 from its bank in order to expand its operations. The firm issued a four-month, 12 percent note for $10,000 to the bank and received

$9,600 in cash because the bank deducted the interest for the entire period in advance. In general journal form, show the entry that would be made to record this transaction and the adjustment for prepaid interest that should be recorded on the firm's worksheet for the year ended December 31, 19X3. Omit explanations.

EXERCISE 12–6
(Obj. 2)

Tutorial

Recording adjustments for accrued and prepaid expense items. On December 31, 19X3, the Notes Payable account at Dale's Furniture Shop had a balance of $20,000. This amount represented funds borrowed on a four-month, 12 percent note from the firm's bank on December 1. Record the journal entry for interest expense on this note that should be recorded on the firm's worksheet for the year ended December 31, 19X3. Omit explanations.

EXERCISE 12–7
(Obj. 3)

Tutorial

Recording adjustments for accrued and deferred income items. For each of the independent situations below, indicate the adjusting entry that must be made on the December 31, 19X3, worksheet. Omit explanations.

a. On December 31, 19X3, the Notes Receivable account at the Carroll Company had a balance of $4,800, which represented a six-month, 10 percent note issued by a customer on August 1.
b. On December 31, 19X3, the Sales Tax Payable account at the Lee Shoe Store had a balance of $645. This balance represented the sales tax owed for the fourth quarter of 19X3. The firm is scheduled to send the amount to the state sales tax agency on January 15, 19X4. At that time the firm will deduct a commission of 2 percent of the tax due, as allowed by state law.
c. During the week ended January 7, 19X3, the Kovacs Publishing Company received $12,000 from customers for subscriptions to its magazine *Modern Business*. On December 31, 19X3, an analysis of the Unearned Subscription Revenue account showed that $6,000 of the subscriptions were earned in 19X3.
d. On September 1, 19X3, the Hart Real Estate Company rented a commercial building to a new tenant and received $15,000 in advance to cover the rent for six months.

EXERCISE 12–8
(Obj. 4)

Completing a 10-column worksheet. Indicate whether each of the accounts that follow would appear in the Income Statement Debit or Credit column or the Balance Sheet Debit or Credit column.

Purchases
Purchases Returns and Allowances
Purchases Discount
Unearned Rent
Subscription Revenue
Calvin Reese, Capital
Income Summary
Accumulated Depreciation—Equipment
Sales Discount

PROBLEMS

PROBLEM SET A

PROBLEM 12–1A
(Obj. 2)

Recording adjustments for accrued and prepaid expense items. On July 1, 19X7, James Walker established his own accounting practice. Selected transactions for the first of July follow.

Instructions

Tutorial

1. Record the transactions on page 1 of the general journal. Omit explanations. Assume that the firm initially records prepaid expenses as assets and unearned income as a liability.
2. Record the adjusting journal entries that must be made on July 31, 19X7, on page 2 of the general journal. Omit explanations but show all necessary computations.

TRANSACTIONS

July 1 Signed a lease for an office and issued Check 101 for $6,000 to pay the rent in advance for six months.

1 Borrowed money from Security National Bank by issuing a four-month, 12 percent note for $9,000; received $8,640 because the bank deducted the interest in advance.

1 Signed an agreement with the Anderson Company to provide accounting and tax services for one year at $2,000 per month; received the entire fee of $24,000 in advance.

1 Purchased office equipment for $7,800 from Office Depot; issued a two-month, 12 percent note in payment. The equipment is estimated to have a useful life of six years and a $600 salvage value. The equipment will be depreciated using the straight-line method.

1 Purchased a one-year insurance policy and issued Check 102 for $960 to pay the entire premium.

3 Purchased office furniture for $8,400 from Contemporary Office Furniture Mart; issued Check 103 for $4,200 and agreed to pay the balance in 60 days. The equipment is estimated to have a useful life of five years and a $600 salvage value. The office furniture will be depreciated using the straight-line method.

5 Purchased office supplies for $1,080 with Check 104. Assume $400 of supplies are on hand July 31, 19X7.

PROBLEM 12–2A
(Obj. 2)

Tutorial

Spreadsheet

Recording adjustments for accrued and prepaid expense items. On July 31, 19X7, after one month of operation, the general ledger of Janet Linz, Attorney, contained the accounts and balances reflected on page 438.

Instructions

1. Prepare a partial worksheet with the following sections: Trial Balance, Adjustments, and Adjusted Trial Balance.
2. Use the data about the firm's accounts and balances to complete the Trial Balance section.
3. Enter the adjustments described below in the Adjustments section. Identify each adjustment with the appropriate letter.
4. Complete the Adjusted Trial Balance section.

ACCOUNTS AND BALANCES

Cash	$11,100 Dr.
Accounts Receivable	650 Dr.
Supplies	430 Dr.
Prepaid Rent	4,500 Dr.
Prepaid Insurance	840 Dr.
Prepaid Interest	200 Dr.
Furniture	5,900 Dr.
Accum. Depr.—Furniture	
Equipment	3,200 Dr.
Accum. Depr.—Equipment	
Notes Payable	9,200 Cr.
Accounts Payable	2,000 Cr.
Interest Payable	
Unearned Legal Fees	1,800 Cr.
Janet Linz, Capital	12,610 Cr.
Janet Linz, Drawing	1,000 Dr.
Legal Fees	4,000 Cr.
Salaries Expense	1,600 Dr.
Utilities Expense	110 Dr.
Telephone Expense	80 Dr.
Supplies Expense	
Rent Expense	
Insurance Expense	
Depr. Expense—Furniture	
Depr. Expense—Equipment	
Interest Expense	

ADJUSTMENTS

a. On July 31 an inventory of the supplies showed that items costing $380 were on hand.
b. On July 1 the firm paid $4,500 in advance for six months of rent.
c. On July 1 the firm purchased a one-year insurance policy for $840.
d. On July 1 the firm paid $200 interest in advance on a four-month note that it issued to the bank.
e. On July 1 the firm purchased office furniture for $5,900. The furniture is expected to have a useful life of five years and a salvage value of $500.
f. On July 1 the firm purchased office equipment for $3,200. The equipment is expected to have a useful life of five years and a salvage value of $800.
g. On July 1 the firm issued a two-month, 12 percent note for $3,200.
h. On July 1 the firm received a legal fee of $1,800 in advance for a one-year period.

PROBLEM 12–3A
(Obj. 1, 2, 3, 4)

Tutorial

Recording adjustments and completing the worksheet. The Plant Emporium is a retail store that sells plants, soil, and decorative pots. On December 31, 19X5, the firm's general ledger contained the accounts and balances shown on the next page.

Instructions

1. Prepare the Trial Balance section of a 10-column worksheet. The worksheet covers the year ended December 31, 19X5.
2. Enter the adjustments below in the Adjustments section of the worksheet. Identify each adjustment with the appropriate letter.
3. Complete the worksheet.

Note: This problem will be required to complete Problem 13-3A.

ACCOUNTS AND BALANCES

Cash	$ 4,700 Dr.
Accounts Receivable	3,100 Dr.
Allowance for Doubtful Accounts	52 Cr.
Merchandise Inventory	11,800 Dr.
Supplies	1,200 Dr.
Prepaid Advertising	960 Dr.
Store Equipment	7,000 Dr.
Accum. Depr.—Store Equipment	1,300 Cr.
Office Equipment	1,600 Dr.
Accum. Depr.—Office Equipment	280 Cr.
Accounts Payable	1,750 Cr.
Social Security Tax Payable	430 Cr.
Medicare Tax Payable	99 Cr.
Federal Unemployment Tax Payable	
State Unemployment Tax Payable	
Salaries Payable	
Peter Dall, Capital	25,711 Cr.
Peter Dall, Drawing	20,000 Dr.
Sales	89,768 Cr.
Sales Returns and Allowances	1,100 Dr.
Purchases	46,400 Dr.
Purchases Returns and Allowances	430 Cr.
Rent Expense	6,000 Dr.
Telephone Expense	590 Dr.
Salaries Expense	14,100 Dr.
Payroll Taxes Expense	1,270 Dr.
Income Summary	
Supplies Expense	
Advertising Expense	
Depr. Expense—Store Equipment	
Depr. Expense—Office Equipment	
Uncollectible Accounts Expense	

ADJUSTMENTS

a–b. Merchandise inventory on December 31, 19X5, is $13,000.

c. During 19X5 the firm had net credit sales of $35,000; the firm estimates that 0.6 percent of these sales will result in uncollectible accounts.

d. On December 31, 19X5, an inventory of the supplies showed that items costing $350 were on hand.

e. On October 1, 19X5, the firm signed a six-month advertising contract for $960 with a local newspaper and paid the full amount in advance.

f. On January 2, 19X4, the firm purchased store equipment for $7,000. At that time, the equipment was estimated to have a useful life of five years and a salvage value of $500.

g. On January 2, 19X4, the firm purchased office equipment for $1,600. At that time the equipment was estimated to have a useful life of five years and a salvage value of $200.

h. On December 31, 19X5, the firm owed salaries of $1,500 that will not be paid until 19X6.

i. On December 31, 19X5, the firm owed the employer's social security (assume 6.5 percent) and medicare (assume 1.5 percent) taxes on the entire $1,500 of accrued wages.

j. On December 31, 19X5, the firm owed federal unemployment tax (assume 1.1 percent) and state unemployment tax (assume 5.4 percent) on the entire $1,500 of accrued wages.

PROBLEM 12–4A
(Obj. 1, 2, 3, 4)

Tutorial GL

Recording adjustments and completing the worksheet. The Nutri-Products Company is a distributor of nutritious snack foods like granola bars. On December 31, 19X3, the firm's general ledger contained the accounts and balances shown below.

Instructions

1. Prepare the Trial Balance section of a 10-column worksheet. The worksheet covers the year ended December 31, 19X3.
2. Enter the adjustments in the Adjustments section of the worksheet. Identify each adjustment with the appropriate letter.
3. Complete the worksheet.

ACCOUNTS AND BALANCES

Cash	$ 15,300 Dr.
Accounts Receivable	17,600 Dr.
Allowance for Doubtful Accounts	210 Cr.
Merchandise Inventory	43,000 Dr.
Supplies	5,200 Dr.
Prepaid Insurance	2,700 Dr.
Office Equipment	3,900 Dr.
Accum. Depr.—Office Equipment	1,400 Cr.
Warehouse Equipment	14,000 Dr.
Accum. Depr.—Warehouse Equipment	4,800 Cr.
Notes Payable—Bank	15,000 Cr.
Accounts Payable	6,100 Cr.
Interest Payable	
Social Security Tax Payable	840 Cr.
Medicare Tax Payable	194 Cr.
Federal Unemployment Tax Payable	
State Unemployment Tax Payable	
Salaries Payable	
Gary Smith, Capital	55,267 Cr.
Gary Smith, Drawing	28,000 Dr.
Sales	326,889 Cr.
Sales Returns and Allowances	5,000 Dr.
Purchases	175,000 Dr.
Purchases Returns and Allowances	4,600 Cr.
Income Summary	

ACCOUNTS AND BALANCES (Continued)

Rent Expense	18,000 Dr.
Telephone Expense	1,100 Dr.
Salaries Expense	80,000 Dr.
Payroll Taxes Expense	6,500 Dr.
Supplies Expense	
Insurance Expense	
Depr. Expense—Office Equipment	
Depr. Expense—Warehouse Equipment	
Uncollectible Accounts Expense	
Interest Expense	

ADJUSTMENTS

a–b. Merchandise inventory on December 31, 19X3, is $42,000.

c. During 19X3 the firm had net credit sales of $280,000; past experience indicates that 0.5 percent of these sales should result in uncollectible accounts.

d. On December 31, 19X3, an inventory of supplies showed that items costing $600 were on hand.

e. On May 1, 19X3, the firm purchased a one-year insurance policy for $2,700.

f. On January 2, 19X1, the firm purchased office equipment for $3,900. At that time the equipment was estimated to have a useful life of five years and a salvage value of $400.

g. On January 2, 19X1, the firm purchased warehouse equipment for $14,000. At that time the equipment was estimated to have a useful life of five years and a salvage value of $2,000.

h. On November 1, 19X3, the firm issued a four-month, 11 percent note for $15,000.

i. On December 31, 19X3, the firm owed salaries of $2,500 that will not be paid until 19X4.

j. On December 31, 19X3, the firm owed the employer's social security (assume 6.5 percent) and medicare (assume 1.5 percent) taxes on the entire $2,500 of accrued wages.

k. On December 31, 19X3, the firm owed the federal unemployment tax (assume 1.1 percent) and the state unemployment tax (assume 5.4 percent) on the entire $2,500 of accrued wages.

PROBLEM SET B

PROBLEM 12–1B (Obj. 2)

Recording adjustments for accrued and prepaid expense items. On June 1, 19X5, June Ortiz established her own advertising firm. Selected transactions for the first of June follow.

Instructions

Tutorial

1. Record the transactions on page 1 of the general journal. Omit explanations. Assume that the firm initially records prepaid expenses as assets and unearned income as a liability.
2. Record the adjusting journal entries that must be made on June 30, 19X5, on page 2 of the general journal. Omit explanations but show all necessary computations.

TRANSACTIONS

June 1 Signed a lease for an office and issued Check 101 for $7,200 to pay the rent in advance for six months.

1 Borrowed money from First National Bank by issuing a three-month, 10 percent note for $8,000; received $7,800 because the bank deducted the interest in advance.

1 Signed an agreement with World of Fashion Clothing Store to provide advertising consulting for one year at $2,500 per month; received the entire fee of $30,000 in advance.

1 Purchased office equipment for $10,800 from Office Furniture Store; issued a three-month, 12 percent note in payment. The equipment is estimated to have a useful life of five years and a $600 salvage value and will be depreciated using the straight-line method.

1 Purchased a one-year insurance policy and issued Check 102 for $1,080 to pay the entire premium.

3 Purchased office furniture for $9,600 from Office Furniture Mart; issued Check 103 for $4,800 and agreed to pay the balance in 60 days. The equipment is estimated to have a useful life of five years and a $600 salvage value and will be depreciated using the straight-line method.

5 Purchased office supplies for $1,400 with Check 104; assume $600 of supplies are on hand June 30, 19X5.

PROBLEM 12–2B (Obj. 2)

Tutorial

Recording adjustments for accrued and prepaid expense items. On September 30, 19X6, after one month of operation, the general ledger of Management Skills Company contained the accounts and balances shown below.

Instructions

1. Prepare a partial worksheet with the following sections: Trial Balance, Adjustments, and Adjusted Trial Balance.
2. Use the data about the firm's accounts and balances to complete the Trial Balance section.
3. Enter the adjustments described below in the Adjustments section. Identify each adjustment with the appropriate letter.
4. Complete the Adjusted Trial Balance section.

ACCOUNTS AND BALANCES

Cash	$13,500 Dr.
Supplies	370 Dr.
Prepaid Rent	2,100 Dr.
Prepaid Advertising	1,200 Dr.
Prepaid Interest	225 Dr.
Furniture	2,800 Dr.
Accum. Depr.—Furniture	
Equipment	4,500 Dr.
Accum. Depr.—Equipment	
Notes Payable	10,300 Cr.
Accounts Payable	2,000 Cr.
Interest Payable	
Unearned Course Fees	11,000 Cr.
Kevin Doyle, Capital	3,365 Cr.

ACCOUNTS AND BALANCES (Continued)

Kevin Doyle, Drawing	1,000 Dr.
Course Fees	
Salaries Expense	800 Dr.
Telephone Expense	60 Dr.
Entertainment Expense	110 Dr.
Supplies Expense	
Rent Expense	
Advertising Expense	
Depr. Expense—Furniture	
Depr. Expense—Equipment	
Interest Expense	

ADJUSTMENTS

a. On September 30 an inventory of the supplies showed that items costing $320 were on hand.
b. On September 1 the firm paid $2,100 in advance for six months of rent.
c. On September 1 the firm signed a six-month advertising contract for $1,200 and paid the full amount in advance.
d. On September 1 the firm paid $225 interest in advance on a three-month note that it issued to the bank.
e. On September 1 the firm purchased office furniture for $2,800. The furniture is expected to have a useful life of five years and a salvage value of $400.
f. On September 3 the firm purchased equipment for $4,500. The equipment is expected to have a useful life of five years and a salvage value of $600.
g. On September 1 the firm issued a two-month, 9 percent note for $2,800.
h. During September the firm received $11,000 in advance. An analysis of the firm's records shows that $3,500 applies to services provided in September and the rest pertains to future months.

PROBLEM 12–3B
(Obj. 1, 2, 3, 4)

Tutorial

Recording adjustments and completing the worksheet. The Toy Palace is a retail store that sells toys, games, and bicycles. On December 31, 19X8, the firm's general ledger contained the accounts and balances shown below.

Instructions

1. Prepare the Trial Balance section of a 10-column worksheet. The worksheet covers the year ended December 31, 19X8.
2. Enter the adjustments below in the Adjustments section of the worksheet. Identify each adjustment with the appropriate letter.
3. Complete the worksheet.

Note: This problem will be required to complete Problem 13-3B.

ACCOUNTS AND BALANCES

Cash	$ 6,900 Dr.
Accounts Receivable	5,300 Dr.
Allowance for Doubtful Accounts	80 Cr.
Merchandise Inventory	34,500 Dr.

ACCOUNTS AND BALANCES (Continued)

Supplies	2,900 Dr.
Prepaid Advertising	1,320 Dr.
Store Equipment	8,200 Dr.
Accum. Depr.—Store Equipment	1,440 Cr.
Office Equipment	2,100 Dr.
Accum. Depr.—Office Equipment	360 Cr.
Accounts Payable	2,150 Cr.
Social Security Tax Payable	1,480 Cr.
Medicare Tax Payable	342 Cr.
Federal Unemployment Tax Payable	
State Unemployment Tax Payable	
Salaries Payable	
Marie Testa, Capital	28,380 Cr.
Marie Testa, Drawing	25,000 Dr.
Sales	260,598 Cr.
Sales Returns and Allowances	4,300 Dr.
Purchases	126,900 Dr.
Purchases Returns and Allowances	1,260 Cr.
Rent Expense	30,000 Dr.
Telephone Expense	1,070 Dr.
Salaries Expense	42,300 Dr.
Payroll Taxes Expense	3,800 Dr.
Income Summary	
Supplies Expense	
Advertising Expense	1,500 Dr.
Depr. Expense—Store Equipment	
Depr. Expense—Office Equipment	
Uncollectible Accounts Expense	

ADJUSTMENTS

a–b. Merchandise inventory on December 31, 19X8, is $36,000.

c. During 19X8 the firm had net credit sales of $110,000. The firm estimates that 0.7 percent of these sales will result in uncollectible accounts.

d. On December 31, 19X8, an inventory of the supplies showed that items costing $700 were on hand.

e. On September 1, 19X8, the firm signed a six-month advertising contract for $1,320 with a local newspaper and paid the full amount in advance.

f. On January 2, 19X7, the firm purchased store equipment for $8,200. At that time the equipment was estimated to have a useful life of five years and a salvage value of $1,000.

g. On January 2, 19X7, the firm purchased office equipment for $2,100. At that time the equipment was estimated to have a useful life of five years and a salvage value of $300.

h. On December 31, 19X8, the firm owed salaries of $1,500 that will not be paid until 19X9.

i. On December 31, 19X8, the firm owed the employer's social security (assume 6.5 percent) and medicare (assume 1.5 percent) taxes on the entire $1,500 of accrued wages.

j. On December 31, 19X8, the firm owed federal unemployment tax (assume 1.1 percent) and state unemployment tax (assume 5.4 percent) on the entire $1,500 of accrued wages.

PROBLEM 12–4B
(Obj. 1, 2, 3, 4)

Tutorial

Recording adjustments and completing the worksheet. Valley Forge Furniture is a retail store that sells reproductions of colonial furniture. On December 31, 19X4, the firm's general ledger contained the accounts and balances shown below.

Instructions

1. Prepare the Trial Balance section of a 10-column worksheet. The worksheet covers the year ended December 31, 19X4.
2. Enter the adjustments below in the Adjustments section of the worksheet. Identify each adjustment with the appropriate letter.
3. Complete the worksheet.

ACCOUNTS AND BALANCES

Cash	$ 15,600 Dr.
Accounts Receivable	18,200 Dr.
Allowance for Doubtful Accounts	180 Cr.
Merchandise Inventory	84,000 Dr.
Supplies	4,900 Dr.
Prepaid Insurance	3,000 Dr.
Store Equipment	5,500 Dr.
Accum. Depr.—Store Equipment	1,960 Cr.
Warehouse Equipment	12,100 Dr.
Accum. Depr.—Warehouse Equipment	4,240 Cr.
Notes Payable	12,000 Cr.
Accounts Payable	16,100 Cr.
Interest Payable	
Social Security Tax Payable	910 Cr.
Medicare Tax Payable	210 Cr.
Federal Unemployment Tax Payable	
State Unemployment Tax Payable	
Salaries Payable	
Ann Kerr, Capital	76,187 Cr.
Ann Kerr, Drawing	30,000 Dr.
Sales	450,203 Cr.
Sales Returns and Allowances	11,000 Dr.
Purchases	275,000 Dr.
Purchases Returns and Allowances	7,600 Cr.
Income Summary	
Rent Expense	24,000 Dr.
Telephone Expense	1,200 Dr.
Salaries Expense	78,000 Dr.
Payroll Taxes Expense	6,900 Dr.
Supplies Expense	
Insurance Expense	
Depr. Expense—Office Equipment	
Depr. Expense—Warehouse Equipment	
Uncollectible Accounts Expense	
Interest Expense	190 Dr.

ADJUSTMENTS

a–b. Merchandise inventory on December 31, 19X4, is $83,000.

c. During 19X4 the firm had net credit sales of $340,000. Past experience indicates that 0.9 percent of these sales should result in uncollectible accounts.

d. On December 31, 19X4, an inventory of supplies showed that items costing $1,100 were on hand.

e. On June 1, 19X4, the firm purchased a one-year insurance policy for $3,000.

f. On January 2, 19X2, the firm purchased store equipment for $5,500. At that time the equipment was estimated to have a useful life of five years and a salvage value of $600.

g. On January 2, 19X2, the firm purchased warehouse equipment for $12,100. At that time the equipment was estimated to have a useful life of five years and a salvage value of $1,500.

h. On November 1, 19X4, the firm issued a three-month, 10 percent note for $12,000.

i. On December 31, 19X4, the firm owed salaries of $1,800 that will not be paid until 19X5.

j. On December 31, 19X4, the firm owed the employer's social security (assume 6.5 percent) and medicare (assume 1.5 percent) taxes on the entire $1,800 of accrued wages.

k. On December 31, 19X4, the firm owed federal unemployment tax (assume 1.1 percent) and state unemployment tax (assume 5.4 percent) on the entire $1,800 of accrued wages.

CHALLENGE PROBLEM

GL

The unadjusted trial balance of Value Mart Discount Store on December 31, 19X3, the end of its accounting period, follows.

VALUE MART DISCOUNT STORE
Trial Balance
December 31, 19X3

Cash	$ 6,475 Dr.
Accounts Receivable	25,000 Dr.
Allowance for Doubtful Accounts	1,000 Cr.
Merchandise Inventory	53,315 Dr.
Store Supplies	1,920 Dr.
Office Supplies	1,475 Dr.
Store Equipment	56,795 Dr.
Accumulated Depreciation—Store Equipment	6,310 Cr.
Office Equipment	13,660 Dr.
Accumulated Depreciation—Office Equipment	2,385 Cr.
Accounts Payable	2,195 Cr.
Salaries Payable	

Social Security Taxes Payable	
Medicare Tax Payable	
Federal Unemployment Tax Payable	
State Unemployment Tax Payable	
John Thomas, Capital	84,000 Cr.
John Thomas, Drawing	15,000 Dr.
Income Summary	
Sales	431,115 Cr.
Sales Returns and Allowances	3,790 Dr.
Purchases	252,715 Dr.
Purchases Returns and Allowances	2,120 Cr.
Purchases Discount	5,385 Cr.
Freight In	3,500 Dr.
Sales Salaries Expense	37,975 Dr.
Rent Expense	18,000 Dr.
Advertising Expense	6,150 Dr.
Store Supplies Expense	
Depreciation Expense—Store Equipment	
Office Salaries Expense	38,740 Dr.
Payroll Taxes Expense	
Uncollectible Accounts Expense	
Office Supplies Expense	
Depreciation Expense—Office Equipment	

Instructions

1. Copy the unadjusted trial balance onto a worksheet and complete the worksheet using the following information.
   a–b. Ending merchandise inventory, $49,680.
   c. Uncollectible accounts expense, $500.
   d. Store supplies on hand December 31, 19X3, $275.
   e. Office supplies on hand December 31, 19X3, $190.
   f. Depreciation on store equipment, $5,500.
   g. Depreciation on office equipment, $1,500.
   h. Accrued sales salaries, $2,000, and accrued office salaries, $500.
   i. Social security tax on accrued salaries, $163; medicare tax on accrued salaries, $38.
   j. Federal unemployment tax on accrued salaries, $28; state unemployment tax on accrued salaries, $135.
2. Journalize the adjusting entries on page 30 of the general journal. Omit explanations.
3. Journalize the closing entries on page 32 of the general journal. Omit explanations.
4. Compute the following:
   a. net sales
   b. net delivered cost of purchases
   c. cost of goods sold
   d. net income or net loss
   e. balance of John Thomas, Capital on December 31, 19X3

CRITICAL THINKING PROBLEM

When Vincent Margolis's father became seriously ill and had to go to the hospital, Vincent stepped in to run the family business, the Margolis Cab Company. Under his father's direction, the cab company was a successful operation and provided ample money to meet the family's needs, including Vincent's college tuition.

Vincent was majoring in psychology in college and knew little about business or accounting, but he was eager to do a good job of running the business in his father's absence. Since all the service performed by the cab company was for cash, Vincent figured that he would do all right as long as the cash account increased. Thus he was delighted to watch the cash balance increase from $15,821 at the beginning of the month to $35,425 at the end of the month—an increase of $19,604. Vincent assumed that the company had made $19,604 during the month he was in charge. He did not understand why the income statement prepared by the company's bookkeeper did not show that amount as income but instead reported a lower amount as net income.

Knowing that you are taking an accounting class, Vincent brings the income statement, shown below, to you and asks if you can explain the difference.

MARGOLIS CAB COMPANY
Income Statement
for the Current Month

Operating Revenue		
Fares Income		$96,467
Operating Expenses		
Salaries Expense	$60,000	
Gasoline and Oil Expense	13,000	
Repairs Expense	2,785	
Supplies Expense	1,134	
Insurance Expense	1,583	
Depreciation Expense	8,500	
Total Operating Expenses		87,002
Net Income		$ 9,465

In addition, Vincent permits you to examine the accounting records, which show that Salaries Payable were $1,340 at the beginning of the month but had increased to $1,620 at the end of the month. The Prepaid Insurance account had decreased $225 during the month and all the supplies had been purchased in a previous month. The balances of the company's other asset and liability accounts showed no changes.

1. Explain the cause of the difference between the increase in the cash account balance and the net income for the month.
2. Prepare a schedule that accounts for this difference.

CHAPTER

13 Financial Statements and Closing Procedures

OBJECTIVES

1. Prepare a classified income statement from the worksheet.
2. Prepare a statement of owner's equity from the worksheet.
3. Prepare a classified balance sheet from the worksheet.
4. Journalize and post the adjusting entries.
5. Journalize and post the closing entries.
6. Prepare a postclosing trial balance.
7. Journalize and post reversing entries.
8. Define the accounting terms new to this chapter.

After the end-of-period adjustments have been determined and recorded on the worksheet, the worksheet itself is completed and the financial statements prepared. These procedures should be carried out as quickly and efficiently as possible because management needs timely information about the results of operations and the financial position of the business.

The financial statements discussed in this chapter are those of Fashion World, a retail merchandising business. The income statement and the balance sheet for this firm are arranged in a classified format and are more elaborate than the financial statements you have learned about previously.

NEW TERMS

Classified financial statement ▪ Current assets ▪ Current liabilities ▪ Current ratio ▪ Gross profit percentage ▪ Inventory turnover ▪ Liquidity ▪ Long-term liabilities ▪ Multiple-step income statement ▪ Plant and equipment ▪ Reversing entries ▪ Single-step income statement

PREPARING THE FINANCIAL STATEMENTS

All the information needed to prepare the financial statements is now assembled on the worksheet. The figures required to present the results of operations for the period are contained in the Income Statement section, and the figures required to report the financial position of the business on the last day of the period are available in the Balance Sheet section.

Fashion World prepares three financial statements at the end of each fiscal period: an income statement, a statement of owner's equity, and a balance sheet. The income statement and the balance sheet are arranged in a **classified** format; that is, revenues, expenses, assets, and liabilities are divided into groups of similar accounts and a subtotal is given for each group. This more elaborate method of presenting financial information makes the statements more meaningful to readers and is widely used.

The Classified Income Statement

OBJECTIVE 1

Prepare a classified income statement from the worksheet.

In a classified income statement, revenues are identified by source and expenses by type. The term **multiple-step income statement** is sometimes used to describe this form of income statement because several subtotals and totals are computed before the net income is presented. The simpler type of income statement that lists all revenues in one section and all expenses in another section is known as a **single-step income statement** because just one computation is necessary to determine the net income. An example of a single-step income statement appears in Chapter 5.

The different sections of the classified income statement are explained below.

Operating Revenue

The first section of the classified income statement contains the revenue from operations for the period—the revenue that is earned from the normal activities of the business. Other income is presented separately in a later section of the statement. In the case of Fashion World, all operating revenue comes from sales of merchandise. The first figure listed in this section is therefore the total sales. Notice that the amount of sales returns and allowances is deducted to find the net sales for the period. Because Fashion World is a retail firm, it does not offer sales discounts to its customers. If it did, the sales discounts would also be treated as a deduction from the total sales. The Operating Revenue section of the classified income statement for Fashion World is shown in Figure 13–1 on page 452.

Cost of Goods Sold

The Cost of Goods Sold section combines the figures for the beginning and ending inventory with all the figures related to purchases in order to determine the cost of the merchandise that was sold during the period. Figure 13–1 shows this section of the income statement.

Merchandise Inventory is the one account that appears on both the income statement and the balance sheet. On the income statement, the figures for the beginning and ending inventory are combined with information about purchases made during the period to determine the cost of goods sold, as shown in Figure 13–1. On the balance sheet, the ending inventory is reported as an asset.

Notice how the merchandise inventory figures are used in the Cost of Goods Sold section of the income statement. The beginning inventory and the net delivered cost of purchases are added to find the total merchandise available for sale during the period. Then the ending inventory is subtracted from the total merchandise available for sale to find the cost of goods sold for the period.

Gross Profit on Sales

The gross profit on sales is the difference between the net sales and the cost of goods sold. This figure is highly important because all operating expenses will be deducted from it. Obviously, if a business is to earn a net income, the gross profit on sales must be great enough to more than cover the operating expenses. The Operating Revenue through the Gross Profit on Sales sections of the classified income statement of Fashion World for the year ended December 31, 19X4, are illustrated in Figure 13–1.

Operating Expenses

Operating expenses are expenses that arise from the normal activities of a business. On the income statement prepared for Fashion World, these expenses are divided into two groups and a subtotal is shown for each group. The selling expenses include all expenses that are directly related to the sale and delivery of goods. The general and administrative expenses cover rent, utilities, the salaries of office employees, and other expenses that are necessary to the conduct of business operations but are not directly connected with the sales function.

Net Income or Net Loss from Operations

The total of the operating expenses for the period is deducted from the gross profit on sales to determine the net income or net loss from operations. Keeping operating and nonoperating income separate makes it possible to appraise the true operating efficiency of the firm. The Operating Revenue through Net Income from Operations sections of the classified income statement of Fashion World for the year ended December 31, 19X4, are illustrated in Figure 13–1.

Other Income and Other Expenses

Any income that is earned from nonoperating sources is reported in the Other Income section. At Fashion World, small amounts of nonoperating income were obtained in 19X4 from interest on notes receivable and from the commission deducted from sales taxes.

Any expenses that are not directly connected with operations appear in the Other Expenses section. A common expense of this type is interest on notes payable or a mortgage payable.

FIGURE 13–1
A Classified Income Statement

FASHION WORLD Income Statement Year Ended December 31, 19X4				
Operating Revenue				
Sales				409 650 00
Less Sales Returns and Allowances				13 000 00
Net Sales				396 650 00
Cost of Goods Sold				
Merchandise Inventory, Jan. 1, 19X4			31 500 00	
Purchases		250 500 00		
Freight In		3 800 00		
Delivered Cost of Purchases		254 300 00		
Less Purchases Returns and Allowances	3 050 00			
Purchases Discounts	3 130 00	6 180 00		
Net Delivered Cost of Purchases			248 120 00	
Total Merchandise Available for Sale			279 620 00	
Less Merchandise Inventory, Dec. 31, 19X4			32 000 00	
Cost of Goods Sold				247 620 00
Gross Profit on Sales				149 030 00
Operating Expenses				
Selling Expenses				
Sales Salaries Expense		69 990 00		
Advertising Expense		7 425 00		
Supplies Expense		4 975 00		
Cash Short		125 00		
Depreciation Expense—Store Equipment		2 100 00		
Total Selling Expenses			84 615 00	
General and Administrative Expenses				
Rent Expense		13 500 00		
Insurance Expense		2 700 00		
Utilities Expense		3 925 00		
Office Salaries Expense		16 500 00		
Payroll Taxes Expense		7 923 00		
Telephone Expense		1 375 00		
Uncollectible Accounts Exp.		630 00		
Depreciation Expense—Office Equipment		600 00		
Total Gen. and Admin. Expenses			47 153 00	
Total Operating Expenses				131 768 00
Net Income from Operations				17 262 00
Other Income				
Interest Income		160 00		
Miscellaneous Income		144 00		
Total Other Income			304 00	
Other Expenses				
Interest Expense			770 00	
Net Nonoperating Expense				466 00
Net Income for Year				16 796 00

Net Income or Net Loss for the Period

The final total on the income statement shows the combined results of all types of revenue and expenses. If this amount is a net loss, it is placed in parentheses. The classified income statement for Fashion World for the year ended December 31, 19X4, reflects a net income of $16,796, as shown in Figure 13–1.

The Statement of Owner's Equity

OBJECTIVE 2

Prepare a statement of owner's equity from the worksheet.

The statement of owner's equity reports the changes that have occurred in the owner's financial interest during the fiscal period. This statement is prepared before the balance sheet so that the amount of the ending capital is available for presentation on the balance sheet. The statement of owner's equity shown in Figure 13–2 was completed at Fashion World for the year ended December 31, 19X4.

FIGURE 13–2
Statement of Owner's Equity

FASHION WORLD
Statement of Owner's Equity
Year Ended December 31, 19X4

Carolyn Wells, Capital, January 1, 19X4		82 921 00
Net Income for Year	16 796 00	
Less Withdrawals for the Year	24 000 00	
Decrease in Capital		7 204 00
Carolyn Wells, Capital, December 31, 19X4		75 717 00

Because the owner made no additional investments during the period, all the information needed for the statement of owner's equity appears on the worksheet. The balance shown for the Capital account in the Balance Sheet section of the worksheet is listed as the beginning capital of $82,921 on the statement of owner's equity. To this figure is added the net income for the period, $16,796, also taken from the worksheet. The amount of withdrawals ($24,000) is obtained from the balance of the Drawing account in the Balance Sheet section of the worksheet. This amount is subtracted on the statement of owner's equity to find the ending capital of $75,717.

If the owner made additional investments during the period, it is necessary to consult the Capital account in the general ledger before preparing the statement of owner's equity. This account provides information about the beginning capital and the amounts invested.

The Classified Balance Sheet

OBJECTIVE 3

Prepare a classified balance sheet from the worksheet.

The classified balance sheet reports the financial position of a firm on a particular date. This type of balance sheet divides the various assets and liabilities into groups, as explained below.

Current Assets

The first section of the classified balance sheet (see Figure 13–3) lists the **current assets,** which consist of cash, items that will normally be converted into cash within one year, and items that will be used up within one year. These items are usually listed in order of **liquidity**—ease of conversion into cash. Current assets are vital to a firm's survival because they provide the funds needed to pay bills and meet expenses.

Plant and Equipment

The next section of the classified balance sheet shows the firm's **plant and equipment**—property that will be used for a long time in the conduct of business operations. Managers must keep a close watch on these assets because they usually represent a very sizable investment and may therefore be difficult and costly to replace.

Notice that three amounts are reported for each item of plant and equipment: the original cost, the accumulated depreciation, and the book value. For the store equipment owned by Fashion World, the original cost is $12,000, the accumulated depreciation is $2,100, and the book value is $9,900. Remember that the book value of an item bears no relation to the market value. It is simply the portion of the original cost that has not been depreciated yet. The Current Assets through the Total Assets sections of the classified balance sheet of Fashion World on December 31, 19X4, are illustrated in Figure 13–3.

Current Liabilities

The third section of the classified balance sheet lists **current liabilities**—the debts that must be paid within one year. These items are usually presented in order of priority of payment. Since the firm's credit reputation depends upon prompt settlement of its debts, management must make sure that funds are available when these obligations become due.

Long-Term Liabilities

Following current liabilities on the classified balance sheet are **long-term liabilities**—debts of the business due more than a year in the future. Although repayment of these obligations may not be due for several years, management must make sure that periodic interest is paid promptly. Mortgages payable, notes payable that extend for more than a year, and loans payable that extend for more than a year are common types of long-term liabilities. Fashion World had no long-term liabilities on December 31, 19X4.

Owner's Equity

Because Fashion World prepares a statement of owner's equity, the firm's balance sheet simply shows the ending capital in the Owner's Equity section. The separate statement of owner's equity reports all information about the changes that occurred in the owner's financial interest during the period. The classified balance sheet of Fashion World on December 31, 19X4, is illustrated in Figure 13–3.

FIGURE 13–3
A Classified Balance Sheet

FASHION WORLD
Balance Sheet
December 31, 19X4

Assets			
Current Assets			
Cash			28,634.00
Petty Cash Fund			100.00
Notes Receivable			1,200.00
Accounts Receivable		26,000.00	
Less Allow. for Doubtful Accts.		730.00	25,270.00
Interest Receivable			160.00
Merchandise Inventory			32,000.00
Prepaid Expenses			
Supplies		1,325.00	
Prepaid Insurance		900.00	
Prepaid Interest		75.00	2,300.00
Total Current Assets			89,664.00
Plant and Equipment			
Store Equipment	12,000.00		
Less Accumulated Depreciation	2,100.00	9,900.00	
Office Equipment	3,500.00		
Less Accumulated Depreciation	600.00	2,900.00	
Total Plant and Equipment			12,800.00
Total Assets			102,464.00
Liabilities and Owner's Equity			
Current Liabilities			
Notes Payable—Trade			2,000.00
Notes Payable—Bank			9,000.00
Accounts Payable			4,129.00
Interest Payable			20.00
Social Security Tax Payable			1,181.50
Medicare Tax Payable			272.50
Employee Income Tax Payable			1,490.00
Fed. Unemployment Tax Pay.			17.00
State Unemployment Tax Pay.			81.00
Salaries Payable			1,500.00
Sales Tax Payable			7,056.00
Total Current Liabilities			26,747.00
Owner's Equity			
Carolyn Wells, Capital			75,717.00
Total Liab. and Owner's Equity			102,464.00

SELF-REVIEW

1. What are classified financial statements?
2. What is the purpose of the income statement?
3. Explain the difference between a single-step income statement and a multiple-step income statement.
4. What is the gross profit on sales?
5. How is net income from operations determined?
6. Why would a factory machine not be considered a current asset? How is the factory machine classified?

Answers to Self-Review

1. Classified financial statements are statements on which the revenues, expenses, assets, and liabilities are divided into groups of similar accounts and a subtotal is given for each group.
2. The purpose of the income statement is to show the results of operations for a specific period of time.
3. The single-step income statement is one in which all revenues are listed in one section and all expenses in another section. The multiple-step income statement has various sections in which subtotals and totals are computed before the net income is presented.
4. The gross profit on sales is the difference between the net sales and the cost of goods sold.
5. The net income from operations is determined by deducting the total of the operating expenses from the gross profit on sales.
6. A factory machine has a life longer than one year and is thus considered a long-term asset that is classified as plant and equipment.

JOURNALIZING AND POSTING THE ADJUSTING ENTRIES

OBJECTIVE 4

Journalize and post the adjusting entries.

The worksheet shows the accounts and the amounts of all adjustments. Thus, once the financial statements have been prepared, the data on the worksheet is used to record and post the adjusting journal entries. These entries are essential if the firm is to have a complete and accurate record of its financial affairs for the period.

Journalizing the Adjusting Entries

Each adjusting entry in the general journal should contain a detailed explanation of how the amount was derived. The explanation should be sufficient to allow another person, such as an auditor, to easily understand what was done and why. The adjusting entries for Fashion World made on the December 31, 19X4, worksheet are shown in Figure 13–4. Trace the data about the adjustments from the worksheet shown in Figure 12–1 to these journal entries.

FIGURE 13–4
Adjusting Entries in the General Journal

GENERAL JOURNAL PAGE 25

DATE		DESCRIPTION	POST. REF.	DEBIT	CREDIT
		Adjusting Entries			
19X4		*(Adjustment a)*			
Dec.	*31*	*Income Summary*	*399*	*31 500 00*	
		Merchandise Inventory	*121*		*31 500 00*
		To transfer beginning			
		inventory to Income			
		Summary			
		(Adjustment b)			
	31	*Merchandise Inventory*	*121*	*32 000 00*	
		Income Summary	*399*		*32 000 00*
		To record ending			
		inventory			
		(Adjustment c)			
Dec.	*31*	*Uncollectible Accounts Exp.*	*556*	*630 00*	
		Allow. for Doubtful Accts.	*112*		*630 00*
		To record estimated loss			
		from uncollectible			
		accounts based on 0.3%			
		of net credit sales of			
		$210,000			
		(Adjustment d)			
	31	*Depr. Exp.—Store Equipment*	*526*	*2 100 00*	
		Accum. Depr.—Store Equip.	*132*		*2 100 00*
		To record depreciation			
		for 19X4, as shown by			
		schedule on file			
		(Adjustment e)			
	31	*Depr. Exp.—Office Equipment*	*559*	*600 00*	
		Accum. Depr.—Office Equip.	*142*		*600 00*
		To record depreciation			
		for 19X4, as shown by			
		schedule on file			
		(Adjustment f)			
	31	*Sales Salaries Expense*	*511*	*1 500 00*	
		Salaries Payable	*229*		*1 500 00*
		To record accrued			
		salaries of part-time			
		salesclerks for Dec. 28–31			

(Continued)

FIGURE 13–4 (Continued)
Adjusting Entries in the General Journal

GENERAL JOURNAL PAGE *26*

DATE		DESCRIPTION	POST. REF.	DEBIT	CREDIT
		Adjusting Entries			
19X4		*(Adjustment g)*			
Dec.	*31*	*Payroll Taxes Expense*	*544*	*120 00*	
		Social Sec. Tax Payable	*221*		*97 50*
		Medicare Tax Payable	*223*		*22 50*
		To record accrued payroll			
		taxes on accrued salaries			
		for Dec. 28–31			
		(Adjustment h)			
	31	*Payroll Taxes Expense*	*544*	*98 00*	
		Fed. Unemployment Tax Pay.	*225*		*17 00*
		State Unemploy. Tax Pay.	*227*		*81 00*
		To record accrued payroll			
		taxes on accrued salaries			
		for Dec. 28–31			
		(Adjustment i)			
	31	*Interest Expense*	*591*	*20 00*	
		Interest Payable	*216*		*20 00*
		To record interest on a			
		2-month, $2,000, 12% note			
		payable dated Dec. 1, 19X4			
		(Adjustment j)			
	31	*Supplies Expense*	*517*	*4975 00*	
		Supplies	*129*		*4975 00*
		To record supplies used			
		(Adjustment k)			
	31	*Insurance Expense*	*536*	*2700 00*	
		Prepaid Insurance	*126*		*2700 00*
		To record expired insurance			
		on 1-year policy for $3,600			
		bought April 1, 19X4			
		(Adjustment l)			
	31	*Interest Expense*	*591*	*150 00*	
		Prepaid Interest	*127*		*150 00*
		To record transfer of 2/3			
		of prepaid interest of			
		$225 for a 3-month,			
		10% note payable issued			
		to bank on Nov. 1, 19X4			

FIGURE 13–4 (Continued)
Adjusting Entries in the General Journal

GENERAL JOURNAL PAGE 27

	DATE		DESCRIPTION	POST. REF.	DEBIT	CREDIT	
1			*Adjusting Entries*				1
2	*19X4*		*(Adjustment* **m***)*				2
3	*Dec.*	*31*	*Interest Receivable*	*116*	*24 00*		3
4			*Interest Income*	*491*		*24 00*	4
5			*To record accrued interest*				5
6			*earned on a 4-month, 12%*				6
7			*note receivable dated Nov.*				7
8			*1, 19X4: $1,200 ×*				8
9			*12/100 × 2/12*				9
10							10
11			*(Adjustment* **n***)*				11
12		*31*	*Sales Tax Payable*	*231*	*144 00*		12
13			*Miscellaneous Income*	*493*		*144 00*	13
14			*To record accrued*				14
15			*commission earned on*				15
16			*sales tax owed for fourth*				16
17			*quarter of 19X4:*				17
18			*Sales Tax Payable $7,200*				18
19			*Commission rate ×0.02*				19
20			*Commission due $ 144*				20
21							21

Posting the Adjusting Entries

The next step in the end-of-period routine is to post the adjusting entries from the general journal to the general ledger accounts involved. This task should be completed promptly because the account balances must be up to date before the closing entries are made. The posting procedure used is the same as the one described in Chapter 5. For example, refer to the account shown below, which reflects the posting of the debit part of Adjustment **f,** recording accrued salaries of part-time salesclerks, from the general journal illustrated in Figure 13–4.

ACCOUNT *Sales Salaries Expense* ACCOUNT NO. *511*

DATE		EXPLANATION	POST. REF.	DEBIT	CREDIT	BALANCE DEBIT	BALANCE CREDIT
19X4							
Dec.	*31*	*Balance*	√			*68 490 00*	
	31	*Adjusting*	*J25*	*1 500 00*		*69 990 00*	

Notice that the word *Adjusting* has been recorded in the Explanation column of the account. This identifies the nature of the entry and distinguishes it from the entries for transactions that occurred during the fiscal period. For the sake of simplicity, the account shown here contains only the balance on December 31 prior to the adjustment. The entries made at the end of each semimonthly payroll period throughout the year have been omitted.

After all adjusting entries are posted, the balances of the general ledger accounts should match the amounts shown in the Adjusted Trial Balance section of the worksheet. In the case of Sales Salaries Expense, the updated balance is $69,990.

JOURNALIZING AND POSTING THE CLOSING ENTRIES

OBJECTIVE 5

Journalize and post the closing entries.

The worksheet is the source of the data for the general journal entries required to close the temporary accounts—the revenue, cost, and expense accounts. Each balance appearing in the Income Statement section of the worksheet is closed to the Income Summary account. The following four-step procedure is used.

1. Close the revenue accounts and all other accounts with credit balances, *except the Income Summary account,* appearing in the Credit column of the Income Statement section of the worksheet. Debit the figures appearing in the Credit column of the Income Statement section of the worksheet and credit the Income Summary account for the total.
2. Close the expense accounts and all other accounts with debit balances, *except the Income Summary account,* appearing in the Debit column of the Income Statement section of the worksheet. Credit the figures appearing in the Debit column of the Income Statement section of the worksheet and debit the Income Summary account for the total.
3. Transfer the balance of the Income Summary account, which represents the net income or net loss for the period, to the owner's Capital account. If there is a net income, debit the Income Summary account and credit the Capital account. If a net loss was incurred, debit the Capital account and credit the Income Summary account.
4. Transfer the balance of the owner's Drawing account to the owner's Capital account. Debit the Capital account and credit the Drawing account.

Journalizing the Closing Entries

The procedures for recording the closing entries for Fashion World are described in detail in the next sections.

Step 1: Closing the Revenue Accounts and Accounts with Credit Balances. Refer to the Income Statement section of the completed worksheet for Fashion World in Figure 12–2. Five items are listed in the Credit column of that section. The first closing entry is made by debiting each account, *except Income Summary,* for the amount shown and crediting Income Summary for the total, $416,134. This entry, which is illustrated below, closes the revenue accounts and other temporary accounts with credit balances.

GENERAL JOURNAL PAGE *28*

DATE		DESCRIPTION	POST. REF.	DEBIT	CREDIT
19X4		*Closing Entries*			
Dec.	*31*	*Sales*	*401*	*409 650 00*	
		Interest Income	*491*	*1 600 00*	
		Miscellaneous Income	*493*	*1 440 00*	
		Purch. Ret. and Allowances	*503*	*3 050 00*	
		Purchases Discount	*504*	*3 130 00*	
		Income Summary			*416 134 00*

Step 2: Closing the Cost and Expense Accounts. Refer again to the worksheet illustrated in Figure 12–2. The Debit column of the Income Statement section shows the amounts for cost and expense accounts and the other temporary accounts with debit balances. The second closing entry is made by debiting Income Summary for the total of these items, $399,838, and crediting each account for its balance, as shown below. The purpose of this entry is to close the cost and expense accounts and other temporary accounts with debit balances.

GENERAL JOURNAL PAGE *28*

DATE		DESCRIPTION	POST. REF.	DEBIT	CREDIT
Dec.	*31*	*Income Summary*	*399*	*399 838 00*	
		Sales Returns and Allow.	*451*		*13 000 00*
		Purchases	*501*		*250 500 00*
		Freight In	*502*		*3 800 00*
		Sales Salaries Expense	*511*		*69 990 00*
		Advertising Expense	*514*		*7 425 00*
		Supplies Expense	*517*		*4 975 00*
		Cash Short or Over	*520*		*125 00*
		Depr. Exp.—Store Equip.	*526*		*2 100 00*
		Rent Expense	*535*		*13 500 00*
		Insurance Expense	*536*		*2 700 00*
		Utilities Expense	*538*		*3 925 00*
		Office Salaries Expense	*541*		*16 500 00*
		Payroll Taxes Expense	*544*		*7 923 00*
		Telephone Expense	*553*		*1 375 00*
		Uncollectible Accts. Exp.	*556*		*630 00*
		Depr. Exp.—Office Equip.	*559*		*600 00*
		Interest Expense	*591*		*770 00*

Step 3: Closing the Income Summary Account. The effect of the first two closing entries is to transfer the results of operations for the period to the Income Summary account. After this data is posted, the balance of the Income Summary account will represent the net income or net loss for the period. Since the entire net income or net loss in a sole proprietorship belongs to the owner, the third closing entry made in this type of business transfers the net income or net loss to the owner's Capital account.

In the case of Fashion World, there is a net income of $16,796 for the fiscal year 19X4. The Income Summary account is therefore debited for $16,796, and the Carolyn Wells, Capital account is credited, as shown below.

GENERAL JOURNAL PAGE *28*

	DATE		DESCRIPTION	POST. REF.	DEBIT	CREDIT	
28	*Dec.*	*31*	*Income Summary*	*399*	*16 7 9 6 00*		28
29			*Carolyn Wells, Capital*	*301*		*16 7 9 6 00*	29
30							30

This entry closes the Income Summary account, and it remains closed until it is used in the end-of-period routine for the next year.

Step 4: Closing the Drawing Account. The final step in the closing process for a sole proprietorship is to transfer the balance of the owner's Drawing account to the owner's Capital account. In the case of Fashion World, the required entry involves a debit to Carolyn Wells, Capital and a credit to Carolyn Wells, Drawing for $24,000, as shown below. This entry closes the Drawing account and updates the Capital account so that its balance will agree with the ending capital reported on the statement of owner's equity and the balance sheet.

GENERAL JOURNAL PAGE *28*

	DATE		DESCRIPTION	POST. REF.	DEBIT	CREDIT	
31	*Dec.*	*31*	*Carolyn Wells, Capital*	*301*	*24 0 0 0 00*		31
32			*Carolyn Wells, Drawing*	*302*		*24 0 0 0 00*	32
33							33

Posting the Closing Entries

The closing entries are posted from the general journal to the general ledger in the usual manner. This process reduces the balances of the temporary accounts to zero, as shown in the following example.

ACCOUNT *Sales Salaries Expense* ACCOUNT NO. *511*

DATE		EXPLANATION	POST. REF.	DEBIT	CREDIT	BALANCE	
						DEBIT	CREDIT
19X4							
Dec.	*31*	*Balance*	√			*68 4 9 0 00*	
	31	*Adjusting*	*J25*	*1 5 0 0 00*		*69 9 9 0 00*	
	31	*Closing*	*J28*		*69 9 9 0 00*	—0—	

The word *Closing* is recorded in the Explanation column of each account involved to identify the nature of these entries.

PREPARING A POSTCLOSING TRIAL BALANCE

OBJECTIVE 6

Prepare a postclosing trial balance.

As soon as the closing entries have been posted, a postclosing trial balance should be prepared to make sure that the general ledger is in balance. Only the accounts that are still open—the asset and liability accounts and the owner's Capital account—appear on the postclosing trial balance. The amounts shown should match those reported on the balance sheet. For example, compare the postclosing trial balance illustrated in Figure 13–5, page 464, with the balance sheet illustrated in Figure 13–3 on page 455.

Of course, if the postclosing trial balance shows that the general ledger is out of balance, the error or errors must be located. Then correcting entries must be journalized and posted. It is essential that the general ledger be in balance before any transactions are recorded for the new fiscal period.

INTERPRETING THE FINANCIAL STATEMENTS

After the financial statements are prepared, accountants, owners, managers, and other interested parties interpret the information shown on the financial statements to evaluate the results of operations and make other intelligent business decisions. Interpreting financial statements involves more than just looking at the numbers. It requires an understanding of the business and the environment in which it operates as well as the nature and limitations of accounting information. A number of percentages and ratios are frequently used for analyzing and interpreting financial statements. Three of these measures are applied to interpreting Fashion World's statements for the year 19X4.

1. The **gross profit percentage** reveals the amount of gross profit from each sales dollar. The gross profit percentage is calculated in the following manner.

$$\frac{\text{Gross profit for year}}{\text{Net sales for year}} = \frac{\$149{,}030}{\$396{,}650} = 0.38 = 38\%$$

   The gross profit percentage for Fashion World reveals that for every dollar of net sales, gross profit amounted to 38 cents.

FIGURE 13–5
Postclosing Trial Balance for Fashion World

FASHION WORLD
Postclosing Trial Balance
December 31, 19X4

ACCOUNT NAME	DEBIT	CREDIT
Cash	28 634 00	
Petty Cash Fund	100 00	
Notes Receivable	1 200 00	
Accounts Receivable	26 000 00	
Allowance for Doubtful Accounts		730 00
Interest Receivable	160 00	
Merchandise Inventory	32 000 00	
Supplies	1 325 00	
Prepaid Insurance	900 00	
Prepaid Interest	75 00	
Store Equipment	12 000 00	
Accumulated Depreciation—Store Equipment		2 100 00
Office Equipment	3 500 00	
Accumulated Depreciation—Office Equip.		600 00
Notes Payable—Trade		2 000 00
Notes Payable—Bank		9 000 00
Accounts Payable		4 129 00
Interest Payable		20 00
Social Security Tax Payable		1 181 50
Medicare Tax Payable		272 50
Employee Income Taxes Payable		1 490 00
Federal Unemployment Tax Payable		17 00
State Unemployment Tax Payable		81 00
Salaries Payable		1 500 00
Sales Tax Payable		7 056 00
Carolyn Wells, Capital		75 717 00
Totals	105 894 00	105 894 00

2. The **current ratio** measures the ability of a firm to pay its current debt. The current ratio is calculated in the following manner.

$$\frac{\text{Current assets}}{\text{Current liabilities}} = \frac{\$89{,}644}{\$26{,}747} = 3.35 \text{ to } 1$$

The current ratio for Fashion World reveals that the firm has \$3.35 in current assets for every dollar of current liabilities.

3. The **inventory turnover** represents the number of times inventory is replaced during an accounting period. Inventory turnover is calculated in the following manner.

$$\frac{\text{Cost of goods sold}}{\text{Average inventory}} = \text{Inventory turnover}$$

$$\text{Average inventory} = \frac{\text{Beginning inventory} + \text{Ending inventory}}{2}$$

$$\text{Fashion World's average inventory} = \frac{\$31{,}500 + \$32{,}000}{2}$$

$$= \$31{,}750$$

$$\text{Fashion World's inventory turnover} = \frac{\$247{,}620}{\$31{,}750} = 7.8 \text{ times}$$

The inventory turnover for Fashion World reveals that inventory had to be replaced approximately eight times during the year.

A detailed discussion of financial statement analysis is presented in Chapters 23 and 24.

JOURNALIZING AND POSTING REVERSING ENTRIES

OBJECTIVE 7

Journalize and post reversing entries.

Certain adjustments made in the current period may lead to recording problems in the new period. Many firms follow a policy of reversing adjustments of this nature at the start of the new period in order to avoid difficulties later. The necessary entries, which are known as **reversing entries,** are first made in the general journal and then posted to the general ledger.

Adjustment **f** recorded at Fashion World provides a good illustration of why reversing entries can be helpful. On December 31, 19X4, the firm owed salaries of $1,500 to its part-time salesclerks. Since the salaries will not be paid until January 19X5, the firm made an adjustment debiting Sales Salaries Expense and crediting Salaries Payable for $1,500 on the December 31 worksheet. This adjustment allowed the amount to be charged as an expense during the correct fiscal year and to be presented accurately as a liability at the end of the period. After the financial statements were prepared, the adjustment for accrued salaries expense was journalized and posted along with the firm's other adjustments.

On January 3, 19X5, when the weekly payroll period for the part-time salesclerks ends, a total of $2,000 is owed to these employees for salaries. However, only $500 of the $2,000 amount pertains to the current year. A busy employee who is journalizing the payroll might easily overlook the fact that $1,500 of the sum was recorded as accrued salaries expense at the end of the previous year. Even if the employee recognizes the item as being related to Adjustment **f,** the situation is complicated because it is necessary to consult the end-of-period records for 19X4 and then properly divide the expense and liability involved between the two fiscal years. This procedure is time consuming, and it can easily lead to errors.

A simple method of avoiding such problems is to make reversing entries before recording any transactions for the new period. Each reversing entry is the exact opposite of the related adjusting entry. The account credited in the adjusting entry is now debited, and the account debited in the adjusting entry is now credited. For example, Salaries Payable is debited and Salaries Expense is credited for $1,500 to reverse Adjustment **f,** as shown below. Notice that the reversing entry is dated as of the start of the new fiscal year—January 1, 19X5.

GENERAL JOURNAL PAGE 25

	DATE		DESCRIPTION	POST. REF.	DEBIT	CREDIT	
1	*19X4*		*Adjusting Entries*				1
39			*(Adjustment f)*				39
40	*Dec.*	*31*	*Sales Salaries Expense*	*511*	*1 5 0 0 00*		40
41			*Salaries Payable*	*229*		*1 5 0 0 00*	41
42							42
1			*Reversing Entries*				1
2	*19X5*						2
3	*Jan.*	*1*	*Salaries Payable*	*229*	*1 5 0 0 00*		3
4			*Sales Salaries Expense*	*511*		*1 5 0 0 00*	4
5							5

The reversing entry guards against any later oversight, eliminates the need for checking old records, and makes it unnecessary to divide the amount of salaries between the two fiscal years when the payroll is recorded on January 3, 19X5.

After the reversing entry is posted, the Salaries Payable account has a zero balance and the Sales Salaries Expense account has a credit balance of $1,500, as shown below. Thus the general journal entry for the $500 of salaries owed to the part-time salesclerks can be made in the normal manner, as reflected below, at the end of the payroll period on January 3, 19X5.

GENERAL JOURNAL PAGE 30

	DATE		DESCRIPTION	POST. REF.	DEBIT	CREDIT	
1	*19X5*						1
2	*Jan.*	*3*	*Sales Salaries Expense*	*511*	*2 0 0 0 00*		2
3			*Cash*	*101*		*2 0 0 0 00*	3
4							4

ACCOUNT *Salaries Payable* ACCOUNT NO. *229*

DATE		EXPLANATION	POST. REF.	DEBIT	CREDIT	BALANCE DEBIT	BALANCE CREDIT
19X4							
Dec.	*31*	*Adjusting*	*J25*		*1500 00*		*1500 00*
19X5							
Jan.	*1*	*Reversing*	*J29*	*1500 00*			*—0—*

ACCOUNT *Sales Salaries Expense* ACCOUNT NO. *511*

DATE		EXPLANATION	POST. REF.	DEBIT	CREDIT	BALANCE DEBIT	BALANCE CREDIT
19X4							
Dec.	*31*	*Balance*	√			*68490 00*	
	31	*Adjusting*	*J25*	*1500 00*		*69990 00*	
	31	*Closing*	*J28*		*69990 00*	*—0—*	
19X5							
Jan.	*1*	*Reversing*	*J29*		*1500 00*		*1500 00*

The credit balance of $1,500 in the Sales Salaries Expense account partially offsets the debit of $2,000 posted from the payroll entry of January 3. The result is a debit balance of $500, which represents the correct amount of expense for 19X5, as shown in the ledger account that follows. Since the Salaries Payable account has no balance after the reversing entry is posted, there is no problem when the payroll is recorded on January 3. Once the posting of the payroll entry is made, this account contains the correct amount of liability.

ACCOUNT *Sales Salaries Expense* ACCOUNT NO. *511*

DATE		EXPLANATION	POST. REF.	DEBIT	CREDIT	BALANCE DEBIT	BALANCE CREDIT
19X4							
Dec.	*31*	*Balance*	√			*68490 00*	
	31	*Adjusting*	*J25*	*1500 00*		*69990 00*	
	31	*Closing*	*J28*		*69990 00*	*—0—*	
19X5							
Jan.	*1*	*Reversing*	*J29*		*1500 00*		*1500 00*
	3		*J30*	*2000 00*		*500 00*	

Identifying Items for Reversal

Not all adjustments need to be reversed. Normally, the adjustments requiring reversal are accrued expense items that will involve future payments of cash and accrued income items that will involve future receipts of cash. Thus there is no need to reverse adjustments for uncollectible accounts, depreciation, and prepaid expenses. Adjustments for prepaid expenses do not require reversal if these items are initially recorded as assets, as is done at Fashion World. However, when prepaid expense items are initially treated as expenses, the end-of-period adjustments for these items must be reversed.

Journalizing Reversing Entries

At Fashion World there are five accounts that require reversal as of January 1, 19X5. The reversing entry for the first of these adjustments—accrued salaries expense—has already been illustrated. The next two adjustments that must be reversed are for accrued payroll taxes expense. The necessary entries, which are shown below, allow the firm to avoid recording problems on January 3, 19X5, when the employer's payroll taxes on the salaries of the part-time salesclerks must be journalized.

GENERAL JOURNAL PAGE 29

	DATE		DESCRIPTION	POST. REF.	DEBIT	CREDIT	
1	19X5						1
2	Jan.	1	Social Security Tax Payable	221	97 50		2
3			Medicare Tax Payable	222	22 50		3
4			Payroll Taxes Expense	544		120 00	4
5			To reverse adjusting entry				5
6			(e) made Dec. 31, 19X4				6
7							7
8		1	Federal Unemploy. Tax Pay.	225	17 00		8
9			State Unemployment Tax Pay.	227	81 00		9
10			Payroll Taxes Expense	544		98 00	10
11			To reverse adjusting entry				11
12			(h) made Dec. 31, 19X4				12
13							13

The next adjustment that requires reversal is the one for accrued interest expense. This adjustment covered one month of interest on a two-month, 12 percent trade note payable for $2,000 that was issued on December 1, 19X4. The $20 of interest that applied to 19X4 was recorded by debiting Interest Expense and crediting Interest Payable. The reversing entry shown below prevents recording difficulties when the note is paid on February 1, 19X5.

GENERAL JOURNAL PAGE *29*

DATE		DESCRIPTION	POST. REF.	DEBIT	CREDIT
Jan.	*1*	*Interest Payable*	*216*	*2 0 00*	
		Interest Expense	*591*		*2 0 00*
		To reverse adjusting entry			
		i *made on Dec. 31, 19X4*			

In addition to the adjustments for accrued expense items, Fashion World had two adjustments for accrued income items at the end of 19X4. The first of these items was accrued interest income on a note receivable. Since the firm will obtain cash for the note and the interest in the new fiscal year, the adjustment must be reversed.

Remember that Fashion World accepted a four-month, 12 percent note for $1,200 from a customer on November 1, 19X4. The interest of $24 for November and December 19X4 was recorded in an adjusting entry that debited Interest Receivable and credited Interest Income. This adjustment is reversed as shown below in order to eliminate any difficulties in recording the receipt of the interest when the note is paid on March 1, 19X5.

GENERAL JOURNAL PAGE *29*

DATE		DESCRIPTION	POST. REF.	DEBIT	CREDIT
Jan.	*1*	*Interest Income*	*491*	*2 4 00*	
		Interest Receivable	*116*		*2 4 00*
		To reverse adjusting entry			
		m *made on Dec. 31, 19X4*			

After the reversing entry is posted, the Interest Receivable account has a zero balance and the Interest Income account has a debit balance of $24, as shown below. When the firm receives a check for $1,248 in payment of the note and the interest on March 1, 19X5, the transaction can be recorded in the normal manner—by debiting Cash for $1,248, crediting Notes Receivable for $1,200, and crediting Interest Income for $48. The $24 debit balance of the Interest Income account partially offsets the credit posting of $48 on March 1. The resulting credit balance of $24 represents the correct amount of interest income on the note for 19X5.

ACCOUNT *Interest Receivable* ACCOUNT NO. *116*

DATE		EXPLANATION	POST. REF.	DEBIT	CREDIT	BALANCE DEBIT	BALANCE CREDIT
19X4							
Dec.	*31*	*Adjusting*	*J27*	*24 00*		*24 00*	
19X5							
Jan.	*1*	*Reversing*	*J29*		*24 00*	*—0—*	

ACCOUNT *Interest Income* ACCOUNT NO. *491*

DATE		EXPLANATION	POST. REF.	DEBIT	CREDIT	BALANCE DEBIT	BALANCE CREDIT
19X4							
Dec.	*31*	*Balance*	√				*136 00*
	31	*Adjusting*	*J27*		*24 00*		*160 00*
	31	*Closing*	*J28*	*160 00*			*—0—*
19X5							
Jan.	*1*	*Reversing*	*J29*	*24 00*		*24 00*	
Mar.	*1*		*CR3*		*48 00*		*24 00*

The second accrued income item that Fashion World had at the end of 19X4 was an accrued commission on the sales tax collected during the fourth quarter. Since no cash will be received in January 19X5 when the sales tax return is filed, there is no need to reverse the adjustment made for the accrued commission.

REVIEW OF THE ACCOUNTING CYCLE

Typical accounting procedures, records, and statements for merchandising businesses have now been discussed in detail. Chapters 11 through 13 presented the end-of-period activities for businesses of this type. Earlier chapters focused on the day-to-day recording process in merchandising businesses. Underlying the various procedures described are the steps of the accounting cycle, which are performed in each fiscal period to classify, record, and summarize financial data and produce needed financial information. These steps are reviewed below.

1. ***Analyze transactions.*** The data about transactions comes into an accounting system from a variety of source documents—sales slips, purchase invoices, credit memorandums, check stubs, and so on. Each document must be analyzed to determine the accounts and amounts affected.
2. ***Journalize the data about transactions.*** The effects of each transaction are recorded in the appropriate journal. Most merchandising businesses use a number of special journals as well as the general journal.

3. ***Post the data about transactions.*** Each transaction is transferred from the journal to the ledger accounts. Typically, a merchandising business has several subsidiary ledgers in addition to the general ledger.
4. ***Prepare a worksheet.*** At the end of each period of operations, a worksheet is prepared. The Trial Balance section of the worksheet is used to prove the equality of the debits and credits in the general ledger. The Adjustments section is used to enter any changes in account balances that may be necessary at the end of the period in order to present a more accurate and complete picture of the firm's financial affairs. The Adjusted Trial Balance section provides a check on the equality of the debits and credits after the adjustments are combined with the original account balances. The Income Statement and Balance Sheet sections allow the accountant to arrange the data needed for the financial statements in an orderly manner so that the statements can be prepared quickly.
5. ***Prepare financial statements.*** A set of formal financial statements is prepared to report information to owners, managers, and other interested parties.
6. ***Journalize and post adjusting entries.*** Adjusting entries are journalized and posted in order to create a permanent record of the changes in account balances that were made on the worksheet when the adjustments were determined.
7. ***Journalize and post closing entries.*** Closing entries are journalized and posted in order to transfer the results of operations to owner's equity and to prepare the revenue, cost, and expense accounts for use in the next period. The closing entries reduce the balances of the temporary accounts to zero.
8. ***Prepare a postclosing trial balance.*** Another trial balance is taken to make sure that the general ledger is still in balance after the adjusting and closing entries have been posted.
9. ***Interpret the financial information.*** The accountant, owners, managers, and other interested parties must interpret the information shown on the financial statements and other less formal financial reports that may be prepared. This information is used to evaluate the results of operations and the financial position of the business and to make decisions.

In addition to the steps listed here, some firms record reversing entries, as discussed previously in this chapter.

The chart shown in Figure 13–6 illustrates the flow of data through an accounting system that uses special journals and subsidiary ledgers. Notice that the system is composed of several smaller areas or subsystems that perform specialized functions.

- The accounts receivable area records transactions involving sales and cash receipts and maintains the accounts with credit customers. This area also handles the billing of credit customers.

FIGURE 13–6
The Flow of Financial Data Through an Accounting System

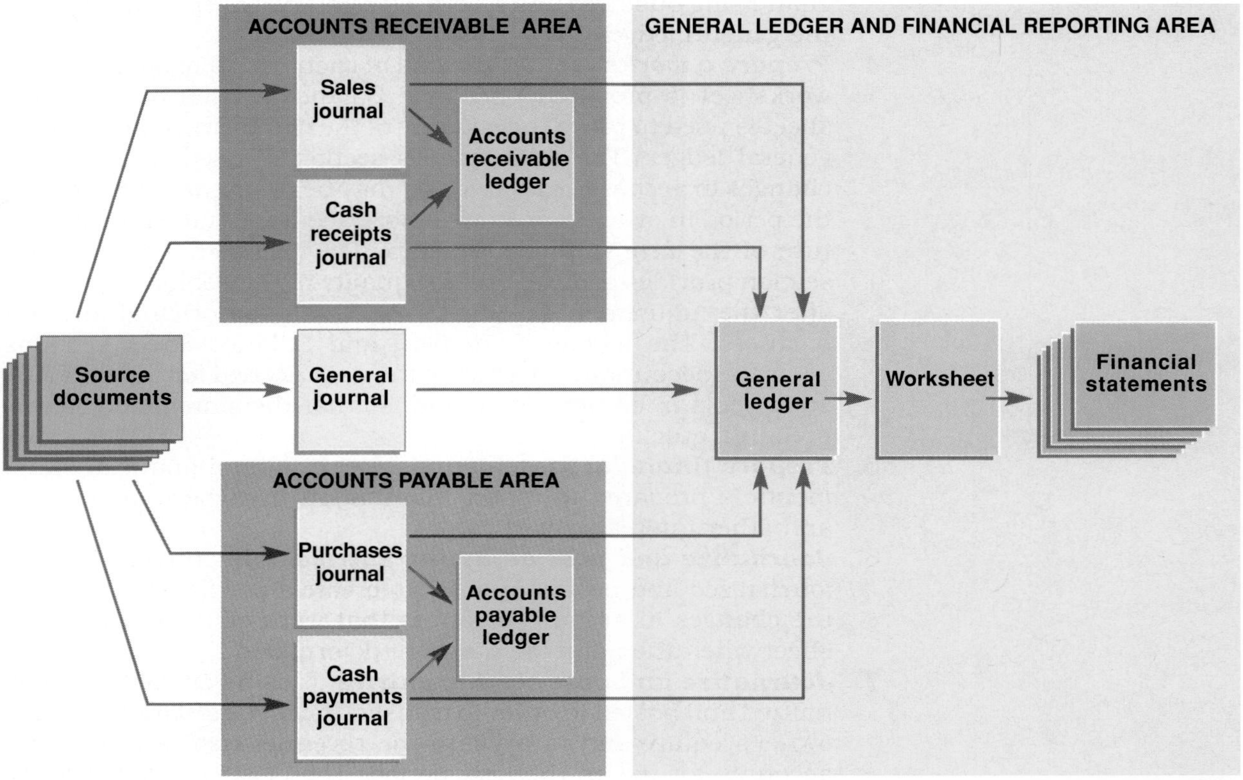

- The accounts payable area records transactions involving purchases and cash payments and maintains the accounts with creditors. This area also issues checks to pay the firm's obligations.
- The general ledger and financial reporting area records transactions that do not belong in the special journals such as credit purchases of plant and equipment, maintains the general ledger accounts, carries out the end-of-period procedures, and prepares financial statements. This area is the focal point for the accounting system because the results of all the firm's transactions eventually flow into the general ledger; and, of course, the general ledger provides the data that is presented on the financial statements.

MANAGERIAL IMPLICATIONS

Managers are keenly interested in receiving timely financial statements, especially the periodic income statement, which shows the results of operations. The worksheet is a very useful device for gathering data about adjustments and for preparing the income statement. Managers are also interested in prompt preparation of the bal-

Information Block: International Accounting

Careers in International Accounting

As U.S. companies expand their operations to other parts of the world, more opportunities are created for careers in international accounting. Today even small businesses may export products to other countries, and their accountants need to understand not only the rules and procedures governing accounting but also the impact of doing business in another country.

Many careers in international accounting offer the opportunity to live and work in another country. If you are interested in such a career, you might have to learn another language. Some of the more significant careers involving international accounting are listed below.

General Accounting

At the Home Office

- Reporting international operations
- Translation of foreign operations
- Allocation of home country expenses to foreign operations
- Geographical analysis of sales, operating income, and assets
- Payroll for international workers

At the Foreign Company

- Reporting financial results to local managers
- Reporting financial results to the home office
- Reporting foreign currency exposure
- Accounting for manufacturing and marketing operations
- Accounting for credit and collections

Cost Accounting

- Setting transfer pricing across international boundaries

Tax Accounting

- Preparing foreign country tax returns
- Allocating expenses between countries
- Preparing U.S. tax returns incorporating foreign company tax information

Data Processing Specialists

- Transmitting data over telephone lines
- Writing software to automate specialized accounting functions

ance sheet because it shows the financial position of the business at the end of the fiscal period.

As soon as the statements are available, managers must carefully study the figures in order to evaluate the firm's operating efficiency and financial strength. A common technique is to compare the data shown on the current statements with the data from previous statements. This procedure places the current amounts in perspective and reveals trends that have developed. In large firms, comparison with the published financial reports of other companies in the same industry is also highly useful.

Classified financial statements are prepared so that managers and others can more easily draw meaningful conclusions from the information on the statements. However, managers must understand the nature and significance of the groupings in order to obtain the proper value from these statements.

Although management is not directly involved in carrying out the end-of-period procedures, the efficiency of these procedures should be of concern to management. Correct adjusting entries must be made if all revenue and expense items are to be recorded and matched in the appropriate period. Similarly, both the adjusting and closing processes must be handled properly if the firm's financial records are to contain complete and accurate information about its affairs during the fiscal year.

The promptness of the closing entries is also important. The sooner the financial records are closed for the old period, the sooner the recording of transactions for the new period can begin. Any significant lag between the time that transactions occur and the time that they are recorded can lead to serious problems. For example, information that management may need on a daily or weekly basis, such as the firm's cash position, will not be available or will not be up to date.

The efficiency of the adjusting and closing procedures also has an effect on the annual audit by the company's public accounting firm. Audits of financial records are greatly speeded up by good end-of-period procedures. For example, detailed explanations in the general journal make it easy for an auditor to understand and check the adjusting entries.

SELF-REVIEW

1. Why is it necessary to journalize and post adjusting entries if the amounts of the adjustments already appear on the worksheet?
2. Why should detailed explanations be provided for all adjusting entries when they are recorded in the general journal?
3. Briefly explain the four steps in the closing procedure for a sole proprietorship merchandising business.
4. Describe the entry that would be made at the Bell Company to close the Income Summary account in each of the following cases.

The owner of the firm is Janet Bell.
   a. There is a net income of $35,000.
   b. There is a net loss of $12,000.

5. After closing entries are posted, which of the following types of accounts will have zero balances?
   a. Asset accounts
   b. Revenue accounts
   c. Owner's Drawing account
   d. Liability accounts
   e. Income Summary account
   f. Cost and expense accounts
   g. Owner's Capital account

Answers to Self-Review

1. It is necessary to journalize and post adjusting entries even though the adjustments already appear on the worksheet so that the financial records for the accounting period are complete.
2. Detailed explanations should be provided for all adjusting entries when they are journalized in order to show how the adjustments were arrived at. Another person, such as an auditor, should be able to easily understand what was done and why.
3. The four steps in the closing procedure for a sole proprietorship merchandising business are as follows.
   a. Debit the revenue accounts and other temporary accounts with credit balances to close them. Credit Income Summary for the total.
   b. Debit the Income Summary account for the total of the balances of the expense accounts and other temporary accounts with debit balances. Credit each account balance listed.
   c. Transfer the balance of the Income Summary account to the owner's Capital account. If there is a net income, debit the Income Summary account and credit the Capital account. If a net loss was incurred, debit the Capital account and credit the Income Summary account.
   d. Transfer the balance of the owner's Drawing account to the owner's Capital account. Debit the Capital account and credit the Drawing account.
4. a. Debit Income Summary and credit Janet Bell, Capital for $35,000.
   b. Debit Janet Bell, Capital and credit Income Summary for $12,000.
5. Revenue accounts, the owner's Drawing account, Income Summary, and the cost and expense accounts will have zero balances.

CHAPTER 13 **Review and Applications**

CHAPTER SUMMARY

As soon as all adjustments have been entered on the worksheet, the worksheet is completed and the financial statements prepared. The first step is to combine the figures in the Trial Balance section with the adjustments in order to obtain an adjusted trial balance. Then each item in the Adjusted Trial Balance columns is extended to the appropriate financial statement section of the worksheet.

When all figures in the Adjusted Trial Balance section have been transferred, the Income Statement columns are totaled and the net income or net loss is determined. The amount of net income or net loss is then entered in the Balance Sheet section. At this point, the total debits must equal the total credits in the Balance Sheet columns.

Next financial statements are prepared from the information on the worksheet. The format of these statements can vary, but many firms prepare classified statements because they provide more meaningful information to readers.

A classified income statement for a merchandising business usually includes the following sections: Operating Revenue, Cost of Goods Sold, Gross Profit on Sales, Operating Expenses, Net Income from Operations, Other Income, Other Expenses, and Net Income for the period. To make the income statement even more useful, operating expenses may be broken down into several categories, such as selling expenses and general and administrative expenses.

On a classified balance sheet, the assets and liabilities are arranged in groups. Assets are usually presented in two groups—current assets and plant and equipment. Liabilities are also divided into two groups—current liabilities and long-term liabilities.

Current assets consist of cash, items that will normally be converted into cash within one year, and items that will be used up within one year. Plant and equipment consists of property that will be used for a long time in the operations of the business. Current liabilities are debts that must be paid within one year, whereas long-term liabilities are due more than a year in the future.

In addition to the income statement and the balance sheet, a statement of owner's equity may be prepared to provide detailed information about the changes in the owner's financial interest during the period. Otherwise, this data is presented in the Owner's Equity section of the balance sheet.

When the year-end worksheet and financial statements have been completed, adjusting entries are recorded in the general journal and posted to the general ledger. The data for these entries comes from the Adjustments section of the worksheet. The next step in the end-of-period procedure is to journalize and post closing entries from the data in the Income Statement section of the worksheet. Then, to make sure that the general ledger is still in balance after the adjusting and closing entries have been posted, a postclosing trial balance is prepared.

At the beginning of each new fiscal period, many firms follow the practice of reversing certain adjustments that were made in the previous period. This is done to avoid recording problems with transactions related to the adjustments that will occur in the new period.

Only adjusting entries for accrued expenses and accrued income need be considered in the reversing process. Furthermore, only those accrued expense and income items that will involve future payments and receipts of cash are likely to cause difficulties later and should therefore be reversed.

The use of reversing entries is optional, but these entries save time, promote efficiency, and help to achieve a proper matching of revenue and expenses in each fiscal period. When reversing entries are recorded, there is no need to examine each transaction to see whether a portion applies to a past period and then divide the amount of the transaction between the two periods.

GLOSSARY OF NEW TERMS

Classified financial statement (p. 450) A format by which revenues and expenses on the income statement, and assets and liabilities on the balance sheet, are divided into groups of similar accounts and a subtotal is given for each group

Current assets (p. 453) Those assets that are liquid or relatively liquid, such as cash, items that will be converted to cash within a year, or items that will be used up within a year

Current liabilities (p. 454) Debts that must be paid within a year

Current ratio (p. 464) A relationship between current assets and current liabilities that provides a measure of a firm's ability to pay its current debts

Gross profit percentage (p. 463) A figure derived by dividing gross profit by net sales to determine the amount of profit from each dollar of sales

Inventory turnover (p. 464) The number of times inventory is purchased and sold during a financial period; the average length of time it takes to move an item from purchase to sale

Liquidity (p. 454) The ease with which an item can be converted to cash

Long-term liabilities (p. 454) Debts that are due more than a year into the future

Multiple-step income statement (p. 450) A type of income statement on which several subtotals and totals are computed before the net income is presented

Plant and equipment (p. 454) Long-term assets; property that will be used for a long time in operating the business

Reversing entries (p. 465) Journal entries made to reverse the effect of certain adjusting entries involving accrued income or accrued expenses to avoid problems in recording future payments or receipts of cash in a new accounting period

Single-step income statement (p. 450) A type of income statement where only one computation—total revenue minus total expenses—is needed to determine net income

REVIEW QUESTIONS

1. What is the difference between operating revenue and other income?
2. What are operating expenses?
3. Which section of the income statement contains information about the purchases made during the period and the beginning and ending merchandise inventory?
4. What is the purpose of the balance sheet?
5. What are current assets? Give four examples of items that would be considered current assets.
6. What is plant and equipment? Give two examples of items that would be considered plant and equipment.
7. How do current liabilities and long-term liabilities differ?
8. What is the advantage of having classified financial statements?
9. What information is provided by the statement of owner's equity?
10. What is the purpose of the postclosing trial balance?
11. What types of accounts appear on the postclosing trial balance?
12. Why are reversing entries helpful?
13. What types of adjustments are reversed?
14. On December 31, 19X3, the Chan Company made an adjusting entry debiting Interest Receivable and crediting Interest Income for $30 of accrued interest. What reversing entry would be recorded for this item as of January 1, 19X4?
15. Various adjustments made at the Smith Company are listed below. Which ones should be reversed?
    a. An adjustment for the estimated loss from uncollectible accounts
    b. An adjustment for depreciation on equipment
    c. An adjustment for accrued salaries expense
    d. An adjustment for accrued payroll taxes expense
    e. An adjustment for accrued interest expense
    f. An adjustment for supplies used
    g. An adjustment for expired insurance
    h. An adjustment for accrued interest income
16. Name the steps of the accounting cycle.

MANAGERIAL FOCUS

1. Why is it important to compare the financial statements of the current year with those of prior years?
2. Should a manager be concerned if the balance sheet shows a large increase in current liabilities and a large decrease in current assets? Explain your answer.
3. The latest income statement prepared at the Wilkes Company shows that net sales increased by 10 percent over the previous year and selling expenses increased by 25 percent. Do you think that management should investigate the reasons for the increase in selling expenses? Why or why not?
4. Why is it useful for management to compare a firm's financial statements with financial information from other companies in the same industry?
5. For the last two years, the income statement of the Fashion Clothing Center, a large retail store, has shown a substantial increase in the merchandise inventory. Why might management be concerned about this development?
6. The Anderson Company had an increase in sales and net income during its last fiscal year, but cash decreased and the firm was having difficulty paying its bills by the end of the year. What factors might cause a shortage of cash even though a firm is profitable?
7. Why should management be concerned about the efficiency of the end-of-period procedures?
8. Why is it important that the closing process be completed promptly?

EXERCISES

EXERCISE 13–1
(Obj. 1)
Tutorial

Classifying income statement items. The accounts shown below appear on the worksheet of the Mayville Appliance Store. Indicate the section of the classified income statement where each account will be reported.

SECTIONS OF CLASSIFIED INCOME STATEMENT

a. Operating Revenue
b. Cost of Goods Sold
c. Operating Expenses
d. Other Income
e. Other Expenses

ACCOUNTS

1. Purchases
2. Salaries Expense
3. Sales
4. Interest Expense
5. Merchandise Inventory
6. Interest Income
7. Freight In
8. Sales Returns and Allowances
9. Utilities Expense
10. Purchases Discount

EXERCISE 13–2 (Obj. 3)

Tutorial

Classifying balance sheet items. The accounts shown below appear on the worksheet of the Mayville Appliance Store. Indicate the section of the classified balance sheet where each account will be reported.

SECTIONS OF CLASSIFIED BALANCE SHEET

a. Current Assets
b. Plant and Equipment
c. Current Liabilities
d. Long-Term Liabilities
e. Owner's Equity

ACCOUNTS

1. Sales Tax Payable
2. Cash
3. John Cortez, Capital
4. Building
5. Accounts Payable
6. Store Supplies
7. Mortgage Payable
8. Prepaid Insurance
9. Delivery Van
10. Accounts Receivable

EXERCISE 13–3 (Obj. 1)

Preparing a classified income statement. The worksheet of the Midtown Shoe Center contains the revenue, cost, and expense accounts listed below. Prepare a classified income statement for this firm for the year ended December 31, 19X8. The merchandise inventory amounted to $27,000 on January 1, 19X8, and $25,200 on December 31, 19X8. The expense accounts numbered 511 through 517 represent selling expenses, and those numbered 531 through 546 represent general and administrative expenses.

ACCOUNTS

401	Sales	$124,000 Cr.
451	Sales Returns and Allowances	3,100 Dr.
491	Miscellaneous Income	110 Cr.
501	Purchases	51,000 Dr.
502	Freight In	900 Dr.
503	Purchases Returns and Allowances	1,500 Cr.
504	Purchases Discount	800 Cr.
511	Sales Salaries Expense	22,000 Dr.
514	Store Supplies Expense	1,100 Dr.
517	Depreciation Expense—Store Equipment	800 Dr.
531	Rent Expense	6,000 Dr.
534	Utilities Expense	1,400 Dr.
537	Office Salaries Expense	10,000 Dr.
540	Payroll Taxes Expense	2,500 Dr.
543	Depreciation Expense—Office Equipment	200 Dr.
546	Uncollectible Accounts Expense	320 Dr.
591	Interest Expense	260 Dr.

EXERCISE 13–4 (Obj. 2)

Preparing a statement of owner's equity. The worksheet of the Midtown Shoe Center contains the owner's equity accounts listed below. Use this data and the net income determined in Exercise 13–3 to prepare a statement of owner's equity for the year ended December 31, 19X8. No additional investments were made during the period.

ACCOUNTS

301	Elaine Erves, Capital	$30,060 Cr.
302	Elaine Erves, Drawing	21,000 Dr.

EXERCISE 13–5
(Obj. 3)

Preparing a classified balance sheet. The worksheet of the Midtown Shoe Center contains the asset and liability accounts listed below. The balance of the Notes Payable account consists of notes that are due within a year. Prepare a balance sheet dated December 31, 19X8. Obtain the ending capital for the period from the statement of owner's equity completed in Exercise 13–4.

ACCOUNTS

101	Cash	$ 5,500 Dr.
107	Change Fund	100 Dr.
111	Accounts Receivable	2,700 Dr.
112	Allowance for Doubtful Accounts	380 Cr.
121	Merchandise Inventory	25,200 Dr.
131	Store Supplies	950 Dr.
133	Prepaid Interest	90 Dr.
141	Store Equipment	5,100 Dr.
142	Accum. Depr.—Store Equipment	800 Cr.
151	Office Equipment	1,600 Dr.
152	Accum. Depr.—Office Equipment	200 Cr.
201	Notes Payable	2,700 Cr.
203	Accounts Payable	1,800 Cr.
216	Interest Payable	30 Cr.
231	Sales Tax Payable	1,240 Cr.

EXERCISE 13–6
(Obj. 5)

Tutorial

Recording closing entries. On December 31, 19X3, the Income Statement section of the worksheet for the Sanders Company contained the information given below. Give the entries that should be made in the general journal to close the revenue, cost, expense, and other temporary accounts.

INCOME STATEMENT

	Debit	Credit
Income Summary	$ 38,000	$ 40,000
Sales		245,000
Sales Returns and Allowances	4,100	
Sales Discount	3,300	
Interest Income		100
Purchases	125,000	
Freight In	1,700	
Purchases Returns and Allowances		1,900
Purchases Discount		2,200
Rent Expense	8,400	
Utilities Expense	2,100	
Telephone Expense	1,300	
Salaries Expense	65,000	
Payroll Taxes Expense	5,150	
Supplies Expense	1,600	
Depreciation Expense	2,400	
Interest Expense	350	
Totals	$258,400	$289,200

Assume further that the owner of the firm is Karen Sanders and that the Karen Sanders, Drawing account had a balance of $26,000 on December 31, 19X3.

EXERCISE 13–7
(Obj. 7)
Tutorial

Journalizing reversing entries. Examine the adjusting entries below and determine which ones should be reversed. Show the reversing entries that should be recorded in the general journal as of January 1, 19X4. Include appropriate explanations.

19X3	(Adjustment *a*)		
Dec. 31	Uncollectible Accounts Exp.	1,800.00	
	Allowance for Doubtful Accts.		1,800.00
	To record estimated loss from uncollectible accounts based on 0.5% of net credit sales, $360,000		
	(Adjustment *b*)		
31	Supplies Expense	2,320.00	
	Supplies		2,320.00
	To record supplies used during 19X3		
	(Adjustment *c*)		
31	Insurance Expense	900.00	
	Prepaid Insurance		900.00
	To record expired insurance on 1-year $2,700 policy purchased on Sept. 1, 19X3		
	(Adjustment *d*)		
31	Depr. Exp.—Store Equipment	7,700.00	
	Accum. Depr.—Store Equip.		7,700.00
	To record depreciation for 19X3		
	(Adjustment *e*)		
31	Office Salaries Expense	680.00	
	Salaries Payable		680.00
	To record accrued salaries for Dec. 29–31		
	(Adjustment *f*)		
31	Payroll Tax Expense	54.00	
	Social Sec. Tax Payable		44.00
	Medicare Tax Payable		10.00
	To record accrued payroll taxes on accrued salaries; Social Security, 6.5% × 680 = $44; Medicare, 1.5% × 680 = $10		
	(Adjustment *g*)		
31	Interest Expense	330.00	
	Interest Payable		330.00
	To record accrued interest on a 4-month, 11% trade note payable dated Oct. 1, 19X3: $12,000 × 11/100 × 3/12 = $330		

	(Adjustment *h*)		
31	Interest Receivable	50.00	
	Interest Income		50.00
	To record interest earned on 6-month, 10% note receivable dated Nov. 1, 19X3: $3,000 × 10/100 × 2/12 = $25		

EXERCISE 13–8 (Obj. 6)

Preparing a postclosing trial balance. The Adjusted Trial Balance section of the worksheet for the Harden Company appears below. The owner made no additional investments during the year. Prepare a postclosing trial balance for the firm on December 31, 19X3.

ACCOUNT	DEBIT	CREDIT
Cash	$ 3,400	
Accounts Receivable	6,800	
Allowance for Doubtful Accounts		$ 20
Merchandise Inventory	31,500	
Supplies	1,190	
Prepaid Insurance	510	
Equipment	8,500	
Accumulated Depr.—Equipment		2,800
Notes Payable		1,750
Accounts Payable		1,450
Social Security Tax Payable		232
Medicare Tax Payable		54
Howard Davis, Capital		38,905
Howard Davis, Drawing	14,000	
Income Summary	30,000	31,500
Sales		128,000
Sales Returns and Allowances	2,400	
Purchases	79,500	
Freight In	900	
Purchases Returns and Allowances		1,750
Purchases Discount		1,150
Rent Expense	3,600	
Telephone Expense	541	
Salaries Expense	20,690	
Payroll Taxes Expense	1,850	
Supplies Expense	600	
Insurance Expense	110	
Depr. Expense—Equipment	1,500	
Uncollectible Accounts Expense	20	
Totals	$207,611	$207,611

PROBLEMS

PROBLEM SET A

PROBLEM 13–1A (Obj. 1, 2, 3)

Preparing classified financial statements. The Micro Circuits Company distributes electronic components to computer manufacturers. The adjusted trial balance data given below is from the firm's worksheet for the year ended December 31, 19X7.

Instructions

1. Prepare a classified income statement for the year ended December 31, 19X7. The expense accounts numbered 511 through 515 represent warehouse expenses, those numbered 521 through 527 represent selling expenses, and those numbered 531 through 549 represent general and administrative expenses.
2. Prepare a statement of owner's equity for the year ended December 31, 19X7. No additional investments were made during the period.
3. Prepare a classified balance sheet as of December 31, 19X7. The mortgage and the loans extend for more than a year.

Account Name	*Debit*	*Credit*
Cash	$ 6,775	
Petty Cash Fund	100	
Notes Receivable	2,700	
Accounts Receivable	13,625	
Allowance for Doubtful Accounts		1,250
Merchandise Inventory	56,000	
Warehouse Supplies	690	
Office Supplies	330	
Prepaid Insurance	1,800	
Land	9,000	
Building	42,000	
Accum. Depr.—Building		12,000
Warehouse Equipment	8,000	
Accum. Depr.—Warehouse Equip.		3,600
Delivery Equipment	11,500	
Accum. Depr.—Delivery Equip.		4,400
Office Equipment	5,000	
Accum. Depr.—Office Equip.		2,250
Notes Payable		4,800
Accounts Payable		10,500
Interest Payable		120
Mortgage Payable		14,000
Loans Payable		3,000
Ruth Newman, Capital (Jan. 1)		99,410
Ruth Newman, Drawing	31,500	
Income Summary	58,500	56,000
Sales		418,400
Sales Returns and Allowances	4,300	

Account Name	*Debit*	*Credit*
Interest Income		370
Merchandise Purchases	192,600	
Freight In	3,200	
Purchases Returns and Allowances		1,860
Purchases Discount		2,540
Warehouse Wages Expense	47,400	
Warehouse Supplies Expense	1,525	
Depr. Exp.—Warehouse Equip.	1,200	
Sales Salaries Expense	64,800	
Travel and Entertainment Exp.	5,125	
Delivery Wages Expense	21,000	
Depr. Exp.—Delivery Equip.	2,200	
Office Salaries Expense	17,400	
Office Supplies Expense	750	
Insurance Expense	1,300	
Utilities Expense	2,400	
Telephone Expense	1,380	
Payroll Taxes Expense	13,500	
Property Taxes Expense	1,150	
Uncollectible Accounts Expense	1,200	
Depr. Expense—Building	2,000	
Depr. Expense—Office Equip.	750	
Interest Expense	1,800	
Totals	$634,500	$634,500

PROBLEM 13–2A (Obj. 1, 2, 3)

Preparing classified financial statements. High-Grade Products distributes automobile parts to service stations and repair shops. The adjusted trial balance data that follows is from the firm's worksheet for the year ended December 31, 19X3.

Instructions

1. Prepare a classified income statement for the year ended December 31, 19X3. The expense accounts numbered 511 through 515 represent warehouse expenses, those numbered 521 through 525 represent selling expenses, and those numbered 531 through 551 represent general and administrative expenses.

2. Prepare a statement of owner's equity for the year ended December 31, 19X3. No additional investments were made during the period.
3. Prepare a classified balance sheet as of December 31, 19X3. The mortgage and the long-term notes extend for more than a year.

Account Name	Debit	Credit	Account Name	Debit	Credit
Cash	$ 43,000		Sales Returns and Allowances	3,700	
Petty Cash Fund	200		Interest Income		240
Notes Receivable	5,000		Purchases	219,000	
Accounts Receivable	50,600		Freight In	4,400	
Allow. for Doubtful Accounts		1,400	Purchases Returns and Allow.		5,780
Interest Receivable	100		Purchases Discount		4,120
Merchandise Inventory	62,000		Warehouse Wages Expense	53,600	
Warehouse Supplies	1,150		Warehouse Supplies Expense	2,400	
Office Supplies	300		Depr. Expense—Ware. Equip.	1,200	
Prepaid Insurance	1,820		Sales Salaries Expense	75,100	
Land	7,500		Travel Expense	11,500	
Building	46,000		Delivery Expense	18,200	
Accum. Depr.—Building		7,200	Office Salaries Expense	42,000	
Warehouse Equipment	9,400		Office Supplies Expense	560	
Accum. Depr.—Ware. Equip.		4,800	Insurance Expense	4,400	
Office Equipment	4,200		Utilities Expense	3,000	
Accum. Depr.—Office Equip.		1,520	Telephone Expense	1,590	
Notes Payable—Short-Term		7,000	Payroll Taxes Expense	15,300	
Accounts Payable		29,500	Building Repairs Expense	1,350	
Interest Payable		150	Property Taxes Expense	6,200	
Notes Payable—Long-Term		5,000	Uncollectible Accounts Expense	1,290	
Mortgage Payable		10,000	Depr. Expense—Building	1,800	
Carl Furjanic, Capital (Jan. 1)		163,510	Depr. Expense—Office Equip.	760	
Carl Furjanic, Drawing	32,000		Interest Expense	1,500	
Income Summary	65,200	62,000	Totals	$797,320	$797,320
Sales		495,100			

PROBLEM 13–3A
(Obj. 4, 5, 7)

Tutorial Spreadsheet

Journalizing adjusting, closing, and reversing entries. Obtain all necessary data from the worksheet prepared for the Nutri-Products Company in Problem 12–4A.

Instructions

1. Record adjusting entries in the general journal as of December 31, 19X3. Use 25 as the first journal page number. Include explanations for the entries.
2. Record closing entries in the general journal as of December 31, 19X3. Include explanations.
3. Record reversing entries in the general journal as of January 1, 19X4. Include explanations.

PROBLEM 13–4A
(Obj. 4, 7)

Journalizing adjusting and reversing entries. The data below concerns adjustments to be made at the Vincent Company.

Instructions

1. Record the adjusting entries in the general journal as of December 31, 19X3. Use 25 as the first journal page number. Include explanations.

2. Record reversing entries in the general journal as of January 1, 19X4. Include explanations.

ADJUSTMENTS

a. On September 1, 19X3, the firm signed a lease for a warehouse and paid rent of $8,400 in advance for a six-month period.
b. On December 31, 19X3, an inventory of supplies showed that items costing $920 were on hand. The balance of the Supplies account was $5,560.
c. A depreciation schedule for the firm's equipment shows that a total of $3,900 should be charged off as depreciation for 19X3.
d. On December 31, 19X3, the firm owed salaries of $2,200 that will not be paid until January 19X4.
e. On December 31, 19X3, the firm owed the employer's social security (6.5 percent) and medicare (1.5 percent) taxes on all accrued salaries.
f. On November 1, 19X3, the firm received a four-month, 10 percent note for $2,700 from a customer with an overdue balance.

PROBLEM SET B

PROBLEM 13–1B
(Obj. 1, 2, 3)

Preparing classified financial statements. Discount Computer Company is a retail store that sells computers and computer supplies. The adjusted trial balance data given below is from the firm's worksheet for the year ended December 31, 19X7.

Instructions

1. Prepare a classified income statement for the year ended December 31, 19X7. The expense accounts numbered 511 through 515 represent warehouse expenses, those numbered 521 through 527 represent selling expenses, and those numbered 531 through 549 represent general and administrative expenses.
2. Prepare a statement of owner's equity for the year ended December 31, 19X7. No additional investments were made during the period.
3. Prepare a classified balance sheet as of December 31, 19X7. The mortgage and the loans extend for more than a year.

Account Name	*Debit*	*Credit*	Account Name	*Debit*	*Credit*
Cash	$ 8,925		Delivery Equipment	14,000	
Petty Cash Fund	100		Accum. Depr.—Delivery Equip.		3,600
Notes Receivable	3,200		Office Equipment	6,000	
Accounts Receivable	16,325		Accum. Depr.—Office Equip.		2,500
Allowance for Doubtful Accounts		2,250	Notes Payable		5,000
Merchandise Inventory	36,000		Accounts Payable		12,800
Warehouse Supplies	750		Interest Payable		240
Office Supplies	730		Mortgage Payable		16,000
Prepaid Insurance	2,200		Loans Payable		4,000
Land	7,000		Shirley Davis, Capital (Jan. 1)		60,490
Building	48,000		Shirley Davis, Drawing	24,000	
Accum. Depr.—Building		12,000	Income Summary	34,000	36,000
Warehouse Equipment	9,000		Sales		430,500
Accum. Depr.—Warehouse Equip.		2,600	Sales Returns and Allowances	3,150	

(Continued)

Account Name	Debit	Credit	Account Name	Debit	Credit
Interest Income		420	Office Salaries Expense	15,900	
Purchases	185,550		Office Supplies Expense	950	
Freight In	2,200		Insurance Expense	1,500	
Purchases Returns and Allowances		1,920	Utilities Expense	2,800	
Purchases Discount		2,350	Telephone Expense	1,380	
Warehouse Wages Expense	39,400		Payroll Taxes Expense	15,100	
Warehouse Supplies Expense	1,790		Property Taxes Expense	1,750	
Depr. Expense—Warehouse Equip.	1,400		Uncollectible Accounts Expense	1,050	
Sales Salaries Expense	70,200		Depr. Expense—Building	3,000	
Travel and Entertainment Expense	6,300		Depr. Expense—Office Equip.	1,020	
Delivery Wages Expense	24,000		Interest Expense	1,600	
Depr. Expense—Delivery Equip.	2,400		Totals	$592,670	$592,670

PROBLEM 13–2B
(Obj. 1, 2, 3)

Preparing classified financial statements. Speedway Cycle Center is a retail firm that sells motorcycles, parts, and accessories. The adjusted trial balance data given below is from the firm's worksheet for the year ended December 31, 19X3.

Instructions

1. Prepare a classified income statement for the year ended December 31, 19X3. The expense accounts numbered 511 through 515 represent warehouse expenses, those numbered 521 through 525 represent selling expenses, and those numbered 531 through 551 represent general and administrative expenses.
2. Prepare a statement of owner's equity for the year ended December 31, 19X3. No additional investments were made during the period.
3. Prepare a classified balance sheet as of December 31, 19X3. The mortgage and the long-term notes extend for more than a year.

Account Name	Debit	Credit	Account Name	Debit	Credit
Cash	$ 6,600		Accounts Payable		16,250
Petty Cash Fund	100		Interest Payable		300
Notes Receivable	3,000		Notes Payable—Long-Term		3,000
Accounts Receivable	27,500		Mortgage Payable		16,000
Allowance for Doubtful Accounts		2,500	Jerry Morgan, Capital (Jan. 1)		100,085
Interest Receivable	100		Jerry Morgan, Drawing	28,000	
Merchandise Inventory	42,500		Income Summary	44,500	42,500
Warehouse Supplies	1,850		Sales		301,451
Office Supplies	900		Sales Returns and Allowances	4,700	
Prepaid Insurance	3,600		Interest Income		360
Land	9,000		Purchases	112,500	
Building	27,000		Freight In	4,800	
Accum. Depr.—Building		4,200	Purchases Returns and Allow.		3,100
Warehouse Equipment	12,000		Purchases Discount		2,170
Accum. Depr.—Warehouse Equip.		2,000	Warehouse Wages Expense	31,750	
Office Equipment	6,400		Warehouse Supplies Expense	2,150	
Accum. Depr.—Office Equip.		900	Depr. Expense—Ware. Equip.	1,200	
Notes Payable—Short-Term		4,000	Sales Salaries Expense	39,550	

(Continued)

Account Name	*Debit*	*Credit*	Account Name	*Debit*	*Credit*
Travel Expense	10,500		Building Repairs Expense	1,550	
Delivery Expense	17,700		Property Taxes Expense	5,850	
Office Salaries Expense	23,000		Uncollectible Accounts Expense	1,310	
Office Supplies Expense	680		Depr. Expense—Building	1,600	
Insurance Expense	4,560		Depr. Expense—Office Equip.	840	
Utilities Expense	3,456		Interest Expense	1,800	
Telephone Expense	1,870		Totals	$498,816	$498,816
Payroll Taxes Expense	14,400				

PROBLEM 13–3B
(Obj. 4, 5, 7)

Tutorial

Journalizing adjusting, closing, and reversing entries. This problem is a continuation of Problem 12–3B. Obtain all necessary data from the worksheet prepared for the Toy Palace in Problem 12–3B.

Instructions

1. Record adjusting entries in the general journal as of December 31, 19X8. Use 25 as the first journal page number. Include explanations for the entries.
2. Record closing entries in the general journal as of December 31, 19X8. Include explanations.
3. Record reversing entries in the general journal as of January 1, 19X9. Include explanations.

PROBLEM 13–4B
(Obj. 4, 7)

Journalizing adjusting and reversing entries. The data below concerns adjustments to be made at the Jorganson Company.

Instructions

1. Record the adjusting entries in the general journal as of December 31, 19X3. Use 25 as the first journal page number. Include explanations.
2. Record reversing entries in the general journal as of January 1, 19X4. Include explanations.

ADJUSTMENTS

a. On August 1, 19X3, the firm signed a one-year advertising contract with a trade magazine and paid the entire amount, $3,000, in advance. Prepaid Advertising has a balance of $3,000.
b. On December 31, 19X3, an inventory of supplies showed that items costing $750 were on hand. The balance of the Supplies account was $3,490.
c. A depreciation schedule for the firm's equipment shows that a total of $2,630 should be charged off as depreciation for 19X3.
d. On December 31, 19X3, the firm owed salaries of $1,600 that will not be paid until January 19X4.
e. On December 31, 19X3, the firm owed the employer's social security (6.5 percent) and medicare (1.5 percent) taxes on all accrued salaries.
f. On October 1, 19X3, the firm received a six-month, 12 percent note for $2,200 from a customer with an overdue balance.

CHALLENGE PROBLEM

The Universal Software Center is a retail firm that sells computer programs for home and business use. On December 31, 19X7, its general ledger contained the accounts and balances shown below.

ACCOUNTS	BALANCES
Cash	$ 6,800 Dr.
Accounts Receivable	13,600 Dr.
Allowance for Doubtful Accounts	40 Cr.
Merchandise Inventory	31,000 Dr.
Supplies	2,380 Dr.
Prepaid Insurance	1,020 Dr.
Equipment	17,000 Dr.
Accumulated Depreciation—Equipment	5,600 Cr.
Notes Payable	3,500 Cr.
Accounts Payable	2,900 Cr.
Social Security Tax Payable	280 Cr.
Medicare Tax Payable	65 Cr.
John Dillon, Capital	46,123 Cr.
John Dillon, Drawing	25,000 Dr.
Sales	256,174 Cr.
Sales Returns and Allowances	4,800 Dr.
Purchases	159,000 Dr.
Freight In	1,800 Dr.
Purchases Returns and Allowances	3,500 Cr.
Purchases Discount	2,300 Cr.
Rent Expense	7,200 Dr.
Telephone Expense	1,082 Dr.
Salaries Expense	46,000 Dr.
Payroll Taxes Expense	3,700 Dr.
Interest Expense	100 Dr.

These accounts had no balances: Interest Payable, Salaries Payable, Income Summary, Supplies Expense, Insurance Expense, Depreciation Expense—Equipment, and Uncollectible Accounts Expense. The data needed for the adjustments on December 31 are as follows:

a–b. Ending Merchandise Inventory, $34,000
c. Uncollectible accounts, 0.6 percent of net credit sales of $115,000
d. Supplies on hand December 31, $550
e. Expired insurance, $595.
f. Depreciation Expense—Equipment, $2,800
g. Accrued interest expense on notes payable, $140
h. Accrued salaries, $800
i. Social Security Tax Payable (6.5 percent) and Medicare Tax Payable (1.5 percent) of accrued salaries

Instructions

1. Prepare a worksheet for the year ended December 31, 19X7.
2. Prepare a classified income statement. The firm does not divide its operating expenses into selling and administrative expenses.
3. Prepare a statement of owner's equity. No additional investments were made during the period.

4. Prepare a classified balance sheet. All notes payable are due within one year.
5. Journalize the adjusting entries.
6. Journalize the closing entries.
7. Journalize the reversing entries.

CRITICAL THINKING PROBLEM

Hillary Francis is the owner of Sweaters Galore, a store specializing in women's and children's sweaters. During the past year, in response to increased demand, Hillary doubled her selling space by expanding into the vacant store next to Sweaters Galore. This expansion has been expensive because of the need to increase inventory and to purchase new store fixtures and equipment. Hillary notes that the company's cash position has gone down, and she is worried about paying for the expansion. Hillary shows you balance sheet data for the current year and last year and asks your opinion on the company's ability to pay for the recent expansion.

	December 31, 19X7		December 31, 19X8	
Assets				
Cash	50,000.00		10,000.00	
Accounts Receivable	15,000.00		30,500.00	
Inventory	35,000.00		78,000.00	
Prepaid Expenses	2,000.00		3,000.00	
Store Fixtures and Equipment	60,000.00		130,000.00	
Total Assets		162,000.00		251,500.00
Liabilities and Owner's Equity				
Liabilities				
Notes Payable (due in 5 years)	30,000.00		80,000.00	
Accounts Payable	44,000.00		57,000.00	
Salaries Payable	6,000.00		6,500.00	
Total Liabilities		80,000.00		143,500.00
Owner's Equity				
Hillary Francis, Capital		82,000.00		108,000.00
Total Liabilities and Owner's Equity		162,000.00		251,500.00

Instructions

1. Prepare classified balance sheets for Sweaters Galore for the years 19X7 and 19X8.
2. Based on the information as presented in the classified balance sheets, what is your opinion of Sweaters Galore's ability to pay its current bills in a timely manner?
3. What is the advantage of a classified balance sheet over a balance sheet that is not classified?

MINI-PRACTICE SET 2

Merchandising Business Accounting Cycle

Fashions for Less is a retail merchandising business that sells brand-name clothing at discount prices. The firm is located in a shopping center near two busy highways. It is owned and managed by Maria Cortez, who started the business five months ago. This project will give you an opportunity to put your knowledge of accounting into practice as you handle the accounting work of Fashions for Less during the month of June 19X4.

INTRODUCTION

Fashions for Less has a monthly accounting period. The firm's chart of accounts is shown below. The journals used to record transactions are the sales journal, purchases journal, cash receipts journal, cash payments journal, and general journal. Postings are made from the journals to the accounts receivable ledger, accounts payable ledger, and general ledger. The employees are paid at the end of the month. A computerized payroll service prepares all payroll records and checks.

INSTRUCTIONS

1. Open the general ledger accounts and enter the balances for June 1, 19X4. Obtain the necessary figures from the postclosing trial balance prepared on May 31, 19X4, which is shown on page 496. (If you are using the *Study Guide and Working Papers,* you will find that the general ledger accounts are already open.)
2. Open the subsidiary ledger accounts and enter the balances for June 1, 19X4. Obtain the necessary figures from the schedule of accounts receivable and schedule of accounts payable prepared on May 31, 19X4, which are on pages 495–496. (If you are using the *Study Guide and Working Papers,* you will find that the subsidiary ledger accounts are already open.)
3. Analyze the transactions for June and record each transaction in the proper journal. (Use 6 as the number for the first page of each special journal and 16 as the number for the first page of the general journal.)
4. Post the individual entries that involve customer and creditor accounts from the journals to the subsidiary ledgers on a daily basis. Post the individual entries that appear in the general journal and in the Other Accounts sections of the cash receipts and cash payments journals to the general ledger on a daily basis.

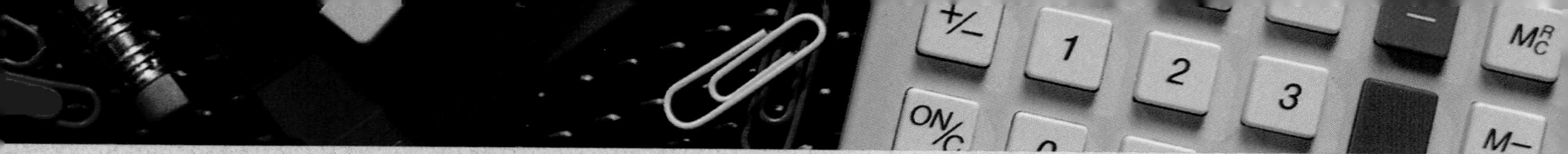

FASHIONS FOR LESS
Chart of Accounts

ASSETS
101 Cash
111 Accounts Receivables
112 Allowance for Doubtful Accounts
121 Merchandise Inventory
131 Supplies
133 Prepaid Insurance
135 Prepaid Advertising
141 Equipment
142 Accumulated Depreciation Equipment

LIABILITIES
203 Accounts Payable
221 Social Security Tax Payable
222 Medicare Tax Payable
223 Employee Income Tax Payable
225 Federal Unemployment Tax Payable
227 State Unemployment Tax Payable
229 Salaries Payable
231 Sales Tax Payable

OWNER'S EQUITY
301 Maria Cortez, Capital
302 Maria Cortez, Drawing
399 Income Summary

REVENUE
401 Sales
402 Sales Returns and Allowances

EXPENSES
501 Merchandise Purchases
502 Freight In
503 Purchases Returns and Allowances
504 Purchases Discount
511 Advertising Expense
514 Depreciation Expense—Equipment
517 Insurance Expense
520 Uncollectible Accounts Expense
523 Payroll Processing Expense
526 Payroll Taxes Expense
529 Rent Expense
532 Salaries Expense
535 Supplies Expense
538 Telephone Expense
541 Utilities Expense

5. Total, prove, and rule the special journals as of June 30.
6. Post the column totals from the special journals to the general ledger accounts.
7. Check the accuracy of the subsidiary ledgers by preparing a schedule of accounts receivable and a schedule of accounts payable as of June 30, 19X4. Compare the totals with the balances of the Accounts Receivable account and the Accounts Payable account in the general ledger.
8. Check the accuracy of the general ledger by preparing a trial balance in the first two columns of a 10-column worksheet. Make sure that the total debits and the total credits are equal.
9. Complete the Adjustments section of the worksheet. Use the following data. Identify each adjustment with the appropriate letter.
   a. During June the firm had net credit of $4,620. From experience with similar businesses, the previous accountant had estimated that 0.8 percent of the firm's net credit sales would result in uncollectible accounts. Record an

adjustment for the expected loss from uncollectible accounts for the month of June.

b. On June 30 an inventory of the supplies showed that items costing $1,420 were on hand. Record an adjustment for the supplies used in June.

c. On May 31 the firm purchased a one-year insurance policy for $4,050. Record an adjustment for the expired insurance for June.

d. On June 1 the firm signed a four-month advertising contract for $1,400 with a local radio station and paid the full amount in advance. Record an adjustment for the expired advertising for June.

e. On January 2 the firm purchased equipment for $41,500. At that time, the equipment was estimated to have a useful life of five years and a salvage value of $4,300. Record an adjustment for depreciation on the equipment for June.

f–g. After a physical inventory, ending inventory was $40,100.

10. Complete the Adjusted Trial Balance section of the worksheet.
11. Determine the net income or net loss for June and complete the worksheet.
12. Prepare a classified income statement for the month ended June 30, 19X4. (The firm does not divide its operating expenses into selling and administrative expenses.)
13. Prepare a statement of owner's equity for the month ended June 30, 19X4.
14. Prepare a classified balance sheet as of June 30, 19X4.
15. Journalize and post the adjusting entries using general journal page 33.
16. Prepare and post the closing entries using general journal page 34.
17. Prepare a postclosing trial balance.

TRANSACTIONS

June 1 Issued Check 521 for $1,600 to pay the monthly rent for the store.

1 Signed a four-month advertising contract for $1,400 with a local radio station; issued check 522 to pay the full amount in advance.

2 Received $235 from Susan Berger, a credit customer, in payment of her account.

2 Issued Check 523 for $8,910 to remit the sales tax owed for May to the state sales tax agency.

2 Issued Check 524 for $3,350.62 to Allen Sportswear, a creditor, in payment of Invoice 9387 ($3,419), less a cash discount ($68.38).

3 Sold merchandise on credit for $1,240 plus sales tax of $62 to Vincent Rizzo, Sales Slip 241.

4 Issued Check 525 for $500 to purchase plastic hangers, shopping bags, and other supplies.

4 Issued Check 526 for $4,273.78 to Zenith Modes, a creditor, in payment of Invoice 5671 ($4,361), less a cash discount ($87.22).

5 Collected $610 on account from Sharon Scott, a credit customer.

5 Accepted a return of merchandise from Vincent Rizzo. The merchandise was originally sold on Sales Slip 241 of June 3; issued Credit Memorandum 18 for $315, which includes sales tax of $15.

5 Issued Check 527 for $735 to Classic Styles, Inc., a creditor, in payment of Invoice 3292 ($750), less a cash discount ($15).

6 Had cash sales of $8,600 plus sales tax of $430 during June 1–6.

8 Keith Larson, a credit customer, sent a check for $416 to pay the balance he owes.

8 Issued Check 528 for $942 to deposit the social security tax ($351), the medicare tax ($81), and the employee income tax ($510) from the May payroll.

9 Sold merchandise on credit for $920 plus sales tax of $46 to Diane Nichols, Sales Slip 242.

10 Issued Check 529 for $1,000 to pay for a newspaper advertisement that appeared in May.

11 Purchased merchandise for $2,410 from Allen Sportswear, Invoice 9422, dated June 8; the terms are 2/10, n/30.

12 Issued Check 530 for $150 to pay freight charges to the trucking company that delivered merchandise from Allen Sportswear on May 27 and June 11.

13 Had cash sales of $5,760 plus sales tax of $288 during June 8–13.

15 Sold merchandise on credit for $970 plus sales tax of $48.50 to Keith Larson, Sales Slip 243.

16 Made a purchase of discontinued merchandise; paid for it immediately with Check 531 for $2,300.

16 Received $243 on account from Vincent Rizzo, a credit customer.

16 Issued Check 532 for $2,361.80 to Allen Sportswear, a creditor, in payment of Invoice 9422 ($2,410) less a cash discount ($48.20).

18 Issued Check 533 for $3,000 to Maria Cortez as a withdrawal for personal use.

20 Had cash sales of $6,400 plus sales tax of $320 during June 15–20.

22 Issued Check 534 for $380 to pay the monthly electric bill.

24 Sold merchandise on credit for $410 plus sales tax of $20.50 to Susan Berger, Sales Slip 244.

25 Purchased merchandise for $1,560 from Classic Styles Inc., Invoice 3418, dated June 23; the terms are 2/10, n/30.

26 Issued Check 535 for $240 to pay the monthly telephone bill.

27 Had cash sales of $6,120 plus sales tax of $306 during June 22–27.

29 Received Credit Memorandum 175 for $215 from Classic Styles Inc. for defective goods that were returned. The original purchase was made on Invoice 3418 on June 25.

29 Sold merchandise on credit for $1,380 plus sales tax of $69 to Sharon Scott, Sales Slip 245.

29 Recorded the June payroll. The records prepared by payroll service show the following totals: earnings, $5,400; social security, $351; medicare, $81; income tax, $510; and net pay $4,458.

29 Recorded the employer's payroll taxes, which were calculated by the payroll service: social security, $351; medicare, $81; federal unemployment tax, $59; and state unemployment tax, $292.

30 Purchased merchandise for $1,150 from Zenith Modes, Invoice 5821, dated June 26; the terms are 1/10, n/30.

30 Issued Check 536 for $4,458 to pay the June payroll.

30 Issued Check 537 for $100 to pay the fee owed to the payroll service for processing the June payroll.

30 Had cash sales of $720 plus sales tax of $36 for June 29 and June 30.

FASHIONS FOR LESS

Schedule of Accounts Payable

May 31, 19X4

Allen Sportswear	*3 4 1 9 00*
Classic Styles Inc.	*7 5 0 00*
Zenith Modes	*4 3 6 1 00*
Total	*8 5 3 0 00*

FASHIONS FOR LESS
Postclosing Trial Balance
May 31, 19X4

ACCOUNT NAME	DEBIT	CREDIT
Cash	30,350.00	
Accounts Receivable	2,594.00	
Allowance for Doubtful Accounts		117.00
Merchandise Inventory	43,700.00	
Supplies	2,200.00	
Prepaid Insurance	4,050.00	
Equipment	41,500.00	
Accumulated Depreciation—Equipment		3,030.00
Accounts Payable		8,530.00
Social Security Tax Payable		351.00
Medicare Tax Payable		81.00
Employee Income Tax Payable		510.00
Federal Unemployment Tax Payable		256.00
State Unemployment Tax Payable		634.00
Sales Tax Payable		8,910.00
Maria Cortez, Capital		101,975.00
Totals	124,394.00	124,394.00

FASHIONS FOR LESS
Schedule of Accounts Receivable
May 31, 19X4

Joyce Andrews	410.00
Susan Berger	235.00
Keith Larson	416.00
Diane Nichols	112.00
Michael O'Mara	568.00
Vincent Rizzo	243.00
Sharon Scott	610.00
Total	2,594.00

College Accounting

PART TWO

U N I T   F I V E

Accounting for Assets and Liabilities

The rules of accounting used by businesses in reporting their financial activities are called generally accepted accounting principles. These principles—often referred to as accounting principles, assumptions, and modifying conventions—make up the body of rules that guide the recording and reporting of financial information that appears in the financial statements. A recognized process is used to develop and modify these principles for contemporary accounting practice. Generally accepted accounting principles are used in all areas of accounting, such as accounts receivable and uncollectible accounts; notes payable and receivable; merchandise inventory; and property, plant, and equipment.

CHAPTER 14

Accounting Principles and Reporting Standards

OBJECTIVES

1. Describe the process used to develop generally accepted accounting principles.
2. Identify, assess, and apply the assumptions that underlie current accounting principles and procedures and the modifying conventions that may alter their application.
3. Define the accounting terms new to this chapter.

In Part 1 you learned how accounting procedures are used to properly record business transactions in a sole proprietorship. You also learned how to prepare an income statement, a statement of owner's equity, and a balance sheet to reflect the net income or net loss of a business and to show its financial condition. These accounting procedures and financial statements are based on accounting principles and rules that have come to be generally accepted by the preparers and users of financial information.

In Part 2 you will gain an understanding of generally accepted accounting principles and financial reporting standards. You will also become familiar with the application of accounting principles and procedures to the operations of partnerships and corporations.

NEW TERMS

Conservatism principle ▪ Consistency principle ▪ Cost basis ▪ Full disclosure principle ▪ Going concern assumption ▪ Historical cost ▪ Matching principle ▪ Materiality principle ▪ Objectivity assumption ▪ Periodicity of income assumption ▪ Qualitative characteristics ▪ Realization principle ▪ Separate entity assumption ▪ Stable monetary unit assumption

THE NEED FOR GENERALLY ACCEPTED ACCOUNTING PRINCIPLES

In a sole proprietorship, adherence to proper accounting rules is important even though the owner is usually deeply involved in the firm's activities and is the person primarily interested in its financial affairs. However, creditors, suppliers, and others must also be able to rely on the financial statements prepared for a sole proprietorship. When the business is a partnership or a corporation, it is even more important that operations be properly accounted for because owners are unlikely to be intimately involved in the activities of the firm. Generally accepted accounting principles make financial statements meaningful and useful, regardless of the type of business organization.

The various needs for reliable financial information can be satisfied only if there are rules, procedures, and principles of accounting that are generally accepted and used. If each company made up its own rules, there could be no basis for comparing the earnings and financial position of different firms. Even the records and reports of a particular company could not be compared for different periods unless accounting principles were applied consistently. In addition, users of financial statements would probably be misinformed and misled.

This chapter discusses generally accepted accounting principles (GAAP) and the basic assumptions and modifying conventions that underlie them. In addition, the chapter describes how accounting principles are developed and put into use. Later chapters examine in detail the application of generally accepted accounting principles.

THE DEVELOPMENT OF GENERALLY ACCEPTED ACCOUNTING PRINCIPLES

OBJECTIVE 1
Describe the process used to develop generally accepted accounting principles.

Many of today's accounting principles were developed over a period of years in response to the changing needs for business reports. The process has worked very much like this: A particular procedure is devised by an accountant as a solution to a specific problem. Then other accountants find the procedure suitable for their problems and start to use it. Eventually the procedure may become widely used and may be recognized by professional accountants, accounting writers, and organizations that are responsible for developing generally accepted accounting principles. Other accounting principles have resulted from a decision by an authoritative, rule-making body to select one of several alternative methods being used in practice. In other cases, rule-making bodies have developed standards on the basis of logic or deductive reasoning because no clearly defined practices were being used to account for certain types of transactions or events.

Accounting principles, or standards, that have "authoritative support" in this country are developed through a cooperative effort between the private (business) sector and the public (governmental) sector of the economy. Currently the main bodies involved are the Securities and Exchange Commission (SEC) in the public sector and the Financial Accounting Standards Board (FASB) in the private sector.

The Securities and Exchange Commission

In 1934 the Securities and Exchange Commission was set up to administer the Securities Act of 1933 and the Securities Exchange Act of 1934. Among other powers, the SEC has authority to define accounting terms and to prescribe accounting principles. The SEC also determines the form and content of accounting reports filed by companies under its jurisdiction. Since all publicly held companies (those whose stocks are traded in the organized securities markets) and all companies with more than a specified number of shareholders or owners are subject to SEC regulations, the SEC is a dominant force in accounting. Historically, however, the SEC has used these powers rather sparingly, preferring to let the accounting profession develop acceptable accounting principles and financial reporting standards.

The Financial Accounting Standards Board

The Financial Accounting Standards Board resulted from efforts by the private sector, especially the American Institute of Certified Public Accountants (AICPA), to develop an organization responsible for formulating financial accounting standards. In 1972 the AICPA, the American Accounting Association, the National Association of Accountants, the Financial Executives Institute, and the Financial Analysts Federation jointly established the Financial Accounting Standards Board (FASB). The FASB is responsible for developing financial accounting standards and principles. By having groups other than the AICPA involved, the organizations that formed the FASB hoped that its rulings would have wide support in the economy.

The FASB receives its funding from the Financial Accounting Foundation, whose trustees are chosen by the member organizations. These trustees are responsible for general oversight of the foundation and for securing financial support through contributions from the private sector. No governmental funds are used. More important, the trustees select the seven members of the Financial Accounting Standards Board. The board members, who develop and issue accounting pronouncements, are full-time employees who generally have distinguished accounting backgrounds.

The authoritative pronouncements of the FASB are known as *Statements of Financial Accounting Standards.* To date, the FASB has issued over 100 statements. As previously pointed out, the Securities and Exchange Commission recognizes these pronouncements as authoritative. The AICPA gives these statements additional support by requiring that its members make sure that the companies whose statements they audit follow the accounting and reporting standards specified in the FASB statements. Any departures from these standards must be justified. Thus the pronouncements of the FASB automatically become generally accepted accounting principles.

One of the FASB's most important current projects is the "conceptual framework project." Its aim is to develop a series of documents that will provide a theoretical framework for financial accounting. These documents will, among other things, perform the following functions.

1. Define the objectives of accounting.
2. Identify users of financial reports and the uses made of these reports.
3. Develop the best possible definition of financial elements such as assets, liabilities, revenues, and expenses.
4. Establish the form and content of financial statements.
5. Develop measurement standards for income and other items.

The documents produced by the conceptual framework project should lead to more logical and concise accounting principles and reporting standards.

To some extent, the conceptual framework project reflects the suggestion by a number of accountants that accounting principles should be arrived at deductively. This means that rules should be based on observations of the general needs and uses of financial accounting. The following steps might be involved in the deductive process.

- *Step 1:* Identify the users of financial reports.
- *Step 2:* Define what uses are made of financial reports.
- *Step 3:* Determine what kinds of accounting information best serve these uses.
- *Step 4:* Define basic assumptions about the society in which business exists and about the nature of business activities and functions.
- *Step 5:* Develop broad principles, standards, or guides for providing the information needed, based on the assumptions that have been made.
- *Step 6:* Develop detailed rules and procedures for implementing the broad principles.

Although completion of the conceptual framework project is expected to require several years, much of the work has been done. Later in this chapter we shall examine the conclusions that have been reached about the identity of the users of financial reports, the uses made of these reports, the objectives of the reports, the types of information that best serve the needs of the users, and the qualitative characteristics of financial reports.

Other Organizations

Other organizations have also played an important role in developing accounting principles. The American Accounting Association is one such group. About half the members of the association are teachers of accounting, and a number of them have written textbooks and articles dealing with accounting principles. Thus, in a variety of ways, the association has been able to stimulate the acceptance of the principles it has developed and perfected over the years.

As early as 1900, the New York Stock Exchange began requiring corporations whose stock and bonds it listed to publish annual reports. Later, quarterly reports were required, and in 1933 the Exchange insisted upon independent audits for all corporations that applied to have their securities listed.

Federal and state government regulatory agencies have prescribed detailed systems of accounting for various public utilities, including the railroad industry and the electric power industry. Such agencies are more concerned with regulation, however, than with the development of accounting principles. Similarly, federal income tax requirements have had an impact on financial accounting even though it is not usually necessary that financial accounting practices and tax accounting practices be the same.

USERS AND USES OF FINANCIAL REPORTS

Financial reports provide information that is important to many different users. However, because some of these users, such as management, tax authorities, and regulatory agencies, have access to the specific information they need from the firm's records, the FASB has concluded that financial reporting rules should concentrate on providing information that is helpful to present and potential investors and creditors in making investment and credit decisions.

In its conceptual framework project, the FASB has also concluded that the information investors and creditors need is information that will help them assess the likelihood of receiving a future cash flow, the amount of such a cash flow, and the time when the cash flow may be received. This conclusion is based on the idea that investors and creditors expect to receive a cash flow directly or indirectly from the business entity, either through the distribution of the company's earnings or through the disposal of their interests for cash. Thus financial report users look for information about profits and about the firm's economic resources (its assets), the claims against those assets (liabilities and owner's equity), and the changes in those assets and in the claims against them. Of course, information about profits appears on the income statement, and information about assets, liabilities, and owner's equity is provided by the balance sheet. Certain analyses of the financial statements also supply meaningful data about the results of operations and the financial condition of a business. The analysis of financial statements is discussed in Chapters 23 and 24 of this textbook.

SELF-REVIEW

1. How do accounting principles originate?
2. Explain the role of the Securities and Exchange Commission (SEC) in developing accounting principles.
3. What are *Statements of Financial Accounting Standards?*
4. Why was the Financial Accounting Standards Board (FASB) formed?
5. Describe the organization of which the FASB is a part.

Answers to Self-Review

1. Many accounting principles are developed over a period of time. When a procedure that is devised to solve a particular problem becomes widely used in the accounting profession, eventually it becomes a generally accepted accounting principle. Other principles result from a decision or selection by a rule-making body.
2. The SEC has the authority to define accounting terms and to prescribe accounting principles. However, it has historically used these procedures sparingly.
3. Issued by the FASB, *Statements of Financial Accounting Standards* are authoritative guidelines for maintaining accounting records.
4. The Financial Accounting Standards Board (FASB) was formed by a number of groups in the private sector to develop financial accounting standards and procedures.
5. The Financial Accounting Foundation, of which the FASB is part, is composed of trustees who are responsible for the general oversight of the foundation, for securing financial support through contributions from the private sector, and for selecting the seven members of the FASB.

THE PRESENT FRAMEWORK OF ACCOUNTING PRINCIPLES

OBJECTIVE 2
Identify, assess, and apply the assumptions that underlie current accounting principles and procedures and the modifying conventions that may alter their application.

The rules of accounting that you have already learned and that you will study in the remaining chapters of this textbook are embodied in what is known today as the **historical-cost** framework of accounting. There are a number of ideas underlying this framework. Some refer to all of these ideas as accounting principles; others refer to them as accounting concepts. The exact term one uses for them is immaterial; the ideas involved are the important elements. For the convenience of discussion, we shall separate the ideas into four categories: (1) qualitative characteristics of financial reports, (2) underlying assumptions, (3) general principles, and (4) modifying conventions.

Qualitative Characteristics of Financial Reports

The FASB has concluded that the information given in financial statements should have several **qualitative characteristics.**

Usefulness

Financial information must be useful to statement readers; otherwise, there is no reason to include it. Usefulness is a rather broad and all-inclusive term and embraces most of the other qualitative characteristics described here.

Relevance

The information shown in the statements must be appropriate for, and have a bearing on, decisions to be made by users of that information.

Reliability

The information shown in the statements must be dependable, that is, free from error and also free from any bias on the part of the preparer.

Verifiability

Financial information is said to be verifiable if it can be reviewed by individuals outside the company who arrive at the same conclusions as the preparers of the statements. Verifiability usually implies that documents such as checks, invoices, and contracts provide supporting evidence for the statements and are available for examination.

Neutrality

The information shown in the statements should not favor one group of users over another group. It should be prepared in such a way that it is helpful to all groups.

Understandability

The information must be presented in a manner that is clear and understandable by readers. However, in preparing financial statements, it is assumed that users have a basic knowledge of business and economics and that they will devote an appropriate amount of time to studying and analyzing the statements.

Timeliness

Financial information covering an accounting period must be presented quickly enough to be useful in making related decisions.

Comparability

The financial statements for a company must be prepared on a basis that permits comparison with the financial statements of other firms and also with similar data of the company for other periods.

Completeness

Financial statements are considered complete if all information that would have a material impact on the decisions of users is presented. The key word in this requirement is "material" since financial statements cannot include every item of information about a company because the cost would be prohibitive and some of the data would not be relevant.

Underlying Assumptions

In applying the present body of accounting theory, accountants have used several assumptions about the economy, business enterprises, and business activities that make accounting principles meaningful. We will refer to these assumptions as (1) the separate entity assumption, (2) the going concern assumption, (3) the stable monetary unit assumption, (4) the objectivity assumption, and (5) the periodicity of income assumption.

Separate Entity Assumption

Accounting records are kept for a particular business organization. The **separate entity** concept assumes that the firm is separate from other businesses and even separate from its owners and creditors. Transactions are recorded in relation to their effects on the business entity. Financial statements summarize these effects for owners, managers, and others. The accounting equation (Assets equal Liabilities plus Owner's Equity) expresses the concept concisely.

It is easy to understand the difference between the business entity and its owners in the case of a corporation such as General Motors because the accounting concept of separation agrees with the legal facts. However, the separate entity concept in accounting applies equally to a sole proprietorship or a partnership, even though owners of these types of businesses are legally liable for all debts of the business and for actions carried out on behalf of the business.

Going Concern Assumption

When periodic financial reports are prepared for a business, it is generally assumed that the firm is a **going concern** and will continue to operate indefinitely. This assumption permits carrying forward a portion of the cost of assets that will be used in future periods or recognizing revenue that will be earned in the future.

Stable Monetary Unit Assumption

Accounting records are kept in terms of money, or a **stable monetary unit.** It is convenient for accountants to assume that the value of money is stable or that changes in its value are not great enough to affect the recorded financial data. The costs of assets purchased many years ago are therefore added to the costs of assets recently purchased, and a total dollar amount is reported.

As a matter of fact, the value of money has changed substantially in recent years. For this reason, many people have questioned the validity of the assumption that money is a stable measure of value. Until recently, however, accounting organizations have been reluctant to recognize changes in the value of the dollar. In the past few years, research committees of the American Accounting Association and a research study sponsored by the American Institute of Certified Public Accountants have suggested that this problem should be recognized and perhaps be reflected in the financial statements or in supplementary statements. In addition, the FASB and the SEC suggest that certain larger companies disclose the impact that price-level changes would have on their financial statements.

Objectivity Assumption

Users of financial reports have a right to expect that the statements are **objective**—that they are unbiased and fair to all parties. In addition, users are entitled to assume that the statements are based on verifiable evidence rather than on opinions. In accounting this is taken to mean that two competent accountants who look at the same evidence would arrive at the same conclusion. However, the concepts of objectivity and verifiability do not eliminate the factor of judgment from accounting. For example, estimates of the useful lives of plant and equipment, selection of depreciation methods, and estimates of salvage value are all largely subjective decisions. These decisions affect the computation of depreciation expense for each fiscal period. Subjective judgments must also be made in many other cases.

Periodicity of Income Assumption

The concept that income should be reported by certain time periods refers to the **periodicity of income.** Accountants realize that the final and correct results of a firm's operations cannot actually be determined until the business has ceased to exist. Only when all assets have been sold and all liabilities settled is it known for certain what is left for the owners and whether they have experienced a gain or a loss. However, owners, managers, and others need some idea of operating results at short intervals. Accountants must therefore have techniques for interim determination of values so that financial statements can be prepared at least yearly for all businesses and as often as monthly for many firms. The accrual basis of accounting is widely used because it allows accountants to provide financial information for each year or other fiscal period.

If yearly statements (or statements prepared at other intervals during the life of the business) are to have validity, it must be assumed that the nature of a firm's activities is such that they do, in fact, lend themselves to reasonable periodic income determination.

General Principles

In deciding how a transaction should be recorded and how its effects should be reported on the financial statements, accountants must keep in mind several basic accounting principles or concepts that serve as guides.

Cost Basis Principle

Business transactions are, almost without exception, recorded on a **cost basis,** which is the amount of money determined through dealings in the market between the business and outsiders. Assets are carried at cost until they are used. At that time the cost (or an appropriate part of it) is charged against revenue. Cost is preferred to some possible alternatives, such as appraisal value, because cost, when determined in an "arm's length" transaction (a transaction with outsiders), is an objective, verifiable measure of economic value. In recent years the cost principle has come under severe criticism. Many people have pointed out that the increased rate of inflation throughout the world makes original costs meaningless. Both the FASB and the SEC have recognized this problem by encouraging certain large companies to disclose the impact of inflation on their financial statements.

Realization Principle

Since accounting reports today focus on the measurement of income for the fiscal period, one critical problem is the determination of the period in which to record revenue and to report it on the income statement. Revenue represents the inflow of new assets resulting from the sale of goods or services. Thus, as a general rule, revenue is recognized when a sale is made or a service is provided to an outsider. The **realization** of revenue occurs at the time new assets are created in the form of money or in claims against others. Thus accountants usually say that revenue should not be recognized until it has been realized.

The realization principle has been the subject of much criticism. For example, it is argued by many people, including some accountants, that if a company owns shares of stock in another corporation and those shares are traded on a stock exchange, the quoted market value of the stock should be recorded in the accounts and any increase in value should be recognized as income. However, under the realization principle, no income is recognized until the increase is realized through sale or exchange. However, a decrease in value might be recognized under our present accounting principles.

The argument usually given for insistence on the realization principle is that an increase in value might be eliminated by a later decrease in value before the asset is sold. Also, the realization principle ensures that objective, verifiable evidence underlies the accounting records.

There have been and still are a number of important exceptions to the general rule that revenue is recognized at the time of sale. One exception, which existed prior to 1988 for tax purposes, involved accounting for installment sales. Under this method the difference between the price of merchandise sold on the installment plan and the cost of the merchandise was credited to a deferred income account at the time of sale. Part of the deferred income was recognized as revenue whenever a collection was made on the installment account receivable. Use of this method was proper when it was not possible to estimate losses from defaults on installments. The Revenue Act of 1987 generally repealed use of the installment method to account for sales of property by dealers made after December 31, 1987.

Another exception to the realization principle that is interesting, but seldom encountered, involves commodities for which there is an assured price and few costs to be incurred in getting the items to market. In this case the revenue may be recognized at the time the commodity is produced. The best example of the recording of revenue when production is completed has historically been in connection with the mining of gold. For many years in this country, gold had a guaranteed market at a fixed price with few after-production costs. Thus the immediate recognition of revenue at the time of production was justified.

Still another, and more complex, exception to the realization principle for reporting revenue is the percentage-of-completion basis for measuring income on long-term construction contracts. For example, a contractor may build a bridge that requires three years to complete. It is not logical to wait until the bridge is entirely finished and report all income in the year of completion. Instead, each year a portion of the estimated profit may be recorded as earned. The profit recorded is based on the portion of the estimated total costs for the project incurred during that year.

Other businesses, especially service firms such as those operated by physicians, attorneys, and accountants, record revenues only when cash is received because of high losses on the outstanding bills owed by patients or clients.

By far the greatest number of businesses follow the general rule that revenue is recognized at the time a sale is made, rather than when cash from the sale is actually received.

Principle of Matching Costs with Revenue

If income is to be properly measured, revenues must be matched against the expired costs incurred in earning those revenues. This concept is referred to as the **matching principle.** To achieve matching, the accountant seeks systematic, rational approaches for determining the period in which costs should be charged against revenues.

Some costs, such as manufacturing costs, can easily be identified with specific products. It is customary to treat these costs as inventory costs and to charge them to cost of goods sold when the products are sold. Other costs, such as office salaries, do not clearly benefit future periods and are charged as expenses when they are incurred. Still other costs benefit many future periods. The accountant therefore seeks to estimate the periods benefitted and to charge the costs as expenses during the periods involved. For example, the cost of a store building is depreciated over its estimated useful life.

Many of the controversial questions in accounting involve determining the period or periods in which a cost should be charged as an expense.

Accrual Principle

Inherent in the realization principle and the matching principle is the *accrual principle,* which you learned about in earlier chapters. As you

Information Block: Communication

Positive or Neutral Messages

To plan and develop effective business communication, business professionals must consider not only the actual message but also the receiver's anticipated reaction to the message. The four reactions that receivers may have to any oral or written message are:

- **Positive.** Positive reactions result when a receiver is happy with a message. Examples of positive messages include a congratulatory message, an invitation, an announcement, or an order.
- **Neutral.** Neutral reactions result when a receiver is neither happy nor unhappy with a message. Examples of neutral messages include an inquiry or a response to an inquiry.
- **Negative.** Negative reactions result when a receiver is definitely unhappy with a message. Examples of negative messages include bad news or a refusal for credit.
- **Mixed.** Mixed reactions result when a receiver is positive or neutral with part of a message and negative with another part. Examples of mixed messages may include sales messages, collection messages, or other messages where a degree of persuasion is necessary.

As you learned in the steps for planning and developing effective communication, your analysis of the receiver will influence the details of your message, your word choice, and your approach. This project fo-

saw in Part 1, sometimes a transaction occurs in one period but the cash involved is not received or paid out until a later period. Under the accrual principle, transactions are recorded in the period in which they occur, rather than in the period when the cash inflow or outflow takes place. For example, suppose that employees work in December but are not paid until January of the following year. Their earnings should be recorded as an expense in December, and the amount owed to them at the end of December should be shown as a liability on the December 31 balance sheet. Similarly, if a firm purchases office supplies in December and uses only a portion of them in that month, the cost should be allocated so that the part used is treated as an expense and the part still on hand is reported as an asset.

Consistency Principle

The **consistency principle** requires that the application of a given accounting procedure be the same from one period to the next in a

cuses on the approach or plan of positive and neutral messages. Later projects focus on negative and persuasive messages.

When an oral or written message will result in a positive or neutral reaction, receivers want to know the news immediately. Therefore, to be effective in positive communication situations, use a direct approach to communicating your message.

1. *Begin with the positive or neutral news.* In a positive/neutral message, your objective is generally the news. Your news is most appropriate in the first sentence or paragraph.
2. *Provide details and explanations.* Your supporting information will provide the receiver with the necessary details or explanations to clearly understand the news. The number of paragraphs may vary from one to three or more, depending on the nature of the news.
3. *Close with a positive statement.* Always end a message with a positive, yet relevant, statement or paragraph. When appropriate, encourage action from the receiver.

Use this plan for positive/neutral messages to achieve your objective in positive/neutral communication situations.

Project: Assume you are interested in securing employment or an internship with a mid- to large-sized company. You want to obtain background information about the company and its overall financial standing before you express interest in employment. Write a letter to the Human Resources Manager asking for a copy of the company's latest annual report. Remember to follow the steps for planning and developing effective business communication and the plan for positive/neutral messages.

particular company. Any lack of consistency would result in financial reports that are not comparable with earlier reports and are therefore misleading.

However, the consistency rule does not mean that no changes in accounting principles or methods can be made. If the application of another accounting method would clearly give a fairer presentation of earnings or financial position, it is proper to change to the new method. Detailed rules have been developed for reporting the effects of the change so that statement users are completely informed.

Full Disclosure Principle

Full disclosure requires that all information that might affect the statement user's interpretation of the profitability and financial position of a business must be disclosed in the business's financial statements or in footnotes to the statements. In recent years there have been numerous lawsuits by statement users against certified public accountants and against companies issuing financial statements.

The lawsuits have charged that the statements of these companies did not disclose facts that would have influenced investor decisions. As a result, accountants are careful to include enough information so that the informed reader can obtain a complete and accurate picture. The financial reports issued by large companies usually include a thorough explanation of the accounting principles and methods that have been used in preparing the statements. The SEC has long maintained that the key element of financial reporting is full disclosure.

Modifying Conventions

Although the basic accounting principles and underlying assumptions provide a means for analyzing each business transaction to determine its proper treatment in the accounts, a number of practical considerations have come to be accepted as limiting or modifying the application of the general principles. Among the most important of these modifying conventions are materiality, conservatism, and industry practice.

Materiality

Materiality concerns the significance of an item in relation to the particular situation of which it is a part. An item of a certain dollar amount might be material in a small company and thus would have to be disclosed. However, the same amount might not be significant in a larger firm and could therefore be combined with other figures or be presented in a different manner on the statements.

Although no hard-and-fast rules for judging materiality have been laid down, an item is usually compared with the firm's net income and with total owner's equity in deciding whether it is material. It is generally accepted that a deviation from normal accounting principles is permissible if the amount is immaterial. For example, a business that has sales of $10 million a year might buy a small tool with a useful life of three years for $50. Practicality dictates that this item be charged as an expense rather than recorded as an asset and then depreciated over its useful life. The amount of this transaction is immaterial in such a large business. Although this example is extreme, it indicates the concept involved.

Conservatism

Accountants have long followed a doctrine of **conservatism,** under which assets are understated rather than overstated if any question exists. Recognition of income is deferred until it is realized, and losses and expenses are recognized as soon as they occur.

Although this convention is still basically accepted by most accountants, an increasing number concede that undue conservatism in the present may make for a lack of conservatism in the future. For example, if too much of the cost of an asset is charged as depreciation expense in the present period, the firm's net income will be conservatively reported and the book value of the asset will be conservatively stated. In later years, during which the asset still performs useful service, the depreciation expense will be understated and the net income will be correspondingly overstated, which is not conservative. Increased accuracy of valuation and timing has come to be more important to many accountants than the old-style conservatism.

Industry Practice

Sometimes accounting practices have become acceptable in certain industries although not generally acceptable in other industries. These exceptions are often created because of tax laws, regulatory requirements, or the high risk involved. For example, in the public utility industry, it has been customary for many years to capitalize, as part of asset costs, all interest expense incurred on money borrowed to build a power plant during the period that the plant is being constructed. This practice developed in the public utility industry because interest capitalization is permitted by regulatory agencies for rate-making purposes. The procedure is now required by the FASB for all industries.

THE IMPACT OF ACCOUNTING PRINCIPLES, ASSUMPTIONS, AND MODIFYING CONVENTIONS

Throughout the remainder of this book, you will find many references to accounting principles, assumptions, and modifying conventions. A thorough knowledge of these concepts will help you to understand how individual transactions are accounted for and why they are handled in a specific way. Often businesses encounter new or unusual transactions that give rise to accounting questions that do not appear to have simple solutions. Almost invariably the solutions to these questions will fall back on the concepts discussed in this chapter. Thus an understanding of these concepts is essential to an understanding of complex accounting issues.

MANAGERIAL IMPLICATIONS

Financial statements are of great importance in managerial decision making. Thus management should understand the basic principles that underlie financial statements. Of particular importance in large firms is the need for comparability between statements so that the management of one firm can compare the results of its operations with those of its competitors. Comparisons of this type are made possible only by the existence of a body of basic accounting assumptions, principles, and conventions that are applied by all businesses.

SELF-REVIEW

1. What is the FASB's conceptual framework project? Why is it important?
2. In what way, if any, are the FASB and the SEC related?
3. Whom does the FASB define as the users of financial reports? Why is this important?
4. In this chapter, nine qualitative characteristics of financial reports were discussed. In your opinion, which of these characteristics is most important? Why?
5. Explain what is meant by the cost basis of accounting.

Answers to Self-Review

1. The conceptual framework project consists of the development of a series of documents by the FASB. The project's purpose is to provide a theoretical framework for financial accounting and reporting, which should lead to more logical and concise accounting principles and reporting standards.
2. The FASB and the SEC are related in that both are responsible for accounting standards and principles—the FASB in the private sector and the SEC in the public sector. In general, the SEC relies on the pronouncements made by the FASB.
3. Financial statements provide information to a wide variety of users. However, the FASB feels that financial statements should concentrate on providing useful information to present and potential investors and creditors in making investment and credit decisions. They feel that financial statements are most important for investors and creditors because these groups do not have specific information from the firm's records enjoyed by the other users of the financial statements such as management, tax authorities, and regulatory agencies.
4. Reliability is the most important characteristic of financial reports. The absence of any of the other characteristics would impair any decision to be made on the basis of a report; however, if the information in the report is not reliable, no sound decision can be made.
5. The cost basis of accounting means that business transactions are recorded at cost, that is, for an amount of money. Assets are carried at cost until they are used, at which point all or part of the cost is charged against revenue.

CHAPTER 14 Review and Applications

CHAPTER SUMMARY

Some of the most important ideas underlying accounting are the cost principle, the realization principle, the matching principle, the accrual principle, the consistency principle, and the full disclosure principle. There are also certain assumptions that have an important influence on accounting. These are the separate entity assumption, the going concern assumption, the stable monetary unit assumption, the objectivity assumption, and the periodicity of income assumption.

In order to obtain greater uniformity and improve reliability, accounting organizations, especially the American Institute of Certified Public Accountants, have taken an active role in developing accounting principles. The ever-increasing interest of government, stockholders, analysts, creditors, and economists in financial reports ensures that there will be continuing progress in the search for accounting principles that will make the reports more meaningful and reliable. Never in the history of accounting has there been such a large and diverse group interested in accounting principles and financial reporting standards. This has led to the formation of the Financial Accounting Standards Board, a private-sector group whose specific task is the development of accounting principles and financial reporting standards. In addition, the federal government plays a role in these matters through the Securities and Exchange Commission, which is the government agency responsible for the reporting standards used by publicly held corporations.

GLOSSARY OF NEW TERMS

Conservatism principle (p. 512) The concept that assets should be understated rather than overstated if any question exists

Consistency principle (p. 510) The concept that applications of accounting procedures should be the same from one period to the next in a particular company

Cost basis (p. 507) The principle that requires assets to be recorded at their original cost

Full disclosure principle (p. 511) All information that might affect the statement user's interpretation of the profitability and financial position of a business must be included in its financial statements

Going concern assumption (p. 506) The assumption that a firm will continue to operate in the future

Historical cost (p. 504) See Cost basis

Matching principle (p. 509) The concept that revenues must be matched against the expired costs incurred in earning those revenues

Materiality principle (p. 512) The significance of an item in relation to the particular situation of which it is a part

Objectivity assumption (p. 507) The idea that financial reports are unbiased and fair to all parties

Periodicity of income assumption (p. 507) The concept that income should be reported by certain time periods

Qualitative characteristics (p. 504) Traits necessary for credible financial statements—usefulness, relevance, reliability, verifiability, neutrality, understandability, timeliness, comparability, and completeness

Realization principle (p. 508) The concept that revenue occurs, and is recorded, at the time new assets are created in the form of money or in claims against others

Separate entity assumption (p. 506) The concept that a firm is separate from other businesses and from its owners and creditors

Stable monetary unit assumption (p. 506) The concept that accounting records are kept in terms of money that is assumed not to fluctuate in value

REVIEW QUESTIONS

1. What is the major strength of, or argument for, the cost basis of accounting?
2. Define realization. Why is the realization concept used?
3. Name three alternatives to the cost basis of accounting.
4. Explain the matching concept.
5. Why is the accrual basis generally the basis required for measuring income?
6. Explain the separate entity assumption.
7. What is the going concern assumption? Explain how this assumption is important to the cost basis of accounting.
8. Is the assumption of a stable monetary unit valid? If not, why is it still used?
9. What is meant by periodicity of income?
10. How does the materiality convention affect day-to-day accounting?
11. What is the conservatism convention? What potential problems are created by this convention?

MANAGERIAL FOCUS

1. Why must management understand the principles, conventions, and assumptions underlying a firm's financial statements?
2. How can the element of personal judgment, which is involved in such matters as selection of depreciation methods and estimates of salvage value and useful life, be minimized to preserve the objectivity of an accounting system?
3. Why might management argue that the historical-cost framework should be abandoned?
4. The management of a firm suggests that all financial statements of debtors report "the current value of assets." What objection do you see to this procedure? What benefits do you see in this procedure?
5. Suppose you are employed as an accountant. An officer of the firm where you work asks why you use generally accepted accounting principles and where these rules come from. Explain the sources of generally accepted accounting principles and the reasons for using them.

EXERCISES

EXERCISE 14–1
(Obj. 2)
Tutorial

Applying various accounting principles and concepts. In each of the cases listed below, respond to the question asked and indicate the accounting principle or concept that applies.

1. The Briggs Corporation paid insurance premiums of $9,000 on December 1, 19X3. These premiums covered a three-year period beginning on that date. What amount should the corporation show as insurance expense for the year 19X3? What accounting principles, conventions, or assumptions support your answer?
2. The Gallo Construction Company signed a contract with a customer on July 1, 19X4. The contract called for the construction of a new building to begin on or before December 31, 19X4, and to be completed by December 31, 19X5. The contract price was $1.6 million, and Gallo estimated that the building would cost $1 million. No work was begun in 19X4. How much income from the project should Gallo report in 19X4? Why?
3. George Mendez buys and sells real estate. On December 31, 19X3, his inventory of property included a tract of undeveloped land for which he had paid $450,000. The fair market value of the land was $600,000 at that date. How much income should Mendez report for 19X3 in connection with this land? Why?

EXERCISE 14–2
(Obj. 2)
Tutorial

Applying various accounting principles and concepts. In each of the cases that follow, respond to the question asked and indicate the accounting principle or concept that applies.

1. The Taylor Company purchased several hundred small tools during 19X3 at a total cost of $2,100. Some of the tools were expected to last for a few weeks, some for several months, and some for several years. Taylor's income for 19X3 will be about $1.5 million. How should Taylor account for the small tools in order to be theoretically correct? As a practical matter, how should Taylor account for these tools? Why?
2. Leo Stern is the sole proprietor of a hardware store. Stern's accountant insists that he keep a detailed record of all amounts of money and merchandise that he takes out of the business for his personal use. Why?
3. At the end of each fiscal period, the accountant for the Marlow Company requires that a careful inventory be made of the office supplies and that the amount on hand be reported as an asset and the amount used during the period be reported as an expense. Why?

EXERCISE 14–3
(Obj. 2)

Tutorial

Applying various accounting principles and concepts. In each of the cases listed below, respond to the question asked and indicate the accounting principle or concept that applies.

1. Three years ago the O'Brien Company purchased a machine for $100,000. The machine is expected to have no salvage value. Nevertheless, O'Brien continues to keep the asset's cost in its accounting records and to depreciate the asset over its 10-year useful life, which will include the next seven years. Why?
2. On January 14 of last year, the Carlson Company purchased some land for $20,000 on which it planned to construct an office building. At the end of the year, the land had increased in value to $26,000. Nevertheless, Carlson recognized no income as a result of the increase in value. Why?
3. The Van Ness Company has decided to charge off as a loss a portion of its accounts receivable that it estimates will be uncollectible. The accounts involved resulted from the current year's sales. What is the reason for this practice?

EXERCISE 14–4
(Obj. 2)

Applying various accounting principles and concepts. In each of the cases listed below, respond to the question asked and indicate the accounting principle or concept that applies.

1. The Hudson Company charges off the cost of all newspaper advertising in the year it is incurred even though the advertising probably results in some sales in later years. Why?
2. The Goldberg Company's net income is about $1 million a year. The company follows the practice of charging to expense all property insurance premiums when paid. Last year approximately $1,200 of these premiums represented amounts applicable to future years. What is the reason for this practice?
3. The Stanley Corporation charges all of its research and development costs to expense when incurred. Why?

EXERCISE 14-5
(Obj. 2)

Tutorial

Applying various accounting principles and concepts. The DeMaio Company sells refrigerators. It grants all customers a 12-month warranty, agreeing to make necessary repairs within the following 12-month period free of charge. At the end of each year, the company estimates the total cost to be incurred during the next period under the warranties for appliances sold during the current period and charges that amount to expense, crediting a liability account. Why?

EXERCISE 14-6
(Obj. 2)

Applying various accounting principles and concepts. At the end of last year, the Stewart Corporation was engaged in defending itself against several major lawsuits. If any of these lawsuits is lost, it would cause a major financial hardship for the corporation. The auditors insisted that the corporation include some discussion of the lawsuits in footnotes to its financial reports. Why?

PROBLEMS

PROBLEM SET A

PROBLEM 14-1A
(Obj. 2)

Tutorial

Applying various accounting principles and concepts. The accounting treatment or statement presentation of various items is discussed below. The items pertain to different businesses and are unrelated.

Instructions

Indicate in each case whether the item has been handled in accordance with generally accepted accounting principles. If so, indicate which of the basic concepts has been followed. If not, indicate which concept has been violated and tell how the item should have been recorded or presented.

1. Included on the balance sheet of the Swift Cleaning Shop is the personal automobile of Martin Webb, the owner.
2. The Fitzgerald Manufacturing Company makes furniture. The cost of a particular chair is $35. However, when the inventory figures are computed for the balance sheet, the amount used for this chair is $68, the normal selling price.
3. On December 1, 19X4, the Ridge Mining Company purchased some highly specialized, custom-made equipment for $400,000. Since the equipment is of no use to anyone else and has no resale value, it is shown on the December 31, 19X4, balance sheet at $1.
4. On December 31, 19X3, the Canfield Corporation valued its inventory according to an acceptable accounting method. On December 31, 19X4, the inventory was valued by a different but also acceptable method, and on December 31, 19X5, the inventory was valued by the method that was used in 19X3.
5. Each year the Evergreen Company values its investments in land at the current market price.
6. In 19X3 the Lomax Corporation had sales of $8 million, all on credit. Statistics of the company for prior years show that losses

from uncollectible accounts are equal to about 1 percent of sales each year. However, the Lomax Corporation charges off part of its accounts receivable as a loss only when a specific account is found to be uncollectible.

7. The Sanders Company owns office equipment that was purchased seven years ago. It is still carried in the firm's accounting records at the original cost. No depreciation has ever been taken on the equipment.

PROBLEM 14–2A (Obj. 2)

Reconstructing an income statement to reflect proper accounting principles. The income statement shown below was sent by Susan Curtis, the owner of Curtis Audio Center, to several of her creditors who had asked for financial statements. The business is a sole proprietorship that sells record players, tape decks, speakers, and other audio equipment. An accountant for one of the creditors looked over the income statement and found that it did not conform to generally accepted accounting principles.

Instructions

Prepare an income statement in accordance with generally accepted accounting principles.

CURTIS AUDIO CENTER
Income Statement
Year Ended December 31, 19X3

Cash Collected from Customers		$460,000
Cost of Goods Sold		
Merchandise Inventory, Jan. 1	$ 50,000	
Payments to Suppliers	290,000	
	$340,000	
Less Merchandise Inventory, Dec. 31	55,000	
Cost of Goods Sold		285,000
Gross Profit on Sales		$175,000
Operating Expenses		
Salary to Owner	$ 18,000	
Salaries to Employees	54,000	
Depreciation Expense	17,500	
Income Tax of Owner	12,200	
Payroll Taxes Expense	8,800	
Advertising and Other Selling Expenses	15,000	
Repairs Expense	6,000	
Office Expense	18,000	
Insurance Expense	3,000	
Interest Expense	8,000	
Utility and Telephone Expense	6,000	
Legal and Audit Expenses	2,000	
Miscellaneous Expense	19,000	
Total Expenses		187,500
Net Income from Operations		($12,500)
Increase in Appraised Value of Land During Year		10,000
Net Loss		($ 2,500)

The following additional information was made available by Curtis.

a. On December 31, 19X3, accounts receivable from customers totaled $22,000. On January 1, 19X3, the receivables totaled $18,000.
b. No effort has been made to charge off worthless accounts. An analysis shows that $900 of the accounts receivable on December 31, 19X3, will never be collected.
c. The beginning and ending merchandise inventories were valued at their estimated selling price. The actual cost of the ending inventory is estimated to be $33,000, and the actual cost of the beginning inventory is estimated at $30,000.
d. On December 31, 19X3, suppliers of merchandise were owed $29,000, while on January 1, 19X3, these debts were $26,000.
e. The owner paid herself a salary of $1,500 per month from the business's funds and charged this amount to an account called Salary to Owner.
f. The owner also withdrew cash from the firm's bank account to pay herself $5,000 interest on her capital investment. This amount was charged to Interest Expense.
g. A check for $12,200 to cover the owner's personal income tax for the previous year was issued from the firm's bank account.
h. Depreciation on assets was computed at 10 percent of the gross profit. An analysis of assets showed that the original cost of the equipment and fixtures totaled $40,000. Their estimated useful life is 10 years with no salvage value. The building had a cost of $75,000. Its useful life is expected to be 25 years with no salvage value.
i. Included in Repairs Expense was a $3,000 payment on December 22 for a new parking lot.
j. The increase in land value was based on an appraisal by a qualified real estate appraiser.

PROBLEM 14–3A
(Obj. 2)

Tutorial

Reconstructing a balance sheet to reflect proper accounting principles. John Johnson owns a small retail store. He recently approached the local bank for a loan to finance a planned expansion of his store. Johnson prepared and submitted the balance sheet shown at the top of page 522 to the bank's loan officer in support of his loan application.

Instructions

1. Identify any errors in the balance sheet and explain why they should be considered errors.
2. Prepare a corrected balance sheet in accordance with generally accepted accounting principles.

The following additional information was made available by John Johnson.

a. The inventory has an original cost of $50,000. It is listed in the balance sheet at what it would cost to purchase today.

JOHNSON'S RETAIL CENTER
Balance Sheet
December 31, 19X4

Assets	
Cash	$ 5,000
Accounts Receivable	16,000
Inventory	56,000
Equipment	10,000
Personal Residence	240,000
Supplies	3,000
Family Auto	10,000
Total Assets	$350,000
Liabilities and Owner's Equity	
Accounts Payable	$ 10,000
Note Payable on Family Car	5,000
Mortgage on House	160,000
John Johnson, Capital	175,000
Total Liabilities and Owner's Equity	$350,000

b. Included in the cash listed on the balance sheet is $2,000 in John Johnson's personal account. The remainder of the cash is in the store's account.

c. The store has a delivery truck that it recently purchased for $20,000. The truck was financed through a bank loan and the bank has legal title to the truck. To date, the store has paid $4,000 on the loan. Of the remaining $16,000 liability, $2,000 is current and the remainder long-term. John did not include the truck or the liability on the balance sheet because it is not owned by either himself or the business.

d. Depreciation allowable to date is $2,000 on the equipment and $1,000 on the truck.

PROBLEM 14–4A (Obj. 2)

Applying various accounting principles and concepts. For each of the situations below, identify the accounting principle that has been violated and explain the nature of the violation.

1. Wilson Builders does not have sufficient current assets for a much-needed loan. Therefore, the company included among its current assets the personal savings account of its owner, James Wilson, since the owner is willing to invest additional cash in the business if necessary.
2. First City Bank incurred large losses on uncollectible oil company loans. On average, these loans call for payments to be received over a period of five years. Therefore, First City Bank is amortizing its losses from the uncollectible oil company loans against the revenue that will be earned over this five-year period.

3. *Phantom of the Opera,* a Broadway play, has sold out in advance for the next two years. These ticket sales were recognized as revenue at the time cash was received from the customers.
4. Upward Bound Investment Service has been sued by clients for engaging in illegal securities transactions. No mention of this lawsuit is included in the company's financial statements, since the suit has not been settled and the company cannot objectively estimate the extent of its liability.
5. Jason Company sold for $300,000 land that was purchased 15 years ago for $75,000. The general price level doubled during this period, so Jason Company restated the cost of the land at $150,000 and recognized a $150,000 gain on the sale of the land.
6. In recent years City Savings Bank has enjoyed increased prosperity due to wise investments and conservative loan policies. The bank recently increased the carrying value of its assets to market value to make its financial statements more reflective of its success in the industry.

PROBLEM SET B

PROBLEM 14–1B
(Obj. 2)

Tutorial

Applying various accounting principles and concepts. The accounting treatment or statement presentation of various items is discussed below. The items pertain to different businesses and are unrelated.

Instructions

Indicate in each case whether the item has been handled in accordance with generally accepted accounting principles. If so, indicate which of the basic concepts has been followed. If not, indicate which concept has been violated and tell how the item should have been recorded or presented.

1. The Dodd Company manufactured some machinery for its own use at a cost of $45,000. The lowest bid from an outsider was $52,000. The company recorded the machinery at $45,000.
2. At the beginning of the year 19X3, the Elmwood Company bought a building for $100,000. At the end of 19X3, the building's value was appraised at $105,000. Since there was an increase in value, the company did not record depreciation on the building.
3. The balance sheet of the Summit Sporting Goods Store reports prepaid insurance at $300, the cash value of the policy on the date when the statement is prepared. The prepaid insurance consists of the last year of a three-year fire insurance policy that originally cost $1,500.
4. The assets listed in the accounting records of the World Travel Agency include the residence of Gail Sims, the owner of the business.
5. On December 31, 19X3, the accounts receivable of the Anderson Company include $500 owed by Earl Haines, who is in the county jail on charges of passing bad checks. The owner of An-

derson Company writes off the amount because he feels certain that the debt will not be paid, even though Haines insists that he will pay after he gets out of jail and obtains a job.

6. The machinery of the Paragon Manufacturing Company has a depreciated cost of $60,000. However, the machinery could not be sold for more than $25,000 today. The owner thinks that the machinery should nevertheless be reported on the balance sheet at $60,000.
7. The Valley Hotel owns certain land purchased about 40 years ago for $10,000. Elizabeth Ford, the owner, thinks that since the price level today is almost three times the price level at the time the land was purchased, the balance of the account for this asset should be increased to reflect the price level change.

PROBLEM 14–2B
(Obj. 2)

Tutorial

Reconstructing an income statement to reflect proper accounting principles. The income statement shown below was prepared by Gary Morgan, the owner of Morgan's Sand and Surf Shop. The business is a sole proprietorship that sells beachwear, surfboards, and skin-diving equipment. An accountant who looked at the income statement told Morgan that it does not conform to generally accepted accounting principles.

Instructions

Prepare an income statement for Morgan's Sand and Surf Shop in accordance with generally accepted accounting principles.

MORGAN'S SAND AND SURF SHOP
Income Statement
Year Ended December 31, 19X4

Cash Receipts from Customers		$265,000
Cost of Goods Sold		
Merchandise Inventory, Jan. 1	$ 24,000	
Payments to Creditors	200,000	
	$224,000	
Less Merchandise Inventory, Dec. 31	30,000	
Cost of Goods Sold		194,000
Gross Profit on Sales		$ 71,000
Expenses		
Salaries Expense	$ 42,000	
Insurance Expense	1,400	
Payroll Taxes Expense	4,600	
Repairs Expense	1,000	
Supplies and Other Office Expenses	6,000	
Advertising and Other Selling Expenses	10,000	
Utilities Expense	2,000	
Interest Expense	3,000	
Total Expenses		70,000
Net Income from Operations		$ 1,000
Increase in Market Value of Store Equipment		3,200
Net Income for Year		$ 4,200

The following additional information was made available by Morgan.

a. On December 31, 19X4, accounts receivable from customers totaled $15,500. On January 1, 19X4, receivables totaled $20,000.
b. On December 31, 19X4, accounts receivable amounting to $800 were expected to be uncollectible.
c. On December 31, 19X4, accounts payable owed to suppliers were $21,000. On January 1, 19X4, the outstanding accounts payable were $12,000.
d. Included in Salaries Expense is $6,000 that Morgan withdrew for his personal use.
e. Included in Interest Expense is $1,200 that Morgan withdrew as interest on his capital investment.
f. Miscellaneous repairs of $500 were charged to Store Equipment during the year. No new equipment was purchased.
g. Morgan explains that since the estimated value of his store equipment has increased by $3,200 during the year, no depreciation expense was recorded. The store equipment has a total value of $33,000 and a total estimated useful life of 10 years with no salvage value.

PROBLEM 14–3B
(Obj. 2)

Tutorial

Reconstructing a balance sheet to reflect proper accounting principles. Earl Wilson owns Wilson Appliance Center. He recently approached the local bank for a loan to finance a planned expansion of his store. Wilson prepared and submitted the balance sheet below to the bank's loan officer in support of his loan application.

Instructions

1. Identify any errors in the balance sheet and explain why they should be considered errors.
2. Prepare a corrected balance sheet in accordance with generally accepted accounting principles.

WILSON APPLIANCE CENTER
Balance Sheet
December 31, 19X4

Assets	
Cash	$ 10,000
Accounts Receivable	23,000
Inventory	32,000
Equipment	15,000
Building	120,000
Land	5,000
Supplies	3,000
Family Auto	10,000
Total Assets	$218,000
Liabilities and Owner's Equity	
Accounts Payable	$ 10,000
Note Payable on Family Car	8,000
Mortgage on Building	75,000
Earl Wilson, Capital	125,000
Total Liabilities and Owner's Equity	$218,000

The following additional information was made available by Wilson.

a. The inventory has an original cost of $28,000. It is listed in the balance sheet at what it would cost to purchase today.
b. Included in the cash listed on the balance sheet is $4,000 in Earl Wilson's personal account. The remainder of the cash is in the store's account.
c. The store has a delivery truck that it recently purchased for $18,000. The truck was financed through a bank loan and the bank has legal title to the truck. To date, the store has paid $5,000 on the loan. Of the remaining $13,000 liability, $3,000 is current and the remainder is long-term. Earl did not include the truck or the liability on the balance sheet because it is not owned by either himself or the business.
d. The building was recently constructed by Earl at a total cost of $75,000, financed with a mortgage on the building. The current portion of the mortgage liability is $3,000 and the remainder is long-term. The building appears on the balance sheet at the current market value of the building. Allowable depreciation on the building to date is $2,000.
e. Depreciation allowable to date on the equipment is $3,000 and on the truck is $2,000.

PROBLEM 14–4B
(Obj. 2)

Applying various accounting principles and concepts. For each of the situations below, identify the accounting principle or concept that has been violated and explain the nature of the violation. If you believe that the treatment is in accordance with generally accepted accounting principles, state this as your position and defend it.

1. Haden Hardware Company follows the practice of charging the purchase of tools with a unit cost of less than $50 to an expense account rather than to an asset account. The average life of the tools is three years.
2. An airline company does not record depreciation on its aircraft because the company's excellent maintenance program keeps the planes in "as good as new" condition.
3. A real estate developer carries an unsold inventory of houses in its accounting records at estimated sales value rather than cost because the developer believes estimated sales value has greater relevance than cost.
4. A lawsuit filed against a company is described in footnotes to the company's financial statements even though the lawsuit was filed with the court shortly after the company's balance sheet date.
5. Nelson Company sold for $200,000 land that was purchased 15 years ago for $75,000. Even though the general price level had doubled during this period, Nelson Company reported a gain of $125,000 on the sale of the land.
6. In recent years City Department Store has enjoyed increased profits due to customer loyalty because of its excellent reputation

of putting the needs of the customer first. The store recently included an account called Goodwill in its assets to make its financial statements more reflective of its success in the industry and to reflect the true worth of the business. The offsetting credit was made to the owner's equity account.

CHALLENGE PROBLEM

Assume that you are an independent CPA performing audits of financial statements. In the course of your work you encounter the independent situations below. Review each of the situations. If you consider the treatment to be in conformity with generally accepted accounting principles and concepts, explain why. If you do not, explain which principle or concept has been violated and how the situation should have been reported.

1. Holiday Towers Hotel recognizes room rental revenue on the date that a reservation is made. For the summer season, many guests make reservations as far as a year in advance of their intended visit.
2. Discount Department Store spends a substantial sum on advertising for various sales promotions during the year. The owner is sure that the advertising will generate revenue in future periods, but he has no idea of how much revenue will be produced or over what period of time it will be earned. In the current year, $600,000 was paid for advertising and all of this amount was charged as an expense in the current period.
3. Erves Equipment Company has constructed special-purpose equipment designed to build other equipment that will be sold to the public. Due to the special nature of this equipment it has virtually no resale value to any other company. Therefore, Erves has charged the entire cost to construct the equipment, $120,000, to expense in the current period.
4. Slidell Company prepares financial statements four times each year. For convenience, these statements are prepared when business is slow and the accounting staff is not busy with other matters. Last year financial statements were prepared for the three-month period ended March 31, the five-month period ended May 31, the nine-month period ended September 30, and the twelve-month period ended December 31.
5. The liabilities of Haley Construction Company are substantially in excess of the company's assets. In order to present a more impressive picture, Carol Haley, the owner of the company, included in the company's balance sheet such personal assets as her savings account, automobile, and real estate investments.
6. The owner of City Autoplex, a metropolitan auto dealership, depreciates metal wastebaskets over a period of five years.

CRITICAL THINKING PROBLEM

The president of Steel Bearings Company, Jeffrey Monroe, recently attended a Chamber of Commerce luncheon where Joe Forrester, one of the county commissioners, spoke about development of a new airport annex and expansion of the highway providing access to what will be the new entrance to the airport. Commissioner Forrester indicated that he expected an upsurge in commercial development along the highway leading to the expanded airport facilities.

Steel Bearings' plant, which was purchased 20 years ago for $200,000, is located on this highway just two miles from the new airport entrance. As a result of the commissioner's optimistic evaluation of future business activity in the area, Jeffrey believes that the plant has easily doubled in value. He instructs the company's bookkeeper, Anita Dunn, to double the value of the plant on the company's books. Anita makes an entry debiting Plant for $200,000 and Capital for $200,000, but she is not certain that this entry conforms to generally accepted accounting principles.

What is your opinion of this situation? Have generally accepted accounting principles been violated? If so, identify specific violations and identify accounting principles to support your opinion.

CHAPTER

15

Accounts Receivable and Uncollectible Accounts

OBJECTIVES

1. Record the losses from uncollectible accounts receivable using the direct charge-off and allowance methods.
2. Write off uncollectible accounts after estimated losses have been recorded.
3. Record the collection of accounts previously written off using the direct charge-off and allowance methods.
4. Properly classify accounts receivable on the financial statements.
5. Define the accounting terms new to this chapter.

Whenever there are credit transactions, some people will inevitably fail to pay their obligations. Businesses try to keep their bad debt losses to a minimum by carefully extending credit and by diligently collecting accounts. However, such losses will occur, and they must be considered an expense of doing business on credit. Two methods are generally used for recognizing losses from uncollectible accounts. This chapter discusses in detail the valuation or adjustment of receivables to reflect such losses.

The operations of Hanson's Sportswear will be used to illustrate the procedures for computing and recording losses from uncollectible accounts. This retail merchandising business provides charge accounts to steady customers who can meet its credit standards.

NEW TERMS

Aging the accounts receivable ▪ Allowance method ▪ Direct charge-off method ▪ Valuation account

DETERMINING LOSSES FROM UNCOLLECTIBLE ACCOUNTS

A firm that extends credit to a customer expects to collect the amount owed in full. If a customer does not pay the account when due, a loss has occurred. The firm may carry the account in its financial records until the account has definitely become uncollectible. At that time the firm must formally recognize the balance owed as a loss.

The Direct Charge-Off Method

OBJECTIVE 1

Record the losses from uncollectible accounts receivable using the direct charge-off and allowance methods.

Suppose Hanson's Sportswear has a customer, Fred Robinson, who has left town without paying his account balance of $125. After exhausting all possibilities of finding Robinson and collecting from him, Hanson's Sportswear writes off the account as a bad debt by the journal entry shown below. Notice that the amount involved is debited to an expense account called Uncollectible Accounts Expense. Other widely used titles for this type of account are Bad Debts Expense and Loss from Uncollectible Accounts.

19X4					
Jan.	*16*	*Uncollectible Accounts Exp.*	*561*	*1 2 5 00*	
		Accounts Rec./Fred Robinson	*111/√*		*1 2 5 00*
		To write off account			
		determined to be			
		uncollectible			

This method of recording uncollectible accounts is called the **direct charge-off method,** under which a firm records losses as they occur. After the accounts known to be uncollectible have been written off, the new balance of Accounts Receivable represents the total of all customer accounts presumed to be collectible. It is likely that other customer accounts in the future will not be collectible, so the balance in the Accounts Receivable account is probably greater than the amount that will actually be obtained from customers.

The Allowance Method

Although businesses may choose the method to use in estimating losses for their financial accounting records, the direct charge-off method must be used, except by certain financial institutions, to record bad debt losses for tax purposes.

Instead of waiting until a particular account proves uncollectible and then recording the loss, it is possible to anticipate losses from uncollectible accounts and to provide for those losses in the period when the sales are made. By doing so, the seller can match the estimated expense for uncollectible accounts against the revenue that the firm has earned during the same accounting period. The use of this procedure is logical because the expense for uncollectible accounts is matched to the sales transactions from which the accounts receivable resulted. In addition, the amount shown on the balance sheet for accounts receivable will more nearly reflect the amount that will ultimately be collected. The practice of providing for losses from uncollectible accounts before specific accounts become uncollectible is often referred to as the **allowance method.** Hanson's Sportswear uses this method.

To record the expense for uncollectible accounts and the sales revenue in the same accounting period, losses likely to result from the accounts receivable must be estimated. Three common ways of estimating the amount of loss from uncollectible accounts are:

1. Taking a percentage of the net credit sales for the period
2. Classifying the accounts receivable into age groups at the end of the period and taking a percentage of each group
3. Taking a percentage of the total accounts receivable outstanding at the end of the period

Taking a Percentage of Credit Sales

A business that has been operating for a number of years may be able to determine an average ratio of losses from uncollectible accounts to credit sales. It can then use this ratio in estimating future losses. To be accurate, the ratio should be based on net credit sales—total credit sales minus the sales returns and allowances on these sales. When sales returns and allowances are few, businesses usually base their estimated losses from uncollectible accounts on total credit sales because this figure is more easily computed. Since Hanson's Sportswear has relatively few sales returns and allowances, its losses from uncollectible accounts are based on total credit sales.

A new firm may use the experience of other firms in the same line of business in making its estimate. Suppose, for example, that Hanson's Sportswear relies on the experience of the previous owner. Using the data from prior years, it is estimated that three-tenths of 1 percent (0.003) of the firm's credit sales will result in uncollectible accounts. Suppose also that during Hanson's Sportswear's first year of operation $300,000 in sales are made on credit. The store's estimated loss from uncollectible accounts is determined by applying the percentage to the credit sales (0.003 × $300,000 = $900). The estimated loss from uncollectible accounts for the period is thus $900. The adjusting entry to record this estimate is shown in general journal form below. The adjustment is actually entered on the worksheet first and is later recorded in the general journal, along with the other adjusting entries.

19X4					
Jan.	*31*	*Uncollectible Accounts Exp.*	*561*	*900 00*	
		Allow. for Doubtful Accts.	*112*		*900 00*
		To record estimated bad debt losses for the fiscal year, based on 0.3% of credit sales of $300,000			

The effect of the debit part of the entry is to charge the estimated loss from uncollectible accounts against the operations of the period.

Information Block: Communication

Negative Messages

Business professionals must make decisions in the best interests of the company. As a result, employees, customers, and associates may receive some business decisions favorably and others unfavorably. When a message is negative, the receiver's reactions may range from mild disappointment, yet acceptance, to extreme anger and hurt.

When an oral or written message will result in a negative reaction, receivers want the sender to use an appropriate tone and to prepare them for the negative news. Most people prefer to learn the reasons that led to a negative decision or the facts involved in unexpected bad news *before* they actually hear the bad news. The receiver is then better able to understand and accept the negative news even though negative reactions may result. Therefore, to be effective in negative communication situations, apply an indirect approach by using the plan that follows for negative messages.

- *Begin with a positive, neutral statement.* Your opening statement is critical; you want to begin with an agreeable, relevant statement. However, you must be careful not to mislead the receiver into thinking that your message is positive news.
- *Provide details and explanations for the decision, using a positive tone.* Your supporting information should provide the receiver with the necessary reasons to clearly understand the negative news. Be careful to avoid stating company policy as the reason; instead, explain why the policy is in effect. The number of paragraphs will vary from one to three or more, depending on the nature of the negative news.
- *Imply or state the negative news.* Your objective, to share the negative news while maintaining the receiver's goodwill, must be appropriately stated. When possible, imply the negative news by stating what you *can* do instead of what you *cannot* do. For example, *"To establish an account, you must have three credit references and an*

The credit part of the entry, Allowance for Doubtful Accounts (sometimes called Allowance for Bad Debts), reflects the estimated shrinkage in the asset accounts receivable. Allowance for Doubtful Accounts is called a **valuation account** because it literally revalues or reappraises the accounts receivable in the light of reasonable expectations. It is shown on the balance sheet as a deduction from Accounts Receivable (illustrated later in the chapter).

average monthly balance of more than $5,000" instead of *"You may not establish an account with us since you have only two credit references and an average monthly balance of $2,000."*

Where the negative news must be explicitly stated, use an appropriate positive tone. Writers often imbed the negative news in the middle of a paragraph or at least in the middle of a message.

- *Offer alternative suggestions when possible.* To emphasize a positive tone in a negative message, offer alternatives in a separate paragraph when they exist. Receivers view other recommendations as helpful in spite of their unfavorable reaction to the negative news. For example, a credit refusal message may offer an alternative to buy merchandise with cash.
- *Close with a positive statement.* Always end a message with a positive, yet relevant, statement or paragraph. When appropriate, encourage action from the receiver.

As compared to positive messages, negative messages are often more difficult to communicate, require more thought and planning to prepare the receiver for the news, and may be somewhat longer. Learn to communicate even the most negative message in a positive manner by using the plan for negative messages.

Project: Assume you are the manager of accounts receivable to Tri-State Accounting, a firm that provides these accounting services for small businesses: tax consulting, computerized financial statements, auditing, and management advisory service. One of your clients, Mr. David Joseph, proprietor of Joseph's Supply Company (93 South Madison Boulevard, Cincinnati, OH 45202-3902) has a three-month overdue account with a balance of $2,050. Previous communication with Mr. Joseph indicated that the firm has a temporary cash-flow problem. In the meantime, Mr. Joseph has asked you to provide tax consultation.

Prepare a message to Mr. Joseph regarding his overdue account and your decision to delay tax consultation until the account is paid. Provide any additional facts to complete your message. Remember to follow the steps for planning and developing effective business communication and the plan for negative messages.

Note that when the estimate of the loss from uncollectible accounts is based on sales, the primary emphasis is on charging as an expense the credit losses that apply to the sales of the period. It is through this process that the accounts receivable can be reported at their expected realizable value. However, valuation is of secondary concern. In other words, the matching principle is being emphasized when the loss from uncollectible accounts is based on sales.

Aging the Accounts Receivable

A procedure called **aging the accounts receivable** also can be used as a guide in estimating probable losses from uncollectible accounts. This procedure involves setting up a schedule on which each account receivable is listed by name and balance owed, as shown in Figure 15–1.

FIGURE 15–1
Schedule of Accounts Receivable by Age

HANSON'S SPORTSWEAR
Schedule of Accounts Receivable by Age
January 31, 19X4

Account	Balance		Current		Past Due—Days					
					1–30		31–60		Over 60	
Susan Alexander	150	00	150	00						
Dorothy Anderson	200	00					150	00	50	00
Thomas Aston	120	00	20	00	100	00				
Jon Barry	80	00	80	00						
Kathryn Bender	82	00	42	00	40	00				
Ann Yoder	48	00					32	00	16	00
Sue Zant	110	00	50	00	60	00				
Martin Zeller	98	00	60	00			38	00		
Totals	11,217	00	8,900	00	1,350	00	592	00	375	00

The data in the accounts is analyzed to determine the age of the various amounts that make up each balance. The column headings of the schedule permit the classification of the amounts according to how long they have been outstanding. The headings may be Current (within the allowed credit period), Past Due 1–30 Days, Past Due 31–60 Days, and Past Due over 60 Days. When a firm breaks down each customer's total debt in this way, it gains a picture of the relative currency of its receivables.

The longer an account is past due, the less likely it is to be collected. For example, past experience at Hanson's Sportswear might indicate that 50 percent of the accounts more than 60 days past due will be uncollectible, whereas the figures for the other age groups are 25 percent for accounts 31–60 days past due, 10 percent for accounts 1–30 days past due, and 1 percent for the current accounts. By applying these percentages to the totals shown on the schedule of accounts receivable by age, the uncollectible accounts expense for the period may be estimated as follows.

Over 60 days past due	0.50 × $ 375.00 =	$187.50
31–60 days past due	0.25 × 592.00 =	148.00
1–30 days past due	0.10 × 1,350.00 =	135.00
Current	0.01 × 8,900.00 =	89.00
Total estimated loss from doubtful accounts		$559.50

Allowance for Doubtful Accounts should then be *adjusted to the needed balance* of $559.50. For example, suppose that Allowance for

Doubtful Accounts has a credit balance of $108 on January 31, prior to adjustment. The account must be credited for $451.50 to bring the balance up to $559.50. The adjustment amount may be seen in the following T-account analysis.

Allowance for Doubtful Accounts			
−		+	
	Bal.	108.00	
	Adj.	451.50	
	Bal.	559.50	

559.50
−108.00
451.50

In the case illustrated above, the adjustment amount is obtained by subtracting the credit balance of $108 from the needed balance of $559.50 to obtain the adjustment amount of $451.50. The following entry is made in the general journal to record this adjustment.

19X4					
Jan.	*31*	*Uncollectible Accounts Exp.*	*561*	*451 50*	
		Allow. for Doubtful Accts.	*112*		*451 50*
		To record adjustment of			
		allowance account to			
		$559.50 needed balance			
		based on aging of			
		accounts receivable			

On the other hand, suppose that Allowance for Doubtful Accounts has a debit balance of $70 as a result of writing off specific accounts. It would then be necessary to credit the account for $629.50 ($70 + $559.50) to bring the balance up to $559.50, the total estimated expense from uncollectible accounts. The adjustment amount may be obtained from the following T-account analysis.

Allowance for Doubtful Accounts			
−		+	
Bal.	70.00		
		Adj.	629.50
		Bal.	559.50

559.50
+ 70.00
629.50

Whatever the amount, the adjusting entry consists of a debit to Uncollectible Accounts Expense and a credit to Allowance for Doubtful Accounts, as previously shown.

When the provision for uncollectible accounts is based on the age of the accounts receivable, the primary concern is the proper valuation of the accounts receivable on the balance sheet. The amount charged as an expense is of secondary concern.

Using a Predetermined Percentage of Accounts Receivable

In some cases it is possible to estimate the necessary balance of Allowance for Doubtful Accounts by applying a single rate, based on past experience, to the total accounts receivable. For example, assume that Hanson's Sportswear's records reflect the information on accounts receivable and actual losses from accounts receivable shown below.

Date	Accounts Receivable Balance	Accounts Receivable Written Off
12/31/X1	$ 9,870	$ 425
12/31/X2	10,250	465
12/31/X3	10,975	515
	$31,095	$1,405

Hanson's Sportswear's average loss over the three-year period has been 4.5 percent.

$$\frac{\text{Average accounts receivable}}{\text{Average accounts written off}} = \frac{1{,}405}{31{,}095} = 0.045 = 4.5 \text{ percent}$$

At the end of 19X4 the balance of Accounts Receivable is $11,217 and the Allowance for Doubtful Accounts has a credit balance of $108. Using the percentage of accounts receivable method to estimate bad debts, the firm would estimate Accounts Receivable of $505 ($11,217 × 0.045) to be uncollectible. The amount of the adjustment is $397 ($505 − $108) since the desired balance in the Allowance for Doubtful Accounts is $505. The adjustment may be obtained from the following T-account analysis.

Allowance for Doubtful Accounts

−	+	
	Bal.	108.00
	Adj.	397.00
	Bal.	505.00

505.00
−108.00
397.00

Because the allowance method matches bad debt losses against revenue of the same period, it is consistent with generally accepted accounting principles and is used by most firms.

In the case illustrated above, the adjustment amount is obtained by subtracting the credit balance of $108 from the needed balance of $505 to obtain the adjustment amount of $397. The general journal entry to record this adjustment is given at the top of page 537.

The percentage of accounts receivable method for determining uncollectible accounts expense is similar to the aging method. When these methods are used, the Allowance for Doubtful Accounts must be adjusted to the needed balance.

19X4					
Jan.	*31*	*Uncollectible Accounts Exp.*	*561*	*397 00*	
		Allow. for Doubtful Accts.	*112*		*397 00*
		To record adjustment of allowance account to $505 needed balance based on aging of accounts receivable			

RECORDING ACTUAL UNCOLLECTIBLE ACCOUNTS

OBJECTIVE 2
Write off uncollectible accounts after estimated losses have been recorded.

As you have seen, under the system of providing for losses before they occur, Uncollectible Accounts Expense is debited and Allowance for Doubtful Accounts credited for the estimated amount of loss. Then, when a particular account proves uncollectible, it is written off. The amount owed is debited to Allowance for Doubtful Accounts. The offsetting credit is to the Accounts Receivable control account in the general ledger and the customer's account in the subsidiary ledger. Suppose Hanson's Sportswear determines that the account of Dorothy Anderson with a balance of $200 is uncollectible. The account is written off by making the following general journal entry.

19X4					
Feb.	*10*	*Allow. for Doubtful Accounts*	*112*	*200 00*	
		Accounts Rec./D. Anderson	*111/√*		*200 00*
		To write off account determined to be uncollectible			

Notice that when losses are provided for in advance, the write-off of a particular customer's account does not involve an entry in Uncollectible Accounts Expense. The expense has already been recorded by means of the adjustment for estimated uncollectible accounts made at the end of the period in which the sale took place.

Normally, Allowance for Doubtful Accounts will have a credit (excess) balance. However, if the losses written off are greater than those estimated in previous accounting periods, Allowance for Doubtful Accounts may show a debit (deficiency) balance until the current adjustment is recorded. If the amount of the estimated loss is based on sales, the existence of the debit balance will not affect the amount of the adjustment. However, if the estimated loss is based on accounts receivable, it will be necessary to credit Allowance for Doubtful Accounts for an amount sufficient to eliminate the debit balance and replace it with the desired credit balance. This means that the adjustment will be greater than the estimated loss from uncollectible accounts for the period.

In other words, if the estimate of the loss is based on sales, do not consider an existing balance in Allowance for Doubtful Accounts when determining the amount of the adjustment. If, however, the estimate of the loss is based on accounts receivable, consider any existing balance in Allowance for Doubtful Accounts when computing the adjustment. In this case, after the adjustment is made, the resulting balance of the allowance account should be the amount of accounts receivable estimated to be uncollectible.

COLLECTING AN ACCOUNT THAT WAS WRITTEN OFF

OBJECTIVE 3

Record the collection of accounts previously written off using the direct charge-off and allowance methods.

Occasionally an account written off as uncollectible is later collected, in whole or in part. Remember Fred Robinson's account that was written off for $125 under the direct charge-off method by a debit to Uncollectible Accounts Expense and a credit to Accounts Receivable/Fred Robinson. Suppose the account is collected in full several months later. Since Robinson's account has already been written off, the general journal entry shown below must be made to reverse the write-off. The cash received is recorded in the cash receipts journal by debiting Cash and crediting Accounts Receivable/Fred Robinson.

19X4					
July	*17*	*Accounts Rec./Fred Robinson*	*111/✓*	*125 00*	
		Uncollectible Accounts Exp.	*561*		*125 00*
		To reverse entry dated			
		Jan. 16 writing off this			
		account collected in full			
		today			

Some accountants prefer to record the amount recovered as a credit to an account called Uncollectible Accounts Recovered, especially when the money is received in a later period than the one in which the write-off was made. The debit part of this entry involves the Accounts Receivable control account in the general ledger and the customer's account in the subsidiary ledger to make sure that all pertinent facts relating to the customer's debt are recorded and can be used for future credit purposes. The collection of the money is recorded in the cash receipts journal in the usual way as a debit to Cash and a credit to Accounts Receivable and the customer's account. The Uncollectible Accounts Recovered account is shown on the income statement under Other Income.

When a firm uses the allowance method to provide for losses, the recovery of an account previously charged off as uncollectible also requires an entry in the general journal to reverse the write-off. For example, the recovery of the $200 balance owed by Dorothy Anderson is recorded in the general journal as follows. Notice that Accounts Receivable/Dorothy Anderson is debited and Allowance for Doubtful Accounts is credited in the reversal process.

Information Block: Computers in Accounting

Processing Computerized Accounts Receivable

Businesses need to maintain accurate, up-to-date balances for each customer's account in the accounts receivable ledger. In a manual accounting system, current balances may not always be available because amounts may not be posted immediately to customers' accounts. With a computerized accounts receivable system, though, transaction data is processed quickly and account balances are instantly updated in both the general and subsidiary ledgers.

How does a computerized accounts receivable system work? First, a master customer file is created. This file contains information about the customer, such as account number, name, address, telephone number, and amount of any credit limit.

When a customer places a credit order, the data is keyed into the computer using an order-entry processing program. This program will create a second file called a *sales transaction log.* This file contains the customer's account number, the items and quantity ordered, and additional data on shipping charges, discount rates, and sales tax. This file will be used with the master file to prepare the sales invoice to be mailed to the customer and the packing slip to be sent to the warehouse to use in filling the order.

The order-entry program will also post the amount of the sale immediately to the customer's account in the subsidiary ledger file and will update the balances for inventory on hand. If a customer returns merchandise to the company, the computer will prepare a credit memorandum for the amount of the sales return and then post the data to the customer's account.

Cash receipts are entered into the computer to create a cash receipts transaction log. This file is used along with the master customer file to post payments on accounts to appropriate subsidiary accounts.

In addition to maintaining current, accurate customer account balances, computerized accounts receivable systems also provide valuable reports to management. These reports include an aged accounts receivable schedule that identifies past-due accounts, a schedule of accounts receivable that lists all customers by name and reports the balance in each account, and a cash receipts report. Additional reports are also available to summarize the amount of cash discounts taken by a customer and the amount of sales returns and allowances.

19X4					
Aug.	19	Accts. Rec./Dorothy Anderson	111/√	200 00	
		Allow. for Doubtful Accts.	112		200 00
		To reverse entry dated			
		Feb. 10 writing off this			
		account collected in full			
		today			

An entry in the cash receipts journal is then made in the usual way to record the collection of the account receivable.

If the amount recovered represents only part of the balance written off, a reversing entry is used to restore *only the amount actually collected* unless the firm is almost certain that the remainder will be paid. For example, if Dorothy Anderson pays only $60 on her $200 balance, the reversing entry in the general journal will be for the smaller amount unless the firm is reasonably sure the additional $140 will be paid.

ACCOUNTING FOR OTHER RECEIVABLES AND BAD DEBT LOSSES

Just as accounts receivable may result in bad debt losses, notes receivable and other receivables may prove uncollectible. Losses from uncollectible notes receivable and other receivables may be recorded as they occur, or they may be estimated and provided for ahead of time in the manner previously described for accounts receivable. The same accounts—Uncollectible Accounts Expense and Allowance for Doubtful Accounts—can be used for losses from all types of receivables.

CLASSIFYING ACCOUNTS RECEIVABLE ON FINANCIAL STATEMENTS

OBJECTIVE 4

Properly classify accounts receivable on the financial statements.

Businesses that use classified financial statements report the accounts related to accounts receivable in different ways depending upon the type of business and the method used to account for uncollectible accounts.

The Income Statement

Uncollectible Accounts Expense appears among the operating expenses on the income statement. If the function of giving credit and collecting accounts rests in the sales department, it is classified as a selling expense. However, in most businesses, the credit function is separated from the sales function. For these businesses, Uncollectible Accounts Expense is usually shown as a general or administrative expense. Some businesses show Uncollectible Accounts Expense as a deduction from sales revenue on the income statement.

The Balance Sheet

If Allowance for Doubtful Accounts is used, the balance in this account at the end of the period represents the amount of accounts receivable estimated to be uncollectible. When the balance sheet is prepared, the balance of Allowance for Doubtful Accounts is deducted from the balance of the Accounts Receivable account, as shown below. The difference is considered the net value of the asset. In this case the net value of the firm's accounts receivable is $10,657.50.

HANSON'S SPORTSWEAR
Balance Sheet
January 31, 19X4

Assets		
Current Assets		
Cash in Bank		10 875 00
Accounts Receivable	11 217 00	
Less Allowance for Doubtful Accounts	559 50	10 657 50

INTERNAL CONTROL OF ACCOUNTS RECEIVABLE

For most companies, Accounts Receivable represents one of the largest assets on the balance sheet. Because of the way in which accounts receivable arise—the delivery of merchandise or services to customers—and because accounts receivable are expected to be converted into cash, internal control is very important.

This control originates with appropriate delegation of authority for approving the extension of credit and an insistence that all credit be properly approved. Detailed procedures must be established to make certain that all sales are properly recorded and that customers' accounts are correctly charged. In addition, every effort must be made to separate the functions of recording the accounts receivable transactions, preparing bills or statements for customers, mailing the bills or statements, and processing the cash received from the customers. This division of responsibility is necessary to make it more difficult for an employee to steal or misuse the company's cash or merchandise and then cover up what was done by making improper entries in the accounts receivable records.

To ensure efficient collection of accounts receivable, customers should be billed regularly and the accounts receivable balances should be aged often. Using the data from the age analysis, management should quickly identify and monitor slow-paying accounts. When accounts are past due, management should promptly investigate the situation and take appropriate action. The responsibility for authorizing charge-offs of uncollectible accounts should be delegated only to selected individuals, and all charge-offs should be approved in writing. Even after accounts have been written off, efforts should be continued to collect them.

MANAGERIAL IMPLICATIONS

It is essential that managers keep informed about the losses from uncollectible accounts. This enables them to determine the effectiveness of the credit policies used by their firms, especially with regard to profitability. Managers must always weigh the cost of losses against the effects of tighter credit policies on sales volume.

Managers should insist that estimated losses from uncollectible accounts be charged against the revenue of the period in which the sales are made in order to get a proper matching of revenues and expenses. This allows a more accurate determination of net income or net loss.

SELF-REVIEW

1. Which method of accounting for bad debts, the direct charge-off or the allowance method, is considered preferable? Why?
2. Which method of accounting for bad debts, the direct charge-off or the allowance method, must be used for tax purposes?
3. How is the book value of Accounts Receivable determined?
4. When an account is written off under the allowance method, does the book value of Accounts Receivable increase or decrease? Why?
5. Nelson Company's bad debt losses are estimated at 1/2 percent of net sales. Net sales for the year are $275,000 and Allowance for Doubtful Accounts has a credit balance of $325. Give the adjusting entry to record bad debt losses for the year.

Answers to Self-Review

1. The allowance method of accounting for bad debts is considered preferable because it is consistent with the matching principle. The allowance method matches bad debt losses during a period against revenue of the same period.
2. Except for certain financial institutions, the direct charge-off method must be used for tax purposes.
3. The book value of Accounts Receivable is determined by subtracting the Allowance for Doubtful Accounts balance from the balance in the Accounts Receivable account.
4. When an account is written off under the allowance method of accounting for bad debt losses, the book value of accounts receivable does not change. This result occurs because the journal entry to write off an account involves a debit to Allowance for Doubtful Accounts and a credit to Accounts Receivable for the same amount. The net result is no change in the book value of Accounts Receivable.
5. The adjusting entry is:

Uncollectible Accounts Expense	1,375	
Allowance for Doubtful Accounts		1,375
To record estimated bad debt expense based on 0.5% of credit sales of $275,000		

CHAPTER 15 Review and Applications

CHAPTER SUMMARY

When credit is extended to customers, uncollectible accounts will inevitably occur. Before receivables can be accurately presented on the balance sheet and net income can be properly measured, the accounts must be studied for possible adjustment to reflect such losses. The losses can be recorded as particular accounts become uncollectible, the direct charge-off method, or an estimate of probable losses can be recorded before they occur, the allowance method. Because the allowance method matches bad debt losses during a period against revenue of the same period, it is consistent with generally accepted accounting principles and is the preferable method.

The estimate of losses from uncollectible accounts may be determined by taking a certain percentage of credit sales. This percentage is usually based on the firm's past experience. The adjustment for the estimated losses is debited to Uncollectible Accounts Expense and credited to Allowance for Doubtful Accounts.

The estimate may also be based on an analysis of the age of the accounts receivable. A different percentage for credit losses is applied to each age group, and the resulting amounts are added together. Then Allowance for Doubtful Accounts is adjusted to the proper balance, and the same amount is charged to Uncollectible Accounts Expense. The adjustment is made in the same way when the estimate of bad debt losses is computed by applying a single rate to the total accounts receivable.

Under the allowance method, when an account actually becomes worthless, it is written off by a debit to Allowance for Doubtful Accounts and a credit to Accounts Receivable and to the customer's account in the subsidiary ledger.

GLOSSARY OF NEW TERMS

Aging the accounts receivable (p. 534) Classifying accounts receivable according to how long they have been outstanding

Allowance method (p. 530) A method of providing for bad debts before specific accounts become uncollectible

Direct charge-off method (p. 530) A method of recording uncollectible accounts at the time they are known to be uncollectible

Valuation account (p. 532) An account, such as Allowance for Doubtful Accounts, whose balance is revalued or reappraised in light of reasonable expectations

REVIEW QUESTIONS

1. Explain the direct charge-off method for recording uncollectible accounts expense.
2. Under what condition would the direct charge-off method be appropriate?
3. What is the major weakness of the direct charge-off method?
4. Name three approaches to measuring uncollectible accounts when the allowance method is used.
5. What is meant by aging the accounts receivable?
6. Explain the purpose of estimating losses from uncollectible accounts and using the allowance method for recording uncollectible accounts.
7. Under the allowance method, what entry is made when a specific customer's account becomes uncollectible?
8. Under the direct charge-off method, what entry is made when a firm collects an account that was previously written off?
9. Explain how to treat the collection of an account receivable that was previously written off if the allowance method is used.
10. When is it logical to base the estimate of uncollectible accounts on gross credit sales rather than on net credit sales?
11. Why is Allowance for Doubtful Accounts sometimes referred to as a valuation account?
12. If a company is primarily interested in matching expenses and revenues each period, would it base its estimate of uncollectible accounts on sales or on accounts receivable? Explain.
13. Suppose that the estimate of uncollectible accounts is based on credit sales and that Allowance for Doubtful Accounts has a debit balance before the adjustment is made. Explain how this situation is handled.
14. How would an accountant show Uncollectible Accounts Expense on the income statement? Explain.

MANAGERIAL FOCUS

1. How do managers appraise the effectiveness of credit policies?
2. What are the advantages of using an analysis of the accounts receivable by age as a guide in estimating losses from uncollectible accounts?
3. Why would managers use the allowance method for recording uncollectible accounts instead of the direct charge-off method?
4. Why is an account receivable that was charged off as uncollectible reinstated if it is later collected?
5. In the Anchor Company, the credit function is delegated to the sales department. In most cases the firm's salespeople are authorized to approve credit for customers. Comment on the desirability of this procedure.

EXERCISES

EXERCISE 15–1 (Obj. 1)

Tutorial

Recording losses under the direct charge-off method. The Lone Star Company uses the direct charge-off method to record uncollectible accounts. On July 29, 19X3, the company learned that Alan Shaw, a customer who owed $380, had been declared bankrupt and that no part of the debt was collectible. Give the general journal entry to write off the account.

EXERCISE 15–2 (Obj. 3)

Recording the collection of an account previously written off. On January 8, 19X4, the Lone Star Company received a check for $60 and a letter from the bankruptcy official handling the affairs of Alan Shaw. The letter stated that the $60 represented a final distribution of Smith's assets to his creditors. Give the general journal entry to partially reverse the write-off recorded in Exercise 15–1.

EXERCISE 15–3 (Obj. 1)

Tutorial

Estimating and recording uncollectible accounts on the basis of total net sales. On December 31, 19X3, certain account balances at the Rogers Company were as follows before end-of-year adjustments.

Accounts Receivable	$ 500,000
Allowance for Doubtful Accounts	2,000 (debit)
Sales	12,000,000
Sales Returns and Allowances	50,000

A further examination of the business's records showed that cash sales during the year were $1.2 million and credit sales were $10.8 million. Of the sales returns and allowances, $10,000 came from cash sales and $40,000 came from credit sales. Assume that the Rogers Company bases its estimate of losses from uncollectible accounts on 0.3 percent of total net sales. Compute the estimated amount of uncollectible account expense for 19X3, and give the general journal entry to record the provision for uncollectible accounts.

EXERCISE 15–4 (Obj. 1)

Tutorial

Estimating and recording uncollectible accounts on the basis of net credit sales. Assume that the Rogers Company bases its estimate of uncollectible accounts expense on 0.4 percent of net credit sales. Compute the estimated amount of uncollectible accounts expense for 19X3 and give the general journal entry to record the provision for uncollectible accounts. Obtain any data that you need for the computation from Exercise 15–3.

EXERCISE 15–5 (Obj. 1)

Tutorial

Estimating and recording uncollectible accounts on the basis of accounts receivable. Assume that the Rogers Company bases its estimate of uncollectible accounts expense on 1.1 percent of accounts receivable. Compute the estimated amount of losses for 19X3 and give the general journal entry to record the provision for uncollectible accounts. Obtain any data that you need for the computation from Exercise 15–3.

EXERCISE 15–6 (Obj. 3)

Recording the collection of an account previously written off under the allowance method. The Schmidt Company uses the allowance method to record uncollectible accounts. On January 1. 19X3, its general ledger showed a balance of $1,220,000 for Accounts Receivable and a credit balance of $12,000 for Allowance for Doubtful Accounts. Assume that on January 8, 19X3, Sam Cole, whose account for $600 had been charged off in 19X1, sent a check to Schmidt for $600 in payment, along with an apology for having been so late. Give the entries in general journal form to reverse the previous write-off of Cole's account and to record the receipt of his check.

EXERCISE 15–7 (Obj. 2)

Recording actual uncollectible amounts under the allowance method. On February 8, 19X3, the Schmidt Company decided that the $800 account of Jean Gray was worthless and should be written off. Give the general journal entry to record the charge-off.

EXERCISE 15–8 (Obj. 3)

Recording the collection of an account previously written off under the allowance method. On July 10, 19X3, Jean Gray paid $800 to the Schmidt Company in settlement of her account, which had been charged off on February 8. Give the entries in general journal form to reverse the previous write-off of Gray's account and to record the receipt of her check.

PROBLEMS

PROBLEM SET A

PROBLEM 15–1A (Obj. 1, 2, 3)

Tutorial GL

Recording uncollectible account transactions under the direct charge-off method. The Bayer Company records uncollectible accounts expenses as they occur. Selected transactions for 19X3 are described below. The accounts involved in these transactions are Notes Receivable, Accounts Receivable, and Uncollectible Accounts Expense. Record each transaction in general journal form.

TRANSACTIONS

Feb. 12 The account receivable of Alan Scott, amounting to $98, is determined to be uncollectible and is to be written off.

Mar. 20 Because of the death of Joan Harris, her note receivable amounting to $300 is considered uncollectible and is to be written off.

June 4 Received $45 from Alan Scott in partial payment of his account, which had been written off on February 12. The cash obtained has already been recorded in the cash receipts journal. There is doubt that the balance of Scott's account will be collected.

July 9 Received $53 from Alan Scott to complete payment of his account, which had been written off on February 12. The cash obtained has already been recorded in the cash receipts journal.

Aug. 14 The account receivable of Robert West, amounting to $80, is determined to be uncollectible and is to be written off.

Sept. 18 Received $100 from the estate of Joan Harris as part of the settlement of affairs. This amount is applicable to the note receivable written off on March 20. The cash obtained has already been recorded in the cash receipts journal.

PROBLEM 15–2A
(Obj. 1, 2, 3, 4)

Tutorial

Estimating and recording uncollectible accounts transactions on the basis of sales. The Plano Feed Company sells farm supplies at both wholesale and retail. The company has found that there is a higher rate of uncollectible accounts from retail credit sales than from wholesale credit sales. Plano computes its estimated loss from uncollectible accounts at the end of each year. The amount is based on the two rates of loss that the firm has developed from experience. Thus a separate computation must be made for each source of sales. The firm uses the percentage of credit sales method.

As of December 31, 19X3, Accounts Receivable has a balance of $186,700, and Allowance for Doubtful Accounts has a debit balance of $36.20. The following table provides a breakdown of the credit sales for the year 19X3 and the estimated rates of loss.

CATEGORY	AMOUNT	ESTIMATED RATE OF LOSS
Wholesale	$908,000	0.6%
Retail	274,300	1.1%

Instructions

1. Compute the estimated amount of uncollectible accounts expense for each of the two categories of credit sales for the year.
2. Prepare an adjusting entry in general journal form to provide for the uncollectible accounts expense before they occur. Use Uncollectible Accounts Expense.
3. Show how Accounts Receivable and Allowance for Doubtful Accounts should appear on the balance sheet of the Plano Feed Company as of December 31, 19X3.
4. On January 30, 19X4, the account receivable of Roy Carter, amounting to $283, is determined to be uncollectible and is to be written off. Record this transaction in the general journal.
5. On June 13, 19X4, the attorneys for Plano Feed Company turned over a check for $283 that they obtained from Roy Carter in settlement of his account, which had been written off on January 30. The money has already been recorded in the cash receipts journal. Make an entry in the general journal to cancel the original write-off.

PROBLEM 15–3A
(Obj. 1, 2, 3)

Tutorial

Estimating and recording uncollectible account transactions on the basis of accounts receivable. The schedule of accounts receivable by age shown on page 548 was prepared for the Garcia Company at the end of the firm's fiscal year on December 31, 19X3.

Instructions

1. Compute the estimated uncollectible accounts at the end of the year using these rates.

Current	1%
1–30 days past due	3%
31–60 days past due	8%
Over 60 days past due	20%

2. As of December 31, 19X3, there is a debit balance of $64.12 in Allowance for Doubtful Accounts. Compute the amount of the

GARCIA COMPANY
Schedule of Accounts Receivable by Age
December 31, 19X3

Account	Balance	Current	Past Due—Days		
			1–30	31–60	Over 60
Anton, Janet	180 00	180 00			
Ardath, Robert	210 00		150 00	60 00	
Aston, Thomas	104 00				104 00
Baltus, Ida	80 00	80 00			
Barton, Leslie	62 00	42 00	20 00		
Bender, Harold	225 00	85 00	100 00	40 00	
Benson, Mary	48 00			32 00	16 00
(All Other Accounts)	10,748 00	9,075 00	1,050 00	360 00	263 00
Totals	11,657 00	9,462 00	1,320 00	492 00	383 00

adjustment for uncollectible accounts expense that must be made as part of the adjusting entries.

3. In general journal form, record the adjustment for the estimated losses. Use Uncollectible Accounts Expense.
4. On February 10, 19X4, the $108 account receivable of Ruth Hall was recognized as uncollectible. Record this entry.
5. On June 12, 19X4, a check for $50 was received from John Casey to apply on his account, which had been written off on November 8, 19X3, as uncollectible. Record the cancellation of the previous write-off in the general journal. The cash obtained has already been entered in the cash receipts journal.
6. Suppose that instead of aging the accounts receivable, the company estimated the uncollectible accounts to be 3 percent of the total accounts receivable on December 31. Give the general journal entry to record the adjustment for estimated losses from uncollectible accounts. Assume that Allowance for Doubtful Accounts has a debit balance of $103.60 before the adjusting entry.

PROBLEM 15–4A
(Obj. 1, 2, 3)

Using different methods to estimate uncollectible accounts. The balances of selected accounts of the Huang Company on December 31, 19X3, are given below. Credit sales were $2,810,000. Returns and allowances on these sales were $60,000.

Accounts Receivable	$ 316,500
Allowance for Doubtful Accounts	380 (credit)
Sales	3,450,000
Sales Returns and Allowances	75,000

Instructions

1. Compute the amount to be charged to Uncollectible Accounts Expense under each of the following different assumptions.
   a. Uncollectible accounts are estimated to be 0.4 percent of net credit sales.
   b. Uncollectible accounts are estimated to be 0.3 percent of total net sales.
   c. Experience has shown that about 2.50 percent of the accounts receivable will prove worthless.

2. Suppose Allowance for Doubtful Accounts has a debit balance of $380 instead of a credit balance, but all other account balances remain the same. Compute the amount to be charged to Uncollectible Accounts Expense under each assumption in item 1.

PROBLEM SET B

PROBLEM 15–1B
(Obj. 1, 2, 3)

Recording uncollectible account transactions under the direct charge-off method. The Fairmont Company records uncollectible accounts expenses as they occur. Selected transactions for 19X3 are described below. The accounts involved are Notes Receivable, Accounts Receivable, and Uncollectible Accounts Expense. Record each transaction in general journal form.

TRANSACTIONS

Jan. 15 The account receivable of Aaron Davis, amounting to $96, is determined to be uncollectible and is to be written off.

Mar. 20 Because of the death of Paul O'Grady, his $250 note receivable is considered uncollectible and is to be written off.

June 4 Received $40 from Aaron Davis in partial payment of his account, which had been written off on January 15. The cash obtained has already been recorded in the cash receipts journal. There is doubt that the balance of Davis's account will be collected.

July 17 Received $56 from Aaron Davis to pay his account, which was written off on January 15. The cash obtained has been recorded in the cash receipts journal.

Sept. 24 Received $105 from the estate of Paul O'Grady as part of the settlement of his affairs. This amount is applicable to the note receivable written off on March 20. The cash obtained has been recorded in the cash receipts journal.

Sept. 30 The account receivable of Helen Hart, amounting to $75, is determined to be uncollectible and is to be written off.

PROBLEM 15–2B
(Obj. 1, 2, 3, 4)

Estimating and recording uncollectible account transactions on the basis of sales. The U-Build Company sells building materials on credit and records sales in three separate revenue accounts. The company's experience has been that each sales category has a different rate of losses from uncollectible accounts. Thus the total that the company charges off for these losses at the end of each accounting period is based on three computations (one computation for each revenue account). The firm uses the percentage of credit sales method.

As of December 31, 19X3, Accounts Receivable has a balance of $234,550, and Allowance for Doubtful Accounts has a credit balance of $2,860. The following table provides a breakdown of the credit sales for the year 19X3 and the estimated rates of loss.

CATEGORY	AMOUNT	ESTIMATED RATE OF LOSS
Plumbing	$625,000	0.9%
Electrical	470,000	1.4%
Hardware	138,000	2.0%

Instructions

1. Compute the estimated amount of losses in uncollectible accounts expense for each of the three categories of credit sales for the year.
2. Prepare an adjusting entry in general journal form to provide for the losses before they occur. Use Uncollectible Accounts Expense.
3. Show how Accounts Receivable and Allowance for Doubtful Accounts should appear on the balance sheet of U-Build Company as of December 31, 19X3.
4. On February 17, 19X4, the account receivable of Linda Ellis, amounting to $344, is determined to be uncollectible and is to be written off. Record the transaction in general journal form.
5. On May 15, 19X4, the attorneys for U-Build Company turned over a check for $344 that they obtained from Linda Ellis in settlement of her account, which had been written off on February 17. The money has already been entered in the cash receipts journal. Make an entry in general journal form to cancel the original write-off.

PROBLEM 15–3B
(Obj. 1, 2, 3)

Tutorial

Estimating and recording uncollectible account transactions on the basis of accounts receivable. The schedule of accounts receivable by age shown below was prepared for the Fashion Clothing Store at the end of the firm's fiscal year on July 31, 19X4.

Instructions

1. Compute the estimated uncollectible accounts at the end of the year using these rates.

Current	1%
1–30 days past due	4%
31–60 days past due	10%
Over 60 days past due	20%

FASHION CLOTHING STORE
Schedule of Accounts Receivable by Age
July 31, 19X4

Account	Balance	Current	Past Due—Days 1–30	31–60	Over 60
Armad, John	127 00	63 00	64 00		
Bates, Steven	236 00	111 00	90 00	35 00	
Cline, Judith	98 00	98 00			
Derr, Allen	19 00	19 00			
Everett, Linda	316 00			208 00	108 00
Foley, Ann	74 00	29 00	45 00		
Gorin, Charles	197 00	68 00	92 00		37 00
Hayes, Frank	252 00	114 00	138 00		
Ivan, Thomas	132 00			132 00	
Jones, Ellen	59 00		59 00		
(All Other Accounts)	5,637 00	2,932 00	1,874 00	453 00	378 00
Totals	7,147 00	3,434 00	2,362 00	828 00	523 00

2. As of June 30, 19X4, there is a debit balance of $113.50 in Allowance for Doubtful Accounts. Compute the amount of the adjustment for uncollectible accounts expense that must be made as part of the adjusting entries.
3. In general journal form, record the adjustment for the estimated losses. Use Uncollectible Accounts Expense.
4. On August 18, 19X4, the account receivable of Thomas Ivan, amounting to $132, was recognized as uncollectible. Record this write-off in the general journal.
5. On September 2, 19X4, a check for $100 was received from Donna Ryan to apply on her account, which had been written off on April 19, 19X3, as uncollectible. Record the cancellation of the previous write-off in the general journal. The cash obtained has already been entered in the cash receipts journal.
6. Suppose that instead of aging the accounts receivable, the company estimated the uncollectible accounts to be 5 percent of the total accounts receivable on July 31. Give the general journal entry to record the adjustment for estimated losses from uncollectible accounts. Assume that Allowance for Doubtful Accounts has a credit balance of $62.50 before the adjusting entry.

PROBLEM 15–4B
(Obj. 1, 2, 3)

Using different methods to estimate uncollectible accounts. The balances of selected accounts of the Murphy Company on December 31, 19X3, are given below. Credit sales amounted to $13 million. The returns and allowances on these sales totaled $69,200.

Accounts Receivable	$ 1,480,000
Allowance for Doubtful Accounts	4,200 (credit)
Sales	16,700,000
Sales Returns and Allowances	90,400

Instructions

1. Compute the amount to be charged to Uncollectible Accounts Expense under each of the following different sets of assumptions.
   a. Uncollectible accounts are estimated to be 0.25 percent of net credit sales.
   b. Uncollectible accounts are estimated to be 0.2 percent of total net sales.
   c. Experience has shown that about 1.75 percent of the accounts receivable are uncollectible.
2. Suppose that Allowance for Doubtful Accounts has a debit balance of $4,200 instead of a credit balance, but all other account balances remain the same. Compute the amount to be charged to Uncollectible Accounts Expense under each of the assumptions listed in the first instruction.

CHALLENGE PROBLEM

Furniture Land, Inc., is a national chain of furniture stores. The company's year-end trial balance for 19X4 reported the information shown on the next page.

	19X4
Accounts Receivable	$1,750,300
Less Allowance for Doubtful Accounts	18,750
	$1,731,550

Assume that net credit sales for 19X4 amounted to $5,333,000, no accounts have been previously written off during the year, and the Allowance for Doubtful Accounts has not yet been adjusted.

Instructions

1. At the end of 19X4 the following accounts receivable were deemed uncollectible:

Andrew Anderson	$ 5,800
Brenda Cosby	2,500
Henderson Office Supply	8,200
Sue King	1,890
William Taylor	2,500
Helen Zeller	1,050
Total	$21,940

   Prepare the 19X4 journal entry necessary to write off the above accounts.
2. Assume that the company uses the percentage of sales method to estimate uncollectible accounts expense. After analyzing the prior year's activities, Furniture Land's management determined that losses from uncollectible accounts for 19X4 should be 1.8 percent of net credit sales. Prepare the necessary adjusting journal entry.
3. Assume that the company uses the aging of accounts receivable method. The information reflected below was furnished by the credit manager for use in calculating the estimated loss from uncollectible accounts:

Receivable Category	**Estimated Loss Rate**	**Amount**
Current	1%	$1,200,000
1–30 days past due	4%	300,000
31–60 days past due	9%	125,300
Over 60 days past due	18%	125,000
Total		$1,750,300

   Prepare the necessary adjusting journal entry.
4. Describe both the direct charge-off method and the allowance method of accounting for uncollectible accounts. Explain why one of the above methods is preferable to the other and why the other method is usually not consistent with generally accepted accounting principles.

CRITICAL THINKING PROBLEM

Marsha Cooper is president of Cooper & Company, a manufacturer of home exercise equipment. For the past eight years, the company has sold its product both to wholesale and to retail dealers of fitness equipment in the northeastern United States. Over the years the company has come to know its customers well, and, while all sales are made on credit, few credit losses have occurred. The company's experience has shown that an annual provision for uncollectible accounts of one quarter of 1 percent of sales is adequate.

This year, Cooper & Company decided to expand and develop a new sales base in the southeastern United States. Marsha was delighted when credit sales of $400,000 were achieved in the new territory during 19X7. To achieve this level of sales and get a foothold in the new territory, though, credit was granted to some customers with questionable credit ratings. Marsha estimated that during the initial period of development losses from uncollectible accounts would be 4 percent of sales in the new territory.

The credit losses connected with sales in the southeast became apparent by the end of 19X7. The following losses from new territory customers were identified.

1. Fitness Plus, Inc., which owed Cooper $8,100, filed for bankruptcy and it was determined that nothing could be collected from the bankrupt firm.
2. Another new customer, Home Gym Equipment Co., which owed Cooper $22,000, entered receivership. The receiver sent Cooper a check for $16,000 and indicated that nothing else could be paid.
3. Deavers Sports Store went out of business and no collection of the $3,700 owed was possible.

Sales in the old territory totaled $2,625,000 for 19X7. Accounts receivable of $6,328 attributed to customers in the old sales territory were determined to be uncollectible and were written off during 19X7.

Instructions

1. Record in general journal form all Cooper & Company transactions described above.
2. Compute the estimated amount of losses from uncollectible accounts for 19X7. Prepare an adjusting entry in general journal form to record the provision for uncollectible accounts. Include both territories in the adjusting entry.
3. Assume that Allowance for Doubtful Accounts had a beginning credit balance of $3,100. Was Cooper & Company's provision for losses from uncollectible accounts adequate? To help with your analysis, set up and post amounts to a T account for Allowance for Doubtful Accounts.

CHAPTER

16

Notes Payable and Notes Receivable

OBJECTIVES

1. Determine whether a business paper or instrument meets all the requirements of negotiability.
2. Calculate the interest on a note.
3. Determine the maturity date of a note.
4. Record routine notes payable transactions.
5. Record the discounting of a note payable to a bank.
6. Record routine notes receivable transactions.
7. Compute the proceeds from a discounted note receivable.
8. Define the accounting terms new to this chapter.

Checks are not the only kind of written order or promise to pay that may be used in financing and settling business transactions. Promissory notes, drafts, and trade acceptances are often used, especially for larger transactions and for obligations that extend for a longer time than the typical open-account credit period.

In this chapter, we discuss the requirements a business document must meet to be a negotiable instrument. We also discuss in detail one of the most common types of negotiable instrument—the promissory note. You will become familiar with handling the promissory note as an asset and as a liability, along with procedures for calculating the maturity date, interest, and maturity value for promissory notes. The computation of interest and the concept of discounting a note payable and a note receivable are also emphasized.

NEW TERMS

Bank draft ▪ Banker's year ▪ Bill of lading ▪ Cashier's check ▪ Commercial draft ▪ Discounting ▪ Draft ▪ Face amount ▪ Interest ▪ Maturity value ▪ Note payable ▪ Note receivable ▪ Principal ▪ Promissory note ▪ Sight draft ▪ Time draft ▪ Trade acceptance

NEGOTIABLE INSTRUMENTS

OBJECTIVE 1
Determine whether a business paper or instrument meets all the requirements of negotiability.

The law dealing with negotiable instruments is a part of the Uniform Commercial Code, which has been adopted by the legislatures of all the states. This law specifies that an instrument must meet the following requirements to be negotiable.

1. It must be in writing and must be signed by the maker (or drawer).
2. It must contain an unconditional promise or order to pay a definite amount of money.
3. It must be payable either on demand or at a future time that is fixed or that can be determined.
4. It must be payable to the order of a specific person or to the bearer.
5. If addressed to a drawee, it must clearly name or identify that person.

Most checks that you write are negotiable instruments because they meet all these requirements. The **promissory note** shown in Figure 16–1 also meets all the requirements of negotiability.

FIGURE 16–1
A Promissory Note

$5,000.00 **Columbus, Ohio** March 18, 19X1

Ninety days **AFTER DATE** We **PROMISE TO PAY**

TO THE ORDER OF Columbia Equipment Company

Five thousand and no/100 - **DOLLARS**

PAYABLE AT City National Bank

VALUE RECEIVED plus interest at rate of 12% per annum

NO. 1 **DUE** June 16, 19X2 Linda Hanson

The 90-day note for $5,000 given by Linda Hanson, the owner of Hanson's Sportswear, to the Columbia Equipment Company is negotiable for the following reasons.

1. It is in writing and is signed by the maker (Linda Hanson for Hanson's Sportswear).
2. It is an unconditional promise to pay a definite sum.
3. It is payable on a date that can be determined exactly.
4. It is payable to a party named in the instrument.

The note also specifies that interest at the rate of 12 percent a year must be paid at maturity. However, this provision is not needed for negotiability, and some notes may not bear interest.

Calculating the Interest on a Note

When a business grants credit by accepting a promissory note, it must wait for payment and thus forego the use of money during the credit period. The party receiving the credit postpones payment and

OBJECTIVE 2
Calculate the interest on a note.

has the use of its own money during the credit period. Since the use of money is a valuable privilege, creditors almost always charge debtors for it. **Interest** is the price charged for the use of money or credit.

The amount of interest for any time period can be determined by using the formula

$I = P \times R \times T$

$$\text{Interest} = \text{Principal} \times \text{Interest Rate} \times \text{Time (in years)}$$

The time period is indicated by a fraction. The exact number of days the note is to run is generally used as the numerator, and 360 is used as the denominator. Although most years have 365 days, 360 is used for convenience. This 360-day period is referred to as a **banker's year.** For instance, the 90-day term of the note shown in Figure 16–1 is expressed as 90/360 of a year. Applying the interest formula to the note, we find that the interest on \$5,000 for 90 days at 12 percent is \$150.

$$\text{Interest} = \$5{,}000 \times 0.12 \times (90/360) = \$150$$

The interest specified in a credit transaction is accounted for separately from the amount of the note. It is recorded as interest expense by the debtor and as interest income by the creditor. We will look at how interest is recorded later in this chapter.

Remember that interest is charged to the party that is receiving goods or services without paying cash upon receipt of those goods or services. Thus a business may have interest either as an income item (if the business is granting credit) or as an expense item (if the business is receiving credit).

The amount shown on the note in Figure 16–1, \$5,000, is called the **principal, face value,** or **face amount.** The total that must be paid when the note becomes due (the principal plus the interest) is known as the **maturity value** of the note. A formula to express this relationship is

$MV = P + I$

$$\text{Maturity value} = \text{Principal} + \text{Interest}$$

The maturity value of Hanson's Sportswear's note to Columbia Equipment Company is \$5,150, or \$5,000 in principal plus \$150 in interest.

Calculating the Maturity Date of a Note

OBJECTIVE 3
Determine the maturity date of a note.

Hanson's Sportswear needs to keep a record of the date that payment is due on its notes payable so the firm will have enough money available to cover the amount owed. The maturity date of the note is determined at the time the note is issued by counting the number of days from the date the note was issued. (The issue date itself is not counted.) For example, a 30-day note issued on January 1 matures 30 days after January 1, which is January 31.

The steps that follow are used to find the maturity date of a note, in this case a 30-day note issued on January 15.

Days remaining in January: 16

1. Determine the number of days the note will run in the month of issue. In this case it will run for 16 remaining days in January (31 – 15).

30-day term − 16 = 14

2. Subtract the number of days the note will run in the month of issue from the total time for which the note was issued. In this case, the remaining time is 14 days (30 − 16). Thus the note will run for 14 days in February.

16 + 14 = 30

3. Prove the computations. Add the previous figures together to see whether they equal the total period of the note in days.

Since the note runs 14 days into February, the maturity date is February 14. Many notes have longer time periods. For example, Hanson's Sportswear's note issued on March 18 to Columbia Equipment Company was for 90 days. The calculation of its maturity date follows.

Days remaining in March: 13

1. Determine the number of days the note will run in the month of issue, in this case 13 days in March (31 − 18).

13 + 30 + 31 = 74

2. Add the total number of days in the following months until the remainder is within one month of the total time period. In this case the 30 days in April and the 31 days in May are added to the 13 remaining days in March, which equals 74 days.

90 − 74 = 16

3. Determine the number of days the note will run in the month in which it matures. In this case the note will run for 16 days in June (90 − 74). Thus the maturity date is June 16.

74 + 16 = 90

4. Prove the computations. Add the previous figures together to see whether they equal the total period of the note in days.

Sometimes the period of a note is described in months instead of days. For example, the note issued to the Columbia Equipment Company might have been for three months rather than for 90 days. When the period is defined in months, the maturity date is determined by counting ahead to the same date the following month or months. For example, three months from March 18 is June 18, regardless of the fact that March and May have 31 days and April has 30 days. No count of the actual days is required.

If a note is issued at the end of a month, there may be no actual date corresponding to the theoretical due date. In that event the note falls due on the first day of the following month. For example, a six-month note given on August 30 would be due on February 30. However, since there is no February 30, the note is due on March 1.

NOTES PAYABLE

A **note payable** is merely written evidence of a debt that says the debtor promises to pay the amount borrowed. Companies issue notes payable for many reasons, for example, to borrow money to expand the business or to buy equipment.

Interest-Bearing Note Given to Purchase an Asset

The interest-bearing note issued by Hanson's Sportswear (Figure 16–1) was created under the following circumstances. On March 18, 19X3, Hanson's Sportswear purchased furniture and store fixtures for $5,000 from the Columbia Equipment Company. Columbia agreed to allow the store 90 days in which to pay for the goods if Hanson's Sportswear would issue a promissory note bearing interest

Many business assets are bought on credit through notes payable.

at 12 percent a year. Columbia accepted this arrangement so that Hanson's Sportswear could pay for the goods later but Columbia could have legal protection for the debt.

Recording the Issuance of a Note Payable

OBJECTIVE 4

Record routine notes payable transactions.

Hanson's Sportswear records the note payable transaction in its accounting records by making a general journal entry as shown below. This entry involves a debit to Furniture and Fixtures and a credit to Notes Payable—Trade.

19X2					
Mar.	*18*	*Furniture and Fixtures*		*5 0 0 0 00*	
		Notes Payable—Columbia			*5 0 0 0 00*
		Issued a 90-day, 12% note			
		for store furnishings to			
		Columbia Equipment Co.			

No entry is made for the interest at the time the note is given. The interest will be recorded later when it is paid.

Recording Payment of the Note and Its Interest

On the maturity date, June 16, Hanson's Sportswear pays the $5,000 principal plus the $150 in interest. This transaction is recorded in general journal form as shown below.

19X2					
June	*16*	*Notes Payable—Columbia*		*5 0 0 0 00*	
		Interest Expense		*1 5 0 00*	
		Cash			*5 1 5 0 00*
		Payment of March 18 note			
		to Columbia Equipment			
		Company			

Renewing or Making a Partial Payment on a Note

Sometimes the firm that has issued a note asks for an extension of time in which to pay. If the note payable is renewed for another period of time, no additional accounting entries are required. The usual accounting entry is made when the note is paid on the deferred maturity date. Obviously, interest would be charged for the entire period of the debt.

You will probably have to pay the interest in order to renew the note.

If only partial payment of a note is made at its maturity, a check is prepared for the amount that is being paid. This amount is endorsed on the note by the payee, or the old note is canceled and a new one is issued for the balance due.

If no agreement exists to the contrary, a noninterest-bearing note that is not paid at maturity begins at that time to bear interest at a rate established by law in each state. The note continues to bear interest until it is paid.

Recording a Discounted Note Payable

OBJECTIVE 5

Record the discounting of a note payable to a bank.

Businesses often borrow money from banks and sign notes payable as evidence of the debts. Banks always charge interest on loans. Like the interest on the note payable to the Columbia Equipment Company, the interest on a bank loan may be paid at maturity. In many cases, however, the bank deducts the interest in advance, and the borrower receives only the difference between the face amount of the note and the interest on it to maturity. This arrangement, which is called **discounting,** works in the following way.

Suppose Hanson's Sportswear arranges to borrow $6,000 at 10 percent from its bank on May 1 by discounting a 30-day note payable. The interest is calculated according to the formula given earlier.

$$\text{Interest} = \text{Principal} \times \text{Rate} \times \text{Time}$$
$$= \$6{,}000 \times 0.10 \times (30/360) = \$50$$

The bank deducts the $50 interest from the $6,000 face amount of the note and Hanson's Sportswear receives the difference, which is $5,950.

$$\text{Proceeds} = \text{Face Amount} - \text{Discount}$$
$$\$5{,}950 = \$6{,}000 - \$50$$

The firm will probably have the bank deposit the proceeds in its checking account.

Recording the Issuance of a Discounted Note

The effect of this transaction is shown below in general journal form. Notes Payable—Bank is credited because the business wishes to distinguish notes payable to banks from notes payable to businesses. Cash is debited for the amount of cash actually received, and Interest Expense is debited for the amount of interest that was deducted.

19X2					
May	*1*	*Cash*		*5 9 5 0 00*	
		Interest Expense		*5 0 00*	
		Notes Payable—Bank			*6 0 0 0 00*
		Record receipt of bank			
		note			

Recording the Payment of a Discounted Note

The maturity date of Hanson's Sportswear's note is May 31. The firm prepares a check for $6,000 on May 31 to pay the note. The accountant debits Notes Payable—Bank and credits Cash to record the payment. Since the interest was deducted in advance by the bank and was recorded at the time the note was issued, no further entry for it is required. Only the face amount of the note is paid at maturity.

19X2				
May	31	*Notes Payable*	6 0 0 0 00	
		Cash		6 0 0 0 00
		Record payment of note		

The Notes Payable Register

If many notes payable are issued, it may be convenient to keep a record of the details by maintaining a notes payable register. This record shows the important information about each note payable on a single line. The information includes the date of the note, the payee, where the note is payable, the time it is to run, its maturity date, its face amount, and the interest rate and amount of interest, if any. At the end of each accounting period, a schedule of notes payable can be prepared by listing the unpaid notes that appear in the notes payable register. The total must agree with the Notes Payable account(s) in the general ledger, as though proving to a control account.

Reporting Notes Payable and Interest Expense

Notes payable represent financial obligations of the business. They appear on the balance sheet as liabilities. As explained earlier, Hanson's Sportswear has set up separate accounts called Notes Payable—Trade and Notes Payable—Bank. Both accounts are shown on the balance sheet. Notes due within one year are usually classified as current liabilities, and notes due in more than one year are classified as long-term liabilities. The notes presented in this chapter are current liabilities. Long-term liabilities are discussed in Chapter 22.

Interest expense usually appears on the income statement as a nonoperating expense. It is listed under Other Expense, and it is deducted from Net Income from Operations, as shown below.

Sales	$50,000
Cost of Goods Sold	35,000
Gross Profit	$15,000
Operating Expenses	8,000
Net Income from Operations	$ 7,000
Other Income	
Other Expense	
Interest Expense	900
Net Income	$ 6,100

SELF-REVIEW

1. List the elements of a negotiable instrument.
2. Compute the maturity date of a 60-day note issued on January 17.
3. Compute the interest on a note payable of $3,000 at 10 percent for 30 days.
4. How much cash will you receive if your business discounts a $5,000, 90-day note payable at the bank at a discount rate of 12 percent?
5. Of what value is a notes payable register?

Answers to Self-Review

1. A negotiable instrument must (a) be in writing and signed by the maker; (b) contain an unconditional promise or order to pay a definite amount of money; (c) be payable on demand or at another time that can be determined; (d) be payable to the order of the bearer; and (e) if addressed to a drawee, be clearly identified.
2. The maturity date of a 60-day note issued on January 17 is computed as follows.

		Total
Days in January (31 − 17)	14	
Days in February	28	42
Days in March	18	60

   The due date is therefore March 18.
3. Interest = \$3,000 × 0.10 × (30/360) = \$25
4. Proceeds = Face Amount − Discount
   Discount = \$5,000 × 0.12 × (90/360) = \$150
   Proceeds = \$5,000 − \$150 = \$4,850
5. A notes payable register is valuable in keeping up with payments, interest, and due dates of liabilities.

NOTES RECEIVABLE

Some firms accept promissory notes from customers. For example, instead of paying cash immediately, a customer may be allowed to use a promissory note to finance a purchase of goods. A note that a firm obtains with a customer's written promise to pay in the future is called a **note receivable.**

A note receivable is an asset, as is any receivable. It represents the promise of a customer (or other party) to pay the debt in the future. In return for not receiving cash immediately, the company issuing the note usually charges interest. However, it can be noninterest-bearing if the parties involved prefer it that way. The methods used to determine maturity dates and interest due on notes receivable are the same as those used for notes payable. Of course, the entries needed to record notes receivable in a firm's accounting records are different from those used to record notes payable.

A firm may accept a note receivable from a customer at the time of a sale or when extending credit on a past-due account. The procedures for handling notes receivable are described in the following typical examples.

Noninterest-Bearing Notes Receivable

Suppose John Rose has an overdue balance of \$500 in his account with Hanson's Sportswear. On April 1, 19X2, Rose offers to give the firm a 30-day, noninterest-bearing note to obtain an extension of time in which to pay. Hanson's Sportswear agrees to this arrange-

Information Block: Communication

Persuasive Messages

In the business world, *persuasion* is a daily occurrence with professionals who manage operations, make decisions, and plan for the future. Many oral and written communication situations require persuasion strategies for appropriate decisions.

A persuasive request may be for money, time, a policy change, cooperation, or a new procedure or approach. Receivers may react positively, neutrally, and/or negatively to all or part of the request. The receiver's anticipated reaction will determine the degree of persuasion needed for the situation. Nevertheless, the communicator's primary objective is to convince the receiver to support the request and to take action.

When an oral or written message will result in a situation where the receiver may or may not want to fulfill a request or make a decision, business professionals should apply an indirect approach to following a plan for persuasive messages.

- *Capture the receiver's attention.* Begin your message with a short, relevant opening sentence or paragraph. Consider opening your message with the request, a question, a quotation, or a relevant fact.
- *Create interest and desire in the request or recommendation.* Share relevant details, descriptions, facts, financial data, and comparisons

ment because a note receivable provides stronger evidence of the debt in the event legal action becomes necessary.

OBJECTIVE 6
Record routine notes receivable transactions.

Recording Receipt of a Noninterest-Bearing Note

Hanson's Sportswear records the receipt of Rose's note in the general journal, as shown below. Notice that a new asset account called Notes Receivable is debited for $500, and Accounts Receivable/John Rose is credited for $500. The credit part of the entry is recorded as Accounts Receivable/John Rose because it must be posted in two places.

19X2					
April	*1*	*Notes Receivable*		*500 00*	
		Accounts Rec./John Rose			*500 00*
		To record 30-day note			

that appeal to the receiver's emotions or logical reasoning. Demonstrate how the receiver or company will benefit from supporting the request. Benefits may be in terms of money, time, profitability, productivity, or sales. This section of a written persuasive message may be two to four paragraphs.

- *Request the receiver to take action.* Since your objective is to persuade the receiver to fulfill your request, state the desired action with confidence and courtesy.

Persuasive communication situations—oral or written—require much planning, receiver analysis, and selection of relevant information to achieve the objective of gaining support for the request. Persuasive messages may be somewhat longer than positive/neutral and negative messages. Develop your communication skills by using the plan for persuasive messages.

Project: Assume you are the financial manager for Piedmont Telephone Company (150 Northern Boulevard, San Diego, CA 92008). With the impact of new technology, the company's needs for capital improvements have increased. You want your superior, Nancy Perez, Chief Financial Officer, to approve the purchase of new computerized equipment. Prepare a persuasive message to Ms. Perez regarding your proposal. Provide any additional facts to complete your message. Remember to follow the steps for planning and developing effective business communication and the plan for persuasive messages.

1. The Accounts Receivable control account must be credited in the general ledger.
2. John Rose's account must be credited in the accounts receivable subsidiary ledger.

As a result of this double-posting procedure, the total of all the balances in the subsidiary ledger will remain equal to the balance of the Accounts Receivable control account in the general ledger.

When Rose pays the note at maturity, an entry will be made in the cash receipts journal. This entry will consist of a debit to Cash and a credit to Notes Receivable. Rose's note will then be marked "Paid" and returned to him.

Calculating the Maturity Date

The maturity date of a note receivable is calculated in the same way as the maturity date of a note payable. In the case of John Rose's note receivable, the 30-day note taken on April 1 will be due on May 1 (29 days in April plus 1 day in May).

Interest-Bearing Notes Receivable

Most firms are willing to meet customers more than halfway to make sales and to retain goodwill. However, a customer who does not settle a bill within the credit period originally agreed upon can usually expect to pay interest on the amount owed in order to receive an extension of credit. Thus promissory notes issued under such conditions are normally interest-bearing. Assume that Hanson's Sportswear agrees to accept a 60-day, 12 percent note for $400 from Laura Morgan to cover her past-due account. The note is dated April 14, 19X2.

Recording an Interest-Bearing Note Receivable

When the business receives the note, an entry is made in the general journal. This entry involves a debit to Notes Receivable for $400 and a credit to Accounts Receivable/Laura Morgan for $400.

19X2					
April	*14*	*Notes Receivable*		*400 00*	
		Accts. Rec./Laura Morgan			*400 00*
		To record a 60-day,			
		12% note			

Calculating Interest, Maturity Date, and Maturity Value

The interest on $400 for 60 days at 12 percent is computed by using the standard interest formula.

$$\text{Interest} = \$400 \times 0.12 \times (60/360) = \$8$$

The maturity date of a note receivable is figured the same way as is that of a note payable.

The maturity date of Morgan's note is June 13. This date is determined as shown below.

Days the note will run in April: 30 − 14 = 16	16 days
Days the note will run in May	31 days
Total days to the end of May	47 days
Days in June to maturity: 60 − 47 = 13	13 days
Total period of the note	60 days

Collecting an Interest-Bearing Note Receivable

Morgan's payment of the note on the maturity date will include the $400 face amount of the note plus $8 interest. Thus the maturity value of the note is $408. Hanson's Sportswear records the collection of the note by debiting Cash for the total amount, crediting Notes Receivable for $400, and crediting Interest Income for $8, as illustrated in general journal form on the next page.

19X2				
June	13	Cash	408.00	
		Notes Rec./Laura Morgan		400.00
		Interest Income		8.00
		Collection of Laura Morgan's note		

Accounting for Partial Collection of a Note

Suppose that Laura Morgan offers to pay half her note if Hanson's Sportswear will renew the balance for an additional 30 days at 12 percent interest. Ordinarily, any payment made on a note is applied first to the interest due. The remaining amount is then applied to the principal owed. In this case Morgan is paying the interest to maturity of the original note, $8, plus half the principal of the note, $200, for a total of $208. The entry to record the transaction consists of a debit to Cash for the total, a credit to Notes Receivable for $200, and a credit to Interest Income for $8, as shown below in general journal form.

19X2				
June	13	Cash	208.00	
		Notes Rec./Laura Morgan		200.00
		Interest Income		8.00
		Collection of part of Laura Morgan's note		

The original note may be endorsed or receipted in part by Hanson's Sportswear to reflect the partial payment. Or the firm may cancel the first note and obtain a new note for the remaining balance from Laura Morgan.

Note Receivable Not Collected at Maturity

If a note is not paid at maturity, the note is said to be "dishonored." It is not proper to carry the amount of a dishonored note in the Notes Receivable account. Suppose Laura Morgan dishonors the note that she issued to Hanson's Sportswear. The firm should transfer the balance she owes out of Notes Receivable and back into Accounts Receivable. This transfer is done by making the general journal entry that follows.

19X2					
June	*13*	*Accounts Rec./Laura Morgan*		*408 00*	
		Notes Receivable			*400 00*
		Interest Income			*8 00*
		To charge back Morgan's			
		dishonored note plus			
		interest to maturity			

If a customer does not pay a note when it is due, it should be noted on the customer's credit history.

Notice that both the Accounts Receivable control account in the general ledger and Morgan's subsidiary account in the accounts receivable ledger must be debited. Since Morgan now owes the original balance of $400 plus $8 interest on the note, each of these accounts is debited for $408. The offsetting credits are to Notes Receivable for the face amount of the note ($400) and to Interest Income for the interest ($8).

After an interest-bearing note is dishonored, interest continues to run on the note. The rate of interest charged is usually specified by law, which in most cases is higher than the original rate shown on the note. In some cases, the parties may agree on a rate different from the statutory rate. A note usually calls for payment by the maker of all attorney's fees and other costs incurred by the holder that result from efforts to collect the obligation.

Notes Received at the Time of a Sale

The notes from Rose and Morgan were obtained when past-due accounts were extended. Hanson's Sportswear does not engage in a type of business in which notes are ordinarily received at the time of sale. If the firm receives an occasional note when a sale is made, the transaction is recorded in the general journal as follows.

19X2					
June	*5*	*Notes Receivable*		*450 00*	
		Sales			*450 00*
		Received 90-day, 10% note			
		from Dave Roberts on			
		sale of goods			

If it is common for a business to receive notes from customers at the time of sale, a special column will be created in the sales journal for debiting Notes Receivable. In this way the total of the notes can be posted to the general ledger in one amount at the end of each month.

Discounting a Note Receivable

One of the advantages of a note receivable over an open account is that the holder of the note can borrow on it by discounting it at a bank. The bank accepts the note and charges interest on its maturity

OBJECTIVE 7
Compute the proceeds from a discounted note receivable.

value at a specified discount (interest) rate for the number of days remaining until maturity. The bank deducts this discount charge in advance, and the seller receives the net proceeds (the maturity value less the discount charge). The bank usually credits the net proceeds to the firm's checking account.

Noninterest-Bearing Note Discounted

Suppose Hanson's Sportswear has to raise cash to meet an obligation at the end of September. The owners decide to discount a 90-day, noninterest-bearing note receivable for $600 that the firm obtained from Peter Ross on July 2. The note is payable on September 30. Hanson's Sportswear turns the note over to the Central State Bank for discounting on August 31. The bank's discount rate is 12 percent. This transaction must be examined carefully because of new elements involved.

Action Before Discounting. Hanson's Sportswear receives the note on July 2. The amount of the note ($600) is debited to the asset account Notes Receivable in a general journal entry. The maturity date is determined to be September 30 (29 days in July + 31 days in August + 30 days in September).

Calculating the Discount and the Proceeds. The method used to determine the discount and the proceeds on the note receivable is similar to that described for a discounted note payable.

1. Determine the maturity value of the note. Since the note from Peter Ross is noninterest-bearing, its maturity value is the same as its face amount—$600.
2. Determine the number of days in the discount period (the number of days from the discount date to the maturity date).

Days the note will run in September to maturity	30 days
Total discount period	30 days

3. Determine the amount of discount to be charged by the bank. This is found by applying the regular interest formula (Interest = Principal × Rate × Time) as shown below. Notice that time in this formula is time left on the note from the date of discounting to maturity date.

$$\begin{aligned}\text{Discount} &= \text{Maturity value} \times \text{Discount rate} \times \text{Discount period}\\ &= \$600 \times 0.12 \times (30/360)\\ &= \$6\end{aligned}$$

▲ **REMEMBER!**
MV − D = PR

4. Determine the proceeds (*PR*)—the amount to be received from the bank. This amount is the maturity value (*MV*) of the note less the amount of the discount (*D*). This relationship may be expressed by the formula $MV - D = PR$. Inserting this discounted note situation into the formula gives $600 − $6 = $594. The proceeds, $594, are deposited to Hanson's Sportswear's checking account by the bank.

Recording the Discounted Note Receivable. When the computations are completed, Hanson's Sportswear records the discounting of the note in general journal form as illustrated below. Notice that two debits are involved—one to Cash for the proceeds ($594) and one to Interest Expense for the amount of the discount ($6). Also notice that the principal of the note ($600) is credited to a new account called Notes Receivable Discounted (a contra asset account) rather than to the Notes Receivable account. On the balance sheet, Notes Receivable Discounted offsets the amount carried as an asset in the Notes Receivable account.

19X2					
Aug.	31	Cash		594 00	
		Interest Expense		6 00	
		Notes Receivable Discounted			600 00
		To record discounting of			
		the Peter Ross note			

Contingent Liability for a Discounted Note. When a note receivable is discounted, it must be endorsed by the party selling or discounting the note. If the maker (in our example, Peter Ross) of the note does not pay it at maturity, the holder (the bank) can then obtain payment from the endorser (Hanson's Sportswear). Hence the endorser has a possible, or contingent, liability amounting to $600. This fact was recorded in Hanson's Sportswear's accounting records by crediting Notes Receivable Discounted. On the balance sheet, the balance of Notes Receivable Discounted is deducted from the balance of Notes Receivable. The difference represents the notes receivable still held, which amount to $1,300 for Hanson's Sportswear.

Notes Receivable	$1,900
Less Notes Receivable Discounted	600
	$1,300

Another commonly used procedure is to show only the net undiscounted notes on the balance sheet and to include a footnote to the financial statements indicating the amount of discounted notes receivable on which the company has a contingent liability.

Discounted Noninterest-Bearing Note Paid at Maturity. At the maturity date, the holder of the discounted note presents it to the maker for payment. If Peter Ross pays the note when the bank presents it to him, Hanson's Sportswear has no further contingent liability. At that time the firm makes a general journal entry to remove the liability.

19X2				
Sept. 30	Notes Receivable Discounted		600 00	
	Notes Receivable			600 00
	Record payment of discounted note of Peter Ross			

Discounted Noninterest-Bearing Note Dishonored at Maturity. If Ross dishonors his note by failing to pay it at maturity, the bank may file a formal protest through a notary public. Hanson's Sportswear then has to pay the bank the maturity value of the note plus the protest fee charged by the notary public. Banks often deduct this amount from the firm's checking account and send a debit memorandum with the dishonored note and the protest form. Assuming that the protest fee is $10 in this case, the resulting entry is a debit to Accounts Receivable/Peter Ross for $610 and a credit to Cash for $610. Notice that the total of the maturity value and the protest fee ($610)—not merely the amount due on the dishonored note—is charged to the Accounts Receivable control account in the general ledger and the customer's account in the subsidiary ledger.

One more entry is required to complete the record of this transaction. By paying the dishonored note, Hanson's Sportswear has removed the contingent liability that was set up when the note was discounted. To eliminate the liability from the firm's accounting records, an entry must be made in the general journal debiting Notes Receivable Discounted and crediting Notes Receivable.

After paying the dishonored note, Hanson's Sportswear would probably contact the maker of the note and then turn the note over to an attorney for collection if payment is not received at once.

Interest-Bearing Note Discounted

The owner of Hanson's Sportswear now decides to increase the firm's available cash by discounting a note received from Kathy Graham on March 3. The principal is $600, the note runs for 60 days, and the interest rate is 10 percent. The maturity date of the note is May 2.

Action Before Discounting. On March 3, when Hanson's Sportswear obtained the note receivable from Kathy Graham, the Notes Receivable account was debited and Accounts Receivable/Kathy Graham was credited.

Calculating the Discount and the Proceeds. On April 2, Hanson's Sportswear arranges to discount Graham's note at the bank at 12 percent.

The discount and the proceeds on the note are computed by following the steps below.

1. Determine the maturity value of the note. We can use the easy formula, $MV = P + I$, to find the maturity value by adding the face amount ($600) and the interest for 60 days at 10 percent ($10). Thus the maturity value of the note is $610.
2. Determine the number of days in the discount period. By counting the days from the discount date to the maturity date, we find that the discount period is 30 days.

Days the note will run in April (30 − 2)	28 days
Days the note will run in May to maturity	2 days
Total discount period	30 days

3. Determine the amount of the discount. The bank will levy its charge of 12 percent on the maturity value ($610) for the discount period (30 days). Putting these figures into the interest formula, Discount = Maturity value × Discount rate × Discount period, gives the discount.

$$\text{Discount} = \$610 \times 0.12 \times (30/360) = \$6.10$$

4. Determine the proceeds. The amount to be received from the bank is $603.90, the maturity value minus the discount charge ($610 − $6.10).

Recording the Discounted Note Receivable. The discounting of the note receivable is recorded at Hanson's Sportswear as shown below in general journal form. This time the entry consists of a debit to Cash and two credits—one to Notes Receivable Discounted and the other to Interest Income.

19X2					
Apr.	*2*	*Cash*		*603 90*	
		Notes Receivable Discounted			*600 00*
		Interest Income			*3 90*
		Discounted Kathy Graham's note			

The credit to Interest Income of $3.90 represents the $10.00 total interest determined in computing the maturity value, less the discount of $6.10 charged by the bank. If the proceeds had been less than the face amount of the note, the difference would have been debited to Interest Expense.

Discounted Interest-Bearing Note Paid at Maturity. If Kathy Graham pays the note at the maturity date, Hanson's Sportswear cancels the contingent liability that was set up at the time the note was discounted. It debits $600 to Notes Receivable Discounted and credits the same amount to Notes Receivable.

19X2				
May	2	*Notes Receivable Discounted*	600 00	
		Notes Receivable		600 00
		Kathy Graham note paid at maturity		

Discounted Interest-Bearing Note Dishonored at Maturity. If Kathy Graham dishonors the note at the maturity date, Hanson's Sportswear must pay the maturity value (the face amount of the note plus the interest) and any protest fee to the bank. The firm charges the entire sum to the Accounts Receivable control account in the general ledger and Graham's account in the accounts receivable subsidiary ledger. An entry is also made to remove the contingent liability by debiting Notes Receivable Discounted and crediting Notes Receivable for the face amount of the note.

The Notes Receivable Register

If a firm has many notes receivable, it may be convenient to set up a notes receivable register. This record has somewhat the same form as the notes payable register discussed earlier in the chapter. Information recorded in the notes receivable register includes the date of the note, the maker, where the note is payable, the time it is to run, the maturity date, the face amount, and the rate and amount of interest, if any. Columns are also provided to record the dates on which notes have been discounted and the banks that are holding the notes.

Reporting Notes Receivable and Interest Income

The Notes Receivable account is a current asset and appears on the balance sheet, usually just below the accounts for Cash and Accounts Receivable. Interest Income is shown on the income statement as Other (Nonoperating) Income. It is listed below Net Income from Operations and added to it. The expense that arises from bank charges on discounted notes is shown in the Interest Expense account. This account also appears below the Net Income from Operations but is deducted. The final sections of an income statement for a firm that has received and paid interest might look like this.

Sales	$50,000
Cost of Goods Sold	35,000
Gross Profit	$15,000
Operating Expenses	8,000
Net Income from Operations	$ 7,000
Other Income and Expenses	
Interest Income	125
Interest Expense	(200)
Net Income	$ 6,925

DRAFTS

A **draft** is a written order that requires the person or business firm addressed to pay a stated sum of money to another party. An ordinary check is one form of draft. Two others are bank drafts and commercial drafts.

Bank Drafts

A **bank draft** is a check written by a bank that orders another bank—one in which it has funds on deposit—to pay the indicated amount to a specified person or business firm. Since a bank draft is more readily accepted than an individual's check, a person may use a bank draft to pay a debt to an out-of-town supplier with whom credit has not been established.

Another type of draft is called a **cashier's check.** This form of draft is prepared by a bank official. It orders the bank to pay the specified amount from its own (the bank's) funds. Like a bank draft, a cashier's check offers greater protection to a creditor than an individual's check. For this reason, cashier's checks are sometimes used to pay bills.

The purchase of a bank draft or cashier's check is recorded in the general journal by debiting the account payable the draft is intended to settle, debiting an expense account for the bank service charge, and crediting Cash. The business issues one of its own checks to the bank to cover the amount of the draft or cashier's check and the amount of the service charge.

For example, suppose a bill for $575 is to be settled by sending the creditor a bank draft instead of a regular check. The bank imposes a service charge of $2 for the draft. The effect of the entry required for the payment is shown here in general journal form.

19X2					
Feb.	5	*Accounts Payable/Brandon Inc.*		575 00	
		Bank Miscellaneous Expenses		2 00	
		Cash			577 00
		Paid Brandon, Inc., bill			
		with bank draft			

Commercial Drafts

A **commercial draft** is issued by a person or business firm to order another person or firm to pay a specified sum of money at a certain time. This instrument is used to take care of special shipment and collection problems.

A **sight draft** is a commercial draft that is payable on presentation. It is honored by payment. No accounting entry (other than a memorandum notation) is made for the issuance of a sight draft. If the draft is honored, the transaction is recorded as a cash receipt.

Sight drafts may be used for collecting accounts receivable, especially past-due accounts. A draft is usually sent for collection to the customer's bank. If the customer does not honor the draft, his or her credit standing at the bank may be injured. Thus a debtor is more likely to honor a draft than a collection letter.

It is also possible to ship goods with a sight draft to obtain cash on delivery. In this situation a business paper called a **bill of lading** is sent to a bank near the customer. A sight draft is attached to the bill of lading. The customer must pay the draft to the bank before getting the bill of lading, which is needed to obtain the goods. The collecting bank sends the money, less its collection fee, to the firm issuing the draft. When the funds arrive, the firm records the transaction as a cash sale and debits an expense account for the collection fee. Transmitting a sight draft with a bill of lading is a common practice when shipments are made to customers with poor credit ratings or to new customers who have not yet established good credit.

A **time draft** differs from a sight draft in that a period of time is allowed for payment. The maturity date of a time draft may be stated in several different ways.

1. The maturity date may be a date specified in the draft.
2. It may be a specified number of days after the date of the draft.
3. It may be a specified number of days after acceptance of the draft.

A time draft requires no accounting entry (other than a memorandum notation) when it is issued. If the person upon whom the instrument is drawn agrees to honor it at maturity, this agreement is indicated by writing "Accepted" on the face of the draft, signing it, and dating it. The accepted draft is then recorded in the accounting records as a note payable and the draft is returned to the drawer, who enters it in the accounting records as a note receivable.

TRADE ACCEPTANCES

A **trade acceptance** is a special form of commercial time draft that arises out of the sale of goods and has this fact noted on its face. The original transaction may be recorded in the same manner as a sale on credit. When the draft has been accepted, it is accounted for as a promissory note. Merchants have found that they have fewer credit losses on trade acceptances than on open-account transactions. Trade acceptances can also be discounted. An example of a trade acceptance is shown in Figure 16–2.

FIGURE 16–2
A Trade Acceptance

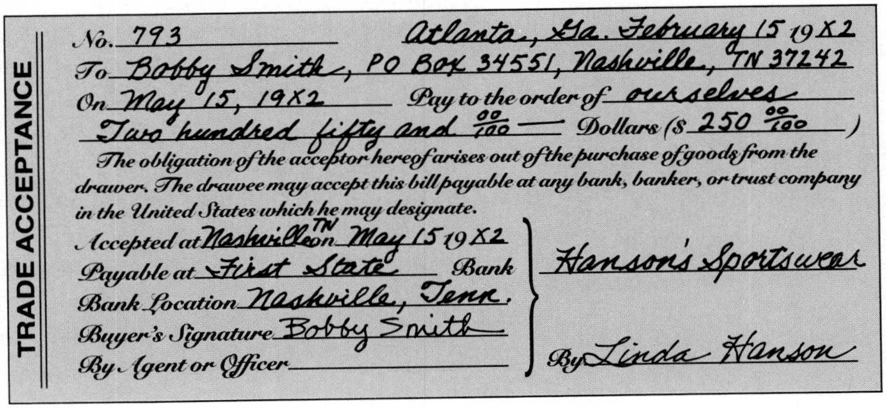
TRADE ACCEPTANCE

No. 793 Atlanta, Ga. February 15 19X2

To Bobby Smith, PO BOX 34551, Nashville, TN 37242

On May 15, 19X2 Pay to the order of ourselves

Two hundred fifty and 00/100 Dollars ($250 00/100)

The obligation of the acceptor hereof arises out of the purchase of goods from the drawer. The drawee may accept this bill payable at any bank, banker, or trust company in the United States which he may designate.

Accepted at Nashville TN on May 15 19X2

Payable at First State Bank

Bank Location Nashville, Tenn.

Buyer's Signature Bobby Smith

By Agent or Officer

Hanson's Sportswear

By Linda Hanson

Information Block: Computers in Accounting

Computer Viruses

Computer viruses are spread from computer to computer via contact with an infected source. The virus is actually a program designed to attach itself to the operating system or application programs on another computer. The virus can then spread quickly to any program used on the infected computer. Some viruses are rather innocuous and cause little if any damage. However, other viruses can be very destructive. The worst of these viruses (with names like DataLock and Disk Killer) destroy all applications and data on the infected system. Regardless of the intent of these viruses, the programmers who create them are engaging in an illegal activity.

In recent years, there have been several "outbreaks" of computer viruses. For example, the Michelangelo virus, thought to have infected thousands of computers, was set to destroy all the data on those machines on March 6, 1992. To counter its effects, many individuals and businesses used special software to detect and erase the virus before it was activated to destroy their data.

Viruses can be spread rather easily. Public bulletin boards and shareware programs were initially responsible for the rapid spread of viruses. Anyone could post an infected shareware program on an electronic bulletin board. Unsuspecting users would download and run the program, releasing the virus to their system. Once infected, the computer and its applications could then infect other programs.

Controlling the spread of viruses has become critical. Special safeguards installed on public bulletin boards and computer systems have reduced but not eliminated the virus threat. Several software development companies have produced software specifically designed to scan and remove viruses from application programs. Software publishers such as Microsoft, Lotus, and others take precautions to verify that the software they sell to their customers is free of viruses. Before the disks are duplicated, the software is scanned for any known viruses and is checked again at various stages of production to determine whether the disk has been infected during the duplication process.

A virus can result in the loss of valuable data. Some precautions that you can take to avoid viruses are: (1) write-protect your disks before inserting them into a disk drive, (2) never boot a computer from a floppy disk that has not been checked for viruses, and (3) test software on a stand-alone computer before using the application on a network.

INTERNAL CONTROL OF NOTES PAYABLE AND NOTES RECEIVABLE

Notes payable must be carefully controlled because they represent financial obligations of the business. Only a limited number of persons should be allowed to obligate the business by signing notes payable. All notes payable should be recorded immediately. Responsibility for prompt payment of interest expense and the principal of the note should be fixed to a specific person or department. Managers should oversee the prompt payment of these obligations to lessen the amount of interest expense and to make sure that the company's credit rating is not hurt by late payment of debts. All paid notes should be marked "Canceled" or "Paid" and kept on file for a reasonable time.

Drafts are essentially checks and must be handled just as carefully as checks. Since notes receivable are negotiable, they have many of the same characteristics as checks. Thus the internal control procedures devised for these instruments must treat them as almost equivalent to cash items. Authority to accept notes must be delegated to specific persons. All notes received must be entered promptly in the appropriate journal and stored securely in a safe or fireproof vault to which access is carefully controlled. In addition, the actual notes on hand must be verified periodically and compared with the amounts shown in the notes receivable register.

Just prior to a note's maturity, its maker should be informed of the approaching due date and the amount owed. If payment is not received on the due date, the maker should be contacted immediately by a responsible person to find out what is happening. Management should review all past-due notes promptly and take necessary steps, including legal action if appropriate, to ensure payment.

MANAGERIAL IMPLICATIONS

Managers should be aware of the possibility of financing operations through the use of short-term notes payable. Since interest is charged for the use of these funds, borrowing should be carefully controlled and limited. The authority to commit the firm to such borrowing should be limited.

Because notes payable and notes receivable are negotiable instruments, they fall under the rules and regulations of the Uniform Commercial Code. The firm's rights, responsibilities, and obligations should be fully understood when dealing with these items.

Another possibility of using negotiable instruments is in connection with sales on credit. These instruments (specifically notes receivable) are especially useful when cash is short. Notes receivable due some time in the future can be discounted to raise cash for current operations. In some cases, past-due accounts can be converted into notes receivable. The notes give more legal protection to the creditor and are more likely to be collected. Because notes and drafts are negotiable, internal control procedures must be developed to safeguard them.

SELF-REVIEW

1. When would you want to have a customer sign a note receivable?
2. What does the phrase *dishonoring a note receivable* mean?
3. If a note receivable with a maturity value of $4,400 is discounted with your bank at 12 percent, with 60 days remaining until its maturity date, how much cash will you receive?
4. What kind of account is Notes Receivable Discounted?
5. What is the most common kind of draft?

Answers to Self-Review

1. When a customer is unable to pay a currently due account receivable, it is wise to have a note receivable signed.
2. The maker of the note does not pay it when it is due.
3. You will receive $4,312 ($4,400 – $88 discount).
4. Notes Receivable Discounted is a contra asset account and is shown on the balance sheet as a reduction of Notes Receivable.
5. The most common type of draft is the check written from an ordinary checking account.

CHAPTER 16 Review and Applications

CHAPTER SUMMARY

Notes payable usually involve interest for the borrower. When a note is given to purchase an asset, the asset account is debited and Notes Payable is credited. When the note is paid at maturity date, Notes Payable is debited for the face of the note, Interest Expense is debited for the amount of interest, and Cash is credited for the total amount paid (principal plus interest).

When money is borrowed from a bank on a note payable, the bank will usually deduct its interest charge immediately from the proceeds of the loan, which is called discounting. The borrower will receive the difference between the discount and the principal as cash. This is recorded by debiting Cash (for the difference between the principal and the discount), debiting Interest Expense (for the amount of the discount), and crediting Notes Payable (for the amount borrowed). Interest Expense is recorded on the income statement below Net Income from Operations in the Other Income/Other Expense area of the statement.

Upon maturity of the note, the full amount of the principal must be repaid. There is no interest payment since the interest was collected by the bank when the loan was made. This is recorded by a debit to Notes Payable and a credit to Cash.

Notes receivable, like notes payable, may be noninterest-bearing or interest-bearing. Most firms will charge interest on granting credit to customers. If the note receivable relates to a sale, the transaction will be recorded by debiting Notes Receivable and crediting Sales. If the note receivable comes into existence because of a customer's failure to pay an accounts receivable, the entry will involve a debit to Notes Receivable and a credit to Accounts Receivable. Any interest that is received upon payment is recorded through a credit to Interest Income, which is reported in the Other Income/Other Expense section of the income statement, below Net Income from Operations.

A firm will usually discount a note receivable because it has an immediate need for cash. Usually the note is discounted at a bank. This transaction is recorded by debiting Cash for the amount of proceeds, crediting Notes Receivable Discounted for the face of the note, and debiting Interest Expense (if the proceeds are less than the principal) or crediting Interest Income (if the proceeds exceed the principal). Notes Receivable Discounted represents a contingent liability of the business. Should the maker of the note receivable fail to pay at maturity, the business will have to pay the bank.

Bank drafts, commercial drafts, and trade acceptances are other types of negotiable instruments sometimes used in business transactions.

GLOSSARY OF NEW TERMS

Bank draft (p. 572) A check written by a bank that orders another bank to pay an indicated amount to a specified party
Banker's year (p. 556) A 360-day period used to calculate interest on a note
Bill of lading (p. 573) A business document that lists goods being sold in a business transaction
Cashier's check (p. 572) A draft on the issuing bank's own funds
Commercial draft (p. 572) A note issued by one party that orders another party to pay a specified sum on a specified date
Discounting (p. 559) Deducting in advance the interest on a note payable or receivable
Draft (p. 572) A written order, such as a check, requiring one party to pay a stated sum of money to another party
Face amount (p. 556) An amount of money indicated to be paid, exclusive of interest or discounts; also called face value
Interest (p. 556) The price charged for the use of money or credit
Maturity value (p. 556) The total amount (principal plus interest) that must be paid when a note comes due
Note payable (p. 557) A liability that represents the debtor's written promise to pay a specified amount at a specified future date
Note receivable (p. 561) An asset that represents the creditor's written promise to pay a specified amount at a specified future date
Principal (p. 556) The amount shown on the face of a note
Promissory note (p. 555) A negotiable instrument that gives evidence of a debt and a promise to pay
Sight draft (p. 572) A commercial draft payable on presentation
Time draft (p. 573) A commercial draft payable at a specified time
Trade acceptance (p. 573) A special commercial time draft used in transactions involving the sale of goods

REVIEW QUESTIONS

1. What are the requirements that must be met in order for a document to be negotiable?
2. What is the face amount of a note? The principal?
3. Why do most notes bear interest?
4. What is meant by "discounting a note payable"?
5. If a note dated March 31 has a three-month term, on what date must the note be paid?
6. Explain how the maturity value of a note is computed.
7. How are notes payable shown on the balance sheet?
8. Are notes payable likely to be given in the purchase of merchandise? The purchase of equipment? The borrowing of money? Why?
9. Explain why records must be kept of the due dates of all notes payable.

10. How does a note receivable differ from an account receivable?
11. How, if at all, does computation of the maturity value of a note receivable differ from that for a note payable?
12. What is a dishonored note receivable?
13. What is meant by "discounting a note receivable"?
14. Explain how to compute the proceeds from discounting a note receivable.
15. When is a discounted note receivable considered a contingent liability?
16. What is a draft?
17. Explain a cashier's check.
18. What is a trade acceptance?

MANAGERIAL FOCUS

1. Why might managers use outside sources of funds for their business operations? How do they acquire these funds?
2. Why should management be familiar with the Uniform Commercial Code's provisions concerning notes?
3. As a manager, would you consider a note received at the time of sale of merchandise to be as collectible as a note received in exchange for a further extension of credit? Explain.
4. As a manager, why would you insist that dishonored notes receivable be charged back to the Accounts Receivable control account?
5. How can notes receivable be used by management as a means of acquiring cash?
6. Assume that you are a member of the internal audit staff at the Signal Company. A review of office practices indicates that the office manager in the accounting department routinely makes the arrangements with the bank for short-term notes payable and signs the notes. How would you evaluate this practice? What changes would you recommend?

EXERCISES

EXERCISE 16–1 (Obj. 3)

Tutorial

Determining the due dates of notes. Find the due date of each of the following notes.

1. A note dated January 11, 19X3, due one year from date
2. A note dated June 8, 19X4, due in 120 days
3. A note dated October 28, 19X3, due three months from date

EXERCISE 16–2 (Obj. 2, 3)

Tutorial

Determining the maturity value of notes. Compute the maturity value for each of the following notes.

1. A note payable with a face amount of $5,000, dated February 10, 19X4, due in 90 days, bearing interest at 10 percent
2. A note payable with a face amount of $2,000, dated May 15, 19X5, due in three months, bearing interest at 12 percent

EXERCISE 16-3
(Obj. 4, 5)

Tutorial

Recording the issuance of notes payable. During 19X4, the Cromwell Company borrowed money at the Valley National Bank on two occasions. On June 3 the company borrowed $6,000, giving a 90-day, 8 percent note, and on December 12 the company discounted at 10 percent a $10,000, 90-day note payable.

1. Give the entries in general journal form to record the issuance of each of the above notes.
2. Give the entries in general journal form to record the issuance of a check in payment of each of the notes.

EXERCISE 16-4
(Obj. 4)

Tutorial

Recording a note given for a purchase of equipment. On July 1, 19X4, the Black Company purchased a microcomputer (office equipment) for $2,200, signing a 90-day, 16 percent note for the entire purchase price. Give the entry in general journal form to record this transaction.

EXERCISE 16-5
(Obj. 4, 6, 7)

Tutorial

Recording the receipt of a note for a past-due account. On February 15, 19X3, the Rose Company received a 90-day note receivable for $2,500 from George Adams, a customer whose account was past due. The note bears interest at 10 percent.

1. Give the entry in general journal form that Rose Company would make to record receipt of the note.
2. Give the entry in general journal form to record the discounting of this note receivable on April 6 at the Second State Bank. The bank charged a discount rate of 13 percent.

EXERCISE 16-6
(Obj. 4, 6)

Tutorial

Recording the payment of a discounted note receivable. In general journal form, give the entry required when a discounted note is paid on the maturity date.

EXERCISE 16-7
(Obj. 4, 6)

Tutorial

Recording a dishonored note receivable. Give the general journal entry required when a maker dishonors a note receivable that you have endorsed and discounted to the bank.

EXERCISE 16-8
(Obj. 3)

Tutorial

Computing the maturity value of notes receivable. Find the maturity value of each of the following notes receivable.

1. A 90-day note, dated February 15, 19X3, with a face value of $12,000, bearing interest at 10 percent
2. A six-month note, dated March 10, 19X3, with a face value of $2,000, bearing interest at 12 percent

EXERCISE 16-9
(Obj. 7)

Computing the proceeds from a discounted note receivable. Assume that the 90-day note described in item 1 of Exercise 16-8 was discounted at a bank on March 17, 19X3. The bank charged a discount rate of 12 percent. Compute the net proceeds.

EXERCISE 16-10
(Obj. 7)

Computing the proceeds from a discounted note receivable. Assume that the six-month note described in item 2 of Exercise 16-8 was discounted at a bank on April 10, 19X3. The bank charged a discount rate of 12 percent. Compute the net proceeds.

PROBLEMS

PROBLEM SET A

PROBLEM 16–1A
(Obj. 2)

Computing interest on notes payable. The notes listed below were issued by several businesses. Find the interest due on each of the following notes, using the interest formula method. Show all calculations.

1. A $1,000 note at 12 percent for 180 days
2. A $2,000 note at 9 percent for four months
3. A $50,000 note at 10 percent for 90 days

PROBLEM 16–2A
(Obj. 2, 3, 4, 5)

Recording transactions involving notes payable. Give the general journal entry to record each of the following transactions.

1. On February 5, 19X3, the Ames Company issued a 180-day, 12 percent note for $16,000 to purchase an automobile.
2. On June 8, 19X3, the Ames Company discounted its own 90-day, noninterest-bearing note with a principal amount of $5,000 at the State Bank. The bank charged a discount rate of 16 percent.
3. The Ames Company paid the February 5 note on its due date.
4. The Ames Company paid the note discounted on June 8 on its due date.

PROBLEM 16–3A
(Obj. 2, 3)

Computing interest and maturity value. The notes received by the O'Malley Manufacturing Company during 19X4 are summarized below. Find the total interest and the maturity value of each note. Show all computations.

DATE	FACE AMOUNT	PERIOD	INTEREST RATE
Jan. 2	$5,000	60 days	12%
May 18	2,000	90 days	13%
Oct. 10	1,200	4 months	10%

PROBLEM 16–4A
(Obj. 7)

Computing the proceeds from discounted notes receivable. The notes receivable held by the Ling Company are summarized below. On July 3, 19X4, Ling discounted all of these notes at the Third State Bank at a discount rate of 13 percent. Find the net proceeds received from discounting each note (19X4 was not a leap year).

NOTE NO.	DATE	FACE AMOUNT	PERIOD	INTEREST RATE
10	Mar. 3, 19X4	$15,000	6 months	12%
8	Feb. 2, 19X4	4,000	1 year	10%
19	June 1, 19X4	1,800	60 days	13%

PROBLEM 16–5A
(Obj. 2, 3, 4, 6, 7)

Recording the receipt, discounting, and payment of notes receivable. On July 16, 19X3, the Arnall Corporation received a 90-day, 12 percent, interest-bearing note from the Arthur Company in settlement of Arthur's past-due account of $2,200. On July 31, Arnall discounted this note at the Fourth National Bank. The bank charged a discount rate of 14 percent. On October 15, Arnall received notice that Arthur had paid the note and the interest on the due date. Give the general journal entries required to record these transactions.

PROBLEM 16-6A (Obj. 1)

Determining elements of a negotiable instrument. Draft a note receivable that includes all the elements of a negotiable instrument.

PROBLEM SET B

PROBLEM 16-1B (Obj. 2)

Computing interest on notes payable. The notes listed below were issued by several businesses. Find the interest due on each of the following notes, using the interest formula method. Show all calculations.

1. A $1,300 note at 12 percent for 90 days
2. A $3,000 note at 8 percent for six months
3. A $20,000 note at 11.5 percent for 75 days

PROBLEM 16-2B (Obj. 2, 3, 4, 5)

Recording transactions involving notes payable. Give the general journal entry to record each of the following transactions.

1. On August 3, 19X3, the Gwen Company issued a 90-day, 11 percent note for $10,000 to purchase a new computer system.
2. The Gwen Company paid the August 3 note when it became due.
3. On November 18, 19X3, the Gwen Company borrowed money from the First State Bank by discounting its own $20,000 note payable. The bank charged a discount rate of 12 percent on this noninterest-bearing note. The note matures in 120 days.
4. The Gwen Company paid the November 18 note when it became due.

PROBLEM 16-3B (Obj. 2, 3)

Computing interest and maturity value. The notes received by the Sung Merchandising Company during 19X3 are summarized below. Find the total interest and the maturity value of each note. Show all computations.

DATE	FACE AMOUNT	PERIOD	INTEREST RATE
Feb. 22	$1,000	30 days	12%
July 8	2,000	60 days	11.25%
Aug. 15	3,200	3 months	12%

PROBLEM 16-4B (Obj. 7)

Computing the proceeds from discounted notes receivable. The notes receivable held by the JRH Company on January 1, 19X4, are summarized below. On January 2, 19X4, JRH discounted all of these notes at the Western National Bank at a discount rate of 14 percent. Find the net proceeds that the firm received from discounting each note (19X4 was not a leap year).

NOTE NO.	DATE	FACE AMOUNT	PERIOD	INTEREST RATE
44	July 1, 19X4	$12,000	1 year	12%
64	Sept. 1, 19X4	8,000	6 months	11%
79	Dec. 1, 19X4	7,500	1 year	13%

PROBLEM 16–5B
(Obj. 2, 3, 4, 6, 7)

Recording the receipt, discounting, and payment of notes receivable. On March 1, 19X3, Jones Discount Stores received a 120-day, 12 percent, interest-bearing note from Central Hospital in settlement of Central's past-due account of $3,000. On April 30 Jones discounted this note at the Bay State Bank. The bank charged a discount rate of 14 percent. On June 29 Jones received notice from the bank that Central had paid the note and the interest.

Instructions

1. Give the entries in general journal form that Jones would make to record all the transactions involving the note from Central.
2. Assume that when the note became due, Central failed to pay it. The bank notified Jones on June 30 and charged Central's account for the maturity value of the note plus a $15 protest fee. Give the entries in general journal form that Jones would make to record the default by the maker of the note.

PROBLEM 16–6B
(Obj. 1)

Drawing up a negotiable instrument. Make up a note payable for $10,000 that will meet all requirements for a negotiable instrument.

CHALLENGE PROBLEM

Joe's Used Cars is owned by Joe Perrot. Mr. Perrot periodically borrows money from Second National Bank. In addition, he allows some customers to sign short-term notes receivable, which he usually discounts at the bank. The bank requires that he endorse all notes receivable that are discounted. Following are selected transactions that occurred in January 19X4.

Instructions

1. Record each of the January transactions in the general journal.
2. Record the additional data in the general journal using the appropriate dates.

TRANSACTIONS

Jan. 15 Mr. Perrot borrows $3,000 from the bank on a note payable. Terms of the note are 12 percent interest and 45 days.

22 Another $4,500 note payable to the bank is discounted immediately. Bank terms on this loan are 10 percent interest and a 90-day due date.

23 A car is sold to Suzanne Carlos for $900 on a note receivable. The terms of this note are 12 percent interest and a 60-day due date.

23 Perrot discounts the Carlos note with the bank. The bank charges a discount rate of 15 percent.

24 David Arnall buys a car for $2,000, paying $1,000 cash and signing a 30-day note for the remainder at 14 percent.

25 Claude Eaves is late paying his account receivable that is due this day. Perrot requires him to sign a 14 percent, 90-day note receivable for the $3,000.

Additional Data

a. Perrot pays all his notes payable on time.
b. Suzanne Carlos defaults on her $900 loan and the bank requires Perrot to honor his endorsement.
c. David Arnall pays his note on time.
d. Claude Eaves pays his note on time.

CRITICAL THINKING PROBLEM

Allen Home Furnishings, a wholesale dealer of country-style home furniture, frequently accepts promissory notes from its customers at the time of sale. Since Allen regularly needs cash to meet its own obligations, it frequently discounts these notes at the bank.

Allen's bookkeeper tells you that he does not bother to credit discounted notes to a Notes Receivable Discounted account. Instead, he makes an entry to debit Cash and Interest Expense and to credit Notes Receivable. He says that using a Notes Receivable Discounted account just makes extra work, and, anyway, once the note is discounted, it becomes the bank's problem.

What is your opinion of the bookkeeper's comments?

CHAPTER 17 Merchandise Inventory

OBJECTIVES

1. Compute inventory cost by applying four commonly used costing methods.
2. Explain the advantages and limitations of each method of inventory costing.
3. Compute inventory value under the lower of cost or market rule.
4. Estimate inventory cost using the gross profit method.
5. Estimate inventory cost using the retail method.
6. Define the accounting terms new to this chapter.

Information about merchandise inventory must be reported on the financial statements at the end of each accounting period. In Part 1 you saw how a small business valued its inventory to provide the necessary data for the financial statements. Larger firms use more complex methods for inventory valuation, and we discuss those methods in this chapter.

You will become familiar with the four procedures that are used to compute the cost of a firm's merchandise inventory: the specific identification method; the average cost method; the first in, first out (FIFO) method; and the last in, first out (LIFO) method. You will also learn about two methods that can be used to estimate the cost of a merchandise inventory: the gross profit and retail methods. The operations of Hanson's Sportswear will again be used as an example.

NEW TERMS

Average cost method ▪ First in, first out (FIFO) method ▪ Gross profit method ▪ Last in, first out (LIFO) method ▪ Lower of cost or market rule ▪ Markdown ▪ Market price ▪ Markon ▪ Markup ▪ Perpetual inventory ▪ Physical inventory ▪ Replacement cost ▪ Retail method ▪ Specific identification method ▪ Weighted average method

THE IMPORTANCE OF INVENTORY VALUATION

Merchandise Inventory is the one account that appears on both the balance sheet and the income statement. Its valuation is important because in many businesses it represents the current asset with the largest dollar amount. At the same time, inventory valuation directly affects the amount of net income or net loss reported for the accounting period.

In most businesses the merchandise inventory at the end of each accounting period is determined by actually counting the number of units of each type of goods on hand and multiplying that number by the appropriate cost per item. This process is known as taking a **physical inventory,** and it is the approach we will use in this chapter. However, in some types of businesses, especially manufacturing businesses, it is desirable to know at all times the number of units and the total cost of each item. The procedure used to gain this information is known as keeping a **perpetual inventory.** Perpetual inventory records are discussed in a later chapter.

If other items remain the same, the larger the ending inventory valuation, the lower the cost of goods sold and the higher the reported net income (or the lower the reported net loss). The smaller the ending inventory valuation, the higher the cost of goods sold and the lower the reported net income (or the higher the reported net loss).

INVENTORY COSTING METHODS

OBJECTIVE 1
Compute inventory cost by applying four commonly used costing methods.

In Part 1 the merchandise inventory of the businesses discussed was valued at the original cost of the items on hand. In such small firms, the valuation of inventory is a relatively simple matter. The stock of merchandise is limited, and the manager is in direct daily contact with operations. Thus the inventory valuation can be based on the specific identification of merchandise, the first method of inventory costing we will discuss.

Specific Identification Method

In many businesses it is possible to keep a record of the purchase price of each item in inventory and therefore to determine the exact cost of the specific merchandise sold, which is the **specific identification method** of inventory valuation. Automobile dealers, art dealers, and merchants who deal with items having a large unit cost or with one-of-a-kind items may account for their inventory by this method. However, this method is not practical for a business such as Hanson's Sportswear, where hundreds of similar items of relatively small unit value—such as shirts, blouses, and sweaters—are carried in the inventory. Furthermore, the purchase cost of many types of items may change during the accounting period. Fortunately, there are several other costing methods that may be utilized depending on the size and needs of the business.

Average Cost Method

If the company's inventory is composed of many similar items, it may be advantageous to use the **average cost method** to value the inventory. With this method, the average cost of all the similar items is used to value the ending inventory. To understand how the average cost method works, study Table 17–1, which provides an analysis of purchases of a certain brand and quality of shirt during the fiscal year January 1 to December 31, 19X3.

TABLE 17–1
Average Cost Method of Inventory Valuation

Explanation	Number of Units	Unit Cost	Total Cost
Beginning inventory, Jan. 1, 19X3	25	$ 8.00	$ 200.00
Purchases			
Feb. 19, 19X3	75	9.00	675.00
May 5, 19X3	50	10.00	500.00
Sept. 29, 19X3	20	12.00	240.00
Total merchandise available for sale	170		$1,615.00
Average cost ($1,615.00 ÷ 170) = $9.50			
Ending inventory, Dec. 31, 19X3 (24 × $9.50)	24		228.00
Cost of goods sold ($1,615 – $228)	146		$1,387.00

Note that the computation begins with the number of units, unit cost, and total cost of the beginning inventory. To these figures are added the amounts of all purchases made during the period. The sum of the units in the beginning inventory and the units purchased represents the total units available for sale. The total cost of the beginning inventory is added to the total cost of each lot purchased to obtain the total cost of the units available for sale. This total cost, $1,615.00, is then divided by the total number of units available to find the average unit cost ($1,615.00 ÷ 170 = $9.50). The value of the ending inventory is established by multiplying the number of units on hand by the average unit cost (24 × $9.50 = $228.00). The cost of goods sold can then be easily determined by subtracting the value of the ending inventory from the total value of the merchandise available for sale ($1,615.00 – $228.00 = $1,387.00). The procedure just described is sometimes referred to as the **weighted average method** because it considers both the number of units in each purchase and the unit purchase price in computing a "weighted average" cost per unit.

The average cost method of inventory valuation is relatively simple to use, but it reflects the limitations of any procedure that involves average figures. The unit cost cannot be related to any tangible unit or lot of merchandise, and it does not reveal price changes as clearly as might be desired. In highly competitive businesses that are subject to significant price and style changes, it is desirable to have a more specific and revealing method of cost determination. Two other popular methods of inventory valuation are the first in, first out method and the last in, first out method.

First In, First Out Method

In most businesses, merchants naturally try to sell the oldest items first. Thus the merchandise on hand at any given time is usually the most recently purchased items. The **first in, first out method** of inventory valuation (usually referred to as **FIFO**) parallels this physical flow of inventory. A point to remember is that the name *FIFO* refers to the cost of the goods sold. Therefore, the cost of the ending inventory is computed by referring to the cost of the latest purchases.

Using the figures from the example in Table 17–1, but applying the FIFO method, we find the cost of the ending inventory of 24 units to be $280, as shown in Table 17–2.

TABLE 17–2
FIFO Method of Inventory Valuation

Explanation	Number of Units	Unit Cost	Total Cost
From purchase of Sept. 29, 19X3	20	$12.00	$240.00
From purchase of May 5, 19X3	4	10.00	40.00
Ending inventory	24		$280.00

The cost of goods sold is then found by subtracting the value of the ending inventory from the total value of the merchandise available for sale, which was previously computed ($1,615 – $280 = $1,335).

Actually, the FIFO method attempts to approximate the results of the specific identification method, even though large and varied stocks of merchandise are involved. While it does not identify specific items, it does distinguish between recent and earlier purchases of stock so that the inventory valuation on the balance sheet will reflect the most recent price levels. This means that the cost of goods sold will reflect the costs applicable to the oldest goods handled during the period. In a time of rising prices, the difference in the cost of goods sold may have a significant impact on the net income to be reported. For example, there is a difference of $52 between the average cost method and the FIFO method in the costing of the 146 shirts sold during the period.

Cost of goods sold, average cost method	$1,387.00
Cost of goods sold, FIFO method	1,335.00
Difference	$ 52.00

Last In, First Out Method

While the FIFO method will result in a more favorable profit picture under the circumstances just discussed, many accountants, owners, and managers hesitate to use it. They believe that the current cost of merchandise should be matched as closely as possible to current sales dollars. They say that failure to do this means the income statement is failing to recognize the higher costs of replacing the sold merchandise. The system of valuation that they consider more conservative and realistic is the **last in, first out (LIFO)** method.

The LIFO method of inventory costing assumes that the most current costs of merchandise purchased should be charged to the cost of goods sold. Thus the value assigned to the ending inventory is the cost of the oldest merchandise on hand during the period. Using the figures from the previous example, but applying the LIFO method, we find the value of the 24 shirts on hand at the end of the period to be $192, as shown in Table 17–3.

TABLE 17–3
LIFO Method of Inventory Valuation

Explanation	Number of Units	Unit Cost	Total Cost
From beginning inventory, Jan. 1, 19X3	24	$8.00	$192.00
Ending inventory, Dec. 31, 19X3	24		$192.00

The cost of goods sold is computed by subtracting $192 from the previously established value of the merchandise available for sale ($1,615 – $192 = $1,423). It is apparent that in a time of rising prices, the relatively lower inventory valuation under the LIFO method tends to increase the reported cost of goods sold and decrease the reported net income. The lower net income will produce a lower income tax liability for the company.

LIFO, just like the other methods of inventory valuation, is not an exact matching of the physical flow of inventory as it is sold, but it is a cost flow assumption used to compute values for ending inventory and cost of goods sold.

COMPARING RESULTS OF INVENTORY COSTING METHODS

The different results obtained for the same example using the average cost, FIFO, and LIFO inventory methods can be seen in Table 17–4.

TABLE 17–4
Comparison of Results of Inventory Costing Methods

Explanation	Units	Unit Cost	Total Cost	Ending Inventory Valuation	Cost of Goods Sold
Beginning inventory, Jan. 1, 19X3	25	$ 8.00	$ 200.00		
Purchases:					
Feb. 19, 19X3	75	$ 9.00	675.00		
May 5, 19X3	50	$10.00	500.00		
Sept. 29, 19X3	20	$12.00	240.00		
Total merchandise available for sale	170		$1,615.00		
1. Average cost method	24	$ 9.50		$228.00	$1,387.00
2. FIFO	20	$12.00	$ 240.00		
	4	$10.00	40.00		
	24		$ 280.00	$280.00	$1,335.00
3. LIFO	24	$ 8.00	$ 192.00	$192.00	$1,423.00

OBJECTIVE 2
Explain the advantages and limitations of each method of inventory costing.

Notice that the ending inventory valuation of the same 24 shirts ranges from a low of $192 when the LIFO method is used to a high of $280 when the FIFO method is used. The average cost method gives a figure in between (as is almost always the case) of $228. Subtracting the ending inventory valuation in each case from the total cost of merchandise available for sale, $1,615, gives a high cost of goods sold of $1,423 with the LIFO method and a low cost of goods sold of

$1,335 with the FIFO method. Again, the average cost method usually gives a figure in between ($1,387 in this situation).

Since price trends are a vital element in any inventory valuation, remember these basic rules.

1. In a period of rising prices, the LIFO method results in a higher reported cost of goods sold and a lower reported net income than the FIFO or average cost method.
2. In a period of falling prices, the LIFO method results in a lower reported cost of goods sold and a higher reported net income than the FIFO or average cost method.
3. Whatever direction prices take, the average cost method results in a reported net income somewhere between the amounts obtained with FIFO and LIFO.

A business cannot change its inventory valuation method at will from one period to the next in order to report the amount of net income it prefers. Following the consistency principle, once the firm adopts a method, it should use that method consistently from one period to the next. Although a firm can generally use one inventory costing method for financial accounting purposes and another for federal income tax purposes, the firm must use the LIFO method for financial accounting if that method is adopted for tax purposes.

SELF-REVIEW

1. What method of inventory costing should be used in an automobile dealership?
2. Give a formula used to compute the average cost of inventory in the average cost method.
3. What does FIFO stand for, and what is the cost flow assumption under this method?
4. Under LIFO, which goods are assumed sold in the period?
5. In a period of inflation, which inventory method (LIFO, FIFO, average cost) will give the lowest income tax expense for the firm?

Answers to Self-Review

1. Specific identification would be the most appropriate method to use in an automobile dealership.
2. The formula is

$$\text{Average cost of inventory} = \frac{\text{Total cost of merchandise available for sale}}{\text{Total number of units available for sale}}$$

3. FIFO stands for first in, first out. This method assumes that the older goods in the inventory were sold during this accounting period.
4. LIFO assumes that the last items purchased were sold during this period.
5. LIFO will produce the highest cost of goods sold, the lowest net income, and thus the lowest income tax expense.

THE LOWER OF COST OR MARKET RULE

OBJECTIVE 3
Compute inventory value under the lower of cost or market rule.

The methods of inventory valuation discussed so far have been based on cost. However, as you learned in Chapter 14, the asset valuation used on the balance sheet should be conservative and should not overstate the asset values. If the **market price** (the price it will cost the business to buy the same item of inventory for resale) of an inventory item declines, the merchant will probably have trouble selling it at the usual increase, or *markon*, above original cost. (**Markon** is the difference between the cost and the established retail price of merchandise.) If the price decline is especially severe, the merchant may even have to sell the item at a loss. Consequently, inventory must be valued at either its original cost or its replacement cost, whichever is lower. This rule is called the **lower of cost or market rule.** As the name of this rule suggests, when the replacement cost of an item is below its original purchase cost, it is necessary to value the inventory at market price (replacement price) instead of cost in order to reflect the lower current value in the firm's financial records.

The market price (or **replacement cost**) for the purpose of applying the rule can be described as the price at which the item could be bought (at the inventory date) through the usual channels and in the usual quantities. In some cases, current market prices are quoted in trade publications. In other cases, a recent purchase may give a price that is reasonably close to the current market price. In still other circumstances, the firm's regular suppliers can provide quotations for use in valuing the goods.

There are two major ways of applying the lower of cost or market rule. The first is to apply it item by item. The second is to use the total cost and the total market value. We will also look at a variation of this second method, finding the lower of total cost or total market on the basis of group classification.

Applying the Lower of Cost or Market Rule by Item

If the lower of cost or market rule is to be applied item by item, the cost is determined for each item in the inventory according to one of the acceptable methods (specific identification, average cost, FIFO, or LIFO). Current replacement cost (market cost) is also determined for each item. Then the basis of valuation (the lower figure) is selected. Finally, the quantity of the item on hand is multiplied by the valuation amount to obtain the total value at the lower of cost or market. The lower value figures for all items are added to determine the value of the inventory as a whole. The application of this rule is illustrated in Table 17–5, with assumed figures for two stock items.

TABLE 17–5
Establishing Lower of Cost or Market Valuation by Item

		Unit Price		Lower of Cost or Market	
Description	Quantity	Cost	Market	Valuation Basis	Amount
Stock #1234	150	$1.00	$1.10	Cost	$150.00
Stock #2765	200	2.50	2.20	Market	440.00
Inventory valuation					$590.00

Information Block: Computers in Accounting

Inventory Control

Whether a business sells only a few products or offers thousands of items, managing the flow of merchandise is essential to gaining control over inventory and quickly responding to customer preferences. Although a business with a small inventory may choose to track its inventory manually, most businesses use computer technology to manage their inventories.

A computerized inventory control system offers several benefits:

- An ability to fill orders faster and more efficiently
- An ability to reduce overstocked or back-ordered items
- An ability to obtain inventory valuations quickly
- Improved inventory planning and control
- An ability to monitor the history of in-store transactions

An inventory control system must accommodate transactions involving purchases and sales. Many software programs are available to record these types of transactions and to generate inventory reports. A small retail store may be able to use software developed for a microcomputer, while a large store such as Wal-Mart or K-Mart would need more sophisticated programs.

A database that contains thousands of entries is needed to track inventory information, such as product description, price, unit cost, units on hand, quantity sold, reorder point, stock-keeping unit, and vendor data. Point-of-sale terminals provide a critical link to the inventory database. As sales transactions are processed using a terminal or a scanner, data about the quantity sold and the units on hand is instantly updated.

Store managers can generate reports to analyze buying trends and to determine which items to reorder. Taking a physical count to identify the items to reorder is unnecessary for a business using an automated inventory control system. Using specialized software, inventory data can be transmitted, via telephone lines or a satellite, from several stores within a chain to a central distribution center for order fulfillment. Within a few days, the merchandise arrives at the store and the database is updated to adjust the quantity-on-hand data for each item. Hand-held scanning devices may be used to facilitate the restocking process.

Applying the Lower of Total Cost or Total Market

Under another method of applying the rule of the lower of cost or market, the total cost and the total market value of the entire inventory are computed. The lower of these total figures is then used as the inventory valuation. This method is illustrated in Table 17–6.

TABLE 17–6
Establishing Lower of Total Cost or Total Market Valuation

Description	Quantity	Unit Price Cost	Unit Price Market	Total Cost	Total Market
Stock #1234	150	$1.00	$1.10	$150.00	$165.00
Stock #2765	200	2.50	2.20	500.00	440.00
				$650.00	$605.00
Inventory valuation, $605.00					

This procedure gives a somewhat less conservative inventory valuation than the item-by-item method if the prices of some items have risen while others have declined. However, advocates of this method justify it on the ground that the total inventory figure is the one that should be presented conservatively. If the market value of the inventory as a whole has not declined below cost, then no adjustment is made and the cost value is presented on the statements.

Applying the Lower of Cost or Market Rule by Groups

A variation on the method discussed above involves classifying inventory items by groups or departments and determining the lower of total cost or total market according to these classifications. The lower figure (cost or market) for each group is added to the lower figures for the other groups to obtain the total inventory valuation. Let's assume that Stock #1234 and Stock #2765 in the preceding example make up group 1 and that Stock #3124 and Stock #4532 make up group 2. The basic computations required for the group total method using these classifications are as shown in Tables 17–7 and 17–8.

TABLE 17–7
Establishing the Lower of Total Cost or Total Market by Groups

Description	Quantity	Unit Price Cost	Unit Price Market	Total Cost	Total Market
Group 1					
Stock #1234	150	$1.00	$1.10	$150.00	$165.00
Stock #2765	200	2.50	2.20	500.00	440.00
Totals, group 1				$650.00	$605.00
Group 2					
Stock #3124	80	$1.70	$1.60	$136.00	$128.00
Stock #4532	150	1.60	1.80	240.00	270.00
Totals, group 2				$376.00	$398.00

Lower of cost or market valuation by group

Group 1	Market	$605.00
Group 2	Cost	376.00
		$981.00

In this case, market ($605) is the lower basis for valuation of the items in group 1, and cost ($376) is the lower basis for valuation of the items in group 2. The combined value of groups 1 and 2 is $981 ($605 + $376). Compare this valuation with the figures obtained from the two other methods as shown in Table 17–8.

TABLE 17–8
A Comparison of Lower of Cost or Market Methods

Lower of Cost or Market by Items			Lower of Total Cost or Total Market		
				Valued at	
Item	Basis	Valuation	Item	Cost	Market
#1234	Cost	$150.00	#1234	$ 150.00	$ 165.00
#2765	Market	440.00	#2765	500.00	440.00
#3124	Market	128.00	#3124	136.00	128.00
#4532	Cost	240.00	#4532	240.00	270.00
		$958.00		$1,026.00	$1,003.00

Using the lower of total cost or total market by groups is a method that produces middle-of-the-road figures. It does not reflect individual fluctuations, as the lower of cost or market by items method does. But it also does not lump together as many value variations as the grand total cost or market figures do. The final choice of one of the three methods will depend on many factors, including the size and variety of the stock of merchandise, the margin of profit on which the business operates, industry practices, and future plans for expansion. Usually, the lower of cost or market by items is used.

INVENTORY ESTIMATION PROCEDURES

Occasionally the managers of a business might want to know the approximate cost of its inventory without taking a physical count and applying one of the costing procedures. For example, if a fire occurs, the business will need to know the cost of the goods destroyed to provide data for insurance and income tax purposes. Similarly, a department manager in a retail store may be permitted to have only a certain amount of money tied up in inventory. Therefore, the manager must be able to estimate the cost of the department's inventory at any time. Two common techniques for estimating inventory are the gross profit method and the retail method.

Gross Profit Method of Inventory Valuation

OBJECTIVE 4
Estimate inventory cost using the gross profit method.

The fundamental assumption of the **gross profit method** is that the rate of gross profit on sales is about the same from period to period. You will recall from earlier chapters that gross profit is equal to sales minus cost of goods sold. The gross profit rate is a percent computed by dividing the gross profit by net sales. This method also assumes that the ratio of cost of goods sold to net sales is relatively constant.

The procedure can be illustrated as follows. Assume that a company's entire merchandise inventory is destroyed by fire on May 26, 19X3, but that its accounting records are preserved. An analysis of the company's income statements for the two preceding years shows that the gross profit rate has been 40 percent of net sales (or that the cost of goods sold has been 60 percent of net sales). The records for the current year provide the following figures.

Inventory (at cost), Jan. 1, 19X3	$ 50,000
Net purchases, Jan. 1 to May 26, 19X3	130,000
Net sales, Jan. 1 to May 26, 19X3	220,000

Computing estimated inventory valuation is a three-step process.

1. The first step is to estimate the cost of goods sold for the period January 1 to May 26. Since sales were $220,000 and the ratio of cost of goods sold to net sales is assumed to be 60 percent, the estimated cost of goods sold is computed as follows: 0.60 × $220,000 = $132,000.
2. The second step is to determine the cost of goods available for sale. This computation is shown below.

Beginning inventory	$ 50,000
Net purchases	130,000
Cost of goods available for sale	$180,000

3. The final step is to compute the estimated ending (destroyed) inventory by subtracting the estimated cost of goods sold ($132,000) from the cost of goods available for sale ($180,000), as shown below.

Cost of goods available for sale	$180,000
Estimated cost of goods sold	132,000
Estimated ending inventory	$ 48,000

Retail Method of Inventory Valuation

OBJECTIVE 5
Estimate inventory cost using the retail method.

A second method of estimating inventories, widely used by retailers, is called the **retail method.** Under this method, inventory is classified into groups of items that have about the same rate of markon.

The beginning inventory is valued both at cost and at retail. At the time merchandise is purchased, it is recorded at cost and its retail value is determined. The retail value of all merchandise available for sale is obtained by adding the retail value of the beginning inventory and the retail value of the new merchandise purchased. Sales are recorded at their retail price in the usual manner. When the total of sales at retail is subtracted from the total retail value of the merchandise available for sale, the difference is the retail value of the ending inventory. This amount is multiplied by the cost ratio (total available for sale at cost ÷ total available for sale at retail) to give the approximate cost of the ending inventory. Using assumed figures, the calculations involved in the application of the retail method of inventory pricing are shown below.

	Cost	Retail
Beginning inventory	$ 3,900	$ 6,500
Purchases	61,000	91,000
Freight	100	
Total merchandise available for sale	$65,000	$97,500
Less sales		79,500
Ending inventory priced at retail		$18,000

Cost ratio = $65,000 ÷ $97,500 = 66 2/3%

Conversion to approximate cost:
Ending inventory at retail × Cost ratio = $18,000 × 0.6667
Ending inventory at cost = $12,000 (rounded)
Cost of goods sold = $65,000 − $12,000 = $53,000

In practice, the application of the retail method of inventory pricing is not quite as simple as this example suggests. Records must be kept of further price increases—**markups**—above the original markons, as well as of markup cancellations. Records must also be kept of **markdowns** below the original markon and of markdown cancellations. The requirements of the retail inventory method are discussed in more detail in intermediate-level accounting textbooks.

When there are many merchandise items of small unit value, as is often the case in retail stores, the retail method of inventory pricing permits a firm to determine the approximate cost of its ending inventory from the financial records. Thus the firm does not have to take a physical inventory. In turn, the ease of determining the inventory value makes it possible for the firm to prepare financial statements easily and often.

Many retail stores take a periodic inventory at retail values, using the sales price marked on the merchandise. This has become more popular as the cost of inventory scanning equipment has become affordable. Then the physical inventory at retail is converted to cost by applying the cost ratio. This is done in the same way as the ending retail inventory computed in the previous example was reduced to cost. Hanson's Sportswear uses this method of valuation because of its simplicity and because of the firm's need to have inventory values available often.

INTERNAL CONTROL OF INVENTORIES

The degree of physical control over inventories must be appropriate for the nature of the goods involved. For example, the type of control system used for an inventory containing small, valuable, easily disposed of items such as jewelry would be greatly different from that used for an inventory made up of lumber. The jewelry would require far more elaborate safeguards than a lumber yard.

Merchandise purchases should be controlled through a voucher system or a similar mechanism. The removal of merchandise from a company's warehouse or premises should be made only on the basis of such documents as sales invoices and shipping orders. A physical inventory should be taken periodically (at least annually) to verify the goods on hand. The procedures used for the physical inventory should include not only techniques that are designed to produce accurate original counts but also techniques for spot-checking the accuracy of the counts. Similarly, the unit cost figures used in computing the inventory should be verified through spot checks. If the

Information Block: Ethics in Accounting

Yes, It's Old, But . . .

P. & A. Webster, Inc., is a manufacturing firm in a medium technology industry. One of their products is called Drill-Tech, an accessory for automated drill presses. Currently about 2,500 units of Drill-Tech are in inventory. Dave Harper, the sales manager with responsibility for Drill-Tech, is evaluated and compensated based on profitability of the division.

At the end of the current fiscal year, Mr. Harper is examining the inventory records. He notices that the Drill-Tech units have not been selling well and that no new units have been produced this year due to the decline in sales. Mr. Harper knows that his sales force has had some difficulty selling this product because of a new process developed by a competitor.

Mr. Harper looks at the annual income statement for his area and notes that the net income is barely at the level that was budgeted for the year. If he decides to write off the Drill-Tech inventory, his division will fall below the target profit. Looking further into the sales records, Mr. Harper notes that 40 units of Drill-Tech were sold this year. He reasons that if 40 were sold this year, more could be sold next year. After all, current customers will eventually have to replace their old Drill-Techs. Mr. Harper must now decide whether to write off the Drill-Tech inventory.

1. What are the ethical issues?
2. What are the alternatives?
3. Who are the affected parties?
4. How do the alternatives affect the parties?
5. What should Mr. Harper do?

company is having an audit performed by outside auditors, it is a generally accepted auditing standard for a member of the auditor's staff to observe the physical counting process of the inventory.

MANAGERIAL IMPLICATIONS

Because inventory makes up a large part of the assets of most businesses, it must be carefully controlled. The inventory costing method chosen by management must be one that is practical, reliable, and as simple as possible to apply. Inventory valuation is very important in computing federal income tax because the value placed on the inventory determines the net income reported. For example, in times of rising prices, the LIFO method is a means of lowering the income tax by charging off a higher cost of goods sold.

The gross profit method of estimating inventory is a valuable tool for approximating the cost of the inventory. It is used in preparing budgets when a physical count cannot be made, and it is used in verifying the reasonableness of the inventory computed under an actual physical count.

Management should consider the retail method of inventory pricing as a means of estimating the cost of goods on hand at any given time. This estimate is especially important in retail businesses where department managers have inventory budgets—specified amounts they are allowed to tie up in inventory. Such managers generally need to know often, sometimes weekly, the amount of inventory that is on hand.

SELF-REVIEW

1. In the phrase *lower of cost or market,* what does market mean?
2. Under what accounting theory is the lower of cost or market computation justified?
3. What two methods of estimating inventory are available to a business where a fire has destroyed most of the inventory?
4. What is the formula for the cost ratio used in the retail method of estimating inventory?
5. How often should inventory be physically counted?

Answers to Self-Review

1. Market refers to the replacement cost of the same item of inventory.
2. The lower of cost or market is justified under the conservatism principle requiring current assets to be stated at their cost or a lower figure if the value has declined.
3. The two methods available to estimate inventory are the retail method and the gross profit method.
4. The cost ratio is computed according to the formula below.

$$\text{Cost ratio} = \frac{\text{Total cost of goods available for sale}}{\text{Total retail value of goods available for sale}}$$

5. Inventory should be physically counted as often as management desires, but at least once a year.

CHAPTER 17 Review and Applications

CHAPTER SUMMARY

There are four common inventory cost flow assumptions. The specific identification method uses the actual purchase price of the specific items in inventory. The average cost method uses the average of the cost of all like items available for sale during the period for valuing the ending inventory. The FIFO method develops the cost of the ending inventory from the cost of later purchases. The LIFO method develops the cost of the ending inventory from the cost of earlier purchases. In a period of rising prices, the LIFO method will result in a lower reported net income than the FIFO method, as well as lower income taxes payable. In a period of falling prices, the LIFO method will result in a higher reported net income. The average cost method will always give a result between the two.

Not all inventory valuation is based on the purchase cost. The rule of lower of cost or market is the most conservative method available. It can be applied to individual items in the inventory, to groups of items, or to the inventory as a whole.

The gross profit method of estimating inventory involves estimating the cost of goods sold by applying a historical cost ratio to the sales of the current period. The estimated cost of goods sold is then subtracted from the cost of goods available for sale to arrive at the estimated ending inventory.

The retail method of inventory pricing uses the retail selling price of the items remaining. The retail value of the inventory is multiplied by the cost ratio of the current period to reach the approximate cost. An estimate of the inventory approximating the lower of cost or market can be obtained by fully considering markups, markup cancellations, markdowns, and markdown cancellations.

GLOSSARY OF NEW TERMS

Average cost method (p. 586) A method of inventory valuation using the average cost of similar items to value the ending inventory

First in, first out (FIFO) method (p. 587) A method of inventory valuation that assumes the oldest merchandise is sold first

Gross profit method (p. 594) A method of estimating inventory based on the assumption that the rate of gross profit on sales is relatively constant from period to period

Last in, first out (LIFO) method (p. 588) A method of inventory valuation that assumes that the most recently purchased merchandise is sold first

Lower of cost or market rule (p. 591) The principle by which inventory is valued at either its original cost or its replacement cost, whichever is lower

Markdown (p. 596) Price decrease from the original markon

Market price (p. 591) The current cost of buying an item of inventory for resale

Markon (p. 591) The difference between the cost and the established retail price of merchandise

Markup (p. 596) A price increase above the original markon

Perpetual inventory (p. 586) Inventory based on a running total of number of units

Physical inventory (p. 586) Inventory based on an actual count of the number of units of each type of goods on hand

Replacement cost (p. 591) See Market price

Retail method (p. 595) A method of estimating inventory cost by applying the ratio of cost to selling price in the current accounting period to the retail price of the inventory

Specific identification method (p. 586) A method of inventory valuation based on the actual cost of each piece of merchandise

Weighted average method (p. 587) See Average cost method

REVIEW QUESTIONS

1. How does the ending merchandise inventory amount appear on both the balance sheet and the income statement?
2. What is a physical inventory?
3. What is a perpetual inventory?
4. Using an illustration, explain the specific identification method of inventory valuation.
5. Is the specific identification method of inventory valuation suitable for a retail grocery store? Why or why not?
6. Explain the assumption underlying the FIFO method. Does this generally agree with the physical flow of merchandise?
7. If prices are rising, will an ending inventory be higher under the LIFO method or the FIFO method? Explain.
8. What is meant by the term market as it is used in the lower of cost or market rule?
9. If a business uses the lower of cost or market method of inventory valuation, how is cost determined?
10. Explain how the lower of cost or market method is applied on a group basis.
11. Is the value of an inventory likely to be lower if the lower of cost or market method is applied on an item-by-item basis, on a group basis, or to the inventory as a whole?
12. Explain the gross profit method of estimating inventories.
13. Suggest two situations in which it might be desirable to estimate inventories without a physical count.
14. Describe how the cost of an ending inventory is estimated under the retail method.

MANAGERIAL FOCUS

1. What are two specific managerial reasons for using the LIFO method of inventory valuation during a period of rising prices?
2. In order to achieve better control over its investment in inventory, the management of a retail store wishes to get an estimate of the cost of inventory at the close of business each week. Outline a procedure to obtain this estimate without actually taking a physical count.
3. In a retail diamond store, what are some specific controls that management must provide over a firm's inventory?
4. The purchasing manager of a retail store has suggested that the company should maintain a perpetual inventory. The controller opposes this suggestion. In your opinion, on what basis does the controller probably oppose the idea?
5. In what special situations are inventory estimation procedures extremely useful?
6. The manager of a retail store has grown concerned about the time taken to count the merchandise on hand each quarter. She argues that too much time is spent on this activity, with a resulting high cost of labor. She suggests that the company need not take a physical inventory at all but could rely on the retail inventory estimation procedure to arrive at the cost of the inventory. Respond to this argument.

EXERCISES

EXERCISE 17-1
(Obj. 1)
Tutorial

Using the various costing methods of inventory valuation. Information about the Joseph Company's inventory of one item during 19X3 is given below. Compute the cost of the ending inventory under: (1) the average cost method, (2) the FIFO method, and (3) the LIFO method.

Explanation	No. of Units	Unit Cost
Beginning inventory, Jan. 1, 19X3	20	$150
Purchases:		
Mar. 19X3	40	155
July 19X3	45	170
Nov. 19X3	30	180
Ending inventory, Dec. 31, 19X3	35	

EXERCISE 17-2
(Obj. 2)

Choosing the method of inventory valuation and the effect on income. Given the following choices—average cost, FIFO, and LIFO—which method will give the lowest net income? Which method will give the highest net income?

EXERCISE 17-3
(Obj. 3)
Tutorial

Using the lower of cost or market method. The following information concerns four items that the Catanzaro Company has in its inventory. Two of these items are in the hardware department, and two are in the household goods department.

	Quantity	Unit Cost	Market Value
Hardware			
Item #101	200	$ 8	$ 9
Item #120	120	30	28
Household goods			
Item #220	90	42	45
Item #229	150	17	16

1. What is the valuation of the ending inventory if the firm uses the lower of cost or market method and applies it on an item-by-item basis?
2. If the company applies the lower of cost or market method on the basis of total cost or total market, what is the value of the ending inventory?
3. If the company elects to apply the lower of cost or market method to inventory groups, what is the value of the ending inventory?

EXERCISE 17–4 (Obj. 4)

Tutorial

Estimating inventory cost under the gross profit method. Use the following data to compute the estimated inventory cost for the Cortez Company under the gross profit method.

Average gross profit rate: 40% of sales
Inventory on January 1 (at cost): $80,000
Purchases from January 1 to date of inventory estimate: $500,000
Net sales for period: $900,000

EXERCISE 17–5 (Obj. 5)

Tutorial

Estimating inventory cost under the retail method. Based on the following data, compute the estimated cost of the ending inventory at the Merrick Company. Use the retail method.

	Cost	Retail
Beginning inventory	$ 50,000	$ 75,000
Purchases	180,000	389,000
Freight	2,000	
Sales		400,000

PROBLEMS

PROBLEM SET A

PROBLEM 17–1A (Obj. 1)

Tutorial Spreadsheet GL

Computing inventory costs under different valuation methods. The following data concerns inventory and purchases at the Americus Company.

Inventory, May 1	150 units at $10.00
Purchases:	
May 6	180 units at $10.50
May 14	160 units at $10.60
May 24	100 units at $10.65
Inventory, May 31	162 units

Instructions Determine the cost of the ending inventory on January 31 under each of the following methods: (1) average cost method; (2) first in, first out (FIFO) method; and (3) last in, first out (LIFO) method. When using the average cost method, compute the unit cost to four decimal places.

PROBLEM 17–2A
(Obj. 1, 3)

Computing inventory costs under different valuation methods and applying the lower of cost or market rule. The following data pertains to Quick 'n Easy wall panels that were in the inventory of the Lookout Building Supply Company during 19X3.

Inventory, Jan. 1	80 units at $24.00
Purchases:	
Jan. 10	50 units at $24.50
July 18	85 units at $25.00
Aug. 12	80 units at $25.30
Inventory, Dec. 31	82 units

Instructions

1. Determine the cost of the inventory on December 31 and the cost of goods sold for the year ending on that date under each of the following valuation methods: (a) FIFO, (b) LIFO, and (c) average cost. When using the average cost method, compute the unit cost to the nearest cent.
2. Assume that the replacement cost of each unit on December 31, 19X3, is $23.90. Using the lower of cost or market rule, find the inventory amount under each of the methods given in item 1 above.

PROBLEM 17–3A
(Obj. 3)

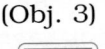

Applying the lower of cost or market rule by different methods. The following data concerns selected inventory items at the Quality Jewelry Company.

	Quantity	Unit Cost	Market Value
Costume Jewelry Department			
Stock No. 101	100	$ 6.00	$ 6.40
Stock No. 102	150	8.80	8.40
Stock No. 103	250	4.00	4.20
Gold Jewelry Department			
Stock No. 401	10	140.00	164.00
Stock No. 402	4	820.00	800.00
Stock No. 403	2	906.00	900.00

Instructions Determine the amount to be reported as the inventory valuation at cost or market, whichever is lower, under each of these methods.

1. Lower of cost or market for each item separately
2. Lower of total cost or total market
3. Lower of total cost or total market by departments

PROBLEM 17–4A
(Obj. 4)

Estimating inventory by the gross profit method. Over the past several years, the Roma Company has averaged a gross profit of 30 percent. At the end of 19X4, the income statement of the company included the information shown at the top of page 604.

Sales		*1750 0 0 0 00*
Cost of Goods Sold:		
Inventory, Jan. 1, 19X4	*120 0 0 0 00*	
Purchases	*1208 0 0 0 00*	
Total Merchandise Available for Sale	*1328 0 0 0 00*	
Less Inventory, Dec. 31, 19X4	*78 0 0 0 00*	
Cost of Goods Sold		*1250 0 0 0 00*
Gross Profit on Sales		*500 0 0 0 00*

Investigation revealed that employees of the company had not taken an actual physical count of the inventory on December 31, 19X4. Instead, they had merely estimated the inventory.

Instructions

Using the gross profit method of inventory estimation, verify the reasonableness (or lack of reasonableness) of the ending inventory shown on the income statement.

PROBLEM 17–5A (Obj. 5) Tutorial

Estimating inventory by the retail method. The August 1 inventory of the Plains Company had a cost of $35,000 and had a retail value of $52,500. During August, merchandise was purchased for $80,000 and marked to sell for $120,000. January sales totaled $150,000.

Instructions

1. Compute the retail value of the ending inventory as of August 31.
2. Compute the approximate cost of the ending inventory.
3. Compute the cost of goods sold during August.

PROBLEM 17–6A (Obj. 1, 2)

Applying the correct method of evaluating inventory. Alexander Brothers sells expensive jewelry. The beginning inventory on June 1 was composed of the following items:

	Cost	Retail
Item #1001 Diamond necklace	$9,000	$22,500
Item #1012 Diamond earrings	5,000	12,500
Item #1013 Diamond ring	5,000	15,000
Item #2300 Emerald set	9,500	22,000
Item #2311 Emerald ring	2,000	5,000

Sales during the month included items #1001 and #1012.

Instructions

1. Determine the best method of valuing the ending inventory.
2. Determine the value of the ending inventory.
3. Determine the cost of goods sold during June.

PROBLEM SET B

PROBLEM 17–1B (Obj. 1) Tutorial

Computing inventory costs under different valuation methods. The data at the top of page 605 concerns inventory and purchases at the Remote Corporation.

Inventory, Jan. 1	180 units at $16.00
Purchases:	
Jan. 8	140 units at $16.05
Jan. 16	120 units at $16.08
Jan. 24	140 units at $16.10
Inventory, Jan. 31	222 units

Instructions Determine the cost of the ending inventory on January 31 under each of the following methods: (1) average cost method; (2) first in, first out (FIFO) method; and (3) last in, first out (LIFO) method. When using the average cost method, compute the unit cost to four decimal places.

PROBLEM 17–2B (Obj. 1, 3)

Computing inventory costs under different valuation methods and applying the lower of cost or market rule. The following data pertains to Model Q laptop computers that were in the inventory of the New Computer Store during the first six months of 19X3.

Inventory, Jan. 1	22 units at $2,500
Purchases:	
Jan. 31	16 units at $2,200
Mar. 10	20 units at $2,150
May 19	20 units at $2,000
Inventory, June 30	18 units

Instructions

1. Determine the cost of the inventory on June 30 and the cost of goods sold for the six-month period ending on that date under each of the following valuation methods: (a) FIFO, (b) LIFO, and (c) average cost. When using the average cost method, compute the unit cost to the nearest cent.
2. Assume that the replacement cost of each unit on June 30, 19X3, is $1,970. Using the lower of cost or market rule, find the inventory amount under each of the methods given in item 1 above.

PROBLEM 17–3B (Obj. 3)

Tutorial

Applying the lower of cost or market rule by different methods. The following data concerns inventory at River City Products, Inc.

	Quantity	Unit Cost	Market Value
Boat Department			
Model 160	12	$ 9,500	$ 9,200
Model 170	9	11,000	11,750
Model 180	8	12,400	13,000
Motor Department			
Model 110	6	1,290	1,350
Model 150	3	1,775	1,750
Model 130	4	1,275	1,350

Instructions Determine the amount that the company should report as the inventory valuation at cost or market, whichever is lower. Use each of the following three valuation methods.

1. Lower of cost or market for each item separately
2. Lower of total cost or total market
3. Lower of total cost or total market by departments

PROBLEM 17–4B
(Obj. 4)

Tutorial

Estimating inventory by the gross profit method. Over the last three years, the Stainless Corporation has averaged 40 percent gross profit. At the end of 19X3, the auditor found the following data in the records of the company.

Sales		*2000 0 0 0 00*
Cost of Goods Sold:		
Inventory, Jan. 1, 19X3	*240 0 0 0 00*	
Purchases	*1200 0 0 0 00*	
Total Merchandise Available for Sale	*1440 0 0 0 00*	
Less Inventory, Dec. 31, 19X3	*380 0 0 0 00*	
Cost of Goods Sold		*1060 0 0 0 00*
Gross Profit on Sales		*940 0 0 0 00*

Inquiry by the auditor revealed that employees of the Regal Corporation had estimated the inventory on December 31, 19X3, instead of taking a complete physical count.

Instructions

Using the gross profit method of inventory estimation, verify the reasonableness (or lack of reasonableness) of the inventory estimate made by the company's employees.

PROBLEM 17–5B
(Obj. 5)

Tutorial

Estimating inventory by the retail method. The DSC Corporation uses the retail method of inventory pricing. As of December 31, 19X4, the firm's records disclosed the following figures about the beginning inventory for the year, the merchandise purchases made during the period, the total merchandise available, and the total sales.

	ACTUAL COST	RETAIL SALES PRICE
Beginning inventory, Jan. 1, 19X4	$ 18,000	$ 27,900
Merchandise purchases during 19X4	200,000	372,100
Freight on purchases	2,000	
Total merchandise available for sale	220,000	400,000
Total Sales During 19X4		375,000

Instructions

1. Compute the retail value of the ending merchandise inventory as of December 31.
2. Compute the approximate cost of the ending merchandise inventory as of December 31.
3. Compute the cost of goods sold during 19X4.

PROBLEM 17–6B
(Obj. 2)

Using the correct inventory valuation method. The Walt Arthur Construction Company built the following houses in 19X3.

	COST	RETAIL
Unit #111	$45,250	$55,000
Unit #113	46,800	56,000
Unit #254	79,000	90,000
Unit #277	72,500	85,000

All the units except #277 were sold during 19X3.

Instructions

1. Determine the appropriate costing method for inventory in this construction business.
2. What value should be reported on the balance sheet for the company for the unsold unit?
3. Determine the cost of goods sold in 19X3.

CHALLENGE PROBLEM

The Advantage Computer Store classifies its computer inventory into three categories—Model S, Model F, and Model Q. Following is data related to January 19X3 inventory transactions.

Hardware	Units	Cost
Inventory, Jan. 1		
S machines	3	$ 590
F machines	6	800
Q machines	2	1,200
Purchases		
Jan. 2		
S machines	2	550
F machines	15	825
Q machines	20	1,100
Jan. 15		
S machines	2	525
F machines	9	825
Q machines	8	1,150
Jan. 27		
F machines	8	850
Q machines	6	1,125

The company uses the LIFO method for inventory valuation purposes. Sales for the month were composed of the following: S machines, 5 units; F machines, 25 units; and Q machines, 30 units.

Instructions

1. Determine the cost of goods sold during the month.
2. Determine the value of the ending inventory.

CRITICAL THINKING PROBLEM

Jane Carter owns a retail pottery outlet that stocks a variety of pottery items such as bowls, flower pots, vases, and tableware, which she purchases from three different pottery manufacturers. Last week an earthquake hit the area, and the inventory was destroyed and the accounting records buried under the debris.

To file an insurance claim for the lost inventory, Ms. Carter needs to reconstruct her records. If she uses the gross profit method to estimate the lost inventory, what financial information does she need to obtain? From what sources can she obtain this information?

CHAPTER 18

Property, Plant, and Equipment

OBJECTIVES

1. Compute the amount that should be recorded as an asset's cost.
2. Compute and record depreciation of property, plant, and equipment by commonly used methods.
3. Classify assets according to which modified accelerated cost recovery system (MACRS) class they fall into for federal income tax purposes.
4. Compute and record depletion of natural resources.
5. Record sales of plant and equipment.
6. Record trade-ins of assets using the income tax method and the fair market value method.
7. Compute and record amortization of intangible assets.
8. Define the accounting terms new to this chapter.

Housing and equipping a modern business often calls for a large investment in property. This chapter explains the accounting procedures and records needed to keep track of the purchase, use, and disposition of property, plant, and equipment—often referred to as fixed assets, capital assets, or long-lived assets. In addition, the accounting treatment of intangible assets such as patents and copyrights, which have no physical characteristics, is examined.

You are already familiar with the straight-line method of computing depreciation for property, plant, and equipment. In this chapter you will learn about other depreciation methods that are widely used in business. You will also learn about the procedures for computing depletion of natural resources and amortization of intangible assets.

NEW TERMS

Accelerated method of depreciation ▪ Amortization ▪ Book value ▪ Capitalized costs ▪ Copyright ▪ Declining-balance method ▪ Depletion ▪ Depreciation ▪ Double-declining-balance method ▪ Fair-market value method ▪ Franchise ▪ Goodwill ▪ Income tax method ▪ Patent ▪ Property, plant, and equipment ▪ Real property ▪ Salvage value ▪ Straight-line method ▪ Sum-of-the-years'-digits method ▪ Tangible personal property ▪ Trademark ▪ Trade name ▪ Units-of-output method

CLASSIFYING PROPERTY, PLANT, AND EQUIPMENT

The category of business assets known as **property, plant, and equipment** includes real property and tangible personal property. Among the **real property** holdings of a business are land, land improvements (such as sidewalks and parking lots), buildings, and other structures attached to the land. **Tangible personal property** consists of machinery, equipment, furniture, and fixtures.

Property, plant, and equipment does not include assets purchased for investment reasons. For example, land purchased for a future building site or land being held for investment would be classified as "other assets" or as "investments," not as property, plant, and equipment. Similarly, intangible assets are not classified as property, plant, and equipment but separately as "intangible assets."

Three aspects of accounting for property, plant, and equipment are examined in this chapter.

1. The costs of acquiring these assets
2. The transfer of the costs of these assets to expense through depreciation or depletion
3. The removal of these assets from the accounting records through retirement, sale, or a trade-in for new assets

THE ACQUISITION OF PROPERTY, PLANT, AND EQUIPMENT

Items of property, plant, and equipment are usually acquired by purchase. The total cost of an asset may actually be made up of several elements, each of which must be debited to the account for that asset. The general rule is that the acquisition cost of an asset includes the net price paid the seller, all transportation and installation costs, and the cost of any adjustments or modifications needed to prepare the asset for use.

Suppose Hanson's Sportswear purchases office equipment at a price of $450 FOB (free on board) the factory, which means that the buyer pays for transportation from the factory. The freight bill is $49.50. When the equipment arrives, the firm decides to have extra features installed on it locally, at a net cost of $100.50. At what cost is the machine entered in the Office Equipment account?

The seller's invoice is the first amount to be debited to the Office Equipment account. The transportation charge is part of the cost of the equipment and should also be debited to Office Equipment. The cost of the changes made to the machine before it is suitable for the intended use is a further charge to its asset account—Office Equipment. When all these charges have been posted to the Office Equipment account, the total acquisition cost of the machine will be $600, as shown below.

Net amount paid to seller	$450.00
Freight	49.50
Minor changes in operating features	100.50
Total acquisition cost of machine	$600.00

In the case of land purchased for a building site, the acquisition cost of the land should include the net costs (less salvage) of removing unwanted buildings and of grading and draining the land. The costs of installing permanent walks or roadways, curbing, gutters, and drainage facilities should be debited to the asset Land Improvements, which would be subject to depreciation.

Land is not depreciated, but improvements to land are depreciated.

When items of property, plant, and equipment are constructed by the company for its own use, interest costs incurred on borrowed funds during the construction period are capitalized or added to the asset account. **Capitalized costs** are all costs recorded as part of an asset's cost and depreciated over an asset's useful life. The amount capitalized is the interest deemed to apply to the average amount of accumulated costs during the period. This topic is covered in detail in more advanced accounting courses.

THE COST OF USING PROPERTY, PLANT, AND EQUIPMENT

OBJECTIVE 1
Compute the amount that should be recorded as an asset's cost.

Several obvious costs are incurred in using assets. Some of these costs include repairs, maintenance, insurance, and taxes. Assets such as buildings and machines have limited useful lives. Their inevitable wear through use in a firm's operations must be taken into account as an additional expense of doing business. Other types of assets such as natural resources are also used up in the course of a firm's operations. Two technical terms are commonly used to distinguish the nature of the expense involved. **Depreciation** is the name given to the periodic allocation of the costs of assets, such as buildings and equipment. The allocation of the costs of natural resources, such as minerals, to the units produced is referred to as **depletion.** In addition, the costs of intangible assets, such as patents, are transferred to expense through amortization, which is discussed later in this chapter. Here we focus on depreciation and depletion.

Depreciation

As noted above, depreciation is the term used in accounting to describe the periodic transfer of acquisition cost to expense for assets such as buildings, machinery, equipment, furniture, and fixtures. This transfer is accomplished by debiting an account called Depreciation Expense. (Note that land is not depreciated because it is assumed that land has an infinite life and does not deteriorate over time.) Four widely used methods of computing the amount of depreciation expense for each time period over the useful life of an asset are described later in this chapter.

OBJECTIVE 2
Compute and record depreciation of property, plant, and equipment by commonly used methods.

Recording Depreciation

Assets that will be used for more than one year are recorded at acquisition cost. The title of the asset should reflect its use—Office Equipment, Vehicles, or Building. The asset is generally shown on the balance sheet at this figure as long as the asset remains in use. Of course, later additions or partial dispositions require an adjustment of the acquisition cost figure.

At the end of each accounting period, the current depreciation is debited to an appropriate expense account and credited to a contra asset account. Usually the title of the contra asset account is Accumulated Depreciation. For example, assume that a business has plant buildings costing $100,000 and an annual depreciation expense of $5,000 is to be recorded for these buildings. The current-year expense for depreciation appears on the worksheet as an adjustment and is later recorded in the general journal as an adjusting entry.

Dec.	31	*Depr. Exp.—Buildings*	5 000 00	
		Accum. Depr.—Buildings		5 000 00
		To record the depreciation		
		for the year		

Assume that this is the first year of use for the asset. The balance sheet presentation at the end of the year after the adjusting entry has been recorded is as follows.

Property, Plant, and Equipment		
Plant Buildings	$100,000	
Less Accumulated Depreciation	5,000	$95,000

The accumulated depreciation account is a contra asset account. Its credit balance, which is opposite to the normal asset account balance, reflects the amount of acquisition cost that has been transferred to expense. In the journal entry above, notice that the asset account is not a part of the adjusting entry. The difference between the acquisition cost shown in the asset account and the balance of the contra account is the **book value,** or net book value, of the asset. In the example shown above, the plant buildings have a book value of $95,000. The book value of the asset is usually not the same as the fair market value of the asset—the price you could sell the asset for on the open market.

▲ REMEMBER!

Book value = Cost − Accumulated depreciation

Since depreciation has a major impact on the assets of a business, the following information must be shown on the financial statements or in accompanying notes to the financial statements.

1. The depreciation expense for the period
2. The balances in the accounts of the depreciable assets, classified according to their nature or their function
3. The accumulated depreciation
4. A general description of the method or methods used in computing depreciation

Computing the Amount of Depreciation Expense

As previously explained, the cost of certain tangible assets is spread over their useful lives through periodic debits to depreciation expense and corresponding credits to a contra asset account, commonly Accumulated Depreciation. The total amount charged to the expense account must not exceed the total cost of the asset less any net salvage value. The **salvage value, residual value,** or **scrap value** is the value that the asset is expected to have at the end of its useful life. The net salvage value is the salvage value less any costs to remove and sell the item.

Four methods of computing depreciation expense are widely used for financial accounting purposes: straight line, declining balance, sum-of-the-years' digits, and units of output. In addition, the modified accelerated cost recovery system (MACRS) is used for federal income tax purposes.

Straight-Line Method. The **straight-line method** (first presented in Chapter 5) is the most widely used method of computing the amount of depreciation expense. Under this method the same amount of depreciation is recorded for each year (or other accounting period) over the useful life of the asset. To obtain the annual depreciation, the acquisition cost less the expected net salvage value is divided by the expected life in years. This relationship is expressed by the following formula.

Acquisition Cost − Net Salvage Value ÷ Useful Life in Years = Annual Depreciation Amount

Suppose an office machine purchased by Hanson's Sportswear at a total cost of $600 is expected to be used for five years and to have a net salvage value of $60 at the end of that time. We can use these figures in the above equation to find the amount of annual depreciation.

$$(\$600 - \$60)/5 = \$540/5 = \$108$$

This example of straight-line depreciation is shown in graph form in Figure 18–1.

FIGURE 18–1
Straight-Line Depreciation

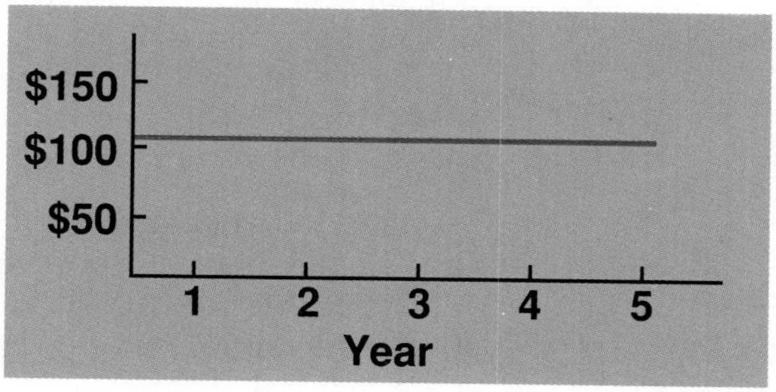

If the firm records depreciation at the end of each fiscal year, $108 is debited to Depreciation Expense—Office Equipment and credited to Accumulated Depreciation—Office Equipment. The monthly amount of the depreciation charge on the office equipment is 1/12 of $108, or $9. Depreciation on a newly acquired asset is usually computed to the nearest month. For example, if the asset had been purchased on September 5, 19X3, depreciation of $45 (5 months × $9) would be recorded as follows for the company's fiscal year ended January 31, 19X4.

Jan.	*31*	*Depr. Exp.—Office Equip.*	45 00	
		Accum. Depr.—Off. Equip.		45 00
		To record fiscal year depreciation for asset purchased September 5, 19X3		

Declining-Balance Method. Under the **declining-balance method** of computing the amount of depreciation expense, the accountant multiplies an appropriate percentage, or factor, by the book value (cost − accumulated depreciation) of an asset at the beginning of each year to obtain the amount of depreciation expense for that year. In the past the percentage allowable on depreciable personal property for income tax purposes (and therefore widely used by business firms) was twice the straight-line rate. The straight-line rate for a five-year asset is 1/5; therefore, the double-declining rate would be 2 × 1/5 or 2/5. Usually this rate is converted to a decimal number for ease of computation; hence the factor in this example becomes 0.40. This method of calculating depreciation is the **double-declining-balance method.** A shortcut formula for calculating the double-declining-balance factor is to apply $2/n$, where n is the useful life of the asset.

When the straight-line method is applied to Hanson's Sportswear's office machine (which has an expected useful life of five years), the yearly depreciation is 1/5, or 20 percent, of the cost minus the net salvage value. The double-declining-balance rate allowable on the same item is twice 20 percent, or 40 percent. Because tax regulations allow the accountant to ignore salvage value when computing depreciation, it is also usually ignored when computing the amount of depreciation for financial accounting purposes.

In the first year, the acquisition cost of $600 is multiplied by 40 percent to give a depreciation expense of $240 for that year. Thus the book value at the beginning of the second year is $360 ($600 − $240), and the depreciation expense for the second year is $144 (40 percent of $360). The depreciation of the office machine under the declining-balance method for the five years of its useful life is shown in Table 18–1.

TABLE 18–1
Depreciation by Declining-Balance Method

Year	Beginning Book Value	Rate, %	Depreciation for Year	Depreciation to Date
1	$600.00	40	$240.00	$240.00
2	360.00	40	144.00	384.00
3	216.00	40	86.40	470.40
4	129.60	40	51.84	522.24
5	77.76	40	31.10	553.34

Ending book value = $46.66

Although no salvage value is used in computing the annual depreciation when the declining-balance method is used, there remains at the end of the five years a book value of $46.66—only slightly less than the estimated salvage value of $60 used under the straight-line method.

The declining-balance method of computing the amount of depreciation expense is referred to as an **accelerated method of depreciation.** It is accelerated in that more depreciation is taken in the early years of the asset's life than under the straight-line method. This can be illustrated by the graph in Figure 18–2.

FIGURE 18–2
Declining-Balance Depreciation

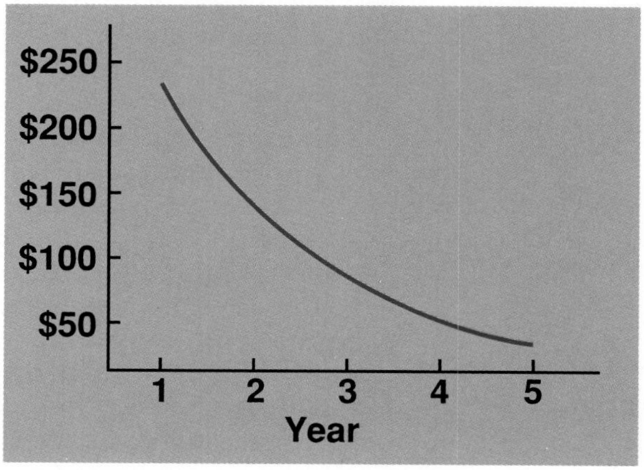

Sum-of-the-Years'-Digits Method. A second accelerated method of depreciation is the **sum-of-the-years'-digits method.** Using this method requires that a fractional part of the depreciable cost of the asset be debited to Depreciation Expense each year; the denominator (bottom part) of the fraction is always the "sum of the years' digits." This amount is found by simply adding together the numbers representing the years of the asset's useful life. For example, the digits for a machine expected to have a useful life of five years are 1, 2, 3, 4, and 5. Thus the sum of the years' digits is 1 + 2 + 3 + 4 + 5, or 15. The numerator (top part) of the fraction for any year is the number of years remaining in the useful life of the asset. Thus for the first year the fraction is 5/15, for the second year it is 4/15, and so on. This fraction is multiplied by the acquisition cost minus the net salvage value of the asset, which, in our office machine example, is $600 – $60, or $540.

The depreciation of the office machine owned by Hanson's Sportswear under the sum-of-the-years'-digits method is shown in Table 18–2, which also compares this method of depreciation with the two methods previously illustrated. Note that both the declining-balance method and the sum-of-the-years'-digits method give higher depreciation charges in the early years of the asset's life and lower charges in the later years. As mentioned earlier, both of these methods represent accelerated methods of depreciation.

TABLE 18–2
Comparison of Depreciation Methods

	Sum-of-the-Years'-Digits Method			Other Methods	
Year	Fraction	Cost Minus Salvage	Depreciation for Year	Declining Balance	Straight Line
1	5/15	$540.00	$180.00	$240.00	$108.00
2	4/15	540.00	144.00	144.00	108.00
3	3/15	540.00	108.00	86.40	108.00
4	2/15	540.00	72.00	51.84	108.00
5	1/15	540.00	36.00	31.10	108.00
Total depreciation, 5 years			540.00	553.34	540.00

Units-of-Output Method. In some situations the useful life of an asset is related more directly to units of work performed by the asset than to the passage of time. In such cases, depreciation can be calculated at the same rate for each unit of output. The expense for any time period is then determined by multiplying the rate for each unit by the number of units produced. This method of computing depreciation is called the **units-of-output method.**

For example, suppose a firm purchases a metal stamping press for $21,000. The press is expected to have a useful life of 1,000,000 stamping impressions and a net salvage value of $1,000 at the end of its useful life. The rate for each stamping is $20,000 ($21,000 − $1,000) divided by 1,000,000, or $0.02. If 50,000 stampings are produced during a period, the depreciation charge is 50,000 × $0.02, or $1,000.

SELF-REVIEW

1. What is depreciation?
2. Name two methods of accelerated depreciation.
3. What accounts are debited and credited when you make the journal entry to record depreciation expense?
4. Give the formula to determine the net book value of an asset.
5. What is the denominator of the fraction used in the sum-of-the-years'-digits method of depreciation for an asset with a useful life of four years?

Answers to Self-Review

1. Depreciation is the process of transferring the acquisition cost of a capital asset to expense over its useful life.
2. Two methods of accelerated depreciation are the declining-balance and the sum-of-the-years'-digits methods.

3. The entry to record depreciation includes a debit to Depreciation Expense and a credit to Accumulated Depreciation.
4. Net book value of an asset equals acquisition cost of the asset minus accumulated depreciation.
5. In the sum-of-the-years'-digits method of computing depreciation for an asset with a four-year life, the denominator will be the sum of 4 + 3 + 2 + 1, or 10.

OBJECTIVE 3
Classify assets according to which modified accelerated cost recovery system (MACRS) class they fall into for federal income tax purposes.

Depreciation for Federal Income Tax Purposes

The depreciation methods previously described are used by businesses in preparing their financial statements. A separate set of rules is prescribed by the Internal Revenue Service to allow businesses to "recover" their capital investment costs for tax purposes. The most recent legislation allows companies to recover their initial investment in capital assets through the modified accelerated cost recovery system (MACRS), which revised the earlier Accelerated Cost Recovery System (ACRS) by extending the recovery period (useful life) for most assets. MACRS applies to assets purchased after December 31, 1986.

Under MACRS, the classification of various items of personal property is based on terms of 3, 5, 7, 10, 15, or 20 years. The costs of residential rental buildings are recovered over 27.5 years. Nonresidential building costs (such as office buildings) are recovered over 31.5 years. A general description of items included in each class of personal property is given below.

- The 3-year class includes few assets. It includes racehorses that are more than 2 years old and other horses more than 12 years old. It excludes automobiles and light-duty trucks.
- The 5-year class includes automobiles, lightweight trucks, computers, and certain other types of special-purpose property.
- The 7-year class includes office furniture and fixtures and most manufacturing equipment.
- The 10-year class includes few business assets since this class pertains mostly to special-purpose property, such as equipment used in the manufacture of food and tobacco products.
- The 15-year class includes telephone distribution plants, sewage treatment plants, and certain types of equipment used in the communications industry.
- The 20-year class includes certain types of farm buildings and municipal sewer systems.

The amount of "recovery" costs allowed in any tax year is determined by multiplying the percentage from the MACRS table for the asset's class life by the original cost, ignoring any salvage value. For example, a five-year asset costing $10,000 (assuming a half-year convention) would be allowed the following cost-recovery deductions on the federal tax return.

Year	Percent	Original Cost	Current Recovery
1	20.00	$10,000	$2,000
2	32.00	10,000	3,200
3	19.20	10,000	1,920
4	11.52	10,000	1,152
5	11.52	10,000	1,152
6	5.76	10,000	576

Note that it takes six years under the MACRS half-year convention for the business to fully "recover" its initial investment of $10,000. The term *half-year convention* refers to the allowance of six months' depreciation expense in the first year of the asset's life, without regard to the purchase date. The exception to this rule, the mid-quarter convention, is applied when more than 40 percent of purchased assets are placed in service in the fourth quarter of a year. A full discussion of determining what convention to follow—half-year or mid-quarter—is beyond the scope of this text. These conventions are discussed in tax courses.

Instead of using ACRS or MACRS rules in effect at the time of the purchase of the asset, a firm can adopt the units-of-output method of depreciation for income tax purposes, if that method is appropriate. Also, a firm can decide to use the straight-line method rather than ACRS or MACRS, but this can be done only on an extended-life basis. For example, assets in the 5-year ACRS class must be depreciated over either 12 years or 25 years.

The original ACRS rules were designed to encourage companies to invest in productive business property by permitting a rapid charge-off of costs, with a resulting tax saving, in the early years of each asset's life. Neither ACRS nor MACRS, however, is suitable as a means of matching the costs of assets with the revenues produced by those assets. Thus they are not acceptable for financial accounting purposes.

Depletion

Natural resources, such as timber, oil, and minerals, are physically removed from the land in the process of production. Their cost is part of the expense of carrying on such operations. As explained already, *depletion* is the term used to describe this expense. Remember that you debit expense accounts—in this case, Depletion Expense—to increase those accounts.

For financial accounting purposes, the amount to be charged for depletion of property such as oil, minerals, or metals is based on cost. However, for federal income tax purposes, the depletion can also be computed as a percentage of gross income from the product sold (based on the sales price). Both the cost depletion and the percentage depletion methods are discussed in the next section.

OBJECTIVE 4
Compute and record depletion of natural resources.

Depletion for Financial Accounting Purposes

Cost depletion is determined in a manner similar to depreciation determined by the units-of-output method. The total cost of, say, a mineral deposit is divided by the estimated number of units in the deposit to give the depletion cost for each unit of the mineral extracted. For example, suppose a firm purchases a clay pit that is estimated to contain 500,000 tons of extractable clay suitable for making brick. The firm pays $50,000 for the clay pit. The depletion cost for each ton of clay is $0.10 ($50,000/500,000 tons). If the firm extracts 60,000 tons of this clay in a particular year, the depletion will be $6,000 (60,000 × $0.10). The adjusting entry to record these facts is shown here.

Dec.	31	Depletion Exp.—Min. Deposits		6 000 00	
		Accum. Deple.—Min. Dep.			6 000 00
		To record the extraction			
		of 60,000 tons			

The balance sheet presentation after making the adjusting entry for the first year of the life of this asset is shown below.

Property, Plant, and Equipment

Mineral Deposits	$50,000	
Less Accumulated Depletion	6,000	$44,000

As shown here, the net book value of the mineral deposits is $44,000 at the end of the year.

Depletion for Federal Income Tax Purposes

For federal income tax purposes, the depletion to be deducted is the larger of cost depletion or percentage depletion. Cost depletion for tax purposes is computed in the same way as it is for financial accounting purposes (see the discussion above). However, the amount of cost depletion computed for each purpose will generally differ because the costs capitalized for financial accounting and tax purposes are not identical. In addition, if percentage depletion is taken on the tax return, the amount taken in one year will reduce the cost on which cost depletion is based in future years.

Percentage depletion is based on a percentage of the gross income from the sale of minerals from a property. The percentage to be used is specified in the tax law for each type of mineral. However, the amount computed by applying the specified percentage to the gross income is limited to either 50 percent or 100 percent of the net income from the property, depending on the type of mineral. Because of the complexity of the rules regarding depletion, the computation of depletion allowable for federal tax purposes is not covered here.

Information Block: Ethics in Accounting

What's Another Five Years?

Sue Tomsovic is the chief financial officer for Ruble Robotics, Inc. The end of the year is near, and Ms. Tomsovic knows that the company plans a public offering of stock early in the next year. She is now trying to estimate annual earnings for the current year, and the numbers do not look good. It appears that net income will be 10 percent lower than last year. Ms. Tomsovic determines that the decrease in net income is the result of several capital acquisitions made early in the year.

Assets purchased in February were classified as five-year assets. Ms. Tomsovic calculates that changing the estimated life of these assets from five to ten years will result in a net income about 3 percent higher than last year, due to the decreased depreciation. The higher net income is needed for the company to have a successful public offering of its stock.

Ms. Tomsovic understands that ensuring the company has sufficient capital to operate is her primary responsibility. As chief financial officer, she can make policy changes as they relate to accounting conventions.

1. What is the ethical issue?
2. What are the alternatives?
3. Who are the affected parties?
4. How do the alternatives affect the parties?
5. What should Ms. Tomsovic do?

THE DISPOSITION OF AN ASSET

OBJECTIVE 5
Record sales of plant and equipment.

Assets that are no longer useful to a business are usually disposed of. They may be sold, traded in, or scrapped. Sometimes useful assets are also sold so the company can purchase better assets. When an asset is disposed of, the following steps are taken to account for the asset in the firm's financial records.

1. The accountant records depreciation to the date of disposition.
2. The accountant closes out (removes) the cost of the asset from the asset account, removes the asset's total accumulated depreciation from the related accumulated depreciation account, records the proceeds realized, and determines and records the gain or loss if any.

The accounting entries necessary to record the sale of an asset under various conditions are illustrated by the following example.

Assume that Hanson's Sportswear has recorded depreciation for its $600 office machine on the straight-line basis for three years at $108 a year, for a total depreciation of $324. Three and a half years after purchasing the machine, management decides to sell it. The first thing the accountant must do is record depreciation up to the date of the sale. The amount to be recorded is $54 for the six months following the last year in which depreciation was recorded. This amount is debited to Depreciation Expense—Office Equipment and credited to Accumulated Depreciation—Office Equipment.

The Office Equipment account has a debit balance of $600 representing the original cost of buying the asset. The Accumulated Depreciation account now has a credit balance of $378 ($324 + $54). The book value (cost minus accumulated depreciation) is $222 ($600 − $378).

Sale at Book Value

Suppose first that the sale is made on credit for an amount equal to the book value of $222. The accountant must do the following.

1. Record the new account receivable of $222 on the books.
2. Close out the balance of $378 in the Accumulated Depreciation account.
3. Close out the cost of the asset sold, $600.

In the general journal, all this can be accomplished in one compound entry, as illustrated below. Since the sale is for the book value, there is no gain or loss to be recorded.

July	*31*	*Accounts Receivable*		*222 00*	
		Accum. Depr.—Office Equip.		*378 00*	
		Office Equipment			*600 00*
		Sale of office machine			
		at book value			

Sale Above Book Value

Suppose that the sales price is $249, which is $27 above the book value. Accounts Receivable is debited for $249. The Accumulated Depreciation account is debited for $378, and the asset account is credited for $600, as before. To complete the entry, a new account called Gain on Sale of Equipment is credited for $27, as shown below.

July	*31*	*Accounts Receivable*		*249 00*	
		Accum. Depr.—Office Equip.		*378 00*	
		Office Equipment			*600 00*
		Gain on Sale of Equipment			*27 00*
		Sale of office machine at			
		gain			

The $27 gain represents the difference between the sales price of $249 and the book value of the equipment, $222. It is shown on the income statement as an item of income, usually under the heading, Other Income.

Sale Below Book Value

Suppose the sale price of the machine is $199. Compared with the book value of $222, this price represents a loss of $23. Accounts Receivable is debited for the agreed-upon sale price of $199. The Accumulated Depreciation account is debited for $378, and the asset account, Office Equipment, is credited for $600. The journal entry is completed with a debit to a new account called Loss on Sale of Equipment for $23. The journal entry given below will record these events.

July	*31*	*Accounts Receivable*		*199 00*	
		Accum. Depr.—Office Equip.		*378 00*	
		Loss on Sale of Equipment		*23 00*	
		Office Equipment			*600 00*
		Sale of office equipment			
		at loss			

The loss is shown on the income statement, usually under the heading, Other Expenses. Many companies use a single account to record both gains and losses on sales of assets. This account is usually called Gains and Losses on Sales of Assets. If gains exceed losses, the account will have a credit balance and will be reported on the income statement in Other Income. If losses exceed gains, the balance is reported in the Other Expenses section of the income statement.

Trade-In of an Asset on a Similar Asset

OBJECTIVE 6

Record trade-ins of assets using the income tax method and the fair market value method.

Businesses often trade old equipment when they purchase new equipment. This type of transaction must be recorded in two steps. First, the depreciation on the piece of equipment being traded in must be brought up to the date of the trade. Second, the trade and the purchase must be recorded. Two methods are used to record this kind of transaction: the income tax method and the fair market value method.

The Income Tax Method

For many years the federal tax laws have provided that when an asset used in business is traded in for a similar asset, no gain or loss is to be recorded on the transaction. The cost of the new asset is recorded at the book value (cost minus accumulated depreciation) of the old asset plus the cash paid for the new asset.

Under the **income tax method,** the accountant must do the following.

1. Credit the asset account for the cost of the old asset that is traded in.

2. Close out the amount in the accumulated depreciation account that relates to the old asset.
3. Record the amount of the cash payment to be made (as a credit to Accounts Payable if a voucher system is used).
4. Record the new asset as the sum of the cash to be paid plus the book value of the old asset that is traded in.

The following examples will illustrate this procedure. A firm trades in a printer that originally cost $950. Depreciation totaling $500 was recorded to the date of the trade-in. The printer is traded for a new model having a list price and fair market value of $1,200. The seller offers an allowance of $500 on the old printer against the list price of the new $1,200 printer. In effect, the trade-in of the old printer produces a gain of $50 (a $500 allowance less the $450 book value) for the purchaser of the new printer. Under the income tax method that gain is not recognized, however. Under that method, the accountant must do the following.

1. Remove the cost of the old asset, $950, from the asset account.
2. Remove the old asset's related accumulated depreciation, $500, from its accumulated depreciation account.
3. Record the $700 cash to be paid ($1,200 list minus $500 trade-in allowance for the old printer) by crediting Accounts Payable.
4. Record the new printer in the financial records at $1,150, which is the sum of the book value of the old asset ($950 − $500) plus the cash to be paid, $700. The necessary journal entry appears below.

Oct.	*31*	*Office Equipment (new)*		*1 1 5 0 00*	
		Accum. Depr.—Off. Equip. (old)		*5 0 0 00*	
		Office Equipment (old)			*9 5 0 00*
		Accounts Payable			*7 0 0 00*
		Trade-in of old printer			
		for new model			

If the seller of the new equipment had made an allowance of only $400 on the trade-in, the purchaser would have realized a loss of $50 ($450 book value of old asset less trade-in allowance of $400). Under *APB Opinion No. 29,* this kind of loss must be recorded, as shown in the next section. However, for income tax purposes, no loss would be recorded; instead the new equipment would have a "tax basis" of $1,250—the total of the book value of the old asset ($450) and the amount of cash paid ($800). In spite of the requirements of *APB Opinion No. 29* to record all losses on trade-ins, many businesses continue to use the income tax method in recording the transaction. This practice is justified on the grounds that such losses are usually immaterial and would involve duplicate record keeping. If the income tax method is used to record this transaction, the following journal entry will be made.

Oct.	31	*Office Equipment (new)*	1 2 5 0 00	
		Accum. Depr.—Off. Equip. (old)	5 0 0 00	
		Office Equipment (old)		9 5 0 00
		Accounts Payable		8 0 0 00
		Trade-in of old printer		
		for new model		

The Fair Market Value Method

As already mentioned, under *APB Opinion No. 29,* if the book value of the old asset exceeds the amount of the trade-in allowance received, the new asset should be recognized at its fair market value and the loss should be recognized. In using the **fair market value method,** the accountant must do the following if the book value of the old asset exceeds the trade-in allowance.

1. Credit the asset account for the cost of the old asset traded in.
2. Close out (by debiting) the amount of depreciation related to the old asset that is in the Accumulated Depreciation account.
3. Record the cash payment to be made.
4. Record the new asset at its fair market value (purchase price).
5. Record a loss (by debiting Loss on Sale of Equipment) equal to the difference between the trade-in allowance given and the book value of the old asset traded.

Assume that this method is used in the case of the printer trade-in discussed above. The journal entry to record this event follows.

If the trade-in value allowed for the old asset exceeds the book value of the old asset, no gain is recognized. Instead, the income tax method must be used to record the transaction.

Oct.	31	*Office Equipment (new)*	1 2 0 0 00	
		Accum. Depr.—Off. Equip. (old)	5 0 0 00	
		Loss on Sale of Equipment	5 0 00	
		Office Equipment (old)		9 5 0 00
		Accounts Payable		8 0 0 00
		Trade-in of old printer		
		for new model		

CLASSIFYING INTANGIBLE ASSETS

In addition to property, plant, and equipment, many businesses have intangible assets. The major types of intangible assets are patents, copyrights, franchises, trademarks, brand names, organizational costs, computer software, and goodwill. With the exception of computer software, these assets usually do not have any physical attributes.

A **patent** is an exclusive right given by the U.S. Patent Office to manufacture and sell an invention for a period of 17 years from the date of the patent grant. A patent may not be renewed; however, a

Information Block: Computers in Accounting

Fixed-Asset Record Keeping

Appropriate and up-to-date depreciation records are needed for accurate financial statement reporting and for income tax reporting purposes. Computer programs are used to maintain subsidiary records for property, plant, and equipment assets.

The calculation of asset depreciation is well suited to the speed and accuracy of the computer. Software provides the various mathematical equations to calculate the amount of depreciation using various methods. When the appropriate information is provided—such as the date of acquisition, cost, salvage value, and estimated useful life—the computer can quickly and accurately calculate the amount of depreciation and print or display depreciation schedules listing the annual depreciation over the asset's useful life.

Two methods are used to maintain subsidiary records. With the first method, a master file is created containing the appropriate data for each individual plant asset. This master file is kept on an auxiliary storage device such as magnetic tape or magnetic disk. When the depreciation program is run, the computer will access this file and calculate the depreciation for the current accounting period. The computer can generate the necessary general journal adjusting entries for depreciation expense and update the general ledger expense accounts and related accumulated depreciation accounts. In addition, the computer updates the subsidiary account for each asset to show its current book value. A depreciation report can be printed to summarize the journal entries and the amounts of individual depreciation expense.

The second method of maintaining asset subsidiary records is to print the depreciation schedule for each plant asset. This hard copy is

new patent may be obtained if significant improvements can be demonstrated in the original idea. The right to the patent may be sold, assigned, or otherwise controlled by the owner.

A **copyright** is the exclusive right granted by the federal government to produce, publish, and sell a literary or artistic work for a period equal to the author's life plus 50 years.

Two types of **franchises** are available to businesspeople. The first type is a right granted by a governmental unit for the business to provide a service to the governmental unit (such as cable television).

then filed for future reference. At the end of each accounting period, the accountant refers to these depreciation schedules to obtain the correct amount of depreciation for the current year. Adjusting entries are then entered into the computer to update the general ledger accounts. An example of a depreciation schedule is shown below.

RUN DATE: 12/31/94

ASSET: MAINFRAME COMPUTER
DATE ACQUIRED: YEAR: 1992 MONTH: 05
COST: $160,000
SALVAGE VALUE: $10,000
ESTIMATED USEFUL LIFE: 10 YEARS
DEPRECIATION METHOD: STRAIGHT LINE

YEAR	DEPRECIATION EXPENSE	ACCUMULATED DEPRECIATION	BOOK VALUE
1992	10,000	10,000	150,000
1993	15,000	25,000	135,000
1994	15,000	40,000	120,000
1995	15,000	55,000	105,000
1996	15,000	70,000	90,000
1997	15,000	85,000	75,000
1998	15,000	100,000	60,000
1999	15,000	115,000	45,000
2000	15,000	130,000	30,000
2001	15,000	145,000	15,000
2002	5,000	150,000	10,000

The second type is an exclusive dealership or an exclusive arrangement between a manufacturer and a dealer or distributor.

Trademarks, trade names, and **brand names** are used to build consumer confidence and loyalty. They can be registered with the U.S. Patent Office. Like other intangible assets, they can be sold, traded, or otherwise controlled by the owner.

Organizational costs are the costs incurred when organizing a business. Examples include attorney's fees, accountant's fees, legal filing fees, and other costs of beginning a business.

Computer software consists of written programs that instruct a computer's hardware to do certain tasks. Software may be developed by the company's employees or purchased from outside the company.

Goodwill represents the value of a business in excess of the value of its identifiable assets. Goodwill is recorded only on the purchase of a business. It usually arises because a business has extraordinary earnings or earnings potential.

THE ACQUISITION OF INTANGIBLE ASSETS

Intangible assets may be produced or developed by the firm, or they may be purchased from other parties. A general rule is that only if it is purchased from other parties is the intangible asset recorded on the books of the firm. Costs incurred internally to develop intangible assets are charged off in the year incurred to an account called Research and Development Expenses. Similarly, costs related to software development by a company should be charged to expense in the year incurred.

AMORTIZING THE COSTS OF INTANGIBLE ASSETS

OBJECTIVE 7

Compute and record amortization of intangible assets.

Most intangible assets have limited legal and economic (useful) lives. Their acquisition costs should be transferred to expense over the shorter of the two lives. **Amortization** is the accounting term used to describe the process of transferring the acquisition cost of intangible assets to expense.

Fewer methods for calculating the amount of amortization of intangible assets exist than for calculating the amount of depreciation of physical assets. The straight-line method is most commonly used, although the units-of-output method is appropriate in some unique situations. In no case should an intangible asset be amortized for a period exceeding 40 years.

The periodic amortization is debited to an expense account (usually Amortization Expense) and credited, by custom, directly to the intangible account. The balance remaining in the intangible asset account is therefore always its book value. For example, suppose a firm purchased a patent for $40,000 and the patent has a remaining economic life of 10 years, even though 12 years remain in its legal life. The amount to be amortized each year would equal $4,000 ($40,000 cost divided by the shorter of economic or legal life, 10 years). The adjusting entry to record a full year's amortization is shown below.

Dec.	*31*	*Amortization Expense—Patent*		*4 000 00*	
		Patent			*4 000 00*
		To record 12 months'			
		amortization of patent			

INTERNAL CONTROL OF PROPERTY, PLANT, AND EQUIPMENT

The internal control of property, plant, and equipment centers on physical safeguards to prevent theft. Regardless of the size of the business or the nature of the assets it owns, most of the following procedures are standard.

1. All purchases of capital assets should be authorized and justified by appropriate personnel.
2. Each asset should be given an identification number to be used for inventory control purposes. If possible, this number should be engraved on the asset.
3. An asset register should be maintained that lists all capital assets, their costs, acquisition dates, location, and any other useful information.
4. Each asset should be assigned to a single person for its safekeeping, maintenance, and operation.
5. A physical inventory should be taken periodically to account for all property, plant, and equipment. This inventory should be compared with the asset register and any differences should be investigated.
6. Procedures should be established to detail the authorizing of asset retirement, sale, or other disposition.

The internal control of intangible assets is usually not as big a problem as the control of physical assets. Internal control procedures consist primarily of safe storage of documents related to the intangibles and protection of the storage location. In addition, firms must constantly be alert for infringement on their copyrights and trademarks. Appropriate legal action is required whenever there is an infringement on an intangible asset.

MANAGERIAL IMPLICATIONS

Property, plant, and equipment usually represent the largest cash investment by the owners of a business. Managers must therefore establish strong internal control systems for these assets to protect the owners' investment. Managers should also understand the differences between the various methods of depreciation and the impact each has on the company financial statements and tax returns. Managers must also study the methods used to record sales and trade-ins of assets because of the different methods used to report these transactions and the different results that impact the financial statements and tax returns.

SELF-REVIEW

1. Under MACRS, what is the recovery period for a nonresidential office complex?
2. When would you have a gain on the disposition of an asset?
3. Under the income tax method of accounting for the trade of one asset for a similar asset, when is a gain or loss recognized?
4. Under current law, what is the life of a copyright?
5. What is the purpose of internal control?

Answers to Self-Review

1. MACRS requires the cost of nonresidential real property to be recovered over 31.5 years.
2. When an asset is disposed of, a gain will result when the value received is greater than the net book value of the asset.
3. A gain or loss is never recognized when trading similar assets under the income tax method.
4. The life of a copyright is the length of the author's life plus 50 years.
5. The purpose of internal control is to safeguard (protect) the business's assets.

CHAPTER 18 Review and Applications

CHAPTER SUMMARY

Property, plant, and equipment are those tangible assets used in carrying out the company's business operations. Depending on the nature of the asset, depreciation or depletion must be included as a current expense. Through these expenses, the asset's original cost is spread over its useful or legal life.

Four widely used methods of computing depreciation are the straight-line method, the declining-balance method, the sum-of-the-years'-digits method, and the units-of-output method. Under current tax law, new assets must be depreciated under the modified accelerated cost recovery system (MACRS).

Depletion is based on cost for financial accounting purposes and is charged to expense on a per-unit-produced basis. For federal income tax purposes, depletion is generally based on a percentage of gross income from production.

Items of property, plant, and equipment are disposed of in various ways. They can be sold outright, scrapped, or traded in on other assets. At the time of sale or trade-in, the asset's depreciation must be brought up to date. If a loss results from a sale or trade, it must be determined and recorded. A gain from a sale is also recorded, but a gain from a trade-in is not.

Except for computer software, intangible assets have no physical characteristics. They are also recorded at cost, but only if acquired in a purchase from outside parties. The original cost is amortized over the shorter of an asset's economic or legal life, usually by the straight-line method. Costs incurred by firms who produce their own intangible assets are charged to Research and Development Expense in the year incurred.

GLOSSARY OF NEW TERMS

Accelerated method of depreciation (p. 614) A method of depreciating asset cost that allocates greater amounts of depreciation to the asset's early years of useful life

Amortization (p. 626) The process of transferring acquisition costs of intangible assets to expense

Book value (p. 611) The excess of the acquisition cost of an asset over its accumulated depreciation, depletion, or amortization

Capitalized costs (p. 610) All costs recorded as part of an asset's costs and depreciated over an asset's useful life

Copyright (p. 624) An intangible asset; an exclusive right granted by the federal government to produce, publish, and sell a literary or artistic work

Declining-balance method (p. 613) An accelerated method of depreciation in which the book value of an asset at the beginning of a year is multiplied by an appropriate percentage to determine depreciation for the year

Depletion (p. 610) Periodic allocation of the cost of a natural resource to expense

Depreciation (p. 610) Periodic allocation of the cost of an asset

Double-declining-balance method (p. 613) A method of depreciation using a rate equal to twice the straight-line rate

Fair-market value method (p. 623) A method of recording the trade-in of an asset that allows a loss to be recognized on the transaction if the book value exceeds the trade-in allowance

Franchise (p. 624) An intangible asset; a right to exclusive dealership granted by a governmental unit or a business entity

Goodwill (p. 626) An intangible asset; the value of a business in excess of the value of its identifiable assets

Income tax method (p. 621) A method of recording the trade-in of an asset according to tax allowances that permit no gain or loss to be recognized on the transaction

Patent (p. 623) An intangible asset; an exclusive right given by the federal government to manufacture and sell an invention

Property, plant, and equipment (p. 609) A category of business assets used in the business's operation and having a life of more than one year

Real property (p. 609) Assets such as land, land improvements, buildings, and other structures attached to the land

Salvage value (p. 612) The value of an asset expected at the end of its useful life; also called residual or scrap value

Straight-line method (p. 612) A method of depreciating asset costs that allocates equal amounts of expense each year (or each accounting period) of an asset's useful life

Sum-of-the-years'-digits method (p. 614) A method of depreciating asset costs by allocating as expense each year a fractional part of the asset's depreciable cost, based on the sum of the digits of the number of years in the asset's useful life

Tangible personal property (p. 609) Assets such as machinery, equipment, furniture, and fixtures having physical existence

Trademark (p. 615) An intangible asset; an exclusive business symbol registered with the U.S. Patent Office

Trade name (p. 625) An intangible asset; an exclusive business name registered with the U.S. Patent Office; also called brand name

Units-of-output method (p. 615) A method of depreciating asset cost on the basis of the number of units produced during each period

REVIEW QUESTIONS

1. What type of assets are included in the category property, plant, and equipment?
2. Distinguish between real property and personal property.
3. Name the most common items that make up the cost of factory equipment.
4. What are capitalized costs?
5. A company purchases some land on which are located several old buildings. The land is bought as the location for a new factory, so the existing buildings must be torn down. Explain how to account for the purchase price and the cost of razing the old buildings.
6. Explain how depreciation, depletion, and amortization differ and how they are similar.
7. What account is debited and what account is credited to record depreciation on office equipment?
8. Is depreciation for federal income tax purposes the same as depreciation for financial accounting purposes? Explain.
9. Which method will give you a higher amount of depreciation expense, straight-line or double-declining-balance?
10. What information related to the company's property, plant, and equipment must be presented in the financial statements and in the notes to the financial statements?
11. Explain how straight-line depreciation is computed.
12. Explain when and how salvage value is taken into account when computing depreciation under the following methods—straight line, declining balance, and sum-of-the-years'-digits.
13. What method is used to compute depletion expense for financial statement purposes for a coal mine operation?
14. What is an intangible asset?
15. Distinguish between the legal life and the economic life of an intangible asset. Which is used in computing amortization?
16. Under the income tax method, what will be the amount assigned to a new asset acquired through a trade-in of an old asset?
17. Explain the steps to record the trade-in of an old asset for a similar new asset under the income tax method.
18. Explain the difference between the income tax method and the fair market value method of recording the trade-in of an old asset for a new asset.
19. What is accelerated depreciation? Which methods discussed in this chapter are accelerated methods of depreciation?

MANAGERIAL FOCUS

1. Assume that you are the accountant at a fabricating plant. One of the vice presidents has asked you why one of the pieces of equipment used in the plant is shown at its original cost when its

value has gone up in the last several years. How do you explain this?

2. Explain why one company might prefer one method of depreciation over another method.
3. Suppose you are on the controller's staff at a large company. You have suggested assigning responsibility for the equipment used by the company to specific individuals. One of the supervisors has objected, saying it is a waste of time. Defend your suggestion to the controller and to the supervisor.
4. Why should management insist on amortizing intangible assets over their useful life instead of their legal life?
5. Generally accepted accounting principles require that all costs incurred for research and development be expensed in the year incurred. An officer of the company wants to amortize these costs. What can you say to explain the GAAP requirement?

EXERCISES

EXERCISE 18–1
(Obj. 1)

Determining the elements that make up the cost of an asset. The following costs were incurred by Ham & Smith, Inc., in connection with the construction of a new office building.

Cost of land	$150,000
Cost to demolish old building	5,000
Cost to construct building	750,000

1. What is the capitalized cost of the land?
2. What is the capitalized cost of the new building?

EXERCISE 18–2
(Obj. 1)
Tutorial

Determining the elements that make up the cost of an asset. The following costs related to a new computer system were incurred by MDH Limited.

Invoice price of computer	$5,500
Cash discount for prompt payment	400
Transportation costs	150
Installation costs	750

What is the capitalized cost of the new computer system?

EXERCISE 18–3
(Obj. 2)

Recording depreciation. For the year ending December 31, 19X4, the Ross Walker Corporation had depreciation totaling $4,000 on its office equipment. Give the general journal entry to record this adjusting entry.

EXERCISE 18–4
(Obj. 2)
Tutorial

Computing depreciation under various methods. The Park Company acquired an asset on January 1, 19X3, at a cost of $55,000. The asset's useful life is five years and its salvage value is $5,000. Compute the first two years of depreciation expense using the straight-line method, the double-declining-balance method, and the sum-of-the-years'-digits method.

EXERCISE 18-5
(Obj. 2)

Tutorial

Computing depreciation under the units-of-output method. The Sheet Company purchased 10 automobiles for its salespeople on January 6, 19X3. The automobiles cost $22,000 each and the expected salvage value is $2,000 per car. The company has been using cost per mile to depreciate its autos. These 10 automobiles are expected to get 50,000 miles each before they are sold outright. During 19X3, 125,000 miles were driven. Compute the 19X3 depreciation expense using the units-of-output method. During 19X4, 195,000 miles were driven. Give the amount of the 19X4 depreciation expense.

EXERCISE 18-6
(Obj. 7)

Tutorial

Computing amortization of patent costs. The Patrick Company purchased a patent on July 4, 19X4, for $42,000. The patent's legal life remaining is 13 years but the Patrick Company feels its economic life is only 10 years. Compute the amount of amortization on the patent for 19X4.

EXERCISE 18-7
(Obj. 4)

Computing depreciation of ore property cost. The Nevada Mining Company purchased a mine in 19X4. Capitalized costs were $900,000. It is estimated that 1.8 million tons of ore will be mined. The company mined 250,000 tons in 19X4. Compute the amount of depletion for 19X2.

EXERCISE 18-8
(Obj. 5)

Tutorial

Recording the sale of an asset. The Hernandez Company owns a truck that cost $35,000. Depreciation totaling $25,000 has been taken on the truck up to the date of its sale, when it is sold for $9,000.

1. Give the journal entry to record the sale.
2. Assume that the truck is sold for $12,000. Give the journal entry to record the sale.

EXERCISE 18-9
(Obj. 6)

Tutorial

Recording the trade-in of an asset for a similar asset. On January 5, 19X3, the Corker Construction Company purchased some construction equipment for $250,000. The equipment's estimated useful life is eight years and its salvage value is $10,000. The company uses the straight-line method of depreciation. On July 7, 19X7, this equipment is traded for new construction equipment that has a price of $300,000. The company pays $200,000 cash and is given a trade-in allowance of $100,000 on the old equipment.

1. Give the general journal entry needed on July 7, 19X7, to record the trade under the income tax method.
2. Give the general journal entry needed on July 7, 19X7, to record the trade under the fair market value method.

EXERCISE 18-10
(Obj. 3)

Classifying assets using the MACRS system. Give the class life each of the following assets would be assigned under the MACRS requirement.

1. Telephones for an office
2. Auto for the president of the company
3. Computer
4. Apartment building
5. Mall

PROBLEMS

PROBLEM SET A

PROBLEM 18–1A
(Obj. 1)

Tutorial

Determining the cost to be capitalized for acquisition of assets. On February 5, 19X5, the Dillon Corporation purchased a site for a new office building for $900,000. An existing building (fair market value of $50,000) had to be razed at a cost of $8,500. Salvage proceeds from the building totaled $3,000. The company also paid $750 attorney fees, $290 recording fees, and $150 for a permit to raze the building. After the building was torn down, the following costs were incurred.

- $8,000 for fill dirt for the site
- $5,000 for leveling of the site
- $32,000 for paving of sidewalks and curbs
- $35,000 for paving a parking lot
- $1,200,000 for building costs of new building.

Instructions

Compute the capitalized costs of (1) the building, (2) the land, and (3) the land improvements.

PROBLEM 18–2A
(Obj. 2)

Tutorial Spreadsheet

Using different depreciation methods and comparing the results. On January 8, 19X4, the Hardy Shop purchased some new equipment for $83,000. The equipment had a useful life of four years and a salvage value of $3,000.

Instructions

Prepare a schedule showing the annual depreciation for the first three years of the asset's life under (1) the straight-line method, (2) the sum-of-the-years'-digits method, and (3) the double-declining-balance method.

PROBLEM 18–3A
(Obj. 2)

GL

Using the straight-line and units-of-output methods of depreciation. On January 3, 19X3, the Molly Corporation purchased factory equipment for $42,000. The equipment had an estimated useful life of five years or 80,000 units of product. The estimated salvage value was $2,000. Actual production for the first three years was 19X3, 20,000 units; 19X4, 24,000 units; and 19X5, 22,000 units.

Instructions

Compute each year's depreciation under (1) the straight-line method and (2) the units-of-output method.

PROBLEM 18–4A
(Obj. 4)

Tutorial

Computing depletion for financial accounting. The Marion Coal Company had total depletable costs of $500,000 for a mine purchased on July 1, 19X3. It is estimated that 650,000 tons of coal are to be mined. During 19X3, 98,000 tons were mined; 150,000 tons were mined in 19X4.

Instructions

Compute the amount of depletion expense for both 19X3 and 19X4 and give the general journal entry to record the depletion.

PROBLEM 18–5A
(Obj. 5, 6)

Tutorial

Recording asset trade-ins and sales. The transactions listed below occurred at the Porter Partnership during the year 19X3.

Instructions

1. Give the entries in general journal form to record the two exchange transactions, using (a) the income tax method and (b) the fair market value method.
2. Give the entries in general journal form to record the sale of the truck, assuming (a) the sales price was $8,000 and (b) the sales price was $10,000. Round your computations to the nearest whole dollar. Use the straight-line method of depreciation.

TRANSACTIONS

Mar. 29 Exchanged a printer (Office Equipment) that had an original cost of $1,100 when purchased on March 5, 19X1, two years earlier. The useful life of the old asset was originally estimated at eight years and the salvage value at $100. The new printer had a sales price of $1,800. Porter gave up the old machine and paid $1,000 cash. The new printer is estimated to have a useful life of five years and a salvage value of $300.

July 23 Exchanged a truck (Vehicles) for a new one that had a sales price of $18,400. Received a trade-in allowance of $6,800 on the old truck, which had been purchased for $15,600 on May 27, 19X1, two years earlier. The life of the old truck was originally estimated at four years and the salvage value at $4,600. Depreciation is recorded using the straight-line method. The life of the new truck is estimated to be four years and it is estimated to have a salvage value of $4,400.

Aug. 27 Sold a truck (Vehicles) for cash. The truck was purchased on January 5, 19X1, for $19,500 and was depreciated on the straight-line basis, using an estimated life of four years and an estimated salvage value of $3,500. Depreciation was last recorded on December 31, 19X2.

PROBLEM 18–6A (Obj. 5, 6)

Recording asset trade-ins and sales. The Red Store purchased four identical machines on January 2, 19X3, paying $750 for each. The useful life of each machine is expected to be six years, with a salvage value of $150 each. The company uses the straight-line method of depreciation. Selected transactions involving the machines follow. The accounts for recording these transactions are also given.

Instructions

1. Record the transactions in general journal form.
2. Assume that the income tax method is to be used, and record the trade-in of machine 4 on August 29, 19X6, under that method.

Round all calculations to the nearest whole dollar.

ACCOUNTS

101 Cash
141 Machinery
142 Accumulated Depreciation—Machinery
495 Gain on Sale of Machinery
541 Depreciation Expense—Machinery
595 Loss on Sale of Machinery
597 Loss on Stolen Machinery

TRANSACTIONS FOR 19X3

Jan. 2 Paid $750 each, in cash, for four machines.
Dec. 31 Recorded depreciation for the year on the four machines.

TRANSACTIONS FOR 19X4

Mar. 31 Machine 1 was stolen; no insurance was carried.
Dec. 31 Recorded depreciation for the year for the three remaining machines.

TRANSACTIONS FOR 19X5

Sept. 30 Sold machine 2 for $600 cash.
Dec. 31 Recorded depreciation for the year on the two remaining machines.

TRANSACTIONS FOR 19X6

June 4 Machine 3 was traded in for a similar machine with a $975 list price and fair market value. A trade-in allowance of $400 was received. The balance was paid in cash.
Aug. 29 Machine 4 was traded in for a similar machine with a $1,000 list price and fair market value. A trade-in allowance of $500 was received. The balance was paid in cash.

PROBLEM 18–7A (Obj. 5)

Recording intangible assets and research and development costs. Selected accounts of the Choo-Choo Manufacturing Company are listed below. Several transactions and events that took place at the company during 19X3 are also given.

Instructions

1. Record the transactions for 19X3 in general journal form.
2. Record amortization of the intangible assets for the year ended December 31, 19X3.

ACCOUNTS

Cash
Product Formulas
Computer Software
Research and Development Expense
Amortization of Product Formulas
Amortization of Computer Software

TRANSACTIONS

1. On July 1 the company paid $36,000 to purchase a product formula. The formula is expected to have a useful life of 60 months.
2. On September 30, 19X3, the company paid $100,000 for a patent having a useful life of 10 years.
3. On October 4, 19X3, the company purchased a unique computer program for $60,000. This program has an estimated useful life of five years.
4. During the year the company recorded various cash expenditures of $150,000 for labor and supplies used in its research department.

PROBLEM SET B

PROBLEM 18–1B (Obj. 1) Tutorial

Determining the costs to be capitalized for acquisition of assets. On July 2, 19X4, the Blue Book Company purchased a site for a new apartment complex for $150,000. Two existing houses, with a total appraised value of $50,000, had to be torn down at a cost of $5,000. Salvage proceeds from these two houses were $7,000. Other costs incurred to purchase the site included $500 in legal fees; $5,500 to pave the sidewalks and patio areas; $950,000 to build the apartments; and $12,000 to pave the parking area. Compute the capitalized costs of (1) the land, (2) the apartment building, and (3) the land improvements.

PROBLEM 18–2B (Obj. 2) Tutorial

Using different depreciation methods and comparing the results. The Fred Corporation purchased a new machine on January 3, 19X3, for $70,000. It is expected to have a useful life of five years and an estimated salvage value of $4,000.

Instructions

Prepare a schedule showing the annual depreciation and accumulated depreciation for each of the first three years of the asset's life under (1) the straight-line method, (2) the sum-of-the-years'-digits method, and (3) the double-declining-balance method.

PROBLEM 18–3B (Obj. 2)

Using the straight-line and units-of-output methods of depreciation. The RPS Systems Company purchased a large delivery truck for $55,000 on January 5, 19X3. The truck's salvage value is estimated at $5,000, and its useful life is five years or 300,000 miles. During 19X3, the truck was driven 45,000 miles and in 19X4, 62,500 miles.

Instructions

Compute the depreciation expense for 19X3 and 19X4 under (1) the straight-line method and (2) the units-of-output method.

PROBLEM 18–4B (Obj. 4) Tutorial

Computing depletion for financial accounting. The Green County Mining Company paid $250,000 for mining rights in 19X3. An estimated total of 125,000 tons of ore are expected to be extracted. During 19X3, 10,000 tons were mined.

Instructions

Compute the amount of depletion taken for income statement purposes in 19X3, and record the amount in the general journal.

PROBLEM 18–5B (Obj. 5, 6) Tutorial

Recording asset trade-ins and sales. The transactions that follow occurred at Home Builders Supply Co. during 19X5. The company uses the straight-line method of depreciation.

Instructions

1. Give the entries in general journal form to record the two exchange transactions, using (a) the income tax method and (b) the fair market value method.
2. Give the entries in general journal form to record the sale of the forklift truck, assuming (a) the sales price was $10,000 and (b) the sales price was $7,000.

TRANSACTIONS

Mar. 2 Exchanged a computer (Office Equipment) that had been purchased for $1,800 on January 3, 19X3. The useful life of the old computer was estimated at five years, with a salvage value of $300. The new computer had a sales price of $2,600. Home Builders gave up the old computer and $1,500 in cash. The new machine has a useful life of four years and a salvage value of $200. Depreciation on the old machine was last recorded on December 31, 19X4.

June 25 Exchanged a delivery truck (Vehicles) for a new one with a list price of $22,000. A trade-in allowance of $5,000 was received on the old truck, which had been purchased on July 3, 19X2, for $23,000. The old truck had an estimated economic life of five years and a salvage value of $3,000. Depreciation on the old truck was last taken on December 31, 19X4.

Aug. 4 Sold a forklift (Warehouse Equipment) for cash. The forklift was purchased on January 2, 19X2, for $18,500 and was depreciated on the straight-line basis, using an estimated life of six years and a salvage value of $500. Depreciation was last taken on December 31, 19X4.

PROBLEM 18–6B
(Obj. 5, 6)

Recording asset trade-ins and sales. The Sandiago Company purchased four identical machines on January 6, 19X3, paying $2,000 for each machine. The useful life of each machine is five years and there is no salvage value expected. The company uses the straight-line method of depreciation. Selected transactions involving the machines are listed below. The necessary accounts for recording these transactions are also given.

Instructions

1. Record the transactions in general journal form.
2. Assume that the income tax method is to be used, and record the trade-in of machine 4 on August 29, 19X6.

ACCOUNTS

101 Cash
141 Machinery
142 Accumulated Depreciation—Machinery
495 Gain on Sale of Machinery
541 Depreciation Expense—Machinery
595 Loss on Sale of Machinery
597 Fire Loss on Machinery

TRANSACTIONS FOR 19X3

Jan. 2 Paid $2,000 each for four machines.
Dec. 31 Recorded depreciation for the year for the four machines.

TRANSACTIONS FOR 19X4

Apr. 1 Machine 1 was destroyed by fire; no insurance was carried.
Dec. 31 Recorded depreciation for the year for the three remaining machines.

TRANSACTIONS FOR 19X5

Sept. 30 Sold machine 2 for $1,000 cash.

Dec. 31 Recorded depreciation for the year for the two remaining machines.

TRANSACTIONS FOR 19X6

June 4 Machine 3 was traded for a similar machine with a $2,200 list price and fair market value. A trade-in allowance of $600 was received. The balance was paid in cash.

Aug. 29 Machine 4 was traded in for a similar machine with a list price of $2,300. A trade-in allowance of $500 was received. The balance was paid in cash.

PROBLEM 18–7B
(Obj. 5)

Recording intangible assets and research and development costs. Selected accounts of the Silicon Valley Electronics Company are listed below. Also given are some transactions and events that took place at the company during 19X3. The company has discovered that it is impossible to estimate accurately the useful life of computer software, so it has adopted an arbitrary policy of amortizing all such costs over a period of 36 months, beginning with the month of acquisition. Similarly, the company has adopted the practice of amortizing all patents over a period of 60 months, beginning with the month of purchase or acquisition.

Instructions

1. Record the transactions that follow for 19X3 in general journal form.
2. Record amortization of the intangible assets for the year ended December 31, 19X3.

ACCOUNTS

Cash
Patents
Computer Software
Research and Development Expense
Amortization of Patents
Amortization of Computer Software

TRANSACTIONS

Mar. 31 Made cash expenditures of $150,000 for research and development costs related to a new patent. This patent was developed in the company's laboratory.

June 30 Made cash expenditures of $65,000 for company personnel to develop computer programs that are to be used in the company's research activities.

Apr. 1 Purchased a patent for $60,000 in cash. The patent is to be used in the company's operations.

Sept. 1 Purchased a completed software program for $14,400 in cash from a computer software supply firm. The software program is to be used in the company's inventory control system.

CHALLENGE PROBLEM

The Parker Systems Company, Inc., develops and sells computer hardware and software. Several transactions that occurred during 19X3 and 19X4 are given below.

Instructions Give the December 31, 19X4, adjusting entries to record all depreciation and amortization costs for the Parker assets. No depreciation was taken on the building or land improvements in 19X3.

TRANSACTIONS

1. The company purchased a building site for $25,000 on July 3, 19X3. A new office building was built on the site for $100,000. Construction was completed on January 3, 19X4. Various other costs included grading and preparing the site, $5,000; paving the parking lot and sidewalks, $20,000; and fencing the back of the property, $5,000. The useful life of the building was estimated at 20 years while the land improvements were estimated at 10 years.
2. On January 3, 19X4, Parker moved into the building. A telephone system costing $3,000 was installed on that date, with an estimated useful life of five years. Office furniture costing $7,000 and having a useful life of seven years was purchased and delivered to the business on January 5, 19X4. The company elected the double-declining-balance method to recover the costs of the telephone system and the furniture.

CRITICAL THINKING PROBLEM

In a review of the annual reports of Updike Corporation and Stuart Corporation, you note that Updike Corporation uses straight-line depreciation and Stuart Corporation uses the declining-balance method.

1. Are these companies violating the generally accepted accounting principle of consistency by using different depreciation methods?
2. If you examined the federal income tax returns of these companies, would you expect the depreciation expense shown on their federal income tax returns to be the same as the depreciation expense shown on their financial statements? Why or why not?
3. Assume that these companies are similar in all respects except for the difference in computing depreciation. Which company would you expect to report the lower net income for financial reporting purposes?
4. Who is responsible for determining the depreciation method used by the company for financial reporting purposes?

U N I T   S I X

Accounting for Partnerships

CHAPTER 19
Accounting for Partnerships

Previous chapters have introduced procedures for accounting for businesses owned by one person, a sale proprietor. Businesses owned by two or more persons who operate the business as co-owners are known as partnerships. Although any type of business may be organized as a partnership, businesses that provide services, such as accounting firms and legal firms, are the most common types of partnerships.

Partnerships are similar to sole proprietorships but have distinct legal characteristics, as well as different advantages and disadvantages. Accounting procedures for partnerships focus on the formation of a partnership, the division of partnership profits and losses among the partners, the admission of a new partner, and the withdrawal of a partner.

CHAPTER

19

Accounting for Partnerships

OBJECTIVES

1. Explain the major advantages and disadvantages of a partnership.
2. State the important provisions that should be included in every partnership agreement.
3. Account for the formation of a partnership.
4. Compute and record the division of net income or loss between partners in accordance with the partnership agreement.
5. Prepare a statement of partners' equities.
6. Account for the revaluation of assets and liabilities prior to the dissolution of a partnership.
7. Account for the sale of a partnership interest.
8. Account for the investment of a new partner in an existing partnership.
9. Account for the withdrawal of a partner from a partnership.
10. Define the accounting terms new to this chapter.

In previous chapters you have learned to account for the business transactions of a sole proprietorship—the most frequently used form of business entity. Although some sole proprietorships are quite large, most of them are relatively small businesses. When a business needs a variety of professional or managerial skills or a large amount of capital, one of two other types of business entities—a partnership or a corporation—is generally used. In this chapter you learn how to account for a partnership's activities. In Chapters 20 and 21 we discuss the corporate form of entity. First let's take a look at the legal characteristics of a partnership and at the advantages and disadvantages of using that type of entity to conduct business.

NEW TERMS

Articles of partnership ▪ Dissolution ▪ Distributive share ▪ General partner ▪ Limited partner ▪ Limited partnership ▪ Liquidation ▪ Memorandum entry ▪ Mutual agency ▪ Partnership ▪ Partnership agreement ▪ Statement of partners' equities ▪ Unlimited liability

THE CHARACTERISTICS OF A PARTNERSHIP

In a partnership two or more persons join together under a written or oral contract as co-owners of a business. The Uniform Partnership Act, adopted by all the states, defines a **partnership** as "an association of two or more persons who carry on as co-owners a business for profit." The partnership form of organization is widely used in small service businesses and in professional fields such as accounting, law, and medicine, where individuals are closely identified with the services provided. Until recent years the codes of ethics of many professional organizations, such as the American Institute of Certified Public Accountants, and the rules of conduct of state regulatory boards and commissions for those professions did not allow practitioners to form corporations. As a result, professional people have historically joined together in partnerships to pool their talents and abilities. Many small merchandising and manufacturing businesses are also operated as partnerships.

Although partnerships are commonly used to pool the talents of professional people, most large manufacturing and merchandising businesses are corporations.

The partnership form of organization has several distinguishing features. Let's look at some of the most important characteristics of this type of business entity.

Advantages of the Partnership

OBJECTIVE 1

Explain the major advantages and disadvantages of a partnership.

Three important advantages to the partnership form of business entity are:

- A partnership permits a pooling of the skills, abilities, and financial resources of two or more individuals.
- A partnership is easy to form at a low cost, especially when compared with a corporation.
- No federal income tax is levied on the net income of a partnership as such. However, the partners must include their shares of the firm's profits when calculating taxable income on their personal income tax returns.

Disadvantages of the Partnership

Limited partnerships have been popular in certain industries, such as oil and gas exploration and real estate development, because of special provisions in the federal income tax laws.

Certain characteristics of partnerships are clearly disadvantages.

- Each partner has **unlimited liability** for the debts of the partnership. This characteristic enhances the credit standing of the firm, but it can be a distinct danger to the individual partners, who stand the chance of losing not only their investments in the business, but also all of their personal assets. In most states it is possible for some partners to have limited liability under closely regulated conditions, and partnerships with one or more limited partners are referred to as **limited partnerships.** The liability of a **limited partner** extends only to that partner's investment in the partnership. State laws generally require that there be at least one **general partner**—a partner who has unlimited liability—in a limited partnership. The partners who have limited liability are prohibited from taking an active role in the management of the business and from having their names in the partnership's title.
- The partnership is a **mutual agency**—that is, each partner may act as agent of the partnership, binding the partnership by the

partner's act so long as those acts are within the normal scope of the partnership's activities.

- A partnership lacks continuity. It has a limited life because if one partner dies or is incapacitated, the existing partnership is dissolved.
- A partnership interest is not freely transferable. The other partners must approve the sale of a partner's interest to a new partner. Upon a transfer of interest, the existing partnership is dissolved and the business can continue only after a new partnership is formed.

Partnership Agreements

OBJECTIVE 2
State the important provisions that should be included in every partnership agreement.

The articles of partnership are also referred to in legal circles as the *articles of copartnership.*
If the agreement does not specify a particular life for the partnership, the business may continue until death or withdrawal of a partner causes dissolution.

It is easy to form a partnership. Two or more partners simply agree to form the business entity by entering into a contract. Although an oral agreement is binding on the partners, they should have an attorney prepare a written **partnership agreement,** referred to legally as **articles of partnership,** to avoid any future misunderstanding about the terms of their arrangement. The partnership agreement may be as simple and brief or as complex and detailed as the partners like. The agreement should always contain as a minimum the following provisions.

1. Names of the partners
2. Name, location, and nature of the business
3. Starting date of the agreement
4. The period of life of the partnership
5. The rights and duties of each partner
6. Amount of capital to be contributed by each partner
7. Drawings by the partners
8. The fiscal year and accounting method
9. Method of allocating income or loss to the partners
10. Procedures to be followed in case of death or incapacitation of a partner, withdrawal of a partner, or other dissolution; similarly, procedures that should be followed in case of liquidation of the business

The partners can include any other items pertinent to the business at the time they draw up their contract. They may also later modify or amend the agreement.

ACCOUNTING FOR THE FORMATION OF A PARTNERSHIP

The accounting records of a partnership contain the same journals and ledgers as those for a sole proprietorship. The same asset, liability, revenue, and expense accounts are also used for both types of entities. The single difference is that in a partnership it is necessary to have a capital account and a drawing account for each partner.

Frequently partnerships are formed when the owner of an existing sole proprietorship "takes in" a partner (or more than one partner) to continue operation of an existing business. The partner entering the business usually invests cash, while the owner of the existing business transfers the noncash assets and the liabilities of the business to the partnership. In other cases the sole owners of two or more existing businesses may combine their operations into a partnership. Sometimes the partners may start a completely new business, with their initial investments being only cash. In every instance where noncash assets are transferred to the partnership, they should be recorded at their fair values, as agreed to by the partners, on the date the assets are transferred. Similarly, all liabilities transferred must be stated at their correct balances at the time of transfer.

To illustrate formation of a partnership, let's look at a partnership formed by Lisa Garcia and Ritchie Rogers. Lisa has operated The Mod Shoppe, a small clothing store that sells T-shirts, jeans, and other casual clothing. To get additional capital and to obtain the talents of Rogers, who has been employed in a shop selling athletic shoes, Lisa offered to make Rogers a partner in the business. Lisa agreed to transfer the assets (except cash) of The Mod Shoppe to the new partnership, which would also assume the liabilities of her firm. Ritchie agreed to invest cash of $15,000 in the business.

The balance sheet of The Mod Shoppe on December 31, 19X2, is shown in Figure 19–1.

FIGURE 19–1
Balance Sheet for a Sole Proprietor

THE MOD SHOPPE
Balance Sheet
December 31, 19X2

Assets		
Cash		700 00
Accounts Receivable	10 800 00	
Less Allowance for Doubtful Accts.	300 00	10 500 00
Merchandise Inventory		59 500 00
Store Equipment	5 000 00	
Less Accumulated Depreciation	4 000 00	1 000 00
Total Assets		71 700 00
Liabilities and Owner's Equity		
Liabilities		
Notes Payable—Bank	20 000 00	
Accounts Payable	18 000 00	
Total Liabilities		38 000 00
Owner's Equity		
Lisa Garcia, Capital		33 700 00
Total Liabilities and Owner's Equity		71 700 00

After an examination of the assets of The Mod Shoppe, Garcia and Rogers agreed to the following:

- Accounts receivable of $800 were definitely uncollectible and should not be transferred to the partnership. In addition, experience showed that $700 of the accounts to be transferred to the partnership was likely to be uncollectible. The estimated net value of the accounts receivable was therefore $9,300.

- The merchandise inventory should be valued at $52,200.
- An equipment dealer's appraisal of the store equipment at $1,500 was a valid and acceptable figure.
- An examination of the liabilities of The Mod Shoppe showed that accrued interest of $200 on the note payable was not recorded on December 31, 19X2. This liability was to be transferred to the partnership, along with the note payable.
- The correct balance of Accounts Payable was only $17,800.

The net assets transferred by Lisa to the partnership were agreed to be $25,000: $9,300 + $52,200 + $1,500 – $20,000 – $200 – $17,800.

Memorandum Entry to Record Formation of Partnership

A memorandum entry merely provides useful information. It does not result in recording monetary amounts in the accounts.

Garcia and Rogers next opened a new set of records covering the operations of the partnership. The first entry in the general journal of this new partnership was a **memorandum entry,** which indicated the name of the business, the names of the partners, and other pertinent information. The memorandum entry to set up the accounting records for Garcia and Rogers' partnership is shown below.

19X3					
Jan.	1	*On this date a partnership*			
		was formed between Lisa			
		Garcia and Ritchie Rogers to			
		carry on a retail clothing			
		business under the name of			
		The Mod Shoppe, according to			
		the terms of the partnership			
		agreement effective this date.			

Notice the reference to the partnership agreement. The agreement provides guidance on questions about the partners' original investments, the division of profits, and other matters.

Investment of Assets and Liabilities by Sole Proprietor

OBJECTIVE 3

Account for the formation of a partnership.

Lisa Garcia's investment consisted of the assets and liabilities of her sole proprietorship. The assets and liabilities transferred were recorded at the amounts previously agreed upon. Her Capital account was credited for the net equity. The journal entry to record the investment is shown on the next page.

Note that the agreed-upon balances of both Accounts Receivable and Allowance for Doubtful Accounts were entered into the records of the partnership. This entry was necessary because all the individual customers' balances, except for those the parties specifically agreed were not collectible, were transferred to the partnership. Since the Accounts Receivable account in the general ledger must agree with the subsidiary ledger, the gross amount must be entered in the control account. Therefore, the Allowance for Doubtful Ac-

19X3				
Jan.	1	Accounts Receivable	10 000 00	
		Merchandise Inventory	52 200 00	
		Store Equipment	1 500 00	
		Allow. for Doubtful Accts.		700 00
		Notes Payable—Bank		20 000 00
		Accounts Payable		17 800 00
		Interest Payable		200 00
		Lisa Garcia, Capital		25 000 00
		Investment of Lisa Garcia		

counts was recorded on the partnership's books at the revised balance of $700.

However, when the owner of a sole proprietorship transfers items of plant and equipment, such as office equipment, to a partnership, only the net agreed-upon value of these assets is recorded in the partnership accounts. The accumulated depreciation accounts begin with zero balances in the partnership's ledger. For partnership accounting purposes, the depreciation previously recorded by the sole proprietor is irrelevant. Depreciation will be recorded by the partnership based on the value at which the assets are recorded, beginning with the date of the transfer.

Investment of Cash by Partner

An investment of cash is recorded by a debit to the Cash account and a credit to the partner's capital account. The receipt of Ritchie Rogers's investment of $15,000 in cash will be recorded in the cash receipts journal. The effect of this investment, in general journal form, is shown below.

19X3				
Jan.	1	Cash	15 000 00	
		Ritchie Rogers, Capital		15 000 00
		Investment of cash by		
		Rogers		

Subsequent Investments and Permanent Withdrawals

Additional investments made by the partners will be recorded in the same manner as the initial investments at the time the partnership was formed. If partners make cash withdrawals from the partnership that are intended to be permanent reductions of capital, the withdrawals are recorded as debits to the partners' capital accounts.

Drawing Accounts

Like sole proprietors, partners in a business need funds with which to pay their living expenses. They may agree to obtain these funds from their business by making current withdrawals against anticipated profits. A drawing account is set up for each partner to record such withdrawals.

For example, assume that the partnership agreement of The Mod Shoppe specified that Lisa Garcia could withdraw up to $1,200 each month and that Ritchie Rogers could withdraw up to $1,000 each month to help defray living expenses. The withdrawals are recorded in the cash payments journal by a credit to Cash and a debit to the drawing accounts. Thus, if Garcia and Rogers withdraw the specified amounts each month for 12 months, on December 31, 19X3, Garcia's drawing account will have a debit balance of $14,400 and Rogers's drawing account will have a debit balance of $12,000.

Partners sometimes have their personal bills paid with business checks. This practice is not sound because it leads to confusion between business transactions and personal ones. If the practice is followed, however, each check written to pay a personal bill must be charged to the appropriate partner's drawing account by an entry in the cash payments journal.

The cost of merchandise withdrawn by a partner from the partnership should be charged to the partner's drawing account and credited to the Purchases account.

It is common for partners to take merchandise from the business for their personal use. The partners generally agree that the cost of merchandise withdrawn should be charged to the partner's drawing account. The credit should be made to the Purchases account rather than to the inventory account. This is because the amount shown as beginning inventory in the current period's cost of goods sold should agree with the amount shown as ending inventory of the prior period. If Garcia withdrew merchandise that cost $80 and had a retail sales price of $110, the withdrawal would be recorded as follows.

19X3					
June	*14*	*Lisa Garcia, Drawing*		*80 00*	
		Purchases			*80 00*
		Cost of merchandise			
		withdrawn by Garcia			

Frequently the partnership calls for salaries to be paid to partners. Such payments are treated as withdrawals, not as expenses of the partnership. They should therefore be charged to the drawing accounts. Salary withdrawals are discussed later in this chapter.

SELF-REVIEW

1. What are the major advantages of the partnership form of business enterprise?
2. What are the major disadvantages of the partnership form of business enterprise?
3. Name eight major topics, other than the names of the partners, that should be included in a partnership agreement.
4. When the assets of a sole proprietorship are transferred to a partnership, at what amount should they be recorded on the partnership's books?

5. How do the accounts of a partnership differ from those of a sole proprietorship?

Answers to Self-Review

1. A partnership offers ease of formation, permits pooling of skills and financial resources, and involves no federal income taxation of the entity itself.
2. The disadvantages of a partnership stem from its inherent characteristics; that is, it brings unlimited liability, mutual agency, lack of continuity, and lack of transferability.
3. Topics to be included: name, location, and nature of business; starting date of the agreement; period of life of the agreement; rights and duties of each partner; amount of capital to be contributed; drawings by the partners; fiscal year and accounting method; method for allocating income or loss; and dissolution and liquidation procedures.
4. Assets should be recorded at their fair market values, as agreed upon by the partners.
5. The accounts are essentially the same, except that there should be a drawing and a capital account for each partner.

ALLOCATING PARTNERSHIP INCOME OR LOSS

The closing procedures followed at the end of a period for a partnership are essentially the same as those used for a sole proprietorship.

1. Revenue accounts are closed into the Income Summary account.
2. Expense accounts are closed into the Income Summary account.
3. The Income Summary account is closed into the partners' capital accounts. (Remember that there is a separate capital account for each partner.)
4. Each partner's drawing account is closed into that partner's capital account.

In closing partnership accounts, however, there is one element in the four-step procedure that you have not previously dealt with. This element is determining, in step 3, the amount of net income or loss to be allocated to each partner. The amount allocated is referred to as the partner's **distributive share.** This term is not to be interpreted as having any relationship to cash distributions. It refers solely to the allocation or division of net income or loss for the period.

Income allocation or division is frequently referred to as the "distribution of income." This allocation does not mean that cash is distributed to the partners.

The partners may agree to divide or allocate the income between themselves in any manner they desire. In reaching that agreement, partners should consider such factors as the amount of time spent in the business by each partner; the skills, expertise, and experience of each partner; and the amount of capital invested by each. An analysis of all the factors involved may lead to a simple allocation based on a fixed ratio, or percentage, or one based on the capital account balances. In other cases, the arrangement may be more complex. Frequently an agreement calls for some or all partners to be allowed salaries for the work they perform and/or to receive an allowance for interest on their capital investments; the remaining net income or loss is then shared according to an agreed-upon ratio or percentage. The partnership agreement should clearly and carefully spell out the basis for allocation so that there will be no misunderstanding among the partners. It is essential to remember that *in the absence of an agreement to the contrary, partners share profits and losses equally.* This practice is true regardless of the amount of time spent by the partners or of the amount of investment of each partner.

Remember that, unless the partnership agreement provides otherwise, net income or loss is allocated equally to the partners.

To illustrate the most common allocation methods, we shall examine the end-of-year procedures for the partnership of Garcia and Rogers in December 19X3. The balances of the partners' Capital accounts and Drawing accounts are shown below in T-account form. The only entries in the Capital accounts during the year are the original investments made when the partnership was formed. The balances in the Drawing accounts reflect the amounts withdrawn for living costs during the year.

Lisa Garcia, Capital 301	
	Dec. 31 Bal. 25,000

Ritchie Rogers, Capital 311	
	Dec. 31 Bal. 15,000

Lisa Garcia, Drawing 302	
Dec. 31 Bal. 14,400	

Ritchie Rogers, Drawing 312	
Dec. 31 Bal. 12,000	

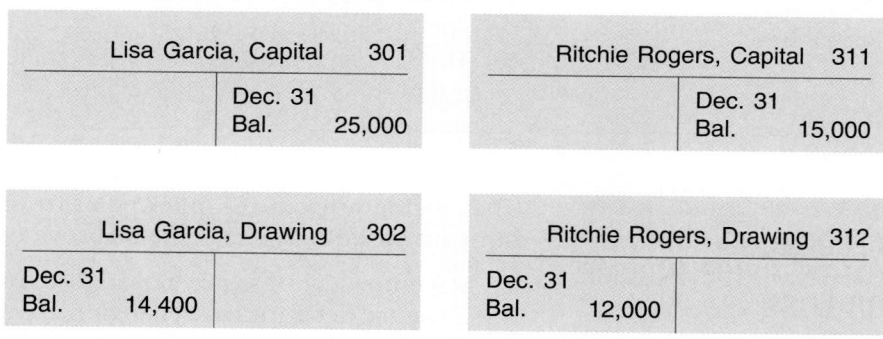

In demonstrating different methods used to allocate net income or loss, we will look at four different arrangements:

1. Net income or loss is allocated on the basis of a fixed ratio.
2. Net income or loss is allocated on the basis of Capital account balances.
3. Each partner is allowed a salary. The balance of net income or loss is allocated in a fixed ratio.
4. Each partner is allowed a salary and also is allowed interest on the capital investment. The partnership agreement does not specify how the balance of net income or loss is to be divided.

Allocation Based on Agreed-Upon Ratio

Assume that after considering such factors as time spent in the business, skills and abilities provided, and capital invested, Garcia and Rogers agreed that net income should be split in the ratio of 3:2 (or 3 to 2) to Garcia and Rogers, respectively. To compute the partners' allocations at year end, we must convert this ratio to either fractions or decimals. Generally it is easier to work with decimals than with fractions. Converting ratios to decimals is a simple process.

OBJECTIVE 4
Compute and record the division of net income or loss between partners in accordance with the partnership agreement.

1. Add the figures given in the ratio:

   Garcia = 3
   Rogers = 2
   Total = 5

2. Express each individual figure as a fractional part of the total number, using the individual figure as the numerator and the total as the denominator:

   Garcia's share = 3/5
   Rogers's share = 2/5

3. Convert each fraction into a percentage by dividing the numerator by the denominator:

   Garcia's share = 3/5 = 0.6
   Rogers's share = 2/5 = 0.4

To compute Garcia's share of net income or loss, simply multiply the total net income or loss by 0.6. Similarly, to compute the net income or loss allocated to Rogers, multiply the total net income or loss by 0.4.

Allocating Net Income

Assume that the balance of the Income Summary account contained a credit balance of $50,000 (net income) after closing the revenue and expense accounts. Garcia's share of net income would be $30,000, and Rogers's share of net income would be $20,000.

Garcia: 0.6 × $50,000 = $30,000
Rogers: 0.4 × $50,000 = $20,000

The general journal entry to close the Income Summary account would thus be as shown below.

19X3					
Dec.	31	*Income Summary*	399	50 000 00	
		Lisa Garcia, Capital	301		30 000 00
		Ritchie Rogers, Capital	311		20 000 00
		To record allocation of			
		net income in ratio of 3:2			

The partners' Drawing accounts are then closed into the capital accounts.

19X3					
Dec.	31	*Lisa Garcia, Capital*	301	14 400 00	
		Lisa Garcia, Drawing	302		14 400 00
	31	*Ritchie Rogers, Capital*	311	12 000 00	
		Ritchie Rogers, Drawing	312		12 000 00

After posting the entries to close the Income Summary account and the partners' drawing accounts, the ledger accounts, in T-account form, will appear as follows.

Income Summary 399			
Dec. 31 Clos.	50,000	Dec. 31 Net Inc.	50,000

Lisa Garcia, Drawing 302			
Dec. 31 Bal.	14,400	Dec. 31 Cl.	14,400

Ritchie Rogers, Drawing 312			
Dec. 31 Bal.	12,000	Dec. 31 Cl.	12,000

Lisa Garcia, Capital 301			
Dec. 31 Draw.	14,400	Dec. 31 Bal.	25,000
		Dec. 31 Inc.	30,000

Ritchie Rogers, Capital 311			
Dec. 31 Draw.	12,000	Dec. 31 Bal.	15,000
		Dec. 31 Inc.	20,000

Allocating Net Loss

Again assume that Garcia and Rogers divide net income or loss in the ratio of 3:2. However, suppose The Mod Shoppe experiences a net loss of $15,000 instead of a net income of $50,000 from the first year's operations. Since the partnership agreement calls for net income or net loss to be divided in the ratio of 3:2, Garcia must absorb $9,000 of the loss (0.6 × $15,000) and Rogers must absorb $6,000 of the loss (0.4 × $15,000). The $15,000 debit balance in the Income Summary account will be closed into the partners' Capital accounts as shown below. The partners' Drawing accounts will also be closed into Capital by the entries shown.

19X3				
Dec.	*31*	*Lisa Garcia, Capital*	9 000 00	
		Ritchie Rogers, Capital	6 000 00	
		Income Summary		15 000 00
	31	*Lisa Garcia, Capital*	14 400 00	
		Lisa Garcia, Drawing		14 400 00
	31	*Ritchie Rogers, Capital*	12 000 00	
		Ritchie Rogers, Drawing		12 000 00

Allocation Based on Capital Account Balances

Allocating net income or loss on the basis of capital account balances is in reality making the allocation on a ratio. However, unlike a fixed ratio (for example, 3:2), the ratio varies from one period to the next, depending on the Capital account balances. Where capital is extremely important in the income-earning process (for example, in a partnership whose business is owning and renting real estate), this allocation basis is quite logical. Where partners' services are the most important factor in earning income (for example, in an accounting firm), the method may not be as appropriate.

To demonstrate how the method works, assume that Garcia and Rogers had agreed that net income or loss should be based on the ratio of capital account balances at the beginning of the year. The beginning balances for Garcia and Rogers were $25,000 and $15,000, respectively. Once again, the allocations may be expressed as a decimal. The decimal is computed by adding together the beginning balances, then expressing each partner's capital as a decimal part of the total.

Garcia's beginning capital	$25,000
Rogers's beginning capital	15,000
Total beginning capital	$40,000

The ratios of the beginning balances, ending balances, or average balances of the partners' capital accounts may be used to allocate income or loss.

Garcia's share of net income or loss will be found by multiplying 0.625 ($25,000/$40,000 = 0.625) by the income or loss. Rogers's share will be found by multiplying 0.375 ($15,000/$40,000 = 0.375) by the net income or loss.

Assuming that the net income for the year 19X3 was $50,000, $31,250 (0.625 × $50,000) will be allocated to Garcia and $18,750 (0.375 × $50,000) will be allocated to Rogers. Assuming withdrawals of $14,400 for Garcia and $12,000 for Rogers, the closing journal entries for this income division agreement are shown below.

19X3				
Dec.	*31*	*Income Summary*	50 000 00	
		Lisa Garcia, Capital		31 250 00
		Ritchie Rogers, Capital		18 750 00
	31	*Lisa Garcia, Capital*	14 400 00	
		Lisa Garcia, Drawing		14 400 00
	31	*Ritchie Rogers, Capital*	12 000 00	
		Ritchie Rogers, Drawing		12 000 00

A loss for the year would be allocated in the same ratio as was net income. The Income Summary account would be credited to close the debit balance into the Capital accounts, as previously illustrated.

Salary Allowances

Salary allowances to partners are solely a part of the income allocation process. They are intended to reward the partners for the time they spend in the business as well as for the expertise and talents they bring to it. For example, Garcia and Rogers agreed that each would devote full time to the business. Garcia felt that her longer experience in the trade should entitle her to a larger share of the profits. Rogers acknowledged Garcia's superior skill and ability, and he conceded that the new business would greatly benefit from Garcia's good reputation and established clientele.

Assume that Garcia and Rogers had agreed that in dividing net income or loss each should receive a salary allowance equal to the amount of monthly withdrawals permitted in their partnership agreement. The balance of net income or loss is to be divided in the ratio of 3:2 between Garcia and Rogers. The withdrawals ($1,200 per month to Garcia and $1,000 each month to Rogers) have been properly charged to the partners' Drawing accounts. The fact that the monthly withdrawals are equal to the salary allowances does not change the nature of the withdrawals. They do not represent salary expense. No payroll taxes or withholdings apply to them. Neither do they appear in the expense section of the income statement. They are simply temporary withdrawals in anticipation of profits.

Remember that salary allowances to partners do not represent expenses of the partnership. They are merely a part of the profit or loss division.

Allocating Net Income

When salary allowances are included in the income or loss distribution formula, the process to close Income Summary requires two steps.

1. The salary allowances are recorded by a debit to Income Summary and a credit to the partners' Capital accounts.
2. The balance in the Income Summary account after the debit entry to record salary allowances is then closed into the partners' Capital accounts on the basis called for in the partnership agreement.

To illustrate the proper treatment of salary allowances in the allocation of net income, assume that the net income of The Mod Shoppe for 19X3, its first year of operations, was $56,400.

1. The first step in recording the division of net income is to record the salary allowances of $14,400 to Garcia and $12,000 to Rogers. The general journal entry to record these allowances is shown below.

19X3					
Dec.	*31*	*Income Summary*	*399*	*26 400 00*	
		Lisa Garcia, Capital			*14 400 00*
		Ritchie Rogers, Capital			*12 000 00*

After the above entry has been posted, the Income Summary account will have a credit balance of $30,000.

Income Summary 399	
Dec. 31	Dec. 31
Sal. All. 26,400	Income 56,400

2. The entry to close the $30,000 credit balance of the Income Summary account is made in the usual way, with $18,000 (0.6 × $30,000) being allocated to Garcia and $12,000 (0.4 × $30,000) being allocated to Rogers.

19X3					
Dec.	*31*	*Income Summary*		*30 0 0 0 00*	
		Lisa Garcia, Capital			*18 0 0 0 00*
		Ritchie Rogers, Capital			*12 0 0 0 00*

To complete the closing process, the partners' Drawing accounts are closed into the Capital accounts in the usual manner.

Allocating Net Loss

Salaries and interest provided in the partnership agreement must be recorded as part of the income or loss allocation computation even though there is a net loss for the year. Assume again that the net loss for The Mod Shoppe in 19X3 was $15,000 and that the profit-sharing agreement called for Garcia to be allowed a salary of $14,400 for the year and Rogers to be allowed a salary of $12,000 for the year.

1. The first entry in recording the income or loss allocation for the year is to record the salary allowances. Salary allowances are always recorded by a debit to the Income Summary account and a credit to the partners' Capital accounts. The following entry would be necessary to record the salary allowances on December 31, 19X3.

19X3					
Dec.	*31*	*Income Summary*	*399*	*26 4 0 0 00*	
		Lisa Garcia, Capital	*301*		*14 4 0 0 00*
		Ritchie Rogers, Capital	*311*		*12 0 0 0 00*

After this entry, the Income Summary account will have a debit balance of $41,400.

Income Summary 399	
Dec. 31	
Loss 15,000	
Dec. 31	
Sal. All. 26,400	

2. The balance of Income Summary must now be closed. The balance of $41,400 is allocated to the partners in the ratio provided for in the partnership agreement. Garcia's Capital account is charged for $24,840 (0.6 × $41,400) and Rogers's Capital account is charged for $16,560 (0.4 × $41,400). The required journal entry follows.

19X3					
Dec.	31	*Lisa Garcia, Capital*	301	24 8 4 0 00	
		Ritchie Rogers, Capital	311	16 5 6 0 00	
		Income Summary	399		41 4 0 0 00

The partners' Drawing accounts are then closed into the Capital accounts in the usual way.

19X3					
Dec.	31	*Lisa Garcia, Capital*	301	14 4 0 0 00	
		Lisa Garcia, Drawing	302		14 4 0 0 00
	31	*Ritchie Rogers, Capital*	311	12 0 0 0 00	
		Ritchie Rogers, Drawing	312		12 0 0 0 00

Let's see how the accounts involved appear (in T-account form) after the closing entries have been posted.

Income Summary 399

Debit		Credit	
Dec. 31 Loss	15,000	Dec. 31 Clos.	41,400
Dec. 31 Sal. All.	26,400		

Lisa Garcia, Capital 301

Debit		Credit	
Dec. 31 Loss	24,840	Dec. 31 Bal.	25,000
Dec. 31 Draw.	14,400	Dec. 31 Sal.	14,400

Ritchie Rogers, Capital 311

Debit		Credit	
Dec. 31 Loss	16,560	Dec. 31 Bal.	15,000
Dec. 31 Draw.	12,000	Dec. 31 Sal.	12,000

Lisa Garcia, Drawing 302

Debit		Credit	
Dec. 31 Bal.	14,400	Dec. 31 Cl.	14,400

Ritchie Rogers, Drawing 312

Debit		Credit	
Dec. 31 Bal.	12,000	Dec. 31 Cl.	12,000

Salary and Interest Allowances

Earlier in this chapter, it was observed that the partners may wish to recognize the importance of differing levels of capital investment by allowing the partners interest on their capital. Assume now that Garcia and Rogers want to reward the partners for their time and skills through salary allowances of $14,400 to Garcia and $12,000 to Rogers. They also wish to recognize the capital investments by allowing each partner interest of 10 percent on the capital balance at the start of the period. Assume that the partnership agreement does not specify how the remaining balance of income or loss is to be allocated. Remember that if the partnership agreement is silent on this matter, the remaining net income or net loss is to be divided equally. The procedure for closing the Income Summary account now must have three steps:

1. Record the salary allowances in the same way as previously illustrated.
2. Record the interest allowances by crediting each partner's capital account for the appropriate amount of interest and debiting Income Summary for the total interest allowed the two partners.
3. Allocate the new balance of Income Summary in the proper ratio.

Let's now examine how this agreement would apply in situations with different levels of income or loss.

Allocation Where Net Income Is Adequate to Cover Allowances

Let's first apply our three-step approach to allocating net income to a situation where the net income is greater than the total allowances for salaries and interest. The necessary journal entries are shown.

1. Record the salary allowances of $14,400 to Garcia and $12,000 to Rogers in the usual manner.

19X3					
Dec.	*31*	*Income Summary*	*399*	*26 400 00*	
		Lisa Garcia, Capital	*301*		*14 400 00*
		Ritchie Rogers, Capital	*311*		*12 000 00*

2. Record the interest allowance. Since the interest to be allowed is simply 10 percent of the beginning Capital balances, the computation is quite simple. You will remember that the formula for computing interest is

$$\text{Interest} = \text{Principal} \times \text{Rate} \times \text{Time}$$

In this case the principal amount is the beginning Capital balance; the rate is 10 percent, or 0.10; and the time is one year. The interest allowance to Garcia is therefore $2,500.

$$\text{Interest} = \$25{,}000 \times 0.10 \times 1 \text{ year}$$
$$= \$2{,}500$$

The interest allowance to Rogers is $1,500.

$$\text{Interest} = \$15{,}000 \times 0.10 \times 1 \text{ year}$$
$$= \$1{,}500$$

The journal entry to record the interest allowance is made in the same way as the entry to record salary allowances. Each partner's Capital account is credited for the amount allowed that partner, and the Income Summary account is debited for the total.

19X3					
Dec.	*31*	*Income Summary*	*399*	*4 0 0 0 00*	
		Lisa Garcia, Capital	*301*		*2 5 0 0 00*
		Ritchie Rogers, Capital	*311*		*1 5 0 0 00*
		To record 10% interest allowance on beginning investments			

At this point the credit balance of the Income Summary account is $19,600.

Income Summary 399			
Dec. 31 Sal.	26,400	Dec. 31 Profit	50,000
Dec. 31 Int.	4,000		

3. The remaining credit balance ($19,600) in the Income Summary account is closed into the Capital accounts in the usual way. Each partner will receive credit for 50 percent of the balance.

19X3					
Dec.	*31*	*Income Summary*	*399*	*19 6 0 0 00*	
		Lisa Garcia, Capital	*301*		*9 8 0 0 00*
		Ritchie Rogers, Capital	*311*		*9 8 0 0 00*

Allocation of Net Loss

Now assume the opposite situation—that The Mod Shoppe suffers a net loss of $15,000 from the first year's operation. The Income Summary account shows this amount as a debit balance after all revenues and expenses have been transferred to it. Even though a loss has occurred, the allowances for salaries and interest must still be made in accordance with the partnership agreement, as in the previous example. The debits of $26,400 for the salary allowances and $4,000 for the interest allowances increase the debit balance of the summary account to $45,400, as shown in the T account below.

Income Summary 399	
Net Loss 15,000	
Dec. 31 Sal. All. 26,400	
Dec. 31 Int. All. 4,000	

The debit balance of $45,400 must be divided between Garcia and Rogers in the ratio of 50:50 since the partnership agreement did not provide otherwise. The entry to close the Income Summary account thus results in a debit of $22,700 to each partner's Capital account and a credit to Income Summary for the total of $45,400.

After this closing entry is posted, the Income Summary account and the partners' Capital accounts appear as shown below in T-account form.

Income Summary 399	
Net Loss 15,000	Dec. 31 Closing 45,400
Dec. 31 Sal. All. 26,400	
Dec. 31 Int. All. 4,000	

Lisa Garcia, Capital 301	
Dec. 31 Loss 22,700	Dec. 31 Sal. All. 14,400
	Dec. 31 Int. All. 2,500

Ritchie Rogers, Capital 311	
Dec. 31 Loss 22,700	Dec. 31 Sal. All. 12,000
	Dec. 31 Int. All. 1,500

Finally, the Drawing accounts will be closed into the Capital accounts in the usual manner.

Profit Less Than Difference Between Partners' Allocations

Now assume that operations of The Mod Shoppe for the year resulted in a net income of only $2,000. The net income appears as a credit balance in the Income Summary account after all the revenues and expenses have been closed into it. The entries to record the salary and interest allowances are made in the usual manner, illustrated previously, by debiting the Income Summary account and crediting the partners' Capital accounts. After the journal entries to record the allowances have been made, the Income Summary account will have a debit balance of $28,400. Since no provision is made in the agreement as to how this balance should be divided, each partner's Capital account will be debited for $14,200 and the Income Summary account credited for $28,400 to close the account. After these entries have been posted, the relevant accounts will appear as follows.

Income Summary		399	
Dec. 31 Sal. All.	26,400	Dec. 31 Income	2,000
Dec. 31 Int. All.	4,000	Dec. 31 Closing	28,400

Lisa Garcia, Capital		301	
Dec. 31 Loss	14,200	Dec. 31 Bal.	25,000
		Dec. 31 Sal. All.	14,400
		Dec. 31 Int. All.	2,500

Ritchie Rogers, Capital		311	
Dec. 31 Loss	14,200	Dec. 31 Bal.	15,000
		Dec. 31 Sal. All.	12,000
		Dec. 31 Int. All.	1,500

You will already have noticed in the above illustration that Rogers's equity suffered a net decrease of $700 ($12,000 + $1,500 − $14,200) as a result of the net income allocation process, even though the partnership actually had net income of $2,000. In effect, Rogers was charged with a loss. On the other hand, Garcia received an allocation of $2,700 of income even though the total net income was only $2,000. These quirks appear because of the relationships between the profit-sharing arrangements and the amount of net income reported.

PARTNERSHIP STATEMENTS

Once the net income or net loss distribution has been completed, the financial statements can be prepared.

Income Statement Presentation

The income statement for a partnership is identical to that for a sole proprietorship, with one exception. It is customary to show on a partnership's income statement how the net income or loss for the year has been divided between the partners. The details of salary allowances, interest allowances, and other allocation factors are generally included.

The schedule of distribution of income or loss, based on the allocation illustrated immediately above, that will appear at the bottom of The Mod Shoppe's income statement for the year ending December 31, 19X3, is shown below. Details of revenues and expenses entering into net income have been omitted in the illustration.

Net Income for Year			$ 2,000
Allocation of Net Income	Garcia	Rogers	Total
Salary Allowance	$14,400	$12,000	$26,400
Interest Allowance	2,500	1,500	4,000
Balance Equally	(14,200)	(14,200)	(28,400)
Totals	$ 2,700	($ 700)	$ 2,000

Balance Sheet Presentation

OBJECTIVE 5
Prepare a statement of partners' equities.

As a general rule, only the final balances of the partners' Capital accounts are shown on the balance sheet. A separate **statement of partners' equities** summarizes the changes that have taken place during the year. The statement of partners' equities contains the beginning capital of each partner, additional investments during the year, each partner's share of net income or net loss, withdrawals, and ending capital. The statement of partners' equities for The Mod Shoppe for the year ending December 31, 19X3, is shown in Figure 19–2. The net income is based on the income previously allocated.

FIGURE 19–2
Statement of Partners' Equities

THE MOD SHOPPE
Statement of Partners' Equities
Year Ended December 31, 19X3

	GARCIA CAPITAL	ROGERS CAPITAL	TOTAL CAPITAL
Capital Balances, Jan. 1, 19X3	0	0	0
Investment During Year	25 000 00	15 000 00	40 000 00
Net Income (Loss) for Year	2 700 00	(700 00)	2 000 00
Totals	27 700 00	14 300 00	42 000 00
Less Withdrawals During Year	14 400 00	12 000 00	26 400 00
Capital Balances, Dec. 31, 19X3	13 300 00	2 300 00	15 600 00

SELF-REVIEW

1. In the absence of an agreement to the contrary, how should partnership profits and losses be allocated between the partners?
2. Name two allowances that are commonly used in allocating net income or loss to the partners.
3. If salary and interest allowances are to be made to the partners, list the three steps in closing the Income Summary account.
4. Explain the difference between the accounting treatment of "salary" payments to partners and "salary allowances" in allocating income or loss.

5. Explain how it might be possible for one partner to receive a profit allocation even though the partnership has a loss for the period.

Answers to Self-Review

1. Profits and losses should be allocated equally between the partners.
2. Salary and interest are two allowances commonly used.
3. (a) Record salary allowances, (b) record interest allowances, (c) close balance of Income Summary.
4. Salary payments are cash payments to be charged to the partners' Drawing accounts. Salary allowances are part of the income or loss allocation and are charged to Income Summary and credited to the partners' Capital accounts.
5. One partner may receive an interest and/or salary allowance considerably larger than the other partner does. Allowances must be made even if there is a loss.

CHANGES IN PARTNERS

The partners in an existing business may change. Former partners may withdraw, sell their interests, or die. New partners may be admitted. You will recall that a partnership has a limited life. Whenever a partner dies or withdraws, or when a new partner is admitted, a **dissolution** of the old partnership occurs, and a new partnership is formed. A dissolution generally has little impact on the business activities of the partnership. On the other hand, when the business is completely terminated, a **liquidation** is said to have occurred. The business ceases to exist, and the partnership agreement is void.

Before the dissolution of a partnership, whether it results from the withdrawal of a partner or from the admission of a new partner, is recorded in the accounting records, two steps should be taken:

1. The accounting records should be closed and the net income or net loss of the period ending on the date of dissolution should be recorded and transferred to the partners' capital accounts in the usual end-of-period manner.
2. Assets and liabilities should be revalued at amounts agreed on by the partners (including any new partner being admitted).

Recording Revaluation of Assets

The partnership agreement usually provides that a revaluation of assets is to be made when the existing partnership is dissolved and the business is to be continued as a new partnership entity. Similarly, all liabilities must be properly recorded. The revaluation is made because differences between the current value of assets and their book values are, in effect, gains or losses resulting from events

OBJECTIVE 6
Account for the revaluation of assets and liabilities prior to the dissolution of a partnership.

Revaluation gains or losses are allocated to the partners in accordance with their income and loss allocation formula.

that occurred during the life of the old partnership. The same rationale applies to adjustments required in recorded liabilities to make the accounts reflect actual liabilities. Those gains and losses should not be shared by the new partner. Frequently the revaluation will require the services of a professional appraiser. Based on the revaluation, the assets are written up or down, and any differences between the book values of the assets and their appraised values are allocated to the old partner's capital accounts. The allocation is made in accordance with the formula used for sharing net income or loss.

For example, assume that the partners of The Sox Place have agreed to admit a new partner, effective with the opening of business on April 1, 19X4. The partners have agreed to revalue the assets of the business following the closing of the accounts on March 31. After the routine closing entries have been made on that date, the summarized balance sheet of The Sox Place appears as shown in Figure 19–3.

FIGURE 19–3
Partnership Balance Sheet

THE SOX PLACE
Balance Sheet
March 31, 19X4

Assets		
Cash		31 000 00
Accounts Receivable	19 000 00	
Less Allowance for Doubtful Accts.	1 000 00	18 000 00
Merchandise Inventory		35 000 00
Land		11 000 00
Total Assets		95 000 00
Liabilities and Owners' Equity		
Liabilities		
Notes Payable—Bank	9 000 00	
Accounts Payable	12 000 00	
Total Liabilities		21 000 00
Owners' Equity		
Rudy Ramirez, Capital	18 000 00	
Kaye Selby, Capital	30 000 00	
Dick Tolliver, Capital	26 000 00	
Total Partners' Equity		74 000 00
Total Liabilities and Owners' Equity		95 000 00

The partners agree that the balance in Allowance for Doubtful Accounts should be increased to $2,000 and that the value of the merchandise inventory is $40,000. The land is appraised at a value of $11,000. The liabilities are properly stated. Thus the net increase in assets is $4,000.

Increase in Merchandise Inventory	$5,000
Decrease in Accounts Receivable (Increase in Allowance for Doubtful Accounts)	(1,000)
Net increase in assets	$4,000

Assume that profits and losses are shared by the partners as follows: Ramirez, 40 percent; Selby, 40 percent; Tolliver, 20 percent. Revaluation of the assets will be recorded as follows.

19X4					
Apr.	1	Merchandise Inventory		5 000 00	
		Allow. for Doubtful Accounts			1 000 00
		R. Ramirez, Capital			1 600 00
		(40% × $4,000)			
		K. Selby, Capital			1 600 00
		(40% × $4,000)			
		D. Tolliver, Capital			800 00
		(20% × $4,000)			
		To record revaluation of assets and allocation of gain to partners			

After the above entry has been posted, the Capital accounts contain the following balances.

Ramirez, Capital	$19,600	($18,000 + $1,600)
Selby, Capital	31,600	($30,000 + $1,600)
Tolliver, Capital	26,800	($26,000 + $800)
Total	$78,000	

Admission of a New Partner

A new partner may be admitted in one of two ways.

1. The new partner may purchase all or part of the interest of an existing partner, making payment directly to the old partner. In this case, no cash or other asset is transferred to the partnership.
2. The new partner may invest cash or other assets directly in the existing partnership.

OBJECTIVE 7
Account for the sale of a partnership interest.

Purchase of an Interest

One way to join an existing partnership is to buy a portion of an old partner's share of capital for an agreed sum. Of course, the prospective partner must have the approval of the old partners. The money or other consideration passes directly from the purchaser to the old partner and does not appear in the accounting records of the partnership.

No assets flow into the partnership when an existing partner sells all or part of that partner's capital interest to a new partner.

Suppose that after the books of The Sox Place have been closed and the assets revalued as shown above, Ramirez sells half his interest in the business to Jack Ussery for $15,000. The $15,000 is paid by Ussery directly to Ramirez. In the accounting records of the partnership, the transfer of half of Ramirez's Capital account balance is recorded by a debit to Ramirez's Capital account for $9,800 and a credit to Ussery's Capital account for the same amount.

The amount paid by the new partner is frequently not the same as the amount credited to that person's Capital account. In the case of The Sox Place, Ussery paid $15,000 but was credited with only $9,800. The price paid for the interest is a matter of bargaining between the parties involved because the value of the interest is a matter of opinion. Circumstances affect the willingness of the buyer and seller to trade at any particular price. The difference between "book value" and the purchase price does not affect the partnership's accounts.

When a new partner is admitted, a new partnership agreement must be entered into.

With the admission of the new partner, the old partnership comes to an end and a new one comes into being. The partners should therefore draw up a new partnership agreement that covers all the usual topics.

OBJECTIVE 8
Account for the investment of a new partner in an existing partnership.

Investment of Assets by a New Partner

A prospective partner may invest money or other property to obtain admission to the partnership while the old partners remain as partners in the business. The new partner's investment, share of ownership in capital, and share of the net income or net loss are matters to be settled among the partners. They are specified in the partnership agreement drawn up for the new organization. The new partner may receive credit for the amount invested or for a greater or lesser amount.

New Partner Given Credit for Amount Invested. Suppose the four parties involved in The Sox Place agree that Ussery will receive a one-fourth interest in the capital of the business on investing cash in an amount equal to one-fourth of the total capital in the new partnership. The three existing partners, whose Capital accounts total $78,000 after the revaluation previously discussed, will own three-fourths of the business. Therefore, the investment needed for Ussery to own one-fourth of the capital must equal $26,000: 3/4 = $78,000; 1/4 = $78,000/3 = $26,000.

The entry to record Ussery's investment is shown below.

19X4				
Apr.	*1*	*Cash*	*26 0 0 0 00*	
		Jack Ussery, Capital		*26 0 0 0 00*
		To record investment of		
		Ussery for one-fourth		
		interest in partnership		

The existing partners may give the new partner credit for an amount greater than the amount invested if they are especially eager to have the new partner in the business.

New Partner Given Credit for More Than Amount Invested. The new partner may be given credit for more than the amount invested. This is frequently done because the new partner has skills that the existing partners are especially eager to have in the business. Suppose, for example, that Ussery had agreed to invest $22,000 for a one-fourth interest in the partnership on April 1, 19X4.

The simplest way to handle such an investment is to first record the cash investment in the usual way by a debit to Cash for $22,000 and a credit to Jack Ussery, Capital, for the same amount. After this entry is posted, the Capital account balances will be as shown below in T-account form.

Rudy Ramirez, Capital 301	
	Apr. 1 Balance 19,600

Kaye Selby, Capital 311	
	Apr. 1 Balance 31,600

Dick Tolliver, Capital 321	
	Apr. 1 Balance 26,800

Jack Ussery, Capital 331	
	Apr. 1 Invest. 22,000

After Ussery's investment is recorded, the total partners' equity, as shown in the above T accounts, is $100,000. It has been agreed that Ussery's Capital account should contain a credit balance equal to one-fourth of the total partners' equity, or $25,000. The $3,000 increase necessary to bring Ussery's Capital account to the agreed-upon balance is usually referred to as a "bonus to the new partner" and is credited to Ussery's Capital account. This credit is offset by debits to the original partners' Capital accounts. The charge for the bonus granted Ussery is allocated to the old partners on the basis of the old profit and loss ratio. Thus the amounts charged to the old partners' accounts will be: Ramirez, $1,200 (0.40 × $3,000); Selby, $1,200 (0.40 × $3,000); and Tolliver, $600 (0.20 × $3,000).

The general journal entry to record the bonus follows.

19X4					
Apr.	*1*	*Rudy Ramirez, Capital*	*301*	*1 2 0 0 00*	
		Kaye Selby, Capital	*311*	*1 2 0 0 00*	
		Dick Tolliver, Capital	*321*	*6 0 0 00*	
		Jack Ussery, Capital	*331*		*3 0 0 0 00*
		To record bonus allowed			
		new partner			

In T-account form, the partners' Capital accounts after the bonus has been recorded will appear as follows.

Rudy Ramirez, Capital 301	
Apr. 1 Ussery bonus 1,200	Apr. 1 Balance 19,600

Kaye Selby, Capital 311	
Apr. 1 Ussery bonus 1,200	Apr. 1 Balance 31,600

Dick Tolliver, Capital 321	
Apr. 1 Ussery bonus 600	Apr. 1 Balance 26,000

Jack Ussery, Capital 331	
	Apr. 1 Invest. 22,000 Apr. 1 Bonus 3,000

New Partner Given Credit for Less Than Amount Invested. Suppose Ussery had agreed to invest $22,000 for a one-fifth interest in the capital of the partnership. The $22,000 investment would first be recorded in the usual way by a debit to Cash and a credit to Jack Ussery, Capital.

After Ussery's cash investment has been recorded, the total owners' equity would be $100,000.

Ramirez	$19,600
Selby	31,600
Tolliver	26,800
Ussery	22,000
Total	$100,000

Ussery's Capital account must ultimately show a credit balance equal to only one-fifth of the total partners' equity of $100,000, or $20,000. The usual method used to adjust Ussery's Capital account to the desired balance of $20,000 is to debit Ussery's Capital account for the $2,000 bonus ($22,000 − $20,000) and to credit this amount to the other partners' Capital accounts. This "bonus allowed the old partners" is credited to their capital accounts in the old 40:40:20 ratio. The entry to record the bonus is shown below.

19X4					
Apr.	*1*	*Jack Ussery, Capital*	*331*	*2,000.00*	
		Rudy Ramirez, Capital	*301*		*800.00*
		Kaye Selby, Capital	*311*		*800.00*
		Dick Tolliver, Capital	*321*		*400.00*
		To record bonus to old partners			

Keep in mind that income or loss in the new partnership is divided in the manner agreed upon by the partners. The Capital account balances may have nothing to do with profit or loss division.

After this entry has been posted, Ussery's Capital account will contain a balance of $20,000, or one-fifth of the total capital of $100,000.

Withdrawal of a Partner

OBJECTIVE 9

Account for the withdrawal of a partner from a partnership.

The partnership agreement should contain provisions specifying the procedures to be followed for the withdrawal of a partner. The partnership agreement for The Sox Place provides that on withdrawal of a partner the assets are to be revalued and the retiring partner is to be paid an amount equal to that partner's capital account after recording the revaluation. Suppose that the partners of The Sox Place agree that Dick Tolliver is to withdraw from the partnership after the close of business on March 31, 19X4, and that he is to receive cash in an amount equal to the balance of his Capital account after revaluation of the assets. Assuming that the proper revaluation of The Sox Place's assets has been carried out on March 31, 19X4, as previously described, the withdrawal of Tolliver will be recorded by the entry that follows.

19X4					
Mar.	31	*Dick Tolliver, Capital*	321	26 8 0 0 00	
		Cash	101		26 8 0 0 00
		To record cash payment made to Tolliver on withdrawal from partnership			

Sometimes the other partners may be willing to pay a partner more than the balance of the partner's capital account when the latter withdraws. In other cases, the withdrawing partner may receive an amount less than his or her capital account balance.

The parties may agree that the withdrawing partner is to receive either more than or less than the balance of that partner's capital account at the time of withdrawal. In this event, the withdrawing partner's capital account is debited for the balance of the account. If the amount withdrawn is greater than the withdrawing partner's capital account balance, the excess is charged to the capital accounts of the remaining partners. The excess will, of course, be allocated to the remaining partners in the ratio in which they share income and losses. If the amount withdrawn is less than the withdrawing partner's capital account balance, the difference is credited to the remaining partners' capital accounts. Once again the allocation is based on the partnership agreement's formula for sharing profits and losses.

To illustrate this point, suppose that after the assets of The Sox Place have been revalued as previously illustrated, Tolliver, whose Capital account balance is $26,800, withdraws. The partners agree to pay Tolliver $30,800 from partnership funds. The $4,000 bonus paid to the retiring partner ($30,800 – $26,800) would be divided between the two remaining partners according to their profit-and-loss ratio of 40:40 (equally). The entry, in general journal form, to record the withdrawal of a partner is shown at the top of the next page.

19X4					
Mar.	31	Dick Tolliver, Capital	321	26 8 0 0 00	
		Rudy Ramirez, Capital	301	2 0 0 0 00	
		Kaye Selby, Capital	311	2 0 0 0 00	
		Cash	101		30 8 0 0 00
		To record cash payment to Tolliver on withdrawal from partnership			

MANAGERIAL IMPLICATIONS

The partnership form of business offers many advantages to the sole proprietor who needs more capital, managerial assistance, or technical help. It is extremely important, however, that individuals who enter into a partnership have a clear understanding about the duties, obligations, rights, and responsibilities of each partner. These points must be clearly and thoroughly covered in a written partnership agreement. Consultation with a lawyer and an accountant is advisable at every stage of the negotiations.

Partners must give serious consideration to the profit-and-loss distribution formula to make sure that each pertinent factor is properly considered. Disputes between partners often arise because the profit-and-loss sharing formula is not clearly understood. Before admitting new partners, the old partners must have the assets and liabilities revalued to make certain that changes in value occurring prior to the new partner's admission are properly allocated to the old partners—the owners when the changes occurred.

SELF-REVIEW

1. Why are the assets and liabilities revalued prior to a dissolution?
2. An existing partner sells one-half of her capital interest to a new partner. Explain the necessary accounting entries.
3. Explain the accounting treatment necessary when a new partner invests more cash than his or her fractional share in the total capital.
4. If a withdrawing partner is paid more than his or her capital account balance, how is the excess accounted for?

Answers to Self-Review

1. The value changes represent gain or loss that should be shared by the old partners, not by the new partnership.
2. The only entry is to transfer one-half of the old partner's capital account to the new partner's capital account.
3. The excess represents a bonus to the old partners to be credited to their capital accounts according to the old profit-and-loss formula.
4. The excess is charged to the other partners' capital accounts, allocated according to their profit-and-loss ratio.

CHAPTER 19 Review and Applications

CHAPTER SUMMARY

A partnership is the joining together of two or more persons under a written or oral contract as co-owners of a business. The major advantages of a partnership are that (1) it permits the pooling of skills, abilities, and resources of two or more people, and (2) a partnership does not pay an income tax on its profits. However, the partners pay income taxes on their shares of profits.

The major disadvantages of a partnership are that (1) the partners are personally liable for all debts of the partnership, (2) any partner can bind the other partners, (3) the business lacks continuity, (4) partners have unlimited liability, and (5) ownership rights are not freely transferable.

Partnerships should always have a written partnership agreement spelling out such details as the amount of initial investment, the duties of each partner, the fiscal year, the accounting method to be used, how profits or losses are to be divided (including any allowances for salaries and interest), how withdrawals are to be handled, the life of the partnership, and other pertinent facts.

When assets and liabilities are contributed to a partnership in exchange for a partnership interest, the assets should be appraised and recorded at the agreed-upon fair market value at the date of transfer. Each partner should have a drawing account and a capital account. Permanent withdrawals are charged to a partner's capital account, and temporary or periodic withdrawals are charged to the partner's drawing account.

The division of partnership profits and losses can be made in any manner agreed to by the partners. If no agreement has been made to the contrary, profits and losses are divided equally by the partners.

Allowances for salaries of partners and interest on their investments are debited to the Income Summary account and credited to the partners' drawing accounts. Actual payments of cash for salary and interest allowances should be charged to the drawing accounts.

The details of the allocation of net income or loss should be shown at the end of the income statement. A statement of partners' equities is used to summarize the changes that have taken place in the capital accounts during the period.

Before a partnership is dissolved, whether by withdrawal of a partner or admission of a new partner, the assets of the business should be revalued and the gain or loss allocated in the old profit-and-loss ratio.

If a new partner purchases a partnership interest from an existing partner, the only entry necessary on the partnership books is to transfer from the old partner's capital account to the new partner's capital account the proper portion of ownership interest sold. A new partner may invest more than or less than that partner's share of book value. If more than book value is invested, the imbalance is usually handled by recording a bonus to the old partners (debiting the new partner's capital account and crediting the old partners' capital accounts). If a new partner invests less than book value, the deficiency is generally handled by recording a bonus to the new partner (crediting the new partner's capital account and debiting the old partners' capital accounts).

When a partner withdraws, the assets and liabilities are revalued and the gain or loss allocated according to the old profit-and-loss agreement. The cash payment is charged to the withdrawing partner's account. If the payment is more or less than the withdrawing partner's capital balance, the difference is debited or credited to the remaining partners according to their profit-and-loss ratio.

GLOSSARY OF NEW TERMS

Articles of partnership (p. 644) A partnership agreement specifying the terms governing the partners' financial relationship and operations of the partnership

Dissolution (p. 662) The legal termination of a partnership

Distributive share (p. 649) The amount of net income or loss allocated to each partner

General partner (p. 643) A member of a partnership who has unlimited liability

Limited partner (p. 643) A member of a partnership whose liability is limited to his or her investment in the partnership

Limited partnership (p. 643) A partnership having one or more limited partners

Liquidation (p. 662) Termination of a business with all assets being distributed and the business discontinued

Memorandum entry (p. 646) An information entry in the general journal

Mutual agency (p. 643) The characteristic of a partnership by which each partner is empowered to act as agent for the partnership, binding the firm by his or her acts

Partnership (p. 643) An association of two or more persons who carry on as co-owners of a business for profit

Partnership agreement (p. 644) A legal contract forming a partnership and specifying certain details of operation

Statement of partners' equities (p. 661) A financial statement prepared to summarize the changes in partners' capital accounts during an accounting period

Unlimited liability (p. 643) The implication that a partner's personal assets as well as the assets of the partnership can be required in payment of the firm's debts

REVIEW QUESTIONS

1. Explain the liability that a general partner has for the debts of a partnership.
2. What is a limited partner?
3. Does a partnership continue to exist after the death of a partner? Explain.
4. Does a partnership pay federal income tax? Explain.
5. Why are assets of an existing proprietorship revalued when they are transferred to a partnership?
6. Is Allowance for Doubtful Accounts brought forward from the general ledger of a sole proprietorship when the firm's assets and liabilities are being transferred to the partnership? Why?
7. How does the balance sheet of a partnership differ from that of a sole proprietorship?
8. Why have limited partnerships become popular in recent years?
9. Are partners' salaries considered to be expenses of the partnership? Explain.
10. Explain how the net income of a partnership is allocated if it is less than the salary and interest allowances.
11. What information appears on a statement of partners' equities?
12. The two partners in a business often pay personal bills by writing checks on the business's bank account. Is this a good business practice? Explain. How should such payments be recorded?
13. Why does the sale of one partner's capital interest not affect the capital accounts of any of the other original partners?

MANAGERIAL FOCUS

1. The owner of an accounting practice is considering establishing a partnership with two other persons to carry on the business. What are the major disadvantages of the partnership form of organization that she should consider in making her decision?
2. Assume that you are the controller of a business operating as a sole proprietorship. The owner tells you that he is considering forming a partnership with two other individuals who would be limited partners. Explain the weakness of this arrangement from the viewpoint of your employer.
3. Your employer is planning to form a partnership with one of his close friends. He explains to you that because he is well acquainted with the prospective partner, there is no need to have a written partnership agreement and he asks your advice. Give him your reaction and the reasons for your recommendation.
4. Your employer is considering investing $25,000 in a partnership. In discussing the advantages and disadvantages of the arrangement, the employer informs you that a friend has told him that his potential loss is limited to the amount invested—$25,000. What are your thoughts on this arrangement?

5. Two partners in a new firm failed to make an agreement about how their profits and losses would be divided. At the end of the first year, one partner argued that the division should be based on the balance of the capital accounts. The other argued that there should be an equal division. Which partner was correct? What advice would you give partners about the importance of a definite agreement about the division of profits and losses?
6. Two individuals who are forming a partnership ask you how they should divide the profits and losses of the business. What factors should you consider in making a recommendation?
7. You work for a partnership. The partnership agreement between the two partners specifies that one partner shall be allowed a monthly drawing of $1,500 and the other a monthly drawing of $1,000. The agreement does not mention salary allowances for the partners. At the end of the year, one partner maintains that a drawing is the same as a salary allowance. They ask your opinion. What do you tell them?
8. At the time that a partner's capital account had a balance of $120,000, she sold one-half of her interest to Mayberry for $79,000. Mayberry tells you, the accountant for the partnership, that his capital account should show a balance of $79,000, the amount that he paid the old partner for the interest. Do you accept this argument? Explain your answer.
9. One of the partners in a partnership, by which you are employed, is retiring from the business. Her capital account has a balance of $128,000. She tells you that she expects to receive a check for $128,000 from the partnership. Explain to her the proper procedure for determining the amount to be paid her.

EXERCISES

EXERCISE 19–1
(Obj. 3)
Tutorial

Recording cash investment in a partnership. Rose Williams invests cash of $82,990 in a newly formed partnership that will operate the WW Exercise Center. In return, Williams receives a one-third interest in the capital of the partnership. In general journal form, record Williams's investment in the partnership.

EXERCISE 19–2
(Obj. 3)
Tutorial

Recording investment of assets and liabilities in a partnership. Kevin Wells operates a sole proprietorship business that sells exercise equipment. Wells has agreed to transfer his assets and liabilities to a partnership that will operate the WW Exercise Center. Wells will own a two-thirds interest in the capital of the partnership. The agreed-upon values of assets and liabilities to be transferred are:

Accounts Receivable, $62,300 (It is agreed that approximately $1,000 of these accounts may be uncollectible.)
Merchandise Inventory, $85,680
Furniture and Fixtures, $33,000
Accounts Payable, $14,000

Record the receipt of the assets and liabilities by the partnership in the general journal.

EXERCISE 19–3 (Obj. 3)

Preparing a balance sheet for a partnership. On July 1, 19X3, Stella Hickman and Gloria Martinez formed the Video Rental Center. The two partners invested cash and other assets and liabilities with the following agreed-upon values.

Stella: Cash, $1,400; Merchandise Inventory, $4,000; Equipment, $18,000; Accounts Payable, $2,400

Gloria: Furniture, $4,000; Cash, $6,500

Stella is to own two-thirds of the capital and Gloria is to own one-third of the capital, but they will split profits and losses equally. Prepare a balance sheet for the partnership just after the assets and liabilities have been transferred to it.

EXERCISE 19–4 (Obj. 4)

Tutorial

Computing the division of net income of a partnership. The partnership agreement of Bella Antonio and Ralph Baker does not indicate how the profits and losses will be shared. Before dividing the net income for 19X3, Bella's Capital account balance was $80,000 and Ralph's Capital balance was $20,000. The net income of their firm for the year ended December 31, 19X3, was $60,000. How much income will be allocated to each partner?

EXERCISE 19–5 (Obj. 4)

Tutorial

Computing and recording division of net income based on fixed ratio. The net income for Mayfair Jewelry Arcade for the year ended December 31, 19X3, was $6,000. The partners, Zeke Johnson and James George, share profits in the ratio of 60 and 40 percent, respectively. Record the general journal entry (or entries) to close the Income Summary account.

EXERCISE 19–6 (Obj. 4)

Computing and recording division of net loss, with no partnership agreement on method of allocation. After revenue and expense accounts of the Quick-Serve Hamburger Shoppe were closed on December 31, 19X3, Income Summary contained a credit balance of $22,600. The Drawing accounts of the two partners, Fred Davis and Suzanne Barnes, showed debit balances of $18,000 and $20,000, respectively. Profits and losses are to be shared equally. Record the general journal entries to close the Income Summary account and the partners' Drawing accounts.

EXERCISE 19–7 (Obj. 4)

Tutorial

Computing and recording division of net income, with salaries allowed. Mark Chew and Anita Delmar are partners who share profits and losses in the ratio of 75 and 25 percent, respectively. Their partnership agreement provides that each of them will be paid a yearly salary of $18,000. The salaries were paid to the partners during 19X3 and were charged to the partners' Drawing accounts. The Income Summary account has a credit balance of $74,000 after revenue and expense accounts are closed at the end of the year. What amount of net income or net loss will be allocated to each partner?

EXERCISE 19–8 (Obj. 4)

Computing and recording allocation of net income, with interest allowed. Rodriquez and Cohen are partners. Their partnership agreement provides that in dividing profits each partner is to be allocated interest at 10 percent of her beginning capital balance. The balance of net income or loss after the interest allowances is to be split in the ratio of 60 and 40 percent to Rodriquez and Cohen, respectively. The beginning capital balances were Rodriquez, $30,000, and Cohen, $60,000. Net income for the year was $60,000. Compute the amount of net income to be allocated to each partner.

EXERCISE 19-9
(Obj. 4)

Tutorial

Computing and recording allocation of net income, with salaries and interest allowed. Tony Rocco and Barbara Pells are partners who share profits and losses in the following manner. Rocco receives a salary of $24,000 and Pells receives a salary of $35,000. These amounts were paid to the partners and charged to the Drawing accounts. Both partners also receive 10 percent interest on their capital balances at the beginning of the year. The balance of any remaining profits or losses is divided equally. The beginning Capital accounts for 19X4 were Rocco, $102,000, and Pells, $127,000. At the end of the year, the partnership had a net income of $72,000.

1. How much net income or loss will be allocated to each partner?
2. Prepare a statement of partners' equities for the partnership of Rocco and Pells for the year 19X4.

EXERCISE 19-10
(Obj. 6)

Tutorial

Recording revaluation of assets prior to dissolution of a partnership. Jane Potter and Nicholas Bronsky are partners who share profits and losses in the ratio of 60 and 40 percent, respectively. On December 31, 19X3, they decide that Bronsky will be allowed to sell one-half of his interest to A. L. Blevins. At that time the balances of the Capital accounts are $125,000 for Potter and $175,000 for Bronsky. The partners agree that before the new partner is admitted, certain assets should be revalued. These assets include merchandise inventory carried at $104,000, to be revalued at $100,000, and a building with a book value of $60,000, to be revalued at $120,000.

1. Record the revaluations in the general journal.
2. What will the Capital balances of the two existing partners be after the revaluation is made?

EXERCISE 19-11
(Obj. 7)

Recording sale of a part interest. Jeanne Quinn and Jessica McDonald are partners who share profits and losses in the ratio of 60 and 40 percent, respectively. The balances of their Capital accounts are Quinn, $90,000, and McDonald, $110,000. With McDonald's agreement, Quinn sells one-half of her interest in the partnership to Rudy Lopez for $80,000. What will the Capital account balances for each of the three partners be after this sale?

EXERCISE 19-12
(Obj. 9)

Recording withdrawal of a partner. Peterson, Quayle, and Rinzulli are partners, sharing profits and losses in the ratio of 30, 40, and 30 percent, respectively. Their partnership agreement provides that if one of them withdraws from the partnership, the assets and liabilities are to be revalued, gain or loss allocated to the partners, and the retiring partner paid the balance of his account. Rinzulli withdraws from the partnership on December 31, 19X3. The capital account balances before recording revaluation are Peterson, $60,000;

Quayle, $60,000; and Rinzulli, $50,000. The effect of the revaluation is to increase Merchandise Inventory by $9,000 and the Building account balance by $5,000. How much cash will be paid to Rinzulli?

PROBLEMS

PROBLEM SET A

PROBLEM 19–1A
(Obj. 3)
Tutorial

Accounting for formation of a partnership. Aaron Cohen operates a small shop that sells fishing equipment. His postclosing trial balance on December 31, 19X4, is as follows.

COHEN'S FISHING SHOP
Postclosing Trial Balance
December 31, 19X4

ACCOUNT NAME	DEBIT	CREDIT
Cash	1 8 0 0 00	
Accounts Receivable	7 5 0 0 00	
Allowance for Doubtful Accounts		8 0 0 00
Merchandise Inventory	22 0 0 0 00	
Furniture and Equipment	13 5 0 0 00	
Accumulated Depreciation		10 5 0 0 00
Accounts Payable		1 5 0 0 00
Aaron Cohen, Capital		32 0 0 0 00
Totals	44 8 0 0 00	44 8 0 0 00

Cohen plans to enter into a partnership with Jill Hebda, effective January 1, 19X5. Profits and losses will be shared equally. Cohen is to transfer all assets and liabilities of his store to the partnership, after revaluation as agreed. Hebda will invest cash equal to Cohen's investment after revaluation. The agreed values are Accounts Receivable (net), $7,000; Merchandise Inventory, $23,000; and Furniture and Equipment, $6,200. The partnership is to operate under the name Cohen and Hebda Outfitters.

Instructions

1. In general journal form, give the entries to record:
   a. The receipt of Cohen's investment of assets and liabilities
   b. The receipt of Hebda's investment of cash
2. Prepare a balance sheet for Cohen and Hebda Outfitters just after the investments.

PROBLEM 19–2A
(Obj. 3)
Tutorial GL

Accounting for formation of a partnership. Jane Hopkins operates a store that sells computer software. Hopkins has agreed to enter into a partnership with Chris DiMaggio, effective January 1, 19X4. The new firm will be called the Superior Software Center. Hopkins is to transfer all assets and liabilities of her firm to the partnership, at the values agreed on. DiMaggio will invest cash that is equal to 80 percent of Hopkins's investment after revaluation. The accounts shown on Hopkins's books and the agreed-on value of assets and liabilities are shown below.

		Balances Shown in Hopkins's Records	Value Agreed to by Partners
Assets Transferred:			
Cash		$ 3,500	$ 3,500
Accounts Receivable	$14,500		
Allowance for Doubtful Accounts	500	14,000	13,400
Merchandise Inventory		84,000	87,000
Furniture and Equipment	28,000		
Accumulated Depreciation	11,500	16,500	17,900
Total Assets		$118,000	$121,800
Liabilities and Owner's Equity Transferred:			
Accounts Payable		10,000	10,000
Jane Hopkins, Capital		$108,000	$111,800

Instructions

1. Give the general journal entries to record the following transactions on the books of the partnership on January 1, 19X4.
   a. Receipt of Hopkins's investment of assets and liabilities
   b. Receipt of DiMaggio's investment of cash
2. Prepare a balance sheet for the partnership as of the beginning of its operations on January 1, 19X4.

PROBLEM 19–3A
(Obj. 4)

Tutorial

Computing and recording the division of net income or loss between partners. Phyllis King and Eli Strait own the All-America Ice Cream Company. The partnership agreement provides that King can withdraw $1,200 a month and Strait $1,800 a month in anticipation of profits. The withdrawals, which are not considered to be salaries, were made each month. Net income and net losses are to be allocated 55 percent to King and 45 percent to Strait. For the year ended December 31, 19X3, the partnership earned a net income of $21,000.

Instructions

1. Prepare general journal entries to:
   a. Close the Income Summary account
   b. Close the partners' Drawing accounts
2. Assume that there was a net loss of $8,000 for the year, instead of a profit of $21,000. Give the general journal entries to:
   a. Close the Income Summary account
   b. Close the partners' Drawing accounts

PROBLEM 19–4A
(Obj. 4, 5)

Tutorial

Computing and recording the division of net income or loss between partners; preparing a statement of partners' equities. Olive Krauss and Newton Rayzor own the Sunland Art Gallery. Their partnership agreement provides for salary allowances of $22,000 for Krauss and $18,000 for Rayzor and for interest of 10 percent on each partner's invested capital at the beginning of the year. The remainder of the net income or loss is to be distributed 40 percent to Krauss and 60 percent to Rayzor. On January 1, 19X3, the Capital account balances were Krauss, $85,000, and Rayzor, $105,000. On December

12, 19X3, Rayzor made a permanent withdrawal of $20,000. The net income for 19X3 was $72,000.

Instructions

1. Prepare the general journal entry on December 12, 19X3, to record the permanent withdrawal by Rayzor.
2. Prepare the general journal entries on December 31, 19X3, to:
   a. Record the salary allowances for the year
   b. Record the interest allowances for the year
   c. Record the division of the balance of net income
   d. Close the Drawing accounts into Capital, assuming that Krauss and Rayzor have withdrawn their full salary allowances
3. Prepare a schedule showing the division of net income to the partners as it would appear on the income statement for 19X3.
4. Prepare a statement of partners' equities showing the changes that took place in the partners' Capital accounts during 19X3.

PROBLEM 19–5A
(Obj. 6, 8, 9)

Tutorial

Accounting for revaluation of assets and liabilities of a partnership, investment of a new partner, and withdrawal of a partner. The balance sheet of City Used Book Store, after the revenue, expense, and partners' Drawing accounts have been closed on December 31, 19X3, follows.

CITY USED BOOK STORE
Balance Sheet
December 31, 19X3

Assets		
Cash		21 000 00
Accounts Receivable		4 000 00
Merchandise Inventory		104 000 00
Equipment	40 000 00	
Allowance for Depreciation—Equipment	24 000 00	16 000 00
Building	100 000 00	
Allowance for Depreciation—Building	80 000 00	20 000 00
Land		9 000 00
Total Assets		174 000 00
Liabilities and Owners' Equity		
Liabilities		
Accounts Payable		99 000 00
Taxes Payable		5 000 00
Total Liabilities		104 000 00
Owners' Equity		
Melody Rohmer, Capital	40 000 00	
Bruce Testa, Capital	15 000 00	
Margaret Shannon, Capital	15 000 00	
Total Owners' Equity		70 000 00
Total Liabilities and Owners' Equity		174 000 00

On that date, Rohmer, Testa, and Shannon agree to admit Amy Vonstorch to the partnership. The partnership agreement among Rohmer, Testa, and Shannon provides that in case of dissolution of the partnership all assets and liabilities should be revalued. Profits and losses are shared in the ratio of 50:25:25, respectively. The agreed-upon values of the assets are:

Accounts Receivable	$ 3,700	Building	$31,000
Merchandise Inventory	99,600	Land	22,000
Equipment	17,000		

All liabilities are properly recorded.

Instructions

1. Give the general journal entries to record revaluation of the assets.
2. Give the general journal entry (or entries) to record Vonstorch's investment of $30,000, assuming that she is to receive capital equal to the amount invested.
3. Give the general journal entry (or entries) to record Vonstorch's investment of $30,000, assuming that she is to receive one-fifth of the capital of the partnership.
4. Give the general journal entry (or entries) to record Vonstorch's investment of $30,000, assuming that she is to receive one-third of the capital of the partnership.
5. Assume that after the revaluation had been recorded, the old partners and Vonstorch decided that their previous agreement should be canceled and that Vonstorch should not become a partner. Instead, the partners agreed that Testa would withdraw from the partnership and be paid cash by the partnership.
   a. Give the general journal entry to record the payment to Testa if he is paid an amount equal to his Capital account balance after the revaluation.
   b. Give the general journal entry to record the payment to Testa if he is paid an amount equal to $3,000 less than his Capital account balance after revaluation.
   c. Give the general journal entry to record the payment to Testa if he is paid an amount equal to $2,400 more than his Capital account balance after revaluation.

PROBLEM 19–6A
(Obj. 7, 8)
Tutorial

Accounting for sale of a partnership interest and investment of a new partner. Valentine Alaoma and Dean Allen, attorneys, operate a law practice. They would like to expand the expertise of their firm. In anticipation of this, they have agreed to admit Angela Blount to the partnership on January 1, 19X3. The Capital account balances on January 1, 19X3, after revaluation of assets, are Alaoma, $90,000, and Allen, $70,000. Net income or net loss is shared equally.

Instructions

Give the entries in general journal form to record the admission of Blount to the partnership on January 1, 19X3, under each of the following independent conditions.

1. Alaoma sells a one-half interest to Blount for $69,000 cash.
2. Alaoma sells a one-half interest to Blount for $42,000 cash.

3. Blount invests $60,000 in the business for a one-fourth interest.
4. Blount invests $62,000 in the business for a 30 percent interest.

PROBLEM SET B

PROBLEM 19–1B (Obj. 3)

Accounting for the formation of a partnership. Maggie O'Hara operates a retail store that sells telephones and answering machines. Her postclosing trial balance on December 31, 19X4, is as follows.

THE PHONE CENTER
Postclosing Trial Balance
December 31, 19X4

ACCOUNT NAME	DEBIT	CREDIT
Cash	6 5 0 0 00	
Accounts Receivable	27 0 0 0 00	
Allowance for Doubtful Accounts		3 0 0 0 00
Merchandise Inventory	84 5 0 0 00	
Furniture and Equipment	30 0 0 0 00	
Accumulated Depreciation		22 0 0 0 00
Accounts Payable		6 0 0 0 00
Maggie O'Hara, Capital		117 0 0 0 00
Totals	148 0 0 0 00	148 0 0 0 00

O'Hara agrees to enter into a partnership with Eloy Gomez, effective January 1, 19X5. Profits and losses will be shared equally. O'Hara is to transfer the assets and liabilities of her store to the partnership, after revaluation as agreed. Gomez will invest cash equal to one-half of O'Hara's investment after revaluation. The agreed-upon values are Accounts Receivable (net), $25,200; Merchandise Inventory, $90,000; and Furniture and Equipment (net), $14,000. The partnership is to operate as the Service Phone Center.

Instructions

1. In general journal form, give the entries to record the following on the books of the partnership:
   a. The receipt of O'Hara's investment of assets and liabilities
   b. The receipt of Gomez's investment of cash
2. Prepare a balance sheet for Service Phone Center just after the investments.

PROBLEM 19–2B (Obj. 3)

Accounting for formation of a partnership. Michael Craig operates a store that sells records, tapes, and CDs. Craig has agreed to enter into a partnership with Delores Argo, effective January 1, 19X4. The new firm will be called the Sound and Sight Emporium. Craig is to transfer the assets and liabilities of his firm to the partnership, at the values agreed on. Argo will invest cash that is equal to Craig's investment after revaluation. The accounts shown on Craig's books and the agreed-on value of assets and liabilities follow.

Instructions

1. Give the general journal entries to record the following transactions on the books of the partnership on January 1, 19X4.

		Balances Shown in Craig's Records	Value Agreed on by Partners
Assets Transferred:			
Cash		$ 3,500	$ 3,500
Accounts Receivable	$ 4,500		
Allowance for Doubtful Accounts	500	4,000	3,400
Merchandise Inventory		48,000	42,000
Furniture and Equipment	27,000		
Accumulated Depreciation	20,500	6,500	11,900
Total Assets		$62,000	60,800
Liabilities and Owner's Equity Transferred:			
Accounts Payable		0	3,000
Michael Craig, Capital		$62,000	$57,800

a. Receipt of Craig's investment of assets and liabilities
b. Receipt of Argo's investment of cash

2. Prepare a balance sheet for the partnership as of the beginning of its operations on January 1, 19X4.

PROBLEM 19–3B (Obj. 4)

Computing and recording the division of net income or loss between partners. John Grasso and Elizabeth Heid operate Modern Suites, a retail furniture store. Under the terms of the partnership agreement, Grasso is authorized to withdraw $1,500 a month and Heid $1,000 a month. The withdrawals, which are not considered to be salaries, were made each month and charged to the Drawing accounts. By agreement, net income or loss is to be allocated two-thirds to Grasso and one-third to Heid. For the year ended December 31, 19X3, the partnership earned a net income of $52,800.

Instructions

1. Prepare general journal entries to:
   a. Close the Income Summary account
   b. Close the partners' Drawing accounts
2. Assume that there had been a net loss of $6,000 instead of net income of $52,800. Give the general journal entries to:
   a. Close the Income Summary account
   b. Close the partners' Drawing accounts

PROBLEM 19–4B (Obj. 4, 5)

Computing and recording the division of net income or loss between partners; preparing a statement of partners' equities. Alexia Lanza and Beth Ludwig operate the Welcome Pad Student Hostel. Their partnership agreement provides for salaries of $30,000 a year for Lanza and $24,000 for Ludwig and for an interest allowance of 10 percent on each partner's invested capital at the beginning of the year. The remainder of the net income or loss is to be distributed equally between the two partners. On January 1, 19X3, the Capital account balances were $52,000 for Lanza and $112,000 for Ludwig. On July 15, 19X3, Ludwig made a permanent withdrawal of capital of $30,000. The net income for 19X3 was $96,400.

Instructions

1. Prepare the general journal entry on July 15, 19X3, to record the permanent withdrawal by Ludwig.
2. Prepare the following general journal entries on December 31, 19X3, to:
   a. Record the salary allowances for the year
   b. Record the interest allowances for the year
   c. Record the division of the balance of net income
   d. Close the Drawing accounts into the Capital accounts, assuming that the partners had withdrawn the full amount of their salary allowances
3. Prepare a schedule showing the division of net income to the partners as it would appear on the income statement for 19X3.
4. Prepare a statement of partners' equities showing the changes that took place in the partners' Capital accounts during the year 19X3.

PROBLEM 19–5B
(Obj. 6, 8, 9)

Accounting for revaluation of assets and liabilities of a partnership, investment of a new partner, and withdrawal of a partner. The balance sheet of Campus Garden Center, after the revenue, expense, and partners' Drawing accounts have been closed on December 31, 19X3, follows.

CAMPUS GARDEN CENTER
Balance Sheet
December 31, 19X3

Assets		
Cash		10 500 00
Accounts Receivable		2 000 00
Merchandise Inventory		52 000 00
Equipment	20 000 00	
Allowance for Depreciation—Equipment	12 000 00	8 000 00
Building	50 000 00	
Allowance for Depreciation—Building	40 000 00	10 000 00
Land		4 500 00
Total Assets		87 000 00
Liabilities and Owners' Equity		
Liabilities		
Accounts Payable		54 500 00
Taxes Payable		2 500 00
Total Liabilities		57 000 00
Owners' Equity		
Joseph Otungu, Capital	15 000 00	
Sean Stewart, Capital	7 500 00	
Steve Riley, Capital	7 500 00	
Total Owners' Equity		30 000 00
Total Liabilities and Owners' Equity		87 000 00

On that date, Otungu, Stewart, and Riley agree to admit John Matson to the partnership. The partnership agreement among Otungu, Stewart, and Riley provides that in case of dissolution of the partnership all assets and liabilities should be revalued. Profits and losses are shared in the ratio of 50:20:30. The agreed-upon values of the assets are given below.

Accounts Receivable	$ 1,700
Merchandise Inventory	49,800
Equipment	7,500
Building	14,500
Land	11,000

All liabilities are properly recorded.

Instructions

1. Give the general journal entries to record revaluation of the assets.
2. Give the general journal entry (or entries) to record Matson's investment of $15,000, assuming that he is to receive credit for the amount invested.
3. Give the general journal entry (or entries) to record Matson's investment of $15,000, assuming that he is to receive one-fifth of the capital of the entity.
4. Give the general journal entry (or entries) to record Matson's investment of $15,000, assuming he is to receive 40 percent of the capital of the entity.
5. Assume that after the revaluation had been recorded, the old partners and Matson decided that their previous agreement should be canceled and that Matson should not become a partner. Instead, the partners agreed that Riley would withdraw from the partnership.
   a. Give the general journal entry to record the payment to Riley if Riley is paid an amount equal to his Capital account balance after the revaluation.
   b. Give the general journal entry to record the payment to Riley if Riley is paid an amount equal to $1,400 less than his Capital account balance after the revaluation.
   c. Give the general journal entry to record the payment to Riley if Riley is paid an amount equal to $2,100 more than his Capital account balance after the revaluation.

PROBLEM 19–6B (Obj. 7, 8)

Accounting for sale of partnership interest and investment of a new partner. Ronnie Bethel and Steven Blackwood are partners in the Madison Advertising Agency. The balances of their Capital accounts on January 2, 19X3, after revaluation of assets were Bethel, $60,000, and Blackwood, $80,000. Profits and losses are shared in the ratio of 55:45 between Bethel and Blackwood. The partners agree to admit Yien Choo to the partnership on January 3.

Instructions

Give the entries in general journal form to record the admission of Choo under each of the following independent conditions.

1. Bethel sells one-half of his interest to Choo for $44,000 in cash.

2. Blackwood sells one-half of his interest to Choo for $32,000 in cash.
3. Choo invests $60,000 in the business for a one-fourth interest.
4. Choo invests $60,000 in the business for a 35 percent interest.

CHALLENGE PROBLEM

For several years Maria Vela had operated the Vela Curio Shop as a sole proprietor. On January 1, 19X3, she agreed to form a partnership with George Papadou to operate the shop under the name College Curio Shop. Pertinent terms of the partnership agreement follow.

a. Vela was to transfer to the partnership the accounts receivable, merchandise inventory, furniture and equipment, and all liabilities of the sole proprietorship in return for a partnership interest of 60 percent of the partnership capital. Assets were appraised and transferred to the partnership at the appraised values.

   Balances in the relevant accounts of Vela's sole proprietorship at the close of business on December 31, 19X2, are shown below.

Accounts Receivable	$30,500 Dr.
Allowance for Doubtful Accounts	1,500 Cr.
Merchandise Inventory	44,000 Dr.
Furniture and Equipment	30,000 Dr.
Allowance for Depr.—Furn. & Equipment	20,000 Cr.
Accounts Payable	6,000 Cr.

   The two parties agreed that there were unrecorded accounts payable of $400 and unrecorded accrued expenses of $200. They also agreed that $500 of the accounts receivable were definitely uncollectible and should not be transferred to the partnership and that the Allowance for Doubtful Accounts should be $1,400. The appraised values of the other assets were Merchandise Inventory, $39,000, and Furniture and Equipment, $8,000.

b. In return for a 40 percent interest in partnership capital, Papadou invested cash in an amount equal to two-thirds of Vela's net investment.
c. Each partner was allowed a salary, payable on the 15th day of each month. Vela's salary was to be $2,000 per month, and Papadou's salary was to be $1,500 per month.
d. The partners were to be allowed interest of 10 percent of their beginning capital balances.
e. No provision was made for profit division, except for the salaries and interest previously discussed.
f. Revenues for the year 19X3 were $400,000 and expenses were $364,000. Payments for salary allowances were charged to the drawing accounts.

Instructions

1. Record the following information in general journal form in the partnership's records.
   a. Receipt of assets and liabilities from Vela
   b. Investment of cash by Papadou
   c. Summary of cash withdrawals for salaries by the two partners during the year
   d. Profit or loss division, including salary and interest allowances, and the closing balance of the Income Summary account, determined on an appropriate basis.
2. Record the journal entry to close the partners' Drawing accounts into the Capital accounts.
3. Open general ledger accounts for the partners' Capital accounts. The account numbers are Maria Vela, Capital, 301, and George Papadou, Capital, 311. Post the journal entries to the Capital accounts.
4. Prepare a schedule showing the division of net income to the partners as it would appear on the income statement for 19X3.
5. Prepare a statement of partners' equities for the year.
6. On January 1, 19X4, the partners agreed to admit Tyrone Cobb as a partner. Cobb is to invest cash of $30,000 for a one-fourth interest in the capital of the partnership. The three parties agree that the book value of assets and liabilities properly reflects their values. Give the general journal entry to record Cobb's investment.

CRITICAL THINKING PROBLEM

Mike Crivelli has operated a successful motorcycle repair business for the past several years. Crivelli thinks his business is almost too successful because he has little time for himself. Crivelli talks to Patricia Flanagan, who is also a motorcycle enthusiast, about joining him in the business. They agree to form a partnership called the CF Motorcycle Repair Shop. They ask for your help in establishing terms for dividing partnership profits and losses.

The partners give you the following information about their plans for the business:

a. Crivelli plans to contribute to the partnership the assets of his sole proprietorship, which have a fair market value of $88,000.
b. Flanagan will invest $120,000 in cash.
c. Crivelli will work full time in the business while Flanagan will work part time and continue her study for a college degree.

What division of profits and losses would you suggest for Crivelli and Flanagan? Assume that CF Motorcycle Repair earned a net income of $56,000 during its first year of operation. Using your proposed plan of profit sharing, prepare a schedule showing the distribution of the first year's net income to the partners.

U N I T   S E V E N

Accounting for Corporations

Almost all large businesses and many small ones adopt the corporate form of organization for carrying on their activities. Legal characteristics of the corporate form differ from those for sole proprietorships and partnerships. The corporate form of organization also has different advantages and disadvantages, as well as some different accounting entries and reports necessary to record and report information specific to a corporation. Some of the special accounting procedures for corporations relate to accounting for federal and state income taxes, various transactions involving capital stock, and the distribution of profits to the corporation's shareholders. Another special procedure relates to accounting for long-term debt, such as bonds payable issued by corporations to finance their business activities.

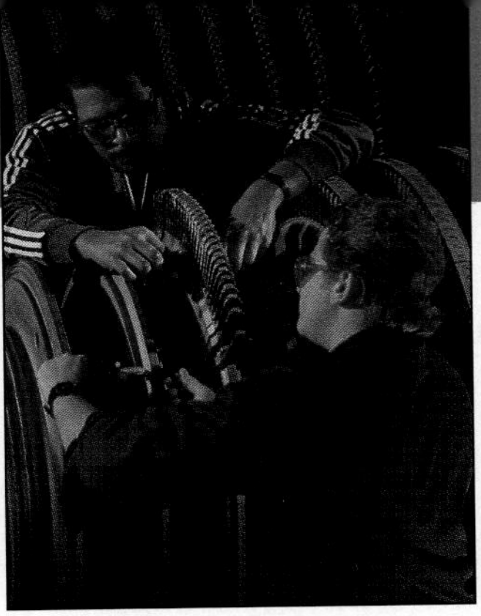

CHAPTER

20

Corporations: Formation and Capital Stock Transactions

OBJECTIVES

1. Explain the characteristics of a corporation.
2. Describe the different types of stock.
3. Compute the number of shares of common stock to be issued on the conversion of convertible preferred stock.
4. Compute dividends payable on stock.
5. Record the issuance of capital stock at par value.
6. Record organization costs.
7. Prepare a Stockholders' Equity section of a corporate balance sheet.
8. Record premium and discount on issuance of stock.
9. Record the issuance of no-par-value stock.
10. Record transactions for stock subscriptions.
11. Explain the capital stock records peculiar to a corporation.
12. Define the accounting terms new to this chapter.

Up to this point, you have studied the operations of two different types of businesses—a sole proprietorship and a partnership. Now we turn to another important form of business organization—the corporation. Although there are many more sole proprietorships and partnerships than corporations, a majority of business transactions involve corporate enterprises. Most businesses that operate on a national or international scale use the corporate form.

In this chapter you will learn the basic characteristics of the corporation, how corporations are formed, the accounting entries necessary to record issuance of capital stock, and the various records needed to manage capital stock. In Chapter 21 you will learn about more complex transactions affecting a corporation's capital structure.

NEW TERMS

Authorized capital stock ▪ Bylaws ▪ Callable preferred stock ▪ Capital stock ledger ▪ Capital stock transfer journal ▪ Common stock ▪ Convertible preferred stock ▪ Corporate charter ▪ Cumulative preferred stock ▪ Liquidation value ▪ Minute book ▪ Noncumulative preferred stock ▪ Nonparticipating preferred stock ▪ No-par value stock ▪ Organization costs ▪ Par value ▪ Participating preferred stock ▪ Preemptive right ▪ Preference dividend ▪ Preferred stock ▪ Registrar ▪ Retained earnings ▪ Shareholder ▪ Stated value ▪ Stock certificate ▪ Stockholders' equity ▪ Subscribers' ledger ▪ Subscription book ▪ Transfer agent

CHARACTERISTICS OF A CORPORATION

OBJECTIVE 1
Explain the characteristics of a corporation.

To understand the legal and accounting characteristics of a corporation, it is helpful to first examine the definition of a corporation. A classic definition was given in 1818 by Chief Justice John Marshall of the United States Supreme Court, who defined the *corporation* as "an artificial being, invisible, intangible, and existing only in contemplation of the law." The corporation is a legal entity, completely separate and apart from its owners. It is created by a **corporate charter** issued by the state government. Since it is a legal entity, it may enter into contracts and own property and is entitled to almost all the rights and privileges of a sole proprietorship or a partnership.

Corporations can have few or many owners. A *privately held* corporation is one that is owned by one or more persons and whose stock is not traded on an organized stock exchange. A *publicly held* corporation has many owners and its stock is traded on an organized stock exchange.

Advantages of the Corporate Form

The corporate form offers the business person some major advantages, as discussed in the following paragraphs.

Limited Liability

Owners of a corporation are not personally liable for the corporation's debts.

You will remember that sole proprietors and general partners in partnerships are personally liable for all debts of the business. However, the owners of a corporation (referred to as **shareholders** or **stockholders** because their ownership is evidenced by shares of stock in the corporation) have no personal liability for the corporation's debts. The corporation's creditors must look to the assets of the firm to satisfy their claims, not to the owners' personal property, even in the event of liquidation. Lending institutions, however, usually require major stockholders in small corporations to give a personal guarantee to repay loans made to the corporation.

Restricted Agency

Ownership of stock in a corporation does not bestow on the owner the right to act on behalf of the corporation.

The mere fact that an individual owns an interest in a corporation conveys no rights whatsoever to that person to take actions on behalf of the business. Instead, the board of directors controls the corporation, and the corporate officers are in direct charge of operations. For example, a person who owns 10,000 shares of the stock of General Motors Corporation has no greater power to act on behalf of GM than a person who has no ownership interest at all.

Continuous Existence

The death of a shareholder or sale of that owner's shares of stock does not dissolve the corporation.

Potential investors are interested in knowing that a firm's operations will continue indefinitely. The death, disability, or withdrawal of an equity owner has no effect on the life of a corporation. Any of these events would lead to dissolution of a sole proprietorship or partnership.

Transferability of Ownership Rights

Owners of a corporation's stock can freely transfer their ownership rights.

The owners can sell their stock without consulting or obtaining the consent of other owners. Shareholders are free to shift their investments at any time, provided they can find buyers for their stock. The organized stock markets, such as the New York Stock Exchange, make it easy to sell or buy interests in corporations whose stocks are "traded." Remember that in a partnership a partner who wishes to sell part of his or her interest to another person must get the permission of the other partners. Remember, too, that the transfer of ownership in a partnership dissolves the existing partnership.

Ease of Raising Capital

A corporation may have thousands, or even millions, of shareholders.

A sole proprietorship has only one owner. A partnership usually has a small number of owners. As a result, the total investment capital that can be raised by these types of entities depends on the wealth of a small group of people. On the other hand, a corporation can have an unlimited number of stockholders. Some corporations have more than a million stockholders, making available a vast pool of capital.

Disadvantages of the Corporate Form

Although the advantages described above are impressive, the corporate form of operation also has certain disadvantages that must be considered.

Corporate Income Tax

Corporations must pay federal income taxes, and sometimes state and local income taxes, on their net income.
Corporations also pay state franchise taxes.

Corporations are subject to certain taxes that are not applied to sole proprietorships and partnerships. For instance, a corporation's profits are subject to federal income taxation. Profits distributed to stockholders in the form of dividends are taxed a second time as part of the personal income of the recipients. The taxation of profits at the corporate level and the subsequent taxation of the profits again when they are distributed as dividends to shareholders is popularly known as *double taxation.* (Under certain conditions a corporation with only a few stockholders can choose not to pay the corporate income tax but instead be treated for tax purposes in much the same way as a partnership.)

State and local governments can also levy income taxes on corporations. In addition, most states require corporations to pay an annual franchise tax for the privilege of carrying on business in the state. In some states, especially those that have no corporate income tax, the franchise tax can be quite onerous.

Governmental Regulation

State governments regulate corporations more closely than they do other business forms.

As artificial entities created by the state government, corporations are subject to any special laws and regulations that the state may impose. In general, the state regulatory bodies exercise closer supervision and control over corporations than they do over sole proprietorships or partnerships. The state laws may prohibit corporations from entering into particular types of transactions or from owning specific types of property. Special reports requiring extra work and cost are frequently required of corporations.

FORMATION OF A CORPORATION

To understand why and how a corporation is formed, place yourself in the shoes of David Webb. Webb has been operating the Webb Office Furniture Company, a retail business, for a number of years as a sole proprietorship. The business currently sells traditional office furniture, but Webb has decided to enlarge the line of products to emphasize computer desks, computer workstations, and other computer-related furniture and equipment. His store will operate under the name Webb Office Workstation, and he hopes, in a few years, to have a chain of office furniture stores in operation.

To expand his activities, Webb needs more operating capital to remodel the store and buy new fixtures, to acquire much larger inventories, and to extend more credit to customers. Several of Webb's friends are willing to invest as partners in his business, but he has put off a decision because he has some doubts about this arrangement. Although he needs the extra funds, he does not want to share operating control of the firm with people who know nothing about the business. Also, he does not wish to go further in debt.

Webb's prospective backers have some doubts, too. They do not mind risking the money they invest, but they wish to avoid responsibility for the debts of the business. Although they do not mind letting Webb run the business, they do want to have some voice in general policy. They would also like to be assured of a reasonable and regular return on their money.

Webb and his friends consult an attorney who specializes in business law and taxation. The lawyer suggests that forming a corporation offers the best solution to their needs, and explains the steps to be taken. Requirements and procedures differ from state to state, but typically the process follows a certain course.

1. One or more persons, referred to as the "organizers" or "promoters," must apply to a state officer, usually the secretary of state, for a charter permitting the proposed corporation to do business. The state charges a fee for the charter.
2. When issued, the charter specifies the exact name, length of life (state laws generally provide for unlimited life), rights and duties, and scope of operations of the corporation. Most corporate charters grant the corporation a rather broad sphere of operations. The charter also sets forth the classes of stock and number of shares in each class that can be issued in exchange for money, property, or services.
3. Shortly after the charter is issued, the organizers meet to elect an acting board of directors. The corporation proceeds to issue shares of stock to individuals who have paid the full amount of the purchase price of the stock. The shareholders then elect permanent directors, usually the same individuals as the acting di-

rectors. The directors or shareholders approve **bylaws** for the corporation. The bylaws provide the guidelines for conducting the corporation's business affairs. The board then selects officers, who hire employees and begin operating the business.

4. The amount received for the capital stock issued by the corporation appears on its balance sheet as part of the owners' equity, which is usually called **stockholders' equity**.

STRUCTURE OF A CORPORATION

When the owners invest in a corporation they buy shares of stock. That is why the owners of the firm are known as shareholders or stockholders. They are issued **stock certificates,** discussed and illustrated later in this chapter, as evidence of their ownership. The owners can participate in stockholders' meetings, elect a board of directors, and vote on certain questions of basic corporate policy.

The members of the board of directors of a corporation are elected by the shareholders. The board sets the general policies of the entity.

The directors formulate general operating policies and are responsible for seeing that the activities of the corporation are carried on. They select officers and other top management personnel to direct everyday operations. The officers hire managers who hire other employees and, along with the officers, make the day-to-day decisions necessary to operate the business.

The officers of a corporation might consist of the president, one or more vice presidents, a secretary, and a treasurer. The top accounting official might be called the controller or chief accountant. As the firm grows, there might be a need for several layers of management, including division managers, department heads, and supervisors. The levels would depend on the nature and complexity of the firm's operations.

The flow of authority in a corporate entity is shown in Table 20–1.

TABLE 20–1
Corporate Structure and Responsibilities

Stockholders	■ Elect directors
Directors	■ Make policies ■ Appoint officers
Officers	■ Carry out policies ■ Hire managers
Managers	■ Oversee and supervise operations
Other employees	■ Perform assigned tasks

SELF-REVIEW

1. List the major advantages of the corporate form of business.
2. What is a corporate charter? By whom is it issued?
3. If a shareholder in a corporation dies, will the corporation continue to exist? Explain.
4. Compare the transferability of shares of stock in a corporation with the transferability of a partner's interest in a partnership.
5. What is a corporate franchise tax?

Answers to Self-Review

1. The major advantages include limited liability, transferability of ownership rights, continuous existence, and the non-agency of owners.
2. The corporate charter is a permit issued by the state government, usually by the secretary of state, creating the corporation.
3. Yes. A corporation is a separate entity with a continuous existence. It is not affected by the death, disability, or withdrawal of individual shareholders.
4. Shareholders are free to sell any stock they own at any time and need no consent of other shareholders. Partners must obtain the consent of other partners to transfer an ownership interest.
5. A corporate franchise tax is a tax levied by the state on corporations for the privilege of carrying on business in the state.

CAPITAL STOCK

The decision about the classes of stock to be offered and the number of shares of each class to be issued must be made before the charter application is filed because the charter approves the issue of specific amounts and types of stock. The promoters usually make certain that the **authorized capital stock**—the number of shares authorized by the charter—is greater than the number of shares they plan to issue in the foreseeable future. In this way, they provide for later increases in the corporation's capital without having to request an amendment of the corporation's charter when there is a need to issue more stock.

Capital Stock Values

A number of different terms are used in referring to the value of capital stock. Three of the most commonly encountered stock values are discussed below.

Par Value

If stock has a par value, that value is specified in the corporate charter.

Par value is a figure selected by the organizers of the corporation to be assigned to each share of stock for accounting purposes. The par value, if any, is specified in the charter. It is almost always $100 or less, but it may be any amount, such as $25, $5, or even less than $1 a share. Stock may be issued for more than par value per share. Generally, however, state laws prohibit the issuance of par-value stock for less than the par value. (This problem is discussed later in the chapter.)

Stated Value

Stated value is a value assigned to no-par stock by the board of directors for accounting and legal purposes.

State laws permit stock to be issued without par value. This type of stock is called **no-par-value stock.** In such cases, the board of directors of the corporation may assign a **stated value** to the stock. The stated value serves much the same purpose as par value.

Market value of stock is the price at which the stock is bought and sold.

Market Value

Market value of stock is the price per share at which stock is bought and sold. After stock has been paid for and issued by the corporation, it may be resold for any price. The sales price of the stock (its market value) may have little relation to par value or stated value.

Classes of Capital Stock

OBJECTIVE 2

Describe the different types of stock.

A corporation may have several different types of stock. Each type, or "class," has different rights and privileges.

Common Stock

If there is only one class of stock, the stock is called **common stock.** Each share of common stock conveys to the owner the same rights and privileges as every other share. In general, these rights are as follows.

1. The right to attend stockholders' meetings.
2. The right to vote in the election of directors and on certain other matters. The owner is entitled to one vote for each share of stock.
3. The right to receive dividends as declared by the board of directors.
4. The right to purchase a proportionate amount of any new stock issued at a later date. This right is referred to as the **preemptive right.**

Preemptive right of shareholders is the right to purchase a proportionate share of any new stock issued at a later date.

If a corporation has two or more classes of stock, one class will be common stock possessing all the rights discussed above, while the other class(es) of stock authorized will have certain preferences over the common shares.

Preferred Stock

Stock that carries special privileges or rights is called preferred stock.

One or more classes of stock may have certain preferred claims on the corporation's profits or on its assets in case of liquidation. They may also carry other special preferences that set them apart from the common stock. This kind of stock is known as **preferred stock.** In receiving special preferences, the owners of preferred stock may lose some of their general rights, such as the right to vote. Unless the charter specifies otherwise, however, preferred stock will have voting rights.

Liquidation Preferences on Preferred Stock. The terms of issue of preferred stock usually provide that in case of liquidation the preferred stockholders have a prior claim on assets. Often a **liquidation value** (usually par value or an amount in excess of par value) is assigned to the preferred stock. This feature means that after the creditors have been paid their claims, the preferred stockholders are paid the specified liquidation value for each share before any assets are distributed to common stockholders. The liquidation value of preferred stock is extended to include any cumulative dividends that may not have been paid. (Cumulative dividends are explained later in this chapter.)

To illustrate the importance of liquidation preferences, assume that a corporation is going out of business. It has paid all liabilities. The company has 10,000 shares of $50 preferred stock outstanding, with a liquidation value of $52 per share, and 50,000 shares of $20 par-value common stock outstanding. If there is only $700,000 to distribute to the shareholders, the preferred stockholders will be paid $520,000 (10,000 shares × $52 per share). The common stockholders will receive the balance of $180,000 ($700,000 – $520,000).

The liquidation preference on all preferred stock should be shown in the Stockholders' Equity section of the balance sheet.

OBJECTIVE 3
Compute the number of shares of common stock to be issued on the conversion of convertible preferred stock.

Convertible Preferred Stock. **Convertible preferred stock** gives its owners the right to convert their shares into common stock after a specified date. Sometimes the conversion terms also specify the last date on which the preferred stock can be converted. The conversion ratio, the number of shares of common stock into which a share of preferred stock can be converted, is specified on the preferred stock certificate. The conversion privilege may help to overcome the reluctance that many investors have to purchasing preferred stock. This reluctance arises because the market value of preferred stock usually does not increase significantly even though the corporation may be quite profitable. Since convertible preferred stock bears a fixed dividend rate and at the same time can be converted into common stock if the value of common stock increases, this type of stock has great appeal.

To better understand the conversion right, assume that a corporation has outstanding 100,000 shares of 12 percent, $25 par-value preferred stock that may be converted into common stock at the rate of three shares of common stock for each share of preferred stock surrendered. The conversion privilege is exercisable on or after January 1, 19X9. Owners of the preferred stock may then exchange any or all of their shares for common stock at the stated ratio. Thus a preferred stockholder with 600 shares could obtain 1,800 shares of common stock by means of the conversion process.

600 shares of preferred
× 3 shares of preferred for each share of common
= 1,800 shares of common

In making the decision to convert the preferred stock into common stock, the stockholders would consider the market prices of the two types of stock, the relative dividends being paid on the common and the preferred stock, and the degree of risk involved.

Callable Preferred Stock. **Callable preferred stock** gives the issuing corporation the right to repurchase the preferred shares from the stockholders at a specified price. The call price is usually substantially greater than the original issue price. The rights are effective after some specified date. Callable stock gives a corporation greater flexibility in controlling its capital structure.

The following example will illustrate the call feature. Assume that on July 12, 19X3, a corporation issued 50,000 shares of 11 percent, $40 par-value preferred stock at $40 a share. The issue terms give the corporation the right to call any part of the preferred stock at any time after December 31, 19X8, for $56 a share. If the corporation has surplus funds available, or if money can be borrowed at substantially less than 11 percent, the corporation may wish to call the preferred stock and retire it.

STOCK DIVIDENDS

The board of directors has wide discretion in distributing corporate earnings as dividends to shareholders.

The right to receive a portion of the corporation's profits is obviously one of the major incentives for investment. Stockholders receive part of a corporation's profits in the form of dividends only when the board of directors declares a dividend. The board of directors has almost complete discretion, subject to certain legal restrictions, in deciding whether to declare a dividend and how much it will be.

Dividends on Preferred Stock

One of the privileges usually accorded preferred stock is a priority with respect to dividends. The exact nature of the priority is established by the terms specified in the corporation's charter. Almost all preferred stock bears a basic or stated dividend rate, called the **preference dividend,** that must be paid each year before a dividend can be paid to common stockholders that year. The dividend rate is generally expressed in dollars-per-share per year, but may instead be expressed as a percentage. Where the dividend is expressed as a percentage, the percentage rate is applied to the par value of the stock to arrive at the dollar amount of the preference dividend each year. For example, the annual dividend on 10 percent preferred stock with a par value of $50 is $5 per share.

Not all preferred stock has a dividend expressed simply in terms of dollars per year or in percentage of par value.

1. **Cumulative preferred stock** conveys to its owners the right to receive the stated preference dividend for both the current year and any prior years in which the stated dividend was not paid before the common stockholders can receive any dividends. On the other hand, for **noncumulative preferred stock,** the stated preference dividend for a particular year must be paid in that year before dividends can be paid to common stockholders. However, if no dividends are declared in one year, the next year represents a fresh start. This type of stock has no continuing rights to dividends for the year in which none were declared.
2. **Nonparticipating preferred stock** allows the preferred stockholders to receive only the preference dividend amount specified on the stock certificate, while **participating preferred stock** allows the preferred stockholders to receive the regular preferred dividend *and* to participate in additional dividends with the common stockholders.

Dividends on Common Stock

Dividends on common stock are paid only after dividend requirements for preferred stock have been met. The fewer the dividend privileges enjoyed by the preferred stockholders, the greater the dividends that the common stockholders can receive, especially in prosperous years.

Comparison of Dividend Provisions

OBJECTIVE 4
Compute dividends payable on stock.

The effects on dividend distributions of various types of stock are best understood by analyzing several alternative plans.

Plan A—Only Common Stock Issued

Assume that a corporation has only one class of stock—common stock. Assume also that 2,500 shares at $100 par value were authorized and were issued and remain outstanding.

Situation 1. The dividend declared by the board of directors depends on the corporate earnings and the need to keep profits (called **retained earnings**) for use in the business. A 6 percent dividend would amount to $15,000 a year (2,500 shares × $100 par value × 0.06).

Situation 2. The board of directors has the right to *pass* the dividend (not pay it) or to declare a smaller dividend if conditions so warrant ($7,500, or 3 percent, instead of $15,000, for instance). If the board does declare a smaller dividend, or even no dividend at all, the stockholders have to be content. Similarly, stockholders may receive a larger dividend if the directors see fit to declare one.

Plan B—Common and Noncumulative, Nonparticipating Preferred Stock Issued

The uncertainty of dividends described in Plan A is a risk of stock ownership that cannot be entirely avoided. However, preferred stock offers advantages that are attractive to certain types of investors. Assume that a corporation has both preferred and common stock issued and outstanding as follows.

Preferred stock, noncumulative, nonparticipating, (12%, $100 par value, 500 shares)	$ 50,000
Common stock ($50 par value, 4,000 shares)	200,000
Total capital stock	$250,000

Situation 1. If the board of directors distributes $17,000, the preferred stockholders will get first consideration. They must receive the regular preference dividend of $6,000 (500 shares × $100/share × 0.12) before any dividends can be paid to common shareholders. This payment will leave $11,000 to be distributed to the common stockholders, who will receive $2.75 a share computed as follows:

Total dividend paid	$17,000
Preference dividend to preferred shareholders	6,000
Remaining dividend to common stockholders	$11,000

$$\text{Dividend per share on common stock} = \frac{\$11{,}000}{4{,}000 \text{ shares}}$$
$$= \$2.75 \text{ per share}$$

Situation 2. If there is only $9,500 to distribute, the preferred stockholders will receive their full 12 percent, or $6,000, and the remaining $3,500 will allow a return of only $0.875 a share on the common stock ($3,500/4,000 shares).

Total dividend paid	$9,500
Preference dividend to preferred stockholders	6,000
Remaining dividend to common stockholders	$3,500

$$\text{Dividend per share on common stock} = \frac{\$3{,}500}{4{,}000 \text{ shares}}$$
$$= \$.0875 \text{ per share}$$

Situation 3. If there is only $4,000 to distribute, the preferred stockholders will receive it all—$8 a share ($4,000/500). The remaining preference dividends owed on the preferred stock ($4 a share) will not be paid since the stock is noncumulative. The common stockholders will receive nothing.

If dividends are not paid on cumulative preferred stock, the unpaid amount must be paid in future years before any dividends can be paid on common stock.

Plan C—Common and Cumulative Preferred Stock Issued

When business conditions are poor, preferred stockholders have a better chance for a return than do common stockholders. However, the preferred stockholders' chances can be further improved if the preferred stock is cumulative. Under this privilege, the $4 balance owed on each share of the 12 percent dividend remaining unpaid in the preceding example will be carried forward as a continuing claim into future periods.

In subsequent years in which dividends are paid, the dividends will be paid in the following sequence:

1. To preferred stockholders for prior-year dividends in arrears
2. To preferred stockholders for the regular preference dividend for the year of payment
3. Any balance to common stockholders

Situation 1. If the board of directors distributes $9,000 in the next year and the preferred stock is cumulative, the distribution will be made as follows:

1. To preferred stockholders for the dividends in arrears (500 shares × $4/share)	$2,000
2. To preferred stockholders for the regular preference dividend	6,000
Total to preferred stockholders	$8,000
3. The balance to common stockholders ($9,000 − $8,000)	$1,000

In preparing financial statements, the total and the per-share amounts of cumulative preferred dividends not previously paid should be shown either on the face of the balance sheet or in footnotes to the statements.

Situation 2. In good years the common stockholders may enjoy very substantial gains. Suppose, for example, the directors decide to distribute $37,500. If there is no balance owed to the preferred stockholders because of the cumulative privilege and if their stock is not participating, they will receive only the regular preference dividend of $6,000 (500 shares × $12/share). The balance of $31,500 will be divided among the common stockholders. The result will be a dividend of $7.875 a share ($31,500/4,000 shares) on the common stock—a return of 15.75 percent on the $50 stated value, greater than the 12 percent return received by the preferred stockholders.

Holders of participating preferred stock may receive more than their regular dividends.

Plan D—Common and Cumulative Participating Preferred Stock Issued

Investors may be induced to purchase preferred stock in a corporation that appears to have the potential for large future profits and dividends, even though present earnings and dividends are low, through the use of participating preferred stock. Under this plan, which is not frequently encountered, dividend distributions are allocated between preferred and common stock as follows:

1. Preferred stockholders receive any dividends in arrears plus their regular specified preference dividend.
2. Next, some specified rate of dividend is paid to owners of common stock.
3. Then the participating preferred stockholders and common stockholders share in additional dividends declared. The exact terms of participation vary.

Because almost all preferred stock is nonparticipating and because the terms of participation differ, we will not illustrate the calculation of dividends on participating preferred stock. In the remainder of this book, it should be assumed that preferred stock is nonparticipating.

Table 20–2 summarizes the dividend rights of the different classes of stock frequently issued by corporations.

REFLECTING CAPITAL STOCK ON THE BALANCE SHEET

The owners' equity in a corporation is called stockholders' equity. The Stockholders' Equity section of the corporate balance sheet usually includes information that identifies the classes of stock, the number of shares authorized and issued for each class, their par values, and any special privileges carried by the stock. The illustration that follows is typical of how the capital stock accounts are presented on the balance sheet.

TABLE 20–2
Dividend Rights of Different Classes of Stock

Type of Stock	Dividend Rights
Noncumulative, nonparticipating preferred stock	■ Has right to receive preference dividend each year before any dividend can be paid on common stock ■ If dividend is passed (not paid) in one year, the amount not paid is not cumulative and does not affect dividend payments in future years
Cumulative preferred stock	■ Has right to receive preference dividend each year before any dividend can be paid on common stock ■ If dividend is passed in one year, the amount not paid carries over and must be paid in subsequent year before any dividend can be paid on common stock
Participating preferred stock	■ Has right to receive preference dividend each year before any dividend can be paid on common stock ■ After preference dividend is paid, any additional dividend up to specified amount is paid to common stockholders ■ After common shareholders have received specified amount, preferred and common stock share in further dividends
Common stock	■ Receives all dividends after dividends have been paid on preferred stock in accordance with contractual obligation

Stockholders' Equity	
Preferred Stock (12% cumulative, $100 par value, 1,000 shares authorized) at Par Value (500 shares issued)	$50,000
Common Stock (no-par value, with stated value of $25, 4,000 shares authorized) at Stated Value (1,000 shares issued)	25,000
Total Stockholders' Equity	$75,000

SELF-REVIEW

1. How does preferred stock differ from common stock?
2. What are liquidation preferences?
3. What is cumulative preferred stock?
4. What is convertible preferred stock?
5. What is callable preferred stock?

Answers to Self-Review

1. Preferred stock may carry certain preferred claims on the corporation's profits or on its assets in case of liquidation, or it may carry other special preferences that set it apart from common stock. Holders of preferred stock may also give up certain rights, such as the right to vote.

2. Liquidation preference refers to the right to be paid a specified liquidation value after creditors have been paid but before any assets are distributed to the common stockholders.
3. Owners of cumulative preferred stock must be paid the stated dividend for the current year and any prior years in which the stated dividend was not paid before the common stockholders can receive any dividends.
4. Convertible preferred stock is preferred stock that can be converted at the option of the owner into common stock under specified conditions.
5. Callable preferred stock means that the issuing corporation retains the right to repurchase the shares from the stockholders at a specified price.

RECORDING STOCK ISSUED AT VARIOUS VALUES

Stock can be issued only after the purchaser has paid for it in full, either with cash, noncash assets, or services rendered. First we will examine a simple situation—the issuance of par-value stock for cash equal to the stock's par value. Then we shall examine the issuance of stock in other types of transactions.

Stock Issued at Par Value

Assume that David Webb and his associates determine that their new corporation, Webb Office Workstation Corporation, will ultimately have capital requirements of $700,000. Based on these requirements, the incorporators decide to use two classes of stock, preferred and common, as shown below.

Preferred Stock (12%, $100 par value, noncumulative and nonparticipating, 2,000 shares)	$200,000
Common Stock ($50 par value, 10,000 shares)	500,000
Total Capital Stock	$700,000

Webb is to transfer the noncash assets and the liabilities of his furniture store to the corporation as of the close of business on December 31, 19X3. Preferred and common stock will be issued to Webb in payment for his equity of $73,400. In addition, Webb will invest cash for 132 shares of common stock to bring his total investment to $80,000. Webb's friends who have agreed to go into the venture with him also agree to invest cash for specified amounts of common stock and preferred stock.

When the charter is received, the accounting records are set up and a memorandum entry is made in the general journal. This entry gives the details of the authorized capital stock.

19X3					
Dec.	*31*	*The Webb Office Workstation Corporation has been organized to market office furniture and related products and to carry on all necessary and convenient related activities. It is authorized to issue 10,000 shares of $50 par-value common stock and 2,000 shares of $100 par-value 12% preferred stock that is noncumulative and nonparticipating.*			

For permanent reference, the data relating to each authorized class of stock is entered on a separate ledger sheet. The information for Webb Office Workstation Corporation might be recorded at the top of the ledger sheets as shown below.

ACCOUNT *Common Stock (Par Value $50 10,000 Shares Authorized)* ACCOUNT NO. *301*

DATE	EXPLANATION	POST. REF.	DEBIT	CREDIT	BALANCE DEBIT	BALANCE CREDIT

ACCOUNT *Preferred Stock (12% Noncumulative, Nonparticipating; $100 Par Value; 2,000 Shares Authorized)* ACCOUNT NO. *311*

DATE	EXPLANATION	POST. REF.	DEBIT	CREDIT	BALANCE DEBIT	BALANCE CREDIT

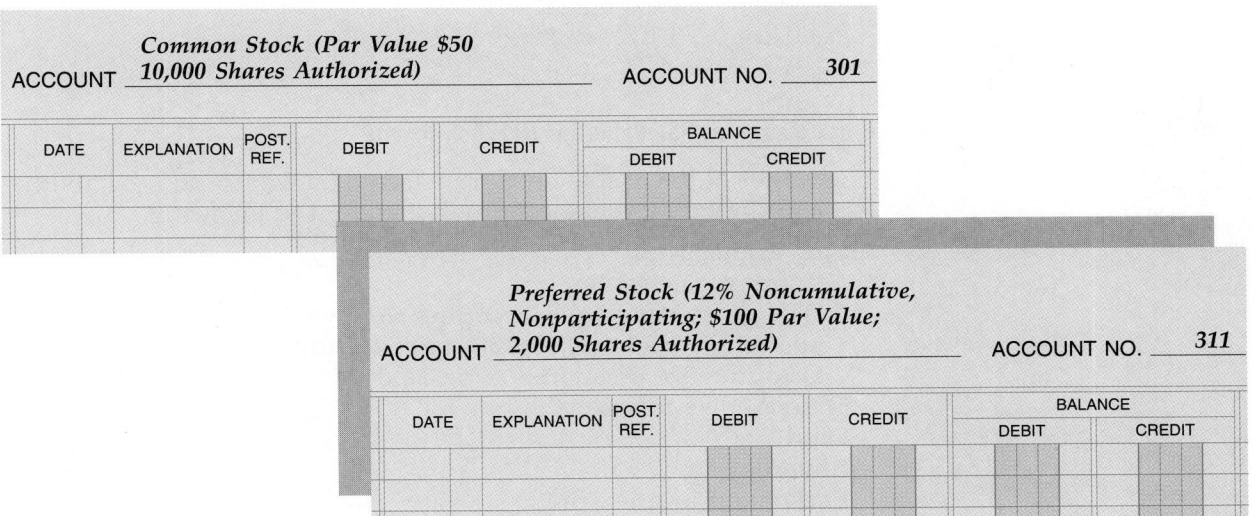

OBJECTIVE 5
Record the issuance of capital stock at par value.

Stock Issued at Par Value for Cash

When stock is issued in return for a cash investment equal to the par value of the shares, the entire amount of cash proceeds is credited to the appropriate capital stock account. Suppose, for example, that Webb and his friends purchase the following number of shares at par value for cash.

	Common Stock Shares	Preferred Stock Shares
David Webb	132	
Robert Novak	200	200
Mary Fields	200	200
John Valdez	100	
Alice Hill	50	

The receipt of cash from each stock purchaser would be recorded in the corporation's cash receipts journal. However, to simplify the illustration, we will show the entry in general journal form for the receipt of cash and the issuance of common stock and preferred stock to Robert Novak only. Cash receipts from the issue of stock to other shareholders would be recorded in similar fashion.

19X3				
Dec.	*31*	*Cash (10,000 + 20,000)*	*30 000 00*	
		Common Stock (200 × $50)		*10 000 00*
		Preferred Stock (200 × $100)		*20 000 00*
		Issuance of stock to Robert Novak: 200 shares of common at par ($50 a share) and 200 shares of preferred at par ($100 a share)		

Stock Issued at Par Value for Noncash Assets

The values of the assets to be transferred by Webb and the liabilities to be assumed by the corporation include the following.

Assets Transferred:	
Accounts Receivable	$ 8,000
(The gross balance of Accounts Receivable on Webb's books is $9,000; uncollectible accounts are estimated to be $1,000)	
Merchandise Inventory	20,000
Land	15,000
Building	36,000
Equipment and Fixtures	4,000
Total Assets	83,000
Liabilities Transferred:	
Accounts Payable	9,600
Net value of assets transferred	$73,400

The acquisition of the assets and liabilities of the Webb Office Furniture Company is now recorded in the accounting records of Webb Office Workstation Corporation, and an entry is made of the stock issued in payment. Webb and the other shareholders agreed that Webb would be issued 400 shares of the $100 par value preferred stock, to be recorded at par value ($40,000). In addition, shares of the $50 par-value common stock are to be issued to Webb for the difference between the net value of the noncash assets received by the corporation and the par value of the 400 shares of preferred stock. Thus 668 shares of common stock are also issued.

Net value of assets transferred	$73,400
Par value of preferred stock issued	
(400 shares × $100/share)	40,000
Par value of common stock to be issued	$33,400

Number of common shares to be issued:
$33,400/$50 per share = 668 shares

All assets, except accounts receivable, are recorded at the appraised value agreed to by the incorporators. The $9,000 balance in the Accounts Receivable control account agrees with the total of the accounts receivable subsidiary ledger. Thus the entire $9,000 balance is recorded in the Accounts Receivable account of the corporation. An Allowance for Doubtful Accounts of $1,000 is recorded to reduce the net carrying value of the accounts to $8,000, the amount estimated to be collectible.

19X3					
Dec.	*31*	*Accounts Receivable*		*9 000 00*	
		Merchandise Inventory		*20 000 00*	
		Land		*15 000 00*	
		Building		*36 000 00*	
		Equipment and Fixtures		*4 000 00*	
		Allow. for Doubtful Accts.			*1 000 00*
		Accounts Payable			*9 600 00*
		Common Stock (668 × 850)			*33 400 00*
		Preferred Stock (400 × 100)			*40 000 00*
		Issuance of stock in payment for net noncash assets of Webb Office Furniture Company, 668 shares of $50 par common stock at $50/share and 400 shares of $100 par preferred stock at $100/share			

It is extremely important to remember that non-cash assets should be recorded at their fair market values.

OBJECTIVE 6
Record organization costs.

Recording Organization Costs

Bringing a new corporation into existence involves a variety of costs, such as legal fees, attorneys' fees, charter fees paid to the state, and the cost of the organizational meeting of the directors. These costs ordinarily are paid soon after the corporation receives its charter. Some of them may be paid through the issue of capital stock. These costs are charged to an intangible asset account, usually called **Organization Costs.** This account is set up initially as an asset rather than an operating expense because it is a necessary cost of bringing the corporation into existence. Since organization costs would have no sales value if the corporation were to liquidate, accountants follow the conservative practice of charging the amount off to expense over a period of several years.

Generally accepted accounting principles permit organization costs to be amortized over a period of up to 40 years. However, these costs are often charged off over a 60-month period, starting in the month the corporation begins operation. This period is commonly used because organization costs can be amortized over a period of not less than 60 months for federal income tax purposes. The amortization procedure will be illustrated in Chapter 21.

Suppose that immediately after the issue of stock to the original shareholders on December 31, the Webb Office Workstation Corporation paid its attorney $1,000 for legal fees, including reimbursement for the charter fee and the cost of drafting and printing the stock certificates. In general journal form, this transaction would be recorded as shown.

19X3					
Dec.	*31*	*Organization Costs*		*1 0 0 0 00*	
		Cash			*1 0 0 0 00*
		Payment of legal fees,			
		charter fee, and cost of			
		engraving stock			
		certificates			

OBJECTIVE 7
Prepare a Stockholders' Equity section of a corporate balance sheet.

Reporting Stockholders' Equity on the Balance Sheet

Immediately following the organization of the Webb Office Workstation Corporation, a balance sheet is prepared (Figure 20–1). This balance sheet reflects the acquisition of the Webb Office Furniture Company by the issuance of stock, the issuance of stock for cash, and the payment of organization costs.

Stock Issued at a Premium

OBJECTIVE 8
Record premium and discount on issuance of stock.

When stock is issued for more than its par value, it is said to have been issued at a premium.

Once the business is launched and its relative success and prospects can be evaluated, investors may feel that its stock is actually worth more or less than par value. For example, if the corporation has potential for earning very attractive profits, investors may understandably be willing to pay more than par value to become stockholders. Similarly, if the dividend rate on the par value of an issue of preferred stock is higher than the rate that could be earned on other investments with similar risk, investors may be willing to pay more than par value for the preferred stock. The amount received by a corporation in excess of the par value of stock is called a *premium.* A premium on preferred stock is usually credited to an account entitled Paid-in Capital in Excess of Par Value—Preferred Stock.

FIGURE 20–1
A Corporate Balance Sheet Prepared after Organization

WEBB OFFICE WORKSTATION CORPORATION
Balance Sheet
December 31, 19X3

Assets		
Current Assets		
Cash		73 1 0 0 00
Accounts Receivable	9 0 0 0 00	
Less Allowance for Doubtful Accounts	1 0 0 0 00	8 0 0 0 00
Merchandise Inventory		20 0 0 0 00
Total Current Assets		101 1 0 0 00
Property, Plant, and Equipment		
Land	15 0 0 0 00	
Building	36 0 0 0 00	
Equipment and Fixtures	4 0 0 0 00	
Total Property, Plant, and Equipment		55 0 0 0 00
Intangible Assets		
Organization Costs		1 0 0 0 00
Total Assets		157 1 0 0 00
Liabilities and Stockholders' Equity		
Current Liabilities		
Accounts Payable		9 6 0 0 00
Stockholders' Equity		
Preferred Stock (12%, $100 par value, 2,000 shares authorized)		
At Par Value (800 shares issued)	80 0 0 0 00	
Common Stock ($50 par value, 10,000 shares authorized)		
At Par Value (1,350 shares issued)	67 5 0 0 00	
Total Stockholders' Equity		147 5 0 0 00
Total Liabilities and Stockholders' Equity		157 1 0 0 00

Suppose that Linda Levy agrees to pay $110 a share, which means she will pay a premium of $10 a share, for 200 shares of the 12 percent, $100 par-value preferred stock of the Webb Office Workstation Corporation. Here is how the transaction would be recorded in general journal form.

19X4				
Mar.	*2*	*Cash*	22 0 0 0 00	
		Preferred Stock		20 0 0 0 00
		Paid-in Capital in Excess of Par Value—Preferred Stock		2 0 0 0 00
		Issuance of 200 shares for $110 per share		

In the Stockholders' Equity section of the balance sheet shown below, the amount of the new account, called Paid-in Capital in Excess of Par Value—Preferred Stock, is added to the par value of the shares issued to show the total paid in by that class of stockholder. (The account title might also be Premium on Preferred Stock or some other name.)

Stockholders' Equity		
Preferred Stock (12%, $100 par value, 2,000 shares authorized)		
At Par Value (1,000 shares issued)	$100,000	
Paid-in Capital in Excess of Par Value	2,000	$102,000

Stock Issued at a Discount

Most states do not permit the issuance of stock at a discount.

Although most states prohibit the issuance of stock at a *discount,* or less than par value, this procedure is permitted in a few states. Corporations sometimes sell their stock at a discount as an inducement to hesitant investors. The technique for recording the sale of stock at a discount is illustrated below. In this example, 50 shares of $100 par-value common stock are issued for $90 a share. Thus the total discount is $500 (50 shares × $10 a share).

Cash	4 500 00	
Discount on Common Stock	500 00	
Common Stock		5 000 00
Issued common stock at discount		

When items are presented in the Stockholders' Equity section of the balance sheet, the discount is shown as a deduction from the credit balance of the related stock account. The difference indicates the amount paid in by that class of stockholder. If both premiums and discounts occur in sales of the same class of stock, the premiums are added and the discounts are deducted separately. The two figures are not combined. For example, assume that the Webb Corporation had already issued 350 shares of common stock at a total premium of $2,000. The Stockholders' Equity section of the balance sheet would appear as follows after issuance of the 50 shares at a discount.

Stockholders' Equity			
Common Stock ($100 par value, 1,000 shares authorized)			
At Par Value (400 shares issued)	$40,000		
Paid-in Capital in Excess of Par Value	2,000	$42,000	
Less Discount on Common Stock		500	$41,500

In states where stock can be issued at a discount, the stockholder generally has a *contingent liability* to pay the amount of the discount if the corporation needs the funds to pay its creditors.

Stock Issued at No Par

As pointed out earlier in this chapter, common stock that is not assigned a par value in the corporate charter is sometimes issued. No-par-value stock provides several theoretical advantages over stock with par value. Two specific advantages are listed below.

1. No-par-value stock can be issued for whatever it will bring, without considering premium or discount. This eliminates the contingent liability that might exist if the stock were sold at a discount.
2. The stock buyer is not misled into thinking that a par-value amount represents the market value of the stock.

OBJECTIVE 9
Record the issuance of no-par-value stock.

No-Par Stock Without Stated Value

We have previously seen that most states allow corporations to issue common stock that has no par value assigned by the charter. Some states have established a minimum stated value that must be assigned to each share of no-par stock. In other states, it is not required that a stated value be assigned the stock, but the board of directors may do so.

If the stock has not been assigned a stated value, the entire amount received on the issue of common shares is credited to the Common Stock account. For example, suppose that Classic Tutoring Corporation is authorized to issue no-par common stock. A stated value has not been assigned the shares. On January 4, 19X4, the corporation issues 1,000 shares to a purchaser who pays $10 per share, and on January 5 it issues 600 shares to a purchaser who pays $11 per share. The two stock issues would be recorded as follows.

19X4					
Jan.	*4*	*Cash (1,000 × $10)*		*10 000 00*	
		Common Stock (1,000 × $10)			*10 000 00*
		Issue of 1,000 shares of			
		no-par common stock at			
		$10 per share			
	5	*Cash (600 × $11)*		*6 600 00*	
		Common Stock (600 × $11)			*6 600 00*
		Issue of 600 shares of			
		no-par common stock at			
		$11 per share			

For accounting purposes, the stated value assigned to no-par stock is treated in the same way as par value.

No-Par Stock with Stated Value

In most cases where no-par stock is issued, a stated value is set by the board of directors, and this stated value is treated as though it were par value. If no-par stock with a stated value is issued for an amount equal to the stated value, the proceeds are credited to the No-Par Common Stock account.

If no-par common stock with a stated value is issued at a price greater than the stated value, the stated value is credited to the Capital Stock account, and any excess received over stated value is treated as a premium. The excess is credited to Paid-in Capital in Excess of Stated Value, or some similar account.

For example, suppose the College Hamburger Corporation is authorized to issue no-par common stock. The board of directors has assigned $50 as the stated value of the stock. On March 1, 19X4, the corporation issues 400 shares of its stock to a purchaser for $52 a share. The stock sale and issue would be recorded as shown below.

19X4					
Mar.	*1*	*Cash (400 × $50)*		*20 8 0 0 00*	
		Common Stock (400 × $50)			*20 0 0 0 00*
		Paid-in Capital in Excess			
		of Stated Value			*8 0 0 00*
		Issue of 400 shares of			
		common stock at $52 per			
		share			

Note the credit of $800 to the Paid-in Capital in Excess of Stated Value account (400 shares × $2 a share). On the balance sheet, this item is added to the amount in the Common Stock account to show the total paid by common stockholders in exactly the same way that Paid-in Capital in Excess of Par Value is shown.

Summary of Recording Rules for Par and No-Par Stock

We have now seen that capital stock may have a par value, it may be true no-par stock, or it may be no-par stock with a stated value. The effects on the capital accounts of issuing each of these three types of stock are summarized in Table 20–3.

TABLE 20–3
Comparison of Rules for Par and No-Par Stock

Par-Value Stock	No-Par Stock	
	Stated Value	No Stated Value
Par value is specified in corporate charter.	Stated value is assigned by directors. Corporate charter indicates that stock is no-par stock.	Corporate charter indicates that stock is no-par stock.
Stock certificate indicates par value.	Stock certificate does not generally show stated value.	Stock certificate shows that stock is no-par stock.
Change in par value requires revision of charter.	Stated value can be changed by directors.	
On issue of stock, par value is credited to Capital Stock account.	On issue of stock, stated value is credited to Capital Stock account.	On issue of stock, entire proceeds are credited to Capital Stock account.

SUBSCRIPTIONS FOR CAPITAL STOCK

OBJECTIVE 10
Record transactions for stock subscriptions.

Some prospective stockholders may not be able to pay immediately for the securities they want to buy. These investors are asked to sign a subscription contract in which they agree to buy the stock at a certain price, to pay for it in accordance with a fixed plan, and to receive the stock when payment is completed. The payment may be due in a single amount at a future date or in installments over a period of time. A stock subscription gives the corporation a receivable from the subscriber and an obligation to hold enough stock for issue when the subscription is paid in full.

Receipt of Subscriptions

Suppose that on April 1, 19X4, the Webb Office Workstation Corporation received a subscription from Doris Martin to purchase 200 shares of $50 par common stock at $50 a share. Martin is to pay for the stock in full on May 1. The corporation also received a subscription from Lewis Nichols to purchase 200 shares of $100 par-value preferred stock at $110 a share. Nichols is to pay for the stock in two equal installments beginning May 1, 19X4, and ending June 1, 19X4. These subscriptions are recorded as shown below.

19X4					
Apr.	1	Subscriptions Rec.—Common		10 000 00	
		Common Stock Subscribed			10 000 00
		Subscription from Doris Martin to buy 200 shares of common stock at par value of $50 a share			
	1	Subscrip. Rec.—Preferred		22 000 00	
		Preferred Stock Subscribed			20 000 00
		Paid-in Capital in Excess of Par Value—Preferred Stock			2 000 00
		Subscription from Lewis Nichols to buy 200 shares of $100 par preferred stock at $110 a share			

Capital Stock Subscribed is shown in the Stockholders' Equity section of the balance sheet.

Notice that separate Subscriptions Receivable accounts are used for each class of stock. Separate accounts must also be kept for the subscribed stock. At the time the contracts are paid in full, the stock will be issued. Until that time, the Stock Subscribed accounts will be presented in the Stockholders' Equity section of the balance sheet as additions to the same class of stock issued. For example, immediately after the receipt of Nichols's stock subscription, the preferred stock listing in the Stockholders' Equity section appears as shown on the next page.

Stockholders' Equity		
Preferred Stock (12%, $100 par value, 2,000 shares authorized)		
At Par Value (1,000 shares issued)	$100,000	
Subscribed (200 shares)	20,000	
Paid-in Capital in Excess of Par Value	2,000	$122,000

Collection of Subscriptions and Issuance of Stock

Stock is issued when payment has been received for the subscription. Stock may be paid for in a single cash payment or in payments over a period of time.

Single Cash Payment

When Martin pays her $10,000 subscription in full on May 1, 19X4, 200 shares of common stock are issued to her. The cash received for this transaction is normally recorded in the cash receipts journal. However, for illustrative purposes, the transaction is shown below in general journal form, followed by an entry to record the issuance of the stock.

19X4				
May	*1*	*Cash*	*10 000 00*	
		Subscrip. Rec.—Common		*10 000 00*
		Received Doris Martin's subscription in full		
	1	*Com. Stock Sub. (200 shares)*	*10 000 00*	
		Common Stock (200 shares)		*10 000 00*
		Issued 200 shares of common stock to Doris Martin		

When these entries have been posted, the Subscriptions Receivable—Common account with Doris Martin is closed and the Common Stock Subscribed account is also closed. The net effect of this series of transactions is to increase the corporation's Cash account by $10,000 and to increase its Common Stock account by the same amount.

Subscriptions Receivable			
Apr. 1	10,000	May 1	10,000

Common Stock Subscribed			
May 1	10,000	Apr. 1	10,000

Cash			
May 1	10,000		

Common Stock			
		May 1	10,000

Installment Payments

Nichols agreed to pay his preferred stock subscription in two monthly installments of $11,000 each, beginning May 1. Each collection will be debited to Cash and credited to the Subscriptions Receivable—Preferred account. When he makes his final payment, the stock will be issued to him. In general journal form, the collection of the final installment and the issuance of the stock would be recorded as shown below.

19X4				
June	*1*	*Cash*	*11 000 00*	
		Sub. Rec.—Preferred		*11 000 00*
		Receipt of final installment from Lewis Nichols on his stock subscription		
	1	*Pref. Stock Subscribed*	*20 000 00*	
		Preferred Stock		*20 000 00*
		Issuance of 200 shares of preferred stock to Lewis Nichols		

As shown in the T accounts below, this series of transactions has resulted in an increase in Cash of $22,000. This amount is offset by a $20,000 increase in the Preferred Stock account for the 200 shares issued to Nichols and a $2,000 increase in the Paid-in Capital in Excess of Par Value—Preferred Stock account.

Cash

Debit		Credit	
May 1	11,000		
June 1	11,000		

Subscriptions Receivable—Preferred

Debit		Credit	
Apr. 1	22,000	May 1	11,000
		June 1	11,000

Preferred Stock Subscribed

Debit		Credit	
June 1	20,000	Apr. 1	20,000

Preferred Stock

Debit		Credit	
		June 1	20,000

Paid-in Capital in Excess of Par Value Preferred Stock

Debit		Credit	
		Apr. 1	2,000

SELF-REVIEW

1. How does a premium on stock arise?
2. Is a discount on stock a usual occurrence? Explain.
3. A corporation issues no-par-value stock with a stated value of $1.50 a share at $28 a share. How is the transaction recorded?
4. How is the issuance of no-par-value stock for cash recorded?
5. What are organization costs? How are they accounted for?

Answers to Self-Review

1. A premium on stock arises when the value received for the stock exceeds its par (or stated) value.
2. No. State laws generally prohibit the issuance of stock at a discount.
3. Debit Cash for $28. Credit Common Stock for $1.50 and Paid-in Capital in Excess of Stated Value for $26.50.
4. If the stock has a stated value, credit the stock account for the stated value. The difference between the amount received and the stated value is premium or discount on stock. If the stock has no stated value, credit the stock account for the entire amount received.
5. Organization costs are the costs incurred in organizing the corporation (for example, charter fees, attorneys' fees, costs of the organization meeting, and expenses of promoters). These costs are recorded in an intangible asset account, Organization Costs, and are then charged off as an expense over a period of time.

SPECIAL CORPORATION RECORDS AND AGENTS

OBJECTIVE 11
Explain the capital stock records peculiar to a corporation.

A corporation must keep detailed records of its stockholders' equity. It must also maintain special corporate records such as minutes of meetings of stockholders and directors, corporate bylaws, stock certificate books, stock ledgers, and stock transfer records.

Minute Book

To keep accurate and complete records of all meetings of stockholders and directors, the corporation maintains a **minute book.** In the minute book, actions taken, directives issued, directors elected, officers elected, and all other matters discussed are formally reported.

Stock Certificate Books

Capital stock is issued by a corporation in the form of a stock certificate. A separate series of stock certificates must be prepared for each class of stock. A corporation that expects to issue relatively few stock certificates may have them prepared in books. Each certificate is numbered consecutively and attached to a stub from which it is separated at the time of issuance. The certificate indicates the class of stock and the number of shares. Certificates become valid when they are properly signed by corporate officers and have the corporate seal affixed to them.

FIGURE 20–2
Stock Certificate and Stub

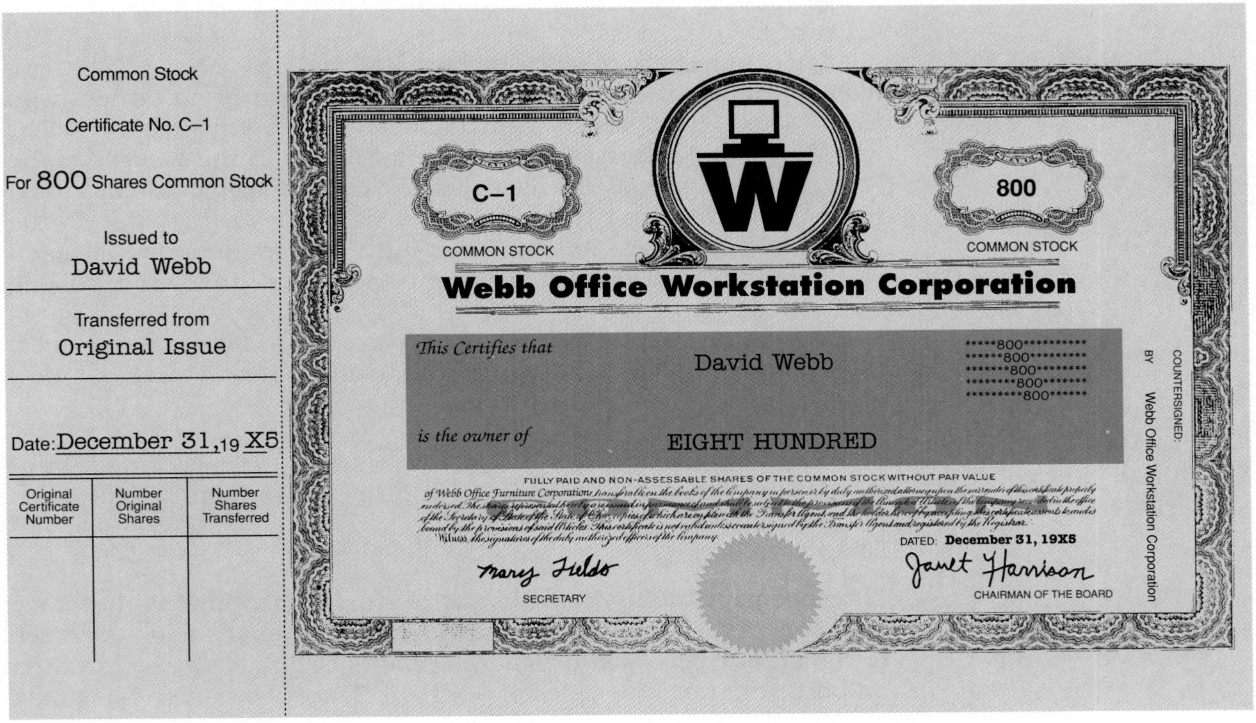

The first common stock certificate of the Webb Office Workstation Corporation is issued to David Webb for 800 shares (132 for cash and 668 for the net assets of the Webb Office Furniture Company). The certificate and stub (before they have been separated) are illustrated in Figure 20–2. (The lower section of the stub is used when stock is transferred.) Certificates for preferred stock are similar to those for common stock.

A capital stock ledger for each class of stock contains a sheet for each shareholder of that class.

Capital Stock Ledger

It is important for the corporation or for an agent acting on its behalf to keep careful records of the number of shares of stock issued and of the names and addresses of the stockholders. This information is needed when dividend checks are mailed, when official notices of stockholders' meetings are sent out, when proxies are solicited, and at other times.

In order to maintain the required information about stockholders, the corporation or its agent sets up a **capital stock ledger,** or **stockholders' ledger,** for each class of stock issued. There is a sheet for each stockholder with the stockholder's name and address, the dates of transactions affecting his or her stock holdings, the certificate numbers, and the number of shares involved in each transaction. The balance shows the number of shares held. The ledger sheets may also include a record of dividends. The stockholders' ledger for a class of stock is a subsidiary to the Capital Stock account for that class. Thus the total shares shown in the stockholders' ledger must agree with the number of shares in the Capital Stock account for that class.

Once a quantity of stock has been issued, new stockholders are likely to obtain their shares by purchasing them from owners who want to sell all or part of their holdings. The buyer pays the seller, and the stock is transferred to the new owner in the records of the corporation. A special journal called the **capital stock transfer journal** is used to record the transaction, which is then posted to the stockholders' ledger. One of these journals is maintained for each class of stock issued by the corporation, and all transfers involving that class of stock are recorded in it.

When stock is sold by one shareholder to another, the stock certificate is surrendered to the corporation and is then canceled. A new certificate is issued to the purchaser.

Records of Stock Subscriptions

The corporation needs two special records to keep track of stock subscriptions: the subscription book and the subscribers' ledger.

Subscription Book

The **subscription book** is a listing of stock subscriptions that have been received. This book is used to record the names and addresses of the subscribers, the number of shares they have agreed to buy, and the amounts and times of payment. The subscription book may consist of the actual stock subscription contracts.

The subscribers' ledger contains an account receivable for each subscriber to stock.

Subscribers' Ledger

A separate subsidiary ledger, the **subscribers' ledger,** is maintained. The subscribers' ledger contains an account receivable for each subscriber. This account is debited for the total amount of the original subscription and credited as payments are made by the subscriber to the corporation. No new principles are involved here. The subscribers' ledger is a subsidiary ledger, and the balances of the individual subscriber accounts must agree with the Subscriptions Receivable control account in the general ledger.

Summary of Stock Control Accounts and Subsidiary Ledgers

The relationship between the most commonly found control accounts and subsidiary ledgers used in keeping records of corporate stock are summarized in Table 20–4.

Special Agents

Corporations whose stock is widely held and actively traded ordinarily do not keep their own stockholder records. Instead, they turn the responsibility for these records over to a transfer agent and a registrar. The bank that is to serve as a transfer agent is often chosen because of its nearness to the stock exchange or the market in which the corporation's stock is expected to be traded. The same bank may also be appointed registrar.

TABLE 20–4
Subsidiary Stock Ledgers

Control Account	Subsidiary Ledger
Common Stock	Common Stockholders' Ledger Contains an account for each owner of common stock and shows shares bought or transferred and the balance of shares owned
Preferred Stock	Preferred Stockholders' Ledger Contains an account for each owner of preferred stock and shows shares bought or transferred and the balance of shares owned
Subscriptions Receivable—Common Stock	Subscribers' Ledger—Common Contains the account receivable for each subscriber to common stock
Subscriptions Receivable—Preferred Stock	Subscribers' Ledger—Preferred Contains an account receivable for each subscriber to preferred stock

Transfer Agent

The **transfer agent** receives the stock certificates being surrendered. (An assignment form on the certificates indicates to whom a new certificate should be issued.) The agent cancels the old certificates, issues the new ones, and makes the necessary entries in the capital stock ledger. When required to do so by the corporation, the agent also prepares lists of stockholders who should receive dividend payments, notices, and other items. The agent may also prepare and mail the dividend checks.

Registrar

The **registrar** accounts for all the stock issued by the corporation and makes sure that the corporation does not issue more shares than are authorized. The registrar receives from the transfer agent all the canceled certificates and all the new certificates issued. The new certificates must be countersigned by the registrar before they are valid.

MANAGERIAL IMPLICATIONS

It is essential that the individuals who are setting up a new firm have a clear idea of the nature of a corporation, its rights and limitations, and how the corporation differs from other forms of business organization. For example, these individuals should know that the corporation is a separate legal entity apart from its owners, that it has continuous existence regardless of changes in ownership, and that owners have limited liability and are free to dispose of their stock without consulting other stockholders. The organizers of a new firm should also understand the corporation's potential disadvantages with reference to the payment of taxes and the regulation of operations.

In order to select the most beneficial capital structure, management should be familiar with the various types of stock that may be used.

It is essential to corporate management that assets acquired through the issue of stock be realistically valued so that the true measure of their worth can be known and so that the corporation's profitability can be properly computed and evaluated.

Management must be sure that capital stock issues are properly accounted for. State laws regarding the issuance of stock at a discount must be carefully observed. Management must also be fully informed about state laws concerning stock subscriptions and must be sure that the accounting records fully reflect all information relating to such transactions.

Management must be certain that it has adequate records to comply with legal requirements and to keep track of stockholder transactions. The bylaws and charter provisions of the corporation must be carefully followed, and minutes must be kept of all meetings of directors and stockholders. Actions of the board of directors, as reported in the corporate minutes, often have accounting effects that must be recognized and acted upon.

SELF-REVIEW

1. Describe the information contained on a stock certificate.
2. What is a stock certificate book?
3. Explain the nature of a capital stock ledger.
4. Describe the information contained in a capital stock transfer journal.
5. What functions are served by the transfer agent?

Answers to Self-Review

1. A stock certificate lists a serial number, the class of stock, and the number of shares. Preferred stock certificates also include the essence of the preferred stock contract.
2. It contains stock certificates attached to stubs. The certificate and its stub are separated at the time the stock is issued.
3. It contains a separate record for each shareholder, showing the number of shares of stock issued, the name and address of the stockholder, and information about transactions affecting the stockholder's shares.
4. It contains the names of shareholders surrendering and receiving shares, the number of shares being surrendered and received, and the certificate number.
5. The transfer agent receives old certificates and cancels them, issues new certificates, and makes entries in the capital stock ledger.

CHAPTER 20 Review and Applications

CHAPTER SUMMARY

A corporation is organized under state law to carry on activities permitted by its charter. Ownership is evidenced by shares of stock. Stockholders owning voting stock elect a board of directors, which selects officers who hire employees and who direct the operations of the business.

The corporate charter specifies the types and amounts of capital stock authorized. The bylaws serve as guides for general operation of the firm, which must be consistent with charter provisions. Stock may have a par value specified in the charter. If it does not have a specified par value, it is called no-par-value stock. Some states require that no-par stock be assigned a stated value, which is used in almost the same way as par value for accounting purposes.

Preferred stockholders enjoy certain privileges, often including priority in the distribution of dividends. Cumulative and participating provisions may give further advantages to the preferred stockholders. In addition, the preferred stock may be convertible into shares of common stock.

Stock may be issued at a premium over par value, but state laws generally prohibit the issuance of stock at a discount (less than par value). In states where stock may be issued at a discount, stockholders may have a contingent liability for the amount of the discount.

Sometimes stock is subscribed to, then paid for and issued at a later date. To record stock subscriptions, a corporation sets up a special subsidiary ledger, called a subscribers' ledger, with a separate account receivable for each subscriber. The individual accounts receivable are controlled by a Subscriptions Receivable account in the general ledger. The stock is issued when the subscription price has been fully paid.

The accounting records of a typical corporation include the usual journals and ledgers kept by any firm. In addition, corporations must keep special records. These records include minute books, stockholders' ledgers, stock certificate books, and stock transfer records.

GLOSSARY OF NEW TERMS

Authorized capital stock (p. 692) The number of shares authorized for issue by a corporation's charter

Bylaws (p. 691) A corporation's guidelines for conducting business affairs

Callable preferred stock (p. 694) Stock that gives the issuing corporation the right of repurchase at a specified price and generally after a specified date

Capital stock ledger (p. 713) A subsidiary ledger that contains a record of each stockholder's purchases, transfers, and current balance of shares owned; also called stockholders' ledger

Capital stock transfer journal (p. 714) A record of stock transfers, used for posting to the stockholders' ledger

Common stock (p. 693) The general class of stock issued when no other class of stock is authorized; each share carries the same rights and privileges as every other share

Convertible preferred stock (p. 694) Preferred stock that conveys the right to convert that stock to common stock after a specified date

Corporate charter (p. 688) A document issued by a state government that establishes a corporation

Cumulative preferred stock (p. 695) Stock requiring that a preference dividend for a year that is not paid in that year be paid in the future before other dividends may be declared

Liquidation value (p. 693) Value applied to preferred stock, usually par value or an amount in excess of par value

Minute book (p. 712) A book in which accurate and complete records of all directors' and stockholders' meetings are kept

Noncumulative preferred stock (p. 695) Stock on which a preference dividend not paid in one year does not accumulate

Nonparticipating preferred stock (p. 695) Stock that conveys the right to a preference dividend amount specified on the face of the stock certificate but to no additional dividends

No-par value stock (p. 692) Stock issued by a corporation without a value assigned by the charter

Organization costs (p. 704) The costs associated with establishing a corporation; an intangible asset account

Par value (p. 692) An amount selected by organizers of a corporation and assigned by the corporate charter to each share of stock for accounting purposes

Participating preferred stock (p. 695) Stock that conveys the right not only to the preference dividend amount but also to a share of other dividends paid

Preemptive right (p. 693) A shareholder's right to purchase a proportionate share of any new stock issued by the corporation

Preference dividend (p. 695) A stated dividend rate for preferred stock that must be paid before dividends can be paid on common stock

Preferred stock (p. 693) A class of stock that conveys certain claims on a corporation's profits or assets in case of liquidation

Registrar (p. 715) A person or institution in charge of the issuance and transfer of stock

Retained earnings (p. 696) Cumulative corporate profits not paid out in dividends

Shareholder (p. 688) A person who owns shares of stock in a corporation; also called stockholders

Stated value (p. 692) The value assigned to stock by a board of directors when stock has been authorized without par value

Stock certificate (p. 691) A document that shows evidence of ownership of shares in a corporation

Stockholders' equity (p. 691) The corporate equivalent of owners' equity

Subscribers' ledger (p. 714) A special ledger that contains an account receivable for each stock subscriber

Subscription book (p. 714) A listing of stock subscriptions

Transfer agent (p. 715) A person or institution that handles all stock transfers and transfer records for a corporation

REVIEW QUESTIONS

1. Name five provisions commonly included in the articles of incorporation.
2. What are the bylaws of a corporation?
3. How are members of a corporate board of directors chosen?
4. If there is only one class of stock, what is it called?
5. How does par value differ from stated value?
6. What is participating preferred stock?
7. How do bonds differ from stock?
8. What is convertible preferred stock?
9. When par-value stock is issued, what amount is credited to the Capital Stock account?
10. Is discount on stock a common occurrence? Explain.
11. What is a stock subscription?
12. How are organization costs classified on the balance sheet?
13. Explain the purpose of the minute book.
14. What role does the registrar serve?
15. What is the control account for accounts in the common stockholders' ledger?

MANAGERIAL FOCUS

1. What legal characteristics of a corporation are of special importance to its management?
2. Would management generally expect to pay a higher rate or a lower rate of dividends on preferred stock than the rate of interest necessary on bonds? Explain.
3. A group of individuals is planning to form a corporation. Explain in general terms the usual steps necessary to do this.
4. Why should the management of a corporation be concerned about the realistic valuation of assets transferred to the firm?
5. Why must the management and directors of a corporation be fully informed about laws and regulations affecting corporations? How can they find out what they need to know?

6. Why would the management of a corporation sell its stock on a subscription basis, considering all the record keeping involved?
7. Is stock issued to the subscriber at the time the subscription agreement is signed? Explain.

EXERCISES

EXERCISE 20–1
(Obj. 4)

Computing dividends payable. The Horowitz Corporation has only one class of stock. There are 100,000 shares outstanding. During 19X3 the corporation's net income after taxes was $290,000. The policy of the corporation is to declare dividends equal to 40 percent of its net income. James Giese owns 1,120 shares of the stock. How much will Giese receive as a dividend on his shares?

EXERCISE 20–2
(Obj. 4)
Tutorial

Computing dividends payable. The Habib Corporation has outstanding 10,000 shares of noncumulative, 14 percent, $60 par-value preferred stock and 100,000 shares of no-par-value common stock.

1. During 19X3 the corporation paid dividends of $72,000. What amount will be paid on each share of preferred stock? What amount will be paid on each share of common stock?
2. During 19X4 the Habib Corporation paid dividends of $420,000. How much will be paid on each share of preferred stock? How much will be paid on each share of common stock?

EXERCISE 20–3
(Obj. 4)
Tutorial

Computing dividends payable. The Chilton Corporation has outstanding 30,000 shares of 14 percent, $50 par-value cumulative preferred stock and 100,000 shares of no-par-value common stock.

1. During 19X3 the corporation distributed dividends of $225,000. What amount will be paid on each share of preferred stock? What amount will be paid on each share of common stock?
2. During 19X4 the corporation distributed dividends of $480,000. What amount will be paid on each share of preferred stock?

EXERCISE 20–4
(Obj. 3)
Tutorial

Converting preferred stock. The Bellows Corporation has outstanding 50,000 shares of $30 par-value preferred stock, issued at an average price of $32 a share. The preferred stock is convertible into common stock at the rate of one-half share of common stock for each share of preferred stock. Louise Jackson owns 400 shares of the preferred stock. During the current year she decides to convert 200 shares into common stock. How many shares of common stock will she receive?

EXERCISE 20–5
(Obj. 5)
Tutorial

Issuing stock for assets. Ruth Jenson, the owner of a sole proprietorship, is planning to incorporate her business. Her capital account has a balance of $164,000 after revaluation of the assets. Her cash account totals $16,000. She will receive 14 percent, $20 par-value preferred stock with a total par value equal to the cash transferred. The balance of her capital is to be exchanged for shares of $10 par-value common stock with a total par value equal to the remaining capital. How many shares of preferred stock should be issued to

Jenson? How many shares of common stock should be issued to Jenson?

EXERCISE 20-6 (Obj. 6)

Amortizing organization costs. The Fernandez Corporation was formed in January 19X4 with organization costs of $2,800.

1. What is the least amount of organization costs to be amortized for the year 19X4?
2. Assume that the Fernandez Corporation wishes to amortize an amount of organization costs equal to the largest amount that can be charged off on its federal income tax return. How much will Fernandez amortize for 19X4?

EXERCISE 20-7 (Obj. 5)

Tutorial

Issuing stock at par value for cash. The Henrich Corporation issued 3,000 shares of $20 par-value common stock and 300 shares of 13 percent, $50 par-value preferred stock for cash at par value. Give the entry in general journal form to record the issuance of the stock.

EXERCISE 20-8 (Obj. 8)

Tutorial

Issuing par-value stock at premium. The Lagos Corporation issued 500 shares of its $20 par-value common stock for cash at $31 a share. Give the entry in general journal form to record the issuance of the stock.

EXERCISE 20-9 (Obj. 9)

Tutorial

Issuing no-par stock for cash. The Ibriham Corporation issued 580 shares of its no-par-value common stock (stated value, $2) for cash at $2.90 a share. Give the entry in general journal form to record the issuance of the stock.

EXERCISE 20-10 (Obj. 10)

Tutorial

Transactions for stock subscriptions. On June 1, 19X4, the Creek Corporation received a subscription from Linda Kelso for 1,000 shares of its $25 par-value common stock at a price of $30 a share.

1. Kelso made a payment of $15.00 per share on the stock at the time of the subscription. Record the entries in general journal form to record receipt of the subscription and the cash payment.
2. Give entries on July 1, 19X4, to record payment of the balance of Kelso's subscription and issuance of the stock.

PROBLEMS

PROBLEM SET A

PROBLEM 20-1A (Obj. 4)

Tutorial

Computing dividends payable. The Atlas Corporation has issued and has outstanding 10,000 shares of $50 par-value common stock and 1,000 shares of $100 par-value 12 percent preferred stock. The board of directors votes to distribute $5,000 as dividends in 19X3, $12,000 in 19X4, and $81,000 in 19X5.

Instructions

Compute the total dividend and the dividend for each share paid to preferred stockholders and common stockholders each year under the following assumed situations. *Case A:* The preferred stock is nonparticipating and noncumulative. *Case B:* The preferred stock is cumulative and nonparticipating.

PROBLEM 20–2A (Obj. 4)

Computing dividends payable. This problem consists of two parts.

Part I

A portion of the Stockholders' Equity section of the Banowitz Corporation's balance sheet as of December 31, 19X5, appears below. Dividends have not been paid for the years 19X3 and 19X4. There has been no change in the number of shares of stock issued and outstanding during these years. Assume that the board of directors of the Banowitz Corporation declares a dividend of $14,000 after completing operations for the year 19X5.

Stockholders' Equity	
Preferred Stock (11% cumulative, $100 par value, 1,000 shares authorized)	
At Par Value (700 shares issued)	$ 70,000
Common Stock (no-par value, with stated value of $50, 5,000 shares authorized)	
At Stated Value (3,000 shares issued)	150,000

Instructions

1. Compute the total amount of the dividend to be distributed to the preferred stockholders.
2. Compute the amount of the dividend to be paid on each share of preferred stock.
3. Compute the total amount of the dividend available to be distributed to the common stockholders.
4. Compute the amount of the dividend to be paid on each share of common stock.
5. Compute the amount of dividends in arrears (if any) that preferred stockholders may expect from future declarations of dividends.

Part II

Use the information given in Part I to solve this part of the problem. Assume that the board of directors of the Banowitz Corporation has declared a dividend of $42,900 instead of $14,000 after operations of the year 19X5 are completed.

Instructions

1. Compute the total amount of the dividend to be distributed to the preferred stockholders.
2. Compute the amount of the dividend to be paid on each share of preferred stock.
3. Compute the total amount of the dividend available to be distributed to the common stockholders.
4. Compute the amount of the dividend to be paid on each share of common stock.
5. Compute the amount of dividends in arrears (if any) that preferred stockholders may expect from future declarations of dividends.

PROBLEM 20–3A (Obj. 5)

Issuing stock for cash and noncash assets at par. Clarice Parker and Sennett Kirk are equal partners in P & K Stereo Center, which sells audio equipment and operates a sound equipment repair service. Parker and Kirk have decided to incorporate the business. The new corporation will be known as Economy Sound Corporation.

The corporation is authorized to issue 1,000 shares of $100 par-value, 12 percent preferred stock that is noncumulative and nonparticipating and 20,000 shares of no-par-value common stock with a stated value of $50 a share. It is mutually agreed that the accounting records of P & K Stereo Center will be closed on December 31, 19X3, and that certain assets will be revalued. The Economy Sound Corporation will then take over all assets and assume all liabilities of the partnership. In payment for the business, the corporation will issue 200 shares of preferred stock to Parker and 200 shares of preferred stock to Kirk, plus a sufficient number of shares of common stock to each partner to equal the balance of the partners' capital accounts. After the partners have recorded the revaluation of their assets immediately prior to the dissolution of their partnership and withdrawn the amounts of cash agreed on, the trial balance of P & K Stereo Center as of December 31, 19X3, appears as shown.

P & K STEREO CENTER
Trial Balance
December 31, 19X3

ACCOUNT NAME	DEBIT	CREDIT
Cash	4 010	
Accounts Receivable	12 720	
Allowance for Doubtful Accounts		4 120
Merchandise Inventory	162 700	
Parts Inventory	10 950	
Land	20 000	
Building	137 870	
Allowance for Depreciation—Building		13 870
Furniture and Equipment	29 350	
Accumulated Depr.—Furn. and Equipment		2 150
Accounts Payable		19 860
Clarice Parker, Capital		168 800
Sennett Kirk, Capital		168 800
Totals	377 600	377 600

Instructions

1. In the corporation's general journal, record a memorandum entry describing the corporation's formation on December 31, 19X3.
2. Record general journal entries as of December 31 to show the takeover of the assets and liabilities of the partnership and the issuance of stock in payment to Parker and Kirk. Use the same account titles that the partnership used for assets and liabilities. Also use two new accounts: Common Stock and Preferred Stock.

PROBLEM 20–4A
(Obj. 5, 6, 7, 9)
Tutorial GL

Issuing stock at par and no-par value, recording organization costs, and drafting Stockholders' Equity section of balance sheet. The Tatum Corporation, a new corporation, took over the assets and liabilities of the T. T. Tatum Retail Company on January 2, 19X3. The assets and liabilities assumed, after appropriate revaluation by Tatum, were as follows.

Cash	$ 500
Accounts Receivable	90,000
Allowance for Doubtful Accounts	(3,000)
Merchandise Inventory	155,000
Accounts Payable	(98,000)
Accrued Expenses Payable	(6,000)

The corporation is authorized to issue 500,000 shares of no-par-value common stock with a stated value of $10 a share and 100,000 shares of $5 par-value preferred stock. The preferred stock bears a stated yearly dividend rate of $0.50 a share. The transactions that follow were entered into at the time the corporation was formed.

Instructions

1. Make general journal entries to record the transactions.
2. Prepare the opening balance sheet as of January 2, 19X3, for the Tatum Corporation.

TRANSACTIONS

Jan. 2 The corporation issued 13,850 shares of common stock to Tatum for his equity in the sole proprietorship business, and the corporation took over Tatum's assets and liabilities.

2 Issued 100 shares of preferred stock to Tatum for his services in organizing the corporation. The agreed-upon value of these services was $500.

2 Issued 1,000 shares of common stock to Alice Hernandez. She paid $10,000 in cash for the stock.

2 Issued 1,000 shares of preferred stock to Julio Rodriquez. He paid $5,000 in cash for the stock.

2 Paid $900 to Samuel Derrin, the attorney who prepared the articles of incorporation and the corporate bylaws, for his services.

PROBLEM 20-5A
(Obj. 5, 6, 7, 8, 10)

Tutorial GL

Issuing stock at par and at premium, recording organization costs, preparing Stockholders' Equity section of balance sheet, and recording stock subscriptions. The Keynote Corporation was organized on July 1, 19X3, to manufacture musical instruments. The firm is authorized to issue 50,000 shares of no-par-value common stock with a stated value of $50 per share and 20,000 shares of $50 par-value, 12 percent preferred stock that is nonparticipating and noncumulative. Selected transactions that took place during July 19X3 follow.

Instructions

1. Set up the following general ledger accounts.

   101 Cash
   114 Subscriptions Receivable—Common Stock
   115 Subscriptions Receivable—Preferred Stock
   301 Common Stock
   302 Common Stock Subscribed
   305 Paid-in Capital in Excess of Par Value—Common
   311 Preferred Stock
   312 Preferred Stock Subscribed
   315 Paid-in Capital in Excess of Par Value—Preferred

2. Record in general journal form the transactions listed below and post them to the general ledger accounts.
3. Prepare the Stockholders' Equity section of a balance sheet for the Keynote Corporation, as of July 31, 19X3.

TRANSACTIONS

July 1 The corporation received its charter. (Make a memorandum entry.)

1 Issued 300 shares of common stock for cash at $50 a share to Alice Clayton.

2 Issued 250 shares of preferred stock for cash at par value to Jacob Green.

5 Issued 150 shares of common stock for cash at $52 to Frank Oliva.

10 Received a subscription for 200 shares of common stock at $53 a share from Diane Norris, payable in two installments due in 10 and 20 days.

12 Received a subscription for 100 shares of preferred stock at $52 a share from Richard Selby, payable in two installments due in 15 and 30 days.

20 Received payment of a stock subscription installment due from Diane Norris (one-half of the purchase price—see July 10 transaction).

27 Received payment of a stock subscription installment due from Richard Selby (one-half of the purchase price—see July 12 transaction).

30 Received the balance due on the stock subscription of July 10 from Diane Norris; issued the stock.

PROBLEM SET B

PROBLEM 20–1B (Obj. 4)

Computing dividends payable. The Alabaster Corporation has issued and has outstanding 2,000 shares of $75 par-value common stock and 2,000 shares of $50 par-value, 10 percent preferred stock. The board of directors votes to distribute $6,000 as dividends in 19X3, $10,000 in 19X4, and $51,000 in 19X5.

Instructions

Compute the total dividend and the dividend for each share to be paid to preferred stockholders and common stockholders each year under the following assumed situations. *Case A:* The preferred stock is nonparticipating and noncumulative. *Case B:* The preferred stock is cumulative and nonparticipating.

PROBLEM 20–2B (Obj. 4)

Computing dividends payable. This problem consists of two parts.

Part I

Tutorial

A portion of the Stockholders' Equity section of the Marino Corporation's balance sheet as of December 31, 19X4, appears below. Dividends have not been paid for the year 19X3. There has been no change in the number of shares of stock issued and outstanding during 19X3 or 19X4. Assume that the board of directors of the corporation declared a dividend of $15,000 after completing operations for the year 19X4.

Stockholders' Equity	
Preferred Stock (10% cumulative, $50 par value, 20,000 shares authorized)	
At Par Value (4,000 shares issued)	$200,000
Common Stock ($25 par value, 35,000 shares authorized)	
At Par Value (10,000 shares issued)	250,000

Instructions

1. Compute the total amount of the dividend to be distributed to the preferred stockholders.
2. Compute the amount of the dividend to be paid on each share of preferred stock.
3. Compute the total amount of the dividend available to be distributed to the common stockholders.
4. Compute the amount of the dividend to be paid on each share of common stock.
5. Compute the amount of dividends in arrears (if any) that preferred stockholders may expect from future declarations of dividends.

Part II Assume that after operations for 19X4 were completed, the board of directors declares a dividend of $84,000 instead of $15,000. Use the information given in Part I to solve this part of the problem.

Instructions

1. Compute the total amount of the dividend to be distributed to the preferred stockholders.
2. Compute the amount of the dividend to be paid on each share of preferred stock.
3. Compute the total amount of the dividend available to be distributed to the common stockholders.
4. Compute the amount of the dividend to be paid on each share of common stock.
5. Compute the amount of dividends in arrears (if any) that preferred stockholders may expect from future declarations of dividends.

PROBLEM 20–3B
(Obj. 5)

Tutorial

Issuing stock at par for cash and noncash assets. Kaye Steele and Kevin King are equal partners in the Steele Music Center, a retail store selling records and tapes. Steele and King have decided to form the Modern Music Corporation to take over the operation of the Steele Music Center on December 31, 19X3. The corporation is authorized to issue 2,000 shares of no-par common stock with a stated value of $50 a share and 1,000 shares of $100 par-value, 12 percent preferred stock that is noncumulative and nonparticipating.

Certain assets are revalued so that the accounts will reflect current values. Steele and King will each receive 100 shares of Modern Music Corporation preferred stock at par value ($100) and sufficient $50 par-value shares of common stock to cover the partners' adjusted net investment in the partnership.

The trial balance shown below was prepared after the firm's accounting records were closed at the end of its fiscal year on December 31, 19X3, and the assets were revalued as agreed on.

STEELE MUSIC CENTER
Trial Balance
December 31, 19X3

ACCOUNT NAME	DEBIT	CREDIT
Cash	6 000	
Accounts Receivable	14 750	
Allowance for Doubtful Accounts		250
Merchandise Inventory	51 000	
Furniture and Equipment	22 900	
Accumulated Depr.—Equipment		1 100
Accounts Payable		13 300
Kaye Steele, Capital		40 000
Kevin King, Capital		40 000
Totals	94 650	94 650

Instructions

1. In the corporation's general journal, record a memorandum entry describing its formation on December 31, 19X3.
2. Make general journal entries as of December 31 to show the takeover of the assets and liabilities of the partnership and the issuance of stock in payment to Kaye Steele and Kevin King. Use the same account titles that the partnership used for assets and liabilities. Also use the following new account titles: Common Stock and Preferred Stock.

PROBLEM 20–4B
(Obj. 5, 6, 7, 9)

Issuing stock at par for cash and noncash assets, issuing stock at premium, recording organization costs, and preparing Stockholders' Equity section of balance sheet. The Staples Corporation, a new corporation, took over the assets and liabilities of the Christine Staples Supply Company on January 2, 19X4. The assets and liabilities assumed, after appropriate revaluation by Staples, were as follows.

Cash	$ 1,000
Accounts Receivable	80,000
Allowance for Doubtful Accounts	(3,000)
Merchandise Inventory	165,000
Accounts Payable	(88,000)
Accrued Expenses Payable	(2,000)

The corporation is authorized to issue 250,000 shares of no-par-value common stock with a stated value of $15 a share and 50,000 shares of $10 par-value preferred stock. The preferred stock bears a preference dividend of $1.20 per share each year. The transactions entered into at the time the corporation was formed follow.

Instructions

1. Prepare general journal entries to record the transactions.
2. Prepare the opening balance sheet as of January 2, 19X4, for the Staples Corporation.

TRANSACTIONS

Jan. 2 The corporation issued to Christine Staples common stock with a stated value equal to her net equity in the sole proprietorship business, and the corporation took over Staples's assets and liabilities.

2 Issued 100 shares of preferred stock to Christine Staples for her services in organizing the corporation. The agreed-upon value of these services was $1,000.

2 Issued 1,000 shares of common stock to Mark Hannah. He paid $15,000 in cash for the stock.

2 Issued 1,000 shares of preferred stock to Frank Petrillo. He paid $10,000 in cash for the stock.

2 Paid $800 to Mary Butler, the attorney who prepared the articles of incorporation and the corporate bylaws, for her services.

PROBLEM 20-5B
(Obj. 5, 6, 7, 8, 10)

Issuing stock at par, issuing stock at a premium, recording organization costs, drafting Stockholders' Equity section of balance sheet, and recording stock subscriptions. Party Time Supply Store Corporation was organized on January 2, 19X3, to operate a chain of party supply stores. The firm is authorized to issue 20,000 shares of $20 par-value common stock and 9,000 shares of $50 par-value, 13 percent preferred stock. The preferred stock is noncumulative and nonparticipating. Selected transactions that took place during January 19X3 are given below.

Instructions

1. Set up the following general ledger accounts.
   101 Cash
   114 Subscriptions Receivable—Common Stock
   115 Subscriptions Receivable—Preferred Stock
   301 Common Stock
   302 Common Stock Subscribed
   305 Paid-in Capital in Excess of Par Value—Common
   311 Preferred Stock
   312 Preferred Stock Subscribed
   315 Paid-in Capital in Excess of Par Value—Preferred
2. Record the transactions listed below in general journal form and post them to the general ledger accounts.
3. Prepare the Stockholders' Equity section of a balance sheet for Party Time Supply Store as of January 31, 19X3.

TRANSACTIONS

Jan. 2 The corporation received its corporate charter. (Make a memorandum entry.)

3 Issued 1,000 shares of common stock for cash at $20 a share to John DeLorenzo.

3 Issued 500 shares of preferred stock for cash at $50 a share to Lynn Hodges.

10 Issued 200 shares of common stock for cash at $21 a share to Mark LaSalle.

10 Received a subscription for 500 shares of common stock at $21 a share from Janet Thompson, payable in two installments due in 5 and 15 days.
14 Received a subscription for 400 shares of preferred stock at $52 a share from George Wesley, payable in two installments due in 10 and 20 days.
15 Received payment of a stock subscription installment due from Janet Thompson (one-half of purchase price—see January 10 transaction).
24 Received payment of a stock subscription installment due from George Wesley (one-half of purchase price—see January 14 transaction).
25 Received the balance due on the stock subscription of January 10 from Janet Thompson; issued the stock.

CHALLENGE PROBLEM

Just after its formation on August 1, 19X4, the ledger accounts of the Beauty Products Corporation contained the following balances.

Accrued Expenses	$ 5,000
Accounts Payable	40,000
Accounts Receivable	22,000
Allowance for Doubtful Accounts	2,000
Building	100,000
Cash	16,000
Common Stock ($25 par)	151,300
Common Stock Subscribed	8,000
Furniture and Fixtures	25,000
Merchandise Inventory	100,000
Notes Payable—Short Term	25,000
Organization Costs	3,000
Paid-in Capital in Excess of Par—Common	6,000
Paid-in Capital in Excess of Par—Preferred	3,000
Preferred Stock (10%, $50 par)	25,000
Preferred Stock Subscribed (10%, $50 par)	10,000
Subscriptions Receivable—Common Stock	4,100
Subscriptions Receivable—Preferred Stock	5,200

The corporation is authorized to issue 50,000 shares of $25 par common stock and 5,000 shares of 10 percent, $50 par preferred stock (noncumulative and nonparticipating).

Instructions

1. Answer the following questions:
   a. How many shares of common stock are outstanding?
   b. How many shares of common stock are subscribed?
   c. How many shares of preferred stock are outstanding?
   d. How many shares of preferred stock are subscribed?

e. At what average price has common stock been subscribed or issued?
f. Assume that no dividends are paid in the first year of the corporation's existence. What are the rights of the preferred stockholders?
g. Assuming that all of the Paid-in Capital in Excess of Par—Common was applicable to the shares of common stock that have been subscribed but not yet issued, what was the subscription price per share of the common stock subscribed?
h. Assuming that the board of directors declared no dividends in 19X4, what amount would have to be paid the preferred stockholders in 19X5 before any dividend could be paid to the common stockholders?

2. Prepare a classified balance sheet for the corporation just after its formation on August 1, 19X4.

CRITICAL THINKING PROBLEM

The Stockholders' Equity section of Atlantic Corporation's balance sheet at the close of the current year follows.

Stockholders' Equity	
Preferred stock (8%, $100 par value, 30,000 shares authorized)	
At Par Value (10,000 shares issued)	$1,000,000
Paid-in Capital in Excess of Par Value	130,000
Common Stock (no-par value, stated value of $5, 200,000 shares authorized)	
At Stated Value	750,000
Paid-in Capital in Excess of Stated Value	3,300,000
Retained Earnings	1,400,000
Total Stockholders' Equity	$6,580,000

1. What is the amount of the annual dividend on the preferred stock? Per share? In total?
2. How many shares of common stock have been issued?
3. What was the average price paid by the stockholders for the preferred stock?
4. What was the average price paid by the stockholders for the common stock?
5. How many shares of common stock are currently outstanding (held by stockholders)?
6. If total dividends of $287,200 were paid to stockholders in the current year, how much was paid to the common stockholders? In total? Per share? Assume that no preferred dividends are in arrears.

C H A P T E R

21

Corporate Earnings and Capital Transactions

O B J E C T I V E S

1. Estimate the federal corporate income tax and prepare journal entries related to income taxes.
2. Compute and record amortization of organization costs.
3. Complete a worksheet for a corporation.
4. Record adjusting and closing entries for a corporation.
5. Prepare an income statement for a corporation.
6. Record the declaration and payment of cash dividends.
7. Record the declaration and issuance of stock dividends.
8. Record stock splits.
9. Record appropriations of retained earnings.
10. Record receipt by a corporation of donated assets.

The principal difference between accounting for a corporation and for a sole proprietorship or a partnership is that the owners' equity accounts for a corporation are more complex. As pointed out in Chapter 20, the owners' equity in a corporation, called stockholders' equity, consists of two major classifications.

1. ***Paid-in capital,*** representing the amount of capital acquired from capital stock transactions
2. *Retained earnings,* representing the accumulated profits retained in the business and not distributed as dividends

We have seen that the fundamental accounting equation, Assets = Liabilities + Owners' Equity, can be restated to reflect the two major types of owners' equity explained above.

Assets = Liabilities + (Paid-in Capital + Retained Earnings)

N E W T E R M S

Appropriation of retained earnings ▪ Book value ▪ Common stock dividend distributable ▪ Declaration date ▪ Deferred income taxes ▪ Donated capital ▪ Extraordinary, nonrecurring items ▪ Paid-in capital ▪ Payment date ▪ Record date ▪ Statement of retained earnings ▪ Statement of stockholders' equity ▪ Stock dividend ▪ Stock split ▪ Stockholders of record ▪ Treasury stock

11. Record the purchase of treasury stock.
12. Prepare financial statements for a corporation.
13. Define the accounting terms new to this chapter.

Several different accounts for each category of stockholders' equity may be needed to reflect different sources of equity. The most important source of paid-in capital is the issuance of capital stock in return for cash or other assets. Chapter 20 discussed transactions involving issuance of stock. In this chapter, we shall examine the most typical transactions affecting retained earnings. In addition, certain transactions that involve both paid-in capital and retained earnings will be analyzed.

CORPORATE INCOME TAXES

OBJECTIVE 1
Estimate the federal corporate income tax and prepare journal entries related to income taxes.

You learned in Chapter 20 that one disadvantage of the corporate form of organization is that corporations must pay federal income taxes and, usually, state income taxes on their profits. Some local governments also levy corporate income taxes.

The income on which the income tax is based may be calculated differently for state, local, and federal tax purposes. In general, however, the basic principles are the same, and in many cases the state or local income tax is based directly on the taxable income shown on the federal income tax return. The procedures used to account for federal taxes and for state and local taxes are identical. For the sake of simplicity, we shall therefore ignore state and local taxes and illustrate the handling of federal taxes only.

Federal Income Tax Rates

Federal income tax rates are changed periodically by Congress. As of this writing, the federal rates are:

- On the first $50,000 of taxable income, 15 percent
- On the next $25,000 of taxable income, 25 percent
- On the next $25,000 of taxable income, 34 percent
- On the next $235,000 of taxable income, 39 percent
- On all taxable income over $335,000, 34 percent

Federal income tax rates are changed periodically.

Some types of income receive special tax treatment. Interest earned on state and local bonds held for investment is not taxed at all. Some expenses also are computed differently for financial accounting and income tax purposes. For example, straight-line depreciation is deducted for financial accounting purposes while accelerated cost recovery system (ACRS) or modified accelerated cost recovery system (MACRS) deductions may be taken on the tax return. In addition, the period for deducting other expenses or the time for reporting income may differ between the tax return and the financial statements. As a result, the income tax rates cannot simply be applied to the financial net income to arrive at the tax owed to the government for the period.

Taxable income often differs from income reported in the financial statements.

Quarterly Tax Estimates

Corporations must prepay their income taxes through quarterly tax deposits.

Corporations are required to estimate their income taxes in advance for each year and to deposit one-fourth of the estimated amount to a federal depository each quarter during the year. Total quarterly deposits must equal at least 90 percent of the tax liability for the year. Penalties are assessed for underpayment or late payment. The due dates of the four deposits for a corporation reporting on the calendar year are April 15, June 15, September 15, and December 15.

The quarterly payments of estimated taxes are debited to Income Tax Expense and credited to Cash. Suppose that early in 19X3 Webb Office Workstation estimated that its tax liability for the year would be $11,000. As a result, a deposit of $2,750 was made each quarter. The entry on April 15 would be as follows.

19X3				
Apr.	*15*	*Income Tax Expense*	2 7 5 0 00	
		Cash		2 7 5 0 00
		Paid quarterly estimate of income taxes		

Income Tax Expense
Apr. 15 2,750
June 15 2,750
Sep. 15 2,750
Dec. 15 2,750

An identical entry would be made for each of the other quarterly payments. At the end of 19X3 the Income Tax Expense account shows a balance of $11,000 before adjusting entries have been made.

This balance of $11,000 is shown in the Trial Balance section of the December 31, 19X3, worksheet of Webb Office Workstation (see Figure 21–1 on pages 738–739).

Year-End Adjustment of Tax Liability

When the books are closed at the end of the year, the income tax is reestimated and the Income Tax Expense account is adjusted.

At the end of the year, when the worksheet is being completed and the financial statements prepared, the tentative tax expense for the year is computed, based on the facts known at that time. The difference between the end-of-year tax computation and the amounts that have been deposited quarterly as estimated taxes represents the additional tax that is unrecorded or the amount by which taxes have been overpaid.

1. If the tax computed at the time the worksheet is completed exceeds the total of quarterly deposits that have been made, an adjustment will be made debiting Income Tax Expense and crediting Income Taxes Payable for the difference. For example, if at the end of 19X3 Webb Office Workstation Corporation computes its tax for the year to be $11,324, the corporation has underpaid its taxes by $324 in quarterly deposits that totaled only $11,000.

Tax liability for the year	$11,324
Quarterly payments	11,000
Additional tax due	$ 324

The necessary adjusting journal entry will be as shown below.

19X3				
Dec.	*31*	*Income Tax Expense*	3 2 4 00	
		Income Tax Payable		3 2 4 00

2. If the tax computed at the end of the year is less than the total of quarterly deposits, the necessary adjustment will result in a debit to Income Tax Refund Receivable and a credit to Income Tax Expense. For example, if Webb made tax deposits of $12,000 during 19X4 and at the end of the year the tax liability is computed to be $10,600, the following entry would be made.

19X4					
Dec.	*31*	*Income Tax Refund Receivable*		*1 4 0 0 00*	
		Income Tax Expense			*1 4 0 0 00*

When the income tax return is filed, the actual tax for the year may differ from the year-end estimate.

Note that the adjustment above is made at the time the worksheet is completed and the financial statements are prepared. Because the tax return is quite complex and there are many differences between taxable income and financial income, the computation made at the time the worksheet is prepared also may be described as an estimate. The final tax return is due on March 15 (although permission is automatically given by the tax authorities to extend this due date). When the return is completed, it is quite likely that the total tax bill will be more than or less than the computation made on December 31. This difference is usually treated as a debit or credit to the Income Tax Expense Account.

To illustrate, suppose that during 19X5 Sanaray Corporation made quarterly deposits for estimated tax totaling $16,000. When the worksheet was prepared, the accountant estimated that the tax expense for the year would be $16,800, so the following adjusting entry was made.

19X5					
Dec.	*31*	*Income Tax Expense*		*8 0 0 00*	
		Income Tax Payable			*8 0 0 00*

Assume further that when the 19X5 tax return was filed on March 15, 19X6, the actual tax for the year was $16,600. A check for $600, the difference between the tax for the year ($16,600) and the amount paid through quarterly deposits ($16,000) was sent to the Internal Revenue Service. The following entry would be made.

19X6					
Mar.	*15*	*Income Tax Payable*		*8 0 0 00*	
		Cash			*6 0 0 00*
		Income Tax Expense			*2 0 0 00*
		Pay balance of federal			
		income tax due			

Note that as a result of these entries, the Income Tax Expense account for 19X6 has been credited for $200 that actually applies to 19X5. However, these differences are generally minor and will not result in a material misstatement of income.

Reporting Income Tax Expense on the Income Statement

Income taxes may be shown as an operating expense or as a deduction from Net Income Before Income Tax.

Income Tax Expense may be shown in the corporate income statement in one of two ways.

1. It may be treated as a deduction from Net Income Before Income Tax at the bottom of the income statement. This is the traditional presentation and is used in this book. For example, refer to the income statement of Webb Office Workstation Corporation (Figure 21–2 later in this chapter), which shows Income Tax Expense as a deduction from Net Income Before Income Tax.
2. Income Tax Expense may be shown as an operating expense to emphasize that taxes represent a cost of doing business. Many larger corporations use this presentation today.

Deferred Income Taxes

As we have already discussed, income reported on the financial statements often does not agree with income reported on the tax return because tax laws do not always follow generally accepted accounting principles. Some common examples are given below.

- The taxpayer may be permitted to deduct an expense on the tax return in the current year even though the expense will not be deducted on the financial statements until a later year.
- An expense may be deductible on the financial statements prior to the time it is deductible on the tax return.
- Income received in advance is almost always taxed in the year received, while for financial accounting purposes it is reported as income over the period to which it applies.

To provide a fair presentation of net income after taxes each year to users of the corporation's financial statements, accountants have developed the concept of **deferred income taxes.** In accordance with this concept, each year they show as an expense on the income statement the ultimate tax liability related to the net income that appears on the income statement that year. The difference between the tax actually paid during the period and the amount that will ultimately be paid on the net income for the period is reported as the deferred tax amount. This most complex and controversial topic is discussed in most intermediate accounting textbooks. In this book, we will assume that the income shown on the income statement and the income reported on the tax return are essentially the same, making the recording of deferred taxes unnecessary.

AMORTIZATION OF ORGANIZATION COSTS

In addition to income tax expense, another item that may be found on the income statement of a corporation but not of a sole proprietorship is Amortization of Organization Costs. You will recall from Chapter 20 that certain costs incurred in forming a corporation are

OBJECTIVE 2
Compute and record amortization of organization costs.

Organization costs are often amortized over a 60-month period because this amortization period is allowed for federal income tax purposes.

capitalized as Organization Costs. These costs include attorneys' fees, expenses of the organizers, the charter fee, and similar items.

Organization costs are amortized over some arbitrary period—frequently a 60-month period beginning with the month in which the corporation begins business. The 60-month period is permitted for federal income tax purposes and is therefore chosen by many corporations as the amortization period for financial accounting. Webb Office Workstation Corporation, which began operations in January 19X4, incurred organization costs of $1,000. The costs were capitalized in the Organization Costs account. The board of directors decides to amortize the costs over a period of 60 months. At the end of each year, 19X4 through 19X8, $200 (12/60 × $1,000) will be charged to Amortization of Organization Costs, an expense account, as part of the adjustment process.

19X4					
Dec.	*31*	*Amortization of Org. Costs*		*200 00*	
		Organization Costs			*200 00*
		Amortize organization			
		costs for 12 months			

The account, Amortization of Organization Costs, may be treated as a part of general and administrative expenses, or it may be shown in a separate category entitled Other Expenses. On the balance sheet on December 31, 19X4, Webb Corporation will show the remaining $800 balance in the Organization Costs account under the heading "Intangible Assets."

COMPLETING THE CORPORATE WORKSHEET

OBJECTIVE 3
Complete a worksheet for a corporation.

The worksheet prepared at the end of the period for a corporation is almost identical to that prepared for a sole proprietorship or a partnership. The major difference results from the necessity to compute and show the income tax adjustment. The worksheet for Webb Office Workstation Corporation for 19X4 is shown in Figure 21–1. Observe that this worksheet has only eight money columns, in contrast to the 10-column worksheets that you have used in previous chapters. It is common for the experienced accountant to omit the Adjusted Trial Balance columns and to enter the adjusted amounts directly in the Income Statement and Balance Sheet sections. The obvious disadvantage of omitting the Adjusted Trial Balance section is that errors in adding and subtracting adjustment amounts are more difficult to detect.

The following steps are used in completing the worksheet. Study the worksheet carefully as you read the description of each step.

Step 1. The trial balance is recorded in the Trial Balance section on the worksheet. To save space, General Expenses and Selling Expenses control accounts, rather than individual expense accounts, have been used in this illustration.

The Trial Balance section contains a few accounts with which you may be unfamiliar, but you will learn about these accounts later.

Step 2. All adjustments except the adjustment to Income Tax Expense are entered in the Adjustments columns on the worksheet. The adjustment to Income Tax Expense is entered later. The adjustments in Figure 21–1 are self-explanatory.

Step 3. The balances of all income and expense amounts, except Income Tax Expense, are extended to the Income Statement section of the worksheet. The totals of the Debit column and the Credit column of the Income Statement section are calculated on a separate paper. The totals are not entered on the worksheet. The difference between the two totals represents the corporation's net income or net loss before income taxes have been considered.

At this point, the Income Statement columns of the worksheet will contain the following information.

All income and expense items except Income Tax Expense are extended to the Income Statement section of the worksheet so that net income before income taxes can be easily computed.

	Income Statement	
	Debit	Credit
Sales		920,000
Purchases	628,000	
Selling Expenses	165,200	
General Expenses	92,305	
Amortization of Organization Costs	200	
Income Summary	100,000	131,000
Totals	985,705	1,051,000

The difference of $65,295 between the total of the Credit column ($1,051,000) and the total of the Debit column ($985,705) is the net income before income tax.

Step 4. Based on the $65,295 of net income determined in step 3 and assuming that there are no differences between financial income and taxable income, we can compute the income tax rounded to the nearest dollar as follows:

Tax on first $50,000 of income @ 15%	$ 7,500
Tax on next $15,295 ($65,295 – $50,000) @ 25%	3,824
Total tax on $65,295	$11,324

The $324 difference between the $11,324 income tax expense for the year and the total of $11,000 that has been paid through quarterly deposits is recorded as an adjustment, with a debit to Income Tax Expense and a credit to Income Tax Payable.

Step 5. After the item to record the additional tax payable of $324 is entered in the Adjustments columns, those columns are totaled. The balance of Income Tax Expense is extended to the Debit column of the Income Statement section of the worksheet.

FIGURE 21–1
A Completed, Eight-Column Worksheet

WEBB OFFICE WORKSTATION CORPORATION
Worksheet
Year Ended December 31, 19X4

ACCOUNT NAME	TRIAL BALANCE		ADJUSTMENTS	
	DEBIT	CREDIT	DEBIT	CREDIT
Cash	9975 00			
Accounts Receivable	86000 00			
Allowance for Doubtful Accounts		180 00		(c) 4400 00
Merchandise Inventory	100000 00		(b) 131000 00	(a) 100000 00
Prepaid Insurance	2800 00			(d) 1400 00
Land	30000 00			
Buildings	36000 00			
Accumulated Depreciation—Buildings		1200 00		(e) 1200 00
Equipment and Fixtures	36000 00			
Accumulated Depr.—Equip. and Fixt.		2000 00		(f) 2000 00
Organization Costs	800 00			(h) 200 00
Accounts Payable		28800 00		
Dividends Payable—Preferred		10800 00		
Dividends Payable—Common		8000 00		
Accrued Expenses Payable				(g) 4100 00
Income Tax Payable				(i) 324 00
Preferred Stock—12%, $100 Par		90000 00		
Paid-in Cap. in Excess of Par—Pref.		6000 00		
Common Stock, $50 Par		100000 00		
Paid-in Cap. in Excess of Par—Common		8000 00		
Retained Earnings		17200 00		
Sales		920000 00		
Purchases	628000 00			
Selling Expenses (control)	157300 00		(c) 4400 00	
			(d) 1000 00	
			(e) 1000 00	
			(f) 1500 00	
General and Adm. Expenses (control)	87105 00		(d) 400 00	
			(e) 200 00	
			(f) 500 00	
			(g) 4100 00	
Amortization of Organization Costs			(h) 200 00	
Income Tax Expense	11000 00		(i) 324 00	
Income Summary			(a) 100000 00	(b) 131000 00
	1,184980 00	1,184980 00	244624 00	244624 00
Net Income After Income Tax				

INCOME STATEMENT		BALANCE SHEET		
DEBIT	CREDIT	DEBIT	CREDIT	
		9 9 7 5 00		1
		86 0 0 0 00		2
			4 5 8 0 00	3
		131 0 0 0 00		4
		1 4 0 0 00		5
		30 0 0 0 00		6
		36 0 0 0 00		7
			2 4 0 0 00	8
		36 0 0 0 00		9
			4 0 0 0 00	10
		6 0 0 00		11
			28 8 0 0 00	12
			10 8 0 0 00	13
			8 0 0 0 00	14
			4 1 0 0 00	15
			3 2 4 00	16
			90 0 0 0 00	17
			6 0 0 0 00	18
			100 0 0 0 00	19
			8 0 0 00	20
			17 2 0 0 00	21
	920 0 0 0 00			22
628 0 0 0 00				23
				24
				25
				26
165 2 0 0 00				27
				28
				29
				30
92 3 0 5 00				31
2 0 0 00				32
11 3 2 4 00				33
100 0 0 0 00	131 0 0 0 00			34
997 0 2 9 00	1,051 0 0 0 00	330 9 7 5 00	277 0 0 4 00	35
53 9 7 1 00			53 9 7 1 00	36
1,051 0 0 0 00	1,051 0 0 0 00	330 9 7 5 00	330 9 7 5 00	37
				38

Step 6. The Debit and Credit columns of the Income Statement section are totaled. The difference between the totals is the Net Income After Taxes for the year.

Step 7. The adjusted balances of the asset, liability, and stockholders' equity accounts are extended to the Balance Sheet columns. The Net Income After Income Tax is extended to the Credit column of the Balance Sheet section. The worksheet is then completed in the same manner as the worksheet for a sole proprietorship.

ADJUSTING AND CLOSING ENTRIES

OBJECTIVE 4
Record adjusting and closing entries for a corporation.

Net Income After Income Taxes is transferred from the Income Summary account to Retained Earnings.

Based on the adjustments shown on the worksheet, the adjusting entries are recorded in the same way as those for a sole proprietorship or a partnership. The closing entries for the corporation also are prepared from the information assembled on the worksheet and recorded in the same way as they are for a sole proprietorship or a partnership, except for the final entry. The last closing entry for a corporation transfers the net income after income taxes (or the net loss) from the Income Summary account to Retained Earnings.

The Retained Earnings account accumulates profits and losses of the business. The December 31, 19X4, entries for Webb Office Workstation Corporation are shown below. They are taken from the worksheet in Figure 21–1. Compare the journal entries to the worksheet to see how the information for the journal entries is prepared.

FIGURE 21–2
Adjusting and Closing Entries

GENERAL JOURNAL PAGE *38*

	DATE		DESCRIPTION	POST. REF.	DEBIT	CREDIT	
1	*19X4*						1
2			*Adjusting Entries*				2
3			*(Entry a)*				3
4	*Dec.*	*31*	*Income Summary*		*100 0 0 0 00*		4
5			*Merchandise Inventory*			*100 0 0 0 00*	5
6							6
7			*(Entry b)*				7
8		*31*	*Merchandise Inventory*		*131 0 0 0 00*		8
9			*Income Summary*			*131 0 0 0 00*	9
10							10
11			*(Entry c)*				11
12		*31*	*Selling Expense (Control)*		*4 4 0 0 00*		12
13			*Allow. for Doubtful Accts.*			*4 4 0 0 00*	13
14							14
15			*(Entry d)*				15
16		*31*	*Selling Expenses (Control)*		*1 0 0 0 00*		16
17			*General Expenses (Control)*		*4 0 0 00*		17
18			*Prepaid Insurance*			*1 4 0 0 00*	18
19							19

(Continued)

FIGURE 21–2 (Continued)
Adjusting and Closing Entries

GENERAL JOURNAL PAGE *38*

DATE	DESCRIPTION	POST. REF.	DEBIT	CREDIT
	(Entry e)			
31	*Selling Expenses (Control)*		1,000.00	
	General Expenses (Control)		200.00	
	Allow. for Depr.—Bldgs.			1,200.00
	(Entry f)			
31	*Selling Expenses (Control)*		1,500.00	
	General Expenses (Control)		500.00	
	Allow. for Depr.—Furn.			
	and Equipment			2,000.00
	(Entry g)			
31	*General Expenses (Control)*		4,100.00	
	Accrued Expenses Payable			4,100.00
	(Entry h)			
31	*Amortization of Org. Costs*		200.00	
	Organization Costs			200.00
	(Entry i)			
31	*Income Tax Expense*		324.00	
	Income Tax Payable			324.00
	Closing Entries			
31	*Sales*		920,000.00	
	Income Summary			920,000.00
31	*Income Summary*		897,029.00	
	Purchases			628,000.00
	Selling Exp. (Control)			165,200.00
	General Exp. (Control)			92,305.00
	Amort. of Org. Costs			200.00
	Income Tax Expense			11,324.00
31	*Income Summary*		53,971.00	
	Retained Earnings			53,971.00

THE CORPORATE INCOME STATEMENT

After the worksheet is completed, the financial statements of the corporation are prepared. At this point, we are concerned with only one financial statement—the income statement. We will postpone examination of the other financial statements because, before we do so, we want to discuss some accounts with which you are not yet familiar.

OBJECTIVE 5
Prepare an income statement for a corporation.

The income statements of most corporations look almost exactly like the income statement of a sole proprietorship. The major difference is that the corporation must pay income taxes, so the corporate income statement contains a deduction for income tax expense.

FIGURE 21–3
A Corporate Income Statement

WEBB OFFICE WORKSTATION CORPORATION
Income Statement
Year Ended December 31, 19X4

Sales		*920 0 0 0 00*
Cost of Goods Sold:		
Inventory, January 1, 19X4	*100 0 0 0 00*	
Purchases	*628 0 0 0 00*	
Goods Available for Sale	*728 0 0 0 00*	
Less Inventory, Dec. 31, 19X4	*131 0 0 0 00*	
Cost of Goods Sold		*597 0 0 0 00*
Gross Profit on Sales		*323 0 0 0 00*
Expenses		
Selling Expenses	*165 2 0 0 00*	
General and Admin. Expenses	*92 3 0 5 00*	
Amortization of Org. Costs	*2 0 0 00*	*257 7 0 5 00*
Net Income Before Income Tax		*65 2 9 5 00*
Income Tax Expense		*11 3 2 4 00*
Net Income After Income Tax		*53 9 7 1 00*

The income statement for Webb Office Workstation for the year ending December 31, 19X4, illustrated in Figure 21–3, is prepared from the worksheet shown in Figure 21–1. Note that Income Tax Expense is deducted from Net Income Before Income Tax to arrive at the final figure, Net Income After Income Tax.

Variations in Income Statement Presentation

The exact form of income statements used by different corporations varies. Some common variations are summarized below.

- Corporations sometimes do not include a gross profit section in their income statements. Instead, the cost of goods sold is treated in the same manner as operating expenses. In this book the traditional income statement with a separate gross profit section will be used.
- As we have already seen, Income Tax Expense may be shown as an operating expense rather than as a deduction from Net Income Before Income Tax. This presentation may be used in order to emphasize that income taxes are a cost of doing business, like any other expense.
- If a gain or loss results from a transaction that is highly unusual, is clearly unrelated to routine operations, and is not expected to occur again in the near future, the gain or loss should be shown in a separate section entitled ***Extraordinary, Nonrecurring***

Items. Such items as gains or losses from fires, floods, or other casualties and gains or losses from the retirement of bonds payable (discussed in Chapter 22) are extraordinary items. These are items that do not occur frequently and that clearly are not related to the normal operations of the business.

An income statement containing extraordinary items is illustrated in Figure 21–4. This statement shows the net income from operations, the income tax expense related to operating income, and the net income from operations after income tax. After this, the gross amount of each extraordinary item of gain or loss is shown. The related effect of the extraordinary gain or loss on income taxes (the amount by which income taxes increased or decreased as a result of the extraordinary gain or loss) is offset against the gross amount of each gain or loss to arrive at the amount of gain or loss "net of taxes."

FIGURE 21–4
An Income Statement Showing Extraordinary Items

BRISTOL CORPORATION
Partial Income Statement
Year Ended December 31, 19X3

Net Income from Operations			
Before Income Taxes			278 220 00
Income Taxes Applicable to			
Operating Income			91 756 00
Net Income from Operations			
After Income Taxes			186 464 00
Extraordinary Gains and Losses			
Add Gain on Condemnation of			
Land by City	10 000 00		
Less Federal Taxes on Gain	3 900 00	6 100 00	
Deduct Tornado Loss on			
Building	8 000 00		
Less Federal Tax Reduction	3 120 00	4 880 00	
Excess of Extraordinary Gains			
over Losses			1 220 00
Net Income for Year			187 684 00

SELF-REVIEW

1. Explain the two major classifications of stockholders' equity.
2. A corporation's taxable income is $120,000. Compute the federal income tax on this income using the rates on page 732.
3. Why is the adjustment to Income Tax Expense not entered on the worksheet at the same time as other adjustments?
4. Explain briefly why "deferred income taxes" arise.
5. What are "extraordinary gains and losses"?

Answers to Self-Review

1. Paid-in capital arises from transactions involving the corporation's capital stock. Retained earnings represent the accumulated profits, less distributions to shareholders.
2. Tax on first $50,000 @ 0.15 = $7,500; tax on next $25,000 @ 0.25 = $6,250; tax on next $25,000 @ 0.34 = $8,500; tax on next $20,000 @ 0.39 = $7,800 for a total of $30,050.
3. The net income before taxes must be determined before the tax liability can be computed. This can be done only after all other adjustments have been entered.
4. Deferred taxes arise because the taxes actually paid during a year may not reflect the ultimate tax that will be paid on the net income reported that year for financial accounting purposes.
5. Extraordinary gains and losses are items that do not result from routine operations, are unusual, and do not regularly recur.

RETAINED EARNINGS

Retained Earnings represents the accumulated profits that may be distributed as dividends to shareholders.

A sole proprietor's capital investment is recorded in the owner's capital account. The net income or net loss for the period and the owner's withdrawals during the period are closed into the capital account. Similarly, the net income, net losses, and withdrawals of a partnership are closed into the partners' capital accounts. Thus for a sole proprietorship or a partnership there is no distinction in the accounting records between different sources of capital, or of reasons for increases or decreases in capital. There are, however, legal and financial distinctions between the different sources and uses of capital of a corporation. This is why the profits and losses of a corporation are accumulated in Retained Earnings, separate and apart from the capital paid in by the stockholders.

The Retained Earnings account does not represent a cash fund.

Stockholders usually expect to receive a portion of the profits of the corporation through dividends. Dividends are charged to the Retained Earnings account. Thus the balance of Retained Earnings reflects the cumulative profits and losses of the corporation, less distributions to stockholders. Certain other transactions may also affect the Retained Earnings account. We will explain some of these transactions later in this chapter. It is important for you to remember that Retained Earnings does not represent a cash fund. Retained earnings are reinvested in inventory, plant and equipment, and various other types of assets. A corporation may have a large cash balance, but no retained earnings. Conversely, it may have a large balance in the Retained Earnings account, but no cash.

Cash Dividends

Shareholders usually receive a share of profits of the corporation through cash dividend distributions. In some corporations the board of directors will establish a policy of making regular cash dividend distributions to stockholders, perhaps at the same amount, or a

OBJECTIVE 6
Record the declaration and payment of cash dividends.

A regular dividend policy helps to stabilize the market price of a corporation's stock.

gradually increasing amount, per share each year. Frequently dividends are paid quarterly or semiannually. Many companies, however, need to retain their earnings to finance growth and reinvestment and do not pay cash dividends. This is especially true in the first several years of a corporation's existence, a time when the company usually grows rapidly and needs to use all available cash in its operations. A regular dividend policy tends to make the stock more attractive to investors and may help avoid sharp fluctuations in the stock's market price.

Dividend Policy

The board of directors of a corporation has broad powers in declaring and paying dividends. The board must weigh two basic considerations in connection with ordinary dividends—their legality and their financial feasibility.

State laws govern the circumstances under which a corporation may declare dividends.

Legality. State laws differ with respect to the conditions under which a board of directors can declare a dividend. In general, the corporation must have accumulated earnings in order to declare and pay dividends. Laws limiting the payment of dividends to stockholders are generally intended to protect the corporation's creditors. The restrictions prevent an impairment of the corporation's capital that would occur if dividends were paid that would reduce total stockholders' equity to an amount less than that originally credited to the paid-in capital accounts.

Financial Feasibility. Even if a corporation has accumulated earnings, the earnings may have been invested in plant and equipment, inventories, or other assets. Although payment of dividends is sometimes made in noncash assets, dividend payments almost always require cash. The board of directors must examine the corporation's financial position and not declare a dividend that would lead to a shortage of cash or to other financial difficulties.

The declaration date is the date on which the directors declare a dividend.

Dates Relevant to Dividends

Three dates are involved in declaring and paying dividends. The first is the **declaration date**—the date of the board of directors' meeting at which formal action is taken to declare the dividend. The dividend declaration is recorded in the corporation's minute book. Once notice of the board's action in declaring a dividend has been given to the stockholders (for example, by an announcement in the newspapers), the corporation has a liability to the stockholders for the amount of the declared dividend. If statements are prepared before the dividend is paid, the amount payable appears on the balance sheet as a current liability.

The names of specific shareholders to receive dividends are determined by ownership on the record date.

The second date is the **record date.** On this date the capital stock ledger is analyzed and a list is made of the stockholders (called **stockholders of record**) to whom dividends will be paid on a still later date, the **payment date.**

Information Block: Ethics in Accounting

They Don't Need It Now

O'Neil Fabrication, Inc. (OFI), is a large U.S.-based steel fabrication company. Recently the company has experienced some difficulty in financing expansion and updating its production facilities. The company is likely to reduce its work force by about 10 percent due to this updating and expansion.

Fred Fry, the treasurer of OFI, is responsible for securing the financing for this project. After dealing with several financial institutions, Fry determines that the cost of borrowing the needed money on the open market or from the financial institutions is too high for OFI.

Declaration of a Cash Dividend

Suppose the board of directors of the Webb Office Workstation Corporation meets on December 1, 19X4, and declares cash dividends of $12 per share on the preferred stock and $4 per share on the common stock. The dividends are payable the following January 15 to stockholders of record on December 31. On the declaration date (December 1, 19X4), the company has 900 shares of preferred stock and 2,000 shares of common stock outstanding. The dividend declaration is recorded as shown below.

19X4					
Dec.	*1*	*Retained Earnings*		*10 8 0 0 00*	
		Dividends Pay.—Preferred			*10 8 0 0 00*
		Dividend declaration of			
		$12 per share on 900			
		shares, payable Jan. 15 to			
		holders of record Dec. 31			
	1	*Retained Earnings*		*8 0 0 0 00*	
		Dividends Pay.—Common			*8 0 0 0 00*
		Dividend declaration of $4			
		per share on 2,000 shares,			
		payable on Jan. 15 to			
		holders of record Dec. 31			

The declaration of a cash dividend reduces stockholders' equity (retained earnings).

Retained Earnings is debited and a separate liability account is credited for the dividends payable to each class of stockholders.

One of Fry's other responsibilities is the management of the employee pension plan. As Fry ponders his options to finance the expansion, Donna O'Neil, the president of OFI, enters his office. Fry summarizes the results of his inquiries into outside funding. O'Neil points out that as the manager of the pension fund Fry could simply authorize a loan for the money from the employee pension fund at a reasonable interest rate (one the company could afford at the current time).

1. What is the ethical issue?
2. What are the alternatives?
3. Who are the affected parties?
4. How do the alternatives affect the parties?
5. What should Fry do?

The dividends payable accounts will appear on the balance sheet as current liabilities on December 31, as shown in the balance sheet presented later in this chapter (Figure 21–6, page 759).

Payment of a Cash Dividend

On the record date, December 31, the accounts in the capital stock ledger are analyzed, and a list is made of the stockholders on that date and the number of shares each owns. This analysis is made to determine the amount of the dividend due each investor. On January 15, the payment date, the dividend checks are issued to the stockholders on the list. The total effect of these checks is shown below.

19X5				
Jan.	*15*	*Dividends Payable—Preferred*	*10 8 0 0 00*	
		Dividends Payable—Common	*8 0 0 0 00*	
		Cash		*18 8 0 0 00*
		Payment of cash dividends		

Stock Dividends

OBJECTIVE 7

Record the declaration and issuance of stock dividends.

A corporation that has accumulated profits may actually be short of cash or unable to pay a cash dividend. In other cases, the board of directors may prefer to make part of the corporation's retained earnings a permanent part of its capital. In this case the board of directors may reward stockholders by declaring a **stock dividend,** which is a distribution of the corporation's own stock on a pro rata basis.

Suppose that on December 3, 19X5, the board of directors of Webb Corporation declares a stock dividend payable the following January 20 to common stockholders of record on December 28, at the rate of one new share of common stock for each ten shares held. On the declaration date, there are 2,000 shares outstanding, so 200 additional shares will be issued.

When a stock dividend is declared, the total amount charged to the Retained Earnings account is the estimated market value of the shares to be issued. Assuming that each share of Webb stock is expected to have a market value of $54, a total of $10,800 (200 shares × $54 market value) would be charged to Retained Earnings. The par value of the shares, $10,000 (200 shares × $50 par), is credited to a new equity account entitled **Common Stock Dividend Distributable.** The $800 excess of the market value over the stated value ($10,800 − $10,000 = $800) is credited to Paid-in Capital in Excess of Par Value—Common Stock. (Some companies credit this excess to a new capital account entitled Paid-in Capital from Common Stock Dividends.) The entry that records the corporation's obligation to issue the new shares of common stock is shown below.

19X5				
Dec.	*3*	*Retained Earnings*	*10 8 0 0 00*	
		Common Stock Dividend		
		Distributable		*10 0 0 0 00*
		Paid-in Capital in Excess of		
		Par Value—Common		*8 0 0 00*
		Declaration of 10% stock		
		dividend, distributable on		
		Jan. 20 to holders of		
		record on Dec. 28		

The Stock Dividend Distributable account is part of stockholders' equity.

The balance in the Common Stock Dividend Distributable account appears on the December 31 balance sheet as a part of Paid-in Capital. It is not shown as a current liability, as was the case with cash dividends payable, but appears in the Stockholders' Equity section with the common stock. This presentation is illustrated below.

Common Stock ($50 par value, 5,000 shares authorized)	
Issued and outstanding, 2,000 shares	$100,000
Distributable as stock dividend, 200 shares	10,000
Paid-in Capital in Excess of Par	800
	$110,800

On December 28 the stockholders' names are listed, along with the number of shares each owns and the number of new shares each is to receive as the stock dividend. For example, Henry Gonzalez, who owns 200 shares of common stock, will receive 20 new shares as his stock dividend.

On January 20, a stock certificate is prepared for each stockholder on the list, and the 200 shares are distributed. This issuance of stock is recorded by the general journal entry that follows.

19X6				
Jan.	20	Common Stock Dividend Distributable	10 0 0 0 00	
		Common Stock		10 0 0 0 00
		Distribution of stock dividend		

A stock dividend does not change the total stockholders' equity, nor does it change the percentage of ownership of any stockholder.

The effect of issuing a stock dividend is to convert a portion of the firm's retained earnings to permanent capital.

Since no assets enter or leave the corporation and no liabilities are involved, the total book value belonging to the owners of common stock is the same as it was before. However, the book value of each share of common stock is less because there are now more shares of common stock outstanding. **Book value** for each share is computed by dividing the total book value applicable to a class of stock by the number of shares outstanding. Each stockholder has the same total book value after the stock dividend as before, but each owns more shares of stock with a proportionately smaller book value per share.

Sometimes a stock's price does not decrease as much after a stock dividend as it theoretically should.

For example, assume that Alice Wilson, who owns 100 shares out of a total of a corporation's 2,000 shares outstanding (100 shares/2,000 shares = 5 percent of the total), receives a 10 percent stock dividend (100 shares × 0.10 = 10 shares) so that her total ownership is now 110 shares. After the stock dividend, a total of 2,200 shares will be outstanding. Her share of ownership is still 5 percent (110 shares/2,200 shares). Since the corporation's assets, liabilities, and profits have not changed, Alice Wilson is in the same ownership position as before, except that she has more shares to show for her 5 percent ownership. In theory, a stock dividend would result in a proportionate reduction in the market value of each share. Sometimes, because a lower price per share may result in a wider market for the shares and because investors associate stock dividends with successful corporations, the stock price will decline less than it should in theory. As a result, the total market value of the shares owned by a stockholder may increase slightly.

Stock Splits

OBJECTIVE 8

Record stock splits.

A stock split results in a reduction of the par value or stated value and the issuance of a proportionately larger number of shares.

In recent years an increasing number of corporations have made **stock splits.** Under this procedure, the corporation issues two or more shares of new stock to replace each share outstanding without making any changes in the capital accounts.

A stock split often is made by the directors because the market price of the stock has increased to such a point that it is relatively difficult to sell the stock. Stock splits ordinarily involve no-par-value stock, but they can be made with par-value stock. If par-value stock is split, the corporation's charter must be amended to change the par value.

To understand a stock split involving no-par stock, assume that the Carson Corporation is authorized to issue 200,000 shares of no-par stock, to which the directors have assigned a stated value of

If par-value stock is split, the corporate charter must be revised to reduce the par value of the shares.

$100 a share. The number of shares actually issued and outstanding is 30,000. On December 1, 19X3, the market price of the stock is $330 a share. The board of directors feels that if the price of the stock were lower, the shares would have a wider market. Accordingly, on that date, the board declares a 4-for-1 split and reduces the stated value to $25 a share. Three new shares are to be issued for each share outstanding. The shares will be issued on December 31, 19X3, to holders of record December 15, 19X3. The result will be that a stockholder who formerly owned one share of stock with a stated value of $100 will own four shares of stock with a stated value of $25 a share. Theoretically, the market price will also decrease to one-fourth of the original market value, or to $82.50 a share. However, as in the case of stock dividends, the new price may be a little higher than the theoretical price. Stockholders realize no income from the stock split, and the balances in the capital accounts of the corporation are unaffected.

On the date of declaration of the stock split, a memorandum notation is made in the general journal of Carson Company.

19X3					
Dec.	*1*	*On this date the board of directors declared a 4-for-1 stock split and reduced the stated value of common stock from $100 to $25 a share. Total outstanding shares will now be 120,000.*			

A stock split does not require a monetary entry in the accounts.

On December 31 another memorandum entry is made in the general journal to note issuance of the new shares.

19X3					
Dec.	*31*	*On this date 90,000 shares of common stock were issued, as declared by the directors on December 1, 19X3.*			

An entry is made in the Common Stock account in the general ledger to indicate that the stated value is now $25 a share and that 120,000 shares are outstanding instead of the original 30,000 shares. It will also be necessary to change the stockholders' records to reflect the number of shares now held by each stockholder.

Appropriations of Retained Earnings

The amount in the Retained Earnings account provides one indication of a corporation's ability to pay dividends because dividends are generally distributions of retained earnings. However, all or part of retained earnings is usually reinvested in plant assets or working capital. Even the cash on hand may be needed for some future transaction. As a result, the directors may find it desirable to restrict divi-

OBJECTIVE 9
Record appropriations of retained earnings.

An appropriation of retained earnings reduces the amount of retained earnings available for dividend declarations.

dend payments. In other cases, distribution of dividends may be restricted by contract—for example, in connection with a bond issue. In still other circumstances, such as when treasury stock is purchased, as discussed later in this chapter, the restriction on dividends may be required by law. How can these limitations be indicated on the financial statements?

One way of presenting such information is by adding a footnote to the balance sheet. The footnote states that management's plans or contractual obligations will probably affect the dividends that will be declared. A more formal way for the board of directors to show this intention is to make an **appropriation of retained earnings** by a formal resolution.

Suppose, for example, that after several years of successful operations, the directors of the Webb Corporation foresee the need to build a warehouse costing $150,000 within the next five years. Construction of the new building will put a financial strain on the corporation. The directors therefore wish to restrict dividend payments and to notify the stockholders that the new storage facility is to be built and that dividends are to be restricted. A resolution is passed at a board meeting on November 5, 19X4, to order the transfer of $30,000 from Retained Earnings to a Retained Earnings Appropriated for Warehouse Construction account. Similar appropriations will be made during each of the next four years.

The resolution appropriating $30,000 in 19X4 for the warehouse would be recorded in the minutes and would serve as the accountant's authorization to make the general journal entry shown below. A similar entry is made during each of the succeeding four years.

19X4					
Nov.	*5*	*Retained Earnings*		*30 0 0 0 00*	
		Ret. Earnings Appropriated			
		for Warehouse Constr.			*30 0 0 0 00*
		Appropriation for construction made by board of directors on Nov. 5			

The balance sheet presentation of Retained Earnings indicates the amounts appropriated and unappropriated. The specific appropriated amounts are listed under the "Appropriated" heading. Assume that Retained Earnings for the Webb Office Workstation Corporation amounted to $66,371 before the first appropriation was made. The following illustration shows how the figures would appear on a balance sheet prepared immediately thereafter.

Retained Earnings	
Appropriated	
Appropriated for Warehouse Construction	$30,000
Unappropriated	36,371
Total Retained Earnings	$66,371

An appropriation of retained earnings does not mean that cash or other assets have been set aside in a fund.

Notice that the Total Retained Earnings figure is the same as before, but it is now divided into two parts—the appropriated portion from which dividends cannot, for the moment at least, be declared and the unappropriated balance available for any purpose. Remember that the balance of retained earnings does not represent a cash balance, nor does appropriating retained earnings provide cash for any desired purpose. The availability of cash therefore influences the timing of the actual work of building the new warehouse.

When the purpose for which an appropriation was made has been accomplished, the appropriation may be transferred back to unappropriated retained earnings.

Assume that cash is available and that the warehouse construction project is completed in 19X9 at a cost of $171,000. The effect of the project has been to increase plant assets by $171,000 and to decrease Cash by that amount. The balance in the Retained Earnings Appropriated for Warehouse Construction account has not been affected. Now that the project is finished, the board of directors can pass another resolution to return the amount of the appropriated retained earnings to unappropriated retained earnings. When such a resolution has been adopted, the entry shown below is made in the general journal, assuming that $30,000 has been appropriated in each of the five prior years.

19X9					
Aug.	*7*	*Ret. Earnings Appropriated for*			
		Warehouse Construction		*150 0 0 0 00*	
		Retained Earnings			*150 0 0 0 00*
		Close appropriations			
		account as ordered by			
		board of directors in			
		meeting of Aug. 7			

The board can use the appropriation technique to notify stockholders of its intention to undertake virtually any type of activity that will affect the amount and probability of dividends. When the purpose for which retained earnings have been appropriated is attained, the board can direct that the reserve account be closed and that the amount be transferred back to Retained Earnings.

SELF-REVIEW

1. What criteria must be met for an item to be classified as extraordinary?
2. What is meant by the date of record? By the declaration date?
3. When a cash dividend is declared, what accounts are debited and credited?
4. What effect does a stock dividend have on an individual shareholder's share of ownership in a corporation?
5. Does an appropriation of retained earnings include a transfer of cash to a restricted account? Explain.

Answers to Self-Review

1. To be classified as extraordinary, an item must be of an unusual nature and occur infrequently.
2. The date of record is the date on which it is determined exactly which shareholders will receive dividends. The owners of stock as of the close of business on that date will receive the dividends. The declaration date is the date on which the board of directors formally declares a dividend.
3. When a cash dividend is declared, the Retained Earnings account is debited and the Dividends Payable account is credited.
4. None. A stock dividend does not change the total stockholders' equity in a corporation nor does it change the ownership of any individual shareholder.
5. No. An appropriation of retained earnings has nothing to do with cash. The appropriation merely indicates that a portion of retained earnings is not available for dividend distribution.

OTHER CAPITAL TRANSACTIONS

Many other transactions affect the stockholders' equity of a corporation. Most of these transactions are encountered infrequently. As the accounting rules related to them are quite technical, they are discussed in advanced accounting texts. There are, however, two other types of transaction that occur often that we address: the donation of assets to a corporation and the purchase by a corporation of treasury stock (shares of its own outstanding stock).

Donations of Capital

OBJECTIVE 10
Record receipt by a corporation of donated assets.

An asset that is donated to the corporation is recorded at its fair market value and is credited to Donated Capital.

Property may be given to a corporation. This often occurs when a community that wishes to attract new industry gives the corporation a plant site, or even a building, as an inducement for the corporation to move to the community. An asset received as a gift is recorded in the accounting records of the corporation at the asset's fair market value. The offsetting credit is made to a paid-in capital account entitled **Donated Capital.**

The general journal entry below indicates how a gift of a plant site valued at $25,000 is recorded by a corporation.

19X7					
Jan.	*2*	*Land*		*25 000 00*	
		Donated Capital			*25 000 00*
		Appraised value of plant			
		site donated by city			

On the balance sheet the Donated Capital account is shown as a new category under paid-in capital, following the accounts related to preferred stock and to common stock.

Information Block: International Accounting

Doing Business in Canada and Mexico

What better place to start doing business internationally than across the border in Canada or Mexico? Many U.S. businesses agree. Total U.S. trade is $171 billion with Canada and $52 billion with Mexico. Both countries are among the top five trading partners with the United States for imports and exports. In fact, the United States, Canada, and Mexico have agreed to the North American Free Trade Agreement, which creates the largest free trade area in the world.

The United States is the principal trading partner with Canada, representing over 70 percent of their total trade. Canada is a major industrialized nation that generally welcomes foreign investment and trade. It has a stable government with moderate inflation and a relatively strong Canadian dollar. The labor force is highly educated and skilled and enjoys a high standard of living. The country has extensive natural resources supplying industries such as fishing, forestry, mining, agriculture, and mineral fuels, as well as a large manufacturing sector, particularly in motor vehicles.

All business forms are acceptable in Canada, including licensing, direct trading, proprietorship, partnership, branch of a U.S. corporation, or a foreign-owned Canadian company. Generally accepted accounting

Treasury Stock

OBJECTIVE 11
Record the purchase of treasury stock.

Treasury stock is a corporation's own capital stock that has been reacquired. The reacquired stock must have been previously paid for in full and issued to a stockholder in order to be considered treasury stock. Any class or type of stock can be reacquired as treasury stock. No dividends, voting rights, or liquidation preferences apply to treasury stock.

There are many reasons why a company might purchase its own stock. Some common reasons are given below.

- The corporation has extra cash and the board of directors thinks that the corporation's own stock is a better investment than other potential investments. The corporation does not pay itself dividends on treasury stock. The stockholders benefit when the corporation repurchases common stock because there will be fewer shares of outstanding stock to share the profits and dividends. If preferred stock is reacquired, the dividends on the stock are no longer payable, thus increasing the amount available to owners of common stock.

principles and practices in Canada are similar to those in the United States because of the close economic ties between the two countries. Both English and French are official languages of business in Canada.

The United States is also the principal trading partner with Mexico, representing 60 to 70 percent of their total trade. U.S. trade with Mexico has been increasing rapidly, with Mexico importing almost as much from the United States as Japan. Mexico has become a desirable country for business because of its low costs, trainable labor force, stable government, favorable investment climate, strong government efforts to reduce inflation, lower trade barriers, and close proximity to the United States. The Mexican literacy rate is 87 percent, one of the highest in Latin America. Typical business forms are Mexican corporations, licensing agreements, joint ventures, and export for resale. Mexican accounting principles are substantially similar to those in the United States, except that financial statements must also be restated to reflect the effects of inflation in Mexico. Spanish is the national language in Mexico.

A hot spot for business has been the area near the U.S.–Mexico border, where 1,500 manufacturing plants have been started by U.S., European, and Japanese businesses. These plants employ half a million Mexicans. The plants buy almost all their new materials and parts from the United States and export their products from Mexico. The automotive industry is betting that Mexico can provide cost savings and superior quality. In a recent year, one million vehicles were produced in Mexico. By the end of the decade, about one in every six automobiles is expected to be produced in Mexico.

- The corporation may wish to use treasury stock to transfer to officers and key employees in connection with incentive plans. If unissued shares were used for this purpose, it would be necessary to ask the stockholders to give up their preemptive rights. However, preemptive rights do not apply to treasury stock.
- Sometimes treasury stock is reacquired to create a demand for the corporation's stock and thus to increase its market value.
- In small, privately held corporations having few owners, the board of directors may vote to purchase the shares of a stockholder who needs cash or of a stockholder who wishes to retire.

To qualify as treasury stock, the reacquired shares must have been fully paid for and issued before being reacquired.

Recording the Purchase of Treasury Stock

When treasury stock is purchased, the Treasury Stock account is debited for the entire amount paid. A separate treasury stock account is kept for each class of stock. For example, the repurchase of 100 shares of $100 par preferred stock for $105 per share in cash on July 10, 19X5, is recorded as follows by Webb Corporation.

19X5					
Jan.	*10*	*Treasury Stock—Preferred*		*10 5 0 0 00*	
		Cash			*10 5 0 0 00*
		Purchased 100 shares of			
		treasury stock			

On the balance sheet, the cost of treasury stock is deducted from the sum of all items in the Stockholders' Equity section (see Figure 21–6 on page 759).

Appropriation of Retained Earnings for Treasury Stock

The purchase of treasury stock reflects a payment to a shareholder and thus reduces capital. In order to protect creditors against stockholder withdrawals disguised as treasury stock purchases, some states require that retained earnings must be appropriated in an amount equal to the cost of treasury stock. As a result of this requirement, if a corporation does not have retained earnings greater than the purchase price, it cannot purchase treasury stock. Thus, if the state in which the Webb Corporation is incorporated requires an appropriation of retained earnings equal to the cost of treasury stock, the following entry would be required.

19X5					
Jan.	*10*	*Retained Earnings*		*10 5 0 0 00*	
		Ret. Earnings Appropriated—			
		Treasury Stock			*10 5 0 0 00*
		To appropriate retained			
		earnings equal to purchase			
		price of preferred			
		treasury stock			

The proper treatment of treasury stock and of retained earnings appropriated because the company holds treasury stock is shown on the December 31, 19X5, balance sheet of Webb Office Workstation Corporation (Figure 21–5).

An Illustrative, Real-Life Case

Many large, well-known corporations have reacquired significant amounts of their own capital stock. The magnitude of the amounts involved is illustrated by Exxon Corporation's stock repurchase plan. The December 31, 1991, balance sheet of the corporation showed that the company had issued 1,813 million shares of its no-par common stock and had reacquired 571 million shares, or 31.5 percent of the total issued, and held them in its treasury. The reacquired shares of common stock were repurchased by the corporation for $16,774 million. Exxon Corporation's total stockholders' equity before deducting the cost of treasury stock was $51,701 million. After deducting the cost of treasury stock, the stockholders' equity was $34,927 million.

FINANCIAL STATEMENTS FOR A CORPORATION

OBJECTIVE 12
Prepare financial statements for a corporation.

Four financial statements are usually prepared for a corporation: the income statement, the statement of retained earnings, the balance sheet, and the statement of cash flows. You have already seen the income statement of Webb Office Workstation Corporation for the year 19X4 (Figure 21–2). Now we move ahead two years to the end of 19X6 and examine the statement of retained earnings and the balance sheet of that corporation. These statements will reflect some of the transactions that you have studied in this chapter. The statement of cash flows will be explained in Chapter 25.

The Statement of Retained Earnings

The statement of retained earnings shows all the changes that have occurred in the retained earnings accounts during the year.

Because of the importance of retained earnings to the corporation and to the stockholders, a **statement of retained earnings** should be presented as part of the financial statements. This statement shows all changes that have occurred in both the appropriated and unappropriated retained earnings accounts during the period.

The statement of retained earnings begins with the balance of Retained Earnings (unappropriated) as of the first day of the period and shows all the changes that have occurred in that account during the period. Then each appropriated retained account is analyzed.

This format is followed in the statement of retained earnings of the Webb Office Workstation Corporation for the year ended December 31, 19X6, which is shown in Figure 21–5 on page 758.

The opening balance of Retained Earnings was $93,571. The net income after taxes ($96,000) for 19X6 is the only increase in retained earnings during the year. The Retained Earnings account balance was reduced by $61,100 as a result of the following:

- Dividends on preferred stock, $9,600
- Dividends on common stock, $11,000
- Appropriation for warehouse construction, $30,000
- Appropriation for treasury stock purchased, $10,500

Note that the statement of retained earnings reconciles each account representing an appropriation of retained earnings. At the end of 19X6, Webb Corporation had two such accounts: Retained Earnings Appropriated for Warehouse Construction and Retained Earnings Appropriated for Treasury Stock.

Since the statement of retained earnings shows changes in each account, only the ending balances of each appropriated retained earnings account and of the unappropriated retained earnings account are shown on the balance sheet.

Many accountants prefer to combine the statement of retained earnings with the income statement. In the combined statement of income and retained earnings, the beginning balance of Retained Earnings is added to the net income after taxes for the period. All

FIGURE 21-5
A Statement of Retained Earnings

WEBB OFFICE WORKSTATION CORPORATION
Statement of Retained Earnings
Year Ended December 31, 19X6

Unappropriated Retained Earnings:			
Balance, January 1, 19X6	93 571 00		
Add: Net Income After Taxes for 19X6	96 000 00	189 571 00	
Deductions:			
Dividends on Preferred Stock	9 600 00		
Dividends on Common Stock	11 000 00		
Transfer to Appropriation for Warehouse Construction	30 000 00		
Transfer to Appropriation for Treasury Stock	10 500 00	61 100 00	
Total Unappropriated Retained Earnings, December 31, 19X6			128 471 00
Appropriated Retained Earnings:			
Appropriated for Warehouse Construction:			
Balance, January 1, 19X6	30 000 00		
Add Appropriation for the Year	30 000 00		
Balance, December 31, 19X6		60 000 00	
Appropriated for Treasury Stock:			
Balance, January 1, 19X6	—0—		
Add Appropriation for the Year	10 500 00		
Balance, December 31, 19X6		10 500 00	
Total Appropriated Retained Earnings, December 31, 19X6			70 500 00
Total Retained Earnings, December 31, 19X6			198 971 00

The statement of stockholders' equity reconciles the beginning and ending balance of each major type of stockholders' equity.

other amounts are shown in the same way as on the separate statement of retained earnings.

Publicly held corporations, and some privately owned corporations, include in their financial reports not only a statement of retained earnings, but also a **statement of stockholders' equity** (often referred to as an *analysis of changes in stockholders' equity*). This statement exists because the Securities and Exchange Commission requires publicly held corporations to disclose the reasons for major changes in equity. Corporations find that the most convenient way to make the required disclosure is to include an analysis reconciling the beginning and ending balance of each of the stockholders' equity accounts. There is, however, no specified form for the statement, and various types of schedules are used.

The Corporate Balance Sheet

In Chapter 20 we illustrated how the corporate balance sheet of Webb Office Workstation Corporation would look just after the firm's formation. Since that time we have discussed a number of other stockholder equity accounts. Let's now see how the corporate balance sheet would appear after considering some of these new accounts. The balance sheet of Webb Office Workstation Corporation on December 31, 19X6, is shown in Figure 21–6.

FIGURE 21–6
An End-of-Year Balance Sheet

WEBB OFFICE WORKSTATION CORPORATION
Balance Sheet
December 31, 19X6

Assets			
Current Assets			
Cash		48 200 00	
Accounts Receivable	123 000 00		
Less Allow. for Doubtful Accounts	4 300 00	118 700 00	
Merchandise Inventory		209 371 00	
Prepaid Insurance		3 000 00	
Total Current Assets			379 271 00
Property, Plant, and Equipment			
Land		30 000 00	
Buildings	36 000 00		
Less Accumulated Depr.—Bldgs.	6 000 00	30 000 00	
Equipment and Fixtures	36 000 00		
Less Accum. Depr.—Equip. and Fixtures	8 000 00	28 000 00	
Total Property, Plant, and Equipment			88 000 00
Intangible Assets			
Organization Costs			2 000 00
Total Assets			467 471 00
Liabilities and Stockholders' Equity			
Current Liabilities			
Accounts Payable		44 000 00	
Dividends Payable—Preferred		9 600 00	
Dividends Payable—Common		11 000 00	
Accrued Expenses Payable		4 800 00	
Income Tax Payable		1 200 00	
Total Current Liabilities			70 600 00

(Continued)

FIGURE 21–6 (Continued)
An End-of-Year Balance Sheet

Stockholders' Equity			
Paid-in Capital			
Preferred Stock (9%, $100			
par value, 10,000 shares authorized)			
Issued 900 Shares (of which			
100 shares are held as treasury stock)	90 000 00		
Paid-in Capital in Excess of			
Par Value—Preferred	6 800 00	96 800 00	
Common Stock ($50 par value, 5,000 shares authorized)			
Issued and Outstanding, 2,200 Shares	110 000 00		
Paid-in Capital in Excess			
of Par Value—Common	1 600 00	111 600 00	
Total Paid-in Capital		208 400 00	
Retained Earnings			
Appropriated			
For Treasury Stock Purchase	10 500 00		
For Warehouse Construction	60 000 00		
Total Appropriated	70 500 00		
Unappropriated	128 471 00		
Total Retained Earnings		198 971 00	
		407 371 00	
Deduct Treasury Stock, Preferred (100 shares at cost)		10 500 00	
Total Stockholders' Equity			396 871 00
Total Liabilities and Stockholders' Equity			467 471 00

The asset accounts on the December 31, 19X6, balance sheet are the same as those on the initial balance sheet shown in Figure 20–1 (page 705). The new liability accounts include Income Tax Payable, Dividends Payable—Preferred, and Dividends Payable—Common. The new accounts in the stockholders' equity section are those related to retained earnings and the Treasury Stock account. Note that the balances shown for unappropriated retained earnings and for the two appropriations of retained earnings are the ending amounts shown for these items on the statement of retained earnings (Figure 21–5).

MANAGERIAL IMPLICATIONS

Managers must understand exactly what enters into the computation of corporate net income. Otherwise, they may not interpret the statement figures correctly and may make unwise decisions.

Managers must also be thoroughly familiar with the legal and accounting aspects of dividends. They need to understand the desirability of developing a dividend policy that gives appropriate consideration to legal requirements and restrictions and to financial feasibility. Stock dividends offer management an opportunity to limit the distribution of cash, while at the same time making a distribution to shareholders. Stock dividends also provide a means for transforming a part of retained earnings into permanent capital. Both stock dividends and stock splits provide the means to reduce the price per share of the company's outstanding stock and, in doing so, to make the stock more marketable.

Managers should know about the use of appropriated accounts to inform stockholders about restrictions on retained earnings. At the same time, they should realize that the mere appropriation of retained earnings does not in any way guarantee that the necessary cash will be on hand.

It is extremely important for management to understand how treasury stock purchases can be used to enhance the value of the stock held by other shareholders. They also need to understand how treasury stock can be used to achieve such objectives as making it possible to offer stock to officers and key employees under stock-purchase plans.

SELF-REVIEW

1. How is capital donated to a corporation?
2. Is treasury stock an asset of the corporation? Explain.
3. What is meant by "appropriating retained earnings"?
4. Does an appropriation of retained earnings represent a cash fund? Explain.
5. What is the relationship between the statement of retained earnings of a corporation and the corporation's balance sheet?

Answers to Self-Review

1. Donated capital usually arises when assets are given to the corporation. For example, a city may give the corporation land on which to build a plant in order to attract the corporation to the city.
2. No. Treasury stock represents assets transferred to shareholders and is therefore a deduction from stockholders' equity.
3. Appropriating retained earnings refers to the placing of restrictions on retained earnings that would otherwise be available for dividends.
4. No. Retained earnings represents net assets (assets minus liabilities). A corporation may have a large balance of retained earnings but no cash.
5. The ending balance of each of the appropriated retained earnings accounts and of the unappropriated retained earnings as shown in the statement of retained earnings appears on the balance sheet.

CHAPTER 21 Review and Applications

CHAPTER SUMMARY

Two major classifications of corporate capital are paid-in capital—representing capital acquired from capital stock transactions—and retained earnings—the accumulated profits and losses of the business.

Corporations pay income taxes to the federal government and to the governments of many states and cities. They are required to prepay their income taxes through quarterly payments during the year. The payments are charged to Income Tax Expense. On the income statement, Income Tax Expense is usually deducted from Net Income Before Taxes to arrive at Net Income After Taxes. Some corporations, however, treat income tax expense in the same way as any operating expense.

Organization costs are amortized over some predetermined period, frequently 60 months because this amortization period is allowed for federal income tax purposes.

The worksheet for a corporation is similar to that for sole proprietorships and partnerships. The net income after taxes is closed into the Retained Earnings account. Retained earnings reflect the accumulated, undistributed profits of the corporation and are the source of dividend distributions. On the date cash dividends are declared, the amount involved is charged to Retained Earnings and credited to Dividends Payable, a current liability account.

Stock dividends represent the issuance of additional shares of common stock to stockholders. Stock dividends do not affect the relative ownership or total book value of the common stockholders or of any one stockholder. It is to be expected that the market price of the shares will decrease in proportion to the number of new shares issued; however, sometimes the market price does not drop as much as it theoretically should. In this case the total market value of a shareholder's stock may increase.

The major financial statements of the corporation are the income statement, the statement of retained earnings, the balance sheet, and the statement of cash flows. In addition, some corporations prepare a statement of stockholders' equity. The statement of retained earnings reconciles the beginning and ending balances of each appropriated retained earnings account and of the unappropriated retained earnings account. The statement of stockholders' equity reconciles the beginning and ending balance of each category of stockholders' equity.

GLOSSARY OF NEW TERMS

Appropriation of retained earnings (p. 751) A formal declaration of an intention to restrict dividends

Book value (p. 749) The value of a share of stock that is calculated by dividing the total equity applicable to a class of stock by the number of shares outstanding

Common stock dividend distributable (p. 748) Equity account used to record par, or stated, value of shares to be issued

Declaration date (p. 745) The date on which the board of directors declares a dividend

Deferred income taxes (p. 735) The difference between the tax actually payable during a period and the amount that will ultimately be paid on net income for the period

Donated capital (p. 753) Capital resulting from the receipt of gifts by a corporation

Extraordinary, nonrecurring items (p. 742) Transactions clearly unrelated to routine operations

Paid-in capital (p. 731) Capital acquired from stock transactions

Payment date (p. 745) The date on which dividends are paid

Record date (p. 745) The date on which the specific stockholders to receive a dividend are determined

Statement of retained earnings (p. 757) A financial statement that shows beginning and ending balances, along with changes that have occurred in both the appropriated and unappropriated retained earnings accounts during the period

Statement of stockholders' equity (p. 758) A financial statement that provides an analysis of changes in equity

Stock dividend (p. 747) Distribution of the corporation's own stock on a pro rata basis

Stock split (p. 749) An increase in the number of shares, which has no effect on capital accounts

Stockholders of record (p. 745) Shareholders to whom dividends are to be paid

Treasury stock (p. 754) A corporation's own capital stock that has been issued, fully paid for, and reacquired

REVIEW QUESTIONS

1. What accounting treatment is recommended for quarterly payments of estimated income taxes?
2. At the end of the year, what entries are necessary if the quarterly tax deposits are more than the income tax as computed at the time the worksheet is completed and the financial statements prepared?
3. Explain the three dates related to declaration and payment of a cash dividend.
4. Compare the effects on stockholders' equity of a cash dividend and a stock dividend.

5. When a stock dividend is declared, what journal entry is made? How is the amount of the dividend measured?
6. How is the Common Stock Dividend Distributable account classified on the balance sheet?
7. Explain the difference between a stock split and a stock dividend.
8. What effect does a stock split have on retained earnings? Explain.
9. What effect does an appropriation have on total retained earnings? Explain.
10. Several years ago a corporation made an appropriation of retained earnings because of a building project. The building project was completed in the current year. What accounting entry will probably be made with respect to the appropriation?
11. As an inducement for Penrol Corporation to locate in Central City, the Penrol Industrial Development Committee gave the corporation a tract of land with a fair market value of $100,000. How is the gift accounted for?
12. What is treasury stock? How is it shown on the balance sheet?
13. What information is shown on the statement of retained earnings?
14. What is the purpose of the statement of stockholders' equity?

MANAGERIAL FOCUS

1. Why would managers be interested in establishing a policy of regular dividend payments?
2. Assume that you are the controller of a corporation. Some members of the board of directors have asked you how the firm can have a large balance in the Retained Earnings account but no cash with which to pay dividends. Explain.
3. A corporation's balance sheet shows Retained Earnings Appropriated for Plant Expansion with a balance of $800,000. Does this mean that the corporation has set aside $800,000 in cash to expand its plant? Explain.
4. Assume that the director of a corporation where you work has asked you how an appropriation of retained earnings will help the corporation accumulate funds to achieve a specific purpose. What explanation would you give to the director?
5. The president of a corporation suggests to the controller that one way to convert retained earnings into permanent capital is to have a stock split. What explanation should the controller give to the president?
6. The management of the O'Riley Corporation wishes to know why its common stock held as treasury stock should not be shown on the balance sheet as an asset since the stock has a ready market value. Explain.
7. Why would the management of a corporation consider using corporate funds to purchase the firm's own outstanding stock?

EXERCISES

EXERCISE 21-1 (Obj. 1)

Estimating corporation income tax. After all revenue and expense accounts, other than Income Tax Expense, have been extended to the Income Statement section of the worksheet of Akim Corporation, the revenues exceed the expenses by $187,000. Using the tax rates given in this chapter, compute the corporation's federal income taxes payable. (Assume that the firm's taxable income is the same as its income for financial accounting purposes.)

EXERCISE 21-2 (Obj. 1)

Tutorial

Recording journal entries related to taxes. A corporation has paid estimated income taxes of $22,000 during the year 19X4. At the end of the year, the corporation's tax bill is computed to be $19,800. Give the general journal entry to adjust the Income Tax Expense account.

EXERCISE 21-3 (Obj. 2)

Tutorial

Amortizing organization costs. Pogo Corporation was formed and began business in June 19X3. Organization costs of $3,000 were incurred in forming the corporation. The board of directors wishes to amortize the costs over the same period as used on the federal income tax return. Give the journal entry on December 31, 19X3, to record amortization for the year.

EXERCISE 21-4 (Obj. 4)

Tutorial

Recording closing of Income Summary. After the revenue and expense accounts were closed into Income Summary on December 31, 19X4, the Income Summary account showed a net loss for the year of $34,000. Give the general journal entry to close the Income Summary account.

EXERCISE 21-5 (Obj. 6)

Tutorial

Recording cash dividends. On November 30, 19X3, the board of directors of the Celebrity Photographic Corporation declared a cash dividend of $1 a share on its 30,000 outstanding shares of common stock. The dividend is payable on December 31, 19X3, to stockholders of record on December 8, 19X3. Give any general journal entries necessary on November 30, December 8, and December 31.

EXERCISE 21-6 (Obj. 7)

Tutorial

Recording a stock dividend. The Warren Corporation had outstanding 50,000 shares of $5 par-value common stock on December 3, 19X3. On that date, it declared a 10 percent common stock dividend distributable on December 30 to stockholders of record on December 15. The estimated market value of the shares at the time of their issue was $12 a share. Give any general journal entries necessary on December 3, December 15, and December 30.

EXERCISE 21-7 (Obj. 8)

Tutorial

Recording a stock split. The Environmental Safety Corporation had outstanding 100,000 shares of no-par-value common stock, with a stated value of $10, on December 1, 19X3. The company voted to split the stock on a 2-for-1 basis, issuing one new share to stockholders for each share presently owned. The estimated market value of the new shares will be $14.50. Give any general journal entry required on December 31.

EXERCISE 21-8 (Obj. 9)

Recording appropriation of retained earnings. On December 31, 19X3, the board of directors of the Akroid Corporation voted to appropriate $50,000 of retained earnings each year for five years to establish a reserve for contingencies. Give the general journal entry on December 31, 19X3, to record the appropriation.

EXERCISE 21-9 (Obj. 9)

Closing appropriation of retained earnings. Because of fears about the outcome of several lawsuits in progress during the years 19X1 through 19X7, Tina Tot Corporation had appropriated retained earnings of $99,000, transferring that amount from the Retained Earnings account to the Retained Earnings Appropriated for Contingencies. In October 19X7 the lawsuits were settled and Tina Tot Corporation paid $66,000 to settle the suits. The board of directors breathed a sigh of relief and on November 1, 19X7, passed a resolution that the appropriation was no longer needed. Give the necessary journal entry on November 1 to close the appropriation account.

EXERCISE 21-10 (Obj. 10)

Recording receipt of property as gift. The city of Oakville contributed to the Van Ness Corporation a tract of land on which to build a plant. When the contribution was made on August 10, 19X3, the land's fair market value was $80,000. Give the general journal entry, if any, necessary to record the contribution.

EXERCISE 21-11 (Obj. 11)

Purchasing treasury stock. On August 31, 19X3, the Miami Corporation had outstanding 100,000 shares of 9 percent preferred stock with a par value of $10. The stock was originally issued for $10.40 a share. On that date the corporation repurchased 4,000 shares of the preferred stock, paying cash of $10.30 per share for the stock. Give the general journal entry to record the repurchase of the treasury stock.

EXERCISE 21-12 (Obj. 12)

Preparing Stockholders' Equity section of balance sheet. The following are selected accounts from the general ledger of Rosco's Pizza Parlor on December 31, 19X4. Show how the corporation's Stockholders' Equity section would appear on the December 31, 19X4, balance sheet.

Common Stock, $50 par, authorized 2,000 shares, issued and outstanding 2,000 shares	$100,000
Paid-in Capital in Excess of Par Value—Common	4,000
Retained Earnings (debit balance)	(17,000)

PROBLEMS

PROBLEM SET A

PROBLEM 21-1A (Obj. 1, 6)

Tutorial GL

Recording federal income tax transactions and cash dividend transactions. Selected transactions of the Davila Corporation during 19X4 are given below. Record them in the general journal.

TRANSACTIONS

Mar. 15 Filed the federal income tax return for 19X3. The total tax for the year was $54,000. During 19X3 quarterly deposits of estimated tax totaling $50,000 had been made. The additional tax of $4,000 was paid with the return. On December 31, 19X3, the accountant had estimated the total tax for 19X3 to be $52,000 and had recorded a liability of $2,000 for federal income tax payable.

Apr. 15 Paid first quarterly installment of $9,000 on 19X4 estimated federal income tax.

May 4 Declared dividend of $0.75 per share on the 15,000 shares of common stock outstanding. The dividend is payable on June 10 to stockholders of record as of May 25.

June 10 Paid dividend declared on May 4.

June 15 Paid second quarterly installment of $9,000 on 19X4 estimated federal income tax.

Sept. 15 Paid third quarterly installment of $9,000 on 19X4 estimated federal income tax.

Nov. 5 Declared cash dividend of $0.77 per share on 15,000 shares of common stock outstanding. The dividend is payable on December 10 to holders of record on November 25.

Dec. 10 Paid dividend declared on November 5.

Dec. 15 Paid fourth quarterly installment of $9,000 on 19X4 estimated income tax.

Dec. 31 In completing the worksheet at the end of the year, the accountant determined that the total income tax for 19X4 was $38,925. The difference between this amount and the total of quarterly deposits is to be recorded as an adjustment.

PROBLEM 21–2A
(Obj. 2, 3, 4, 5, 12)

Tutorial

Amortizing organization costs, completing a corporate worksheet, recording adjusting and closing entries, preparing an income statement and balance sheet. The Jabaar Corporation has been authorized to issue 3,000 shares of 13 percent noncumulative, nonparticipating preferred stock with a par value of $100 a share and 200,000 shares of common stock with a par value of $10 a share. As of December 31, 19X3, 800 shares of preferred stock and 18,000 shares of common stock have been issued. A condensed trial balance as of December 31, 19X3, is provided on page 768.

Instructions

1. Enter the December 31, 19X3, trial balance on an eight-column worksheet. Provide three lines for the Selling Expenses Control account and three lines for the General Expenses Control account. Total and rule the Trial Balance columns.
2. Enter the necessary adjustments on the worksheet, based on the following data for December 31:
   a. Ending merchandise inventory is $55,000. Close the beginning inventory and set up the ending inventory.
   b. Depreciation of buildings is $6,250 ($5,000 is selling expense; $1,250 is general expense).
   c. Depreciation of equipment is $12,500 ($9,000 is selling expense; $3,500 is general expense).

d. Accrued expenses are $3,000 ($2,000 is selling expense; $1,000 is general expense).
e. Amortization of organization costs is $200.
f. The balance in the Allowance for Doubtful Accounts is deemed to be adequate.
g. The $34,000 balance in Income Tax Expense represents the quarterly tax deposits. Adjust the Income Tax Expense account, using the following procedure.
   (1) Extend the adjusted income and expense items to the Income Statement columns. Using this data, compute the net income before taxes.

JABAAR CORPORATION
Trial Balance (Condensed)
December 31, 19X3

ACCOUNT NAME	DEBIT	CREDIT
Cash	34 245 00	
Accounts Receivable	83 900 00	
Allowance for Doubtful Accounts		1 000 00
Income Tax Refund Receivable		
Inventory	50 000 00	
Land	50 000 00	
Buildings	200 000 00	
Accumulated Depreciation—Buildings		18 750 00
Equipment	125 000 00	
Accumulated Depreciation—Equipment		12 500 00
Organization Costs	640 00	
Accounts Payable		57 610 00
Dividends Payable—Preferred		10 400 00
Dividends Payable—Common		5 000 00
Accrued Expenses Payable		
Preferred Stock—13%		80 000 00
Paid-in Capital in Excess of Par Value—Preferred		8 000 00
Common Stock		180 000 00
Retained Earnings		64 000 00
Sales (Net)		560 275 00
Purchases	300 000 00	
Selling Expenses Control	81 400 00	
General Expenses Control	38 350 00	
Amortization of Organization Costs		
Income Tax Expense	34 000 00	
Income Summary		
Totals	997 535 00	997 535 00

(2) Assuming that taxable income is the same as net income before income taxes, use the tax rates given in this chapter to compute the federal income tax. Round the computed tax to the nearest whole dollar. Ignore state and local income taxes.

3. Complete the worksheet as shown in the text.
4. Prepare a condensed income statement for the year.
5. Prepare a balance sheet as of December 31, 19X3. The balance of Retained Earnings on January 1, 19X3, was $79,400. All dividends for the year were declared on December 5, 19X3, and are payable January 4, 19X4.
6. Journalize the adjusting and closing entries on December 31. Explanations are not required.

PROBLEM 21–3A
(Obj. 6, 7, 9, 12)

Recording cash dividends, stock dividends, and appropriation of retained earnings; preparing statement of retained earnings. The stockholders' equity accounts of College Video Arcades Corporation on January 1, 19X3, contained the following balances.

Preferred Stock (10%, $50 par value, 2,000 shares authorized)		
Issued and Outstanding, 600 Shares	$30,000	
Paid-in Capital in Excess of Par Value—Preferred	1,200	$ 31,200
Common Stock ($20 par value, 10,000 shares authorized)		
Issued and Outstanding, 5,000 Shares		100,000
Retained Earnings		98,000
Total Stockholders' Equity		$229,200

The corporation's transactions affecting stockholders' equity during 19X3 follow.

Instructions

1. Set up a ledger account (381) for Retained Earnings and record the January 1, 19X3, balance.
2. Record the transactions given below in general journal form. Use the account titles as in the chapter. Post these entries to the Retained Earnings account only.
3. Prepare a statement of retained earnings for the year 19X3.

TRANSACTIONS

June 15 The board of directors declared a semiannual dividend of 5 percent on the preferred stock, payable on July 15 to stockholders of record on June 30.

July 15 Paid the dividend on the preferred stock.

Dec. 15 The board of directors declared a semiannual dividend of 5 percent on the preferred stock, payable on January 8, 19X4, to stockholders of record on December 31, 19X3, and a cash dividend of $3 per share on common stock, payable on January 8, 19X4, to stockholders of record on December 31, 19X3. Make separate entries.

Dec. 15 The board of directors declared a 5 percent common stock dividend to be distributed to the common stockholders of record on December 31, 19X3. The new shares are to be issued on January 15, 19X4. A market price of $52 a share is expected for the new shares of common stock that the corporation will issue.

Dec. 31 Because of the poor economic outlook, the board of directors created an "appropriation of retained earnings for contingencies" of $40,000.

Dec. 31 The Income Summary account contained a debit balance of $6,000. The board had anticipated a net loss for the year and no quarterly deposits of estimated income taxes were made, so income taxes may be ignored.

PROBLEM 21-4A
(Obj. 6, 8, 9, 10, 12)

Tutorial

Recording cash dividends, stock splits, appropriations of retained earnings, donated assets; preparing the Stockholders' Equity section of the balance sheet. The Stockholders' Equity section of the balance sheet of the Ellis Corporation on January 1, 19X4, is shown below along with transactions for the year 19X4.

Stockholders' Equity		
Preferred Stock (14% cumulative, $20 par value, 100,000 shares authorized)		
Issued and outstanding, 2,000 shares	$40,000	
Paid-in Capital in Excess of Par Value	4,000	$ 44,000
Common Stock (no-par value, stated value of $25, 100,000 shares authorized)		
Issued and outstanding, 1,000 shares	25,000	
Paid-in Capital in Excess of Stated Value	5,000	30,000
Total Paid-in Capital		$ 74,000
Retained Earnings		90,000
Total Stockholders' Equity		$164,000

Instructions

1. Open the stockholders' equity accounts in the general ledger and enter the beginning balances. In addition to the accounts listed, open the following accounts:

   Donated Capital
   Treasury Stock—Preferred
   Retained Earnings Appropriated for Treasury Stock Purchased

2. Record the transactions in general journal form.
3. Post the transactions to the stockholders' equity accounts.
4. Prepare the Stockholders' Equity section of the balance sheet.

TRANSACTIONS

Jan. 23 Repurchased 1,000 shares of the outstanding preferred stock for $23,000 in cash. The stock is to be held as treasury stock. State law requires that an amount of retained earnings equal to the cost of treasury stock held must be appropriated. Record the purchase and the appropriation of retained earnings.

Mar. 1 Declared a 2-for-1 stock split of common stock. Each shareholder is to receive one new share for each share held. Stated value is reduced to $12.50 per share. Date of record is March 15. Date of issue of new shares is April 1.

April 1 Issued new shares called for by split.

June 15 Declared cash dividend on preferred stock of 7 percent to be paid on July 5 to holders of record on June 28.

July 5 Paid cash dividend on preferred stock.

Aug. 25 Purchased 200 shares of outstanding preferred stock at $22 per share to be held as treasury stock. Appropriated retained earnings equal to cost of the treasury stock.

Dec. 15 Declared cash dividend on preferred stock of 7 percent to be paid on January 5 to holders of record on December 28.

Dec. 15 Declared cash dividend of $1 per share on common stock to be paid on January 5 to holders of record on December 28.

Dec. 15 Accepted title to a tract of land with a fair market value of $95,000 from the City of Midville. The tract is to be used as a building site for the corporation's new factory.

Dec. 31 The net income after taxes for the year is $34,000. Give the entry to close the Income Summary account.

PROBLEM SET B

PROBLEM 21-1B
(Obj. 1, 6)

Tutorial

Recording federal income tax and cash dividend transactions. Selected transactions of the City Health Center, Inc., during 19X5 are given below. Record them in the general journal.

TRANSACTIONS

Mar. 15 Filed the federal tax return for 19X4. The total tax for the year was $65,000. Estimated tax deposits of $60,000 had been made during the year, and on December 31, 19X4, the accountant had accrued an additional liability of $6,000. Paid the additional $5,000 due.

Apr. 15 Paid first quarterly installment of $17,000 on 19X5 estimated federal income tax.

June 1 Declared dividend of $1.00 per share on the 22,000 shares of common stock outstanding. The dividend is payable on June 30 to holders of record on June 15.

June 15 Paid second quarterly installment of $17,000 on 19X5 estimated federal income tax.

June 30 Paid dividend declared on June 1.

Sept. 15 Paid third quarterly installment of $17,000 on 19X5 estimated federal income tax.

Nov. 20 Declared cash dividend of $1.05 per share on the 22,000 shares of common stock outstanding. The dividend is payable on December 18 to stockholders of record on December 1.

Dec. 15 Paid fourth quarterly installment of $17,000 on 19X5 estimated federal income tax.

Dec. 31 In completing the worksheet at the end of the year, the accountant determined that the total income tax for 19X5 was $62,000. The difference between this amount and the quarterly deposits is to be recorded as an adjustment.

PROBLEM 21–2B
(Obj. 2, 3, 4, 5, 12)

Tutorial

Amortizing organization costs; completing a corporate worksheet; recording adjusting and closing entries; preparing an income statement and balance sheet. The Luker Antiques Corporation has been authorized to issue 5,000 shares of 12 percent noncumulative, nonparticipating preferred stock with a par value of $100 a share and 5,000 shares of common stock with a stated value of $100 a share. As of December 31, 19X3, 400 shares of preferred stock and 200 shares of common stock have been issued and are outstanding. Dividends are paid quarterly on the preferred stock. A condensed trial balance as of December 31, 19X3, follows.

LUKER ANTIQUES CORPORATION
Trial Balance (Condensed)
December 31, 19X3

ACCOUNT NAME	DEBIT	CREDIT
Cash	10 265 00	
Accounts Receivable	27 400 00	
Allowance for Doubtful Accounts		130 00
Merchandise Inventory	37 460 00	
Land	18 000 00	
Building	44 000 00	
Accumulated Depreciation—Building		4 000 00
Equipment	39 000 00	
Accumulated Depreciation—Equipment		11 000 00
Organization Costs	120 00	
Accounts Payable		11 325 00
Dividends Payable—Preferred		1 200 00
Accrued Expenses Payable		
Income Tax Payable		
Preferred Stock—12%		40 000 00
Paid-in Capital in Excess of Par—Preferred		3 000 00
Common Stock		20 000 00
Retained Earnings		43 085 00
Sales (Net)		222 290 00
Purchases	110 000 00	
Selling Expenses Control	43 185 00	
General Expenses Control	20 000 00	
Amortization of Organization Costs		
Income Tax Expense	6 600 00	
Income Summary		
Totals	356 030 00	356 030 00

Instructions

1. Enter the December 31 trial balance on an eight-column worksheet. Provide four lines for the Selling Expenses Control account and three lines for the General Expenses Control account. Total and rule the Trial Balance columns.
2. Enter the necessary adjustments on the worksheet, based on the following data for December 31:
   a. Ending merchandise inventory is $40,000. Close the beginning inventory and set up the ending inventory.
   b. Allowance for Doubtful Accounts should be adjusted to a balance of $750 (debit Selling Expenses).
   c. Depreciation of the building is $2,000 ($1,800 is selling expense; $200 is general expense).
   d. Depreciation of equipment is $3,000 ($1,500 is selling expense; $1,500 is general expense).
   e. Accrued expenses are $1,800 ($500 is selling expense; $1,300 is general expense).
   f. Amortization of organization costs is $80.
   g. The $6,600 balance in Income Tax Expense represents the quarterly tax deposits. Adjust the Income Tax Expense account, using the following procedure.
      (1) Extend the adjusted income and expense items to the Income Statement columns. Using this data, compute the net income before income taxes.
      (2) Assuming that taxable income is the same as net income before income taxes, use the tax rates given in this chapter to compute the federal income tax. Round the computed tax to the nearest whole dollar. Ignore state and local income taxes.
3. Complete the worksheet as shown in the text.
4. Prepare a condensed income statement for the year.
5. Prepare a balance sheet as of December 31, 19X3. The balance of Retained Earnings on January 1, 19X3, was $47,885. The only dividends declared during 19X3 were dividends on preferred stock.
6. Journalize the adjusting and closing entries on December 31, 19X3. Explanations are not required.

PROBLEM 21–3B
(Obj. 6, 7, 9, 11)

Tutorial

Recording cash dividends, stock dividends, appropriation of retained earnings; preparing statement of retained earnings. The stockholders' equity accounts of McDougall's Hamburger Corporation on January 1, 19X2, contained the balances shown below.

Preferred Stock (12%, $100 par value, 1,000 shares authorized)		
Issued and Outstanding, 500 Shares		$50,000
Common Stock (no-par, $50 stated value, 5,000 shares authorized)		
Issued and Outstanding, 2,000 Shares	$100,000	
Paid-in Capital in Excess of Stated Value	4,000	104,000
Retained Earnings		95,000
Total Stockholders' Equity		$249,000

The corporation's transactions affecting stockholders' equity during 19X2 are given below. The worksheet at the end of 19X2 showed a net loss of $8,000.

Instructions

1. Set up a ledger account (381) for Retained Earnings and record the January 1, 19X2, balance.
2. Record the following transactions in general journal form. Use the account titles used in the textbook. No explanations are required. Post these entries to the Retained Earnings account only.
3. Prepare a statement of retained earnings for the year 19X2.

TRANSACTIONS

June 15 The board of directors declared a semiannual 6 percent cash dividend on preferred stock and a cash dividend of $3 a share on common stock. Both are payable July 12 to stockholders of record July 1. (Make a compound entry.)

July 12 Paid the cash dividends.

Aug. 15 The board of directors declared a 10 percent common stock dividend to be distributed on September 12 to common stockholders of record on September 1. The stock is expected to have a market value of $58 a share when issued.

Sept. 12 Distributed the common stock dividend.

Dec. 15 The board of directors declared a semiannual 6 percent cash dividend on the preferred stock and a cash dividend of $2 a share on the common stock. Both dividends are payable January 12 to stockholders of record on December 31. (Make a compound entry.)

Dec. 15 The board of directors directed that retained earnings of $20,000 be appropriated each year for the next four years to purchase a new computer system. Title the account "Retained Earnings Appropriated for Equipment Acquisition." Record the appropriation for 19X2.

Dec. 31 Closed the debit balance in Income Summary.

PROBLEM 21–4B
(Obj. 6, 8, 9, 10, 12)

Tutorial

Recording cash dividends, stock splits, appropriation of retained earnings, and donated assets; preparing the Stockholders' Equity section of the balance sheet. The Stockholders' Equity section of the Curtis Corporation's balance sheet on January 1, 19X4, is given below, along with selected transactions for 19X4.

Stockholders' Equity		
Preferred Stock (10%, $50 par value, 10,000 shares authorized)		
Issued and Outstanding, 500 Shares	$25,000	
Paid-in Capital in Excess of Par Value	2,000	$27,000
Common Stock (no-par value, $50 stated value, 10,000 shares authorized)		
Issued and Outstanding, 900 Shares	$45,000	
Paid-in Capital in Excess of Stated Value	1,500	46,500
Retained Earnings		82,475
Total Stockholders' Equity		$155,975

Instructions

1. Set up general ledger accounts for the stockholders' equity items and enter the given balances. In addition to the accounts listed, open the following accounts:

   Retained Earnings Appropriated for Treasury Stock Purchased
   Donated Capital
   Treasury Stock—Preferred

2. Record the transactions listed below in general journal form.
3. Post the general journal entries to the stockholders' equity accounts only.
4. Prepare the Stockholders' Equity section of the balance sheet as of December 31, 19X4.

TRANSACTIONS

Feb. 6 The corporation reacquired 60 shares of preferred stock, paying $53 a share, and set up an appropriation of retained earnings equal to cost of treasury stock purchased, as required by state law.

Mar. 1 Declared a 4-for-1 split of common stock and reduced the stated value to $12.50 per share. Each shareholder is to receive three new shares for each share held. Date of record is March 20. Date of issue is April 1.

Apr. 1 Issued new shares of common stock called for by split.

June 20 The board of directors declared a cash dividend of 5 percent on the preferred stock outstanding. The dividend is payable July 5 to holders of record on June 28.

July 5 Paid cash dividends on preferred stock.

Nov. 10 Purchased 100 shares of the corporation's own preferred stock to be held as treasury stock, paying $51 per share. Appropriated retained earnings equal to cost of the shares.

Dec. 17 The board of directors declared the semiannual cash dividend of 5 percent on preferred stock and a $1 per share cash dividend on common stock. Both dividends are payable to stockholders of record on December 28 and are payable on January 8. Make separate entries.

Dec. 17 Received land valued at $40,000 as a gift from a neighboring city. The corporation has agreed to build a new factory in this location.

Dec. 31 The Income Summary account contained a credit balance of $21,000 after income tax. Give the entry to close the account.

CHALLENGE PROBLEM

The Stockholders' Equity section of the balance sheets of Alto Corporation on December 31, 19X3, and December 31, 19X4, along with other selected account balances on the two dates, follow. (Certain information is missing from the statements.)

	19X4	19X3
Stockholders' Equity		
Paid-in Capital		
Preferred Stock (8 percent, $50 par, authorized 2,000 shares)		
Issued	$ 40,000	$ 34,000
Paid-in Capital in Excess of Par Value—Preferred	300	-0-
Common Stock ($10 par value, 100,000 shares authorized)		
Issued	400,000	350,000
Paid-in Capital in Excess of Par Value—Common	10,000	-0-
Total Paid-in Capital	$450,300	$384,000
Retained Earnings:		
Appropriated for Plant Expansion	$125,000	$125,000
Appropriated for Treasury Stock	20,000	-0-
Unappropriated	320,000	300,000
Total Retained Earnings	$465,000	$425,000
	$915,300	$809,000
Less Treasury Stock—Preferred	20,000	-0-
Total Stockholders' Equity	$895,000	$809,000

During the year the following transactions, other than net income or loss after taxes, affected stockholders' equity:

a. A stock dividend was declared on common stock and issued in February 19X4. No other common stock was issued during the year.
b. A cash dividend of $2 a share was declared and paid on common stock in December 19X4.
c. The Treasury Stock—Preferred was purchased at par value in January 19X4.
d. Additional preferred stock was issued for cash in March 19X4.
e. The yearly cash dividend of $4 per share was declared and paid on preferred stock outstanding as of December 3, 19X4.

Instructions Answer the following questions.

1. How many shares of preferred stock were outstanding on December 31, 19X4?
2. How many shares of common stock were issued as a stock dividend during 19X4?
3. What was the market value per share of common stock at the time the stock dividend was declared?
4. How many shares of preferred stock were purchased as treasury stock?
5. What was the sales price per share of the preferred stock issued during the year?

6. How many shares of preferred stock were issued for cash during 19X4?
7. What was the total cash dividend on preferred stock during the year?
8. What was the total cash dividend on common stock?
9. What was the corporation's net income or loss after taxes during 19X4?

CRITICAL THINKING PROBLEM

Techcom, Inc., has the following stockholders' equity on September 30, 19X6.

Common Stock (100,000 shares issued)	$ 500,000
Paid-in Capital in Excess of Par	1,500,000
Retained Earnings	1,700,000
Total Stockholders' Equity	$3,700,000

For the past three years, Techcom has paid dividends of $1.80 per share. After thorough consideration of the corporation's current position, the board of directors declared a 20 percent stock dividend on October 1, 19X6, in place of the $1.80 cash dividend. Before the end of the year and after the stock dividend was distributed, however, the board declared a cash dividend of $1.50 per share.

In September 19X6 before the stock dividend was declared, Alva Thompson purchased 5,000 shares of Techcom, Inc., stock for $48 per share. Now Ms. Thompson is concerned because she had purchased the stock expecting $1.80 per share dividend only to learn that the dividend has been reduced to $1.50 per share. How would you answer the following questions concerning this investment?

1. What could have caused Techcom's board of directors to declare a stock dividend rather than a cash dividend in October?
2. How did the book value of Ms. Thompson's stock prior to the stock dividend compare with the book value of the stock after the stock dividend?
3. Why does the market value of the stock ($48) differ from the book value of the stock?
4. How does the total amount of cash dividends differ between the $1.80 per share and the $1.50 per share?
5. The market price of the stock fell to $40 after the stock dividend was announced. Does this reduction in market price represent a loss to Alva Thompson?
6. What do you think would have happened to the market price of the stock if the board of directors had not reduced the amount of the cash dividend per share of stock?

CHAPTER

22 Long-Term Bonds

OBJECTIVES

1. Explain the various types of bonds.
2. Explain the advantages and disadvantages of using bonds as a method of financing.
3. Record the issuance of bonds.
4. Record the payment of interest on bonds.
5. Record the accrual of interest on bonds.
6. Compute and record the periodic amortization of a bond premium.
7. Compute and record the periodic amortization of a bond discount.
8. Record the transactions of a bond sinking fund.
9. Record an increase or decrease in Retained Earnings Appropriated for Bond Retirement.
10. Record retirement of bonds payable.
11. Define the accounting terms new to this chapter.

As you have seen, corporations may obtain needed funds by selling stock. Corporations may also obtain the money they require for expansion or operating needs in other ways. A corporation may secure funds by obtaining a loan for an intermediate period (two to five years) through signing a note payable. Notes that have a maturity date of more than one year are classified as long-term debt.

A cash loan may also be obtained by issuing a long-term note that is secured by a mortgage on specific assets such as land, buildings, or equipment. More frequently, **mortgage loans** are created when land, buildings, and equipment are initially acquired and a note is given for part of the purchase price. The mortgage gives the lender the right to bring legal action to seize and sell the property pledged as security if either the principal or the current interest is not paid when due. Interest may be payable annually, but it is usually paid at shorter intervals over the life of the loan. Repayment of the principal may be in a lump sum at a future date or in installments over the life of the loan.

When a corporation has a greater need for long-term funds, it frequently obtains those funds by issuing bonds.

NEW TERMS

Bearer bonds ▪ Bond indenture ▪ Bond issue costs ▪ Bond sinking fund ▪ Bonds payable ▪ Call price ▪ Callable bonds ▪ Carrying value of bonds ▪ Collateral trust bonds ▪ Convertible bonds ▪ Coupon bonds ▪ Debentures ▪ Discount on bonds payable ▪ Face interest ▪ Leveraging ▪ Mortgage loan ▪ Premium on bonds payable ▪ Registered bonds ▪ Secured bonds ▪ Serial bonds ▪ Straight-line amortization ▪ Trading on the equity

FINANCING THROUGH BONDS

Bonds payable are long-term debt instruments that are written promises to pay the principal borrowed at a specified future date. Interest is due at a fixed rate that is payable annually, semiannually, or quarterly over the life of the bond. Bonds are similar to notes payable, but the contract involved is much more formal than that involved in a note payable and the bonds evidencing the debt are easily transferred by one owner (or bondholder) to another creditor.

TYPES OF BONDS

OBJECTIVE 1

Explain the various types of bonds.

Bonds are frequently classified on the basis of certain broad characteristics. The following three factors are most commonly considered when classifying and describing bonds.

1. Are the bonds secured by collateral, or are they unsecured?
2. Are the bonds registered or unregistered?
3. Do all the bonds mature (fall due) on the same date, or does a portion of the issue mature each year over a period of several years?

Secured and Unsecured Bonds

When a corporation pledges specific assets to guarantee payment, bonds are said to be secured.

Bonds are called **secured bonds** if specific property is pledged to secure the claims of the bondholders. If the bonds are not paid when due, the bondholder can seize the assets and sell them. A bond contract, referred to as a **bond indenture,** is prepared and a trustee, frequently an investment banker, who acts to protect the bondholders' interests when necessary, is named. In the case of default, for example, the trustee takes legal steps to sell the pledged property and pay off the bonds. The bonds may be identified according to the nature of the property pledged and the year of maturity—for example, "First Mortgage 10 Percent Real Estate Bonds Payable, 19X5," or "Collateral Trust 14 Percent Bonds Payable, 19X2."

Collateral trust bonds involve the pledge of securities, such as the stocks or bonds of other companies.

Unsecured bonds are called debentures.

Bonds backed only by the general credit of the corporation are called **debentures.** They involve no pledge of specific property that the bondholders can seize to satisfy their claims. However, the bondholders do have some protection in case of liquidation because the claims of creditors, including bondholders, rank above those of stockholders. Creditors must be paid in full before stockholders can receive anything.

Registered and Unregistered Bonds

If bonds are registered, the name of each owner is listed in the corporation's records. Interest is paid by check to the registered owner.

Bonds issued to a particular individual whose name is listed in the corporation's records are **registered bonds.** Ownership is transferred by completing an assignment form and having the change of ownership entered in the corporation's records. Interest is paid by check to each registered bondholder. The corporation must maintain a detailed subsidiary ledger, similar to the stockholders' ledger, for registered bonds. This ledger lets the corporation know at all times who owns the bonds and is therefore entitled to receive interest payments.

The corporation does not know the names of owners of its bearer bonds. To collect interest, the owner "clips" a coupon and deposits it in a bank.

Some bonds do not require that the names of the owners be registered. These bonds have individual coupons attached for each interest payment. These coupons are, in effect, checks payable to the bearer. On or after each interest date, the bondholder detaches a coupon from the bond and presents it to a bank for payment. **Coupon bonds** are transferred by delivery, and no record of the owner's identity is kept by the corporation. Coupon bonds are often referred to as **bearer bonds** because the holder, or bearer, is assumed to be the owner. Because of the requirement that the interest payer send the Internal Revenue Service a form showing each payee's name, tax identification number, address, and amount of interest paid, coupon bonds are issued infrequently by corporations today. State and local governmental units, however, continue to issue coupon bonds because interest on such bonds is not taxable.

Single-Maturity and Serial-Maturity Bonds

Most bond indentures call for all the bonds to have the same maturity date (that is, become payable on the same day). However, an issue of bonds may be payable over a period of years. In this case, the bonds are referred to as **serial bonds.** For example, a corporation may issue serial bonds totaling $1 million, dated January 1, 19X3, with $200,000 face amount of the bonds maturing each year, beginning on January 1, 19Y3, ten years later. The corporation may find it easier to retire bonds on a serial basis rather than having all the bonds fall due on the same date.

Other Characteristics of Bonds Payable

There are certain other characteristics of corporate bonds of which you should be aware. Bonds are issued in various denominations, but a face value—the denomination specified on the contract—of $1,000 is typical.

Convertible bonds may be converted into common stock at the option of the bondholder.

Some bonds are **convertible,** which gives the owner the right to convert the bonds into common stock under specified conditions. For example, an indenture dated January 1, 19X4, may give the holder of a 20-year, $1,000 bond the right to convert the bond into 50 shares of the corporation's common stock at any time after January 1, 19Y4. If the price of the stock is $20 per share or more, the owner of the bonds is likely to convert them into stock.

Bonds are frequently callable. **Callable bonds** give the issuing corporation the right to require the holders to surrender the bonds for payment before their maturity date. Usually the **call price,** the amount the corporation must pay for the bond when it is called and redeemed, is slightly above the par value. If interest rates decline below the face rate on the bonds or if the corporation has excess cash, it may call all or part of the bonds and retire them.

For example, assume that on October 1, 19X2, Snow Corporation issues 20-year bonds having a face value of $100,000 and maturing October 1, 19Z2. Under the terms of the indenture, Snow can call the bonds at any time after October 1, 19Y2, at a call price of 102 of face value. The bonds are called by Snow on October 1, 19Y3. Smittel, an owner of bonds with a par value of $40,000, must surrender the bonds and will be paid $40,800 ($1.02 \times \$40,000$).

STOCK VERSUS BONDS AS A FINANCING METHOD

In practice, the funds for investment in corporate assets are often raised through varying combinations of common stock, preferred stock, and bonds. In deciding whether to issue additional stock or to use bonds payable in raising funds, management must consider several factors. You can readily grasp some of those factors by studying Table 22–1, a comparison of bonds and capital stock.

TABLE 22–1
Stock and Bonds Compared

Capital Stock	Bonds Payable
Capital stock is permanent capital. There is no debt to be repaid.	Bonds payable are debt. When the bonds fall due, the debt must be repaid.
Because the stock is permanent capital, it is classified as stockholders' equity.	Because the bonds represent debt, they are classified as long-term liabilities.
Dividends are not legally required on common stock. The requirements on preferred stock depend on the contract.	Interest must be paid on the bonds.
Dividends are not deductible for income tax purposes.	Interest is deducted in arriving at the taxable income.
Preference dividends on preferred stock are usually slightly higher than interest rates on bonds because there is more risk associated with preferred stock.	Interest rates on bonds are slightly lower than dividend on preferred stock.

OBJECTIVE 2
Explain the advantages and disadvantages of using bonds as a method of financing.

In deciding whether to use bonds as a financing medium or to issue additional stock, the factors summarized in the table must be considered. A basic question in deciding to issue bonds payable to obtain funds is whether the company can earn a rate of return on the assets acquired with the proceeds from the bonds that is greater than the interest rate paid on the bonds. This factor is a most important consideration, as you will see from the following discussion.

Bonds payable are long-term debts evidenced by formal documents and are easily transferred by one creditor to another.

Suppose a newly formed corporation has chosen to use both common stock and bonds payable to provide total capital of $250,000 to acquire assets. The owners invest $125,000 for common stock and are able to borrow the other $125,000 by issuing bonds payable for cash. The bonds bear interest at the rate of 10 percent per year. Assume further that the corporation's net income, before interest and before taxes, is $55,000 and that the corporate income tax rate is 20 percent. Let's compute the rate of profit on the stockholders' investment.

Amount available to stockholders:	
Net income before bond interest	$55,000
Bond interest expense (10% × $125,000)	12,500
Net income before income taxes	$42,500
Income tax expense (20% × $42,500)	8,500
Net income after taxes	$34,000

The net income after taxes is available to the common stockholders. Since the stockholders have invested $125,000 in the business, we can say that they have earned 27.2 percent profit on their equity ($34,000 ÷ $125,000).

Let's see what they would have earned if the full $250,000 had been raised through the form of common stock.

Net income before taxes (there is no bond interest)	$55,000
Income tax expense (20% × $55,000)	11,000
Net income after income taxes	$44,000

Now let's compute the rate of profit on the stockholders' equity of $250,000:

Rate of profit = $44,000 profit ÷ $250,000 investment
= 17.6 percent

Note that although the total net income available to the stockholders is larger if the stockholders provide all the capital ($44,000 versus $34,000), the rate of profit on the amount they invest in stock is much higher if they use bond financing for half the needed funds (27.2 percent versus 17.6 percent).

Using borrowed funds to earn a profit greater than the interest that must be paid on the borrowing is called trading on the equity, or leveraging.

The increase in the rate of profit on stockholders' equity if bonds are used is due to the fact that the company's profits are higher than the contract rate of interest on the bonds. This situation is called **trading on the equity,** or **leveraging.** In lean years such financing may be dangerous from the stockholders' standpoint because the prior fixed claim of bond interest expense may leave little or nothing for dividends to the stockholders. Moreover, even when the firm operates at a loss, the bondholders' interest must be paid in full. In addition, the principal amount of the debt must also be paid when the bonds fall due.

For example, if the net income before bond interest and income tax had been only $10,000, the use of bonds payable would have resulted in a net loss for the corporation.

Net income before bond interest	$10,000
Bond interest expense (10% × $125,000)	12,500
Net loss	($ 2,500)

SELF-REVIEW

1. Explain the difference between secured bonds and debenture bonds.
2. What are registered bonds? Coupon bonds?
3. What is a convertible bond?
4. Why would a corporation wish to issue callable bonds?
5. Name two disadvantages of raising capital through the issue of bonds payable rather than through the issue of preferred stock.

Answers to Self-Review

1. Secured bonds are bonds that have specific assets pledged as security. If the corporation does not pay the principal and interest, the bondholders may take possession of the property. Debenture bonds have no specific assets pledged to secure payment.
2. Registered bonds are bonds whose owners are registered in the records of the corporation. Interest is paid each payment date to the registered owner. Coupon bonds are not registered. The corporation does not know the names of owners of the bonds. To collect interest, the owner clips a coupon from the bond and deposits it in the bank.
3. A convertible bond is one that may be converted into common stock, under specified conditions, at the option of the owner.
4. If interest rates decrease, or if the corporation has extra cash, the corporation can redeem the bonds if they are callable.
5. Two disadvantages of raising capital through the issue of bonds payable are that (a) interest must be paid and (b) the face amount must be repaid at maturity.

ACCOUNTING FOR BOND ISSUE AND INTEREST

OBJECTIVE 3

Record the issuance of bonds.

Suppose the Mirabel Unpainted Furniture Corporation decides to issue $100,000 face value of 11 percent bonds, maturing in 10 years, with interest payable semiannually. (The contractual interest specified on the bond is called the **face interest.**) This means that each April 1 and October 1, the bondholders will be paid interest equal to 5 1/2 percent of the face value of the bonds they own. Each bond is to have a par value of $1,000 and, at 11 percent, a face interest amount of $110 per year. Half the authorized bonds are to be sold immediately. The remainder will be held for future needs. The bonds are registered, so interest checks will be issued to the individual bondholders on interest payment dates. The bonds are unsecured.

Bonds Issued at Face Value

On April 1, 19Y1, the issue date, Mirabel sells $50,000 of its bonds at face value for cash. The corporation records this transaction by debiting Cash and crediting an account called 11% Bonds Payable, 19Z1 (indicating the maturity date 10 years later).

19Y1				
		Cash	*50 000 00*	
		11% Bonds Payable, 19Z1		*50 000 00*
		Issued bonds at face value		

After the entry is posted, the ledger account for the bonds appears as follows.

ACCOUNT *11% Bonds Payable, 19Z1* ACCOUNT NO. *261*
(Authorized $100,000; Interest April 1, October 1)

DATE		EXPLANATION	POST. REF.	DEBIT	CREDIT	BALANCE DEBIT	BALANCE CREDIT
19Y1							
Apr.	*1*		*J4*		*50 0 0 0 00*		*50 0 0 0 00*

Bonds payable are shown on the balance sheet as long-term liabilities.

Notice that the amount of bonds authorized is recorded as a memorandum item in the ledger account. In the balance sheet the bonds payable are listed as long-term liabilities. (Bonds that mature within the next year from the balance sheet date will be shown as current liabilities.) Both the amount authorized and the amount issued are shown. One of three methods is generally used to present the bonds on the balance sheet.

1. The value of the bonds authorized is shown. The amount unissued is deducted from the amount authorized to arrive at the face value of the bonds issued. This presentation is illustrated in the section of the balance sheet shown below.

Long-Term Liabilities		
11% Bonds Payable, Due April 1, 19Z1		
Authorized	$100,000	
Less Unissued	50,000	
Issued		$50,000

2. The face value of the bonds authorized is shown as a parenthetical note. Only the par value of the bonds issued is extended to the money columns of the balance sheet.

Long-Term Liabilities	
11% Bonds Payable, Due April 1, 19Z1	$50,000
(Bonds with a face value of $100,000 are authorized, of which bonds with a par value of $50,000 are unissued.)	

3. Many corporations show in the balance sheet only the bonds that have been issued. A footnote to the statements gives details of the bonds authorized and issued. This approach is especially common when more than one bond issue is outstanding.

OBJECTIVE 4
Record the payment of interest on bonds.

Payment of Interest

On October 1 the interest for six months at 11 percent becomes due on the $50,000 of bonds issued. The entry to record the payment is illustrated in general journal form below.

19X1					
Oct.	*1*	*Bond Interest Expense*		*2 7 5 0 00*	
		Cash			*2 7 5 0 00*
		Paid semiannual bond interest			

Information Block: International Accounting

The Multinational Company

Multinational companies are those that have organizations and operations in other countries. They have manufacturing plants, service operations, and sales organizations in various parts of the world. These companies are global in the sense that they are organized and managed without respect to national boundaries. Their products are tailored to local markets. They may engage in exports from the United States, joint ventures, licensing arrangements, and other ventures.

U.S. multinational companies typically form their foreign operations as foreign corporations, branches of a U.S. corporation, or partnerships or joint ventures organized under either the laws of a state or a foreign country. The foreign corporation is organized and operated in the country where the product is sold or business is transacted. The branch is generally organized under the laws of a particular state and will do business abroad by means of an unincorporated organization located in a foreign country. The principal considerations for selecting the form of organization are the nature of the business activity, local laws, risk of liability, and tax considerations.

The international structure of McDonald's includes 1,101 foreign company-operated restaurants, 1,586 foreign franchises, and 967 foreign affiliates in 1991. Markets in England, Canada, and Germany represent 75 percent of total company-operated restaurants outside the United States. Markets in Canada, Germany, Australia, Japan, and France represent 75 percent of franchised restaurants outside the United States. Restaurants operated by foreign affiliates are primarily located in Japan and the Pacific countries.

International joint ventures are numerous. Dow Chemical and Sumitomo Chemical have combined operations in Japan to make high-performance plastics for medical equipment and motor vehicles. Sun Microsystems formed a joint venture with Fuji/Xerox in Japan, and Ford Motor Company has an alliance with Volkswagen in Portugal. These examples are a few of the increasing number of joint ventures being formed by companies that want to do business in a global marketplace.

A special bank account may be opened for writing interest checks if there are many holders of the corporation's bonds payable.

Since some bond owners may not present their interest checks promptly for payment, it may be convenient to transfer the amount of cash needed to pay the interest to a special bank account. Individual interest checks are then written on the bond interest account. This practice is almost always used when a corporation has many bondholders and therefore numerous outstanding checks. Use of a special account for paying bond interest makes it easier to reconcile the firm's bank accounts and to keep records of interest checks that have not been presented for payment.

OBJECTIVE 5

Record the accrual of interest on bonds.

Accrual of Interest

On December 31, 19Y1, when the fiscal year ends for the Mirabel Unpainted Furniture Corporation, bond interest of $1,375 has accrued for three months since the bond interest was last paid on October 1 ($\$50{,}000 \times 0.11 \times 3/12$). An adjusting entry is made on that date as shown below.

19Y1					
Dec.	*31*	*Bond Interest Expense*		*1 375 00*	
		Bond Interest Payable			*1 375 00*
		Accrued interest for 3			
		months			

Bond Interest Expense is usually shown as a "nonoperating expense" or "other expense."

When the adjusting entry has been posted, the Bond Interest Expense account has a balance of $4,125, the correct amount of interest for the nine months the bonds have been outstanding since their issuance. Bond Interest Expense is usually listed under nonoperating expenses or other expenses on the income statement.

ACCOUNT *Bond Interest Expense* ACCOUNT NO. *692*

DATE		EXPLANATION	POST. REF.	DEBIT	CREDIT	BALANCE	
						DEBIT	CREDIT
19Y1							
Oct.	*1*		*J1*	*2 750 00*		*2 750 00*	
Dec.	*31*		*J1*	*1 375 00*		*4 125 00*	

Entries for Second-Year Interest

Assuming that the same bonds remain outstanding during all of the second year, 19Y2, the following entries would be required to record bond interest transactions.

The adjusting entry to record accrued interest is reversed on the first day of the following period.

1. January 1: Like other adjusting entries to record accrued entries, the $1,375 entry for accrued interest made on December 31 must be reversed. The reversing entry is made in the general journal,

debiting Bond Interest Payable and crediting Bond Interest Expense for $1,375.

2. April 1: Record the payment of interest for six months, $2,750, by debiting Bond Interest Expense and crediting Cash for that amount.
3. October 1: Record the payment of interest for six months, $2,750, by debiting Bond Interest Expense and crediting Cash for that amount.
4. December 31: Record accrued interest for three months, $1,375, by debiting Bond Interest Expense and crediting Bond Interest Payable.

After these four entries have been posted, the Bond Interest Expense for 19Y2 will appear as shown below.

ACCOUNT *Bond Interest Expense* ACCOUNT NO. *692*

DATE		EXPLANATION	POST. REF.	DEBIT	CREDIT	BALANCE DEBIT	BALANCE CREDIT
19Y2							
Jan.	*1*	*Reversing*	*J1*		*1 375 00*		*1 375 00*
Apr.	*1*		*J4*	*2 750 00*		*1 375 00*	
Oct.	*1*		*J10*	*2 750 00*		*4 125 00*	
Dec.	*31*		*J12*	*1 375 00*		*5 500 00*	

Notice that the balance in the Bond Interest Expense account on December 31 is $5,500, which is the correct amount of interest incurred for one year on the $50,000 of bonds issued (11% × $50,000).

Bonds Issued at a Premium

If the market rate of interest on the day that bonds are issued is lower than the face rate of interest, the bonds will sell at a premium.

Two years after the first bonds were sold, the Mirabel Unpainted Furniture Corporation decides to issue another $20,000 of the $100,000 authorized bonds. Although interest rates have fallen to 10 percent in the two years since the first bonds were issued, the interest rate specified on the bonds remains fixed at 11 percent. Each $1,000 bond will therefore earn $110 interest each year. Bondholders will naturally be attracted by the favorable interest rate offered and will probably be willing to pay more than $1,000 for each bond in order to earn $110 interest. Under these conditions, the $20,000 of bonds are sold on April 1, 19Y3, at a market quotation of 105.4. (Bond prices are quoted in terms of percent of face value.) These bonds are therefore issued for $1,054 each (105.4 percent of $1,000 face), yielding a total of $21,080 in cash (20 × $1,054). The $1,080 received for the bonds in excess of their face value ($21,080 − $20,000) is a **premium on bonds payable** received from investors because the contract rate of interest on the bonds is above the market rate of interest at the time they are sold. This transaction is recorded in general journal form as follows.

19Y3				
Apr.	*1*	*Cash*	*21 0 8 0 00*	
		11% Bonds Payable, 19Z1		*20 0 0 0 00*
		Premium on Bonds Payable		*1 0 8 0 00*
		Issued bonds at 105.4		

OBJECTIVE 6
Compute and record the periodic amortization of a bond premium.

Premium on bonds payable is amortized over the period from date of issue of the bonds until date of maturity.

Amortization of Bond Premium

The issuing corporation must write off, or amortize, the premium paid by the bond purchasers over the period from the issue date through the date of maturity. Amortizing the premium will reduce the amount shown on the income statement as bond interest expense. In this case the bonds are 10-year bonds sold two years (24 months) after their authorization date, leaving an eight-year (96-month) period over which to amortize the premium.

A common method for computing the monthly or yearly amortization is **straight-line amortization.** Under the straight-line method, an equal part of the premium is amortized each month. (A method that is preferable if the amount computed under it is substantially different from that computed under the straight-line approach is the effective interest method. The effective-interest method is discussed in most intermediate accounting texts. In this book, we will assume that the straight-line method is appropriate and will use it in all computations.) On a straight-line basis, the amortization amounts to $135 a year ($1,080 ÷ 8 years) or $11.25 a month ($1,080 ÷ 96 months).

On October 1, 19Y3, Mirabel will record the interest paid on the $70,000 of bonds outstanding and will record amortization of the premium received on $20,000 of these bonds, using the straight-line method. The bond premium reduces the amount of interest expense over the life of the bonds.

Bond premium reduces the interest expense over the period the bonds are outstanding.

The bond interest paid in cash for the six-month period April 1 to October 1 is $3,850 ($70,000 × 0.11 × 6/12).

The total amount of bond interest paid includes $2,750 for the $50,000 of bonds first issued and $1,100 for the $20,000 issued two years later, on April 1, 19Y3. The $67.50 amortization of bond premium on October 1 is for six months at $11.25 a month.

19Y3				
Oct.	*1*	*Bond Interest Expense*	*3 8 5 0 00*	
		Cash		*3 8 5 0 00*
		Payment of semiannual interest on $70,000 of bonds		
	1	*Premium on Bonds Payable*	*6 7 50*	
		Bond Interest Expense		*6 7 50*
		Amortization on $20,000 of bonds for six months		

Adjusting and Reversing Entries

On December 31, 19Y3, an adjusting entry is required for three months' interest on the entire $70,000 of bonds outstanding and for amortization of premium for the three months, October 1 through December 31, on $20,000 of bonds. Interest payable on the $70,000 of bonds is $1,925 ($70,000 × 0.11 × 3/12). The amortization of the premium amounts to $33.75 ($11.25 × 3). In the entry shown below, Premium on Bonds Payable is debited for $33.75 and Bond Interest Payable is credited for $1,925. The difference of $1,891.25 is charged to Bond Interest Expense.

19Y3					
Dec.	*31*	*Bond Interest Expense*		*1 8 9 1 25*	
		Premium on Bonds Payable		*3 3 75*	
		Bond Interest Payable			*1 9 2 5 00*
		Accrue interest and			
		amortize premium for			
		three months			

On January 1 of the following year, this adjusting entry will be reversed, as shown later in this chapter. The entries on each April 1 and October 1 for interest and amortization will be the same as the one previously illustrated for October 1, 19Y3. The adjusting and reversing entries will be repeated at the end of each year.

Bonds Issued at a Discount

If the market rate of interest is greater than the face rate on the bonds, the bonds will sell at a discount.

Suppose that the Mirabel Unpainted Furniture Corporation decides to issue another $20,000 of bonds on April 1, 19Y4, a year after the preceding issue. If the prevailing interest rates on other investments have risen to 12 percent since the last sale of bonds, investors will no longer be willing to pay a premium for an investment paying only 11 percent. In fact, they will not be interested in buying the bonds at par value either. Instead, they may offer only $953.17 for each $1,000, 11 percent bond. When bonds are issued for less than face value, they are said to have been issued at a **discount.**

Bond prices are expressed as a percentage of face value. Thus, if Mirabel Corporation sells its bonds at 95.317, the cash it receives for the $20,000 par-value bonds is $19,063.40 (0.95317 × $20,000). The discount is $936.60 ($20,000.00 − $19,063.40). The entry to record issuance of the bonds is shown in general journal form.

19Y4					
Apr.	*1*	*Cash*		*19 0 6 3 40*	
		Discount on Bonds Payable		*9 3 6 60*	
		11% Bonds Payable			*20 0 0 0 00*
		Issue bonds at 95.317			

OBJECTIVE 7

Compute and record the periodic amortization of a bond discount.

The bond discount represents an increase in bond interest over the period the bonds will be outstanding.

Amortization of Bond Discount

The bonds issued on April 1, 19Y4, have seven years to run, and the \$936.60 discount must be amortized over this period. Amortizing the discount will increase the bond interest expense shown on the income statement. On a straight-line basis, the amortization will be \$133.80 a year (\$936.60 ÷ 7 years) or \$11.15 per month (\$936.60 ÷ 84 months). The October 1, 19Y4, interest payment on the \$90,000 of bonds outstanding will be \$4,950 (\$90,000 × 11% × 1/2).

The premium on the bonds issued in 19Y3 will be amortized as previously illustrated. A new entry is required to amortize \$66.90 of the discount for half of a year (\$133.80 ÷ 2). This entry debits Bond Interest Expense and credits Discount on Bonds Payable for \$66.90; the discount increases the actual cost of borrowing. The following general journal entry summarizes the cash payment and the amortization of premium and discount.

19X4					
Oct.	*1*	*Bond Interest Expense*		*4 9 4 9 40*	
		Premium on Bonds Payable		*6 7 50*	
		Discount on Bonds Payable			*6 6 90*
		Cash			*4 9 5 0 00*
		Interest payment and amortization of premium and discount for six months			

Adjusting and Reversing Entries

On December 31, 19Y4, an adjusting entry is made to accrue \$2,475 of interest payable for three months on \$90,000 of bonds (\$90,000 × 11% × 3/12). Bond discount amortization of \$33.45 (3/12 × \$133.80) is added, and bond premium amortized for three months, \$33.75 (3 × \$11.25), is subtracted from this figure. What remains is a debit of \$2,474.70 to Bond Interest Expense. The adjusting entry is illustrated below. This entry, of course, is reversed on the first day of the following year.

19Y4					
Dec.	*31*	*Bond Interest Expense*		*2 4 7 4 70*	
		Premium on Bonds Payable		*3 3 75*	
		Discount on Bonds Payable			*3 3 45*
		Bond Interest Payable			*2 4 7 5 00*
		Accrue interest on \$90,000 of bonds, amortize premium on \$20,000 of bonds, and amortize discount on \$20,000 of bonds for three months			

Balance Sheet Presentation of Bond Premium and Discount

The Premium on Bonds Payable account has a credit balance that should be shown on the balance sheet as an addition to the face value of bonds payable, under the heading "Long-Term Liabilities." The Discount on Bonds Payable account has a debit balance that should be subtracted from the face value of the bonds payable. When there is both a discount and a premium on a bond issue, the two are combined and shown on the balance sheet as a single net figure. For example, on December 31, 19Y4, Mirabel Corporation has a net premium on bonds payable of $7.50.

Unamortized discount ($936.60 – $100.35) =	$836.25
Unamortized premium ($1,080.00 – $236.25) =	843.75
Net unamortized premium	$ 7.50

The method of reporting bonds payable and the related discount or premium on the balance sheet is illustrated below for the Mirabel Unpainted Furniture Corporation on December 31, 19Y4.

Long-Term Liabilities	
11% Bonds Payable, Due April 1, 19Z1 (authorized $100,000 par value, less $10,000 par value unissued)	$90,000.00
Net Premium on Bonds Payable	7.50
Net Liability	$90,007.50

The balance of the Bonds Payable account plus that of the Premium on Bonds Payable account (or minus that of the Discount on Bonds Payable account) is referred to as the book value, or the **carrying value,** of the bonds.

Bonds Issued Between Interest Dates

The preceding examples were for bonds that were issued on interest payment dates. In practice, however, bonds are often issued between interest dates. The new owner will nevertheless be paid for the entire interest period when he or she receives the interest check or surrenders the interest coupon on the interest payment date. Consequently, when bonds are sold between interest dates, the purchaser pays the seller for the interest accrued to the day of purchase.

When bonds are issued between interest payment dates, the accrued interest is paid to the corporation by the purchaser.

Recording Issuance of the Bonds

Suppose the Mirabel Unpainted Furniture Corporation sells its remaining $10,000 face value bonds on July 1, 19Y4. At this time the prevailing interest rate has again changed. Purchasers of the bonds are now willing to pay face value for the bonds, plus accrued interest from April 1 to July 1, 19Y4—a period of three months. Interest for three months at 11 percent on $10,000 is $275 ($10,000 × 0.11 × 3/12), and the total cash actually received at the time the bonds are issued is $10,275 ($10,000 + $275). On October 1 Mirabel will pay interest of $550 ($10,000 × 0.11 × 6/12) for the full six-month interest period, April 1 to October 1. At that time, the $550 paid will be charged to interest expense. For that reason, when the bonds are issued and interest is paid for the period April 1 to July 1 by the buyer, the interest received by the corporation is credited to Bond Interest Expense. In that way, when the interest is paid in October, the amount paid can be charged to Bond Interest Expense. The net interest expense will be $275 ($550 − $275). The entry to record sale of the bonds is shown below.

19Y4				
July	*1*	*Cash*	*10 2 7 5 00*	
		Bond Interest Expense		*2 7 5 00*
		11% Bonds Payable, 19Z1		*10 0 0 0 00*
		Issuance of bonds at face plus accrued interest for three months		

Remember that bond discount or premium is amortized over the period from the date the bonds are issued until the date of maturity.

Amortization of Discount or Premium

If bonds are issued at a discount or a premium between interest dates, the discount or premium is amortized over the time remaining from the date of issue to the date of maturity. Suppose, for example, that on March 1, 19X4, a corporation issues $50,000 face value, 9 percent, 10-year bonds, dated January 1, 19X1, and maturing January 1, 19Y1, with interest payments due on January 1 and July 1 of each year. The bonds are issued at 102.5, plus accrued interest. The necessary entry is shown in general journal form below.

19X4				
Mar.	*1*	*Cash*	*52 0 0 0 00*	
		Bond Interest Expense		*7 5 0 00*
		9% Bonds Payable, 19Y1		*50 0 0 0 00*
		Premium on Bonds Payable		*1 2 5 0 00*
		Issued $100,000 of 9% bonds at 102.5 plus accrued interest for two months		

On July 1, 19X4, the date of the first interest payment, the amount of the bond premium to amortize will be $121.95, assuming a straight-line method of amortization.

Total premium	$1,250
Number of months from date of issue to date of maturity (March 1, 19X4, to January 1, 19Y1)	82
Amortization each month ($1,250 ÷ 82)	$15.24
Amortization from March 1, 19X4, to July 1, 19X4 ($15.24 × 4)	$60.96

The entry to record payment of the interest and amortization of the premium on July 1, 19X4, follows.

To calculate interest:

$50,000 × 0.09 × 10 = $45,000

$45,000 ÷ 20 periods = $2,250

19X4				
July	1	*Bond Interest Expense*	2 1 8 9 04	
		Premium on Bonds Payable	6 0 96	
		Cash		2 2 5 0 00
		Semiannual interest on 9% bonds and amortization of bond premium for four months		

Accounting for Bond Issue Costs

Costs related to issuing bonds are treated as additional discount or as a reduction of premium.

In issuing bonds, a corporation incurs **bond issue costs.** These costs include such items as legal and accounting fees and printing costs. Bond issue costs reduce the proceeds of borrowing and increase the effective interest rate. Consequently, they may be accounted for as discount (or as a reduction of premium) on the bonds and amortized over the period the bonds are outstanding. Alternatively, bond issue costs may be charged to expense in the period when they are incurred.

SELF-REVIEW

1. What factor or factors would cause bonds to be sold at a discount?
2. Explain the straight-line method for amortizing bond discount or premium.
3. How is bond discount shown on the balance sheet?
4. Why is the amortization of bond premium offset against interest expense?
5. Ten-year bonds, dated January 1, 19X1, with a face value of $300,000 are issued at 102.32 on May 1, 19X1. How much premium will be amortized on the interest payment date, July 1, 19X1?

Answers to Self-Review

1. Bonds sell at a discount when the face interest rate is less than the market rate of interest on similar investments on the date of the sale.
2. Under the straight-line amortization method, an equal amount of discount or premium is amortized each month from the date of issue until the date of maturity.
3. Discount on bonds payable is shown on the balance sheet as a deduction from the face value of the bonds.
4. Bond premium is a device to adjust the face amount of interest to the market interest at the date of issuance. Thus the premium is directly related to interest expense.
5. The premium to be amortized is $120 (2/116 × $300,000 × 0.0232).

ACCUMULATING FUNDS TO RETIRE BONDS

When the bond issue matures on April 1, 19Z1, the Mirabel Unpainted Furniture Corporation will have to pay bondholders the face amount of their bonds, a total of $100,000, in cash. The premium and discount will be completely amortized at the time of the last interest payment on April 1, 19Z1. Careful planning is needed to make sure that the required money will be available to pay off the bonds on the maturity date. In order to ensure the availability of cash, the corporation may voluntarily set up a **bond sinking fund** or it may be required to do so by its contract with the bondholders.

Bond Sinking Fund

OBJECTIVE 8
Record the transactions of a bond sinking fund.

A bond sinking fund is a planned fund established to accumulate assets to pay off bonds when they mature.

Suppose the corporation is to accumulate $20,000 a year in the bond sinking fund for each of the last five years that the bonds are outstanding. The cash put into the fund will be invested, and the net earnings of the fund will reduce the amount that the corporation will have to add each year after the first. For example, the bond sinking fund is started on April 1, 19Y6, by transferring $20,000 in cash to it. This $20,000 is immediately invested to earn interest. During the next year, $2,800 is earned on the investments made by the sinking fund, and an expense of $50 is incurred in operating the fund. This leaves net earnings of $2,750 for the year. On April 1 of the second year, only $17,250 ($20,000 − $2,750) needs to be added to the fund. This procedure is repeated each year, so that at the end of the fifth year the fund should have accumulated the $100,000 needed to pay off the bonds.

Entries for the first transfer of cash to the fund on April 1, 19Y6; the net earnings for the period ending April 1, 19Y7; the transfer of cash to the fund on April 1, 19Y7; and the final retirement of the bonds at the end of the fifth year are shown below.

19Y6				
Apr.	*1*	*Bond Sinking Fund*	*20 000 00*	
		Cash		*20 000 00*
		First annual installment		
		in bond sinking fund		

19Y7				
Apr.	*1*	*Bond Sinking Fund*	*2 750 00*	
		Income from Sinking Fund		*2 750 00*
		Net income earned by		
		bond sinking fund for year		
	1	*Bond Sinking Fund*	*17 250 00*	
		Cash		*17 250 00*
		Second annual installment		
		($20,000 less $2,750		
		income earned for year		

19Z1				
Apr.	*1*	*11% Bonds Payable, 19Z1*	*100 0 0 0 00*	
		Bond Sinking Fund		*100 0 0 0 00*
		Retirement of bonds		

To simplify the illustration above, it was assumed that the sinking fund is managed by an outside trustee who makes the necessary detailed entries to record the fund transactions. If the corporation handled the bond sinking fund itself, additional entries would be required to show the investment of the fund's cash, the receipt of earnings, and the payment of fund expenses.

Other procedures may be used to finance the sinking fund. For example, an assumption may be made about the rate of earnings of the sinking fund and a constant amount contributed each period, which when added to the earnings will equal the required balance. If earnings exceed or are less than the rate assumed, the periodic contributions will be adjusted.

The bond sinking fund is reported under the heading "Investments" in the Assets section of the balance sheet. Investments are usually shown before Property, Plant, and Equipment.

Retained Earnings Appropriated for Bond Retirement

OBJECTIVE 9

Record an increase or decrease in retained earnings appropriated for bond retirement.

The fact that retained earnings are restricted for bond retirement does not mean that a bond retirement fund has been established.

As further protection for the bondholders and as a clear indication to the stockholders that retained earnings are being kept in the business and dividends are being restricted to make it more probable that funds will be available to pay the bonds at maturity, the bond contract may require that dividend payments be restricted by appropriations of retained earnings while the bonds are outstanding. Even if the bond contract does not require an appropriation, retained earnings may be appropriated by order of the board of directors.

If such an appropriation of retained earnings is made by the directors of the Mirabel Unpainted Furniture Corporation, an entry might be recorded to appropriate $20,000 a year during each of the last five years of the life of the bonds. The firm might also adopt some other schedule of appropriations. When the bonds have been retired (paid off), the balance in the appropriated retained earnings account is returned to the Retained Earnings account. The entries shown below are to make an appropriation on April 1, 19Y6. Similar entries would be made each year for the next four years and to eliminate the appropriation when the bonds are paid. The Retained Earnings Appropriated for Bond Retirement account would be shown under the heading "Appropriated Retained Earnings" on the balance sheet.

19Y6				
Apr.	*1*	*Retained Earnings*	*20 0 0 0 00*	
		Retained Earnings		
		Appropriated for Bond		
		Retirement		*20 0 0 0 00*
		Set up appropriation		

19Z1	*Retained Earnings Appropriated for Bond Retirement*	100 0 0 0 00	
	Retained Earnings		100 0 0 0 00
	Close out appropriation account		

RETIREMENT OF BONDS

OBJECTIVE 10
Record retirement of bonds payable.

Bonds payable are usually retired at the maturity date, but they may be retired prior to that date. We discuss both instances in the paragraphs that follow.

Retirement on Due Date

The retirement of Mirabel's bonds by payment from the sinking fund has been illustrated. If there had been no bond sinking fund, the corporation would have recorded the retirement on the maturity date by debiting 11% Bonds Payable, 19Z1, and crediting Cash.

Early Retirement

Under certain circumstances a corporation may retire some or all of its bonds before maturity. Early retirement may be made because the corporation has surplus cash, interest costs have decreased, or interest rates are expected to decrease. In any case, the corporation may decide to purchase the bonds on the open market, or, if the bonds are callable, the corporation may require the holders to surrender their bonds for cash.

When bonds are retired prior to maturity, the bondholders are paid the agreed-upon price for the bonds plus the accrued interest to the date of purchase. The following two steps are taken to record the purchase and retirement.

The first step in recording retirement of bonds payable prior to maturity is to bring the amortization of discount or premium up to date.

1. Amortize discount or premium on the bonds being retired for the period from the date of the last amortization entry to the date of retirement.
2. Remove the book value of the bonds being retired and record gain or loss equal to the difference between the book value of the bonds and their repurchase price. Debit Bond Interest Expense for any interest accrued at the date of retirement. Credit Cash for the total of the interest and the repurchase price of the bonds.

Any significant gain or loss on early retirement of bonds is shown as an extraordinary gain or loss. If the amount is not significant, it may be shown under Other Income or Other Expense.

To illustrate the early retirement of bonds, we will assume that on January 1, 19X1, the Drake Corporation issued $1 million face value of its 10 percent, 20-year bonds, maturing January 1, 19Z1, with interest payable on January 1 and July 1 of each year. The bonds were issued at 102.4, so a premium of $24,000 was recorded. The premium is being amortized on a straight-line basis at $100 a month ($24,000 ÷ 240 months). The amortization is therefore $600 for each six-month interest payment period ($100 × 6).

On July 1, 19X6, after the interest was paid and the premium was amortized, the account balances related to the bonds were as shown below.

10% Bonds Payable, 19Z1		$1,000,000
Premium on Bonds Payable:		
Original premium	$24,000	
Amortized July 1, 19X1, to July 1, 19X6 ($24,000 × 66 months ÷ 240 months)	6,600	17,400

On September 1, 19X6, the corporation purchased and retired $300,000 face value of the bonds—30 percent of the total outstanding. The bonds were purchased on the open market at 101 plus accrued interest. The bondholders were therefore paid $303,000 ($300,000 × 1.01) for the bonds, plus $5,000 interest accrued for two months ($300,000 × 10% × 2/12). The necessary entries follow the two-step procedure outlined above.

1. Record amortization of premium on the bonds being retired. The amortization for the period July 1 to September 1, 19X6, is $60, computed as shown.

Total original premium on all bonds	$24,000
Portion of premium applicable to bonds being retired, $300,000 ÷ $1,000,000	
Period of amortization, 2 months out of original total of 240 months	
Amortization	
$300,000 ÷ $1,000,000 × $24,000 × 2/240	$60

19X6				
Sept.	*1*	*Premium on Bonds Payable*	*60 00*	
		Bond Interest Expense		*60 00*
		Amortize premium for two months		

The difference between the book value of the bonds being retired and the purchase price is a gain or loss.

2. The calculations for step 2 follow.
   a. The face value and unamortized premium on the bonds retired are removed. The unamortized premium on $300,000 of bonds being retired is $5,160, computed as follows:

Unamortized premium after amortization on July 1, 19X6: 30% × $17,400	$5,220
Less amortization for July and August, recorded above	60
Balance	$5,160

b. The net gain on the retirement is $2,160:

Cost of bonds being retired		$303,000
Book value of bonds being retired:		
Face value	$300,000	
Premium on bonds	5,160	$305,160
Gain on retirement		$ 2,160

c. Interest Expense is debited for the amount of interest paid the bondholders at date of retirement ($300,000 × 10% × 2/12 = $5,000).

d. Cash is credited for the total paid for the bonds and the interest ($303,000 + $5,000 = $308,000).

The entry to record the retirement of the bonds is shown in general journal form below.

19X6				
Sept.	*1*	*10% Bonds Payable, 19Z1*	*300 000 00*	
		Premium on Bonds Payable	*5 160 00*	
		Bond Interest Expense	*5 000 00*	
		Cash		*308 000 00*
		Gain on Early Retirement of Bonds		*2 160 00*
		Retirement of bonds at 101 plus accrued interest		

MANAGERIAL IMPLICATIONS

One of the most critical decisions that management must make is in choosing the proper method for obtaining money. This means that managers must know the advantages and disadvantages of using bonds and stock. A thorough understanding of different characteristics of bonds that may be used is required. For example, such choices as registered versus bearer bonds, secured versus debenture bonds, convertible bonds, and callable bonds must be considered. Bond sinking funds and the appropriation of retained earnings provide tools for management to use in assuring that when bonds fall due funds are available for their retirement. A thorough understanding of such features as call provisions and an appreciation of the opportunity to retire bonds before their maturity date enable management to arrange a more flexible financing structure and to reduce financing costs.

SELF-REVIEW

1. What is a bond sinking fund?
2. What purpose does an appropriation of retained earnings for bond retirement serve?
3. Why would a corporation purchase its own bonds on the open market and retire them?
4. How should gain or loss on retirement of bonds be shown on the income statement?
5. What entry, or entries, will be made when bonds are retired at maturity?

Answers to Self-Review

1. A bond sinking fund is used to accumulate funds to pay off bonds when they mature. The fund may be required by the bond indenture or it may be voluntarily established.
2. The appropriation is intended to protect the bondholders. It clearly indicates that dividends are being restricted because of a future need to pay off the bonds.
3. Bonds may be retired prior to maturity because management has surplus cash, it wants to save interest costs, or it expects interest costs to decrease.
4. Gain or loss on bond retirement is shown as an extraordinary item if the amount is significant. Otherwise, it is shown as Other Income or Other Expense.
5. When bonds are redeemed at maturity, Bonds Payable is debited and Cash (or Bond Sinking Fund) is credited.

CHAPTER 22 Review and Applications

CHAPTER SUMMARY

Long-term borrowing may be accomplished through the issuance of bonds. A bond is a written promise to repay a certain sum at a future date. It bears interest that is usually payable annually or semiannually at a specified rate. Bonds may be secured by the pledge of specific assets as security, or they may be unsecured. Unsecured bonds are known as debenture bonds. Some bonds are registered, with the owner listed in the records of the corporation. Others are bearer bonds with interest coupons attached.

Corporations sometimes issue convertible bonds, which may be converted into common stock under specified terms at the election of the bondholder. Also, bonds are sometimes callable under specified terms at the election of the corporation.

Bonds may be issued at face value, at a premium, or at a discount. If the face rate on the bonds exceeds the market rate of interest at the time the bonds are issued, the bonds will be issued at a premium. If the market rate of interest exceeds the face rate on the bonds, the bonds will be issued at a discount.

The premium or discount is amortized over the period beginning with the date the bonds are issued and ending with the date of maturity. The amortization each period is treated as an adjustment of the interest expense for that period. When bond interest dates do not coincide with the end of the fiscal year, an adjustment is made for accrued bond interest at the end of the year. The adjustment is reversed at the beginning of the next year. When bonds are issued between interest dates, the purchaser pays for any accrued interest up to the date of purchase.

A bond sinking fund may be used to accumulate the cash required to pay bonds at maturity. In addition, an appropriation of retained earnings for bond retirement may be established and increased by debits to the Retained Earnings account and credits to Retained Earnings Appropriated for Bond Retirement account. An appropriation indicates that an amount of retained earnings is not available for dividends because of the need to accumulate funds with which to pay off the bonds.

When bonds are retired prior to maturity, the difference between the book value (face value, plus premium or minus discount) and the repurchase price is treated as gain or loss on retirement of bonds. The gain or loss is shown as an extraordinary item on the income statement if the amount is material. Otherwise, it may be shown as Other Income or Other Expense.

GLOSSARY OF NEW TERMS

Bearer bonds (p. 780) See Coupon bonds

Bond indenture (p. 779) A bond contract

Bond issue costs (p. 793) Costs incurred in issuing bonds, such as legal, printing, and accounting fees

Bond sinking fund (p. 794) A planned fund established to accumulate assets and to pay off bonds when they mature

Bonds payable (p. 779) Long-term debt instruments that are written promises to repay the principal, and any interest, at a specified time

Call price (p. 780) The set price the corporation must pay in redeeming, or calling, bonds

Callable bonds (p. 780) Bonds that can be recalled before their maturity date by the issuing corporation

Carrying value of bonds (p. 791) The balance of the Bonds Payable account plus or minus the bond premium or discount; also called book value of bonds

Collateral trust bonds (p. 779) Bonds secured by the pledge of securities, such as bonds or stock of another company

Convertible bonds (p. 780) Bonds that give the holder the right to convert the bonds into common stock under specified conditions

Coupon bonds (p. 780) Unregistered bonds that can be transferred by delivery and bear coupons that are, in effect, checks payable

Debentures (p. 779) Unsecured bonds backed only by a company's general credit

Discount on bonds payable (p. 789) The excess of the face value over the price received by the corporation for a bond

Face interest (p. 783) The contractual interest specified on the bond

Leveraging (p. 782) Using borrowed funds to earn a profit greater than the interest that must be paid on the borrowing

Mortgage loan (p. 778) A long-term debt created when a note is given as part of the purchase price for land, buildings, or equipment

Premium on bonds payable (p. 787) The excess of the price paid over the face value of a bond

Registered bonds (p. 779) Bonds issued to a particular purchaser listed in the company's records

Secured bonds (p. 779) Bonds for which specific property is pledged as collateral

Serial bonds (p. 780) Bonds issued at one time but maturing at different times over a period of years

Straight-line amortization (p. 788) A method of amortizing the premium or discount on bonds payable in equal amounts each month over the life of the bond

Trading on the equity (p. 782) See Leveraging

REVIEW QUESTIONS

1. What is the meaning of collateral trust?
2. What is a bond indenture?
3. How is the Bonds Payable account classified on the balance sheet?
4. Are authorized, unissued bonds shown on the balance sheet? If so, where?
5. Why might a company use a special bank account for paying bond interest?
6. In a bond indenture dated January 1, 19X1, Shapiro Corporation authorized the issuance of $500,000 face value, 12 percent, 20-year bonds payable. No bonds were issued until July 1, 19X3, when bonds with a face value of $200,000 were issued. At that time, the market rate of interest on similar debt was 10 percent. Would the issue price of the bonds be greater than, or less than, face value? Explain.
7. Why is a bond premium or discount amortized as part of the adjustment process at the end of the year?
8. Why is the year-end adjusting entry for amortization of a bond premium or discount reversed at the start of the new year?
9. How are the legal costs and other costs related to issuing bonds accounted for?
10. Explain how bond accrued interest is handled when bonds are issued between interest payment dates.
11. What is a bond sinking fund?
12. What is the relationship between a bond sinking fund and an appropriation of retained earnings for bond retirement? Explain.
13. Explain the accounting treatment necessary when bonds are retired before maturity.

MANAGERIAL FOCUS

1. Under what circumstances would it be wise for corporate management to obtain long-term funds by issuing bonds instead of selling stock?
2. Which type of bonds would give management greater flexibility in formulating and controlling a corporation's financial affairs?
3. Under what circumstances would it be wise for management to issue additional common stock rather than to issue bonds to meet long-term capital needs?
4. Why would management repurchase and retire a corporation's bonds prior to their maturity?
5. The board of directors of Cohen Corporation is considering authorization of a new bond issue. The controller of the corporation suggests that the bonds contain a provision that they are callable

at 101.6 at any time beginning five years after the date of the bond contract. What does this mean? What would be the advantage of such a provision?

EXERCISES

EXERCISES 22-1 THROUGH 22-3. The Chandy Corporation issued $50,000 of its 12 percent bonds payable on March 1, 19X1. The bonds were issued at face value. Interest is payable semiannually on September 1 and March 1.

EXERCISE 22-1 Tutorial (Obj. 3)

Issuing bonds. Give the entry in general journal form to record the issuance of the bonds on March 1, 19X1.

EXERCISE 22-2 (Obj. 4)

Paying interest on bonds payable. Give the entry in general journal form to record the interest payment by Chandy on September 1, 19X1.

EXERCISE 22-3 (Obj. 4)

Accruing interest on bonds. Give the entry to accrue bond interest on Chandy's bonds on December 31, 19X1.

EXERCISES 22-4 THROUGH 22-6. The Krauss Corporation was authorized to issue $1,000,000 of 12 percent bonds. On April 1, 19X2, the corporation issued bonds with a face value of $90,000 at a price of 102.4. The bonds mature 10 years from the date of issue. Interest is payable semiannually on October 1 and April 1. Legal and printing costs related to the bond issue were $1,200. These costs are to be treated as a discount or a reduction of premium.

EXERCISE 22-4 Tutorial (Obj. 3)

Recording issuance of bonds. Give the entry in general journal form to record the issuance of the bonds on April 1, 19X2.

EXERCISE 22-5 Tutorial (Obj. 6)

Computing amortization of premium on bonds. Using the data given above, what amount of premium will be amortized by Krauss Corporation on October 1, 19X2, assuming that straight-line amortization is used?

EXERCISE 22-6 (Obj. 4, 5, 6)

Recording adjusting entry for bond interest and premium. Using the data given above, give the adjusting entry that would be made by Krauss Corporation on December 31, 19X2, to record accrued interest and to amortize the premium.

EXERCISE 22-7 (Obj. 7)

Recording transactions of a bond sinking fund. Give the entry, in general journal form, to record each of the following transactions.

1. On December 31, 19X4, Wheaton Corporation established a bond sinking fund by depositing $40,000 with the fund trustee.
2. On December 31, 19X4, Wheaton recorded $8,800 net income from its bond sinking fund for the year.
3. On January 2, 19X5, Wheaton made a deposit of $31,200 into the bond sinking fund.

EXERCISE 22-8 (Obj. 9)

Appropriating retained earnings for bond retirement. Record the appropriation of $80,000 of retained earnings on December 31,

19X8, by the Bermuda Corporation to establish an appropriations for bond retirement.

EXERCISE 22-9
(Obj. 10)
Tutorial

Retiring bonds before maturity. On March 1, 19X3, the Tarik Bey Corporation issued $80,000 of its 12 percent bonds, maturing 10 years later, on March 1, 19Y3. Interest is payable semiannually on September 1 and March 1. The issue price was 96.4. Interest and amortization have been recorded through March 1, 19X7, four years after the bonds were issued. On June 1, 19X7, the corporation repurchased and retired $40,000 face value of the bonds at a purchase price of 99.8, plus accrued interest. Give the entry in general journal form to record the repurchase and retirement.

PROBLEMS

PROBLEM SET A

PROBLEM 22-1A
(Obj. 3, 4, 5)
Tutorial

Issuing bonds; bond interest transactions. The board of directors of the Student Computer Services Corporation authorized the issuance of $1,000,000 face value, 10-year, 12 percent bonds dated April 1, 19X1, and maturing on April 1, 19Y1. Interest is payable semiannually on April 1 and October 1. The Student Computer Services Corporation uses the calendar year as its fiscal year. The bond transactions that occurred in 19X1 and 19X2 follow.

Instructions

Record the given transactions in general journal form. Use the account titles given in the chapter.

TRANSACTIONS FOR 19X1

Apr. 1 Issued $40,000 of bonds at face value.
Oct. 1 Paid the semiannual interest on the bonds issued.
Dec. 31 Recorded the adjusting entry for the accrued bond interest.
Dec. 31 Closed the Bond Interest Expense account into the Income Summary account.

TRANSACTIONS FOR 19X2

Jan. 1 Reversed the adjusting entry made on December 31, 19X1.
Apr. 1 Issued $50,000 face value of bonds at face value.
1 Paid the interest for six months on the bonds previously issued.
Oct. 1 Paid the interest for six months on the outstanding bonds.
Dec. 31 Recorded the adjusting entry for the accrued bond interest.
31 Closed the Bond Interest Expense account into the Income Summary account.

PROBLEM 22-2A
(Obj. 3, 4, 5, 6)
Tutorial

Issuing bonds; recording interest transactions and amortization of premium. The board of directors of Ohio Valley Record Shops, Inc., authorized the issuance of $2,000,000 face value of 10-year, 14 percent bonds dated April 1, 19X1, and maturing on April 1, 19Y1. Interest is payable semiannually on April 1 and October 1. The corporation did not immediately issue the bonds because funds were not currently needed. The transactions that took place in 19X3 and 19X4 are shown below.

Instructions

1. Record the given transactions in general journal form. Use the account titles given in the chapter.
2. Prepare the Long-Term Liabilities section of the corporation's balance sheet on December 31, 19X3.

TRANSACTIONS FOR 19X3

Feb. 1 Issued $20,000 face value bonds for $20,196, plus accrued interest.

Apr. 1 Paid the semiannual interest on the outstanding bonds and amortized the bond premium. (Make two entries. Use the straight-line method to compute the amortization.)

Oct. 1 Paid the semiannual interest on the outstanding bonds and amortized the bond premium. (Make two entries.)

Dec. 31 Recorded the adjusting entry for accrued interest and amortization of the bond premium for three months. (Make one entry.)

31 Closed the Bond Interest Expense account into the Income Summary account.

TRANSACTIONS FOR 19X4

Jan. 1 Reversed the adjusting entry made on December 31, 19X3.

PROBLEM 22–3A
(Obj. 3, 4, 5, 7)

Tutorial GL

Issuing bonds; recording bond interest transactions and amortization of discount. The board of directors of the Paris Corporation authorized the issuance of $400,000 face value, 10-year, 10 percent bonds, dated March 1, 19X1, and maturing on March 1, 19Y1. Interest is payable semiannually on September 1 and March 1. The transactions that occurred in 19X1 and 19X2 are shown below.

Instructions

1. Record the given transactions in general journal form. Use the account titles given in the chapter.
2. Prepare the Long-Term Liabilities section of the corporation's balance sheet on December 31, 19X1.

TRANSACTIONS FOR 19X1

May 1 Issued bonds with a face value of $50,000 for $49,070, plus accrued interest. Paid issue costs of $250 on bonds.

Sept. 1 Paid the semiannual bond interest and amortized the discount for four months. (Make two entries. Use the straight-line method to compute the amortization.)

Dec. 31 Recorded an adjusting entry to accrue the interest and to amortize the discount. (Make one entry.)

31 Closed the Bond Interest Expense account into the Income Summary account.

TRANSACTIONS FOR 19X2

Jan. 1 Reversed the adjusting entry made on December 31, 19X1.

Mar. 1 Paid the semiannual bond interest and amortized the discount on the outstanding bonds.

PROBLEM 22–4A
(Obj. 8, 9, 10)
Tutorial

Recording bond sinking fund transactions, retained earnings appropriated for bond retirement, and retirement of bonds. Super High Tech Corporation has outstanding $100,000 of its 11 percent bonds payable, dated January 1, 19X1, and maturing on January 1, 19Z1, 20 years later. The corporation is required under the bond contract to transfer $3,740 to a sinking fund each year. The directors have also voted to restrict retained earnings by transferring $5,000 each year over the life of the bond issue to a Retained Earnings Appropriated for Bond Retirement account. The pertinent account balances on January 1, 19X5, were Bond Sinking Fund, $15,850, and Retained Earnings Appropriated for Bond Retirement, $20,000. Transactions that took place at the end of 19X5 are shown below.

Instructions

1. Prepare entries in general journal form to record the transactions described.
2. Show how the Bond Sinking Fund account and the Retained Earnings Appropriated for Bond Retirement account would be presented on the balance sheet as of December 31, 19X5. (Assume that the ending balance of the Retained Earnings—Unappropriated account after the December 31 appropriation was $45,572.)
3. Assuming that the Bond Sinking Fund account had a balance of $100,000 on January 1, 19Z1, give the entry in general journal form to record retirement of the bonds.

TRANSACTIONS

Dec.	31	The annual bond sinking fund deposit was made.
	31	The annual appropriation of retained earnings was recorded.
	31	The bond sinking fund trustee reported $18,900 of net income on the sinking fund investments for the year.

PROBLEM 22–5A
(Obj. 10)

Retiring bonds payable prior to maturity. On April 1, 19X1, the Santana Corporation issued $50,000 face value, 14 percent bonds at 98.8. The bonds are dated April 1, 19X1, and mature 20 years later. The discount is amortized on each interest payment date. The interest is payable semiannually on April 1 and October 1. On March 1, 19X6, the corporation purchased one-half of the outstanding bonds from the bondholders and retired them. The purchase price was 99.2, plus accrued interest for five months.

Instructions

1. Give the entry in general journal form to amortize the discount on the bonds being retired (five months' amortization). Use the straight-line method.
2. Give the entry in general journal form to record the repurchase and retirement of the bonds. (Use the Loss on Early Retirement of Bonds account.)

PROBLEM SET B

PROBLEM 22–1B (Obj. 3, 4, 5)

Tutorial

Issuing bonds; bond interest transactions. The board of directors of National Pizza Corporation authorized the issuance of $1,000,000 face value of 10 percent bonds dated May 1, 19X2. The bonds will mature on May 1, 19Y2. The interest is payable semiannually on May 1 and November 1. The bond transactions that occurred in 19X2 and 19X3 are shown below.

Instructions

Record the given transactions in general journal form. Use the account titles given in the chapter.

TRANSACTIONS FOR 19X2

May 1 Issued $60,000 of bonds at face value.
Nov. 1 Paid the semiannual bond interest on the outstanding bonds.
Dec. 31 Recorded the adjusting entry to accrue the interest on the bonds issued.
31 Closed the Bond Interest Expense account into the Income Summary account.

TRANSACTIONS FOR 19X3

Jan. 1 Reversed the adjusting entry of December 31, 19X2.
May 1 Paid the semiannual bond interest.
Nov. 1 Paid the semiannual bond interest.
1 Issued $10,000 of bonds at face value.
Dec. 31 Recorded the adjusting entry to accrue the interest on all bonds issued.
31 Closed the Bond Interest Expense account into the Income Summary account.

PROBLEM 22–2B (Obj. 3, 4, 5, 6)

Tutorial

Issuing bonds; recording interest transactions and amortization of premium. The board of directors of Creative Computer Schools, Inc., authorized issuance of $2,000,000 of 12 percent bonds. Each bond has a face value of $1,000 and is in registered form. The interest is payable semiannually on May 1 and November 1. The bonds are dated May 1, 19X1, and mature 10 years later, on May 1, 19Y1. Because the funds to be raised were not immediately needed, no bonds were issued until 19X3. The transactions that occurred in 19X3 and 19X4 are shown below.

Instructions

1. Record the given transactions in general journal form. Use the account titles given in the chapter.
2. Prepare the Long-Term Liabilities section of the corporation's balance sheet on December 31, 19X3.

TRANSACTIONS FOR 19X3

Feb. 1 Issued $50,000 of bonds at face value, plus accrued interest.
May 1 Paid the semiannual interest on the bonds issued.
1 Issued $50,000 of bonds at 103.4 less a $500 broker's fee. (Treat the broker's fee as a reduction from the premium.)

Nov. 1 Paid the semiannual interest on the bonds.
1 Recorded the amortization of the premium on the bonds sold on May 1, using the straight-line method.
Dec. 31 Recorded the adjusting entry to accrue interest on the bonds issued and to amortize the premium for two months.
31 Closed the Bond Interest Expense account into the Income Summary account.

TRANSACTIONS FOR 19X4
Jan. 1 Reversed the adjusting entry of December 31, 19X3.

PROBLEM 22–3B
(Obj. 3, 4, 5, 7)

Tutorial

Issuing bonds; recording bond interest transactions and amortization of discount. The board of directors of Jordanian Corporation authorized the issuance of $500,000 face value of 10 percent bonds. The bonds mature 10 years from their issue date of May 1, 19X1. The interest is payable semiannually on May 1 and November 1. Because the funds were not immediately needed, no bonds were issued until 19X4. The transactions that occurred in 19X4 and 19X5 are shown below.

Instructions

1. Record the given transactions in general journal form. Use the account titles given in the chapter.
2. Prepare the Long-Term Liabilities section of the corporation's balance sheet on December 31, 19X4.

TRANSACTIONS FOR 19X4
May 1 Issued $50,000 of bonds at 99, less a broker's fee of $500. (Treat the broker's fee as part of the discount on the bonds.)
Nov. 1 Paid the semiannual bond interest.
1 Amortized the discount on the bonds issued.
Dec. 31 Recorded the adjusting entry to accrue the interest on the bonds issued and to amortize the discount for two months. (Make one entry.)
31 Closed the Bond Interest Expense account into the Income Summary account.

TRANSACTIONS FOR 19X5
Jan. 1 Reversed the adjusting entry of December 31, 19X4.

PROBLEM 22–4B
(Obj. 8, 9, 10)

Tutorial

Recording bond sinking fund transactions, retained earnings appropriated for bond retirement, and retirement of bonds. Video Products Corporation has outstanding $60,000 face value of 12 percent bonds payable dated January 1, 19X1, and maturing January 1, 19Y3, 12 years later. The corporation is required under the bond contract to transfer $4,100 each year to a sinking fund. The directors have also voted to restrict retained earnings by transferring $5,000 each year to a Retained Earnings Appropriated for Bond Retirement account. On January 1, 19X6, the pertinent account balances are Bond Sinking Fund, $22,100, and Retained Earnings Appropriated for Bond Retirement, $25,000. Transactions that took place at the end of 19X6 follow.

Instructions

1. Prepare entries in general journal form to record the end-of-year transactions in 19X6.
2. Show how the Bond Sinking Fund account and the Retained Earnings Appropriated for Bond Retirement account would appear on the balance sheet as of December 31, 19X6. (Assume that the balance of the Retained Earnings—Unappropriated account after the transaction given was $84,957.)
3. Assuming that the Bond Sinking Fund account had a balance of $60,000 on January 1, 19Y3, give the entry in general journal form to record payment of the amount due and the retirement of the bonds.

TRANSACTIONS FOR 19X6

Dec. 31 The annual bond sinking fund deposit was made.
31 The annual appropriation of retained earnings was recorded.
31 The bond sinking fund trustee reported a net income of $2,884 on the sinking fund investments for the year.

PROBLEM 22–5B
(Obj. 10)

Retiring bonds payable prior to maturity. On February 1, 19X1, Spring Break Tours Corporation issued $60,000 face value, 12 percent bonds at 98.2. The bonds were dated February 1, 19X1, and mature 20 years later. The discount is to be amortized on each interest payment date. The interest is payable semiannually on February 1 and August 1. On September 1, 19X4, the corporation purchased $30,000 face value of the bonds from the bondholders and retired them. The purchase price was 98.

Instructions

1. Give the entry in general journal form to amortize the discount on the bonds being retired (one month's amortization) on September 1, 19X4.
2. Give the entry in general journal form to record the repurchase and retirement of the bonds. (Use the Gain on Retirement of Bonds account.)

CHALLENGE PROBLEM

On December 31, 19X0, the equity accounts of Eddie Mata Corporation contained the following balances.

Common Stock ($20 par, 100,000 shares authorized) 30,000 shares issued and outstanding	600,000
Retained Earnings	600,000

For the year 19X0 the corporation had net income before income taxes of $230,000, income taxes of $80,000, and net income after taxes of $150,000. The corporation's marginal tax rate is 39 percent.

Construction of a new plant at a cost of $600,000 is planned. The corporation's president, who owns 60 percent of the corporation's common stock, estimates that the plant would result in an increased net income of approximately $150,000 before interest and taxes. The financial vice president is less optimistic and forecasts that the increase in income before interest and taxes would be only $100,000.

Management is considering two possibilities for financing:

a. Issuance of 12,000 additional shares of common stock for $50 per share
b. Issuance of $600,000 face amount, 15-year, 10 percent bonds payable, secured by a mortgage lien on the plant

Instructions

1. Assuming that profits from existing operations will remain the same and that the president's estimate of net income from the new plant is correct, prepare a two-column table that shows for each of the proposed financing plans the items listed below.
   a. Total net income before interest and tax
   b. Total bond interest
   c. Total income tax
   d. Total income after tax
   e. Present income after tax
   f. Increase/decrease in total income after bond interest and tax
   g. Present earnings per share of common stock (Compute earnings per share by dividing the net income after taxes by the number of shares of common stock outstanding.)
   h. Estimated earnings per share of common stock under the proposed plan.
   i. Ratio of net income after income taxes for 19X0 to total stockholders' equity on December 31, 19X0 (divide net income for 19X0 by total stockholders' equity on December 31, 19X0.)
   j. Ratio of net income after income taxes to total stockholders' equity if the plant is constructed. Use the following formula:

$$\frac{\text{Estimated total net income}}{\text{Present stockholders' equity (\$1,200,000) + Additional common stockholders' equity resulting from new financing}}$$

2. Construct a similar table, assuming the financial vice president's estimate of earnings is correct.
3. Write a brief comment on the results of your analysis.

CRITICAL THINKING PROBLEM

Next-Day Air Express Company currently has $2,000,000 of 10 percent, 20-year bonds outstanding. The bonds were issued at par value and will mature in 15 years. Interest rates have dropped to 8 percent, and the president of the company wants to know whether it would be a good idea for the company to buy back the outstanding 10 percent bonds and issue new 15-year bonds with an 8 percent interest rate.

1. How much money would Next-Day Air Express save in interest payments if new, 8 percent bonds were issued?
2. Under what circumstances would this action be advantageous for Next-Day Air?

MINI-PRACTICE SET 3

Corporation Accounting Cycle

This project will give you an opportunity to apply your knowledge of accounting principles and procedures to a corporation. You will handle the accounting work of the Accent Corporation for 19X5.

INTRODUCTION

The chart of accounts and account balances of the Accent Corporation on January 1, 19X5, are shown on the next page. The Accent Corporation *does not* use reversing entries.

INSTRUCTIONS

1. Open the general ledger accounts and enter the balances for January 1, 19X5. Obtain the necessary figures from the chart of accounts on page 812.
2. Analyze the transactions given below and on the pages that follow, and then record them in the general journal. Use 1 as the number of the first journal page.
3. Post the journal entries to the general ledger accounts.
4. Prepare a worksheet for the year ended December 31, 19X5.
5. Prepare a summary income statement for the year ended December 31, 19X5.
6. Prepare a statement of retained earnings for the year ended December 31, 19X5.
7. Prepare a balance sheet as of December 31, 19X5.
8. Journalize and post the adjusting entries as of December 31, 19X5.
9. Journalize and post the closing entries as of December 31, 19X5.

SELECTED TRANSACTIONS FOR 19X5

Jan. 4 Issued 9,000 shares of 12 percent preferred stock for $12 a share. (The corporation has been authorized to issue 25,000 shares of preferred stock.)

15 Paid estimated income taxes of $14,700 accrued at the end of 19X4.

Apr. 1 Paid semiannual bond interest on the 10-year, 10-percent bonds payable and amortized the premium for the period since October 1, 19X4. (The interest and premium were recorded as of December 31, 19X4; the entry was not reversed.) The bonds were issued on October 1, 19X3, at a price of 110, and they mature on October 1, 19Y3. Use straight-line amortization.

ACCENT CORPORATION Chart of Accounts/Account Balances			
Account Number	Account Name	Debit	Credit
101	Cash	$ 72,185	
103	Accounts Receivable	161,910	
104	Allowance for Doubtful Accounts		$ 2,960
105	Subscriptions Receivable on Common Stock		
121	Interest Receivable		
131	Merchandise Inventory	136,170	
141	Land	50,000	
151	Buildings	150,000	
152	Accumulated Depreciation—Buildings		15,000
161	Furniture and Equipment	61,000	
162	Accumulated Depreciation—Furniture & Equip.		12,200
181	Organization Costs	9,000	
202	Accounts Payable		134,600
203	Interest Payable		2,500
205	Estimated Income Taxes Payable		14,700
206	Dividends Payable—Preferred Stock		
207	Dividends Payable—Common Stock		
211	10-Year, 10% Bonds Payable		100,000
212	Premium on 10% Bonds Payable		8,750
301	12% Preferred Stock ($10 Par, 25,000 Shares Authorized)		
302	Paid-In Capital in Excess of Par—Preferred Stock		
303	Common Stock (No Par, $20 Stated Value, 100,000 Authorized)		60,000
304	Paid-In Capital in Excess of Stated Value—Common Stock		70,000
305	Common Stock Subscribed		
306	Common Stock Dividend Distributable		
311	Retained Earnings Appropriated for Plant Expansion		
312	Retained Earnings—Unappropriated		219,555
343	Treasury Stock—Preferred		
399	Income Summary		
401	Sales		
501	Purchases		
601	Operating Expenses		
701	Interest Income		
751	Interest Expense		
753	Organization Costs Amortized		
801	Income Tax Expense		
		$640,265	$640,265

July 1 Accent Corporation's board of directors declared a cash dividend of $0.60 a share on the common stock. The dividend is payable on July 25 to stockholders of record as of July 15.

25 Paid the cash dividend on the common stock.

Aug. 10 A purchaser of 400 shares of preferred stock issued on January 4 asked the corporation to repurchase the shares. The corporation repurchased the stock for $11.75 a share. The stock is to be held by the corporation until it can be resold to another purchaser.

Oct. 1 Paid the semiannual bond interest and recorded amortization of the bond premium.

Dec. 1 Because of its good cash position and current bond prices, Accent Corporation repurchased and retired $20,000 par value of the 10-percent bonds that it has outstanding. The repurchase price was 98, plus accrued interest.

15 Accent Corporation's board of directors declared a cash dividend of $1.20 a share on the outstanding preferred stock. This dividend is payable on January 10 to stockholders of record as of December 31.

15 Accent Corporation's board of directors also declared a 15-percent stock dividend on the outstanding common stock. The new shares are to be distributed on January 10 to stockholders of record as of December 31. At the time the dividend was declared, the common stock had a fair market value of $95 a share.

30 Received a subscription for 500 shares of Accent Corporation's common stock at $100 a share from the company's president. Received cash equal to one-half the purchase price on the date of subscription. The balance of the purchase price is to be paid in two equal installments on January 15 and January 31, 19X6. (The subscriber will not be entitled to the stock dividend previously declared on the outstanding shares of common stock.)

30 Because the management of Accent Corporation foresees the need to expand a warehouse the firm owns, the board of directors has restricted future dividend payments. Record the appropriation of $30,000 of retained earnings for plant expansion.

SUMMARY OPERATING TRANSACTIONS FOR 19X5

Journalize the following summary transactions using December 31, 19X5, as the record date.

1. Total sales of merchandise for the year were $3,050,000. All sales were on credit.
2. Total collections on accounts receivable during the year were $2,860,000.

3. Total purchases of merchandise for the year were $1,710,000. All purchases were on credit.
4. Total operating expenses incurred during the year were $612,000. (Debit Operating Expense and credit Accounts Payable.)
5. Total cash payments on accounts payable during the year were $1,942,000.
6. Total accounts receivable charged off as uncollectible during the year were $5,610. (Accent Corporation uses the allowance method to record uncollectible accounts.)

DATA FOR YEAR-END ADJUSTMENTS

1. The balance of Allowance for Doubtful Accounts should be adjusted to equal 1 percent of the balance of Accounts Receivable. (Debit Operating Expenses.)
2. Depreciation on the buildings should be recorded. (Debit Operating Expenses.) The firm uses the straight-line method and an estimated life of 20 years to compute this adjustment.
3. Depreciation on furniture and equipment should be recorded. (Debit Operating Expenses.) The firm uses the straight-line method and an estimated life of 10 years to compute this adjustment.
4. Accrued interest on the outstanding bonds payable of Accent Corporation should be recorded and the premium amortized.
5. The amortization of organization costs for the year should be recorded. The Accent Corporation was formed on January 1, 19X3. Organization costs of $15,000 were incurred at the time and are being amortized over a 60-month period.
6. The ending merchandise inventory is $138,700.

OTHER DATA

Estimated federal income taxes are to be recorded using the tax rates given on page 732.

UNIT EIGHT

Financial Reporting and Analysis

The visible result of accounting activities is the preparation of financial statements. For financial statements to be useful, they must be analyzed and the information interpreted. There are two major types of statement analysis. One type of analysis is the comparison of items on the statements of one period with the corresponding items on the statements of other periods. A second form of analysis is the comparison of items on a statement to some base amount to establish a relationship that is usually expressed as a ratio or a percentage.

Of special importance in analyzing the changes in the financial condition of a business is the statement of cash flows. This statement reflects the changes in the company's cash balance during the accounting period and includes changes caused by profit or loss, the buying or selling of long-term assets, and various financing transactions.

CHAPTER

23

Statement Analysis: Comparative Statements

OBJECTIVES

1. Use vertical analysis techniques to analyze a comparative income statement.
2. Use vertical analysis techniques to analyze a comparative balance sheet.
3. Use horizontal analysis techniques to analyze a comparative income statement.
4. Use horizontal analysis techniques to analyze a comparative balance sheet.
5. Use horizontal and vertical analysis techniques to analyze a comparative statement of retained earnings.
6. Use trend analysis to evaluate financial statements.
7. Interpret the results of the statement analyses by comparison with industry averages.
8. Define the accounting terms new to this chapter.

Financial statements are designed to help owners, managers, creditors, and other interested parties make intelligent business decisions. The statement reader must know what the figures on the statements mean and how to analyze and interpret the data in a logical and systematic manner. For example, does a net income of *X* dollars mean a good, poor, or average performance? Do the financial statements represent an improvement over the last period and the last several periods? Do the figures indicate that the firm is being run efficiently?

To assist the reader in interpreting business data, financial statements are usually presented in comparative form. **Comparative statements** are financial statements presented side by side for two or more years. In this chapter, you will see how the figures on comparative statements can be used for vertical analysis and horizontal analysis. In the following chapter we will discuss how relationships between individual items on the financial statements are used to measure the profitability, financial strength, and liquidity of the company. The financial statements of the Mirabel Unpainted Furniture Corporation will provide the basis for discussion in both chapters.

NEW TERMS

Common-size statements ▪ Comparative statements ▪ Horizontal analysis ▪ Industry averages ▪ Ratio analysis ▪ Trend analysis ▪ Vertical analysis

THE PHASES OF STATEMENT ANALYSIS

Sound conclusions can be drawn from financial statements only when the meaning of the figures contained in them is completely understood. An analysis must be made of key items and key relationships before the results can be evaluated. The figures are usually analyzed in a two-step procedure:

1. Differences, percentages, and ratios are computed.
2. The findings are interpreted.

The Computation Phase

The first step in statement analysis is the computation phase. The required computations are made by using simple arithmetic processes and can be learned rather quickly. Three basic calculations are used.

The computational phase of statement analysis involves computing percentages and ratios between various statement items.

1. The relationship of each item on a financial statement to some base amount on that statement is computed. This process is referred to as **vertical analysis.** It is customary to express each item on the income statement as a percentage of net sales for the fiscal period covered by the statement. Similarly, each item on the balance sheet is expressed as a percentage of total assets.
2. Dollar amounts of changes and percentages of changes in individual items in the financial statements from year to year are computed. This approach is called **horizontal analysis.**
3. Relationships between various items in the annual financial statements are computed. This procedure, referred to as **ratio analysis,** may involve two items on the same statement or items on different statements. Ratio analysis is discussed in Chapter 24.

The Interpretation Phase

The second step in statement analysis, the interpretation phase, is more difficult. A thorough understanding of financial statements and a knowledge of the operations of the individual business and of the industry in which the business operates are necessary for the analyst to become proficient at interpreting financial statements. The interpretation phase is also the more important step because it is necessary for an understanding of the significance of the percentages and ratios computed. Yardsticks against which computations can be compared help to provide an understanding of the results of operations.

The interpretation phase involves understanding and explaining the percentages and ratios computed.

The most frequent comparisons are made using the same ratios or percentages for prior years, budgets or goals of the company, and/or ratios and percentages achieved by other companies in the industry.

VERTICAL ANALYSIS OF FINANCIAL STATEMENTS

Having completed this brief overview of the statement analysis process, let us now turn to the techniques of vertical analysis of financial statements, beginning with the comparative income statement of Mirabel Unpainted Furniture Corporation for the years 19Y3 and 19Y2, shown in Figure 23–1. For purposes of analysis, the items on this statement are rounded to the nearest whole dollar.

FIGURE 23–1
A Comparative Income Statement: Vertical Analysis

MIRABEL UNPAINTED FURNITURE CORPORATION
Comparative Income Statement (Vertical Analysis)
Years Ended December 31, 19Y3 and 19Y2

	Amounts		Percent of Net Sales	
	19Y3	19Y2	19Y3	19Y2
Revenue				
Sales	3241578	2970530	100.7	100.7
Less Sales Returns and Allowances	22496	19390	0.7	0.7
Net Sales	3219082	2951140	100.0	100.0
Cost of Goods Sold				
Merchandise Inventory, Jan. 1	285100	253700	8.8*	8.6
Purchases (Net)	1982488	1808270	61.6	61.3
Freight In	15000	13000	0.5	0.4
Total Merchandise Available for Sale	2282588	2074970	70.9	70.3
Less Merchandise Inventory, Dec. 31	300000	285100	9.3	9.6*
Cost of Goods Sold	1982588	1789870	61.6	60.7
Gross Profit on Sales	1236494	1161270	38.4	39.3
Operating Expenses				
Selling Expenses (Schedule A)	719346	706032	22.3	23.9
Administrative Expenses (Schedule B)	288952	260501	9.0	8.8
Total Operating Expenses	1008298	966533	31.3	32.7*
Net Income from Operations	228196	194737	7.1	6.6
Other Income				
Gain on Sale of Equipment	1000	—0—		
Interest Income	355	722		
Total Other Income	1355	722		
Total Income for Year	229551	195459	7.1	6.6
Other Expenses				
Bond Interest Expense	6774	4400	0.2	0.1
Other Interest Expense	475	2300		0.1
Total Other Expenses	7249	6700	0.2	0.2
Net Income Before Income Taxes	222302	188759	6.9	6.4
Income Tax Expense	69950	56870	2.2	1.9
Net Income After Income Taxes	152352	131889	4.7	4.5

*Adjusted

Information Block: Communication

Business Reports

Managers in every organization use reports to gather essential information for solving problems and making decisions. Business professionals analyze financial statements and other documents to detect problem areas in the business. This analysis and interpretation is then communicated to management in a written or oral business report.

A *business report* is an objective, organized presentation of essential information for analyzing and evaluating situations. To ensure ample preparation time for a business report, determine the target due date and any specific requirements. The quality of the resulting decisions will be largely dependent on the quality and timeliness of the information in the business report.

Business reports may be formal or informal. *Formal reports* (or long reports) generally involve major investigations and result in a lengthy, formal presentation. *Informal reports* (or short reports) are common in organizations and may be oral and/or written. Informal oral reports may be communicated in meetings or small- or large-group discussions. Whether written or oral, the sender presents the problem being analyzed, the supporting information (facts, figures, charts), an analysis of the information, a summary, conclusions, and recommendations.

To prepare an effective written or oral business report, follow these guidelines.

1. Apply the steps for planning and developing effective business communication.
2. Apply the appropriate plan for positive/neutral, negative, or persuasive messages. As with all other communication, the plan for the business report is dependent upon the anticipated receiver reaction.

Vertical Analysis of the Income Statement

OBJECTIVE 1

Use vertical analysis techniques to analyze a comparative income statement.

Notice the descriptive heading on the comparative income statement. The third line indicates the periods covered by the statement. The year 19Y3 is the more recent year and is presented in the column to the left, with the figures for the earlier year, 19Y2, in the column to the right. The presentation is made in condensed form. The details of the selling expenses and administrative expenses are shown in separate schedules, illustrated later in this chapter, so that significant changes in individual expenses will be readily apparent to the statement reader.

3. To enhance readability of written business reports, consider using short, descriptive headings to separate the topics within the report. Generally the outline topics are useful as headings for the actual report. As with the block letter format and the memorandum format, place the headings at the left margin. To differentiate the heading levels, use all uppercase letters, uppercase and lowercase letters, underlines, or different type styles.
4. To enhance written and oral business reports, consider whether portions of the report will be more effective if the information is displayed in a graphic. A graphic may be a table, chart, diagram, drawing, or financial statements. In oral presentations, graphics may be displayed on transparencies, slides, or videos.

Project: Assume you are a financial manager for a company of your choice. Using an annual report from that company, prepare an informal business report to your instructor. Use the memorandum format with headings and at least one graphic. All information in the report must be factual. Applying your knowledge of accounting concepts and practices (capital structure, stock, inventory, depreciation, and so on), address any relevant topics, including those listed below.

- Analyze and interpret the financial statements.
- Identify the strengths and weaknesses of the company.
- Identify the existing and potential problem areas.
- Project the likelihood of the company's future success.
- Provide a summary of your findings.
- Identify your conclusions or recommendations.

Remember to follow the steps for planning and developing effective business communication.

Computing the percentage relationship of each item on the income statement with net sales, or each item on the balance sheet with total assets, is called vertical analysis.

In vertical analysis of the income statement, it is customary to express items on the statement as a percentage of the *net sales* figure. In each column the net sales figure is used as the base, or 100 percent. Every figure in the column is expressed as a percentage of net sales. To compute an item's percentage of net sales, divide the amount of that item by the amount of net sales (amount ÷ net sales = percentage of net sales). For example, in 19Y3, the cost of goods sold is shown in the comparative income statement as 61.6 percent of net sales, computed as follows.

$$\frac{\text{Cost of goods sold}}{\text{Net sales}} = \frac{\$1{,}982{,}588}{\$3{,}219{,}082} = 0.6159, \text{ or } 61.59 \text{ percent, which is rounded to } 61.6 \text{ percent}$$

In statement analysis, it is customary to compute percentages to the nearest one-tenth of a percent.

In making computations such as these, it is customary to carry the division one place further than needed to show the answer and then round off. In analyzing statements, the usual practice is to round off percentages to the nearest one-tenth of a percent. The computation in the example above is made to the fourth decimal (0.6159). That decimal fraction is converted to a percentage by moving the decimal point two places to the right (61.59 percent). The percentage is then rounded to the nearest one-tenth of a percent; hence, 61.59 is rounded to 61.6.

Note in the comparative income statement in Figure 23–1 that gross sales are larger than 100 percent ($3,241,578 ÷ $3,219,082 = 100.7 percent in 19Y3, for example) because of Sales Returns and Allowances, which are 0.7 percent of net sales in 19Y3.

In vertical statement analysis, the percentages may be added and subtracted.

You will observe that the percentage figures may be added and subtracted, giving highly informative subtotals and final total percentages of change.

Because of the procedure used for rounding off, the individual percentages may not add up to 100 percent. In this case one or more percentages may be adjusted arbitrarily until the total equals 100 percent. However, if the difference is more than a very slight amount, it is probable that an error has been made, and all the computations should be checked before adjusting any of the figures. Several percentages, marked by asterisks, have been adjusted on the comparative income statement seen in Figure 23–1.

In common-size statements, percentages (of net sales on the income statement and of assets on the balance sheet) are shown instead of dollar amounts.

When each item on a statement is expressed as a percentage of some common base figure on the statement, the result is called a **common-size statement.** The last two columns in the comparative income statement may be referred to as a *comparative common-size statement.*

Percentages obtained by vertical analysis of the income statement are especially useful when they are compared with the percentages of the same company for prior years. It is helpful to make comparisons with several years to detect trends, but even year-to-year comparisons are useful. For example, the comparative income statement of the Mirabel Unpainted Furniture Corporation shows that gross profit on sales was 39.3 percent in 19Y2, but decreased to 38.4 percent in 19Y3. This decrease probably resulted from problems with pricing policies or with purchasing procedures. A comparison with the **industry average** might be very revealing. For example, if trade association publications reveal that the average gross profit for the industry is 41.7 percent, a more detailed analysis of Mirabel's business activities would certainly be justified. The corporation's lower-than-average margin of gross profit may be attributed to peculiarities of its operations, its local competition, or other factors. However, the unfavorable comparison with the industry average is at least an indication of the need for further examination.

Vertical Analysis of the Balance Sheet

OBJECTIVE 2
Use vertical analysis techniques to analyze a comparative balance sheet.

In vertical analysis of the balance sheet, each item is expressed as either a percentage of total assets or a percentage of total liabilities and stockholders' equity.

$$\frac{\text{Individual asset item}}{\text{Total assets}} = \text{Percent of total assets}$$

$$\frac{\text{Individual liability or equity item}}{\text{Total liabilities and stockholders' equity}} = \text{Percent of total liabilities and stockholders' equity}$$

A comparative balance sheet for the Mirabel Unpainted Furniture Corporation is presented in Figure 23–2, page 824, with the results of vertical analysis shown. Amounts are shown in the first two money columns. The pair of columns on the right is used to record each item as a percentage of total assets for each year, the later year on the left and the earlier year on the right. For instance, on December 31, 19Y3, the cash balance was $72,860 and the total assets were $779,144. Thus the cash balance is found to be 9.4 percent of total assets in 19Y3.

$$\frac{\text{Cash}}{\text{Total assets}} = \frac{\$72{,}860}{\$779{,}144} = 0.0935 = 9.4 \text{ percent}$$

The same procedure is applied to each item in turn.

You will recall that a characteristic of the vertical process is that the percentages can be added and subtracted down the column to give 100 percent on the line for total assets and also on the line for total liabilities and stockholders' equity. In making the computations and rounding off percentages, it may be necessary, as with vertical analysis of income statements, to adjust one or more of the figures to obtain an even 100 percent for each total.

Vertical analysis percentages of the balance sheet are very useful when they are compared with the percentages of the same company for previous years and with those of other companies in the same industry. Changes in the percentages may reveal situations that need investigation. For example, the comparative balance sheet of the Mirabel Unpainted Furniture Corporation shows that cash has decreased from 15.9 percent of total assets in 19Y2 to 9.4 percent of total assets in 19Y3. The accountant would be quick to realize that this decline may mean a future problem and would take steps to find out exactly why the decrease occurred.

FIGURE 23–2
A Comparative Balance Sheet: Vertical Analysis

MIRABEL UNPAINTED FURNITURE CORPORATION Comparative Balance Sheet (Vertical Analysis) December 31, 19Y3 and 19Y2	Amounts on December 31		Percent of Total Assets	
	19Y3	19Y2	19Y3	19Y2
Assets				
Current Assets				
Cash	72860	100187	9.4	15.9
Accounts Receivable (Net)	198184	168184	25.4	26.8
Merchandise Inventory	300000	285100	38.5	45.4
Prepaid Insurance	5700	2600	0.7	0.4
Other Prepayments	5500	2500	0.7	0.4
Total Current Assets	582244	558571	74.7	88.9
Property, Plant, and Equipment				
Land	30000	30000	3.9	4.8
Building	120000	—0—	15.4	
Less Accumulated Depreciation	2000	—0—	0.3	
Net Book Value—Building	118000	—0—	15.1	
Equipment and Fixtures	103200	83600	13.3*	13.3
Less Accumulated Depreciation	54300	44000	7.0	7.0
Net Book Value—Equipment and Fixtures	48900	39600	6.3	6.3
Total Property, Plant, and Equipment	196900	69600	25.3	11.1
Total Assets	779144	628171	100.0	100.0
Liabilities and Stockholders' Equity				
Current Liabilities				
Accounts Payable	113326	92300	14.5	14.7
Income Tax Payable	17000	14000	2.2	2.2
Accrued Liabilities	14446	17530	1.9	2.8
Total Current Liabilities	144772	123830	18.6	19.7
Long-Term Liabilities				
Long-Term Notes Payable	—0—	10000		1.6
11% Bonds Payable, 19Z1	70000	40000	9.0	6.4
Premium on Bonds Payable	979	—0—	0.1	
Total Long-Term Liabilities	70979	50000	9.1	8.0
Total Liabilities	215751	173830	27.7	27.7
Stockholders' Equity				
12% Pref. Stock ($100 par, 2,000 shares auth.)				
Issued and Outstanding, 1,000 shares	100000	100000	12.8	15.9
Paid-in Capital in Excess of Par Value	6000	6000	0.8	1.0
Com. Stock ($50 stated value, 10,000 shares auth.)				
Issued and Outstanding: 3,200 shares in 19Y3, 3,000 shares in 19Y2	160000	150000	20.5	23.9
Paid-in Capital in Excess of Stated Value	29000	19000	3.7	3.0
Retained Earnings (Schedule C)	268393	179341	34.5*	28.5
Total Stockholders' Equity	563393	454341	72.3	72.3
Total Liabilities and Stockholders' Equity	779144	628171	100.0	100.0

* Adjusted

SELF-REVIEW

1. How does vertical analysis differ from horizontal analysis?
2. When a vertical analysis is made of the income statement, what item serves as the base for the percentage calculations?
3. Why are the financial statement items of one period compared with those of the prior period?
4. How does the computation phase of statement analysis differ from the interpretation phase?
5. What is a common-size statement?

Answers to Self-Review

1. Vertical analysis refers to a comparison of items on an individual financial statement. Horizontal analysis refers to a comparison of data for the current period with data of a prior period.
2. Vertical analysis of the income statement is based on net sales.
3. This comparison often reveals significant changes that need to be investigated.
4. The computation phase involves simple mathematical computations. The interpretation phase considers what caused relationships or changes and what can be done to improve the relationships or changes.
5. Common-size statements express each item on the income statement as a percent of net sales and each item on the balance sheet as a percent of total assets. Dollar amounts are not given for the items.

HORIZONTAL ANALYSIS OF FINANCIAL STATEMENTS

Comparing an item on a financial statement with the same item for past years is called horizontal analysis.

Financial statements for two or more periods may be evaluated by means of horizontal analysis in which the items on each line are compared to determine the change in dollar amounts. In addition, the percentage of the change may be shown (with the earlier figures used as the base).

Horizontal Analysis of the Income Statement

OBJECTIVE 3

Use horizontal analysis techniques to analyze a comparative income statement.

Let's examine how a horizontal analysis is made, starting with the comparative income statement of Mirabel Corporation for 19Y3 and 19Y2, shown in Figure 23–3. We will subsequently examine the horizontal analysis of the balance sheet.

Each figure in the 19Y3 statement is compared with the corresponding figure on the 19Y2 statement, the amount of change is shown, and the percentage of change is shown. For example, look at the sales figures on the comparative income statement.

FIGURE 23–3
A Comparative Income Statement: Horizontal Analysis

MIRABEL UNPAINTED FURNITURE CORPORATION
Comparative Income Statement (Horizontal Analysis)
Years Ended December 31, 19Y3 and 19Y2

	Amounts		*Increase or (Decrease) During 19Y3*	
	19Y3	*19Y2*	*Amount*	*Percent*
Revenue				
Sales	3241578	2970530	271048	9.1
Less Sales Returns and Allowances	22496	19390	3106	16.0
Net Sales	3219082	2951140	267942	9.1
Cost of Goods Sold				
Merchandise Inventory, Jan. 1	285100	253700	31400	12.4
Merchandise Purchases (Net)	1982488	1808270	174218	9.6
Freight In	15000	13000	2000	15.4
Total Merchandise Available for Sale	2282588	2074970	207618	10.0
Less Merchandise Inventory, Dec. 31	300000	285100	14900	5.2
Cost of Goods Sold	1982588	1789870	192718	10.8
Gross Profit on Sales	1236494	1161270	75224	6.5
Operating Expenses				
Selling Expenses (Schedule A)	719346	706032	13314	1.9
General Expenses (Schedule B)	288952	260501	28451	10.9
Total Operating Expenses	1008298	966533	41765	4.3
Net Income from Operations	228196	194737	33459	17.2
Other Income				
Gain on Sale of Equipment	1000	—0—	1000	
Interest Income	355	722	(367)	(50.8)
Total Other Income	1355	722	633	87.7
Total Income for Year	229551	195459	34092	17.4
Other Expenses				
Bond Interest Expense	6774	4400	2374	54.0
Other Interest Expense	475	2300	(1825)	(79.3)
Total Other Expenses	7249	6700	549	8.2
Net Income Before Income Taxes	222302	188759	33543	17.8
Income Tax Expense	69950	56870	13080	23.0
Net Income After Income Taxes	152352	131889	20463	15.5

The gross sales for 19Y3 are greater than those for 19Y2. The amount of increase is found by subtracting the 19Y2 gross sales from the 19Y3 gross sales.

Sales for 19Y3	$3,241,578
Sales for 19Y2	−2,970,530
Increase	$ 271,048

In preparing horizontal percentage analyses, the old year is always used as the base for computing the percentage of change.

The percentage of increase is found by dividing the amount of increase ($271,048) by the amount of sales ($2,970,530) for the base year, 19Y2. (The base year is always the old year.) The increase is found to be 9.1 percent.

$$\frac{\text{Increase in sales}}{\text{Sales for base year}} = \frac{\$271{,}048}{\$2{,}970{,}530} = 9.12 \text{ percent}$$

All the other figures on the comparative statements have been analyzed in the same manner. If the amount for the second year is less than that for the base year, the percentage decrease is still calculated in the same manner. For example, the comparative statements show that Other Interest Expense decreased by $1,825 during 19Y3.

The percentage of decrease is again found by dividing the change in amount ($1,825) by the amount for the base year ($2,300 in 19Y2). The change is a decrease of 79.3 percent from 19Y2.

$$\frac{\text{Amount of decrease}}{\text{Amount in base year}} = \frac{(\$1{,}825)}{\$2{,}300} = 79.3 \text{ percent}$$

Note that decreases are shown in parentheses as they probably would be shown in a formal report. They might be presented in italics or parentheses in a printed report.

Horizontal statement analysis shows at a glance the changes that occurred between two years and points out relationships that merit further examination.

Interpretation of the Percentages

The amounts of increase or decrease can be added or subtracted in the column from top to bottom and will give correct subtotals at each point. However, the percentages of change cannot be added or subtracted from top to bottom. Each percentage relates only to the line on which it appears. If the amount of change is zero, there is no percentage of change.

A study of each item on the comparative income statement quickly reveals the changes that occurred between the two years. Some important changes in Mirabel Corporation's income statement from 19Y2 to 19Y3 are seen to include the following.

In horizontal analysis, the amounts in the Increase or Decrease columns can be added or subtracted vertically, but the percentages of change cannot be.

1. Gross sales and net sales were both up 9.1 percent.
2. Cost of goods sold increased 10.8 percent.
3. Gross profit on sales increased 6.5 percent.
4. Operating expenses increased 4.3 percent.
5. Net income from operations increased 17.2 percent.
6. Income taxes were up by 23.0 percent.
7. Net income after income taxes was 15.5 percent higher.

Horizontal analysis is especially useful in calling attention to relationships that bear further investigation. For example, although the increase in net sales for 19Y3 over 19Y2 was only 9.1 percent, the increase in cost of goods sold was 10.8 percent. An alert manager would call for pertinent facts to determine the reasons for the disproportionate increase in cost of goods sold.

Management would be interested in learning in greater detail why general expenses showed an increase of 10.9 percent during 19Y3, while selling expenses increased only 1.9 percent. This would call for an analysis of each selling expense and each general expense.

The analyst is interested in both the amount of change and the percentage change in each item. Percentages of change may be misleading in the case of small amounts.

It should be kept in mind that percentages of increase or decrease can be misleading when small amounts are involved. For example, Mirabel's interest income decreased from $722 in 19Y2 to $355 in 19Y3, a decrease of 50.8 percent. However, in terms of actual dollars, the amount is immaterial. On the other hand, even a small percentage change for an item involving many dollars is important because of the sizable amount. No percentage change is computed when there is no amount for the base period, as happened with the gain on the sale of equipment that is reported for 19Y3 on Mirabel's comparative income statement. Actually, some analysts prefer to omit items like this gain from their computations even if data for a base period is available because the changes are usually not meaningful for such items.

As noted previously, the process of interpretation is easier if some basis of comparison is available, such as a company budget or industry average data. Significant, or out-of-line, changes should be investigated in detail and the reasons evaluated.

Horizontal and Vertical Analysis of Operating Expenses

On the income statement illustrated in Figure 23–3, operating expenses were shown as two subtotals—Selling Expenses and General Expenses. The details of selling and general expenses are included in supplemental schedules. An analysis of the comparative schedule of selling expenses for Mirabel Corporation is shown in Figure 23–4. A similar analysis, not shown, would be made of general expenses.

Notice that the results of both horizontal and vertical analysis are given in the schedule. The vertical analysis percentages relate to net sales, as they would if the details of these expenses had been presented on the income statement. The horizontal analysis is completed in the usual manner. The arithmetic follows the pattern previously discussed, as does the interpretation of these figures.

Horizontal Analysis of the Balance Sheet

OBJECTIVE 4
Use horizontal analysis techniques to analyze a comparative balance sheet.

A firm's balance sheets for two or more periods can be presented in comparative form to permit a detailed horizontal analysis. A comparative balance sheet showing the Mirabel Unpainted Furniture Corporation's financial position on December 31 of 19Y3 and 19Y2 is illustrated in Figure 23–5 on page 830.

FIGURE 23–4
Horizontal and Vertical Analysis of Selling Expenses

Schedule A

MIRABEL UNPAINTED FURNITURE CORPORATION
Comparative Schedule of Selling Expenses
Years Ended December 31, 19Y3 and 19Y2

	Amounts		*Percent Of Net Sales*		*Percent of Increase or (Decrease) During 19Y3*	
	19Y3	*19Y2*	*19Y3*	*19Y2*	*Amount*	*Percent*
Sales Salaries	382600	375200	11.9	12.7	7400	2.0
Sales Commissions	42000	38000	1.3	1.3	4000	10.5
Payroll Taxes—Sales Staff	46600	42300	1.5*	1.4	4300	10.2
Employee Fringe Benefits	31600	38300	1.0	1.3	(6700)	(17.5)
Freight Out and Deliveries	28870	22750	0.9	0.8	6120	26.9
Advertising	94630	98100	2.9	3.3	(3470)	(3.5)
Sales Supplies	10307	13960	0.3	0.5	(3653)	(26.2)
Rent	22000	22000	0.7	0.7	—0—	
Utilities	9039	7820	0.3	0.3	1219	15.6
Insurance	9800	9300	0.3	0.3	500	5.4
Repairs and Maintenance	1800	3102	0.1	0.1	(1302)	(42.0)
Depreciation	8300	6200	0.2*	0.2	2100	33.9
Travel and Entertainment	12000	9600	0.3*	0.3	2400	25.0
Other Taxes	7800	7600	0.2	0.3	200	2.6
Miscellaneous	12000	11800	0.4	0.4	200	1.7
Total Selling Expenses	719346	706032	22.3	23.9	13314	1.9

*Adjusted

The calculations involved are the same as those for a horizontal analysis of income statements. The amounts are compared line by line. For example, the accountant computes the difference between the amounts for Cash ($100,187 − $72,860) and finds that there is a decrease of $27,327. The percentage of change is determined by dividing the amount of change by the base-year (19Y2) amount: $27,327 ÷ $100,187 = 27.3 percent. Every line is analyzed in the same manner.

HORIZONTAL AND VERTICAL ANALYSIS OF THE STATEMENT OF RETAINED EARNINGS

OBJECTIVE 5

Use horizontal and vertical analysis techniques to analyze a comparative statement of retained earnings.

Both horizontal and vertical analysis techniques are used in preparing the comparative statement of retained earnings, as shown in the comparative statement in Figure 23–6, page 831. In the vertical analysis of the statement of retained earnings each item is expressed as a percent of total liabilities and stockholders' equity. Combined analysis may also be used for the income statement and balance sheet in order to have all the pertinent information available on one page for each statement.

FIGURE 23–5
A Comparative Balance Sheet: Horizontal Analysis

MIRABEL UNPAINTED FURNITURE CORPORATION
Comparative Balance Sheet (Horizontal Analysis)
December 31, 19Y3 and 19Y2

	Amounts on December 31		*Increase or (Decrease) During 19Y3*	
	19Y3	*19Y2*	*Amount*	*Percent*
Assets				
Current Assets				
Cash	72860	100187	(27327)	(27.3)
Accounts Receivable (Net)	198184	168184	30000	17.8
Merchandise Inventory	300000	285100	14900	5.2
Prepaid Insurance	5700	2600	3100	119.2
Other Prepayments	5500	2500	3000	120.0
Total Current Assets	582244	558571	23673	4.2
Property, Plant, and Equipment				
Land	30000	30000	—0—	
Building	120000	—0—	120000	
Less Accumulated Depreciation	2000	—0—	2000	
Net Book Value—Building	118000	—0—	118000	
Equipment and Fixtures	103200	83600	19600	23.4
Less Accumulated Depreciation	54300	44000	10300	23.4
Net Book Value—Equip. and Fixtures	48900	39600	9300	23.5
Total Property, Plant, and Equip.	196900	69600	127300	182.9
Total Assets	779144	628171	150973	24.0
Liabilities and Stockholders' Equity				
Current Liabilities				
Accounts Payable	113326	92300	21026	22.8
Income Tax Payable	17000	14000	3000	21.4
Accrued Liabilities	14446	17530	(3084)	(17.6)
Total Current Liabilities	144772	123830	20942	16.9
Long-Term Liabilities				
Long-Term Notes Payable	—0—	10000	(10000)	(100.0)
11% Bonds Payable, 19Z1	70000	40000	30000	75.0
Premium on Bonds Payable	979	—0—	979	100.0
Total Long-Term Liabilities	70979	50000	20979	42.0
Total Liabilities	215751	173830	41921	24.1
Stockholders' Equity				
12% Preferred Stock ($100 par, authorized, 2,000 shares)				
Issued and Outstanding, 1,000 shares	100000	100000	—0—	
Paid-in Capital in Excess of Par	6000	6000	—0—	
Common Stock (no par, $50 stated value, authorized, 10,000 shares)				
Issued and Outstanding: 3,200 shares in 19Y3, 3,000 shares in 19Y2	160000	150000	10000	6.7
Paid-in Capital in Excess of Stated Value	29000	19000	10000	52.6
Retained Earnings (Schedule C)	268393	179341	89052	49.7
Total Stockholders' Equity	563393	454341	109052	24.0
Total Liabilities and Stockholders' Equity	779144	628171	150973	24.0

FIGURE 23–6
A Comparative Statement of Retained Earnings: Horizontal and Vertical Analysis

Schedule C

MIRABEL UNPAINTED FURNITURE CORPORATION
Comparative Statement of Retained Earnings
Years Ended December 31, 19Y3 and 19Y2

	Amounts on December 31		*Percent of Total Assets*		*Increase or (Decrease) During 19Y3*	
	19Y3	*19Y2*	*19Y3*	*19Y2*	*Amount*	*Percent*
Balance, Jan. 1	179341	114742	23.0	18.3	64599	56.3
Additions						
Net Income After Income Taxes	152352	131889	19.6	21.0	20463	15.5
Total	331693	246631	42.6	39.3	85062	34.5
Deductions						
Dividends—Preferred	12000	12000	1.5	1.9	—0—	
Dividends—Common	51300	55290	6.6	8.8	(3990)	(7.2)
Total	63300	67290	8.1	10.7	(3990)	(5.9)
Balance, Dec. 31	268393	179341	34.5*	28.6*	89052	49.7

*Adjusted

▲ REMEMBER!

A single worksheet combining both horizontal and vertical analysis of a statement saves work. In addition, the combined statement makes it easier to detect items that need further investigation.

The analysis is interpreted in the same manner as previously described for the balance sheet. Mirabel's net income in 19Y3 was 19.6 percent of its total assets, slightly lower than in 19Y2. Total dividends were 8.1 percent of total assets in 19Y3, as compared with 10.7 percent in 19Y2. Retained earnings increased by 49.7 percent during 19Y3.

TREND ANALYSIS OF FINANCIAL STATEMENTS

OBJECTIVE 6

Use trend analysis to evaluate financial statements.

Trend analysis involves comparing amounts, percentages, or ratios over a period of several years.

It has been pointed out that comparing ratio and percentage relationships of the current year with those of the immediately preceding year is a normal procedure and is helpful. However, comparisons between only two years may be misleading and are not adequate to indicate long-term trends. It is far better to use a technique called **trend analysis** to make comparisons of selected ratios and percentages over several years. Often a period of five years is chosen.

We will give only one example of trend analysis out of dozens that might be chosen. Let's concentrate on the gross profit percentage. We have seen that the percentage of gross profit to net sales of Mirabel decreased from 39.3 percent in 19Y2 to 38.4 percent in 19Y3. It is obvious that a higher gross profit percentage generally is desirable, so the decrease would probably be evaluated as unfavorable. A com-

Information Block: International Accounting

Accounting for and Reporting International Operations

Most accountants working for U.S. companies are trained in the United States and are not prepared for the many problems that arise in international business transactions. It is easy to assume that what is done in this country is also done in other countries, but that is not necessarily the case. Accountants who work in international accounting must learn different accounting methods as well as how to communicate with people of different cultures and perhaps in a language other than English. Accountants will also face challenges with foreign economic systems, currencies, inflation rates, governmental regulations, legislation, and taxes.

Accountants working for multinational companies will become involved in many areas never encountered in their work for domestic companies. Some of the most significant areas where accountants are likely to become involved include foreign company reporting, geographical spread of sales, operating income and assets, allocation of home country expenses to foreign subsidiaries, differences in accounting principles and disclosures, statutory audit requirements in foreign countries, translation of foreign currencies into U.S. dollars, foreign tax reporting, foreign currency exposure reporting, and transfer prices for goods and ser-

parison with the percentages of several prior years would be very helpful in making an evaluation. Suppose, for example, that the following condensed analysis of gross profit was made for the five-year period ending with 19Y3.

	19Y3	19Y2	19Y1	19Y0	19X9
Net Sales	3,219,082	2,951,140	2,770,000	2,620,600	2,370,000
Cost of Goods Sold	1,982,588	1,789,870	1,656,460	1,540,913	1,388,820
Gross Profit	1,236,494	1,161,270	1,113,540	1,079,687	981,180
Percentage of gross profit to sales	38.4	39.3	40.2	41.2	41.4

In looking at the data over five years, it becomes clear that the decrease in percentage from 19Y2 to 19Y3 is not merely a random occurrence. It reflects a trend that has been present each year and calls for the urgent attention of management. Management would need to obtain other facts, talk with responsible personnel, and observe other trends before arriving at a solution to the problem.

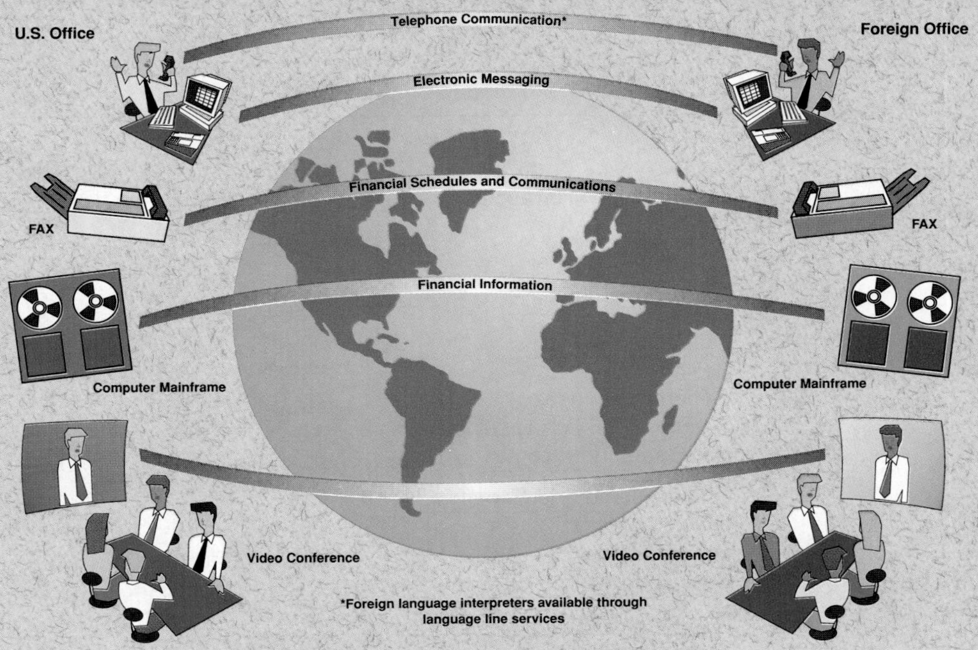

CHART A
Modes of International Communication

vices crossing international boundaries.

Accountants can communicate accounting information quickly with recent advances in technology. These advances include facsimile machines, computer links over telephone lines, electronic messaging, video conferencing, and language-line services that provide translation of foreign languages over the telephone line. Chart A shows several means of international communication.

The comparison of percentages and ratios over a period of time makes it possible to ask similar questions about all aspects of operations of the company. It is in the area of analyzing operating data that the accountant makes the most valuable contribution to the success of the business.

COMPARISON WITH INDUSTRY AVERAGES

OBJECTIVE 7
Interpret the results of the statement analyses by comparison with industry averages.

Almost all trade associations make surveys of their members to obtain financial and other data. The information gathered is converted to a uniform presentation, usually in common-size statements, arranged by groups of companies according to their size (usually sales volume or total assets). The income statement items are expressed as a percent of net sales and balance sheet items as a percent of total assets. The common-size statements may be presented for only one year or for a period of years.

Let's look at a broad example of how the management of Mirabel Unpainted Furniture Corporation might evaluate the corporation in comparison with others in the industry. Highly condensed data from

TABLE 23–1
Comparison of Trade Data

	Percentage of Net Sales			
	Mirabel Corp.		Industry Average	
	19Y3	19Y2	19Y3	19Y2
Revenue				
Sales	100.7	100.7	100.4	100.5
Returns and Allowances	0.7	0.7	0.4	0.5
Net Sales	100.0	100.0	100.0	100.0
Cost of Goods Sold	61.6	60.7	58.3	58.4
Gross Profit on Sales	38.4	39.3	41.7	41.6
Operating Expenses				
Selling Expenses	22.3	23.9	24.4	23.4
General Expenses	9.0	8.8	6.2	6.1
Total Operating Expenses	31.3	32.7	30.6	29.5
Net Operating Income	7.1	6.6	11.1	12.1
Other Income and Expenses				
Other Income	–0–	–0–	.2	.2
Other Expenses	(0.2)	(0.2)	(0.5)	(0.5)
Net Other Income or (Exp.)	(0.2)	(0.2)	(0.3)	(0.3)
Net Income Before Income Tax	6.9	6.4	10.8	11.8

Financial statement ratios and percentages are published by trade associations, financial reporting companies, and government agencies.

Mirabel's income statement and the data provided by the trade association about companies of the same general sales level of Mirabel are shown in Table 23–1.

Note that in the illustration income tax expense has been omitted. This is often done in practice because some companies that are included in the trade averages are sole proprietorships, some are partnerships, and still others are corporations. It might not be appropriate for a corporate entity to make a comparison of its net income after income taxes with the statements of a group of entities, some of whom do not pay taxes.

Because of differences in accounting procedures and classifications, types of entities, financing methods, and operations, comparisons with industry data must be made carefully.

You can easily see why the comparison illustrated would be of interest to management, owners, and other interested parties. It appears that Mirabel's operations are not as efficient or as profitable as those of its competitors. Not only is its rate of gross profit lower (and, as we have seen, on a downward trend), but the ratio of Mirabel's expenses to its net sales is higher than that of others in the industry. Mirabel's general expenses are especially out of line. The end result is that Mirabel's ratio of net income to sales is much lower than that of its competitors in each of the two years. Mirabel's management would wish to immediately determine the causes of its relatively poor showing.

In making comparisons with industry averages, several factors associated with industry-wide data must be kept in mind.

1. Different businesses keep different types of accounts and do not classify items in a consistent manner.

2. No two businesses are exactly alike. There are differences in the merchandise sold, the type of customers served, and the method of financing used (owners' equity versus borrowed funds). Some businesses elect to purchase fixed assets, while others lease all or a part of such assets and equipment.
3. The industry figures may include data from corporate entities, partnerships, and sole proprietorships. Although instructions accompanying the request for information sent by the trade association to its members contain instructions about how to treat salary allowances, benefits for owners, and other items, there is a great deal of inconsistency in their presentation. In a closely held corporation, the owners may have a practice of paying very high salaries to themselves, while a similar corporation may pay the owners very low salaries.

In spite of these problem areas, common-size statements provided by trade associations or commercial financial service companies are of extreme importance to business managers in evaluating their own operations in comparison to others. They are of special value in making comparisons of data not affected by the variables listed above.

USING THE COMPUTER IN STATEMENT ANALYSIS

The great advantage of computers is that they can do massive numbers of computations in seconds, or even in fractions of a second. It is abundantly clear that a large part of financial statement analysis, especially vertical analysis and horizontal analysis, consists of arithmetic exercises—principally subtracting and dividing.

Spreadsheet programs make short work of the computational phase of statement analysis. Almost all companies using the computer for accounting purposes have computer-generated statements using spreadsheet formats. In making horizontal analyses, it is a simple matter to instruct the computer to subtract the amount for the second year from the amount for the first year and enter the difference in a column. A second instruction tells the computer to divide each difference computed in the step above by the amount of that item as shown in the base period and enter the percentage in a second column. Similarly, in making vertical analyses, it takes only a few seconds to instruct the computer to divide each item on the statement for each year by the total assets for that year. The computer responds in seconds. Think of the drudgery that is thereby eliminated.

MANAGERIAL IMPLICATIONS

Statement analysis is extremely important to managers in detecting problem areas and areas of strength in a business. Comparison of current data with the data of prior years indicates trends that may be either favorable or unfavorable. Percentage analysis figures can be compared with industry percentages and with percentages of prior years to detect variations that require prompt investigation.

SELF-REVIEW

1. In horizontal analysis of the balance sheet, how is the percentage of change determined?
2. In comparing an older company and a newer one, in which company would property, plant, and equipment be likely to represent a higher percentage of total assets? Why?
3. Why is comparison with industry averages important in analyzing financial statements?
4. Name several factors that may cause misleading results when comparing percentage figures of a specific company to industry averages.
5. Over a period of five years, a company's sales have increased by approximately 10 percent per year. During the same period, its gross profit has increased by about 8 percent per year. Is this favorable or unfavorable? Explain.

Answers to Self-Review

1. The percentage of change is calculated by first subtracting an amount from the base-year amount and then dividing the difference by the base-year amount.
2. The newer company would probably have a higher ratio because its book value is likely to be higher (less depreciation has been charged off) and its assets are likely to be newer, which means they were acquired at higher price levels than those acquired in earlier years by the older company.
3. Such comparisons point out areas in which the business is performing either better or worse than average. The areas showing poorer performance can be investigated to determine the reason.
4. Different accounting methods, different types of entities, different ages of assets, and different financing methods may impair comparability.
5. This situation is probably undesirable unless management has deliberately adopted a policy of reducing prices to increase volume. The question that must be raised is whether this situation has led to increased profitability.

CHAPTER 23 Review and Applications

CHAPTER SUMMARY

The two steps in financial statement analysis are computation and interpretation. The computation process includes the calculation of percentages and ratios. The interpretation process involves direct comparison with other figures (prior statements, budgets, or industry averages) and determination of what the comparisons imply about the financial position of the business at the end of the period.

The comparative statement is a convenient form for the presentation of figures for analysis and appraisal. Amount and percentage comparisons can be made both horizontally and vertically. Horizontal analysis involves the comparison of items from one year to the next. Vertical analysis involves expressing each item as a percentage of some base amount on that statement. Net sales is used as the base for all income statement items, while total assets serves as the base for comparing all balance sheet items.

GLOSSARY OF NEW TERMS

Common-size statements (p. 822) Financial statements with items expressed as percentages of a base figure, usually net sales or total assets, on the statement rather than as dollar amounts

Comparative statements (p. 817) Financial statements presented side by side for two or more years

Horizontal analysis (p. 818) Computing the relationship of changes in individual items from year to year

Industry averages (p. 822) Financial ratios and percentages reflecting averages for similar companies

Ratio analysis (p. 818) Computing relationships between various items in the year's financial statements

Trend analysis (p. 831) Comparing dollar amounts or percentages over several periods

Vertical analysis (p. 818) Computing the relationship between each item on a financial statement to some base amount on that statement, usually net sales or total assets

REVIEW QUESTIONS

1. What is horizontal analysis of the balance sheet?
2. In horizontal analysis it is common to omit a calculation of percentage change when there is no base period amount. Why?
3. What is meant by vertical analysis of the income statement?

4. Why do percentages in the Increase or Decrease column of a horizontal analysis of a comparative statement not add up to 100?
5. Of what use to the financial statement analyst are industry-wide statements?
6. Would you, as an analyst, be satisfied with comparative percentages for only two years? Why?
7. Why would a short-term creditor be interested in the analysis of a company's income statement?
8. What are common-size statements?
9. If a company's net sales and its cost of goods sold both increase by 10 percent from 19X2 to 19X3, would gross profit on sales also increase by 10 percent? Explain.
10. The vertical analysis of Geronimo Corporation's balance sheets for the past five years show that the percent of inventory to total assets has increased each year. Comment on this situation.
11. In a vertical analysis of the statement of retained earnings, what is the base for comparing each item on the statement?
12. Which is more important: a large change in percentage or a large change in dollar amount? Explain.

MANAGERIAL FOCUS

1. Suppose a vertical analysis of the income statement shows an item to be 18 percent of net sales. How would this information be used in order to make it meaningful? With what would it be compared?
2. In 19X3 the cost of goods sold was 66 percent of net sales. For 19X2 the same item was 63 percent, and for 19X1 it was 60 percent. What recommendations would you make about items or activities that should be investigated further?
3. In deciding whether an increase in accounts receivable during the current year is desirable or undesirable, what factors should management consider?
4. Management is concerned that over a three-year period a company's balance sheets show that the total stockholders' equity has changed from 56 percent to 51 percent to 43 percent of total equities. What factors might explain this trend?
5. A company's income statements reveal that its net income after taxes has been 4.3 percent of net sales for each of the past three years. During that time the industry average has been about 7 percent. What types of questions would management want answered in seeking an explanation for this difference?
6. A company's net sales increased by 35 percent from one year to the next year. During that period selling expenses increased by 41 percent. Is this desirable? Explain.

EXERCISES

Use the comparative income statement and the comparative balance sheet for Niagara Corporation to solve Exercises 23–1 through 23–7.

NIAGARA CORPORATION
Comparative Income Statement
Years Ended December 31, 19X3 and 19X2

	19X3	19X2
Sales	1 2 4 0 0 0 0	1 0 2 0 0 0 0
Less Sales Returns and Allowances	4 0 0 0 0	2 0 0 0 0
Net Sales	1 2 0 0 0 0 0	1 0 0 0 0 0 0
Cost of Goods Sold	9 0 0 0 0 0	7 0 0 0 0 0
Gross Profit on Sales	3 0 0 0 0 0	3 0 0 0 0 0
Selling Expenses	1 4 5 0 0 0	1 3 0 0 0 0
General Expenses	8 5 0 0 0	8 0 0 0 0
Total Expenses	2 3 0 0 0 0	2 1 0 0 0 0
Net Income Before Income Taxes	7 0 0 0 0	9 0 0 0 0
Income Tax Expense	1 2 5 0 0	1 8 8 5 0
Net Income After Income Taxes	5 7 5 0 0	7 1 1 5 0

NIAGARA CORPORATION
Comparative Balance Sheet
December 31, 19X3 and 19X2

	19X3	19X2
Assets		
Cash	5 0 0 0 0	7 8 0 0 0
Accounts Receivable (Net)	1 8 0 0 0 0	1 3 5 0 0 0
Inventory	3 0 0 0 0 0	2 3 7 0 0 0
Buildings (Net)	9 5 0 0 0	1 0 0 0 0 0
Equipment (Net)	8 5 0 0 0	8 0 0 0 0
Land	2 0 0 0 0	2 0 0 0 0
Total Assets	7 3 0 0 0 0	6 5 0 0 0 0
Liabilities and Stockholders' Equity		
Liabilities		
Accounts Payable	1 8 0 0 0 0	1 4 0 0 0 0
Other Current Liabilities	2 0 0 0 0	2 0 0 0 0
Bonds Payable	1 0 0 0 0 0	8 0 0 0 0
Total Liabilities	3 0 0 0 0 0	2 4 0 0 0 0
Stockholders' Equity		
Common Stock ($20 par)	2 0 0 0 0 0	2 0 0 0 0 0
Retained Earnings	2 3 0 0 0 0	2 1 0 0 0 0
Total Stockholders' Equity	4 3 0 0 0 0	4 1 0 0 0 0
Total Liabilities and Stockholders' Equity	7 3 0 0 0 0	6 5 0 0 0 0

EXERCISE 23-1 (Obj. 1) Tutorial

Vertical analysis of income statement. Using the comparative income statement, prepare a vertical analysis of all items from sales through gross profit on sales for the years 19X3 and 19X2.

EXERCISE 23-2 (Obj. 2) Tutorial

Vertical analysis of balance sheet. Prepare a vertical analysis of all asset items on the comparative balance sheet for years 19X3 and 19X2.

EXERCISE 23-3 (Obj. 3) Tutorial

Horizontal analysis of income statement. Using the comparative income statement, prepare a horizontal analysis of all items from sales through gross profit on sales for 19X3 and 19X2.

EXERCISE 23-4 (Obj. 3) Tutorial

Horizontal analysis of income statement. Using the comparative income statement, prepare a horizontal analysis of all items from operating expenses through net income after income tax for 19X3 and 19X2.

EXERCISE 23-5 (Obj. 4) Tutorial

Horizontal analysis of balance sheet. Prepare a horizontal analysis of all asset items on the comparative balance sheet for years 19X3 and 19X2.

EXERCISE 23-6 (Obj. 7)

Comparison with industry averages. Suppose that you, as a financial analyst, found that for companies in the same industry and of the same general size as the Niagara Corporation net income after income taxes averaged 7 percent of net sales in both 19X3 and 19X2. Evaluate the Niagara Corporation's net income after taxes for both years.

EXERCISE 23-7 (Obj. 2, 7)

Vertical analysis of balance sheet; comparison with industry averages. Assume that for companies in the same industry and of the same general size as the Niagara Corporation stockholders' equity was 55 percent of total liabilities and stockholders' equity in 19X3 and 53 percent of total liabilities and stockholders' equity in 19X2. Write brief comments about the ratio of stockholders' equity to total liabilities and stockholders' equity at the Niagara Corporation each year in comparison with the industry figures.

PROBLEMS

PROBLEM SET A

PROBLEM 23-1A (Obj. 1, 2, 3, 4) Tutorial Spreadsheet

Horizontal and vertical analysis of income statement and balance sheet. The High Five Corporation sells auto parts through a retail store that it operates. The firm's comparative income statement and balance sheet for the years 19X2 and 19X1 are shown on pages 841–842.

Instructions

1. Prepare both a horizontal and a vertical analysis of the statements. Carry all calculations to two decimal places, and then round to one decimal place. (Leave all vertical analysis percentages unadjusted in this problem.)
2. Make written comments about any of the results that seem worthy of investigation.

HIGH FIVE CORPORATION
Comparative Income Statement
Years Ended December 31, 19X2 and 19X1

	19X2	19X1
Revenue		
Sales	516950	506950
Less Sales Returns and Allowances	2810	2650
Net Sales	514140	504300
Cost of Goods Sold		
Merchandise Inventory, Jan. 1	42200	40000
Purchases	293570	290752
Total Merchandise Available for Sale	335770	330752
Less Merchandise Inventory, Dec. 31	45970	42200
Cost of Goods Sold	289800	288552
Gross Profit on Sales	224340	215748
Operating Expenses		
Selling Expenses		
Sales Salaries Expense	70108	73930
Payroll Taxes Expense—Sales	7850	8000
Other Selling Expenses	6600	4900
Total Selling Expenses	84558	86830
General Expenses		
Officers' Salaries Expense	54000	54000
Office Employees' Salaries Expense	18000	16000
Payroll Taxes Expense—Administrative	7850	7600
Depreciation Expense	5100	4860
Other General Expenses	1656	1828
Total General Expenses	86606	84288
Total Operating Expenses	171164	171118
Net Income Before Income Taxes	53176	44630
Income Tax Expense	8294	6695
Net Income After Income Taxes	44882	37935

PROBLEM 23–2A (Obj. 1, 2, 3, 4, 5)

Horizontal and vertical analysis of balance sheet, income statement, and statement of retained earnings. The Brasseau Products Corporation sells paper plates, napkins, and other supplies to fast-food restaurants. Its comparative income statement, schedule of selling expenses, balance sheet, and statement of retained earnings for the years 19X2 and 19X1 are shown on pages 843–844.

HIGH FIVE CORPORATION
Comparative Balance Sheet
December 31, 19X2 and 19X1

	19X2	19X1
Assets		
Current Assets		
Cash	57944	53578
Accounts Receivable (Net)	84914	90848
Merchandise Inventory	45970	42200
Prepaid Insurance	2000	3980
Supplies on Hand	210	370
Total Current Assets	191038	190976
Property, Plant, and Equipment		
Land	60400	10400
Building and Equipment	83000	83000
Less Accumulated Depreciation	32130	23830
Net Book Value	50870	59170
Total Property, Plant, and Equipment	111270	69570
Total Assets	302308	260546
Liabilities and Stockholders' Equity		
Current Liabilities		
Accounts Payable	49576	39421
Salaries Payable	1360	1120
Payroll Taxes Payable	2652	2526
Income Tax Payable	2294	2195
Total Liabilities	55882	45262
Stockholders' Equity		
Common Stock (par value, $20, authorized, 10,000 shares)		
Issued and Outstanding, 6,000 shares	120000	120000
Retained Earnings	126426	95284
Total Stockholders' Equity	246426	215284
Total Liabilities and Stockholders' Equity	302308	260546

Instructions

1. Prepare both a horizontal and a vertical analysis of the statements. Carry all calculations to two decimal places and then round to one decimal place. (Leave all vertical analysis percentages unadjusted in this problem.)
2. Make written comments about any of the results that seem worthy of investigation.

BRASSEAU PRODUCTS CORPORATION
Comparative Income Statement
Years Ended December 31, 19X2 and 19X1

	19X2	19X1
Revenue		
Sales	6530000	5932000
Less Sales Returns and Allowances	30000	32000
Net Sales	6500000	5900000
Cost of Goods Sold	4548000	4242000
Gross Profit on Sales	1952000	1658000
Operating Expenses		
Selling Expenses (Schedule A)	992000	859500
General Expenses	621500	538500
Total Operating Expenses	1613500	1398000
Net Operating Income	338500	260000
Other Income		
Gain on Sale of Investments	4000	—0—
Total Income for Year	342500	260000
Other Deductions		
Interest Expense	45000	45000
Loss on Disposal of Equipment	4000	—0—
Total Other Deductions	49000	45000
Net Income Before Income Taxes	293500	215000
Income Tax Expense	97700	67000
Net Income After Income Taxes	195800	148000

BRASSEAU PRODUCTS CORPORATION
Comparative Statement of Retained Earnings
Years Ended December 31, 19X2 and 19X1

	19X2	19X1
Balance, Jan. 1	398500	356750
Additions		
Net Income After Income Taxes	195800	148000
Total	594300	504750
Deductions		
Dividends—Preferred Stock	50000	50000
Dividends—Common Stock	83300	56250
Total Deductions	133300	106250
Balance, Dec. 31	461000	398500

(Continued)

BRASSEAU PRODUCTS CORPORATION Comparative Balance Sheet December 31, 19X2 and 19X1	19X2	19X1
Assets		
Current Assets		
Cash	389000	413500
Accounts Receivable (Net)	817500	610000
Merchandise Inventory	1500000	1250000
Prepaid Insurance	21000	26000
Total Current Assets	2727500	2299500
Property, Plant, and Equipment		
Plant and Equipment	447500	420000
Less Accumulated Depreciation	136500	105000
Total Property, Plant, and Equipment	311000	315000
Investments	—0—	100000
Total Assets	3038500	2714500
Liabilities and Stockholders' Equity		
Current Liabilities		
Accounts Payable	755500	622000
Estimated Income Taxes Payable	24000	16000
Other Payables	188000	128000
Total Current Liabilities	967500	766000
Long-Term Liabilities		
15% Bonds Payable	300000	300000
Total Liabilities	1267500	1066000
Stockholders' Equity		
10% Preferred Stock ($50 par, authorized, 20,000 shares)		
Issued and Outstanding, 10,000 shares	500000	500000
Common Stock ($80 par value, authorized, 20,000 shares)		
Issued and Outstanding, 10,000 shares	800000	750000
Premium on Common Stock	10000	—0—
Retained Earnings (Schedule C)	461000	398500
Total Stockholders' Equity	1771000	1648500
Total Liabilities and Stockholders' Equity	3038500	2714500

PROBLEM SET B

PROBLEM 23–1B
(Obj. 1, 2, 3, 4)

Tutorial

Horizontal and vertical analysis of income statement and balance sheet. The Molina Corporation sells business supplies through a retail store that it operates. The firm's comparative income statement and balance sheet for the years 19X3 and 19X2 follow.

Instructions

1. Prepare both a horizontal and a vertical analysis of the two statements. Carry all calculations to two decimal places and then round to one place. (Leave all vertical analysis percentages unadjusted in this problem.)
2. Make written comments about any of the results that seem worthy of investigation.

MOLINA CORPORATION
Comparative Income Statement
Years Ended December 31, 19X3 and 19X2

	19X3	19X2
Revenue		
Sales	385196	317630
Less Sales Returns and Allowances	1847	1655
Net Sales	383349	315975
Cost of Goods Sold		
Merchandise Inventory, Jan. 1	60112	72560
Purchases	249879	207422
Total Merchandise Available for Sale	309991	279982
Less Merchandise Inventory, Dec. 31	64396	60112
Cost of Goods Sold	245595	219870
Gross Profit on Sales	137754	96105
Operating Expenses		
Selling Expenses		
Sales Salaries Expense	22429	20550
Payroll Taxes Expense—Sales	2600	2300
Depreciation Expense	2156	1720
Delivery Expense	2511	2115
Advertising Expense	10393	8380
Other Selling Expenses	2372	1915
Total Selling Expenses	42461	36980
General Expenses		
Officers' Salaries Expense	19000	18000
Office Employees' Salaries Expense	13720	9360
Payroll Taxes Expense—General	3913	3575
Depreciation Expense	752	683
Other Office Expense	1625	1435
Uncollectible Accounts Expense	337	240
Total General Expenses	39347	33293
Total Operating Expenses	81808	70273
Net Income from Operations	55946	25832
Other Income		
Interest Income	275	385
Total Income for Year	56221	26217
Other Expense		
Organization Costs Written Off	300	300
Net Income Before Income Taxes	55921	25917
Income Tax Expense	8980	7730
Net Income After Income Taxes	46941	18187

(Continued)

MOLINA CORPORATION
Comparative Balance Sheet
December 31, 19X3 and 19X2

	19X3	19X2
Assets		
Current Assets		
Cash	44997	22833
Notes Receivable	6000	9500
Accounts Receivable (Net)	54327	40909
Interest Receivable	120	240
Merchandise Inventory	64396	60112
Prepaid Insurance	2177	2640
Supplies on Hand	1725	628
Total Current Assets	173742	136862
Property, Plant, and Equipment		
Land	35000	15000
Building	98450	98450
Less Accumulated Depreciation	28286	26218
Net Book Value	70164	72232
Store Equipment	58900	51700
Less Accumulated Depreciation	30575	25045
Net Book Value	28325	26655
Office Equipment	7351	6895
Less Accumulated Depreciation	4411	3659
Net Book Value	2940	3236
Total Property, Plant, and Equipment	136429	117123
Intangible Assets		
Organization Costs	600	900
Total Assets	310771	254885
Liabilities and Stockholders' Equity		
Current Liabilities		
Accounts Payable	41736	20235
Dividends Payable—Preferred Stock	4500	4500
Dividends Payable—Common Stock	3000	2000
Income Tax Payable	2250	1200
Salaries Payable	3126	1353
Employee Income Taxes Payable	1244	1390
Payroll Taxes Payable	1175	217
Total Liabilities	57031	30895

(Continued)

Stockholders' Equity		
Paid-in Capital		
Preferred Stock (10%, noncumulative, nonparticipating, $75 par value, 1,000 shares authorized)		
Issued and Outstanding, 1,000 shares	75000	75000
Common Stock ($25 par value, 1,000 shares authorized)		
Issued and Outstanding, 1,000 shares	25000	25000
Total Paid-in Capital	100000	100000
Retained Earnings		
Appropriated for Purchase of New Building	25000	20000
Unappropriated	128740	103990
Total Retained Earnings	153740	123990
Total Stockholders' Equity	253740	223990
Total Liabilities and Stockholders' Equity	310771	254885

PROBLEM 23–2B
(Obj. 1, 2, 3, 4, 5)

Horizontal and vertical analysis of balance sheet, income statement, and statement of retained earnings. The Cowhide Corporation sells high-quality leather boots, vests, and jackets. Its comparative income statement, balance sheet, and statement of retained earnings for the years 19X2 and 19X1 follow.

Instructions

1. Prepare both a horizontal and a vertical analysis of the three statements. Carry all calculations to two decimal places and then round to one decimal place. (Leave all vertical analysis percentages unadjusted in this problem.)
2. Make written comments about any of the results that seem worthy of investigation.

COWHIDE CORPORATION
Comparative Income Statement
Years Ended December 31, 19X2 and 19X1

	19X2	19X1
Revenue		
Net Sales	1950000	1770000
Cost of Goods Sold		
Merchandise Inventory, Jan. 1	375000	390000
Purchases	1349400	1257600
Total Merchandise Available for Sale	1724400	1647600
Less Merchandise Inventory, Dec. 31	360000	375000
Cost of Goods Sold	1364400	1272600
Gross Profit on Sales	585600	497400

(Continued)

Comparative Income Statement (Continued)

Operating Expenses		
Selling Expenses		
Sales Salaries Expense	184800	158850
Payroll Taxes Expense—Sales	20000	15800
Rent Expense	19800	18000
Delivery Expense	13500	12300
Advertising Expense	15300	10800
Depreciation Expense	5000	4800
Other Selling Expense	39200	37300
Total Selling Expenses	297600	257850
General Expenses		
Officers' Salaries Expense	90000	74000
Office Employees' Salaries Expense	20000	20000
Payroll Taxes Expense—Administrative	12000	10400
Uncollectible Accounts Expense	14550	12600
Rent Expense	4000	4000
Depreciation Expense	4450	4200
Other General Expenses	41450	36350
Total General Expenses	186450	161550
Total Operating Expenses	484050	419400
Net Income from Operations	101550	78000
Other Expenses		
Bond Interest Expense	9000	9000
Net Income Before Income Taxes	92550	69000
Income Tax Expense	19720	12250
Net Income After Income Taxes	72830	56750

COWHIDE CORPORATION
Comparative Balance Sheet
December 31, 19X2 and 19X1

	19X2	*19X1*
Assets		
Current Assets		
Cash	173550	124050
Accounts Receivable (Net)	207000	183000
Merchandise Inventory	360000	375000
Prepaid Insurance	6300	7800
Total Current Assets	746850	689850

(Continued)

Property, Plant, and Equipment		
Furniture and Equipment	134250	126000
Less Accumulated Depreciation	40950	31500
Total Property, Plant, and Equipment	93300	94500
Total Assets	840150	784350
Liabilities and Stockholders' Equity		
Current Liabilities		
Accounts Payable	187950	177600
Estimated Income Taxes Payable	39000	25500
Other Payables	27300	21900
Total Current Liabilities	254250	225000
Long-Term Liabilities		
10% Bonds Payable	90000	90000
Total Liabilities	344250	315000
Stockholders' Equity		
6% Preferred Stock ($100 par value, authorized 2,000 shares)		
Issued and Outstanding, 1,500 shares	150000	150000
Common Stock (no par value, 2,000 shares authorized)		
Issued and Outstanding, 1,000 shares	225000	225000
Retained Earnings	120900	94350
Total Stockholders' Equity	495900	469350
Total Liabilities and Stockholders' Equity	840150	784350

COWHIDE CORPORATION
Comparative Statement of Retained Earnings
Years Ended December 31, 19X2 and 19X1

	19X2	*19X1*
Balance, Jan. 1	94350	69100
Additions		
Net Income for Year	72830	56750
Total	167180	125850
Deductions		
Dividends—Preferred Stock	9000	9000
Dividends—Common Stock	37280	22500
Total Deductions	46280	31500
Balance Dec. 31	120900	94350

CHALLENGE PROBLEM

Condensed balance sheets and income statements for Exxon Corporation, one of the largest corporations in the United States, for the years 1991 and 1990 are shown below. These reports have been condensed and simplified from the corporation's annual Form 10K for 1990, filed with the U.S. Securities and Exchange Commission.

EXXON CORPORATION
Balance Sheet
December 31, 1991 and 1990
(Millions of Dollars)

	1991	1990
Assets		
Current Assets		
Cash and cash equivalents	1496	1332
Other marketable securities	91	47
Notes and accounts receivable, less estimated doubtful amounts	8540	9574
*Inventories (total)**	6081	6386
Prepaid taxes and expenses	804	997
Total current assets	17012	18336
Investments and advances	4408	4385
Property, plant, and equipment, at cost, less accumulated depreciation and depletion	63864	62688
Other assets, including intangibles, net	2276	2298
Total Assets	87560	87707
Liabilities		
Current Liabilities		
Notes and loans payable	4460	6090
Accounts payable and accrued liabilities	14079	15611
Income taxes payable	2315	2324
Total current liabilities	20854	24025
Long-term debt	8582	7687
Annuity reserves and accrued liabilities	7152	6810
Deferred income tax liabilities	12449	12568
Other noncurrent liabilities	3596	3562
Total Liabilities	52633	54652

(Continued)

Shareholders' Equity		
Preferred stock without par value (authorized 200 million shares)		
1991, 14 million shares outstanding	867	
1990, 15 million shares outstanding		955
Common stock without par value (authorized 2 billion shares, 1,813 issued)	2822	2822
Earnings reinvested	46483	44286
*Other items (net)**	1529	1501
Common stock held in treasury, at cost (571 million shares in 1991, 568 million shares in 1990)	(16774)	(16509)
Total Shareholders' Equity	34927	33055
Total Liabilities and Shareholders' Equity	87560	87707

*This net figure reflects the combination of items appearing on the Exxon balance sheet.

EXXON CORPORATION
Consolidated Statements of Income
Years Ending December 31, 1991 and 1990
(Millions of Dollars)

	1991	1990
Revenue		
Sales and other operating revenue, including excise taxes	115068	115794
Earnings from equity interests and other revenue	1424	1146
	116492	116940
Costs and Other Deductions		
Crude oil and product purchases	46847	50746
Operating expenses	13487	11995
Selling, general, and administrative expenses	7881	7776
Depreciation and depletion	4824	5545
Exploration expenses, including dry holes	914	957
Interest expense	810	1300
Income taxes	2918	3170
Excise taxes	12221	10275
Other taxes and duties	20823	19894
*Other deductions**	167	272
Total deductions	110892	111930
Net Income	5600	5010

*The name of this classification has been changed from that appearing on the Exxon income statement.

Instructions

1. Prepare a combined horizontal and vertical analysis of the comparative balance sheet of Exxon Corporation.
2. Prepare a combined horizontal and vertical analysis of the comparative income statement of Exxon Corporation.
3. Exxon Corporation is involved in many business activities, the major ones being petroleum exploration, refining, and petrochemicals production. It operates in dozens of countries throughout the world and is clearly a massive company.
   a. Explain how these factors complicate the task of analyzing the financial statements of the company.
   b. Suggest some other types of information that would help an analyst interpret the statements of Exxon Corporation.

CRITICAL THINKING PROBLEM

Jake Hecht, the accountant for Simon Corporation, was asked to make a presentation at a Saturday meeting of the board of directors concerning the corporation's year-end financial position. While flying to the meeting on Saturday morning, Mr. Hecht checked the papers in his briefcase and realized he had left the income statement on his desk back at the office. Since he knew there would not be enough time for anyone to get to the office and fax him a copy of the statement, he examined the rest of the material in his briefcase to see what information was available.

A review of the statement of retained earnings revealed that net income after income taxes for the year was $126,000. From some notes he had made for his presentation, he knew that the corporation's gross profit on sales was 40 percent and net income as a percentage of net sales was 7 percent. The income tax rate for the corporation is 40 percent, and Mr. Hecht also remembers that the selling and administrative expenses were the same amount. With this information, he was able to reconstruct the income statement for the corporation before the plane reached its destination.

Instructions

Using the same information given above, prepare an income statement for Simon Corporation for the current year. To get started, first list the major headings for a condensed income statement. Then, starting with the net income figure, work to fill in the dollar amounts based on the percentage relationships given.

CHAPTER

24

Statement Analysis: Measuring Profitability, Financial Strength, and Liquidity

OBJECTIVES

1. Compute and interpret financial ratios that measure profitability, operating results, and efficiency.
2. Compute and interpret financial ratios that measure financial strength.
3. Compute and interpret financial ratios that measure liquidity.
4. Recognize certain shortcomings in financial statement analysis.
5. Define the accounting terms new to this chapter.

Management, creditors, stockholders, and other financial statement users are interested in assessing the profitability, the financial strength, and the liquidity of a business. In making this assessment, they not only make horizontal and vertical analyses of the statements, they compute ratios that help explain the company's financial condition and results. In Chapter 23 you learned how the figures on comparative statements can be used for vertical analysis and horizontal analysis. In this chapter we explain how relationships between individual items on the financial statements can be expressed in ratios that can then be used in the analyst's interpretation of the statements.

The comparative financial statements of the Mirabel Unpainted Furniture Corporation, as illustrated in Chapter 23, will again provide the basis for the discussion. In the remainder of this chapter, you will learn about the ratios that are most widely used to analyze a firm's financial statements and measure its profitability, financial strength, and liquidity.

NEW TERMS

Accounts receivable turnover ▪ Acid-test ratio ▪ Asset turnover ▪ Average collection period ▪ Current ratio ▪ Leveraged buyout ▪ Liquidity ▪ Price-earnings ratio ▪ Quick assets ▪ Ratio analysis ▪ Return on common stockholders' equity ▪ Working capital

RATIO ANALYSIS

The relationship between two items may be expressed either as a ratio (for example, 2 to 1, or 2:1) or as a rate (usually stated as a percentage). In Chapter 23 we saw that both vertical and horizontal analyses involve computation of percentages. In this chapter we refer to the relationship between two amounts as **ratio analysis** whether the result is expressed as a ratio or as a percentage. The major purpose of ratio analysis is to give the statement reader a clear idea of the relationship between two items. Ratios are computed for items on the same financial statement or on statements for different years.

The ratios discussed in this text are the most important ones used by investors, creditors, and managers. The selection and classification of ratios are somewhat arbitrary. However, many analysts find it useful to classify financial ratios in the following three groups.

- Ratios measuring profitability, operating results, and efficiency
- Ratios measuring financial strength and equity protection
- Ratios measuring current position and liquidity

RATIOS MEASURING PROFITABILITY, OPERATING RESULTS, AND EFFICIENCY

OBJECTIVE 1

Compute and interpret financial ratios that measure profitability, operating results, and efficiency.

The profitability of a corporation is measured by net income. However, a dollar figure for net income is not a sufficiently revealing yardstick. An income of $100,000 for the year might be excellent for a small company, but for a large corporation this amount would be completely unsatisfactory. The analyst needs to consider the sales of the company, the nature of its operations, the assets used in earning the income, the stockholders' equity, and many other factors in determining whether the net income is adequate. A number of ratios have been developed for testing the adequacy of a company's profit.

Rate of Return on Sales

The rate of return on sales is a measure of managerial efficiency and profitability. It is computed by dividing net income by net sales.

$$\frac{\text{Net income}}{\text{Net sales}} = \text{Rate of return on net sales}$$

The profitability of a company cannot be evaluated merely by the dollar amount of the profit.

Often the figure for net income before taxes is used because income taxes depend on factors that are not related to sales. Since the Mirabel Unpainted Furniture Corporation has relatively little other income or other expense affecting the tax liability, net income after income taxes is used in making the computation. In 19Y2, the rate of net income on net sales at Mirabel was 4.5 percent. In 19Y3, the figure increased to 4.7 percent.

$$\frac{\text{Net income after income taxes}}{\text{Net sales}} = \overset{\text{19Y3}}{\frac{\$152,352}{\$3,219,082}}, \text{ or } 4.7\%$$

$$\overset{\text{19Y2}}{\frac{\$131,889}{\$2,951,140}}, \text{ or } 4.5\%$$

The rate of return on sales measures what part of each sales dollar is net income to the shareholders. It is a basic measure of operating efficiency and profitability.

Generally, the higher the rate of return on sales, the more satisfactory the operation of the business. A comparison with the rates of past years can reveal a trend. For example, the improvement in the rate of net income on net sales from 4.5 percent in 19Y2 to 4.7 percent in 19Y3 for the Mirabel Corporation indicates a small but favorable change. Note in the previous chapter that when we compared Mirabel's income statement to the industry average it was less than average.

Rate of Return on Common Stockholders' Equity

The activities of a corporation are carried on to earn a profit for the shareholders. Preferred shareholders are entitled to the amount of dividends provided for in the preferred stock contract. The remainder of earnings belong to the common shareholders. Therefore, the rate of return on common stockholders' equity (often called the **return on common stockholder's equity**) is a key measure of how well the corporation is achieving its goal of making a profit for the shareholders. This rate is computed by dividing net income available to common stockholders by the total equity of the common stock.

$$\frac{\text{Net income available to common stock}}{\text{Common stockholders' equity}} = \text{Return on common stockholders' equity}$$

Now let's see how the two amounts in the ratio—(1) net income available to common stockholders and (2) the total equity of the common stock—are determined.

Step 1: Compute income available to common stockholders. The net income available to common stockholders of Mirabel Corporation during 19Y3 and 19Y2 is computed as shown below.

	19Y3	19Y2
Net Income After Income Taxes	$152,352	$131,889
Less Dividend Requirements on 12% Preferred Stock	12,000	12,000
Income Available to Common Stock	$140,352	$119,889

Another key measure of profitability is the rate of net income on stockholders' equity.

Step 2: Compute the equity of common stockholders. In making this computation, some analysts use only the common stockholders' equity at the end of the year. Other analysts use an average of the beginning and ending common stockholders' equity. The analyst can even compute an average common stockholders' equity based on the amount at the end of each month or each quarter if the necessary figures are available. Mirabel uses the total common stockholders' equity at the end of the year to compute the rate of return on common stockholders' equity. Since the preferred stock of Mirabel is noncumulative and nonparticipating and has no liquidation preference except its par value, the preferred stock's book value is the par value of the outstanding shares, $100,000 each year. The book value of the common stock is calculated as follows.

	19Y3	19Y2
Total Stockholders' Equity	$563,393	$454,341
Less Preferred Stock Equity	100,000	100,000
Common Stockholders' Equity	$463,393	$354,341

Step 3: Compute the rate of return on common stockholders' equity.

19Y3

$$\frac{\text{Net income on common stock}}{\text{Common stockholders' equity}} = \frac{\$140{,}352}{\$463{,}393}\text{, or } 30.3\%$$

19Y2

$$\frac{\$119{,}889}{\$354{,}341}\text{, or } 33.8\%$$

A comparison with rates of prior years can indicate a significant trend. A constantly decreasing rate over a period of years would be cause for alarm. Similarly, a comparison with the industry average can indicate whether the firm's rate of return is in line with that of other companies in the industry. For example, if the average rate of return on common stockholders' equity in the industry is 20.2 percent, Mirabel's performance is very good.

Earnings per Share of Common Stock

Earnings per share is a basic measure of the profitability of a stockholder's shares, especially when compared with the market value of the share.

Earnings per share of common stock is an especially important factor to the stockholders because it measures the amount of profit accruing to each share of stock owned. Earnings per share of common stock is computed by dividing the earnings available to the owners of the common stock by the weighted average number of shares outstanding during the year.

$$\frac{\text{Earnings available to common stockholders}}{\text{Average number of shares of common stock outstanding during year}} = \text{Earnings per share}$$

It is often necessary to first compute the earnings available to the common stockholders and the average number of shares of common stock outstanding.

The necessary steps in computing the earnings per share on Mirabel Corporation's common stock are shown below.

Step 1: Subtract the dividend requirements on preferred stock from the Net Income After Income Tax amount. This figure gives us the income available to the owners of the common stock.

	19Y3	19Y2
Net Income After Income Taxes	$152,352	$131,889
Less Dividend Requirements on 12% Preferred Stock	12,000	12,000
Income Available to Common Stock	$140,352	$119,889

Step 2: Determine the average number of shares of common stock outstanding during the year. An analysis of Mirabel's common stock account reveals that 3,000 shares were outstanding throughout the year 19Y3 and that 200 additional shares were issued on October 1, 19Y3. Thus the weighted average number of shares outstanding for 19Y3 was 3,050 shares, calculated as follows.

3,000 shares × 12 months =	36,000 shares
200 shares × 3 months =	600 shares
Total	36,600 shares

$$\text{Average} = \frac{36{,}600 \text{ shares}}{12} = 3{,}050 \text{ shares}$$

Throughout all of 19Y2, 3,000 shares were outstanding, so the average for that year was 3,000 shares.

Step 3: Divide the net income available to common stock by the average number of shares of common stock outstanding during the year. The result of this computation shows us that earnings per common share were $46.02 in 19Y3 and $39.96 in 19Y2.

19Y3

$$\frac{\text{Net income available to common stock}}{\text{Average number of shares outstanding}} = \frac{\$140{,}352}{3{,}050 \text{ sh.}}, \text{ or } \$46.02$$

19Y2

$$\frac{\$119{,}889}{3{,}000 \text{ sh.}}, \text{ or } \$39.96$$

Perhaps no other analytical measure is watched more closely by analysts, stockholders, creditors, and others than earnings per share. The earnings per share for the year is of importance to stockholders, especially when compared with the current market value of each share (the *price-earnings ratio*, discussed below). A comparison with other companies in the industry is relatively meaningless because of the differences in par value, market value, and other factors. A comparison with earnings per share for the same company in prior years can be meaningful because it may show a trend, but changes in the number of shares outstanding and other elements that might lead to distortions in the ratio must be considered.

Price-Earnings Ratio

The **price-earnings ratio** compares the present market value of a corporation's common stock with earnings per share of that stock.

$$\frac{\text{Current market value per share}}{\text{Earnings per share}} = \text{Price-earnings ratio}$$

For example, if a corporation's common stock is selling at $44 a share (current market value) and its earnings are $4 a share for the year, the price-earnings ratio is 11 to 1.

$$\frac{\text{Current market value per share}}{\text{Earnings per share}} = \frac{\$44}{\$4} = 11 \text{ to } 1$$

Information Block: Communication

Oral Presentations

Professionals must apply written, oral, and nonverbal communication skills in the business environment. While many professionals are comfortable with *written* presentations, others are extremely anxious about *oral* presentations. By focusing on planning, preparation, and practice, business professionals can develop effective oral communication skills.

Oral communication skills are essential in sharing and securing information, persuading others, making recommendations, developing positive rapport, and building confidence levels. Whether the situation is a small or large group discussion, a conference, a one-on-one meeting, a telephone call, a conference call, or a teleconference, communicators must pay particular attention to the factors described below.

- *Appearance.* Just as business professionals form impressions from the appearance of a written document, professionals form impressions from the speaker's appearance *before* a word is heard. Dress appropriately to achieve the best first impression.
- *Nonverbal communication.* An individual's nonverbal communication is critical to the overall effectiveness of the oral presentation. Appropriate posture and eye contact demonstrate confidence. To achieve a comfortable atmosphere and to express interest in the topic and audience, the professional maintains a pleasant facial expression and limits hand movements to relaxed, natural motions.
- *Voice quality.* Voice makes a critical impact on the effectiveness of an oral presentation. The tone of voice, volume, speaking rate, and speaking ability will either enhance the message or distract the receiver.
- *Listening skills.* While some presentations may be formal speeches, many oral communication situations involve discussion time. When

The price-earnings ratio depends in large part on expectations of future profitability, which cause stock prices to increase or decrease.

This comparison is one indicator of the attractiveness of the stock as an investment at its present market value. Investors' interpretations of price-earnings ratios are largely dependent on their expectations for the future and on the amount they are willing to pay for stock because of those expectations. For privately held companies (those companies whose shares are not traded in the financial markets), price-earnings ratios are not relevant because there is no readily available market value for the shares.

discussions are appropriate, communicators must exhibit superb listening skills to lead the discussion, encourage participation, and keep the discussion on track.

To overcome stage fright or other anxieties, business professionals follow these guidelines for effective presentations.

1. Use the steps for planning and developing effective business communication to prepare the oral presentation.
2. Use an appropriate plan for a positive/neutral, negative, or persuasive message.
3. Prepare relevant visual aids, such as transparencies, slides, videos, and handouts, to enhance and support the presentation. Check that any visual aid is readable from the audience.
4. Prepare notes for the presentation.
5. Practice the presentation. If time is critical, check the length of the presentation.
6. Deliver the presentation with confidence (using notes as needed), encouraging and leading discussions as relevant.
7. Seek constructive criticism from other professionals to build on strengths and learn from mistakes.

With planning, preparation, and practice, you will achieve effective communication in your oral presentations.

Project: Following the guidelines for effective oral presentations, prepare an oral presentation for your class regarding the company you analyzed for the communication project in Chapter 23. Follow these guidelines.

1. Limit your presentation to three minutes or less.
2. Use at least one visual aid.
3. Present an overview or summary of the company.
4. Identify the company's strengths and weaknesses from an accounting perspective.
5. Draw conclusions and make recommendations.

Yield on Common Stock

Although the price-earnings ratio is valuable in helping the investor measure the return on the current value of the stock investment, it does not measure the relationship between the cash income realized as dividends by the stockholder and the market value of each share. For a publicly held corporation, whose market value is easily determined and whose stock may be freely bought and sold, this is important. The yield on common stock is computed by dividing the yearly dividend per share by the current market value of the share.

$$\frac{\text{Dividend paid per share}}{\text{Current market price per share}} = \text{Yield on common stock}$$

For example, if the price of a share of common stock is $60 and the corporation is paying an annual dividend of $6, the yield is 10 percent.

$$\frac{\text{Dividend paid per share}}{\text{Current price per share}} = \frac{\$6 \text{ per share}}{\$60 \text{ per share}} = 0.10, \text{ or } 10 \text{ percent}$$

Rate of Return on Total Assets

The rate of return on total assets measures how efficiently the total assets have been utilized in the business.

The rate of return on total assets measures the rate of return on the assets used by a company. In recent years this rate has become an important tool in judging managerial performance, in measuring the effectiveness of the assets used, and in evaluating proposed capital expenditures. This rate of return is computed by dividing net income before interest and taxes by total assets.

$$\frac{\text{Net income before interest and income taxes}}{\text{Total assets}} = \text{Rate of return on total assets}$$

Some analysts use the average of the assets at the beginning and end of the year in making the computation. If monthly figures are available, the average assets based on the monthly figures can be used. Other analysts use only the ending amount of assets or only the beginning amount of assets in the computation.

If the amounts are large, it is preferable to exclude from the net income figure revenue arising from nonoperating sources, such as dividend income and interest income from bond investments, so that only the net income from normal business operations is used. In this case the assets used in earning the nonoperating income are excluded from the asset base. In evaluating the profitability of assets, net income before interest and income taxes should be used. As a result, the rate measures how effectively management has used the assets at its disposal, regardless of the source used to finance the acquisitions. Once again, the resulting computations are meaningful only if compared with rates of prior years and with the industry average.

The Mirabel Unpainted Furniture Corporation uses net income before income taxes and year-end total assets to compute the rate of return on its assets.

19Y3

$$\frac{\text{Net income before interest and income taxes}}{\text{Total assets (end of year)}} = \frac{\$222{,}302}{\$779{,}144}, \text{ or } 28.5\%$$

19Y2

$$\frac{\$188{,}759}{\$628{,}171}, \text{ or } 30\%$$

Asset Turnover

The ratio of net sales to total assets measures the effective use of assets in making sales. This ratio, usually called the **asset turnover,** is computed by dividing net sales by total assets.

$$\frac{\text{Net sales}}{\text{Total assets}} = \text{Asset turnover}$$

In this computation, assets that are not used in producing sales, primarily investments, are excluded from total assets. Again, end-of-year total assets, average assets based on beginning and ending totals, or assets based on monthly averages may be used. Mirabel uses its net sales and its total assets at the end of each year to compute the asset turnover ratio.

	19Y3	19Y2
$\frac{\text{Net sales}}{\text{Total assets}} =$	$\frac{\$3{,}219{,}082}{\$779{,}144}$, or 4.1 to 1	$\frac{\$2{,}951{,}140}{\$628{,}171}$, or 4.7 to 1

Generally the higher the asset turnover rate, the more effectively the assets of the company are being used. A low turnover in comparison with the industry average shows that the assets are too great for the sales volume of the company. Once again, the trend of this ratio is of interest primarily because it indicates whether asset growth is accompanied by corresponding sales growth. If sales increase proportionately more than total assets, this ratio increases (a generally favorable indication).

SELF-REVIEW

1. Name three ratios that are often used in evaluating profitability.
2. What does the ratio of net income to stockholders' equity measure?
3. What is meant by yield on common stock? Why is this ratio not meaningful for most small companies?
4. What does the ratio of net income to total assets measure?
5. In general, would it be preferable to have a higher or a lower asset turnover? Explain.

Answers to Self-Review

1. Return on net sales, return on stockholders' equity, return on assets, and earnings per share are all common measures of profitability.
2. It measures the rate of profit being earned by the corporation on the net assets provided by the stockholders.
3. The yield on common stock is the rate of cash dividends earned by stockholders on the market value of each share. For small companies, there is usually no established market value.
4. This ratio measures how effectively total assets are being used by management to make a profit.
5. A higher asset turnover usually suggests that assets are being used more effectively in generating sales.

RATIOS MEASURING FINANCIAL STRENGTH AND EQUITY SAFETY

OBJECTIVE 2
Compute and interpret financial ratios that measure financial strength.

A number of ratios are useful in measuring the financial strength of a corporation and the protection afforded to long-term creditors and owners. Some of the ratios involve profitability, and other ratios indicate relationships between balance sheet accounts.

Number of Times Bond Interest Earned

Both the bondholders and the stockholders of a corporation are interested in the margin of safety that net income provides for the required bond interest payments. The computation of times bond interest is earned is used widely to measure this safety. The ratio is computed by dividing the net income before bond interest and before income tax by the amount of cash required to pay annual interest on the bonds outstanding at the end of the year.

$$\frac{\text{Net income before income tax and bond interest}}{\text{Cash required to pay bond interest}} = \text{Times bond interest earned}$$

Let's see how the ratio is computed for Mirabel Corporation.

Step 1: Compute the net income available for bond interest. This is the amount of net income before income tax and bond interest. To compute the net income before income tax and bond interest, it is necessary only to add the bond interest expense back to the net income before income taxes.

In 19Y3 Mirabel had bond interest expense of $6,774, consisting of $6,875 interest paid, less $101 bond premium amortized during the year on the $30,000 of bonds issued on April 1. In 19Y2 the bond interest expense was the interest on the $40,000 of bonds outstanding for the entire year. There was no premium or discount to amortize, so the bond interest expense was $4,400 (11% × $40,000).

The net income available for bond interest for each year is computed as shown below.

	19Y3	19Y2
Net Income Before Income Tax	$222,302	$188,759
Add Bond Interest Expense	6,774	4,400
Available for Bond Interest	$229,076	$193,159

Step 2: Compute the cash requirement for bond interest on bonds outstanding at the end of each year. In determining the cash required for future bond interest payment, the cash interest on bonds outstanding at the end of the year is used. The bond interest requirement at the end of 19Y3 is $7,700, which is 11 percent of the $70,000 of bonds outstanding at the end of the year. The cash requirement for 19Y2 was $4,400.

19Y3: $70,000 × 11% = $7,700
19Y2: $40,000 × 11% = $4,400

Step 3: Compute the ratio.

19Y3

$$\frac{\text{Net income before bond interest}}{\text{Bond interest requirement}} = \frac{\$229{,}076}{\$7{,}700}, \text{ or } 29.8 \text{ times}$$

19Y2

$$\frac{\$193{,}159}{\$4{,}400}, \text{ or } 43.9 \text{ times}$$

Mirabel's bondholders apparently had little to worry about in either year as far as their interest payment was concerned.

Number of Times Preferred Dividends Earned

The owners of preferred stock are also interested in the probable regularity of their dividend payments. This factor can be measured to some extent by the number of times preferred dividends are earned, computed by dividing net income after taxes by the amount required to pay the preferred dividends.

$$\frac{\text{Net income after income taxes}}{\text{Amount required for preferred dividends}} = \begin{array}{l}\text{Times preferred}\\ \text{dividends earned}\end{array}$$

At Mirabel the dividends on the preferred stock totaled $12,000 for each year, so the following computations are made.

19Y3

$$\frac{\text{Net income after income taxes}}{\text{Preferred dividends}} = \frac{\$152{,}352}{\$12{,}000}, \text{ or } 12.7 \text{ times}$$

19Y2

$$\frac{\$131{,}889}{\$12{,}000}, \text{ or } 11.0 \text{ times}$$

The number of times that preferred dividends were earned increased from 11.0 times in 19Y2 to 12.7 times in 19Y3, giving the preferred stockholders even more protection. A comparison of this ratio with the industry average is of little value, but a comparison with prior years at the same company would be very useful.

Ratio of Stockholders' Equity to Total Equities

The liabilities and stockholders' equity of a corporation are referred to as its total equities. The ratio of stockholders' equity to total equities measures the portion of total capital provided by the stockholders and indicates the protection afforded creditors against possible losses. For obvious reasons, creditors are particularly interested in the cushion provided. The ratio of stockholders' equity to total equities is computed by dividing stockholders' equity by total equities or by total assets.

$$\frac{\text{Stockholders' equity}}{\text{Total equities}} = \text{Ratio of stockholders equities to total equities}$$

The ratios of stockholders' equity to total equities of the Mirabel Unpainted Furniture Corporation at the end of 19Y3 and 19Y2 are shown below.

19Y3

$$\frac{\text{Stockholders' equity}}{\text{Total equities}} = \frac{\$563{,}393}{\$779{,}144}, \text{ or } 0.72 \text{ to } 1$$

19Y2

$$\frac{\$454{,}341}{\$628{,}171}, \text{ or } 0.72 \text{ to } 1$$

In both 19Y3 and 19Y2, Mirabel's stockholders were providing 72 cents of each dollar of total equities. Clearly, the more capital provided by the stockholders, the greater the protection to creditors. The ratio of stockholders' equity to total equities varies widely from industry to industry, and a comparison with the industry average is important in determining a desirable ratio for a particular firm.

Ratio of Stockholders' Equity to Total Liabilities

The ratio of stockholders' equity to total liabilities is a measure of the security provided to creditors.

Another way of expressing the same relationship as in the preceding ratio is to compute the ratio of stockholders' equity to total liabilities, which is also known as the ratio of *owned capital to borrowed capital.* It is determined by dividing stockholders' equity by total liabilities.

$$\frac{\text{Stockholders' equity}}{\text{Total liabilities}} = \text{Ratio of stockholders' equity to total liabilities}$$

The ratios of stockholders' equity to total liabilities of the Mirabel Unpainted Furniture Corporation at the end of 19Y3 and 19Y2 are shown below.

19Y3

$$\frac{\text{Total stockholders' equity}}{\text{Total liabilities}} = \frac{\$563{,}393}{\$215{,}751}, \text{ or } 2.61 \text{ to } 1$$

19Y2

$$\frac{\$454{,}341}{\$173{,}830}, \text{ or } 2.61 \text{ to } 1$$

A low ratio of stockholders' equity to total liabilities can be very dangerous. It may result in an inability of the corporation to make interest and principal payments on its debts.

This ratio reveals that in both 19Y3 and 19Y2 Mirabel's stockholders were providing $2.61 of capital for each dollar provided by creditors. Again, the greater the share of capital provided by stockholders, the less the risk for creditors.

In the 1980s there were many leveraged buyouts. In a **leveraged buyout** the purchasers of a business buy the stock, having the corporation agree to pay the sellers. The result is that the debt created by the purchase is a debt of the corporation. In many cases the corporate debt, usually bearing an interest rate much higher than the rate on high-quality debt, makes up a large part of the total equity of the corporation. In the mid-1980s and early 1990s, for instance, many corporations went into bankruptcy because they could not meet the interest and principal payments on the debts. The balance sheets of these corporations would reflect an abnormally low ratio of stockholders' equity to total liabilities.

Ratio of Property, Plant, and Equipment to Long-Term Liabilities

The ratio of property, plant, and equipment to long-term liabilities measures the security afforded holders of long-term debts if assets are pledged as collateral for the debts. When the assets are not pledged as collateral, this ratio indicates the potential ability to borrow on the assets. The ratio is computed by dividing the book value of property, plant, and equipment by total long-term liabilities.

$$\frac{\text{Book value of property, plant, and equipment}}{\text{Long-term liabilities}}$$

Ideally, the present fair market value of the property, plant, and equipment rather than its book value should be used in the computation since these amounts more adequately measure the protection afforded long-term creditors in the event of liquidation. However, market value is almost never available to the financial statement reader outside the company, so the book value must be used in most cases. The ratio for the Mirabel Corporation was 2.8 to 1 for 19Y3 and 1.4 to 1 for 19Y2, as shown below.

19Y3

$$\frac{\text{Book value of property, plant, and equipment}}{\text{Long-term liabilities}} = \frac{\$196{,}900}{\$70{,}979}, \text{ or 2.8 to 1}$$

19Y2

$$\frac{\$69{,}600}{\$50{,}000}, \text{ or 1.4 to 1}$$

The large increase from 19Y2 to 19Y3 was due mostly to the fact that Mirabel constructed a new building in 19Y3 at a cost of $120,000, while increasing its long-term liabilities only $20,000 through the issue of $30,000 of bonds payable and the retirement of $10,000 of long-term notes payable. Comparisons with the ratios of prior years and with the industry average can be helpful because they place the company's figures in perspective.

Book Value per Share of Stock

Book value per share of stock is a commonly used measure of the financial strength underlying each share of stock and is frequently reported in financial journals. It represents the amount that each share would receive in case of liquidation if the assets were sold for exactly the recorded value. Obviously, book value has little meaning in many cases because the recorded value of assets may be quite different from their market value.

Book value per share of stock does not indicate how much the owner of a share of stock would receive if the assets were sold and the corporation liquidated.

If there is only one class of stock outstanding, the book value of each share is found by simply dividing total stockholders' equity by the number of shares outstanding. If more than one class of stock is outstanding, the relative rights of the various classes must be considered in computing the book value of each. The book value of preferred stock is computed first; then any remaining balance of stockholders' equity is divided by the number of common shares.

$$\frac{\text{Common stockholders' equity}}{\text{Number of common shares}} = \text{Book value per share of common stock}$$

Several special considerations, such as dividends in arrears on cumulative stock and liquidation preferences, must be given to preferred stock.

Since the Mirabel Unpainted Furniture Corporation has outstanding both preferred stock and common stock, the following steps are required to compute the book value per share of common stock.

Step 1: Compute the claims of preferred stockholders. The preferred stock of Mirabel Corporation involves no cumulative dividends nor special liquidation provisions. In case of liquidation, the owner of a share of this preferred stock will receive only its par value. Its book value is therefore the same as its par value, $100 a share. There were 1,000 shares outstanding during both 19Y3 and 19Y2, so the claims of the preferred stockholders for both years total $100,000.

Step 2: Deduct the claims of preferred stockholders from total stockholders' equity to compute the claims of common stockholders. The common stock is entitled to receive all of the difference between the total stockholders' equity and the portion assigned to the preferred stock. The claims of common stockholders of Mirabel Corporation for 19Y3 and 19Y2 are shown below.

	19Y3	19Y2
Stockholders' Equity	$563,393	$454,341
Less Preferred Stock Equity	100,000	100,000
To Common Stockholders	$463,393	$354,341

Step 3: Divide the total claims of common stockholders by the number of shares of common stock outstanding. Mirabel had 3,200 shares of common stock outstanding on December 31, 19Y3, and 3,000 shares outstanding on December 31, 19Y2. The book value of each share is computed as shown below.

19Y3

$$\frac{\text{Claims of common stockholders}}{\text{Common shares outstanding}} = \frac{\$463{,}393}{3{,}200}, \text{ or } \$144.81$$

19Y2

$$\frac{\$354{,}341}{3{,}000}, \text{ or } \$118.11$$

This computation indicates that the book value of Mirabel's common stock increased in 19Y3 by $26.70 a share, from $118.11 to $144.81.

SELF-REVIEW

1. What does the computation of the number of times bond interest is earned measure?
2. Explain how to compute the ratio of owned capital to borrowed capital.
3. Explain how to compute the book value per share of common stock.
4. Explain how to compute the times preferred dividends earned ratio.
5. What does the ratio of property, plant, and equipment to long-term liabilities measure?

Answers to Self-Review

1. The number of times bond interest is earned is a measure of the safety of bond interest payments.
2. The ratio is determined by dividing the stockholders' equity by the total liabilities.
3. The value is determined by dividing the total stockholders' equity (or the balance of stockholders' equity after book value of preferred stock is deducted from total stockholders' equity) by the number of common shares outstanding.
4. The ratio is determined by dividing net income after taxes by the amount required to pay the preferred dividends.
5. It measures the security provided long-term creditors.

RATIOS MEASURING LIQUIDITY

OBJECTIVE 3
Compute and interpret financial ratios that measure liquidity.

The ability of a company to pay its currently maturing debts is of critical importance to short-term creditors, long-term creditors, and the stockholders. Many companies have failed because they lacked the ability to pay their debts when due, known as **liquidity,** even though they were profitable and had long-term financial strength. The analyst therefore computes various ratios to evaluate a company's present liquidity.

Amount of Working Capital

Working capital is often used to refer to the excess of current assets over current liabilities. This measure is sometimes referred to as net working capital.

Working capital is a fundamental measure of the ability of a company to meet its current obligations and represents the margin of security afforded short-term creditors. Working capital is used in this text to describe the excess of current assets over current liabilities.

$$\text{Current assets} - \text{Current liabilities} = \text{Working capital}$$

Some accountants and analysts refer to the excess of current assets over current liabilities as *net working capital.* Mirabel's working capital in 19Y3 was $437,472, an increase of $2,731 over 19Y2.

	19Y3	19Y2	Increase or (Decrease)
Current assets	$582,244	$558,571	$23,673
Current liabilities	144,772	123,830	20,942
Working capital	$437,472	$434,741	$ 2,731

Current Ratio

The current ratio is a key measure of a company's ability to pay its current liabilities.

Although working capital is a very important element in the analysis of liquidity, the absolute amount of working capital has little meaning by itself. The dollar amount of working capital for a large corporation obviously will be far greater than that for a small business, but it is difficult to judge how adequate the amount is without more information. The **current ratio,** the ratio of current assets to current liabilities, is a key measure in determining a firm's ability to pay current debts and is a good measure of the adequacy of working capital.

$$\frac{\text{Current assets}}{\text{Current liabilities}} = \text{Current ratio}$$

The computation of the current ratio for Mirabel is:

$$\frac{\text{Current assets}}{\text{Current liabilities}} = \overset{\text{19Y3}}{\frac{\$582{,}244}{\$144{,}772}}, \text{ or } 4:1 \qquad \overset{\text{19Y2}}{\frac{\$558{,}571}{\$123{,}830}}, \text{ or } 4.5:1$$

Mirabel had $4 of current assets for each dollar of current liabilities in 19Y3 compared with $4.50 for each dollar in 19Y2.

The magnitude of a desirable current ratio varies widely from industry to industry and even from company to company within an industry. Nevertheless, there is a popular rule of thumb that a current ratio of at least 2 to 1 is desirable in retail and manufacturing businesses. It must be clearly understood that the 2-to-1 ratio is merely a general guide and is not applicable to all businesses.

From the viewpoint of a short-term creditor, generally the higher the current ratio, the greater the protection afforded. However, a company can easily have too high a current ratio. A very high current ratio usually results from having unneeded current assets on hand that are not earning income, large sums of money tied up in accounts receivable that may prove uncollectible, or inventories that contain many obsolete items or are greater than required to conduct normal operations.

Acid-Test Ratio

Quick assets are cash, receivables, and other "near-cash" assets.

Although the current ratio measures a company's ability to meet current liabilities out of existing current assets, it is not a measure of immediate liquidity. For example, a considerable period of time may be necessary to sell the inventories and convert them into cash in the normal course of business operations. Immediate liquidity is measured by the **acid-test ratio.** This ratio is computed by dividing the total of the "near-cash" assets (or **quick assets**)—cash, receivables, and marketable securities—by the current liabilities.

$$\frac{\text{Cash + receivables + marketable securities}}{\text{Current liabilities}} = \text{Acid-test ratio}$$

Mirabel's calculations for 19Y3 and 19Y2 are given below.

	19Y3		19Y2	
Cash	$ 72,860		$100,187	
Accounts Receivable	198,184		168,184	
Total quick assets / Current liabilities	= $271,044 / $144,772,	or 1.87:1	$268,371 / $123,830,	or 2.17:1

The acid-test ratio shows that Mirabel had $1.87 of quick assets for each dollar of current liabilities in 19Y3 compared with $2.17 for each dollar in 19Y2. Although a general rule of thumb is that the acid-test ratio should be at least 1 to 1, the preferred ratio varies widely from industry to industry. Such factors as due dates of current liabilities, composition of quick assets, and various operating factors must be considered in evaluating the adequacy of the ratio. Comparisons with the industry average and with the company's ratio in prior years can be helpful.

Inventory Turnover

It is important that a firm's inventory be turned over rapidly, so that excess amounts of working capital are not tied up in unnecessary merchandise. Since the cost of the merchandise that has been moved during the year is shown on the income statement as the cost of goods sold, the inventory turnover is easily determined. The ratio is computed by dividing the cost of goods sold during the period by the average inventory on hand.

$$\frac{\text{Cost of goods sold}}{\text{Average inventory}} = \text{Inventory turnover}$$

This ratio measures the number of times the average inventory had to be replaced during the period. Obviously, the higher the turnover, the less time that has elapsed between the date of purchase and the date of sale.

In general, a high inventory turnover indicates a tight control over the level of inventory on hand.

Ideally, the average inventory amount should be based on monthly figures. However, the outside analyst often has available only the inventory figures for the beginning and end of the fiscal year. In using the end-of-year inventory figure, the analyst must remember that usually the inventory at that time is near the lowest level of the entire year. Hence, using the beginning and ending inventory figures for the year produces an inventory average that may not be at all typical of the inventory during the other months.

The calculations for the Mirabel Unpainted Furniture Corporation are as follows.

	19Y3
Inventory, Jan. 1	$285,100
Inventory, Dec. 31	300,000
Totals	$585,100
Average Inventory	$585,100 ÷ 2 = $292,550

$$\frac{\text{Cost of goods sold}}{\text{Average inventory}} = \frac{\$1{,}982{,}588}{\$292{,}550}, \text{ or 6.8 times}$$

19Y2

Inventory, Jan. 1	$253,700	
Inventory, Dec. 31	285,100	
Totals	$538,800	

$$\frac{\$1{,}789{,}870}{\$269{,}400}, \text{ or 6.6 times}$$

Average Inventory $538,800 ÷ 2 = $269,400

The typical inventory turnover varies widely from one type of business to another.

Obviously, the inventory turnover ratio varies widely between industries. A bakery would expect to have an almost daily turnover, while dealers in some durable goods might have a turnover of only two times a year. Thus comparisons with the industry average and the company's ratios in prior years are very important.

Accounts Receivable Turnover

A company should collect accounts and notes receivable as quickly as possible. Prompt collection reduces the amount of working capital tied up in receivables, as well as the likelihood that accounts will become uncollectible. The **accounts receivable turnover** is a measure of the reasonableness of the accounts outstanding. This ratio is computed by dividing net credit sales by the average trade receivables, including notes arising from sales transactions.

$$\frac{\text{Net credit sales}}{\text{Average receivables}} = \text{Accounts receivable turnover}$$

As in the case of the inventory turnover, it is desirable to use monthly balances in computing the average receivables, but analysts outside the company usually do not have access to monthly figures and must rely on an average of the balances at the beginning and end of the fiscal year. Also, analysts outside the company normally must use the net amount of all sales since they have no way of telling what part of the sales were made on credit. The computations for the Mirabel Unpainted Furniture Corporation are shown below. (It is assumed that the accounts receivable on January 1, 19Y2, were $158,000 and that net credit sales were $1,910,812 in 19Y3 and $1,645,800 in 19Y2.)

Step 1: Compute average accounts receivable. Since the average accounts receivable for Mirabel is based on the average of the receivables at the beginning and end of the year, the average is computed by adding together the two amounts and then dividing the total by two.

	19Y3
Accounts Receivable, Jan. 1	$168,184
Accounts Receivable, Dec. 31	198,184
Totals	$366,368

$$\text{Average accounts receivable} = \frac{\$366{,}368}{2}, \text{ or } \$183{,}184$$

19Y2

$$\begin{array}{r} \$158{,}000 \\ 168{,}184 \\ \hline \$326{,}184 \end{array} \qquad \frac{\$326{,}184}{2}, \text{ or } \$163{,}092$$

Step 2: Divide credit sales by average accounts receivable. The computations for Mirabel show that the accounts receivable turnover in 19Y3 was 10.4 times and in 19Y2 it was 10.1 times.

19Y3

$$\frac{\text{Net credit sales}}{\text{Average accounts receivable}} = \frac{\$1{,}910{,}812}{\$183{,}184}, \text{ or } 10.4 \text{ times}$$

19Y2

$$\frac{\$1{,}645{,}800}{\$163{,}092}, \text{ or } 10.1 \text{ times}$$

The average collection period, or number of days' sales in receivables, is an important measure of the efficiency of the credit and collections functions in a business.

The accounts receivable turnover is often expressed in a more meaningful and useful way as the **average collection period** of accounts receivable. The computation is made by dividing the average accounts receivable by the average daily credit sales.

$$\frac{\text{Average accounts receivable}}{\text{Average daily credit sales}} = \text{Average collection period}$$

Step 1: Compute the average amount of net credit sales per day. (Total net credit sales for year ÷ 365 days.)

19Y3

$$\frac{\text{Net credit sales}}{365} = \frac{\$1{,}910{,}812}{365}, \text{ or } \$5{,}235 \text{ per day}$$

19Y2

$$\frac{\$1{,}645{,}800}{365}, \text{ or } \$4{,}509 \text{ per day}$$

Step 2: Compute the average accounts receivable. As computed above, the average accounts receivable was $183,184 in 19Y3 and $163,092 in 19Y2.

Step 3: Divide the average accounts receivable by the average daily net credit sales.

19Y3

$$\frac{\text{Average accounts receivable}}{\text{Average daily net credit sales}} = \frac{\$183{,}184}{\$5{,}235}, \text{ or } 35.0 \text{ days}$$

19Y2

$$\frac{\$163{,}092}{\$4{,}509}, \text{ or } 36.2 \text{ days}$$

The Mirabel Unpainted Furniture Corporation required approximately 35 days to collect accounts during 19Y3 compared with 36

Information Block: International Accounting

Performance Evaluation of Foreign Operations

Evaluating the performance of foreign operations is complicated by different accounting standards, corporate pricing differences across international boundaries, and fluctuations in foreign currency rates. U.S. companies that have foreign operations are generally required to maintain accounting records using the currency and accounting standards of the local country. These records are used for local accounting and tax reporting. A second set of records may be kept to conform to U.S. accounting practices and is translated into U.S. dollars. This set of records is used by the U.S.-based corporation for reporting and internal management. These two sets of records may be very different from one another.

Multinational companies use a number of different criteria to evaluate performance of their foreign operations. The primary decision is whether to measure performance in the local, foreign environment or to translate it into U.S. dollars. A significant number of multinational companies evaluate profit performance in the local country, freeing the finan-

days in 19Y2. As a rule of thumb, the average collection period should not exceed the net credit period plus one-third. Since Mirabel's terms are net 30 days, the figures show that it is below the maximum of 40 days suggested by the general rule.

One reason that age of the accounts receivable is important is the need for cash to carry on business operations. The longer that receivables remain uncollected, the less cash is available. Another important consideration is that the older an account becomes, the less likely it is to be collected.

OTHER RATIOS

By definition, a ratio is computed by dividing one number by another. Since there are a great many numbers on financial statements, there is almost no limit to the ratios that might be developed. Each analyst has his or her own set of preferred ratios to follow, and financial writers use many more than have been presented here. The key ratios vary from industry to industry. However, the ratios discussed in this chapter are among those most often used by accountants.

cial results from problems of varying exchange rates. The largest percentage of U.S. multinational companies, however, use profit and return on assets after translation into U.S. dollars as the most important financial measures.

In addition to profit, other financial measures include sales, cash flow available for remittance to the U.S. company, return on equity, and market share.

The table that follows shows the U.S. and foreign operating results for McDonald's for 1991.

McDonald's Geographic Financial Information, 1991 (In millions of dollars)

	U.S.		Outside U.S.		Total	
	$	%	$	%	$	%
Systemwide sales	12.5	63	7.4	37	19.9	100
Operating income	1.0	59	.7	41	1.7	100
% of sales		8		10		9
Total assets	6.2	55	5.1	45	11.3	100
% return on assets		16		14		15
Average annual growth rate*						
% of sales		8		18		11
Operating income		8		23		12

*Based on past 10 years

SOME PRECAUTIONARY NOTES ON STATEMENT ANALYSIS

OBJECTIVE 4
Recognize shortcomings in financial statement analysis.

The astute financial analyst knows to consider many factors when analyzing a company and comparing it with other companies.

Some ratios may be misleading if one does not understand that the accounts reflect historical costs rather than current market values.

An analyst of financial statements must keep in mind a number of significant points that to some extent limit the benefits of the analysis. One of the most important points is that financial statements reflect book values. Book values depend on original cost and on the accounting policies followed. For example, suppose one mining company decides to capitalize as an asset cost the amount spent for developing its mineral properties. Thus its asset accounts will include all these capitalized costs less depletion taken. Another mineral producer decides to charge all such costs to expense, showing none as an asset. Obviously, the statements of the two companies are not comparable. Similarly, differences in depreciation policies—including useful life and methods of computing depreciation—will produce widely varying book values. In many cases the market values of assets, especially of land and buildings, are quite different from the book values. For example, suppose a corporation purchased land for $50,000 a number of years ago and carries the land in its accounting records at that amount. The land is worth $500,000 on the date of the balance sheet. An analyst's interpretation of this statement might be considerably different if the land were carried at its current market value of $500,000 rather than $50,000.

Another point is that accounting assumes that the dollar is a stable monetary unit, although this assumption is far from correct. The financial statements of all but the newest firms actually contain a mixture of dollars with different purchasing power. Changes in the general price level mean that the recorded book values of assets represent dollars with different purchasing power and do not represent dollars with today's purchasing power. Therefore, the significance of the dollar amounts is somewhat uncertain.

We have already discussed the problems in comparing the financial data of different companies arising from the fact that different companies use different financing methods, classify expenses differently, have different policies for paying owner-employees, and operate as different types of entities (partnerships, sole proprietorships, and corporations). Only if these limitations arising from accounting policies and methods and from organizational differences are clearly understood can statement analysis be helpful in evaluating the financial affairs of a business.

SUMMARY OF RATIOS

In this chapter we have examined many ratios that are commonly used by analysts in evaluating a business. Let's summarize these ratios, how they are computed, and what they indicate or mean.

TABLE 24–1
Summary of Ratios Used in Statement Analysis

Ratio	Equation	Performance Measured
Ratios That Measure Profitability and Efficiency		
Rate of return on net sales	$\frac{\text{Net income after taxes}}{\text{Net sales}}$	Percentage of each sales dollar that reflects net income
Rate of return on common stockholders' equity	$\frac{\text{Net income after taxes} - \text{Preferred dividend requirements}}{\text{Equity of common stockholders}}$	Rate of return on book value of common stock
Earnings per share of common stock	$\frac{\text{Net income after taxes} - \text{Preferred dividend requirements}}{\text{Average number of shares of common stock outstanding during year}}$	Income accruing on each share of common stock
Price-earnings ratio	$\frac{\text{Price per share of common stock at end of year}}{\text{Earnings per share of common stock}}$	Value of a share of common stock compared with income accruing to that share
Yield on common stock	$\frac{\text{Cash dividend per share of common stock}}{\text{Market value per share of common stock}}$	Cash income (dividend) from a share of common stock as a percentage of the market value of the share
Rate of return on total assets	$\frac{\text{Net income before interest and income tax}}{\text{Total assets}}$	Efficiency of management in utilizing assets, regardless of how they were financed
Asset turnover	$\frac{\text{Net sales}}{\text{Total assets}}$	Effectiveness of management in using assets to generate sales

TABLE 24–1 (continued)
Summary of Ratios Used in Statement Analysis

Ratios That Measure Financial Strength		
Times bond interest earned	Net income before bond interest and income taxes / Cash bond interest requirement	Security afforded bondholders
Times preferred dividends earned	Net income after taxes / Preferred dividend requirement	Security afforded preferred stockholders for dividend requirements
Ratio of stockholders' equity to total equities	Stockholders' equity / Total equities	Portion of assets provided by stockholders and therefore security afforded creditors
Ratio of stockholders' equity total liabilities	Stockholders' equity / Total liabilities	Owners' capital compared with liability; measures security afforded creditors
Ratio of property, plant, and equipment to long-term liabilities	Book value of property, plant, and equipment / Long-term liabilities	Security afforded long-term liabilities
Book value per share of common stock	Total stockholders' equity − Equity of preferred stock / Number of common shares outstanding	Amount owner of each share would receive if assets were sold for their book value and the corporation were liquidated
Ratios That Measure Liquidity and Solvency		
Amount of working capital	Current assets − Current liabilities	Dollar amount of security provided short-term creditors
Current ratio	Current assets / Current liabilities	Ability of business to pay current debts out of current assets
Acid-test ratio	Cash + Receivables + Marketable securities / Current liabilities	Immediate liquidity or short-run debt-paying ability
Inventory turnover	Cost of goods sold / Average merchandise inventory	Effectiveness of control of inventory for sales volume
Accounts receivable turnover	Sales / Average accounts receivable	Speed with which sales on account are collected
Days' sales in receivables	Average accounts receivable / Average daily sales	Average number of days required to collect sales on account

MANAGERIAL IMPLICATIONS

Management must understand relationships between various items on the financial statements if the statements are to be of maximum use in running the business. Statement analysis assists management in identifying areas of operations that are weak and need management's attention.

Management must know not only how to compute ratios, but how to interpret them and how the ratios are interrelated. For example, a low inventory turnover compared with the industry average may reflect obsolete goods, overstocking of merchandise, poor purchasing procedures, or other operating inefficiencies. As another example, a low current ratio should serve as a warning that the company is facing a liquidity problem. In addition, a low current ratio combined with a low ratio of stockholders' equity to total equities may mean that the company is undercapitalized. Similarly, many other ratios taken alone or in combination can be of great use to the skillful manager in detecting and correcting problems.

It is important that management depend on the accountant to play a key role in making these interpretations. The accountant understands what enters into each item on the financial statement and should provide prompt assistance to management in analyzing and interpreting the accounting reports.

SELF-REVIEW

1. What is liquidity?
2. Why does working capital represent the margin of security afforded short-term creditors?
3. How is the current ratio computed?
4. How is immediate liquidity measured?
5. Why is it useful to know the inventory turnover of a company?

Answers to Self-Review

1. Liquidity is the ability of a business to pay its currently maturing debts in the very near future.
2. Working capital is a fundamental measure of the amount available to a company to pay its current obligations if the current assets can be converted into cash.
3. The current ratio is computed by dividing the current assets by the current liabilities.
4. Immediate liquidity is measured by the acid-test ratio.
5. If the inventory turnover is too low, it suggests that the amounts tied up in the inventory are excessive for the sales volume being generated.

CHAPTER 24 Review and Applications

CHAPTER SUMMARY

Stockholders, creditors, management, financial analysts, and many other groups are interested in a company's profitability, its long-term financial strength and equity protection, and its current position and liquidity. To help in measuring these important factors, comparisons can be made between items on the financial statements. The resulting ratios can be compared with ratios for prior years in order to observe trends and with those of other companies in the industry.

In using financial ratios, several cautions must be kept in mind, especially when comparing the ratios of one business with those of others. Different companies use different accounting methods, which may impair the comparability of data. Also, the operations of no two companies are exactly the same: there are different mixes of products sold, different organizational structures, and different types of entities. Finally, financial statements reflect historical costs, rather than current market values. All of these factors may reduce the usefulness of data. Nevertheless, skillful analysis of statements makes it possible to evaluate not only the past operations of a company, but also to assess its future operations.

GLOSSARY OF NEW TERMS

Accounts receivable turnover (p. 870) The ratio of net credit sales to average receivables

Acid-test ratio (p. 868) A measure of immediate liquidity, the ratio of quick assets to current liabilities

Asset turnover (p. 861) The ratio of net sales to total assets

Average collection period (p. 871) The ratio of average accounts receivable to average daily credit sales, or the number of days' sales in receivables

Current ratio (p. 868) The ratio of current assets to current liabilities

Leveraged buyout (p. 864) Purchasing a business by acquiring the stock and obligating the business to pay the debt incurred

Liquidity (p. 867) The ability to pay debts when due

Price-earnings ratio (p. 857) The ratio of the current market value of common stock to earnings per share of the stock

Quick assets (p. 868) Cash and noncash assets, such as receivables and marketable securities, that can be converted quickly to cash

Ratio analysis (p. 854) A study of the relationship between two amounts

Return on common stockholders' equity (p. 855) The ratio of net income available to common stockholders to total equity of the common stock

Working capital (p. 867) The excess of current assets over current liabilities

REVIEW QUESTIONS

1. Why is the rate of net income on stockholders' equity an important measure to stockholders?
2. What is the procedure for measuring earnings per share of common stock?
3. In order for the computation of earnings per share to be meaningful, with which figures must it be compared?
4. How is inventory turnover computed?
5. Why is the inventory turnover computed by an analyst outside the company likely to be higher than actual turnover? Does this distort the meaning of the computation?
6. What are the procedures for determining the average collection period of accounts receivable?
7. How does the acid-test ratio differ from the current ratio?
8. Why would an analyst be interested in a firm's turnover of assets?
9. What does the accounts receivable turnover measure?
10. Why is it more useful to know the number of days' sales in receivables than the turnover of receivables?
11. As a rule of thumb, what is the minimum desired current ratio?
12. Why does the fact that accounting records are kept on the basis of historical cost sometimes cause difficulties for an analyst of financial statements?
13. Does the analyst outside a company or inside a company have the advantage in analyzing financial statements? Explain.
14. In general, a higher current ratio is favorable because it reflects a greater ability to meet currently maturing obligations. However, management should become concerned if the current ratio becomes too high. Why?
15. Why would the rate of a corporation's net income on sales and the rate of net income on stockholders' equity be of interest and concern to the owners of the corporation's bonds payable?

MANAGERIAL FOCUS

1. Assume that a director of a corporation where you work asks why the rate of return on assets is considered an important tool for judging managerial effectiveness. What explanation would you provide?

2. The current ratio in the company for which you work is 3 to 1. The average for other firms in the industry is 1.6 to 1. Management has asked you to evaluate this ratio. Summarize the questions that you would like to have answered before making your evaluation.
3. Your management has expressed concern that you, as controller of the company, have been providing management with too many ratio analyses. They have asked you to give only three ratios that indicate profitability, three that reflect financial strength, and three that reflect liquidity. In addition, they wish to know what you would compare each ratio with in making an evaluation. In a brief summary, provide the information requested.
4. Suppose that you are the controller for a company that has an inventory turnover of eight times a year while the industry average is only six times a year. One of the officers asks you whether this is a favorable situation for the company. How would you evaluate the situation?
5. In looking at an analysis of financial statements that you have prepared for your employer, a member of management points out that the rate of gross profit on sales has declined in each of the past three years. Management has asked you to explain and evaluate the reasons for this situation. What other ratios might be useful in making your analysis?

EXERCISES

Note: Use the comparative income statement and comparative balance sheet given below for Niagara Corporation in solving Exercises 24–1 through 24–13.

NIAGARA CORPORATION
Comparative Income Statement
Years Ended December 31, 19X3 and 19X2

	19X3	19X2
Sales	1 240 000	1 020 000
Less Sales Returns and Allowances	40 000	20 000
Net Sales	1 200 000	1 000 000
Cost of Goods Sold	900 000	700 000
Gross Profit on Sales	300 000	300 000
Selling Expenses	145 000	130 000
General Expenses	85 000	80 000
Total Expenses	230 000	210 000
Net Income Before Income Taxes	70 000	90 000
Income Tax Expense	12 500	18 850
Net Income After Income Taxes	57 500	71 150

NIAGARA CORPORATION
Comparative Balance Sheet
December 31, 19X3 and 19X2

	19X3	19X2
Assets		
Cash	50000	78000
Accounts Receivable (Net)	180000	135000
Inventory	300000	237000
Buildings (Net)	95000	100000
Equipment (Net)	85000	80000
Land	20000	20000
Total Assets	730000	650000
Liabilities and Stockholders' Equity		
Liabilities		
Accounts Payable	180000	140000
Other Current Liabilities	20000	20000
Bonds Payable, 19Y6	100000	80000
Total Liabilities	300000	240000
Stockholders' Equity		
Common Stock ($20 par)	200000	200000
Retained Earnings	230000	210000
Total Stockholders' Equity	430000	410000
Total Liabilities and Stockholders' Equity	730000	650000

EXERCISE 24–1 (Obj. 1)
Rate of net income on stockholders' equity. Compute the rate of net income on average stockholders' equity for 19X3 and 19X2. Retained Earnings on January 1, 19X2, was $178,850.

EXERCISE 24–2 (Obj. 1)
Rate of net income on assets. Compute Niagara Corporation's rate of net income before income taxes on total assets for 19X3 and 19X2. (Base the calculation on total ending assets for each year.)

EXERCISE 24–3 (Obj. 1)
Asset turnover. Compute Niagara's asset turnover for 19X3 and 19X2. (Base the calculation on total ending assets for each year.)

EXERCISE 24–4 (Obj. 1)
Tutorial
Earnings per share of common stock. Compute Niagara's earnings per share of common stock for 19X3 and 19X2. (Net income after tax for 19X2 was $71,150.)

EXERCISE 24–5 (Obj. 2)
Ratio of stockholders' equity to total equities. Compute Niagara's ratio of stockholders' equity to total equities on December 31, 19X3, and December 31, 19X2.

EXERCISE 24–6 (Obj. 1)
Price-earnings ratio. Assuming that Niagara's common stock on December 31, 19X3, was $104 per share, compute the price-earnings ratio of Niagara's common stock on December 31, 19X3.

EXERCISE 24–7 (Obj. 2)

Ratio of stockholders' equity to total liabilities. Compute Niagara Corporation's ratio of stockholders' equity to total liabilities on December 31, 19X3.

EXERCISE 24–8 (Obj. 2)

Book value per share. Compute the net book value per share of Niagara Corporation's common stock on December 31, 19X3.

EXERCISE 24–9 (Obj. 3)

Acid-test ratio. Compute Niagara Corporation's acid-test ratio as of December 31 of each year.

EXERCISE 24–10 (Obj. 3)

Tutorial

Current ratio. Compute Niagara Corporation's current ratio on December 31 of each year.

EXERCISE 24–11 (Obj. 3)

Working capital. Compute Niagara's working capital on December 31 each year.

EXERCISE 24–12 (Obj. 3)

Inventory turnover. Compute Niagara Corporation's inventory turnover for 19X3.

EXERCISE 24–13 (Obj. 3)

Number of days' sales in accounts receivable. Compute the number of days' sales in the ending accounts receivable on December 31, 19X3, for Niagara Corporation.

PROBLEMS

PROBLEM SET A

PROBLEM 24–1A (Obj. 1, 2, 3)

Compute various ratios and compare ratios with industry averages.

Part I

Tutorial | Spreadsheet

Using the financial statements for the High Five Corporation given in Problem 23-1A, calculate each of the following ratios or measures for the years 19X2 and 19X1.

1. The rate of net income after income taxes on net sales.
2. The rate of net income on total stockholders' equity.
3. The dividend yield per share of common stock. A dividend of $2.29 a share was paid in 19X2, and a dividend of $2 a share was paid in 19X1. The market values were $21 a share in 19X2 and $18.50 a share in 19X1.
4. The rate of net income before interest and income taxes on total assets.
5. The ratio of net sales to total assets.
6. The ratio of net sales to total property, plant, and equipment.
7. The ratio of stockholders' equity to total equities.
8. The ratio of stockholders' equity to total liabilities.
9. The book value per share of common stock.
10. The current ratio.
11. The acid-test ratio.
12. The number of days' sales in average receivables. The net accounts receivable totaled $82,662 on December 31, 19X0.
13. The merchandise inventory turnover.

Part II Selected ratios for other companies in the same industry as the High Five Corporation are given below. Using this data and the ratios you computed in Part I, make brief written comments or suggestions about any areas of strength or weakness for High Five Corporation.

1. Rate of net income on stockholders' equity, 21.4 percent
2. Stockholders' equity to total liabilities, 2.2 to 1
3. Net sales to total assets, 3.1 to 1
4. Merchandise inventory turnover, 3.2 times

PROBLEM 24–2A
(Obj. 1, 2, 3)

Tutorial GL

Compute various ratios. Using the financial statements for the Brasseau Products Corporation in Problem 23-2A, calculate each of the following ratios or measures for 19X2 and 19X1.

1. The rate of net income after income taxes on net sales.
2. The rate of net income on ending stockholders' equity.
3. The earnings per share of common stock, assuming that the preferred stock is nonparticipating and noncumulative.
4. The dividend yield per share of common stock. A dividend of $8.33 a share was paid in 19X2, and a dividend of $6 a share was paid in 19X1. The market values were $58 a share in 19X2 and $60 a share in 19X1.
5. The rate of net income before interest and income taxes on total assets.
6. The asset turnover.
7. The ratio of net sales to total property, plant, and equipment.
8. The ratio of stockholders' equity to total equities.
9. The ratio of stockholders' equity to total liabilities.
10. The book value per share of common stock, assuming that the preferred stock is noncumulative, nonparticipating, and has no liquidation premium.
11. The ratio of property, plant, and equipment (net) to long-term liabilities.
12. The current ratio.
13. The acid-test ratio.
14. The number of days' sales in receivables. The net accounts receivable totaled $554,000 on December 31, 19X0.
15. The merchandise inventory turnover. The merchandise inventory on January 1, 19X1, was $1,385,000.

PROBLEM 24–3A
(Obj. 1, 2, 3)

Compute and interpret various ratios. Condensed financial statements for South Side Corporation and East End Corporation for 19X1 are given on the next page.

Instructions

1. Compute the following ratios for each company.
   a. Rate of net income on net sales
   b. Rate of net income before interest and taxes on total assets at end of year
   c. Rate of net income after income taxes on stockholders' equity at the end of the year

Income Statements
Year Ended December 31, 19X1

	South Side Corp.	East End Corp.
Sales	6000000	6000000
Cost of Goods Sold	3600000	3600000
Gross Profit on Sales	2400000	2400000
Operating Expenses	1000000	1000000
Net Income from Operations	1400000	1400000
Interest Expense	180000	—0—
Net Income Before Income Tax	1220000	1400000
Income Tax	410000	470000
Net Income After Income Tax	810000	930000

Balance Sheets
December 31, 19X1

	South Side Corp.	East End Corp.
Assets		
Current Assets	800000	1000000
Plant and Equipment	1600000	1400000
Total Assets	2400000	2400000
Liabilities and Stockholders' Equity		
Liabilities		
Current Liabilities	400000	400000
Bonds Payable	1600000	—0—
Total Liabilities	2000000	400000
Stockholders' Equity		
Common Stock ($50 par value)	200000	1000000
Retained Earnings	200000	1000000
Total Stockholders' Equity	400000	2000000
Total Liabilities and Stockholders' Equity	2400000	2400000

d. Earnings per share of common stock
e. Ratio of stockholders' equity to total equities
f. Current ratio
g. Asset turnover
h. Book value per share of common stock

2. Comment on the similarities and differences in the ratios computed for the two companies, pointing out the major factor that causes differences.
3. In which corporation would stock ownership be riskier? Explain.
4. Would you consider the extension of short-term credit to South Side or East End riskier? Explain.

PROBLEM SET B

PROBLEM 24–1B (Obj. 1, 2, 3)

Compute various ratios and compare ratios with industry averages.

Part I

Tutorial

Using the financial statements for the Molina Corporation given in Problem 23–1B, calculate each of the following ratios or measures for the years 19X3 and 19X2.

1. The rate of net income after income taxes on net sales
2. The rate of net income on ending stockholders' equity
3. The earnings per share of common stock, assuming that the preferred stock is noncumulative and nonparticipating
4. The dividend yield per share of common stock. A dividend of $35.58 a share was paid in 19X3, and a dividend of $22.50 a share was paid in 19X2. The market values were $148 a share in 19X3 and $116 a share in 19X2.
5. The rate of net income before interest and income taxes on total assets.
6. The ratio of net sales to total assets.
7. The ratio of net sales to total property, plant, and equipment.
8. The times preferred dividends earned ratio.
9. The ratio of stockholders' equity to total equities.
10. The ratio of stockholders' equity to total liabilities.
11. The book value per share of common stock, assuming that the preferred stock has no liquidation premium.
12. The current ratio.
13. The acid-test ratio.
14. The number of days' sales in average receivables. The net accounts receivable totaled $38,743 on December 31, 19X1.
15. The merchandise inventory turnover.

Part II

Selected ratios for other companies in the same industry as the Molina Corporation are given below. Using these ratios and the ratios you computed in Part I, make brief written comments about any areas of Molina's operations that should be examined by management.

1. Rate of net income on net sales, 8.1 percent
2. Net sales to total assets, 2.4 to 1
3. Days' sales in accounts receivable, 22.1 days
4. Merchandise inventory turnover, 5.8 times
5. Current ratio, 1.8 to 1
6. Net sales to total property, plant, and equipment, 4.3 to 1

PROBLEM 24–2B
(Obj. 1, 2, 3)

Tutorial

Compute various ratios. Using the financial statements for the Cowhide Corporation given in Problem 23-2B, calculate each of the following ratios or measures for 19X2 and 19X1.

1. The rate of net income after income taxes on net sales.
2. The rate of net income on ending stockholders' equity.
3. The earnings per share of common stock, assuming that the preferred stock is nonparticipating and noncumulative.
4. The dividend yield per share of common stock. A dividend of $37.28 a share was paid on each share outstanding all year in 19X2, and a dividend of $22.50 a share was paid in 19X1. The market values were $186 a share in 19X2 and $116 in 19X1.
5. The rate of net income before interest and income taxes on total assets.
6. The ratio of net sales to total assets other than investments.
7. The ratio of net sales to total property, plant, and equipment.
8. The ratio of stockholders' equity to total equities.
9. The ratio of stockholders' equity to total liabilities.
10. The book value per share of common stock, assuming that the preferred stock is noncumulative, nonparticipating, and has no liquidation premium.
11. The ratio of property, plant, and equipment (net) to long-term liabilities.
12. The current ratio.
13. The acid-test ratio.
14. The number of days' sales in average receivables. The net accounts receivable totaled $177,000 on December 31, 19X0.
15. The merchandise inventory turnover.

PROBLEM 24–3B
(Obj. 1, 2, 3)

Compute and interpret various ratios. Condensed financial statements for Abbott Corporation and Costello Corporation for 19X1 are given below.

Income Statements
Year Ended December 31, 19X1

	Abbott Corp.	*Costello Corp.*
Sales	9000000	9000000
Cost of Goods Sold	6000000	6000000
Gross Profit on Sales	3000000	3000000
Operating Expenses	1500000	1500000
Net Income from Operations	1500000	1500000
Interest Expense	220000	—0—
Net Income Before Income Tax	1280000	1500000
Income Tax	435000	510000
Net Income After Income Tax	845000	990000

Balance Sheets
December 31, 19X1

	Abbott Corp.	Costello Corp.
Assets		
Current Assets	1000000	1200000
Plant and Equipment	1600000	1400000
Total Assets	2600000	2600000
Liabilities and Stockholders' Equity		
Liabilities		
Current Liabilities	300000	350000
Bonds Payable	1800000	—0—
Total Liabilities	2100000	350000
Stockholders' Equity		
Common Stock ($50 par value)	250000	1000000
Retained Earnings	250000	1250000
Total Stockholders' Equity	500000	2250000
Total Liabilities and Stockholders' Equity	2600000	2600000

Instructions

1. Compute the following ratios for each company.
   a. Rate of net income on net sales
   b. Rate of net income before interest and income taxes on total assets at end of year
   c. Rate of net income on stockholders' equity at end of year
   d. Earnings per share of common stock
   e. Ratio of stockholders' equity to total equities
   f. Current ratio
   g. Asset turnover
   h. Book value per share of common stock
2. Comment on the similarities and differences in the ratios computed for the two companies, pointing out the major factor that causes differences.
3. In which corporation would stock ownership be riskier? Explain.
4. Would you consider the extension of short-term credit to Abbott Corporation or to Costello Corporation riskier? Explain.

CHALLENGE PROBLEM

The condensed comparative income statement and balance sheet for Pilgrim Bay Merchandising Corporation for the years 19X5 and 19X4 follow.

Instructions Compute the missing amounts or percentages.

	December 31, 19X5	December 31, 19X4	Increase or (Decrease) Amount	Percent
Net Sales	800,000	?	84,000	?
Cost of Merchandise Sold	?	416,000	47,000	?
Gross Profit on Sales	?	?	?	?
Operating Expenses				
Selling Expenses	?	?	?	?
General Expenses	?	96,000	(2,000)	?
Total Operating Expenses	?	240,000	?	?
Net Income Before Income Tax	?	?	?	?
Income Tax Expense	?	10,000	?	2.5
Net Income After Income Tax	?	?	(1,875)	?

	December 31, 19X5	December 31, 19X4	Increase or (Decrease) Amount	Percent
Assets				
Current Assets				
Cash	?	10,000	?	4.0
Accounts Receivable	60,000	?	?	25.0
Merchandise Inventory	?	?	17,900	
Total Current Assets	?	?	?	?
Property, Plant, and Equipment				
Land, Buildings, Equipment	?	60,000	30,400	
Less Accumulated Depreciation	18,675	?	?	25.0
Net Book Value, Property, Plant, and Equipment	?	?	?	?
Total Assets	?	?	?	?
Liabilities and Stockholders' Equity				
Current Liabilities				
Accounts Payable	?	?	?	31.8
Accrued Expenses	8,000	?	2,000	?
Total Current Liabilities	?	?	?	?
Stockholders' Equity				
Common Stock ($50 par value)	?	50,000	?	0.0
Retained Earnings	?	?	?	?
Total Stockholders' Equity	?	?	?	?
Total Liabilities and Stockholders' Equity	?	?	?	?

Other information:

Dividends per share	$6	
Inventory turnover (based on ending inventory)	8 times	
Asset turnover (based on ending assets)	4 times	
Acid-test ratio		1.25 to 1

CRITICAL THINKING PROBLEM

Robert Carter, a wholesale distributor of air conditioning and heating equipment, has been approached by two heating contractors who want to purchase merchandise from him on net 30-day credit terms. He shows you the following financial data about the two firms and asks for your help in evaluating their liquidity and ability to pay short-term debt.

	Admiral Heating and Plumbing	Best Heating & Cooling, Inc.
Net Credit Sales	$350,000	$590,000
Cost of Goods Sold	279,000	436,800
Cash	4,080	10,100
Accounts Receivable	36,400	54,900
Inventory	62,000	78,000
Accounts Payable	49,100	50,000
Salaries Payable	1,500	

Instructions For each company, compute the (1) current ratio, (2) acid-test ratio, (3) inventory turnover, and (4) accounts receivable turnover. Evaluate each company's ability to pay short-term debt and advise Carter on whether or not he should sell to these companies on credit.

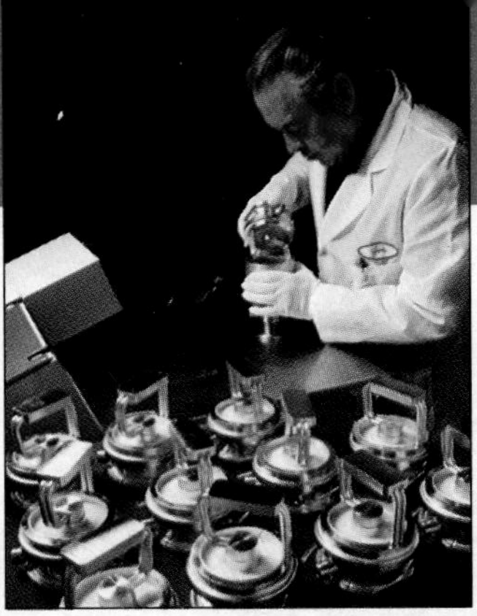

CHAPTER 25

The Statement of Cash Flows

OBJECTIVES

1. Distinguish between operating, investing, and financing activities.
2. Compute cash flows from operating activities.
3. Compute cash flows from investing activities.
4. Compute cash flows from financing activities.
5. Prepare a statement of cash flows.
6. Define the accounting terms new to this chapter.

In previous chapters of this book, three major financial statements for corporations were explained and illustrated: the income statement, the balance sheet, and the statement of retained earnings. Some corporations also prepare a statement of stockholders' equity. One additional statement is required to complete the set of annual financial statements for a corporation—the statement of cash flows.

NEW TERMS

Cash ▪ Cash equivalents ▪ Direct method ▪ Financing activities ▪ Indirect method ▪ Investing activities ▪ Operating activities ▪ Operating assets and liabilities ▪ Statement of cash flows

THE IMPORTANCE OF A STATEMENT OF CASH FLOWS

The published financial statements of corporations must include a **statement of cash flows.** The purpose of the statement of cash flows is to provide relevant information about the cash receipts and cash payments of a business entity during a fiscal period. Creditors (bondholders, noteholders, other lenders, and suppliers of goods and services) clearly look to a corporation's cash flows as the source for payment of interest and payment of debts. Investors who purchase stock in a corporation do so because they expect to receive a competitive rate of return on their investment. This return on investment is ultimately in the form of dividends, which are paid from corporate profits.

Management also is interested in cash flows. It must make plans to obtain cash to meet payrolls, to pay suppliers, and to meet other obligations. In planning future cash inflows and outflows, it is very helpful to analyze cash flows of the past. Past cash flows give an indication of the sources and uses of cash in the future.

THE MEANING OF CASH

To qualify as a cash equivalent, an asset must be readily convertible into a known amount of cash.

To be classified as a cash equivalent, a short-term investment must fall due within three months from the date the investment was acquired.

Before the statement of cash flows is examined, it is necessary to understand the use of the word *cash* in the context of a statement of cash flows. The statement reflects both cash in the usual sense of the word and cash equivalents.

Cash and **cash equivalents** consist of currency, bank accounts, and short-term, highly liquid investments, such as certificates of deposit, that are easily convertible into known amounts of cash. Generally, if a short-term investment is to qualify as a cash equivalent, the investment must fall due within three months from the date the investment was acquired by the corporation. Thus a certificate of deposit acquired by a corporation on September 1, 19Y2, and maturing on March 1, 19Y3, would not be considered a cash equivalent on the December 31, 19Y2, balance sheet because the maturity date is more than three months from the date the certificate was acquired. Examples of commonly found cash equivalents are U.S. Treasury bills and money market funds.

SOURCES AND USES OF CASH

OBJECTIVE 1
Distinguish between operating, investing, and financing activities.

Cash inflows from services rendered or merchandise sold are the main sources of cash from operating activities.

The purchase of assets such as land, buildings, equipment, and securities of other corporations represents use of cash in investing activities.

Financing activities involve dealings with creditors and stockholders who provide cash to the corporation.

In the statement of cash flows, cash receipts and cash payments must be classified under three general headings. Although these classifications will be examined in greater detail later, they are briefly described below.

1. Cash flows from **operating activities.** Routine business operations result in cash inflows and cash outflows. The most common transactions that give rise to cash inflows from operating activities include (a) the sale of merchandise or services for cash, (b) the collection of accounts receivable created by the sale of merchandise or services, and (c) miscellaneous sources, such as interest income. Similarly, cash outflows from operations commonly result from (a) paying expenses at the time they are incurred and (b) paying accounts payable created when merchandise is purchased or operating expenses are incurred and credited to accounts payable.
2. Cash flows from **investing activities.** Investing activities are those transactions that involve the acquisition of assets (cash outflow) or disposal of assets (cash inflow) such as bonds of other corporations, land, buildings, and equipment. These assets are not purchased for resale and are not normally consumed in operations within one year.
3. Cash flows from **financing activities.** Financing activities involve transactions between a corporation and those who provide cash to the corporation to carry on its activities. Note that interest expense is considered a part of operating, not financing, activities.

   The following financing activities result in cash inflows.

   a. Issuing capital stock for cash
   b. Issuing bonds for cash
   c. Borrowing cash by issuing or discounting a note payable
   d. Resale of treasury stock

The following financing activities result in cash outflows.

a. Paying a note payable or a bond payable
b. Purchasing treasury stock
c. Paying cash dividends on stock

Table 25–1 summarizes the sources and uses of cash.

TABLE 25–1
The Sources and Uses of Cash in a Corporation

	Sources of Cash	Uses of Cash
Operating Activities	Sale of merchandise	Pay for merchandise
	Sale of services	Pay taxes
	Interest income	Pay salaries and wages
	Dividend income	Pay interest expense
	Miscellaneous income	Pay for other expenses
Investing Activities	Sale of land, buildings, or equipment	Pay for purchase of land, buildings, or equipment
	Sale of investment in bonds or other securities	Pay for purchase of investments in bonds or other securities
	Collection of debts acquired from sale of long-term assets	
Financing Activities	Issuance of common stock	Pay cash dividends on common stock
	Issuance of preferred stock	Pay cash dividends on preferred stock
	Issuance of bonds payable	Repay bond indebtedness
	Borrowing through issue or discounting of notes payable	Repay notes payable or other borrowing
	Resale of treasury stock	Purchase treasury stock

SELF-REVIEW

1. What are cash and cash equivalents?
2. What are the three types of activities for which cash flow must be shown in a statement of cash flows?
3. What are investing activities?
4. What are financing activities?
5. Is short-term borrowing by discounting a note payable a financing activity? Explain.

Answers to Self-Review

1. Cash and cash equivalents include currency, bank accounts, and short-term liquid investments that are easily convertible into cash.
2. Operating, investing, and financing activities are shown in a statement of cash flows.
3. Investing activities involve the acquisition or disposal of assets—such as bonds of other corporations, land, buildings, and equipment—not normally consumed in operations within one year.

4. Financing activities are transactions between the corporation and those who provide cash. (Interest expense is not considered a part of financing activities.)
5. Yes. This activity is one of financing the business—obtaining cash for carrying on its activities.

CASH FLOWS STATEMENT

In preparing the statement of cash flows, the accountant depended largely on Mirabel Corporation's income statement, schedule of operating expenses, and statement of retained earnings for the year 19Y3 and on its comparative balance sheet for December 31, 19Y3. These statements appear in Figures 25–1 through 25–4.

FIGURE 25–1
The Income Statement

MIRABEL UNPAINTED FURNITURE CORPORATION
Income Statement
Year Ended December 31, 19Y3

Revenue		
Sales	3241 5 7 8 00	
Less Sales Returns and Allowances	22 4 9 6 00	
Net Sales		3219 0 8 2 00
Cost of Goods Sold		
Merchandise Inventory, Jan. 1	285 1 0 0 00	
Purchases (Net)	1982 4 8 8 00	
Freight In	15 0 0 0 00	
Total Merchandise Available for Sale	2282 5 8 8 00	
Less Merchandise Inventory, Dec. 31	300 0 0 0 00	
Cost of Goods Sold		1982 5 8 8 00
Gross Profit on Sales		1236 4 9 4 00
Operating Expenses		
Selling Expenses (see schedule)	719 3 4 6 00	
General Expenses (see schedule)	288 9 5 2 00	
Total Operating Expenses		1008 2 9 8 00
Net Income from Operations		228 1 9 6 00
Other Income		
Gain on Sale of Equipment	1 0 0 0 00	
Interest Income	3 5 5 00	
Total Other Income		1 3 5 5 00
Total Income for Year		229 5 5 1 00
Other Expenses		
Bond Interest Expense	6 7 7 4 00	
Other Interest Expense	4 7 5 00	
Total Other Expenses		7 2 4 9 00
Net Income Before Income Taxes		222 3 0 2 00
Income Tax Expense		69 9 5 0 00
Net Income After Income Taxes		152 3 5 2 00

FIGURE 25–2
The Schedule of Operating Expenses

MIRABEL UNPAINTED FURNITURE CORPORATION
Schedule of Operating Expenses
Year Ended December 31, 19Y3

Selling Expenses		
Sales Salaries	382 6 0 0 00	
Sales Commissions	42 0 0 0 00	
Payroll Taxes—Sales Staff	46 6 0 0 00	
Employee Fringe Benefits	31 6 0 0 00	
Freight Out and Deliveries	28 8 7 0 00	
Advertising	94 6 3 0 00	
Sales Supplies	10 3 0 7 00	
Rent	22 0 0 0 00	
Utilities	9 0 3 9 00	
Insurance	9 8 0 0 00	
Repairs and Maintenance	1 8 0 0 00	
Depreciation	8 3 0 0 00	
Travel and Entertainment	12 0 0 0 00	
Other Taxes	7 8 0 0 00	
Miscellaneous	12 0 0 0 00	
Total Selling Expenses		719 3 4 6 00
General Expenses		
Officers' Salaries	158 7 5 9 00	
Office Employees' Salaries	57 0 0 0 00	
Payroll Taxes—Administrative Staff	23 8 0 0 00	
Office Supplies	15 6 3 3 00	
Postage, Copying, and Miscellaneous	3 8 0 0 00	
Uncollectible Accounts Expense	5 3 6 0 00	
Rent	8 0 0 0 00	
Depreciation	6 4 0 0 00	
Other Taxes	4 8 0 0 00	
Utilities	5 4 0 0 00	
Total General Expenses		288 9 5 2 00
Total Operating Expenses		1,008 2 9 8 00

The statement of cash flows reconciles the beginning and ending balances of cash and cash equivalents.

The comparative balance sheet (Figure 25–4) shows the net change in each balance sheet item during 19Y3. The statement of cash flows ties together the income statement for 19Y3 (Figure 25–1) and the changes that have occurred in the noncash items on the balance sheet and the changes in retained earnings (Figure 25–3) during the year. The statement of cash flows accounts for changes in the balances of every noncash asset, liability, and stockholders' equity account.

FIGURE 25–3
The Statement of Retained Earnings

MIRABEL UNPAINTED FURNITURE CORPORATION
Comparative Statement of Retained Earnings
Years Ended December 31, 19Y3 and 19Y2

	Amounts 19Y3	Amounts 19Y2	Increase or (Decrease) During 19Y3
Balance, January 1	179341	114742	64599
Additions			
Net Income After Income Taxes	152352	131889	20463
Total	331693	246631	85062
Deductions			
Dividends—Preferred	12000	12000	—0—
Dividends—Common	51300	55290	(3990)
Balance, December 31	268393	179341	89052

FIGURE 25–4
The Comparative Balance Sheet

MIRABEL UNPAINTED FURNITURE CORPORATION
Comparative Balance Sheet
December 31, 19Y3 and 19Y2

	Amounts 19Y3	Amounts 19Y2	Increase or (Decrease) During 19Y3
Assets			
Current Assets			
Cash	72860	100187	(27327)
Accounts Receivable (Net)	198184	168184	30000
Merchandise Inventory	300000	285100	14900
Prepaid Insurance	5700	2600	3100
Other Prepaid Expenses	5500	2500	3000
Total Current Assets	582244	558571	23673
Property, Plant, and Equipment			
Land	30000	30000	—0—
Buildings	120000	—0—	120000
Less Accumulated Depreciation	2000	—0—	2000
Net Book Value—Buildings	118000	—0—	118000
Equipment and Fixtures	103200	83600	19600
Less Accumulated Depreciation	54300	44000	10300
Net Book Value—Equipment and Fixtures	48900	39600	9300
Total Property, Plant, and Equipment	196900	69600	127300
Total Assets	779144	628171	150973

(Continued)

Liabilities and Stockholders' Equity			
Current Liabilities			
Accounts Payable	113326	92300	21026
Estimated Income Taxes Payable	17000	14000	3000
Accrued Liabilities	14446	17530	(3084)
Total Current Liabilities	144772	123830	20942
Long-Term Liabilities			
Long-Term Notes Payable	—0—	10000	(10000)
11% Bonds Payable, 19Z1	70000	40000	30000
Premium on Bonds Payable	979	—0—	979
Total Long-Term Liabilities	70979	50000	20979
Total Liabilities	215751	173830	41921
Stockholders' Equity			
12% Preferred Stock, $100 Par Value	100000	100000	—0—
Paid-in Capital in Excess of Par Value	6000	6000	—0—
Common Stock, $50 Par Value	160000	150000	10000
Paid-in Capital in Excess of Par Value	29000	19000	10000
Retained Earnings	268393	179341	89052
Total Stockholders' Equity	563393	454341	109052
Total Liabilities and Stockholders' Equity	779144	628171	150973

On Mirabel's balance sheet, the only item considered to be either cash or a cash equivalent is the amount shown as Cash. The firm's cash balance was $100,187 on December 31, 19Y2, and $72,860 on December 31, 19Y3, showing a decrease of $27,327 in cash during the year. The statement of cash flows will show the factors that caused this change.

Now let's look at how the figures on Mirabel's cash flows statement shown in Figure 25–5, page 908, are obtained.

CASH FLOWS FROM OPERATING ACTIVITIES

OBJECTIVE 2

Compute cash flows from operating activities.

The first section of Mirabel's statement of cash flows (Figure 25–5) shows that $135,893 was provided by operating activities. The cash inflows and outflows from operating activities are of vital concern to management, creditors, investors, and other parties interested in a corporation's financial affairs. Since cash flows from operating activities are closely related to net income, the starting point in the analysis of the cash flows from operating activities is the net income after income taxes, as shown on the income statement for the period (Figure 25–1). Mirabel's 19Y3 net income after taxes was $152,352. The

The starting point for analyzing cash flows from operations is the net income after taxes, as shown on the income statement.

Cash Flows from Operating Activities section of the cash flows statement explains why the net cash flow from operations differs from the amount of net income after taxes.

The accrual basis of accounting must be used when recording transactions and preparing the balance sheet and the income statement. Therefore, the net income shown in the income statement does not reflect solely cash received and cash paid out. To prepare the section of the statement of cash flows that reports the cash flows from operating activities, the net income amount must be adjusted for the noncash items.

Several types of income and expense items reported on the income statement for a period do not involve cash inflows or cash outflows during that period. Let's analyze those items on Mirabel Corporation's income statement as shown in Figure 25–1.

Expense and Income Items Involving Long-Term Assets and Liabilities

Usually, some expense and income items on the income statement result from adjustments related to long-term assets or long-term liabilities and do not involve cash operating inflows or outflows in the current year. To arrive at the cash flow from operations, it is necessary to add or subtract these amounts from the net income reported. Look at Mirabel's statement of cash flows (page 908) to see how the following items are handled on the statement.

Depreciation Expense

Depreciation, depletion, and other charges related to long-term assets or liabilities must be added to net income to arrive at net cash inflow.

Depreciation, depletion, or amortization expense shown on an income statement does not require a cash outlay in the year the expense is deducted. Instead, it represents a reduction in property, plant, and equipment. The property, plant, and equipment was acquired either in the current period or some prior period in an investing activity.

Mirabel's 19Y3 schedule of operating expenses (Figure 25–2, page 893) shows that depreciation of $14,700 was deducted. This amount includes $8,300 from the Selling Expenses schedule and $6,400 from the General Expenses schedule. The depreciation expense was recorded by the following journal entry.

19Y3					
Dec.	*31*	*Depreciation Expense (Selling)*		*8 3 0 0 00*	
		Depreciation Expense (General)		*6 4 0 0 00*	
		Accumulated Depreciation			*14 7 0 0 00*

Note that the depreciation expense did not involve a cash outflow in 19Y3. As a result, the net income of $152,352 reported in the income statement does not reflect the actual net cash inflow from operations. As shown in the statement of cash flows the depreciation expense of $14,700 must be "added back" to the net income in computing the cash inflow from operations.

Amortization of Premium on Bonds Payable

Bond Interest Expense of $6,774 is shown on the income statement (Figure 25–1). However, this figure does not show the actual outflow for interest because the Bond Interest Expense account reflects both the cash paid and the amortization of $101 of premium on the bonds. That amount of amortization was debited to Premium on Bonds Payable and credited to Bond Interest Expense during the year. The entries related to bond interest that were made during the year may be summarized by the following journal entry.

	Bond Interest Expense	6 774 00	
	Premium on Bonds Payable	101 00	
	Cash		6 875 00

Note that the actual cash outflow for interest was $6,875—not the amount of $6,774 shown as bond interest expense in the income statement. Since the balance of Bond Interest Expense in the income statement understates the actual cash outflow by $101 (the amount of the premium amortized), in the statement of cash flows on page 908 the $101 is deducted from net income in arriving at the net cash flow from operations.

Gain or Loss on Sale of Equipment

A gain on the sale of long-term assets must be deducted from net income, and a loss on sale of long-term assets must be added to net income, in computing cash flow from operations.

One other item related to long-term assets appears in Mirabel's income statement (Figure 25–1). This is a gain of $1,000 on the sale of equipment. This gain resulted from the sale for $2,700 of equipment with a net book value of $1,700 (cost of $4,100 less accumulated depreciation of $2,400). At the time of sale, the following entry was made.

	Cash	2 700 00	
	Accum. Depr.—Equipment	2 400 00	
	Equipment		4 100 00
	Gain on Sale of Equipment		1 000 00

The sale of equipment is not a part of the routine operating activities of the business. The gain of $1,000 is a part of the $2,700 in cash received from the asset sale. As we will see later, the entire $2,700 will be included in cash inflows from investing activities. It is therefore necessary to remove (deduct) the $1,000 of gain on sale of equipment from the net income figure in arriving at the net cash inflow provided by operations.

Adjustments such as those for depreciation and gain on the sale of equipment, described above, remove from net income the effects of noncash expense and income items that have resulted from prior investing activities. Adjustments such as the one for amortization of premium on bonds payable remove the effects of noncash items that have resulted from prior financing activities.

Income and Expense Items Involving Changes in Current Assets and Current Liabilities

Changes in most noncash current assets and in current liabilities are related to the routine operations of the business and are reflected in net income. Current assets and current liabilities are often referred to as **operating assets and liabilities.** Let's assume for the moment that all the changes in Mirabel's current assets and current liabilities resulted from routine operating activities. Let's first see how increases in current assets are reflected in cash flows from operations. We shall then examine, in turn, the effects of decreases in current assets, increases in current liabilities, and decreases in current liabilities.

Increases in Current Assets

Increases in current assets such as accounts receivable, merchandise inventory, and prepaid expenses must be deducted from net income to arrive at cash flow from operations.

If a current asset, other than cash or cash equivalents, increased as a result of operations, some of the net income reported was not converted to cash during the period. Mirabel's statement of cash flows (Figure 25–5) shows several adjustments resulting from increases in current assets.

Increase in Accounts Receivable. The $30,000 adjustment to net income to arrive at cash flows from operations can be traced to the change in Mirabel's Accounts Receivable account reflected in the comparative balance sheet (Figure 25–4, page 894).

	Accounts Receivable
Balance, December 31, 19Y3	$198,184
Balance, December 31, 19Y2	168,184
Increase during year	$ 30,000

This increase of $30,000 in accounts receivable suggests that cash collections on accounts during the year were $30,000 less than the amounts charged to accounts receivable when sales were made during the year. The $30,000 increase in the Accounts Receivable account represents an amount that was not received in cash during the year, although it represents sales made and included in computing net income. The accounts receivable increase, therefore, must be deducted from net income to arrive at the cash flow from operating activities, as shown in the statement of cash flows (Figure 25–5).

Increase in Merchandise Inventory. The $14,900 adjustment to net income for the inventory increase shown in the statement of cash flows also can be traced to Mirabel's comparative balance sheet (Figure 25–4).

	Merchandise Inventory
Balance, December 31, 19Y3	$300,000
Balance, December 31, 19Y2	285,100
Increase during year	$ 14,900

The increase of $14,900 in the account balance during the year indicates that Mirabel not only purchased merchandise equal to the cost of goods sold during the year, but also purchased an additional amount equal to the increase in inventory. Thus the inventory increase must be deducted from net income to determine the net cash inflow from operations, as shown in Mirabel's statement of cash flows.

Increase in Prepaid Insurance. Like the increases in accounts receivable and merchandise inventory, the $3,100 adjustment for the increase in prepaid insurance shown in the cash flows statement can be traced to the comparative balance sheet on page 894. The balance sheet shows the following for Prepaid Insurance.

	Prepaid Insurance
Balance, December 31, 19Y3	$5,700
Balance, December 31, 19Y2	2,600
Increase during year	$3,100

The increase of $3,100 in the Prepaid Insurance account balance during the year indicates that Mirabel spent $3,100 more for prepaid insurance than was charged to expense and deducted in arriving at the net income figure for the year. As a result, net income does not reflect the full amount paid (cash outflow) for insurance premiums. As shown in the cash flows statement, the $3,100 must be deducted from net income to determine the net cash provided by operations.

Increase in Other Prepaid Expenses. The statement of cash flows shows a deduction from net income of $3,000, representing a decrease in other prepaid expenses, in computing cash flows from operating activities. This decrease is reflected in the comparative balance sheet, which shows the following balances.

	Other Prepaid Expenses
Balance, December 31, 19Y3	$5,500
Balance, December 31, 19Y2	2,500
Increase during year	$3,000

The increase in other prepaid expenses, like the increase in prepaid insurance, means that more cash was paid for the items involved than is reflected in the expense accounts. Since the expense accounts understate the cash outflow involved, the net income figure overstates the net cash inflow from operations.

Decreases in Current Assets

Decreases in most current assets must be added to net income to arrive at the cash flow from operations.

A decrease in a noncash current asset generally signifies that the cash flow from operating activities was greater than the net income. Therefore, in computing cash flow from operations, the decrease must be added to the net income for the period. The comparative balance sheet for Mirabel Corporation (Figure 25–4) shows that all current assets increased during 19Y3. To illustrate how decreases in current assets affect cash flows from operations, assume that at the beginning of the year the balance of a company's Prepaid Insurance account was $2,500 and at the end of the year the balance was zero. The income statement for the year shows Insurance Expense of $4,000. This includes the reduction in prepaid insurance during the year. The effect of the reduction in prepaid insurance is shown in the following journal entry.

Insurance Expense		2 5 0 0 00	
Prepaid Insurance			2 5 0 0 00

Note that the $2,500 reduction in Prepaid Insurance that is reflected in insurance expense did not require a cash outlay during the year. Consequently, the $2,500 must be added to net income in order to determine the actual cash flow from operating activities.

Increases in Current Liabilities

Increases in current liabilities also must be added to net income to determine the actual cash flow. Mirabel Corporation's statement of cash flows shows that in computing net cash provided by operating activities, increases in the following current liability accounts have been added to net income.

Increase in accounts payable	$21,026
Increase in income taxes payable	$ 3,000

Increase in Accounts Payable. The adjustment in the statement of cash flows for the increase in accounts payable can be traced to the comparative balance sheet (Figure 25–4). The balance sheet shows the following balances for Mirabel's Accounts Payable account.

	Accounts Payable
Balance, December 31, 19Y3	$113,326
Balance, December 31, 19Y2	92,300
Increase during year	$ 21,026

The increase of $21,026 in Accounts Payable indicates that purchases were made, or expenses were incurred, and were deducted in computing net income but were not paid in cash. The company still owes this amount. The effect of the change in accounts payable can be expressed in the form of a hypothetical journal entry.

Purchases and Expenses		21 0 2 6 00	
Accounts Payable			21 0 2 6 00

Since the amount of $21,026 was deducted in arriving at net income, but did not require a cash expenditure, that amount must be added to net income to arrive at the cash flow generated from operating activities.

Increase in Income Taxes Payable. The addition to net income of $3,000 for the increase in income taxes payable to arrive at cash flows from operations also can be traced to the comparative balance sheet.

	Income Taxes Payable
Balance, December 31, 19Y3	$17,000
Balance, December 31, 19Y2	14,000
Increase during year	$ 3,000

Increases in current liabilities must be added to net income, and decreases must be subtracted from net income, to arrive at cash flow from operations.

This increase in income taxes payable means that the actual cash paid for taxes during the year was $3,000 less than the $69,950 that was recorded in the Income Tax Expense account appearing on the income statement. To arrive at the net cash provided by operating activities, the $3,000 must be added to the amount of net income.

Decreases in Current Liabilities

As we have seen above, an increase in a current liability must be added to net income to determine the cash flow from operating activities. Conversely, a decrease in a current liability necessitates a deduction from the reported net income in order to arrive at the net cash provided by operating activities. Look at the adjustment of $3,084 on Mirabel's statement of cash flows (Figure 25–5). This adjustment reflects a decrease in accrued liabilities during 19Y3, as shown in the comparative balance sheet.

	Accrued Liabilities
Balance, December 31, 19Y3	$14,446
Balance, December 31, 19Y2	17,530
Increase during year	$ 3,084

This decrease means that cash of $3,084 was used to reduce accrued liabilities during the year. Presumably, those liabilities resulted from operations so the cash used to reduce the debt reflects a cash flow related to operations. The $3,084 must be deducted from net income to arrive at the net cash inflow from operating activities.

Summary of Effects of Changes in Current Assets and Current Liabilities

Let's summarize how the reported net income must be adjusted for increases and decreases in current assets and current liabilities in computing the net cash flow from operations.

	Add to Net Income	Deduct from Net Income
Increase in current liability	X	
Decrease in current liability		X
Increase in current asset		X
Decrease in current asset	X	

Effect of Net Loss on Cash Flow from Operations

Even if the income statement reflects a net loss, rather than net income, for the year, the loss is reported under cash flows from operating activities in the statement of cash flows. The following illustration shows how a net loss would appear in the statement.

Cash flows from operating activities		
Net loss (from income statement)		(16,000)
Adjustments to reconcile net loss to net cash used by operating activities		
Depreciation	4,000	
Increase in inventory	(6,000)	
Decrease in accounts receivable	3,000	
Increase in accounts payable	2,000	
Decrease in income tax payable	(9,000)	(6,000)
Net cash outflow from operating activities		(22,000)

SELF-REVIEW

1. A corporation's income statement shows a loss of $10,000 on the sale of a building. How would the loss be treated in computing net cash flow from operations?
2. The income statement shows depreciation expense of $34,000. How, if at all, would this expense be reflected in computing net cash flow from operations?
3. During the year, the balance of notes payable increased from $50,000 to $85,000. How, if at all, would this balance be reflected in computing net income from operations?
4. During the year, accounts payable increased from $50,000 to $85,000. How, if at all, would this balance be reflected in computing net income from operations?

Answers to Self-Review

1. The loss does not relate to operating activities and must be added back to net income.
2. Depreciation expense does not reflect a cash outlay, so it must be added back to net income.
3. An increase in notes payable does not affect cash flow from operations, unless the notes were credited when merchandise inventory or other operating assets were purchased.
4. The increase in accounts payable must be added to net income to arrive at cash flow from operations.

Information Block: Computers in Accounting

Protecting Confidential Information

Accountants often need to send confidential financial statements and other data, such as employee salary information, to corporate headquarters using an electronic mail service. Appropriate precautions should be taken to prevent others from illegally or inadvertently accessing this information during the transmission, storage, and retrieval process.

Large businesses and government agencies have long relied on complex security and data encryption systems to protect their sensitive data. For many personal computer users, however, the protection of confidential data is often an overlooked aspect of computer use.

With the proliferation of the microcomputer and vast communication networks, data security is becoming an increasingly important concern for both small and large businesses. Many kinds of sensitive data are communicated via electronic mail both nationally and internationally. How can the sender be certain that the data being sent is protected from unauthorized access? In addition, what measures are available to the receiver to verify the origin and authenticity of electronic mail?

The need for data security is critical to all forms of business. Advances in data encryption technology have lowered the cost and complexity of protecting data, making protection more affordable for all businesses. Digital signatures combined with public and private keys (passwords) form the basis of this technology. Prior to transmitting data, the sender uses a password to protect the data. The data is encoded using complex algorithms to secure the message. Only the receiver, using the appropriate password to decode the data, can access the information.

Security concerns are not limited to the electronic transfer of data. Documents and other sensitive information stored on floppy and hard disks are also subject to the same protection requirements. Safeguards are needed to protect against unauthorized access to sensitive information. Personal computers may be equipped with built-in locks requiring the user to use a key to unlock the computer before it can be turned on. Such measures do not prevent access to information on unattended computers, so data encryption must be combined with other solutions to provide a total data security system.

CASH FLOWS FROM INVESTING ACTIVITIES

OBJECTIVE 3
Compute cash flows from investing activities.

We have already seen that investing activities are transactions involving the acquisition or disposal of assets that a business will not consume or use in its routine operations in a short period of time.

For example, a cash purchase of equipment or a cash purchase of shares of stock of another corporation would be an investing activity involving a cash outflow. On the other hand, the purchase of merchandise inventory for resale, the purchase of supplies, and the prepayment of insurance premiums are examples of operating activities, rather than investing activities, because the items acquired will normally be consumed in operations within a short period of time.

Cash Outflows from Investing Activities

Investing activities are transactions that involve the acquisition or disposal of assets that will not be used up or consumed in routine operations in a short time.

Most investing activities involve cash outflows.

The most common cash outflows from investing activities are cash payments for purchases of property, plant, and equipment and for purchases of the stocks and bonds of other corporations.

Mirabel Corporation's comparative balance sheet (Figure 25–4) shows that the asset Buildings increased by $120,000 during 19Y3 (from $0 to $120,000). An analysis of the entries in that account shows that the increase resulted from the purchase of a building for $120,000 in cash during the year. An analysis of the ledger accounts also shows that during 19Y3 Mirabel purchased equipment and fixtures for $23,700 in cash. Both of these expenditures represent cash outflows from investing activities and are shown as such in the statement of cash flows (Figure 25–5).

Cash Inflows from Investing Activities

Most cash inflows from investing activities reflect the sale of land, buildings, equipment, or investments in securities of other corporations.

By their nature, most transactions involving investing activities result in cash outflows. However, there are also cash inflows from investing activities. Cash received from the sale of used equipment and from the sale of an investment in the bonds of another corporation would be cash inflows from investing activities. If payments are received on the principal of mortgages or notes obtained in connection with the sale of plant and equipment in prior years, the amounts received are treated as cash inflows from investing activities.

Mirabel had only one cash inflow from investing activities in 19Y3. During the year, the corporation sold some used equipment for $2,700 in cash. The original cost of the equipment was $4,100, and depreciation totaling $2,400 had been taken in prior years. As we have already seen, a gain of $1,000 was recognized on the sale and reported on the income statement (Figure 25–1).

Sales price (cash inflow)		$2,700
Asset cost	$4,100	
Depreciation taken	2,400	1,700
Gain on sale		$1,000

The statement of cash flows shows the $2,700 received from the sale of the equipment as a cash inflow from investing activities. (Treatment of the gain reported on the income statement was discussed earlier in this chapter in the section dealing with cash flows from operating activities.)

At this point, the $12,300 increase in accumulated depreciation ($10,300 on the equipment and fixtures and $2,000 on the building) has been accounted for. The total accumulated depreciation on December 31, 19Y2 ($44,000), and the total accumulated depreciation on December 31, 19Y3 ($56,300), are reconciled as follows.

Accumulated Depreciation, Dec. 31, 19Y2:		
On equipment and fixtures	$44,000	
On buildings	-0-	$44,000
Add: Depreciation expense for year		14,700
Total		$58,700
Less: Accumulated depreciation on assets sold		(2,400)
Total accumulated depreciation, Dec. 31, 19Y3		$56,300

The net change of $19,600 in the Equipment and Fixtures account has also been explained, and the beginning and ending balances can be reconciled as follows.

Balance, Equipment and Fixtures, Dec. 31, 19Y2	$ 83,600
Add: Purchases during 19Y3	23,700
Total	$107,300
Less: Cost of equipment sold during 19Y3	4,100
Balance, Equipment and Fixtures, Dec. 31, 19Y3	$103,200

The section entitled Cash Flows from Investing Activities in Mirabel's statement of cash flows shows that net cash of $141,000 was used in investing activities during 19Y3. This section of the statement reflects the transactions discussed above.

CASH FLOWS FROM FINANCING ACTIVITIES

OBJECTIVE 4
Compute cash flows from financing activities.

As we have already seen, some financing activities produce cash inflows while others produce cash outflows. Let's look first at the activities that produce cash inflows.

Cash Inflows from Financing Activities

Cash inflows from investing activities usually reflect long-term or short-term borrowing or the sale of treasury stock.

The most important cash inflows from financing activities include (1) the proceeds of cash investments by stockholders and (2) the proceeds of short-term and long-term borrowing. Specifically, amounts received from the original issue of preferred stock or common stock, the resale of treasury stock, the issue of bonds payable, and the issue of long-term notes are all examples of cash inflows from financing activities. This category also includes cash received from short-term borrowings through the issue or discounting of notes payable.

An analysis of Mirabel's statements and accounts shows the following cash inflows from financing activities in 19Y3.

Proceeds of Cash Investments by Stockholders

The Stockholders' Equity section of the balance sheet in Figure 25–4 shows that during 19Y3 Mirabel's Common Stock account and Paid-in Capital in Excess of Par Value account increased as follows.

	Common Stock	Paid-in Capital in Excess of Par
Balance, December 31, 19Y3	$160,000	$29,000
Balance, December 31, 19Y2	150,000	19,000
Increase during year	$ 10,000	$10,000

An analysis of the two accounts reveals that during 19Y3 Mirabel issued 200 shares of $50 stated-value common stock for $100 a share. The stock issuance resulted in a cash inflow of $20,000, as shown in the statement of cash flows (Figure 25–5).

Proceeds of Short-Term and Long-Term Borrowing

The comparative balance sheet on page 894 also shows that during the year 19Y3 the Bonds Payable account increased by $30,000 and the Premium on Bonds Payable increased by $979.

	Bonds Payable	Premium on Bonds Payable
Balance, December 31, 19Y3	$70,000	$979
Balance, December 31, 19Y2	40,000	-0-
Increase during year	$30,000	$979

An analysis of the two accounts shows that during the year, the company issued 11 percent bonds payable with a principal amount of $30,000. These bonds were issued for $31,080, which indicates that the bonds were sold at a premium of $1,080. The cash received, $31,080, is reported on the statement of cash flows as a cash flow from financing activities. A portion of the premium, in the amount of $101, was amortized during 19Y3, but this does not affect cash flows from financing activities.

The change of $30,000 in 11% Bonds Payable shown by the comparative balance sheet is fully explained by the par value of the new bonds issued during 19Y3. The change of $979 in Premium on Bonds Payable is thus recorded as shown below.

Balance of Premium on Bonds Payable, Dec. 31, 19Y2	$ -0-
Premium on bonds issued in 19Y3	1,080
Less: Premium amortized in 19Y3	(101)
Balance of Premium on Bonds Payable, Dec. 31, 19Y3	$ 979

Cash Outflows from Financing Activities

Cash outflows from financing activities result from the repayment of notes payable, bonds payable, and other debt obligations; the purchase of treasury stock; and the retirement of outstanding preferred stock. The payment of cash dividends on common or preferred stock is also considered to be an outflow of cash from a financing activity. Interest expense, however, is not treated as an outflow of cash from a financing activity but is considered to be an outflow of cash that results from an operating activity.

In 19Y3 Mirabel had the following cash outflows from financing activities.

Payment of Long-Term Notes

The corporation's comparative balance sheet (Figure 25–4) shows a decrease of $10,000 in the Long-Term Notes Payable account during 19Y3.

	Long-Term Notes Payable
Balance, December 31, 19Y3	$ –0–
Balance, December 31, 19Y2	10,000
Net decrease during year	$10,000

An analysis of the account reveals that this decrease resulted from the payment of a long-term note for $10,000 when it became due during the year. Payment of the $10,000 is shown in the statement of cash flows (Figure 25–5) as a cash outflow from financing activities.

Mirabel did not acquire cash through short-term borrowing during 19Y3, nor did it repay any short-term loans during that year. However, the fact that neither the 19Y2 nor the 19Y3 balance sheet shows short-term notes payable does not necessarily mean that there were no such transactions. For example, if the corporation had borrowed $4,000 by signing a three-month note payable on March 1, 19Y3, and had repaid the note on June 1, 19Y3, the note would not appear on either balance sheet. Yet it represents both an inflow and an outflow of cash from financing activities during the year and should be shown as both in the Cash Flows from Financing Activities section of the statement of cash flows.

Payment of Cash Dividends

During the year Mirabel paid cash dividends of $12,000 on its preferred stock and cash dividends of $51,300 on its common stock, as shown in the statement of retained earnings (Figure 25–3, page 894). These amounts are included in the statement of cash flows as a part of cash flows from financing activities.

As a result of these inflows and outflows, net cash of $22,220 was used in Mirabel's financing activities in 19Y3. This amount is shown in the statement of cash flows.

PREPARING A STATEMENT OF CASH FLOWS

OBJECTIVE 5

Prepare a statement of cash flows.

The cash flows from the three types of business activities (operating, investing, and financing) are combined to arrive at the net change in cash and cash equivalents for the year. The net change is then combined with the beginning balance of cash and cash equivalents to reconcile the ending balance of cash and cash equivalents. The statement of cash flows for Mirabel shows that the net change in the company's cash and cash equivalents for the year was a decrease of $27,327, that the beginning balance on January 1, 19Y3, was $100,187, and that the ending balance on December 31, 19Y3, was $72,860.

FIGURE 25–5
The Statement of Cash Flows

MIRABEL UNPAINTED FURNITURE CORPORATION
Statement of Cash Flows
Year Ended December 31, 19Y3

Cash Flows from Operating Activities		
Net income (per income statement)		152 3 5 2 00
Adjustments to reconcile net income to net cash provided by operating activities:		
Depreciation expense	14 7 0 0 00	
Amortization of premium on bonds payable	(1 0 1 00)	
Gain on sale of equipment	(1 0 0 0 00)	
Changes in operational noncash current assets and current liabilities:		
Increase in accounts receivable	(30 0 0 0 00)	
Increase in inventories	(14 9 0 0 00)	
Increase in prepaid insurance	(3 1 0 0 00)	
Increase in other prepaid expenses	(3 0 0 0 00)	
Increase in accounts payable	21 0 2 6 00	
Increase in income taxes payable	3 0 0 0 00	
Decrease in accrued liabilities	(3 0 8 4 00)	
Total adjustments		(16 4 5 9 00)
Net cash provided by operating activities		135 8 9 3 00)
Cash Flows from Investing Activities		
Proceeds from sale of equipment	2 7 0 0 00	
Purchase of building	(120 0 0 0 00)	
Purchase of equipment and fixtures	(23 7 0 0 00)	
Net cash used in investing activities		(141 0 0 0 00)
Cash Flows from Financing Activities		
Proceeds from issue of common stock	20 0 0 0 00	
Proceeds from issue of bonds payable	31 0 8 0 00	
Payment of long-term debt	(10 0 0 0 00)	
Payment of dividends on preferred stock	(12 0 0 0 00)	
Payment of dividends on common stock	(51 3 0 0 00)	
Net cash used in financing activities		(22 2 2 0 00)
Net Decrease in Cash and Cash Equivalents		(27 3 2 7 00)
Cash and cash equivalents, Jan. 1, 19Y3		100 1 8 7 00
Cash and cash equivalents, Dec. 31, 19Y3		72 8 6 0 00

Note: During the year payments for income taxes were $66,950 and payments for interest expense were $7,350.

Direct and Indirect Methods of Preparing the Statement of Cash Flows

There are two widely accepted methods of reporting cash generated from operating activities on the statement of cash flows: the indirect and direct methods. The statement discussed and illustrated in this chapter was prepared by the **indirect method.** Under this method, net income is treated as the primary source of cash in the operating section of the statement of cash flows and is adjusted for changes in current assets and liabilities associated with net income, noncash expenses, and other items. This method of presentation is used by a large majority of corporations, probably due to the simplicity of its approach.

Under the direct method of reporting sources and uses of cash, the cash receipts and expenditures for each category of outlay are shown.

Under the **direct method** of reporting operating activities, all revenue and expenses reported on the income statement are adjusted in the operating section of the statement of cash flows by reporting cash received or paid out for each item. The direct method is preferred by the Financial Accounting Standards Board. Using the direct method, a corporation reports cash flows from operating activities in two major classes: gross cash receipts and gross cash payments. The FASB suggests classifications such as the following for reporting cash inflows and outflows.

- Cash collected from customers
- Interest and dividends received
- Cash paid to employees and other suppliers of goods or services, including suppliers of insurance and advertising
- Interest paid
- Income taxes paid

The categories listed above are merely examples. Corporations that use the direct method are encouraged to provide further breakdowns of operating cash receipts and cash payments—breakdowns that are meaningful and feasible. The direct method is not commonly used because many businesses do not have easily available records of the amount of cash payments for each class of expenditures, especially when the voucher system is used.

Most corporations use the indirect method of reporting cash flows, the same form as used in this textbook.

A statement of cash flows based on the direct method must be accompanied by a reconciliation of net income to the net cash provided by operating activities. It is necessary to prepare a separate schedule containing the details of the reconciliation process. This schedule reports the same information in the same form as the cash flow from operations shown in the statement of cash flows prepared according to the indirect method. Thus the direct method requires additional work, which is probably another reason why many corporations avoid that method of preparing the statement.

The procedures for using the direct method to prepare the statement of cash flows are discussed in detail in intermediate accounting textbooks.

Disclosures Required in the Statement of Cash Flows

If the indirect method is used, the interest and income taxes paid during the period must be separately disclosed.

Various disclosures are sometimes required as addenda to the statement of cash flows. We have seen that a separate schedule of reconciliation is necessary in reporting cash flow from operations if the direct method is used to prepare the statement. If the indirect method of presentation is used, the amount of interest and income taxes paid during the period must be reported in notes accompanying the statement. The note at the bottom of Mirabel's statement of cash flows (Figure 25–5) shows that cash payments for income taxes were $66,950 and cash payments for interest were $7,350.

If there are major transactions that affect financing but do not involve cash flows, the details should be shown in notes to the statement of cash flows.

It also may be necessary to report information about noncash investing and financing activities to provide complete information to statement readers. For example, if a corporation issued bonds payable with a par value of $100,000 and received in return land with a fair market value of $100,000, the transaction would not involve cash and thus would not appear in the statement of cash flows. Nevertheless, this is an important financing and investing transaction, and it should be included in disclosures related to the statement of cash flows. Another important transaction of this type would be the conversion of bonds payable into common stock.

MANAGERIAL IMPLICATIONS

Cash flow is of vital importance to management. Cash must be available to meet operating expenses and pay debts promptly. The statement of cash flows is of tremendous help to management in analyzing the operations of the company for the current period, in planning future operations, in forecasting cash needs, in arranging proper financing, and in planning dividend payments. It is also extremely useful in determining how well the company will be able to meet its currently maturing obligations. The analysis of past cash flows provided in the statement of cash flows gives management the basis for making those future estimates and plans necessary to keep the company solvent and profitable.

SELF-REVIEW

1. During the year, a corporation sold certain equipment for $100,000, recording a loss of $8,000. How should this transaction be shown in the statement of cash flows?
2. Where on the statement of cash flows should a dividend paid on preferred stock be shown?
3. Where on the statement of cash flows should a payment of interest expense be shown?
4. During the year, a corporation issued $100,000 of bonds payable in return for land with a fair market value of $100,000. Explain how this should be shown in the statement of cash flows.

Answers to Self-Review

1. The $100,000 cash received should be shown as an inflow of cash from investing activities. The $8,000 loss would be added back to net income to arrive at cash flow from operations.
2. Dividends are shown as cash used in financing activities.
3. Interest expense is a part of the cash flows from operations, included in net income. The amount of cash payments for interest must be shown in a note to the statement of cash flows.
4. This transaction would not be reflected in the body of the statement of cash flows, but should be disclosed in footnotes to the statement.

CHAPTER 25 Review and Applications

CHAPTER SUMMARY

A complete set of published financial statements for a corporation must include a statement of cash flows. This statement shows the sources and uses of cash during the year. The activities of a corporation are divided into three categories on the statement of cash flows: operating, investing, and financing activities. Cash inflows and outflows from transactions related to each type of activity are shown in the statement, along with the net cash inflow or outflow for that type of activity.

The first section of the statement of cash flows involves operating activities—the carrying on of buying, selling, and administrative activities. This section of the statement begins with the net income as shown in the income statement. In order to arrive at the net cash flow provided by operating activities, the net income amount is adjusted for noncash items that were used to calculate net income.

The most common items to be added to net income are (1) depreciation, (2) losses on sales of assets, (3) amortization of bond discount, (4) decreases in current assets, and (5) increases in current liabilities. The most common items to be deducted from net income are (1) gains on sales of assets, (2) amortization of bond premium, (3) increases in current assets, and (4) decreases in current liabilities.

The second section of the statement of cash flows discloses investing activities. Cash inflows from investing activities frequently result from cash sales of items of property, plant, and equipment and cash sales of the stocks and bonds of other corporations held as investments. Cash outflows from investing activities, on the other hand, result from cash purchases of plant and equipment and cash purchases of the stocks and bonds of other corporations.

The third section of the statement discloses cash flows from financing activities. These activities may reflect transactions between a corporation and its stockholders. Cash inflows often result from the issuance of common stock or preferred stock or the sale of treasury stock. Typical cash outflows from stockholder transactions are dividend payments and the purchase of treasury stock. Other financing activities involve the corporation and its creditors. Inflows of cash result from issuing bonds payable for cash and from borrowing money by issuing or discounting notes payable. Cash outflows result when notes payable or bonds payable are repaid. Interest paid on debt is treated as the result of an operating activity.

There are two methods of preparing the statement of cash flows—the direct method and the indirect method. Most corporations use the indirect method, because the statement is easier to prepare when this method is used. However, the Financial Accounting Standards Board encourages use of the direct method.

Some major transactions that do not involve cash should be disclosed in notes to the statement of cash flows. For example, the creation of a mortgage payable in connection with the acquisition of fixed assets does not involve cash. Nevertheless, it is an important element involving the finances of the company and should be disclosed.

GLOSSARY OF NEW TERMS

Cash (p. 890) An asset defined as currency or holdings in a bank account

Cash equivalents (p. 890) Assets that are readily convertible into a known amount of cash

Direct method (p. 909) A means of reporting sources and uses of cash under which all revenue and expenses reported on the income statement are adjusted in the operating section of the statement of cash flows by reporting cash received or paid out for each item

Financing activities (p. 890) Transactions (except for interest expense) that involve dealings with creditors and stockholders who provide cash to the corporation, other than interest expense

Indirect method (p. 908) A means of reporting cash generated from operating activities by treating net income as the primary source of cash in the operating section of the statement of cash flows and adjusting that amount for noncash expenses, changes in current assets and current liabilities associated with net income, and other items

Investing activities (p. 890) Transactions that involve the acquisition or disposal of long-lived assets

Operating activities (p. 890) Routine business transactions—selling goods or services and incurring expenses

Operating assets and liabilities (p. 898) Current assets and current liabilities used in routine operations

Statement of cash flows (p. 889) A financial statement that shows a business's inflows and outflows of cash during a fiscal period

REVIEW QUESTIONS

1. What is the purpose of the statement of cash flows?
2. Where is information obtained for preparing the statement of cash flows?
3. Give two examples of cash inflows from investing activities.
4. Give two examples of cash outflows from investing activities.
5. Give two examples of cash outflows from financing activities.
6. Give two examples of cash inflows from financing activities.

7. What are cash and cash equivalents?
8. Is an investment in a corporate bond maturing 120 days after the purchase date a cash equivalent? Explain.
9. A corporation's income statement shows a gain of $12,000 on the sale of plant and equipment. In computing the net cash provided by operating activities, how would this $12,000 be treated?
10. A corporation's income statement shows bond interest expense of $32,500. Amortization of the discount on the bonds during the year was $1,200. What is the amount of cash outflow for bond interest expense?
11. Explain the difference between the direct method and the indirect method of preparing the statement of cash flows.
12. On January 1, 19X3, the balance of the Accounts Payable account was $23,000. On December 31, 19X3, the balance was $31,800. How, if at all, would this change be reflected in the statement of cash flows?
13. On January 1, 19X3, the balance of the Accrued Income Taxes Payable account was $35,000. On December 31, 19X3, the balance was $19,400. How, if at all, would this change be shown in the statement of cash flows?

MANAGERIAL FOCUS

1. How can the statement of cash flows help management to arrange for proper financing?
2. A corporation's income statement shows a net income of $5,000 after income taxes for the year. Its statement of cash flows shows that its cash balance increased by $240,000. An analysis of the statement of cash flows indicates the following: net cash outflow from operating activities, $320,000; net cash inflow from financing activities, $200,000; and net cash inflow from investing activities, $360,000. The president of the corporation has commented, "Even though the company's profit is small, it is clear, based on our positive cash flow, that we are doing quite well." Do you agree with this comment? Why or why not?
3. A member of the board of directors of a corporation has suggested that because the statement of cash flows and the income statement are so similar, there is no need to prepare the income statement. How would you respond to this suggestion?
4. Assume that you are the accountant for a company and you are preparing the statement of cash flows for the year. Should the cash proceeds of $102,000 from a short-term note payable discounted in May of this year be included in the statement? The note was repaid in October. Would it be preferable to simply ignore both the loan and the repayment because it might confuse management to show both? Explain your conclusions.
5. Assume that you are the credit manager for a manufacturing company. A potential customer has applied for an open-account

credit line. Explain how a statement of cash flows for the potential customer would be of help to you in evaluating that firm's short-term debt-paying ability.

EXERCISES

EXERCISE 25–1 (Obj. 1)

Tutorial

Effects of transactions on cash flows. What effect would each of the following transactions have on the statement of cash flows?

1. The sum of $8,000 in cash was received from the sale of used office equipment that originally cost $18,000. Depreciation of $12,000 had been taken on the asset up to the date of the sale. The resulting $2,000 gain was shown on the income statement.
2. The sum of $97,000 in cash was received from the sale of investments in the stock of another corporation. The stock had a book value of $108,000. The $11,000 loss on the sale was shown on the income statement.

EXERCISE 25–2 (Obj. 2)

Tutorial

Cash flow from operating activities. The following data is summarized from the income statement of the Hall Corporation for the year ended December 31, 19X3. Using this data and ignoring changes in current assets and current liabilities, prepare a schedule of cash flows from operating activities for the year. (Use Figure 25–5 as a model for this schedule.)

HALL CORPORATION
Income Statement
Year Ended December 31, 19X3

Sales		2,000,000 00
Cost of Goods Sold		1,200,000 00
Gross Profit on Sales		800,000 00
Operating Expenses		
Depreciation	31,000 00	
Other Selling Expenses	560,000 00	
Other Administrative Expenses	220,000 00	811,000 00
Net Loss from Operations		(11,000 00)
Bond Interest Expense		
Cash Interest	30,000 00	
Amortization of Discount	1,500 00	31,500 00
Net Loss for Year		(42,500 00)

EXERCISE 25–3 (Obj. 2)

Tutorial

Cash flow from operating activities. The current assets and current liabilities of the Salina Corporation on December 31, 19X4 and 19X3, are listed below. The corporation's net income for 19X4 was $80,000. Included in its expenses was depreciation of $12,200. Prepare a schedule of the cash flows from operating activities for 19X4. (Use Figure 25–5 as a model for this schedule.)

	Dec. 31, 19X4	Dec. 31, 19X3
Cash	$ 80,000	$ 60,000
Accounts Receivable (Net)	110,000	85,000
Prepaid Expenses	12,000	14,000
Merchandise Inventory	92,000	76,000
Accounts Payable	104,000	100,000
Notes Payable (Borrowing)	20,000	–0–

EXERCISE 25–4 (Obj. 2)

Cash flow from operating activities. The income statement of the Eloy Corporation showed net income of $68,000 for 19X2. The firm's beginning inventory was $42,000, and its ending inventory was $48,000. Accounts payable were $31,000 on January 1 and $23,000 on December 31. Compute the net cash provided by the firm's operating activities during the year.

EXERCISE 25–5 (Obj. 2)

Cash flow from operating activities. The following information is taken from the income statement of the DeMaris Corporation for 19X3.

Sales		$650,000
Cost of Goods Sold		400,000
Gross Profit on Sales		$250,000
Operating Expenses		
Depreciation	$ 10,000	
Other Operating Expenses	180,000	190,000
Net Income from Operations		$ 60,000

Additional information relating to account balances at the beginning and end of the year appears below.

	Jan. 1, 19X3	Dec. 31, 19X3
Accounts Receivable	$54,000	$60,000
Merchandise Inventory	28,000	33,000
Accrued Liabilities	6,000	2,500
Accounts Payable	18,000	12,000

Determine the cash flows from operations for 19X3.

EXERCISE 25–6 (Obj. 3)

Cash flow from investing activities. The following transactions occurred at the Salerno Corporation in 19X8. Use this information to compute the company's net cash flow from investing activities.

1. The company issued 200 shares of its own $50 par-value common stock for land with a fair market value of $14,000.
2. The company gave its president a loan of $20,000 and obtained a 12 percent note receivable, dated December 22, 19X8, and maturing two years later.
3. The company sold a used truck for $3,000 in cash. The original cost of the truck was $17,000. Depreciation of $12,000 had been deducted.

EXERCISE 25–7 (Obj. 3)

Cash flow from investing activities. The transactions below occurred at the Kopp Company in 19X3. Use this information to compute the company's net cash flow from investing activities.

1. The company purchased a new building for $90,000. A down payment of $10,000 was made. The balance is due in four equal annual installments (plus interest) beginning July 1, 19X4.
2. The company bought 100 shares of its own preferred stock for $12,000.
3. The company purchased as a short-term investment $10,000 par value of the Abel Corporation's 12 percent bonds, maturing in six years. The purchase price was $9,800.

EXERCISE 25-8
(Obj. 4)

Cash flow from financing activities. The following transactions occurred at the Paris Company in 19X3. Use this information to compute the company's net cash flow from financing activities for the year.

1. Holders of $100,000 par-value 10 percent bonds surrendered the bonds for redemption and were paid $102,000 in cash. The unamortized discount on these bonds as of the date of redemption was $600.
2. Cash interest of $27,000 was paid on bonds during the year. The bond discount amortized was $300.
3. Cash dividends of $23,000 were paid on common stock during the year.

EXERCISE 25-9
(Obj. 4)

Cash flow from financing activities. The following transactions occurred at the Affiliated Company in 19X5. Use this information to compute the company's net cash flow from financing activities for the year.

1. The company reacquired as treasury stock 400 shares of its outstanding common stock, paying a total of $51,000 for the shares.
2. On December 18 the company borrowed $40,000 from the bank, signing a 90-day, 11 percent note payable.

PROBLEMS

PROBLEM SET A

PROBLEM 25-1A
(Obj. 1, 2, 3, 4, 5)

Prepare a statement of cash flows. A comparative balance sheet for the Delmar Corporation on December 31, 19X3 and 19X2, follows. Certain additional information about the firm's financial activities during 19X3 is also given below.

Instructions

Prepare a statement of cash flows for 19X3. Additional information for 19X3 follows.

a. Had a $13,000 net loss.
b. Recorded $6,000 in depreciation.
c. Issued bonds payable with a par value of $10,000 at par and received cash.

DELMAR CORPORATION
Comparative Balance Sheet
December 31, 19X3 and 19X2

	19X3	19X2
Assets		
Cash	30000	25000
Accounts Receivable (Net)	50000	40000
Merchandise Inventory	80000	75000
Property, Plant, and Equipment	90000	80000
Less: Accumulated Depreciation	(26000)	(20000)
Total Assets	224000	200000
Liabilities and Stockholders' Equity		
Liabilities		
Accounts Payable	55000	40000
Bonds Payable	90000	80000
Total Liabilities	145000	120000
Stockholders' Equity		
Common Stock, No-Par Value	62000	50000
Retained Earnings	17000	30000
Total Stockholders' Equity	79000	80000
Total Liabilities and Stockholders' Equity	224000	200000

d. Received $12,000 in cash for the issue of an additional 1,000 shares of no-par-value common stock.
e. Purchased equipment for $10,000 in cash.

PROBLEM 25–2A
(Obj. 1, 2, 3, 4, 5)
Tutorial

Prepare a statement of cash flows. Postclosing trial balance data and certain other financial data for the Morales Company as of December 31, 19Y7 and 19Y6, follow.

Instructions

Prepare a statement of cash flows for 19Y7. Additional information for 19Y7 follows.

a. Sold common stock for $80,000 in cash.
b. Had a net income of $28,200 after income taxes.
c. Sold additional bonds payable for $40,000 cash at par value.
d. Completed a major addition to the building for $20,000 in cash.
e. Bought additional land for $12,000. Paid $2,000 in cash; the balance is a mortgage.
f. Paid common stock dividends of $3,900 in cash.
g. Amortized organization costs of $2,000.

Account Name	19Y7 Debit	19Y7 Credit	19Y6 Debit	19Y6 Credit
Cash	$ 210,000		150,000	
Accounts Receivable (Net)	195,700		193,500	
Inventory	419,250		410,525	
Prepaid Expenses	5,500		4,000	
Land	43,500		31,500	
Building	230,000		210,000	
Accum. Depr.—Building		$ 82,500		$ 75,000
Organization Costs	4,000		6,000	
Notes Payable—Trade		20,000		30,000
Accounts Payable		138,250		150,000
Payroll Taxes Payable		19,875		17,500
Income Taxes Payable		15,000		55,000
Mortgage Payable, 19Y9		130,000		120,000
13% Bonds Payable, 19Z5		270,000		230,000
Common Stock		320,000		240,000
Retained Earnings		112,325		88,025
Totals	$1,107,950	$1,107,950	$1,005,525	$1,005,525

PROBLEM 25–3A
(Obj. 1, 2, 3, 4, 5)

Preparing a statement of cash flows. The condensed income statement and comparative balance sheet of the DeMoss Corporation as of December 31, 19X5 and 19X4, follows. Other financial data is also given.

Instructions

Prepare a statement of cash flows for 19X5. Additional information for 19X5 includes:

a. No items of property, plant, and equipment were disposed of during the year.
b. Paid cash for the additions to property, plant, and equipment during the year.
c. Paid dividends on the common stock in cash during the year.
d. Issued common stock at par value for cash.
e. Paid cash to retire the mortgages when they became due.

DeMOSS CORPORATION
Condensed Income Statement
Year Ended December 31, 19X5

Revenues	1050 000 00
Costs and Expenses	
Cost of Goods Sold	500 000 00
Salaries Expense	125 000 00
Depreciation Expense	50 000 00
Advertising Expense	25 000 00
Utilities Expense	25 000 00
Total Costs and Expenses	725 000 00
Net Income Before Income Taxes	325 000 00
Income Tax Expense	100 000 00
Net Income After Income Taxes	225 000 00

DeMOSS CORPORATION
Comparative Balance Sheet
December 31, 19X5 and 19X4

	19X5	19X4
Assets		
Cash	8 000	15 000
Accounts Receivable	37 000	25 000
Inventories	60 000	50 000
Prepaid Advertising	10 000	5 000
Property, Plant, and Equipment	675 000	500 000
Less: Accumulated Depreciation	(175 000)	(125 000)
Total Assets	615 000	470 000
Liabilities and Stockholders' Equity		
Liabilities		
Accounts Payable	12 000	20 000
Salaries Payable	30 000	20 000
Unearned Rental Income	5 000	12 000
Income Taxes Payable	25 000	15 000
Mortgages Payable	–0–	45 000
Total Liabilities	72 000	112 000
Stockholders' Equity		
Common Stock	150 000	125 000
Retained Earnings	393 000	233 000
Total Stockholders' Equity	543 000	358 000
Total Liabilities and Stockholders' Equity	615 000	470 000

PROBLEM 25–4A
(Obj. 1, 2, 3, 4, 5)

Prepare a statement of cash flows. The comparative balance sheet for the Nahid Corporation as of December 31, 19X8 and 19X7, is shown below, followed by the condensed income statement. Other financial data for 19X8 is also given.

Instructions

Prepare a statement of cash flows for 19X8. Additional information for 19X8 follows.

a. Acquired land at a cost of $100,000; paid one-half of the purchase price in cash and issued common stock for the balance.
b. Sold used equipment for $5,000 in cash. The original cost was $80,000; depreciation of $60,000 had been taken. The remaining change in the Building and Equipment account represents a purchase of equipment for cash.
c. Issued bonds payable at par value for cash.
d. Sold bond investments costing $30,000 at no gain or loss during the year; acquired other bond investments for cash.
e. Paid cash dividends on the common stock.

NAHID CORPORATION
Comparative Balance Sheet
December 31, 19X8 and 19X7

	19X8	19X7
Assets		
Cash	50000	45000
Accounts Receivable	150000	200000
Inventory	280000	390000
Prepaid Advertising	20000	10000
Land	200000	100000
Building and Equipment	380000	250000
Less: Accumulated Depreciation	(100000)	(120000)
Investment in City Corp. Bonds	70000	50000
Total Assets	1050000	925000
Liabilities and Stockholders' Equity		
Liabilities		
Accounts Payable	400000	340000
Income Taxes Payable	-0-	10000
Bonds Payable	100000	75000
Total Liabilities	500000	425000
Stockholders' Equity		
Common Stock	150000	100000
Retained Earnings	400000	400000
Total Stockholders' Equity	550000	500000
Total Liabilities and Stockholders' Equity	1050000	925000

NAHID CORPORATION
Condensed Income Statement
Year Ended December 31, 19X8

Revenues	1000 0 0 0 00
Costs and Expenses	
Cost of Goods Sold	500 0 0 0 00
Depreciation Expense	40 0 0 0 00
Selling and Administrative Expenses	350 0 0 0 00
Interest Expense	25 0 0 0 00
Loss on Sale of Equipment	15 0 0 0 00
Income Tax Expense	20 0 0 0 00
Total Costs and Expenses	950 0 0 0 00
Net Income for Year	50 0 0 0 00

PROBLEM SET B

PROBLEM 25–1B
(Obj. 1, 2, 3, 4, 5)

Tutorial

Prepare a statement of cash flows. A comparative balance sheet for the Ngooi Corporation as of December 31, 19X4 and 19X3, and certain additional information about the firm's financial activities during 19X4 are given below.

Instructions

Use this data to prepare a statement of cash flows for 19X4. Additional information for 19X4 includes:

a. Sold used machinery for $9,000 in cash. The original cost was $10,000, and the accumulated depreciation was $3,000; included is the gain of $2,000 in net income.
b. Purchased new machinery for $20,000. Of this amount, $10,000 was paid in cash; the balance of $10,000 is carried in Accounts Payable and falls due in January 19X5.
c. Had a net loss of $4,000.
d. Paid cash dividends of $10,000.
e. Recorded $8,000 in depreciation.

NGOOI CORPORATION
Comparative Balance Sheet
December 31, 19X4 and 19X3

	19X4	19X3
Assets		
Cash	7 000	13 000
Accounts Receivable (Net)	20 000	17 000
Merchandise Inventory	23 000	25 000
Property, Plant, and Equipment	70 000	60 000
Less: Accumulated Depreciation	(25 000)	(20 000)
Total Assets	95 000	95 000
Liabilities and Stockholders' Equity		
Liabilities		
Accounts Payable	20 000	16 000
Stockholders' Equity		
Common Stock, No-Par Value	55 000	45 000
Retained Earnings	20 000	34 000
Total Stockholders' Equity	75 000	79 000
Total Liabilities and Stockholders' Equity	95 000	95 000

PROBLEM 25–2B
(Obj. 1, 2, 3, 4, 5)
Tutorial

Prepare a statement of cash flows. Postclosing trial balance data and other financial data for the Sterling Corporation as of December 31, 19X9 and 19X8, follow.

Instructions

Prepare a statement of cash flows for 19X9. Additional information for 19X9 follows.

a. Sold an unused building lot for $15,000 in cash; the lot originally cost $10,000.
b. Constructed a new building for $50,000, of which $20,000 was paid in cash and $30,000 is a long-term mortgage payable.
c. Issued $50,000 of 12 percent bonds payable, maturing in 19Y8, for cash at par.
d. Sold common stock for $70,000 in cash.
e. Had a net income of $63,600 after income taxes.
f. Paid common stock dividends of $13,000 in cash.
g. Amortized organization costs of $2,000.

	19X9		19X8	
Account Name	Debit	Credit	Debit	Credit
Cash	$ 253,500		$ 152,400	
Accounts Receivable (Net)	196,300		188,700	
Inventory	381,000		395,000	
Prepaid Expenses	6,200		4,800	
Land	64,000		74,000	
Buildings	250,000		200,000	
Accum. Depr.—Buildings		$ 65,000		$ 60,000
Organization Costs	4,000		6,000	
Notes Payable—Short-Term		–0–		50,000
Accounts Payable		137,300		162,500
Payroll Taxes Payable		17,200		15,800
Income Taxes Payable		25,400		23,100
Mortgages Payable—Long-Term		110,000		80,000
12% Bonds Payable, 19Y8		250,000		200,000
Common Stock		290,000		220,000
Retained Earnings		260,100		209,500
Totals	$1,155,000	$1,155,000	$1,020,900	$1,020,900

PROBLEM 25–3B
(Obj. 1, 2, 3, 4, 5)

Preparing a statement of cash flows. The comparative balance sheet of the Santiago Corporation as of December 31, 19X3 and 19X2, is shown below. The condensed income statement and other financial data for 19X3 also appear below.

Instructions

Prepare a statement of cash flows for 19X3. Additional information for 19X3 follows.

a. Depreciation totaling $30,000 is included in expenses.
b. Sold land for $35,000 in cash; the land, which is included in plant and equipment, had a cost of $35,000.

c. Acquired a building with a fair market value of $100,000 by issuing common stock.
d. Purchased equipment for $200,000 in cash.
e. Declared dividends totaling $85,000. Some dividends were paid in cash during 19X3; others are payable as of January 5, 19X4.
f. Issued common stock at par value for cash.
g. Issued notes payable for cash.

SANTIAGO CORPORATION
Comparative Balance Sheet
December 31, 19X3 and 19X2

	19X3	19X2
Assets		
Cash	150000	100000
Accounts Receivable (Net)	460000	290000
Merchandise Inventory	330000	210000
Prepaid Expenses	50000	25000
Plant and Equipment	565000	300000
Less: Accumulated Depreciation	(55000)	(25000)
Total Assets	1500000	900000
Liabilities and Stockholders' Equity		
Liabilities		
Accounts Payable	265000	220000
Accrued Liabilities	70000	65000
Dividends Payable	35000	—0—
Notes Payable, due 19X8	250000	—0—
Total Liabilities	620000	285000
Stockholders' Equity		
Common Stock, No-Par Value	600000	450000
Retained Earnings	280000	165000
Total Stockholders' Equity	880000	615000
Total Liabilities and Stockholders' Equity	1500000	900000

SANTIAGO CORPORATION
Condensed Income Statement
Year Ended December 31, 19X3

Sales	3200 0 0 0 00
Cost of Goods Sold	(2500 0 0 0 00)
Expenses	(500 0 0 0 00)
Net Income for Year	200 0 0 0 00

PROBLEM 25–4B (Obj. 1, 2, 3, 4, 5)

Prepare a statement of cash flows. The comparative balance sheet for the My-Favorite Corporation as of December 31, 19X5 and 19X4, is shown below, as are the condensed income statement and other financial data for 19X5.

MY-FAVORITE CORPORATION
Comparative Balance Sheet
December 31, 19X5 and 19X4

	19X5	19X4
Assets		
Current Assets		
Cash	60000	54000
Accounts Receivable	90000	60000
Inventories	165000	87000
Total Current Assets	315000	201000
Plant and Equipment		
Equipment	150000	120000
Less: Accumulated Depreciation	(66000)	(45000)
Net Plant and Equipment	84000	75000
Total Assets	399000	276000
Liabilities and Stockholders' Equity		
Current Liabilities		
Notes Payable	60000	45000
Accounts Payable	36000	30000
Income Taxes Payable	18000	12000
Total Current Liabilities	114000	87000
Long-Term Liabilities		
Bonds Payable	-0-	45000
Total Liabilities	114000	132000
Stockholders' Equity		
Common Stock	204000	120000
Retained Earnings	81000	24000
Total Stockholders' Equity	285000	144000
Total Liabilities and Stockholders' Equity	399000	276000

MY-FAVORITE CORPORATION Condensed Income Statement Year Ended December 31, 19X5	
Revenues	*630 000 00*
Costs and Expenses	
Cost of Goods Sold	*302 000 00*
Depreciation Expense	*31 000 00*
Selling and Administrative Expenses	*190 000 00*
Interest Expense	*3 000 00*
Income Tax Expense	*13 000 00*
Loss on Sale of Equipment	*18 000 00*
Total Costs and Expenses	*557 000 00*
Net Income for Year	*73 000 00*

Instructions Prepare a statement of cash flows for 19X5. Additional information for 19X5 follows.

a. Sold used equipment for $12,000 in cash. The original cost was $40,000; accumulated depreciation was $10,000. The remainder of the change in the Equipment account represents equipment purchased for cash during the year.
b. Issued notes payable with a par value of $60,000 during the year. Certain other notes were paid off during the year. The bonds payable were retired at maturity.
c. Declared dividends and paid them in cash during the year.
d. Issued common stock at par value for cash.

CHALLENGE PROBLEM

The HighFlyer Corporation was formed and began business on December 31, 19X4, when Cecil Crow transferred merchandise inventory with a value of $20,000, cash of $20,000, accounts receivable of $20,000, and accounts payable of $20,000 to the corporation in exchange for common stock with a par value of $20 per share. The common stock was recorded at par.

The company's statement of cash flows for 19X4 is shown below.

Instructions Based on the data supplied, prepare the December 31, 19X4, balance sheet for the corporation.

HIGHFLYER CORPORATION
Statement of Cash Flows
Year Ended December 31, 19X4

Cash Flows from Operating Activities		
Net income		30 0 0 0 00
Adjustments:		
Depreciation of building	3 0 0 0 00	
Depreciation of machinery	2 0 0 0 00	
Increase in accounts receivable	(18 0 0 0 00)	
Increase in inventory	(15 0 0 0 00)	
Increase in prepaid insurance	(3 0 0 0 00)	
Increase in accounts payable	16 0 0 0 00	
Increase in income taxes payable	5 0 0 0 00	(10 0 0 0 00)
Net cash flow provided by operations		20 0 0 0 00
Cash Flows from Investing Activities		
Purchase of land	(10 0 0 0 00)	
Purchase of building	(40 0 0 0 00)*	
Purchase of equipment	(20 0 0 0 00)	
Net cash used by investing activities		(70 0 0 0 00)
Cash Flows from Financing Activities		
Issuance of common stock at $22/share	44 0 0 0 00	
Borrowing at bank by issuance of note payable	30 0 0 0 00	
Payment on principal of bank note	(20 0 0 0 00)	
Net cash flow provided by financing activities		54 0 0 0 00
Net increase in cash balance		4 0 0 0 00
Cash balance, January 1, 19X4		20 0 0 0 00
Cash balance, December 31, 19X4		24 0 0 0 00

**Note:* A building was acquired at a cost of $180,000. Cash of $40,000 was paid, and a mortgage payable of $140,000 was given for the balance.

CRITICAL THINKING PROBLEM

Alan Altman, the bookkeeper for the Hemingway Lighting Corporation, asks for your help in identifying whether the following transactions should be reported on the corporation's statement of cash flows. Prepare a list for Altman indicating whether or not each transaction should be reported on the statement. If the transaction should appear on the statement, indicate whether it should be classified as a financing activity, an investing activity, or an operating activity. If the transaction should not be part of the statement of cash flows, explain why not.

1. Paid cash dividends on the common stock.
2. Purchased short-term U.S. Treasury bills for cash.
3. Issued common stock for cash.
4. Collected on accounts receivable from a customer.
5. Paid federal income taxes due.
6. Borrowed cash, signing a short-term note that was repaid before the end of the year.
7. Issued long-term bonds for cash; proceeds to be used to purchase new equipment for plant.
8. Distributed a stock dividend on common stock.
9. Prepaid six months of rent on warehouse storage facilities at the end of the year.
10. Used proceeds from bond issue to purchase new equipment for plant.
11. Paid suppliers amounts due on accounts payable.
12. Received principal payments on note receivable held in connection with sale of building last year.

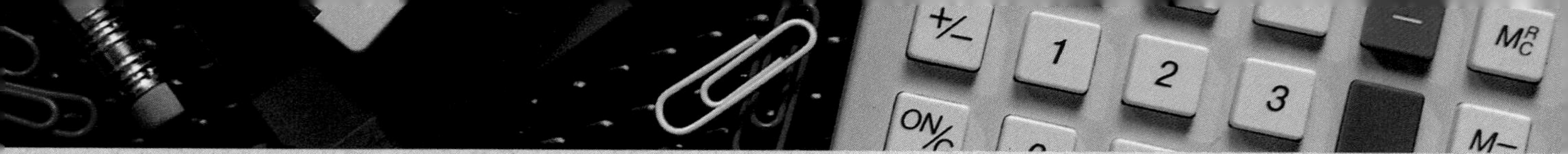

MINI-PRACTICE SET FOUR

Financial Analysis and Decision Making

This project will give you an opportunity to evaluate financial statements and to make decisions based on the information presented in the financial statements of the Hudson Corporation.

The background information on Hudson Corporation, its financial statements, and the instructions for completing Mini-Practice Set 4 *are found in the* Study Guides and Working Papers, Part 2.

College Accounting

PART THREE

UNIT NINE

Responsibility and Cost Accounting

The financial statements that you have studied previously in this textbook reported the overall results of operations of the business entity and its financial position. This information is useful to owners, creditors, management, and other interested parties. However, these financial statements do not provide all the information needed about individual operating segments of a business and about individual products, especially in manufacturing operations.

Other accounting techniques and analyses that provide more detailed information are the voucher system, departmental accounting procedures, the job order and process systems of accounting for manufacturing activities, the use of standard costs in evaluating manufacturing operations, and cost-revenue analysis for making business decisions.

CHAPTER

26 Internal Control and the Voucher System

OBJECTIVES

1. Explain the general principles of internal control.
2. Explain how the voucher system facilitates internal control.
3. Prepare vouchers.
4. Record vouchers in a voucher register.
5. Record payment of approved vouchers.
6. Record transactions for partial payments in a voucher register.
7. Record payments for notes payable in a voucher register.
8. Record payments involving purchases returns and allowances in a voucher register.
9. Use alternative methods to record purchases and purchases discounts.
10. Define the accounting terms new to this chapter.

Every business should have a well-planned system of internal control to ensure accuracy, honesty, and efficiency in the handling of its resources and the recording of its transactions. The exact control procedures used vary somewhat according to the size of a firm and the nature of its operations. However, all systems of internal control are based on certain fundamental principles. This chapter discusses the underlying principles of internal control for purchases and cash payments. It also explains and illustrates the voucher system, a widely used method of controlling liabilities and payments. You will see how the system operates at the Chicago Corporation, a retail merchandising business.

NEW TERMS

Check register ▪ Internal control system ▪ Net of discount ▪ Payment voucher ▪ Schedule of vouchers payable ▪ Tickler file ▪ Unpaid vouchers file ▪ Voucher register ▪ Voucher system

THE IMPORTANCE OF INTERNAL CONTROL

OBJECTIVE 1
Explain the general principles of internal control.

Losses to American business from employee carelessness, inaccuracy, and improper handling of assets are estimated to total billions of dollars a year. No business is immune to this hazard, and to ignore it may mean the difference between a profitable operation and complete failure. Accountants recommend that all firms, no matter their size, establish effective internal control procedures. These procedures are designed to protect the resources and financial records of a business. However, they also benefit the employees because they limit the temptation to misuse assets and they pinpoint responsibility, which prevents suspicion from falling on honest employees.

From the discussion up to this point, it is clear that an **internal control system** has three basic purposes:

1. To safeguard assets
2. To achieve efficient processing of transactions
3. To ensure the accuracy and reliability of financial records

A key element of good internal control is that the system be organized and operated so that the work of one person provides a check on the work of another, with minimum duplication of effort. If a business has enough employees to permit the necessary separation of duties, a strong system of internal control can be established. If the number of employees is small, internal control will be weaker and will have to be supplemented by more careful supervision.

In previous chapters you learned about a variety of procedures that are used to control purchases, cash receipts, cash payments, petty cash, and banking activities. Accountants follow certain principles in developing these and other control procedures.

No one person should be in complete charge of any business transaction.

1. No one person should be in complete charge of all phases of any important business transaction. Neither should one person be responsible for both the transaction itself and the recording of the transaction. Two or more employees should be assigned to every major operation, and the work of one should be checked against the work of the other at some point in the routine.

A person who handles cash should not also be the person who records it.

2. The individuals who handle cash and other valuable assets should not be the same as those who have responsibility for recording the assets.
3. Every employee should be trained to do his or her job and should also understand why the job or procedure is to be performed in the specified manner.

A good internal control system includes provisions for all employees to take annual vacations, during which time their work is carried out by other people.

4. Only capable and experienced personnel of demonstrated reliability should be assigned to key positions in the internal control system. Unannounced changes in these assignments are desirable. Annual vacations should be required for each employee, and his or her regular work should be performed by other employees during vacations.
5. All transactions should be backed by adequate documentation.
6. Prenumbered forms should be used for documents produced within the business, such as purchase orders, sales invoices, and checks. All document numbers must be accounted for.

Prenumbered forms should be used for all such documents as purchase orders, sales invoices, and checks.

7. The business should maintain a strong audit trail by providing references to source documents in accounting entries, cross-referencing entries that appear in different records, and keeping documents on file for a specified period of time. In this way, every transaction can be traced through the accounting system to its origin.
8. Whenever appropriate, the controls built into forms, records, and operating routines should be supplemented by electronic or mechanical devices to gain maximum protection. For example, electronic cash registers and locked storerooms make theft or mishandling of assets more difficult.
9. Management should review and evaluate the established system of internal control frequently to make sure that it is operating as planned and continues to provide adequate safeguards.

A company's outside accountants should periodically review the company's internal control procedures.

10. Periodically, the company's internal control procedures should be reviewed by a public accounting firm to assess their effectiveness. As an outsider, the public accounting firm can provide a more detached evaluation; and because of its broad experience, the public accounting firm is better able to locate weaknesses and design improved procedures. This evaluation is a normal part of the annual audit of the company's records by the public accountant, who relies to a large extent on internal controls to assure the integrity and accuracy of the figures reported on the financial statements.

THE VOUCHER SYSTEM AS A TOOL OF INTERNAL CONTROL

OBJECTIVE 2
Explain how the voucher system facilitates internal control.

Most large businesses rely on a voucher system to control cash payments.

The **voucher system** is a method of controlling liabilities and cash payments that is based on the use of a form called a **voucher.** This form is prepared to authorize the payment of all obligations. Under the voucher system, all payments, except for small disbursements from petty cash, are made by check, and no check is issued without a properly approved voucher that is backed by suitable documentation. The voucher is the focal point for a series of tight controls built into the system.

The voucher method of internal control is most appropriate for medium-sized and large businesses. As a business gets larger, the owner finds it increasingly difficult to be involved in all of the firm's transactions. As a result, the voucher system becomes of increasing importance as the firm grows in size. It is also a good control tool for small business, although the amount of paperwork involved and the number of different individuals required to carry out the procedures correctly may make it more difficult for a small business to use the system efficiently.

CONTROLS INVOLVED IN A VOUCHER SYSTEM

Several controls are built into a voucher system. Some of these procedures have already been discussed in connection with the purchases journal and cash payments journal.

Under a voucher system, no check is written without a properly approved voucher.

1. No liabilities are incurred without prior authorization. For example, a properly approved purchase order is required for each credit purchase of merchandise.
2. All payments are made by check, except for payments made from carefully controlled special-purpose cash funds such as a petty cash fund.
3. No check is issued without a properly approved voucher to authorize payment.
4. Vouchers are required to set up and replenish cash funds used within the business as well as to cover bills and invoices received from outside parties.
5. All bills and invoices are carefully verified before they are approved for payment.
6. Only designated employees who are experienced and responsible are allowed to approve bills and invoices for payment.
7. Approved bills and invoices are attached to the corresponding vouchers to provide supporting documentation.
8. The accounting entries for vouchers and payments are made by someone other than the person who approves the payments.
9. Still another person signs the checks and mails them to creditors.
10. All paid vouchers are kept on file for a specified period of time, along with the supporting documentation.

SELF-REVIEW

1. Why is there a need for internal control over business operations?
2. Division of responsibility is one of the most important principles of internal control. How is this principle put into practice?
3. Would it be advisable to have the accounts receivable clerk open incoming mail and make out receipts for checks received? Explain.
4. Why should all documents be prenumbered?
5. When carrying out the audit of a company's records, does the public accountant examine the system of internal control? Explain.

Answers to Self-Review

1. Effective internal control increases efficiency and reduces the possibility of errors and improper use of the company's assets.
2. The principle of division of duties is put into effect by attempting to ensure that no one individual is responsible for all phases of a transaction.
3. No. The accounts receivable clerk might be tempted to remove a check, keep it for personal use, and cover the shortage with an entry in the accounts receivable records.

4. Prenumbered documents are easily accounted for; if a document is deliberately or accidentally removed and destroyed, its absence will be detected.
5. Yes. The auditor relies to a great extent on the integrity of the internal control system to help assure that the numbers in the financial statements are reliable and correct.

THE VOUCHER SYSTEM IN OPERATION

OBJECTIVE 3
Prepare vouchers.

Let's now see how the voucher system operates by examining the system used by the Chicago Corporation, a retail merchandising corporation.

As noted already, the voucher system requires that a voucher be prepared and approved before any obligation is paid or before any sum is used to set up or replenish a cash fund for the business. Vouchers are often numbered consecutively throughout the year or for an even longer period. However, the Chicago Corporation uses a two-part number—the number to the left of the dash representing the month and the number to the right showing the sequence within the month. Thus Voucher 2–01 identifies the first voucher prepared in February.

Voucher 2–01 was issued on February 1, 19X3, to authorize a payment of $1,250 to the Commercial Realty Company for the monthly rent on the store. Two other vouchers prepared on February 1 were Voucher 2–02 for $100 issued to the cashier, Domingo Reuben, to establish a change fund, and Voucher 2–03 for $75 issued to the office clerk, Susan Bates, to establish a petty cash fund. The specific employees were named as the payees of these two vouchers to pinpoint responsibility for the change fund and the petty cash fund.

The next voucher issued by the firm, Voucher 2–04, which authorizes payment of an invoice for merchandise, provides a good illustration of the procedures typical of those used to prepare and approve vouchers. Let's see how the system operates in practice.

Voucher 2–04 covers goods received on February 1, 19X3. The merchandise was purchased on open account from Gulf Wholesale Clothiers. Let's examine each step followed by Chicago Corporation in handling this transaction.

Step 1: Verifying Receipt of the Merchandise. The clerk who opened the mail used a rubber stamp to place a verification block on the invoice, as shown in Figure 26–1. Then she passed the invoice along to Steven Casey, co-owner and store manager. Casey compared the quantities listed on the invoice with the quantities that appear on a receiving report filled out when the shipment arrived. Casey placed a check mark next to each quantity on the invoice and entered his initials in the appropriate area of the verification block.

FIGURE 26–1
Purchase Invoice

GULF WHOLESALE CLOTHIERS
123 Ponce DeLeon Avenue
Atlanta, GA 30308

INVOICE NO. R 47651

SOLD TO CHICAGO CORPORATION
246 Summit Drive
Houston, TX 77047

Date February 1, 19X3
Customer's Order Number 19-34
Terms 2/10, n/30

Quantity	Description	Unit Price	Amount
10	Corduroy Suits D-4786	✓90.00	✓ 900.00
4	Pairs, Denim Jeans P-537	✓25.00	✓ 100.00
1	Denim Jacket J-34	✓20.14	✓ 20.14
			✓1,020.14
	Less 20%		✓ 204.03
			✓ 816.11
	Less 10%		✓ 81.61
			✓ 734.50

VERIFICATIONS	
QUANTITIES RECEIVED	SC
PRICES CHARGED	TS
EXTENSIONS AND TOTAL	SB

Step 2: Verifying Prices. Casey gave the invoice to John Silvertree, one of the owners, who compared it with a copy of the purchase order originally issued to the supplier to make certain that the prices listed did not exceed those specified when the order was placed. He checked off each unit price on the invoice and entered his initials in the verification block to show that the prices charged were correct.

Step 3: Verifying Computations. The office clerk, Susan Bates, checked the computations on the invoice to make sure they were accurate. She multiplied the quantity of each item by its unit price to verify the extensions. Then she added the extensions and calculated trade discounts to verify the total. She placed a check mark next to each amount on the invoice as its accuracy was verified. Then she entered her initials in the verification block. At that point, the invoice appeared as shown in Figure 26–1.

The same careful verification procedure is used for all bills and invoices received by the business. Of course, if an error is discovered, it is reported to the creditor immediately so that a correction can be made.

Step 4: Preparing and Approving a Voucher. Once a bill or invoice is determined to be accurate, it provides the basis for preparing a voucher, sometimes called a **payment voucher,** to authorize payment when due. The voucher shown in Figure 26–2 (Voucher No. 2–04) was issued for the invoice from Gulf Wholesale Clothiers. After preparing this voucher, the accounting clerk at the Chicago Corporation attached the verified invoice to the voucher and the two documents were given to the store manager, who compared the invoice and the voucher and then signed the voucher to approve payment.

FIGURE 26–2
Payment Voucher

CHICAGO CORPORATION

Payment Voucher

NO. 2–04

PAYEE: Gulf Wholesale Clothiers
123 Ponce DeLeon
Atlanta, GA 30308

Voucher Date Feb. 1, 19X3
Terms 2/10, n/30
Discount Date Feb. 11, 19X3
Date Due March 2, 19X3

Invoice Date	Invoice Number	DESCRIPTION	AMOUNT
Feb. 1, 19X3	R-47651	Suits, Jeans, and Jacket	$734 50
			$734 50

DISTRIBUTION	
ACCT. NO.	AMOUNT
501	$734.50

Price O.K. JS
Material Received S.C
Extensions O.K. SB
Gross Amount $734.50
Discount
Net Paid
Approved for Pay. Steven Casey
Paid by Ck. No. Date

Notice that the Distribution section of the voucher shows the number (501) of the account to be debited (Purchases) and the amount ($734.50). This information is used in making an accounting entry for the voucher. No account to be credited is specified because vouchers are normally credited to Accounts Payable. However, it is sometimes necessary to credit additional accounts. In that case, it is customary to enter all debits and credits in the Distribution section of the voucher.

Step 5: Recording and Filing the Unpaid Voucher. After a voucher is approved, it is entered in an accounting record called the voucher register, which is discussed in greater detail below. Then if the voucher is not payable immediately, it is placed in an **unpaid voucher file,** according to its due date. This file is also sometimes called the **tickler file** because the file serves as a reminder of the amounts to be paid each day. The file of unpaid vouchers thus represents the accounts payable of the business, and no formal accounts payable subsidiary ledger is necessary.

Step 6: Paying a Voucher. When a voucher is due for payment, a check is issued for the amount involved. This sum is recorded on the voucher along with the check number and the date. (Notice that the voucher shown in Figure 26–2 has space for this information in the lower right corner.) The payment of the voucher is entered in the **check register.**

Step 7: Filing a Paid Voucher. Vouchers that have been paid are stamped "Paid" and then placed in a paid vouchers file, usually in numerical order. However, in some cases, paid vouchers are filed according to the name of the payee to permit easier reference and to avoid duplication of payment.

Division of Responsibility

Note that at Chicago Corporation one person (the accounting clerk) prepares the voucher, a second person (Casey, the store manager) approves the voucher, a third person (Bates, the office clerk) prepares the check, and a fourth person (Silvertree, one of the owners) signs the check and mails it. Division of responsibility must be carefully planned by a firm if its voucher system is to provide the desired amount of control.

USING THE VOUCHER REGISTER

OBJECTIVE 4
Record vouchers in a voucher register.

After vouchers are prepared and approved, they are entered in the voucher register in numerical order. This record provides a detailed listing of the vouchers issued each month and indicates the accounts that should be debited and credited for the transactions involved. The **voucher register** is a journal, very similar to the purchases journal, used to record liabilities arising from business transactions.

The completed voucher register of Chicago Corporation for February 19X3 is shown in Figure 26–3, pages 940–941. Notice that the voucher register contains space for entering the date and number of each voucher, the name of the payee, and the debit and credit amounts. Entries for some of the vouchers shown in the register are discussed below. For the sake of efficiency, separate columns are provided to record vouchers for the accounts that are used most often. These columns speed up the initial entry of the vouchers and permit summary postings at the end of the month. Debits and credits to accounts not used frequently are recorded in the Other Accounts section. Columns are also provided for entering the date each voucher is paid and the number of the check issued for the payment.

Each voucher entered in the voucher register is credited to Accounts Payable.

When entries are made in the voucher register, the amount of each voucher is credited to Accounts Payable. However, some transactions also require credits to other accounts. For example, refer to the entry for Voucher 2–14 in the voucher register. This voucher was issued for the net pay of Susan Bates, the office clerk, for the semimonthly period ended February 15. The total of her salary ($600) was debited to Office Salaries Expense. To record the taxes withheld from this sum, $39 was credited to Social Security Tax Payable, $9 was credited to Medicare Tax Payable, and $45 was credited to Employee Income Tax Payable. The net amount due Bates ($507) was credited to Accounts Payable. Similar entries are made for the earnings, deductions, and net pay of other employees. Since there are several entries to the accounts involving payrolls during each month, special columns are set up for recording the credits.

On February 28, Vouchers 2–27 and 2–28 were issued for payments to John Silvertree and Steven Casey, the owners, for personal withdrawals. The voucher register entries show that the amounts were debited to the two partners' drawing accounts.

All entries in the Other Accounts section of the voucher register are posted individually to the accounts.

During the month, all entries in the Other Accounts section of the voucher register are posted individually to the appropriate accounts in the general ledger. At the end of the month, the voucher register is totaled, proved, and ruled. Then the totals of all columns except the columns in the Other Accounts section are posted to the general ledger.

The voucher register replaces the purchases journal.

In a firm that uses the voucher system, there is no need for a purchases journal. The voucher register contains columns that permit the recording of purchases of merchandise on credit.

USING THE CHECK REGISTER

OBJECTIVE 5

Record payment of approved vouchers.

When the voucher system is used, all checks written result in a debit to Accounts Payable.

In the voucher system used by the Chicago Corporation, the function of classifying expenditures is performed by entries in the voucher register. The actual payment of cash is always made to settle a specific voucher that was previously recorded in the voucher register as an account payable. Therefore, each check issued under the voucher system results in a debit to Accounts Payable and a credit to Cash. If the payment is for goods purchased on credit, it may also require a credit to Purchases Discount. The necessary entry is made in the check register, which takes the place of a cash payments journal.

The check register is shown in Figure 26–4, page 942. Notice that it provides space for recording the date, check number, payee's name, voucher number, and amount of each payment. The checks are entered in numerical order.

The first entries in the check register cover the payment of Vouchers 2–01, 2–02, and 2–03 on February 1. These entries simply involve a debit to Accounts Payable and a credit to Cash. However, the entry made on February 10 for the payment of Voucher 2–04 also includes a credit to Purchases Discount. This voucher was issued when the firm received an invoice from Gulf Wholesale Clothiers for goods purchased on credit.

The Chicago Corporation uses the procedure described in Chapter 9 to handle cash discounts on purchases. Invoices are recorded at their total price. If a discount is taken, the amount of discount is credited to Purchases Discount. Purchases discounts are shown on the income statement as a reduction in the cost of purchases.

In accordance with this procedure, the full amount of the invoice from Gulf Wholesale Clothiers ($734.50) was used in preparing a voucher, even though the invoice has terms of 2/10, n/30 and the company expected to take advantage of the discount. Thus the entry in the voucher register resulted in a credit of $734.50 to Accounts Payable.

FIGURE 26–3
A Voucher Register

VOUCHER REGISTER

DATE		VOU. NO.	PAYABLE TO	PAID		ACCOUNTS PAYABLE CREDIT	SOC. SECURITY TAX PAYABLE CREDIT	MEDICARE TAX PAYABLE CREDIT	EMP. INC. TAX PAYABLE CREDIT
				DATE	CK. NO.				
Feb.	1	2–01	Commercial Realty Co.	2/01	101	1,250.00			
	1	2–02	Domingo Reuben	2/01	102	100.00			
	1	2–03	Susan Bates	2/01	103	75.00			
	1	2–04	Gulf Wholesale Clothiers	2/10	108	734.50			
	3	2–05	Graham Paper Company			189.50			
	5	2–06	Office Suppliers Co.			57.75			
	9	2–07	Kelly & Smith, Attys.			200.00			
	10	2–08	G. Thompson, CPA			75.00			
	10	2–09	Burke Clothing Company	2/19	114	5,240.00			
	10	2–10	Southern Express Co.	2/11	109	56.35			
	10	2–11	Fashions, Inc.	2/19	115	4,937.00			
	10	2–12	Fast Truckers	2/11	110	82.50			
	10	2–13	Moore Insurance Agency			240.00			
	12	2–14	Susan Bates	2/15	111	507.00	39.00	9.00	45.00
	15	2–15	Domingo Reuben	2/15	112	596.00	45.50	10.50	48.00
	15	2–16	Alfred White	2/15	113	608.00	45.50	10.50	36.00
	18	2–17	Better Box Company			95.00			
	25	2–18	City Water Supply			12.50			
	25	2–19	State Utilities Company			157.25			
	27	2–20	Gulf Wholesale Clothiers			3,465.00			
	27	2–21	Central Telephone Co.			76.75			
	28	2–22	Star-Herald Papers			329.75			
	28	2–23	Jiffy Delivery Co.			245.00			
	28	2–24	Susan Bates	2/28	116	507.00	39.00	9.00	45.00
	28	2–25	Domingo Reuben	2/28	117	596.00	45.50	10.50	48.00
	28	2–26	Alfred White	2/28	118	608.00	45.50	10.50	36.00
	28	2–27	John Silvertree	2/28	119	1,000.00			
	28	2–28	Steven Casey	2/28	120	975.00			
	28	2–29	Susan Bates	2/28	121	57.05			
						23,072.90	260.00	60.00	258.00
						(205)	(221)	(222)	(223)

PAGE 3

PURCHASES DEBIT	FREIGHT IN DEBIT	STORE SUPPLIES DEBIT	OTHER ACCOUNTS: ACCOUNT TITLE	POST. REF.	DEBIT	CREDIT
			Rent Expense	542	1,250.00	
			Change Fund	106	100.00	
			Petty Cash Fund	105	75.00	
734.50						
		189.50				
			Office Supplies	125	57.75	
			Professional Services Expenses	554	200.00	
			Professional Services Expenses	554	75.00	
5,240.00						
	56.35					
4,937.00						
	82.50					
			Prepaid Insurance	126	240.00	
			Office Salaries Expense	551	600.00	
			Sales Salaries Expense	521	700.00	
			Sales Salaries Expense	521	700.00	
		95.00				
			Utilities Expense	543	12.50	
			Utilities Expense	543	157.25	
3,465.00						
			Miscellaneous Office Expense	553	76.75	
			Advertising Expense	522	329.75	
			Delivery Expense	532	245.00	
			Office Salaries Expense	551	600.00	
			Sales Salaries Expense	521	700.00	
			Sales Salaries Expense	521	700.00	
			John Silvertree, Drawing	301	1,000.00	
			Steven Casey, Drawing	311	975.00	
	12.55	13.45	*Advertising Expense*	522	12.00	
			Office Supplies	125	19.05	
14,376.50	151.40	297.95			8,825.05	
(501)	(506)	(129)			(X)	

FIGURE 26–4
A Check Register

CHECK REGISTER PAGE 3

DATE		CK. NO.	PAYABLE TO	VOU. NO.	ACCOUNTS PAYABLE DEBIT	PURCHASES DISCOUNT CREDIT	CASH CREDIT
19X3							
Feb.	1	101	Commercial Reality Co.	2–01	1 2 5 0 00		1 2 5 0 00
	1	102	Domingo Reuben	2–02	1 0 0 00		1 0 0 00
	1	103	Susan Bates	2–03	7 5 00		7 5 00
	10	108	Gulf Wholesale Clothiers	2–04	7 3 4 50	1 4 69	7 1 9 81
	28	119	John Silvertree	2–27	1 0 0 0 00		1 0 0 0 00
	28	120	Steven Casey	2–28	9 7 5 00		9 7 5 00
	28	121	Susan Bates	2–29	5 7 05		5 7 05
					20 9 2 9 40	2 6 8 23	20 6 6 1 17
					(205)	(512)	(101)

When purchases are recorded at their gross amounts, discounts taken are recorded in the accounts.

Since the invoice was paid by the necessary date, the firm was able to take the 2 percent cash discount, which amounted to \$14.69 (\$734.50 × 0.02). A check for \$719.81 (\$734.50 − \$14.69) was issued to Gulf Wholesale Clothiers. The full amount of the invoice (\$734.50) was debited to Accounts Payable to close out the liability that was previously set up in the voucher register entry. The amount of the discount (\$14.69) was credited to Purchases Discount, and the amount actually paid (\$719.81) was credited to Cash. The effect of this entry, expressed in general journal form, follows.

19X3					
Feb.	10	Accounts Payable		7 3 4 50	
		Purchases Discounts			1 4 69
		Cash			7 1 9 81

Refer to the entry in the check register to see how this payment was actually recorded in the register.

As in the case of other special journals, at the end of each month the check register is totaled, proved, and ruled. Then the totals are posted to the general ledger accounts indicated in the column headings.

PREPARING A SCHEDULE OF VOUCHERS PAYABLE

Remember that no accounts payable subsidiary ledger is maintained when the voucher system is used. The file of unpaid vouchers takes the place of this ledger. At the end of each month, a **schedule of**

vouchers payable is prepared from the items in the file. This schedule provides a listing of all amounts owed for unpaid vouchers, as shown in Figure 26–5.

FIGURE 26–5
A Schedule of Vouchers Payable

THE CHICAGO CORPORATION Schedule of Vouchers Payable February 28, 19X3		
Voucher Number	Payable to	Amount
2–05	Graham Paper Company	$ 189.50
2–06	Office Suppliers Co.	57.75
2–07	Kelly & Smith, Attorneys	200.00
2–08	G. Thompson, CPA	75.00
2–13	Moore Insurance Agency	240.00
2–17	Better Box Company	95.00
2–18	City Water Company	12.50
2–19	State Utilities Company	157.25
2–20	Gulf Wholesale Clothiers	3,465.00
2–21	Central Telephone Company	76.75
2–22	Star-Herald Papers	329.75
2–23	Jiffy Delivery Company	245.00
	Total	$5,143.50

The file of unpaid vouchers takes the place of the accounts payable subsidiary ledger.

The schedule of unpaid vouchers should be checked against the entries in the voucher register.

After the schedule is prepared, it should be checked against the entries in the voucher register to be certain that it includes all vouchers that have not been marked "Paid." Then the total of the schedule should be compared with the balance of the Accounts Payable account in the general ledger to make sure that the two figures are equal.

On February 28, 19X3, the Accounts Payable account of the Chicago Corporation appeared as shown below. The beginning balance in the account on February 1 was $3,000. The next two amounts are totals posted from the voucher register and the check register at the end of the month. These entries are identified by the abbreviations *VR* and *CR* in the Posting Reference column. Notice that the final balance of the account ($5,143.50) agrees with the total of the schedule of vouchers payable.

ACCOUNT *Accounts Payable* ACCOUNT NO. *205*

DATE		EXPLANATION	POST. REF.	DEBIT	CREDIT	BALANCE DEBIT	BALANCE CREDIT
19X3							
Feb.	*1*	*Balance*	√				*3 000 00*
	28		*VR1*		*23 072 90*		*26 072 90*
	28		*CR1*	*20 929 40*			*5 143 50*

SELF-REVIEW

1. Division of responsibility is one of the most important principles of internal control. How is this principle put into practice?
2. What is the purpose of the voucher?
3. What is the purpose of the voucher register?
4. When a voucher is entered in the voucher register, what account is normally credited?
5. What ledger does the unpaid vouchers file replace?

Answers to Self-Review

1. Division of responsibility is put into practice by assigning two or more employees to every major operation. For example, a person handling cash should not have responsibility for recording cash.
2. The voucher is to ensure that no check is issued without proper authorization and is backed by appropriate documentation.
3. The voucher register provides a journal in which to record every approved voucher. Entries are posted to the accounts affected.
4. Each voucher normally results in a credit to accounts payable.
5. The unpaid vouchers file replaces the accounts payable subsidiary ledger.

TRANSACTIONS REQUIRING SPECIAL TREATMENT

As long as invoices are received, verified, vouchered, and paid in the normal manner, businesses using the voucher system can efficiently handle a large volume of transactions. However, the procedures are rather rigid, and certain infrequent transactions are awkward to record. Here are some typical examples.

FIGURE 26–6
A Voucher Register (Partial)

VOUCHER REGISTER

DATE		VOU. NO.	PAYABLE TO	PAID DATE	PAID CK. NO.	ACCOUNTS PAYABLE CREDIT	SOC. SECURITY TAX PAYABLE CREDIT	MEDICARE TAX PAYABLE CREDIT	EMP. INC. TAX PAYABLE CREDIT
19X3									
Apr.	4	4–08	Office Suppliers	Canc.	V4-33	4 000 00			
					V4-34				
	30	4–33	Office Suppliers	4/30	208	2 000 00			
	30	4–34	Office Suppliers			2 000 00			

Partial Payments

OBJECTIVE 6

Record transactions for partial payments in a voucher register.

When partial payment of a previously recorded voucher is to be made, two or more new vouchers must be prepared.

After a voucher has been prepared for the full amount of an invoice, a firm may arrange to pay the debt in two or more installments. For instance, suppose the Chicago Corporation bought furniture and fixtures costing $4,000 on April 4, 19X3, and Voucher 4–08 was prepared to cover the purchase. Being short of cash at the end of April, the firm arranged to pay half the amount at that time and to pay the other half at the end of May.

The original voucher (4–08) is canceled by issuing two new vouchers (4–33 and 4–34). The new vouchers are recorded in the voucher register separately, each entry involving a credit of $2,000 to the Accounts Payable account in the usual manner. However, each entry also involves a debit of $2,000 to Accounts Payable, which is recorded in the Other Accounts Debit column to cancel the original voucher. (The original debit of $4,000 to the Furniture and Fixtures account is not affected.) In general journal form, the effect of the entry is shown below.

19X3					
April	*4*	*Accounts Payable*		*4 0 0 0 00*	
		Accounts Payable			*2 0 0 0 00*
		Accounts Payable			*2 0 0 0 00*

The actual entry in the voucher register is shown in Figure 26–6. The cancellation is noted in the Date column of the Paid section of the voucher register on the line where Voucher 4–08 (the original voucher) was recorded, and the new voucher numbers are entered in the Check Number column, as illustrated.

PAGE *5*

PURCHASES DEBIT	FREIGHT IN DEBIT	STORE SUPPLIES DEBIT	OTHER ACCOUNTS: ACCOUNT TITLE	POST. REF.	DEBIT	CREDIT
			Furniture and Fixtures	*131*	*4 0 0 0 00*	
			Accounts Payable	*205*	*2 0 0 0 00*	
			Accounts Payable	*205*	*2 0 0 0 00*	

The first new voucher (4–33) is paid on April 30, and the second new voucher (4–34) is filed for payment at the end of May. The entries for payment are made in the check register in the usual way.

Notes Payable

OBJECTIVE 7

Record payments for notes payable in a voucher register.

The Chicago Corporation owes $10,000 to the First National Bank on a 9 percent, 60-day note, dated February 1, 19X3. When the note becomes due on April 2, a voucher must be prepared to authorize payment of $10,150 (the $10,000 face value of the note plus $150 interest). In general journal form, the following entry is necessary to record the voucher that must be prepared to authorize payment.

19X3					
April	*2*	*Notes Payable—Bank*		*10 000 00*	
		Interest Expense		*150 00*	
		Accounts Payable			*10 150 00*

Look at the voucher register in Figure 26–7 to see how the entry is actually recorded in the register. After the voucher is recorded in the register, a check for $10,150 is issued and entered in the check register to settle the obligation. This entry is recorded in the usual manner.

Another recording problem involving notes payable arises after a voucher is prepared for an invoice in the normal manner. Suppose the firm arranges to issue a note payable to the supplier as a means of postponing payment. The amount owed is no longer an account payable so a general journal entry is made debiting Accounts Payable (thus canceling the original voucher) and crediting Notes Payable—Trade. The date of the note is recorded in the Date column of the Paid

FIGURE 26–7
A Voucher Register (Partial)

VOUCHER REGISTER

DATE		VOU. NO.	PAYABLE TO	PAID DATE	PAID CK. NO.	ACCOUNTS PAYABLE CREDIT	SOC. SECURITY TAX PAYABLE CREDIT	MEDICARE TAX PAYABLE CREDIT	EMP. INC. TAX PAYABLE CREDIT
19X3									
Apr.	*2*	*4–04*	*First National Bank*	*4/2*	*201*	*10 150 00*			

section. In the Check Number column, the words *By note* are entered. When the time comes for payment, a new voucher is prepared for the note (plus interest, if any).

Purchases Returns and Allowances

OBJECTIVE 8
Record payments involving purchases returns and allowances in a voucher register.

If goods that are for some reason unsatisfactory are received, either the items are returned to the supplier or they are kept and an allowance is obtained from the supplier. In either case, the amount finally owed to the supplier is less than the amount of the original invoice. In Chapter 8 you learned how to account for purchases returns and allowances. Now let's see how returns and allowances are handled if the voucher system is being used.

If the original invoice has already been vouchered and entered in the voucher register, the accounting records must be adjusted. For example, suppose that on March 2 the Chicago Corporation receives an invoice for $750 for goods purchased from Madison Wholesalers. Voucher 3–05 is prepared for the invoice. Then, on March 8, an allowance of $50 is made by the supplier to cover goods damaged in transit. The revised amount owed for the invoice is therefore $700. Either of two methods may be used to record a return or allowance.

Either of two methods may be used to record purchases returns and allowances under the voucher system.

Method 1. On March 8, when the allowance is made, a new voucher can be issued crediting Accounts Payable for $700, the revised amount. Accounts Payable will also be debited for $750 to cancel the original voucher (3–05), and Purchases Returns and Allowances will be credited for $50. In general journal form, the effect of the entry is as shown below.

19X3					
Mar.	*8*	*Accounts Payable*		*750 00*	
		Purch. Returns and Allow.			*50 00*
		Accounts Payable			*700 00*

PAGE *5*

PURCHASES DEBIT	FREIGHT IN DEBIT	STORE SUPPLIES DEBIT	OTHER ACCOUNTS ACCOUNT TITLE	POST. REF.	DEBIT	CREDIT
			Notes Payable—Bank	*201*	*10 000 00*	
			Interest Expense	*591*	*150 00*	

FIGURE 26–8
A Voucher Register (Partial)

VOUCHER REGISTER

DATE		VOU. NO.	PAYABLE TO	PAID DATE	PAID CK. NO.	ACCOUNTS PAYABLE CREDIT	SOC. SECURITY TAX PAYABLE CREDIT	MEDICARE TAX PAYABLE CREDIT	EMP. INC. TAX PAYABLE CREDIT
19X3									
Mar.	2	3–05	Madison Wholesalers	Canc.	V3-12	750 00			
	8	3–12	Madison Wholesalers			700 00			

The entry for the new voucher (3–12) would actually appear in the voucher register as shown in Figure 26–8. Observe that a notation is also made on the line for Voucher 3–05 to indicate that it has been canceled by Voucher 3–12.

Method 2. Some accountants use a simpler method for handling this type of adjustment. Since the voucher register for March was not closed and posted before the allowance was agreed upon, the original entry can be corrected by making a notation for the $50 allowance on the same line as the original voucher entry, as shown in Figure 26–9. The notation is circled to indicate that it represents a reduction in the firm's accounts payable and its cost of purchases.

FIGURE 26–9
A Voucher Register (Partial)

VOUCHER REGISTER

DATE		VOU. NO.	PAYABLE TO	PAID DATE	PAID CK. NO.	ACCOUNTS PAYABLE CREDIT	SOC. SECURITY TAX PAYABLE CREDIT	MEDICARE TAX PAYABLE CREDIT	EMP. INC. TAX PAYABLE CREDIT
19X3									
						(50 00)			
Mar.	2	3–05	Madison Wholesalers			750 00			
						(50 00)			
	31		Totals			19 980 00			
						(205)			

PAGE *4*

Purchases Debit	Freight In Debit	Store Supplies Debit	Other Accounts: Account Title	Post. Ref.	Debit	Credit
750 00						
			Accounts Payable	*205*	*750 00*	
			Purchases Returns and Allow.	*509*		*50 00*

The adjustment is recorded on the original voucher, and when the invoice becomes due, payment is made for the net amount. At the end of the month, the figures that are circled in each column of the voucher register are totaled separately from the original figures. The $50 total for returns and allowances for the month, shown in Figure 26–9, is posted as a debit to Accounts Payable and a credit to Purchases Returns and Allowances, thereby accomplishing the same result as the first method. Note, however, that the second method can be used only if the revision is made *before* the voucher register has been closed for the month.

PAGE *4*

Purchases Debit	Freight In Debit	Store Supplies Debit	Other Accounts: Account Title	Post. Ref.	Debit	Credit
(50 00)						
750 00						
(50 00)						
15 960 00					*5 000 00*	*200 00*
					(X)	*(X)*

FIGURE 26–10
A Voucher Register (Partial)

VOUCHER REGISTER

DATE		VOU. NO.	PAYABLE TO	PAID DATE	PAID CK. NO.	ACCOUNTS PAYABLE CREDIT	SOC. SECURITY TAX PAYABLE CREDIT	PURCHASES DEBIT
19X3								
Feb.	*1*	*2–04*	*Gulf Wholesale Clothiers*	*2/10*	*108*	*719 81*		*719 81*

Recording Purchases Discounts Lost

OBJECTIVE 9
Use alternative methods to record purchases and purchases discounts.

For better internal control over cash payments, purchases may be recorded at net price after discounts. Discounts not taken are reflected in the accounts.

The procedures described in previous chapters for recording both purchases and cash discounts are commonly used. However, there is a possible disadvantage in using those procedures if a good system of internal control is to be developed. If, due to inefficiency, a discount is not taken because an invoice is not paid promptly, the accounting records will not reveal the loss of the discount under the system discussed earlier in this text. To overcome this shortcoming, many accountants record vouchers for purchases in such a way that discounts *not taken* will stand out for investigation. Under this procedure, discounts taken are not separately stated in the accounts, while discounts not taken are noted in a Discounts Lost account.

Under this procedure, purchase invoices are recorded in the voucher register **net of discount.** The amount used for the entry is the invoice price minus the cash discount that may be taken. If the invoice is paid within the discount period, the check is drawn for the exact amount of the original voucher. On the other hand, if the invoice is paid too late to take the discount, the total amount of the invoice must be paid. This sum will be larger than the amount of the original voucher. The difference is recorded in the check register by debiting an account called Discounts Lost. The balance of this account is presented in the Cost of Goods Sold section of the income statement as an addition to Purchases.

To illustrate how this procedure for recording purchases and cash discounts works, assume that on February 1 the Chicago Corporation received the invoice for a purchase of $734.50 from Gulf Wholesale Clothiers with terms of 2/10, n/30. The purchase is recorded in the voucher register at the net amount ($734.50 − $14.69 = $719.81), as shown in Figure 26–10.

When payment is made within the discount period, it is recorded in the check register in the usual way, as illustrated in Figure 26–11. If the payment is made too late to take the discount, the amount of discount lost is recorded in the check register and management's attention will immediately be directed to this failure. The check register entry shown in Figure 26–12 reflects the lost discount.

FIGURE 26–11
A Check Register (Partial)

CHECK REGISTER — PAGE 3

DATE		CK. NO.	PAYABLE TO	VOU. NO.	ACCOUNTS PAYABLE DEBIT	PURCHASES DISCOUNTS CREDIT	CASH CREDIT
19X3							
Feb.	10	108	Gulf Wholesale Clothiers	2–04	7 1 9 81		7 1 9 81

FIGURE 26–12
A Check Register (Partial)

CHECK REGISTER — PAGE 3

DATE		CK. NO.	PAYABLE TO	VOU. NO.	ACCOUNTS PAYABLE DEBIT	PURCHASES DISCOUNTS LOST DEBIT	CASH CREDIT
19X3							
Feb.	10	116	Gulf Wholesale Clothiers	2–04	7 1 9 81	1 4 69	7 3 4 50

MANAGERIAL IMPLICATIONS

Because of its nature, cash is easily lost, stolen, or misused. The protection of cash and other assets is vital to successful business operations and should be a major concern of management. Only a well-planned system of internal control can provide the necessary safeguards, and management must work with the accountant to establish and maintain such a system. Aside from protecting assets, a good system of internal control produces other important benefits. It helps to ensure efficient processing of transactions and accurate preparation of financial records, to prevent liabilities from being incurred without proper authorization, and to protect honest employees from suspicion by pinpointing responsibility.

The voucher system is invaluable to management because of the tight control it provides over liabilities and cash payments. Every transaction is carefully recorded, checked, and documented. Responsibility is clear and definite all along the line.

Although most companies record purchases of merchandise at the gross invoice price, this procedure has one managerial deficiency. Discounts that are taken are recorded in the accounts, but discounts that are not taken do not appear separately in the records. An alternative procedure that management should consider is to record invoices at the net amount payable after considering potential discounts. Then, if discounts are not taken and the company pays the full invoice price, the discounts lost will be recorded. This affords management a means for detecting inefficiencies, errors, and other causes of failure to take discounts.

SELF-REVIEW

1. How is a partial payment of a voucher recorded in the voucher register?
2. A 30-day note payable is given in settlement of a voucher that has been recorded in the voucher register. How is this transaction handled in the accounting records?
3. What two methods may be used in a voucher system to record purchases returns and allowances after a voucher for the purchase has been entered in the voucher register?
4. If a company records purchase invoices at their gross amounts, how is the cash discount taken on an invoice recorded?
5. If a company records purchases invoices at their net amounts, after considering cash discounts, how is the cash discount taken on an invoice recorded?

Answers to Self-Review

1. Two new vouchers are prepared—one for the amount to be paid immediately and another for the balance of the amount of the original voucher.
2. A general journal entry is made debiting Accounts Payable and crediting Notes Payable. In the Paid section of the voucher register a notation is made to indicate settlement "by note."
3. (a) A new voucher is prepared and entered in the voucher register. Accounts Payable is credited for the new amount owed, Purchases Returns and Allowances is credited for the amount of the return or allowance, and Accounts Payable is debited for the amount of the old voucher. (b) If the return occurs before the register is totaled and posted, a notation entry for the amount of the return or allowance can be entered just above the original amounts in the voucher register and circled. The total of the circled amounts is posted as a debit to Accounts Payable and a credit to Purchases Returns and Allowances.
4. Under this system discounts are recorded in the check register at the time the voucher is paid. The discount is subtracted from Purchases in the Cost of Goods Sold section of the income statement.
5. Under this entry there is no record in the accounts of discounts taken. Only discounts lost are recorded.

CHAPTER 26 **Review and Applications**

CHAPTER SUMMARY

Internal control is important for every business, no matter what its size. Each step in the accounting process of a firm should be planned to ensure accuracy, honesty, and efficiency. An essential technique for achieving these goals is to divide responsibility so that every major accounting routine involves two or more employees and the work of one person can be checked against that of another person. In addition to division of responsibility, accountants use a number of other widely recognized techniques to design internal control procedures for a business.

The voucher system is employed by many firms to control their liabilities and cash payments. A voucher is prepared for each expenditure. After careful verification and examination, the voucher is approved. The voucher is recorded in the voucher register as a credit to Accounts Payable and a debit to the appropriate account. The voucher is then placed with other approved vouchers in an unpaid vouchers file. When a check is issued to pay the voucher, an entry is recorded in the check register, debiting Accounts Payable and crediting Cash. A notation is made in the voucher register showing the date paid and the check number. The voucher is then transferred to a paid vouchers file. At the end of each month, a schedule of vouchers payable is prepared.

Certain transactions such as purchases returns and allowances, partial payments, and notes payable may require special treatment when they are recorded under the voucher system.

Traditionally, most companies record purchases at gross invoice price. Then, if cash discounts are taken, the difference between the original purchase price and the net amount paid is recorded as discounts taken and is shown on the income statement as a reduction of Purchases in the Cost of Goods Sold section. In some firms, purchases are recorded net of discount. Then, if payments are not made within the discount period, the discounts lost will be recorded and will stand out so that they can be investigated.

GLOSSARY OF NEW TERMS

Check register (p. 938) The record of cash payments of vouchers

Internal control system (p. 932) A system designed to safeguard assets, achieve efficient processing of transactions, and ensure accuracy and reliability of financial records

Net of discount (p. 950) The invoice price minus the cash discount offered

Payment voucher (p. 936) See Voucher

Schedule of vouchers payable (p. 942) A listing of all amounts owed for unpaid vouchers

Tickler file (p. 937) A file with vouchers filed by due date

Unpaid voucher file (p. 937) A file to hold vouchers until they are due to be paid, often filed by due date

Voucher (p. 933) A form used to authorize payment of an obligation

Voucher register (p. 938) A journal used to record vouchers issued by a business

Voucher system (p. 933) A record-keeping system that requires a written authorization (the voucher) for each amount to be paid, thus controlling liabilities and cash payments

REVIEW QUESTIONS

1. Why is there a need for internal control over business operations?
2. What is the voucher system?
3. Why is the voucher system more appropriate for medium-sized and large businesses than small businesses?
4. A number of different controls are built into the voucher system. Briefly describe five of these controls.
5. What steps are usually followed in verifying an invoice before a voucher is prepared?
6. What is the purpose of the check register?
7. What information is presented on the schedule of vouchers payable?
8. Under the voucher system, how is the balance of the Accounts Payable account proved at the end of each month?
9. In what order are vouchers filed in the unpaid vouchers file?
10. What types of transactions often require special treatment in the voucher system?
11. A voucher for $3,000 was recorded in the voucher register in March. In April a 60-day note payable was given to settle the open account. How is this transaction recorded?
12. What is the purpose of recording invoices net of discount?
13. When an invoice that was recorded net of discount is paid after the discount period has ended, what accounts are debited and credited in the check register entry?
14. How is the Discounts Lost account presented on the income statement?

MANAGERIAL FOCUS

1. Assume you are the newly hired controller of the Renoir Company and have suggested that the firm adopt the voucher system. The president has asked you to provide a brief analysis of the

advantages and disadvantages of this system. How would you respond?

2. The personnel manager of the Renoir Company is concerned that the employees will view the installation of the voucher system as a sign of mistrust. How can this system be explained to the employees as providing benefits to them as well as to the business?
3. How can the management of a firm avoid unnecessary red tape as a by-product of its search for adequate internal controls?
4. In a small business there may be only one or two experienced and reliable employees capable of assuming key positions in an internal control system. Is it impractical to introduce internal controls in this situation? Why or why not?
5. The president of Ace Company received a letter from one of the companies from which Ace purchases merchandise. The letter expressed surprise that although Ace usually pays all invoices shortly after the due date the company does not take advantage of all cash discounts available. The president asks you to design a system to routinely report discounts not taken. Describe the procedures you would recommend.

EXERCISES

EXERCISE 26–1
(Obj. 3, 4, 5)

Tutorial

Record vouchers and payment of vouchers. Record the following transactions for 19X3 for Eastern Electronics Company in general journal form, assuming that purchases are recorded at the gross invoice price. On the line above each journal entry, indicate the name of the journal or register in which the transaction would actually be recorded. Omit explanations.

TRANSACTIONS

Sept. 3 Purchased merchandise from Allied Corporation for $12,000; terms, 2/10, n/30; Voucher 9–01. (Record purchases at gross invoice price.)

Sept. 5 Received bill for $640 from City Utility Company for utilities; prepared Voucher 9–02.

Sept. 12 Paid Allied Corporation for purchase of September 3 (Voucher 9–01), less 2 percent discount.

Sept. 15 Purchased office equipment from City Office Supply Company for $3,000, giving 60-day, 10-percent note payable for total purchase price.

EXERCISE 26–2
(Obj. 7)

Tutorial

Record notes payable given to settle invoice when voucher system is used. Frenchman Clothing Company uses the voucher system. Selected transactions that occurred during 19X6 are given below. Record these transactions in general journal form. Omit explanations. On the line above the general journal entry, indicate the name of the journal or register in which the voucher would be recorded.

TRANSACTIONS

May 3 Purchased merchandise from Riviera Manufacturing Company for $14,000; terms are net/15 days; prepared Voucher 5–05. (Record purchases at gross invoice price.)

May 14 Reached an agreement with Riviera Manufacturing Company, giving a three-month, 14-percent note, for the $14,000 owed on Voucher 5–05.

Aug. 14 Prepared Voucher 8–13 for the amount of note and principal owed Riviera Manufacturing Company for the note of May 14.

EXERCISE 26–3
(Obj. 9)
Tutorial

Record purchase and payment of invoice (discount taken) when purchases are recorded at gross invoice price. In general journal form, record the following transactions of Eastern Electronics Company during September 19X3. Omit explanations. On the line above the general journal entry, indicate the name of the journal or register in which the voucher would be recorded.

TRANSACTIONS

Sept. 10 Purchased merchandise for $4,000 from Central Manufacturing Company; terms are 3/10, n/30. (Record the purchase at gross invoice price.)

Sept. 18 Paid Eastern Electronics for invoice of September 10, deducting cash discount.

EXERCISE 26–4
(Obj. 9)
Tutorial

Record purchase and payment of invoice (discount not taken) when purchases are recorded at gross amount. In general journal form, record the following transactions of Eastern Electronics Company during September 19X3. Omit explanations. On the line above the general journal entry, indicate the name of the journal or register in which the voucher would be recorded.

TRANSACTIONS

Sept. 12 Purchased merchandise for $2,000 from Ajax Supply Corporation; terms are 2/10, n/30. (Record the purchase at gross invoice price.)

Sept. 30 Paid Ajax Supply Corporation for invoice of September 12.

EXERCISE 26–5
(Obj. 9)
Tutorial

Record purchases and payment of invoices when purchases are recorded at net amount. In general journal form, record the following transactions of Sally's Jean Shop during June 19X4. Omit explanations. On the line above the general journal entry, indicate the name of the journal or register in which the voucher would be recorded.

TRANSACTIONS

June 4 Purchased merchandise for $1,200 from Western Clothing Manufacturing Company; terms are 2/10, n/30. (Record the purchase at net invoice price.)

June 12 Paid Western Clothing for invoice of June 4, less discount.

EXERCISE 26–6
(Obj. 9)
Tutorial

Record purchase and payment of invoice (discount not taken) when purchases are recorded at net amount. In general journal form, record the following transactions of Ray's Video Shop during July 19X4. Omit explanations. On the line above the general journal entry, indicate the name of the journal or register in which the voucher would be recorded.

TRANSACTIONS

July 6 Purchased merchandise for $2,000 from Northstar Supply Company; terms are 1/10, n/30. (Record the purchase at net invoice price.)

July 31 Paid Northstar for invoice of July 6.

PROBLEMS

PROBLEM SET A

PROBLEM 26–1A
(Obj. 3, 4, 5, 6)

Tutorial | Spreadsheet

Recording transactions in the voucher register and the check register. Transactions of the Salem Medical Supply Company during the first two weeks of September 19X5 are listed below, along with selected accounts from the firm's general ledger.

Instructions

1. Record the transactions in a voucher register like the one shown in Figure 26–3 and a check register like the one shown in Figure 26–4. This firm enters invoices at their total price.
2. Foot and prove the voucher register and the check register.

GENERAL LEDGER ACCOUNTS

Cash	Paul Lund, Drawing
Prepaid Insurance	Purchases
Office Supplier	Freight In
Warehouse Equipment	Purchases Discounts
Office Equipment	Rent Expense
Accounts Payable	Utilities Expense

TRANSACTIONS

Sept. 1 Prepared Voucher 9–01 for $3,240 owed to United Hospital Products for a purchase of merchandise; the terms are 2/10, n/30.

2 Prepared Voucher 9–02 for $900 owed to Reed Business Properties, Inc., for the monthly rent; paid the voucher by Check 3710.

3 Prepared Voucher 9–03 for $625 owed to the Kelso Corporation for new storage bins for the warehouse; paid the voucher by Check 3711.

6 Prepared Voucher 9–04 for $5,400 owed to Dow Medical Equipment for a purchase of merchandise; the terms are 2/10, n/30.

6 Prepared Voucher 9–05 for $136 owed to the Interstate Trucking Company for a freight charge on a purchase of merchandise; paid the voucher by Check 3712.

8 Prepared Voucher 9–06 for $1,260 owed to the Ramos Insurance Agency for a one-year insurance policy.

9 Issued Check 3713 to pay Voucher 9–01 less the cash discount of 2 percent.
10 Prepared Voucher 9–07 for $128 owed to the Customers Power Company for electricity; paid the voucher by Check 3714.
12 Prepared Voucher 9–08 for $2,773 owed to the Allen Drug Company for a purchase of merchandise ($2,700) and a freight charge ($73); the terms are 1/10, n/30.
14 Prepared Voucher 9–09 for $1,000 for a cash withdrawal by the owner for personal use; paid the voucher by Check 3715.
15 Issued Check 3716 to pay Voucher 9–04 less the cash discount of 2 percent.

PROBLEM 26–2A (Obj. 3, 4, 5, 6)

Tutorial

Recording transactions in the voucher register and the check register; recording purchases returns and allowances and notes payable. Transactions that occurred at the Cut-Rate Hardware Company, a retail business, during August 19X7 are listed below, along with selected accounts from the firm's general ledger.

Instructions

1. Record the transactions in a voucher register like the one shown in Figure 26–3, a check register like the one shown in Figure 26–4, and a general journal. This firm enters invoices at their total price.
2. Total, prove, and rule the voucher register and the check register.
3. Prepare a schedule of vouchers payable on August 31, 19X7. Obtain the necessary information from the voucher register.

GENERAL LEDGER ACCOUNTS

Cash	Freight In
Store Supplies	Purchases Returns and Allowances
Office Supplies	Purchases Discounts
Store Equipment	Sales Salaries Expense
Office Equipment	Advertising Expense
Notes Payable	Rent Expense
Accounts Payable	Office Salaries Expense
Social Security Tax Payable	Sales Salaries Expense
Medicare Tax Payable	Utilities Expense
Employee Income Tax Payable	Telephone Expense
Purchases	

TRANSACTIONS

Aug. 1 Prepared Voucher 8–01 for $1,650 owed to Cayman Properties for the monthly rent; paid the voucher by Check 5101.
2 Purchased office equipment for $1,900 from the O'Day Supply Company, giving a noninterest-bearing 30-day note.
3 Prepared Voucher 8–02 for $215 owed to the ABC Supply Company for office supplies; the terms are n/30.
4 Prepared Voucher 8–03 for $600 owed to the Bay Company for store fixtures; the terms are n/30.

5 Prepared Voucher 8–04 for $208 owed to the Interstate Trucking Company for freight on merchandise purchased.
6 Paid Voucher 8–04 by Check 5102.
8 Prepared Voucher 8–05 for $2,250 to the Chan Toy Company for a purchase of merchandise; the terms are 2/10, n/30.
9 Purchased a laser printer (office equipment) for $1,500 from the Micro Equipment Company; the terms are $500 cash with the balance due in 30 days. Vouchers 8–06 and 8–07 were prepared for the two installments; issued Check 5103 for $500 to pay Voucher 8–06.
10 Prepared Voucher 8–08 for $6,000 to the Gold Medal Plumbing Supply Company for a purchase of merchandise; the terms are 2/10, n/30.
15 Received a credit memorandum for $100 from the Gold Medal Plumbing Supply Company for a return of damaged merchandise. (Make a circled entry in the voucher register over the entry for Voucher 8–08.)
16 Issued Check 5104 to pay Voucher 8–05 less the 2 percent discount.
18 Prepared Voucher 8–09 for $180 owed to the *City Tribune* for advertising; paid the voucher by Check 5105.
19 Prepared Voucher 8–10 for $225 owed to the Eastern Trucking Company for freight on merchandise purchased.
20 Issued Check 5106 to pay Voucher 8–10.
20 Issued Check 5107 to pay Voucher 8–08 less the return and the 2 percent discount.
25 Prepared Voucher 8–11 for $4,150 owed to Pine Lumber Company for a purchase of merchandise; the terms are 2/10, n/30.
27 Prepared Voucher 8–12 for $350 owed to City Utilities for electricity used in the store during the month; paid the voucher by Check 5108.
28 Prepared Voucher 8–13 for $100 to the Central Telephone Company for telephone service during the month; paid the voucher by Check 5109.
31 Prepared Voucher 8–14 for $1,900 note payable of August 2 owed to the O'Day Supply Company; paid the voucher by Check 5110.
31 Prepared Voucher 8–15 for Jane Perry, the sales clerk, for her salary of $1,600, less $104 deducted for social security tax, $24 for medicare tax, and $98 income tax; paid the voucher by Check 5111. Prepared Voucher 8–16 for Nikita Moffitt, the office clerk, for his salary of $1,200, less $78 deducted for social security tax, $18 for medicare tax, and $84 deducted for income tax; paid the voucher by Check 5112.

PROBLEM 26–3A (Obj. 9) Tutorial

Alternative methods for recording purchases and purchases discounts. On April 10, 19X3, the Hilton Shoppe Company purchased merchandise from the Kuhn Corporation. The total invoice price was $1,800, and the terms were 3/20, n/60.

Instructions

1. Record the purchase made by Hilton Shoppe Company in general journal form, assuming the following conditions.
   a. Hilton records purchases at the total invoice price.
   b. Hilton records purchases at the net invoice price.
2. Suppose that Hilton Shoppe Company paid the invoice on April 28. Record the payment in general journal form, assuming the following conditions.
   a. Hilton recorded the purchase at the total invoice price.
   b. Hilton recorded the purchase at the net invoice price.
3. Suppose that Hilton Retail Company paid the invoice on June 7 (after the discount period). Record the payment in general journal form, assuming the following conditions.
   a. Hilton recorded the purchase at the total invoice price.
   b. Hilton recorded the purchase at the net invoice price.

PROBLEM SET B

PROBLEM 26–1B
(Obj. 2, 3, 4, 5, 6)

Tutorial

Recording transactions in the voucher register and the check register. Transactions of the Telewide Corporation during the first two weeks of March 19X3 are listed below, along with selected accounts from the firm's general ledger.

Instructions

1. Record the transactions in a voucher register like the one shown in Figure 26–3 and a check register like the one shown in Figure 26–4. This firm enters invoices at their total price.
2. Foot and prove the voucher register and the check register.

GENERAL LEDGER ACCOUNTS

Cash	Ruth McCabe, Drawing
Store Supplies	Purchases
Office Supplies	Freight In
Store Equipment	Purchases Discounts
Office Equipment	Rent Expense
Accounts Payable	Utilities Expense

TRANSACTIONS

Mar. 1 Prepared Voucher 3–01 for $1,585 owed to Ace Products, Inc., for a purchase of merchandise; the terms are 2/10, n/30.

2 Prepared Voucher 3–02 for $600 owed to the Malibu Real Estate Corporation for the monthly rent on the store; paid the voucher by Check 1225.

4 Prepared Voucher 3–03 for $150 owed to Safety Business Systems for office file cabinets; paid the voucher by Check 1226.

5 Prepared Voucher 3–04 for $730 owed to the Keller Company for a purchase of merchandise; the terms are 2/10, n/30.

5 Prepared Voucher 3–05 for $26 owed to State Trucking Inc. for a freight charge on a purchase of merchandise; paid the voucher by Check 1227.
7 Prepared Voucher 3–06 for $295 owed to the Barnes Paper Company for store supplies; the terms are n/30.
9 Issued Check 1228 to pay Voucher 3–01 less the cash discount of 2 percent.
11 Prepared Voucher 3–07 for $136 owed to the Atlantic Power Company for electricity; paid the voucher by Check 1229.
12 Prepared Voucher 3–08 for $1,492 owed to the Harvest Corporation for a purchase of merchandise ($1,440) and a freight charge ($52); the terms are n/30.
14 Issued Check 1230 to pay Voucher 3–04 less the cash discount of 2 percent.
15 Prepared Voucher 3–09 for $800 for a cash withdrawal by the owner for personal use; paid the voucher by Check 1231.

PROBLEM 26–2B
(Obj. 3, 4, 5, 6)

Tutorial

Recording transactions in the voucher register and the check register; recording purchases returns and allowances and notes payable transactions. Transactions that occurred at the Alfonso Book Bazaar, a retail business, during August 19X3 are listed below, along with selected accounts from the firm's general ledger.

Instructions

1. Record the transactions in a voucher register like the one shown in Figure 26–3, a check register like the one shown in Figure 26–4, and a general journal. This firm enters invoices at their total price.
2. Total, prove, and rule the voucher register and the check register.
3. Prepare a schedule of vouchers payable. Obtain the necessary information from the voucher register.

GENERAL LEDGER ACCOUNTS

Cash	Purchases
Store Supplies	Freight In
Office Supplies	Purchases Returns and Allowances
Store Equipment	Purchases Discounts
Office Equipment	Sales Salaries Expense
Notes Payable	Advertising Expense
Accounts Payable	Rent Expense
Social Security Tax Payable	Office Salaries Expense
FICA Tax Payable	Sales Salaries Expense
Medicare Tax Payable	Utilities Expense
Employee Income Tax Payable	Telephone Expense

TRANSACTIONS

Aug. 1 Prepared Voucher 8–01 for $900 owed to the Jordan Realty Company for the monthly rent; paid the voucher by Check 1101.

2 Purchased office equipment for $1,900 from the Micro Systems Company, giving a noninterest-bearing 30-day note.
3 Prepared Voucher 8–02 for $55 owed to the ABC Supply Company for office supplies; the terms are n/30.
4 Prepared Voucher 8–03 for $500 owed to the York Company for building new fixtures in the store; the terms are n/30. (Debit Store Equipment.)
5 Prepared Voucher 8–04 for $188 owed to the Mountain Trucking Company for freight on merchandise purchased.
6 Paid Voucher 8–04 by Check 1102.
8 Prepared Voucher 8–05 for $1,000 owed to the Schwartz Tool Company for a purchase of merchandise; the terms are 2/10, n/30.
9 Purchased a used cash register (Store Equipment) for $500 from the Town Equipment Company; the terms are $200 cash, with the balance due in 30 days. Vouchers 8–06 and 8–07 were prepared for the two installments. Issued Check 1103 for $200 to pay Voucher 8–06.
10 Prepared Voucher 8–08 for $3,000 owed to the Bates Toy Company for a purchase of merchandise; the terms are 2/10, n/30.
12 Prepared Voucher 8–09 for $145 owed to the Marsh Company for store supplies; the terms are n/30.
15 Received a credit memorandum for $100 from the Bates Toy Company for a return of damaged merchandise. (Make a circled entry in the voucher register over the entry for Voucher 8–08.)
16 Issued Check 1104 to pay Voucher 8–05 less the 2 percent discount.
18 Prepared Voucher 8–10 for $80 owed to the *Weekend News* for advertising; paid the voucher by Check 1105.
19 Prepared Voucher 8–11 for $156.40 owed to the Mountain Trucking Company for freight on merchandise purchased.
20 Issued Check 1106 to pay Voucher 8–11.
20 Issued Check 1107 to pay Voucher 8–08 less the return and the 2 percent discount.
25 Prepared Voucher 8–12 for $2,150 owed to Electronic Games Inc. for a purchase of merchandise; the terms are 2/10, n/30.
27 Prepared Voucher 8–13 for $166 owed to City Utilities for electricity used in the store during the month; paid the voucher by Check 1108.
28 Prepared Voucher 8–14 for $74 owed to the Central Telephone Company for telephone service during the month; paid the voucher by Check 1109.
31 Prepared Voucher 8–15 for the $1,900 note payable of August 2 owed to the Micro Systems Company; paid the voucher by Check 1110.

31 Prepared Voucher 8–16 for John Perry, the salesclerk, for his salary of $1,400, less $91 deducted for social security tax, $21 for medicare tax, and $84 income tax; paid the voucher by Check 1111. Prepared Voucher 8–17 for Mary Hernandez, the office clerk, for her salary of $1,200, less $78 deducted for social security tax, $18 for medicare tax, and $44 deducted for income tax; paid the voucher by Check 1112.

PROBLEM 26–3B
(Obj. 9)

Tutorial

Alternative methods for recording purchases and purchases discounts. On March 1, 19X3, City Retailers purchased merchandise from the Marino Corporation. The total invoice price was $2,000, and the terms were 2/10, n/30.

Instructions

1. Record the purchase made by City Retailers in general journal form, assuming the following conditions.
   a. City Retailers records purchases at the total invoice price.
   b. City Retailers records purchases at the net invoice price.
2. Suppose that City Retailers paid the invoice on March 9. Record the payment in general journal form, assuming these conditions:
   a. City Retailers recorded the purchase at the total invoice price.
   b. City Retailers recorded the purchase at the net invoice price.
3. Suppose that City Retailers paid the invoice on March 30 (after the discount period). Record the payment in general journal form, assuming the following conditions.
   a. City Retailers recorded the purchase at the total invoice price.
   b. City Retailers recorded the purchase at the net invoice price.

CHALLENGE PROBLEM

In June of 19X9, the first month of operations of Yuma Specialty Equipment Sales Corporation, the purchases of merchandise that are given below were entered in the voucher register.

Instructions

1. Prepare a cost of goods sold schedule for June, assuming that Yuma Corporation records purchases at their total invoice price and that purchases discounts taken are treated as other income.
2. Prepare a schedule of vouchers payable on June 30, 19X9, assuming that purchases are recorded at total invoice price. All vouchers other than those for purchases have been paid.
3. Prepare a cost of goods sold schedule for June, assuming that Yuma Corporation records purchases at their net invoice price.
4. Prepare a schedule of vouchers payable on June 30, 19X9, assuming that purchases are recorded at net invoice price. All vouchers other than those for purchases have been paid.

TRANSACTIONS

June 1 Issued Voucher 6–01, payable to Phoenix Electronics Corporation, for $18,000; terms, 2/10, n/30 (paid on June 10).

2 Issued Voucher 6–04, payable to Tucson Equipment Corporation, for $12,000; terms, 2/10, n/30 (paid on June 21).

5 Issued Voucher 6–08, payable to Prescott Supply Company, for $16,000; terms, n/30.

20 Issued Voucher 6–15, payable to Phoenix Electronics Corporation, for $20,000; terms, 2/10, n/30 (paid on June 30).

25 Issued Voucher 6–26, payable to Bilko Corporation, for $10,000; terms, 2/20, n/30.

27 Issued Voucher 6–31, payable to Santa Fe Equipment Supply Company, for $14,000; terms, 3/10, n/30.

On June 30 an inventory was taken. The inventory consisted of all the merchandise purchased on June 27 and June 25, one-half of the merchandise purchased on June 20, and one-fourth of the merchandise purchased on June 2.

CRITICAL THINKING PROBLEM

Agnes Glenn, a college accounting major, has just been hired to work part time in the treasurer's office of the local museum. On her first day of work, her boss, Mrs. Bowman, the treasurer, calls Agnes into her office to explain the operations of the office and to describe her duties. The treasurer's office is small—with just two full-time employees other than Mrs. Bowman.

Mrs. Bowman explains that Nancy is in charge of all cash collections. She opens the mail, sets aside for deposit any donation checks, and distributes the rest of the mail to the appropriate persons. When the museum entrance fees are turned over to her each afternoon, she counts the money and prepares the bank deposit. It is usually too late to take the money to the bank so Nancy locks it in her desk overnight. After returning from the bank the next morning, Nancy enters the amount of the deposit in the cash receipts journal and files the deposit slip. Once a month, Nancy prepares a summary of cash receipts for the president of the museum.

Edith, the other full-time employee, handles the museum payroll. She collects the time cards at the end of the week, makes the payroll calculations, prepares the payroll checks, and enters the payroll data in the appropriate records. To save time, the office uses a machine that prints a facsimile signature on each check. The check-signing machine is kept out of sight behind a door in Mrs. Bowman's office, which, Mrs. Bowman explains, prevents unauthorized persons from using the machine and also eliminates the need for Edith to unlock and lock the machine each time she uses it.

As the part-timer in the office, Agnes's job will be to assist the others and fill in when they are on vacation. When Nancy goes on vacation or is absent from work, Agnes will be required to prepare the bank deposit and take it to the bank. Mrs. Bowman says that the student who used to have the job objected to taking the deposit to the bank because of a fear of being robbed, a fear Mrs. Bowman dismisses, saying such things are usually an "inside job."

Agnes explains that she has no experience with payroll, but Mrs. Bowman assures her she has only to follow what Edith does and she will soon learn what she needs to know. In addition to filling in for Nancy and Edith, Agnes is to help Mrs. Bowman prepare financial statements and close the books.

When Agnes gets home from her first day on the job, she is not sure she wants to go back. If she is robbed on the way to the bank, she will likely be accused of being involved. If she makes a mistake, how will it be discovered? This office does not seem to do anything the way Agnes learned in her accounting classes.

Instructions Evaluate the internal control system of the treasurer's office. Identify the strong and weak points of the system. What suggestions would you make to improve it?

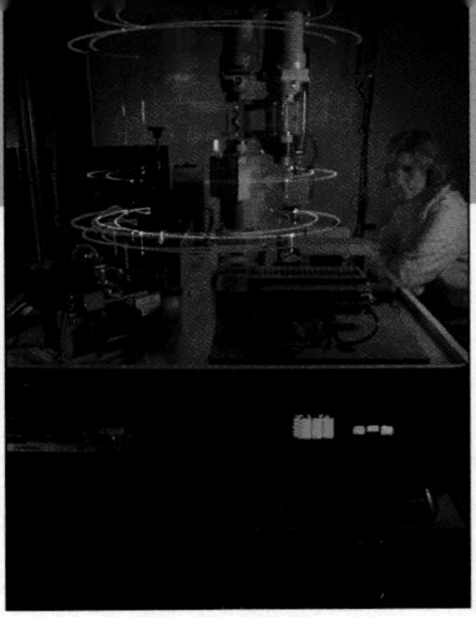

CHAPTER

27 Departmentalized Profit and Cost Centers

OBJECTIVES

1. Explain profit centers and cost centers.
2. Prepare the Gross Profit section of a departmental income statement.
3. Explain and identify direct and indirect departmental expenses.
4. Choose the basis for allocation of indirect expenses and compute the amounts to be allocated to each department.
5. Prepare a departmental income statement showing the contribution margin and net income for each department.
6. Use a departmental income statement in making decisions such as whether to close a department.
7. Define the accounting terms new to this chapter.

In Parts 1 and 2 of this book we examined financial accounting concepts and procedures. Emphasis was placed on the analysis and accumulation of accounting data and the reporting of that data in financial statements. Four basic financial statements were presented: the income statement, the balance sheet, the statement of retained earnings (for a corporation), and the statement of cash flows. All of these statements are historical in nature. They report the results of financial transactions that occurred in the past. However, if management is to properly carry out the functions of planning and control, it must have forward-looking information and analyses in addition to historical data. Historical data alone will not be enough.

In this chapter and later chapters, you will see how financial data can be used to assess the efficiency of current operations and determine the profitability of individual business segments and individual products. You will also see how financial data is used in planning future operations.

NEW TERMS

Contribution margin ▪ Cost center ▪ Direct expenses ▪ Indirect expenses ▪ Managerial accounting ▪ Profit center ▪ Responsibility accounting ▪ Semidirect expenses ▪ Transfer price

MANAGERIAL ACCOUNTING

Traditional financial statements may not contain adequate information for managing a business.

Basic financial statements are limited in that they summarize the activities and financial position of a business as a whole, while most management decisions are made about individual activities or segments of a business. For example, the income statement, although useful, is inadequate to answer questions such as these.

- Should a machine be replaced?
- How much profit was made on an order from a certain customer?
- Is a particular department of the business operating profitably?
- Should the firm discontinue a certain product?
- What price should be set for a new product?

The answers to such questions are provided by an area of accounting that is usually known as managerial accounting. **Managerial accounting** provides financial information about individual segments, activities, or products of a business. In Part 3 of this book we examine a number of topics that illustrate the broad scope of managerial accounting. First, the measurement of profit for a common type of business segment, departments, is covered. Next, we examine the methods used to determine and analyze the costs involved in the manufacture of products. We also discuss the use of manufacturing budgets and standard costs in controlling a manufacturing business. Then we examine the ways in which management analyzes cost and revenue data to make decisions. Finally, the financial budgeting process—the planning of profits, financial position, capital outlays, and cash flow—is illustrated.

Management is more interested in the future than in the past.

Although management is interested in the results of past operations, it is even more interested in the future. Typically, a forecast or estimate for the future begins with an analysis of what has occurred in the past. For example, an estimate of future sales usually begins with an analysis of past sales. Similarly, an estimate of future expenses begins with an analysis of past expenses. Decisions about such matters as pricing also use information from past accounting records as a basis for future action. Thus Part 3 of this book deals with the use of historical data in decision making and in controlling costs and profits.

PROFIT CENTERS AND COST CENTERS

OBJECTIVE 1

Explain profit centers and cost centers.

Profit centers have both revenues and costs.

Managerial accounting is concerned with segments of a business. These segments are often referred to as *centers*. The accounting information related to each center is accumulated and analyzed separately from the information for other centers. There are two types of centers for accounting purposes—profit centers and cost centers. The two are similar, with one important exception. For a **profit center,** both revenue and cost data are accumulated to measure profit, whereas for a **cost center,** only cost data is accumulated and no attempt is made to ascribe profit to the center.

Typically, profit centers are revenue-producing segments that sell products or services to customers outside the business. For example, in a clothing store the coat, dress, suit, and shoe departments may all be separate profit centers. Sales and costs related to each

A cost center is an operating center that incurs costs but does not have revenues.

A transfer price is the price at which a product is transferred from one segment of a business to another segment of the same business.

department are accumulated and matched, and a "profit" is computed for the center. Similarly, each store in a chain of stores owned by one company or each branch sales office may be treated as a profit center. Sometimes, however, a segment of a company is considered a profit center even though it does not sell products or services to outside customers. For example, the segment of an oil company that produces crude oil from the ground may be treated as a profit center even though the oil it produces is not sold directly to outside customers but is merely transferred to the company's refinery. In cases such as this, the revenue from the segment's activities is the **transfer price** of its product—the price at which the segment's goods are transferred to another segment of the company. In this chapter we examine the methods used to measure the profitability of revenue-producing departments, the most common type of profit center.

In accounting for cost centers, the emphasis is on cost control.

As we have noted, cost centers are those segments of a business that do not directly earn revenue. Cost centers often represent areas of a business that merely provide services to other segments of the firm. The emphasis in accounting for cost centers is therefore on cost control rather than on profit measurement. For example, the purchasing department of a company does not produce revenue directly; it merely performs a service for other departments that do earn revenue. The purpose of accounting for the purchasing department as a separate unit is to measure the costs of its operations and to provide a basis for controlling those costs. Other typical cost centers might be the data processing department, the maintenance department, the storeroom, the research laboratory, and the accounting department. In later chapters we will examine how costs are accumulated and analyzed for service departments such as these.

RESPONSIBILITY ACCOUNTING

Responsibility accounting provides information that will help in evaluating each segment of a business and pinpoint responsibility for results.

A common theme underlying both profit centers and cost centers is the idea of **responsibility accounting.** The basic principle underlying responsibility accounting is that management should be able to evaluate the performance of each segment of the business and pinpoint responsibility for its financial results. With this type of system, internal accounting reports provide detailed data for each cost center and profit center so that management can determine how efficiently the individual segments are functioning. This type of information is essential if management is to control current operations effectively and develop sound plans for the future.

SELF-REVIEW

1. What is the role of historical costs in making forecasts or estimates of future costs?
2. What is a profit center? What is a cost center?
3. What are the logical profit centers in a retail store?
4. How could a segment of a business that does not sell products or services be considered a profit center?
5. What is responsibility accounting?

Answers to Self-Review

1. Forecasts or estimates of future costs usually begin with historical costs. Future costs can be more accurately anticipated if past costs are known.
2. A profit center is a business segment that has both revenues and expenses. A cost center incurs expenses but does not have revenues.
3. In a retail store, departments that sell similar items to customers outside the business would be logical profit centers.
4. Some cost centers render services or make products that are transferred to other centers in the same company. In such cases a hypothetical revenue, or transfer price, is attributed to the goods or services transferred. This price permits measuring a "profit" for the center.
5. Responsibility accounting is the development of accounting records that measure profit or cost control for a business segment that is the responsibility of a specific person.

DEPARTMENTALIZED OPERATIONS

When a business is organized into separate departments, it is necessary to provide accounting information about each department.

When the operations of a business include more than one type of sales or service activity, managers and owners want to know how much each activity is contributing to the firm's net income or net loss. If all sales are combined, information on revenue by type of activity will not be available unless each sales transaction is analyzed and the results of each activity are summarized whenever such data is needed. Obviously, this procedure is tedious and inefficient.

Experienced accountants plan in advance to meet requests for such information. They first determine what data will be required. Then they set up a system for gathering the information. If management needs a detailed record of the profits provided by the different types of merchandise handled, accounts must be set up to departmentalize the related revenue and expenses. This segmentation is done when the accountant plans the business's chart of accounts.

For example, suppose the Esquire Men's Store has been in the business of selling men's clothing for two years. On January 1, 19X4, the company adds a shoe department. After studying the planned organizational structure and operations, the accountant redesigned the firm's system of financial records to gather departmentalized data concerning the following items.

Gross profit
- Operating revenues
- Cost of goods sold
- Gross profit on sales

Operating expenses
Net income from operations

Gross Profit Section of a Departmental Income Statement

OBJECTIVE 2
Prepare the Gross Profit section of a departmental income statement.

To determine departmental gross profit, the accountant determines for each department the amount of each element entering into the computation. For example, the gross sales, sales returns and allowances, sales discounts, purchases, purchases returns and allowances, and beginning and ending inventories for each department are determined.

Departmental Accounts in the General Ledger

The basic source for the information that goes into the income statement is the related general ledger accounts. The departmental information may be easily accumulated in the ledger accounts in one of two ways.

A separate sales account may be maintained for each department, or a single sales account with individual columns for each department may be maintained.

1. A separate general ledger account for each element may be maintained for each department. For example, the Esquire Men's Store has two sales departments, Clothing and Shoes, so two different sales accounts are maintained.

   401 Sales—Clothing
   402 Sales—Shoes

   Similar separate departmentalized accounts are kept for each other element entering into the gross profit calculation. Obviously, if there were several departments, the number of general ledger accounts would soon become unwieldy. This situation is even further exaggerated because separate departmental accounts would also be kept for operating expenses that apply specifically to individual departments.
2. One way to avoid maintaining a large number of general ledger accounts is to maintain one ledger account for each element entering into gross profit, while also keeping a record of the amounts applicable to each department. This information is often kept by having "analysis" columns in the ledger accounts. The analysis columns show the amounts applicable to each department. Then information for departmental income statements can be obtained easily from the analysis columns in the accounts.

Recording Sales and Purchases by Departments

When a departmental income statement is to be prepared, the books of original entry are departmentalized where possible. For example, the sales journal and the voucher register provide special columns for each department.

When the sales account is departmentalized, the sales journal must show information for each department.

At the Esquire Men's Store, sales on credit are recorded in a sales journal containing a separate Sales column for each department. The procedures for recording sales invoices in a departmentalized sales journal are exactly the same as those you have already learned for a nondepartmentalized business.

Postings are made daily from the sales journal to the individual accounts receivable ledger accounts.

The posting procedure is also similar to the procedure you learned previously for nondepartmentalized sales journals. Each day, postings are made to the individual customer accounts in the accounts receivable ledger. At the end of each month, the sales journal is totaled and the total sales of each department for the month are posted in one summary figure to the departmental Sales account in the general ledger. For example, as shown in Figure 27–1, the debits to the individual accounts for Esquire's customers—Ryder, Brueker, and Christy—are posted immediately. At the end of the month, the totals of the Accounts Receivable column, the Sales Tax Payable column, and the two Sales columns are posted to the general ledger account.

FIGURE 27–1
A Departmental Sales Journal

SALES JOURNAL PAGE 1

DATE		SALES SLIP NO.	CUSTOMER'S NAME	POST. REF.	ACCOUNTS RECEIVABLE DEBIT	SALES TAX PAYABLE CREDIT	SALES—CLOTHING CREDIT	SALES—SHOES CREDIT
19X4								
Jan.	2	2178	Rena Ryder	√	24 41	71	23 70	
	2	2179	Abraham Brueker	√	18 54	54		18 00
	2	2180	George Christy	√	39 04	1 14	21 40	16 50
	31		Totals		34 680 00	1 080 00	29 000 00	4 600 00
					(111)	(231)	(401.1)	(401.2)

Similar individual columns for the different departments will be included in other special journals in cases where there are numerous transactions specifically identified with individual departments. For example, the voucher register would have separate columns for recording purchases of clothing and shoes, and the sales returns and allowances journal would have separate columns for the sales departments.

Merchandise Inventories

When the merchandise inventory is counted, the inventory in each department is accumulated separately so that the departmental cost of goods sold can be computed. As a result, both the beginning and ending inventories in each department are known.

A Sample Gross Profit Section

The gross profit section of the departmental income statement of Esquire Men's Store for the year ending December 31, 19X4, is shown in Figure 27–2.

FIGURE 27–2
Departmental Income Statement (Partial)

ESQUIRE MEN'S STORE
Income Statement (Partial)
Year Ended December 31, 19X4

	Clothing	*Shoes*	*Total*
Operating Revenues			
Sales	568366	223230	791596
Less Sales Returns and Allowances	9165	2918	12083
Net Sales	559201	220312	779513
Cost of Goods Sold			
Merchandise Inventory, Jan. 1, 19X4	130000	—0—	130000
Purchases	366350	144350	510700
Freight In	5470	1710	7180
Delivered Cost of Purchases	371820	146060	517880
Less: Purchases Returns and Allowances	1650	480	2130
Purchases Discounts	8699	1397	10096
Total Deductions	10349	1877	12226
Net Delivered Cost of Purchases	361471	144183	505654
Total Merchandise Available for Sale	491471	144183	635654
Less Merchandise Inventory, Dec. 31, 19X3	112000	20000	132000
Cost of Goods Sold	379471	124183	503654
Gross Profit on Sales	179730	96129	275859

Operating Expenses Section of a Departmental Income Statement

The procedures used to record and account for operating expenses depend on whether the item involved is a direct expense or an indirect (or semidirect) expense.

OBJECTIVE 3
Explain and identify direct and indirect departmental expenses.

Direct Expenses

Some operating expenses can be identified directly with an individual department and are therefore referred to as **direct expenses.** It is often possible to charge direct expenses to the appropriate departments at the time the expenses are incurred. For example, at the Esquire Men's Store, each salesclerk works in only one department. Thus the salaries expense for these employees can be charged directly to the proper departments throughout the fiscal year. Similarly, advertising costs at the Esquire Men's Store are identified with specific departments and charged directly to those departments throughout the fiscal year. Other direct expenses, such as cash short and over and delivery expense, also can be charged to the departments as the expenses are incurred.

Expenses that can be identified directly with a department are referred to as *direct expenses.*

The direct expenses of Esquire Men's Store for the year ended December 31, 19X4, are shown in Figure 27–3.

FIGURE 27–3
Schedule of Direct Departmental Expenses

ESQUIRE MEN'S STORE
Schedule of Direct Departmental Expenses
Year Ended December 31, 19X4

	Clothing Department	*Shoe Department*	*Total*
Sales Salaries Expense	49600	36000	85600
Advertising Expense	10470	3317	13787
Store Supplies Expense	6268	2240	8508
Cash Short or Over	90	54	144
Delivery Expense	5680	2040	7720
Total Direct Expenses	72108	43651	115759

Indirect and Semidirect Expenses

All the accounts that have been set up on a departmental basis in the discussion so far have one important common characteristic. These revenue and expense items can be easily and directly assigned to a specific department when a transaction is initially recorded.

Not all operating costs are direct expenses, however. Some expenses cannot be directly assigned to particular departments when the transactions occur and are initially recorded. Even though some expenses cannot be directly assigned to specific departments when the costs are incurred, they are closely related to departmental activities and can be allocated among the departments on a meaningful basis at the end of the accounting period. For example, the depreciation on store equipment and the cost of insurance for store equipment and merchandise inventory bear a close relationship to individual sales departments and can be allocated to each of these departments on a very meaningful basis. Some accountants consider costs such as depreciation and insurance to be direct expenses. Others feel it more appropriate to set up a new category known as **semidirect expenses.**

Semidirect expenses are expenses that cannot be directly assigned to individual departments but are closely related to individual departments.

Many operating expenses cannot be allocated to specific departments on the basis of a measurable activity that closely correlates activity and expense. Operating expenses that cannot be readily related to activity within a department are referred to as **indirect expenses.** At the end of the accounting period, indirect expenses are allocated on the most logical basis possible to the sales departments.

Expenses that cannot be readily related to activity in departments are called *indirect expenses.*

For example, items such as postage and stationery used in the office are operating expenses, but if they are allocated to sales departments, the allocation must be done on a somewhat arbitrary basis. Later in this chapter you will see how indirect and semidirect expenses are allocated to permit the calculation of net income from operations for each sales department.

No attempt is made to allocate semidirect or indirect expenses to sales departments at the time the expenses are incurred.

The accountant for Esquire Men's Store does not distinguish between semidirect and indirect expenses. All such expenses of the company are referred to as indirect expenses. The amounts taken from the Adjusted Trial Balance columns of the company's worksheet on December 31, 19X4, follow.

Indirect Expenses	
Insurance Expense	$ 6,180
Custodial Wages Expense	10,240
Rent Expense	12,000
Utilities Expense	11,888
Office Salaries Expense	33,600
Payroll Taxes Expense	14,357
Other Office Expenses	1,609
Professional Services Expense	1,550
Taxes and Licenses	2,652
Uncollectible Accounts Expense	1,338
Depr. Expense—Furn. and Fixtures	920
Depr. Expense—Office Equipment	430
Total Indirect Expenses	$96,764

OBJECTIVE 4
Choose the basis for allocation of indirect expenses and compute the amounts to be allocated to each department.

Allocating Semidirect and Indirect Expense Items

The process of allocating semidirect and indirect items takes place after all adjusting entries have been made and the Adjusted Trial Balance section of the worksheet has been completed. As a basis for making the allocation of each expense, the accountant seeks to find some factor to which the expense level is logically related and that can be measured for each department. Let's see how the accountant goes about allocating the indirect costs of the Esquire Men's Store.

Insurance Expense. Insurance premiums are allocated to separate departments in proportion to the value of the furniture, fixtures, and inventory that are directly involved in the unit's operations. To simplify the computations, the accountant for the Esquire Men's Store uses the ending inventory amount and the cost (before depreciation) of the furniture and fixtures. On December 31, 19X4, the clothing department had furniture and fixtures that cost $7,200 and inventory of $112,000—a total of $119,200. The shoe department had furniture and fixtures of $2,000 and inventory of $20,000—a total of $22,000. On the basis of the total assigned asset value of $141,200, the accountant allocates insurance expense of $6,180 for the year to each department as shown in Table 27–1.

TABLE 27–1
Allocation of Insurance Expense

Asset Item	Clothing Department	Shoe Department	Percent		Total Insurance Expense		Amount Allocated to Each Department
Merchandise inventory	$112,000	$20,000					
Furniture and fixtures	7,200	2,000					
Total clothing	$119,200	$22,000	84.4	×	$6,180	=	$5,215.92
Total shoes	22,000		15.6	×	6,180	=	964.08
Combined totals	$141,200		100.0				$6,180.00

Because cost allocations are somewhat arbitrary, allocated expenses are often rounded to the nearest whole dollar on departmental income statements. The accountant for Esquire Men's Store follows this practice. As a result, on the departmental income statement shown later in the chapter (Figure 27–5), the insurance expense for the clothing department is shown as $5,216, and the insurance expense for the shoe department is shown as $964.

Custodial Wages Expense. The cost of the work of the custodian is closely related to the space occupied by each department. The custodian's wages are allocated to the two operating departments according to their floor area. The data and computations are as follows.

Department	Basis: Square Feet	Percent		Total Custodial Wages Expense		Amount Allocated to Each Department
Clothing	3,600	90	×	$10,240	=	$ 9,216
Shoes	400	10	×	10,240	=	1,024
Totals	4,000	100				$10,240

The amounts allocated to the clothing department, $9,216, and to the shoe department, $1,024, are shown in the departmental income statement (Figure 27–5).

Rent Expense. Rent expense is also allocated to the two departments in proportion to the space occupied by each. Thus 90 percent of the $12,000 in rent expense, or $10,800, is allocated to the clothing department, and 10 percent, or $1,200, is allocated to the shoe department, as shown in the income statement in Figure 27–5.

Utilities Expense. Again, space occupied is a logical basis to use for allocating the utilities expense. Thus $10,699 (90 percent of $11,888) is assigned to the clothing department, and $1,189 (10 percent of $11,888) is assigned to the shoe department. Both items are recorded as debits in the departmental income statement columns.

Office Salaries Expense. Office salaries expense is allocated according to the total sales made by each department. The data and computations, rounded to the nearest whole dollar, are shown below.

Department	Basis: Total Sales	Percent		Total Office Salaries Expense		Amount Allocated to Each Department
Clothing	$568,366	71.8	×	$33,600	=	$24,125
Shoes	223,230	28.2	×	33,600	=	9,475
Totals	$791,596	100.0				$33,600

Payroll Taxes Expense. Payroll taxes expense is allocated on the basis of the total salaries and wages (including allocated custodial wages and office salaries) assigned to each department. The computations made to assign the total salaries and wages to each department follow.

	Total	Clothing Department	Shoe Department
Sales salaries	$ 85,600	$49,600	$36,000
Custodial wages (allocated)	10,240	9,216	1,024
Office salaries (allocated)	33,600	24,125	9,475
Totals	$129,440	$82,941	$46,499

After the total salaries and wages are assigned, the payroll taxes are allocated to the departments, as illustrated in the following schedule.

Department	Basis: Total Salaries and Wages	Percent		Total Payroll Taxes Expense		Amount Allocated to Each Department
Clothing	$ 82,941	64.077	×	$14,357	=	$ 9,200
Shoes	46,499	35.923	×	14,357	=	5,157
Totals	$129,440	100.0				$14,357

Some companies prefer to treat payroll taxes on sales salaries as direct departmental expenses.

The procedure used by the Esquire Men's Store to allocate payroll taxes expense results in an approximation because not all salaries and wages are fully subject to payroll taxes. (Note that the percentage used has been carried to three decimal places.) If it is considered necessary to have more precise tax figures for each department, the accountant must analyze the earnings of each employee to determine the exact amount of payroll taxes on that employee's earnings. Then, by identifying the department to which the employee's earnings were charged, the precise amount of payroll tax expense applicable to each department can be determined. Many companies treat the payroll taxes on sales salaries as direct expenses and set up a departmentalized account in which to record them as they are incurred.

Other Office Expenses. At the Esquire Men's Store, postage, stationery, and a variety of other small items for office use are debited to an account called Other Office Expenses. The proportion of total sales in each department is used as the basis for allocating the $1,609 balance of Other Office Expenses. Of this amount, 71.8 percent, or $1,155, is assigned to clothing, and 28.2 percent, or $454, is assigned to shoes.

Professional Services Expense. Total sales are used as a basis for allocating the balance of Professional Services Expense, which amounts to $1,550. Of this figure, 71.8 percent, or $1,113, is assigned to the clothing department, and 28.2 percent, or $437, is assigned to the shoe department.

Taxes and Licenses. The most significant tax for the Esquire Men's Store is the property tax, which is levied on merchandise inventory and other assets. Allocation can therefore be reasonably based on the combined total value of the ending merchandise inventory and the furniture and fixtures in each of the operating departments. As you saw when insurance expense was allocated, 84.4 percent of the total asset value is in the clothing department and 15.6 percent is in the shoe department. Thus the $2,652 balance of the Taxes and Licenses account is allocated as follows: $2,238 to the clothing department and $414 to the shoe department.

Uncollectible accounts expense should be allocated on the basis of net credit sales if it is feasible to do so.

Uncollectible Accounts Expense. As a result of an aging of the accounts receivable balance on December 31, 19X4, an additional $1,338 was added to the allowance account and charged to Uncollectible Accounts Expense. The uncollectible accounts expense is to be allocated on the basis of credit sales, because there are no losses from cash sales. Preferably the allocation would be based on net credit sales, but because of the time required to determine which returns are from cash sales and which from credit sales, the accountant for Esquire Men's Store uses gross sales on account to make the allocation. An analysis of the sales journal shows that credit sales were $348,000 for the clothing department and $97,500 for the shoe department. The amount of the estimated uncollectible accounts expense that should be allocated to each department is therefore computed as follows.

Department	Basis: Credit Sales	Percent		Total Uncollectible Accounts Expense		Allocated to Each Department
Clothing	$348,600	78.1	×	$1,338	=	$1,045
Shoes	97,500	21.9	×	1,338	=	293
Totals	$446,100	100.0				$1,338

Depreciation on store furniture and fixtures may be treated as an indirect cost or as a direct departmental cost.

Depreciation Expense—Furniture and Fixtures. The assets used to compute depreciation for furniture and fixtures are identified with specific departments. Thus depreciation expense on these assets can be directly allocated. As shown earlier, the furniture and fixtures in the clothing department had an original cost of $7,200 and those in the shoe department had a cost of $2,000. Depreciation is computed at 10 percent per year, so depreciation of $720 is allocated to the clothing department and $200 is allocated to the shoe department, as shown in the income statement in Figure 27–5.

Depreciation Expense—Office Equipment. Depreciation on the office equipment is allocated according to each department's total sales—the basis used for allocating office salaries and other office expenses. The amount of depreciation on the office equipment is $430, of which 71.8 percent, or $309, is allocated to the clothing department and extended to the income statement Debit column for the clothing department, and 28.2 percent, or $121, is allocated to the shoe department.

Nondepartmentalized Expenses

Accounts that are not related to store operations, such as interest income and interest expense, are not allocated to individual departments.

Revenue and expenses that do not apply to the company's operations are not allocated to the departments. For example, interest income and interest expense are related to financing of the business, rather than to its operating activities. Generally, all items that appear under the headings Other Income and Other Expenses on the income statement are treated as nondepartmental items.

Other expense accounts for the Esquire Men's Store for 19X4, which will not be allocated to sales departments, are shown in Figure 27–4.

FIGURE 27–4
Schedule of Other Income and Other Expenses

ESQUIRE MEN'S STORE
Schedule of Other Income and Other Expenses
Year Ended December 31, 19X4

Other Income		
Miscellaneous Income		470 00
Other Expenses		
Interest Expense		987 00
Net Other Expense		517 00

SELF-REVIEW

1. Why would a company prefer to use an analysis ledger sheet for recording sales rather than using separate accounts for the sales of each department?
2. What are direct expenses?

3. How does the recording process for most direct expenses differ from that for indirect expenses?
4. Why are indirect expenses allocated to departments?
5. What is a logical basis for allocating property insurance expense to departments?

Answers to Self-Review

1. An analysis ledger sheet permits the recording of all sales in a single account rather than in separate accounts, which is more convenient.
2. Direct expenses are operating expenses that can be identified directly with individual departments.
3. Direct expenses are usually charged to individual departmental accounts at the time they are incurred. Indirect expenses must be allocated at the end of the fiscal period.
4. Indirect expenses are allocated to departments to attempt to measure profitability of each department.
5. Property insurance should logically be allocated on the basis of the total value of insured assets in each department.

PREPARING THE DEPARTMENTAL INCOME STATEMENT

OBJECTIVE 5
Prepare a departmental income statement showing the contribution margin and net income for each department.

The excess of gross profit over the direct departmental expenses is called the *contribution margin.*

The income statement of Esquire Men's Store for the year ended December 31, 19X4, is shown in Figure 27–5, page 980. Note that the statement contains several features that have not been previously encountered in this text.

First, net income is computed for each department. Second, a new intermediate income figure entitled "Contribution Margin" is introduced. **Contribution margin** is the difference between a department's gross profit on sales and its direct expenses. It is the amount that the department has earned or produced above its own direct costs. This amount is available to help meet the indirect or general expenses of running the business and to provide a net income from operations. A department that more than meets its direct expenses (or has a positive contribution margin) is contributing something toward increasing the net income of the business (or decreasing its net loss).

Departmental Net Income

The final departmental net income figure may not be appropriate for making certain managerial decisions.

There are two principal objections to using the final departmental net income figure in making business decisions, as, for example, in deciding whether a particular department that shows a net loss for the year should be eliminated. One objection to using the departmental net income figure in making such a decision is the difficulty of determining the department's fair share of indirect or general expense items. The second objection is more important: if the particular department were eliminated, many of the indirect expenses allocated to it would not be eliminated. They would have to be absorbed by the remaining departments. Actually, in making managerial decisions,

FIGURE 27–5
A Departmental Income Statement

ESQUIRE MEN'S STORE
Income Statement
Year Ended December 31, 19X4

	Clothing	Shoes	Total
Operating Revenues			
Sales	568366	223230	791596
Less Sales Returns and Allowances	9165	2918	12083
Net Sales	559201	220312	779513
Cost of Goods Sold			
Merchandise Inventory, Jan. 1, 19X4	130000	—0—	130000
Purchases	366350	144350	510700
Freight In	5470	1710	7180
Delivered Cost of Purchases	371820	146060	517880
Less: Purchases Returns and Allowances	1650	480	2130
Purchases Discounts	8699	1397	10096
Total Deductions	10349	1877	12226
Net Delivered Cost of Purchases	361471	144183	505654
Total Merchandise Available for Sale	491471	144183	635654
Less Merchandise Inventory, Dec. 31, 19X3	112000	20000	132000
Cost of Goods Sold	379471	124183	503654
Gross Profit on Sales	179730	96129	275859
Operating Expenses			
Direct Expenses			
Sales Salaries Expense	49600	36000	85600
Advertising Expense	10470	3317	13787
Store Supplies Expense	6268	2240	8508
Cash Short or Over	90	54	144
Delivery Expense	5680	2040	7720
Total Direct Expenses	72108	43651	115759
Contribution Margin	107622	52478	160100
Indirect Expenses			
Insurance Expense	5216	964	6180
Custodial Wages Expense	9216	1024	10240
Rent Expense	10800	1200	12000
Utilities Expense	10699	1189	11888
Office Salaries Expense	24125	9475	33600
Payroll Tax Expense	9200	5157	14357
Other Office Expenses	1155	454	1609
Professional Services Expense	1113	437	1550
Taxes and Licenses	2238	414	2652
Uncollectible Accounts Expense	1045	293	1338
Depr. Expense—Furn. and Fixtures	720	200	920
Depr. Expense—Office Equipment	309	121	430
Total Indirect Expenses	75836	20928	96764
Net Income from Operations	31786	31550	63336
Other Income			
Miscellaneous Income			470
Other Expense			
Interest Expense			987
Net Other Expense			517
Net Income for the Year			62819

more attention should be paid to contribution margin figures and less to net income by departments.

Contribution Margin

OBJECTIVE 6
Use a departmental income statement in making decisions such as whether to close a department.

The contribution margin for a department is often a useful figure in making managerial decisions.

As already noted, if one department is eliminated, other departments have to absorb many, if not all, of the indirect expenses without the help provided by any positive contribution margin of the department. On the other hand, if the direct expenses of a department exceed its gross profit on sales, the unit is reducing the net income of the business as a whole (or increasing its net loss). The business would then be more profitable if the department with the negative contribution margin were eliminated.

As can readily be seen, the concept of the contribution margin is important to business owners and managers because it provides them with valuable assistance in making decisions. Unfortunately, contribution margin figures are not provided in many traditional accounting reports.

PREPARING THE DEPARTMENTAL BALANCE SHEET

The balance sheet of a departmentalized firm is prepared from the Balance Sheet section of the worksheet in exactly the same manner as was shown in previous chapters.

MANAGERIAL IMPLICATIONS

It is essential for managers to know not only the total gross profit of a business but also the gross profit for each department. Departmentalized data shows managers which departments are most profitable and which are losing money or have low profit margins. Once alerted, managers can take proper steps to improve the profit picture. Department heads can then be told specifically what revenue or expense items should receive special attention.

Managers are keenly interested in the operations of each department. Departments that are less profitable may undergo policy changes or may be closed, and profitable departments may be expanded. The data shown on the departmentalized income statement helps managers to evaluate and control the operations of each unit. Similarly, managers are very much interested in prompt preparation of the balance sheet, which shows the financial condition of the business. Current statements and supporting schedules provide up-to-date information that managers need to run a company.

The contribution margin is very important in making managerial decisions. This figure is the amount by which the gross profit of a department exceeds its direct expenses and contributes toward the indirect expenses and net income from operations. Decisions to retain, eliminate, expand, or contract a segment of the business are properly based on the contribution margin analysis of the department or product involved.

Net income analysis has many shortcomings and should be used only with the greatest care in making decisions. The net income figure for a department is, at best, an estimate. Furthermore, managers must consider that many of the indirect expenses would not be eliminated by the decision to curtail or discontinue the operations of a department.

SELF-REVIEW

1. What two ways may be used to record departmental data about the gross profit items in the general ledger?
2. How do direct departmental expenses differ from indirect expenses?
3. How does the accountant choose a basis for allocating indirect expenses to sales departments?
4. How is a department's contribution margin computed?
5. Give two reasons why it may be improper to use departmental net income to make a decision about terminating a department's operations.

Answers to Self-Review

1. A separate general ledger account—for example, a Sales account—may be maintained for each department. Alternatively, a single general ledger account—for example, a single Sales account—may be maintained, but with a separate record of the amount for each department.
2. Direct expenses are those that can be directly related to a specific department at the time the expenses are incurred. Indirect expenses cannot be directly related to a specific department but must be allocated to departments on some logical basis.
3. In allocating indirect expenses, the accountant seeks to find some basis that seems to be correlated with the amount of expense and that can be measured for each department.
4. A department's contribution margin is computed by subtracting the department's direct expenses from its gross profit.
5. Departmental net income may be inappropriate as a basis for making some business decisions because it reflects indirect expenses, which are imprecisely allocated. Also, a large part of indirect expenses may continue without change if a department is discontinued.

CHAPTER 27

Review and Applications

CHAPTER SUMMARY

The basic financial statements summarize the financial operations and position of the business as a whole. They often do not provide all of the accounting information necessary in running a business. Instead, more information is needed about individual segments and activities of the business. Information about individual segments, activities, and products is provided by managerial accounting.

One common type of managerial information is data about the operating centers of a business. Some operating centers are called profit centers because they generate both revenues and expenses. Other operating centers are called cost centers because they incur expenses in providing services but do not produce revenues.

In many retail stores, revenue and cost centers are referred to as departments. When a business becomes departmentalized, separate accounts for sales, inventory, and other elements of the cost of goods sold are established because separate information is needed for each department. This may be done by setting up departmental accounts in the ledger or by using analysis ledger account sheets having separate columns for each department. The sales journal, voucher register, and other records of original entry must also be arranged to gather transaction data by departments.

In addition, separate accounts or departmental analysis ledger sheets may be set up for those expenses that can be assigned directly to a specific department. Other expenses must be allocated to the departments on some predetermined basis at the end of the accounting period. Expenses that are allocated on a logical basis closely related to use are sometimes referred to as semidirect expenses. Those expenses that must be allocated on a more arbitrary basis are called indirect expenses. Many accountants refer to both type of expenses as indirect expenses.

A departmental income statement is prepared. The income statement should show the contribution margin of each department as well as a final net income figure after allocation of all expenses. The contribution margin for a department is especially helpful in making managerial decisions about the department.

GLOSSARY OF NEW TERMS

Contribution margin (p. 979) The difference between a department's gross profit on sales and its direct operating expenses

Cost center (p. 967) A business segment that incurs costs but does not produce revenue

Direct expenses (p. 972) Operating expenses that can be specifically identified with an individual department

Indirect expenses (p. 973) Operating expenses that cannot be readily related to activity within an individual department

Managerial accounting (p. 967) An emphasis in accounting that provides financial information about individual segments, activities, or products of a business

Profit center (p. 967) A business segment that produces revenue

Responsibility accounting (p. 968) An emphasis in accounting that provides information for evaluating each segment of a business and pinpointing responsibility

Semidirect expenses (p. 973) Expenses that cannot be directly assigned to an individual department but can be closely related to that department's operations on some logical basis

Transfer price (p. 968) The price at which one business segment's goods are transferred to another segment of the business

REVIEW QUESTIONS

1. How does managerial accounting differ from financial accounting?
2. Why does managerial accounting focus on the future?
3. What is responsibility accounting?
4. Is departmental accounting a form of responsibility accounting? Explain.
5. Why would a retail operation such as a clothing store departmentalize its records?
6. What is the contribution margin?
7. How does a departmentalized income statement differ from one that is not departmentalized?
8. The Esquire Men's Store, which was discussed in this chapter, allocates payroll tax expense on the basis of the total payroll for each department. What is the weakness of this method? What is its advantage?
9. Explain the difference between semidirect and indirect expenses.
10. Suggest a logical basis for allocating each of the following indirect expenses.
    a. Janitorial wages
    b. Heating and lighting
    c. Repairs to office equipment
    d. General institutional advertising
11. Why is interest expense not allocated to departments?

MANAGERIAL FOCUS

1. Of what value in managerial control is the identification of purchases returns and allowances by department?

2. If one department consistently has a comparatively large amount of cash short in its operations, what management action might be appropriate?
3. Why is it better for managers to use contribution margin analysis rather than net income analysis when deciding whether to retain, expand, or contract operations?
4. How does a firm's accountant determine the reasonable basis to be used in allocating a specific indirect expense? Should management be concerned about the basis used?
5. The management of a store with three sales departments plans to install a bonus system for department managers. Do you think the bonus system should be based on each department's contribution margin or on the department's net income after allocating all administrative expenses? Explain.

EXERCISES

Information for Exercises 27–1 through 27–4. Selected financial data, as of December 31, 19X3, for Today's Fashions, a retail store, follows.

Credit sales
- Women's clothing, $320,000
- Men's clothing, $484,000

Total sales
- Women's clothing, $400,000
- Men's clothing, $600,000

Sales returns and allowances
- Women's clothing
  - Credit sales, $3,200
  - Cash sales, $600
- Men's clothing
  - Credit sales, $1,800
  - Cash sales, $340

Floor space occupied
- Women's clothing, 8,200 sq ft
- Men's clothing, 1,800 sq ft

Book value of inventory and equipment
- Women's clothing, $120,000
- Men's clothing, $60,000

EXERCISE 27–1
(Obj. 4)
Tutorial

Computing the amount of indirect expense to be allocated to a department. Today's Fashions' insurance expense for the year totaled $4,500 and is to be allocated on the basis of the book value of the inventory and equipment in each department. Compute the amount to be allocated to each department.

EXERCISE 27–2
(Obj. 4)
Tutorial

Computing the amount of indirect expense to be allocated to a department. The total custodial expense for the year at Today's Fashions was $9,200. Compute the amount to be allocated to each department, using floor space occupied as the basis for the allocation.

EXERCISE 27–3 (Obj. 4)

Tutorial

Computing the amount of indirect expense to be allocated to a department. The total office expense for the year at Today's Fashions was $61,000. Compute the amount to be allocated to each department, using total sales as the basis for the allocation.

EXERCISE 27–4 (Obj. 4)

Tutorial

Computing the amount of indirect expense to be allocated to a department. The uncollectible accounts expense at Today's Fashions is estimated to be 1/2 of 1 percent of net credit sales. Compute the amount to be allocated to each department.

EXERCISE 27–5 (Obj. 5)

Preparing a departmental income statement showing contribution margin and net income for each department. Data related to the income and expenses of Bigun Company for the year ending December 31, 19X4, are shown below.

Allocated indirect expenses	
Jewelry department	$23,000
China department	16,000
Interest income	800
Gross profit	
Jewelry department	98,000
China department	74,000
Direct expenses	
Jewelry department	77,000
China department	40,000

Prepare a partial departmental income statement showing the contribution margin and net income of each department.

EXERCISE 27–6 (Obj. 6)

Using departmental income statements in making decisions. Data from the departmental income statement of the Thorp Company for the year ended December 31, 19X4, is given below. Assuming that a department's direct expenses can be eliminated if it is closed, what factors should management consider when deciding whether to close department 1?

	Dept. 1	Dept. 2	Total
Net sales	$398,000	$600,000	$998,000
Cost of goods sold	250,000	350,000	600,000
Gross profit on sales	$148,000	$250,000	$398,000
Direct expenses	120,000	190,000	310,000
Contribution margin	$ 28,000	$ 60,000	$ 88,000
Indirect expenses	50,000	20,000	70,000
Net income (or loss)	$ (22,000)	$ 40,000	$ 18,000

EXERCISE 27–7 (Obj. 5)

Preparing a departmental income statement showing contribution margin and net income of departments. Using the data given in Exercise 27–6, prepare an income statement for the company if department 1 is closed.

EXERCISE 27–8 (Obj. 6) **Using a departmental income statement in making decisions.** Using the data given in Exercise 27–6, would you recommend closing department 1? Why or why not?

PROBLEMS

PROBLEM SET A

PROBLEM 27–1A (Obj. 4, 5) **Allocating indirect expenses to departments and preparing a departmental income statement.** Selected information from the adjusted trial balance of the Mayfair Shoe Closet as of December 31, 19X3, is shown below.

Merchandise Inventory, Jan. 1		
Department A	$ 50,000	
Department B	10,000	$ 60,000
Merchandise Inventory, Dec. 31		
Department A	48,000	
Department B	10,500	58,500
Sales		
Department A	240,000	
Department B	274,618	514,618
Sales Returns and Allowances		
Department A	1,400	
Department B	1,200	2,600
Merchandise Purchases		
Department A	161,420	
Department B	163,000	324,420
Freight In		
Department A	12,450	
Department B	3,650	16,100
Purchases Returns and Allowances		
Department A	–0–	
Department B	1,500	1,500
Sales Salaries Expense		
Department A	24,000	
Department B	25,600	49,600
Advertising Expense		
Department A	10,000	
Department B	8,000	18,000
Store Supplies Expense		
Department A	3,832	
Department B	1,606	5,438
Cash Short or Over		
Department A	40	
Department B	80	120
Insurance Expense		3,000
Custodial Wages Expense		6,500
Rent Expense		7,500

Utilities Expense	3,600
Office Salaries Expense	11,800
Payroll Taxes Expense	6,794
Other Office Expenses	1,400
Uncollectible Accounts Expense	2,570
Depr. Expense—Furniture and Fixtures	1,550
Depr. Expense—Office Equipment	320
Interest Income	96
Interest Expense	240

Instructions

Prepare a departmental income statement for the year ended December 31, 19X3. The bases for allocating indirect expenses are given below. (*Note:* Because allocations are not precise, round each allocated amount to the nearest whole dollar.) Show all allocations in a neat and orderly form.

1. Insurance expense: in proportion to the total of the furniture and fixtures (the gross assets before depreciation) and the ending inventory in the departments. These totals are as follows.

Department A	$59,200
Department B	14,800
Total	$74,000

2. Custodial wages expense, rent expense, and utilities expense: on the basis of floor space occupied, as follows.

Department A	1,200 square feet
Department B	400 square feet
Total	1,600 square feet

3. Office salaries expense, other office expenses, and depreciation expense for office equipment: on the basis of the gross sales in each department.
4. Uncollectible accounts expense: on the basis of net sales in each department.
5. Payroll taxes expense: on the basis of the total salaries and wages (including allocated salaries and wages) of each department.
6. Depreciation expense for furniture and fixtures: in proportion to cost of furniture and fixtures in each department. These costs are as follows.

Department A	$11,200
Department B	4,300

PROBLEM 27–2A (Obj. 5, 6)

Preparing a departmental income statement and using the statement in making a business decision. Lola's Greenhouse sells plants, fertilizers, and other garden products. The store has three departments: green products, chemicals, and implements. Certain information about the revenues and expenses of the departments for the year ended December 31, 19Y3, is given below. Indirect expenses have been allocated on bases similar to those discussed and illustrated in the text.

	Green Products	Chemicals	Implements
Allocated indirect expenses	$12,000	$20,000	$10,000
Beginning merchandise inventory	8,000	22,000	22,000
Direct expenses	17,000	12,000	18,000
Ending merchandise inventory	6,000	24,000	8,200
Purchases	53,000	70,000	35,000
Purchases returns and allowances	500	100	100
Sales	99,400	95,000	60,000
Sales returns and allowances	1,500	400	400

Instructions

1. Prepare a departmental income statement showing the contribution margin and the net profit for each department.
2. Based solely on accounting information, would you recommend that any departments be closed? Explain.
3. What information, other than accounting data, would you suggest the owners consider in deciding whether to close any departments?

PROBLEM SET B

PROBLEM 27–1B
(Obj. 4, 5)

Allocating indirect expenses and preparing a departmental income statement. Selected information from the adjusted trial balance of the Midway Art Supply Center as of December 31, 19X3, is shown below.

Merchandise Inventory, Jan. 1		
Department A	$ 75,000	
Department B	15,000	$ 90,000
Merchandise Inventory, Dec. 31		
Department A	72,000	
Department B	15,750	87,750
Sales		
Department A	360,000	
Department B	411,927	771,927
Sales Returns and Allowances		
Department A	1,600	
Department B	1,300	2,900
Purchases		
Department A	242,130	
Department B	244,500	486,630
Freight In		
Department A	18,675	
Department B	5,475	24,150
Purchases Returns and Allowances		
Department A	-0-	
Department B	2,250	2,250
Sales Salaries Expense		
Department A	36,000	
Department B	38,400	74,400

Advertising Expense		
Department A	15,000	
Department B	12,000	27,000
Store Supplies Expense		
Department A	5,748	
Department B	2,409	8,157
Cash Short or Over		
Department A	60	
Department B	120	180
Insurance Expense		4,500
Janitorial Services Expense		9,750
Rent Expense		11,250
Utilities Expense		5,400
Office Salaries Expense		17,700
Payroll Taxes Expense		10,191
Other Office Expenses		2,100
Uncollectible Accounts Expense		1,550
Depr. Expense—Furniture and Fixtures		2,325
Depr. Expense—Office Equipment		480
Interest Income		360

Instructions Prepare a departmental income statement for the year ended December 31, 19X3. The bases for allocating indirect expenses are given below. (*Note:* Because allocations are not precise, round each allocated amount to the nearest whole dollar.) Show all allocations in a neat and orderly form.

1. Insurance expense: in proportion to the total of the furniture and fixtures (the gross assets before depreciation) and the ending inventory in the departments. These totals are as follows.

Department A	$ 90,000
Department B	22,500
Total	$112,500

2. Janitorial services expense, rent expense, and utilities expense: on the basis of floor space occupied, as follows.

Department A	1,600 square feet
Department B	800 square feet
Total	2,400 square feet

3. Office salaries expense, other office expenses, and depreciation expense for office equipment: on the basis of the gross sales in each department.
4. Uncollectible accounts expense: on the basis of net sales in each department.
5. Payroll taxes expense: on the basis of the total salaries and wages (including allocated salaries and wages) of each department.

6. Depreciation expense for furniture and fixtures: in proportion to cost of furniture and fixtures in each department. These costs are as follows.

Clothing	$16,800
Shoes	6,450

PROBLEM 27–2B
(Obj. 5, 6)

Preparing a departmental income statement and using the statement in making a business decision. Tram Nieu's College Supply has three departments: school supplies, books, and casual clothing, such as T-shirts and warm-up suits. Certain information about the revenues and expenses of the departments for the month ending November 30, 19X3, is given below. Indirect expenses have been allocated on bases similar to those discussed and illustrated in the text.

	School Supplies	Books	Clothing
Allocated indirect expenses	$ 5,000	$ 3,000	$ 8,000
Beginning merchandise inventory	15,000	44,000	13,200
Direct expenses	8,000	12,000	3,000
Ending merchandise inventory	9,000	48,000	8,200
Purchases	13,000	70,000	5,000
Purchases returns and allowances	100	700	–0–
Sales	26,400	95,000	20,000
Sales returns and allowances	1,500	400	100

Instructions

1. Prepare a departmental income statement showing the contribution margin and the net profit for each department.
2. Based solely on accounting information, would you recommend that any departments be closed? Explain.
3. What information, other than accounting data, would you suggest the owners consider in deciding whether to close any departments?

CHALLENGE PROBLEM

Meg's Handicraft Outlet Store has three sales departments: stitchery, carvings, and art. The store's condensed income statement for the year ended December 31, 19X8, is shown below.

The proprietor has asked her auditor whether she should close the art department and the carvings department. In the opinion of both the proprietor and the auditor, if the art department were discontinued, it might be possible to reduce the total indirect expenses to $9,500 and if the carvings department were closed, it might be possible to reduce indirect expenses by $1,500. In the opinion of the proprietor, if the art department were discontinued, sales in the stitchery department would decrease—probably by as much as $5,000. A decrease of $5,000 in sales in the stitchery department

MEG'S HANDICRAFT OUTLET STORE
Condensed Income Statement
Year Ended December 31, 19X8

	Stitchery	*Carvings*	*Art*
Sales	40000	24000	16000
Cost of Goods Sold	20000	15000	11000
Gross Profit	20000	9000	5000
Operating Expenses			
Direct Expenses	8000	4000	4000
Indirect Expenses	5000	3000	2000
Total Operating Expenses	13000	7000	6000
Net Profit	7000	2000	(1000)

would probably result in a reduction of that department's direct expenses by $1,000. The proprietor also thinks that closing the art department would have no effect on the sales of carvings and that closing the carvings department would have no effect on sales of either stitchery or art.

Instructions

1. Based on the preceding information, what would the estimated total profit or loss be if the art department were closed?
2. What would the estimated total profit or loss be if the carvings department were closed?
3. What advice would you give the proprietor?

CRITICAL THINKING PROBLEM

At a recent staff meeting of the Van Gogh Art Supply Store, the question of how expenses are allocated to each department was raised. Since year-end bonuses are awarded to the managers on the basis of departmental net income from operations, the discussion was lively.

Susan Connor, manager of the framing department, said that each department should be charged only with the expenses directly related to the department. She indicated that while managers can influence the sales and direct expenses in their departments, they have little control over many of the indirect expenses such as depreciation, office salaries, and taxes.

Bill Yeakel, manager of the fine art department, argued that all expenses—direct and indirect—should be allocated. "After all," he said, "all the revenue is allocated to each department, so why not allocate all the expenses? The store could not operate if it did not incur the indirect expenses." He also stated that many of the indirect expenses, such as insurance and cleaning services, could be allocated on a meaningful basis.

Evaluate these comments.

CHAPTER

28 Accounting for Manufacturing Activities

OBJECTIVES

1. Prepare a statement of cost of goods manufactured.
2. Explain the basic components of manufacturing cost.
3. Prepare an income statement for a manufacturing business.
4. Prepare a balance sheet for a manufacturing business.
5. Prepare a worksheet for a manufacturing business.
6. Record the end-of-period adjusting entries for a manufacturing business.
7. Record closing entries for a manufacturing business.
8. Record reversing entries for a manufacturing business.
9. Define the accounting terms new to this chapter.

Previous chapters explained and illustrated the accounting principles and procedures used by businesses engaged in the sale of services and merchandise. In those chapters it was assumed that the merchandising firms purchased their inventories from manufacturers or wholesalers. If a business engages in manufacturing as well as selling activities, additional accounts are needed to classify the cost elements involved in manufacturing operations.

In this chapter you will learn about the basic components of manufacturing cost and the accounts used to record these components. You will also see how the accounts related to manufacturing cost are presented in the statement of cost of goods manufactured. Then the end-of-period procedures for manufacturing businesses are explained and illustrated.

NEW TERMS

Direct labor ▪ Direct materials ▪ Indirect labor ▪ Indirect materials and supplies ▪ Manufacturing overhead ▪ Raw materials ▪ Statement of cost of goods manufactured ▪ Work in process

ACCOUNTING FOR MANUFACTURING COSTS

As you have seen, a merchandising business purchases merchandise to be resold in the same condition and form, but at a profit. On the other hand, a manufacturing company purchases raw materials and converts these materials into finished goods to be sold at a profit. This difference is reflected in the income statement of the two types of businesses. You can see the similarity and difference by examining the two partial income statements that follow.

XYZ MERCHANDISING COMPANY
Partial Income Statement
Year Ended December 31, 19X3

Revenue		
Sales (net)		*492 000 00*
Cost of Merchandise Sold		
Merchandise Inventory, Jan. 1	*28 000 00*	
Purchases (net)	*287 000 00*	
Merchandise Available for Sale	*315 000 00*	
Less Merchandise Inventory, Dec. 31	*26 000 00*	
Cost of Merchandise Sold		*289 000 00*
Gross Profit on Sales		*203 000 00*

JIMINEZ MANUFACTURING CORPORATION
Partial Income Statement
Year Ended December 31, 19X3

Revenue		
Sales (net)		*492 000 00*
Cost of Goods Sold		
Finished Goods Inventory, Jan. 1	*28 000 00*	
Cost of Goods Manufactured	*287 000 00*	
Total Goods Available for Sale	*315 000 00*	
Less Finished Goods Inventory, Dec. 31	*26 000 00*	
Cost of Goods Sold		*289 000 00*
Gross Profit on Sales		*203 000 00*

In the income statement of a manufacturing company, the line item "Cost of Goods Manufactured" replaces "Purchases."

Note that the major difference in the two partial statements is that for a manufacturing business "Cost of Goods Manufactured" replaces "Purchases."

Let's look more closely at the components that make up the cost of goods manufactured in the financial statements of a manufacturing concern. We will examine the accounts and financial statements of the Jiminez Manufacturing Corporation, which specializes in the production of wooden tables. Jiminez's manufacturing process therefore involves the acquisition and use of raw materials such as lumber, nails, glue, paint, and varnish. These materials are cut, shaped, assembled, painted, and polished in the factory, finally emerging as finished products ready for sale.

The Statement of Cost of Goods Manufactured

OBJECTIVE 1
Prepare a statement of cost of goods manufactured.

Periodically the financial data related to manufacturing operations are summarized in a financial report called a **statement of cost of goods manufactured,** which supports the Cost of Goods Sold figure shown on the income statement. The Jiminez Manufacturing Corporation's statement of cost of goods manufactured for the year ended December 31, 19X3, is shown in Figure 28–1.

FIGURE 28–1
A Statement of Cost of Goods Manufactured

JIMINEZ MANUFACTURING CORPORATION
Statement of Cost of Goods Manufactured
Year Ended December 31, 19X3

Work in Process Inventory, Jan. 1			(5) 10,500.00
Raw Materials			
Raw Materials Inventory, Jan. 1		26,000.00	
Materials Purchases	144,000.00		
Less Purchases Discounts	(3,000.00)		
Net Purchases		141,000.00	
Total Materials Available		167,000.00	
Less Raw Materials Inventory, Dec. 31		25,000.00	
Raw Materials Used		(1) 142,000.00	
Direct Labor		(2) 81,000.00	
Manufacturing Overhead			
Indirect Labor	16,763.00		
Payroll Taxes—Factory	12,159.00		
Utilities—Factory	8,558.00		
Repairs and Maintenance—Factory	6,815.00		
Indirect Materials and Supplies	6,808.00		
Depreciation—Factory Building	750.00		
Depreciation—Factory Equipment	2,400.00		
Insurance—Factory	4,530.00		
Property Taxes—Factory	6,217.00		
Total Manufacturing Overhead		(3) 65,000.00	
Total Manufacturing Cost			(4) 288,000.00
Total Work in Process for Year			298,500.00
Less Work in Process Inventory, Dec. 31			(6) 11,500.00
Cost of Goods Manufactured			(7) 287,000.00

OBJECTIVE 2
Explain the basic components of manufacturing cost.

The Components of Manufacturing Costs

In the statement of cost of goods manufactured (Figure 28–1) the three essential components of manufacturing cost (**4**) are the raw materials used (**1**), the direct labor (**2**), and the manufacturing overhead (**3**). Let's now examine each category of manufacturing cost.

Raw Materials. A major component of manufacturing cost is **raw materials**—the cost of materials placed into production. As you have seen, presentation of data about the cost of raw materials in the Raw Materials section of the statement of cost of goods manufactured is much like the presentation previously used in the Cost of Goods Sold section of the income statement for a merchandising business. The computation starts with the beginning inventory of raw materials, $26,000. Then the amount of net purchases of raw materials, $141,000, is determined by subtracting purchases discounts of $3,000 from gross purchases of $144,000. The next step is to add the beginning inventory of raw materials and the net purchases to find the total materials available, $167,000. Finally, the ending inventory, $25,000, is subtracted to determine the raw materials used, $142,000. Although the routine looks familiar, there are some important points of difference and certain of the items on the statement need an explanation.

Direct materials are all items that go into a product and become part of it.

Indirect materials are items that are used in manufacturing a product but do not become part of the product.

1. The beginning and ending inventories consist of raw materials rather than the merchandise that would be found in the inventory of a merchandising firm.
2. All references to materials in this section (raw materials, materials purchases, and materials available) are related to direct materials only. **Direct materials** are all the items that go into a product and become part of it. For example, the direct materials in a table would include the wood, hardware, glue, and paint or varnish.
3. Other materials such as sandpaper and steel wool may be used in the work on the products being manufactured, but these do not become part of the product. Therefore, they are called **indirect materials and supplies,** and the costs of these items used are listed in the Manufacturing Overhead section of the statement. Cleaning materials, lubricants, and other supplies used in general factory operations and maintenance are also treated as indirect materials and supplies on the statement of cost of goods manufactured. Some firms treat insignificant direct materials, such as glue, as though they were indirect materials.

Direct labor costs are the costs of personnel who work directly on the product being manufactured.

Direct Labor. On the statement of cost of goods manufactured, direct labor appears as a single total, $81,000. This figure is obtained from the Direct Labor account, based upon payroll records and procedures similar to those described in Chapters 10 and 11. **Direct labor** costs are the costs of personnel who work directly on the product as it is being manufactured. In the factory operated by the Jiminez Manufacturing Corporation, such personnel would include workers who saw and shape the lumber, assemble the pieces into tables, and finish or paint them.

All labor used in the manufacturing process that is not direct labor is classified as indirect labor.

All other factory labor is listed as **indirect labor** in the Manufacturing Overhead section of the statement. Indirect labor includes the wages of personnel such as the following:

1. Workers who transport materials from one place to another or are employed in the raw materials storeroom
2. Repair and maintenance workers and janitorial workers
3. Supervisors who see that the work is done properly but do not work directly on the product

Manufacturing overhead is composed of all manufacturing costs other than direct materials and direct labor.

Manufacturing Overhead. **Manufacturing overhead** includes all the costs of manufacturing operations that are not classified as direct materials or direct labor. In addition to indirect materials and supplies and indirect labor, manufacturing overhead might include utilities, depreciation of factory buildings and equipment, repair and maintenance of buildings and equipment, insurance, property taxes, and payroll taxes on factory wages. The Manufacturing Overhead section of Jiminez's statement of cost of goods manufactured contains a listing of typical overhead costs.

Products that have been started in the production process but are not completed are referred to as work in process.

Work in Process

The total manufacturing cost—$288,000, shown as item **(4)** on the statement of cost of goods manufactured (Figure 28–1)—includes all raw materials used, all direct labor costs incurred, and all manufacturing overhead applicable to the current production period. However, this figure does not represent the total cost of goods manufactured because it does not reflect the following two essential facts.

1. Not all products finished during the period are started from raw materials during the period. There is usually a carryover of partially completed units from the previous period. The partially completed units are referred to as **work in process.** The beginning inventory of work in process of Jiminez Corporation, item **(5)** on the statement of cost of goods manufactured illustrated in Figure 28–1, had a cost of $10,500.
2. Not all products that enter the manufacturing process during the period are fully completed at the end of the period. At the end of the period, there is usually an ending inventory of work in process. An estimate is made of the costs of raw materials, direct labor, and manufacturing overhead that apply to the work in process. On the statement of cost of goods manufactured, the $11,500 estimated cost of the work in process inventory at the end of the period, item **(6)**, is subtracted from the total of the beginning work in process and the costs added during the current period. The balance, $287,000, shown as item **(7)** on the statement (Figure 28–1), is the cost of all goods on which manufacturing was completed during the period.

The Income Statement for a Manufacturing Concern

OBJECTIVE 3

Prepare an income statement for a manufacturing business.

The cost of goods sold may differ from the cost of goods manufactured because of beginning and ending inventories of finished goods.

As you saw earlier in this chapter, the income statement for a manufacturing concern is almost identical to that for a merchandising business. The major difference is that on the income statement of a manufacturing concern the heading "Cost of Goods Manufactured" replaces "Purchases." Thus the cost of goods manufactured that is explained in detail in the statement of cost of goods manufactured becomes, in turn, one of the key figures required in the Cost of Goods Sold section of the income statement. This amount, $287,000, is shown on the income statement in Figure 28–2.

The cost of goods sold is not the same as the cost of goods manufactured because two additional facts must be taken into account in computing the former.

1. Not all finished products sold are actually made during the period. There is usually a carryover of finished stock from the previous period (the beginning inventory of finished goods).
2. Not all products made during the period are actually sold during the period (the ending inventory of finished goods).

At the end of each accounting period, an inventory of the finished goods on hand is taken. In the income statement shown in Figure 28–2, the cost of goods manufactured, $287,000, is added to the

FIGURE 28–2
Income Statement for a Manufacturing Concern

JIMINEZ MANUFACTURING CORPORATION
Income Statement
Year Ended December 31, 19X3

Revenue		
Sales		*495 0 0 0 00*
Less Sales Returns and Allowances		*3 0 0 0 00*
Net Sales		*492 0 0 0 00*
Cost of Goods Sold		
Finished Goods Inventory, Jan. 1	*28 0 0 0 00*	
Cost of Goods Manufactured	*287 0 0 0 00*	
Total Goods Available for Sale	*315 0 0 0 00*	
Less Finished Goods Inventory, Dec. 31	*26 0 0 0 00*	
Cost of Goods Sold		*289 0 0 0 00*
Gross Profit on Sales		*203 0 0 0 00*
Operating Expenses		
Selling Expenses (Control)	*85 0 0 0 00*	
Administrative Expenses (Control)	*88 0 0 0 00*	
Total Operating Expenses		*173 0 0 0 00*
Net Income Before Income Taxes		*30 0 0 0 00*
Income Tax Expense		*4 5 0 0 00*
Net Income After Income Taxes		*25 5 0 0 00*

beginning inventory, $28,000, to obtain the total finished goods available for sale, $315,000. Then the ending inventory, $26,000, is subtracted, and the difference (which has previously been used to fill customers' orders) represents the cost of goods sold, $289,000.

The income statement for Jiminez is typical of those prepared for manufacturing businesses. For the sake of simplicity, in this income statement the details of selling expenses and administrative expenses are not given. Instead, Selling Expenses Control and Administrative Expenses Control accounts have been used.

The Balance Sheet for a Manufacturing Concern

OBJECTIVE 4

Prepare a balance sheet for a manufacturing business.

The balance sheet of a manufacturing business contains three inventory accounts: raw materials, work in process, and finished goods.

The balance sheet for a manufacturing business differs little from a balance sheet prepared for a merchandising business. The only new accounts on the balance sheet of Jiminez Manufacturing Corporation, shown in Figure 28–3, are the inventory accounts: Raw Materials Inventory, Work in Process Inventory, and Finished Goods Inventory. These accounts replace the merchandise inventory account of a merchandising business.

SELF-REVIEW

1. What are direct materials?
2. What are indirect materials?
3. What is direct labor cost?
4. What is meant by work in process?
5. How does the cost of goods manufactured relate to the income statement?

Answers to Self-Review

1. Direct materials are materials that go into the manufacture of the finished product and become a part of it.
2. Indirect materials are those materials that are used in the manufacturing process but do not become a part of the finished product.
3. Direct labor cost is the cost of those employees who are working directly on the product being manufactured.
4. Work in process represents items that have been started into production but are not yet completed.
5. The cost of goods manufactured becomes a part of the Total Goods Available for Sale in the income statement.

FIGURE 28–3
Balance Sheet for a Manufacturing Concern

JIMINEZ MANUFACTURING CORPORATION
Balance Sheet
December 31, 19X3

Assets			
Current Assets			
Cash			41 000 00
Accounts Receivable		55 300 00	
Less Allowance for Doubtful Accounts		1 100 00	54 200 00
Inventories			
Raw Materials		25 000 00	
Work in Process		11 000 00	
Finished Goods		26 000 00	62 000 00
Prepaid Expenses			
Prepaid Insurance		1 800 00	
Supplies on Hand		800 00	2 600 00
Total Current Assets			159 800 00
Property, Plant, and Equipment			
Land		7 450 00	
Factory Building	30 500 00		
Less Accumulated Depreciation	2 750 00	27 750 00	
Factory Equipment	38 500 00		
Less Accumulated Depreciation	7 700 00	30 800 00	
Office Equipment	18 000 00		
Less Accumulated Depreciation	8 000 00	10 000 00	
Total Property, Plant, and Equipment			76 000 00
Total Assets			235 800 00
Liabilities and Stockholders' Equity			
Current Liabilities			
Accounts Payable			43 600 00
Salaries and Wages Payable			1 000 00
Estimated Income Taxes Payable			700 00
Social Security Taxes Payable			800 00
Medicare Tax Payable			100 00
Employee Income Tax Payable			700 00
Total Liabilities			46 900 00
Stockholders' Equity			
Common Stock (no-par value, stated value $50; 10,000 shares authorized)			
At Stated Value (2,000 shares issued)	100 000 00		
Paid-in Capital in Excess of Stated Value	23 000 00		
Total Paid-in Capital		123 000 00	
Retained Earnings		65 900 00	
Total Stockholders' Equity			188 900 00
Total Liabilities and Stockholders' Equity			235 800 00

THE ACCOUNTING CYCLE FOR A MANUFACTURING BUSINESS

The financial statements presented in Figures 28–1 through 28–3 reflect the end results of the accounting cycle for a manufacturing concern. We have not yet discussed the other steps in the manufacturing company's accounting cycle. The steps in that accounting cycle are exactly the same as those in the cycle for a merchandising concern (discussed in Chapter 13).

1. Transactions are analyzed.
2. The data about transactions are journalized.
3. The entries are posted from the journals to the ledger accounts.
4. A trial balance is taken and a worksheet is completed.
5. Financial statements are prepared.
6. Adjusting entries are journalized and posted.
7. Closing entries are journalized and posted.
8. A postclosing trial balance is prepared.
9. Reversing entries are journalized and posted.
10. Financial information is interpreted.

Although the accounts used by a manufacturing business differ slightly, the first three steps in the cycle are exactly like those of any other business. However, the manufacturing worksheet does differ.

To facilitate preparation of the statement of cost of goods manufactured, the worksheet has special columns for items that appear on the statement.

You have seen that a new financial statement, a statement of cost of goods manufactured, is prepared for manufacturing operations. The worksheet for a manufacturing business must be constructed to facilitate preparation of the statement of cost of goods manufactured. Thus an additional pair of columns in which to assemble the figures needed for the statement of cost of goods manufactured is added to the worksheet. Refer to Figure 28–4 to see the arrangement of the columns as we go through the completion of the worksheet for Jiminez Manufacturing Corporation.

Completing the Worksheet

OBJECTIVE 5

Prepare a worksheet for a manufacturing business.

At the end of the accounting period, after all transactions have been journalized and posted and a trial balance taken, the worksheet must be completed. The first step is to enter the trial balance in the first two money columns of the worksheet.

The usual practice is to enter all the general ledger accounts in the trial balance on the worksheet.

Entering the Trial Balance on the Worksheet

When the original trial balance is entered on the worksheet, all the general ledger accounts, except the summary accounts, are normally listed. In this way, accounts that have no balances will be in the proper order when the adjustments are recorded later.

Note that there are several new accounts that do not appear in the trial balance of a merchandising business. These accounts are unique to manufacturing activities.

1. The three inventory accounts: Raw Materials Inventory, Work in Process Inventory, and Finished Goods Inventory

FIGURE 28–4
The Worksheet for a Manufacturing Concern

JIMINEZ MANUFACTURING COMPANY
Worksheet
Year Ended December 31, 19X3

	ACCOUNT NAME	TRIAL BALANCE		ADJUSTMENTS		ADJUSTED TRIAL BALANCE	
		DEBIT	CREDIT	DEBIT	CREDIT	DEBIT	CREDIT
1	Cash	41 000 00				41 000 00	
2	Accounts Receivable	55 300 00				55 300 00	
3	Allow. for Doubtful						
4	Accounts		116 00		(g) 984 00		1 100 00
5	Raw Materials Inv.	26 000 00		(b) 25 000 00	(a) 26 000 00	25 000 00	
6	Work in Process Inv.	10 000 00		(d) 11 000 00	(c) 10 000 00	11 000 00	
7	Finished Goods Inv.	28 000 00		(f) 26 000 00	(e) 28 000 00	26 000 00	
8	Prepaid Insurance	3 700 00			(h) 1 900 00	1 800 00	
9	Supplies on Hand			(i) 800 00		800 00	
10	Land	7 450 00				7 450 00	
11	Factory Building	30 500 00				30 500 00	
12	Accum. Depr.—Bldg.		2 000 00		(j) 750 00		2 750 00
13	Factory Equipment	38 500 00				38 500 00	
14	Acc. Depr.—F. Equip.		5 300 00		(j) 2 400 00		7 700 00
15	Office Equipment	18 000 00				18 000 00	
16	Acc. Depr.—O. Equip.		7 000 00		(j) 1 000 00		8 000 00
17	Accounts Payable		43 600 00				43 600 00
18	Sal. and Wages Pay.				(k) 1 000 00		1 000 00
19	Income Tax Payable				(m) 700 00		700 00
20	Social Sec. Tax Pay.		735 00		(l) 65 00		800 00
21	Medicare Tax Pay.		85 00		(l) 15 00		100 00
22	Emp. Inc. Tax Pay.		700 00				700 00
23	Com. Stock, No Par		100 000 00				100 000 00
24	Paid-in Capital in						
25	Ex. of Stated Value		23 000 00				23 000 00
26	Retained Earnings		40 400 00				40 400 00
27	Sales		495 000 00				495 000 00
28	Sales Ret. & Allow.	3 000 00				3 000 00	
29	Materials Purchases	144 000 00				144 000 00	
30	Purchases Discounts		3 000 00				3 000 00
31	Direct Labor	80 120 00		(k) 880 00		81 000 00	
32	Indirect Labor	16 643 00		(k) 120 00		16 763 00	
33	Payroll Taxes—Fact.	12 079 00		(l) 80 00		12 159 00	
34	Utilities—Factory	8 558 00				8 558 00	
35	Rep. & Maint.—Fact.	6 815 00				6 815 00	
36	Indirect Mat. & Sup.	7 608 00			(i) 800 00	6 808 00	
37	Depr.—Factory Bldg.			(j) 750 00		750 00	
38	Depr.—Factory Equip.			(j) 2 400 00		2 400 00	
39	Insurance—Factory	2 730 00		(h) 1 800 00		4 530 00	
40	Prop. Taxes—Fact.	6 217 00				6 217 00	

COST OF GOODS MANUFACTURED		INCOME STATEMENT		BALANCE SHEET		
DEBIT	CREDIT	DEBIT	CREDIT	DEBIT	CREDIT	
				41,000.00		1
				55,300.00		2
						3
					1,100.00	4
				25,000.00		5
				11,000.00		6
				26,000.00		7
				1,800.00		8
				800.00		9
				7,450.00		10
				30,500.00		11
					2,750.00	12
				38,500.00		13
					7,700.00	14
				18,000.00		15
					8,000.00	16
					43,600.00	17
					1,000.00	18
					700.00	19
					800.00	20
					100.00	21
					700.00	22
					100,000.00	23
						24
					23,000.00	25
					40,400.00	26
			495,000.00			27
		3,000.00				28
144,000.00						29
	3,000.00					30
81,000.00						31
16,763.00						32
12,159.00						33
8,558.00						34
6,815.00						35
6,808.00						36
750.00						37
2,400.00						38
4,530.00						39
6,217.00						40

(Continued)

FIGURE 28–4 (Continued)
The Worksheet for a Manufacturing Concern

JIMINEZ MANUFACTURING COMPANY
Worksheet
Year Ended December 31, 19X3

	ACCOUNT NAME	TRIAL BALANCE DEBIT	TRIAL BALANCE CREDIT	ADJUSTMENTS DEBIT	ADJUSTMENTS CREDIT	ADJUSTED TRIAL BALANCE DEBIT	ADJUSTED TRIAL BALANCE CREDIT
41	*Selling Exp. (Control)*	85 000 00				85 000 00	
42	*Admin. Exp. (Control)*	85 916 00		(g) 984 00			
43				(h) 100 00			
44				(j) 1 000 00		88 000 00	
45	*Income Tax Expense*	3 800 00		(m) 700 00		4 500 00	
46	*Manufact. Summary*			(a)26 000 00	(b)25 000 00	26 000 00	25 000 00
47				(c)10 000 00	(d)11 000 00	10 000 00	11 000 00
48	*Income Summary*			(e)28 000 00	(f)26 000 00	28 000 00	26 000 00
49		720 936 00	720 936 00	135 614 00	135 614 00	789 850 00	789 850 00
50	*Cost of Goods*						
51	*Manufactured*						
52							
53	*Net Income*						
54							
55							

2. The other accounts related to manufacturing costs, including the Direct Labor account and the various manufacturing overhead accounts
3. The Manufacturing Summary account

Earlier in this chapter you learned about the three inventory accounts. The other accounts for manufacturing costs are easy to understand. They are the accounts that appear on the statement of cost of goods manufactured as Direct Labor and Manufacturing Overhead.

The Manufacturing Summary account is also easy to understand. You will remember that in the worksheet for a merchandising business (and also for a manufacturing business) there is an Income Summary account, into which all items that appear on the income statement are closed. The Manufacturing Summary account serves a similar purpose: all items that appear in the statement of cost of goods manufactured are closed into that account. Then the balance of the account, representing the cost of goods manufactured, is closed into Income Summary.

All items that appear on the statement of cost of goods manufactured are transferred to the Manufacturing Summary account.

Entering Adjusting Entries on the Worksheet

Adjusting entries are made in the Adjustments columns of the worksheet in the same way as they are for a merchandising concern. Each

COST OF GOODS MANUFACTURED		INCOME STATEMENT		BALANCE SHEET		
DEBIT	CREDIT	DEBIT	CREDIT	DEBIT	CREDIT	
		85 000 00				41
						42
						43
		88 000 00				44
		4 500 00				45
26 000 00	25 000 00					46
10 000 00	11 000 00					47
		28 000 00	26 000 00			48
326 000 00	39 000 00					49
						50
	287 000 00	287 000 00				51
326 000 00	326 000 00	495 500 00	521 000 00	255 350 00	229 850 00	52
		25 500 00			25 500 00	53
		521 000 00	521 000 00	255 350 00	255 350 00	54
						55

The adjusting entries on the worksheet of a manufacturing company are made in the same way as are those for a merchandising company.

adjusting entry on Jiminez's worksheet in Figure 28–4 is identified by a letter for cross-reference. Examination of the trial balance figures and related information for the Jiminez Manufacturing Corporation shows the need for certain entries peculiar to manufacturing operations, as well as for a number of standard adjustments. The adjustments for Jiminez are reviewed below. Carefully follow each item discussed, and trace its treatment on the worksheet. Remember that in the Jiminez Corporation all selling and administrative expenses are recorded in the control accounts rather than in individual expense accounts.

Ending Inventories. Two of the inventory accounts, Raw Materials and Work in Process, appear on the statement of cost of goods manufactured. Therefore, they must be reflected in the Manufacturing Summary account.

Entries **(a)** and **(b)** reflect the adjustment of the Raw Materials Inventory account. First, in entry **(a)**, the account is credited for $26,000, the beginning inventory. This amount is recorded as a debit to the Manufacturing Summary account. Then, in entry **(b)**, the ending inventory of raw materials is recorded as a debit to the Raw Materials Inventory account and a credit to the Manufacturing Summary account. Note the similarity of these two entries to those made to adjust Merchandise Inventory for a merchandising business.

Entries **(c)** and **(d)** are made to adjust the Work in Process Inventory account. Since the work in process inventory appears on the statement of cost of goods manufactured, the adjustments are made through the Manufacturing Summary account. As in the case of raw materials, the inventory account is credited for the beginning balance and is debited for the ending balance, with the offsetting debit and credit being entered in the Manufacturing Summary account.

Finally, the Finished Goods Inventory account is adjusted by entries **(e)** and **(f)**. These entries are identical to those for adjusting the Merchandise Inventory account on the worksheet of a merchandising company.

Uncollectible Accounts. Entry **(g)** is made to record the uncollectible accounts expense, estimated to be 0.2 percent of net sales, or $984 (0.002 × $492,000).

Expired Insurance. Entry **(h)** records insurance expired during the year. Expired insurance includes $1,800 on assets related to manufacturing (equipment, buildings, and inventories) and $100 on office equipment.

Supplies on Hand. Entry **(i)** records the adjustment for supplies on hand. At the Jiminez Manufacturing Corporation, when manufacturing supplies are purchased they are charged to Indirect Materials and Supplies, a manufacturing overhead account. This procedure is usually followed by manufacturing companies because most of the supplies purchased are consumed in a short time. Supplies used in selling and in administrative activities are charged to the Selling Expenses Control and Administrative Expenses Control accounts. At the end of December, factory supplies are on hand that cost $800, and small amounts of sales supplies and office supplies are on hand. Adjustment **(i)** debits the asset account Supplies on Hand for $800 and credits the overhead account Indirect Materials and Supplies for the same amount. The value of the sales supplies and office supplies is considered too small to justify an adjusting entry.

Depreciation. Entry **(j)** records the adjustment for depreciation on assets for the year.

1. On the factory building, $750
2. On the factory equipment, $2,400
3. On the office equipment, $1,000

Accrued Salaries and Wages. On December 31 accrued wages are $880 for direct labor and $120 for indirect labor. These accruals are recorded by entry **(k)**.

Payroll Taxes on Accrued Payroll. Entry **(l)** records payroll taxes on the $1,000 accrued wages of factory workers at the end of the year. All of the workers have already earned the maximum amount subject to federal and state unemployment tax rules. Therefore, only the $65 accrual for social security tax (0.065 × $1,000) and $15 accrual for medicare tax (0.015 × $1,000) must be recorded.

Income Tax Payable. The federal income tax is estimated to be 15 percent of the net taxable income. Based on an analysis of income and expense accounts in the trial balance, adjustment data, and other data affecting taxable income, the estimated taxable income before taxes is $30,000. Therefore, the estimated income tax for the year is $4,500. During the year $3,800 had been paid through estimated tax payments. As a result, $700 of additional taxes must be accrued on December 31. The accrual is recorded on the worksheet as entry (**m**).

Preparing the Adjusted Trial Balance on the Worksheet

After the adjustments discussed above are entered on the worksheet, the Adjustments columns are totaled. The adjustments are then combined with the original trial balance amounts and the new amounts are extended to the Adjusted Trial Balance columns in exactly the same way that they are handled on a worksheet for a merchandising company. Note that both the debit and credit entries made to the Manufacturing Summary and Income Summary accounts to adjust the inventory amounts are extended to the Trial Balance columns. These extensions are made because both the beginning and ending inventory amounts will appear on the cost of goods manufactured statement and the income statement.

The Debit and Credit columns are added to prove the equality of the debits and credits. Some accountants prefer to omit the Adjusted Trial Balance columns from the worksheet to reduce the number of columns in the worksheet. If these columns are omitted, the adjusted balances are extended to the appropriate statement columns.

Completing the Financial Statement Columns

Since three major financial statements—the statement of cost of goods manufactured, the income statement, and the balance sheet—are prepared for a manufacturing business, the worksheet contains three sets of columns for extending items from the adjusted trial balance. All items that will appear on the balance sheet are extended to the Balance Sheet columns. Similarly, items appearing on the income statement and the statement of cost of goods manufactured are extended to the appropriate columns.

The excess of the Debit column over the Credit column in the Cost of Goods Manufactured section represents the cost of goods manufactured.

After the account balances are extended from the Adjusted Trial Balance columns to the statement of cost of goods manufactured columns, the Debit column in the Cost of Goods Manufactured shows a total of $326,000 and the Credit column shows a total of $39,000. The difference in the two columns, $287,000, represents the cost of goods manufactured. This amount is entered in the Credit column of the Cost of Goods Manufactured section. Since the cost of goods sold appears on the income statement, the $287,000 is also extended to the Debit column of the Income Statement section. The two columns in the Cost of Goods Manufactured section are then totaled and double ruled.

The Debit and Credit columns of the Income Statement section of the worksheet are also totaled. The difference between the $495,500 total of the Debit column and the $521,000 total of the Credit column represents the net income for the period. The worksheet is then completed in exactly the same way as the worksheet for a merchandising business.

Preparing the Financial Statements

We have already explained and illustrated the statement of cost of goods manufactured, the income statement, and the balance sheet for Jiminez Manufacturing Corporation for the year ended December 31, 19X3. Those statements were prepared directly from the worksheet illustrated in Figure 28–4. In the interest of space, the statement of retained earnings was not illustrated. It would be prepared in exactly the same way as would one for a merchandising corporation.

Completing the Accounting Cycle

As soon as the financial statements have been prepared, the accountant completes the final phases of the accounting cycle. Four steps must be taken.

1. Adjusting entries are recorded in the general journal and posted to the general ledger.
2. Closing entries are recorded in the general journal and posted to the general ledger.
3. A postclosing trial balance is prepared.
4. Reversing entries are recorded at the beginning of the next period of operations.

OBJECTIVE 6
Record the end-of-period adjusting entries for a manufacturing business.

Recording and Posting Adjusting Entries

The adjustments that were recorded on the worksheet (Figure 28–4) must now be journalized and posted. The procedures are the same as those previously used for merchandising firms. The adjusting entries required at the Jiminez Manufacturing Corporation are shown in the general journal illustrated in Figure 28–5. The identification letter accompanying each adjusting entry is the same as the letter used for the adjustment on the worksheet. For the sake of brevity, explanations have been omitted in the journal entries illustrated.

FIGURE 28–5
Adjusting Entries

19X3		*(Adjustment a)*			
Dec.	*31*	*Manufacturing Summary*		*26 0 0 0 00*	
		Raw Materials Inventory			*26 0 0 0 00*
		(Adjustment b)			
	31	*Raw Materials Inventory*		*25 0 0 0 00*	
		Manufacturing Summary			*25 0 0 0 00*

(Continued)

FIGURE 28–5 (Continued)
Adjusting Entries

19X3		*(Adjustment c)*		
Dec.	*31*	*Manufacturing Summary*	*10 0 0 0 00*	
		Work in Process Inventory		*10 0 0 0 00*
		(Adjustment d)		
	31	*Work in Process Inventory*	*11 0 0 0 00*	
		Manufacturing Summary		*11 0 0 0 00*
		(Adjustment e)		
	31	*Income Summary*	*28 0 0 0 00*	
		Finished Goods Inventory		*28 0 0 0 00*
		(Adjustment f)		
	31	*Finished Goods Inventory*	*26 0 0 0 00*	
		Income Summary		*26 0 0 0 00*
		(Adjustment g)		
	31	*Administrative Exp. Control*	*9 8 4 00*	
		Allowance for Doubtful		
		Accounts		*9 8 4 00*
		(Adjustment h)		
	31	*Insurance—Factory*	*1 8 0 0 00*	
		Administrative Exp. Control	*1 0 0 00*	
		Prepaid Insurance		*1 9 0 0 00*
		(Adjustment i)		
	31	*Supplies on Hand*	*8 0 0 00*	
		Indirect Materials and		
		Supplies		*8 0 0 00*
		(Adjustment j)		
	31	*Depreciation—Factory Bldg.*	*7 5 0 00*	
		Depreciation—Factory Equip.	*2 4 0 0 00*	
		Administrative Exp. Control	*1 0 0 0 00*	
		Accum. Depr.—Fact. Bldg.		*7 5 0 00*
		Accum. Depr.—Fact. Equip.		*2 4 0 0 00*
		Accum. Depr.—Office Equip.		*1 0 0 0 00*
		(Adjustment k)		
	31	*Direct Labor*	*8 8 0 00*	
		Indirect Labor	*1 2 0 00*	
		Sal. and Wages Payable		*1 0 0 0 00*
	31	*(Adjustment l)*		
		Payroll Taxes—Factory	*8 0 00*	
		Social Security Tax Pay.		*6 5 00*
		Medicare Tax Payable		*1 5 00*

(Continued)

FIGURE 28–5 (Continued)
Adjusting Entries

19X3		(Adjustment m)		
Dec.	31	Income Tax Expense	7 0 0 00	
		Income Tax Payable		7 0 0 00

OBJECTIVE 7
Record closing entries for a manufacturing business.

Recording Closing Entries

As discussed earlier in this chapter, all elements of manufacturing cost are drawn together in the Manufacturing Summary account. The beginning and ending inventories of raw materials and work in process were entered in the Manufacturing Summary account as part of the adjusting entries. The remaining accounts reflecting elements of manufacturing costs are closed into the Income Summary as part of the closing process. The balance of the Manufacturing Summary account (actually the cost of goods manufactured) is then transferred to the Income Summary account. Next, all income and expense accounts are closed into the Income Summary account. The balance of the Income Summary account, reflecting net income or net loss after taxes, is transferred to Retained Earnings. A more detailed explanation of the procedure follows.

Closing Accounts into Manufacturing Summary. Refer to the Cost of Goods Manufactured section of the worksheet in Figure 28–4.

1. The Credit column serves as a guide for the first closing entry. The subtotal, $39,000, represents the sum of two ending inventory accounts (Raw Materials Inventory and Work in Process Inventory) and Purchases Discounts. Since the beginning inventories were closed out and the ending inventories opened as part of the adjusting entries, only the Purchases Discounts account must be closed into Manufacturing Summary.

19X3				
Dec.	31	Purchases Discounts	3 0 0 0 00	
		Manufacturing Summary		3 0 0 0 00

2. The Debit column is the guide for the second closing entry. The total of $326,000 includes all manufacturing costs, including the beginning inventories of raw materials and work in process. The amounts representing the inventories have already been transferred to the Manufacturing Summary account in adjusting entries (**a**) and (**b**). No further entry is necessary in the inventory accounts.

19X3				
Dec.	31	Manufacturing Summary	290 000 00	
		Materials Purchases		144 000 00
		Direct Labor		81 000 00
		Indirect Labor		16 763 00
		Payroll Taxes—Factory		12 159 00
		Utilities—Factory		8 558 00
		Repairs and Maint.—Fact.		6 815 00
		Indirect Mat. and Sup.		6 808 00
		Depr.—Factory Building		750 00
		Depr.—Factory Equipment		2 400 00
		Insurance—Factory		4 530 00
		Property Taxes—Factory		6 217 00

ACCOUNT *Manufacturing Summary* ACCOUNT NO. *398*

DATE		EXPLANATION	POST. REF.	DEBIT	CREDIT	BALANCE DEBIT	BALANCE CREDIT
19X3							
Dec.	31	Adj. a		26 000 00		26 000 00	
	31	Adj. b			25 000 00	1 000 00	
	31	Adj. c		10 000 00		11 000 00	
	31	Adj. d			11 000 00	—0—	—0—
	31	Closing			3 000 00		3 000 00
	31	Closing		290 000 00		287 000 00	

Closing Revenue and Expense Accounts into Income Summary. The entries to close the revenue and expense accounts into Income Summary are almost identical to those for a merchandising concern. Refer to the Income Statement section of the Jiminez Manufacturing Corporation's worksheet, Figure 28–4.

1. The Credit column total of $521,000 includes the revenue account Sales and the ending finished goods inventory. The finished goods inventory was recorded as part of the adjusting entries. Therefore, the only account in the credit column that requires closing is the Sales account.

19X3				
Dec.	31	Sales	495 000 00	
		Income Summary		495 000 00

2. Each item in the Debit column of the Income Statement section, except the beginning balance of finished goods, is closed into Income Summary. This entry includes the Cost of Goods Manufac-

tured, $287,000, which has been closed into Manufacturing Summary.

19X3				
Dec.	31	Income Summary	467 500 00	
		Sales Returns and Allow.		3 000 00
		Selling Expense Control		85 000 00
		General Expense Control		88 000 00
		Income Tax Expense		4 500 00
		Manufacturing Summary		287 000 00

At this point all revenue and expense accounts have been closed. The balance in the Income Summary account, $25,500, therefore represents the net income after income taxes.

ACCOUNT *Income Summary* ACCOUNT NO. *399*

DATE		EXPLANATION	POST. REF.	DEBIT	CREDIT	BALANCE DEBIT	BALANCE CREDIT
19X3							
Dec.	31	Adj. e		28 000 00		28 000 00	
	31	Adj. f			26 000 00	2 000 00	
	31	Closing			495 000 00		493 000 00
	31	Closing		467 500 00			25 500 00

Closing Income Summary. The balance of the Income Summary account is now closed into Retained Earnings.

19X3				
Dec.	31	Income Summary	25 500 00	
		Retained Earnings		25 500 00

Preparing the Postclosing Trial Balance

After adjusting and closing entries have been posted to the ledger accounts, a postclosing trial balance is taken to prove that the adjusting and closing entries were posted correctly. The ledger account balances should agree completely with those listed in the Balance Sheet section of the worksheet. Because there are no new concepts in the postclosing trial balance for a manufacturing company, the concept is not illustrated here.

OBJECTIVE 8
Record reversing entries for a manufacturing business.

Recording the Reversing Entries

In Chapter 13 you learned that it is efficient and convenient to reverse certain adjusting entries at the beginning of a new accounting period. The goal is to begin the new fiscal period with balances in the accounts that will be debited and credited in routine entries during the new period. The same reversing procedures will be followed with the accounts of the Jiminez Manufacturing Corporation. In most cases the adjusting entries to be reversed are those made for accrued expenses and accrued income. In addition, if an expenditure is initially charged to expense and then adjusted at the end of the year to record a deferred amount, a reversing entry will normally be made.

Refer again to the adjusting entries illustrated in Figure 28–5. Consider the effect of each in turn. Only the following adjustments require reversing entries.

1. Adjustment (**i**) records the ending inventory of manufacturing supplies. Because the firm initially records purchases of supplies as an expense, the asset account Supplies on Hand should not have a balance during a fiscal period. To remove the balance from the account, the adjustment is reversed.

19X4				
Jan.	*1*	*Indirect Materials and Sup.*	*800 00*	
		Supplies on Hand		*800 00*

2. Adjustment (**k**) for the accrued factory wages is, like other entries recording accrued expenses, reversed.

19X4				
Jan.	*1*	*Salaries and Wages Payable*	*1,000 00*	
		Direct Labor		*880 00*
		Indirect Labor		*120 00*

3. Adjustment (**l**) for the accrued payroll taxes likewise must be reversed.

19X4				
Jan.	*1*	*Social Security Taxes Pay.*	*65 00*	
		Medicare Tax Payable	*15 00*	
		Payroll Taxes—Factory		*80 00*

After these reversing entries have been posted, the transactions of the new period can be recorded in the usual manner without having to consider the effect of the adjustments made in the prior period. The use of reversing entries therefore saves time and helps to prevent errors in the new period.

MANAGERIAL IMPLICATIONS

To plan and control operations, managers need reliable accounting data about the costs of doing business. In a manufacturing firm, managers must be alert to control the costs involved in producing goods. The periodic statement of cost of goods manufactured provides detailed information about both the total cost of manufacturing and individual cost elements. Managers use this data to evaluate past performance and to guide future operations so that the firm can obtain the greatest profit.

Efficient procedures must be used in preparing financial statements. The worksheet allows the accountant to summarize and classify information so that the formal statements can be drawn up more easily and more quickly.

The use of reversing entries enables accounting personnel to handle later transactions in the normal manner without regard to any adjustments made at the end of the preceding period. This decreases the possibility of oversight or error.

SELF-REVIEW

1. What column headings are found on the worksheet for a manufacturing business?
2. How does the worksheet for a manufacturing business differ from one for a merchandising firm?
3. How are the beginning and ending inventories of raw materials and work in process handled on the worksheet?
4. Does the Manufacturing Summary account have a balance during the fiscal period? Explain.
5. Into which account is the Manufacturing Summary account closed?

Answers to Self-Review

1. The column headings found on a worksheet for a manufacturing business are Trial Balance, Adjustments, Adjusted Trial Balance, Cost of Goods Manufactured, Income Statement, and Balance Sheet.
2. The major way in which a manufacturing worksheet differs is in the addition of the Cost of Goods Manufactured columns.
3. The balances of the beginning inventories of raw materials and work in process are entered in the Adjustments columns as credits to the two inventory accounts and debits to the Manufacturing Summary account. The ending inventories of raw materials and work in process are entered in the Adjustments columns as debits to the inventory accounts and credits to the Manufacturing Summary account.
4. The Manufacturing Summary account has no balance during the fiscal period. The account is used only during the closing process.
5. The Manufacturing Summary account is closed into the Income Summary account.

CHAPTER 28 Review and Applications

CHAPTER SUMMARY

The costs of manufacturing operations are recorded in new accounts that fall into three classifications: raw materials, direct labor, and manufacturing overhead. Inventory accounts are required for raw materials, work in process, and finished goods. The Finished Goods Inventory account shows the cost of the completed products ready for sale and thus corresponds to the Merchandise Inventory account of a merchandising business.

A corporation that manufactures goods prepares a balance sheet, income statement, and statement of retained earnings similar to those of any other corporation. In addition, a statement of cost of goods manufactured is prepared to show the results of the manufacturing activities. The total cost of goods manufactured appears on the income statement as part of the Cost of Goods Sold, corresponding to the merchandise purchases on the income statement of a merchandising business.

The worksheet for a manufacturing business is similar in most respects to one for a merchandising firm, but it has an additional pair of columns in which to record the figures that appear on the cost of goods manufactured statement.

The worksheet supplies all the information needed to prepare the statement of cost of goods manufactured, the income statement, and the balance sheet. To prepare a statement of retained earnings, the Retained Earnings account in the general ledger must be analyzed to obtain the necessary details.

All accounts relating to the cost of goods manufactured are closed into the Manufacturing Summary account. Its final balance, representing the cost of goods manufactured, is closed into the Income Summary account. All items in the Income Statement section of the worksheet are closed into Income Summary. The final closing entry transfers the net income after income taxes to the Retained Earnings account.

After the accounting records are adjusted and closed, a postclosing trial balance is prepared. At the beginning of the new period, certain adjusting entries are reversed.

GLOSSARY OF NEW TERMS

Direct labor (p. 996) Costs attributable to personnel who work directly on the product being manufactured

Direct materials (p. 996) All items that go into a product and become a part of it

Indirect labor (p. 997) Cost attributable to personnel who support production but are not directly involved in the manufacture of a product; for example, supervisory, repair and maintenance, and janitorial staff

Indirect materials and supplies (p. 996) Materials that may be used in manufacturing a product but do not become a part of the product itself

Manufacturing overhead (p. 997) All manufacturing costs that are not classified as direct materials or direct labor

Raw materials (p. 996) The materials placed into production

Statement of cost of goods manufactured (p. 995) A financial report showing details of the cost of goods completed during the accounting period

Work in process (p. 997) Partially completed units in the production process

REVIEW QUESTIONS

1. How do the accounting problems of a manufacturing business differ from those of a merchandising business?
2. What procedure is used on the statement of cost of goods manufactured to arrive at the cost of raw materials used?
3. What is indirect labor?
4. It is possible that one company might consider an item, such as paint, as one of its direct materials, while another company with identical manufacturing processes might classify the item as one of its indirect materials. Why?
5. How would the wages of the employee who issues materials from the factory storeroom be classified?
6. What is manufacturing overhead?
7. Why does the figure for total manufacturing cost not equal the cost of goods manufactured?
8. Name the three inventory accounts found in the chart of accounts of a manufacturing business and explain each one.
9. How is the work in process inventory determined?
10. Give five examples of manufacturing overhead items.
11. What is the relationship between the cost of goods manufactured and the income statement?
12. What is the source of the information for preparing the journal entry to close manufacturing cost accounts into the Manufacturing Summary account?
13. Are the financial statements prepared after the closing entries are posted? Explain.
14. Is the statement of cost of goods manufactured prepared before or after the income statement? Explain.

MANAGERIAL FOCUS

1. Why do managers need special manufacturing records and a separate end-of-period statement reporting the costs involved in producing goods?
2. How can an inventory be taken if work in process items are in varying stages of completion at the end of the accounting period?
3. Why might management want direct labor costs separated from indirect labor costs?
4. Why should management not use the statement of cost of goods manufactured alone as a means of measuring efficiency and controlling manufacturing costs?
5. In this chapter we said that the value of the sales supplies and office supplies on hand at the end of the period is considered too small to justify an adjusting entry. If a director were to question this omission as a matter of policy (arguing that the accounting records should show everything), what would you say?

EXERCISES

EXERCISE 28–1 (Obj. 1)

Cost of goods manufactured statement (partial). The following selected items appeared on the worksheet of the Lonberg Company on December 31, 19X4. From this information, prepare the section of the statement of cost of goods manufactured relating to the cost of raw materials used.

	Debit	Credit
Finished Goods Inventory	$ 68,000	$78,000
Work in Process Inventory	98,000	92,000
Raw Materials Inventory	56,000	61,000
Materials Purchases	670,000	
Purchases Returns and Allowances		1,000
Freight In (on Materials Purchases)	16,000	

EXERCISE 28–2 (Obj. 2)

Tutorial

Components of manufacturing cost. The Howard Company's beginning raw materials inventory was $224,000. Its net purchases for the period were $721,000, and its ending raw materials inventory was $197,000. What was its cost of raw materials used?

EXERCISE 28–3 (Obj. 2)

Tutorial

Components of manufacturing cost. The Danville Company's total manufacturing cost for a year was $1,844,000. Its manufacturing overhead was $300,000, and its cost of raw materials used was $833,000. What was its direct labor cost for the year?

EXERCISE 28–4 (Obj. 2)

Tutorial

Components of manufacturing cost. Which of the following items would not appear on the statement of cost of goods manufactured?

1. Amortization of organization costs

2. Depreciation of factory building
3. Taxes on factory building

EXERCISE 28–5 (Obj. 2) Tutorial

Components of manufacturing cost. Which of the following items would not be shown on the statement of cost of goods manufactured?

1. Finished goods inventory
2. Raw materials inventory
3. Work in process inventory

EXERCISE 28–6 (Obj. 2)

Components of manufacturing cost. Which of the following items should not be included in the Manufacturing Overhead section of the statement of cost of goods manufactured?

1. Factory insurance
2. Payroll taxes on the wages of factory employees
3. Freight charges on purchases of raw materials

EXERCISE 28–7 (Obj. 2)

Components of manufacturing cost. Which of the following items would be included in the Manufacturing Overhead section of the statement of cost of goods manufactured?

1. Raw materials used
2. Indirect materials and supplies
3. Direct labor
4. Repairs to factory building
5. Advertising expense
6. Delivery expense
7. Depreciation of factory equipment
8. Repairs to delivery equipment
9. Office supplies expense

EXERCISE 28–8 (Obj. 6) Tutorial

Adjusting entries. Using the data given in Exercise 28–1, make the general journal entry to record adjustments for inventory accounts.

EXERCISE 28–9 (Obj. 5)

Worksheet for a manufacturing business. Which of the following account balances would not be extended to the Cost of Goods Manufactured section of the worksheet?

1. Insurance on factory building
2. Payroll taxes on factory wages
3. Utilities for factory
4. Salary of factory storeroom clerk
5. Insurance on raw materials in factory storeroom
6. Insurance on finished goods
7. Salary of factory superintendent
8. Salary of accounts receivable clerk
9. Payroll taxes on sales salaries
10. Freight out

EXERCISE 28–10 (Obj. 6, 7) Tutorial

Adjusting, closing, and reversing entries. Information about certain account balances in the trial balance of the Navaho Corporation on December 31, 19X4, follows.

a. Balance in Raw Materials Inventory account, December 31, $34,000, reflecting beginning balance; physical count on December 31, $43,000
b. Balance in Prepaid Insurance account, $14,000; insurance expired, $9,300
c. Balance in Direct Labor account, $84,000; accrued direct labor, $300
d. Balance in Factory Supplies on Hand account, $8,000; physical count shows supplies on hand, $500

Record the following in the general journal.

1. Adjusting entries required
2. Closing entries required
3. Reversing entries on January 1, 19X5

PROBLEMS

PROBLEM SET A

PROBLEM 28–1A
(Obj. 1, 3)

Tutorial

Preparing a statement of cost of goods manufactured and an income statement. The Oester Manufacturing Company makes picture frames. Selected account balances for this firm on December 31, 19X3, the end of its fiscal year, are given below. Data about the beginning and ending inventories are also given.

Instructions

1. Prepare a statement of cost of goods manufactured for 19X3.
2. Prepare an income statement for 19X3.

Accounts	Balances
Sales	$498,138
Sales Returns and Allowances	1,782
Materials Purchases	141,000
Direct Labor	80,000
Indirect Labor	17,000
Payroll Taxes—Factory	11,198
Utilities—Factory	8,433
Repairs and Maintenance—Factory	9,391
Indirect Materials and Supplies	7,000
Depreciation—Factory Building	1,000
Depreciation—Factory Equipment	2,208
Insurance—Factory	2,700
Property Taxes—Factory	5,000
Sales Salaries Expense	26,225
Payroll Taxes Expense—Selling	2,710
Delivery Expense	20,740
Advertising Expense	11,710
Miscellaneous Selling Expenses	31,248
Officers' Salaries Expense	55,000
Office Salaries Expense	17,325
Payroll Taxes Expense—Administrative	8,915
Other Administrative Expenses	5,110
Income Tax Expense	4,800

Inventory Data	Jan. 1, 19X3	Dec. 31, 19X3
Finished Goods Inventory	$34,500	$32,000
Work in Process Inventory	23,000	24,950
Raw Materials Inventory	27,000	26,980

PROBLEM 28-2A
(Obj. 1, 3)

Tutorial | Spreadsheet

Preparing a statement of cost of goods manufactured and an income statement. The data that follows is for the Chung Corporation, which makes specialized tools.

Instructions

1. Prepare a statement of cost of goods manufactured for the year ended December 31, 19Y4.
2. Prepare an income statement for the same period.

	Jan. 1, 19Y4	Dec. 31, 19Y4
Finished Goods Inventory	$40,000	$ 35,000
Raw Materials Inventory	20,000	20,500
Work in Process Inventory	11,000	11,200
Depreciation—Factory Building and Equipment		4,420
Direct Labor		109,875
Freight In		2,000
Indirect Labor		20,125
Indirect Materials and Supplies		3,470
Insurance—Factory		3,120
Materials Purchases		130,000
Office Salaries Expense		18,000
Officers' Salaries Expense		30,000
Other Office Expenses		14,500
Payroll Taxes Expense—Administrative		5,200
Payroll Taxes—Factory		14,870
Payroll Taxes Expense—Selling		5,960
Utilities—Factory		5,963
Property Taxes—Factory		3,220
Purchases Returns and Allowances		2,410
Repairs and Maintenance—Factory		8,145
Sales		501,000
Sales Salaries Expense		50,080
Advertising Expense		4,000
Other Selling Expenses		19,600
Miscellaneous Administrative Expenses		8,000
Income Tax Expense		5,785

PROBLEM 28-3A
(Obj. 1, 3, 4, 5, 6, 7, 8)

Tutorial

Preparing a statement of cost of goods manufactured, an income statement, a statement of retained earnings, and a balance sheet; completing the worksheet; recording adjusting, closing, and reversing entries. Electroco Corporation manufactures parts for cassette players. The Trial Balance section of its worksheet and other year-end data are given below.

Instructions

1. Prepare a 12-column manufacturing worksheet for the fiscal year ended December 31, 19X3. Enter the trial balance in the first two columns.

2. Using the data given, enter the adjustments. Then complete the worksheet. Label all inventory adjustments as "**a.**"
3. Prepare a statement of cost of goods manufactured.
4. Prepare an income statement.
5. Prepare a statement of retained earnings. Additional data needed is as follows.
   a. Balance of Retained Earnings on January 1 was $164,272.
   b. Dividends declared and paid on common stock during the year amounted to $6,400.
   c. There were no changes in any other stockholders' equity accounts.
6. Prepare a balance sheet as of December 31, 19X3. There are 25,000 shares of no-par common stock, stated value of $1 per share, outstanding out of 100,000 shares authorized.
7. Record the adjusting entries shown on the worksheet in general journal form. For each journal entry, use the letter that identifies the adjustment on the worksheet. Use the letter "a" for all inventory adjustments, but make a separate entry for each inventory adjustment. Do not give explanations for entries in this problem.
8. Prepare the closing entries for all accounts involved in the cost of goods manufactured.
9. Prepare the closing entries for all revenue and expense accounts and the Manufacturing Summary account.
10. Prepare the closing entry to close the Income Summary account.
11. Journalize the reversing entries. Date all of these entries January 1, 19X4.

ELECTROCO PRODUCTS CORPORATION
Trial Balance
Year Ended December 31, 19X3

ACCOUNT NAME	DEBIT	CREDIT
Cash	20 685 00	
Accounts Receivable	41 274 00	
Allowance for Doubtful Accounts		76 00
Raw Materials Inventory	11 725 00	
Work in Process Inventory	16 000 00	
Finished Goods Inventory	42 560 00	
Prepaid Insurance	3 320 00	
Factory Supplies on Hand	2 870 00	
Land	15 000 00	
Factory Building	98 450 00	
Accum. Depr.—Factory Building		24 150 00
Factory Machines	51 700 00	
Accum. Depr.—Factory Machines		19 875 00
Office Equipment	6 895 00	
Accum. Depr.—Office Equipment		2 976 00

(Continued)

ACCOUNT NAME	DEBIT	CREDIT
Accounts Payable		15 2 3 5 00
Salaries and Wages Payable		
Income Tax Payable		
Social Security Tax Payable		1 0 0 00
Medicare Tax Payable		2 0 00
Employee Income Tax Payable		6 0 0 00
Common Stock		25 0 0 0 00
Retained Earnings		170 6 9 3 00
Sales		354 6 7 9 00
Sales Returns and Allowances	1 6 5 5 00	
Materials Purchases	91 0 0 0 00	
Purchases Returns and Allowances		3 8 0 00
Freight In	1 2 2 5 00	
Direct Labor	76 0 0 0 00	
Indirect Labor	7 2 5 0 00	
Payroll Taxes—Factory	9 6 7 5 00	
Heat, Light, and Power—Factory	4 2 7 5 00	
Repairs and Maintenance—Factory	1 0 2 5 00	
Indirect Materials and Supplies		
Depr.—Factory Building		
Depr.—Factory Machines		
Insurance—Factory		
Property Taxes—Factory	2 8 5 0 00	
Sales Salaries Expense	26 7 5 0 00	
Payroll Taxes Expense—Sales	2 7 2 0 00	
Delivery Expense	4 1 1 5 00	
Advertising Expense	10 4 8 0 00	
Uncollectible Accounts Expense		
Miscellaneous Selling Expense	3 9 1 5 00	
Officers' Salaries Expense	28 0 0 0 00	
Office Salaries Expense	21 3 6 0 00	
Payroll Taxes Expense—Admin.	5 5 7 5 00	
Depr. Expense—Office Furniture		
Other Administrative Expenses	1 4 3 5 00	
Income Tax Expense	4 0 0 0 00	
Manufacturing Summary		
Income Summary		
Totals	613 7 8 4 00	613 7 8 4 00

YEAR-END DATA

a. Physical inventories taken on December 31, 19X3, show $14,982 of raw materials on hand and $30,112 of finished goods on hand. The work in process inventory is estimated to be $13,200 on the same date.

b. It is estimated that $916 of the accounts receivable may not be collectible.

c. Of the prepaid insurance, $1,680 covering the factory building and equipment has expired.
d. A physical inventory discloses $628 of factory supplies unused at the end of the period.
e. Depreciation expense for the year is as follows: $2,068 on the factory building, $5,170 on the factory machines, and $683 on the office furniture. (Make a compound entry.)
f. Payroll accruals at the end of the period include $800 of direct labor and $200 of indirect labor.
g. Payroll taxes on accrued wages are social security, 6.5 percent, and medicare tax, 1.5 percent.
h. The total income tax for the year is $4,300.

PROBLEM SET B

PROBLEM 28–1B
(Obj. 1, 3)
Tutorial

Preparing a statement of cost of goods manufactured and an income statement. The Snook Manufacturing Company makes equipment for billiard tables. Selected account balances (listed alphabetically) for this firm on December 31, 19X4, the end of its fiscal year, are given below. Data about the beginning and ending inventories is also shown.

Instructions

1. Prepare a statement of cost of goods manufactured for 19X4.
2. Prepare an income statement for 19X4.

Accounts	Balances
Depreciation—Factory Building and Equipment	$ 13,000
Depreciation Expense—Office Furniture and Equipment	1,500
Direct Labor	40,000
Freight In	1,000
Income Tax Expense	2,250
Indirect Labor	16,000
Indirect Materials and Supplies	3,000
Insurance—Factory	1,600
Materials Purchases	82,000
Office Salaries Expense	22,000
Officers' Salaries Expense	30,000
Other Administrative Expenses	7,000
Other Selling Expenses	22,000
Payroll Taxes Expense—Administrative	5,200
Payroll Taxes Expense—Selling	3,000
Payroll Taxes—Factory	6,000
Property Taxes Expense—Administrative	800
Property Taxes—Factory	2,900
Purchases Returns and Allowances	900
Repairs and Maintenance Expense—Factory	1,380
Repairs and Maintenance Expense—Office	200
Sales	295,000
Sales Returns and Allowances	1,430
Sales Salaries Expense	28,000
Utilities—Factory	4,000

Inventory Data	Jan. 1, 19X4	Dec. 31, 19X4
Finished Goods Inventory	$ 8,200	$ 9,000
Work in Process Inventory	6,600	8,900
Raw Materials Inventory	11,000	13,300

PROBLEM 28-2B
(Obj. 1, 3)

Tutorial

Preparing a statement of cost of goods manufactured and an income statement. Balances of selected accounts, listed in alphabetical order, at the end of 19X3 for the Klondike Corporation follow. Information about beginning and ending inventories is also given.

Instructions

1. Prepare a statement of cost of goods manufactured for the year ended December 31, 19X3.
2. Prepare an income statement for the same period.

Account Balances	
Delivery Expense	14,000
Depreciation—Factory Building and Equipment	6,135
Direct Labor	142,735
Freight In	4,250
Income Tax Expense	9,000
Indirect Labor	24,620
Indirect Materials and Supplies	4,287
Insurance—Factory	4,335
Materials Purchases	177,500
Materials Purchases Returns and Allowances	610
Miscellaneous Selling Expenses	19,700
Office Salaries Expense	18,000
Officers' Salaries Expense	30,000
Other Office Expenses	20,500
Payroll Taxes Expense—Administrative	5,250
Payroll Taxes Expense—Selling	3,085
Payroll Taxes—Factory	18,862
Property Taxes—Factory	6,178
Repairs and Maintenance—Factory	6,233
Sales	603,400
Sales Returns and Allowances	2,745
Sales Salaries Expense	28,000
Utilities—Factory	6,841

Inventory Data	Jan. 1, 19X3	Dec. 31, 19X3
Finished Goods Inventory	$35,000	$33,500
Raw Materials Inventory	19,500	18,800
Work in Process Inventory	14,500	14,300

PROBLEM 28-3B
(Obj. 1, 3, 4, 5, 6, 7, 8)

Tutorial

Preparing a statement of cost of goods manufactured, an income statement, a statement of retained earnings, and a balance sheet; completing the worksheet; recording adjusting, closing, and reversing entries. The Neptune Manufacturing Corporation produces fishing rods, reels, and lines. The Trial Balance section of its worksheet and other year-end data are given below.

Instructions

1. Prepare a 12-column manufacturing worksheet for the fiscal year ended December 31, 19X4. Enter the trial balance in the first two columns.
2. Using the data given, enter the adjustments and complete the worksheet. Label all inventory adjustments as "a."
3. Prepare a statement of cost of goods manufactured.
4. Prepare an income statement.
5. Prepare a statement of retained earnings. Additional data follows:
   a. Balance of Retained Earnings, January 1, was $47,646
   b. Dividends declared and paid on common stock were $6,000.
6. Prepare a balance sheet as of December 31, 19X4.
7. Record the adjusting entries shown on the worksheet in general journal form. For each journal entry, use the letter that identifies the adjustment on the worksheet.
8. Prepare the closing entries for all accounts involved in the cost of goods manufactured.
9. Prepare the closing entries for all revenue and expense accounts and the Manufacturing Summary account.
10. Prepare the closing entry to close the Income Summary account.
11. Journalize the reversing entries. Date all the reversing entries January 1, 19X5.

NEPTUNE MANUFACTURING CORPORATION
Worksheet (Partial)
Year Ended December 31, 19X4

ACCOUNT NAME	DEBIT	CREDIT
Cash	14 389 00	
Accounts Receivable	51 000 00	
Allowance for Doubtful Accounts		76 00
Raw Materials Inventory	12 000 00	
Work in Process Inventory	10 000 00	
Finished Goods Inventory	20 000 00	
Prepaid Insurance	2 195 00	
Factory Supplies on Hand	3 795 00	
Land	5 200 00	
Factory Building	41 500 00	
Accum. Depreciation—Factory Building		8 140 00
Factory Machinery	13 000 00	
Accum. Depreciation—Factory Machinery		5 200 00
Office Equipment	12 000 00	
Accum. Depreciation—Office Equipment		3 600 00
Accounts Payable		16 345 00
Salaries and Wages Payable		
Income Tax Payable		
Social Security Tax Payable		900 00
Medicare Tax Payable		222 00
Employee Income Tax Payable		100 00

(Continued)

ACCOUNT NAME	DEBIT	CREDIT
Common Stock		*60 0 0 0 00*
Retained Earnings		*41 6 4 6 00*
Sales		*384 4 7 5 00*
Sales Returns and Allowances	*1 3 2 5 00*	
Materials Purchases	*72 2 5 0 00*	
Purchases Returns and Allowances		*6 5 0 00*
Direct Labor	*81 2 4 5 00*	
Indirect Labor	*17 9 8 7 00*	
Payroll Taxes—Factory	*11 9 1 5 00*	
Utilities—Factory	*3 9 4 1 00*	
Repairs and Maintenance—Factory	*4 7 4 2 00*	
Indirect Materials and Supplies Used		
Depreciation—Factory Building		
Depreciation—Factory Equipment		
Insurance—Factory		
Property Taxes—Factory	*3 2 2 5 00*	
Sales Salaries Expense	*32 4 5 0 00*	
Payroll Taxes Expense—Sales	*4 0 0 0 00*	
Uncollectible Accounts Expense		
Other Selling Expenses	*29 9 6 5 00*	
Officers' Salaries Expense	*37 5 0 0 00*	
Office Salaries Expense	*18 0 0 0 00*	
Payroll Taxes Expense—Admin.	*6 3 0 0 00*	
Other Office Expenses	*5 4 3 0 00*	
Income Tax Expense	*6 0 0 0 00*	
Manufacturing Summary		
Income Summary		
Totals	*521 3 5 4 00*	*521 3 5 4 00*

YEAR-END DATA

a. Ending inventories: finished goods, $21,100; work in process, $10,250; and raw materials, $13,300
b. Estimated uncollectible accounts: increase Allowance for Doubtful Accounts to 3 percent of Accounts Receivable
c. Expired insurance, $2,050; debit the Insurance—Factory account for the amount of the necessary adjustment
d. Factory materials and supplies on hand, $185
e. Depreciation for the year: on factory building, $2,000; on factory machinery, $1,300; and on office equipment, $1,200
f. Accrued factory wages: direct labor, $475; indirect labor, $125
g. Accrued payroll taxes: social security, $39; medicare tax, $9
h. Total income tax expense for the year, $6,500

CHALLENGE PROBLEM

Certain information about the statement of cost of goods manufactured and the income statement for the year ended December 31,

19X3, for Schwartz Products Company, a sole proprietorship, is given below.

Beginning inventory of finished goods, 90 percent of ending inventory	
Work in process inventory, January 1, 120 percent of ending inventory	
Net income (10% of net sales)	$40,000
Raw materials inventory, January 1	35,000
Turnover of finished goods, based on ending inventory	6 times
Direct labor costs	80,000
Manufacturing overhead, 120 percent of direct labor costs	
Work in process inventory, December 31	15,000
Raw materials inventory, December 31	30,000
Operating expenses, 15 percent of net sales	

Instructions Prepare a statement of cost of goods manufactured and an income statement for the year.

CRITICAL THINKING PROBLEM

In January of the current year, Audrey Watson started a business manufacturing canvas backpacks called Trailblazer Backpacks. Watson was so busy with the manufacturing side of the business that she did not take time to set up detailed accounting records; the business checkbook was her only record of accounting transactions. When cash came in, she deposited the receipts in the bank, and when invoices were due, she wrote checks to pay them. Now it is the end of the year and Watson would like to know how the business did during its first year of operation.

Watson asks for your help in summarizing the first year's operations. A review of the checkbook yields the following information.

- Raw materials purchases paid for totaled $28,000.
- Wages paid to employees totaled $36,000, with payroll taxes relating to their wages of $3,240.
- Factory supplies cost $6,730.
- Utility bills paid totaled $4,270.
- Repairs to factory equipment were $2,500.
- Rent of $21,000 was paid on the factory building.

Discussions with Watson disclose that $2,000 of raw materials have been received and used in the manufacturing process but have not yet been paid for because the invoice for the purchase is not due until next year. Watson has determined depreciation on the factory equipment for the year to be $3,850. An inventory taken on the last day of the year showed $6,600 of raw materials on hand, $1,300 of backpacks partially completed, and $4,200 of finished backpacks waiting to be sold.

Instructions Prepare a statement of cost of goods manufactured for the current year for Trailblazer Backpacks.

CHAPTER

29
Job Order Cost Accounting

OBJECTIVES

1. Explain how a job order cost accounting system operates.
2. Journalize the purchase and issuance of direct and indirect materials.
3. Maintain perpetual inventory records.
4. Record labor costs incurred and charge labor into production.
5. Compute overhead rates and apply overhead to jobs.
6. Compute overapplied or underapplied overhead and report it in the financial statements.
7. Maintain job order cost sheets.
8. Record the cost of jobs completed and the cost of goods sold under a perpetual inventory system.
9. Define the accounting terms new to this chapter.

Up to this point we have discussed the basic accounting records and financial statements used by manufacturing businesses. These firms must also have other types of records that allow them to gather detailed information about the costs involved in making each product. In this chapter and later chapters, you will see how cost accounting systems are set up to provide such data.

In this chapter, we discuss one of the most common types of cost accounting systems—the job order cost system. The Northwest Manufacturing Corporation, which makes tables, is used as an example. You will learn how Northwest accounts for materials, labor, and overhead under the job order cost system. You will also learn how overhead application rates are calculated and applied.

NEW TERMS

Finished goods subsidiary ledger ▪ Job order ▪ Job order cost accounting ▪ Job order cost sheet ▪ Just-in-time system ▪ Manufacturing overhead ledger ▪ Materials requisition ▪ Overapplied overhead ▪ Overhead application rate ▪ Perpetual inventory system ▪ Process cost accounting ▪ Producing departments ▪ Production order ▪ Raw materials ledger card ▪ Raw materials subsidiary ledger ▪ Service departments ▪ Standard costs ▪ Time tickets ▪ Underapplied overhead ▪ Work in process subsidiary ledger

THE NEED FOR A COST ACCOUNTING SYSTEM

A cost accounting system makes it possible to determine the cost of each unit produced and helps management control costs.

The procedures illustrated in the preceding chapter are useful to a manufacturing business in computing the overall cost of making its products during the period. They provide for the recording of manufacturing costs—direct materials, direct labor, and manufacturing overhead costs—and for the preparation of financial statements reflecting these costs. However, they have two shortcomings. First, unless a single product is manufactured and unless all goods worked on during the period are completed, the procedures described do not make it possible to determine the cost of each unit produced. Second, since costs are assembled and classified only at the end of the accounting period, the procedures described do not help in keeping a close watch on cost behavior and in controlling costs when they get out of line. Since the Northwest Manufacturing Corporation makes several products and normally has work in process at the end of the accounting period, this firm needs a more specialized accounting system to determine the cost of each unit produced.

TYPES OF COST ACCOUNTING SYSTEMS

Two principal systems of cost accounting are used to determine the cost of each unit manufactured: job order cost accounting and process cost accounting. A third type, standard cost accounting, may be used with either of the other two systems as a control on the efficiency of performance.

Job Order Cost Accounting

Under a job order cost accounting system, unit costs are determined for products manufactured under each job order.

Under the **job order cost accounting** system, each "batch" of goods is produced under a **production order,** usually called a **job order.** Unit costs of items manufactured are determined for each separate production order. Specifically, unit costs are determined by dividing the total costs incurred on a particular order by the number of units produced. This system is a logical choice for businesses that produce what each customer wants on special order—for example, a firm that manufactures custom draperies for homeowners or that manufactures machine tools to be used by an automobile manufacturing plant. In addition, a company that produces more than one product in batches rather than on a continuous basis would logically choose the job order cost system. For example, a firm that manufactures four types of standardized chairs for use in churches and schools, and ships the chairs directly from the factory floor to the purchasers, should use the job order cost system.

Process Cost Accounting

Under the process cost system, unit cost of a product is computed by adding the unit costs in each producing department.

Under the **process cost accounting** system, the total cost of a unit of product is found by adding the unit costs in each department through which the product passes while it is being manufactured. This type of cost accounting system resembles a departmentalized accounting system for a merchandising business. Separate cost records are kept for the various producing departments and service departments. **Producing departments** perform work directly on the product. **Service departments** assist in production but do not perform work on the actual product. The process cost accounting system is usually applied to situations in which there are continuous operations on standard types of products. For example, a cement plant, or a flour-milling company, or a manufacturer of cake mixes would use the process cost accounting system.

Standard Cost Accounting

Standard costs reflect what the costs are expected to be under efficient operating conditions.

Standard costs are a measure of what costs should be in an efficient operation. They permit a firm to determine what its costs should be. Managers can then compare actual costs with predetermined standard costs to determine the efficiency of the firm's performance. As previously mentioned, standard costs may be incorporated into either a job order cost accounting system or a process cost accounting system.

COST FLOWS IN A JOB ORDER COST SYSTEM

Since the Northwest Manufacturing Corporation makes several types of tables and customers order the various types in different quantities, Northwest does not have a continuous manufacturing process. The company therefore uses the job order cost system. This system is designed to facilitate recording costs related to the four phases of operations of a manufacturing business:

1. Procurement—obtaining materials, labor, and services necessary for the manufacturing process
2. Production—the actual use of materials, labor, and services on the factory floor
3. Warehousing—the handling and storing of finished goods
4. Selling—removal of finished goods from the storeroom as orders are filled.

Figure 29–1 summarizes the flow of costs through these phases of activity when the job order cost accounting system is used.

FIGURE 29–1
Flow of Costs Through Four Phases of Manufacturing

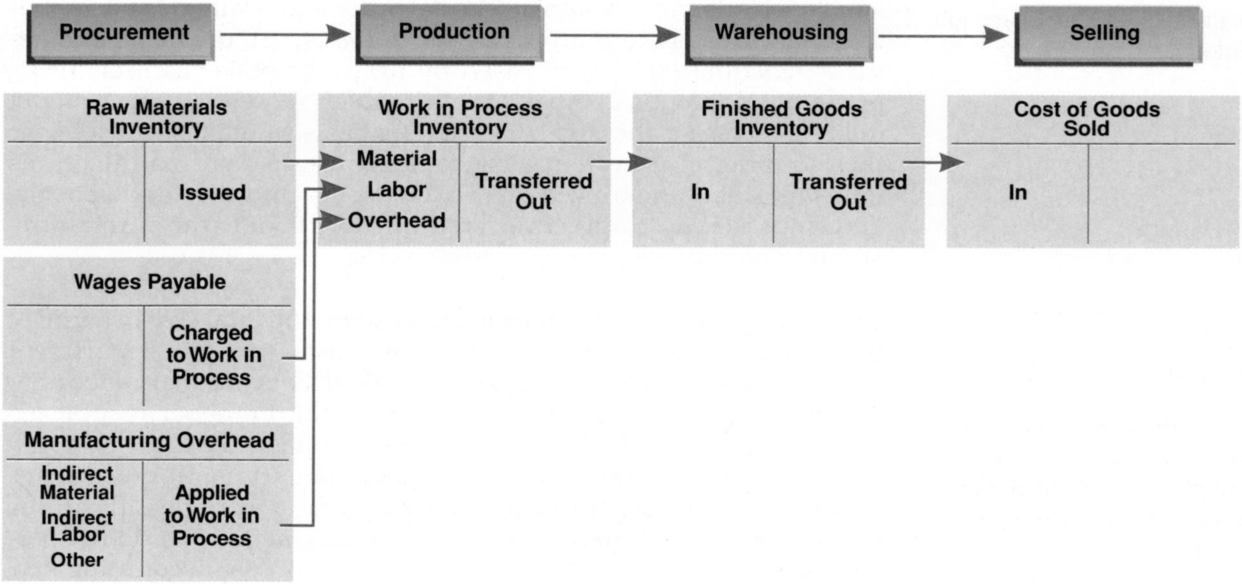

The journal entries necessary to record the flow of manufacturing costs through the accounts will be discussed in detail later. First, let's examine the nature of the three inventory accounts—Raw Materials, Work in Process, and Finished Goods—and how they fit into the flow of costs shown in Figure 29–1. The key to understanding job order cost accounting is in understanding how perpetual inventory accounts work.

The Perpetual Inventory System

When a cost accounting system is used, perpetual inventory records are kept for raw materials, work in process, and finished goods.

In manufacturing operations, taking physical inventories of raw materials, work in process, and finished goods before financial statements are prepared at the end of the accounting period is impractical and expensive. Instead, a perpetual inventory system is used. The **perpetual inventory system** shows the inventories on hand at all times. The system includes the following typical procedures for each of the three principal inventories.

Raw Materials Inventory

Raw materials and supplies of all kinds are recorded in one inventory account called Raw Materials Inventory in the manner described below.

1. All raw materials and manufacturing supplies purchased are recorded in the Raw Materials Inventory account.
2. The costs of direct materials used are removed from the Raw Materials Inventory account and transferred to the Work in Process account.
3. The costs of indirect materials and supplies used are removed from the Raw Materials Inventory account and transferred to the Manufacturing Overhead account.

As a result of recording the costs of all materials purchased and of all materials used during the period, the balance of the Raw Materials Inventory account at the end of any accounting period should reflect the cost of materials and supplies on hand.

Beginning inventory of raw materials	xxx.xx
Add purchases during period	xxx.xx
Total available for use	xxx.xx
Deduct materials used during year	xxx.xx
Ending inventory of raw materials	xxx.xx

At least once a year, a physical inventory should be taken to check the accuracy of the recorded inventory. In the event of a difference, the records should be adjusted to agree with the physical inventory figure.

Work in Process Inventory

The Work in Process Inventory account is charged for direct materials issued for production, as discussed above. The flowchart in Figure 29–1 shows that Work in Process Inventory is also debited for

The balance in the Work in Process Inventory account at the end of the period reflects the cost of work still incomplete at that time.

labor and manufacturing overhead charged into production. Thus all manufacturing costs placed into production during the accounting period are recorded in the Work in Process account.

As work is completed, the related costs are removed from the Work in Process Inventory account and transferred to the Finished Goods Inventory account. The balance in the Work in Process Inventory account at the end of the period should therefore reflect the cost of work still incomplete at that time.

Beginning inventory of work in process	xxx.xx
Add direct materials, direct labor, and manufacturing overhead charged to production	xxx.xx
	xxx.xx
Deduct cost of goods completed	xxx.xx
Ending inventory of work in process	xxx.xx

Finished Goods Inventory

As goods are completed, they are moved from the producing departments to the finished goods storeroom. Their cost will be removed from the Work in Process Inventory account and transferred to the Finished Goods Inventory account.

As goods are sold, their cost will be determined and removed from the Finished Goods Inventory account and transferred to the Cost of Goods Sold account.

The balance of the Finished Goods Inventory account at the end of the period should equal the cost of the finished goods on hand.

Beginning inventory of finished goods	xxx.xx
Add cost of goods manufactured	xxx.xx
	xxx.xx
Deduct cost of goods sold	xxx.xx
Ending inventory of finished goods	xxx.xx

This balance should be checked by taking a physical inventory at least once a year.

Just-in-Time Inventory Systems

Some manufacturing companies that produce goods solely on a special-order basis attempt to eliminate altogether raw materials inventory records. This is accomplished by ordering raw materials to arrive just in time to be placed into production. For this reason the system is called a **just-in-time system.** When the goods arrive, they are moved immediately to the factory floor and charged directly to work in process. As a result, there is no need for a raw materials inventory account nor for a subsidiary raw materials ledger. (This subsidiary ledger is discussed in the following section.)

The advantages of a just-in-time system are obvious.

1. It eliminates having working capital tied up in inventory.
2. It reduces the space necessary for inventory storage.
3. It reduces inventory carrying costs such as storeroom personnel, insurance, and record-keeping costs.

The risks of a just-in-time system are also obvious. If for some reason raw materials are not delivered promptly, the entire manufacturing operations may be shut down. Or, if raw materials are unsatisfactory or are damaged in the manufacturing process, production may temporarily come to a halt. Clearly, the system is risky unless the source of supply is highly dependable.

SELF-REVIEW

1. Why is a cost accounting system needed?
2. What is a job order cost accounting system? When is a job order cost accounting system appropriate?
3. What is a process cost accounting system? Under what conditions would a process cost accounting system be appropriate?
4. Explain a standard cost system.
5. What is a producing department? A service department?

Answers to Self-Review

1. A cost accounting system is needed to determine the cost of each unit that is manufactured. It also helps management keep a close watch on cost behavior and control costs when they get out of line.
2. A job order accounting system is one in which the unit costs of production are determined for each separate production order. It is appropriate for businesses that produce each customer's order as a special order or that produce orders for their products in batches rather than in a continuous operation.
3. A process cost system is one in which the total cost of a unit of product is found by adding the unit costs in each department through which the product passes during the manufacturing process. This system is usually appropriate in situations in which there are continuous operations on standard types of product.
4. A standard cost system allows a firm to determine what its costs should be. Actual costs are compared with predetermined standard costs, which reflect efficient performance. This system may be incorporated into either a job order cost system or a process cost accounting system.
5. A producing department is one in which work is performed directly on the product created. A service department assists in production but does not perform work on the actual product.

A JOB ORDER COST ACCOUNTING SYSTEM

OBJECTIVE 1

Explain how a job order cost accounting system operates.

Installing the job order cost system includes setting up the three required inventory accounts—Raw Materials, Work in Process, and Finished Goods—and appropriate subsidiary accounts. It also requires the development of procedures to record costs incurred, costs of items placed in production, and the transfer of products to finished goods.

Perpetual Inventory Accounts

In a perpetual inventory system, each inventory account is supported by a subsidiary ledger.

Each of the three inventory accounts serves as a perpetual inventory record, and each is supported by a subsidiary ledger. The **raw materials subsidiary ledger** contains a record for each of the different types of raw materials and manufacturing supplies used by the firm.

The **work in process subsidiary ledger** includes a job order cost sheet for each job being worked on. The **finished goods subsidiary ledger** contains a perpetual record for each of the different types of finished products.

Accounting for Materials

OBJECTIVE 2

Journalize the purchase and issuance of direct and indirect materials.

As you have already seen, under the job order cost system the perpetual inventory account, Raw Materials Inventory, reflects all transactions related to materials and supplies.

Purchases of Materials

Purchases of raw materials and supplies are debited to the Raw Materials Inventory account. Typically, a special column entitled Raw Materials Inventory Debit is set up in the voucher register. All transactions involving purchases of materials and supplies are entered in that column.

Assume that at the end of January, purchases of materials and manufacturing supplies for the month, as shown by the total of the Raw Materials Inventory Debit column in the Northwest Manufacturing Corporation's voucher register, amounted to $12,000. The journal entry to record materials purchases for January is shown below.

19Y2					
Jan.	*31*	*Raw Materials Inventory*		*12 0 0 0 00*	
		Accounts Payable			*12 0 0 0 00*
		Cost of materials and			
		supplies purchased during			
		January			

Raw Materials Ledger

For internal control purposes, all purchases of materials by Northwest must be made through the use of prenumbered purchase orders. When the materials and supplies are received, they are checked, counted, and weighed. They are then sent to the storeroom with a report showing what was received. A copy of this receiving report is compared with the supplier's invoice and with the purchase order that was issued by Northwest before the invoice is approved for payment. Data regarding prices and quantities received is obtained from these two records for entry in the individual **raw materials ledger card** that is kept for each item. A typical raw materials ledger card with several transactions posted to it is shown in Figure 29–2. This card is for material XTO-14, a panel unit. Look at the first entry on the card.

FIGURE 29–2
A Raw Materials Ledger Card

RAW MATERIALS LEDGER CARD
(FIFO Cost Method)

ITEM: Brace NUMBER: XTO-14

DATE		REF.	RECEIVED			ISSUED			BALANCE		
			UNITS	PRICE	AMOUNT	UNITS	PRICE	AMOUNT	UNITS	PRICE	AMOUNT
19Y2 Jan.	3	PO-3	150	1.00	150.00				150	1.00	150.00
	8	R-24				100	1.00	100.00	50	1.00	50.00
	12	PO-14	150	1.10	165.00				{50 / 150	1.00 / 1.10	215.00
	17	R-51				{50 / 50	1.00 / 1.10	105.00	100	1.10	110.00
	24	PO-32	100	1.15	115.00				{100 / 100	1.10 / 1.15	225.00
	29	R-90				100	1.10	110.00	100	1.15	115.00

The card shows no balance for material XT0-14 at the beginning of the month. On January 3, 150 panel units were purchased on Purchase Order PO–3 for $1 each. After this transaction, these 150 units are reflected in the Balance section of the ledger card.

OBJECTIVE 3
Maintain perpetual inventory records.

Materials may be withdrawn from the storeroom only on completion of a materials requisition.

Materials Requisition

Materials or supplies are issued by the storeroom only upon presentation of a **materials requisition** signed by someone authorized to withdraw such items. The materials requisition describes the item needed and the quantity and shows the job or purpose for which it is needed. Jobs are ordinarily identified by a job order number, assigned when production on the job begins. The raw materials ledger clerk prices the items listed on the materials requisition. The materials requisition is used by the storeroom clerk in recording materials issued on the individual raw materials ledger cards.

A requisition for Northwest Manufacturing Corporation covering the issuance of 100 units of material XT0-14 on January 8 is shown in Figure 29–3.

FIGURE 29–3
A Materials Requisition Form

MATERIALS REQUISITION

No. R-24

Charge to Account No. 122
Job No. J-5 Date Jan. 8, 19 Y2

Quantity	Description	Unit Cost	Total Cost
100	Panels XTO-14	1.00	100.00

Authorized by	Issued by	Received by
J. Sinclair	E. Layden	T. Santos

Now look at the second entry on the raw materials ledger card in Figure 29–2. This entry shows the issuance on Requisition R–24 of 100 panel units. These units cost $1 each. After this transaction, 50 units are on hand at a cost of $1 per unit.

The raw materials ledger clerk later summarizes the requisitions issued during a week or other operating period. This summary of requisitions issued classifies the direct materials costs by jobs and identifies the supplies and indirect materials involved. It is also the basis for charges to the job order cost sheets (described later) and for a journal entry to record materials issued. This entry debits Work in Process Inventory for the cost of direct materials placed into production, debits Manufacturing Overhead for the cost of indirect materials and supplies issued, and credits Raw Materials Inventory for the total.

For example, assume that Northwest Manufacturing Corporation summarizes materials requisitions at the end of each month. The total materials and supplies issued for the month of January 19Y2 were $9,500 ($9,000 for direct materials and $500 for supplies). The entry to record materials and supplies issued appears in general journal form below.

19Y2					
Jan.	*31*	*Work in Process Inventory*		*9 000 00*	
		Manufacturing Overhead		*500 00*	
		Raw Materials Inventory			*9 500 00*
		Cost of materials and supplies issued during month			

Pricing Basis

In Chapter 17 you learned that there are a number of different methods for determining the value of merchandise inventory. Each method yields significantly different total figures. The most commonly used methods are FIFO, LIFO, and average cost. These same methods are also used in pricing the raw materials inventory. The method used in pricing materials can have an important effect on the final product cost figures obtained. Each company establishes a definite pricing policy after discussion by the accountant with management.

Northwest Manufacturing Corporation uses the FIFO basis of accounting. Look again at the raw materials ledger card for material XTO-14 in Figure 29–2 to see how purchases and issues of materials are entered in the ledger card when the FIFO method is used.

- The third entry, on January 12, reflects the purchase, on Purchase Order PO-14, of an additional 150 units at a cost of $1.10 per unit. After this transaction, there are 200 units on hand.

Since the company is using the FIFO method of inventory pricing, the units on hand are identified with specific purchases. There are 50 units from the purchase of January 3, at a cost of $1 per unit, and 150 units from the purchase of January 12, at a cost of $1.10 per unit.

- The fourth entry in the card reflects the issuance of 100 units on January 17. Remember that under the FIFO system, the first items "in" (purchased) are assumed to be the first items "out" (issued). The 100 units issued are therefore assumed to consist of items purchased in the following sequence:

50 units from the purchase of January 8 (all units purchased on the order have now been issued)	
50 units × $1.00 per unit	$ 50.00
50 units from purchase of January 12	
50 units × $1.10 per unit	55.00
Total 100 units	$105.00

The 100 units remaining on hand are assumed to have come from the last purchase—the purchase of January 12. The balance of item XTO-14 on hand after the issuance on January 17 is therefore $110 (100 units × $1.10 per unit).

Purchases Discounts

When a perpetual inventory system is used for raw materials, the accountant must decide whether the cost of these materials is to be entered in the inventory accounts at the invoice price or at the net invoice price after purchase discounts are deducted.

If the net invoice price after discount is used, the net amount is entered in the purchases journal or voucher register in the manner discussed in Chapter 26. It is then necessary to compute the amount of discount applicable to each item on the invoice so that the net cost of each item can be identified. This procedure is usually rather time-consuming.

To avoid computing the amount of discount applicable to each item, the accountant at the Northwest Manufacturing Corporation decides to record raw materials at their gross invoice price. When raw materials are recorded at gross price under the perpetual inventory system, the purchases discounts may be treated either as other income or as a reduction in the cost of goods sold for the period. Northwest chooses the latter procedure, which is the preferred method.

Accounting for Labor

OBJECTIVE 4

Record labor costs incurred and charge labor into production.

The payroll accounting procedures used in manufacturing activities are the same as those you have learned for a merchandising concern in Chapters 10 and 11 of this book. However, factory labor costs are identified as being either direct labor (charged to Work in Process Inventory) or indirect labor (charged to Manufacturing Overhead). Payrolls are summarized and recorded weekly or monthly. Each summary includes a breakdown of labor costs for the payroll period.

The factory labor costs that Northwest Manufacturing Corporation incurred during January 19Y2 are given below.

Payroll Period Labor	Direct Labor	Indirect Labor	Total
Jan. 8	$1,200	$ 200	$1,400
15	1,300	250	1,550
22	1,200	225	1,425
29	1,100	525	1,625
Totals	$4,800	$1,200	$6,000

The monthly entry to record this payroll data is shown below as it would appear in general journal form.

19Y2				
Jan.	31	Work in Proc. Inv. (Dir. Labor)	4 8 0 0 00	
		Mfg. Overhead (Indirect Labor)	1 2 0 0 00	
		Social Security Tax Payable		3 9 0 00
		Medicare Tax Payable		9 0 00
		Employee Income Tax Pay.		6 1 0 00
		Salaries & Wages Payable		4 9 1 0 00
		Total labor costs for January		

In addition to recording the time when they enter and leave the plant, workers who perform direct labor prepare a series of **time tickets** to account for all time spent in the plant. Each such worker completes a separate time ticket indicating the starting and stopping time for any job on which he or she works. If the worker is idle for part of the day, a time ticket designating "idle time" is prepared so that the cost of this time can be charged appropriately. Idle time is generally charged to manufacturing overhead. If, however, the idle time is due solely to the specifications or peculiarities of the job being worked on, the costs related to the idle time may be charged to that individual job. A typical time ticket appears in Figure 29–4.

A cost clerk computes the total time shown on the time ticket and applies the worker's rate to obtain the cost of the labor. Labor time tickets are sorted by jobs and summarized at the end of each payroll period for entry on the individual job order cost sheets (as shown in Figure 29–5 later in the chapter). The total charged to all the cost sheets must agree with the amounts debited to Work in Process Inventory for direct labor as the payrolls are recorded.

Although the labor time ticket illustrated in Figure 29–4 is designed for manual written entries, many factories use automated systems for recording the time spent by an employee on each task. Each employee is issued an identification card. At the time the employee begins work on a specific job, he or she inserts the identification card into a register. The job being worked on is recorded and the

FIGURE 29–4
Labor Time Ticket

LABOR TIME TICKET

Name Martin Davidson Date January 7, 19 Y2

Description of work	
Assembling tables	Time started 8:00
	Time stopped 10:20
	Hours worked 2 1/3
	Rate of pay $9.00
	Total charge $21.00
Charge Job No. J-5	

Approved J. Sinclair

register automatically records the time the employee began work. Similarly, when the employee has finished working on that job, the identification card is again inserted into the register and the ending time of work on the job is recorded. The beginning and ending times are used by a computer system to automatically compute the charge to be made to each job.

Accounting for Manufacturing Overhead

OBJECTIVE 5
Compute overhead rates and apply overhead to jobs.

As you learned in Chapter 28, manufacturing overhead encompasses all manufacturing costs except direct materials and direct labor. Common overhead items include indirect labor, indirect materials, depreciation of factory building and equipment, insurance, utilities, property taxes, repairs and maintenance, and payroll taxes on factory labor. Overhead costs may be entered in the accounting records in various ways. Northwest Manufacturing Corporation uses a very common method. The company's general ledger contains an account called Manufacturing Overhead. A subsidiary ledger, the **manufacturing overhead ledger,** contains a sheet for each type of overhead item. The overhead costs incurred are debited to the control account, and the details are posted to the appropriate individual subsidiary ledger accounts.

We have already seen that in January Northwest incurred indirect materials costs (supplies) of $500 and indirect labor costs of $1,200. Both these amounts were charged to the Manufacturing Overhead account. In January the company also incurred overhead costs amounting to $2,425 in addition to indirect materials and indirect labor. The entry to summarize these costs is given in general journal form below.

19Y2				
Jan.	*31*	*Manufacturing Overhead*	2 4 2 5 00	
		Accounts Payable and other		
		accounts		2 4 2 5 00
		Overhead for January		

Under the job order cost system, the manufacturing overhead cannot be assigned to a product by simply dividing the total overhead by units of product because each job may cover a different kind of product and should therefore have different amounts of overhead assigned to it. Instead, the company determines an **overhead application rate** and "applies" overhead to jobs using this rate.

Basing Overhead Application on Direct Labor Costs

Methods for applying overhead to specific jobs vary from company to company. Under one widely used method, an estimate is made of the overhead costs for the coming year. A similar estimate is also made of the direct labor costs for the coming year. Estimated total overhead is divided by estimated total direct labor costs to get a predetermined overhead application rate. As direct labor is charged to jobs from summaries of labor time tickets, the overhead rate is multiplied by the direct labor costs. The resulting figure is the amount of overhead to be charged to each job. This method is used by Northwest.

For example, suppose that estimates for the coming year include expected total direct labor costs of \$60,000 and total manufacturing overhead costs of \$45,000. The predetermined overhead application rate is computed to be 75 percent of direct labor costs.

$$\frac{\text{Estimated overhead costs}}{\text{Estimated direct labor costs}} = \frac{\$45{,}000}{\$60{,}000}$$
$$= 75\% \text{ application rate}$$

In January direct labor costs charged to jobs totaled \$4,800. Applying overhead to jobs at the rate of 75 percent of direct labor costs results in charges of \$3,600. This data is recorded in general journal form below.

19Y2				
Jan.	*31*	*Work in Process Inventory*	*3 6 0 0 00*	
		Manuf. Overhead Applied		*3 6 0 0 00*
		Overhead applied to jobs in January at 75% of direct labor costs		

Overapplied or Underapplied Overhead

OBJECTIVE 6
Compute overapplied or underapplied overhead and report it in the financial statements.

Notice that the entry recording the application of overhead to jobs debits Work in Process Inventory and credits Manufacturing Overhead Applied. At the end of each month, the total of the credits recorded in the Manufacturing Overhead Applied account is compared with the total of the debits (actual costs incurred) recorded in the Manufacturing Overhead account for that month. These debits represent the actual overhead costs incurred during the month. If the total of the credits in the applied account is greater, overhead has been **overapplied.** If the total of the debits in the control account is greater, overhead has been **underapplied.** In January the total of the debits in the control account is greater, reflecting an underapplied amount of $525, as shown below.

Actual manufacturing overhead (Debits):		
Indirect materials and supplies	$ 500	
Indirect labor	1,200	
Other overhead costs	2,425	
Total charged to manufacturing overhead		$4,125
Manufacturing overhead applied (Credits)		3,600
Underapplied overhead in January		$ 525

At the end of each month during the year, if the balance of the Manufacturing Overhead control account exceeds the balance of the Manufacturing Overhead Applied account, the difference represents the cumulative underapplied overhead to date. Any underapplied amount is shown on the *monthly* balance sheets as a deferred charge. If the balance of the control account is less than the balance of the applied account, there is a cumulative overapplied amount for the year to date. Any overapplied amount is shown as a deferred credit. This amount is deferred because the application rate is an average based on estimates for the year and may not balance precisely from month to month.

At the end of the year, the Overhead Applied account is closed into the Manufacturing Overhead account. The resulting balance in the Manufacturing Overhead account represents the underapplied or overapplied overhead for the year. The balance of the underapplied or overapplied overhead for the year is normally closed out to the Cost of Goods Sold account. The overapplied or underapplied amount appears as an adjustment to the Cost of Goods Sold amount on the income statement. This subject is treated in detail in cost accounting textbooks.

Basing Overhead Application on Direct Labor Hours

Another commonly used method for applying overhead is based on direct labor hours. For example, assume that the accountant for Northwest expected that 6,000 direct labor hours would be worked in the coming year and that overhead costs would be $45,000. The overhead application rate would be $7.50 per direct labor hour, as shown below.

$$\frac{\text{Estimated overhead costs}}{\text{Estimated direct labor hours}} = \frac{\$45{,}000}{6{,}000} = \$7.50 \text{ per hour}$$

Therefore, if in January 600 direct labor hours were worked, the total direct overhead applied would be $4,500 (600 hours × $7.50 per hour).

SELF-REVIEW

1. When direct materials are issued from the storeroom, what entries are made in the subsidiary records?
2. What is a receiving report?
3. What is a raw materials ledger card?
4. What entry is made for indirect materials issued from the storeroom?
5. What is a time ticket?

Answers to Self-Review

1. Direct materials issued from the storeroom are entered on the raw materials ledger card for the material. Also a posting will be made from the summary of materials requisitions to the Materials section of the job order cost sheet.
2. The receiving report is a record of materials and supplies received.
3. A raw materials ledger card is an individual record kept for each item in the inventory. It shows quantities and costs of items purchased, quantities and costs of items issued, and costs and quantities of items on hand.
4. Indirect materials issued are entered on the raw materials inventory cards. Periodically, based on the summary of materials requisitions, the cost of indirect materials will be charged to the Manufacturing Overhead account and credited to the Raw Materials Inventory account.
5. A time ticket is a record used by workers to account for all time spent in the plant.

The Job Order Cost Sheet

OBJECTIVE 7
Maintain job order cost sheets.

A job order cost sheet is a subsidiary record showing all the manufacturing costs charged to a specific job.

Each new job started in production is assigned a number for identification and reference. A **job order cost sheet** is also set up for the job at this time. The cost sheets for all jobs currently in production constitute a subsidiary ledger that supports the Work in Process Inventory account in the general ledger. The recording procedure gathers together all cost elements.

1. Charges for direct materials are posted to the Materials section of the job order cost sheet from summaries of materials requisitions.
2. Charges for direct labor are posted to the Labor section from summaries of the labor time tickets.
3. As labor costs are posted, overhead is computed at the established application rate and recorded in the Overhead Applied section.
4. When the job is completed, the costs are totaled and divided by the number of units produced to determine the unit cost. The job order cost sheet for Job J–5, started and completed during the month of January, is illustrated in Figure 29–5. Notice that the

FIGURE 29-5
A Job Order Cost Sheet

JOB ORDER COST SHEET

For Stock X
Customer's Name
Address
Item X123 - Tables

Job. No. J-5 Date –
Started Jan. 3, 19Y2
Completed Jan. 15, 19Y2
Quantity 25 (ordered) 25 (completed)

MATERIALS		LABOR		OVERHEAD APPLIED			SUMMARY	
Date	Amount	Date	Amount	Date	Rate	Amount	Item	Amount
Jan. 8	200 00	Jan. 8	116 00	Jan. 8	75%	87 00	Materials	$250 00
15	50 00	15	55 10	15	75%	41 33	Labor	171 10
							Overhead	128 33
							Total	$549 43
							Unit Cost	$ 21 977
							Comments:	
Totals	250 00		171 10			128 33		

information at the top of the sheet shows the job number and the nature of the product being manufactured, its starting and completion dates, and the number of units produced. Northwest's costs for materials and direct labor are posted weekly, and overhead is applied weekly on the basis of 75 percent of direct labor costs. All three costs are then summarized and divided by the units produced to determine the unit cost, as shown in the Summary section of the job order cost sheet.

Accounting for Work Completed

OBJECTIVE 8
Record the cost of jobs completed and the cost of goods sold under a perpetual inventory system.

As each job is completed during the month, the products involved are transferred to finished goods. When the related job order cost sheet is totaled, it supplies the data about quantity, unit cost, and total cost required for posting to the appropriate card in the finished goods subsidiary ledger. This ledger uses the same ledger card forms as the raw materials subsidiary ledger previously illustrated.

At the end of the month, a summary of completed jobs is prepared and an entry is made to transfer the total cost from the Work in Process Inventory account to the Finished Goods Inventory account.

19Y2					
Jan.	31	*Finished Goods Inventory*		14,200 00	
		Work in Process Inventory			14,200 00
		Cost of jobs completed during January			

Accounting for Cost of Goods Sold

As goods are sold, sales invoices are prepared for the customers. The cost of each order is entered as a memorandum on the office copy of the invoice. This cost information comes from the finished goods ledger card for each product. Later the information noted on the invoice copy is used to record credits on the finished goods ledger cards for quantities sold and their costs. At the end of the month, the total cost of goods sold is determined from a summary of the information entered on the invoice copies and is recorded as shown below.

19Y2				
Jan.	31	*Cost of Goods Sold*	12 000 00	
		Finished Goods Inventory		12 000 00
		Cost of goods sold during January		

On the income statement the balance of the Cost of Goods Sold account and the adjustment for underapplied or overapplied overhead are shown as illustrated below.

Sales		$200,000
Cost of Goods Sold (per ledger account)	$148,000	
Add Underapplied Manufacturing Overhead	2,100	
Cost of Goods Sold (adjusted)		150,100
Gross Profit on Sales		$ 49,900

The accountant may prefer to show all the details of actual manufacturing cost, including actual overhead incurred, on the statement of cost of goods manufactured rather than treat the underapplied or overapplied overhead as an adjustment of cost of goods sold.

SUMMARY OF COST FLOW THROUGH INVENTORY ACCOUNTS

The flow of costs through the three inventory accounts (Raw Materials, Work in Process, and Finished Goods) and the Cost of Goods Sold can be seen in the accounts illustrated below.

The Northwest Manufacturing Corporation had inventories of raw materials and finished goods on January 1, 19Y2. There was, however, no beginning inventory of work in process. The three perpetual inventory accounts and the Cost of Goods Sold account are shown below as they appear at the end of January. The entries in the accounts reflect the posting of the journal entries that have been discussed in this chapter.

ACCOUNT *Raw Materials Inventory* ACCOUNT NO. *121*

DATE		EXPLANATION	POST. REF.	DEBIT	CREDIT	BALANCE DEBIT	BALANCE CREDIT
19Y2							
Jan.	1	Balance	√			22 340 00	
	31		J1	12 000 00		34 340 00	
	31		J1		9 500 00	24 840 00	

ACCOUNT *Work in Process Inventory* ACCOUNT NO. *122*

DATE		EXPLANATION	POST. REF.	DEBIT	CREDIT	BALANCE DEBIT	BALANCE CREDIT
19Y2							
Jan.	*31*	*Materials*	*J1*	*9 0 0 0 00*		*9 0 0 0 00*	
	31	*Labor*	*J1*	*4 8 0 0 00*		*13 8 0 0 00*	
	31	*Overhead*					
		Applied	*J1*	*3 6 0 0 00*		*17 4 0 0 00*	
	31	*To Fin.*					
		Goods	*J1*		*14 2 0 0 00*	*3 2 0 0 00*	

ACCOUNT *Finished Goods Inventory* ACCOUNT NO. *126*

DATE		EXPLANATION	POST. REF.	DEBIT	CREDIT	BALANCE DEBIT	BALANCE CREDIT
19Y2							
Jan.	*1*	*Balance*	√			*16 0 0 0 00*	
	31		*J1*	*14 2 0 0 00*		*30 2 0 0 00*	
	31		*J1*		*12 0 0 0 00*	*18 2 0 0 00*	

ACCOUNT *Cost of Goods Sold* ACCOUNT NO. *560*

DATE		EXPLANATION	POST. REF.	DEBIT	CREDIT	BALANCE DEBIT	BALANCE CREDIT
19Y2							
Jan.	*31*		*J1*	*12 0 0 0 00*		*12 0 0 0 00*	

MANAGERIAL IMPLICATIONS

The job order cost system keeps managers informed of the cost of manufacturing specific orders or batches of goods and therefore permits the computation of the cost per unit of product. The use of an overhead application rate helps to develop a more consistent unit cost from month to month because the effects of unusual expenses or variations in monthly volume of output are averaged over the entire year. In addition, computation of unit costs helps management in evaluating and maintaining efficiency.

Perpetual inventory procedures help in keeping management informed about the exact amounts tied up in inventories. In this way they serve as useful tools for inventory control.

SELF-REVIEW

1. What is an overhead application rate?
2. Why is an overhead application rate necessary under the job order cost accounting system?
3. How is underapplied or overapplied manufacturing overhead disposed of at the end of the year?
4. What use is made of the totals on a job order cost sheet?
5. Under the perpetual inventory method, what journal entries are made for sales and cost of goods sold?

Answers to Self-Review

1. An overhead application rate is a predetermined rate for assigning overhead to each job—usually on the basis of either direct labor hours or direct labor cost.
2. An overhead application rate is necessary because different jobs cover different kinds of products and should therefore have different amounts of overhead assigned to them.
3. At the end of the year, underapplied or overapplied overhead is closed. It is usually shown in the Cost of Goods Sold section of the income statement.
4. The totals on the job order cost sheet are used as the basis of entries on the finished goods ledger sheet. Also, the totals provide a basis for making the journal entry to transfer cost of completed jobs from Work in Process to Finished Goods.
5. Sales are recorded by debiting Accounts Receivable and crediting Sales. The cost of goods sold is recorded by debiting Cost of Goods Sold and crediting Finished Goods Inventory.

CHAPTER 29 Review and Applications

CHAPTER SUMMARY

Under the job order cost system, each of three inventory accounts—Raw Materials Inventory, Work in Process Inventory, and Finished Goods Inventory—is operated as a perpetual inventory record. The raw materials ledger, which is subsidiary to the Raw Materials Inventory account, contains a ledger card for each raw material. Job cost sheets function as a subsidiary ledger supporting the Work in Process Inventory account in the general ledger. Similarly, the finished goods ledger contains a record for each type of finished goods. It serves as a subsidiary to the Finished Goods Inventory account.

Raw materials are issued upon presentation of a written requisition that shows the number of the job for which direct materials will be used, and that job is charged with the proper cost. A requisition for indirect materials or supplies will be charged to the proper overhead account. Time tickets provide a basis for charging direct labor to the specific job. Manufacturing overhead is assigned to jobs on the basis of an application rate that is commonly related to direct labor costs or to direct labor hours. Underapplied or overapplied overhead is carried forward from month to month. The net underapplied or overapplied overhead at the end of the year is closed out, usually as an adjustment to Cost of Goods Sold on the income statement.

As each job is completed, the cost sheet furnishes data needed for transferring costs from the Work in Process Inventory account to the Finished Goods Inventory account. The cost of each order is also entered on the office copy of the sales invoice. At the end of the month, the cost of goods sold is determined by summarizing this data. Then the transfer entry is recorded in the general journal.

GLOSSARY OF NEW TERMS

Finished goods subsidiary ledger (p. 1034) A perpetual record for each of the different types of finished products

Job order (p. 1029) A specific order for a specific batch of manufactured items

Job order cost accounting (p. 1029) A cost accounting system whereby unit costs of manufactured items are determined for each separate production order

Job order cost sheet (p. 1042) A subsidiary record of all manufacturing costs charged to a specific job

Just-in-time system (p. 1032) An inventory system whereby raw materials are ordered so as to arrive just in time to be placed into production

Manufacturing overhead ledger (p. 1039) A subsidiary ledger that contains a record for each overhead item

Materials requisition (p. 1035) A form that describes the item needed, the quantity needed, and the job for which the item is needed

Overapplied overhead (p. 1041) A result of applied overhead exceeding the actual overhead costs

Overhead application rate (p. 1040) The rate at which the estimated cost of overhead is charged to each job

Perpetual inventory system (p. 1031) An inventory system that shows inventories on hand at all times

Process cost accounting (p. 1029) A cost accounting system whereby unit costs of manufactured items are determined by totaling unit costs in each production department

Producing departments (p. 1029) Departments within a manufacturing firm that perform work directly on a product

Production order (p. 1029) See Job order

Raw materials ledger card (p. 1034) A record showing details of receipts and issues for a type of raw material

Raw materials subsidiary ledger (p. 1034) A ledger containing the raw materials ledger cards

Service departments (p. 1029) Departments within a manufacturing firm that assist in production but do not work directly on the product

Standard costs (p. 1030) A cost accounting system that establishes standards for expected costs for materials, labor, and overhead for each unit of product

Time tickets (p. 1038) Forms used to record hours worked and jobs performed

Underapplied overhead (p. 1041) A result of actual overhead costs exceeding applied overhead

Work in process subsidiary ledger (p. 1034) A ledger containing the job order cost sheets

REVIEW QUESTIONS

1. What is a perpetual inventory?
2. What information does a job order cost sheet contain?
3. When direct materials are issued from the storeroom, what entries are made in the subsidiary records?
4. What is a receiving report?
5. What is a materials requisition?
6. What does the Raw Materials Inventory account show?
7. What entry is made for indirect materials issued from the storeroom?
8. What is idle time? How is the cost of idle time accounted for?

9. Name the sources of postings to the job order cost sheet.
10. What account is debited and what account is credited when manufacturing overhead is applied?
11. Name five common manufacturing overhead costs.
12. Why is an overhead application rate used?
13. What account is debited and what account is credited when completed goods are transferred from factory floor to the finished goods storeroom?

MANAGERIAL FOCUS

1. The president of your company, a fairly large manufacturing concern, suggests that it would be more efficient to discontinue the job of storeroom clerk and to let factory workers enter the storeroom and select their own materials. Comment on this suggestion.
2. Assume that you are an accountant at a manufacturing firm. At the end of one year, there is a large overapplied overhead amount. How would you explain to management why this balance might exist?
3. Why should management insist that a physical inventory be taken once a year even though perpetual inventory records are kept?
4. From an administrative standpoint, why is direct labor cost a simple basis to use for the application of manufacturing overhead?
5. In general, would managers prefer to see overapplied or underapplied overhead? Why?

EXERCISES

Data for Exercises 29–1 through 29–4. During October 19X6 the Nash Manufacturing Company purchased and issued the following materials and supplies. Use October 31 as the date for all entries.

PURCHASES		ISSUES FROM STOREROOM	
Direct materials	$40,900	Direct materials	$38,725
Manufacturing supplies	2,050	Manufacturing supplies	1,018

EXERCISE 29–1 (Obj. 2)

Tutorial

Journalizing purchase of direct materials. Give the entry in general journal form to record the cost of the direct materials purchased.

EXERCISE 29–2 (Obj. 2)

Journalizing purchase of indirect materials. Give the entry in general journal form to record the cost of the manufacturing supplies purchased during October by Nash.

EXERCISE 29–3 (Obj. 2)

Journalizing issuance of direct materials. Give the entry in general journal form to record the cost of the direct materials issued by Nash during October.

EXERCISE 29–4
(Obj. 2)

Journalizing issuance of indirect materials. Give the entry in general journal form to record the cost of the manufacturing supplies issued by Nash during October.

EXERCISE 29–5
(Obj. 4)
Tutorial

Recording labor costs incurred. A payroll summary prepared at the Nash Manufacturing Company showed the following figures for October 19X6.

Direct labor costs incurred	$16,040
Indirect labor costs incurred	2,160
Social security tax withheld	1,183
Medicare tax withheld	273
Income tax withheld	1,662

Give the October 31 entry in general journal form to record the labor costs incurred.

EXERCISE 29–6
(Obj. 5)
Tutorial

Computing alternative overhead rates; applying overhead to jobs. The Lupe Corporation is considering two methods for applying overhead. One method is to base the rate on direct labor costs, and the other method is to base the rate on the number of direct labor hours. Estimated data for the next year, 19X5, is shown below.

Estimated direct labor costs	$1,200,000
Estimated direct labor hours	150,000 hours
Estimated overhead costs	$600,000

1. What would be the overhead application rate based on direct labor costs?
2. What would be the overhead application rate based on direct labor hours?
3. During 19X5, Job X5 was started and finished, requiring 700 hours of direct labor. What would be the amount of overhead applied to the job if an overhead rate based on direct labor hours is used?

EXERCISE 29–7
(Obj. 5)

Applying overhead. The McNulty Corporation's direct labor costs were $90,160 in 19X2. Assuming that the corporation applies overhead at the rate of 75 percent of direct labor costs, give the general journal entry on December 31 summarizing the overhead applied by McNulty during 19X2.

EXERCISE 29–8
(Obj. 5)

Applying overhead. During 19X2 the McNulty Corporation began and completed Job SO-465. Costs entered on the job order cost sheet for this job were $9,810 for materials and $6,900 for labor.

1. Assuming that the overhead rate is 75 percent of direct labor, compute the amount of overhead that should be applied to the job.
2. Compute the total cost of the job.

EXERCISE 29–9
(Obj. 6)

Computing overapplied or underapplied overhead. For the year 19X2 the McNulty Corporation's actual overhead costs were $263,610, and its applied overhead was $264,820.

1. Did the firm have overapplied or underapplied overhead for the year?
2. What amount was overapplied or underapplied?

EXERCISE 29–10
(Obj. 8)

Tutorial

Recording cost of goods completed and cost of goods sold. The records of the Gulfport Corporation for 19X3 show that it completed goods costing $96,280 and that it had a cost of goods sold of $99,600. Give the entries in general journal form on December 31, 19X3, to record the cost of goods completed and the cost of goods sold for the year.

PROBLEMS

PROBLEM SET A

PROBLEM 29–1A
(Obj. 2, 4, 5, 6, 8)

Tutorial

Recording purchase and issuance of direct and indirect materials, recording labor costs, applying overhead, computing overapplied or underapplied overhead, recording cost of jobs completed and cost of goods sold. The cost data given below is for the Andrea Specialty Company, a maker of sports trophies, for the month of March 19X3.

COST DATA

a. Raw materials and supplies costing $29,000 were purchased.
b. The summary of materials requisitions shows that materials and supplies costing $24,000 were issued for use in jobs. Direct materials accounted for $22,400, and the balance consisted of indirect materials and supplies.
c. The payroll summary shows that direct labor costs were $11,000 and indirect labor costs were $2,000. Social security tax withheld was $845, medicare tax withheld was $195, and income tax deductions were $1,225.
d. Manufacturing overhead of $5,625 was incurred in addition to indirect materials and indirect labor. (Credit Accounts Payable.)
e. The predetermined overhead application rate is 80 percent of direct labor costs.
f. The summary of completed jobs shows that the cost of these jobs amounted to $35,500.
g. The summary of sales invoices shows that goods costing $28,800 were sold on credit for $46,000.

Instructions

1. Prepare general journal entries to record each item of cost data given. Use the account titles listed in the textbook.
2. Compute the amount of overapplied or underapplied overhead for the month.
3. Prepare a partial income statement for the month of March. Adjust the cost of goods sold for the amount of any overapplied or underapplied overhead.

PROBLEM 29–2A
(Obj. 2, 4, 5, 6, 8)

Recording purchase and issuance of direct and indirect materials, recording labor costs, applying overhead, computing overapplied or underapplied overhead, recording cost of jobs completed and cost of goods sold. In July 19X4 the Snook Pool Table Corporation had the transactions given below in connection with its manufacturing operations.

COST DATA

a. Raw materials costing $62,000 were purchased.
b. Raw materials costing $56,000 were used: direct materials, $52,400; indirect materials, $3,600.
c. Factory wages of $64,000 were incurred: direct labor, $45,270; indirect labor, $18,730. Social security tax deductions were $4,160, medicare tax deductions were $960, and income tax deductions were $6,160.
d. Other overhead costs of $9,210 were incurred. (Credit Accounts Payable.)
e. Estimated manufacturing overhead costs were applied to jobs in production at the rate of 70 percent of direct labor costs.
f. Finished goods costing $81,000 were transferred from the factory floor to the warehouse.
g. The cost of goods sold was $77,300.
h. Customers were billed $99,720 for goods sold.

Instructions

1. Prepare general journal entries to record each item of cost data given. Use the account titles listed in the textbook.
2. Compute the amount of overapplied or underapplied overhead for the month.
3. Prepare a partial income statement for the month of July. Adjust the Cost of Goods Sold figure for any overapplied or underapplied overhead.

PROBLEM 29–3A
(Obj. 5, 6, 7, 8)

Tutorial GL

Maintaining job order cost sheets, applying overhead to jobs, computing overapplied or underapplied overhead, recording cost of jobs completed and cost of goods sold. The Osage Cabinet Company builds cabinets and book shelves. On January 1, 19X3, one job (C–123) was in progress. The order is from Metro Apartment Corporation and was begun on December 19, 19X2. Costs accumulated to date on that job are materials, $3,750; labor, $1,720; and overhead, $860. During January the following costs were incurred in production work on Job C–123 and on Jobs S–28 and C–124, which were started on January 5, 19X3.

	Materials	Labor	Items	Quantity
Job C–123	$1,080	$1,380	X-10 Cabinets	120
Job S–28	6,020	3,100	X45 Shelves	200
Job C–124	4,050	840	X07 Cabinets	80

Job S–28 is being manufactured for State Furniture Outlets and Job C–124 is for stock.

Manufacturing overhead is applied at the rate of 50 percent of direct labor costs. During January actual manufacturing overhead costs of $2,990 were incurred. Job C–123 was completed on January 18 and was delivered to the customer. The sales price was $16,800.

Instructions

1. Prepare job order cost sheets for the three jobs. Enter the beginning balances applicable to Job C–123.
2. Post the costs of the materials and labor for January to the job order cost sheets.
3. Compute the overhead amounts that should be applied to the three jobs worked on during the month, and enter these amounts on the job cost sheets.
4. Give the entry in general journal form to transfer the cost of the job completed from work in process to finished goods.
5. Compute the amount of underapplied or overapplied overhead for January.

PROBLEM SET B

PROBLEM 29–1B
(Obj. 2, 4, 5, 6, 8)

Tutorial

Recording purchase and issuance of direct and indirect materials, recording labor costs, applying overhead, computing overapplied or underapplied overhead, recording cost of jobs completed and cost of goods sold. The cost data given below is for Huron Company, a manufacturer of hand-crafted jewelry, for May 19X4.

COST DATA

a. Materials purchased, $68,000.
b. Materials issued to production, $61,000: direct materials, $59,800; indirect materials, $1,200.
c. Payroll: direct labor, $24,000; indirect labor, $6,000; social security tax deducted, $1,950; medicare tax deducted, $900; income tax deducted, $1,464.
d. Manufacturing overhead of $12,000 was incurred in addition to indirect materials and indirect labor. (Credit Accounts Payable.)
e. Manufacturing overhead is applied to production at a predetermined rate of 75 percent of direct labor costs.
f. Jobs costing $81,000 were completed and transferred to finished goods.
g. Finished goods costing $69,000 were sold and billed to customers at $91,000.

Instructions

1. Prepare general journal entries to record each item of cost data given. Use the account titles listed in the textbook.
2. Compute the amount of overapplied or underapplied overhead for the month.
3. Prepare a partial income statement for the month of December. Adjust the cost of goods sold for any overapplied or underapplied overhead.

PROBLEM 29–2B
(Obj. 2, 4, 5, 6, 8)

Recording purchase and issuance of direct and indirect materials, recording labor costs, applying overhead, computing overapplied or underapplied overhead, recording cost of jobs completed

and cost of goods sold. In June 19X5 the Electronic Games Corporation had the following manufacturing transactions.

COST DATA

a. Raw materials costing $57,700 were purchased.
b. Raw materials costing $60,900 were used: direct materials, $57,875; indirect materials, $3,025.
c. Factory wages of $57,000 were incurred: direct labor, $39,570; indirect labor, $17,430; social security tax deducted, $3,705; medicare tax deducted, $855; and income tax deducted, $6,080.
d. Other overhead costs amounting to $11,000 were incurred. (Credit Accounts Payable.)
e. Estimated manufacturing overhead costs were applied to jobs in production at the rate of 80 percent of direct labor costs.
f. Finished goods costing $93,000 were transferred to the warehouse.
g. Goods costing $76,000 were sold and billed to customers for $98,420.

Instructions

1. Prepare general journal entries to record each item of cost data given. Use the account titles listed in the textbook.
2. Compute the amount of overapplied or underapplied overhead for the month.
3. Prepare a partial income statement for the month of June. Adjust the cost of goods sold for any overapplied or underapplied overhead.

PROBLEM 29–3B
(Obj. 5, 6, 7, 8)

Tutorial

Maintaining job order cost sheets, applying overhead to jobs, computing overapplied or underapplied overhead, recording cost of jobs completed and cost of goods sold. The Botts Corporation makes camping trailers. On January 1, 19Y2, two jobs, TRX–4 and SRX–1, were in progress. The costs accumulated to date on these jobs are shown below. Job TRX–4 involves three TRX trailers being built for Outdoor Camping Corporation. Job SRX–1 involves two SRX trailers being built for Recreation USA. Both jobs were begun on November 28, 19Y1.

	Job TRX–4	Job SRX–1
Materials	$18,500	$14,100
Labor	4,100	2,650
Overhead	2,460	1,590

During January the following costs were incurred in production work on the two existing jobs and on a new job, TRX–5, which involves two TRX trailers being constructed for the company's own stock. Job TRX–5 was begun on January 13.

	Job TRX–4	Job SRX–1	Job TRX–5
Materials	$1,300	$2,640	$13,670
Labor	1,800	1,750	1,060

Manufacturing overhead is applied at the rate of 60 percent of direct labor costs. During January actual manufacturing overhead costs of $2,997 were incurred. Jobs TRX–4 and SRX–1 were completed on January 15, 19Y2. The sales price of Job TRX–4 was $41,300, and the sales price of Job SRX–1 was $37,600.

Instructions

1. Prepare job order cost sheets for the three jobs. Enter the beginning balances applicable to Jobs TRX–4 and SRX–1.
2. Post the costs of the materials and labor for January to the job order cost sheets.
3. Compute the overhead amounts that should be applied to the three jobs worked on during January, and enter these amounts on the job order cost sheets.
4. Give the entry in general journal form to transfer the costs of the two jobs completed from work in process to finished goods.
5. Compute the amount of underapplied or overapplied overhead for January.

CHALLENGE PROBLEM

Custer's Manufacturing Company manufactures one product. All materials are added at the beginning of production. On January 1, 19X8, one job, No. X7–21, was in process, with the following accumulated costs:

Materials	$6,000
Direct labor	2,000
Manufacturing overhead	1,000
Total	$9,000

The beginning finished goods inventory on January 1, 19X8, was $12,000.

The following additional data is given for the month of January.

Total labor costs incurred	$13,000
Total cost of completed Job X7–21	13,500
Total materials costs incurred	15,000

In addition, Job X8–1 was begun and completed during the month. Its costs included materials of $8,000 and labor of $7,000. Job X8–2 was begun during the month and was in process at the end of the month. During the month, sales were $42,500 and the gross profit rate was 40 percent.

Instructions

1. For Jobs X7–21, X8–1, and X8–2, calculate the cost of materials, labor, and overhead for the month of January to find the total cost of each job.
2. Prepare a schedule of cost of goods sold for the month of January.

CRITICAL THINKING PROBLEM

The job order cost sheets for the Lucas Manufacturing Company show the following information about special orders for September and October of the current year.

	Manufacturing Costs		
Job Number	September	October	Status of Job
S–688	$6,900		Sold, 10/3
S–689	3,240		Completed, 9/27
S–690	1,450	$2,890	Completed, 10/8
S–691	780	3,740	Sold, 10/10
S–692	520	6,040	Sold, 10/16
O–693		5,340	Sold, 10/22
O–694		3,100	Completed, 10/20
O–695		4,130	In process, 10/31
O–696		1,200	In process, 10/31

Lucas Manufacturing prices its jobs to make a 40 percent gross profit on sales. Operating expenses for October totaled $10,276, and the company's income tax rate is 25 percent of net income before income taxes.

Instructions

1. From this data, compute the following:
   a. Work in Process Inventory, October 1
   b. Finished Goods Inventory, October 1
   c. Cost of Goods Sold for October
   d. Work in Process Inventory, October 31
   e. Finished Goods Inventory, October 31
   f. Sales for October
2. Prepare a condensed income statement for Lucas Manufacturing Company for the month of October.

CHAPTER 30

Process Cost Accounting

OBJECTIVES

1. Compute equivalent production to express the amount of work accomplished with no beginning work in process inventory.
2. Prepare a cost of production report for producing departments with no beginning work in process inventory.
3. Compute the unit cost of manufacturing under the process cost accounting system.
4. Record costs incurred and the flow of costs as products move through the manufacturing process and are sold.
5. Compute equivalent production and prepare a cost of production report with a beginning inventory of work in process.
6. Define the accounting terms new to this chapter.

In the previous chapter the basic principles and procedures of job order cost accounting were discussed. You saw how such a system is used to gather and determine the cost of each item produced. In this chapter you will learn how a process cost accounting system operates. The operations of the Redwine Manufacturing Corporation, which produces laminated trays, will provide the basis for our discussion.

NEW TERMS

Average method of process costing ▪ Cost of production report ▪ Equivalent production ▪ Process cost accounting system

THE PROCESS COST ACCOUNTING SYSTEM

In operations where a single product is manufactured and production is continuous, the **process cost accounting system** is generally used. The process cost system has many of the same features as the job order cost system (see Chapter 29). The flow of costs is almost exactly like that shown in Figure 29–1, and the same Raw Materials Inventory and Finished Goods Inventory accounts are used. There are, however, several significant differences. One such difference is that there is no need to maintain job order cost sheets when a process cost accounting system is used because products are not made in batches or by order. Another major difference is that under process cost accounting a separate Work in Process account is maintained for each department. All costs for materials and labor are identified with specified producing departments as the costs are incurred, and they are charged to the departmental Work in Process accounts.

Under the process cost system, all costs incurred during a period are divided by the production for the period in order to compute a unit cost.

Overhead costs are identified with each producing and service department. The accumulated overhead costs for service departments are allocated on some logical basis to the producing departments at the end of the month. Consequently, all manufacturing costs are charged to the departmental Work in Process accounts at the end of each month. The monthly costs assigned to each producing department are then allocated to the units of product worked on in the department that month, and a cost per unit of product in that department is computed. Thus a process cost accounting system may be viewed as a monthly average cost system because all costs incurred during the month are divided by all units produced that month in the department. As products are transferred from one department to another, the related costs are also transferred. Knowledge of the flow of products in the manufacturing process helps the accountant plan the necessary recording procedures for all producing and service activities.

Redwine's factory operation has two producing departments: the laminating department and the finishing department. All products go through the laminating department. Then trays to be sold in a rough, unpainted state are moved directly to the finished goods storeroom and are recorded in the Finished Goods Inventory account. Other trays go to the finishing department and from there to the finished goods storeroom. This flow of goods is shown in Figure 30–1.

FIGURE 30–1
Flow of Goods in a Factory Operation

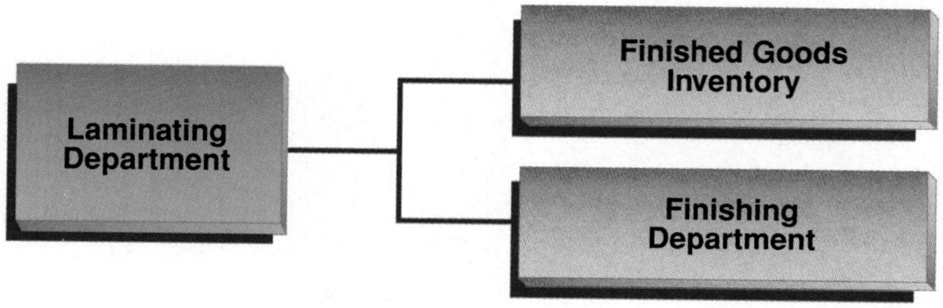

Analyzing Process Cost Data

Let's see how the process cost accounting system used by the Redwine Manufacturing Corporation is put into effect. We begin by examining the data for the first month's operation. Assume that transactions involving materials, labor, and overhead for January have been recorded and departmentalized. Assume, also, that costs of all service departments have been allocated to the producing departments that benefit from the services rendered. The allocated service department costs are treated as overhead of the producing department. A record has been kept of products started, completed, and still in process in each department. The stage of completion of the ending work in process has been estimated. Table 30–1 tells the story in summary form, using three headings—Costs, Quantities, and Stage of Completion—for the month of January 19Y4.

TABLE 30–1
Departmental Cost Data for January 19Y4

	Laminating Department	Finishing Department
Costs		
Materials	$13,000.00	$ 910.00
Labor	6,240.00	2,340.00
Manufacturing Overhead	4,875.00	1,690.00
Total Costs	$24,115.00	$4,940.00
Quantities		
Started in Production	4,000	–0–
Transferred In from Prior Department	–0–	2,700
Transferred Out to Next Department	2,700	–0–
Transferred Out to Finished Goods	1,000	2,500
Work in Process—Ending	300	200
Stage of Completion—Ending Work in Process		
Materials	Complete	1/2
Labor	2/3	1/2
Manufacturing Overhead	2/3	1/2

In the Quantities section of the table, note that of the 4,000 units started in production in the laminating department, 2,700 were transferred to the finishing department and 1,000 were transferred to finished goods for sale as unpainted trays. This transfer leaves 300 trays still in process in the laminating department. The Stage of Completion section indicates that all the required materials have been issued and two-thirds of the labor and overhead have been added to the 300 trays in process.

A similar review of the data in the column for the finishing department reveals that of the 2,700 units transferred in from the laminating department, only 2,500 were completed and transferred to finished goods. Two hundred trays were left in process in the finishing department at the end of the period, to which one-half of the materials, labor, and overhead have been added.

Now that the total costs and the number of units of product worked on in each department are known, it might seem that the cost for each type of tray can be found by dividing the total cost for each cost element by the number of units. However, this calculation would not be correct because some of the units are not complete. The equivalent production must be established before meaningful unit costs can be computed.

Determining Equivalent Production

OBJECTIVE 1

Compute equivalent production to express the amount of work accomplished with no beginning work in process inventory.

The equivalent production technique shows the amount of work accomplished, expressed in terms of equivalent whole units. Simply stated, **equivalent production** represents the estimated number of units that could have been started and completed with the same effort and cost incurred in the department during the month. Thus if two units were started during the period and only one-half of the materials has been added to each, one unit could have been started and completed using those materials.

Using the departmental quantity data given in Table 30–1, we can compute the equivalent production in each department. Let's first calculate equivalent units for the laminating department.

In computing equivalent production, accountants frequently consider labor and overhead to be at the same stage of completion.

Calculating Equivalent Units for Laminating Department

Separate computations must be made for the three elements of production (materials, labor, and overhead) whenever the states of completion of the three elements in the work in process inventory are different. The schedule in Table 30–1 shows that in the laminating department labor and overhead in the ending inventory are at the same stage of completion; thus the same equivalent units of production will apply to both of these elements. However, the stage of completion for materials is different, requiring a separate calculation. As you read the following two paragraphs, look at Table 30–2, which illustrates the calculations for the laminating department.

For materials, the equivalent units of production in the ending work in process total 4,000 units (3,700 + 300) because all the mate-

TABLE 30–2
Computation of Equivalent Production: Laminating Department

Materials		
Units Transferred Out		
To Next Department: 100% × 2,700 units	2,700	
To Finished Goods: 100% × 1,000 units	1,000	
Total Transferred Out		3,700
Work in Process: 100% × 300 units		300
Equivalent Units of Production for Materials		4,000
Labor and Manufacturing Overhead		
Units Transferred Out		
To Next Department: 100% × 2,700 units	2,700	
To Finished Goods: 100% × 1,000 units	1,000	
Total Transferred Out		3,700
Work in Process: 2/3 × 300 units		200
Equivalent Units of Production for Labor and Overhead		3,900

rials have been issued not only for the 3,700 units transferred out of the department, but also for the 300 trays in process.

On the other hand, the 300 units in process in the laminating department are only two-thirds completed as to labor and manufacturing overhead. Adding two-thirds of the labor and overhead to 300 units is equivalent to adding all the materials to 200 completed units (2/3 × 300). The total equivalent units of production for labor and overhead in the department are determined by adding the 200 units in ending work in process to the 3,700 units completed and transferred out of the department. On this basis, equivalent units of production total 3,900 units for labor and manufacturing overhead.

Calculating Equivalent Units for Finishing Department

In the finishing department, materials, labor, and manufacturing overhead are at the same stage of completion (one-half). Therefore, only one computation of equivalent units of production is necessary for the department (see Table 30–3). The 200 trays that are half-completed as to materials, labor, and manufacturing overhead are equivalent to 100 completed units (1/2 × 200). This figure is added to the 2,500 units actually completed to obtain a total equivalent production of 2,600 units for each of the three elements of cost.

TABLE 30–3
Computation of Equivalent Production: Finishing Department

Materials, Labor, and Manufacturing Overhead	
Units Transferred Out: 100% × 2,500 units	2,500
Work in Process: 1/2 × 200 units	100
Equivalent Units of Production for Materials, Labor, and Overhead	2,600

Preparing the Cost of Production Report

OBJECTIVE 2
Prepare a cost of production report for producing departments with no beginning work in process inventory.

With the basic data on costs, quantities, and equivalent production assembled for the month of January, a cost of production report can now be prepared. The **cost of production report** summarizes all costs charged to each department during the month and shows how these costs are assigned to the goods transferred out of the department and those still in process. A commonly used form of this report, illustrated in Table 30–4, page 1062, provides separate sections to summarize quantities and costs. In turn, each section is composed of two parts that reconcile the totals to be accounted for with the totals actually accounted for.

OBJECTIVE 3
Compute the unit cost of manufacturing under the process cost accounting system.

Calculating Costs for the Laminating Department

Let's now look at January's cost of production report for the laminating department shown in Table 30–4. The first section, the Quantity Schedule, shows the units to be accounted for (a) and explains what happened to these units (b).

The second section is entitled Cost Schedule. Its first part (c) shows the total cost of each cost element, the unit cost that results from dividing the total cost of each element by the appropriate equivalent production units (previously computed), and the cumulative cost total. (In practice, the equivalent production units and computations are not shown in the report. The usual report has only two columns, Total Cost and Unit Cost.)

The total of costs accounted for must equal the cumulative total cost for the department.

The second part of the Cost Schedule section (d) accounts for the various costs in two groups. First it shows the cost of units completed through this department and transferred out. Then it presents the cost of the ending inventory of work in process. The sum of these two amounts equals the cumulative cost total shown in the Costs to Be Accounted For portion. As shown in the cost of production report, the ending work in process for each cost element (materials, labor, and overhead) is computed by multiplying the equivalent production units in process for each cost element by the unit cost for that element. The total work in process is found by adding the costs of the three elements.

There are 300 equivalent units for materials in work in process and the unit cost is $3.25. Multiplying these figures gives the total

TABLE 30–4
Cost of Production Report, January 19Y4: Laminating Department

Quantity Schedule			Units		
(a) Quantity to Be Accounted For					
Started in Production			4,000		
Total to Be Accounted For			4,000		
(b) Quantity Accounted For					
Transferred Out to Next Department			2,700		
Transferred Out to Finished Goods			1,000		
Work in Process—Ending			300		
Total Accounted For			4,000		
Cost Schedule	Total Cost		E.P. Units		Unit Cost
(c) Costs to Be Accounted For					
Costs in Current Department					
Materials	$13,000.00	÷	4,000	=	$3.25
Labor	6,240.00	÷	3,900	=	1.60
Manufacturing Overhead	4,875.00	÷	3,900	=	1.25
Cumulative Cost Total	$24,115.00				$6.10
(d) Costs Accounted For					
Transferred Out to Next Department	$16,470.00	=	2,700	×	$6.10
Transferred Out to Finished Goods	6,100.00	=	1,000	×	6.10
Total Costs Transferred Out	$22,570.00				
Work in Process—Ending					
Materials	$ 975.00	=	300	×	$3.25
Labor	320.00	=	200	×	1.60
Manufacturing Overhead	250.00	=	200	×	1.25
Total Work in Process	$ 1,545.00				
Total Costs Accounted For	$24,115.00				

materials cost in the ending work in process inventory—$975 (300 × $3.25). For labor, the equivalent units total 200 (300 × 2/3). Multiplying 200 equivalent units by the unit cost of $1.60 gives a total cost for labor of $320. For manufacturing overhead, 200 equivalent units are multiplied by the $1.25 unit cost to get a total of $250. When the three cost elements are added, the result is a value of $1,545 ($975 + $320 + $250) for the total ending work in process inventory of the department, as shown in the cost of production report in Table 30–4.

Calculating Costs for the Finishing Department

A cost of production report for the second producing department, the finishing department, is shown in Table 30–5. In the Quantity Schedule section, the quantity to be accounted for (a) consists of units transferred in from the prior department. In turn, these units are accounted for (b) as transferred to finished goods or as still in process at the end of the month. Note that there is a new item in the first part (c) of the Cost Schedule section. Under Costs to Be Ac-

TABLE 30–5
Cost of Production Report, January 19Y4: Finishing Department

Quantity Schedule			Units		
(a) Quantity to Be Accounted For					
Transferred In from Prior Department			2,700		
Total to Be Accounted For			2,700		
(b) Quantity Accounted For					
Transferred Out to Finished Goods			2,500		
Work in Process—Ending			200		
Total Accounted For			2,700		

Cost Schedule	Total Cost		E.P. Units		Unit Cost
(c) Costs to Be Accounted For					
Costs in Prior Department	$16,470.00	÷	2,700	=	$6.10
Costs in Current Department					
Materials	$ 910.00	÷	2,600	=	$0.35
Labor	2,340.00	÷	2,600	=	0.90
Manufacturing Overhead	1,690.00	÷	2,600	=	0.65
Total Current Department Costs	$ 4,940.00				$1.90
Cumulative Cost Total	$21,410.00				$8.00
(d) Costs Accounted For					
Transferred Out to Finished Goods	$20,000.00	=	2,500	×	$8.00
Work in Process—Ending					
Costs in Prior Department	$ 1,220.00	=	200	×	$6.10
Costs in Current Department					
Materials	35.00	=	100	×	$0.35
Labor	90.00	=	100	×	0.90
Manufacturing Overhead	65.00	=	100	×	0.65
Total Work in Process	$ 1,410.00				
Total Costs Accounted For	$21,410.00				

counted For, the $16,470 cost of the 2,700 units transferred into the finishing department from the laminating department is shown under Costs in Prior Department.

If there is no beginning inventory of work in process, the total cost to be accounted for in a department is the total of (1) costs transferred in from the prior department and (2) costs incurred in the current department.

Costs in the current department (the finishing department) are listed next. Each cost element (material, labor, and overhead) is divided by the 2,600 equivalent units previously computed (see Table 30–3) to obtain the unit cost figures. Total costs in the current department ($4,940) are then added to total costs in the prior department ($16,470) to get the cumulative cost total ($21,410). Unit costs for prior department costs ($6.10) and for costs added in the current department ($1.90) are added to obtain the figure of $8 for the cumulative unit cost of both departments.

The total of (1) the cost of products transferred out of a department and (2) the cost of ending work in process in the department must equal the total costs charged to the department.

Again, the costs are accounted for in two parts. The first part shows the cost of the 2,500 units completed and transferred out to finished goods. These units are valued at $20,000 ($8 a unit × 2,500 units). The next computation shows the cost elements relating to the work in process inventory. A new element appears in this computation—the costs in the prior department of $6.10 a unit. Applying this cost to the ending inventory of 200 units (which is complete with respect to the work of the prior department) results in a total value of $1,220 ($6.10 × 200). Current department costs are determined by multiplying the 100 equivalent units for each cost element (200 × 1/2) by the unit cost, as shown. The total costs in the current department that are applicable to the ending inventory of work in process are therefore materials, $35; labor, $90; and overhead, $65. Total cost of the ending work in process inventory is $1,410. The total costs transferred out ($20,000) plus the ending work in process inventory ($1,410) yields the total cost accounted for, $21,410. This figure, in turn, equals the cumulative cost total, determined in the first part of the Cost Schedule section (Table 30–5).

Recording Cost Flows

OBJECTIVE 4
Record costs incurred and the flow of costs as products move through the manufacturing process and are sold.

The flow of costs in the accounting records follows the flow of production.

1. All direct materials costs and direct labor costs are charged to the departmental Work in Process accounts.
2. Overhead costs incurred are charged to the Manufacturing Overhead control account and are entered on the departmental overhead sheets for each department.
3. At the end of the month the costs of the service departments are allocated to the producing departments.
4. Finally, the Manufacturing Overhead control account is closed into the departmental Work in Process accounts.

Let's look at the journal entries to summarize flows in the manufacturing operations of Redwine Corporation for January 19Y4.

Charging Costs to Work in Process

Debits to the departmental work in process accounts of Redwine Manufacturing Corporation are made during the month as follows.

1. Materials issued to production are recorded by debiting the departmental Work in Process accounts and crediting Raw Materials Inventory.

19Y4				
Jan.	*31*	*Work in Process—Lam. Dept.*	*13 0 0 0 00*	
		Work in Process—Fin. Dept.	*9 1 0 00*	
		Raw Materials Inventory		*13 9 1 0 00*
		Charge materials to production		

2. Labor is debited to the departmental Work in Process accounts and credited to Salaries and Wages Payable and other liability accounts.

19Y4				
Jan.	*31*	*Work in Process—Lam. Dept.*	*6 2 4 0 00*	
		Work in Process—Fin. Dept.	*2 3 4 0 00*	
		Social Security Tax Payable		*5 5 7 70*
		Medicare Tax Payable		*1 2 8 70*
		Employee Income Tax Pay.		*7 2 0 00*
		Salaries and Wages Payable		*7 1 7 3 60*
		Salaries and wages for month		

3. As we have already seen, when manufacturing overhead costs are incurred they are debited to the Manufacturing Overhead account, a control account, in the general ledger. At the same time, they are entered in subsidiary manufacturing overhead ledger sheets for each department. Then at the end of the month the overhead costs of all service departments are allocated to the producing departments. After this allocation, the total of the overhead ledger sheets for the producing departments will equal the total of all manufacturing overhead costs that have been incurred during the month. This total will also equal the balance in the Manufacturing Overhead control account.
4. Finally, the balance in the Manufacturing Overhead control account is closed into the departmental Work in Process accounts.

Assuming that the total overhead for the month is $6,565 and that $4,875 is to be assigned to the laminating department and $1,690 to the finishing department, we can make the following journal entry to charge the overhead into production. (For the sake of simplicity, entries to record manufacturing costs at the time they are incurred have been omitted.)

19Y4				
Jan.	31	Work in Process—Lam. Dept.	4 8 7 5 00	
		Work in Process—Fin. Dept.	1 6 9 0 00	
		Manufacturing Overhead		6 5 6 5 00
		Charge overhead to work in process		

Recording Transfers of Products out of Departments

Entries for material, labor, and overhead costs are posted to the Work in Process accounts. In turn, these accounts supply the data needed for the cost of production reports.

The cost of goods transferred from the laminating department to the finishing department and to finished goods inventory is shown in the cost of production report for the laminating department seen in Table 30–4. (Remember that in the Redwine factory some trays are not processed in the finishing department but are transferred in rough, unpainted form from the laminating department directly to the finished goods inventory.) Based on the cost of production report for the laminating department, an entry is made in the general journal to transfer costs from the laminating department to the finishing department and to finished goods. An entry is also made to transfer the cost of goods completed in the finishing department to the Finished Goods Inventory account, using the figures shown in the cost of production report for the finishing department.

19Y4				
Jan.	31	Work in Process—Fin. Dept.	16 4 7 0 00	
		Finished Goods Inventory	6 1 0 0 00	
		Work in Proc.—Lam. Dept.		22 5 7 0 00
		Cost of goods transferred out of laminating dept. in January		
	31	Finished Goods Inventory	20 0 0 0 00	
		Work in Proc.—Fin. Dept.		20 0 0 0 00
		Cost of goods completed in January		

After the above entries have been posted, the departmental Work in Process accounts appear as shown below. Note that each ending balance agrees with the amount shown in the departmental cost of production report.

ACCOUNT *Work in Process—Laminating Department* ACCOUNT NO. 122

DATE		EXPLANATION	POST. REF.	DEBIT	CREDIT	BALANCE DEBIT	BALANCE CREDIT
19Y4							
Jan.	31	Materials	J1	13 000 00		13 000 00	
	31	Labor	J1	6 240 00		19 240 00	
	31	Overhead	J1	4 875 00		24 115 00	
	31	Trans. Out	J1		22 570 00	1 545 00	

ACCOUNT *Work in Process—Finishing Department* ACCOUNT NO. 123

DATE		EXPLANATION	POST. REF.	DEBIT	CREDIT	BALANCE DEBIT	BALANCE CREDIT
19Y4							
Jan.	31	Materials	J1	910 00		910 00	
	31	Labor	J1	2 340 00		3 250 00	
	31	Overhead	J1	1 690 00		4 940 00	
	31	Prior Dept.	J1	16 470 00		21 410 00	
	31	Trans. Out	J1		20 000 00	1 410 00	

Recording Sale of Finished Goods

The final step in the month's flow of costs is to record the sale of finished goods. Suppose Redwine's sales during January totaled $29,500 and the cost of the goods sold amounted to $18,750. The entry to record the sales requires a debit to Accounts Receivable and a credit to Sales for the selling price. A second entry is made to record the cost of goods sold, debiting Cost of Goods Sold and crediting Finished Goods Inventory for $18,750. These entries are illustrated below in general journal form.

19Y4					
Jan.	31	Accounts Receivable		29 500 00	
		Sales			29 500 00
		Record sales on credit			
		for January			
		Cost of Goods Sold		18 750 00	
		Finished Goods Inventory			18 750 00
		Cost of goods sold in			
		January			

After the above entries have been posted, the ledger accounts for Finished Goods Inventory and Cost of Goods Sold appear as follows. The illustration assumes a beginning balance of $32,000 for Finished Goods Inventory.

ACCOUNT *Finished Goods Inventory* ACCOUNT NO. *126*

DATE		EXPLANATION	POST. REF.	DEBIT	CREDIT	BALANCE DEBIT	BALANCE CREDIT
19Y4							
Jan.	*1*	*Balance*	✓			*32 0 0 0 00*	
	31		*J1*	*6 1 0 0 00*		*38 1 0 0 00*	
	31		*J1*	*20 0 0 0 00*		*58 1 0 0 00*	
	31		*J1*		*18 7 5 0 00*	*39 3 5 0 00*	

ACCOUNT *Cost of Goods Sold* ACCOUNT NO. *560*

DATE		EXPLANATION	POST. REF.	DEBIT	CREDIT	BALANCE DEBIT	BALANCE CREDIT
19Y4							
Jan.	*31*		*J1*	*18 7 5 0 00*		*18 7 5 0 00*	

SELF-REVIEW

1. Why may a process cost accounting system be referred to as an average cost system?
2. What information is contained in the Quantity Schedule section of a cost of production report?
3. In one firm, goods are transferred from the cleaning department to the mixing department. The costs transferred in April 19X3 totaled $86,000. Show the journal entry to record the transfer.
4. What entry is made to record the transfer of finished goods from the final producing department to the finished goods inventory?
5. In one company some of the units processed in a department are sold without further processing. Other units, which are identical, are transferred to a second department for further processing. How will this affect the computations on the cost of production report?

Answers to Self-Review

1. All costs for each manufacturing element (materials, labor, and overhead) incurred during the month are added together and divided by the equivalent units of production for that element during the month. Costs incurred for each element are, in a sense, averaged.
2. The first part of the Schedule shows the units to be accounted for. The second part shows what happened to the units.
3. Work in Process—Mixing Department is debited for $86,000; Work in Process—Cleaning Department is credited for $86,000.
4. The entry to record the transfer of finished goods from the factory floor to the warehouse is a debit to Finished Goods Inventory and a credit to the Work in Process account of the final department.

5. The Costs Accounted For section of the cost of production report will require two lines for products transferred out of the department. One line will be Transferred Out to Next Department and the second will be Transferred Out to Finished Goods. The total of the two amounts would equal Total Costs Transferred Out.

THE BEGINNING WORK IN PROCESS INVENTORY

OBJECTIVE 5

Compute equivalent production and prepare a cost of production report with a beginning inventory of work in process.

In January Redwine had no beginning inventories of work in process. In the second and later months, however, beginning inventories are a normal part of business operations, being brought forward as the ending inventories of the preceding month. Data covering the performance of both of Redwine's producing departments for the second month is summarized in Table 30–6. Note that the costs of the beginning work in process inventory are shown first, broken down by department and cost element.

TABLE 30–6
Departmental Production and Cost Data for February 19Y4

	Laminating Department	Finishing Department
Costs		
Work in Process—Beginning		
Costs in Prior Department		$1,220.00
Costs in Current Department		
Materials	$ 975.00	35.00
Labor	320.00	90.00
Manufacturing Overhead	250.00	65.00
Current Department Costs—February		
Materials	13,380.00	1,130.50
Labor	6,565.00	2,839.50
Manufacturing Overhead	4,850.00	1,919.50
Total Costs	$26,340.00	$7,299.50
Quantities		
Work in Process—Beginning	300	200
Started in Production	4,050	–0–
Transferred In from Prior Department	–0–	3,000
Transferred Out to Next Department	3,000	–0–
Transferred Out to Finished Goods	1,200	3,100
Work in Process—Ending	150	100
Stage of Completion—Work in Process		
Beginning Inventory		
Materials	Complete	1/2
Labor	2/3	1/2
Manufacturing Overhead	2/3	1/2
Ending Inventory		
Materials	Complete	1/2
Labor	1/3	1/2
Manufacturing Overhead	1/3	1/2

Determining Equivalent Production

Under the average cost system, the cost of each element in beginning work in process is added to the cost of that element during the month.

The equivalent production computations for the second month are worked out just as they were for the first month. The beginning inventory does not complicate the situation at all since the **average method of process costing** is used here. This method simply combines the beginning inventory figure of each cost element with the cost incurred for that element during the current period. The equivalent production computations for February are summarized in Table 30–7.

TABLE 30–7
Computation of Equivalent Production for February 19Y4

Laminating Department		
Materials		
Units Transferred Out		
To Next Department	3,000	
To Finished Goods	1,200	4,200
Work in Process—Ending: 100% × 150 units		150
Equivalent Production for Materials		4,350
Labor and Manufacturing Overhead		
Units Transferred Out		
To Next Department	3,000	
To Finished Goods	1,200	4,200
Work in Process—Ending: 1/3 × 150 units		50
Equivalent Production for Labor and Overhead		4,250
Finishing Department		
Prior Department Costs: 100% × 3,200 units		3,200
Materials, Labor, and Manufacturing Overhead		
Units Transferred Out		3,100
Work in Process—Ending: 1/2 × 100 units		50
Equivalent Production for Materials, Labor, and Overhead		3,150

Preparing the Cost of Production Report

With the data for February assembled and the equivalent production figures computed, the next step is to prepare the cost of production report. This report is illustrated in Table 30–8 as it would normally be prepared, showing both departments in one presentation. (The total cost and unit cost figures appear without the detailed computations that were shown in the January reports.)

Quantity Schedule

Again, the Quantity Schedule section is almost self-explanatory. The beginning inventory of work in process plus the units started in production or received from the prior department during the period make up the total to be accounted for (a). These units are either transferred out or remain in process at the end of the period (b).

Cost Schedule

For the first time, a beginning inventory (c) appears for the laminating department. The unit costs in this department are determined by adding the beginning inventory and the current period costs for each cost element and then dividing the total by the equivalent production for that element. For instance, materials costs are computed by adding $975, (d), and $13,380, (f), to obtain $14,355. Dividing this num-

TABLE 30–8
Cost of Production Report, February 19Y4

	Laminating Department		Finishing Department	
Quantity Schedule		Units		Units
(a) Quantity to Be Accounted For				
Work in Process—Beginning		300		200
Started in Production		4,050		–0–
Transferred In from Prior Department		–0–		3,000
Total to Be Accounted For		4,350		3,200
(b) Quantity Accounted For				
Transferred Out to Next Department		3,000		–0–
Transferred Out to Finished Goods		1,200		3,100
Work in Process—Ending		150		100
Total Accounted For		4,350		3,200
Cost Schedule	Total Cost	Unit Cost	Total Cost	Unit Cost
Costs to Be Accounted For				
Costs in Prior Department				
Work in Process—Beginning	–0–	–0–	$ 1,220.00	
Transfers In—Current Month	–0–	–0–	18,360.00	
Total Prior Department Cost			$19,580.00	$6.12
Costs in Current Department				
(c) Work in Process—Beginning				
(d) Materials	975.00		$ 35.00	
(e) Labor	320.00		90.00	
Manufacturing Overhead	250.00		65.00	
Current Period Costs				
(f) Materials	13,380.00	$3.30	1,130.50	0.37
(g) Labor	6,565.00	1.62	2,839.50	0.93
Manufacturing Overhead	4,850.00	1.20	1,919.50	0.63
Total Current Department Cost	$26,340.00	$6.12	$ 6,079.50	8.05
Cumulative Total Cost	$26,340.00	$6.12	$25,659.50	8.05
Costs Accounted For				
(h) Transferred Out to Next Department	$18,360.00	$6.12	–0–	–0–
Transferred Out to Finished Goods	7,344.00	6.12	$24,955.00	8.05
Total Costs Transferred Out	$25,704.00		$24,955.00	
(i) Work in Process—Ending				
Costs in Prior Department			608.00*	6.12
Costs in Current Department				
Materials	$ 495.00	3.30	18.50	0.37
Labor	81.00	1.62	46.50	0.93
Manufacturing Overhead	60.00	1.20	31.50	0.63
Total Work in Process	$ 636.00		$ 704.50	
Total Costs Accounted For	$26,340.00		$25,659.50	

*Adjusted $4.00 for rounding error.

ber by 4,350 equivalent units gives the unit cost of $3.30. For labor, $320, (e), is added to $6,565, (g), to get total labor cost of $6,885. Dividing by 4,250 equivalent units gives the unit cost of $1.62. The same procedure is followed for manufacturing overhead. The total unit cost for the department is $6.12.

The last part of the Cost Schedule section for the laminating department appears exactly as it did in January (Table 30–4). Quantities transferred (h) to the finishing department or to finished goods are multiplied by the $6.12 unit cost figure to get the total cost transferred out. The ending work in process inventory (i) is computed by multiplying the equivalent production units for each cost element by the unit cost for that element, as shown below.

Laminating Department	
Materials	150 units fully completed × $3.30 = $495
Labor	150 units × 1/3 completed × $1.62 = $ 81
Manufacturing Overhead	150 units × 1/3 completed × $1.20 = $ 60

Under the average cost method, the beginning inventory amount for each cost element is added to the amount of that cost element incurred during the current period.

It is customary to round unit costs to the nearest whole cent or tenth of a cent.

For the finishing department, two items are shown under Costs in Prior Department. The beginning inventory amount ($1,220) is added to the cost transferred in during the current period ($18,360), and the total of $19,580 is divided by the total units (3,200) to get an average unit cost of $6.12 (rounded to the nearest cent) for the work in the prior department. The actual prior department cost is $6.11875, but the unit cost has been rounded to $6.12. Depending on the number of units involved, it is customary to round unit costs to the nearest whole cent or tenth of a cent. Assume that the accountant of Redwine has chosen to compute unit costs to the nearest whole cent. As seen later in this discussion, rounding will require an adjustment in the schedule of costs accounted for.

Current department unit costs are computed as they were for the laminating department. First, consider the cost of materials. The beginning inventory figure, $35.00, is added to the current-period amount, $1,130.50, to obtain a total materials cost of $1,165.50. This total is divided by the 3,150 equivalent units of materials to obtain the unit cost of $0.37 ($1,165.50 ÷ 3,150). Manufacturing overhead computations are handled in the same manner. The procedure used to account for the costs of the finishing department is the same as the procedure used for the laminating department. The cost of goods completed is computed by multiplying the 3,100 units completed by the unit cost of $8.05. The ending work in process balance for each cost element is found by multiplying the equivalent units by the cost per unit.

Earlier it was pointed out that the unit cost shown in the finishing department for Prior Department Cost was rounded to the nearest whole cent. In many cases, costs of materials, labor, and overhead may also be rounded. The accountant for Redwine Corporation has elected to use a commonly followed procedure of reducing the ending work in process inventory by $4 to offset the rounding error. The necessary adjustment is computed as follows.

Work in process—prior department costs, based on rounded cost of \$6.12 per unit (100 × \$6.12)	\$612.00
Total prior department costs less costs transferred out [\$19,580 − (3,100 × \$6.12)]	608.00
Adjustment of ending work in process—prior department costs	\$ 4.00

Recording Cost Flows

The ending work in process inventory of one period becomes the beginning work in process inventory of the following period.

Entries to summarize the February costs and transfers are shown below. Following the journal entries, the departmental Work in Process accounts are shown as they appear after these entries have been posted. Note that the beginning balances of the Work in Process accounts are the same as the ending balances for January. The balances shown in the accounts at the end of February correspond to the amounts shown on the February cost of production report illustrated in Table 30-8.

19Y4				
Feb.	*28*	*Work in Process—Lam. Dept.*	*13,380.00*	
		Work in Process—Fin. Dept.	*1,130.50*	
		Raw Materials Inventory		*14,510.50*
		Charge materials to production		
	28	*Work in Process—Lam. Dept.*	*6,565.00*	
		Work in Process—Fin. Dept.	*2,839.50*	
		Social Security Tax Payable		*611.30*
		Medicare Tax Payable		*141.07*
		Employee Income Tax Pay.		*794.00*
		Salaries and Wages Payable		*7,858.13*
		Salaries and wages for month		
	28	*Work in Process—Lam. Dept.*	*4,850.00*	
		Work in Process—Fin. Dept.	*1,919.50*	
		Manufacturing Overhead		*6,769.50*
		Charge overhead to work in process		
	28	*Work in Process—Fin. Dept.*	*18,360.00*	
		Finished Goods Inventory	*7,344.00*	
		Work in Proc.—Lam. Dept.		*25,704.00*
		Cost of goods transferred out of laminating dept. in Feb.		
	28	*Finished Goods Inventory*	*24,955.00*	
		Work in Process—Fin. Dept.		*24,955.00*
		Costs of goods completed in Feb.		

ACCOUNT *Work in Process—Laminating Department* ACCOUNT NO. *122*

DATE		EXPLANATION	POST. REF.	DEBIT	CREDIT	BALANCE DEBIT	BALANCE CREDIT
19Y4							
Feb.	28	Balance	√			1 5 4 5 00	
	28	Materials	J1	13 3 8 0 00		14 9 2 5 00	
	28	Labor	J1	6 5 6 5 00		21 4 9 0 00	
	28	Overhead	J1	4 8 5 0 00		26 3 4 0 00	
	28	Trans. Out	J1		25 7 0 4 00	6 3 6 00	

ACCOUNT *Work in Process—Finishing Department* ACCOUNT NO. *123*

DATE		EXPLANATION	POST. REF.	DEBIT	CREDIT	BALANCE DEBIT	BALANCE CREDIT
19Y4							
Feb.	28	Balance	√			1 4 1 0 00	
	28	Materials	J1	1 1 3 0 50		2 5 4 0 50	
	28	Labor	J1	2 8 3 9 50		5 3 8 0 00	
	28	Overhead	J1	1 9 1 9 50		7 2 9 9 50	
	28	Prior Dept.	J1	18 3 6 0 00		25 6 5 9 50	
	28	Trans. Out	J1		24 9 5 5 00	7 0 4 50	

Recording the Sale of Finished Goods

Assume that sales totaling $40,000 are made during February and that the cost of goods sold is $25,500. Entries in general journal form to record the sales and the transfer of costs from Finished Goods Inventory to Cost of Goods Sold follow.

19Y4					
Feb.	28	Accounts Receivable		40 0 0 0 00	
		Sales			40 0 0 0 00
		Record sales on credit for Feb.			
	28	Cost of Goods Sold		25 5 0 0 00	
		Finished Goods Inventory			25 5 0 0 00
		Cost of goods sold in Feb.			

The ledger accounts for Finished Goods Inventory and Cost of Goods Sold, after the February entries have been posted, are shown on page 1075.

ACCOUNT *Finished Goods Inventory* ACCOUNT NO. *126*

DATE		EXPLANATION	POST. REF.	DEBIT	CREDIT	BALANCE DEBIT	BALANCE CREDIT
19Y4							
Feb.	1	Balance	√			39 350 00	
	28		J1	7 344 00		46 694 00	
	28		J1	24 955 00		71 649 00	
	28		J1		25 550 00	46 099 00	

ACCOUNT *Cost of Goods Sold* ACCOUNT NO. *560*

DATE		EXPLANATION	POST. REF.	DEBIT	CREDIT	BALANCE DEBIT	BALANCE CREDIT
19Y4							
Feb.	28		J1	25 550 00		25 550 00	

MANAGERIAL IMPLICATIONS

Managers must be provided with accurate and up-to-date cost data about the products manufactured so they can intelligently set prices, evaluate efficiency, and make appropriate operating decisions to improve profits. A firm should probably seek the aid of a specially trained cost accountant to develop a cost accounting system that will accurately and speedily yield the required data. The process cost system yields this information when there is only one product being manufactured and it is manufactured on a continuous basis. Use of the process cost system provides a manufacturing cost for each unit, which is useful in pricing products, controlling costs, and making decisions, when the same product is produced on an ongoing basis. The average cost method of handling beginning inventories of work in process simplifies calculation of the costs per unit.

SELF-REVIEW

1. How does a cost of production report with a beginning inventory of work in process differ from a report that shows no beginning inventory?
2. How is the cost of an equivalent unit for labor determined when there is a beginning inventory and the average method of handling the beginning inventory is used?
3. How are the costs transferred in from a prior department treated in the cost of production report?

4. What is the source of the information in the Costs to Be Accounted For section of a cost of production report?
5. A company uses the process cost accounting system. It has two service departments. How will the costs of the service departments enter into the cost of an equivalent unit for the producing departments?

Answers to Self-Review

1. When there is a beginning work in process inventory, both the quantities and the costs for this inventory must be accounted for. The costs per equivalent unit must consider the beginning inventory of each element as well as the costs added during the current period.
2. The amount of labor cost in the beginning work in process inventory must be added to the labor costs incurred during the current period. The total is divided by the equivalent units of production to arrive at the labor cost per unit.
3. The costs transferred in from the prior department must be treated as a "cost to be accounted for" in the department to which the product is transferred.
4. The current month's costs to be accounted for in the cost of production report are taken from the departmental Work in Process accounts. The details of beginning inventory of work in process can be determined from the cost of production report of the prior month.
5. At the end of the month, the costs of service departments are allocated to the overhead of the producing departments.

CHAPTER 30 Review and Applications

CHAPTER SUMMARY

The process cost accounting system is commonly used when only one product is manufactured in a department and production is on a continuous basis, rather than in batches or specific jobs. Under the process cost system, a work in process inventory account is set up for each producing department. Costs of materials and labor are charged directly to the departmental Work in Process accounts. Manufacturing overhead is recorded in the Manufacturing Overhead control account in the general ledger and in the manufacturing overhead subsidiary ledger. In the subsidiary ledger, a departmental cost sheet is set up for each producing and each service department. At the end of the month, the costs accumulated for service departments are allocated on some logical basis to the producing departments.

A cost of production report is prepared at the end of the month to give full details about costs and quantities. The equivalent production unit technique is used to convert ending work in process to equivalent finished production. Then the costs for each equivalent unit of materials, labor, and manufacturing overhead are computed. The value of goods transferred out of the department, as well as of work in process inventories, is determined on the basis of the equivalent units of production for each cost element. The costs of the goods transferred from one department to another are charged to the receiving department and removed from the Work in Process account of the first department.

If there is a beginning work in process inventory, the same basic process cost accounting procedures are followed. When the average cost method is used, the beginning inventory of each cost element is added to the costs incurred during the current month for that element. For example, the beginning inventory of materials is added to the cost of materials put into production during the current period. The equivalent units of production are computed for each element in the same manner as when there was no beginning inventory of work in process. The unit cost for each element is determined by dividing the total cost of that element by the equivalent units of production for the element. The cost of product transferred out of the department and the cost of the ending work in process are then computed in the usual manner.

GLOSSARY OF NEW TERMS

Average method of process costing (p. 1070) A method of costing based on combining the beginning inventory figure of each cost element with the cost incurred for that element in the current period

Cost of production report (p. 1061) A summary of all costs charged to each department during the period and how those costs are accounted for

Equivalent production (p. 1060) The estimated number of units that could have been started and completed during the same time period and with the same effort and cost

Process cost accounting system (p. 1058) A method of accounting in which costs are accumulated for each process or department and then transferred on to the next process or department.

REVIEW QUESTIONS

1. Why are job order cost sheets not used in the process cost accounting system?
2. What are equivalent units of production?
3. In a cost of production report, what items are found in the Costs to Be Accounted For section?
4. How is the ending work in process inventory computed in a process cost accounting system?
5. Will the same equivalent units always be used for materials, labor, and overhead? Explain.
6. Will the amount shown as a department's ending inventory of work in process on the cost of production report agree with the work in process for the department in the general ledger after adjusting and closing entries have been posted? Explain.
7. Why is it not necessary to use an overhead application rate when the process cost accounting system is employed?
8. Why may the process cost accounting system be unsatisfactory when several different products are being manufactured in the same department?
9. How does accounting for the raw materials inventory and the finished goods inventory differ under the process cost accounting system and the job order cost accounting system?
10. Explain what is meant by "the average method" of accounting for beginning work in process inventories in a process cost system.
11. Explain how to compute the equivalent production for labor when there is a beginning work in process inventory for the period, assuming that the average cost method is used.

MANAGERIAL FOCUS

1. The directors of the firm where you work ask you to explain whether the job order cost accounting system or the process cost accounting system provides the more accurate costs for each unit of product. What will you tell them?

2. What are the benefits to management of perpetual inventories?
3. How would managers use the cost of labor for each equivalent unit to help control costs?
4. Why would a comparison of the cost per equivalent unit of each cost element (materials, labor, and overhead) for the current month with that of the preceding month be useful to management?
5. A member of management in the company that employs you asks why it is necessary to convert production to equivalent units when determining the cost of each unit of product produced under the process cost accounting system. Explain.

EXERCISES

(*Note:* Omit explanations for all journal entries.)

Data for Exercises 30–1 Through 30–3. Information about production in the grinding department of the Cruz Manufacturing Company for May 19X3 follows.

Beginning inventory, work in process	–0–
Transferred in from prior department	12,000 units
Transferred out to next department	8,400 units
Ending inventory, work in process	3,600 units
Stage of completion of ending work in process:	
Prior department costs	100%
Materials	60%
Labor and overhead	40%

EXERCISE 30–1
(Obj. 1)
Tutorial

Computing equivalent production for prior department costs with no beginning inventory. Compute the equivalent units of production for the prior department costs for the month of May for Cruz Manufacturing Company.

EXERCISE 30–2
(Obj. 1)
Tutorial

Computing equivalent production for materials with no beginning inventory. Compute the equivalent units of production for materials for the month of May.

EXERCISE 30–3
(Obj. 1)
Tutorial

Computing equivalent production for labor and overhead with no beginning inventory. Compute the equivalent units of production for labor and overhead for the month of May.

EXERCISE 30–4
(Obj. 1, 3)
Tutorial

Computing equivalent production for materials and unit cost of materials with no beginning work in process. On May 1, 19X4, there was no beginning inventory in the grinding department, the first department, of the Han Corporation. During the month, production was started on 2,000 units. The total cost of materials was $18,400. All materials were placed in production at the start of the manufacturing process in the department. During the month, 1,600 units were transferred to the next department and 400 units were still in process at the end of the month.

1. What is the cost per equivalent unit for materials?
2. What is the cost of materials in the goods transferred to the next department?
3. What is the cost of materials in the ending work in process inventory?

Data for Exercises 30–5 and 30–6. The cooking department is the first manufacturing department of the ReMark Corporation. On May 1, 19X4, the beginning inventory in this department consisted of 2,000 units. Costs for the beginning work in process were as follows.

Materials (100% complete)	$15,000
Labor (75% complete)	9,000
Overhead (75% complete)	3,000

During the month, 10,000 units were started in production with the following costs:

Materials	$75,240
Labor	61,664
Overhead	19,776

During the month, 10,400 units were completed and transferred to the next department, and 1,600 units were still in process at the end of the month. To these 1,600 units, all materials had been added and 80 percent of labor and overhead had been added.

EXERCISE 30–5 (Obj. 3, 5) **Computing equivalent production for materials and cost per equivalent unit with beginning work in process.**

1. Compute the equivalent production for materials for ReMark Corporation for May.
2. Compute the cost per equivalent unit for materials for May.
3. Compute the cost of materials in the work transferred out of the department during the month.
4. Compute the cost of materials in the ending work in process at the end of the month.

EXERCISE 30–6 (Obj. 3, 5) **Computing equivalent production for overhead and cost per equivalent unit with beginning work in process.**

1. Compute the equivalent production for overhead for May.
2. Compute the cost per equivalent unit for overhead for May.
3. Compute the cost of overhead in the goods transferred to the next department.
4. Compute the cost of overhead in the ending work in process inventory.

Data for Exercises 30–7 Through 30–9. In North Lake Corporation, production is started in the forming department. The work is then transferred to the finishing department where goods are completed and then transferred to the finished goods storeroom. Data about the company's costs during February 19X3 follows.

Material costs placed into production	
Forming department	$50,000
Finishing department	1,200
Direct labor costs	
Forming department	3,000
Finishing department	10,000
Taxes withheld from employees' earnings:	
Social security tax withheld	845
Medicare tax withheld	195
Employees' income tax withheld	1,100
Overhead costs	
Forming department	12,500
Finishing department	6,000

During the month, products costing $34,000 were transferred from the forming department to the finishing department; goods costing $48,000 were transferred from the finishing department to finished goods inventory; and goods that cost $52,000 were sold on account for $71,000.

EXERCISE 30–7
(Obj. 4)

Recording costs incurred in production. Give the journal entries on February 28 to summarize the following:

1. Materials placed into production
2. Labor costs charged into production
3. Overhead costs charged into production

EXERCISE 30–8
(Obj. 4)

Recording transfer of product between departments and from work in process to finished goods. Give the general journal entries on February 28 to record the following events during February.

1. Transfer of product from the forming department to the finishing department
2. Transfer of finished goods from the finishing department to the finished goods inventory

EXERCISE 30–9
(Obj. 4)

Recording cost of goods completed. Give general journal entries to record the following events during February.

1. Sale of goods
2. Cost of goods sold

PROBLEMS

PROBLEM SET A

PROBLEM 30–1A
(Obj. 1)
Tutorial

Computing equivalent production with no beginning work in process. The Eastern Garden Cart Company manufactures a single type of garden cart. The monthly production report for January 19X3 follows.

EASTERN GARDEN CART COMPANY Monthly Production Report for January 19X3			
	Molding Department	Assembly Department	Completion Department
Quantities			
Started In Production—Current Month	1,620	–0–	–0–
Transferred In from Prior Department	–0–	1,500	1,420
Transferred Out to Next Department	1,500	1,420	–0–
Transferred Out to Finished Goods	–0–	–0–	1,360
Work in Process—Ending	120	80	60
Stage of Completion—Ending Work in Process			
Materials	Complete	Complete	25%
Labor	50%	75%	25%
Overhead	50%	75%	25%

Instructions Prepare the equivalent production computations for each department.

PROBLEM 30–2A (Obj. 1, 2, 3, 4)

Tutorial

Computing equivalent production, preparing a cost of production report, computing unit costs, and recording flow of cost through manufacturing process and sale. The Student Artistic Curtain Corporation has two producing departments—the fabricating department and the assembly department. The data given below is from the firm's records for the month of January 19X3. There were no beginning inventories.

	Fabricating Department	Assembly Department
Costs		
Materials	$40,800	$ 9,500
Labor	24,200	22,200
Manufacturing Overhead	12,100	7,400
Total Costs	$77,100	$39,100
Quantities		
Beginning Inventories	–0–	–0–
Started in Production	24,000	–0–
Transferred In from Fabricating Department	–0–	20,000
Transferred Out to Assembly Department	20,000	–0–
Transferred Out to Finished Goods	–0–	18,000
Work in Process—Ending	4,000	2,000
Stage of Completion—Ending Work in Process		
Materials	Complete	1/2
Labor	1/2	1/4
Manufacturing Overhead	1/2	1/4

Instructions

1. In general journal form, record the flow of costs that follow. Date all entries January 31, 19X3.
   a. The issuance of materials to each department

b. The monthly payroll for the producing departments; taxes withheld: social security, $3,016; medicare, $696; employee income tax, $3,800
c. The distribution of manufacturing overhead to each department

2. Prepare equivalent production computations for each department.
3. Prepare a cost of production report for each department.
4. Record the following in general journal form.
   a. The transfer of goods from the fabricating department to the assembly department
   b. The transfer of completed goods from the assembly department to the finished goods storeroom
   c. Sales on credit for $99,580; goods cost $78,000

PROBLEM 30–3A
(Obj. 5)

Computing equivalent production and preparing a cost of production report with a beginning work in process. The Nature's Formula Corporation adds all materials at the beginning of production. On June 1, 19X4, 1,000 gallons of its product were in production in the first department. During the month of June, 12,000 gallons were put into production. On June 30, 2,000 gallons were still in production. The ending inventory is estimated 60 percent complete as to labor and overhead. Cost data for the month follows.

	Materials	Labor	Overhead
Beginning Inventory of Work in Process	$ 4,050	$ 852	$ 1,720
Added During June	50,550	11,958	23,900

Instructions

Prepare a cost of production report for the month of June, assuming that the average cost method is used.

PROBLEM 30–4A
(Obj. 5)

Computing equivalent production and preparing a cost of production report when there is beginning work in process. The data that follows appears in the records of the Augusta Corporation for the month of July 19X3.

	Cooking Department	Blending Department
Costs		
Work in Process—Beginning		
Costs in Prior Department	$ -0-	$ 2,680
Costs in Current Department		
Materials	2,720	200
Labor	880	240
Manufacturing Overhead	440	120
Current Department Costs—July		
Materials	20,400	6,872
Labor	13,640	14,864
Manufacturing Overhead	7,480	7,496
Total Costs	$45,560	$32,552

(Continued)

Quantities		
Work in Process—Beginning	200	100
Started in Production	1,500	–0–
Transferred In from Fabricating Department	–0–	1,600
Transferred Out to Assembly Department	1,600	–0–
Transferred Out to Finished Goods	–0–	1,300
Work in Process—Ending	100	400
Stage of Completion—Work in Process		
Beginning Inventory		
Materials	Complete	1/2
Labor	1/2	1/4
Manufacturing Overhead	1/2	1/4
Ending Inventory		
Materials	Complete	Complete
Labor	1/2	3/4
Manufacturing Overhead	1/2	3/4

Instructions

1. Prepare equivalent production computations for each department.
2. Prepare a cost of production report for both departments in a form similar to the one shown in Table 30–8. Carry the unit cost computations to three places when necessary and round off to the nearest whole cent. Any adjustment necessary because of rounding should be made to the ending inventory of work in process.

PROBLEM SET B

PROBLEM 30–1B (Obj. 1)

Computing equivalent production when there is no beginning work in process. The West Fork Company manufactures a popular type of plastic bathroom basin unit. The monthly production report for February 19X3 follows.

WEST FORK COMPANY
Production Report for February 19X3

	Molding Department	Assembly Department	Completion Department
Quantities			
Started in Production—Current Month	720	–0–	–0–
Transferred In from Prior Department	–0–	600	560
Transferred Out to Next Department	600	560	–0–
Transferred Out to Finished Goods	–0–	–0–	530
Work in Process—Ending	120	40	30
Stage of Completion—Ending Work in Process			
Materials	Complete	Complete	66 2/3%
Labor	50%	75%	66 2/3%
Overhead	50%	75%	66 2/3%

Instructions

Prepare the equivalent production computations for each department for the month.

PROBLEM 30–2B
(Obj. 1, 2, 3, 4)

Computing equivalent production, preparing a cost of production report, computing unit costs, and recording flow of cost through manufacturing process and sale. The Modern Toy Company began business in January 19X3. It manufactures a single product. The product is started in the fabricating department and is completed in the assembly department. Data for the month of January 19X3 follows.

	Fabricating Department	Assembly Department
Costs		
Materials	$32,800	$ 4,550
Labor	15,600	11,700
Manufacturing Overhead	12,168	8,450
Total Costs	$60,568	$24,700
Quantities		
Started in Production	4,100	–0–
Transferred In from Prior Department	–0–	3,600
Transferred Out to Next Department	3,600	–0–
Transferred Out to Finished Goods	–0–	3,100
Work in Process—Ending	500	500
Stage of Completion—Ending Work in Process		
Materials	Complete	30%
Labor	60%	30%
Manufacturing Overhead	60%	30%

Instructions

1. In general journal form, record the flow of costs indicated below. Date all entries January 31, 19X3.
   a. The issuance of materials to each producing department
   b. The monthly payroll for the producing departments; withholding taxes: social security, $1,774.50; medicare, $409.50; employee income tax, $1,890
   c. The distribution of manufacturing overhead to each producing department
2. Prepare equivalent production computations for each department.
3. Prepare a cost of production report for each department.
4. Record the following in general journal form.
   a. The transfer of goods from the fabricating department to the assembly department
   b. The transfer of completed goods from the assembly department to the finished goods storeroom
   c. Sales on credit for $99,300; goods cost $73,000

PROBLEM 30–3B
(Obj. 5)

Computing equivalent production and preparing a cost of production report when there is beginning work in process. The Athenia Chemical Company manufactures a pharmaceutical chemical. All materials are put into process at the beginning of production. On January 1, 19X3, 4,000 pounds of the product were in process in the first department. During the month of January, 36,000 pounds were put into production. On January 31, 6,000 pounds were still in production. The ending inventory is estimated to be complete as to materials and two-thirds complete as to labor and overhead. Cost data for the month is as follows.

	Materials	Labor	Overhead
Beginning Inventory of Work in Process	$ 8,000	$ 3,600	$ 1,800
Added During January	72,000	33,260	17,200

Instructions Compute equivalent production and prepare a cost of production report for the month of January, assuming that the average cost method is used.

PROBLEM 30–4B (Obj. 5) **Computing equivalent production and preparing a cost of production report when there is beginning work in process.** The Menzies Manufacturing Company uses a process cost system. Data from this system for June 19Y3 follows.

	Cooking Department	Blending Department
Costs		
Work in Process—Beginning		
Costs in Prior Department	$ –0–	$21,815.00
Costs in Current Department		
Materials	5,400.00	2,225.00
Labor	1,800.00	1,825.00
Manufacturing Overhead	1,425.00	1,450.00
Current Department Costs—June		
Materials	77,100.00	25,337.50
Labor	63,875.00	20,225.00
Manufacturing Overhead	51,825.00	16,925.00
Total Costs	$201,425.00	$89,802.50
Quantities		
Work in Process—Beginning	2,500	4,000
Started in Production	35,000	–0–
Transferred In from Prior Department	–0–	34,500
Transferred Out to Next Department	34,500	–0–
Transferred Out to Finished Goods	–0–	35,000
Work in Process—Ending	3,000	3,500
Stage of Completion—Work in Process		
Beginning Inventory		
Materials	Complete	3/4
Labor	2/5	3/4
Manufacturing Overhead	2/5	3/4
Ending Inventory		
Materials	Complete	1/2
Labor	1/3	1/2
Manufacturing Overhead	1/3	1/2

Instructions

1. Prepare equivalent production computations for both departments.
2. Prepare a cost of production report for both departments in a form similar to the one shown in Table 30–8. Use the average cost basis. Carry the unit cost computations to three places when necessary and round off to the nearest cent. The adjustment for any rounding should be made to the ending work in process amounts.

CHALLENGE PROBLEM

Selected data about the operations of the reforming department, the first department, of Gnochi Manufacturing Company for the month of October 19X4 are given below.

At the beginning of the month, there were 2,000 units in process in the department, with total cost of $49,400. Material costs of $31,800 were included in the beginning work in process inventory of $49,400. During the month, the total cost of the 17,000 units transferred to the next department was $471,920. This total included labor costs of $7.76 per unit and total materials costs of $272,000, in addition to manufacturing overhead. Costs incurred during the month included overhead of $70,000. At the end of the month an estimated two-thirds of labor and overhead had been added to the 3,000 units in process. All materials are added at the start of production.

Instructions

1. Compute the equivalent units of production for the month.
2. Prepare a cost of production report for the department for the month.

CRITICAL THINKING PROBLEM

Florida Beverage Company makes a fruit juice punch from a blend of citrus products. The continuous production operation starts in the first department (mixing) where the fruit is crushed and blended. It then moves to the second department (bottling) where the fruit juice is vacuum-sealed in glass bottles. Finally, in the last department (packaging), the product is packed six bottles to a box and the boxes are sealed, ready for shipping to supermarkets around the country.

Instructions Prepare a flowchart to show the flow of costs through the perpetual inventory accounts of Florida Beverage Company. Indicate with arrows the direction of the cost flow through the T accounts.

CHAPTER

31 Controlling Manufacturing Costs: Standard Costs

OBJECTIVES

1. Explain how fixed, variable, and semivariable costs change as the level of manufacturing activity changes.
2. Use the high-low point method to determine the fixed and variable components of a semivariable cost.
3. Prepare a fixed budget for manufacturing costs.
4. Develop a flexible budget for manufacturing costs.
5. Develop standard costs per unit of product.
6. Compute the standard costs of products manufactured during the period and determine cost variances between actual costs and standard costs.
7. Compute the amounts and analyze the nature of variances from standard for raw materials, labor, and manufacturing overhead.
8. Define the accounting terms new to this chapter.

Traditionally manufacturing firms have used either the job order cost system or the process cost system to determine the unit cost of the goods they produce. Cost accounting has been regarded as a means of measuring the historical costs of goods manufactured. However, accountants are becoming increasingly concerned about the control of manufacturing costs and the development of cost data that will provide more useful information for making managerial decisions. Information that is based on the variability of costs—how costs change as the volume of output changes—is essential if costs are to be controlled and decisions are to be made properly. In this chapter, you will learn how cost variability can be measured. You will also learn how a knowledge of cost behavior is used to develop **budgets** (operating plans expressed in monetary units) and standard costs (what costs should be under defined conditions) for products manufactured. Finally, you will learn how to analyze differences between the actual costs and standard costs. In our study of manufacturing costs, we use as an example the activities of Atlantic Corporation, a mid-sized manufacturer of toys. Atlantic uses the job order cost system.

NEW TERMS

Budget ▪ Budget performance report ▪ Controllable overhead variance ▪ Cost variance ▪ Fixed budget ▪ Fixed costs ▪ Flexible budget ▪ High-low point method ▪ Labor efficiency variance ▪ Labor rate variance ▪ Labor time variance ▪ Manufacturing cost budget ▪ Materials price variance ▪ Materials quantity variance ▪ Mixed costs ▪ Relevant range of activity ▪ Semivariable costs ▪ Spending variance ▪ Standard cost card ▪ Standard costs ▪ Unused capacity ▪ Variable costs ▪ Variance analysis ▪ Volume variance

COST BEHAVIOR

OBJECTIVE 1
Explain how fixed, variable, and semivariable costs change as the level of manufacturing activity changes.

Manufacturing costs can be classified as (1) variable, (2) fixed, and (3) semivariable. An understanding of each of these terms is essential to cost analysis.

Variable Costs

Variable costs are those costs that vary, in total, in direct proportion to the volume of production.

Variable costs are those costs that vary *in total* in direct proportion to changes in the volume of work done or the level of activity. The best examples of variable costs are direct materials and direct labor. If the direct materials cost for one unit of product is $2, then the materials cost in 1,000 units of product should be $2,000 (1,000 × $2), and the materials cost in 5,000 units should be $10,000 (5,000 × $2). Similarly, if direct labor cost is $3 per unit of product, the total labor cost for manufacturing 2,500 units is expected to be $7,500, and the total labor cost for manufacturing 4,000 units should be $12,000 (4,000 units × $3). Note that the term *variable* refers to the *total* cost for the item involved. The cost *per unit* of material or labor does not change as output changes. It is the total cost of material or labor that changes (is variable).

Fixed Costs

The total amount of fixed costs for a period does not change merely because the volume of output changes.

As the volume of output increases, the fixed cost per unit of output decreases.

Fixed costs are costs that do not change *in total* as the volume of output or activity changes. For example, the salary of the factory manager does not usually change from month to month merely because the number of units produced or the number of hours of direct labor was greater or fewer during the second month. Note that although fixed costs do not change in total as the level of activity changes, the cost per unit does change. For example, if factory supervisory salaries are $4,000 for the month, the cost will be $2 per direct labor hour if 2,000 hours are employed ($4,000 ÷ 2,000 hours), but only $1.67 per hour if 2,400 hours are worked ($4,000 ÷ 2,400 hours).

Semivariable Costs

OBJECTIVE 2
Use the high-low point method to determine the fixed and variable components of a semivariable cost.

Semivariable costs vary in some degree with the volume of activity, but not in direct proportion to it.

Semivariable costs, sometimes called **mixed costs,** are those costs that vary in some degree with the volume of activity but not in direct proportion to it. A semivariable cost contains a basic fixed element that does not change merely because the activity or volume changes; it also contains a variable component that does vary with changes in activity or volume.

A good example of a semivariable cost is the cost of utilities consumed in the factory. Light, heat, and cooling will be necessary if the factory operates, regardless of how many hours of direct labor are employed during the month. The portion of utility costs to provide these basic services tends to be fixed in total. At the same time, however, power may be used to operate machines used in production. This part of the utility costs will likely vary in proportion to the number of direct labor hours employed or the number of units produced.

Many manufacturing overhead costs are semivariable in nature.

The high-low point method is often employed to analyze the fixed and variable components in semivariable costs.

To prepare budgets, to measure efficiency, to develop standard costs, and to analyze the differences between actual costs and standard costs, it is necessary to separate semivariable costs into their fixed and variable components. There are many ways to do this. A simple method that is commonly used and generally gives a reasonable approximation of the fixed and variable components in a semivariable cost is the **high-low point method.**

The steps in applying the high-low point method are listed below.

1. The cost and production data for the months of highest and lowest production during the past year are determined.
2. The difference between the number of hours of direct labor in the months of highest and lowest production is determined. The difference between the costs for those two months is also determined.
3. The difference in costs, computed in step 2, is divided by the difference in direct labor hours, also computed in step 2. The result is the variable cost per direct labor hour.
4. The fixed cost for a month is then computed by deducting the variable cost from the total cost in a month chosen. (The variable cost is the cost per direct labor hour, computed in step 3, multiplied by the number of hours of direct labor worked during the month selected.)

To illustrate this commonly used method, let's assume that an analysis of units produced and the costs of utilities in Atlantic Corporation's factory during each month of 19X1 have been determined from the records, which show the following data for the year.

Month	Direct Labor Hours	Utilities Cost
January	2,400	$2,960
February	2,160	2,864
March	2,580	3,032
April	2,800	3,124
May	2,900	3,160
June	2,600	3,042
July	2,200	2,880
August	2,040	2,804
September	2,120	2,858
October	2,200	2,910
November	2,060	2,836
December	1,800	2,720

The variable costs of $0.40 per hour and the fixed costs of $50 per month are computed by applying the steps previously described.

1. May and December are the high and low months of activity.
2. The differences in labor hours and in utility costs for these months are computed as follows.

Month	Direct Labor Hours	Utilities Cost
May	2,900	$3,160
December	1,800	2,720
Difference	1,100	$ 440

3. The difference in the utilities cost is divided by the difference in labor hours to arrive at the variable cost of $0.40 per hour ($440 ÷ 1,100 hours).
4. The fixed costs may be computed by using the data for the month of May, for example.

Total cost	$3,160
Less variable costs (2,900 hours × $0.40 per hour)	1,160
Fixed costs	$2,000

A similar analysis would be made for each semivariable factory overhead cost.

The major advantage of using the high-low point method to separate semivariable costs into their fixed and variable components is its simplicity. There is, however, a danger in using only the data for the single high month and the single low month. The behavior of costs for other months may be inconsistent with these two months. Some accountants will therefore make a similar computation using the month of second highest activity and the month of second lowest activity. The result of this computation is compared with the results of the computation using the high and low activity months. If the two results are similar, the high-low computation will be used. If the results are not similar, the high-low point method may not be appropriate. Other, more complex methods for analyzing the fixed and variable cost components of semivariable costs are discussed in cost accounting textbooks.

SELF-REVIEW

1. What is a fixed cost?
2. Explain this statement: A variable cost remains fixed per unit.
3. Why is it important to analyze semivariable costs to determine the fixed and variable components?
4. Explain briefly the high-low point method.
5. What is the effect of an increase in the level of activity on (a) fixed costs per unit of activity, (b) total variable costs for the period, and (c) variable cost per unit?

Answers to Self-Review

1. A fixed cost is one that remains constant in total during the period and does not change merely because the level of activity changes.

2. A variable cost is one whose total varies in direct proportion to the level of activity, yet the cost per unit of activity remains the same within the usual range of activity level.
3. To control costs and measure efficiency it is necessary to be able to measure what costs should be at any level of activity. This requires an analysis of fixed and variable costs.
4. Under the high-low point method, the activity and cost of the highest month of activity in a year are compared with the activity and cost during the month of lowest activity. The difference in cost is divided by the difference in activity to measure the variable cost per unit of activity.
5. (a) As the level of activity increases, the fixed cost per unit decreases. (b) As the level of activity increases, the total variable cost increases. (c) There is no change in variable cost per unit as the activity level changes.

PREPARATION OF THE FIXED BUDGET

OBJECTIVE 3

Prepare a fixed budget for manufacturing costs.

An important tool in controlling manufacturing costs is the **manufacturing cost budget,** a budget for each manufacturing cost for the budget period. A well-run manufacturing company prepares a detailed budget for each year and for each month within the year. In preparing the budget for manufacturing operations, the accountant employs the concepts of cost behavior discussed earlier in this chapter.

To illustrate techniques used for budgeting manufacturing costs, suppose that Atlantic Corporation uses the job order cost system. Atlantic's operating management plans to produce various products requiring 1,000 direct labor hours during the month of January 19X2. The budgets for raw materials and direct labor are developed by analyzing the costs of the specific products that are to be manufactured. The budgeted amounts for direct materials and direct labor are relatively easy to compute. First, the amounts of direct materials and of direct labor needed to produce the quantity and variety of products planned are determined. Then unit costs of the materials expected to be used and of the labor rates to be paid are applied to determine the direct materials and direct labor budgets.

For example, suppose that several products are to be manufactured during the budget period. One of the products is a decorated toy car. During the budget period, 500 units of the car are to be produced. An analysis shows that materials costs are expected to be $6 per car. The total materials cost budgeted for this product during the month therefore is $3,000. Similar computations are made for all other products to be manufactured. The materials costs expected for each line of product are then added to arrive at the materials budget for the period. Similar computations are made for direct labor costs.

The budget for manufacturing costs is not as easy to compute as the budgets for direct materials and direct labor. As you have seen, some manufacturing overhead costs are purely variable, some are purely fixed, and some are semivariable. In preparing the budget for manufacturing overhead, it is therefore necessary to analyze the cost behavior of each manufacturing overhead item.

Assume that Atlantic's direct labor budget calls for 1,000 hours to be worked each month and that labor costs will be $10 per hour. Assume also that the accountant for the Atlantic Corporation has analyzed manufacturing overhead using the high-low point method and has determined that the cost behavior of each item is as shown below.

	Fixed Costs per Month	Variable Costs per Hour
Supervision & Clerical Wages	$3,000	$-0-
Other Indirect Labor		2.00
Payroll Taxes and Fringe Benefits	600	2.40
Manufacturing Supplies	100	0.20
Depreciation	2,300	
Repairs and Maintenance	500	0.50
Insurance and Taxes	400	-0-

A fixed budget shows the budgeted costs for the level of activity expected for the period.

On the basis of this information, the accountant for Atlantic has prepared the budget shown in Figure 31-1 for manufacturing costs for the month of January 19X2. This budget is based on the assumption that expected total direct materials costs are $20,000 and that 1,000 direct labor hours will be employed at a cost of $10 per hour. Since the budget represents only one level of expected activity—1,000 direct labor hours—it is referred to as a **fixed budget.**

FIGURE 31-1
A Fixed Budget of Manufacturing Costs

ATLANTIC CORPORATION
Budget of Manufacturing Costs
Month Ended January 31, 19X2

Direct Materials		20,000.00
Direct Labor		10,000.00
Manufacturing Overhead		
Supervision and Clerical Wages	3,000.00	
Other Indirect Labor (1,000 × $2)	2,000.00	
Payroll Taxes and Fringe Benefits		
[$600 + (1,000 × $2.40)]	3,000.00	
Manufacturing Supplies		
[$100 + (1,000 × $0.20)]	300.00	
Depreciation	2,300.00	
Repairs and Maintenance		
[$500 + (1,000 × $0.50)]	1,000.00	
Insurance and Taxes	400.00	
Total Manufacturing Overhead		12,000.00
Total Manufacturing Cost		42,000.00

A budget performance report compares actual costs for a period with the budgeted costs for that period.

It is important to know not only the amount by which actual costs differed from budgeted costs, but also *why* there was a difference.

When analyzing differences between actual costs and budgeted costs for a period, it is necessary to consider whether the actual hours worked are more than or less than the hours assumed when the budget was prepared.

Although a budget serves many purposes, a key one is to provide a basis for measuring performance. It is logical that management wishes to know as quickly as possible whether the manufacturing cost budget has been "met." Management is especially eager to know how well manufacturing costs have been controlled. As soon as actual manufacturing costs have been accumulated and reported for the month of January, the accountant will prepare a **budget performance report** comparing actual costs incurred with the monthly budget. Atlantic's budget performance report for manufacturing costs for the month of January 19X2 is shown in Figure 31–2.

Atlantic's budget performance report shows that there are numerous differences between the amount budgeted for various items and the actual cost incurred for those items. Note that in some cases actual costs exceeded the amounts budgeted, while in other cases the budgeted costs were larger. The amounts by which actual costs of materials and labor were under the amounts budgeted are quite large. Although management is generally pleased when actual costs are less than those budgeted and displeased when costs are over budget, it is necessary to determine why costs were over or under budget before the results can be evaluated.

One of the first considerations must be whether the number of hours worked during the month was either more than or less than the hours planned in the budget. For example, if the number of hours worked in Atlantic's factory is very close to 1,000, then the fixed budget may be a meaningful tool against which to compare actual costs. However, if the number of hours worked is materially

FIGURE 31–2
A Budget Performance Report

ATLANTIC CORPORATION
Manufacturing Cost Budget Performance Report
Month of January 19X2

	Budget	*Actual*	*Over*	*Under*
Direct Materials	20000	19206		794
Direct Labor	10000	9595		405
Manufacturing Overhead				
Supervision and Clerical Wages	3000	3000	—0—	—0—
Other Indirect Labor	2000	1980		20
Payroll Taxes and Fringe Benefits	3000	2915		85
Manufacturing Supplies	300	315	15	
Depreciation	2300	2300	—0—	—0—
Repairs and Maintenance	1000	1050	50	
Insurance and Taxes	400	400	—0—	—0—
Total Manufacturing Overhead	12000	11960	65	105
Total Manufacturing Cost	42000	40761	65	1,304

greater or less than the number of hours anticipated when the budget was prepared, the fixed budget loses some of its usefulness as a means of measuring efficiency and cost control. Suppose, for example, that an examination of production records for January shows that only 960 hours were worked and that 940 units were produced. It is logical to assume that since the number of units produced was substantially less than the number budgeted, then actual costs for materials and labor should be less than those budgeted. It is relatively easy to determine the costs that would have been budgeted for direct materials and direct labor at any level of activity because those two costs are generally considered to be variable costs. However, estimating the amount of overhead that would have been budgeted for the actual level of activity achieved is more complex. In order to provide management with a more useful tool for estimating and controlling manufacturing overhead costs, a flexible manufacturing overhead budget is often prepared.

PREPARATION OF THE FLEXIBLE BUDGET

OBJECTIVE 4
Develop a flexible budget for manufacturing costs.

The flexible budget shows budgeted costs at several different levels of activity.

The **flexible budget** is a budget showing the estimated costs at various levels of activity. The flexible budget is especially helpful when the level of activity fluctuates widely from month to month because it shows what costs should be at a level of activity near the actual level. Although there are many approaches to preparing a flexible budget for manufacturing overhead, a common procedure is to show separately the fixed and variable portions of each item of manufacturing overhead. A budget is prepared for several levels of activity, depending on the range of monthly fluctuations in production experienced by the company. The range of activity at which the factory is likely to operate is referred to as the **relevant range of activity.** For example, separate columns might be prepared showing budgeted overhead for the level of expected activity and for levels of 90 percent, 95 percent, 105 percent, and 110 percent of the expected activity. Atlantic's flexible budget for January 19X2 for the expected level of activity of 1,000 direct labor hours, for 95 percent of expected activity (950 labor hours), and for 105 percent of expected activity (1,050 hours) is presented in Figure 31–3, page 1096.

It is obvious that a flexible budget cannot be prepared for every possible number of hours of activity. Nevertheless, the flexible budget prepared for several activity levels is extremely helpful for planning purposes. In addition, it is useful for getting an overview of how well manufacturing overhead costs are being controlled. For example, comparing the results for an actual activity level of 960 hours with the flexible budget for 950 hours will give a reasonable indication of how well costs are being controlled.

Efficiency and cost control can be evaluated by comparing actual overhead costs with the budget for the level of operations attained.

For a more precise measure of efficiency and cost control, however, a comparison of actual overhead costs with the budget for the level of operations actually attained is more meaningful. Using the fixed and variable cost data previously developed, it is a simple matter to prepare a budget for Atlantic's actual activity of 960 hours, as shown in the overhead budget performance report in Figure 31–4.

FIGURE 31–3
A Flexible Budget of Manufacturing Costs

ATLANTIC CORPORATION
Flexible Budget for Manufacturing Overhead
For Month of January 19X2

	Activity Level		
Number of direct labor hours	950	1000	1050
Percent of expected activity	95	100	105
Variable Costs			
Other Indirect Labor	1900	2000	2100
Payroll Taxes and Fringe Benefits	2280	2400	2520
Manufacturing Supplies	190	200	210
Repairs and Maintenance	475	500	525
Total Variable Costs	4845	5100	5355
Fixed Costs			
Supervision and Clerical Wages	3000	3000	3000
Payroll Taxes and Fringe Benefits	600	600	600
Manufacturing Supplies	100	100	100
Depreciation	2300	2300	2300
Repairs and Maintenance	500	500	500
Insurance and Taxes	400	400	400
Total Fixed Costs	6900	6900	6900
Total Manufacturing Overhead	11745	12000	12255

FIGURE 31–4
A Budget Performance Report

ATLANTIC CORPORATION
Manufacturing Overhead Budget Performance Report
Month Ended January 31, 19X2

	Budget for 960 Hours	*Actual*	*Over*	*Under*
Supervision and Clerical Wages	3000	3000	—0—	—0—
Other Indirect Labor (960 × $2)	1920	1980	60	
Payroll Taxes and Fringe Benefits [$600 + (960 × $2.40)]	2904	2915	11	
Manufacturing Supplies [$100 + (960 × $0.20)]	292	315	23	
Depreciation	2300	2300	—0—	—0—
Repairs and Maintenance [$500 + (960 × $0.50)	980	1050	70	
Insurance and Taxes	400	400	—0—	—0—
Total Manufacturing Overhead	11796	11960	164	

Note that every variance shown in the report is unfavorable, although no single item is greatly out of line.

SELF-REVIEW

1. What is a fixed budget?
2. What is the weakness in using a fixed budget as a cost control tool?
3. What is a flexible budget?
4. What is meant by the relevant range of activity?
5. A company prepared a flexible budget showing expected costs at 95, 100, and 105 percent of budgeted activity. Actual activity was 114 percent of that budgeted. What steps should the company take in analyzing cost control at the end of the month?

Answers to Self-Review

1. A fixed budget is a budget showing expected costs at only one level of production activity.
2. If the level of production activity is substantially different from the level anticipated in the fixed budget, the actual and budgeted costs will not be related to comparable bases.
3. A flexible budget is a budget showing expected costs at more than one level of activity.
4. The relevant range of activity is the range of activity at which the company expects to operate during a month or year.
5. To analyze how well costs were controlled, a new budget should be prepared based on 114 percent, the level of activity actually attained.

THE USE OF STANDARD COSTS AS A CONTROL TOOL

Standard costs reflect what costs should be for the work done during the period under normal, efficient operating conditions.

Standard costs may actually be entered in the accounts or they may be used only for making comparisons with actual costs.

An even more useful tool to control manufacturing costs is a system of standard costs. Standard costs reflect what costs *should be* for the units of product manufactured during the period under normal, efficient operating conditions. If standard costs are to be used as the basis for measuring the efficiency and effectiveness of operations, the standards must be achievable. If they are set artificially high and cannot be obtained, individuals involved will become discouraged and demoralized, with the result that they may make no attempt to achieve the standards set.

Some companies actually enter standard costs into the accounts, using either the job order cost system or the process cost system. This procedure is discussed in cost accounting textbooks. Other companies record only historical costs in the accounts but compare the actual costs with standards in order to measure efficiency and to achieve tighter control over manufacturing costs. In the following discussion, we assume that standard costs are *not* entered into the accounts but are developed and used only for analytical purposes.

Let's see how the knowledge of cost behavior can be used for setting manufacturing standards and comparing actual results with standard costs, again using the manufacturing operations of the Atlantic Corporation as our model. Remember that the Atlantic Corporation uses the job order cost accounting system.

Developing Standard Costs

To develop the standard cost of a specific unit of product, standards must be developed for each element of a product, including materials, labor, and overhead.

Developing Raw Materials Standards

Material cost standards are determined by engineers and the purchasing department.

1. Determine the standard quantity (the number of units that should be used) of each type of raw material required to manufacture one unit of finished product. That quantity is determined by the engineers who designed the item and prepared its specifications. Where engineering personnel have not been involved, it may be necessary to base the quantity of materials requirement on past experience in manufacturing the product.
2. Determine the standard cost (what the cost should be) per unit of raw material for each type of raw material required in manufacturing the product. These costs can be determined by the purchasing department, whose personnel should be familiar with market sources and prices. It may be necessary to rely on the catalogs of suppliers and on past experience in setting standard costs per unit. The accountant will multiply the standard hourly rates by the standard hours required to determine the total standard labor cost per unit.
3. Multiply the standard quantity of each raw material per unit of finished product by the standard cost per unit of raw material.

Developing Direct Labor Standards

Standard labor time is often provided by production engineers. Labor rates are generally provided by the personnel department.

1. Determine the standard quantity (the number of hours) of each type of labor necessary to produce one unit of finished product. The types of labor and the number of hours of each type required to make a product can be determined by production engineers through time and motion studies. Approximate data can be developed from experience if records are kept of what was produced and what labor was consumed in the production process.

The setting of standard wage rates is generally a function of the personnel department.

2. Determine the standard cost (what the cost should be) per hour of labor for each type of labor used in manufacturing the product. Wage rate information can be furnished by the personnel department or obtained from contracts with unions. Again, historical information and knowledge of current wage rates and expected changes in rates may be utilized in establishing standard rates per hour. The accountant can apply the wage rates to the quantities of labor specified in order to develop the standard costs for the labor involved in each product.
3. Multiply the standard number of hours of labor per unit of finished product by the standard rate per hour for that type labor.

Developing Manufacturing Overhead Standards

Multiply the overhead application rate per hour by the standard number of hours of direct labor per unit of finished product. If the overhead application rate is based on direct labor costs, the standard overhead for a unit of finished product will be the application rate multiplied by the standard labor cost for the unit of product. When standard costs are used, the amount of overhead that should be charged to each unit of product is worked out in advance, in the same manner as the standards for materials and labor are developed. Although the result is stated in terms of dollars for each unit, the standard overhead cost per unit of product is usually based on the overhead application rate used in assigning overhead costs to products.

Consider this process as applied to Atlantic Corporation. Suppose that prior to the start of each year Atlantic Corporation, which uses the job order cost accounting system, prepares a manufacturing overhead budget for the year based on an analysis of fixed and variable costs. Suppose further that the summary below reflects Atlantic's manufacturing overhead cost budget for 19X2, based on a projection that 12,000 direct labor hours will be worked during the year.

Budgeted manufacturing overhead	
Fixed manufacturing overhead	$ 82,800
Variable manufacturing overhead, 12,000 hours × $5.10 per hour	61,200
Total budgeted manufacturing overhead	$144,000

Atlantic's manufacturing overhead application rate is based on direct labor hours. Using the budgeted manufacturing overhead costs of $144,000 and the expectation that 12,000 direct labor hours will be employed during the year, we find that the overhead application rate is $12.00 per hour ($144,000 ÷ 12,000 hours).

Preparing a Standard Cost Card

OBJECTIVE 5

Develop standard costs per unit of product.

The standard cost card shows the standard costs for labor, materials, and overhead for each unit of product.

To be of use in measuring effectiveness and in controlling costs, standard costs must be reduced to a per-unit basis. Then, if the actual cost per unit of product is compared with the standard cost of that unit of product, a measure of cost control is readily available. To facilitate the comparison of actual cost per unit of product with the standard cost per unit, a **standard cost card** is prepared. The standard cost card shows the standard costs for materials, labor, and overhead per unit of product.

For example, the standard cost card for each spinning top—Product ST 24—produced by Atlantic Corporation is shown in Figure 31–5, page 1100. The standards for materials cost per unit and labor cost per unit have been developed for each top, using the procedures previously described. The standard overhead cost per unit is based on the fact that each top should require one-tenth hour of direct labor and that the manufacturing overhead rate is applied at the rate of $12 per hour.

FIGURE 31-5
A Standard Cost Card

STANDARD COST CARD

Item: Decorated Toy — Product ST 24

Materials	
Base material: 1 pound @ \$1.90/lb.	\$1.90
Finishing material: 2 ounces @ \$0.05/ounce	.10
Total materials	\$2.00
Labor	
1/10 hour @ \$10/hour	\$1.00
Manufacturing Overhead	
1/10 hour @ \$12 per hour	\$1.20
Total Standard Cost per Unit	\$4.20

Notice the details of costs under the three main classifications—materials, labor, and manufacturing overhead. Under the heading "Materials," the quantity and cost of each type of material required are listed, and the total standard materials cost is determined.

Under the heading "Labor," the hours required for each unit of product are shown. If more than one type of labor—for example, cutting and shaping labor, assembling labor, and finishing labor—were required, the number of standard hours and the standard rate per hour for each kind of labor would be shown.

As we have already seen, Atlantic Corporation applies manufacturing overhead at the rate of \$12 per direct labor hour. Since each unit of product requires one-tenth hour of direct labor, the standard manufacturing overhead rate per hour is \$1.20 (\$12.00 × 1/10 hour). This amount is shown on the standard cost card.

Comparing Actual and Standard Costs

OBJECTIVE 6
Compute the standard costs of products manufactured during the period and determine cost variances between actual costs and standard costs.

Let's see now how management can use the standard cost data for a product in measuring efficiency and cost control. In doing so, we will again consider the standard cost of Atlantic's decorated toy, product ST 24. Data from the job order cost sheet for Job Order X2–16, under which 1,400 units of the product were manufactured, follows.

Job X2–16
Product: Decorated toy ST 24
Number of units manufactured: 1,400

Manufacturing costs:	
Materials:	
Base material, 1,425 pounds @ \$1.88 per pound	\$2,679
Finishing material, 2,750 ounces, @ \$.052 per ounce	143
Total materials	\$2,822
Direct labor: 130 hours @ \$10.10 per hour	1,313
Manufacturing overhead: 130 hours @ \$12.00 per hour	1,560
Total manufacturing costs	\$5,695

The accountant is now able to compare the actual cost of Job X2–16 with the standard cost for the 1,400 units produced to see how well costs were controlled in manufacturing the units. The difference between the total standard cost and the total actual cost is called the **cost variance.** The comparison shows that the actual cost of the job is $185 less than the standard cost of the 1,400 units.

Standard cost of 1,400 units: 1,400 units × $4.20 per unit	$5,880
Manufacturing costs charged to job	5,695
Variance	$ 185

Since the actual cost is less than the standard cost of the job, the variance is favorable. If the actual cost had exceeded the standard cost, the variance (difference) would have been unfavorable.

Analyzing Variances Between Standard and Actual Costs

OBJECTIVE 7

Compute the amounts and analyze the nature of variances from standard for raw materials, labor, and manufacturing overhead.

Although computation of the total variance is interesting information and is helpful in measuring how well costs have been controlled, to be truly useful in measuring efficiency and controlling costs the variance between actual and standard cost for each cost element (materials, labor, and overhead) must be computed and analyzed.

Analyzing Materials Variances

The summary of costs charged to Job X2–16 was shown previously. The accountant can now compare the actual quantity and unit cost of each type of material consumed on the job with the standard quantity and standard unit costs for the materials consumed on the job. The results of that comparison follow.

	Standard			Actual			Favorable (Unfavor.) Variance
	Quantity	Unit Cost	Total Cost	Quantity	Unit Cost	Total Cost	
Base Material	1,400	1.90	2,660	1,425	1.88	2,679	(19)
Finished Material	2,800	0.05	140	2,750	0.052	143	(3)
Totals			2,800			2,822	(22)

The preceding summary provides the information that the accountant needs to analyze the factors that caused the actual cost of materials to exceed the standard cost by $22. Differences between the total standard cost and the actual cost of each type of material may be the result of a difference in quantities used, a difference in unit cost, or a combination of both. The process by which the accountant determines the amount of variance resulting from each of these two factors is called **variance analysis.**

That portion of the total variance between (1) actual cost of a raw material used on a job and (2) the standard cost of that material resulting from the fact that the *quantity* of raw materials consumed was more or less than the standard quantity allowable for the job is referred to as the **materials quantity variance** (or **materials usage**

variance). That portion of the total variance resulting from the fact that the unit price paid for the raw material was more than or less than the standard price per unit of the material is called the **materials price variance.** The computations involved in determining the variances are quite simple.

The difference between the actual quantity of materials consumed and the standard quantity for the units produced creates a quantity variance.

Determining Materials Quantity Variance. The quantity variance for a raw material is the difference between (1) the quantity actually consumed and (2) the standard quantity for the units produced, multiplied by (3) the standard cost of the raw material item. The quantity variances for the two raw materials used on Job X2–16 are computed as shown.

Base Material	
Actual quantity	1,425 pounds
Standard quantity (1,400 units × 1 lb./unit)	1,400 pounds
Excess base material used	25 pounds
× standard price per pound	$ 1.90
Unfavorable quantity variance	$47.50

Since the quantity of base material exceeded the standard quantity allowed for the job, the quantity variance is unfavorable.

Finishing Material	
Actual quantity	2,750 ounces
Standard quantity (1,400 units × 2 oz./unit)	2,800 ounces
Underusage of finishing material	50 ounces
× standard price per ounce	$0.05
Favorable quantity variance	$2.50

Because fewer ounces of finishing material were required to complete the job than were allowed for the job based on the standard, the quantity variance for this material is favorable.

The materials quantity variance is a good measure of how well the production manager and factory employees are controlling the waste of materials. Quantity variances often result because there are more or fewer defective goods than anticipated when the materials quantity standard was set.

The material price variance arises because the actual price per unit paid for materials differs from the standard price per unit.

Determining Materials Price Variance. The price variance for a raw material is the difference between (1) its actual price and (2) its standard price, multiplied by (3) the actual quantity consumed. The price variances for the materials consumed on Job X2–16 are shown.

Base Material	
Actual price per pound	$ 1.88
Standard price per pound	1.90
Amount per pound by which actual price was less than standard	0.02
× Actual number of pounds consumed	1,425
Favorable materials price variance	$28.50

Since the actual price per pound for the base material was less than the standard price, a favorable price variance resulted.

Finishing Material	
Actual price per ounce	$0.052
Standard price per ounce	0.050
Amount per ounce by which actual price exceeded standard price	0.002
× Actual number of ounces consumed	2,750
Unfavorable material price variance	$ 5.50

Responsibility for materials price variance usually rests with the purchasing department.

Responsibility for materials price variances usually rests with the purchasing department. There is normally little that the manufacturing department can do to control the prices paid per unit for raw materials.

Summary of Materials Variance Analysis. The materials variances for Job X2–16 are summarized as follows.

	Favorable or (Unfavorable) Variance	
Base Material		
Quantity variance	$(47.50)	
Price variance	28.50	$(19.00)
Finishing Material		
Quantity variance	2.50	
Price variance	(5.50)	$(3.00)
Total material variance		$(22.00)

Analyzing Labor Variance

The total labor variance for Job X2–16 is $87.

Actual labor costs, 130 hours @ $10.10/hour	$1,313
Standard labor costs, 1,400 units × 1/10 hour per unit × $10 per hour	1,400
Favorable labor variance	$ 87

As in the case of materials, the total labor variance can be separated into two components: (1) a labor time (or efficiency) variance and (2) a labor rate variance. The labor time variance is similar to the materials quantity variance and the labor rate variance is similar to the materials quantity variance.

The labor time variance measures that part of the variance resulting from using more than or less than standard time for the goods manufactured.

Determining Labor Time Variance. The **labor time variance** (or **labor efficiency variance**) is found by determining the difference between the actual hours required on the job and the standard labor hours allowed for the job. This difference is then multiplied by the standard cost per hour. Let's make the computation for Atlantic's Job X2–16.

Actual hours required	130
Standard hours allowed (1,400 units × 1/10 hour per unit)	140
Excess of standard hours over actual hours	10
× standard rate per hour	$ 10.00
Favorable labor time variance	$100.00

Normally factory management is responsible for labor time variances.

Since Job X2–16 required fewer hours than allowed by the standard, the labor usage variance is favorable. In general, the responsibility for labor time variances rests with the production manager. If, however, the personnel department has the authority to choose and hire factory employees, a portion of the labor time variance may be the direct result of the employees hired. In that event, at least part of the time variance may be attributed to the personnel department.

The labor rate variance is similar to the materials price variance.

Determining Labor Rate Variance. The **labor rate variance** is computed in the same manner as the materials price variance. The difference between (1) the actual labor rate per hour and (2) the standard labor rate per hour is multiplied by (3) the actual number of hours required to complete the job. For Job X2–16, the labor rate variance is $13.

Actual rate per hour	$10.10
Standard rate per hour	10.00
Amount per hour by which actual rate was more than standard	.10
× Actual number of hours worked	130
Unfavorable labor rate variance	$(13)

The personnel department has basic responsibility for wage rate variances.

Generally, the personnel department is responsible for control of the labor rate variance. However, labor costs per hour may also result from decisions made by operating personnel. For example, the decision to work overtime on a job may result in some wages being at one and one-half the normal rate. Also, operating managers may not wisely assign personnel to jobs. Labor market conditions or wage scales set in union contracts may at times make it difficult to hire workers at the standard rates.

Summary of Direct Labor Variance Analysis. We can now see the source of the total direct labor variance of $87.

Favorable labor time variance	$100
Unfavorable labor rate variance	(13)
Favorable total labor variance	$ 87

Analyzing Manufacturing Overhead Variance

The manufacturing overhead variance cannot be analyzed in the same manner as can the variances for materials and labor since it is not feasible to determine the "actual" manufacturing overhead for any individual job. Manufacturing overhead is charged to jobs on the basis of a predetermined rate. Normally the overhead is applied on the basis of direct labor hours or on the basis of direct labor costs. For example, Atlantic Corporation applies manufacturing overhead at the rate of $12 per direct labor hour. If the number of hours worked on a particular job order is greater than the standard hours allowed, the job will automatically be charged with an amount of overhead greater than the standard allowed for the units produced. Similarly, if the number of direct labor hours required to complete a job is less than standard, a favorable overhead variance will result. In the case of Job X2–16, the applied overhead charged to the job and the standard overhead are as shown below.

Applied overhead:	
Actual hours (130) × rate per hour ($12)	$1,560
Standard overhead: 1,400 units × $1.20 per unit	1,680
Favorable overhead variance	$ 120

Because of the inability to determine the actual overhead costs related to any individual job, it is customary to make no further analysis of the overhead variance. Instead of making an analysis of overhead variances for each individual job, an analysis is made of the variance between total overhead for the period (usually a month) and the total standard overhead of all products manufactured during the period. Later we will see how this approach to overhead analysis might be used by Atlantic Corporation. First, let's summarize the variances for Job X2–16.

Unfavorable materials quantity variance ($47.50 – $2.50)	$(45)
Favorable materials price variance ($28.50 – $5.50)	23
Favorable labor time variance	100
Unfavorable labor rate variance	(13)
Favorable overhead variance	120
Total variance	$185

The variances listed explain the difference of $185 between actual manufacturing costs and standard manufacturing costs, as shown above.

Analysis of Monthly Overhead Variances. Assume that the production and cost data for September 19X2 for Atlantic Corporation are as follows.

Total standard hours for goods manufactured	900
Total hours actually required for work done	880
Manufacturing overhead applied to products	
900 hours × $12 per hour	$10,800
Manufacturing costs incurred:	
Fixed costs	$ 6,900
Variable costs	$ 5,180

Based on this data, a comparison of actual overhead costs with standard overhead allowed for the units produced during the month reveals an unfavorable total overhead variance of $1,280.

Actual manufacturing costs incurred	$ 12,080
Standard overhead for work products manufactured:	
900 hours × $12 per hour	10,800
Unfavorable overhead variance	$(1,280)

A number of different approaches may be used to analyze the variance between actual manufacturing overhead and standard overhead for the work performed during the period. The Atlantic Corporation separates the total overhead variance into two types of variances: the *controllable* variance and the *volume* variance. This is accomplished by comparing both actual costs and standard costs with a common figure—overhead computed under a flexible budget based on the standard hours allowed for the units produced.

The **controllable overhead variance** is a comparison between (1) the actual overhead costs incurred and (2) the flexible budget allowance for standard hours for the work performed. The computation of the controllable overhead variance for Atlantic's manufacturing activities for September 19X2 follows.

Actual costs		$ 12,080
Flexible budget for 900 hours, the standard hours for the goods manufactured:		
Fixed costs	$6,900	
Variable costs (900 hours × $5.10 per hour)	4,590	
Total budget for 900 hours		11,490
Unfavorable controllable variance		$(590)

The controllable variance measures how well factory management controlled costs.

The controllable variance is given that name because it represents a variance that is controllable by factory management. Sometimes the controllable variance is referred to as the **spending variance.** It is of critical importance in measuring operating efficiency because it compares the actual costs incurred with *what the costs should have been for the units produced.* The difference measures how well factory managers have controlled costs.

The **volume variance** is the difference between (1) the standard overhead for the units produced during the period and (2) the flexible overhead budget allowance for the units manufactured. To understand the volume variance, let's look again at how the standard overhead cost rate for Atlantic Corporation was established. As you have seen, Atlantic's standard cost for manufacturing overhead is $12 per direct labor hour. This is based on the assumption that 12,000 direct labor hours will be worked during the year (1,000 hours each month). It is also based on the assumption that fixed costs for the year will be $82,800 ($6,900 per month). Thus the total standard cost of $12 per hour consists of two amounts.

Variable costs, $5.10 per hour	$ 5.10
Fixed costs ($6,900/1,000 hours)	6.90
Total overhead rate per hour	$12.00

If the standard hours for the work performed during the month exactly equal the 1,000 hours expected and on which the standard cost rate was based, budgeted and standard costs will be equal.

Budgeted costs:		
Fixed costs	$6,900	
Variable costs (1,000 hrs. × $5.10)	5,100	$12,000
Standard costs: (1,000 hrs. × $12)		12,000
Difference		–0–

If, however, the standard hours for the work performed do not exactly equal the expected volume on which standards were based, a volume variance will result. For Atlantic Corporation, the overhead volume variance for September 19X2 is computed as follows.

Standard cost:		
Fixed costs (900 hours × $6.90 per hour)	$6,210	
Variable costs (900 hours × $5.10 per hour)	4,590	
Total standard cost		$10,800
Budgeted cost:		
Fixed costs	$6,900	
Variable costs (900 hours × $5.10 per hour)	4,590	
Total budgeted costs		11,490
Unfavorable overhead volume variance		$ 690

Note that the entire difference between the standard cost and the budgeted costs of the units manufactured is attributable to the fixed cost element. Because 900 direct labor hours were allowed for the units manufactured while 1,000 hours were used in computing the standard cost per hour, there are 100 hours of **unused capacity** (the excess of budgeted hours over standard hours). As a result, $690 of the budgeted overhead (100 hours × $6.90 per hour) was not charged into production. The variable element in both the budget and the standard cost is the same, $4,590.

The volume variance results because some of the productive capacity is not used during the month.

If the standard hours for the units produced during the month had exceeded the number of hours used in setting the standard (1,000 hours per month), the budgeted fixed costs would have been less than the fixed costs included in the total standard allowance for the work done. For example, if the standard labor time for the units produced during the month had been 1,050 hours, the total standard cost would have exceeded the budgeted fixed costs by $345. This would be described as a favorable volume variance. Note that the standard variable costs and the budgeted variable costs are identical in the comparison below.

Standard cost for the units produced:		
Fixed overhead, 1,050 hrs. × $6.90 per hour	$7,245	
Var. overhead, 1,050 hrs. × $5.10 per hour	5,355	$12,600
Flexible budget for 1,050 hours:		
Fixed overhead	$6,900	
Variable overhead (1,050 hours × $5.10/hour)	5,355	12,255
Favorable volume variance		$ 345

The volume variance generally cannot be controlled by factory management. It arises because the fixed overhead included in the overhead rate is based on an assumed number of hours of production. Factory management has little control over either the volume of goods produced or the volume used in setting the standard overhead rate.

MANAGERIAL IMPLICATIONS

A knowledge of cost behavior is important to management in controlling costs, in planning for the future, and in making business decisions. An understanding of the benefits and the weaknesses of fixed budgets and how some of those weaknesses can be overcome by constructing variable budgets is important in planning and controlling manufacturing costs. The flexible budget affords a means for management to evaluate how well costs have been controlled, regardless of the volume of production activity.

Another useful tool for evaluating efficiency and control of costs is the use of standard costs. Actual costs for the materials and labor used on a job or in manufacturing a product are compared with standards. Standard costs reflect what costs should be when based on efficient, yet attainable, operating conditions. Variances between actual costs and standard costs can then be analyzed to determine what factors caused the variances. The analysis of standard cost variances can help pinpoint the responsibility for those variances. For example, materials price variances are usually the responsibility of the purchasing department, while materials quantity variances are the responsibility of factory management. Similarly, labor rate variances are generally the responsibility of the personnel department, while labor time variances are normally the responsibility of the factory management. By analyzing the variance between standard manufacturing overhead and actual manufacturing overhead, it is possible to determine whether a variance resulted from unused production capacity or from the effectiveness with which costs were controlled.

SELF-REVIEW

1. What is a standard cost card?
2. Explain how to compute the quantity variance for materials consumed on a job.
3. Explain how to compute the rate variance for labor used on the job.
4. Why is it not possible to analyze overhead variances for a job in the same manner that materials and labor are analyzed?
5. What causes an overhead volume variance to exist?

Answers to Self-Review

1. A standard cost card is a form that shows the standard cost of materials, labor, and overhead for a unit of product.

2. The quantity variance is computed in two steps: (1) compute the difference between the actual number of units of a material consumed and the standard quantity of that material for the job and (2) multiply the difference in quantity by the standard cost per unit.
3. The rate variance for labor is computed by multiplying the difference between (1) the standard rate per hour and (2) the actual rate per hour by (3) the actual number of hours employed.
4. Since the actual overhead incurred on a job cannot be known, it is not possible to analyze the overhead variances in the same way that material and labor costs are analyzed.
5. An overhead volume variance exists because the overhead application rate is based on a volume different from the actual volume of production. As a result, the amount charged to work in process for fixed overhead may be either more than or less than actual fixed costs.

CHAPTER 31 Review and Applications

CHAPTER SUMMARY

To prepare budgets of manufacturing costs and to control those costs, accountants and managers must understand how costs behave as the volume of manufacturing activity increases or decreases. Cost behavior is expressed in terms of variability. Some costs, known as variable costs, tend to vary in direct proportion to the level of activity. Other costs remain relatively constant within the range of activity level at which the factory is likely to operate. These costs are known as fixed costs. Still other costs tend to vary to some extent with changes in the volume of activity, but not in direct proportion. An element of these costs is fixed, while another element is variable. These costs are known as semivariable costs. Various techniques have been developed to separate the fixed and the variable components of semivariable costs. A common, and simple, approach for analyzing semivariable costs is the high-low point method.

An important business tool for planning manufacturing activities and for controlling costs is the budget. A budget that shows the anticipated costs during a designated future period—usually a month, quarter, or year—for one level of production is called a fixed budget. At the end of the period, actual results are compared with the budget and differences are noted and investigated.

If the production volume is materially different from the volume assumed in preparing the budget, some of the budgeted figures (the variable and semivariable costs) will not be meaningful. For this reason, manufacturing companies often prepare flexible budgets. Flexible budgets show what the budgeted costs should be at several levels of activity, centered around the anticipated level of activity. Then, at the end of the period, actual results can be compared with more meaningful budgeted amounts.

Another important tool used in controlling manufacturing costs and evaluating efficiency is standard costs. Costs reflecting efficient, yet attainable, levels of performance are developed for each element of materials, labor, and overhead. A standard cost card for each product, showing the standard cost for each type of materials and labor and for manufacturing overhead, is prepared. At the end of the accounting period, actual costs related to the product are compared with the standard costs allowed for each unit. Variances between standard cost and actual cost are then computed and analyzed.

The total variance between the actual cost and standard cost of material is separated into two components: a materials quantity variance and a materials price variance. Similarly, the total labor cost variance is separated into two components: a labor time variance and a labor rate variance. Manufacturing overhead variances cannot be easily computed on a per-job or per-unit basis, especially under the job order cost accounting system, because it is very difficult to determine the actual overhead cost applicable to a job or to a unit of product. Instead, the variance between total actual overhead and total standard overhead for the month is separated into two components—the controllable variance and the volume variance—and analyzed. The controllable variance measures how well costs were controlled for the volume of production attained. The volume variance reflects the fixed costs that were not absorbed by the products manufactured, based on standard time allowed for completing the work.

GLOSSARY OF NEW TERMS

Budget (p. 1088) An operating plan expressed in monetary units

Budget performance report (p. 1094) A comparison of actual costs and budgeted costs

Controllable overhead variance (p. 1106) The difference between actual overhead costs incurred and the flexible budget allowance for the work performed

Cost variance (p. 1101) The difference between the total standard cost and the total actual cost

Fixed budget (p. 1093) A budget representing only one level of expected activity

Fixed costs (p. 1089) Costs that do not vary in total as the volume of work changes

Flexible budget (p. 1095) A budget showing estimated costs at various levels of activity

High-low point method (p. 1090) A method of determining the fixed and the variable components of a semivariable cost

Labor efficiency variance (p. 1103) See Labor time variance

Labor rate variance (p. 1104) That portion of the variance attributable to the fact that the actual labor rate per hour was more or less than the standard labor rate

Labor time variance (p. 1103) The variance due to the difference between the actual hours spent on the job and the standard labor hours allowed for the job

Manufacturing cost budget (p. 1092) A budget made for each manufacturing cost for the budget period

Materials price variance (p. 1102) That portion of the variance attributable to the fact that the actual unit price paid for raw material was more or less than the standard unit price

Materials quantity variance (p. 1101) That portion of the variance attributable to the fact that actual quantity of material used was more or less than the standard quantity

Materials usage variance (p. 1101) See Materials quantity variance

Mixed costs (p. 1089) See Semivariable costs
Relevant range of activity (p. 1095) The range of activity at which a factory is expected to operate
Semivariable costs (p. 1089) Costs that vary in some degree but not in direct proportion to the volume of work
Spending variance (p. 1106) See Controllable overhead variance
Standard cost card (p. 1099) A form showing the standard costs for materials, labor, and overhead per unit of product
Unused capacity (p. 1107) Excess of budgeted hours over standard hours for the work done
Variable costs (p. 1089) Costs that vary in total in direct relation to changes in volume of work done
Variance analysis (p. 1101) A process to determine the variance in quantities used and/or in unit costs
Volume variance (p. 1106) The difference between the standard overhead for the units produced and the flexible overhead budget allowance

REVIEW QUESTIONS

1. What is a fixed cost?
2. Explain how variable costs per unit change as the level of activity changes.
3. What are semivariable costs?
4. Briefly explain the high-low point method for analyzing semivariable costs.
5. Define relevant range of activity.
6. What is a budget?
7. What is included in a budget performance report?
8. What is a flexible budget?
9. What is the advantage of using a flexible budget?
10. What are standard costs?
11. How are standards set for materials?
12. Who provides information about wage rates in setting labor standards?
13. Explain how to compute the quantity variance for materials.
14. What does the price variance for materials show?
15. Why is a comparison of applied overhead, based on direct labor cost, and standard overhead not a useful procedure in controlling costs?
16. What two variances make up the total labor variance?
17. Which manager would more likely be responsible for materials usage variances?
18. Explain why there may be an overhead volume variance.
19. What does the overhead spending variance reflect?

MANAGERIAL FOCUS

1. How would the distinction between fixed and variable costs help management in forecasting cash needs for the business?
2. Explain how a flexible budget can be used by management to help control costs.
3. Briefly explain to management the reasons why variances between actual and standard costs of materials may exist.
4. The accountant for Delmar Corporation has noticed that historically, when there have been favorable labor rate variances, there have been unfavorable labor time variances. What factors may explain this phenomenon?
5. In a large company the overall wage structure is determined by the personnel department. However, the manager of each producing department has limited control over the rates paid individual workers. Who would be responsible for labor rate variances?
6. Explain how determination of standard costs enables managers to pinpoint responsibility for inefficient performance.

EXERCISES

EXERCISE 31–1 (Obj. 2)

Using the high-low point method. Grant Company's records show the following data for the four quarters of 19Y3.

Quarter	Direct Labor Hours	Utilities Cost
First	10,200	$1,520
Second	14,600	1,960
Third	12,800	1,780
Fourth	13,000	1,800

Compute the fixed and variable elements of utilities, using the high-low point method.

EXERCISE 31–2 (Obj. 4)

Developing a flexible budget for overhead. In Delmonico Corporation's factory, fixed indirect labor costs are $10,000 per month. Variable indirect labor costs are $1.25 per direct labor hour. The budget for the month of January 19X3 calls for employment of 10,000 direct labor hours. Compute the flexible budget amounts for indirect labor costs at the following levels of activity: 100 percent of budget, 95 percent of budget, and 105 percent of budget.

EXERCISE 31–3 (Obj. 5)

Developing standard costs per unit of product. In preparing the standard cost for each unit of product 21, the company's only product, the accountant for London Manufacturing Company has developed the following data for the year 19X3.

Total budgeted production, 20,000 units

Raw material:

Four units of raw material are required for each unit of finished goods. The cost of each unit of raw material is $3.

Labor:

Two hours of direct labor are required for each unit of finished goods. The labor rate per hour is $12.50.

Manufacturing overhead:

Budgeted overhead for 20,000 units of finished goods is $160,000.

Compute the standard cost per unit of product, showing the standard cost of materials, labor, and overhead.

Data for Exercises 31–4 through 31–11.

The standard cost card for a unit of product at the Leslie Corporation shows the following information.

Materials: 8 gallons at $2 a gallon	$16
Labor: 1/2 hour at $8 an hour	4
Overhead: 50% of direct labor	2
Total	$22

During the month of February 19X3, Job X1144 was completed. Four thousand units were produced from the job. The actual costs were as shown below.

Materials: 32,500 gallons at $1.98 a gallon	$64,350
Labor: 1,900 hours at $8.20 an hour	15,580
Overhead applied: 50% of direct labor	7,790
Total	$87,720

EXERCISE 31–4 (Obj. 6) Tutorial

Computing total variance between standard costs and actual costs. Calculate the total variance between the actual cost and the standard cost in February.

EXERCISE 31–5 (Obj. 7) Tutorial

Computing total variance for raw materials. Calculate the total variance for materials in February.

EXERCISE 31–6 (Obj. 7) Tutorial

Computing quantity variance for materials. Calculate the quantity variance for materials in February.

EXERCISE 31–7 (Obj. 7) Tutorial

Computing price variance for materials. Calculate the price variance for materials in February.

EXERCISE 31–8 (Obj. 7) Tutorial

Computing total variance for labor. Calculate the total variance for labor in February.

EXERCISE 31–9 (Obj. 7)

Computing quantity variance for labor. Calculate the quantity variance for labor in February.

EXERCISE 31–10 (Obj. 7)

Computing rate variance for labor. Calculate the rate variance for labor in February.

EXERCISE 31–11 (Obj. 7)

Computing total overhead variance. Calculate the total variance for overhead in February.

EXERCISE 31–12 (Obj. 7)

Analyzing overhead variance. Ace Company's standard costs were based on the assumption that 10,000 units of product would be produced each month. Each unit of product requires one hour of labor. Fixed overhead costs are $10,000 per month and variable costs are $4 per direct labor hour. Each unit of product requires one hour of direct labor. The standard overhead cost per hour is therefore $5. During the month, 10,400 units were produced, requiring 10,500 hours of direct labor. Total overhead cost was $51,800. Compute (1) the overhead controllable variance and (2) the overhead volume variance.

PROBLEMS

PROBLEM SET A

PROBLEM 31–1A (Obj. 2)

Analyzing semivariable costs using the high-low point method. The accountant of the McEnroe Manufacturing Company has compiled the following information about the direct labor hours and the indirect labor costs for each month of 19X3.

Month	Direct Labor Hours	Indirect Labor Costs
January	2,300	$6,220
February	2,100	5,940
March	1,800	5,520
April	1,975	5,765
May	2,035	5,910
June	2,240	6,120
July	2,475	6,465
August	2,420	6,300
September	2,360	6,304
October	2,340	6,276
November	2,510	6,514
December	2,400	6,360

Instructions

1. Compute the monthly fixed costs and the variable costs per hour, using the high-low point method.
2. Compute the estimated total indirect labor cost if 2,200 hours of direct labor are employed during a month.

PROBLEM 31–2A (Obj. 3, 4)

Preparing a fixed budget and flexible overhead budget. The accountant for Durango Products Company has analyzed the manufacturing overhead costs for the company's assembly department. The fixed and variable costs follow.

	Variable Cost Element per Hour	Monthly Fixed Cost Element
Indirect labor	$0.80	$1,000
Payroll taxes	0.86	75
Indirect materials	0.16	100
Power and water	0.24	320
Depreciation	—	920
Taxes and insurance	—	370
Repairs	0.12	100

Instructions

1. Prepare a flexible budget for the department for the month of April 19X4, assuming that the expected production is for 2,000 direct labor hours. The flexible budget should show costs for production levels of 90 percent and 110 percent of the expected production level of 2,000 hours.
2. Assume that during the month of April, actual production was 1,680 hours. Actual costs for the month were as follows.

Indirect labor	$2,416
Payroll taxes	1,516
Indirect materials	380
Power and water	698
Depreciation	920
Taxes and insurance	370
Repairs	380

   a. Prepare a departmental monthly overhead performance report comparing actual costs with the budget allowance for the number of hours worked.
   b. Which of the costs appear to be well controlled?
   c. Which of the costs appear to be out of line?

PROBLEM 31–3A
(Obj. 7)

Tutorial

Analyzing materials variances. The Franco Chemical Company manufactures a product called Tectate, which requires three raw materials. Production is in batches of 1,050 gallons of raw materials that yield only 1,000 gallons of finished product. (Some evaporation of the base occurs, but the amount of evaporation varies slightly from batch to batch.) The firm uses standard costs as a control device. Its standard costs for materials for each batch of Tectate have been established as follows.

Material	Quantity	Standard Cost per Gallon	Standard Cost per Batch
Inert base	850 gal.	$ 0.20	$170.00
Acid	160 gal.	1.60	256.00
Activator	40 gal.	10.25	410.00
Total standard cost		$12.05	$836.00

1,050 gal.

The output is packaged in 50-gallon drums. During the month of July 19X3, 300 drums of Tectate were produced. There was no beginning or ending inventory of work in process. The materials actually used during July are listed below.

Material	Quantity	Cost per Gallon
Inert base	12,840 gal.	$ 0.21
Acid	2,390 gal.	1.56
Activator	612 gal.	10.10

Instructions

1. Compute the total variance between the actual cost of the materials used during July and the standard cost of the materials. Also compute the total variance for each type of material.
2. Analyze the variances for each type of material for the month.

PROBLEM 31–4A (Obj. 7)

GL

Analyzing material and labor variances. The Sydney Manufacturing Company makes a product that is processed through two departments: assembling and finishing. All materials are added in the first department. During the month of June 19X4, 10,000 units of the product were made. Standard costs and actual costs for materials and labor are given below.

STANDARD COSTS

Raw materials	
Framing: 10 square feet at $0.20 a square foot	$2.00
Filler: 14 pounds at $0.06 a pound	0.84
Standard materials cost per unit	$2.84
Direct labor	
Assembling dept.: 1/4 hour at $6.80 an hour	$1.70
Finishing dept.: 1/10 hour at $8.00 an hour	0.80
Standard direct labor cost per unit	$2.50

ACTUAL COSTS

Raw materials	
Framing: 100,500 square feet at $0.196/square foot	$19,698.00
Filler: 138,900 pounds at $0.061 a pound	8,479.00
Total actual materials cost	$28,177.00
Direct labor	
Assembling dept.: 2,580 hours at $7.00 an hour	$18,060.00
Finishing dept.: 980 hours at $8.05 an hour	7,889.00
Total actual direct labor cost	$25,949.35

Instructions

1. Prepare a comparison of the actual cost of materials with the standard cost of materials for the 10,000 units of product. Then prepare an analysis of the materials variances.
2. Prepare a comparison of the actual cost of labor with the standard cost of labor for the 10,000 units of product. Then prepare an analysis of the labor variances.

PROBLEM 31–5A (Obj. 7)

Analyzing manufacturing overhead variance. The Rising Star Manufacturing Company produces one product and uses the process cost accounting system. At the end of each month, it compares its actual costs with standard costs. The manufacturing overhead standard rate is $5 per unit of product. It is based on a monthly normal volume of 8,000 units, requiring 4,000 direct labor hours, and on normal monthly budgeted costs at that volume as shown below.

Fixed costs	$24,000
Variable costs	16,000
Total	$40,000

During the month of April 19X4, the company produced 6,800 units of the product, requiring 3,290 direct labor hours. Actual manufacturing overhead costs for the month included fixed costs of $24,000 and variable costs of $14,280.

Instructions

1. Compute the total variance between actual and standard overhead costs for the month of April. Indicate whether the variance is favorable or unfavorable.
2. Separate the variance into its component parts—controllable and volume—and indicate whether each is favorable or unfavorable.

PROBLEM SET B

PROBLEM 31–1B (Obj. 2)

Tutorial

Analyzing semivariable costs using the high-low point method. The accountant of the Javier Manufacturing Company has compiled the following information about the direct labor hours and utility costs for each month of 19X4.

Month	Direct Labor Hours	Utility Costs
January	2,570	$2,030
February	2,895	2,195
March	3,280	2,630
April	3,745	2,885
May	3,860	2,930
June	4,190	3,185
July	4,288	3,300
August	3,810	3,010
September	3,679	2,895
October	3,542	2,895
November	3,018	2,840
December	2,400	2,413

Instructions

1. Compute the monthly fixed costs (rounded to nearest whole dollar) and the variable costs per hour (rounded to nearest whole cent), using the high-low point method.
2. Compute the estimated total indirect labor cost if 3,600 hours of direct labor are employed during the month.

PROBLEM 31–2B
(Obj. 3, 4)

Preparing a fixed budget and flexible overhead budget. Huang Corporation manufactures a single product, requiring one-half hour of labor for each unit of product. The budgeted output for 19X4 is 60,000 units. Fixed and variable overhead cost data are as follows.

	Variable Cost Element per Hour	Yearly Fixed Cost Element
Indirect labor	$ .80	$36,000
Payroll taxes	1.32	3,500
Indirect materials	.16	1,600
Power and water	.24	3,600
Depreciation	—	10,000
Taxes and insurance	—	3,500
Repairs	.12	2,000

Instructions

1. Prepare a flexible budget for the department for the year 19X4. The flexible budget should show costs for production levels of 90 percent, 100 percent, and 110 percent of the expected production level of 60,000 units (30,000 hours).
2. Assume that during the year 19X4 actual production was 28,900 hours. Actual costs for the month were as follows.

Indirect labor	$60,200
Payroll taxes	41,730
Indirect materials	6,275
Power and water	10,480
Depreciation	10,000
Taxes and insurance	3,500
Repairs	5,200

   a. Prepare a departmental monthly overhead performance report comparing actual costs with the budget allowance for the number of hours worked.
   b. Which of the costs appear to be well controlled?
   c. Which of the costs appear to be out of line?

PROBLEM 31–3B
(Obj. 7)
Tutorial

Analyzing materials variances. The Mesa Verde Synthetics Company manufactures a product called Syntex, which requires three raw materials. Production is in batches of 2,000 pounds of materials. Waste sometimes occurs and is thrown away. The firm uses standard costs as a control device. Its standard costs for materials for each batch of Syntex have been established as follows.

Material	Quantity	Standard Cost per Pound	Standard Cost per Batch
Plastic base	1,800 lb.	$0.15	$270
Tint	100 lb.	0.20	20
Hardener	100 lb.	0.25	25
Totals	2,000 lb.		$315

The output is packaged in containers of 25 pounds each. During the month of February 19X3, 2,400 containers of Syntex were produced. There was no beginning or ending inventory of work in process. The materials actually used during February are listed below.

Material	Quantity	Total Cost
Plastic base	55,300 lb.	$8,460.90
Tint	3,012 lb.	587.34
Hardener	3,100 lb.	806.00

Instructions

1. Compute the total variance between the actual cost of the materials used during February and the standard cost of the materials. Also compute the total variance for each type of material.
2. Analyze the variances for each type of material for the month.

PROBLEM 31–4B
(Obj. 7)

Analyzing material and labor variances. The Aaron Products Company makes a product that is processed through two departments: cutting and assembly. All materials are added in the first department. During the month of August 19X3, 9,000 units of the product were made. Standard costs and actual costs for materials and labor are given below.

STANDARD COSTS

Raw materials	
Panel units, 4 units at $4.20 per unit	$16.80
Assembly sets: 4 sets at $0.20 per unit	0.80
Standard materials cost per unit	$17.60
Direct labor	
Cutting dept.: 1/6 hour at $14.40 per hour	$ 2.40
Assembly dept.: 1/4 hour at $16.00 per hour	4.00
Standard direct labor cost per unit	$ 6.40

ACTUAL COSTS

Raw materials	
Panel units: 36,200 units at $4.24 per unit	$153,488.00
Assembly sets: 36,100 sets at $0.19 per unit	6,859.00
Total actual materials cost	$160,347.00
Direct labor	
Cutting dept.: 1,504 hours at $14.60 per hour	$ 21,958.40
Assembly dept.: 2,200 hours at $15.90 per year	34,980.00
Total actual direct labor cost	$ 56,938.40

Instructions

1. Prepare a comparison of the actual cost of materials with the standard cost of materials for the 9,000 units of product. Then prepare an analysis of the materials variances.
2. Prepare a comparison of the actual cost of labor with the standard cost of labor for the 9,000 units of product. Then prepare an analysis of the labor variances.

PROBLEM 31–5B
(Obj. 7)

Analyzing manufacturing overhead variance. The Gerhardt Manufacturing Company produces one product and uses the process cost accounting system. At the end of each month, it compares its actual costs with standard costs. The manufacturing overhead standard rate is $6 per unit of product. It is based on a monthly normal volume of 10,000 units, requiring 2,500 direct labor hours, and on normal monthly budgeted costs at that volume as shown.

Fixed costs	$20,000
Variable costs	40,000
Total	$60,000

During the month of June 19X3, the company produced 8,200 units of the product, requiring 2,050 direct labor hours. Actual manufacturing overhead costs for the month included fixed costs of $20,000 and variable costs of $33,260.

Instructions

1. Compute the total variance between actual and standard overhead costs for the month of June. Indicate whether the variance is favorable or unfavorable.
2. Separate the variance into its component parts—controllable and volume—and indicate whether each is favorable or unfavorable.

CHALLENGE PROBLEM

The Yoshita Corporation manufactures one product. Standard costs for each unit of the product are given below.

Materials, 12 gallons @ $0.80	$ 9.60
Direct labor, 2 hours @ $12	24.00
Manufacturing overhead, 1 hour @ $8	8.00
Total standard costs per unit	$41.60

During the month of May 19X3, 1,500 units of product were manufactured. At the end of the month, the following data was available.

a. The total materials variance was $824 unfavorable.
b. The materials quantity variance was $400 unfavorable.
c. The labor rate variance was $501.12 unfavorable.
d. Actual hours worked amounted to 3,132.
e. The overhead volume variance was $800 unfavorable.
f. The total overhead variance was $450 unfavorable.

Instructions

Answer the following questions. Show all computations.

1. What was the actual total materials cost?
2. How many units of raw material were used?
3. What was the amount of materials price variance?
4. What was the actual labor rate per hour?

5. What was the actual labor cost for the month?
6. What was the amount of labor time variance?
7. What was the total budgeted overhead for the hours allowed for the units produced?
8. What was the amount of controllable overhead variance?

CRITICAL THINKING PROBLEM

Wear-Rite Company, a manufacturer of sports shoes, uses a standard cost system to help management analyze and control costs. When Helen Stavros, the cost accountant for the company, started to analyze the labor variances for October, she discovered that some of the data had inadvertently been destroyed.

From a review of the data available, Helen learns that the total labor cost variance for October was $1,160 favorable and that the standard labor rate was $8 per hour. A cost-of-living adjustment in the workers' hourly rate caused an unfavorable labor price variance of $0.20 per hour. Total standard labor hours for October's output of shoes was 6,500 hours.

Determine the actual number of labor hours worked in October. (*Hint:* First compute the actual labor rate per hour. Then set up an equation representing the computation of the total labor variance of $1,160.)

CHAPTER

32

Cost-Revenue Analysis for Decision Making

OBJECTIVES

1. Explain the basic steps in the decision-making process.
2. Prepare income statements based on absorption costing and direct costing.
3. Analyze the profits of segments of a business using the contribution approach.
4. Determine relevant cost and revenue data for decision-making purposes.
5. Apply an appropriate decision process in five situations:
   a. Pricing products in special cases
   b. Deciding whether to purchase new equipment
   c. Deciding whether to discontinue a product
   d. Deciding whether to make or to buy a part
   e. Deciding whether to replace equipment
6. Define the accounting terms new to this chapter.

Managers are constantly making business decisions, and most of these decisions rely heavily on financial information and analyses. In many instances accountants play a key role in the decision-making process. Managers require as much measurable data, properly analyzed, as is possible to handle. It is the accountant's job to gather the necessary financial data, analyze it, and present it to management in a manner that will permit effective and efficient decision making.

Many business situations require the analysis of cost and revenue data before a decision can be reached. In this chapter, you will learn how to evaluate data when the decision process involves cost and revenue considerations. You will also learn how these steps are applied to some common types of business decisions.

NEW TERMS

Absorption costing ▪ Common costs ▪ Contribution margin ▪ Controllable fixed costs ▪ Differential cost ▪ Direct costing ▪ Incremental cost ▪ Manufacturing margin ▪ Marginal income ▪ Opportunity cost ▪ Sunk cost ▪ Variable costing

THE DECISION PROCESS

OBJECTIVE 1
Explain the basic steps in the decision-making process.

The decision-making process used in business generally involves the following six steps.

1. Define the problem.
2. Identify workable alternatives.
3. Determine relevant cost and revenue data.
4. Evaluate the cost and revenue data.
5. Consider any nonfinancial factors that should be taken into account.
6. Make a decision.

Many types of decisions that must be made in business are most efficiently handled through the process just outlined. Managers use financial information not only to help identify a problem but also to help reach decisions for solving the problem. Using cost and revenue data, managers must attempt to measure the difference in profitability among the various alternatives for solving a problem or making a decision.

Direct Costing Versus Absorption Costing

OBJECTIVE 2
Prepare income statements based on absorption costing and direct costing.

As the use of accounting data in making business decisions has increased, accountants have become more and more concerned with developing meaningful cost information. One aspect of manufacturing costs that has received special attention is the relationship between fixed manufacturing costs and the volume of goods produced. Similar attention has also been given to the relationship between selling and administrative expenses and the volume of sales.

As you learned in Chapter 31, some manufacturing costs are *fixed;* that is, they do not vary in total during a period even though the volume of goods manufactured may be higher or lower than anticipated. Similarly, some selling and administrative expenses are fixed. Examples are depreciation of office equipment, rent on the office building, salaries and related expenses for officers, and many other office expenses.

Some other manufacturing costs tend to vary in total directly with the volume of manufacturing activity. These are referred to as *variable* costs. Some selling and administrative expenses also tend to vary in direct proportion to the sales volume (expressed either in units or in dollars). Sales commissions, delivery expense, the loss from uncollectible accounts, and certain other expenses tend to be variable.

Many manufacturing costs are *semivariable;* that is, they have characteristics of both fixed and variable costs. The cost of utilities in a factory is a typical example of a semivariable cost. Many selling and administrative expenses are also semivariable.

Under the concept of direct costing, all fixed manufacturing overhead costs are charged to expense in the period in which they are incurred.

Some accountants contend that because fixed costs are not dependent on the quantity of goods produced, they should not be applied or allocated to specific units of product manufactured. Fixed costs generally relate to the development of the capacity to produce goods, not to the actual production. Therefore, these accountants argue, fixed manufacturing costs should be written off as current expenses of the period in which they are incurred and should not be included as part of the cost of goods manufactured during the period. Only variable costs—those that vary in total with the volume of production—should be considered in computing the costs of the goods manufactured. This procedure is referred to as **direct costing,** or **variable costing.** Direct costing is not acceptable for financial reporting purposes, but it is widely used in making business decisions.

Absorption Costing

Under **absorption costing,** all manufacturing costs, including fixed costs, become part of the cost of goods manufactured. To illustrate the use of absorption costing, let's assume that the Dumas Manufacturing Corporation has divided all its manufacturing costs into fixed and variable elements. Data pertaining to the firm's operations for its first year of business is summarized below.

Beginning inventory of finished goods	-0-
Units produced (no work in process inventories)	10,000
Units sold	7,000
Units in ending inventory of finished goods	3,000
Sales price for each unit	$30
Variable manufacturing costs—materials, labor, and variable overhead	$12 per unit manufactured
Variable selling and administrative expenses	$2 per unit sold
Fixed manufacturing costs for the year	$60,000
Fixed selling and administrative expenses	$49,980

Under absorption costing, all manufacturing costs, including fixed overhead, are treated as part of the cost of goods manufactured.

A condensed income statement using absorption costing, including the cost of goods manufactured, appears in Figure 32–1.

FIGURE 32–1
An Income Statement Using Absorption Costing

DUMAS MANUFACTURING CORPORATION
Income Statement
Year Ended December 31, 19X3

Sales (7,000 units at $30)	210 000 00
Cost of Goods Sold	
Variable Manufacturing Costs (10,000 × $12)	120 000 00
Fixed Manufacturing Costs	60 000 00
Total Cost of Goods Mfgd. ($180,000/10,000 = $18/unit)	180 000 00
Less Finished Goods Inventory, Dec. 31 (3,000 × $18)	54 000 00
Cost of Goods Sold	126 000 00
Gross Profit on Sales	84 000 00
Selling and Administrative Expenses	
Variable Expenses (7,000 × $2)	14 000 00
Fixed Expenses	49 980 00
Total Selling and Administrative Expenses	63 980 00
Net Income for Year	20 020 00

Direct Costing Illustrated

The statement shown in Figure 32–2 reflects the same data but uses a direct costing approach. Note the four steps used in drafting that statement.

The excess of net sales over the cost of goods sold, based on variable costs only, is the *manufacturing margin.*

1. The cost of goods sold is computed. Only the variable manufacturing costs are reflected in the cost of goods manufactured and in the finished goods inventory figures.
2. The cost of goods sold is computed from sales to determine the **manufacturing margin.**
3. The variable operating expenses are deducted to arrive at the **marginal income** on sales.
4. The fixed manufacturing costs and the fixed selling and administrative expenses are deducted to arrive at the net income for the year.

The statement in Figure 32–2 illustrates only one of several different arrangements that might be used.

FIGURE 32–2
An Income Statement Using Direct Costing

DUMAS MANUFACTURING CORPORATION
Income Statement
Year Ended December 31, 19X3

Sales (7,000 units at $30)		210 0 0 0 00
Cost of Goods Sold		
Variable Manufacturing Costs (10,000 × $12)	120 0 0 0 00	
Less Finished Goods Inventory, Dec. 31		
(3,000 × $12)	36 0 0 0 00	
Cost of Goods Sold		84 0 0 0 00
Manufacturing Margin		126 0 0 0 00
Variable Selling and Administrative Expenses		
(7,000 × $2)		14 0 0 0 00
Marginal Income on Sales		112 0 0 0 00
Fixed Costs and Expenses		
Fixed Manufacturing Costs	60 0 0 0 00	
Fixed Selling and Administrative Expenses	49 9 8 0 00	109 9 8 0 00
Net Income for Year		2 0 2 0 00

Under absorption costing, some fixed overhead is deferred as part of the inventory of finished goods.

When absorption costing is used, a portion of the fixed manufacturing overhead is deferred to future periods as part of the inventory value. If the number of units in the ending inventory increases, the amount of fixed overhead deferred increases under absorption costing. However, under direct costing, all the fixed overhead is charged off as a current expense, so an increase in finished goods inventory

If the finished goods inventory increases during the period, the reported net income will be larger under absorption costing than under direct costing.

does not result in deferral of additional fixed costs. As a result, the net income reported under absorption costing will be greater than that under direct costing if the inventory increases during the period. In a period when the inventory level decreases, a smaller net income will be reported under absorption costing. This effect of inventory changes on net income resulting from increases or decreases in the deferred fixed cost is the main argument used by those who prefer direct costing over absorption costing. They point out that under absorption costing, fixed manufacturing costs are being deferred as an asset (inventory). However, the fixed costs incurred during a period do not in any way benefit the future because future fixed costs must nevertheless be incurred in the future.

The Concept of Contribution Margin

OBJECTIVE 3

Analyze the profits of segments of a business using the contribution approach.

Under the contribution margin approach, the contribution margin—the excess of revenues over variable costs—is computed for the segment being analyzed.

Most cost-revenue analysis involves calculation of the **contribution margin,** the excess of revenues over variable costs of the activity or business segment being analyzed. You have already seen an application of this approach in analyzing departmental profitability in Chapter 27. Most decisions concerning segments of a business (such as branches, products, machines, and so on) also involve contribution analysis. One of the advantages of this approach is that it avoids arbitrary and often meaningless allocations of common costs. **Common costs** are those not directly traceable to a segment. The profitability of a segment is judged by its contribution toward covering the common costs of the business and producing a profit.

Under the contribution margin approach, the contribution margin is calculated for the business segment being studied. The controllable fixed costs of the segment are then deducted from this margin to determine the segment's contribution to the overall profit of the business. The **controllable fixed costs** are those that the segment manager can control. The company's common costs are not allocated in computing the contribution margin. They are deducted from the total of all segment contributions to determine the company's profit.

Sound decisions about adding, keeping, or eliminating a particular segment of the business can be made more easily by using the contribution approach. If a segment produces a contribution margin, it is helping to meet companywide fixed costs and perhaps a profit for the firm. Failure of a segment to generate a contribution margin would certainly cause management to consider eliminating it from the business. Plans for any new segment should show that it can produce a contribution margin if it is to be considered favorably by management.

In addition to the concept of contribution margin, there are certain other cost concepts that are very important in analyzing the facts that pertain to a decision-making situation. These concepts provide ways of classifying costs that are useful for decision making.

The Concept of Relevant Costs

As pointed out in Chapter 31, for planning purposes, relevant costs are future or expected costs. Historical costs are irrelevant except to the extent that they serve as a basis for estimating future outlays. In

OBJECTIVE 4
Determine relevant cost and revenue data for decision-making purposes.

Generally, only costs that will change as a result of a decision are relevant in making the decision.

Sunk costs are those costs that have been incurred and will not change as a result of a decision.

addition, only those costs that will change as a result of a decision are relevant.

If a decision must be made to replace a machine, the book value of the existing machine is a historical cost and therefore irrelevant. The cost of the new machine, however, is relevant. If a decision must be made to close a warehouse, the salaries of the warehouse personnel are relevant if these workers will be terminated when the warehouse closes. The nonrefundable prepaid rent on the warehouse for the remainder of the year is irrelevant since it has been paid and cannot be recovered.

A historical cost that has been incurred and thus is irrelevant for decision-making purposes is called a **sunk cost.** The prepaid rent on the warehouse and the cost of the existing machine discussed above are both sunk costs.

The Concept of Differential Costs

Differential cost is the difference in cost between one alternative and another.

In decision making, management always compares two or more alternatives. Even in deciding on the acquisition of a machine where only one bid has been received from possible suppliers, management has two alternatives: to accept the bid or to reject it. A **differential cost** is the difference in cost between one alternative and another. For example, the difference in cost between using a hand-operated press and an automated press would be a differential cost. While the term **incremental cost** is often used interchangeably with differential cost, incremental cost actually means only an *increase* in cost from one alternative to another. For example, if it costs $6,000 to produce 20 units and $7,800 to produce 30 units, the incremental cost of producing the additional 10 units is $1,800.

The Concept of Opportunity Cost

Opportunity costs are potential earnings or benefits foregone because a certain course of action is taken.

Not all costs used in decision making appear in the accounting records of a business. **Opportunity cost** is the potential earnings or benefits foregone because a certain course of action is taken. For example, assume that the management of a firm must decide between purchasing additional equipment and investing in top-grade securities. The opportunity cost of a decision to purchase the equipment is the estimated amount of the interest or dividends lost on the securities that could have been purchased had the funds been used for that purpose instead of being applied to the purchase of the equipment.

Later in this chapter we examine the concepts of contribution margin, relevant costs, differential costs, and opportunity costs by applying those concepts to specific cases.

SELF-REVIEW

1. How are fixed manufacturing costs handled under absorption costing? Under direct costing?
2. In a period when the finished goods inventory decreases, will the reported profit be greater under absorption costing or under direct costing? Explain.

3. What are marginal revenues? Incremental costs?
4. What are relevant costs?
5. Why are sunk costs ignored in most managerial decisions?

Answers to Self-Review

1. Under absorption costing, a portion of the fixed manufacturing overhead is deferred to future periods as part of the inventory cost. Under direct costing, all fixed overhead is charged off as a current expense of the period when it is incurred.
2. Profit reported will be greater under the direct costing method. Under direct costing, all fixed manufacturing costs are charged to current expense, while under absorption costing they are treated as part of cost of goods manufactured.
3. Marginal revenues are revenues that change as a result of a decision. Incremental costs are the increases in a total cost that will result from selecting one alternative instead of another.
4. Relevant costs are future or expected costs that will be incurred as a result of a specific decision.
5. Most managers ignore sunk costs because they have already been incurred and will not change as a result of the decision being considered.

USING COST-REVENUE ANALYSIS TO MAKE DECISIONS

Managers use cost-revenue analysis to aid in decision making in many different situations. Five common situations will be discussed here: (1) pricing products in special cases, (2) purchasing new equipment, (3) retaining or discontinuing a product, (4) making or buying a part, and (5) replacing old equipment.

Product Pricing in Special Situations

OBJECTIVE 5a

Apply an appropriate decision process in pricing products in special cases.

The concept of direct costing is extremely useful in setting prices of products in special situations.

Direct costing helps to clarify cost-volume-profit relationships that assist management in making operating decisions and controlling costs. For example, direct costing is often useful in setting prices, especially when special offers from potential customers to buy the company's product are being considered. Direct costing is also helpful in deciding whether to buy or manufacture an item or a part, in scheduling production, and in making many other decisions.

To illustrate one use of direct costing, we will assume that the Dumas Manufacturing Corporation receives an offer from a foreign customer to purchase 1,000 units of its product at $18 a unit. (Information about Dumas Corporation's cost behavior appears on page 1126.) In addition to the usual manufacturing costs, the units sold under the contract would bear the usual selling and administrative expenses. There would also be packaging and shipping costs of $1 a unit. The company has adequate manufacturing capacity to take the special order without endangering its regular production and its ability to take care of steady customers. Management must now analyze the financial aspects of the special order.

In most managerial decisions of this type, consideration must be given to the marginal revenues and incremental costs rather than to total cost computed under the absorption cost approach. A review of the data given on page 1125 shows that the total average unit cost of Dumas's product is currently $27.14.

Manufacturing costs ($180,000 ÷ 10,000 units)	$18.00
Selling and administrative expenses ($63,980 ÷ 7,000 units)	9.14
Total average unit cost	$27.14

The first reaction of many business managers to an offer of $18 would be to compare the suggested sales price of $18 with an average total cost of $27.14 plus the additional packaging and shipping costs of $1 a unit and conclude that a loss of $9.14 a unit would be incurred. However, closer consideration must be given to the marginal revenues and incremental costs. The use of direct costing clarifies the situation considerably, since the incremental (variable) costs are already computed under this method. Although the present total average manufacturing, selling, and administrative cost is $27.14, the additional incremental cost of each of the 1,000 units under the special order would be only $15.

Variable manufacturing costs	$12
Variable selling and administrative expenses	2
Additional packaging and shipping costs	1
Total incremental cost for each unit	$15

Thus the acceptance of the special order would result in an estimated additional profit to the firm of $3 a unit ($18 − $15), or a total of $3,000 for the 1,000 units.

In making decisions in special pricing situations, many factors other than costs and selling price must be considered.

The analysis of special pricing situations must be approached very carefully and consideration given to all relevant factors. In the above example the special order could be taken only if sufficient capacity were available and if the special price on the order did not jeopardize sales to other customers. Furthermore, federal laws that prohibit price differentials, unless they can be justified by cost savings, must not be violated.

Purchasing New Equipment

OBJECTIVE 5b

Apply an appropriate decision process in deciding whether to purchase new equipment.

The management of the Logan Manufacturing Company is considering the purchase of a new machine that will improve the productivity of its factory employees. The machine would cost $22,500 and has an estimated useful life of 10 years, with no anticipated salvage value. The firm's accountant has gathered the relevant data about the two alternatives, as shown in Table 32–1.

TABLE 32–1
Cost and Revenue Data Needed for an Analysis of the Effects of Purchasing a New Machine

	If Machine Is Not Bought	If Machine Is Bought
Annual sales (in units)	8,000	8,000
Sales price (per unit)	$ 30.00	$ 30.00
Cost of machine		22,500.00
Other cost data:		
Materials (per unit)	12.00	12.00
Labor (per unit)	9.00	8.25
Variable overhead (per unit)	3.00	3.00
Fixed overhead (per year)	18,000.00	19,800.00*

*Includes depreciation of $2,250 a year for the new machine and the effects of certain other changes in fixed costs.

In evaluating the proposed purchase, one method is to estimate the net income under each alternative and compute the difference. Another method is for management to look only at the differential cost and revenue data. Using a contribution approach, the net income under each alternative is determined as shown in Table 32–2.

TABLE 32–2
Analysis of the Effects of Purchasing a New Machine (Based on Annual Income)

	If Machine Is Not Bought	If Machine Is Bought	Difference
Annual sales	$240,000	$240,000	
Variable costs			
Materials	$ 96,000	$ 96,000	
Labor	72,000	66,000	$6,000
Manufacturing overhead	24,000	24,000	
Total variable costs	$192,000	$186,000	
Contribution margin	$ 48,000	$ 54,000	
Fixed costs	18,000	19,800	(1,800)
Net income	$ 30,000	$ 34,200	$4,200

The analysis shows that there is an annual savings of $4,200 each year if the machine is bought. Notice that the sales revenue, the cost of materials, and the variable overhead costs remain the same for both alternatives. However, the cost of labor and the fixed overhead costs change. The results of this analysis would seem to indicate that the company should purchase the new machine, but other factors, such as employee morale and the quality of the product, must be considered before making a final decision. In this case a study of the situation leads to the conclusion that employee morale will improve and that there will be no change in product quality. Management therefore decides to purchase the new machine.

Retaining or Discontinuing a Product

After reviewing the firm's income statement for 19X3, the management of the Logan Manufacturing Company had to decide whether to discontinue product C. The company's analysis of results of opera-

OBJECTIVE 5c
Apply an appropriate decision process in deciding whether to discontinue a product.

tions for 19X3 shows that this product incurred a loss of $7,050, as shown in Figure 32–3.

FIGURE 32–3
An Income Statement, Absorption Costing

LOGAN MANUFACTURING COMPANY
Income Statement
Year Ended December 31, 19X3

	Product A	Product B	Product C	Total
Sales	15000	27000	33000	75000
Cost of Goods Sold	7125	9900	33750	50775
Gross Profit on Sales	7875	17100	(750)	24225
Operating Expenses	3000	4050	6300	13350
Net Income (or Loss)	4875	13050	(7050)	10875

Other relevant data about the three products made by the Logan Manufacturing Company is as follows.

	Product A	Product B	Product C
Units sold	1,000	1,200	2,000
Sales price (per unit)	$15.00	$22.50	$16.50
Variable manufacturing costs (per unit)	3.75	4.50	12.00
Variable operating expenses (per unit)	2.25	1.50	1.80
Fixed manufacturing costs (per year)	3,375	4,500	9,750
Fixed selling and administrative expenses (per year)	750	2,250	2,700

In analyzing the profitability of product C, it is useful to prepare an income statement based on direct costing. This income statement would show the data in Figure 32–4.

In deciding whether to discontinue a product, it must be kept in mind that many fixed costs assigned to the product will continue even if the product is discontinued.

The analysis given above indicates that since product C contributes $5,400 toward the firm's fixed costs and net income, discontinuing it will reduce the net income by $5,400 if all fixed costs that have been allocated to the product continue. An income statement based on direct costing, showing the net income of the Logan Company if product C is discontinued, appears in Figure 32–5.

While other relevant factors should be considered, the quantitative (measurable) analysis indicates that product C should not be discontinued.

FIGURE 32–4
An Income Statement, Direct Costing

LOGAN MANUFACTURING COMPANY
Income Statement
Year Ended December 31, 19X3

	Product A	Product B	Product C	Total
Sales	15000	27000	33000	75000
Variable Costs				
Manufacturing	3750	5400	24000	33150
Operating	2250	1800	3600	7650
Total Variable Costs	6000	7200	27600	40800
Contribution Margin	9000	19800	5400	34200
Fixed Costs				
Manufacturing	3375	4500	9750	17625
Operating	750	2250	2700	5700
Total Fixed Costs	4125	6750	12450	23325
Net Income (or Loss)	4875	13050	(7050)	10875

FIGURE 32–5
An Income Statement, Direct Costing

LOGAN MANUFACTURING COMPANY
Income Statement
Year Ended December 31, 19X3

	Product A	Product B	Total
Sales	15000	27000	42000
Variable Costs			
Manufacturing	3750	5400	9150
Operating	2250	1800	4050
Total Variable Costs	6000	7200	13200
Contribution Margin	9000	19800	28800
*Fixed Costs**			
Manufacturing	7554	10071	17625
Operating	1425	4275	5700
Total Fixed Costs	8979	14346	23325
Net Income	21	5454	5475

*Allocated on the basis of the original departmental fixed costs.

Making or Buying a Part

OBJECTIVE 5d
Apply an appropriate decision process in deciding whether to make or to buy a part.

A manufacturing company is sometimes faced with a decision about whether to purchase from a supplier a part to be used in manufacturing its product or to manufacture the part in its own facilities. For example, suppose that the Logan Manufacturing Company now purchases a part for $15 a unit. The company uses 12,000 of these items each year. The part could be made in the company's molding department.

The molding department has a capacity of 20,000 direct labor hours a year. This department has been operating at an annual level of 15,000 hours for several years. Its labor costs are $12 an hour, and its variable manufacturing overhead costs are $6 an hour. Annual fixed costs for the department total $90,000. The estimated cost of materials is $6.60 for each part. Four parts can be produced during each hour.

In deciding whether to manufacture or to purchase a product, fixed costs are generally ignored.

The data can be analyzed on the basis of unit cost or annual total cost. If the unit cost approach is used, there is a savings of $3.90 a part if Logan manufactures the part itself. The total savings on a unit cost basis are $46,800 a year (12,000 parts × $3.90). The necessary computations are shown in Table 32–3. Notice that the fixed manufacturing overhead costs are not considered because these costs remain the same whether the part is bought or made.

TABLE 32–3
Analysis of the Effects of Making or Buying a Part

Cost to purchase part		$15.00
Cost to manufacture part		
Variable costs only		
Materials	6.60	
Labor (1/4 hour at $12 an hour)	3.00	
Mfg. overhead (1/4 hour at $6 an hour)	1.50	11.10
Differential cost (savings per unit if part is manufactured)		$ 3.90

Replacing Equipment

OBJECTIVE 5e
Apply an appropriate decision process in deciding whether to replace equipment.

The process used to reach a decision about replacing old equipment is much like that used to evaluate a proposed purchase of new machinery. It is important to understand, however, that when a decision is made about whether to replace existing equipment, the equipment's book value is not considered because it is a sunk cost. (Book value equals the original cost less accumulated depreciation. As discussed previously in this chapter, sunk costs are costs that were incurred in the past and have no impact on future decisions.) Whether the existing equipment is replaced or not, its book value will be charged off against revenue. The only difference is whether it is charged off immediately or over a period of years. If the equipment is not replaced, the book value is written off against revenue over future years as depreciation. If the equipment is replaced, the book value is written off against revenue immediately. Any salvage value of the old equipment may be treated as an offset against the new equipment.

In deciding whether to replace old equipment, the book value of the old asset can be ignored.

Assume that the Logan Manufacturing Company purchased the factory machine discussed earlier in this chapter. Five years later an equipment supplier tells the company that a new model is available. This model, which is priced at $18,750, has an estimated useful life of five years with no salvage value. The new machine is more efficient and should reduce labor costs at Logan from $8.25 to $7.125 a unit. It should also reduce variable manufacturing overhead costs from $3 to $2.625 a unit. The supplier is not offering a trade-in allowance for the old equipment, and the old equipment has no resale value.

One useful method of evaluating the proposed replacement is to compare the net income that would be earned under the two alternatives during the next five years. This period represents the remaining useful life of the old machine and the estimated useful life of the new machine. The analysis given in Table 32–4 assumes production and sale of 8,000 units a year at $30 a unit and shows net income of $171,000 if the machine is retained, compared with net income of $212,250 if the machine is replaced.

TABLE 32–4
Analysis of the Effects of Replacing an Old Machine (Based on Five-Year Total Income)

	If Machine Is Retained	If Machine Is Replaced	Difference
Sales	$1,200,000	$1,200,000	–0–
Variable costs			
Materials	$ 480,000	$ 480,000	
Labor	330,000	285,000	$45,000
Manufacturing overhead	120,000	105,000	15,000
Total variable costs	$ 930,000	$ 870,000	$60,000
Contribution margin	$ 270,000	$ 330,000	$60,000
Fixed costs	$ 99,000	$ 106,500	$ 7,500
Write-off of book value of old machine		11,250	11,250
Total	$ 99,000	$ 117,750	$18,750
Net income	$ 171,000	$ 212,250	$41,250

This analysis indicates a savings of $41,250 over the five-year period as a result of replacing the equipment. The change in the fixed costs represents the difference between the depreciation charge on the old machine ($11,250 over the next five years) and that on the new machine ($18,750 over the next five years). If the new machine is purchased, depreciation will be discontinued on the old machine and begun on the new one; and the book value of the old machine ($11,250) must be written off as a loss.

The savings from the replacement of the old machine can also be calculated on an annual basis by subtracting the depreciation on the new machine from the annual variable cost reductions in labor and overhead. Under this approach, the book value of the old machine—a sunk cost—is totally ignored. The necessary computations are shown in Table 32–5, page 1136.

The cases discussed in this chapter provide just a few examples of the many decision-making situations that occur in business each day. No matter what their size, most companies are faced with similar situations in the normal course of their operations. The accountant who understands cost-revenue analysis can greatly assist management in reaching logical decisions that will increase the company's profitability. In addition to the factors that have been discussed, the accountant must consider other very important elements—for example, the income tax effects of decisions made and

TABLE 32–5
Analysis of the Effects of Replacing an Old Machine (Based on Net Annual Savings)

Variable cost reductions	
Labor ($8.25 – $7.125)	$1.125 per unit
Manufacturing overhead ($3.00 – $2.625)	0.375 per unit
Total	$1.500 per unit
Total variable cost reduction (8,000 units × $1.50)	$12,000
Less annual depreciation on new machine ($18,750 ÷ 5 years)	3,750
Net annual savings from replacement of old machine	$ 8,250
Net savings for five years ($8,250 × 5):	41,250

the timing of resulting cash receipts and expenditures. Because of the time value of money (the compound interest factor), the timing of cash flows is especially important in making decisions. These factors are discussed in most cost accounting texts.

MANAGERIAL IMPLICATIONS

An understanding of cost and revenue behavior is critical in managerial decision making today. Although a firm's accountant usually gathers and analyzes the necessary data, management must be familiar with such concepts as sunk costs, relevant costs, differential costs, opportunity costs, and contribution margin in order to intelligently assess the data and make logical decisions.

Most decisions involve making a choice between at least two alternative courses of action. Accounting information provides useful data on the effects of the alternative choices on revenues and costs. In making the decision, management must be concerned with the differential revenues and differential costs—the amount of increase or decrease in revenue and costs—that can be expected in choosing one course of action as compared with the other course of action.

Cost-revenue analysis provides management with a highly useful tool for evaluating the financial effects of decisions before they are made. As a general rule, in making operating decisions management must be concerned about future costs and revenues resulting from their decisions. Sunk costs are usually irrelevant in those decisions.

SELF-REVIEW

1. In what circumstances would direct costing be of help to management in setting the prices of products?
2. What is the contribution approach to management decision analysis?
3. In making a decision to replace equipment, what consideration is given to the book value of the old equipment?
4. Should management automatically reject an offer by a potential customer to purchase some of the company's product at a price less than total manufacturing cost of the product? Explain.
5. Give some reasons why a company might decide to purchase a part that is used in its finished product rather than manufacture the part.

Answers to Self-Review

1. Direct costing is of help in special pricing situations when the company has idle capacity and has the opportunity to acquire additional business at special prices. The lower prices must be legal and must not interfere with existing business.
2. The contribution approach to analysis compares the impact of the proposed action on incremental revenues and incremental costs.
3. In making such decisions, the book value of old equipment is a sunk cost and can be ignored.
4. Acceptance of an order for less than total cost may be considered if the company has idle capacity, the price exceeds variable costs, the pricing would be legal, and the special order would not interfere with existing business.
5. It may be cheaper to purchase a part than to manufacture it; purchase may be necessary in order to assure supply; there may be a need to purchase one part in order to get favorable terms on other parts or supplies, and it may simplify the hiring of personnel or the handling of raw materials.

CHAPTER 32

Review and Applications

CHAPTER SUMMARY

Management is constantly involved in decision making. Many of these decisions require financial data, which must be gathered and analyzed by the accountant. The decision process usually consists of the following steps: defining the problem, identifying workable alternatives, determining relevant cost and revenue data, evaluating the cost and revenue data, considering any nonfinancial factors that should be taken into account, and making a decision.

A useful tool in decision making, especially for the pricing of products in special situations, is direct costing. When direct costing is used, only the variable manufacturing costs are considered as part of the cost of goods manufactured. The cost of goods sold, based solely on variable costs, is subtracted from net sales to arrive at the manufacturing margin. Variable selling and administrative expenses are deducted from the manufacturing margin to determine the marginal income on sales. Finally, fixed manufacturing costs and fixed selling and administrative expenses are subtracted from the marginal income on sales to compute the net income for the period.

Although direct costing is often used for internal analysis and in decision making, it is not acceptable for income tax reporting or in published financial statements.

Relevant costs, those costs that should be considered in making a decision, are usually future costs. Sunk costs are historical costs and are therefore generally not relevant to business decisions. An important part of decision analysis usually involves determining differential costs—the differences in cost among the various alternatives. Often the contribution approach is used in evaluating the data that results from the analysis.

Typical business decisions involve purchasing new equipment; adding, retaining, or discontinuing a product; replacing old equipment; making or buying parts; and setting prices for products.

GLOSSARY OF NEW TERMS

Absorption costing (p. 1125) The traditional accounting procedure of charging all manufacturing costs, including fixed costs, to the cost of goods manufactured

Common costs (p. 1127) Costs not directly traceable to one segment of a business activity

Contribution margin (p. 1127) The excess of revenues over variable costs

Controllable fixed costs (p. 1127) Costs that can be controlled by management

Differential cost (p. 1128) The difference in cost between one alternative and another

Direct costing (p. 1125) Writing off all fixed manufacturing costs as current expenses of the period in which they are incurred

Incremental cost (p. 1128) An increase in cost resulting from an increase in production

Manufacturing margin (p. 1126) The excess of net sales over the cost of goods sold, based on variable costs only

Marginal income (p. 1126) The difference between the variable operating expenses and the manufacturing margin

Opportunity cost (p. 1128) Potential earnings or benefits foregone because a certain decision was made

Sunk cost (p. 1128) A cost that has already been incurred and that will not change as a result of a decision

Variable costing (p. 1125) See Direct costing

REVIEW QUESTIONS

1. What is a contribution margin?
2. What is absorption costing?
3. What is the major difference between direct costing and absorption costing?
4. Is absorption costing or direct costing more useful in making decisions? Why?
5. What is the manufacturing margin?
6. Explain the meaning of marginal income on sales.
7. What are differential costs?
8. Explain opportunity costs.
9. What are sunk costs?
10. Suggest some nonmeasurable data that might be considered in deciding to replace existing equipment with new equipment.
11. Why might management be reluctant to accept a special order for its products at less than the normal price even though such an order would be legal and would be profitable?
12. Suppose that a company is considering the purchase of new equipment. The old equipment will be sold when the new equipment is acquired. How should the proceeds from the sale of the old equipment be considered in the analysis of the effects of the purchase?
13. Why do the analyses presented in this chapter focus on future costs rather than on past costs? Does this mean that historical costs are useless? Explain.
14. Why might employee morale be a factor in deciding whether to replace existing equipment with new equipment?
15. In general, it would be inappropriate to operate a segment of the business if the revenues from that segment do not exceed the

variable costs of the segment. Suggest one circumstance where, however, the segment might be continued even though there is a negative contribution margin.

MANAGERIAL FOCUS

1. The vice president of the manufacturing company for which you are the accountant has suggested to the sales manager that all prices should be established on the basis of direct costing. Respond to this suggestion.
2. What types of information are needed to decide whether to discontinue or retain a product line that appears to be losing money because it is selling for less than its cost (when costs are computed under absorption costing)?
3. Assume that the company where you are employed has a substantial amount of unused plant capacity. A foreign company has offered to purchase a large quantity of your company's product, but at a price of 10 percent less than the product's normal selling price. What types of information are needed to arrive at a decision about whether to accept the order?
4. Suppose that your company is considering the purchase of a new machine for use in its production process. The cost of the machine is $250,000. If the purchase is made, an old machine currently in use will be scrapped. It has no net salvage value because its removal cost is equal to its gross salvage amount. The old machine has a book value of $100,000, and management is reluctant to take the loss that would result if this machine is scrapped. Discuss the types of information that management would need to make a decision about purchasing the new asset. Give special attention to the problem of the old asset's book value.
5. Suppose that your company has been manufacturing a part used in its finished product. The total manufacturing cost of the part is $38.40. An outside supplier has offered to provide the part for $32. Describe the measurable data that management would need in making a decision about whether to accept the supplier's offer.

EXERCISES

Data for Exercises 32–1 and 32–2. The Portland Corporation has divided all of its costs and expenses into fixed and variable components. Data for the company's first year of operations follows.

Beginning inventory of finished goods	–0–
Units produced (no work in process)	6,000
Units sold	4,000
Units in ending inventory of finished goods	2,000
Sales price	$100 per unit

Variable manufacturing costs	$40 for each unit manufactured
Variable selling and administrative expenses	$16 per unit sold
Fixed manufacturing costs for year	$112,020
Fixed selling and administrative expenses for year	$100,000

EXERCISE 32–1 (Obj. 2)

Applying absorption costing.

1. Calculate the cost of goods manufactured for the year, assuming that the company uses absorption costing.
2. Calculate the ending inventory of finished goods, assuming that the company uses absorption costing.
3. Compute the cost of goods sold, assuming that the company uses absorption costing.
4. Calculate the net income for the year, assuming that the company uses absorption costing.

EXERCISE 32–2 (Obj. 2)

Applying direct costing.

1. Calculate the ending inventory of finished goods, assuming that the company uses direct costing.
2. Calculate the manufacturing margin for the year, assuming that the company uses direct costing.
3. Calculate the net income for the year, assuming that the company uses direct costing.

EXERCISE 32–3 (Obj. 3)

Identifying relevant costs. Anderson Company is considering the replacement of existing equipment with new equipment. The old equipment has a book value of $120,000 and a remaining useful life of eight years. The new equipment would cost $440,000 and have a useful life of eight years with an estimated salvage value of $40,000. The annual production of 10,000 units would not be changed. The new equipment would reduce direct labor costs by $10 a unit and would reduce variable overhead costs by $2 a unit. Other fixed costs would increase by $60,000 a year. Of the information just given, what items are "relevant" to the decision to replace the equipment?

EXERCISE 32–4 (Obj. 3, 5a)

Determining relevant costs and making a pricing decision. Assume that the Jacobs Corporation, which now sells its product for $100 per unit, has an opportunity to sell 1,000 units in a foreign country for $68 a unit. The order will not affect its current sales, all of which are domestic. Freight and shipping costs of $10 a unit would be incurred on the foreign order. Current variable manufacturing costs are $40 per unit manufactured, and variable selling and administrative costs are $16 per unit sold. Included in variable selling expenses is a sales commission of $2 per unit, which would not apply to the foreign order. Fixed manufacturing costs are $112,000 per year and fixed selling and administrative expenses are $100,000 per year. The company is now manufacturing and selling 6,000 units per year. What would be the effect on profits if the special order is taken? Show all calculations.

EXERCISE 32–5
(Obj. 3, 4, 5a)

Tutorial

Selecting relevant data, determining contribution margin of segment, and making a pricing decision. The standard cost sheet for a product made by the Polanski Corporation shows the following data.

Direct materials	$ 70.00
Direct labor (4 hours at $10.50/hour)	42.00
Manufacturing overhead	
Variable costs (2 hours at $14/hour)	28.00
Fixed costs (2 hours at $21/hour)	42.00
Total standard cost	$182.00

The product normally sells for $210. The company is presently operating at only slightly over 55 percent of capacity.

1. A foreign chain of discount stores has offered to purchase 2,000 units of the product for $175 a unit. Shipping costs would be $2 a unit. Special packaging would be needed and would cost $4 a unit more than the normal packaging. There would be no other variable selling or administrative expenses. Should the order be accepted? (Show all calculations.)
2. Ignoring all factors except those given above, what is the least amount that the Polanski Corporation could profitably accept for a special order of 2,000 units?

EXERCISE 32–6
(Obj. 3, 5b)

Selecting relevant data and deciding whether to purchase equipment. The Permian Company is considering the purchase of a new factory machine at a cost of $50,000. The machine would perform a function that is now being performed primarily by hand. The new machine would have a life of five years and would produce 10,000 units a year (the current output). Direct labor costs would be reduced by $0.92 a unit and variable overhead costs would be reduced by $0.46 a unit. Fixed costs, other than depreciation, would increase by $4,000 a year. Should the machine be purchased? What is the impact on net income of the decision?

Data for Exercises 32–7 and 32–8. The Denovian Company provides the following data about one of its products.

Sales (15,000 units at $40)	$600,000
Cost of goods sold	562,500
Gross profit on sales	$ 37,500
Operating expenses	112,500
Net loss	$ (75,000)

Additional information about the company's costs and expenses follows.

Variable costs	
Manufacturing costs	$30 per unit
Operating expenses	$5 per unit
Fixed costs	
Manufacturing costs	$112,500
Operating expenses	$37,500

EXERCISE 32–7
(Obj. 3, 4, 5c)

Tutorial

Selecting relevant data, determining contribution margin of a segment, and deciding whether to discontinue a product. Assume that if the product is discontinued, fixed manufacturing costs will decrease $50,000 a year. Fixed operating expenses will not change. Based on the information that has been given, would you suggest that Denovian discontinue the product? By what amount would the company's overall net income or net loss change if the product is discontinued?

EXERCISE 32–8
(Obj. 3, 4, 5c)

Selecting relevant data, determining contribution margin of a segment, and deciding whether to discontinue a product. Assume that Denovian's fixed manufacturing costs will decrease by $75,000 and fixed operating expenses will decrease by $25,000 if the product is discontinued. Should the product be discontinued? By what amount will the company's net income or net loss change if the product is discontinued?

Data for Exercises 32–9 and 32–10. The Tuscaloosa Corporation is manufacturing a part used in its finished product. The costs for each unit of the part are as follows.

Direct materials		$16.00
Direct labor		12.00
Manufacturing overhead		
Variable costs	$2.00	
Fixed costs	6.00	8.00
Total cost		$36.00

The fixed overhead is based on $600,000 of fixed costs to manufacture 100,000 parts a year. If the part is not manufactured, fixed costs will be reduced by approximately $140,000 a year.

EXERCISE 32–9
(Obj. 3, 4, 5d)

Tutorial

Selecting relevant data, determining contribution margin of a segment, and deciding whether to make or to buy a part. The firm has an opportunity to purchase the part from an outside company for $29.80 a unit. Should Tuscaloosa accept the offer or should it continue to manufacture the part?

EXERCISE 32–10
(Obj. 3, 4, 5d)

Selecting relevant data, determining contribution margin of a segment, and deciding whether to make or buy a part. Assume that Tuscaloosa Corporation can purchase the part from an outside supplier for $34.20 a unit. Should Tuscaloosa continue to manufacture the part, or should it purchase the part?

PROBLEMS

PROBLEM SET A

PROBLEM 32–1A
(Obj. 2)

Preparing income statements based on absorption costing and direct costing. The data shown below pertains to the operations of the Alcalde Products Corporation for the year ended December 31, 19X3. The company manufactures computer keyboards.

DATA FOR 19X3

Sales	2,400 units @ $60/unit
Variable manufacturing costs	2,500 units @ $30/unit
Variable selling and administrative expenses	$5/unit
Fixed manufacturing costs	$20,000
Fixed selling and administrative expenses	$18,000
Finished goods inventory, January 1, 19X4	300 units
Finished goods inventory, December 31, 19X4	400 units

Instructions

1. Prepare an income statement for the year using the absorption costing approach. Assume that the 300 units in the beginning inventory of finished goods had a cost of $38 per unit.
2. Prepare an income statement for the year using the direct costing approach. Assume that the 300 units in the beginning inventory of finished goods cost $30 per unit.
3. Explain the reason for the difference between the net income or loss computed under the two methods.

PROBLEM 32–2A
(Obj. 2, 3, 4, 5a)

Preparing an income statement based on direct costing, choosing relevant data, determining contribution margin of a segment, and making a pricing decision. The Red Horse Corporation began operations in 19X4 to manufacture a single product. Relevant data for the year follows. There are no work in process inventories.

OPERATING DATA FOR 19X4

Quantities	
Beginning inventories, finished goods	-0-
Units produced during the year	5,000
Units sold during the year	1,200
Costs	
Direct materials ($20 a unit)	$100,000
Direct labor ($24 a unit)	120,000
Variable factory overhead ($6 a unit)	30,000
Fixed factory overhead	60,000
Variable selling and administrative expenses ($11 a unit)	13,200
Fixed selling and administrative expenses	32,000
Selling price for each unit	100

Instructions

1. Prepare an income statement for 19X2, using direct costing.
2. Assume that the company has an opportunity to sell 200 units of the product in a foreign country for $60 a unit. No fixed or variable selling and administrative expenses would be incurred in connection with these units except shipping costs of $2 a unit and miscellaneous administrative expenses of $0.25 a unit. The company has idle capacity, and the order would not affect present markets. Would it be profitable for the company to accept the order? Show all computations.

PROBLEM 32–3A
(Obj. 3, 4, 5b)

Tutorial

Choosing relevant data, determining contribution margin of a segment, and deciding whether to purchase equipment. The Ponder Company makes a single product that it sells to retail stores. The firm's polishing department uses hand labor to perform its work on all products. A proposal has been made by the company's vice president to acquire machinery that will perform most of the functions of this department. The polishing department has consistently produced 100,000 units a year, and that is the estimated production for the foreseeable future. A summary of the manufacturing costs of the department follows.

Direct materials	$ 25,000
Direct labor	1,000,000
Manufacturing overhead	
Variable costs	150,000
Fixed costs	100,000

The machinery being considered will cost $1,400,000 and have an estimated useful life of five years, with no salvage value. The machinery will cause the following changes in costs.

a. Direct labor will decrease by $3.50 a unit.
b. Indirect materials will decrease by $0.15 a unit.
c. Power will increase by $0.52 a unit.
d. Repairs will increase by $3,000 a year.
e. Taxes and insurance will increase by $7,000 a year.
f. Departmental supervision will decrease by $9,000 a year.
g. Interest expense will increase by an average of $50,000 a year.

Instructions

1. Prepare an analysis showing the effect on net income of purchasing the equipment.
2. What other factors should be considered in making the decision?

PROBLEM 32–4A
(Obj. 3, 4, 5c)

Tutorial

Choosing relevant data, determining contribution margin of a segment, and deciding whether to discontinue a product. The data given below is taken from the budgeted income statement of the Pressley Corporation for 19X4. It shows the projected net income or loss for each of the firm's three products. Management is concerned about the budgeted loss for product C and wants to discontinue it.

	Product A	Product B	Product C	Total
Sales	$25,000	$90,000	$15,000	$130,000
Cost of goods sold				
Direct materials	$ 3,000	$15,000	$ 2,000	$ 20,000
Direct labor	5,000	20,000	4,000	29,000
Mfg. overhead	2,500	10,000	2,000	14,500
Total	$10,500	$45,000	$ 8,000	$ 63,500
Gross profit on sales	$14,500	$45,000	$ 7,000	$ 66,500
Operating expenses	10,000	25,000	9,000	44,000
Net income (or loss)	$ 4,500	$20,000	($ 2,000)	$ 22,500

Materials and labor are variable costs. Total manufacturing overhead is applied at 50 percent of the direct labor cost. Variable overhead is 10 percent of the direct labor cost. Fixed overhead totals $11,600 a year. Operating expenses include variable costs at 20 percent of sales dollars. Fixed operating expenses total $18,000. The fixed overhead costs and fixed operating expenses are expected to continue if product C is eliminated.

Instructions

1. Prepare an analysis indicating the effects of discontinuing product C.
2. What other factors should be considered in arriving at a decision to discontinue product C?

PROBLEM 32–5A
(Obj. 3, 5d)

Tutorial

Choosing relevant data and deciding whether to make or buy a part. The Woodstock Equipment Corporation is currently manufacturing a part that goes into its main product. Each year 2,000 of these parts are used. Cost data for the past year that relates to the 2,000 parts is given below. Fixed costs are allocated on the basis of direct labor hours. An outside company has offered to supply the part for $43 a unit, plus a shipping charge of $3 a unit. The plant now used by Woodstock to manufacture the part would not be used to capacity within the foreseeable future if the part is purchased outside.

Direct materials	$47,000
Direct labor	50,000
Variable overhead costs	2,200
Fixed overhead costs	4,000

Instructions

1. Prepare an analysis comparing the unit cost of manufacturing the part with the unit cost of purchasing it.
2. What other factors are important in making the decision to accept or reject the offer?

PROBLEM 32–6A
(Obj. 3, 5e)

Choosing relevant data and deciding whether to replace an asset. The Rocky Mountain Products Corporation makes magnetic coils. The firm is considering the replacement of a machine used in its factory. The new machine will cost $350,000 and have an estimated useful life of 10 years. The existing machine has a book value of $75,000 and could be used for 10 more years. Operating costs related to the two machines are as follows.

	Old Machine	New Machine
Direct labor	$193,000	$147,000
Supervisory labor	15,000	15,000
Power	97,000	74,000
Other overhead	19,000	10,000

In addition, if the new machine is purchased, interest expense each year will average $17,500 and the new machine would be depreciated over a 10-year period.

Instructions

1. Compute the difference in income if the proposed change is made. Assume that sales will remain the same and that the only additional fixed cost will be the depreciation on the new machine.
2. What other factors should be considered in making the decision?

PROBLEM SET B

PROBLEM 32–1B (Obj. 2)

Preparing income statements based on absorption costing and direct costing. The data that follows pertains to the operations of the Jersey City Products Corporation for the year ended December 31, 19X4. The firm makes medicine cabinets.

DATA FOR 19X4	
Sales	1,200 units @ $80/unit
Variable manufacturing costs	1,000 units @ $25/unit
Variable selling and administrative expenses	$5/unit
Fixed manufacturing costs	$25,000
Fixed selling and administrative expenses	$18,000
Finished goods inventory, January 1, 19X4	400 units
Finished goods inventory, December 31, 19X4	200 units

Instructions

1. Prepare an income statement for the year using the absorption costing approach. Assume that the 400 units in the beginning inventory of finished goods had a cost of $50 per unit.
2. Prepare an income statement for the year using the direct costing approach. Assume that the 400 units in the beginning inventory of finished goods cost $25 per unit.
3. Explain the reason for the difference between the net income or loss computed by the two different methods.

PROBLEM 32–2B (Obj. 2, 3, 4, 5a)

Preparing an income statement based on direct costing, choosing relevant data, determining contribution margin of a segment, and making a pricing decision. Verde Corporation began operations in 19X3 to manufacture a single product. Relevant data for the year follows. There are no work in process inventories.

OPERATING DATA FOR 19X3	
Quantities	
Beginning inventories, finished goods	–0–
Units produced during the year	3,000
Units sold during the year	2,250
Costs	
Direct materials ($20 a unit)	$60,000
Direct labor ($8 a unit)	24,000
Variable factory overhead ($2 a unit)	6,000
Fixed factory overhead	18,000
Variable selling and administrative expenses ($2 a unit)	4,500
Fixed selling and administrative expenses	10,000
Selling price for each unit	42

Instructions

1. Prepare an income statement for 19X3, using direct costing.
2. Assume that the company has an opportunity to sell 1,000 units of the product in a foreign country for $36 a unit. No fixed or variable selling and administrative expenses would be incurred in connection with these units except shipping costs of $2 a unit and extra record-keeping costs of $0.50 a unit. The company has idle capacity, and the order would not affect present markets. Would it be profitable for the company to accept the order? Show all computations.

PROBLEM 32–3B
(Obj. 3, 4, 5b)

Choosing relevant data, determining contribution margin of a segment, and deciding whether to purchase equipment. The Fairfield Company makes doors, which it sells to home builders. The firm's finishing department is not mechanized. Employees use hand tools to finish the product. The factory superintendent has proposed that the firm acquire an electric-powered machine to perform some of the finishing functions. Presently, 4,000 units a year are manufactured and sold. A summary of the manufacturing costs of the finishing department follows.

Direct materials	$40,000
Direct labor	50,000
Manufacturing overhead	
Variable costs	4,000
Fixed costs	10,000

The machine being considered will cost $80,000 and have a useful life of five years, with no salvage value. The machine will cause the following changes in costs.

a. Direct labor will decrease by $5 a unit.
b. Indirect materials will decrease by $0.10 a unit.
c. Power will increase by $0.10 a unit.
d. Repairs will increase by $400 a year.
e. Taxes and insurance will increase by $800 a year.
f. Interest expense will increase by an average of $4,000 a year.

Instructions

1. Prepare an analysis showing the effect on net income of purchasing the equipment.
2. What other factors should be considered in making the decision?

PROBLEM 32–4B
(Obj. 3, 4, 5c)

Choosing relevant data, determining contribution margin of a segment, and deciding whether to discontinue a product. The data that follows is taken from the budgeted income statement of the Almagorda Technology Corporation for 19X3. It shows the projected net income or loss for each of the firm's three products. Management is concerned about the budgeted loss for product M and wants to discontinue the product.

Materials and labor are variable costs. Manufacturing overhead is applied at 50 percent of the direct labor cost. Variable overhead is 10 percent of the direct labor cost. Fixed overhead totals $87,000 a

	Product K	Product L	Product M	Total
Sales	$187,500	$675,000	$112,500	$975,000
Cost of goods sold				
Direct materials	$ 22,500	$112,500	$15,000	$150,000
Direct labor	37,500	150,000	30,000	217,500
Mfg. overhead	18,750	75,000	15,000	108,750
Total	$ 78,750	$337,500	$60,000	$476,250
Gross profit on sales	$108,750	$337,500	$52,500	$498,750
Operating expenses	75,000	187,500	67,500	330,000
Net income (or loss)	$ 33,750	$150,000	($15,000)	$168,750

year. Operating expenses include variable costs at 20 percent of sales dollars. Fixed operating expenses total $135,000. The fixed overhead costs and fixed operating expenses are expected to continue if product M is eliminated.

Instructions

1. Prepare an analysis indicating the effects of discontinuing product M.
2. What other factors should be considered in arriving at a decision to discontinue product M?

PROBLEM 32–5B
(Obj. 3, 5d)

Choosing relevant data and deciding whether to make or buy a part. The Goodnight Electrical Equipment Company is currently manufacturing a part that goes into its main product. Each year 1,500 of these parts are used. Cost data for the past year that relates to the 1,500 parts is given below. Fixed costs are allocated on the basis of direct labor hours. An outside company has offered to supply the part at $66 a unit, plus a shipping charge of $2 a unit. The plant capacity now used by Goodnight to manufacture the part would not be used in the foreseeable future if the part is purchased outside.

Variable costs	
Direct materials	$79,500
Direct labor	34,020
Variable overhead	4,005
Fixed overhead costs	7,500

Instructions

1. Prepare an analysis comparing the unit cost of manufacturing the part with the unit cost of purchasing it.
2. What other factors are important in making the decision to accept or reject the offer?

PROBLEM 32–6B
(Obj. 3, 5e)

Choosing relevant data and deciding whether to replace an asset. The McAtee Mill Works makes building products. The firm is considering the replacement of a machine used in its manufacturing operations with a new machine that will cost $280,000 and have an estimated life of seven years. The existing machine has a book value of $45,000 and could be used for seven more years. It has no salvage value. Operating costs related to the two machines are as follows.

	Old Machine	New Machine
Direct labor	$200,000	$160,000
Power	34,000	19,000
Other overhead	18,000	14,000

Instructions

1. Compute the difference in income if the proposed change is made. Assume that sales will remain the same and that the only additional fixed cost will be the depreciation on the new machine. In addition, interest costs over the life of the new asset will average $12,000 per year if the new machine is purchased.
2. What other factors should be considered in making the decision?

CHALLENGE PROBLEM

Beauty Belle Suppliers distributes beauty and barber supplies to retail stores, beauty shops, and barber shops. Early in 19X5, officers of the company decided to develop and market a line of shampoos and hair conditioners under their own private brand. They contracted with another company to manufacture and package the products. After several months, officers of Beauty Belle became quite concerned over the profitability of the new line. An analysis of operations is shown below.

	Fixed Costs per Month	Percent of Selling Price per Unit
Average cost of products		30
Average cost of containers and packaging		10
Average freight in		2
Average delivery costs		6
Sales commissions		10
Advertising expenses		
Variable		5
Fixed	$600	
Warehousing costs		
Variable		3
Fixed	$600	
Other costs		
Variable		2
Fixed	$400	

In November 19X5 sales were only $2,400. Several officers in the company have suggested that the line of products should be discontinued.

Instructions

1. Based on the information above, what is the amount of income or loss for November?
2. Based on the information above only, should the venture be discontinued? The fixed costs are allocated costs and will not be eliminated by discontinuing the venture.
3. What questions, other than those related to the information given above, should be asked by the officers to arrive at a decision on whether or not to discontinue the product line?
4. What sales volume would be necessary to pay all variable costs and cover the allocated fixed costs?

CRITICAL THINKING PROBLEM

The cost accountant for Elias Manufacturing Company has prepared the analysis given below of the profitability of each of the firm's three products. All fixed costs are allocated costs and are not related to specific products.

	Product A	Product B	Product C	Total
Sales	$9,900	$22,400	$16,800	$49,100
Cost of goods sold	4,700	8,780	18,480	31,960
Gross profit on sales	$5,200	$13,620	$ (1,680)	$17,140
Operating expenses	2,170	3,360	3,690	9,220
Net income (or loss)	$3,030	$10,260	$ (5,370)	$ 7,920
Units sold	1,100	1,400	2,100	
Sales price per unit	$9.00	$16.00	$8.00	
Variable cost of goods sold per unit	$2.70	$3.30	$7.15	
Variable operating expenses per unit	$1.20	$1.35	$1.10	

Management has been considering several options concerning the company's product mix to reduce or eliminate the loss on product C. The company's president has asked you to prepare an analysis of the effects on the company's net income before taxes for each of the following proposals. Consider each proposal independently; no changes would occur in the other products.

PROPOSALS

1. Discontinue product C.
2. Increase the sales price of product C to $9. Marketing analysis indicates that the increase in price will cause a decrease in sales of product C to 1,800 units.
3. Discontinue product C and use the resulting plant capacity to produce a new product, product D. Marketing studies estimate that 1,600 units could be sold at $9.50 each. The variable costs and expenses per unit of product D are estimated to be $7.80.

APPENDIX

Other Record Systems: Combination Journal and One-Write Systems

Most small businesses have just a few employees and can devote only a limited amount of time to the preparation of accounting records. To serve the needs of these businesses, record systems are available that have special time-saving and labor-saving features but still produce all the necessary financial information for management. Three examples of such systems are discussed in this appendix.

Small firms play an important role in our economy today. In fact, almost half of the businesses in the United States are classified as small firms. Despite their limited size, these businesses need good accounting systems that can produce accurate and timely information.

SYSTEMS USING THE COMBINATION JOURNAL

The **combination journal** provides the cornerstone for a simple yet effective accounting system in many small firms. As its name indicates, this journal combines features of the general journal and the special journals in a single record.

If a small business has enough transactions to make the general journal difficult to use but too few transactions to make it worthwhile to set up special journals, the combination journal offers a solution. It has many of the advantages of the special journals but provides the simplicity of a single journal. Like the special journals, the combination journal contains separate amount columns for the accounts used most often to record a firm's transactions. These columns speed up the initial entry of transactions and permit summary postings at the end of the month. Most transactions can be recorded on a single line, and the need to write account titles is minimized.

Other Accounts columns allow the recording of transactions that do not fit into any of the special columns. These columns are also used for entries that would normally appear in the general journal, such as adjusting and closing entries.

Some small firms use only a combination journal and a general ledger in their accounting systems. Others need one or more subsidiary ledgers in addition to the general ledger.

Designing a Combination Journal

To function effectively, a combination journal must be designed to meet the specific needs of a firm. For a new business, the firm must first develop an appropriate chart of accounts. Next a decision must be made about which accounts are likely to be used often enough in recording daily transactions to justify special columns in the journal.

Consider the combination journal, shown in Illustration 1, that is used by Hi-Class Cleaners, a small retail business that provides drycleaning services. In designing this journal before the business

ILLUSTRATION 1
A Combination Journal

COMBINATION JOURNAL

DATE		CK. NO.	EXPLANATION	POST. REF.	CASH DEBIT	CASH CREDIT	ACCOUNTS RECEIVABLE DEBIT	ACCOUNTS RECEIVABLE CREDIT
19X3								
Jan.	*3*	*101*	*Rent for month*			*1000 00*		
	5		*Sandy Carter*	√			*160 00*	
	6		*United Chemicals, Inc.*	√				
	7		*Cash sales*		*1218 00*			
	7	*102*	*Payroll*			*1040 00*		
	10		*Renee Davis*	√	*145 00*			*145 00*
	12		*City Products Corporation*	√				
	13		*Thomas Richey*	√	*170 00*			*170 00*
	14		*Cash sales*		*1475 00*			
	14	*103*	*Payroll*			*1040 00*		
	17		*Gloria Williams*	√			*110 00*	
	18		*Alvarez Company*	√				
	19	*104*	*Telephone service*			*125 00*		
	20		*Mary McAllen*	√	*64 00*			*64 00*
	20		*Fred Turner*	√			*33 00*	
	21		*Cash sales*		*1650 00*			
	21	*105*	*Payroll*			*1040 00*		
	24		*Ace Plastic Bags*	√				
	25		*Roger DeKoven*	√			*56 00*	
	26	*106*	*Quality Products, Inc.*	√		*420 00*		
	28		*Cash sales*		*1325 00*			
	28	*107*	*Payroll*			*1040 00*		
	30		*Note issued for purchase*					
			of cleaning equipment					
	31		*Leslie Stewart*	√			*41 00*	
	31		*Totals*		*6047 00*	*5705 00*	*400 00*	*379 00*
					(101)	*(101)*	*(111)*	*(111)*

opened, the firm established a Cash section with Debit and Credit columns because it was known that the business would constantly be receiving cash from customers and paying out cash for expenses and other obligations. The firm also set up Accounts Receivable and Accounts Payable sections with Debit and Credit columns because the firm was planning to offer credit to qualified customers and would make credit purchases of supplies and other items.

After further analysis, the owner realized that the business would have numerous entries for the sale of services and the payment of employee salaries. Columns were set up for recording credits to Sales and debits to Salaries Expense. Finally, the owner set up an

PAGE 1

ACCOUNTS PAYABLE		SALES CREDIT	SALARIES EXPENSE DEBIT	OTHER ACCOUNTS			
DEBIT	CREDIT			ACCOUNT TITLE	POST. REF.	DEBIT	CREDIT
				Rent Expense	511	1 000 00	
		160 00					
	210 00			*Supplies*	121	210 00	
		1 218 00					
			1 040 00				
	90 00			*Supplies*	121	90 00	
		1 475 00					
			1 040 00				
		110 00					
	800 00			*Equipment*	131	800 00	
				Telephone Expense	514	125 00	
		33 00					
		1 650 00					
			1 040 00				
	145 00			*Supplies*	121	145 00	
		56 00					
420 00							
		1 325 00					
			1 040 00				
				Equipment	131	1 500 00	
				Notes Payable	201		1 500 00
		41 00					
420 00	1 245 00	6 068 00	4 160 00			3 870 00	1 500 00
(202)	(202)	(401)	(517)			(X)	(X)

Other Accounts section in the journal to take care of transactions that cannot be entered in the special columns.

Recording Transactions in the Combination Journal

The combination journal shown in Illustration 1 contains the January 19X3 transactions of Hi-Class Cleaners. Notice that most entries for these transactions require only a single line and involve the use of just the special columns. The entries for major types of transactions are explained in the following paragraphs.

Payment of Expenses

During January, Hi-Class Cleaners issued checks to pay three kinds of expenses: rent, telephone service, and employee salaries. Notice how the payment of the monthly rent on January 3 is recorded in the combination journal. Since no special column has been set up for Rent Expense, the debit part of this entry appears in the Other Accounts section. The offsetting credit appears in the Cash Credit column. The payment of the monthly telephone bill on January 19 was recorded in a similar manner. However, when employee salaries were paid on January 7, 14, 21, and 28, both parts of the entries could be made in special columns. Because the firm has a weekly payroll period, the owner set up a separate column in the combination journal for debits to Salaries Expense.

Sales on Credit

On January 5, 17, 20, 25, and 31, Hi-Class Cleaners sold services on credit. The necessary entries were made in two special columns of the journal—the Accounts Receivable Debit column and the Sales Credit column.

Cash Sales

Entries for the firm's weekly cash sales were recorded on January 7, 14, 21, and 28. Again, special columns were used—the Cash Debit column and the Sales Credit column.

Cash Received on Account

When Hi-Class Cleaners collected cash on account from credit customers on January 10, 13, and 20, the transactions were entered in the Cash Debit column and the Accounts Receivable Credit column.

Purchases of Supplies on Credit

Because the firm's combination journal includes a Supplies Debit column and an Accounts Payable Credit column, all purchases of supplies on credit can be recorded in special columns. Refer to the entries made on January 6, 12, and 24.

Purchases of Equipment on Credit

On January 18, Hi-Class Cleaners bought some store equipment on credit. Since there is no special column for equipment, the debit part of the entry was made in the Other Accounts section. The offsetting credit appears in the Accounts Payable Credit column.

Payments on Account

Any payments made on account to creditors are recorded in two special columns—Accounts Payable Debit and Cash Credit, as shown in the entry of January 26.

Issuance of a Promissory Note

On January 30, Hi-Class Cleaners purchased new cleaning equipment and issued a promissory note to the seller. Notice that both the debit to Equipment and the credit to Notes Payable had to be recorded in the Other Accounts section.

Posting from the Combination Journal

One of the advantages of the combination journal is that it simplifies the posting process. All amounts in the special columns can be posted to the general ledger on a summary basis at the end of the month. Only the figures that appear in the Other Accounts section require individual postings to the general ledger during the month. Of course, if the firm has subsidiary ledgers, individual postings must also be made to these ledgers.

Daily Postings

The procedures followed at Hi-Class Cleaners will illustrate the techniques used to post from the combination journal. Each day any entries appearing in the Other Accounts section are posted to the proper accounts in the general ledger. For example, refer to Illustration 1. The amounts listed in the Other Accounts Debit and Credit columns were posted individually during the month. The account numbers recorded in the Posting Reference column of the journal show that the postings have been made.

Because Hi-Class Cleaners has subsidiary ledgers for accounts receivable and accounts payable, individual postings were also made on a daily basis to these ledgers. As each amount was posted, a check mark was placed in the Accounts Receivable or Accounts Payable section of the combination journal.

End-of-Month Postings

At the end of the month, the combination journal is totaled, proved, and ruled. Then the totals of the special columns are posted to the general ledger. Proving the combination journal involves a comparison of the column totals to make sure that total debits and credits are equal. The following procedure is used.

Proof of Combination Journal	
	Debits
Cash Debit Column	$ 6,047
Accounts Receivable Debit Column	400
Accounts Payable Debit Column	420
Salaries Expense Debit Column	4,160
Other Accounts Debit Column	3,870
Total Debits	$14,897
	Credits
Cash Credit Column	$ 5,705
Accounts Receivable Credit Column	379
Accounts Payable Credit Column	1,245
Sales Credit Column	6,068
Other Accounts Credit Column	1,500
Total Credits	$14,897

After the combination journal is proved, all column totals except those in the Other Accounts section are posted to the appropriate general ledger accounts. As each total is posted, the account number is entered beneath the column in the journal. Notice that an **X** is used to indicate that the column totals in the Other Accounts section are not posted.

Typical Uses of the Combination Journal

The combination journal is used most often in small professional offices and small service businesses. It is less suitable for merchandising businesses but is sometimes used in firms of this type if they are very small and have only a limited number of transactions.

The combination journal may be ideal to record the transactions that occur in a professional office, such as the office of a doctor, lawyer, accountant, or architect. However, special journals are more efficient if transactions become very numerous or are too varied.

The use of the combination journal to record the transactions of Hi-Class Cleaners has already been illustrated. The combination journal may be advantageous for a small service business, provided that the volume of transactions does not become excessive and the nature of the transactions does not become too complex.

Disadvantages of the Combination Journal

If the variety of transactions is so great that many different accounts are required, the combination journal will not work well. Either the business will have to set up so many columns that the journal will become unwieldy, or it will be necessary to record so many transactions in the Other Accounts columns that little efficiency will result. As a general rule, if the transactions are numerous enough to merit the use of special journals, any attempt to substitute the combination journal is a mistake. Remember that each special journal can be designed for maximum efficiency in recording transactions.

ONE-WRITE SYSTEMS

The **one-write,** or **pegboard, system** is another type of record system designed to increase the efficiency of accounting work in small businesses and small professional offices. This system allows the preparation of several records at the same time without rewriting the data. It is used most often for accounts payable, accounts receivable, and payroll—areas where there are many repetitive transactions that must be entered in several different records.

Illustration 2 indicates how a one-write system for accounts receivable operates. This system is intended to handle sales on credit, cash received on account, and sales returns and allowances. It permits a transaction to be simultaneously journalized, posted to the customer's account, and recorded on the statement of account that will be sent to the customer at the end of the month.

A flat writing board called a **pegboard** is used to hold the records that will be prepared. First, the journal page is placed on the board. Then, the ledger sheet for the customer is positioned over the journal page, and the customer's statement of account is placed on top of the ledger sheet. The forms are arranged so that the first unused line of each is over the first unused line of the previous record. A clamp at

ILLUSTRATION 2
A One-Write Accounting System

PEGBOARD: Holds forms in place.

JOURNAL: Journal sheet is placed on bottom.

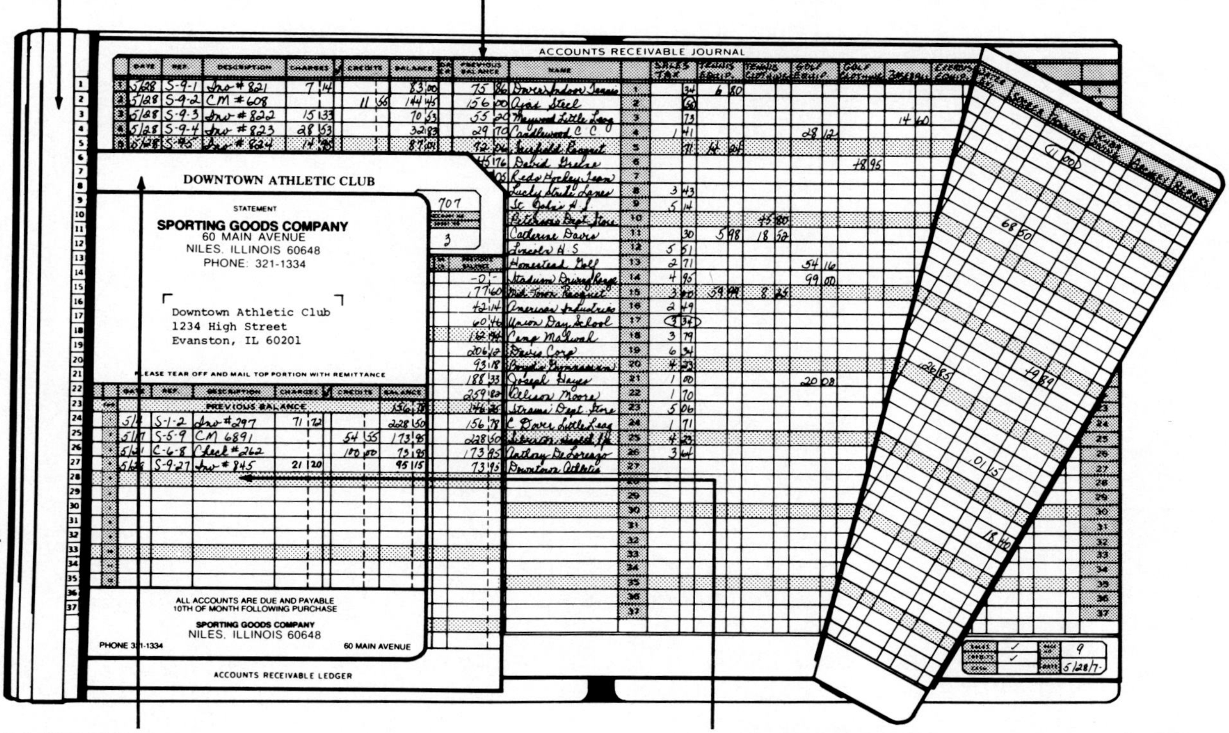

Courtesy of McBee Systems

LEDGER ACCOUNT: First customer's account is placed in position. First unused line of account is positioned over first unused line of journal.

STATEMENT OF ACCOUNT: Customer's statement of account is positioned on pegboard so that the first unused line of the statement is on top of writing line to be used on ledger account.

one side of the board keeps the forms securely in place. Some boards of this type have pegs along the sides to hold the forms—hence, the use of the term "pegboard."

When an entry is made on the form at the top of the pegboard, the data is reproduced on all the other forms at the same time. This is accomplished by having carbon paper between the forms or by using forms that are printed on NCR (no carbon required) paper, which is chemically treated to allow the transfer of entries from one sheet to another.

One-write systems can save a substantial amount of time and effort in the preparation of accounting records in small businesses and small professional offices.

MICROCOMPUTER ACCOUNTING SYSTEMS

Microcomputer accounting systems offer the greatest opportunity for efficient preparation of financial records in small firms. Because of their relatively low prices and ease of use, these systems are spreading rapidly. Not only do they save considerable time and effort by performing many tasks automatically, but they provide management with a wider range of information more quickly than manual accounting systems. Information Blocks on computerized accounting systems appear throughout this text.

Glossary

Absorption costing (p. 1125) The traditional accounting procedure of charging all manufacturing costs, including fixed costs, to the cost of goods manufactured.

Accelerated method of depreciation (p. 614) A method of depreciating asset expense that allocates greater amounts of depreciation to the asset's early years of useful life.

Account balance (p. 55) The difference between the amounts recorded on the two sides of an account.

Account-form balance sheet (p. 126) A balance sheet that lists assets on the left side and liabilities and owner's equity on the right side; *see also* Report-form balance sheet.

Accounting (p. 4) The process by which financial information about a business is recorded, classified, summarized, interpreted, and communicated to owners, managers, and other interested parties.

Accounting cycle (p. 85) A series of steps performed during each accounting period to classify, record, and summarize data for a business to produce needed financial information.

Accounting system (p. 4) A process designed to accumulate, classify, and summarize financial data.

Accounts (p. 52) Written records of a business's assets, liabilities, and owner's equity.

Accounts payable (p. 25) Amounts a company must pay in the future.

Accounts payable ledger (p. 239) A ledger reflecting individual accounts for all creditors.

Accounts receivable (p. 29) Claims for future collection from customers.

Accounts receivable ledger (p. 187) A subsidiary ledger that contains credit customer accounts.

Accounts receivable turnover (p. 870) The ratio of net credit sales to average receivables.

Accrual basis (p. 410) A system of accounting by which all revenues and expenses are matched and reported on statements for the applicable period, regardless of when the cash related to the transaction is received or paid.

Accrued expenses (p. 418) Expense items that related to the current period but that have not yet been paid for and do not yet appear in the accounts.

Accrued income (p. 422) Revenue earned but not yet received and recorded.

Acid-test ratio (p. 868) A measure of immediate liquidity; the ratio of quick assets to current liabilities.

Adjusting entries (p. 114) Journal entries made to record business transactions that are not recorded during the accounting period.

Adjustments (p. 114) *See* Adjusting entries.

Aging the accounts receivable (p. 534) Classifying accounts receivable according to how long they have been outstanding.

Allowance method (p. 530) A method of providing for bad debts before specific accounts become uncollectible.

Amortization (p. 626) The process of transferring acquisition costs of intangible assets to expense.

Appropriation of retained earnings (p. 751) A formal declaration of an intention to restrict dividends.

Articles of partnership (p. 644) A partnership agreement specifying the terms governing the partners' financial relationship and operation of the partnership.

Asset turnover (p. 861) The ratio of net sales to total assets.

Assets (p. 26) Property owned by a business.

Audit trail (p. 87) A chain of references that makes it possible to trace information through the accounting system.

Auditing (p. 5) The review of financial information to assess its fairness and adherence to generally accepted accounting principles.

Auditor's report (p. 16) An independent accountant's review of a firm's financial information.

Authorized capital stock (p. 692) The number of shares authorized for issue by a corporation's charter.

Average collection period (p. 871) The ratio of average accounts receivable to average daily credit sales, or the number of days' sales in receivables.

Average cost method (p. 586) A method of inventory

valuation using the average cost of similar items to value the ending inventory.

Average method of process costing (p. 1070) A method of costing based on combining the beginning inventory figure of each cost element with the cost incurred for that element in the current period.

Balance ledger form (p. 93) A ledger account form that shows the balance of the account after each entry is posted.

Balance sheet (p. 26) A formal report of a business's financial condition on a certain date; reports the assets, liabilities, and owner's equity of the business.

Bank draft (p. 572) A check written by a bank that orders another bank to pay an indicated amount to a specified party.

Bank reconciliation statement (p. 299) A process of proving that all differences between the bank balance and the checkbook balance are accounted for.

Banker's year (p. 556) A 360-day period used to calculate interest on a note.

Bearer bonds (p. 780) *See* Coupon bonds.

Bill of lading (p. 573) A business document that lists goods being sold in a business transaction.

Blank endorsement (p. 292) A signature transferring ownership of a check without specifying to whom or for what purpose.

Bond indenture (p. 779) A bond contract.

Bond issue costs (p. 793) Costs incurred in issuing bonds, such as legal, printing, and accounting fees.

Bond sinking fund (p. 794) A planned fund established to accumulate assets and to pay off bonds when they mature.

Bonding (p. 288) Insurance against losses through employee theft or mishandling of funds.

Bonds payable (p. 779) Long-term debt instruments that are written promises to repay the principal, and any interest, at a specified time.

Book value (pp. 117, 611, 749) That portion of an asset's original cost that has not yet been depreciated; the excess of the acquisition cost of an asset over its accumulated depreciation, depletion, or amortization; the value of a share of stock, calculated by dividing the total value applicable to a class of stock by the number of shares outstanding.

Break even (p. 36) A point at which revenue equals expenses.

Budget (p. 1088) An operating plan expressed in monetary units.

Budget performance report (p. 1094) A comparison of actual costs and budgeted costs.

Business transaction (p. 22) A financial event that changes the resources of a business.

Bylaws (p. 691) A corporation's guidelines for conducting business affairs.

Call price (p. 780) The set price the corporation must pay in redeeming, or calling, bonds.

Callable bonds (p. 780) Bonds that can be recalled before their maturity date by the issuing corporation.

Callable preferred stock (p. 694) Stock that gives the issuing corporation the right of repurchase at a specified price and generally after a specified date.

Canceled check (p. 294) A check paid by the bank on which it was drawn.

Capital (p. 23) Financial investment in a business; also called equity.

Capital stock ledger (p. 713) A subsidiary ledger that contains a record of each stockholder's purchases, transfers, and current balance of shares owned; also called stockholders' ledger.

Capital stock transfer journal (p. 714) A record of stock transfers, used for posting to the stockholders' ledger.

Capitalized costs (p. 610) All costs recorded as part of an asset's costs and depreciated over the asset's useful life.

Carrying value of bonds (p. 791) The balance of the Bonds Payable account plus or minus the bond premium or discount; also called book value of bonds.

Cash (pp. 265, 890) In accounting, currency, coins, checks, money orders, and funds on deposit in a bank; an asset defined as currency or holdings in a bank account.

Cash discounts (p. 235) Discounts offered for payment received in a specified period of time.

Cash equivalents (p. 890) Assets that are readily convertible into a known amount of cash.

Cash payments journal (p. 277) A special journal used to record transactions involving the payment of cash.

Cash receipts journal (p. 265) A special journal used to record transactions involving the receipt of cash.

Cash register proof (p. 266) A verification that the amount of currency and coins in a cash register agrees with the amount shown on the audit tape.

Cash short or over (p. 267) An account used to record any discrepancies between the amount of currency and coins in the cash register and the amount shown on the audit tape.

Cashier's check (p. 572) A draft on the issuing bank's own funds.

Certified public accountant (CPA) (p. 5) An independent accountant who provides accounting services to the public for a fee.

Charge-account sales (p. 201) Sales made through the use of open-account credit or one of various types of credit cards.

Chart of accounts (p. 69) A list of the accounts used by a business to record its financial transactions.

Check (p. 291) A written order signed by an authorized person instructing a bank to pay a specific sum of money to a designated payee.

Check register (p. 938) The record of payment of vouchers.

Chronological order (p. 86) Organized on a day-by-day basis.

Classification (p. 52) A means of identifying each account as an asset, liability, or owner's equity account.

Classified financial statement (p. 450) A format by which revenues and expenses on the income statement, and assets and liabilities on the balance sheet, are divided into groups of similar accounts and a subtotal is given for each group.

Closing entries (p. 146) Entries made in the general journal to transfer the results of operations to owner's equity and to prepare the revenue, expense, and drawing accounts for use in the next accounting period.

Collateral trust bonds (p. 779) Bonds secured by the

pledge of an asset, such as bonds or stock of another company.

Commercial draft (p. 572) A note issued by one party that orders another party to pay a specified sum on a specified date.

Commission basis (p. 337) A method of paying employees according to a percentage of sales.

Common costs (p. 1127) Costs not directly traceable to one segment of a business activity.

Common stock (p. 693) The general class of stock issued when no other class of stock is authorized; each share carries the same rights and privileges as every other share.

Common stock dividend distributable (p. 748) Equity account used to record par, or stated value, of shares to be issued.

Common-size statements (p. 822) Financial statements with items expressed as percentages of some common base figure on the statement rather than as dollar amounts.

Comparative statements (p. 817) Statements having financial data for two or more years presented side by side.

Compensation record (p. 353) *See* Individual earnings record.

Compound entry (p. 91) A journal entry that contains more than one debit or credit.

Conservatism principle (p. 512) The concept that assets should be understated rather than overstated if any question exists.

Consistency principle (p. 510) The concept that applications of accounting procedures should be the same from one period to the next in a particular company.

Contra asset account (p. 117) An asset account with a credit balance and thus contrary to the balance of its related asset account.

Contra revenue account (p. 190) An account with a debit balance, which is contrary to the normal balance for a revenue account.

Contribution margin (p. 1127) The difference between a department's gross profit on sales and its direct operating expenses; the excess of revenues over variable costs.

Control account (p. 193) An account that links a subsidiary ledger and the general ledger, since its balance summarizes the balances of the accounts in the subsidiary ledger.

Controllable fixed costs (p. 1127) Costs that can be controlled by management.

Controllable overhead variance (p. 1106) The difference between actual overhead costs incurred and the flexible budget allowance for the work performed.

Convertible bonds (p. 780) Bonds that give the holder the right to convert the bonds into common stock under specified conditions.

Convertible preferred stock (p. 694) Preferred stock that conveys the right to convert that stock to common stock after a specified date.

Copyright (p. 624) An intangible asset; an exclusive right granted by the federal government to produce, publish, and sell a literacy or artistic work.

Corporate charter (p. 688) A document issued by state government that establishes a corporation.

Corporation (p. 12) A publicly or privately owned business entity that is separate from its owners and has a legal right to do business in its own name; stockholders are not responsible for the debts or taxes of the business.

Correcting entry (p. 98) A journal entry made to correct an erroneous entry.

Cost basis (p. 507) The principle that requires assets to be recorded at their original cost.

Cost center (p. 967) A business segment that incurs costs but does not produce revenue.

Cost of production report (p. 1061) A summary of all costs charged to each department during the period and how those costs are to be accounted for.

Cost variance (p. 1101) The difference between the total standard cost and the total actual cost.

Coupon bonds (p. 780) Unregistered bonds that can be transferred by delivery and bearer coupons that are, in effect, checks payable.

Credit (p. 65) An entry on the right side of an account.

Credit memorandum (pp. 189, 295) A note verifying that a customer's account is being reduced by the amount of a sales return or sales allowance, plus any sales tax that may have been involved; also, a form that explains any amount other than a deposit that is added to a checking account.

Creditor (p. 9) One to whom money is owed.

Cumulative preferred stock (p. 695) Stock requiring that a preference dividend for a year that is not paid in that year be paid in the future before other dividends may be declared.

Current assets (p. 453) Those assets that are liquid or relatively liquid, such as cash, items that will be converted to cash within a year, or items that will be used up within a year.

Current liabilities (p. 454) Debts that must be paid within a year.

Current ratio (pp. 464, 868) A relationship between current assets and current liabilities that provides a measure of a firm's ability to pay its current debts.

Debentures (p. 779) Unsecured bonds backed only by a company's general credit.

Debit (p. 65) An entry on the left side of an account.

Debit memorandum (p. 296) A form that explains any amount (other than a paid check) that is deducted from a checking account.

Declaration date (p. 745) The date on which the board of directors declares a dividend.

Declining-balance method (p. 613) An accelerated method of depreciation in which the book value of an asset at the beginning of the year is multiplied by an appropriate percentage to determine depreciation for the year.

Deferred expenses (p. 420) *See* Prepaid expenses.

Deferred income (p. 423) Income received before it is earned.

Deferred income taxes (p. 735) The difference between the tax actually paid during a period and the amount that will ultimately be paid on net income for the period.

Depletion (p. 610) Periodic allocation of the cost of a natural resource.

Deposit in transit (p. 297) A deposit reaching the bank too late to be shown on the monthly bank statement.

Deposit slip (p. 293) A form prepared to record the deposit of cash or checks to a bank account; also called deposit ticket.

Depreciation (pp. 116, 610) Allocation of the cost of a long-term asset to operations during its expected useful life.

Differential cost (p. 1128) The difference in cost between one alternative and another.

Direct charge-off method (p. 530) A method of recording uncollectible accounts at the time they are known to be uncollectible.

Direct costing (p. 1125) Writing off all fixed manufacturing costs as current expenses of the period in which they are incurred.

Direct expenses (p. 972) Operating expenses that can be directly indentified with an individual department.

Direct labor (p. 996) Costs attributable to personnel who work directly on the product being manufactured.

Direct materials (p. 996) All items that go into a product and become a part of it.

Direct method (p. 909) A means of reporting sources and uses of cash. All revenue and expenses reported on the income statement are adjusted in the operating section of the statement of cash flows by reporting cash received or paid out for each item.

Discount on bonds payable (p. 789) The excess of the face value over the price received by the corporation for a bond.

Discounting (p. 559) Deducting in advance the interest on a note payable or receivable.

Discussion memorandum (p. 13) An explanation of a topic under consideration by the Financial Accounting Standards Board.

Dishonored check (p. 296) A check returned to the depositor because of insufficient funds in the drawer's account; also called an NSF check.

Dissolution (p. 662) The legal termination of a partnership.

Distributive share (p. 649) The amount of net income or loss allocated to each partner.

Donated capital (p. 753) Capital resulting from the receipt of gifts by a corporation.

Double-declining-balance method (p. 613) A method of depreciation using a rate equal to twice the straight-line rate.

Double-entry system (p. 65) An accounting system that involves recording the effects of each transaction as debits and credits.

Draft (p. 572) A written order, such as a check, requiring one party to pay a stated sum of money to another party.

Drawee (p. 291) The bank on which a check is written.

Drawer (p. 291) The person or firm issuing a check.

Drawing account (p. 64) A special type of owner's equity account set up to record the owner's withdrawal of cash from the business.

Economic entity (p. 9) A business or organization whose major purpose is to make a profit for its owners.

Employee (p. 333) One who is under the control and direction of the employer and is paid a salary or wage.

Employee's Withholding Allowance Certificate, Form W-4 (p. 341) A form used to claim exemption allowances.

Employer's Quarterly Federal Tax Return, Form 941 (p. 375) Preprinted government form used by the employer to report payroll tax information to the Internal Revenue Service.

Endorsement (p. 292) A written authorization that transfers ownership of a check.

Entity (p. 9) Anything having its own separate identity, such as an individual, a town, a university, or a business.

Equity (p. 23) An owner's financial interest in a business.

Equivalent production (p. 1060) The estimated number of units that could have been started and completed during the same time period and with the same effort and cost.

Exempt employees (p. 346) Salaried employees not subject to the Wage and Hour Law.

Expense (p. 28) An outflow of cash, use of other assets, or the incurring of a liability.

Experience rating system (p. 384) A system that rewards an employer by reducing the firm's unemployment tax, for maintaining steady employment conditions.

Exposure draft (p. 16) A proposed solution to a problem being considered by the Financial Accounting Standards Board.

Extraordinary, nonrecurring items (p. 742) Transactions clearly unrelated to routine operations.

Face amount (p. 556) An amount of money indicated to be paid, exclusive of interest or discounts; also called face value.

Face interest (p. 783) The contractual interest specified on the bond.

Fair market value (p. 37) The present worth of an asset or the price the asset would bring if sold on the open market.

Fair-market value method (p. 623) A method of recording the trade-in of an asset that allows a loss to be recognized in the transaction if the book value exceeds the trade-in allowance.

Federal Tax Deposit Coupon, Form 8109 (p. 370) Preprinted government form that accompanies an employer's deposit of various taxes.

Federal unemployment taxes (FUTA) (p. 335) Taxes levied by the federal government, against employers, to benefit unemployed workers.

Financial statements (p. 4) Periodic reports of a firm's financial position or operating results.

Financing activities (p. 890) Transactions that involve dealings with creditor and stockholders who provide cash to the corporation, other than interest expense.

Finished goods subsidiary ledger (p. 1034) A perpetual record for each of the different types of finished products.

First in, first out (FIFO) method (p. 587) A method of inventory valuation that assumes the oldest merchandise is sold first.

Fixed budget (p. 1093) A budget representing only one level of expected activity.

Fixed costs (p. 1089) Costs that do not vary in total as the volume of work changes.

Flexible budget (p. 1095) A budget showing estimated costs at various levels of activity.

Footing (p. 55) A small penciled figure at the base of an amount column that is the sum of the entries in the column.

Franchise (p. 624) An intangible asset; a right to exclusive dealership granted by a governmental unit or a business entity.

Freight In (p. 232) An account showing transportation charges for items purchased.

Full disclosure principle (p. 511) All information that might affect the statement user's interpretation of the profitability and financial position of a business must be included in its financial statements.

Full endorsement (p. 292) A signature transferring a check to a specific person, firm, or bank.

Fundamental accounting equation (p. 28) The relationship between assets and liabilities plus owner's equity.

General journal (p. 86) A financial record for entering all types of business transactions.

General ledger (p. 93) A permanent, classified record of all accounts used in a firm's operation; a record of final entry.

General partner (p. 643) A member of a partnership who has unlimited liability.

Generally accepted accounting principles (p. 13) Accounting standards developed and applied by professional accountants.

Going concern assumption (p. 506) The assumption that a firm will continue to operate in the future.

Goodwill (p. 626) An intangible asset; the value of a business in excess of the value of its identifiable assets.

Governmental accounting (p. 5) Accounting work performed for a federal, state, or local governmental unit.

Gross profit method (p. 594) A method of estimating inventory based on the assumption that the rate of gross profit on sales is relatively constant from period to period.

Gross profit percentage (p. 463) A figure derived by dividing gross profit by net sales to determine the amount of profit from each dollar of sales.

High-low points method (p. 1090) A method of determining the fixed and the variable components of a semivariable cost.

Historical cost (p. 504) *See* Cost basis.

Horizontal analysis (p. 818) Computing the relationship of changes in individual items from year to year.

Hourly-rate basis (p. 337) A method of paying employees according to a stated rate of pay per hour.

Income statement (p. 34) A formal report of business operations covering a specific period of time; also called a profit and loss statement or a statement of income and expenses.

Income summary account (p. 146) A special owner's equity account that is used to summarize the results of operations and that is used only in the closing process.

Income tax method (p. 621) A method of recording the trade-in of an asset according to tax allowances that permit no gain or loss to be recognized on the transaction.

Incremental cost (p. 1128) An increase in cost resulting from an increase in production.

Independent contractor (p. 333) One who is paid to carry out a specific job outside the direct control of a company.

Indirect expenses (p. 973) Operating expenses that cannot be readily related to activity within an individual department.

Indirect labor (p. 997) Cost attributable to personnel who support production but are not directly involved in the manufacture of a product; for example, supervisory, repair and maintenance, and janitorial staff.

Indirect materials and supplies (p. 996) Materials that may be used in manufacturing a product but do not become a part of the product itself.

Indirect method (p. 908) A means of reporting cash generated from operating activities. Net income is treated as the primary source of cash in the operating section of the statement of cash flows. That amount is adjusted for noncash expenses, changes in current assets and liabilities associated with net income, and other items.

Individual earnings record (p. 353) An employee record posted from the payroll register.

Industry averages (p. 822) Financial data collected from a number of companies in an industry, allowing comparison of like companies within an industry.

Interest (p. 556) The price charged for the use of money or credit.

Internal control system (p. 932) A system of safeguards designed to protect assets, achieve efficient processing of transactions, and ensure accuracy and reliability of financial records.

Inventory sheet (p. 413) A form used to list the volume and type of goods a firm has in stock.

Inventory turnover (p. 464) The number of times inventory is purchased and sold during a financial period; the average length of time it takes to move an item from purchase to sale.

Investing activities (p. 890) Transactions that involve the acquisition or disposal of assets.

Invoice (pp. 199, 230) A customer billing for merchandise bought on credit; supplier's bill for items ordered and shipped.

Job order (p. 1029) A specific order for a specific batch of manufactured items.

Job order cost accounting (p. 1029) A cost accounting system whereby unit costs of manufactured items are determined for each separate production order.

Job order cost sheet (p. 1042) A subsidiary record of all manufacturing costs charged to a specific job.

Journal (p. 86) The record of original entry.

Journalizing (p. 86) Recording transactions in a journal.

Just-in-time system (p. 1032) An inventory system whereby raw materials are ordered so as to arrive just in time to be placed into production.

Labor efficiency variance (p. 1103) *See* Labor time variance.
Labor rate variance (p. 1104) That portion of the variance attributable to the fact that the actual labor rate per hour was more or less than the standard labor rate.
Labor time variance (p. 1103) The difference between the actual hours spent on the job and the standard labor hours allowed for the job.
Last in, first out (LIFO) method (p. 588) A method of inventory valuation that assumes that the most recently purchased merchandise is sold first.
Ledger (p. 92) The record of final entry.
Leveraged buyout (p. 864) Purchasing a business by acquiring the stock and obligating the business to pay the debt.
Leveraging (p. 782) Using borrowed funds to earn a profit greater than the interest that must be paid on the borrowing.
Liabilities (p. 26) Debts or obligations of a business.
Limited partner (p. 643) A member of a partnership whose liability is limited to his or her investment in the partnership.
Limited partnership (p. 643) A partnership having one or more limited partners.
Liquidation (p. 662) Termination of a business with all assets being distributed and the business discontinued.
Liquidation value (p. 693) Value applied to preferred stock, usually par value or an amount in excess of par value.
Liquidity (pp. 454, 867) The ease with which an item can be converted to cash; the ability to pay debts when due.
List price (p. 197) An established retail price.
Long-term liabilities (p. 454) Debts that are due more than a year into the future.
Lower of cost or market rule (p. 591) The principle by which inventory is valued at either its original cost or its replacement cost, whichever is lower.

Management advisory services (p. 5) Services designed to help clients improve their information systems or their business performance.
Managerial accounting (p. 5) Accounting work carried on by an accountant employed by a single business in industry; an emphasis in accounting that provides financial information about individual segments, activities, or products of a business.
Manufacturing business (p. 179) A business that sells goods that it has produced.
Manufacturing cost budget (p. 1092) A budget made for each manufacturing cost for the budget period.
Manufacturing margin (p. 1126) The excess of net sales over the cost of goods sold, based on variable costs only.
Manufacturing overhead (p. 997) All manufacturing costs that are not classified as direct materials or direct labor.
Manufacturing overhead ledger (p. 1039) A subsidiary ledger that contains a record for each overhead item.
Marginal income (p. 1126) The difference between the variable operating expenses and the manufacturing margin.
Markdown (p. 596) Price decrease from the original markon.
Market price (p. 591) The current cost of buying an item of inventory for resale.
Markon (p. 591) The difference between the cost and the established retail price of merchandise.
Markup (p. 596) A price increase above the original markon.
Matching principle (p. 509) The concept that revenues must be matched against the expired costs incurred in earning those revenues.
Materiality principle (p. 512) The significance of an item in relation to the particular situation of which it is a part.
Materials price variance (p. 1102) That portion of the variance attributable to the fact that the actual unit price paid for raw material was more or less than the standard unit price.
Materials quantity variance (p. 1101) That portion of the variance attributable to the fact that actual quantity of material used was more or less than the standard quantity.
Materials requisition (p. 1035) A form that describes the item needed, the quantity needed, and the job for which the item is needed.
Materials usage variance (p. 1101) *See* Materials quantity variance.
Maturity value (p. 556) The total amount (principal plus interest) that must be paid when a note comes due.
Medicare tax (p. 334) A tax levied on employees and employers to provide medical benefits for elderly persons.
Memorandum entry (p. 646) An information entry in the general journal.
Merchandise inventory (p. 180) The stock of goods a merchandising business keeps on hand.
Merchandising business (p. 179) A business that sells goods purchased for resale.
Merit rating system (p. 384) *See* Experience rating system.
Minute book (p. 712) A book in which accurate and complete records of all directors' and stockholders' meeting are kept.
Mixed accounts (p. 410) Accounts that contain elements of both assets and expenses or both liabilities and revenue.
Mixed costs (p. 1089) *See* Semivariable costs.
Mortgage loan (p. 778) A long-term debt created when a note is given as part of the purchase price for land, buildings, or equipment.
Multiple-step income statement (p. 450) A type of income statement on which several subtotals and totals are computed before the net income is presented.
Mutual agency (p. 643) The characteristic of a partnership by which each partner is empowered to act as agent for the partnership, binding the firm by his or her acts.

Negotiable (p. 291) A financial instrument whose ownership can be transferred from one person to another.

Net income (p. 35) The result of an excess of revenue over expenses.
Net loss (p. 36) The result of an excess of expenses over revenue.
Net of discount (p. 950) The invoice price minus the cash discount.
Net price (p. 197) The list price less all trade discounts.
Net sales (p. 192) The difference between the balance in the Sales account and the balance in the Sales Returns and Allowances account.
No-par value stock (p. 692) Stock issued by a corporation without a value assigned by the charter.
Noncumulative preferred stock (p. 695) Stock on which a preference dividend not paid in one year does not accumulate.
Nonparticipating preferred stock (p. 695) Stock that conveys the right to a preference dividend amount specified on the face of the stock certificate but to no additional dividends.
Normal balance (p. 56) The increase side of an account.
Note payable (p. 557) A liability that represents the debtor's promise to pay a specified amount at a specified future date.
Note receivable (p. 561) An asset that represents the creditor's promise to pay a specified amount at a specified future date.

Objectivity assumption (p. 507) The idea that financial reports are unbiased and fair to all parties.
On account (p. 25) An arrangement to allow payment at a later date; also called a charge account, or open-account credit.
Open-account credit (p. 200) A system that allows the sale of services or goods with the understanding that payment will be made at a later date.
Operating activities (p. 890) Routine business transactions—selling goods or services and paying expenses.
Operating assets and liabilities (p. 898) Current assets and current liabilities.
Opportunity cost (p. 1128) Potential earnings or benefits foregone because a certain decision was made.
Organization costs (p. 704) The costs associated with establishing a corporation; an intangible asset account.
Outstanding checks (p. 297) Checks that have been issued but that have not yet been paid by the bank on which the checks are drawn.
Overapplied overhead (p. 1041) A result of applied overhead exceeding the actual overhead costs.
Overhead application rate (p. 1040) The rate at which the costs of overhead items are charged to each job.
Owner's equity (p. 26) The financial interest of the owner of a business; also called proprietorship, or net worth.

Paid-in capital (p. 731) Capital acquired from stock transactions.
Par value (p. 692) An amount selected by organizers of a corporation and assigned by the corporate charter to each share of stock for accounting purposes.
Participating preferred stock (p. 695) Stock that conveys the right to the preference dividend amount but also to a share of other dividends paid.
Partnership (pp. 10, 643) A business entity owned by two or more people who are legally responsible for the debts and taxes of the business.
Partnership agreement (p. 644) A legal contract forming a partnership and specifying certain details of operation.
Patent (p. 623) An intangible asset; an exclusive right given by the federal government to manufacture and sell an invention.
Payee (p. 291) The person or firm to whom a check is payable.
Payment date (p. 745) The date on which dividends are actually paid.
Payment voucher (p. 936) *See* Voucher.
Payroll register (p. 347) A record of payroll information for each employee for the pay period.
Periodicity of income assumption (p. 507) The concept that income should be reported by certain time periods.
Permanent account (p. 72) An account that is kept open from one accounting period to the next.
Perpetual inventory (p. 586) Inventory based on a running total of number of units.
Perpetual inventory system (p. 1031) An inventory system that shows inventories on hand at all times.
Petty cash analysis sheet (p. 285) A form used to record transactions involving petty cash.
Petty cash fund (p. 265) A special-purpose fund set up to handle payments involving small amounts of money.
Petty cash voucher (p. 284) A form used to record the payments made from a petty cash fund.
Physical inventory (p. 586) Inventory based on an actual count of the number of units of each type of goods on hand.
Piece-rate basis (p. 337) A method of paying employees according to the number of units produced.
Plant and equipment (p. 454) Long-term assets; property that will be used for a long time in operating the business.
Postclosing trial balance (p. 154) A statement that is prepared to prove the equality of total debits and credits after the closing process is completed.
Postdated check (p. 294) A check dated some time in the future.
Posting (p. 92) Transferring data from a journal to a ledger.
Preemptive right (p. 693) A shareholder's right to purchase a proportionate share of any new stock issued by the corporation.
Preference dividend (p. 695) A stated dividend rate for preferred stock that must be paid before dividends can be paid on common stock.
Preferred stock (p. 693) A class of stock that conveys certain claims on a corporation's profits or assets in case of liquidation.
Premium on bonds payable (p. 787) The excess of the price paid over the face value of a bond.
Prepaid expenses (p. 116) Expense items acquired and paid for in advance of their use, such as rent or insurance.
Price-earnings ratio (p. 857) The ratio of the current market value of common stock to earnings per share of the stock.
Principal (p. 556) The amount shown on the face of a note.

Process cost accounting (p. 1029, 1058) A method of accounting in which costs are accumulated for each process or department and then transferred on to the next process or department.
Producing departments (p. 1029) Departments within a manufacturing firm that perform work directly on a product.
Production order (p. 1029) *See* Job order.
Profit center (p. 967) A business segment that produces revenue.
Promissory note (pp. 268, 555) A written promise to pay a specified amount of money on a specific date; a negotiable instrument that gives evidence of a debt and a promise to pay.
Property, plant, and equipment (pp. 416, 609) Long-term assets that are used in the operation of a business and are subject to depreciation (except for land, which is not depreciated).
Public accountants (p. 5) Members of firms that perform accounting services for other businesses.
Purchase allowance (p. 240) A price reduction from the amount originally billed.
Purchase discount (p. 235) A cash discount offered to customers buying goods for payment within a specified period.
Purchase invoice (p. 234) A bill received for goods purchased.
Purchase order (p. 230) An order to the supplier of goods specifying items needed, quantity, price, and credit terms.
Purchase requisition (p. 230) A list sent to the purchasing department showing goods to be ordered.
Purchase return (p. 240) Return of unsatisfactory goods.
Purchases (p. 232) An account used to record the cost of goods bought for resale during a period.
Purchases discounts (p. 278) A reduction in the cost of items purchased given as a result of large-volume purchases or to encourage quick payment of an invoice; also, the account used to record reductions in the cost of purchases.
Purchases journal (p. 232) A special journal used to record the purchase of goods on credit.

Qualitative characteristics (p. 504) Traits necessary for credible financial statements: usefulness, relevance, reliability, verifiability, neutrality, understandability, timeliness, comparability, and completeness.
Quick assets (p. 868) Cash and non-cash assets, such as receivables and marketable securities, that can quickly be converted to cash.

Ratio analysis (pp. 818, 854) Computing relationships between various items on the financial statements.
Raw materials (p. 996) The materials placed into production.
Raw materials ledger card (p. 1034) A record showing details of receipts and issues for a type of raw material.
Raw materials subsidiary ledger (p. 1034) A ledger containing the raw materials ledger cards.
Real property (p. 609) Assets such as land, land improvements, buildings, and other structures attached to the land.
Realization principle (p. 508) The concept that revenue occurs, and is recorded, at the time new assets are created in the form of money or in claims against others.
Receiving report (p. 230) A form showing quantity and condition of goods received.
Record date (p. 745) The date on which the specific stockholders to receive a dividend are determined.
Registered bonds (p. 779) Bonds issued to a particular purchaser listed in the company's records.
Registrar (p. 715) A person or institution in charge of the issuance and transfer of stock.
Relevant range of activity (p. 1095) The range of activity at which a factory is expected to operate.
Replacement cost (p. 591) *See* Market price.
Report-form balance sheet (p. 126) A balance sheet that lists the asset accounts first, followed by the liabilities and owner's equity.
Responsibility accounting (p. 968) An emphasis in accounting that provides information for evaluating each segment of a business and pinpointing responsibility for its financial results.
Restrictive endorsement (p. 292) A signature that transfers a check to a specific party for a stated purpose.
Retail business (p. 179) A business that sells directly to individual consumers.
Retail method (p. 595) A method of estimating inventory cost by applying the ratio of cost to selling price in the current accounting period to the retail price of the inventory.
Retained earnings (p. 696) Corporate profits not paid out in dividends.
Return on common stockholders' equity (p. 855) The ratio of net income available to common stockholders to total equity of the common stock.
Revenue (p. 28) An inflow of money or other assets that results from the sales of goods or services or from the use of money or property; also called income.
Reversing entries (p. 465) Journal entries made to reverse the effect of certain adjusting entries involving accrued income or accrued expenses, to avoid problems in recording future payments or receipts of cash in a new accounting period.

Salary basis (p. 337) A method of paying employees according to an agreed-upon weekly or monthly rate.
Sales allowance (p. 189) A reduction in the price originally charged to customers for goods or services.
Sales discount (pp. 235, 268) A supplier's reduction in price from the amount originally billed, usually offered to encourage quick payment.
Sales invoice (p. 234) A supplier's billing document.
Sales journal (p. 180) A special journal used to record sales of merchandise on credit.
Sales return (p. 189) A firm's acceptance of a return of goods from a customer.
Salvage value (pp. 116, 612) An item's value to a firm at the end of the item's useful life—that is, its value as used goods or scrap.
Schedule of accounts payable (p. 242) A list of all balances owed to creditors.
Schedule of accounts receivable (p. 193) A listing of all balances of the accounts in the accounts receivable subsidiary ledger.

Schedule of vouchers payable (p. 942) A listing of all amounts owed for unpaid vouchers.

Secured bonds (p. 779) Bonds to which specific property is pledged as collateral.

Semidirect expenses (p. 973) Expenses that cannot be directly assigned to an individual department but can be closely related to that department's operations on some logical basis.

Semivariable costs (p. 1089) Costs that vary in some degree but not in direct proportion to the volume of work.

Separate entity assumption (pp. 10, 506) The concept that a firm is separate from other businesses and from its owners and creditors.

Serial bonds (p. 780) Bonds issued at one time but maturing at different times over a period of years.

Service business (p. 179) A business that sells services.

Service charge (p. 296) A fee charged by a bank to cover the costs of maintaining accounts and providing services.

Service departments (p. 1029) Departments within a manufacturing firm that assist in production but do not work directly on the product.

Shareholder (p. 688) A person who owns shares of stock in a corporation; also called stockholder.

Sight draft (p. 572) A commercial draft payable on presentation.

Single-step income statement (p. 450) A type of income statement where only one computation—total revenue minus total expenses—is needed to determine net income.

Slide (p. 69) An accounting error involving a misplaced decimal point.

Social entity (p. 9) A nonprofit organization (a city, public school, or public hospital).

Social Security Act (p. 334) A federal act providing certain benefits for employees and their families; officially the Federal Insurance Contributions Act.

Social security tax (p. 334) A tax imposed by the Federal Insurance Contribution Act and collected on employee earnings to provide retirement and disability benefits; also called FICA tax.

Sole proprietorship (p. 9) A business entity owned by one person who is legally responsible for the debts and taxes of the business.

Special journal (p. 180) A journal used to record only one type of transaction.

Specific identification method (p. 586) A method of inventory valuation based on the actual cost of each piece of merchandise.

Spending variance (p. 1106) *See* Controllable overhead variance.

Stable monetary unit assumption (p. 506) The concept that accounting records are kept in terms of money that is assumed not to fluctuate in value.

Standard cost accounting (p. 1030) A cost accounting system that establishes standards for expected costs for materials, labor, and overhead for each unit of product.

Standard cost card (p. 1099) A form showing the standard costs for materials, labor, and overhead per unit of product.

State unemployment taxes (SUTA) (p. 335) Taxes levied by a state government, against employers, to benefit unemployed workers.

Stated value (p. 692) The value assigned to stock by a board of directors when stock has been authorized without par value.

Statement of account (p. 267) A form sent to a firm's customers showing transactions during the month and the balance owed.

Statement of cash flows (p. 889) A financial statement that shows a business's inflows and outflows of cash during a fiscal period.

Statement of cost of goods manufactured (p. 995) A financial report showing details of the cost of goods completed during the accounting period.

Statement of owner's equity (p. 37) A formal report of changes that occurred in the owner's financial interest during a reporting period.

Statement of partners' equities (p. 661) A financial statement prepared to summarize the changes in partners' capital accounts during an accounting period.

Statement of retained earnings (p. 757) A financial statement that shows beginning and ending balances, along with changes that have occurred in both the appropriated and unappropriated retained earnings accounts during the period.

Statement of stockholders' equity (p. 758) A financial statement that provides an analysis of changes in equity.

Statements of Financial Accounting Standards (p. 13) Accounting principles established by the Financial Accounting Standards Board.

Stock (p. 12) Certificates that represent ownership of a corporation.

Stock certificate (p. 691) A document that shows evidence of ownership of shares in a corporation.

Stock dividend (p. 747) Distribution of the corporation's own stock on a pro rata basis.

Stock split (p. 749) An increase in the number of shares, which has no effect on the capital accounts.

Stockholders (p. 12) The owners of a corporation; also called shareholders.

Stockholders of record (p. 745) Shareholders to whom dividends are to be paid.

Stockholders' equity (p. 691) The corporate equivalent of owners' equity, which is the amount invested in the capital stock of the corporation.

Straight-line amortization (p. 788) A method of amortizing the premium or discount on bonds payable in equal amounts over the life of the bond.

Straight-line depreciation (p. 116) Allocation of an asset's cost in equal amounts to each accounting period of the asset's useful life.

Straight-line method (p. 612) A method of depreciating asset costs that allocates equal amounts of expense each year (or each accounting period) of an asset's useful life.

Subscribers' ledger (p. 714) A special ledger that contains an account receivable for each stock subscriber.

Subscription book (p. 714) A listing of stock subscriptions.

Subsidiary ledger (p. 180) A ledger dedicated to accounts of a single type and showing details to support a general ledger account.

Sum-of-the-years'-digits method (p. 614) A method of depreciating asset costs. Each year a fractional part of the asset's depreciable cost is allocated as an expense, based on the sum of the digits of the number of years in the asset's useful life.

Sunk cost (p. 1128) A cost that has already been incurred and that will not change as a result of a decision.

T account (p. 52) A type of account, resembling a T, used to analyze the effects of a business transaction.

Tangible personal property (p. 609) Assets such as machinery, equipment, furniture, and fixtures having physical existence.

Tax accounting (p. 5) A service that involves tax compliance and tax planning.

Tax-exempt wages (p. 339) Earnings in excess of the base amount set by the Social Security Act.

Temporary account (p. 72) An account whose balance is transferred to another account at the end of an accounting period.

Ticker file (p. 937) A file with vouchers filed by due date.

Time and a half (p. 334) Rate of pay for employee work in excess of 40 hours a week.

Time draft (p. 573) A commercial draft payable at a specified time.

Time tickets (p. 1038) Forms used to record hours worked and jobs performed.

Trade acceptance (p. 573) A special commercial time draft used in transactions involving the sale of goods.

Trade discount (p. 197) A reduction from list price.

Trade name (p. 625) An intangible asset; an exclusive business name registered with the U.S. Patent Office.

Trademark (p. 615) An intangible asset; an exclusive business symbol registered with the U.S. Patent Office; also called brand name.

Trading on the equity (p. 782) *See* Leveraging.

Transfer agent (p. 715) A person or institution that handles all stock transfers and transfer records for a corporation.

Transmittal of Income and Tax Statements, Form W-3 (p. 380) Preprinted government form submitted with W-2 forms to the Social Security Administration.

Transportation In (p. 232) *See* Freight In.

Transposition (p. 69) An accounting error involving misplaced digits in a number.

Treasury stock (p. 754) A corporation's own capital stock that has been issued, fully paid for, and reacquired.

Trend analysis (p. 831) Comparing dollar amounts or percentages over several accounting periods to determine patterns.

Trial balance (p. 66) A statement to test the accuracy of total debits and credits after transactions have been recorded.

Underapplied overhead (p. 1041) A result of actual overhead costs exceeding applied overhead.

Unearned income (p. 423) *See* Deferred income.

Unemployment insurance program (p. 384) A program that provides unemployment compensation through a tax levied on employers.

Units-of-output method (p. 615) A method of depreciating asset cost on the basis of an assigned rate of production over the asset's useful life.

Unlimited liability (p. 643) The implication that personal assets as well as business assets can be required in payment of the firm's debts.

Unpaid vouchers file (p. 937) A file to hold vouchers until they are due to be paid.

Unused capacity (p. 1107) Excess of budgeted hours over standard hours for the work done.

Valuation account (p. 532) An account, such as Allowance for Doubtful Accounts, whose balance is revalued or reappraised in light of reasonable expectations.

Variable costing (p. 1125) *See* Direct costing.

Variable costs (p. 1089) Costs that vary in total in direct relation to volume of work done.

Variance analysis (p. 1101) A process to determine the variance in quantities used and/or in unit costs.

Vertical analysis (p. 818) Computing the relationship between each item on a financial statement and some base amount on that statement.

Volume analysis (p. 1106) The difference between the standard overhead for the units produced and the flexible overhead budget allowance.

Voucher (p. 933) A form used to authorize payment of an obligation.

Voucher register (p. 938) A journal used to record vouchers issued by a business.

Voucher system (p. 933) A record-keeping system that requires a written authorization (the voucher) for each amount to be paid, thus controlling liabilities and cash payments.

Wage and Tax Statement, Form W-2 (p. 378) Preprinted government form that contains information about an employee's earnings and tax withholdings for the year.

Wage-bracket table method (p. 341) A simple method to determine the amount of federal income tax to be withheld, using a table provided by the government.

Weighted average method (p. 587) *See* Average cost method.

Wholesale business (p. 197) A business that manufactures or distributes goods to retail businesses or large consumers such as hotels and hospitals.

Withdrawals (p. 32) Funds taken from the business by the owner for personal use.

Withholding statement (p. 378) *See* Wage and Tax Statement, Form W-2.

Work in process (p. 997) Partially completed units in the production process.

Work in process subsidiary ledger (p. 1034) A ledger containing the job order cost sheets.

Workers' compensation insurance (p. 335) Insurance to reimburse employees for job-related injuries or illnesses, or to compensate their families if death occurs in the course of their employment.

Working capital (p. 867) The excess of current assets over current liabilities.

Worksheet (p. 113) A form used to gather all data needed at the end of an accounting period to prepare financial statements.

Index